P9-DUM-083

JAMES E. MILLER, JR.
Professor of English, University of Chicago. Fulbright Lecturer in Naples and Rome, 1958–59, and in Kyoto, Japan, 1968. President of the National Council of Teachers of English, 1970. Awarded a Guggenheim fellowship, 1969–70. Author of *Quests Surd and Absurd: Essays in American Literature; Theory of Fiction: Henry James;* and *Word, Self, Reality: The Rhetoric of Imagination.*

ROBERT HAYDEN
Professor of English, University of Michigan. Formerly Bingham Professor of English, University of Louisville, Visiting Poet, University of Washington, and Professor of English, Fisk University. Recipient of the Hopwood Award, the Grand Prix de la Poesie of the First World Festival of Negro Arts, Dakar, and the Russell Loines Award. Author of *A Ballad of Remembrance; Selected Poems,* and *Words in the Mourning Time.*

ROBERT O'NEAL
Professor of Humanities, San Antonio College. Formerly Chairman and Professor of English, San Antonio College. Author of *Teachers' Guide to World Literature for the High School, NCTE,* and *English for You.*

The

UNITED STATES

in Literature

America Reads

The
UNITED STATES
In Literature

THE GLASS MENAGERIE *EDITION*

Editorial direction: LEO B. KNEER
Development: DOROTHY KOEBER
with Joel Goldberger, Bruce Holmes,
and Gordon Hull
Design: ROBERT AMFT
Production: MARY KVATSAK
Picture editor: MARGARET LUKACS

SCOTT, FORESMAN AND COMPANY

COVER: WHERE THE TWO CAME TO THEIR FATHER, Painting by Navaho
Artist Jeff King, recorded by Maud Oakes, Bollingen Series I (c) 1943, 1969 by
Princeton University Press, Reprinted by permission of Princeton University Press

ISBN: 0-673-03427-5

Copyright © 1973, 1968, 1963, 1957, 1952 by
Scott, Foresman and Company, Glenview, Illinois 60025.
All Rights Reserved. Philippines Copyright 1973 by Scott,
Foresman and Company. Printed in the United States of America.
Regional offices of Scott, Foresman and Company are located in
Dallas, Texas; Glenview, Illinois; Oakland, New Jersey;
Palo Alto, California; Tucker, Georgia; and London, England.

CONTENTS

INTRODUCING AMERICAN LITERATURE

PAGE 2A

THE AMERICAN LITERARY TRADITION*

1607 / 1899

PAGE 1C

JAMES THURBER

THE LAST FLOWER

PAGE 2C

---

chapter one
PLANTERS AND PURITANS

PAGE 18 C

---

*THIS SECTION IS ALSO AVAILABLE IN A SOFTBOUND EDITION

chapter two
FOUNDERS OF THE NATION
PAGE 50 C

chapter three
EARLY NATIONAL PERIOD
PAGE 82 C

contd.

chapter four
RENAISSANCE
PAGE 126C

chapter five
END OF AN ERA

PAGE 176 C

THE TWENTIETH CENTURY

chapter seven
THE NEW SHORT STORY

PAGE 2 M

POETRY: DEVELOPMENTS AND DEPARTURES

POETRY *contd.*

chapter eleven
MODERN DRAMA
PAGE 278 M

TENNESSEE WILLIAMS
THE GLASS MENAGERIE
PAGE 280 M

LITERARY TECHNIQUES, FORMS, GENRES, AND ELEMENTS

SPECIAL FEATURES

TWENTIETH CENTURY AMERICAN POETRY BY ROBERT HAYDEN

WORD STUDIES

INTRODUCING
AMERICAN
LITERATURE

The writers gathered together in this opening chapter have all won literary prizes of one kind or another: Nobel, Pulitzer, or National Book Award. Such prizes do not, of course, insure excellence, but they do indicate wide recognition and rightfully command critical attention.

When William Faulkner won the Nobel prize in 1950, he delivered a short speech that has become a classic statement of the role of the writer in contemporary culture.

William Faulkner Nobel Acceptance Speech

I feel that this award was not made to me as a man, but to my work—a life's work in the agony and sweat of the human spirit, not for glory and least of all for profit, but to create out of the materials of the human spirit something which did not exist before. So this award is only mine in trust. It will not be difficult to find a dedication for the money part of it commensurate with the purpose and significance of its origin. But I would like to do the same with the acclaim too, by using this moment as a pinnacle from which I might be listened to by the young men and women already dedicated to the same anguish and travail, among whom is already that one who will some day stand here where I am standing.

Our tragedy today is a general and universal physical fear so long sustained by now that we can even bear it. There are no longer problems of the spirit. There is only the question: When will I be blown up? Because of this, the young man or woman writing today has forgotten the problems of the human heart in conflict with itself which alone can make good writing because only that is worth writing about, worth the agony and the sweat.

He must learn them again. He must teach himself that the basest of all things is to be afraid; and, teaching himself that, forget it forever, leaving no room in his workshop for anything but the old verities and truths of the heart, the old universal truths lacking which any story is ephemeral and doomed—love and honor and pity and pride and compassion and sacrifice. Until he does so, he labors under a curse. He writes not of love but of lust, of defeats in which nobody loses anything of value, of victories without hope and, worst of all, without pity or compassion. His griefs grieve on no universal bones, leaving no scars. He writes not of the heart but of the glands.

Until he relearns these things, he will write as though he stood among and watched the end of man. I decline to accept the end of man. It is easy enough to say that man is immortal simply because he will endure: that when the last dingdong of doom has clanged and faded from the last worthless rock hanging tideless in the last red and dying evening, that even then there will still be one more sound: that of his puny inexhaustible voice, still talking. I refuse to accept this. I believe that man will not merely endure: he will prevail. He is immortal, not because he alone among creatures has an inexhaustible voice, but because he has a soul, a spirit capable of compassion and sacrifice and endurance. The poet's, the writer's, duty is to write about these things. It is his privilege to help man endure by lifting his heart, by reminding him of the courage and honor and hope and pride and compassion and pity and sacrifice which have been the glory of his past. The poet's voice need not merely be the record of man, it can be one of the props, the pillars to help him endure and prevail. □

Nobel Prize Speech from THE FAULKNER READER, by William Faulkner. Copyright 1954 by William Faulkner. Reprinted by permission of Random House, Inc.

from

The Way to Rainy Mountain

N. Scott Momaday
illustrations by Al Momaday

PROLOGUE

THE journey began one day long ago on the edge of the northern Plains. It was carried on over a course of many generations and many hundreds of miles. In the end there were many things to remember, to dwell upon and talk about.

"You know, everything had to begin. . . ." For the Kiowas the beginning was a struggle for existence in the bleak northern mountains. It was there, they say, that they entered the world through a hollow log. The end, too, was a struggle, and it was lost. The young Plains culture of the Kiowas withered and died like grass that is burned in the prairie wind. There came a day like destiny; in every direction, as far as the eye could see, carrion lay out in the land. The buffalo was the animal representation of the sun, the essential and sacrificial victim of the Sun Dance. When the wild herds were destroyed, so too was the will of the Kiowa people; there was nothing to sustain them in spirit. But these are idle recollections, the mean and ordinary agonies of human history. The interim was a time of great adventure and nobility and fulfillment.

Tai-me came to the Kiowas in a vision born of suffering and despair. "Take me with you," Tai-me said, "and I will give you whatever you want." And it was so. The great adventure of the Kiowas was a going forth into the heart of the continent. They began a long migration from the headwaters of the Yellowstone River eastward to the Black Hills and south to the Wichita Mountains. Along the way they acquired horses, the religion of the Plains, a love and possession of the open land. Their nomadic soul was set free. In alliance with the Comanches they held dominion in the southern Plains for a hundred years. In the course of that long migration they had come of age as a people. They had conceived a good idea of themselves; they had dared to imagine and determine who they were.

In one sense, then, the way to Rainy Mountain is preeminently the history of an idea, man's idea of himself, and it has old and essential being in language. The verbal tradition by which it has been preserved has suffered a deterioration in time. What remains is fragmentary: mythology, legend, lore, and hearsay—and of course the idea itself, as crucial and complete as it ever was. That is the miracle.

The journey herein recalled continues to be made anew each time the miracle comes to mind, for that is peculiarly the right and responsibility of the imagination. It is a whole journey, intricate with motion and meaning; and it is made with the whole memory, that experience of the mind which is legendary as well as historical, personal as well as cultural. And the journey is an evocation of three things in particular: a landscape that is incomparable, a time that is gone forever, and the human spirit, which endures. The imaginative experience and the historical express equally the traditions of man's reality. Finally, then, the journey recalled is among other things the revelation of one way in which these traditions are conceived, developed, and interfused in the human mind. There are on the way to Rainy Mountain many landmarks, many journeys in the one. From the beginning the migration of the Kiowas was an expression of the human spirit, and that expression is most truly made in terms of wonder and delight: "There were many people, and oh, it was beautiful. That was the beginning of the Sun Dance. It was all for Tai-me, you know, and it was a long time ago."

From THE WAY TO RAINY MOUNTAIN by N. Scott Momaday. © The University of New Mexico Press, 1969. Reprinted by permission.

INTRODUCTION

A single knoll rises out of the plain in Oklahoma, north and west of the Wichita Range. For my people, the Kiowas, it is an old landmark, and they gave it the name Rainy Mountain. The hardest weather in the world is there. Winter brings blizzards, hot tornadic winds arise in the spring, and in summer the prairie is an anvil's edge. The grass turns brittle and brown, and it cracks beneath your feet. There are green belts along the rivers and creeks, linear groves of hickory and pecan, willow and witch hazel. At a distance in July or August the steaming foliage seems almost to writhe in fire. Great green and yellow grasshoppers are everywhere in the tall grass, popping up like corn to sting the flesh, and tortoises crawl about on the red earth, going nowhere in the plenty of time. Loneliness is an aspect of the land. All things in the plain are isolate; there is no confusion of objects in the eye, but *one* hill or *one* tree or *one* man. To look upon that landscape in the early morning, with the sun at your back, is to lose the sense of proportion. Your imagination comes to life, and this, you think, is where Creation was begun.

I returned to Rainy Mountain in July. My grandmother had died in the spring, and I wanted to be at her grave. She had lived to be very old and at last infirm. Her only living daughter was with her when she died, and I was told that in death her face was that of a child.

I like to think of her as a child. When she was born, the Kiowas were living the last great moment of their history. For more than a hundred years they had controlled the open range from the Smoky Hill River to the Red, from the headwaters of the Canadian to the fork of the Arkansas and Cimarron. In alliance with the Comanches, they had ruled the whole of the southern Plains. War was their sacred business, and they were among the finest horsemen the world has ever known. But warfare for the Kiowas was preeminently a matter of disposition rather than of survival, and they never understood the grim, unrelenting advance of the U.S. Cavalry. When at last, divided and ill-provisioned, they were driven onto the Staked Plains in the cold rains of autumn, they fell into panic. In Palo Duro Canyon they abandoned their crucial stores to pillage and had nothing then but their lives. In order to save themselves, they surrendered to the soldiers at Fort Sill and were imprisoned in the old stone corral that now stands as a military museum. My grandmother was spared the humiliation of those high gray walls by eight or ten years, but she must have known from birth the affliction of defeat, the dark brooding of old warriors.

Her name was Aho, and she belonged to the last culture to evolve in North America. Her forebears came down from the high country in western Montana nearly three centuries ago. They were a mountain people, a mysterious tribe of hunters whose language has never been positively classified in any major group. In the late seventeenth century they began a long migration to the south and east. It was a journey toward the dawn, and it led to a golden age. Along the way the Kiowas were befriended by the Crows, who gave them the culture and religion of the Plains. They acquired horses, and their ancient nomadic spirit was suddenly free of the ground. They acquired Tai-me, the sacred Sun Dance doll, from that moment the object and symbol of their worship, and so shared in the divinity of the sun. Not least, they acquired the sense of destiny, therefore courage and pride. When they entered upon the southern Plains they had been transformed. No longer were they slaves to the simple necessity of survival; they were a lordly and dangerous society of fighters and thieves, hunters and priests of the sun. According to their origin myth, they entered the world through a hollow log. From one point of view, their migration was the fruit of an old prophecy, for indeed they emerged from a sunless world.

Although my grandmother lived out her long life in the shadow of Rainy Mountain, the immense landscape of the continental interior lay like memory in her blood. She could tell of the Crows, whom she had never seen, and of the Black Hills, where she had never been. I wanted to see in reality what she had seen more perfectly in the mind's eye, and traveled fifteen hundred miles to begin my pilgrimage.

Yellowstone, it seemed to me, was the top of the world, a region of deep lakes and dark timber, canyons and waterfalls. But, beautiful as it is, one might have the sense of confinement there. The skyline in all directions is close at hand, the high wall of the woods and deep cleavages of shade. There is a perfect freedom in the mountains, but it belongs to the eagle and the elk, the badger and the bear. The Kiowas reckoned their stature by the distance they could see, and they were bent and blind in the wilderness.

Descending eastward, the highland meadows are a

stairway to the plain. In July the inland slope of the Rockies is luxuriant with flax and buckwheat, stonecrop and larkspur. The earth unfolds and the limit of the land recedes. Clusters of trees, and animals grazing far in the distance, cause the vision to reach away and wonder to build upon the mind. The sun follows a longer course in the day, and the sky is immense beyond all comparison. The great billowing clouds that sail upon it are shadows that move upon the grain like water, dividing light. Farther down, in the land of the Crows and Blackfeet, the plain is yellow. Sweet clover takes hold of the hills and bends upon itself to cover and seal the soil. There the Kiowas paused on their way; they had come to the place where they must change their lives. The sun is at home on the plains. Precisely there does it have the certain character of a god. When the Kiowas came to the land of the Crows, they could see the dark lees of the hills at dawn across the Bighorn River, the profusion of light on the grain shelves, the oldest deity ranging after the solstices. Not yet would they veer southward to the caldron of the land that lay below; they must wean their blood from the northern winter and hold the mountains a while longer in their view. They bore Tai-me in procession to the east.

A dark mist lay over the Black Hills, and the land was like iron. At the top of a ridge I caught sight of Devil's Tower upthrust against the gray sky as if in the birth of time the core of the earth had broken through its crust and the motion of the world was begun. There are things in nature that engender an awful quiet in the heart of man; Devil's Tower is one of them. Two centuries ago, because they could not do otherwise, the Kiowas made a legend at the base of the rock. My grandmother said:

Eight children were there at play, seven sisters and their brother. Suddenly the boy was struck dumb; he trembled and began to run upon his hands and feet. His fingers became claws, and his body was covered with fur. Directly there was a bear where the boy had been. The sisters were terrified; they ran, and the bear after them. They came to the stump of a great tree, and the tree spoke to them. It bade them climb upon it, and as they did so it began to rise into the air. The bear came to kill them, but they were just beyond its reach. It reared against the tree and scored the bark all around with its claws. The seven sisters were borne into the sky, and they became the stars of the Big Dipper.

From that moment, and so long as the legend lives, the Kiowas have kinsmen in the night sky. Whatever they were in the mountains, they could be no more. However tenuous their well-being, however much they had suffered and would suffer again, they had found a way out of the wilderness.

My grandmother had a reverence for the sun, a holy regard that now is all but gone out of mankind. There was a wariness in her, and an ancient awe. She was a Christian in her later years, but she had come a long way about, and she never forgot her birthright. As a child she had been to the Sun Dances; she had taken part in those annual rites, and by them she had learned the restoration of her people in the presence of Tai-me. She was about seven when the last Kiowa Sun Dance was held in 1887 on the Washita River above Rainy Mountain Creek. The buffalo were gone. In order to consummate the ancient sacrifice—to impale the head of a buffalo bull upon the medicine tree—a delegation of old men journeyed into Texas, there to beg and barter for an animal from the Goodnight herd. She was ten when the Kiowas came together for the last time as a living Sun Dance culture. They could find no buffalo; they had to hang an old hide from the sacred tree. Before the dance could begin, a company of soldiers rode out from Fort Sill under orders to disperse the tribe. Forbidden without cause the essential act of their faith, having seen the wild herds slaughtered and left to rot upon the ground, the Kiowas backed away forever from the medicine tree. That was July 20, 1890, at the great bend of the Washita. My grandmother was there. Without bitterness, and for as long as she lived, she bore a vision of deicide.

Now that I can have her only in memory, I see my grandmother in the several postures that were peculiar to her: standing at the wood stove on a winter morning and turning meat in a great iron skillet; sitting at the south window, bent above her beadwork, and afterwards, when her vision failed, looking down for a long time into the fold of her hands; going out upon a cane, very slowly as she did when the weight of age came upon her; praying. I remember her most often at prayer. She made long, rambling prayers out of suffering and hope, having seen many things. I was never sure that I had the right to hear, so exclusive were they of all mere custom and company. The last time I saw her she prayed standing by the side of her bed at night, naked to the waist, the light of a kerosene lamp moving upon her dark skin. Her long, black hair, always drawn and braided in the day, lay upon her shoulders and against her breasts like a shawl. I do not speak Kiowa, and I never understood her prayers, but there was something inherently sad in the sound, some merest hesitation upon the syllables of sorrow. She began in a high and descending pitch, exhausting her breath to silence; then again and again—and always the same intensity of effort, of something that is, and is not, like urgency in the human voice. Transported so in the dancing light among the shadows of her room, she seemed beyond the reach of time. But that was illusion; I think I knew then that I should not see her again.

Houses are like sentinels in the plain, old keepers of the weather watch. There, in a very little while,

wood takes on the appearance of great age. All colors wear soon away in the wind and rain, and then the wood is burned gray and the grain appears and the nails turn red with rust. The windowpanes are black and opaque; you imagine there is nothing within, and indeed there are many ghosts, bones given up to the land. They stand here and there against the sky, and you approach them for a longer time than you expect. They belong in the distance; it is their domain.

Once there was a lot of sound in my grandmother's house, a lot of coming and going, feasting and talk. The summers there were full of excitement and reunion. The Kiowas are a summer people; they abide the cold and keep to themselves, but when the season turns and the land becomes warm and vital they cannot hold still; an old love of going returns upon them. The aged visitors who came to my grandmother's house when I was a child were made of lean and leather, and they bore themselves upright. They wore great black hats and bright ample shirts that shook in the wind. They rubbed fat upon their hair and wound their braids with strips of colored cloth. Some of them painted their faces and carried the scars of old and cherished enmities. They were an old council of warlords, come to remind and be reminded of who they were. Their wives and daughters served them well. The women might indulge themselves; gossip was at once the mark and compensation of their servitude. They made loud and elaborate talk among themselves, full of jest and gesture, fright and false alarm. They went abroad in fringed and flowered shawls, bright beadwork and German silver. They were at home in the kitchen, and they prepared meals that were banquets.

There were frequent prayer meetings, and great nocturnal feasts. When I was a child I played with my cousins outside, where the lamplight fell upon the ground and the singing of the old people rose up around us and carried away into the darkness. There were a lot of good things to eat, a lot of laughter and surprise. And afterwards, when the quiet returned, I lay down with my grandmother and could hear the frogs away by the river and feel the motion of the air.

Now there is a funeral silence in the rooms, the endless wake of some final word. The walls have closed in upon my grandmother's house. When I returned to it in mourning, I saw for the first time in my life how small it was. It was late at night, and there was a white moon, nearly full. I sat for a long time on the stone steps by the kitchen door. From there I would see out across the land; I could see the long row of trees by the creek, the low light upon the rolling plains, and the stars of the Big Dipper. Once I looked at the moon and caught sight of a strange thing. A cricket had perched upon the handrail, only a few inches away from me. My line of vision was such that the creature filled the moon like a fossil. It had gone there, I thought, to live and die, for there, of all places, was its small definition made whole and eternal. A warm wind rose up and purled like the longing within me.

The next morning I awoke at dawn and went out on the dirt road to Rainy Mountain. It was already hot, and the grasshoppers began to fill the air. Still, it was early in the morning, and the birds sang out of the shadows. The long yellow grass on the mountain shone in the bright light, and a scissortail hied above the land. There, where it ought to be, at the end of a long and legendary way, was my grandmother's grave. Here and there on the dark stones were ancestral names. Looking back once, I saw the mountain and came away.

THE SETTING OUT[1]

I

You know, everything had to begin, and this is how it was: the Kiowas came one by one into the world through a hollow log. They were many more than now, but not all of them got out. There was a woman whose body was swollen up with child, and she got stuck in the log. After that, no one could get through, and that is why the Kiowas are a small tribe in number. They looked all around and saw the world. It made them glad to see so many things. They called themselves *Kwuda,* "coming out."

They called themselves Kwuda *and later* Tepda, *both of which mean "coming out." And later still they took the name* Gaigwu, *a name which can be taken to indicate something of which the two halves differ from each other in appearance. It was once a custom among Kiowa warriors that they cut their hair on the right side of the head only and on a line level with the lobe of the ear, while on the left they let the hair grow long and wore it in a thick braid wrapped in otter skin. "Kiowa" is indicated in sign language by holding the hand palm up and slightly cupped to the right side of the head and rotating it back and forth from the wrist. "Kiowa" is thought to derive from the softened Comanche form of* Gaigwu.

I remember coming out upon the northern Great Plains in the late spring. There were meadows of blue and yellow wildflowers on the slopes, and I could see the still, sunlit plain below, reaching away out of sight. At first there is no discrimination in the eye, nothing but the land itself, whole and impenetrable. But then smallest things begin to stand out of the depths—herds and rivers and groves—and each of these has perfect being in terms of distance and of silence and of age. Yes, I thought, now I see the earth as it really is; never again will I see things as I saw them yesterday or the day before.

II

They were going along, and some were hunting. An antelope was killed and quartered in the meadow. Well, one of the big chiefs came up and took the udders of that animal for himself, but another big chief wanted those udders also, and there was a great quarrel between them. Then, in anger, one of these chiefs gathered all of his followers together and went away. They are called *Azatanhop,* "the udder-angry travelers off." No one knows where they went or what happened to them.

This is one of the oldest memories of the tribe. There have been reports of a people in the Northwest who speak a language that is similar to Kiowa.

In the winter of 1848–49, the buffalo ranged away from easy reach, and food was scarce. There was an antelope drive in the vicinity of Bent's Fort, Colorado. According to ancient custom, antelope medicine was made, and the Kiowas set out on foot and on horseback—men, women, and children— after game. They formed a great circle, inclosing a large area of the plain, and began to converge upon the center. By this means antelope and other animals were trapped and killed, often with clubs and even with the bare hands. By necessity were the Kiowas reminded of their ancient ways.

One morning on the high plains of Wyoming I saw several pronghorns in the distance. They were moving very slowly at an angle away from me, and they were almost invisible in the tall brown and yellow grass. They ambled along in their own wilderness dimension of time, as if no notion of flight could ever come upon them. But I remembered once having seen a frightened buck on the run, how the white rosette of its rump seemed to hang for the smallest fraction of time at the top of each frantic bound—like a succession of sunbursts against the purple hills.

---

1. Each episode of the journey is narrated in three voices: the legendary, the historical, and the contemporary.

Before there were horses the Kiowas had need of dogs. That was a long time ago, when dogs could talk. There was a man who lived alone; he had been thrown away, and he made his camp here and there on the high ground. Now it was dangerous to be alone, for there were enemies all around. The man spent his arrows hunting food. He had one arrow left, and he shot a bear; but the bear was only wounded and it ran away. The man wondered what to do. Then a dog came up to him and said that many enemies were coming; they were close by and all around. The man could think of no way to save himself. But the dog said: "You know, I have puppies. They are young and weak and they have nothing to eat. If you will take care of my puppies, I will show you how to get away." The dog led the man here and there, around and around, and they came to safety.

A hundred years ago the Comanche Ten Bears re-marked upon the great number of horses which the Kiowas owned. "When we first knew you," he said, "you had nothing but dogs and sleds." It was so; the dog is primordial. Perhaps it was dreamed into being.

The principal warrior society of the Kiowas was the Ka-itsenko, "Real Dogs," and it was made up of ten men only, the ten most brave. Each of these men wore a long ceremonial sash and carried a sacred arrow. In time of battle he must by means of this arrow impale the end of his sash to the earth and stand his ground to the death. Tradition has it that the founder of the Ka-itsenko had a dream in which he saw a band of warriors, outfitted after the fashion of the society, being led by a dog. The dog sang the song of the Ka-itsenko, then said to the dreamer: "You are a dog; make a noise like a dog and sing a dog song."

There were always dogs about my grandmother's house. Some of them were nameless and lived a life of their own. They belonged there in a sense that the word "ownership" does not include. The old people paid them scarcely any attention, but they should have been sad, I think, to see them go.

Long ago there were bad times. The Kiowas were hungry and there was no food. There was a man who heard his children cry from hunger, and he went out to look for food. He walked four days and became very weak. On the fourth day he came to a great canyon. Suddenly there was thunder and lightning. A voice spoke to him and said, "Why are you following me? What do you want?" The man was afraid. The thing standing before him had the feet of a deer, and its body was covered with feathers. The man answered that the Kiowas were hungry. "Take me with you," the voice said, "and I will give you whatever you want." From that day Tai-me has belonged to the Kiowas.

The great central figure of the kado, or Sun Dance, ceremony is the taime. This is a small image, less than 2 feet in length, representing a human figure dressed in a robe of white feathers, with a head-dress consisting of a single upright feather and pendants of ermine skin, with numerous strands of blue beads around its neck, and painted upon the face, breast, and back with designs symbolic of the sun and moon. The image itself is of dark-green stone, in form rudely resembling a human head and bust, probably shaped by art like the stone fetishes of the Pueblo tribes. It is preserved in a rawhide box in charge of the hereditary keeper, and is never under any circumstances exposed to view except at the annual Sun Dance, when it is fastened to a short upright stick planted within the medicine lodge, near the western side. It was last exposed in 1888.—Mooney

Once I went with my father and grandmother to see the Tai-me bundle. It was suspended by means of a strip of ticking from the fork of a small cere-monial tree. I made an offering of bright red cloth, and my grandmother prayed aloud. It seemed a long time that we were there. I had never come into the presence of Tai-me before—nor have I since. There was a great holiness all about in the room, as if an old person had died there or a child had been born.

A long time ago there were two brothers. It was winter, and the buffalo had wandered far away. Food was very scarce. The two brothers were hungry, and they wondered what to do. One of them got up in the early morning and went out, and he found a lot of fresh meat there on the ground in front of the tipi. He was very happy, and he called his brother outside. "Look," he said. "Something very good has happened, and we have plenty of food." But his brother was afraid and said: "This is too strange a thing. I believe that we had better not eat that meat." But the first brother scolded him and said that he was foolish. Then he went ahead and ate of the meat all by himself. In a little while something awful happened to him; he began to change. When it was all over, he was no longer a man; he was some kind of water beast with little short legs and a long, heavy tail. Then he spoke to his brother and said: "You were right, and you must not eat of that meat. Now I must go and live in the water, but we are brothers, and you ought to come and see me now and then." After that the man went down to the water's edge, sometimes, and called his brother out. He told him how things were with the Kiowas.

some awful commotion beneath the surface

During the peyote ritual a fire is kept burning in the center of the tipi, inclosed within a crescent-shaped altar. On top of the altar there is a single, sacred peyote. After the chief priest utters the opening prayer, four peyotes are given to each celebrant, who eats them one after another. Then, in turn, each man sings four sacred songs, and all the while there is the sound of the rattle and the drum—and the fitful, many-colored glare of the fire. The songs go on all through the night, broken only by intervals of prayer, additional distributions of peyote, and, at midnight, a peculiar baptismal ceremony.

Mammedaty was a peyote man, and he was therefore distinguished by these things: a necklace of beans, a beaded staff and rattle, an eagle-bone whistle, and a fan made from the feathers of a water bird. He saw things that other men do not see. Once a heavy rain caused the Washita River to overflow and Rainy Mountain Creek to swell and "back up." Mammedaty went to the creek, near the crossing, to swim. And while he was there, the water began strangely to move against him, slowly at first, then fast, in high, hard waves. There was some awful commotion beneath the surface, and Mammedaty got out of the water and ran away. Later he went back to that place. There was a wide swath in the brush of the bank and the tracks of a huge animal, leading down to the water's edge.

THE GOING ON

If an arrow is well made, it will have tooth marks upon it. That is how you know. The Kiowas made fine arrows and straightened them in their teeth. Then they drew them to the bow to see if they were straight. Once there was a man and his wife. They were alone at night in their tipi. By the light of the fire the man was making arrows. After a while he caught sight of something. There was a small opening in the tipi where two hides were sewn together. Someone was there on the outside, looking in. The man went on with his work, but he said to his wife: "Someone is standing outside. Do not be afraid. Let us talk easily, as of ordinary things." He took up an arrow and straightened it in his teeth; then, as it was right for him to do, he drew it to the bow and took aim, first in this direction and then in that. And all the while he was talking, as if to his wife. But this is how he spoke: "I know that you are there on the outside, for I can feel your eyes upon me. If you are a Kiowa, you will understand what I am saying, and you will speak your name." But there was no answer, and the man went on in the same way, pointing the arrow all around. At last his aim fell upon the place where his enemy stood, and he let go of the string. The arrow went straight to the enemy's heart.

The old men were the best arrowmakers, for they could bring time and patience to their craft. The young men—the fighters and hunters—were willing to pay a high price for arrows that were well made.

When my father was a boy, an old man used to come to Mammedaty's house and pay his respects. He was a lean old man in braids and was impressive in his age and bearing. His name was Cheney, and he was an arrowmaker. Every morning, my father tells me, Cheney would paint his wrinkled face, go out, and pray aloud to the rising sun. In my mind I can see that man as if he were there now. I like to watch him as he makes his prayer. I know where he stands and where his voice goes on the rolling grasses and where the sun comes up on the land. There, at dawn, you can feel the silence. It is cold and clear and deep like water. It takes hold of you and will not let you go.

The Kiowa language is hard to understand, but, you know, the storm spirit understands it. This is how it was: Long ago the Kiowas decided to make a horse; they decided to make it out of clay, and so they began to shape the clay with their hands. Well, the horse began to be. But it was a terrible, terrible thing. It began to writhe, slowly at first, then faster and faster until there was a great commotion everywhere. The wind grew up and carried everything away; great trees were uprooted, and even the buffalo were thrown up into the sky. The Kiowas were afraid of that awful thing, and they went running about, talking to it. And at last it was calm. Even now, when they see the storm clouds gathering, the Kiowas know what it is: that a strange wild animal roams on the sky. It has the head of a horse and the tail of a great fish. Lightning comes from its mouth, and the tail, whipping and thrashing on the air, makes the high, hot wind of the tornado. But they speak to it, saying "Pass over me." They are not afraid of *Man-ka-ih*, for it understands their language.

At times the plains are bright and calm and quiet; at times they are black with the sudden violence of weather. Always there are winds.

A few feet from the southwest corner of my grandmother's house, there is a storm cellar. It will be there, I think, when the house and the arbor and the barn have disappeared. There are many of those crude shelters in that part of the world. They conform to the shape of the land and are scarcely remarkable: low earthen mounds with heavy wooden trapdoors that appear to open upon the underworld. I have seen the wind drive the rain so hard that a grown man could not open the door against it, and once, descending into that place, I saw the whole land at night become visible and blue and phosphorescent in the flash of lightning.

whipping and thrashing on the air

XVIII

You know, the Kiowas are a summer people. Once upon a time a group of young men sat
down in a circle and spoke of mighty things. This is what they said: "When the
fall of the year comes around, where does the summer go? Where does it live?" They
decided to follow the sun southward to its home, and so they set out on horseback.
They rode for days and weeks and months, farther to the south than any Kiowa had ever
gone before, and they saw many strange and wonderful things. At last they came to the
place where they saw the strangest thing of all. Night was coming on, and they were
very tired of riding; they made camp in a great thicket. All but one of them went
right to sleep. He was a good hunter, and he could see well in the moonlight. He
caught sight of something: men were all about in the trees, moving silently from limb
to limb. They darted across the face of the full moon, *and he saw that they were small
and had tails!* He could not believe his eyes, but the next morning he told the others
of what he had seen. They only laughed at him and told him not to eat such a large
supper again. But later, as they were breaking camp, a certain feeling came over
them all at once: they felt that they were being watched. And when they
looked up, the small men with tails began to race about in the limbs
overhead. That is when the Kiowas turned around and came away; they had
had quite enough of that place. They had found the sun's home after
all, they reasoned, and they were hungry for the good buffalo
meat of their homeland.

*It is unnecessary to dilate on the revolution made
in the life of the Indian by the possession of the horse.
Without it he was a half-starved skulker
in the timber, creeping up on foot toward the unwary
deer or building a brush corral with infinite
labor to surround a herd of antelope, and seldom
venturing more than a few days' journey from home.
With the horse he was transformed into the daring
buffalo hunter, able to procure in a single day enough
food to supply his family for a year, leaving
him free then to sweep the plains with his war parties
along a range of a thousand miles.—Mooney*

he was
transformed into
a daring buffalo hunter

*Some of my earliest memories are of the summers on Rainy Mountain Creek,
when we lived in the arbor, on the north side of my grandmother's house. From
there you could see downhill to the pecan grove, the dense, dark growth along
the water, and beyond, the long sweep of the earth itself, curving out on the
sky. The arbor was open on all sides to the light and the air and the sounds
of the land. You could see far and wide even at night, by the light of the moon;
there was nothing to stand in your way. And when the season turned and it was
necessary to move back into the house, there was a sense of confinement and
depression for a time. Now and then in winter, when I passed by the arbor on
my way to draw water at the well, I looked inside and thought of the summer.
The hard dirt floor was dark red in color—the color of pipestone.*

THE CLOSING IN

XX

Once there was a man who owned a fine hunting horse. It was black and fast and afraid of nothing. When it was turned upon an enemy it charged in a straight line and struck at full speed; the man need have no hand upon the rein. But, you know, that man knew fear. Once during a charge he turned that animal from its course. That was a bad thing. The hunting horse died of shame.

In 1861 a Sun Dance was held near the Arkansas River in Kansas. As an offering to Tai-me, a spotted horse was left tied to a pole in the medicine lodge, where it starved to death. Later in that year an epidemic of smallpox broke out in the tribe, and the old man Gaapiatan sacrificed one of his best horses, a fine black-eared animal, that he and his family might be spared.

I like to think of old man Gaapiatan and his horse. I think I know how much he loved that animal; I think I know what was going on in his mind: If you will give me my life and the lives of my family, I will give you the life of this black-eared horse.

XXII

Mammedaty was the grandson of Guipahgo, and he got on well most of the time. But, you know, one time he lost his temper. This is how it was: There were several horses in a pasture, and Mammedaty wanted to get them out. A fence ran all the way around and there was just one gate. There was a lot of ground inside. He could not get those horses out. One of them led the others; every time they were driven up to the gate, that one wheeled and ran as fast as it could to the other side. Well, that went on for a long time, and Mammedaty burned up. He ran to the house and got his bow and arrows. The horses were running in single file, and he shot at the one that was causing all that trouble. He missed, though, and the arrow went deep into the neck of the second horse.

In the winter of 1852–53, a Pawnee boy who had been held as a captive among the Kiowas succeeded in running away. He took with him an especially fine hunting horse, known far and wide as Guadaltseyu, "Little Red." That was the most important event of the winter. The loss of that horse was a hard thing to bear.

Years ago there was a box of bones in the barn, and I used to go there to look at them. Later someone stole them, I believe. They were the bones of a horse which Mammedaty called by the name "Little Red." It was a small bay, nothing much to look at, I have heard, but it was the fastest runner in that whole corner of the world. White men and Indians alike came from far and near to match their best animals against it, but it never lost a race. I have often thought about that red horse. There have been times when I thought I understood how it was that a man might be moved to preserve the bones of a horse— and another to steal them away.

EPILOGUE

During the first hours after midnight on the morning of November 13, 1833, it seemed that the world was coming to an end. Suddenly the stillness of the night was broken; there were brilliant flashes of light in the sky, light of such intensity that people were awakened by it. With the speed and density of a driving rain, stars were falling in the universe. Some were brighter than Venus; one was said to be as large as the moon.

That most brilliant shower of Leonid meteors has a special place in the memory of the Kiowa people. It is among the earliest entries in the Kiowa calendars, and it marks the beginning as it were of the historical period in the tribal mind. In the preceding year Tai-me had been stolen by a band of Osages, and although it was later returned, the loss was an almost unimaginable tragedy; and in 1837 the Kiowas made the first of their treaties with the United States. The falling stars seemed to image the sudden and violent disintegration of an old order.

But indeed the golden age of the Kiowas had been short-lived, ninety or a hundred years, say, from about 1740. The culture would persist for a while in decline, until about 1875, but then it would be gone, and there would be very little material evidence that it had ever been. Yet it is within the reach of memory still, though tenuously now, and moreover it is even defined in a remarkably rich and living verbal tradition which demands to be preserved for its own sake. The living memory and the verbal tradition which transcends it were brought together for me once and for all in the person of Ko-sahn.

A hundred-year-old woman came to my grandmother's house one afternoon in July. Aho was dead; Mammedaty had died before I was born. There were very few Kiowas left who could remember the Sun Dances; Ko-sahn was one of them; she was a grown woman when my grandparents came into the world. Her body was twisted and her face deeply lined with age. Her thin white hair was held in place by a cap of black netting, though she wore braids as well, and she had but one eye. She was dressed in the manner of a Kiowa matron, a dark, full-cut dress that reached nearly to the ankles, full, flowing sleeves, and a wide, apron-like sash. She sat on a bench in the arbor so concentrated in her great age that she seemed extraordinarily small. She was quiet for a time—she might almost have been asleep—and then she began to speak and to sing. She spoke of many things, and once she spoke of the Sun Dance:

My sisters and I were very young; that was a long time ago. Early one morning they came to wake us up. They had brought a great buffalo in from the plain. Everyone went out to see and to pray. We heard a great many voices. One man said that the lodge was almost ready. We were told to go there, and someone gave me a piece of cloth. It was very beautiful. Then I asked what I ought to do with it, and they said that I must tie it to the Tai-me tree. There were other pieces of cloth on the tree, and so I put mine there as well.

When the lodge frame was finished, a woman—sometimes a man—began to sing. It was like this:

> *Everything is ready.*
> *Now the four societies must go out.*
> *They must go out and get the leaves,*
>   *the branches for the lodge.*

And when the branches were tied in place, again there was singing:

> *Let the boys go out.*
> *Come on, boys, now we must get the earth.*

The boys began to shout. Now they were not just ordinary boys, not all of them; they were those for whom prayers had been made, and they were dressed in different ways. There was an old, old woman. She had something on her back. The boys went out to see. The old woman had a bag full of earth on her back. It was a certain kind of sandy earth. That is what they must have in the lodge. The dancers must dance upon the sandy earth. The old woman held a digging tool in her hand. She turned towards the south and pointed with her lips. It was like a kiss, and she began to sing:

> *We have brought the earth.*
> *Now it is time to play;*
> *As old as I am, I still have the*
>   *feeling of play.*

That was the beginning of the Sun Dance. The dancers treated themselves with buffalo medicine, and slowly they began to take their steps . . . And all the people were around, and they wore splendid things—beautiful buckskin and beads. The chiefs wore necklaces, and their pendants shone like the sun. There were many people, and oh, it was beautiful! That was the beginning of the Sun Dance. It was all for Tai-me, you know, and it was a long time ago.

It was—all of this and more—a quest, a going forth upon the way to Rainy Mountain. Probably Ko-sahn too is dead now. At times, in the quiet of evening, I think she must have wondered, dreaming, who she was. Was she become in her sleep that old purveyor of the sacred earth, perhaps, that ancient one who, old as she was, still had the feeling of play? And in her mind, at times, did she see the falling stars?

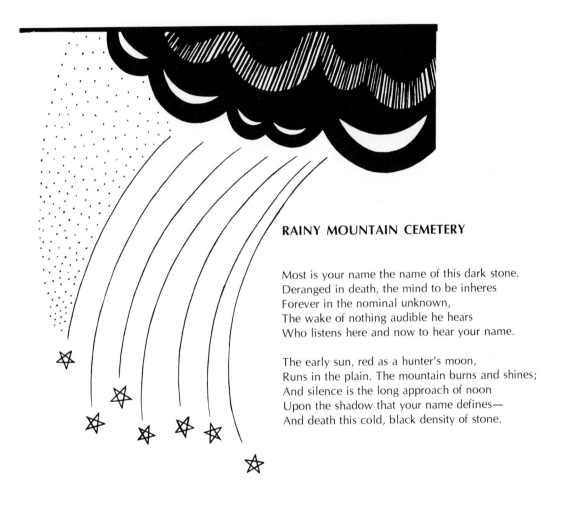

RAINY MOUNTAIN CEMETERY

Most is your name the name of this dark stone.
Deranged in death, the mind to be inheres
Forever in the nominal unknown,
The wake of nothing audible he hears
Who listens here and now to hear your name.

The early sun, red as a hunter's moon,
Runs in the plain. The mountain burns and shines;
And silence is the long approach of noon
Upon the shadow that your name defines—
And death this cold, black density of stone.

DISCUSSION

Many literary genres are to be found in Momaday's *The Way to Rainy Mountain*. Prose carries the narrative, with bits of poetry assisting. The long journey of the Kiowas, from western Montana to the great northern Plains of Oklahoma, is an epic subject. To these genres Momaday adds timeless interludes of myth, bits of half-remembered legend, flashes of true history, a personal history made up of strongly-felt recollections from his boyhood, and intimate domestic scenes from the lives of an almost vanished people. This unusual blending of fact, fiction, and imagination provides a deeply moving narrative.

"The journey began one day long ago on the edge of the northern Plains," Momaday begins, and the reader is in the presence of **epic.** It was an epic journey that Aeneas (in Virgil's *Aeneid*) undertook to found another Troy. It was an epic journey that is described in the Biblical Exodus, in which the children of Israel wander for forty years in search of a new homeland. "They entered the world through a hollow log," the Kiowas believed, and Momaday has put the reader in the presence of myth. **Myth** is a narrative that explains how things came to be—how the world was created, how mankind was made or entered the world, how horses or stars were formed—stories of the mysteries of creation that could have no recorded history.

Legend, another part of the compound material Momaday uses, deals with events close to the mythical past, but based at least in part on the deeds of a historical hero. An example of legend may be found in Part II of *The Way to Rainy Mountain*, in the conflict of the chiefs over the antelope. The event is history, but dim, an event half-forgotten but passed on from generation to generation.

History, unlike myth or legend, has something approximating a date, a date that is like a peg to hang an event on. We can find an example of true history in Part III, because it begins "A hundred years ago . . ." and so has become a little more exact than legend.

Personal history is about events within the author's lifetime, including hearsay. It is more narrow than the great body of myth and legend, since no one person knows the entire story of his tribe or family from personal experience. He may only give us his recollections, or quote ancient history, myth, and legend he has collected from older members of his society. Such personal history begins to be interwoven early in this Kiowa epic. When we read in Part I, "I remember coming out upon the northern Great Plains in the late spring," the reader is in the personal presence of the author. It is through his eyes that we gain something more valuable, perhaps, than that gained through history or its older forms: we gain personal glimpses of domestic scenes, of homelife intimately lived—his grandmother at prayer——or the re-creation of ancient life as it must have been, in the story of the arrow-maker and his wife.

Momaday has gone deeply into the re-creation of a vanished American culture, far beyond the early colonial legends about the Indians around Plymouth and far beyond the romanticized images of Longfellow's *Hiawatha*. This depth of feeling and meaning derive from his perspective *inside* the culture he writes about: it belongs to him and he belongs to it.

FOR EXPLORATION

1. Think about these statements from Momaday's Prologue and discuss whether you agree with them: *(a)* "In the course of that long migration they had come of age as a people." *(b)* "The imaginative experience and the historical express equally the traditions of man's reality."

2. Much can be learned about a writer by examining his choice of metaphors and similes. Momaday usually draws them from his personal experience, or adapts them to his material. The first simile we read in Momaday's writing appears in the second paragraph of the Prologue: "The young Plains culture of the Kiowas withered and died like grass that is burned in the prairie wind." Examine Momaday's metaphors and similes in terms of what they contribute to the effectiveness of the action described.

3. Find examples from other sources of: *(a)* myths; *(b)* legends; *(c)* personal history. Compare these examples with examples from Momaday. What do they have in common? How do they differ?

CREATIVE RESPONSE

1. Use whatever resources you can find to explore your own past. Parents will help, and grandparents will remember even more. Other relatives may surprise you with their lore about you and your ancestors. Write an account of your past (and that of your ancestors), drawing together as many anecdotes, legends, and stories as you are able to gather, casting them in the form that seems appropriate. Use *The Way to Rainy Mountain* as a model.

2. Select one of the stories or episodes from *The Way to Rainy Mountain* and dramatize or reenact it, with or without a script. Several students might work together on a script and a dramatization.

3. Provide photographic illustrations or accompaniment for the account of your past.

HARPER & ROW

UNIVERSITY OF CALIFORNIA, BERKELEY

BERKELEY · DAVIS · IRVINE · LOS ANGELES · RIVERSIDE · SAN DIEGO · SAN FRANCISCO  SANTA BARBARA · SANTA CRUZ

DEPARTMENT OF COMPARATIVE LITERATURE

DWINELLE HALL
BERKELEY, CALIFORNIA 94720

19 January 1972

Mr. James E. Miller, Jr.
Department of English
The University of Chicago
Chicago, Illinois 60637

Dear Mr. Miller:

The Kiowa folktales in The Way to Rainy Mountain were originally
printed, privately, at Santa Barbara, California under the title
The Journey of Tai-me. Later I thought of adding the commentaries.
It seemed to me that the tales in themselves, good as they were,
needed somehow to be revealed in another way. I did not want the
tales to be thought of as verbal artifacts; I wanted to indicate
that they were part of a rich, vital tradition of human thought and
expression. By proceeding through the three voices, the mythical,
the historical, and the personal from the prehistoric to the
contemporary it was possible, I think, to suggest an evolution of
storytelling and to illustrate the relationship between the oral
and written traditions.

I used as a principle of organization in The Way to Rainy Mountain
the device of the journey, the migration of the Kiowas from western
Montana to the Southern Plains. When the idea of the book was still
germinating in my mind I made that journey myself, partly to fix the
landscape in my imagination and partly to realize, almost in terms
of ritual, my heritage. It was a great experience, and I shall never
forget it.

Yours sincerely,

N. Scott Momaday

NSM:ae

Navarre Scott Momaday   1934 /

N. Scott Momaday was born in Lawton, Oklahoma, the son
of artists and educators. His father, who illustrated *The Way
to Rainy Mountain*, is the distinguished contemporary
Kiowa painter and art teacher Alfred Morris Momaday. His
mother, Natachee Scott Momaday, is a novelist and writer
of juvenile fiction as well as an artist and teacher.

Momaday spent his childhood on a number of Indian
reservations. He did his undergraduate work at the Univer-
sity of New Mexico and received his Ph.D. from Stanford
University. He now lives in California where he teaches
English and comparative literature at the University of
California, Berkeley.

Although his most recent publications have been fiction
and prose, Momaday has said that he thinks of himself
primarily as a poet. It was in poetry that he was awarded
a Stanford University Creative Writing Fellowship in 1959.
In 1968 a publishing house suggested he submit some
poetry; instead he sent them a novel, *House Made of Dawn*.
It is the story of an Indian veteran of World War II who,
returning to the Southwest, is unable to cope with the
expectations of two opposing cultures. *House Made of
Dawn* won the 1969 Pulitzer Prize.

The
First Seven Years

Bernard Malamud

FELD, the shoemaker, was annoyed that his helper, Sobel, was so insensitive to his reverie that he wouldn't for a minute cease his fanatic pounding at the other bench. He gave him a look, but Sobel's bald head was bent over the last as he worked and he didn't notice. The shoemaker shrugged and continued to peer through the partly frosted window at the near-sighted haze of falling February snow. Neither the shifting white blur outside, nor the sudden deep remembrance of the snowy Polish village where he had wasted his youth could turn his thoughts from Max the college boy, (a constant visitor in the mind since early that morning when Feld saw him trudging through the snowdrifts on his way to school) whom he so much respected because of the sacrifices he had made throughout the years—in winter or direst heat—to further his education. An old wish returned to haunt the shoemaker: that he had had a son instead of a daughter, but this blew away in the snow for Feld, if anything, was a practical man. Yet he could not help but contrast the diligence of the boy, who was a peddler's son, with Miriam's unconcern for an education. True, she was always with a book in her hand, yet when the opportunity arose for a college education, she had said no she would rather find a job. He had begged her to go, pointing out how many fathers could not afford to send their children to college, but she said she wanted to be independent. As for education, what was it, she asked, but books, which Sobel, who diligently read the classics, would as usual advise her on. Her answer greatly grieved her father.

A figure emerged from the snow and the door opened. At the counter the man withdrew from a wet paper bag a pair of battered shoes for repair. Who he was the shoemaker for a moment had no idea, then his heart trembled as he realized, before he had thoroughly discerned the face, that Max himself was standing there, embarrassedly explaining what he wanted done to his old shoes. Though Feld listened eagerly, he couldn't hear a word, for the opportunity that had burst upon him was deafening.

He couldn't exactly recall when the thought had occurred to him, because it was clear he had more than once considered suggesting to the boy that he go out with Miriam. But he had not dared speak, for if Max said no, how would he face him again? Or suppose Miriam, who harped so often on independence, blew up in anger and shouted at him for his meddling? Still, the chance was too good to let by: all it meant was an introduction. They might long ago have become friends had they happened to meet somewhere, therefore was it not his duty—an obligation—to bring them together, nothing more, a harmless connivance to replace an accidental encounter in the subway, let's say, or a mutual friend's introduction in the street? Just let him once see and talk to her and he would for sure be interested. As for Miriam, what possible harm for a working girl in an office, who met only loud-mouthed salesmen and illiterate shipping clerks, to make the acquaintance of a fine scholarly boy? Maybe he would awaken in her a desire to go to college; if not—the shoemaker's mind at last came to grips with the truth—let her marry an educated man and live a better life.

When Max finished describing what he wanted done to his shoes, Feld marked them, both with enormous holes in the soles which he pretended not to notice, with large white-chalk x's, and the rubber heels, thinned to the nails, he marked with o's, though it troubled him he might have mixed up the letters. Max inquired the price, and the shoemaker cleared his throat and asked the boy, above Sobel's insistent hammering, would he please

Reprinted with the permission of Farrar, Straus & Giroux, Inc. and Eyre & Spottiswoode (Publishers) Ltd. from THE MAGIC BARREL by Bernard Malamud, copyright © 1950, 1958 by Bernard Malamud.

step through the side door there into the hall. Though surprised, Max did as the shoemaker requested, and Feld went in after him. For a minute they were both silent, because Sobel had stopped banging, and it seemed they understood neither was to say anything until the noise began again. When it did, loudly, the shoemaker quickly told Max why he had asked to talk to him.

"Ever since you went to high school," he said, in the dimly-lit hallway, "I watched you in the morning go to the subway to school, and I said always to myself, this is a fine boy that he wants so much an education."

"Thanks," Max said, nervously alert. He was tall and grotesquely thin, with sharply cut features, particularly a beak-like nose. He was wearing a loose, long slushy overcoat that hung down to his ankles, looking like a rug draped over his bony shoulders, and a soggy, old brown hat, as battered as the shoes he had brought in.

"I am a business man," the shoemaker abruptly said to conceal his embarrassment, "so I will explain you right away why I talk to you. I have a girl, my daughter Miriam—she is nineteen—a very nice girl and also so pretty that everybody looks on her when she passes by in the street. She is smart, always with a book, and I thought to myself that a boy like you, an educated boy—I thought maybe you will be interested sometime to meet a girl like this." He laughed a bit when he had finished and was tempted to say more but had the good sense not to.

Max stared down like a hawk. For an uncomfortable second he was silent, then he asked, "Did you say nineteen?"

"Yes."

"Would it be all right to inquire if you have a picture of her?"

"Just a minute." The shoemaker went into the store and hastily returned with a snapshot that Max held up to the light.

"She's all right," he said.

Feld waited.

"And is she sensible—not the flighty kind?"

"She is very sensible."

After another short pause, Max said it was okay with him if he met her.

"Here is my telephone," said the shoemaker, hurriedly handing him a slip of paper. "Call her up. She comes home from work six o'clock."

Max folded the paper and tucked it away into his worn leather wallet.

"About the shoes," he said. "How much did you say they will cost me?"

"Don't worry about the price."

"I just like to have an idea."

"A dollar—dollar fifty. A dollar fifty," the shoemaker said.

At once he felt bad, for he usually charged two twenty-five for this kind of job. Either he should have asked the regular price or done the work for nothing.

Later, as he entered the store, he was startled by a violent clanging and looked up to see Sobel pounding with all his might upon the naked last. It broke, the iron striking the floor and jumping with a thump against the wall, but before the enraged shoemaker could cry out, the assistant had torn his hat and coat from the hook and rushed out into the snow.

So Feld, who had looked forward to anticipating how it would go with his daughter and Max, instead had a great worry on his mind. Without his temperamental helper he was a lost man, especially since it was years now that he had carried the store alone. The shoemaker had for an age suffered from a heart condition that threatened collapse if he dared exert himself. Five years ago, after an attack, it had appeared as though he would have either to sacrifice his business upon the auction block and live on a pittance thereafter, or put himself at the mercy of some unscrupulous employee who would in the end probably ruin him. But just at the moment of his darkest despair, this Polish refugee, Sobel, appeared one night from the street and begged for work. He was a stocky man, poorly dressed, with a bald head that had once been blond, a severely plain face and soft blue eyes prone to tears over the sad books he read, a young man but old—no one would have guessed thirty. Though he confessed he knew nothing of shoemaking, he said he was apt and would work for a very little if Feld taught him the trade. Thinking that with, after all, a landsman,[1] he would have less to fear than from a complete stranger, Feld took him on and within six weeks the refugee rebuilt as good a shoe as he, and not long thereafter expertly ran the business for the thoroughly relieved shoemaker.

Feld could trust him with anything and did, frequently going home after an hour or two at the store, leaving all the money in the till, knowing Sobel would guard every cent of it. The amazing thing was that he demanded so little. His wants were few; in money he wasn't interested—in nothing but books, it seemed—which he one by one lent to Miriam, together with his profuse, queer written comments, manufactured during his lonely rooming house evenings, thick pads of commentary which the shoemaker peered at and twitched his shoulders over as his daughter, from her fourteenth year, read page by sanctified page, as if the word of God were inscribed on them. To protect Sobel, Feld himself had to see that he received more than he asked for. Yet his conscience bothered him for not insisting that the assistant accept a better wage than he was getting, though Feld had honestly told him he could earn a handsome salary if he worked elsewhere, or maybe opened a place of his own. But the assistant answered, somewhat ungraciously, that he was not interested in going elsewhere, and though Feld frequently asked himself what keeps him here? why does he stay? he finally answered it that the man, no doubt because of his terrible experiences as a refugee, was afraid of the world.

After the incident with the broken last, angered by Sobel's behavior, the shoemaker decided to let him stew for a week in the rooming house, although his own strength was taxed dangerously and the business suffered. However, after several sharp nagging warnings from both his wife and daughter, he went finally in search of Sobel, as he had once before, quite

recently, when over some fancied slight—Feld had merely asked him not to give Miriam so many books to read because her eyes were strained and red—the assistant had left the place in a huff, an incident which, as usual, came to nothing for he had returned after the shoemaker had talked to him, and taken his seat at the bench. But this time, after Feld had plodded through the snow to Sobel's house—he had thought of sending Miriam but the idea became repugnant to him—the burly landlady at the door informed him in a nasal voice that Sobel was not at home, and though Feld knew this was a nasty lie, for where had the refugee to go? still for some reason he was not completely sure of—it may have been the cold and his fatigue—he decided not to insist on seeing him. Instead he went home and hired a new helper.

Having settled the matter, though not entirely to his satisfaction, for he had much more to do than before, and so, for example, could no longer lie late in bed mornings because he had to get up to open the store for the new assistant, a speechless, dark man with an irritating rasp as he worked, whom he would not trust with the key as he had Sobel. Furthermore, this one, though able to do a fair repair job, knew nothing of grades of leather or prices, so Feld had to make his own purchases; and every night at closing time it was necessary to count the money in the till and lock up. However, he was not dissatisfied, for he lived much in his thoughts of Max and Miriam. The college boy had called her, and they had arranged a meeting for this coming Friday night. The shoemaker would personally have preferred Saturday, which he felt would make it a date of the first magnitude, but he learned Friday was Miriam's choice, so he said nothing. The day of the week did not matter. What mattered was the aftermath. Would they like each other and want to be friends? He sighed at all the time that would have to go by before he knew for sure. Often he was tempted to talk to Miriam about the boy, to ask whether she thought she would like his type—he had told her only that he considered Max a nice boy and had suggested he call her—but the one time he tried she snapped at him—justly—how should she know?

At last Friday came. Feld was not feeling particularly well so he stayed in bed, and Mrs. Feld

---

1. *landsman*, a fellow countryman.

thought it better to remain in the bedroom with him when Max called. Miriam received the boy, and her parents could hear their voices, his throaty one, as they talked. Just before leaving, Miriam brought Max to the bedroom door and he stood there a minute, a tall, slightly hunched figure wearing a thick, droopy suit, and apparently at ease as he greeted the shoemaker and his wife, which was surely a good sign. And Miriam, although she had worked all day, looked fresh and pretty. She was a large-framed girl with a well-shaped body, and she had a fine open face and soft hair. They made, Feld thought, a first-class couple.

Miriam returned after 11:30. Her mother was already asleep, but the shoemaker got out of bed and after locating his bathrobe went into the kitchen, where Miriam, to his surprise, sat at the table, reading.

"So where did you go?" Feld asked pleasantly.

"For a walk," she said, not looking up.

"I advised him," Feld said, clearing his throat, "he shouldn't spend so much money."

"I didn't care."

The shoemaker boiled up some water for tea and sat down at the table with a cupful and a thick slice of lemon.

"So how," he sighed after a sip, "did you enjoy?"

"It was all right."

He was silent. She must have sensed his disappointment, for she added, "You can't really tell much the first time."

"You will see him again?"

Turning a page, she said that Max had asked for another date.

"For when?"

"Saturday."

"So what did you say?"

"What did I say?" she asked, delaying for a moment—"I said yes."

Afterwards she inquired about Sobel, and Feld, without exactly knowing why, said the assistant had got another job. Miriam said nothing more and began to read. The shoemaker's conscience did not trouble him; he was satisfied with the Saturday date.

During the week, by placing here and there a deft question, he managed to get from Miriam some information about Max. It surprised him to learn that the boy was not studying to be either a doctor or lawyer but was taking a business course leading to a degree in accountancy. Feld was a little disap-

pointed because he thought of accountants as bookkeepers and would have preferred "a higher profession." However, it was not long before he had investigated the subject and discovered that Certified Public Accountants were highly respected people, so he was thoroughly content as Saturday approached. But because Saturday was a busy day, he was much in the store and therefore did not see Max when he came to call for Miriam. From his wife he learned there had been nothing especially revealing about their meeting. Max had rung the bell and Miriam had got her coat and left with him— nothing more. Feld did not probe, for his wife was not particularly observant. Instead, he waited up for Miriam with a newspaper on his lap, which he scarcely looked at so lost was he in thinking of the future. He awoke to find her in the room with him, tiredly removing her hat. Greeting her, he was suddenly inexplicably afraid to ask anything about the evening. But since she volunteered nothing he was at last forced to inquire how she had enjoyed herself. Miriam began something non-committal but apparently changed her mind, for she said after a minute, "I was bored."

When Feld had sufficiently recovered from his anguished disappointment to ask why, she answered without hesitation, "Because he's nothing more than a materialist."

"What means this word?"

"He has no soul. He's only interested in things."

He considered her statement for a long time but then asked, "Will you see him again?"

"He didn't ask."

"Suppose he will ask you?"

"I won't see him."

He did not argue; however, as the days went by he hoped increasingly she would change her mind. He wished the boy would telephone, because he was sure there was more to him than Miriam, with her inexperienced eye, could discern. But Max didn't call. As a matter of fact he took a different route to school, no longer passing the shoemaker's store, and Feld was deeply hurt.

Then one afternoon Max came in and asked for his shoes. The shoemaker took them down from the shelf where he had placed them, apart from the other pairs. He had done the work himself and the soles and heels were well built and firm. The shoes had been highly polished and somehow looked better than new. Max's Adam's apple went up once when he saw them, and his eyes had little lights in them.

"How much?" he asked, without directly looking at the shoemaker.

"Like I told you before," Feld answered sadly. "One dollar fifty cents."

Max handed him two crumpled bills and received in return a newly-minted silver half dollar.

He left. Miriam had not been mentioned. That night the shoemaker discovered that his new assistant had been all the while stealing from him, and he suffered a heart attack.

Though the attack was very mild, he lay in bed for three weeks. Miriam spoke of going for Sobel, but sick as he was Feld rose in wrath against the idea. Yet in his heart he knew there was no other way, and the first weary day back in the shop thoroughly convinced him, so that night after supper he dragged himself to Sobel's rooming house.

He toiled up the stairs, though he knew it was bad for him, and at the top knocked at the door. Sobel opened it and the shoemaker entered. The room was a small, poor one, with a single window facing the street. It contained a narrow cot, a low table and several stacks of books piled haphazardly around on the floor along the wall, which made him think how queer Sobel was, to be uneducated and read so much. He had once asked him, Sobel, why you read so much? and the assistant could not answer him. Did you ever study in a college someplace? he had asked, but Sobel shook his head. He read, he said, to know. But to know what, the shoemaker demanded, and to know, why? Sobel never explained, which proved he read much because he was queer.

Feld sat down to recover his breath. The assistant was resting on his bed with his heavy back to the wall. His shirt and trousers were clean, and his stubby fingers, away from the shoemaker's bench, were strangely pallid. His face was thin and pale, as if he had been shut in this room since the day he had bolted from the store.

"So when you will come back to work?" Feld asked him.

To his surprise, Sobel burst out, "Never."

Jumping up, he strode over to the window that looked out upon the miserable street. "Why should I come back?" he cried.

"I will raise your wages."

"Who cares for your wages!"

The shoemaker, knowing he didn't care, was at at a loss what else to say.

"What do you want from me, Sobel?"

"Nothing."

"I always treated you like you was my son."

Sobel vehemently denied it. "So why you look for strange boys in the street they should go out with Miriam? Why you don't think of me?"

The shoemaker's hands and feet turned freezing cold. His voice became so hoarse he couldn't speak. At last he cleared his throat and croaked, "So what has my daughter got to do with a shoemaker thirty-five years old who works for me?"

"Why do you think I worked so long for you?" Sobel cried out. "For the stingy wages I sacrificed five years of my life so you could have to eat and drink and where to sleep?"

"Then for what?" shouted the shoemaker.

"For Miriam," he blurted—"for her."

The shoemaker, after a time, managed to say, "I pay wages in cash, Sobel," and lapsed into silence. Though he was seething with excitement, his mind was coldly clear, and he had to admit to himself he had sensed all along that Sobel felt this way. He had never so much as thought it consciously, but he had felt it and was afraid.

"Miriam knows?" he muttered hoarsely.

"She knows."

"You told her?"

"No."

"Then how does she know?"

"How does she know?" Sobel said, "because she knows. She knows who I am and what is in my heart."

Feld had a sudden insight. In some devious way, with his books and commentary, Sobel had given Miriam to understand that he loved her. The shoemaker felt a terrible anger at him for his deceit.

"Sobel, you are crazy," he said bitterly. "She will never marry a man so old and ugly like you."

Sobel turned black with rage. He cursed the shoemaker, but then, though he trembled to hold it in, his eyes filled with tears and he broke into deep sobs. With his back to Feld, he stood at the window, fists clenched, and his shoulders shook with his choked sobbing.

Watching him, the shoemaker's anger diminished. His teeth were on edge with pity for the man, and his eyes grew moist. How strange and sad that a refugee, a grown man, bald and old with his miseries, who had by the skin of his teeth escaped Hitler's incinerators,[2] should fall in love, when he had got to America, with a girl less than half his age. Day after day, for five years he had sat at his bench, cutting and hammering away, waiting for the girl to become a woman, unable to ease his heart with speech, knowing no protest but desperation.

"Ugly I didn't mean," he said half aloud.

Then he realized that what he had called ugly was not Sobel but Miriam's life if she married him. He felt for his daughter a strange and gripping sorrow, as if she were already Sobel's bride, the wife, after all, of a shoemaker, and had in her life no more than her mother had had. And all his dreams for her—why he had slaved and destroyed his heart with anxiety and labor—all these dreams of a better life were dead.

The room was quiet. Sobel was standing by the window reading, and it was curious that when he read he looked young.

"She is only nineteen," Feld said brokenly. "This is too young yet to get married. Don't ask her for two years more, till she is twenty-one, then you can talk to her."

Sobel didn't answer. Feld rose and left. He went slowly down the stairs but once outside, though it was an icy night and the crisp falling snow whitened the street, he walked with a stronger stride.

But the next morning, when the shoemaker arrived, heavy-hearted, to open the store, he saw he needn't have come, for his assistant was already seated at the last, pounding leather for his love. □

2. *Hitler's incinerators*, the ovens used by the Nazis for the mass-disposal of their victims' bodies.

DISCUSSION

Through his fiction, Malamud enters a world where life is hard and people really work and struggle for money and a bit of happiness. This literature comes from the American ghetto, the ghetto that prosperous Americans often ignore. It is a crowded place, filled with people fiercely and desperately fighting their condition, first- and second-generation Americans whose culture is still largely that of central or Eastern Europe. Though their lives are grim, Malamud finds dignity, charm, and humor in his characters.

"The First Seven Years" suggests the Biblical story of Jacob, who worked two seven-year periods to win Rachel (Genesis 29: 13–31). It is composed with the restraint that only a fine literary artist can manage. The reader never sees Sobel and Miriam together; they communicate intellectually through the world of books, and by a certain mutual sympathy that father Feld cannot even dimly understand. This love story, oddly enough, uses the time-worn device of the "eternal triangle," in which two men sue for a girl's favors. But in Malamud's hands the device is anything but time-worn. The reader never sees the three together; the rivalry is there, crucial to the outcome of the story, but never obvious.

FOR EXPLORATION

1. Of Malamud's four characters, Feld, Sobel, Miriam, and Max, which do you feel is the central one—which one most comes to life, which one can you most easily visualize?
2. Malamud's personages, though American, emerge as foreign in slight traces of mannerisms, speech, and attitudes. Cite what you noticed as "foreign."
3. Do you feel that your reading of Malamud's short story will influence you to observe lives such as these characters lived more sympathetically, with a knowledge that even "obscure destinies" are deep, complex, and interesting? Discuss.
4. (a) What lesson about life does Feld learn from the events he seeks to control? (b) Do you think it was Malamud's intention to present such a lesson, or did he intend to just observe and entertain?

CREATIVE RESPONSE

Malamud lets Feld make a discovery:

"Then he realized that what he had called ugly was not Sobel but Miriam's life if she married him. He felt for his daughter a strange and gripping sorrow, as if she were already Sobel's bride, the wife, after all, of a shoemaker, and had in her life no more than her mother had had."

Is this the attitude of all parents: wanting better lives for their children? What obligations do parents have with respect to their children? To what extent do they really know what would most satisfy the ambitions of the coming generation? Discuss these questions with your friends and their parents if possible. Then write an account of your views.

JILL KREMENTZ

Bernard Malamud   1914 /

Bernard Malamud was born and raised in Brooklyn, the son of Russian immigrants. He graduated from City College of New York and then in 1940, while earning his M.A. at Columbia University, began teaching evening English classes at his old high school. In 1949 he joined the English department of Oregon State University and in his twelve years there wrote a number of books. *The Assistant*

(1958), a novel about a poor New York Jewish shop-keeper and his assistant, is an acknowledged masterpiece. *The Magic Barrel* (1959), a collection of short stories which included "The First Seven Years," won the National Book Award. *The Fixer* (1966) won both the National Book Award and the Pulitzer Prize.

Malamud is painstaking in his work, constantly revising and rewriting. He has said, "But I know it's finished when I can no longer stand working on it. Valéry [a French poet and essayist] said that a work of art is never completed—it's abandoned."

The Nobel Prize

The Pulitzer Prize

The National Book Awards

NOBEL PRIZE MEDAL—NOBEL FOUNDATION

Nobel Prize   Alfred Nobel was the Swedish inventor of dynamite, and he realized with considerable guilt the destructive force he had let loose into the world. When he died in 1896, he attempted to atone for what he had done by leaving a fortune to Sweden for the establishment of the Nobel prizes for achievement in various sciences, for contribution to peace, and for distinguished work in literature. The Nobel prize for literature amounts to about $40,000 and results usually in international acclaim. Writers from a great variety of countries have won, including not only the well-known Western countries but also India, Japan, Chile, and Iceland. The awarding of the prize inevitably becomes at times a political issue, deepening the political tensions of the time. In 1958 the Russian poet-novelist Boris Pasternak, whose *Dr. Zhivago* could not be published in his own country, was unable to travel to Stockholm to accept the prize awarded him. And again in 1971, the Russian novelist Alexander Solzhenitsyn won the Nobel prize for works unpublished in Russia, and did not appear to accept the prize for fear that he would not be allowed to return to his homeland, source of his literary inspiration. Seven Americans have won the Nobel prize: Sinclair Lewis, novelist, 1930; Eugene O'Neill, dramatist, 1936; Pearl Buck, novelist, 1938; T. S. Eliot, poet, 1948; William Faulkner, novelist, 1949; Ernest Hemingway, novelist, 1954; and John Steinbeck, novelist, 1962. Though some of these writers were more talented than others, all of these Nobel laureates were seriously dedicated writers who made a significant contribution to America in their social and cultural criticism as well as in their occasional celebration and praise.

Pulitzer Prize   The Pulitzer Prize is purely national, and was established by the will of Joseph Pulitzer, newspaper owner, on his death in 1911. Pulitzer's life was a peculiarly American success story. He was born in Hungary and was recruited in Hamburg, Germany, for the Union Army during the Civil War. After the war he became a reporter and worked his way up in journalism to become owner of the *St. Louis Post Dispatch* and the *New York World.*

He left his considerable fortune to Columbia University for the development of a journalism school and for the establishment of Pulitzer Prizes to be awarded for achievement in journalism, music, and literature. The first awards were made in 1917. The prizes in literature are $500, and are awarded for fiction, poetry, drama, history, and biography. Although the awards carry with them fame and distinction, it is astonishing how many former winners are now forgotten, their works unread. It is interesting to note, for example, that although Hemingway and Faulkner published their greatest works, now considered classics, during the 1920's and 1930's, they did not win Pulitzer Prizes until the 1950's, and then with works that are not counted among their best. But though there have been misses in the awarding of the Pulitzer Prize, there have also been hits. If the award cannot be taken with absolute faith in its critical judgment, neither can it be dismissed as meaningless. It is best to regard it with critical caution.

National Book Awards   Probably established to help correct the occasional misjudgments of the Pulitzer Prizes, the National Book Awards were originated in 1950 by a number of publishing and bookseller organizations. Prizes of $1,000 are awarded in a number of literary categories, including fiction, poetry, history, and philosophy. A brief comparison of the fiction winners on the two lists, Pulitzer and National Book Award, shows the usefulness of having more than a single award. For example, in fiction for 1953, Ernest Hemingway won a Pulitzer Prize for *The Old Man and the Sea,* while Ralph Ellison won a National Book Award for *Invisible Man.* Both writers and both works were eminently worthy of recognition.

Although controversies will no doubt continue to be generated about the rightness or justness of decisions in the granting of literary awards, it seems on the whole better to risk occasional errors in recognition than to grant no recognition of writers at all. The controversies themselves provide occasions for useful literary revaluations and reassessments.

Auto Wreck

Karl Shapiro

Its quick soft silver bell beating, beating,
And down the dark one ruby flare
Pulsing out red light like an artery,
The ambulance at top speed floating down
5 Past beacons and illuminated clocks
Wings in a heavy curve, dips down,
And brakes speed, entering the crowd.
The doors leap open, emptying light;
Stretchers are laid out, the mangled lifted
10 And stowed into the little hospital.
Then the bell, breaking the hush, tolls once,
And the ambulance with its terrible cargo
Rocking, slightly rocking, moves away,
As the doors, an afterthought, are closed.

15 We are deranged, walking among the cops
Who sweep glass and are large and
      composed.
One is still making notes under the light.
One with a bucket douches ponds of blood
Into the street and gutter.
20 One hangs lanterns on the wrecks that cling,
Empty husks of locusts, to iron poles.

Our throats were tight as tourniquets,
Our feet were bound with splints, but now
Like convalescents intimate and gauche,
25 We speak through sickly smiles and warn
With the stubborn saw of common sense,
The grim joke and the banal resolution.
The traffic moves around with care,
But we remain, touching a wound
30 That opens to our richest horror.

Already old, the question Who shall die?
Becomes unspoken Who is innocent?
For death in war is done by hands;
Suicide has cause and stillbirth, logic.
35 But this invites the occult mind,
Cancels our physics with a sneer,
And spatters all we knew of denouement
Across the expedient and wicked stones.

Copyright 1942 and renewed 1970 by Karl Shapiro. Reprinted from
POEMS 1940–1953, by Karl Shapiro, by permission of Random
House, Inc.

DISCUSSION

The **language of poetry** tends to be different from the language of prose, even though both draw on the same supply of words. Poetic language is usually more compact. The sentences are normally more evocative in that they suggest far more than they literally say. The language of poetry relies heavily on the suggestive or **connotative** meanings of words rather than the literal or **denotative** meanings (the meanings found in dictionaries). For example, when the ambulance arrives in "Auto Wreck," its bell is "beating, beating," a word suggesting urgency and haste. After the ambulance has been loaded with the victims, the bell "tolls once," a word that suggests grief and possible death.

Poetry is filled with **images**—words and phrases that appeal to the senses of sight, sound, touch, taste, and smell. The lines often have their own quality (aside from their meaning) in their rhythms and sound repetitions, as in their **rhymes** (end sound repeated), or **alliteration** (initial consonants repeated; line 2: "*bell beating, beating*"), or **assonance** (vowel sound repeated; line 1: "*Its* qu*i*ck soft s*i*lver).

Most characteristic of the language of poetry, however, is the use of one thing to describe another. "Auto Wreck" is filled with such comparisons. In lines 2 and 3, the ruby beacon of the ambulance is described as "Pulsing out red light like an artery." Since the comparison is made with the use of "like," it is called **simile**. Sometimes the comparison is made without the use of any such connective at all, as in lines 20–21: the "One [of the cops] hangs lanterns on the wrecks that cling, / Empty husks of locusts, to iron poles." In such cases the comparison is called a **metaphor**.

FOR EXPLORATION

1. Find a passage in the poem that strikes you as particularly vivid and analyze the elements of language in it that contribute to the effect: the imagery, the rhythm or sound repetitions, the metaphors or similes, the words with particularly rich connotative meaning.

2. Explain the metaphor presented in the last two lines of stanza 3.

3. Relate the fourth paragraph of Karl Shapiro's letter to the last stanza of the poem. How is death by accident different from death in war or by suicide or in stillbirth?

CREATIVE RESPONSE

Describe in evocative language an event which has frightened, horrified, or had some other powerful emotional effect on you.

COURTESY OF THE AUTHOR

"Auto Wreck" seems to be my most popular poem. I don't mind really.

Its genesis is partly imaginary, partly composite, partly based on observation, like most poems. Notice that there are no sounds of pain or anguish in the poem. The people are silent, as in a silent film. Even the ambulance bell has a soft almost beautiful music. The accident is at night and the "arterial" light of the ambulance comes and goes through the darkness. And everything is somewhat in slow motion.

The bystander (the poet) is dissociated from the scene and merely wonders at its meaning and its horror. I watched the police wash the blood down the gutters and sweep away the broken glass, and the rest. I had a particular accident in mind, and the poem was written after witnessing a particularly bad one one midnight in Baltimore, but I drew upon similar scenes such as everyone has experienced from time to time.

The questions asked towards the end of the poem have a certain grisly banality, the very kind of question that loved ones would ask. Why? Why? For given another second there would be no accident.

Incidentally, the first line is a deliberate wrenching of an iambic pentameter line, with two reversed feet at the end, "beating, beating". I think the device works well, considering the subject.

I hope these remarks will help.

* victims

Sincerely,

Karl Shapiro

Karl Shapiro 1913 /

Born in Baltimore, Karl Shapiro grew up wanting to write poetry. So strong was his interest that he neglected his studies at the University of Virginia to work on his verses. His second volume of verse, *V-Letter and Other Poems*, poems of World War II, was awarded the Pulitzer Prize in 1945. In 1946 he was appointed Consultant in Poetry at the Library of Congress.

Shapiro has also won fame as critic and editor. From 1950 to 1956 he was editor of *Poetry* and from 1956 to 1966 he was editor of *The Prairie Schooner*. He is now professor of English at the Chicago Circle Campus of the University of Illinois.

Did You Ever Dream Lucky?

Ralph Ellison

AFTER the hurried good-bys the door had closed and they sat at the table with the tragic wreck of the Thanksgiving turkey before them, their heads turned regretfully toward the young folks' laughter in the hall. Then they could hear the elevator open and shut and the gay voices sinking swiftly beneath the floor and they were left facing one another in a room suddenly quiet with disappointment. Each of them, Mary, Mrs. Garfield, and Portwood, missed the young roomers, but in his disappointment Portwood had said something about young folks being green and now Mary was challenging him.

"Green," she said, "shucks, you don't know nothing about green!"

"Just wait a minute now," Portwood said, pushing back from the table, "Who don't? Who you talking about?"

"I'm talking about you," Mary said. "Them chillun is gone off to the dance, so I *must* be talking 'bout you. And like I *shoulda* said, you don't even know green when you see it."

"Let me get on out of here," Portwood said, getting up. "Mrs. Garfield, she's just tuning up to lie. I can't understand why we live here with an ole lying woman like her anyway. And contentious with it too. Talking 'bout *I* don't know nothing 'bout green. Why, I been meeting green folks right at the dam' station for over twenty-five years. . . ."

"Sit down, man. Just sit on back down," said Mary, placing her hand upon the heavy cut-glass decanter. "You got nowhere in this whole wide world to go— probably cause you make so much noise with your mouth . . ."

Mrs. Garfield smiled with gentle amusement. She'd been through it all before. A retired cook whose husband was dead, she had roomed with Mary almost as long as Portwood and knew that just as this was his way of provoking Mary into telling a story, it was Mary's way of introducing the story

she would tell. She watched Mary cut her eyes from Portwood's frowning face to look through the window to where, far beyond the roofs of Harlem, mist-shrouded buildings pierced the sky. It was raining.

"It's gon' be cold out there on the streets this winter," Mary said. "I guess you know all about that."

"Don't be signifying at me," Portwood said. "You must aim to *lie* me into the streets. Well, I ain't even thinking about moving."

"You'll move," Mary said. "You'll be glad to move. And you still won't know nothing 'bout green."

"Then you tell us, Miss Mary," Mrs. Garfield said. "Don't pay Portwood any mind."

Portwood sat down, shaking his head hopelessly. "Now she's bound to lie. Mrs. Garfield, you done *guaranteed* she go' lie. And just look at her," he said, his voice rising indignantly, "sitting there looking like a lady preacher or something!"

"Portwood, I done tole you 'bout your way of talking," Mary began, but suddenly the stern façade of her face collapsed and they were all laughing.

"Hush, y'all," Mary said, her eyes gleaming. "Hush!"

"Don't try to laugh out of it," Portwood said, "I maintain these youngsters nowadays is green. They black and trying to git to heaven in a Cadillac. They think their education proves that we old southern folks is fools who don't know nothing 'bout life or loving or nothing 'bout living in the world. They green, I tell you! How we done come this far and lived this long if we didn't learn nothing 'bout life? Answer me that!"

"Now, Portwood," Mrs. Garfield said gently, "They're not that bad, the world just looks different to their eyes."

"Don't tell me, I see 'em when they get off the trains. Long as I been a Red Cap I've seen thousands of 'em, and dam' nigh everyone of 'em is green. And just cause these here is rooming with you, Moms, don't make 'em no different. Here you done fixed this fine Thanksgiving dinner and they caint hardly finish it for rushing off somewhere. Too green to be polite. Don't even know there ain't no other ole

"*Did You Ever Dream Lucky?*" by Ralph Ellison. Reprinted by permission of William Morris Agency, Inc., on behalf of the author. Copyright © 1954 by Ralph Ellison.

fool woman like you renting rooms in Harlem who'll treat 'em like kinfolks. Don't tell me 'bout . . ."

"Shh," Mrs. Garfield said, as the sound of voices leaving the elevator came to them, "they might be coming back."

They listened. The voices grew gaily up the hall, then, blending with a remote peal of chimes, faded beyond a further wall. Mrs. Garfield sighed as they looked at one another guiltily.

"Shucks," Portwood said, "by now they just about beating the door down, trying to get into that dance. Like I was telling y'all . . ."

"Hush, Portwood!" Mary said. "What *green?*" She said, singing full-throatedly now, her voice suddenly folk-toned and deep with echoes of sermons and blue trombones, "Lawd, *I* was green. That's what I'm trying to tell you. Y'all hear me? *I, Me, Mary Raaaam-bo*, was green."

"You telling me?" Portwood laughed. "Is you telling *me?*" Nevertheless he leaned forward with Mrs. Garfield now, surrendering once more to Mary's once-upon-a-time antiphonal spell, waiting to respond to her stated theme: green.

"Here y'all," she said, beckoning for their glasses with one hand and lifting the decanter with the other. "Git some wine in y'all's stomachs so's it can warm y'all's old-time blood."

They drank ceremoniously with lowered eyes, waiting for Mary's old contralto to resume its flight, its tragic-comic ascendence.

"Sho, I was green," she continued. "Green as anybody what ever left the farm and come to town. Shucks, here you criticizing those youngsters for rushing to the dance 'cause they hope to win that auto—that ain't nothing, not to what I done. Cause like them chillun and everybody else, I was after money. And I was full grown, too. Times was hard. My husband had done died and I couldn't get nothing but part-time work and didn't nobody have enough to eat. My daughter Lucy and me couldn't even afford a ten cents movies so we could go forget about it. So Lawd, this evening we're sitting in the window watching the doings down in the streets. Y'all know how it gits round here in the summertime, after it has been hot all day and has cooled off a bit: Folks out strolling or hanging on the stoops and hollering out the windows, chillun yelling and ripping and romping and begging for pennies to buy that there shaved ice with the red sirup poured over it. Dogs barking—y'all know how it is round here

in the summertime. All that talk and noise and Negroes laughing loud and juke boxes blaring and like-a-that. Well, it's 'bout that time on one of them kinda days, and one of them store-front churches is just beginning to jump. You can hear them clapping their hands and shouting and the tambourines is a-shaking and a-beating, and that ole levee camp trombone they has is going *Wah-wah, Wah-wah, Wah-wah-wah!* Y'all know, just like it really has something to do with the good Lawd's business— when all of a sudden two autos decides to see which is the toughest."

"A wreck?" Portwood said. "What the newspapers call a *collision?*"

"That's it." Mary said, sipping her wine, "one of the biggest smashups you ever seen. Here we is up in the window on the fourth floor and it's happening right down below us. Why, it's like two big bulls has done charged and run head-on. I tell you, Mrs Garfield, it was something! Here they is," she said, shifting two knives upon the cloth, "one's coming thisa way, and the other's coming thata way, and when they gits right here, WHAM! They done come together and something flies out of there like a cannon ball. Then for a second it gets real quiet. It's like everybody done stopped to take a breath at the same time—all except those clapping hands and tambourines and that ole nasty-mouthed trombone (that fool was sounding like he done took over and started preaching the gospel by now). Then, Lawd," she said, rocking forward for emphasis, "*glass* is falling, *dust* is rising, *women* is screaming—Oh, such a commotion. Then all of a sudden all you can hear is Negroes' feet slapping the sidewalks . . ."

"Never mind them feet," Portwood said, "what was it that flew out of there?"

"I'm fixing to tell you now, fool. When the cars come together me and Lucy sees that thing bust outa there like a comet and fly off to one side somewhere. Lucy said, 'Mama, did you see what I seen?' 'Come on, chile,' I says, 'Let's us get ourselfs on down there!' And good people, that's when we started to move! Lawd, we flew down them stairs. I didn't even take time to pull off my apron or my house shoes. Just come a-jumping. Oh, it was a sight, I tell you. Everybody and his brother standing round trying to see if anybody was killed and measuring the skid marks and waiting for the ambulance to come—the man coulda died before that ambulance got there——"

"Well, how about it, Moms, was anybody hurt?"

"Yes, they was, but I ain't your mama, an ole rusty Negro like you! Sho' they was hurt. One man was all cut up and bleeding and the other knocked cold as a big deep freeze. They thought he was dead.

"But me and Lucy don't waste no time with none of that. We gets busy looking for what we seen shoot out of them cars. I whispers, 'Chile, where did it hit?' And she points over near the curb. And sho 'nough, when I starts slow-dragging my leg along the gutter my foot hits against something heavy, and when I hears it clink together my heart almost flies out of my mouth . . ."

"My Lord, Miss Mary! What was it?" Mrs. Garfield said, her eyes intense. "You don't mean to tell me it was——"

Mary gave her a flat look. "I'm goin' to tell you," she said, taking a taste of wine. "I give y'all my word I'm gon' tell you—I calls to Lucy, 'Gal, come over here a minute,' justa looking 'round to see if anybody'd seen me. And she come and I whispers to her, 'Now don't let on we found anything, just get on the other side of me and make like you trying to kick me on the foot. Go on, gal,' I says, 'Don't argue with me—And watch out for my bunion!' And Lawd, she kicks that bag and this time I'm sho, 'cause I hear that sweet metal-like sound. 'What you think it is?' I says and she leans close to me, eyes done got round as silver dollars, says, 'Mother' (always called me *mother* steada 'mama,' when she was excited or trying to be proper or something) says, 'Mother, that's money!' 'Shhh, fool,' I tole her, 'you don't have to tell *eve'y*body.'

" 'But, Mother, what are we going to do?'

" 'Just stand still a secon',' I says. 'Just quiet down. Don't move. Take it easy! Make out like you watching what they doing over yonder with those cars. Gimme time to figure this thing out . . .' "

She laughed. "Lawd, I was sweating by the gallon. Here I am standing in the street with my foot on a bag full of somebody's money! I don't know what to do. By now the police is all around us and I don't know when whichever one of them men who was hurt is gonna rise up and start yelling for it. I tell you, I musta lost five pounds in five minutes, trying to figure out the deal."

"Miss Mary, I wish I could have seen you," Mrs. Garfield said.

"Well, I'm glad you didn't; I was having trouble enough. Oh it was agonizing. Everytime somebody walks toward us I almost faint. And Lucy, she's turning this-away and that-away, real fast, like she's trying to invent a new dance. 'Do something, Mother,' she says. 'Please hurry up and do something!' Till finally I caint stand it and just flops down on the curbstone and kicks the bag kinda up under my skirts. Lawd, today!" she sang, then halted to inspect Portwood, who, with his head on his arms, laughed in silent glee. "What's the matter with you, fool?"

"Go on, tell the lie," Portwood said. "Don't mind poor me. You really had larceny in your heart that day."

"Well," Mary grinned, "more 'bout this time old Miz Brazelton, a meddlesome ole lady who lived across the hall from me, she comes up talking 'bout 'Why Miss Mary, don't you know a woman of your standing in the community oughtn't to be sitting on the curb like some ole common nobody?' Like all Mary Rambo's got to do is worry 'bout what somebody might think about her—I looks and I knows the only way to git rid of the fool is to bawl her out. 'Look here, Miz Brazelton,' I says, 'this here's my own ole rusty tub I'm sitting on and long as I can haul it 'round without your help I guess I can put it down wherever I please . . .' "

"You a rough woman, Moms," Portwood said with deep resonance, his face a judicial frown. "Rough!"

"I done tole you 'bout calling me Moms!" Mary warned.

"Just tell the lie," Portwood said. "Then what happen?"

"I know that type," Mrs. Garfield said. "With them you do sometimes have to be radical."

"You know it too?" Mary said. "Radical sho is the word. You shoulda seen her face. I really didn't want to hurt that ole woman's feelings, but right then I had to git shed of the fool.

"Well, she leaves and I'm still sitting there fighting with myself over what I oughta do. Should I report what we'd found, or just take it on upstairs? Not that I meant to be dishonest, you know, but like everybody else in New York if something-for-nothing comes along, I wanted to be the one to git it. Besides, anybody fool enough to have that much money riding around with him in a car *deserves* to lose it."

"He sho dam' do," Portwood said. "He *dam*' sho do!"

"Well, all at once Lucy shakes me and here comes the ambulance, justa screaming.

" 'Mother, we better go, ' Lucy says. And me I don't know *what* to do. By now the cops is pushing folks around and I knows soon as they see me they bound to find out what kinda egg this is I'm nesting on. Then all of a sudden it comes over me that I'm still wearing my apron! Lawd, I reaches down and touches that bag and my heart starts to going ninety miles a minute. It feels like a heapa money! And when I touches that thick cloth bag you can hear it clinking together. 'Lucy, chile,' I whispers, 'stand right in front of me while the ole lady rolls this heavy stuff up in her apron . . .' "

"Oh, Miss Mary," Mrs. Garfield said, shaking her head, "You'd given in to the devil."

"I'm in his arms, girl, in his hairy arms! And Lucy in on the deal. She's hurrying me up and I picks up that bag and no sooner'n I do, here comes a cop!"

"Oh my Jesus, Miss Mary!" cried Mrs. Garfield.

"Woman," said Mary, "you don't know; you have no *idea*. He's one of these tough-looking, young cops, too. One of them that thinks he has to beat you up just to prove he's in command of things. Here he comes, swinging up to Lucy like a red sledge hammer, telling folks to move along—Ain't seen *me*, cause I'm still sitting down. And when he comes up to Lucy I starts to moaning like I'm sick: 'Please, mister officer,' I says, kinda hiding my face, 'we just fixin' to leave.' Well, suh, his head shoots round Lucy like a turkey gobbler's and he sees me. Says, 'What's the matter, madam, wuz you in this wreck?' —and in a real nice voice too. Then Lucy—Lawd, that Lucy was smart; up to that time I didn't know my chile could lie. But Lucy looks the cop dead in the eye and says, 'Officer, we be going in a minute. My mother here is kinda nauchus from looking at all that blood.' "

"Oh, Miss Mary, she didn't say that!"

"She sho did, and it worked! Why the cop bends down and tries to help me to my feet and I says, 'Thank you, officer, just let me rest here a second and I be all right.' Well, suh, he leaves us and goes on off. But by now I got the bag in my apron and gets up moaning and groaning and starts out across the street, kinda bent over like, you know, with Lucy helping me along. Lawd, that bag feels like a thousand pounds. And everytime I takes a step it gets heavier. And on top of that, looks like we never going to cross the street, cause everybody in the block is stopping us to ask what's wrong: 'You sick Miss Mary?'; 'Lucy, what done happen to your mother?'; 'Do she want a doctor?'; 'Po' thing, she done got herself over-excited'—and all likea that. Shucks! I'm overexcited, all right, that bag's 'bout to give me a nervous breakdown!

"When we finally make it up to the apartment, I'm so beat that I just flops into a chair and sits there panting. Don't even take the bag outa my apron, and Lucy, she's having a fit. 'Open it up, Mother, let's see what's in it,' she says. But I figures we better wait, cause after all, they might miss the money and come searching for it. You see, after I done worked so hard gitting it up there, I had decided to keep it sho 'nough . . .'

"You had given in to the devil," Mrs. Garfield said.

"Who?" said Mary, reaching for the wine, "I'm way, *way* past the giving-in stage."

"This world is surely a trial," Mrs. Garfield mused. "It truly is."

"And you can say that again," said Mary, "cause it's the agonizing truth."

"What did you do then, Miss Mary?"

"Pass me your glass, Portwood," Mary said, reaching for the decanter.

"Never mind the wine," said Portwood, covering his glass with his hand. "Get back to what *happened!*"

"Well, we goes to the bathroom—wait, don't say it!" she warned, giving Portwood a frown. "We goes to the bathroom and I gits up on a chair and drops that bag dead into the flush box."

"Now Miss Mary, really!"

"Girl, yes! I knowed wouldn't nobody think to look for it up there. It coulda been hid up in heaven somewhere. Sho! I dropped it in there, then I sent Lucy on back downstairs to see if anybody'd missed it. She musta hung 'round there for over an hour. Police and the newspaper people come and made pictures and asked a heapa questions and everything, but nothing 'bout the bag. Even after the wreckers come and dragged that pile of brand new junk away—still nothing 'bout the bag."

"Everything going in y'all's favor," Portwood said.

"Uhhuh, everything going our way."

"Y'all had it made, Moms," Portwood said, "Why you never tole this lie before?"

"The devil is truly powerful," Mrs. Garfield said, "Almost as powerful as the Lord. Even so, it's strange nobody missed that much money!"

"Now that's what me and Lucy thought . . ."

Portwood struck the table, "What I want to know is how much money was in the bag?"

"I'm coming to that in a second," Mary said.

"Yeah, but why you taking so long?"

"Who's telling this lie, Portwood, me or you?" said Mary.

"You was 'til you got off the track."

"Don't forget your manners, Portwood," Mrs. Garfield said.

"I'm not, but looks like to me y'all think money ought to be as hard to get in a lie somebody's telling as it is to get carrying folks' bags."

"Or as 'tis to git you to hush your mouth," said Mary. "Anyway, we didn't count it right then. We was scaird. I knowed I was doing wrong, holding on to something wasn't really mine. But that wasn't stopping me."

"Y'all was playing a little finders-keepers," Portwood said, resting back.

"Yeah, and concentrating on the keeping part."

"But why didn't you just *look* at the money, Miss Mary?"

"'Cause we mighta been tempted to spend some of it, girl."

"Yeah, and y'all mighta give yourself away," Portwood said.

"Ain't it the truth! And that bag was powerful enough as it was. It was really working on us. Me and Lucy just sitting 'round like two ole hens on a nest, trying to guess how much is in it. Then we tries to figure whether it was dollars or fifty-centies. Finally we decides that it caint be less'n five or ten dollar gold pieces to weigh so much."

"But how on earth could you resist looking at it?" Mrs. Garfield said.

"Scaird, chile; scaird. We was like a couple kids who somebody's done give a present and tole 'em it would disappear if they opened it before Christmas. And know something else, neither one of us ever had to go to the bathroom so much as when us had that bag up there in that flush box. I got to flushing it just to hear it give out that fine clinking sound."

Portwood groaned. "I knew you was gon' lie," he said. "I *knowed* it."

"Hush, man, hush!" Mary laughed. "I know our neighbors musta got sick and tired of hearing us flush that thing. But I tell you, everytime I pulled the chain it was like ringing up money in the cash register! I tell you, it was disintegrating! Whew! I'd go in there and stay a while and come out. Next thing I know there'd be Lucy going in. Then we got shamed and started slipping past one another. She'd try to keep hid from me, and me from her. I tell you, that stuff was working on us like a dose of salts! Why, after a few days I got so I couldn't work, just sat 'round thinking 'bout that doggone bag. And naturally, I done most of my thinking up there on the throne."

"Didn't I tell you she was tuning up to lie," Portwood laughed. "If she don't stop I'm dead gon' call the police."

"This here's the agonizing truth I'm telling y'all," said Mary.

"I wouldn't have been able to stand it, Miss Mary. I would have had to get it over with."

"They shoulda been looking for it by now," Portwood said, "all that money."

"That's what us thought," said Mary. "And we got to figuring why they didn't. First we figgers maybe it was because the man who was hurt so bad had died. But then we seen in the papers that he got well . . ."

"Maybe they was gangsters," Portwood said.

"Yeah, we thought of that too; gangsters or bootleggers."

"Yeah, yeah, either one of them coulda been carrying all that money—or gamblers even."

"Sho they could. Me and Lucy figgered that maybe they thought the cops had took the money or that they was trying to find it theyselves on the q.t., y'know."

"Miss Mary, you were either very brave or very reckless."

"Neither one, girl," Mary said, "just broke and hungry. And don't talk about brave, shucks, we was scaird to answer the doorbell at night. Let me tell you, we was doing some tall figuring. Finally I got so I couldn't eat and Lucy couldn't sleep. We was evil as a coupla lady bears at cubbing time."

"You just couldn't stand all that prosperity, huh, Moms?"

"It was a burden, all right. And everytime we pulled the chain it got a few dollars more so."

Mrs. Garfield smiled. "Mr. Garfield often said that the possession of great wealth brought with it the slings and arrows of outrageous responsibility."

"Mrs. Garfield," Mary mused, "you know you had you a right smart man in him? You really did. And looks like when you got stuff saved up like that you got the responsibility of keeping some of it circulating. Even without looking at it we got to figuring how to spend it. Lucy, she wants to go into business. Why she *almost* persuaded me to see about buying a building and opening a restaurant! And as if *that* wasn't enough trouble to git into, she decides she's goin' take the third floor and open her a beauty shop. Oh, we had it all planned!'' She shook her head.

"And y'all still ain't looked at it," Portwood said.

"Still ain't seen a thing."

"Dam!"

"You had marvelous self-control," Mrs. Garfield said.

"Yeah, I did," Mary said, "until that day Lucy went to the dentist. Seems I just couldn't hold out no longer. Seems like I got to thinking 'bout that bag and couldn't stop. I looked at the newspaper and all those ads. Reminded me of things I wanted to buy; looked out the window and saw autos; I tried to read the Bible and as luck would have it I opened it to where it says something 'bout 'Store ye up riches in heaven,' or 'Cast your bread upon the waters.' It really had me on a merry-go-round. I just had to take a peep! So I went and pulled down all the shades and started the water running in the tub like I was taking me a bath—turned on every faucet in the house—then I climbed up there with a pair of scissors and reached in and raised that bag up and just looked at it awhile.

"It had done got *cooold!* It come up *cooold,* with the water dripping off it like some old bucket been deep down in a well. Done turned green with canker, y'all!! I just couldn't resist it no longer. I really couldn't, I took them scissors and snipped me a piece outa that bag and took me a good, *looong* look. And let me tell you, dear people, after I looked I was so excited I had to get down from there and put myself to bed. My nerves just couldn't take it . . .''

"It surely must have been an experience, Miss Mary."

"Woman, you don't know. You really don't know. You hear me? *I had to go to bed!*''

"Heck, with that much money you could afford to go to bed," said Portwood.

"Wait, le'me tell you. I'm laying up there moaning and groaning when here come Lucy and she's in one of her talking moods. Soon as I seen her I knowed pretty soon she was going to want to talk 'bout that bag and I truly dreaded telling her that I'd done looked into it without her. I says, 'Baby, I don't feel so good. You talk to me later' . . . But y'all think that stopped her? Shucks, all she does is to go get me a bottle of cold beer she done brought me and start to running her mouth again. And, just like I knowed she was gon' do, she finally got round to talking 'bout that bag. What ought we to buy *first,* she wants to know. Lawd, that pore chile, whenever she got her mind set on a thing! Well suh, I took me a big swoller of beer and just lay there like I was thinking awhile.''

"You were really good companions," Mrs. Garfield said, "There is nothing like young people to make life rich and promising. Especially if they're your own children. If only Mr. Garfield and I . . .''

"Mrs. Garfield, let her finish this lie," Portwood said, "*then* we can talk about you and Mr. Garfield.''

"Oh, of course," Mrs. Garfield said, "I'm sorry, Miss Mary, you know I didn't really mean to interrupt.''

"Pay that pore fool no min'," Mary said. "I wish I had Lucy with me right this minit!''

"Is this lie about money or chillun?" Portwood said. "Y'all here 'bout to go serious. I want to know what you tole Lucy *then.* What did y'all start out to buy?''

"If you hadn't started monkeying with Mrs. Garfield you'da learned by now," Mary said. "Well, after I lay there and thought awhile I tole her, 'Well, baby, if you want to know the truth 'bout what I think, I think we oughta buy us an auto.'

"Well suh, you coulda knocked her over with a feather. 'A car!' she says, 'why Mother, I didn't know you was interested in a car. We don't want to be like these ole ignorant Negroes who buy cars and don't have anything to go with it and no place to keep it,' she says. Says, 'I'm certainly surprised at you, Mother. I never would've dreamed you wanted a *car,* not the very first thing.'

"Oh, she was running off a mile a minute. And looking at me like she done caught me kissing the preacher or the iceman or somebody! 'We want to be practical,' she says. 'We don't want to throw our money away . . .'

"Well, it almost killed me. 'Lucy, honey,' I says, 'that's just what your mama's trying to do, be practical. That's why I say let's git us an auto.'

"'But, Mama,' she says, 'a car isn't practical at all.'

"'Oh yes it is,' I says, 'Cause how else is we gon' use two sets of auto chains?'"——

"And do y'all know," said Mary, sitting up suddenly and balancing the tips of her fingers on her knees, her face a mask of incredulity, "I had to hop outa bed and catch that chile before she swayed dead away in a faint!"

"Yeah," Portwood laughed, falling back in his chair, "and you better hop up from there and catch me."

Mrs. Garfield's voice rose up girlishly, "Oh Miss Mary," she laughed, "you're just fooling."

Mary's bosom heaved, "I wish I was, girl," she said. "I sho wish I was."

"How 'bout that? Tire chains," Portwood said. "All that larceny for some dam' tire chain!"

"Fool," said Mary, "didn't I tell you you didn't know nothing 'bout green? There I was thinking I done found me a bird nest on the ground. C'mon now," she said chuckling at the gullibility of all mankind, "let's us finish the wine."

Portwood winked at Mrs. Garfield. "Hey, Moms, tell us something . . ."

"I ain't go' tell you again that I ain't yo' mama," said Mary.

"I just want you to tell us one last thing. . ."

Mary looked at him warily, "What is it? I got no more time for your foolishness now, I got to git up from here and fix for them chillun."

"Never mind them youngsters," said Portwood, "just tell us if you ever dreamed lucky?"

Mary grinned, "Ain't I just done tole you?" she said, "Sho I did, but I woke up cold in hand. Just the same though," she added thoughtfully, "I still hope them youngsters win that there auto."

"Yes," Mrs. Garfield said. "And wouldn't it be a comfort, Miss Mary? Just to know that they *can* win one, I mean . . . ?"

Mary said that it certainly would be.

THE END

DISCUSSION

Ellison's short story is almost entirely in monologue, with a sort of chorus of commentators almost in the tradition of classical Greek theater. Ellison offers us a meeting with a born storyteller, Mary, who is masterful at the tricks of creating suspense, arousing and maintaining interest at high pitch, and keeping the audience alert with flashes of characterization and humor.

Though humor is undeniable in this ghetto story, just as in Malamud's "The First Seven Years," another feeling persists underneath the self-mockery and gaiety. That emotion is one of frustration, of expectation, and of disillusionment among a deprived people for whom great dreams never quite come true—a frustration that is felt so often they can even learn to laugh at it.

FOR EXPLORATION

1. Try analyzing how Mary keeps alive her hearers' interest in her tale—keeps them wanting more.
2. (a) How do Mary's hearers encourage the development of the narrative? (b) What effect do their comments have on the reader? (c) How do their comments reveal their own personalities?
3. (a) What are the comic elements in this story? the tragic elements? (b) What effect does the combination have upon the story?
4. Why is Mary's story called a "lie," even by herself?
5. At the completion of Mary's narrative, Portwood asks her if she "ever dreamed lucky." Mary replies, "Sho I did, but I woke up cold in hand." What do you think the expression "cold in hand" means?

PICTORIAL PARADE INC.

CREATIVE RESPONSE

Try the art of oral storytelling. Borrow some of Mary's methods, and tell the class the "story" of something that happened to you: a surprise, a disappointment, a significant encounter.

Ralph Waldo Ellison   1914 /

Ralph W. Ellison, essayist, short-story writer, novelist, sculptor, folklorist, lecturer, and erstwhile musician, was born and raised in Oklahoma City. Ellison's father, who hoped his son would someday become a poet, named him after Ralph Waldo Emerson (an appellation, incidentally, that Ellison claims he has never learned to live with). And though the young Ellison was a voracious reader of the sort of books that nourish the imaginations of millions of boys, music, not literature, was his first love. The Oklahoma City in which he grew up was overflowing with jazz musicians. Many of these artists were idolized by Ellison and his friends, who saw jazz as the one sure means of self-expression open to their race.

In 1933, Ellison went to Tuskegee Institute in Alabama to study music; he wanted, at that time, to become a composer. While in his second year at Tuskegee, he read T. S. Eliot's *The Waste Land,* a long pessimistic poem and a masterpiece of its type. This encounter with Eliot's genius was, according to Ellison, the beginning of his gradual transition from musical to literary composition.

While music has now become a secondary thing in Ellison's life, he has never lost his interest in it. And it was his early training in that art which prepared him for the rigorous devotion to craft that is required of every good writer. Three themes dominate Ellison's work: the place of Negro literature and folklore in American life; Negro musical expression, especially jazz and the blues; and the relationship between American Negro culture and North American culture as a whole.

It is the last of these themes which serves as the foundation of *Invisible Man,* Ellison's only novel and most highly acclaimed work to date. This novel, which combines convincing realism with weird fantasies and symbolic events, won the National Book Award for 1952. In 1956, it was judged by a *Book Week* magazine poll of some two hundred authors, critics, and editors "the most distinguished single work" published in the last twenty years.

The Sculptor's Funeral

Willa Cather

A group of the townspeople stood on the station siding of a little Kansas town, awaiting the coming of the night train, which was already twenty minutes overdue. The snow had fallen thick over everything; in the pale starlight the line of bluffs across the wide, white meadows south of the town made soft, smoke-colored curves against the clear sky. The men on the siding stood first on one foot and then on the other, their hands thrust deep into their trousers pockets, their overcoats open, their shoulders screwed up with the cold; and they glanced from time to time toward the southeast, where the railroad track wound along the river shore. They conversed in low tones and moved about restlessly, seeming uncertain as to what was expected of them. There was but one of the company who looked as though he knew exactly why he was there, and he kept conspicuously apart; walking to the far end of the platform, returning to the station door, then pacing up the track again, his chin sunk in the high collar of his overcoat, his burly shoulders drooping forward, his gait heavy and dogged. Presently he was approached by a tall, spare, grizzled man clad in a faded Grand Army suit, who shuffled out from the group and advanced with a certain deference, craning his neck forward until his back made the angle of a jackknife three-quarters open.

"I reckon she's a-goin' to be pretty late again to-night, Jim," he remarked in a squeaky falsetto. "S'pose it's the snow?"

"I don't know," responded the other man with a shade of annoyance, speaking from out an astonishing cataract of red beard that grew fiercely and thickly in all directions.

The spare man shifted the quill toothpick he was chewing to the other side of his mouth. "It ain't likely that anybody from the East will come with the corpse, I s'pose," he went on reflectively.

"I don't know," responded the other, more curtly than before.

"It's too bad he didn't belong to some lodge or other. I like an order funeral myself. They seem more appropriate for people of some reputation," the spare man continued, with an ingratiating concession in his shrill voice, as he carefully placed his toothpick in his vest pocket. He always carried the flag at the G.A.R.[1] funerals in the town.

The heavy man turned on his heel without replying and walked up the siding. The spare man shuffled back to the uneasy group. "Jim's ez full ez a tick, ez ushel," he commented commiseratingly.

Just then a distant whistle sounded, and there was a shuffling of feet on the platform. A number of lanky boys, of all ages, appeared as suddenly and slimily as eels wakened by the crack of thunder; some came from the waiting room, where they had been warming themselves by the red stove, or half asleep on the slat benches; others uncoiled themselves from baggage trucks or slid out of express wagons. Two clambered down from the driver's seat of a hearse that stood backed up against the siding. They straightened their stooping shoulders and lifted their heads, and a flash of momentary animation kindled their dull eyes at that cold, vibrant scream, the world-wide call for men. It stirred them like the note of a trumpet; just as it had often stirred the man who was coming home tonight, in his boyhood.

The night express shot, red as a rocket, from out the eastward marshlands and wound along the river

---

1. *G.A.R.*, Grand Army of the Republic, an organization of those veterans who fought for the North during the Civil War.

ROBERT RAUCHENBERG. "HYMNAL," 1955—COURTESY OF MR. AND MRS. MICHAEL SONNABEND, PARIS

shore under the long lines of shivering poplars that sentineled the meadows, the escaping steam hanging in gray masses against the pale sky and blotting out the Milky Way. In a moment the red glare from the headlight streamed up the snow-covered track before the siding and glittered on the wet, black rails. The burly man with the disheveled red beard walked swiftly up the platform toward the approaching train, uncovering his head as he went. The group of men behind him hesitated, glanced questioningly at one another, and awkwardly followed his example. The train stopped, and the crowd shuffled up to the express car just as the door was thrown open, the spare man in the G.A.R. suit thrusting his head forward with curiosity. The express messenger appeared in the doorway, accompanied by a young man in a long ulster and a traveling cap.

"Are Mr. Merrick's friends here?" inquired the young man.

The group on the platform swayed and shuffled uneasily. Philip Phelps, the banker, responded with dignity: "We have come to take charge of the body. Mr. Merrick's father is very feeble and can't be about."

"Send the agent out here," growled the express messenger, "and tell the operator to lend a hand."

The coffin was got out of its rough box and down on the snowy platform. The townspeople drew back enough to make room for it and then formed a close semicircle about it, looking curiously at the palm leaf[2] which lay across the black cover. No one said anything. The baggageman stood by his truck, waiting to get at the trunks. The engine panted heavily, and the fireman dodged in and out among the wheels with his yellow torch and long oil-can, snapping the spindle boxes. The young Bostonian, one of the dead sculptor's pupils who had come with the body, looked about him helplessly. He turned to the banker, the only one of that black, uneasy, stoop-shouldered group who seemed enough of an individual to be addressed.

"None of Mr. Merrick's brothers are here?" he asked, uncertainly.

The man with the red beard for the first time stepped up and joined the group. "No, they have not come yet; the family is scattered. The body will be taken directly to the house." He stooped and took hold of one of the handles of the coffin.

"Take the long hill road up, Thompson; it will be easier on the horses," called the liveryman as the undertaker snapped the door of the hearse and prepared to mount to the driver's seat.

Laird, the red-bearded lawyer, turned again to the stranger. "We didn't know whether there would be anyone with him or not," he explained. "It's a long walk, so you'd better go up in the hack." He pointed to a single battered conveyance, but the young man replied stiffly: "Thank you, but I think I will go up with the hearse. If you don't object," turning to the undertaker, "I'll ride with you."

They clambered up over the wheels and drove off in the starlight up the long, white hill toward the town. The lamps in the still village were shining from under the low, snow-burdened roofs; and beyond, on every side, the plains reached out into emptiness, peaceful and wide as the soft sky itself, and wrapped in a tangible, white silence.

When the hearse backed up to a wooden sidewalk before a naked, weather-beaten frame house, the same composite, ill-defined group that had stood upon the station siding was huddled about the gate. The front yard was an icy swamp, and a couple of warped planks, extending from the sidewalk to the door, made a sort of rickety footbridge. The gate hung on one hinge, and was opened wide with difficulty. Steavens, the young stranger, noticed that something black was tied to the knob of the front door.

The grating sound made by the casket, as it was drawn from the hearse, was answered by a scream from the house; the front door was wrenched open, and a tall, corpulent woman rushed out bareheaded into the snow and flung herself upon the coffin, shrieking: "My boy, my boy! And this is how you've come home to me!"

As Steavens turned away and closed his eyes with a shudder of unutterable repulsion, another woman, also tall, but flat and angular, darted out of the house and caught Mrs. Merrick by the shoulders, crying sharply: "Come, come, Mother; you mustn't go on like this!" Her tone changed to one of obsequious solemnity as she turned to the banker. "The parlor is ready, Mr. Phelps."

The bearers carried the coffin along the narrow boards, while the undertaker ran ahead with the coffin-rests. They bore it into a large unheated room

---

2. *the palm leaf.* The palm leaf is the traditional symbol of victory or triumph. As it is used here, it implies that the sculptor, Harvey Merrick, had been awarded a significant decoration for achievement in the arts.

that smelled of dampness and disuse and furniture polish, and set it down under a hanging lamp ornamented with jingling glass prisms and before a Rogers group[3] of John Alden and Priscilla, wreathed with smilax. Henry Steavens stared about him with the sickening conviction that there had been some horrible mistake and that he had somehow arrived at the wrong destination. He looked at the clover-green Brussels, the fat plush upholstery, among the hand-painted china plaques and panels and vases, for some mark of identification—for something that might once conceivably have belonged to Harvey Merrick. It was not until he recognized his friend in the crayon portrait of a little boy in kilts and curls, hanging above the piano, that he felt willing to let any of these people approach the coffin.

"Take the lid off, Mr. Thompson. Let me see my boy's face," wailed the elder woman between her sobs. This time Steavens looked fearfully, almost beseechingly into her face, red and swollen under its masses of strong, black, shiny hair. He flushed, dropped his eyes, and then, almost incredulously, looked again. There was a kind of power about her face—a kind of brutal handsomeness, even; but it was scarred and furrowed by violence, and so colored and coarsened by fiercer passions that grief seemed never to have laid a gentle finger there. The long nose was distended and knobbed at the end, and there were deep lines on either side of it; her heavy black brows almost met across her forehead, her teeth were large and square and set far apart— teeth that could tear. She filled the room; the men were obliterated, seemed tossed about like twigs in an angry water, even Steavens felt himself being drawn into the whirlpool.

The daughter—tall, raw-boned woman in crepe, with a mourning comb in her hair which curiously lengthened her long face—sat stiffly upon the sofa, her hands, conspicuous for their large knuckles folded in her lap, her mouth and eyes drawn down, solemnly awaiting the opening of the coffin. Near the door stood a mulatto woman, evidently a servant in the house, with a timid bearing and an emaciated face pitifully sad and gentle. She was weeping silently, the corner of her calico apron lifted to her eyes, occasionally suppressing a long quivering sob. Steavens walked over and stood beside her.

Feeble steps were heard on the stairs, and an old man, tall and frail, odorous of pipe smoke, with shaggy, unkempt gray hair and a dingy beard, tobac-

co-stained about the mouth, entered uncertainly. He went slowly up to the coffin and stood rolling a blue cotton handkerchief between his hands, seeming so pained and embarrassed by his wife's orgy of grief that he had no consciousness of anything else.

"There, there, Annie, dear, don't take on so," he quavered timidly, putting out a shaking hand and awkwardly patting her elbow. She turned with a cry and sank upon his shoulder with such violence that he tottered a little. He did not even glance toward the coffin, but continued to look at her with a dull, frightened, appealing expression, as a spaniel looks at the whip. His sunken cheeks slowly reddened and burned with miserable shame. When his wife rushed from the room, her daughter strode after with set lips. The servant stole up to the coffin, bent over it for a moment, and then slipped away to the kitchen, leaving Steavens, the lawyer, and the father to themselves. The old man stood trembling and looking down at his dead son's face. The sculptor's splendid head seemed even more noble in its rigid stillness than in life. The dark hair had crept down upon the wide forehead; the face seemed strangely long, but in it there was not that repose we expect to find in the faces of the dead. The brows were so drawn that there were two deep lines above the beaked nose, and the chin was thrust forward defiantly. It was as though the strain of life had been so sharp and bitter that death could not at once wholly relax the tension and smooth the countenance into perfect peace—as though he were still guarding something precious and holy, which might even yet be wrested from him.

The old man's lips were working under his stained beard. He turned to the lawyer with timid deference: "Phelps and the rest are comin' back to set up with Harve, ain't they?" he asked. "Thank'ee, Jim, thank'ee." He brushed the hair back gently from his son's forehead. "He was a good boy, Jim; always a good boy. He was ez gentle ez a child and kindest of 'em all—only we didn't none of us ever onderstand him." The tears trickled slowly down his beard and dropped upon the sculptor's coat.

"Martin! Martin! Oh, Martin! come here," his wife wailed from the top of the stairs. The old man started timorously: "Yes, Annie, I'm coming." He turned away, hesitated, stood for a moment in miser-

---

3. *Rogers group*, a small piece of statuary executed by the American sculptor, John Rogers (1829–1904).

able indecision; then reached back and patted the dead man's hair softly, and stumbled from the room.

"Poor old man, I didn't think he had any tears left. Seems as if his eyes would have gone dry long ago. At his age nothing cuts very deep," remarked the lawyer.

Something in his tone made Steavens glance up. While the mother had been in the room, the young man had scarcely seen anyone else; but now, from the moment he first glanced into Jim Laird's florid face and bloodshot eyes, he knew that he had found what he had been heartsick at not finding before— the feeling, the understanding that must exist in someone, even here.

The man was red as his beard, with features swollen and blurred by dissipation, and a hot, blazing blue eye. His face was strained—that of a man who is controlling himself with difficulty—and he kept plucking at his beard with a sort of fierce resentment. Steavens, sitting by the window, watched him turn down the glaring lamp, still its jangling pendants with an angry gesture, and then stand with his hands locked behind him, staring down into the master's face. He could not help wondering what link there could have been between the porcelain vessel and so sooty a lump of potter's clay.

From the kitchen an uproar was sounding; when the dining-room door opened, the import of it was clear. The mother was abusing the maid for having forgotten to make the dressing for the chicken salad which had been prepared for the watchers. Steavens had never heard anything in the least like it; it was injured, emotional, dramatic abuse, unique and masterly in its excruciating cruelty, as violent and unrestrained as had been her grief of twenty minutes before. With a shudder of disgust the lawyer went into the dining room and closed the door into the kitchen.

"Poor Roxy's getting it now," he remarked when he came back. "The Merricks took her out of the poorhouse years ago; and if her loyalty would let her, I guess the poor old thing could tell tales that would curdle your blood. She's the mulatto woman who was standing in here a while ago, with her apron to her eyes. The old woman is a fury; there never was anybody like her for demonstrative piety and ingenious cruelty. She made Harvey's life a hell for him when he lived at home; he was so sick ashamed of it. I never could see how he kept himself sweet."

"He was wonderful," said Steavens slowly, "wonderful; but until tonight I have never known how wonderful."

"That is the true and eternal wonder of it, anyway; that it can come even from such a dung heap as this," the lawyer cried, with a sweeping gesture which seemed to indicate much more than the four walls within which they stood.

"I think I'll see whether I can get a little air. The room is so close I am beginning to feel rather faint," murmured Steavens, struggling with one of the windows. The sash was stuck, however, and would not yield, so he sat down dejectedly and began pulling at his collar. The lawyer came over, loosened the sash with one blow of his red fist and sent the window up a few inches. Steavens thanked him, but the nausea which had been gradually climbing into his throat for the last half-hour left him with one desire—a desperate feeling that he must get away from this place with what was left of Harvey Merrick. Oh, he comprehended well enough now the quiet bitterness of the smile that he had seen so often on his master's lips!

He remembered that once, when Merrick returned from a visit home, he brought with him a singularly feeling and suggestive bas-relief of a thin, faded old woman, sitting and sewing something pinned to her knee; while a full-lipped, full-blooded little urchin, his trousers held up by a single gallows, stood beside her, impatiently twitching her gown to call her attention to a butterfly he had caught. Steavens, impressed by the tender and delicate modeling of the thin, tired face, had asked him if it were his mother. He remembered the dull flush that had burned up in the sculptor's face.

The lawyer was sitting in a rocking chair beside the coffin, his head thrown back and his eyes closed. Steavens looked at him earnestly, puzzled at the line of the chin, and wondering why a man should conceal a feature of such distinction under that disfiguring shock of beard. Suddenly, as though he felt the young sculptor's keen glance, Jim Laird opened his eyes.

"Was he always a good deal of an oyster?" he asked abruptly. "He was terribly shy as a boy."

"Yes, he was an oyster, since you put it so," rejoined Steavens. "Although he could be very fond of people, he always gave one the impression of being detached. He disliked violent emotion; he was reflective, and rather distrustful of himself—except, of course, as regarded his work. He was sure enough there. He distrusted men pretty thoroughly and women even more, yet somehow without believing ill of them. He was determined, indeed, to believe the best; but he seemed afraid to investigate."

"A burnt dog dreads the fire," said the lawyer grimly, and closed his eyes.

Steavens went on and on, reconstructing that whole miserable boyhood. All this raw, biting ugliness had been the portion of the man whose mind was to become an exhaustless gallery of beautiful impressions—so sensitive that the mere shadow of a poplar leaf flickering against a sunny wall would be etched and held there forever. Surely, if ever a man had the magic word in his finger tips, it was Merrick. Whatever he touched, he revealed its holiest secret; liberated it from enchantment and restored it to its pristine loveliness. Upon whatever he had come in contact with, he had left a beautiful record of the experience—a sort of ethereal signature; a scent, a sound, a color that was his own.

Steavens understood now the real tragedy of his master's life; neither love nor wine, as many had conjectured, but a blow which had fallen earlier and cut deeper than anything else could have done—a shame not his, and yet so unescapably his, to hide in his heart from his very boyhood. And without—the frontier warfare; the yearning of a boy, cast ashore upon a desert of newness and ugliness and sordidness, for all that is chastened and old, and noble with traditions.

At eleven o'clock the tall, flat woman in black crepe announced that the watchers were arriving, and asked them to "step into the dining room." As Steavens rose, the lawyer said dryly: "You go on—it'll be a good experience for you, doubtless; as for me, I'm not equal to that crowd tonight; I've had twenty years of them."

As Steavens closed the door after him he glanced back at the lawyer, sitting by the coffin in the dim light, with his chin resting on his hand.

The same misty group that had stood before the door of the express car shuffled into the dining room. In the light of the kerosene lamp they separated and became individuals. The minister, a pale, feeble-looking man with white hair and blond chin whiskers, took his seat beside a small side table and placed his Bible upon it. The Grand Army man sat down behind the stove and tilted his chair back comfortably against the wall, fishing his quill toothpick from his waistcoat pocket. The two bankers, Phelps and Elder, sat off in a corner behind the dinner table, where they could finish their discussion of the new usury law and its effect on chattel security loans. The real-estate agent, an old man with a smiling, hypocritical face, soon joined them. The coal and lumber dealer and the cattle shipper sat on opposite sides of the hard-coal burner, their feet on the nickelwork. Steavens took a book from his pocket and began to read. The talk around him ranged through various topics of local interest while the house was quieting down. When it was clear that the members of the family were in bed, the Grand Army man hitched his shoulders and, untangling his long legs, caught his heels on the rounds of his chair.

"S'pose there'll be a will, Phelps?" he queried in his weak falsetto.

The banker laughed disagreeably, and began trimming his nails with a pearl-handled pocketknife.

"There'll scarcely be any need for one, will there?" he queried in his turn.

The restless Grand Army man shifted his position again, getting his knees still nearer his chin. "Why, the ole man says Harve's done right well lately," he chirped.

The other banker spoke up. "I reckon he means by that Harve ain't asked him to mortgage any more farms lately, so as he could go on with his education."

"Seems like my mind don't reach back to a time when Harve wasn't bein' edycated," tittered the Grand Army man.

There was a general chuckle. The minister took out his handkerchief and blew his nose sonorously. Banker Phelps closed his knife with a snap. "It's too bad the old man's sons didn't turn out better," he remarked with reflective authority. "They never hung together. He spent money enough on Harve to stock a dozen cattle farms, and he might as well have poured it into Sand Creek. If Harve had stayed at home and helped nurse what little they had, and gone into stock on the old man's bottom farm, they might all have been well fixed. But the old man had to trust everything to tenants and was cheated right and left."

"Harve never could have handled stock none," interposed the cattleman. "He hadn't it in him to be sharp. Do you remember when he bought Sander's mules for eight-year-olds, when everybody in town knew that Sander's father-in-law give 'em to his wife for a wedding present eighteen years before, an' they was full-grown mules then?"

Everyone chuckled, and the Grand Army man rubbed his knees with a spasm of childish delight.

"Harve never was much account for anything practical, and he shore was never fond of work," began the coal and lumber dealer. "I mind the last time he was home; the day he left, when the old man was out to the barn helpin' his hand hitch up to take Harve to the train, and Cal Moots was patchin' up the fence; Harve, he come out on the step and sings out, in his ladylike voice, 'Cal Moots! Cal Moots! please come cord my trunk.'"

"That's Harve for you," approved the Grand Army man. "I kin hear him howlin' yet, when he was a big feller in long pants and his mother used to whale him with a rawhide in the barn for lettin' the cows get foundered in the cornfield when he was drivin' 'em home from pasture. He killed a cow of mine that-a-way onct—a pure Jersey and the best milker I had, an' the old man had to put up for her. Harve, he was watchin' the sun set acrost the marshes when the anamile got away; he argued that sunset was on-common fine."

"Where the old man made his mistake was sending the boy East to school," said Phelps, stroking his goatee and speaking in a deliberate, judicial tone. "There was where he got his head full of trapseing to Paris and all such folly. What Harve needed, of all people, was a course in some first-class Kansas City business college."

The letters were swimming before Steavens' eyes. Was it possible that these men did not understand, that the palm on the coffin meant nothing to them? The very name of their town would have remained forever buried in the postal guide had it not been now and again mentioned in the world in connection with Harvey Merrick's. He remembered what his master had said to him on the day of his death, after the congestion of both lungs had shut off any probability of recovery, and the sculptor had asked his pupil to send his body home. "It's not a pleasant place to be lying while the world is moving and doing and bettering," he had said with a feeble smile, "but it rather seems as though we ought to go back to the place we came from, in the end. The townspeople will come in for a look at me; and after they have had their say, I shan't have much to fear from the judgment of God!"

The cattleman took up the comment. "Forty's young for a Merrick to cash in; they usually hang on pretty well. Probably he helped it along with whiskey."

"His mother's people were not long-lived, and Harvey never had a robust constitution," said the minister mildly. He would have liked to say more. He had been the boy's Sunday-school teacher and had been fond of him; but he felt that he was not in a position to speak. His own sons had turned out badly, and it was not a year since one of them had made his last trip home in the express car, shot in a gambling house in the Black Hills.

"Nevertheless, there is no disputin' that Harve frequently looked upon the wine when it was red, also variegated, and it shore made an oncommon fool of him," moralized the cattleman.

Just then the door leading into the parlor rattled loudly and everyone started involuntarily, looking relieved when only Jim Laird came out. His red face was convulsed with anger, and the Grand Army man ducked his head when he saw the spark in his blue, bloodshot eye. They were all afraid of Jim; he was a drunkard but he could twist the law to suit his client's needs as no other man in all western Kansas could do, and there were many who tried. The lawyer closed the door gently behind him, leaned back against it, and folded his arms cocking his head a little to one side. When he assumed this attitude in the courtroom, ears were always pricked up, as it usually foretold a flood of withering sarcasm.

"I've been with you gentlemen before," he began in a dry, even tone, "when you've sat by the coffins of boys born and raised in this town; and, if I remember rightly, you were never any too well satisfied when you checked them up. What's the matter, anyhow? Why is it that reputable young men are as scarce as millionaires in Sand City? It might almost seem to a stranger that there was, some way, something the matter with your progressive town. Why did Reuben Sayer, the brightest young lawyer you ever turned out, after he had come home from the university as straight as a die, take to drinking and forge a check and shoot himself? Why did Bill Merrit's son die of the shakes in a saloon in Omaha? Why was Mr. Thomas' son, here, shot in a gambling house? Why did young Adams burn his mill to beat the insurance companies and go to the pen?"

The lawyer paused and unfolded his arms, laying one clenched fist quietly on the table. "I'll tell you why. Because you drummed nothing but money and knavery into their ears from the time they wore knickerbockers; because you carped away at them as you've been carping here tonight, holding our friends Phelps and Elder up to them for their models, as our grandfathers held up George Washington and John Adams. But the boys, worse luck, were young, and raw at the business you put them to; and how could they match coppers with such artists as Phelps and Elder? You wanted them to be successful rascals; they were only unsuccessful ones—that's all the difference. There was only one boy ever raised in this borderland between ruffianism and civilization who didn't come to grief, and you hated Harvey Merrick more for winning out than you hated all the other boys who got under the wheels. Lord! Lord, how you did hate him! Phelps, here, is fond of saying that he could buy and sell us all out any time he's a mind to; but he knew Harve wouldn't have given a tinker's damn for his bank and all his cattle farms put together; and a lack of appreciation, that way, goes hard with Phelps.

"Old Nimrod, here, thinks Harve drank too much; and this from such as Nimrod and me!

"Brother Elder says Harve was too free with the old man's money—fell short in filial consideration, maybe. Well, we can all remember the very tone in which brother Elder swore his own father was a liar, in the county court; and we all know that the old man came out of that partnership with his son as bare as a sheared lamb. But maybe I'm getting personal, and I'd better be driving ahead at what I want to say."

The lawyer paused a moment, squared his heavy shoulders, and went on: "Harvey Merrick and I went to school together, back East. We were dead in earnest, and we wanted you all to be proud of us someday. We meant to be great men. Even I, and I haven't lost my sense of humor, gentlemen, I meant to be a great man. I came back here to practice, and I found you didn't in the least want me to be a great man. You wanted me to be a shrewd lawyer—oh, yes! Our veteran here wanted me to get him an increase of pension, because he had dyspepsia; Phelps wanted a new county survey that would put the widow Wilson's little bottom farm inside his south line; Elder wanted to lend money at five per cent a month, and get it collected; old Stark here wanted to wheedle old women up in Vermont into investing their annuities in real-estate mortgages that are not worth the paper they are written on. Oh, you needed me hard enough, and you'll go on needing me!

"Well, I came back here and became the damned shyster you wanted me to be. You pretend to have some sort of respect for me; and yet you'll stand up and throw mud at Harvey Merrick, whose soul you couldn't dirty and whose hands you couldn't tie. Oh, you're a discriminating lot of Christians! There have been times when the sight of Harvey's name in some Eastern paper has made me hang my head like a whipped dog; and again, times when I liked to think of him off there in the world, away from all this hog wallow, climbing the big, clean upgrade he'd set for himself.

"And we? Now that we've fought and lied and sweated and stolen, and hated as only the disappointed strugglers in a bitter, dead little Western town know how to do, what have we got to show for it? Harvey Merrick wouldn't have given one sunset over your marshes for all you've got put together, and you know it. It's not for me to say why in the inscrutable wisdom of God, a genius should ever have been called from this place of hatred and bitter waters; but I want this Boston man to know that the drivel he's been hearing here tonight is the only tribute any truly great man could have from such a lot of sick, side-tracked, burnt-dog, land-poor sharks as the here-present financiers of Sand City—upon which town may God have mercy!"

The lawyer thrust out his hand to Steavens as he passed him, caught up his overcoat in the hall, and had left the house before the Grand Army man had had time to lift his ducked head and crane his long neck about at his fellows.

Next day Jim Laird was drunk and unable to attend the funeral services. Steavens called twice at his office, but was compelled to start East without seeing him. He had a presentiment that he would hear from him again, and left his address on the lawyer's table; but if Laird found it, he never acknowledged it. The thing in him that Harvey Merrick had loved must have gone underground with Harvey Merrick's coffin; for it never spoke again, and Jim got the cold he died of driving across the Colorado mountains to defend one of Phelps' sons who had got into trouble out there by cutting government timber. □

DISCUSSION

In "The Sculptor's Funeral," **setting** and **character,** two elements in the building of a successful short story, are especially notable. In Willa Cather's story each element reinforces the other; neither without the other could contribute fully to the narrative.

Setting must be more than physical description. Willa Cather could have said about Sand City that "it was small, ugly, wintry, isolated and provincial." Instead she relates those ideas incidental to the action; she selects one fact after another to let us both see and feel, sharply, the meanness and the provincialism of this western hamlet. Nighttime, snow, mud, the long curve of the railroad track that leads *from* civilization, the small knot of men isolated on the railroad siding—these begin to let the reader know what Sand City is like.

The setting is further developed through her use of **characterization.** We are introduced to a gallery of local people —the war veteran, the banker, the lawyer, the minister, the cattleman. Each in his own way, through his dialect or the conversational topics he chooses or simply by his manner, reflects the town's attitudes.

The principal character who causes the nature of Sand City to be revealed is, oddly enough, hardly present. Merrick the sculptor is dead. But Merrick represents the life beyond Sand City. By the standards of his hometown he was not a success; the palm-wreath tribute on his coffin is ignored by his fellow townsmen. Merrick's world portrays Sand City through contrast.

Next to inform us about the hamlet is Henry Steavens, Merrick's representative both in Boston and in Sand City. Steavens becomes our eyes. Like us, he sees Merrick's birthplace for the first time, and quickly forms his (and our) judgments.

Following Steavens, and after a long delay in the story, another character comes swiftly to life—Jim Laird the lawyer. He verbally lays bare the soul of Sand City. The revelation has been gradual, but detailed, sharp, built up not by just one observer but by many.

FOR EXPLORATION

1. (a) Read again Cather's description of the Merrick house. (beginning page A 40, column b, paragraph 3) How does the house reflect generally what we know about the town? (b) What does it tell us about the boyhood of the sculptor?

2. (a) Why is the author so unsympathetic and even harsh in her presentation of the Merrick family: mother, father, and sister? (b) What do these character-drawings contribute to the life story of Merrick the son?

3. Is Jim Laird the only one in Sand City who came close to understanding Merrick's life aims?

4. Do you feel the tongue-lashing Laird delivers to the mourners is justified? Or is his address as unfair and one-sided as the mourner's comments about Merrick? Discuss.

CREATIVE RESPONSE

1. A Biblical proverb says that "a prophet is without honor in his own country." Discuss this proverb as it applies to Merrick—and to people you know about.

2. Laird states: ". . . you hated Harvey Merrick more for winning out than you hated all the other boys who got under the wheels." (page 45 A, column a, paragraph 1) Is this a typical expression of human nature? Explore the truth of it based on your own experience or observation of human attitudes.

-THE BETTMANN ARCHIVE, INC.

Willa Cather   1873 / 1947

Though born in Virginia, Willa Cather spent much of her youth in a rural Nebraska pioneer community. She lived on a ranch and, since there were no schools nearby, was taught the English classics and Latin at home by her two grandmothers. Her neighbors were also ranchers, most of them foreign-born or second-generation Americans. It was these people and the Midwest landscape which would dominate much of her writing.

The Cather family moved to Red Cloud, Nebraska, in time for Willa to attend high school, following which she worked her way through the state university. After college, while working as a reporter, she began writing first poetry and then short stories.

"The Sculptor's Funeral" appeared first in early 1905 in *McClures Magazine* (of which she later became managing editor) and then later that year in her first collection of stories, *The Troll Garden.*

Success came with such classics as *O Pioneers* (1913) and *My Antonia* (1918), novels which grew from memories of her Nebraska childhood. In 1923 she won the Pulitzer Prize for *One of Ours*, a story of World War I. *Death Comes for the Archbishop* (1927), a chronicle of two priests and the spiritual pioneering of the Catholic Church in New Mexico, is considered her masterpiece.

Some critics have characterized her work as being aloof and lacking immediacy. Others regard the restraint and dignity of her writing as timeless. She herself said she reached her objective when she stopped trying to write and began to remember.

Gwendolyn Brooks

PIANO AFTER WAR

On a snug evening I shall watch her fingers,
Cleverly ringed, declining to clever pink,
Beg glory from the willing keys. Old hungers
Will break their coffins, rise to eat and thank.
5 And music, warily, like the golden rose
That sometimes after sunset warms the west,
Will warm that room, persuasively suffuse
That room and me, rejuvenate a past.
But suddenly, across my climbing fever
10 Of proud delight—a multiplying cry.
A cry of bitter dead men who will never
Attend a gentle maker of musical joy.
Then my thawed eye will go again to ice.
And stone will shove the softness from my face.

DISCUSSION

"Piano After War" and "Mentors" are Parts I and II of a double sonnet and must be read in terms of each other. In both poems, the speaker turns from a situation implicit with warmth, comfort, and pleasantness to something harsh and cold but of profound significance. To whom does the speaker turn in "Piano After War"? in "Mentors"?

"piano after war" and "mentors" from SELECTED POEMS by Gwendolyn Brooks. Copyright, 1945 by Gwendolyn Brooks Blakely. Reprinted by permission of Harper & Row, Publishers, Inc.

FOR EXPLORATION

1. (a) Is the interpretation of these two poems necessarily limited by the title of the first? (b) What might the "War" be? (c) Should "War" be interpreted broadly or narrowly? (d) If you interpret "War" broadly, who might some of the "bitter dead men" be?
2. What is a mentor?
3. (a) To what does the word "their" in line 1 of "Mentors" refer? (b) What does the speaker mean in line 2? (c) What does the speaker say he will do to honor the dead?
4. Who is the "her" in line 11 of "Mentors"?
5. Explain the reference to "midnight" in the last line of "Mentors." Why does it belong to both the speaker and the dead men?
6. How many contrasts can you find in these two poems?

MENTORS

For I am rightful fellow of their band.
My best allegiances are to the dead.
I swear to keep the dead upon my mind,
Disdain for all time to be overglad.
5 Among spring flowers, under summer trees,
By chilling autumn waters, in the frosts
Of supercilious winter—all my days
I'll have as mentors those reproving ghosts.
And at that cry, at that remotest whisper,
10 I'll stop my casual business. Leave the banquet.
Or leave the ball—reluctant to unclasp her
Who may be fragrant as the flower she wears,
Make gallant bows and dim excuses, then quit
Light for the midnight that is mine and theirs.

HARPER & ROW

Gwendolyn Brooks   1917 /

For all but one month of her life Gwendolyn Brooks has lived on the South Side of Chicago. Her early attempts at writing were encouraged by her family, all of whom were interested in the arts. After graduation from Wilson Junior College in Chicago, she did editorial work on a magazine and secretarial work. While she was working she took a writing course, submitted one of her poems to *Poetry* magazine, and was delighted to have it accepted.

After her initial success, fame came rapidly. Her first volume of poetry, *A Street in Bronzeville* (1945), led to both an American Academy of Arts and Letters award and a Guggenheim Fellowship. Her second book of poems, *Annie Allen*, won the Pulitzer Prize for poetry in 1950. In 1968, the same year *In the Mecca* was published, she was named successor to the late Carl Sandburg as Poet Laureate of Illinois. In 1971 a group of new Black poets, in recognition of her influence, support, and encouragement, published a collection of their works entitled *To Gwen with Love.*

Critics have praised Miss Brooks' poetry for its directness, its naturalness, and the way in which it views commonplace situations in an original manner.

I walk down the garden-paths,
And all the daffodils
Are blowing, and the bright blue squills.
I walk down the patterned garden-paths
5 In my stiff, brocaded gown.
With my powdered hair and jeweled fan,
I too am a rare
Pattern. As I wander down
The garden-paths.
10 My dress is richly figured,
And the train
Makes a pink and silver stain
On the gravel, and the thrift
Of the borders.
15 Just a plate of current fashion,
Tripping by in high-heeled, ribboned shoes.
Not a softness anywhere about me,
Only whalebone and brocade.
And I sink on a seat in the shade
20 Of a lime-tree. For my passion
Wars against the stiff brocade.
The daffodils and squills
Flutter in the breeze
As they please.
25 And I weep;
For the lime-tree is in blossom
And one small flower had dropped upon my
    bosom.

And the plashing of waterdrops
In the marble fountain
30 Comes down the garden-paths.
The dripping never stops.
Underneath my stiffened gown
Is the softness of a woman bathing in a marble
    basin,
A basin in the midst of hedges grown
35 So thick, she cannot see her lover hiding,
But she guesses he is near,
And the sliding of the water
Seems the stroking of a dear
Hand upon her.
40 What is Summer in a fine brocaded gown!
I should like to see it lying in a heap upon the
    ground.
All the pink and silver crumpled up on the ground.

I would be the pink and silver as I ran along the
    paths,
And he would stumble after,
45 Bewildered by my laughter.
I should see the sun flashing from his sword hilt
    and the buckles on his shoes.
I would choose
To lead him in a maze along the patterned paths,
A bright and laughing maze for my heavy-booted
    lover.
50 Till he caught me in the shade,
And the buttons of his waistcoat bruised my body
    as he clasped me
Aching, melting, unafraid.
With the shadows of the leaves and the sundrops,
And the plopping of the waterdrops,

PATTERNS

Amy Lowell

"Patterns" by Amy Lowell from THE COLLECTED POEMS OF AMY LOWELL. Copyright, 1955, by Houghton Mifflin Company. Reprinted by permission of the publisher, Houghton Mifflin Company.

All about us in the open afternoon—
I am very like to swoon
With the weight of this brocade,
For the sun sifts through the shade.

Underneath the fallen blossom
In my bosom,
Is a letter I have hid.
It was brought to me this morning by a rider from
      the Duke.[1]
"Madam, we regret to inform you that Lord
      Hartwell
Died in action Thursday se'nnight."[2]
As I read it in the white, morning sunlight,
The letters squirmed like snakes.
"Any answer, Madam," said my footman.
"No," I told him.
"See that the messenger takes some refreshment.
No, no answer."
And I walked into the garden,
Up and down the patterned paths,
In my stiff, correct brocade.
The blue and yellow flowers stood up proudly in
      the sun,
Each one.
I stood upright too,
Held rigid to the pattern
By the stiffness of my gown.
Up and down I walked,
Up and down.

In a month he would have been my husband.
In a month, here, underneath this lime,
We would have broke the pattern;
He for me, and I for him,
He as Colonel, I as Lady,
On this shady seat.
He had a whim
That sunlight carried blessing.
And I answered, "It shall be as you have said."
Now he is dead.

In Summer and in Winter I shall walk
Up and down
The patterned garden-paths
In my stiff, brocaded gown.
The squills and daffodils
Will give place to pillared roses, and to asters, and
      to snow.
I shall go
Up and down,
In my gown.
Gorgeously arrayed,
Boned and stayed.
And the softness of my body will be guarded from
      embrace
By each button, hook, and lace.
For the man who should loose me is dead,
Fighting with the Duke in Flanders,
In a pattern called a war.
Christ! What are patterns for?

---

1. *the Duke*, probably John Churchill, Duke of Marlborough
(1650–1722), commander of the united English and Dutch armies
during the War of the Spanish Succession (1701–1714). The initial
campaign was fought in Belgium and adjoining countries.
2. *se'nnight*, an archaic word meaning a period of seven days and
nights. Within the context of the poem it means that Lord Hartwell
died a week ago Thursday.

DISCUSSION

"Patterns" is a **narrative poem.** It is a fairly simple story, and a common one—the story of love unfulfilled because of death. The action of the narrative is only gradually revealed in the poem. As readers of the poem, we witness the woman walking in her formal garden, longing for the presence of her absent lover. We do not realize until near the end of the poem what has caused the lover's absence— his death in war. We then discover that they were engaged to be married within a month. The interest in the poem is thus sustained not only by the action, but by the order in which details of the action are revealed to the reader.

But even more than the action, the **motif** of "patterns" helps organize the poem and sustain the interest. A motif is a pattern itself—a recurring element in a work of literature that gathers meaning as it appears and reappears. The very title of this poem calls attention to this motif in "Patterns," and as the poem progresses, more and more patterns appear, until almost all existence appears to be a pattern and pattern comes to suggest all the restraint and restriction that prevents emotional fulfillment in life. After we finish reading this poem, the visual image that is likely to stay with us is related to this motif—a patterned garden with a patterned lady walking up and down in a meaningless pattern, unable to break out of the prison of her patterns.

FOR EXPLORATION

1. What is the season and how is the season appropriate to the narrative?
2. In what sense is the woman "a rare Pattern"?
3. In line 83, the speaker says, "We would have broke the pattern." What does she mean?
4. Near the end of the poem, why does the speaker refer to the war as a "pattern"?

CREATIVE RESPONSE

At the end of "Patterns," the speaker asks: "Christ! What are patterns for?" Write a brief answer in reply to her question.

THE BETTMANN ARCHIVE, INC.

Amy Lowell   1874 / 1925

Amy Lowell was born into one of the wealthiest and most distinguished families of Massachusetts. Her grandfather had founded the cotton-manufacturing town of Lowell. Her grandfather's cousin was the poet James Russell Lowell (see page C 182). Her brothers were Percival Lowell, the astronomer, and Abbott Lawrence Lowell, for many years president of Harvard. Amy was educated privately and traveled widely.

Not until she was twenty-eight years old did Amy Lowell decide seriously to become a poet, and then she studied for eight years before publishing a line. Her first volume of poetry, *A Dome of Many-Colored Glass* (1912), was conventional, and echoed the melodies of older poets. Soon after its publication Miss Lowell joined the Imagists, a

group of poets who believed in the use of free-verse forms, freedom to write about any subject, and, above all, the use of the exact word to create strong and concrete images. Miss Lowell's second volume of poetry, *Sword Blades and Poppy Seeds* (1914), brilliantly incorporated these beliefs; *Men, Women, and Ghosts* (1916), in which "Patterns" first appeared, showed that in addition to being a craftsman of note she was also a superb storyteller.

The "new poetry" of the Imagists was bitterly ridiculed. Miss Lowell traveled across the country for ten years, reading and lecturing. Gradually scorn gave way to acceptance, and by the time she died in 1925 her poetry held an honored place. She was posthumously awarded the Pulitzer Prize in 1926 for *What's O'Clock*.

The Oyster and the Pearl

William Saroyan

Characters

HARRY VAN DUSEN, *a barber*
CLAY LARRABEE, *a boy on Saturday*
VIVIAN MCCUTCHEON, *a new schoolteacher*
CLARK LARRABEE, CLAY'S *father*
MAN, *a writer*
ROXANNA LARRABEE, CLAY'S *sister*
GREELEY, CLAY'S *pal*
JUDGE APPLEGARTH, *a beachcomber*
WOZZECK, *a watch repairer*
ATTENDANT, *a man from the gasoline station*

Scene: HARRY VAN DUSEN'S *barbershop in O.K.-by-the-Sea, California, population 909. The sign on the window says: Harry Van Dusen, Barber. It's an old-fashioned shop, crowded with stuff not usually found in barbershops . . .* HARRY *himself, for instance. He has never been known to put on a barber's white jacket or to work without a hat of some sort on his head: a stovepipe, a derby, a western, a homburg, a skullcap, a beret, or a straw, as if putting on these various hats somewhat expressed the quality of his soul, or suggested the range of it.*
On the walls, on shelves, are many odds and ends, some apparently washed up by the sea, which is a block down the street: abalone and other shells, rocks, pieces of driftwood, a life jacket, rope, sea plants. There is one old-fashioned chair.
When the play begins, HARRY *is seated in the chair. A boy of nine or ten named* CLAY LARRABEE *is giving him a haircut.* HARRY *is reading a book, one of many in the shop.*

"The Oyster and the Pearl" is reprinted from PERSPECTIVES 4, Summer 1953, by permission of the author. Copyright 1953 by William Saroyan. This play was first presented on February 4, 1953, on the TV-Radio Workshop's television program, "Omnibus."

CLAY. Well, I did what you told me, Mr. Van Dusen. I hope it's all right. I'm no barber, though. (He begins to comb the hair.)

HARRY. You just gave me a haircut, didn't you?

CLAY. I don't know *what* you'd call it. You want to look at it in the mirror? (He holds out a small mirror.)

HARRY. No thanks. I remember the last one.

CLAY. I guess I'll never be a barber.

HARRY. Maybe not. On the other hand, you may turn out to be the one man hidden away in the junk of the world who will bring merriment to the tired old human heart.

CLAY. Who? Me?

HARRY. Why not?

CLAY. Merriment to the tired old human heart? How do you do that?

HARRY. Compose a symphony, paint a picture, write a book, invent a philosophy.

CLAY. Not me! Did you ever do stuff like that?

HARRY. I did.

CLAY. What did you do?

HARRY. Invented a philosophy.

CLAY. What's that?

HARRY. A way to live.

CLAY. What way did you invent?

HARRY. The *Take-it-easy way.*

CLAY. That sounds pretty good.

HARRY. All philosophies *sound* good. The trouble with mine was, I kept forgetting to take it easy. Until one day. The day I came off the highway into this barbershop. The barber told me the shop was for sale. I told him all I had to my name was eighty dollars. He sold me the shop for seventy-five, and threw in the haircut. I've been here ever since. That was twenty-four years ago.

CLAY. Before I was born.

HARRY. Fifteen or sixteen years before you were born.

CLAY. How old were you then?

HARRY. Old enough to know a good thing when I saw it.

CLAY. What did you see?

HARRY. O.K.-by-the-Sea, and this shop—the proper place for me to stop. That's a couplet. Shakespeare had them at the end of a scene, so I guess that's the end of this haircut. (He gets out of the chair, goes to the hat tree, and puts on a derby.)

CLAY. I guess I'd never get a haircut if you weren't in town, Mr. Van Dusen.

HARRY. Nobody would, since I'm the only barber.

CLAY. I mean, free of charge.

HARRY. I give you a haircut free of charge, you give me a haircut free of charge. That's fair and square.

CLAY. Yes, but you're a barber. You get a dollar a haircut.

HARRY. Now and then I do. Now and then I don't.

CLAY. Well, anyhow, thanks a lot. I guess I'll go down to the beach now and look for stuff.

HARRY. I'd go with you but I'm expecting a little Saturday business.

CLAY. This time I'm going to find something *real good,* I think.

HARRY. The sea washes up some pretty good things at that, doesn't it?

CLAY. It sure does, except money.

HARRY. What do you want with money?

CLAY. Things I need.

HARRY. What do you need?

CLAY. I want to get my father to come home again. I want to buy Mother a present. . .

HARRY. Now, wait a minute, Clay, let me get this straight. Where *is* your father?

CLAY. I don't know. He went off the day after I got my last haircut, about a month ago.

HARRY. What do you mean, he went off?

CLAY. He just picked up and went off.

HARRY. Did he say when he was coming back?

CLAY. No. All he said was, "Enough's enough." He wrote it on the kitchen wall.

HARRY. Enough's enough?

CLAY. Yeah. We all thought he'd be back in a day or two, but now we know we've got to *find* him and *bring* him back.

HARRY. How do you expect to do that?

CLAY. Well, we put an ad in the *The O.K.-by-the Sea Gull.* . . that comes out every Saturday.

HARRY (opening the paper). This paper? But your father's not in town. How will he see an ad in this paper?

CLAY. He *might* see it. Anyhow, we don't know what else to do. We're living off the money we saved from the summer we worked, but there ain't much left.

HARRY. The summer you worked?

CLAY. Yeah. Summer before last, just before we moved here, we picked cotton in Kern County. My father, my mother, and me.

HARRY (indicating the paper). What do you say in your ad?

CLAY (*looking at it*). Well, I say. . . Clark Larrabee. Come home. Your fishing tackle's in the closet safe and sound. The fishing's good, plenty of cabezon, perch, and bass. Let bygones be bygones. We miss you. Mama, Clay, Roxanna, Rufus, Clara.

HARRY. That's a good ad.

CLAY. Do you think if my father reads it, he'll come home?

HARRY. I don't know, Clay. I hope so.

CLAY. Yeah. Thanks a lot for the haircut, Mr. Van Dusen.

(CLAY *goes out.* HARRY *takes off the derby, lathers his face, and begins to shave with a straight-edge razor. A pretty girl in a swimming suit comes into the shop, closing a colorful parasol. She has long blond hair.*)

HARRY. Miss America, I presume.

THE GIRL. Miss McCutcheon.

HARRY. Harry Van Dusen.

THE GIRL. How do you do.

HARRY (*bowing*). Miss McCutcheon.

THE GIRL. I'm new here.

HARRY. You'd be new anywhere—brand-new, I might say. Surely you don't live here?

THE GIRL. As a matter of fact, I do. At any rate, I've been here since last Sunday. You see, I'm the new teacher at the school.

HARRY. You are?

THE GIRL. Yes, I am.

HARRY. How do you like it?

THE GIRL. One week at this school has knocked me for a loop. As a matter of fact, I want to quit and go home to San Francisco. At the same time I have a feeling I ought to stay. What do you think?

HARRY. Are you serious? I mean, in asking me?

THE GIRL. Of course I'm serious. You've been here a long time. You know everybody in town. Shall I go, or shall I stay?

HARRY. Depends on what you're looking for. I stopped here twenty-four years ago because I decided I wasn't looking for anything any more. Well, I was mistaken. I *was* looking, and I've found exactly what I was looking for.

THE GIRL. What's that?

HARRY. A chance to take my time. That's why I'm still here. What are *you* looking for, Miss McCutcheon?

THE GIRL. Well. . .

HARRY. I mean, besides a husband. . .

THE GIRL. I'm not looking for a husband. I expect a husband to look for me.

HARRY. That's fair.

THE GIRL. I'm looking for a chance to teach.

HARRY. That's fair too.

THE GIRL. But this town! . . . The children just don't seem to care about anything—whether they get good grades or bad, whether they pass or fail, or anything else. On top of that, almost all of them are unruly. The only thing they seem to be interested in is games, and the sea. That's why I'm on my way to the beach now. I thought if I could watch them on a Saturday I might understand them better.

HARRY. Yes, that's a thought.

THE GIRL. Nobody seems to have any sensible ambition. It's all fun and play. How can I teach children like that? What can I teach them?

HARRY. English.

THE GIRL. Of course.

HARRY (*drying his face*). Singing, dancing, cooking. . .

THE GIRL. Cooking? . . . I must say I expected to see a much older man.

HARRY. Well! Thank you!

THE GIRL. Not at all.

HARRY. The question is, Shall you stay, or shall you go back to San Francisco?

THE GIRL. Yes.

HARRY. The answer is, Go back while the going's good.

THE GIRL. Why? I mean, a moment ago I believed you were going to point out why I ought to stay, and then suddenly you say I ought to go back. Why?

HARRY (*after a pause*). You're too good for a town like this.

THE GIRL. I am not!

HARRY. Too young and too intelligent. Youth and intelligence need excitement.

THE GIRL. There are *kinds* of excitement.

HARRY. Yes, there are. You need the big-city kind. There isn't an eligible bachelor in town.

THE GIRL. You seem to think all I want is to find a husband.

HARRY. But only to teach. You want to teach him to become a father, so you can have a lot of children of your own—to teach.

THE GIRL. (*She sits almost angrily in the chair and*

speaks very softly.) I'd like a poodle haircut if you don't mind, Mr. Van Dusen.

HARRY. You'll have to get that in San Francisco, I'm afraid.

THE GIRL. Why? Aren't you a barber?

HARRY. I am.

THE GIRL. Well, this is your shop. It's open for business. I'm a customer. I've got money. I want a poodle haircut.

HARRY. I don't know how to give a poodle haircut, but even if I knew how, I wouldn't do it.

THE GIRL. Why not?

HARRY. I don't give women haircuts. The only women who visit this shop bring their small children for haircuts.

THE GIRL. I want a poodle haircut, Mr. Van Dusen.

HARRY. I'm sorry, Miss McCutcheon. In my sleep, in a nightmare, I would *not* cut your hair.

(The sound of a truck stopping is heard from across the street.)

THE GIRL (*softly, patiently, but firmly*). Mr. Van Dusen, I've decided to stay, and the first thing I've got to do is change my appearance. I don't fit into the scenery around here.

HARRY. Oh, I don't know—if I were a small boy going to school, I'd say you look just right.

THE GIRL. You're just like the children. They don't take me seriously, either. They think I'm nothing more than a pretty girl who is going to give up in despair and go home. If you give me a poodle haircut I'll look more—well, plain and simple. I plan to dress differently, too. I'm determined to teach here. You've got to help me. Now, Mr. Van Dusen, the shears, please.

HARRY. I'm sorry, Miss McCutcheon. There's no need to change your *appearance* at all.

(CLARK LARRABEE comes into the shop.)

HARRY. You're next, Clark. (HARRY *helps* MISS MC-CUTCHEON *out of the chair. She gives him an angry glance.*)

THE GIRL (*whispering*). I won't forget this rudeness, Mr. Van Dusen.

HARRY (*also whispering*). Never whisper in O.K.-by-the-Sea. People misunderstand. (*Loudly.*) Good day, Miss.

(MISS MCCUTCHEON opens her parasol with anger and leaves the shop. CLARK LARRABEE has scarcely noticed her. He stands looking at HARRY'S junk on the shelves.)

HARRY. Well, Clark, I haven't seen you in a long time.

CLARK. I'm just passing through, Harry. Thought I might run into Clay here.

HARRY. He was here a little while ago.

CLARK. How is he?

HARRY. He's fine, Clark.

CLARK. I been working in Salinas. Got a ride down in a truck. It's across the street now at the gasoline station.

HARRY. You've been home, of course?

CLARK. No, I haven't.

HARRY. Oh?

CLARK (*after a slight pause*). I've left Fay, Harry.

HARRY. You got time for a haircut, Clark?

CLARK. No thanks, Harry. I've got to go back to Salinas on that truck across the street.

HARRY. Clay's somewhere on the beach.

CLARK (*handing* HARRY *three ten-dollar bills*). Give him this, will you? Thirty dollars. Don't tell him I gave it to you.

HARRY. Why not?

CLARK. I'd rather he didn't know I was around. Is he all right?

HARRY. Sure, Clark. They're *all* O.K. I mean. . .

CLARK. Tell him to take the money home to his mother. (*He picks up the newspaper,* The Gull.)

HARRY. Sure, Clark. It came out this morning. Take it along.

CLARK. Thanks. (*He puts the paper in his pocket.*) How've things been going with *you*, Harry?

HARRY. Oh, I can't kick. Two or three haircuts a day. A lot of time to read. A few laughs. A few surprises. The sea. The fishing. It's a good life.

CLARK. Keep an eye on Clay, will you? I mean— well, I *had* to do it.

HARRY. Sure.

CLARK. Yeah, well. . .That's the first money I've been able to save. When I make some more, I'd like to send it here, so you can hand it to Clay, to take home.

HARRY. Anything you say, Clark.

(There is the sound of the truck's horn blowing.)

CLARK. Well. . . (*He goes to the door.*) Thanks, Harry, thanks a lot.

HARRY. Good seeing you, Clark.

(CLARK LARRABEE goes out. HARRY watches him. A truck shifting gears is heard, and then the sound of the truck driving off. HARRY picks up a book, changes hats, sits down in the chair and begins to read. A MAN *of forty or so, well dressed, rather swift, comes in.)*

THE MAN. Where's the barber?

HARRY. I'm the barber.

THE MAN. Can I get a haircut, real quick?

HARRY (getting out of the chair). Depends on what you mean by real quick.

THE MAN (sitting down). Well, just a haircut, then.

HARRY (putting an apron around the MAN). O.K. I don't believe I've seen you before.

THE MAN. No. They're changing the oil in my car across the street. Thought I'd step in here and get a haircut. Get it out of the way before I get to Hollywood. How many miles is it?

HARRY. About two hundred straight down the highway. You can't miss it.

THE MAN. What town is this?

HARRY. O.K.-by-the Sea.

THE MAN. What do the people do here?

HARRY. Well, I cut hair. Friend of mine named Wozzeck repairs watches, radios, alarm clocks, and sells jewelry.

THE MAN. Who does he sell it to?

HARRY. The people here. It's imitation stuff mainly.

THE MAN. Factory here? Farms? Fishing?

HARRY. No. Just the few stores on the highway, the houses further back in the hills, the church, and the school. You a salesman?

THE MAN. No, I'm a writer.

HARRY. What do you write?

THE MAN. A little bit of everything. How about the haircut?

HARRY. You got to be in Hollywood tonight?

THE MAN. I don't have to be anywhere tonight, but that was the idea. Why?

HARRY. Well, I've always said a writer could step into a place like this, watch things a little while, and get a whole book out of it, or a play.

THE MAN. Or if he was a poet, a sonnet.

HARRY. Do you like Shakespeare's?

THE MAN. They're just about the best in English.

HARRY. It's not often I get a writer in here. As a matter of fact you're the only writer I've had in here in twenty years, not counting Fenton.

THE MAN. Who's he?

HARRY. Fenton Lockhart.

THE MAN. What's he write?

HARRY. He gets out the weekly paper. Writes the whole thing himself.

THE MAN. Yeah. Well. . . How about the haircut?

HARRY. O.K.

(HARRY puts a hot towel around the man's head.

MISS MCCUTCHEON, carrying a cane chair without one leg and without a seat, comes in. With her is CLAY with something in his hand, a smaller boy named GREELEY with a bottle of sea water, and ROXANNA with an assortment of shells.)

CLAY. I got an oyster here, Mr. Van Dusen.

GREELEY. Miss McCutcheon claims there ain't a big pearl in it.

HARRY (looking at MISS MCCUTCHEON). Is she willing to admit there's a little one in it?

GREELEY. I don't know. I know I got sea water in this bottle.

MISS MCCUTCHEON. Mr. Van Dusen, Clay Larrabee seems to believe there's a pearl in this oyster he happens to have found on the beach.

CLAY. I didn't happen to find it. I went looking for it. You know Black Rock, Mr. Van Dusen? Well, the tide hardly ever gets low enough for a fellow to get around to the ocean side of Black Rock, but a little while ago it did, so I went around there to that side. I got to poking around and I found this oyster.

HARRY. I've been here twenty-four years, Clay, and this is the first time I've ever heard of anybody finding an oyster on our beach—at Black Rock, or anywhere else.

CLAY. Well, I did, Mr. Van Dusen. It's shut tight, it's alive, and there's a pearl in it, worth at least three hundred dollars.

GREELEY. A big pearl.

MISS MCCUTCHEON. Now, you children listen to me. It's never too soon for any of us to face the truth, which is supposed to set us free, not imprison us. The truth is, Clay, you want money because you need money. The truth is also that you have found an oyster. The truth is also that there is no pearl in the oyster.

GREELEY. How do you know? Did you look?

MISS MCCUTCHEON. No, but neither did Clay, and inasmuch as only one oyster in a million has a pearl in it, truth favors the probability that this is not the millionth oyster. . . the oyster with the pearl in it.

CLAY. There's a big pearl in the oyster.

MISS MCCUTCHEON. Mr. Van Dusen, shall we open the oyster and show Clay and his sister Roxanna and their friend Greeley that there is no pearl in it?

HARRY. In a moment, Miss McCutcheon. And what's that you have?

MISS MCCUTCHEON. A chair, as you see.

HARRY. How many legs does it have?

MISS MCCUTCHEON. Three of course. I can count to three, I hope.

HARRY. What do you want with a chair with only three legs?

MISS MCCUTCHEON. I'm going to bring things from the sea the same as everybody else in town.

HARRY. But everybody else in town *doesn't* bring things from the sea—just the children, Judge Applegarth, Fenton Lockhart, and myself.

MISS MCCUTCHEON. In any case, the same as the children, Judge Applegarth, Fenton Lockhart, and you. Judge Applegarth? Who's he?

HARRY. He judged swine at a county fair one time, so we call him Judge.

MISS MCCUTCHEON. Pigs?

HARRY. Swine's a little old-fashioned but I prefer it to pigs, and since both words mean the same thing——Well, I wouldn't care to call a man like Arthur Applegarth a pig judge.

MISS MCCUTCHEON. Did he actually judge swine, as you prefer to put it, at a county fair, one time? Did he even do *that*?

HARRY. Nobody checked up. He *said* he did.

MISS MCCUTCHEON. So that entitled him to be called Judge Applegarth?

HARRY. It certainly did.

MISS MCCUTCHEON. On that basis, Clay's oyster has a big pearl in it because he *says* so, is that it?

HARRY. I didn't say that.

MISS MCCUTCHEON. Are we living in the Middle Ages Mr. Van Dusen?

GREELEY. No, this is 1953, Miss McCutcheon.

MISS MCCUTCHEON. Yes, Greeley, and to illustrate what I mean, that's water you have in that bottle. Nothing else.

GREELEY. *Sea* water.

MISS MCCUTCHEON. Yes, but there's nothing else in the bottle.

GREELEY. No, but there's little things in the water. You can't see them now, but they'll show up later. The water of the sea is full of things.

MISS MCCUTCHEON. Salt, perhaps.

GREELEY. No. *Living* things. If I look hard I can see some of them now.

MISS MCCUTCHEON. You can *imagine* seeing them. Mr. Van Dusen, are you going to help me or not?

HARRY. What do you want me to do?

MISS MCCUTCHEON. Open the oyster of course, so Clay will see for himself that there's no pearl in

it. So he'll begin to face reality, as he should, as each of us should.

HARRY. Clay, do you mind if I look at the oyster a minute?

CLAY (*handing the oyster to* HARRY). There's a big pearl in it, Mr. Van Dusen.

HARRY (*examining the oyster*). Clay . . . Roxanna . . . Greeley . . . I wonder if you'd go down the street to Wozzeck's. Tell him to come here the first chance he gets. I'd rather he opened this oyster. I might damage the pearl.

CLAY, GREELEY, *and* ROXANNA. O.K., Mr. Van Dusen. (*They go out.*)

MISS MCCUTCHEON. What pearl? What in the world do you think you're trying to do to the minds of these children? How am I ever going to teach them the principles of truth with an influence like yours to fight against?

HARRY. Miss McCutcheon. The people of O.K.-by-the-Sea are all poor. Most of them can't afford to pay for the haircuts I give them. There's no excuse for this town at all, but the sea is here, and so are the hills. A few people find jobs a couple of months every year North or South, come back half dead of homesickness, and live on next to nothing the rest of the year. A few get pensions. Every family has a garden and a few chickens, and they make a few dollars selling vegetables and eggs. In a town of almost a thousand people there isn't one rich man. Not even one who is well-off. And yet these people are the richest I have ever known. Clay doesn't really want money, as you seem to think. He wants his father to come home, and he thinks money will help get his father home. As a matter of fact his father is the man who stepped in here just as you were leaving. He left thirty dollars for me to give to Clay, to take home. His father and his mother haven't been getting along. Clark Larrabee's a fine man. He's not the town drunk or anything like that but having four kids to provide for he gets to feeling ashamed of the showing he's making, and he starts drinking. He wants his kids to live in a good house of their own, wear good clothes, and all the other things fathers have always wanted for their kids. His wife wants these things for the kids, too. They don't have these things, so they fight. They had one too many fights about a month ago, so Clark went off—he's working in Salinas. He's either going to keep moving away from his family, or he's going to come back. It all depends on—well, I don't know what. This oyster maybe. Clay maybe. (*Softly.*) You and me maybe.

(*There is a pause. He looks at the oyster.* MISS MCCUTCHEON *looks at it, too.*)

HARRY. Clay believes there's a pearl in this oyster for the same reason you and I believe whatever *we* believe to keep *us* going.

MISS MCCUTCHEON. Are you suggesting we play a trick on Clay, in order to carry out your mumbo-jumbo ideas?

HARRY. Well, maybe it *is* a trick. I know Wozzeck's got a few pretty good-sized cultivated pearls.

MISS MCCUTCHEON. You plan to have Wozzeck pretend he has found a pearl in the oyster when he opens it, is that it?

HARRY. I plan to get three hundred dollars to Clay.

MISS MCCUTCHEON. Do you *have* three hundred dollars?

HARRY. Not quite.

MISS MCCUTCHEON. What about the other children who need money? Do you plan to put pearls in oysters for them, too? Not just here in O.K.-by-the-Sea. Everywhere. This isn't the only town in the world where people are poor, where fathers and mothers fight, where families break up.

HARRY. No, it isn't, but it's the only town where I live.

MISS MCCUTCHEON. I give up. What do you want me to do?

HARRY. Well, could you find it in your heart to be just a little less sure about things when you talk to the kids—I mean, the troubled ones? You can get Clay around to the truth easy enough just as soon as he gets his father home.

(ARTHUR APPLEGARTH *comes in.*)

HARRY. Judge Applegarth, may I present Miss McCutcheon?

THE JUDGE (*removing his hat and bowing low*). An honor, Miss.

MISS MCCUTCHEON. How do you do, Judge.

HARRY. Miss McCutcheon's the new teacher at the school.

THE JUDGE. We are honored to have you. The children, the parents, and—the rest of us.

MISS MCCUTCHEON. Thank you Judge. (*To* HARRY, *whispering.*) I'll be back as soon as I change my clothes.

HARRY (*whispering*). I told you not to whisper.

MISS MCCUTCHEON (*whispering*). I shall expect you to give me a poodle haircut.

HARRY (*whispering*). Are you out of your mind?

MISS MCCUTCHEON (*aloud*). Good day, Judge.

THE JUDGE (*bowing*). Good day, Miss.

(*While he is bent over he takes a good look at her knees, calves, ankles, and bow-tied sandals.*)

(MISS MCCUTCHEON *goes out.* JUDGE APPLEGARTH *looks from the door to* HARRY.)

THE JUDGE. She won't last a month.

HARRY. Why not?

THE JUDGE. Too pretty. Our school needs an old battle-ax, like the teachers we had when we went to school, not a bathing beauty. Well, Harry, what's new?

HARRY. Just the teacher, I guess.

THE JUDGE. You know, Harry, the beach isn't what it used to be—not at all. I don't mind the competition we're getting from the kids. It's just that the quality of the stuff the sea's washing up isn't good any more. (*Goes to door*)

HARRY. I don't know. Clay Larrabee found an oyster this morning.

THE JUDGE. He did? Well, one oyster don't make a stew, Harry. On my way home I'll drop in and let you see what I find.

HARRY. O.K., Judge.

(*The* JUDGE *goes out.* HARRY *comes to life suddenly and becomes businesslike.*)

HARRY. Now, for the haircut! (*He removes the towel he had wrapped around the* WRITER'S *head.*)

THE WRITER. Take your time.

HARRY. (*He examines the shears, clippers, and combs.*) Let's see now.

(*The* WRITER *turns and watches. A gasoline station* ATTENDANT *comes to the door.*)

THE ATTENDANT (*to the* WRITER). Just wanted to say your car's ready now.

THE WRITER. Thanks.

(*The* ATTENDANT *goes out.*)

THE WRITER. Look. I'll tell you what. How much is a haircut?

HARRY. Well, the regular price is a dollar. It's too much for a haircut, though, so I generally take a half or a quarter.

THE WRITER (*getting out of the chair*). I've changed my mind. I don't want a haircut after all, but here's a dollar just the same.

(*He hands* HARRY *a dollar, and he himself removes the apron.*)

HARRY. It won't take a minute.

THE WRITER. I know.

HARRY. You don't have to pay me a dollar for a hot towel. My compliments.

THE WRITER. That's O.K. *(He goes to the door.)*

HARRY. Well, take it easy now.

THE WRITER. Thanks. *(He stands a moment, thinking, then turns.)* Do you mind if I have a look at that oyster?

HARRY. Not at all.

(The WRITER *goes to the shelf where* HARRY *has placed the oyster, picks it up, looks at it thoughtfully, puts it back without comment, but instead of leaving the shop he looks around at the stuff in it. He then sits down on a wicker chair in the corner, and lights a cigarette.)*

THE WRITER. You know, they've got a gadget in New York now like a safety razor that anybody can give anybody else a haircut with.

HARRY. They have?

THE WRITER. Yeah, there was a full-page ad about it in last Sunday's *Times*.

HARRY. Is that where you were last Sunday?

THE WRITER. Yeah.

HARRY. You been doing a lot of driving.

THE WRITER. I like to drive. I don't know, though— those gadgets don't always work. They're asking two-ninety-five for it. You take a big family. The father could save a lot of money giving his kids a haircut.

HARRY. Sounds like a great idea.

THE WRITER. Question of effectiveness. If the father gives the boy a haircut the boy's ashamed of, well, that's not so good.

HARRY. No, a boy likes to get a professional-looking haircut all right.

THE WRITER. I thought I'd buy one, but I don't know.

HARRY. You got a big family?

THE WRITER. I mean for myself. But I don't know— there's something to be said for going to a barbershop once in a while. No use putting the barbers out of business.

HARRY. Sounds like a pretty good article, though.

THE WRITER *(getting up lazily)*. Well, it's been nice talking to you.

*(*WOZZECK, *carrying a satchel, comes in, followed by* CLAY, ROXANNA, *and* GREELEY.*)*

WOZZECK. What's this all about, Harry?

HARRY. I've got an oyster I want you to open.

WOZZECK. That's what the kids have been telling me.

ROXANNA. *He* doesn't believe there's a pearl in the oyster, either.

WOZZECK. Of course not! What foolishness!

CLAY. There's a *big* pearl in it.

WOZZECK. O.K., give me the oyster. I'll open it. Expert watch repairer, to open an oyster!

HARRY. How much is a big pearl worth, Louie?

WOZZECK. Oh, a hundred. Two hundred, maybe.

HARRY. A very big one?

WOZZECK. Three, maybe.

THE WRITER. I've looked at that oyster, and I'd like to buy it. *(To* CLAY.*)* How much do you want for it?

CLAY. I don't know.

THE WRITER. How about three hundred?

GREELEY. Three hundred dollars?

CLAY. Is it all right, Mr. Van Dusen?

HARRY. *(He looks at the* WRITER, *who nods.)* Sure it's all right.

(The WRITER *hands* CLAY *the money.)*

CLAY *(looking at the money and then at the* WRITER*).* But suppose there ain't a pearl in it?

THE WRITER. There *is*, though.

WOZZECK. Don't you want to open it first?

THE WRITER. No, I want the whole thing. I don't think the pearl's stopped growing.

CLAY. He says there *is* a pearl in the oyster, Mr. Van Dusen.

HARRY. I think there is, too, Clay; so why don't you just go on home and give the money to your mother?

CLAY. Well . . . I *knew* I was going to find something good today!

(The children go out. WOZZECK *is bewildered.)*

WOZZECK. Three hundred dollars! How do you know there's a pearl in it?

THE WRITER. As far as I'm concerned, the whole thing's a pearl.

WOZZECK *(a little confused)*. Well, I got to get back to the shop, Harry.

HARRY. Thanks for coming by.

*(*WOZZECK *goes out. The* WRITER *holds the oyster in front of him as if it were an egg, and looks at it carefully, turning it in his fingers. As he is doing so,* CLARK LARRABEE *comes into the shop. He is holding the copy of the newspaper that* HARRY *gave him.)*

CLARK. We were ten miles up the highway when I happened to see this classified ad in the paper. *(He hands the paper to* HARRY *and sits down in the chair.)* I'm going out to the house, after all. Just for the weekend of course, then back to work in Salinas again. Two or three months, I think I'll have enough to come back for a long time. Clay come by?

HARRY. No. I've got the money here.

CLARK. O.K., I'll take it out myself, but first let me have the works—shave, haircut, shampoo, massage.

HARRY (*putting an apron on* CLARK). Sure thing, Clark. (*He bends the chair back, and begins to lather* CLARK'S *face.*)

(MISS MCCUTCHEON, *dressed neatly, looking like another person almost, comes in.*)

MISS MCCUTCHEON. Well?

HARRY. You look fine, Miss McCutcheon.

MISS MCCUTCHEON. I don't mean that. I mean the oyster.

HARRY. Oh, that! There *was* a pearl in it.

MISS MCCUTCHEON. I don't believe it.

HARRY. A *big* pearl.

MISS MCCUTCHEON. You might have done me the courtesy of waiting until I had come back before opening it.

HARRY. Couldn't wait.

MISS MCCUTCHEON. Well, I don't believe you, but I've come for my haircut. I'll sit down and wait my turn.

HARRY. Mr. Larrabee wants the works. You'll have to wait a long time.

MISS MCCUTCHEON. Mr. Larrabee? Clay's father? Roxanna's father?

(CLARK *sits up.*)

HARRY. Clark, I'd like you to meet our new teacher, Miss McCutcheon.

CLARK. How do you do.

MISS MCCUTCHEON. How do you do, Mr. Larrabee. (*She looks bewildered.*) Well, perhaps some other time, then, Mr. Van Dusen.

(*She goes out.* CLARK *sits back.* JUDGE APPLEGARTH *stops at the doorway of the shop.*)

THE JUDGE. Not one thing on the beach, Harry. Not a blessed thing worth picking up and taking home.

(JUDGE APPLEGARTH *goes on. The* WRITER *looks at* HARRY.)

HARRY. See what I mean?

THE WRITER. Yeah. Well . . . so long. (*He puts the oyster in his coat pocket.*)

HARRY. Drop in again any time you're driving to Hollywood.

THE WRITER. Or away.

(*He goes out.*)

CLARK (*after a moment*). You know, Harry, that boy of mine, Clay . . . well, a fellow like that, you can't just go off and leave him.

HARRY. Of course you can't, Clark.

CLARK. I'm taking him fishing tomorrow morning. How about going along, Harry?

HARRY. Sure, Clark. Be like old times again. (*There is a pause.*)

CLARK. What's all this about an oyster and a pearl?

HARRY. Oh, just having a little fun with the new teacher. You know, she came in here and asked me to give her a poodle haircut? A poodle haircut! I don't believe I remember what a poodle *dog* looks like, even.

THE END

But what we really want to know is how I happened to write
the play: well, you must surely know there is no real answer,
an accurate answer isn't possible: a writer writes, period.
The rest is mystery, as the saying is. A man knows how to write
and he wants to write, or he must, and so he writes. The forms
vary, but it comes to the same thing: sitting there and putting
the stuff on paper. Among your students may be one or two who
are writers: they will write. And you may report to them if you
like that I don't even know grammar, since it is the truth.
I punctuate entirely on the basis of clarity, for instance.
Now, specific answers to your specific questions. (1) I happened
to write the play because I had a program of writing short plays
at that time. (2) It happened to be about a small town by the sea
because that's where I was living. (3) I frequently saw kids on
the beach excited about stuff they had found, and that may have
given me the idea of a kid finding an oyster, which in itself
is quite an event, although the California beaches have plenty
of mussels. I used to gather mussels off the rocks at low tide
and cook them and eat them. I once found an oyster myself, and
that may have figured in the play, for any oyster can mean the
<u>hope</u> of a pearl, since pearls come only from oysters. The barber
shop in the play is there because I like barber shops, and barbers,
and they figure in quite a few of my stories. The barber is a
kind of poet, and frequently slightly eccentric, certainly free
and independent when he owns and operates his own shop. The rest
is the consequence of the way I write in any case: the consequence
of myself. (4) The play took its own course, pretty much as all
of my writing does, once I have gone to work: a small boy, an
oyster, a barber, and soon a little of the whole world and all
of the human race is involved in the thing, somehow. I never knew
while I was writing precisely how the play was going to develop
and how it was going to end--because I was working, and I had
started and finished a lot of different pieces of work over the
years in precisely the same manner. Now, if there is an implication
here that something special and very important took place in the
writing of the little play, that is an accident entirely, and
the consequence of my trying to answer your questions. I do not
think it is astonishing that a writer writes. That's his work.
The astonishing thing is that he doesn't write better, most likely.

I hope the foregoing proves useful to you, but most of all
to your students, and especially to the one or two who may be
writers. It's a good trade, in some ways almost as good as being
a barber.

william Saroyan

DISCUSSION

There are no characters in Saroyan's little play that we cannot recognize. Most of them fit into our own experience. Saroyan uses these characters to develop a **plot.** A plot is an action formed from a series of connected, related events. In the case of *The Oyster and the Pearl,* the **climax** or high point of the plot seems to be the moment when the writer from New York pays the boy Clay $300 for the oyster—without even opening it to see if there is really a big pearl inside. The important questions that hovered over the action are suddenly all resolved, and Clay is in a position to help his father come home—and the father sees Clay's ad in the newspaper and actually decides to come home. But there is one question that remains—was there a pearl in the oyster?

FOR EXPLORATION

1. In the opening scene Harry Van Dusen tells Clay that he "may turn out to be the one man hidden away in the junk of the world who will bring merriment to the tired old human heart." Explain how this description actually characterizes Van Dusen himself.

2. *(a)* Contrast Miss McCutcheon's and Mr. Van Dusen's attitudes toward life, pointing out specific speeches throughout the play which express their philosophies. *(b)* How does the oyster bring these two philosophies into focus? *(c)* What additional viewpoints are revealed by the attitudes of Wozzeck, the Judge, Greeley, and the Writer?

3. Why does the author never reveal whether or not there is an actual pearl in the oyster?

CREATIVE RESPONSE

Suppose Saroyan elected to have the pearl opened. Rewrite the final scene.

PIX, INC.

William Saroyan   1908 /

William Saroyan has won fame as short-story writer, novelist, and playwright. "The Daring Young Man on the Flying Trapeze" (1934) launched him on a successful career as a writer of short stories. His poignant story of family life, *The Human Comedy* (1942), established him as a successful novelist. And *The Time of Your Life* won a Pulitzer Prize for drama in 1940.

The son of Armenian parents, Saroyan was born in Fresno, California. As a boy he was a voracious reader. At thirteen he left school and at one time or another worked as a telegraph messenger, newsboy, farm laborer, and office clerk. All of these experiences together with his reading supplied material for his short stories, novels, and plays. The excerpt from his letter on the preceding page sheds light on the writing of "The Oyster and the Pearl."

OFFICIAL U.S. AIR FORCE PHOTO

The Death of the Ball Turret Gunner

From my mother's sleep I fell into the State,
And I hunched in its belly till my wet fur froze.
Six miles from earth, loosed from its dream of life,
I woke to black flak and the nightmare fighters.
When I died they washed me out of the turret with a hose.

Randall Jarrell

Reprinted with the permission of Farrar, Straus & Giroux, Inc. from
THE COMPLETE POEMS by Randall Jarrell, copyright © 1945, 1969 by
Mrs. Randall Jarrell.

DISCUSSION

"The Death of the Ball Turret Gunner" is a **lyric poem,** traditionally defined as a short, subjective poem that expresses an individual emotion, attitude, or thought. Jarrell's poem fulfills this definition admirably, and with great power. In reading the poem, one feels the effect of a single sensibility concentrating on a single subject in a mood of bitterness and revulsion. After the shock fades, the bitterness lingers on.

Jarrell's poem might be described as an antiwar poem, which is simply another way of saying that it takes as its **theme** the brutality and horror of war. It is sometimes useful to discriminate between **subject** and theme in a work. The subject is what a literary work is about, while the theme expresses an attitude toward that subject. The subject of this poem is war, and its theme is the cruelty of war and its barbaric consequences.

FOR EXPLORATION

1. What does Jarrell mean in the second line?
2. In line 3, in what sense is the speaker "loosed from [the earth's] dream of life"?
3. Explain the shock of the last line.

CREATIVE RESPONSE

Try composing four lines about a condition other than war which would provide a reason for the fifth line. Change the word "turret" in line 5 if necessary.

Randall Jarrell   1914 / 1965

Randall Jarrell once metaphorically described a good poet as "someone who manages, in a lifetime of standing out in thunderstorms, to be struck by lightning five or six times; a dozen or two dozen times and he is great." Jarrell managed his share of the lightning.

He was born and raised in Tennessee. After college and graduate studies, he began teaching and writing poetry. In 1942 he entered the Army Air Corps. The poetry that grew out of the war years was characteristically stark and almost violent; at times it had an atmosphere of fantasy. a muted, dreamlike air. *Little Friend, Little Friend* (1945) and *Losses* (1948) brought Jarrell recognition and influence.

In 1946 Jarrell returned to teaching and also acted as literary editor to *The Nation*. A collection of critical essays, *Poetry and the Age* (1953) was a major achievement.

From 1956 to 1958 Jarrell left teaching to serve as Poetry Consultant to the Library of Congress, and in 1961 he won the National Book Award for *The Woman at the Washington Zoo*, a volume of poetry and translations.

PHOTO BY PAT ALSPAUGH, GREENSBORO, N.C.

from

BABBITT

Sinclair Lewis

CHAPTER III

I

To George F. Babbitt, as to most prosperous citizens of Zenith, his motor car was poetry and tragedy, love and heroism. The office was his pirate ship but the car his perilous excursion ashore.

Among the tremendous crises of each day none was more dramatic than starting the engine. It was slow on cold mornings; there was the long, anxious whirr of the starter; and sometimes he had to drip ether into the cocks of the cylinders, which was so very interesting that at lunch he would chronicle it drop by drop, and orally calculate how much each drop had cost him.

This morning he was darkly prepared to find something wrong, and he felt belittled when the mixture exploded sweet and strong, and the car didn't even brush the door-jamb, gouged and splintery with many bruisings by fenders, as he backed out of the garage. He was confused. He shouted "Morning!" to Sam Doppelbrau with more cordiality than he had intended.

Babbitt's green and white Dutch Colonial house was one of three in that block on Chatham Road. To the left of it was the residence of Mr. Samuel Doppelbrau, secretary of an excellent firm of bathroom-fixture jobbers. His was a comfortable house with no architectural manners whatever; a large wooden box with a squat tower, a broad porch, and glossy paint yellow as a yolk. Babbitt disapproved of Mr. and Mrs. Doppelbrau as "Bohemian." From their house came midnight music and obscene laughter; there were neighborhood rumors of bootlegged whisky and fast motor rides. They furnished Babbitt with many happy evenings of

discussion, during which he announced firmly. "I'm not straitlaced, and I don't mind seeing a fellow throw in a drink once in a while, but when it comes to deliberately trying to get away with a lot of hell-raising all the while like the Doppelbraus do, it's too rich for my blood!"

On the other side of Babbitt lived Howard Littlefield, Ph.D., in a strictly modern house whereof the lower part was dark red tapestry brick, with a leaded oriel, the upper part of pale stucco like spattered clay, and the roof red-tiled. Littlefield was the Great Scholar of the neighborhood; the authority on everything in the world except babies, cooking, and motors. He was a Bachelor of Arts of Blodgett College, and a Doctor of Philosophy in economics of Yale. He was the employment-manager and publicity-counsel of the Zenith Street Traction Company. He could, on ten hours' notice, appear before the board of aldermen or the state legislature and prove, absolutely, with figures all in rows and with precedents from Poland and New Zealand, that the street-car company loved the Public and yearned over its employees; that all its stock was owned by Widows and Orphans; and that whatever it desired to do would benefit property-owners by increasing rental values, and help the poor by lowering rents. All his acquaintances turned to Littlefield when they desired to know the date of the battle of Saragossa, the definition of the word "sabotage," the future of the German mark, the translation of "*hinc illæ lach-*

From BABBITT by Sinclair Lewis, copyright, 1922, by Harcourt Brace Jovanovich, Inc.; renewed, 1950, by Sinclair Lewis. Reprinted by permission of Harcourt Brace Jovanovich, Inc., and Jonathan Cape, Ltd. for the Estate of Sinclair Lewis.

rimæ,"[1] or the number of products of coal tar. He awed Babbitt by confessing that he often sat up till midnight reading the figures and footnotes in Government reports, or skimming (with amusement at the author's mistakes) the latest volumes of chemistry, archeology, and ichthyology.

But Littlefield's great value was as a spiritual example. Despite his strange learnings he was as strict a Presbyterian and as firm a Republican as George F. Babbitt. He confirmed the business men in the faith. Where they knew only by passionate instinct that their system of industry and manners was perfect, Dr. Howard Littlefield proved it to them, out of history, economics, and the confessions of reformed radicals.

Babbitt had a good deal of honest pride in being the neighbor of such a savant, and in Ted's[2] intimacy with Eunice Littlefield. At sixteen Eunice was interested in no statistics save those regarding the ages and salaries of motion-picture stars, but—as Babbitt definitively put it—"she was her father's daughter."

The difference between a light man like Sam Doppelbrau and a really fine character like Littlefield was revealed in their appearances. Doppelbrau was disturbingly young for a man of forty-eight. He wore his derby on the back of his head, and his red face was wrinkled with meaningless laughter. But Littlefield was old for a man of forty-two. He was tall, broad, thick; his gold-rimmed spectacles were engulfed in the folds of his long face; his hair was a tossed mass of greasy blackness; he puffed and rumbled as he talked; his Phi Beta Kappa key shone against a spotty black vest; he smelled of old pipes; he was altogether funereal and archidiaconal; and to real-estate brokerage and the jobbing of bathroom-fixtures he added an aroma of sanctity.

This morning he was in front of his house, inspecting the grass parking between the curb and the broad cement sidewalk. Babbitt stopped his car and leaned out to shout "Mornin'!" Littlefield lumbered over and stood with one foot up on the running-board.

"Fine morning," said Babbitt, lighting—illegally early—his second cigar of the day.

"Yes, it's a mighty fine morning," said Littlefield.

"Spring coming along fast now."

"Yes, it's real spring now, all right," said Littlefield.

"Still cold nights, though. Had to have a couple blankets, on the sleeping-porch last night."

"Yes, it wasn't any too warm last night," said Littlefield.

"But I don't anticipate we'll have any more real cold weather now."

"No, but still, there was snow at Tiflis, Montana, yesterday," said the Scholar, "and you remember the blizzard they had out West three days ago—thirty inches of snow at Greeley, Colorado—and two years ago we had a snow-squall right here in Zenith on the twenty-fifth of April."

"Is that a fact! Say, old man, what do you think about the Republican candidate? Who'll they nominate for president? Don't you think it's about time we had a real business administration?"

"In my opinion, what the country needs, first and foremost, is a good, sound, business-like conduct of its affairs. What we need is—a business administration!" said Littlefield.

"I'm glad to hear you say that! I certainly am glad to hear you say that! I didn't know how you'd feel about it, with all your associations with colleges and so on, and I'm glad you feel that way. What the country needs—just at this present juncture—is neither a college president nor a lot of monkeying with foreign affairs, but a good—sound—economical—business—administration, that will give us a chance to have something like a decent turnover."

"Yes. It isn't generally realized that even in China the schoolmen are giving way to more practical men, and of course you can see what that implies."

"Is that a fact! Well, well!" breathed Babbitt, feeling much calmer, and much happier about the way things were going in the world. "Well, it's been nice to stop and parleyvoo a second. Guess I'll have to get down to the office now and sting a few clients. Well, so long, old man. See you tonight. So long."

II

They had labored, these solid citizens. Twenty years before, the hill on which Floral Heights was spread, with its bright roofs and immaculate turf and amazing comfort, had been a wilderness of rank second-growth elms and oaks and maples. Along the precise streets were still a few wooded vacant

---

1. *hinc illæ lachrimæ*, a Latin phrase meaning "hence, those tears."
2. *Ted*, Babbitt's son.

lots, and the fragment of an old orchard. It was brilliant to-day; the apple boughs were lit with fresh leaves like torches of green fire. The first white of cherry blossoms flickered down a gully, and robins clamored.

Babbitt sniffed the earth, chuckled at the hysteric robins as he would have chuckled at kittens or at a comic movie. He was, to the eye, the perfect office-going executive—a well-fed man in a correct brown soft hat and frameless spectacles, smoking a large cigar, driving a good motor along a semi-suburban parkway. But in him was some genius of authentic love for his neighborhood, his city, his clan. The winter was over; the time was come for the building, the visible growth, which to him was glory. He lost his dawn depression; he was ruddily cheerful when he stopped on Smith Street to leave the brown trousers, and to have the gasoline-tank filled.

The familiarity of the rite fortified him: the sight of the tall red iron gasoline-pump, the hollow-tile and terra-cotta garage, the window full of the most agreeable accessories—shiny casings, spark-plugs with immaculate porcelain jackets, tire-chains of gold and silver. He was flattered by the friendliness with which Sylvester Moon, dirtiest and most skilled of motor mechanics, came out to serve him. "Mornin', Mr. Babbitt!" said Moon, and Babbitt felt himself a person of importance, one whose name even busy garagemen remembered—not one of these cheap-sports flying around in flivvers. He admired the ingenuity of the automatic dial, clicking off gallon by gallon; admired the smartness of the sign: "A fill in time saves getting stuck—gas to-day 31 cents"; admired the rhythmic gurgle of the gasoline as it flowed into the tank, and the mechanical regularity with which Moon turned the handle.

"How much we takin' to-day?" asked Moon, in a manner which combined the independence of the great specialist, the friendliness of a familiar gossip, and respect for a man of weight in the community, like George F. Babbitt.

"Fill 'er up."

"Who you rootin' for for Republican candidate, Mr. Babbitt?"

"It's too early to make any predictions yet. After all, there's still a good month and two weeks—no, three weeks—must be almost three weeks—well, there's more than six weeks in all before the Republican convention, and I feel a fellow ought to keep an open mind and give all the candidates a show—

look 'em all over and size 'em up, and then decide carefully."

"That's a fact, Mr. Babbitt."

"But I'll tell you—and my stand on this is just the same as it was four years ago, and eight years ago, and it'll be my stand four years from now—yes, and eight years from now! What I tell everybody, and it can't be too generally understood, is that what we need first, last, and all the time is a good, sound business administration!"

"By golly, that's right!"

"How do those front tires look to you?"

"Fine! Fine! Wouldn't be much work for garages if everybody looked after their car the way you do."

"Well, I do try and have some sense about it." Babbitt paid his bill, said adequately, "Oh, keep the change," and drove off in an ecstasy of honest self-appreciation. It was with the manner of a Good Samaritan that he shouted at a respectable-looking man who was waiting for a trolley car, "Have a lift?" As the man climbed in Babbitt condescended, "Going clear down-town? Whenever I see a fellow waiting for a trolley, I always make it a practice to give him a lift—unless, of course, he looks like a bum."

"Wish there were more folks that were so generous with their machines," dutifully said the victim of benevolence.

"Oh, no, 'tain't a question of generosity, hardly. Fact, I always feel—I was saying to my son just the other night—it's a fellow's duty to share the good things of this world with his neighbors, and it gets my goat when a fellow gets stuck on himself and goes around tooting his horn merely because he's charitable."

The victim seemed unable to find the right answer. Babbitt boomed on:

"Pretty punk service the Company giving us on these carlines. Nonsense to only run the Portland Road cars once every seven minutes. Fellow gets mighty cold on a winter morning, waiting on a street corner with the wind nipping at his ankles."

"That's right. The Street Car Company don't care a damn what kind of a deal they give us. Something ought to happen to 'em."

Babbitt was alarmed. "But still, of course it won't do to just keep knocking the Traction Company and not realize the difficulties they're operating under, like these cranks that want municipal ownership. The way these workmen hold up the Company for high wages is simply a crime, and of course the burden falls on you and me that have to pay a seven-cent fare! Fact, there's remarkable service on all their lines—considering."

"Well—" uneasily.

"Darn fine morning," Babbitt explained. "Spring coming along fast."

"Yes, it's real spring now."

The victim had no originality, no wit, and Babbitt fell into a great silence and devoted himself to the game of beating trolley cars to the corner: a spurt, a tail-chase, nervous speeding between the huge yellow side of the trolley and the jagged row of parked motors, shooting past just as the trolley stopped—a rare game and valiant.

And all the while he was conscious of the loveliness of Zenith. For weeks together he noticed nothing but clients and the vexing To Rent signs of rival brokers. To-day, in mysterious malaise, he raged or rejoiced with equal nervous swiftness, and to-day the light of spring was so winsome that he lifted his head and saw.

He admired each district along his familiar route to the office: The bungalows and shrubs and winding irregular driveways of Floral Heights. The one-story shops on Smith Street, a glare of plate-glass and new yellow brick; groceries and laundries and drug-stores to supply the more immediate needs of East Side housewives. The market gardens in Dutch Hollow, their shanties patched with corrugated iron and stolen doors. Billboards with crimson goddesses nine feet tall advertising cinema films, pipe tobacco, and talcum powder. The old "mansions" along Ninth Street, S.E., like aged dandies in filthy linen; wooden castles turned into boarding-houses, with muddy walks and rusty hedges, jostled by fast-intruding garages, cheap apartment-houses, and fruitstands conducted by bland, sleek Athenians. Across the belt of railroad-tracks, factories with high-perched water-tanks and tall stacks—factories producing condensed milk, paper boxes, lighting-fixtures, motor cars. Then the business center, the thickening darting traffic, the crammed trolleys unloading, and high doorways of marble and polished granite.

It was big—and Babbitt respected bigness in anything; in mountains, jewels, muscles, wealth, or words. He was, for a spring-enchanted moment, the lyric and almost unselfish lover of Zenith. He thought of the outlying factory suburbs; of the Chaloosa River with its strangely eroded banks; of the orchard-dappled Tonawanda Hills to the North, and all the fat dairy land and big barns and comfortable herds. As he dropped his passenger he cried, "Gosh, I feel pretty good this morning!"

III

Epochal as starting the car was the drama of parking it before he entered his office. As he turned from Oberlin Avenue round the corner into Third Street, N.E., he peered ahead for a space in the line of parked cars. He angrily just missed a space as a rival driver slid into it. Ahead, another car was leaving the curb, and Babbitt slowed up, holding out his hand to the cars pressing on him from behind, agitatedly motioning an old woman to go ahead, avoiding a truck which bore down on him from one side. With front wheels nicking the wrought-steel bumper of the car in front, he stopped, feverishly cramped his steering-wheel, slid back into the vacant space and, with eighteen inches of room, manœuvered to bring the car level with the curb. It was a virile adventure masterfully executed. With satisfaction he locked a thief-proof steel wedge on the front wheel, and crossed the street to his real-estate office on the ground floor of the Reeves Building.

The Reeves Building was as fireproof as a rock and as efficient as a typewriter; fourteen stories of yellow pressed brick, with clean, upright, unornamented lines. It was filled with the offices of lawyers, doctors, agents for machinery, for emery wheels, for wire fencing, for mining-stock. Their gold signs shone on the windows. The entrance was too modern to be flamboyant with pillars; it was quiet, shrewd, neat. Along the Third Street side were a Western Union Telegraph Office, the Blue Delft Candy Shop, Shotwell's Stationery Shop, and the Babbitt-Thompson Realty Company.

Babbitt could have entered his office from the street, as customers did, but it made him feel an insider to go through the corridor of the building and enter by the back door. Thus he was greeted by the villagers.

The little unknown people who inhabited the Reeves Building corridors—elevator-runners, starter, engineers, superintendent, and the doubtful-looking lame man who conducted the news and cigar stand —were in no way city-dwellers. They were rustics, living in a constricted valley, interested only in one another and in The Building. Their Main Street was the entrance hall, with its stone floor, severe marble ceiling, and the inner windows of the shops. The liveliest place on the street was the Reeves Building Barber Shop, but this was also Babbitt's one embarrassment. Himself, he patronized the glittering Pompeian Barber Shop in the Hotel Thornleigh, and every time he passed the Reeves shop—ten times a day, a hundred times—he felt untrue to his own village.

Now, as one of the squirearchy, greeted with honorable salutations by the villagers, he marched into his office, and peace and dignity were upon him, and the morning's dissonances all unheard.

They were heard again, immediately.

Stanley Graff, the outside salesman, was talking on the telephone with tragic lack of that firm manner which disciplines clients: "Say, uh, I think I got just the house that would suit you—the Percival House, in Linton. . . . Oh, you've seen it. Well, how'd it strike you? . . . Huh? . . . Oh," irresolutely, "oh, I see."

As Babbitt marched into his private room, a coop with semi-partition of oak and frosted glass, at the back of the office, he reflected how hard it was to find employees who had his own faith that he was going to make sales.

There were nine members of the staff, besides Babbitt and his partner and father-in-law, Henry Thompson, who rarely came to the office. The nine were Stanley Graff, the outside salesman—a youngish man given to cigarettes and the playing of pool; old Mat Penniman, general utility man, collector of rents and salesman of insurance—broken, silent, gray; a mystery, reputed to have been a "crack" real-estate man with a firm of his own in haughty Brooklyn; Chester Kirby Laylock, resident salesman out at the Glen Oriole acreage development—an enthusiastic person with a silky mustache and much family; Miss Theresa McGoun, the swift and rather pretty stenographer; Miss Wilberta Bannigan, the thick, slow, laborious accountant and file-clerk; and four freelance part-time commission salesmen.

As he looked from his own cage into the main room Babbitt mourned, "McGoun's a good stenog., smart's a whip, but Stan Graff and all those bums—" The zest of the spring morning was smothered in the stale office air.

Normally he admired the office, with a pleased surprise that he should have created this sure lovely thing; normally he was stimulated by the clean new-

ness of it and the air of bustle; but to-day it seemed flat—the tiled floor, like a bathroom, the ocher-colored metal ceiling, the faded maps on the hard plaster walls, the chairs of varnished pale oak, the desks and filing-cabinets of steel painted in olive drab. It was a vault, a steel chapel where loafing and laughter were raw sin.

He hadn't even any satisfaction in the new water-cooler! And it was the very best of water-coolers, up-to-date, scientific, and right-thinking. It had cost a great deal of money (in itself a virtue). It possessed a non-conducting fiber ice-container, a porcelain water-jar (guaranteed hygienic), a dripless non-clogging sanitary faucet, and machine-painted decorations in two tones of gold. He looked down the relentless stretch of tiled floor at the water-cooler, and assured himself that no tenant of the Reeves Building had a more expensive one, but he could not recapture the feeling of social superiority it had given him. He astoundingly grunted, "I'd like to beat it off to the woods right now. And loaf all day. And go to Gunch's again to-night, and play poker, and cuss as much as I feel like, and drink a hundred and nine-thousand bottles of beer."

He sighed; he read through his mail; he shouted "Msgoun," which meant "Miss McGoun"; and began to dictate.

This was his own version of his first letter:

"Omar Gribble, send it to his office, Miss Mc-Goun, yours of twentieth to hand and in reply would say look here, Gribble, I'm awfully afraid if we go on shilly-shallying like this we'll just naturally lose the Allen sale, I had Allen up on carpet day before yesterday and got right down to cases and think I can assure you—uh, uh, no, change that: all my experience indicates he is all right, means to do business, looked into his financial record which is fine—that sentence seems to be a little balled up, Miss McGoun; make a couple sentences out of it if you have to, period, new paragraph.

"He is perfectly willing to pro rate the special assessment and strikes me, am dead sure there will be no difficulty in getting him to pay for title insurance, so now for heaven's sake let's get busy—no, make that: so now let's go to it and get down—no, that's enough—you can tie those sentences up a little better when you type 'em, Miss McGoun—your sincerely, etcetera."

This is the version of his letter which he received, typed, from Miss McGoun that afternoon:

BABBITT-THOMPSON REALTY CO.
Homes for Folks
Reeves Bldg., Oberlin Avenue & 3d. St., N.E.
Zenith

Omar Gribble, Esq.,
576 North American Building,
Zenith.

Dear Mr. Gribble:
Your letter of the twentieth to hand. I must say I'm awfully afraid that if we go on shilly-shallying like this we'll just naturally lose the Allen sale. I had Allen up on the carpet day before yesterday, and got right down to cases. All my experience indicates that he means to do business. I have also looked into his financial record, which is fine.

He is perfectly willing to pro rate the special assessment and there will be no difficulty in getting him to pay for title insurance.

So let's go!
Yours sincerely,

As he read and signed it, in his correct flowing business-college hand, Babbitt reflected, "Now that's a good, strong letter, and clear's a bell. Now what the— I never told McGoun to make a third paragraph there! Wish she'd quit trying to improve on my dictation! But what I can't understand is: why can't Stan Graff or Chet Laylock write a letter like that? With punch! With a kick!"

The most important thing he dictated that morning was the fortnightly form-letter, to be mimeographed and sent out to a thousand "prospects." It was diligently imitative of the best literary models of the day; of heart-to-heart-talk advertisements, "sales-pulling" letters, discourses on the "development of Will-power," and hand-shaking house-organs, as richly poured forth by the new school of Poets of Business. He had painfully written out a first draft, and he intoned it now like a poet delicate and distrait:

SAY, OLD MAN!
I just want to know can I do you a whaleuva favor? Honest! No kidding! I know you're interested in getting a house, not merely a place where you

hang up the old bonnet but a love-nest for the wife and kiddies—and maybe for the flivver out beyant (be sure and spell that b-e-y-a-n-t, Miss McGoun) the spud garden. Say, did you ever stop to think that we're here to save you trouble? That's how we make a living—folks don't pay us for our lovely beauty! Now take a look:

Sit right down at the handsome carved mahogany escritoire and shoot us in a line telling us just what you want, and if we can find it we'll come hopping down your lane with the good tidings, and if we can't, we won't bother you. To save your time, just fill out the blank enclosed. On request will also send blank regarding store properties in Floral Heights, Silver Grove, Linton, Bellevue, and all East Side residential districts.
Yours for service,

P.S.—Just a hint of some plums we can pick for you—some genuine bargains that came in to-day:
SILVER GROVE.—Cute four-room California bungalow, a.m.i., garage, dandy shade tree, swell neighborhood, handy car line. $3700, $780 down and balance liberal, Babbitt-Thompson terms, cheaper than rent.

DORCHESTER.—A corker! Artistic two-family house, all oak trim, parquet floors, lovely gas log, big porches, colonial, HEATED ALL-WEATHER GARAGE, a bargain at $11,250.

Dictation over, with its need of sitting and thinking instead of bustling around and making a noise and really doing something, Babbitt sat creakily back in his revolving desk-chair and beamed on Miss McGoun. He was conscious of her as a girl, of black bobbed hair against demure cheeks. A longing which was indistinguishable from loneliness enfeebled him. While she waited, tapping a long, precise pencil-point on the desk-tablet, he half identified her with the fairy girl of his dreams. He imagined their eyes meeting with terrifying recognition; imagined touching her lips with frightened reverence and— She was chirping, "Any more, Mist' Babbit?" He grunted, "That winds it up, I guess," and turned heavily away.

For all his wandering thoughts, they had never been more intimate than this. He often reflected, "Nev' forget how old Jake Offutt said a wise bird never goes love-making in his own office or his own home. Start trouble. Sure. But—"

In twenty-three years of married life he had peered uneasily at every graceful ankle, every soft shoulder; in thought he had treasured them; but not once had he hazarded respectability by adventuring. Now, as he calculated the cost of repapering the Styles house, he was restless again, discontented about nothing and everything, ashamed of his discontentment, and lonely for the fairy girl. □

DISCUSSION

Sinclair Lewis' *Babbitt* is one of the best known of modern satires, and has been so popular that the word *Babbitt* has come to stand in the American language for an un-cultivated, crude, banal American businessman whose empty life has been given over to a meaningless pursuit of elusive wealth: a "booster" without depth or sensitivity. **Satire** is one of the oldest literary forms, and is sometimes called a *genre* (a form such as a novel, sonnet, play) that stands by itself, and sometimes a *mode* (comedy, tragedy, allegory) that can appear in any of the genres. In the case of *Babbitt*, for example, the genre is the novel, while the mode is satire: *Babbitt* is a satiric novel. Satire criticizes through ridicule. It may criticize a society, a person, a class of persons, a culture, a philosophy, a book, an event.

Satire is written against something, and it may be only lightly funny and gentle, or it may be bitterly grim and grotesque in its wit and hostility. But it is always written in reaction—humorous disbelief, revulsion, disgust, or hatred—against something.

Satire may be of different kinds. A **burlesque** ridicules by exaggeration, often mocking its subject through the use of **caricature.** Caricature is usually a humorous attack on a characteristic or trait of the subject being satirized. Probably the most familiar form of caricature is the political cartoon. Whether in art or literature, caricature follows the formula of exaggerating selected features. Available to the writer are such devices as: **hyperbole,** the deliberate exaggeration of a figure of speech ("She's as old as the hills"); the **stereotype** figure (everyone's idea of an old-maid aunt or a Hollywood starlet or the big banker); the **cliché,** stock phrases so timeworn that they themselves have become stereotypes (filthy rich, bright as a penny, nutty as a fruitcake, far out, groovy).

Sinclair Lewis in *Babbitt* has employed all these elements of satire to make his comment upon the "typical" middle-class American businessman. Later in the anthology you will study other forms of satire.

FOR EXPLORATION

1. Give your general impression of Babbitt as Lewis draws him. (Your impression may be merely a collection of adjectives that will express your likes and dislikes for the character.)

2. Find quotations from the selection that exemplify the satirical elements Lewis uses to characterize Babbitt, Littlefield, or Doppelbrau.

3. Do you feel the attitudes of these three men are evident in American society today? Explain.

4. *(a)* What features has the artist caricatured in the cartoon of Babbitt on page A 66? *(b)* Would you have chosen differently? Explain.

5. Lewis uses proper names with devastating satirical effect. Comment on the connotations of the following names: Zenith, Floral Heights, Pompeian Barber Shop, Laylock. What other proper names does Lewis use connotatively?

CREATIVE RESPONSE

1. Discuss Babbitt's diction—his use of clichés and slang, as caricature. Make a list of them. Then observe your own language and write an account of terms and phrases that might be used to satirize you.

2. Study the letter Babbitt writes in column a, on page 71 A. Assume you have received the letter and compose an answer.

Sinclair Lewis   1885 / 1951

In 1930 Sinclair Lewis became the first American to receive the Nobel Prize—"for his powerful and vivid art of description, and his ability to use wit and humor in the creation of original characters." Thus Lewis rounded out a decade during which he was acknowledged the foremost man of letters in the United States. He had risen to sudden fame ten years earlier with the publication of *Main Street* (1920), a novel that satirized the stupidity and ignorance of the typical American small town. *Babbitt* (1922) added to his fame. *Arrowsmith* (1925), the story of a young doctor who struggles against the quacks and charlatans of science and medicine, won him the Pulitzer Prize in 1926. Several other novels including *Dodsworth* (1929) were published during this ten years of magnificent production. Although Lewis continued to write until his death, he never again attained the peak he had reached in the 1920's.

Sinclair Lewis was born in Sauk Center, Minnesota, the son of a country doctor. Restless and energetic, he interrupted his studies at Yale University to free lance in New York. Later he wandered about the country working on various newspapers and continuously trying to write. He had published five conventional and mediocre novels before *Main Street* showed for the first time his great gifts: his storytelling ability, his flair for mimicry of speech, his powers of photographic description, and humor which ranged from gentle irony to biting satire.

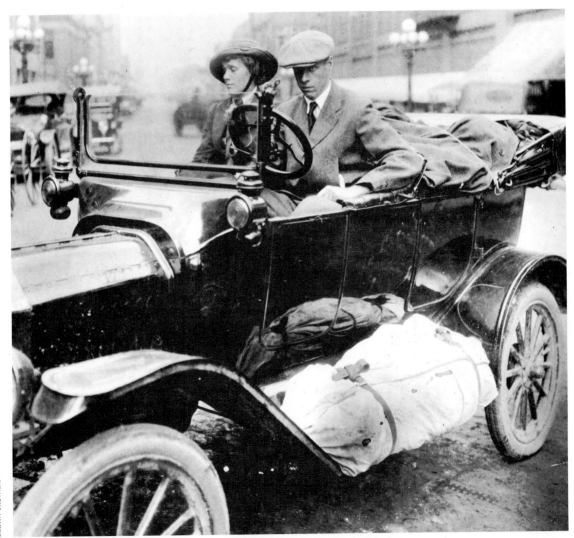

-BROWN BROTHERS

HANS NAMUTH

Starting from his home in Sag Harbor, Long Island, in 1960, John Steinbeck—along with his French poodle, Charley, as his sole traveling companion— sought to rediscover America. Having thought that he had lost touch with his native land, he equipped a brand-new pickup truck for long-distance camping, named it after Don Quixote's horse, Rocinante, and set out on a reflective journey that took him through most of the country.

In the selection below, we join the author as he begins his return journey from California by way of the Mojave Desert.

from

Travels with Charley

John Steinbeck

IT would be pleasant to be able to say of my travels with Charley, "I went out to find the truth about my country and I found it." And then it would be such a simple matter to set down my findings and lean back comfortably with a fine sense of having discovered truths and taught them to my readers. I wish it were that easy. But what I carried in my head and deeper in my perceptions was a barrel of worms. I discovered long ago in collecting and classifying marine animals that what I found was closely intermeshed with how I felt at the moment. External reality has a way of being not so external after all.

This monster of a land, this mightiest of nations, this spawn of the future, turns out to be the macrocosm of microcosm me. If an Englishman or a Frenchman or an Italian should travel my route, see what I saw, hear what I heard, their stored pictures would be not only different from mine but equally different from one another. If other Americans reading this account should feel it true, that

agreement would only mean that we are alike in our Americanness.

From start to finish I found no strangers. If I had, I might be able to report them more objectively. But these are my people and this my country. If I found matters to criticize and to deplore, they were tendencies equally present in myself. If I were to prepare one immaculately inspected generality it would be this: For all of our enormous geographic range, for all of our sectionalism, for all of our interwoven breeds drawn from every part of the ethnic world, we are a nation, a new breed. Americans are much more American than they are Northerners, Southerners, Westerners, or Easterners. And descendants of English, Irish, Italian, Jewish, German, Polish are essentially American. This is not patriotic whoop-

From TRAVELS WITH CHARLEY In Search of America by John Steinbeck. Copyright © 1961, 1962 by The Curtis Publishing Company, Inc. Copyright © 1962 by John Steinbeck. Reprinted by permission of The Viking Press, Inc. and William Heinemann Ltd.

de-do; it is carefully observed fact. California Chinese, Boston Irish, Wisconsin German, yes, and Alabama Negroes, have more in common than they have apart. And this is the more remarkable because it has happened so quickly. It is a fact that Americans from all sections and of all racial extractions are more alike than the Welsh are like the English, the Lancashireman like the Cockney, or for that matter the Lowland Scot like the Highlander. It is astonishing that this has happened in less than two hundred years and most of it in the last fifty. The American identity is an exact and provable thing.

Starting on my return journey, I realized by now that I could not see everything. My impressionable gelatin plate was getting muddled. I determined to inspect two more sections and then call it a day—Texas and a sampling of the Deep South. From my reading it seemed to me that Texas is emerging as a separate force and that the South is in the pain of labor with the nature of its future child still unknown. And I have thought that such is the bitterness of the labor that the child has been forgotten.

This journey had been like a full dinner of many courses, set before a starving man. At first he tries to eat all of everything, but as the meal progresses he finds he must forgo some things to keep his appetite and his taste buds functioning.

I bucketed Rocinante out of California by the shortest possible route—one I knew well from the old days of the 1930s. From Salinas to Los Banos, through Fresno and Bakersfield, then over the pass and into the Mojave Desert, a burned and burning desert even this late in the year, its hills like piles of black cinders in the distance, and the rutted floor sucked dry by the hungry sun. It's easy enough now, on the high-speed road in a dependable and comfortable car, with stopping places for shade and every service station vaunting its refrigeration. But I can remember when we came to it with prayer, listening for trouble in our laboring old motors, drawing a plume of steam from our boiling radiators. Then the broken-down wreck by the side of the road was in real trouble unless someone stopped to offer help. And I have never crossed it without sharing something with those early families foot-dragging through this terrestrial hell, leaving the white skeletons of horses and cattle which still mark the way.

The Mojave is a big desert and a frightening one. It's as though nature tested a man for endurance and constancy to prove whether he was good enough to get to California. The shimmering dry heat made visions of water on the flat plain. And even when you drive at high speed, the hills that mark the boundaries recede before you. Charley, always a dog for water, panted asthmatically, jarring his whole body with the effort, and a good eight inches of his tongue hung out flat as a leaf and dripping. I pulled off the road into a small gulley to give him water from my thirty-gallon tank. But before I let him drink I poured water all over him and on my hair and shoulders and shirt. The air is so dry that evaporation makes you feel suddenly cold.

I opened a can of beer from my refrigerator and sat well inside the shade of Rocinante, looking out at the sun-pounded plain, dotted here and there with clumps of sagebrush.

About fifty yards away two coyotes stood watching me, their tawny coats blending with sand and sun. I knew that with any quick or suspicious movement of mine they could drift into invisibility. With the most casual slowness I reached down my new rifle from its sling over my bed—the .222 with its bitter little high-speed, long-range stings. Very slowly I brought the rifle up. Perhaps in the shade of my house I was half hidden by the blinding light outside. The little rifle has a beautiful telescope sight with a wide field. The coyotes had not moved.

I got both of them in the field of my telescope, and the glass brought them very close. Their tongues lolled out so that they seemed to smile mockingly. They were favored animals, not starved, but well furred, the golden hair tempered with black guard hairs. Their little lemon-yellow eyes were plainly visible in the glass. I moved the cross hairs to the breast of the right-hand animal, and pushed the safety. My elbows on the table steadied the gun. The cross hairs lay unmoving on the brisket. And then the coyote sat down like a dog and its right rear paw came up to scratch the right shoulder.

My finger was reluctant to touch the trigger. I must be getting very old and my ancient conditioning worn thin. Coyotes are vermin. They steal chickens. They thin the ranks of quail and all other game birds. They must be killed. They are the enemy. My first shot would drop the sitting beast, and the other would whirl to fade away. I might very well pull him down with a running shot because I am a good rifleman.

And I did not fire. My training said, "Shoot!" and

my age replied, "There isn't a chicken within thirty miles, and if there are any they aren't my chickens. And this waterless place is not quail country. No, these boys are keeping their figures with kangaroo rats and jackrabbits, and that's vermin eat vermin. Why should I interfere?"

"Kill them," my training said. "Everyone kills them. It's a public service." My finger moved to the trigger. The cross was steady on the breast just below the panting tongue. I could imagine the splash and jar of angry steel, the leap and struggle until the torn heart failed, and then, not too long later, the shadow of a buzzard, and another. By that time I would be long gone—out of the desert and across the Colorado River. And beside the sagebrush there would be a naked, eyeless skull, a few picked bones, a spot of black dried blood and a few rags of golden fur.

I guess I'm too old and too lazy to be a good citizen. The second coyote stood sidewise to my rifle. I moved the cross hairs to his shoulder and held steady. There was no question of missing with that rifle at that range. I owned both animals. Their lives were mine. I put the safety on and laid the rifle on the table. Without the telescope they were not so intimately close. The hot blast of light tousled the air to shimmering.

Then I remembered something I heard long ago that I hope is true. It was unwritten law in China, so my informant told me, that when one man saved another's life he became responsible for that life to the end of its existence. For, having interfered with a course of events, the savior could not escape his responsibility. And that has always made good sense to me.

Now I had a token responsibility for two live and healthy coyotes. In the delicate world of relationships, we are tied together for all time. I opened two cans of dog food and left them as a votive.

I have driven through the Southwest many times, and even more often have flown over it—a great and mysterious wasteland, a sun-punished place. It is a mystery, something concealed and waiting. It seems deserted, free of parasitic man, but this is not entirely so. Follow the double line of wheel tracks through sand and rock and you will find a habitation somewhere huddled in a protected place, with a few trees pointing their roots at under-earth water, a patch of starveling corn and squash, and strips of jerky hanging on a string. There is a breed of desert men, not hiding exactly but gone to sanctuary from the sins of confusion.

At night in this waterless air the stars come down just out of reach of your fingers. In such a place lived the hermits of the early church piercing to infinity with unlittered minds. The great concepts of oneness and of majestic order seem always to be born in the desert. The quiet counting of the stars, and observation of their movements, came first from desert places. I have known desert men who chose their places with quiet and slow passion, rejecting the nervousness of a watered world. These men have not changed with the exploding times except to die and be replaced by others like them.

And always there are mysteries in the desert, stories told and retold of secret places in the desert mountains where surviving clans from an older era wait to re-emerge. Usually these groups guard treasures hidden from the waves of conquest, the golden artifacts of an archaic Montezuma, or a mine so rich that its discovery would change the world. If a stranger discovers their existence, he is killed or so absorbed that he is never seen again. These stories have an inevitable pattern untroubled by the question, If none return, how is it known what is there? Oh, it's there all right, but if you find it you will never be found.

And there is another monolithic tale which never changes. Two prospectors in partnership discover a mine of preternatural richness—of gold or diamonds or rubies. They load themselves with samples, as much as they can carry, and they mark the place in their minds by landmarks all around. Then, on the way out to the other world, one dies of thirst and exhaustion, but the other crawls on, discarding most of the treasure he has grown too weak to carry. He comes at last to a settlement, or perhaps is found by other prospecting men. They examine his samples with great excitement. Sometimes in the story the survivor dies after leaving directions with his rescuers, or again he is nursed back to strength. Then a well-equipped party sets out to find the treasure, and it can never be found again. That is the invariable end of the story—it is never found again. I have heard this story many times, and it never changes. There is nourishment in the desert for myth, but myth must somewhere have its roots in reality.

And there are true secrets in the desert. In the war of sun and dryness against living things, life has its secrets of survival. Life, no matter on what level,

DUNES BY EDWARD WESTON, COURTESY OF THE ART INSTITUTE OF CHICAGO

must be moist or it will disappear. I find more interesting the conspiracy of life in the desert to circumvent the death rays of the all-conquering sun. The beaten earth appears defeated and dead but it only appears so. A vast and inventive organization of living matter survives by seeming to have lost. The gray and dusty sage wears oily armor to protect its inward small moisture. Some plants engorge themselves with water in the rare rainfall and store it for future use. Animal life wears a hard, dry skin or an outer skeleton to defy the desiccation. And every living thing has developed techniques for finding or creating shade. Small reptiles and rodents burrow or slide below the surface or cling to the shaded side of an outcropping. Movement is slow to preserve energy, and it is a rare animal which can or will defy the sun for long. A rattlesnake will die in an hour of full sun. Some insects of bolder inventiveness have

devised personal refrigeration systems. Those animals which must drink moisture get it at second hand —a rabbit from a leaf, a coyote from the blood of a rabbit.

One may look in vain for living creatures in the daytime, but when the sun goes and the night gives consent, a world of creatures awakens and takes up its intricate pattern. Then the hunted come out and the hunters, and hunters of the hunters. The night awakes to buzzing and to cries and barks.

When, very late in the history of our planet, the incredible accident of life occurred, a balance of chemical factors, combined with temperature, in quantities and in kinds so delicate as to be unlikely, all came together in the retort of time and a new thing emerged, soft and helpless and unprotected in the savage world of unlife. Then processes of change and variation took place in the organisms, so that one kind became different from all others. But one ingredient, perhaps the most important of all, is planted in every life form—the factor of survival. No living thing is without it, nor could life exist without this magic formula. Of course, each form developed its own machinery for survival, and some failed and disappeared while others peopled the earth. The first life might easily have been snuffed out and the accident may never have happened again—but, once it existed, its first quality, its duty, preoccupation, direction, and end, shared by every living thing, is to go on living. And so it does and so it will until some other accident cancels it. And the desert, the dry and sun-lashed desert, is a good school in which to observe the cleverness and the infinite variety of techniques of survival under pitiless opposition. Life could not change the sun or water the desert, so it changed itself.

The desert, being an unwanted place, might well be the last stand of life against unlife. For in the rich and moist and wanted areas of the world, life pyramids against itself and in its confusion has finally allied itself with the enemy non-life. And what the scorching, searing, freezing, poisoning weapons of non-life have failed to do may be accomplished to the end of its destruction and extinction by the tactics of survival gone sour. If the most versatile of living forms, the human, now fights for survival as it always has, it can eliminate not only itself but all other life. And if that should transpire, unwanted places like the desert might be the harsh mother of repopulation. For the inhabitants of the desert are well trained and well armed against desolation. Even our own misguided species might re-emerge from the desert. The lone man and his sun-toughened wife who cling to the shade in an unfruitful and uncoveted place might, with their brothers in arms—the coyote, the jackrabbit, the horned toad, the rattlesnake, together with a host of armored insects—these trained and tested fragments of life might well be the last hope of life against non-life. The desert has mothered magic things before this. □

DISCUSSION

A good writer has the gift for expanding a simple incident into a major statement about the human condition. What is the incident Steinbeck uses?

FOR EXPLORATION

1. Discuss Steinbeck's statement, "In the delicate world of relationships, we are tied together for all time." (page 77 A, column a, paragraph 4)
2. What implications does this statement have for our behavior toward each other? for our treatment of the world we live in?

CREATIVE RESPONSE

Steinbeck thinks that "The desert, being an unwanted place, might well be the last stand of life against unlife." (page 79 A, column a, paragraph 1) Of what other environments might this be true?

John Steinbeck   1902 / 1968

Born in Salinas, California, Steinbeck grew up in a rich but strike-tormented valley where the plight of agricultural and factory workers made a deep impression on him. Between 1919 and 1925 he intermittently attended Stanford University, taking whatever courses attracted him. After leaving Stanford, he worked for a while as a newspaper reporter in New York City. His first three books were financial failures, and he was forced to fall back on such jobs as hod-carrying, surveying, and fruit picking. His literary popularity began in 1935 with a book that is said to have been rejected by nine publishers: this was *Tortilla Flat*, a series of stories about Mexican-Americans on the Monterey Peninsula. His short novel, *Of Mice and Men*, became a best seller in 1937; his novel dealing with the plight of migratory workers, *The Grapes of Wrath* (1939), earned the Pulitzer Prize in letters in 1940. In 1962 he was awarded the Nobel Prize for literature.

GARAGE LIGHTS BY STUART DAVIS—COLLECTION OF THE MEMORIAL ART GALLERY OF THE UNIVERSITY OF ROCHESTER, MARION STRATTON GOULD FUND

American Literature   Unlike the literature of, say, Italy, France, or England, the literature of the United States passed through a period of acute identity crisis early in its existence. It strongly felt the need to demonstrate its differences from the literature of the mother country, England, while it everywhere betrayed its resemblances. In actuality, the struggle for literary independence lasted long beyond the struggle for political independence (declared in 1776 and won in 1783). Although there were some signs of literary growth in the early nineteenth century (in such writers as Irving, Cooper, and Poe), it was not until the middle of that century that the country began to discover its genuine literary identity, in the work of such masters as Melville, Thoreau, Whitman, and Twain. And it was not until the middle of the twentieth century that the United States reached its international literary maturity, with writers like Hemingway, Faulkner, Frost, and Eliot, writers who set the literary pace not only in America but abroad as well. Throughout its development, however, American literature has continued its keen interest in its own selfhood and in the American identity. And as a literature that looks to itself and to its sources, it present myriad facets to the reader—facets that include not only the common experience, but also the Indian experience, the Black experience, the Jewish experience, as well as the Irish, the German, the Oriental, and many more. Some American literature praises America, some criticizes, while much simply is realistic. Whatever its subject, tone, or thrust, American literature is the American expression. If we would understand ourselves, we must read about ourselves, our civilization, culture, and country, as imaginatively embodied and presented by our own writers.

THE
AMERICAN
LITERARY
TRADITION

1607 / 1899

This section begins a view of nearly
three centuries of American literature.
Because the concern of literature universally
has been the nature and experience of man,
his human and moral values,
this literary chronology opens with a view
of society by James Thurber, an
author of our own century.
Deceptively simple,
THE LAST FLOWER is a profound
and ironic history,
reflecting the unique and inevitable
sanity / madness of mankind.

JAMES THURBER —HENRI CARTIER-BRESSON (C) MAGNUM

THE
LAST
FLOWER

A parable in

pictures by

James Thurber

In case readers wish to own personal copies of *The Last Flower*,
they may be purchased from Harper and Row.

THE LAST FLOWER. Copyright © 1939 James Thurber. Copyright ©
1967 Helen W. Thurber and Rosemary Thurber Sauers. Published
by Harper and Row, New York.

FOR ROSEMARY

*IN THE WISTFUL HOPE THAT HER WORLD
WILL BE BETTER THAN MINE*

WORLD WAR XII, AS EVERYBODY KNOWS,

BROUGHT ABOUT THE COLLAPSE OF CIVILIZATION

2.

TOWNS, CITIES, AND VILLAGES DISAPPEARED
FROM THE EARTH

3.

ALL THE GROVES AND FORESTS WERE DESTROYED

4.

AND ALL THE GARDENS

5.

AND ALL THE WORKS OF ART

6.

MEN, WOMEN, AND CHILDREN BECAME LOWER THAN THE LOWER ANIMALS

7.

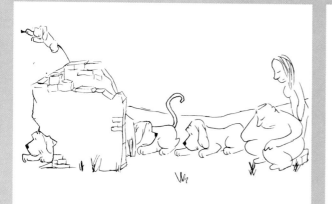

DISCOURAGED AND DISILLUSIONED, DOGS DESERTED THEIR FALLEN MASTERS

8.

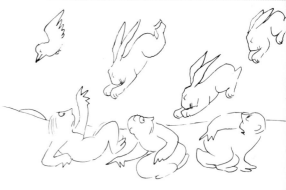

EMBOLDENED BY THE PITIFUL CONDITION OF THE FORMER LORDS OF THE EARTH, RABBITS DESCENDED UPON THEM

9.

BOOKS, PAINTINGS, AND MUSIC DISAPPEARED
FROM THE EARTH, AND HUMAN BEINGS
JUST SAT AROUND, DOING NOTHING

10.

YEARS AND YEARS WENT BY

11.

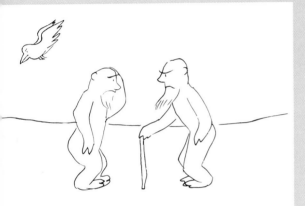

EVEN THE FEW GENERALS WHO WERE LEFT
FORGOT WHAT THE LAST WAR HAD DECIDED

12.

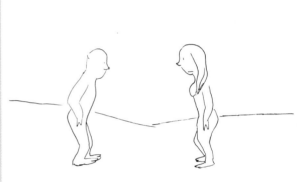

BOYS AND GIRLS GREW UP TO STARE AT EACH OTHER
BLANKLY, FOR LOVE HAD PASSED FROM THE EARTH

13.

ONE DAY A YOUNG GIRL WHO HAD NEVER
SEEN A FLOWER CHANCED TO COME
UPON THE LAST ONE IN THE WORLD

14.

SHE TOLD THE OTHER HUMAN BEINGS
THAT THE LAST FLOWER WAS DYING

15.

THE ONLY ONE WHO PAID ANY ATTENTION
TO HER WAS A YOUNG MAN SHE
FOUND WANDERING ABOUT

16.

TOGETHER THE YOUNG MAN AND THE GIRL
NURTURED THE FLOWER AND IT BEGAN
TO LIVE AGAIN

17.

ONE DAY A BEE VISITED THE FLOWER,
AND A HUMMINGBIRD

18.

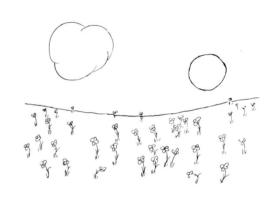

BEFORE LONG THERE WERE TWO FLOWERS, AND
THEN FOUR, AND THEN A GREAT MANY

19.

GROVES AND FORESTS FLOURISHED AGAIN

20.

THE YOUNG GIRL BEGAN TO TAKE
AN INTEREST IN HOW SHE LOOKED

21.

THE YOUNG MAN DISCOVERED THAT
TOUCHING THE GIRL WAS PLEASURABLE

22.

LOVE WAS REBORN INTO THE WORLD

23.

THEIR CHILDREN GREW UP STRONG AND HEALTHY
AND LEARNED TO RUN AND LAUGH

24.

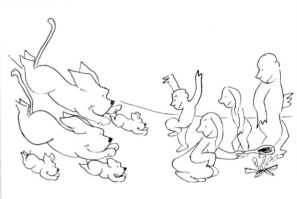

DOGS CAME OUT OF THEIR EXILE

25.

THE YOUNG MAN DISCOVERED, BY PUTTING ONE
STONE UPON ANOTHER, HOW TO BUILD A SHELTER

26.

PRETTY SOON EVERYBODY WAS BUILDING SHELTERS

27.

28. TOWNS, CITIES, AND VILLAGES SPRANG UP

29. SONG CAME BACK INTO THE WORLD

30. AND TROUBADOURS AND JUGGLERS

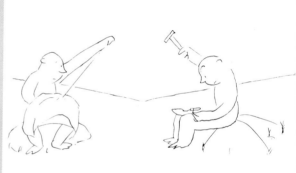

31. AND TAILORS AND COBBLERS

AND PAINTERS AND POETS

33. AND SCULPTORS AND WHEELWRIGHTS

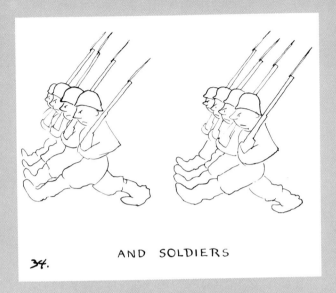

AND SOLDIERS

34.

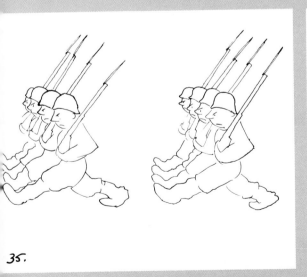

35.

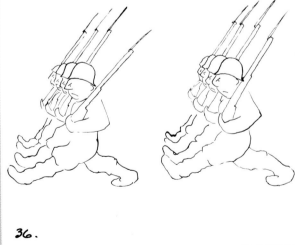

36.

AND   LIEUTENANTS AND CAPTAINS

37.

AND GENERALS AND MAJOR-GENERALS

38.

39.

AND LIBERATORS

SOME PEOPLE WENT ONE PLACE TO LIVE,
AND SOME ANOTHER

40.

BEFORE LONG, THOSE WHO WENT TO LIVE IN THE VALLEYS
WISHED THEY HAD GONE TO LIVE IN THE HILLS

41.

AND THOSE WHO HAD GONE TO LIVE IN THE HILLS
WISHED THEY HAD GONE TO LIVE IN THE VALLEYS

42.

THE LIBERATORS, UNDER THE GUIDANCE OF GOD,
SET FIRE TO THE DISCONTENT

43.

SO PRESENTLY THE WORLD WAS AT WAR AGAIN
44.

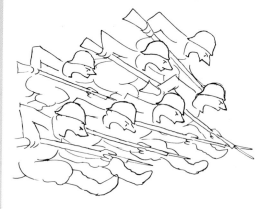

45.

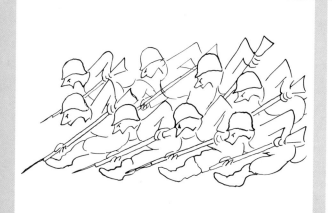

46.

THIS TIME THE DESTRUCTION WAS SO COMPLETE...
47.

THAT NOTHING AT ALL WAS LEFT IN THE WORLD

48.

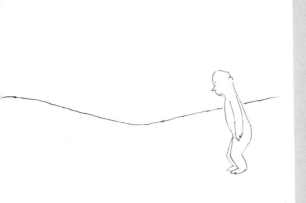

EXCEPT ONE MAN

49.

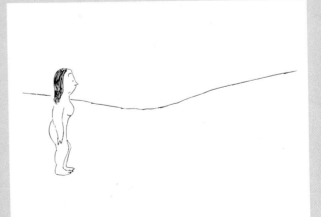

AND ONE WOMAN

50.

AND ONE FLOWER

PLANTERS
AND PURITANS

EARLY PLOW—OWNED BY THE HENRY FORD MUSEUM

THE ENDLESS SERMON: DETAIL FROM A MINISTER'S GRAVESTONE, 1769

William Bradford

1590 / 1657

from

THE HISTORY OF PLYMOUTH PLANTATION

From OF PLYMOUTH PLANTATION, by William Bradford, edited by
Samuel Eliot Morison. Copyright 1952 by Samuel Eliot Morison.
Reprinted by permission of Alfred A. Knopf, Inc.

OF THEIR VOYAGE, AND HOW THEY PASSED THE SEA; AND OF THEIR SAFE ARRIVAL AT CAPE COD

September 6. These troubles being blown over, and now all being compact together in one ship, they put to sea again with a prosperous wind, which continued divers days together, which was some encouragement unto them; yet, according to the usual manner, many were afflicted with seasickness. And I may not omit here a special work of God's providence. There was a proud and very profane young man, one of the seamen, of a lusty, able body, which made him the more haughty; he would alway be contemning the poor people in their sickness and cursing them daily with grievous execrations; and did not let to tell them that he hoped to help to cast half of them overboard before they came to their journey's end, and to make merry with what they had; and if he were by any gently reproved, he would curse and swear most bitterly. But it pleased God before they came half seas over, to smite this young man with a grievous disease, of which he died in a desperate manner, and so was himself the first that was thrown overboard. Thus his curses light on his own head, and it was an astonishment to all his fellows for they noted it to be the just hand of God upon him.

After they had enjoyed fair winds and weather for a season, they were encountered many times with cross winds and met with many fierce storms with which the ship was shroudly[1] shaken, and her upper works made very leaky; and one of the main beams in the midships was bowed and cracked, which put them in some fear that the ship could not be able to perform the voyage. So some of the chief of the company, perceiving the mariners to fear the sufficiency of the ship as appeared by their mutterings, they entered into serious consultation with the master and other officers of the ship, to consider in time of the danger, and rather to return than to cast themselves into a desperate and inevitable peril. And truly there was great distraction and difference of opinion amongst the mariners themselves; fain would they do what could be done for their wages' sake (being now near half the seas over) and on the other hand they were loath to hazard their lives too desperately. But in examining of all opinions, the master and others affirmed they knew the ship to be strong and firm under water; and for the buckling of the main beam, there was a great iron screw the passengers brought out of Holland, which would raise the beam into his place; the which being done, the carpenter and master affirmed that with a post put under it, set firm in the lower deck and otherways bound, he would make it sufficient. And as for the decks and upper works, they would caulk them as well as they could, and though with the working of the ship they would not long keep staunch, yet there would otherwise be no great danger, if they did not overpress her with sails. So they committed themselves to the will of God and resolved to proceed.

In sundry of these storms the winds were so fierce and the seas so high, as they could not bear a knot of sail, but were forced to hull[2] for divers days together. And in one of them, as they thus lay at hull in a mighty storm, a lusty young man called John Howland,[3] coming upon some occasion above the gratings was, with a seele[4] of the ship, thrown into sea; but it pleased God that he caught hold of the topsail halyards which hung overboard and ran out at length. Yet he held his hold (though he was sundry fathoms under water) till he was hauled up by the same rope to the brim of the water, and then with a boat hook and other means got into the ship again and his life saved. And though he was something ill with it, yet he lived many years after and became a profitable member both in church and commonwealth. In all this voyage there died but one of the passengers, which was William Butten, a youth, servant to Samuel Fuller, when they drew near the coast.

---

1. *shroudly,* a now archaic form of shrewdly, in this sense meaning harshly or injuriously.
2. *to hull,* to drift with the wind using very little sail.
3. *John Howland.* Howland became an influential member of the Massachusetts Bay Colony.
4. *seele,* the pitch or roll of a ship.

But to omit other things (that I may be brief) after long beating at sea they fell with that land which is called Cape Cod, the which being made and certainly known to be it, they were not a little joyful. After some deliberation had amongst themselves and with the master of the ship, they tacked about and resolved to stand for the southward (the wind and weather being fair) to find some place about Hudson's River for their habitation. But after they had sailed that course about half the day, they fell amongst dangerous shoals and roaring breakers, and they were so far entangled therewith as they conceived themselves in great danger; and the wind shrinking upon them withal, they resolved to bear up again for the Cape and thought themselves happy to get out of those dangers before night overtook them, as by God's good providence they did. And the next day they got into the Cape Harbor[5] where they rid in safety. . . .

. . . Being thus arrived in a good harbor, and brought safe to land, they fell upon their knees and blessed the God of Heaven who had brought them over the vast and furious ocean, and delivered them from all the perils and miseries thereof, again to set their feet on the firm and stable earth, their proper element. And no marvel if they were thus joyful, seeing wise Seneca[6] was so affected with sailing a few miles on the coast of his own Italy, as he affirmed, that he had rather remain twenty years on his way by land than pass by sea to any place in a short time, so tedious and dreadful was the same unto him.

But here I cannot but stay and make a pause, and stand half amazed at this poor people's present condition; and so I think will the reader, too, when he well considers the same. Being thus passed the vast ocean, and a sea of troubles before in their preparation (as may be remembered by that which went before), they had now no friends to welcome them nor inns to entertain or refresh their weather-beaten bodies; no houses or much less towns to repair to, to seek for succour. It is recorded in Scripture as a mercy to the Apostle[7] and his shipwrecked company, that the barbarians showed them no small kindness in refreshing them, but these savage barbarians, when they met with them (as after will appear) were readier to fill their sides full of arrows than otherwise. And for the season it was winter, and they that know the winters of that country know them

to be sharp and violent, and subject to cruel and fierce storms, dangerous to travel to known places, much more to search an unknown coast. Besides, what could they see but a hideous and desolate wilderness, full of wild beasts and wild men—and what multitudes there might be of them they knew not. Neither could they, as it were, go up to the top of Pisgah[8] to view from this wilderness a more goodly country to feed their hopes; for which way soever they turned their eyes (save upward to the heavens) they could have little solace or content in respect of any outward objects. For summer being done, all things stand upon them with a weather-beaten face, and the whole country, full of woods and thickets, represented a wild and savage hue. If they looked behind them, there was the mighty ocean which they had passed and was now as a main bar and gulf to separate them from all the civil parts of the world. If it be said they had a ship to succour them, it is true; but what heard they daily from the master and company? But that with speed they should look out a place (with their shallop) where they would be, at some near distance; for the season was such as he would not stir from thence till a safe harbor was discovered by them, where they would be, and he might go without danger; and that victuals consumed apace but he must and would keep sufficient for themselves and their return. Yea, it was muttered by some that if they got not a place in time, they would turn them and their goods ashore and leave them. Let it also be considered what weak hopes of supply and succour they left behind them, that might bear up their minds in this sad condition and trials they were under; and they could not but be very small. It is true, indeed, the affections and love of their brethren at Leyden was cordial and entire towards them, but they had little power to help them or themselves; and how the case stood between them

---

5. *Cape Harbor,* Provincetown Harbor at the tip of Cape Cod.
6. *Seneca,* a famous Roman poet and tragedian.
7. *a mercy to the Apostle.* The allusion is to Paul's shipwreck on Malta in Acts 28:2: "And the natives showed us unusual kindness, for they kindled a fire and welcomed us all, because it had begun to rain and was cold."
8. *up to the top of Pisgah.* Pisgah, now known as Mt. Nebo, lies just to the northeast of the Dead Sea in Jordan. Bradford alludes to Moses' and the Hebrews' climb of Mt. Pisgah before continuing on their journey to the Promised Land in Numbers 21:18–20: "And from the wilderness they went on to Mat'tanah, and from Mat'tanah to Nahal'iel, and from Nahal'iel to Bamoth, and from Bamoth to the valley lying in the region of Moab by the top of Pisgah which looks down upon the desert."

and the merchants at their coming away hath already been declared.

What could now sustain them but the Spirit of God and His grace? May not and ought not the children of these fathers rightly say: "Our fathers were Englishmen which came over this great ocean, and were ready to perish in this wilderness; but they cried unto the Lord, and He heard their voice and looked on their adversity,"[9] etc. "Let them therefore praise the Lord, because He is good: and His mercies endure forever," "Yea, let them which have been redeemed of the Lord, shew[10] how He hath delivered them from the hand of the oppressor. When they wandered in the desert wilderness out of the way, and found no city to dwell in, both hungry and thirsty, their soul was overwhelmed in them. Let them confess before the Lord His lovingkindness and His wonderful works before the sons of men."[11]   ☐

---

9. *He . . . adversity*, Deut. 26:5, 7.
10. *shew* (shō), variant of show.
11. *Let them confess . . . before the sons of men*, Ps. 107:1–5, 8.

THE PILGRIMS MEET THE INDIANS

All this while the Indians came skulking about them, and would sometimes show themselves aloof off, but when any approached near them, they would run away. And once they stole away their tools where they had been at work, and were gone to dinner. But about the 16 of March, a certain Indian came boldly amongst them, and spoke to them in broken English, which they could well understand but marveled at it. At length they understood by discourse with him, that he was not of these parts, but belonged to the eastern parts where some English ships came to fish,[1] with whom he was acquainted and could name sundry of them by their names, amongst whom he had got his language. He became profitable to them in acquainting them with many things concerning the state of the country in the east parts where he lived, which was afterwards profitable unto them; as also of the people here, of their names, number, and strength, of their situation and distance from this place, and who was chief amongst them. His name was Samoset; he told them also of another Indian whose name was Squanto, a native of this place, who had been in England and could speak better English than himself. Being, after some time of entertainment and gifts, dismissed, a while after he came again, and 5 more with him, and they brought again all the tools that were stolen away before, and made way for the coming of their great sachem, called Massasoit; who, about 4 or 5 days after, came with the chief of his friends and other attendance, with the aforesaid Squanto. With whom, after friendly entertainment, and some gifts given him, they made a peace with him (which hath now continued this 24 years) in these terms.

1. That neither he nor any of his should injure or do hurt to any of their people.

2. That if any of his did any hurt to any of theirs, he should send the offender, that they might punish him.

3. That if anything were taken away from any of theirs, he should cause it to be restored; and they should do the like to him.

4. If any did unjustly war against him, they would aid him; if any did war against them, he should aid them.

5. He should send to his neighbors confederates to certify them of this, that they might not wrong them, but might be likewise comprised in the conditions of peace.

6. That when their men came to them, they should leave their bows and arrows behind them.

After these things he returned to his place called

---

1. *where some English ships came to fish*, probably the fishing grounds stretching from northeastern Maine to Newfoundland known as the Grand Banks.

Sowans, some 40 miles from this place, but Squanto continued with them, and was their interpreter, and was a special instrument sent of God for their good beyond their expectation. He directed them how to set their corn, where to take fish, and to procure other commodities, and was also their pilot to bring them to unknown places for their profit, and never left them till he died. He was a native of this place, and scarce any left alive besides himself. He was carried away with divers others by one Hunt, a master of a ship, who thought to sell them for slaves in Spain. But he got away for England, and was entertained by a merchant in London, and employed to Newfoundland and other parts, and lastly brought hither into these parts by one Mr. Dermer, a gentleman employed by Sir Ferdinando Gorges[2] and others for discovery and other designs in these parts.   □

---

2. *Sir Ferdinando Gorges* (gôr′jəs), a man instrumental in forming the Plymouth Company. Before the Pilgrims left England, he had sent exploratory parties to America.

DISCUSSION

William Bradford's *The History of Plymouth Plantation* is best termed a **chronicle** or **diary,** a nonfictional literary genre which presents an accurate record of events in their chronological order.

FOR EXPLORATION

Of Their Voyage . . .

1. If you were going to explore an unknown region such as another planet, you might also want to keep a diary of your adventures. Disregarding some of the more obvious differences, would your chronicle bear any resemblance to Bradford's in its essential content?
2. Does the new world as described by Bradford impress you as a friendly or unfriendly place to settle? Support your answer.
3. Today, we tend to idealize nature and natural beauty. What is Bradford's view of nature?
4. An **allusion** is "a brief, often indirect reference to a person, place, event, or work of art which the author assumes the reader will recognize." In the above selection, William Bradford makes use of a number of Biblical allusions, two of which are footnoted at length in the text. Find these and explain why and how they are used by the author.

The Pilgrims Meet the Indians

1. One of the six terms of peace agreed upon by the Pilgrims and Indians is called a mutual defense pact. Give the number of the term that correctly identifies this type of treaty.
2. The Pilgrims were members of a religious sect that we today call Puritan. They were known to have been a piously religious people with a firm belief in God's control over man's destiny. Utilizing both Bradford selections, give evidence for this statement.
3. Never desiring his work to be published, Bradford kept his chronicle for essentially practical reasons. (a) In what ways would his diary be of interest to future colonists? (b) How might it aid them in their attempt to settle the wilderness?

William Bradford 1590/1657

While a boy in England, William Bradford joined a religious group (the Puritans, Roundheads, Calvinists) believing in separation from the Church of England and went with the group for an eleven-year stay in Holland. He was still with the group when it sailed on the historic *Mayflower* and landed at Plymouth in December 1620. He assumed the position of principal leader of the colony and was chosen governor for some thirty times. His *History of Plymouth Plantation, 1620–1647*, was probably not intended for publication, and, indeed, was not published until 1856, when the manuscript was found in the library of the Bishop of London. It remains a primary source for our information about the early days of the "pilgrims."

Captain John Smith

1579/1631

CAPTAIN SMITH AMONG THE INDIANS

THE winter [of 1607] approaching, the rivers became so covered with swans, geese, ducks, and cranes, that we daily feasted with good bread, Virginia peas, pumpkins, putchamins, fish, fowl, and diverse sorts of wild beasts as fat as we could eat them, so that none of our tuftaffety humorists[1] desired to go for England.

But our comedies never endured long without a tragedy; some idle exceptions being muttered against Captain Smith for not discovering the head of Chickahamania River, and taxed by the Council to be too slow in so worthy an attempt. The next voyage he proceeded so far that with much labor by cutting of trees asunder he made his passage; but when his barge could pass no farther, he left her in a broad bay out of danger of shot, commanding none should go ashore till his return: himself with two English and two savages went up higher in a canoe, but he was not long absent but[2] his men went ashore, whose want of government gave both occasion and opportunity to the savages to surprise one George Cassen, whom they slew, and much failed not[3] to have cut off the boat and all the rest.

Smith, little dreaming of that accident, being got to the marshes at the river's head, twenty miles in the desert, had his two men slain (as is supposed) sleeping by the canoe, whilst himself by fowling sought them victual; who, finding he was beset with two hundred savages, two of them he slew, still defending himself with the aid of a savage his guide, whom he bound to his arm with his garters and used him as a buckler; yet he was shot in his thigh a little and had many arrows that stuck in his clothes but no great hurt, till at last they took him prisoner.

When this news came to Jamestown, much was their sorrow for his loss, few expecting what ensued.

Six or seven weeks those barbarians kept him prisoner, many strange triumphs and conjurations they made of him, yet he so demeaned himself amongst them, as he not only diverted them from

surprising the fort, but procured his own liberty, and got himself and his company such estimation amongst them, that those savages admired him more than their own Quiyouckosucks.[4] The manner how they used and delivered him is as follows.

The savages having drawn from George Cassen whither Captain Smith was gone, prosecuting that opportunity they followed him with three hundred bowmen, conducted by the King of Pamaunkee, who in divisions searching the turnings of the river, found Robinson and Emry[5] by the fireside; those they shot full of arrows and slew. Then finding the Captain, as is said, that used the savage that was his guide as his shield (three of them being slain and divers others so galled) all the rest would not come near him. Thinking thus to have returned to his boat, regarding them as he marched more than his way, slipped up to the middle in an oozy creek and his savage with him; yet durst they not come to him till being near dead with cold, he threw away his arms. Then according to their composition[6] they drew him forth and led him to the fire, where his men were slain. Diligently they chafed his benumbed limbs.

He demanding for their captain, they showed him Opechankanough, King of Pamaunkee, to whom he gave a round ivory double compass dial.[7] Much they marveled at the playing of the fly and needle, which they could see so plainly, and yet not touch it because of the glass that covered them. But when he demonstrated by that globelike jewel the roundness of the earth, the skies, the sphere of the sun, moon, and stars, and how the sun did chase the night round about the world continually; the greatness of the land and sea, the diversity of nations, variety of complexions, and how we were to them antipodes, and many other suchlike matters, they all stood as amazed with admiration. Notwithstanding, within an hour after they tied him to a tree, and as many as could stand about him prepared to shoot him, but

---

1. *tuftaffety humorists*, critical, elegant gentlemen who prided themselves on following their whims (humors) and behaving in an unusual or eccentric fashion. Tuftaffeta was a fashionable silk fabric which had a pattern formed by tufts.
2. *but*, until.
3. *much failed not*, almost succeeded.
4. *Quiyouckosucks* (kwē youk′ō suks), god before whose images the Indians of this region made offerings for rain.
5. *Robinson and Emry*, the two men mentioned as slain in a preceding paragraph. Smith was hunting nearby.
6. *composition*, agreement.
7. *round ivory double compass dial*. This primitive type of compass was a ball containing liquid on which a magnetic needle floated.

the King holding up the compass in his hand, they all laid down their bows and arrows, and in a triumphant manner led him to Orapaks, where he was after their manner kindly feasted and well used.

At last they brought him to Meronocomoco, where was Powhatan, their emperor. Here more than two hundred of these grim courtiers stood wondering at him, as he had been a monster; till Powhatan and his train had put themselves in their great braveries. Before a fire upon a seat like a bedstead, he sat covered with a great robe, made of raccoonskins, and all the tails hanging by. On either hand did sit a young wench of sixteen or eighteen years, and along on each side the house, two rows of men, and behind them as many women, with all their heads and shoulders painted red; many of their heads bedecked with the white down of birds; but every one with something.

At his entrance before the King, all the people gave a great shout. The Queen of Appamatuck was appointed to bring him water to wash his hands, and another brought him a bunch of feathers, instead of a towel, to dry them. Having feasted him after their best barbarous manner they could, a long consultation was held; but the conclusion was, two great stones were brought before Powhatan: then as many as could laid hands on him, dragged him to them, and thereon laid his head, and being ready with their clubs to beat out his brains, Pocahontas, the King's dearest daughter, when no entreaty could prevail, got his head in her arms, and laid her own upon his to save him from death: whereat the emperor was contented he should live to make him hatchets, and her bells, beads, and copper; for they thought him as well of all occupations as themselves. For the King himself will make his own robes, shoes, bows,

arrows, pots; plant, hunt, or do anything so well as the rest.

Two days after, Powhatan having disguised himself in the most fearfullest manner he could, caused Captain Smith to be brought forth to a great house in the woods, and there upon a mat by the fire to be left alone. Not long after, from behind a mat that divided the house, was made the most dolefullest noise he ever heard; then Powhatan, more like a devil than a man, with some two hundred more as black as himself, came unto him and told him now they were friends and presently he should go to Jamestown to send him two great guns and a grindstone, for which he would give him the country of Capahowosick, and forever esteem him as his son Nantaquoud.

So to Jamestown with twelve guides Powhatan sent him. That night they quartered in the woods, he still expecting (as he had done all this long time of his imprisonment) every hour to be put to one death or other, for all their feasting. But almighty God, by His divine providence, had mollified the hearts of those stern barbarians with compassion. The next morning betimes they came to the fort, where Smith having used the savages with what kindness he could, he showed Rawhunt, Powhatan's trusty servant, two demi-culverins and a millstone to carry Powhatan: they found them somewhat too heavy; but when they did see him discharge them, being loaded with stones, among the boughs of a great tree loaded with icicles, the ice and branches came so tumbling down that the poor savages ran away half dead with fear. But at last we regained some conference with them, and gave them such toys; and sent to Powhatan, his women, and children such presents, and gave them in general full content.

DISCUSSION

The personality of a writer almost always comes through his work. The reader, however, must be discriminating lest he draw inferences that may not be valid; he must consider the author's purpose. From reading the *Generall Historie*, Captain John Smith would seem to be no more than a colorful adventurer and soldier of fortune. But one of the main purposes of Captain Smith's *Historie* was to attract settlement in the New World for the Virginia Company. Involved in the organization and promotion of the expedition, Smith had a definite interest in its success. His accounts, therefore, take on somewhat the aspect of advertisement, offering adventure, fame, and fortune to the lucky participant.

FOR EXPLORATION

1. The fascination of the Europeans with this barbaric new land tended to encourage a chronicler to embellish incidents or descriptions. Do you find anything unbelievable in Smith's account? Explain.

2. Would you say that Captain Smith was a modest man? If not, what circumstances would have encouraged a boastful nature?

3. (*a*) Judging from the selection, what qualities of leadership did Captain Smith possess? (*b*) In what ways does he show an understanding of his captors?

4. In most works of the colonial period tribute is paid to God's mercy and power. (*a*) Find the example in Smith's account, and discuss the validity of the idea expressed.

(*b*) In what ways does Smith's tribute to God compare with Bradford's?

5. A critic has written: "Of all the Indian tales of early America, that of Captain John Smith's rescue by Pocahontas is the most famous and the most symbolic. That Smith probably made it up matters little; it tells us still what the English wanted to think about themselves and about the people they were to displace." (*a*) In what way is the tale symbolic? (*b*) What does the second sentence of the statement mean? (*c*) Do you agree or disagree with the statement? Explain.

6. What contrasts in both form and content do you find in John Smith's and William Bradford's accounts of the New World?

THE CREATIVE RESPONSE

Find the literary sketch of the Indian Squanto in William Bradford's *The Pilgrims Meet the Indians* (page 23 C). Try your hand at a short fictional biography (one or two paragraphs) making this unheralded American come to life.

John Smith 1579/1631

John Smith led the expedition that established in 1607 the first permanent British colony in America, in Jamestown, Virginia. Smith remained in Virginia until 1609, and during that period wrote his first book (the first book written in America), an account of his experiences, *A True Relation* (1607). Later travels and explorations in the new country resulted in still other accounts written in part to encourage colonization, including *The Generall Historie of Virginia, New England, and the Summer Isles* (1624).

Anne Bradstreet

c. 1612 / 1672

UPON THE BURNING OF OUR HOUSE
July 10th, 1666

In silent night when rest I took,
For sorrow near I did not look,
I waken'd was with thund'ring noise
And piteous shrieks of dreadful voice.
5 That fearful sound of fire and fire,
Let no man know is my desire.

I, starting up, the light did spy,
And to my God my heart did cry
To strengthen me in my distress
10 And not to leave me succorless.
Then coming out beheld a space,
The flame consume my dwelling place.

And, when I could no longer look,
I blest his Name that gave and took,
15 That laid my goods now in the dust:
Yea so it was, and so 'twas just.
It was his own: it was not mine;
Far be it that I should repine.

He might of all justly bereft,
20 But yet sufficient for us left.
When by the ruins oft I past,
My sorrowing eyes aside did cast,
And here and there the places spy
Where oft I sat, and long did lie.

25 Here stood that trunk, and there that chest;
There lay that store I counted best:
My pleasant things in ashes lie,

And them behold no more shall I.
Under thy roof no guest shall sit,
30 Nor at thy table eat a bit.

No pleasant tale shall e'er be told,
Nor things recounted done of old.
No candle e'er shall shine in thee,
Nor bridegroom's voice ere heard shall be.
35 In silence ever shalt thou lie;
Adieu, adieu; all's vanity.

Then straight I gin my heart to chide,
And did thy wealth on earth abide?
Didst fix thy hope on mould'ring dust,
40 The arm of flesh didst make thy trust?
Raise up thy thoughts above the sky
That dunghill mists away may fly.

Thou hast an house on high erect,
Fram'd by that mighty Architect,
45 With glory richly furnished,
Stands permanent tho' this be fled.
It's purchased, and paid for too
By him who hath enough to do.

A prize so vast as is unknown,
50 Yet, by his gift, is made thine own.
There's wealth enough, I need no more;
Farewell my pelf, farewell my store.
The world no longer let me love,
My hope and treasure lies above.

DISCUSSION

One can imagine how sacred home was in the colonial period when Anne Bradstreet wrote this verse: a place of refuge against hostile Indians and bitter weather; a bit of order in an alien wilderness. But what is most interesting about Bradstreet's poem is not so much the poignancy with which she describes her own personal disaster, the burning of her house, but the manner in which she reconciles her loss with her deep belief in God's wisdom.

FOR EXPLORATION

1. Today, we try to find logical explanations for unfortunate disasters of this nature. Does the poet, anywhere in the poem, attempt to place blame for her troubles?

2. (*a*) Cite lines from the text which show the affection the poet feels for objects that were in her home and the pleasant memories that her house suggested to her. (*b*) In the sixth stanza Bradstreet's attitude toward her home changes. Identify the line of that stanza that best summarizes her feelings.

3. Bradstreet speaks of *two* homes in the poem. (*a*) Identify the nominal owner of each home. (*b*) In the philosophical sense of the poem, identify the *true* owner of both homes. Explain.

4. In line 52 the poet uses the word "pelf." Find the meaning of this word and explain its use in the poem. Does the poet use the word connotatively or denotatively?

Anne Bradstreet   c. 1612 / 1672

At the age of eighteen, Anne Bradstreet came to America with her husband, settling in the Massachusetts Bay Colony. She had received a better education than most women of her day, and in spite of the demands made on her as a housewife (mother of eight children) in a frontier community, she found time to write poetry. Her first volume of poems was published in London, entitled *The Tenth Muse Lately Sprung Up in America* (1650). Some of her best, less bookish, and more personal poems appeared in a volume after her death, published in Boston in 1678.

JABEZ HOWLAND HOUSE

William Byrd II

1674 / 1744

from

A PROGRESS TO THE MINES IN THE YEAR 1732

In the fall of 1732, Byrd, a member of the Virginia plantation aristocracy, made an extended trip to inspect his frontier mining properties and to collect what information he could about the manufacture of iron. He stopped to visit with various planters along his way; on September 27 he reached the home of Colonel Alexander Spotswood, the owner and operator of some iron mines. Colonel Spotswood had formerly been colonial governor of Virginia (1710-1722), and in his attempt to limit the power of the Council had been vigorously opposed by Byrd. Judging from Byrd's description of their visit, the controversy in which the two men had engaged did not affect their mutual respect and friendship.

27th. . . . I came into the main country road that leads from Fredericksburg to Germanna, which last place I reached in ten miles more. This famous town consists of Colonel Spotswood's enchanted castle on one side of the street, and a baker's dozen of ruinous tenements on the other, where so many German families had dwelt some years ago; but are now removed ten miles higher, in the fork of Rappahannock, to land of their own. There had also been a chapel about a bowshot from the Colonel's house, at the end of an avenue of cherry trees, but some pious people had lately burnt it down, with intent to get another built nearer to their own homes. Here I arrived about three o'clock, and found only Mrs. Spotswood at home, who received her old acquaintance with many a gracious smile. I was carried into a room elegantly set off with pier glasses, the largest of which came soon after to an odd misfortune. Amongst other favorite animals that cheered this lady's solitude, a brace of tame deer ran familiarly about the house, and one of them came to stare

at me as a stranger. But unluckily spying his own figure in the glass, he made a spring over the tea table that stood under it and shattered the glass to pieces, and falling back upon the tea table, made a terrible fracas among the china. This exploit was so sudden and accompanied with such a noise that it surprised me, and perfectly frightened Mrs. Spotswood. But 'twas worth all the damage to show the moderation and good humor with which she bore this disaster.

In the evening the noble Colonel came home from his mines, who saluted me very civilly, and Mrs. Spotswood's sister, Miss Theky, who had been to meet him *en cavalier*,[1] was so kind too as to bid me welcome. We talked over a legend[2] of old stories, supped about nine, and then prattled with the ladies till it was time for a traveler to retire. In the meantime I observed my old friend to be very uxorious, and exceedingly fond of his children. This was so opposite to the maxims he used to preach up before he was married that I could not forbear rubbing up the memory of them. But he gave a very good-natured turn to his change of sentiments, by alleging that whoever brings a poor gentlewoman into so solitary a place, from all her friends and acquaintance, would be ungrateful not to use her and all that belongs to her with all possible tenderness.

28th. We all kept snug in our several apartments till nine, except Miss Theky, who was the housewife of the family. At that hour we met over a pot of coffee, which was not quite strong enough to give us the palsy. After breakfast the Colonel and I left the ladies to their domestic affairs and took a turn in the garden, which has nothing beautiful but three terrace walks that fall in slopes one below another. I let him understand that besides the pleasure of paying him a visit I came to be instructed by so great a master in the mystery of making of iron, wherein he had led the way, and was the Tubal Cain of Virginia.[3] He corrected me a little there, by assuring me he was not only the first in this country,[4] but the first in North America, who had erected a regular furnace.[5] That they ran altogether upon bloomeries

---

1. *en cavalier* (än kä väl yā′), on horseback. [*French*]
2. *legend,* legion, or great number.
3. *the Tubal Cain* (tyü′bəl kān) *of Virginia.* Tubal Cain is mentioned in the Bible (Genesis 4:22) as ''an instructor of artificers in brass and iron.'' He is regarded as the inventor of the metal-working arts.
4. *country,* colony.
5. *a regular furnace,* a real plant for removing the iron from the ore and for reheating it for shaping into various forms.

in New England and Pennsylvania,[6] till his example had made them attempt greater works. But in this last colony, they have so few ships to carry their iron to Great Britain that they must be content to make it only for their own use, and must be obliged to manufacture it when they have done. That he hoped he had done the country very great service by setting so good an example. That the four furnaces now at work in Virginia circulated a great sum of money for provisions and all other necessaries in the adjacent counties. That they took off a great number of hands from planting tobacco and employed them in works that produced a large sum of money in England to the persons concerned, whereby the country is so much the richer.

Then I inquired after his own mines, and hoped, as he was the first engaged in this great undertaking, that he had brought them to the most perfection. He told me he had iron in several parts of his great tract of land, consisting of 45,000 acres. But that the mine he was at work upon was thirteen miles below Germanna. That his ore (which was very rich) he raised a mile from his furnace, and was obliged to cart the iron, when it was made, fifteen miles to Massaponox, a plantation he had upon Rappahannock River; but that the road was exceeding good, gently declining all the way, and had no more than one hill to go up in the whole journey. For this reason his loaded carts went it in a day without difficulty. He said it was true his works were of the oldest standing, but that his long absence in England, and the wretched management of Mr. Greame, whom he had entrusted with his affairs, had put him back very much. . . . That his furnace stood still a great part of the time, and all his plantations ran to ruin. That indeed he was rightly served for committing his affairs to the care of a mathematician, whose thoughts were always among the stars.

Our conversation on this subject continued till dinner, which was both elegant and plentiful. The afternoon was devoted to the ladies, who showed me one of their most beautiful walks. They conducted me through a shady lane to the landing, and by the way made me drink some very fine water that issued from a marble fountain and ran incessantly. Just behind it was a covered bench, where Miss Theky often sat and bewailed her maiden state. Then we proceeded to the river, which is the south branch of Rappahannock, about fifty yards wide, and so rapid that the ferryboat is drawn over by a chain, and therefore called the Rapidan. At night we drank prosperity to all the Colonel's projects in a bowl of rack punch, and then retired to our devotions.

29th. Having employed about two hours in retirement, I sallied out at the first summons to breakfast, where our conversation with the ladies, like whip sillabub, was very pretty, but had nothing in it. This it seems was Miss Theky's birthday, upon which I made her my compliments, and wished she might live twice as long a married woman as she had lived a maid. I did not presume to pry into the secret of her age, nor was she forward to disclose it, for this humble reason, lest I should think her wisdom fell short of her years.

Then the Colonel and I took another turn in the garden, to discourse farther on the subject of iron. He was very frank in communicating all his dearbought experience to me, and told me very civilly he would not only let me into the whole secret, but would make a journey to James River, and give me his faithful opinion of all my conveniences. For his part he wished there were many more ironworks in the country, provided the parties concerned would preserve a constant harmony among themselves, and meet and consult frequently, what might be for their common advantage.

30th. The sun rose clear this morning, and so did I, and finished all my little affairs by breakfast. It was then resolved to wait on the ladies on horseback, since the bright sun, the fine air, and the wholesome exercise, all invited us to it. We forded the river a little above the ferry, and rode six miles up the neck to a fine level piece of rich land, where we found about twenty plants of ginseng with the scarlet berries growing of the top of the middle stalk. The root of this is of wonderful virtue in many cases, particularly to raise the spirits and promote perspiration, which makes it a specific in colds and coughs. The Colonel complimented me with all we found, in return for my telling him the virtues of it. We were all pleased to find so much of this king of plants so near the Colonel's habitation, and growing too upon his own land; but were, however, surprised to find it upon level ground, after we had been told it grew

6. *they ran altogether upon bloomeries in New England and Pennsylvania.* A bloomery was the first forge in an ironworks where the metal, already separated from the ore, was made into lumps of iron. The manufacturers of New England and Pennsylvania had only bloomeries as contrasted with Colonel Spotswood's more modern furnace.

only upon the north side of stony mountains. I carried home this treasure, with as much joy, as if every root had been a graft of the Tree of Life,[7] and washed and dried it carefully. This airing made us as hungry as so many hawks, so that between appetite and a very good dinner, 'twas difficult to eat like a philosopher. In the afternoon the ladies walked me about amongst all their little animals, with which they amuse themselves, and furnish the table; the worst of it is, they are so tenderhearted, they shed a silent tear every time any of them are killed. At night the Colonel and I quitted the threadbare subject of iron, and changed the scene to politics. . . . Our conversation was interrupted by a summons to supper, for the ladies, to show their power, had by this time brought us tamely to go to bed with our bellies full, though we both at first declared positively against it. So very pliable a thing is frail man when women have the bending of him.

7. *Tree of Life,* a tree in the Garden of Eden. According to its description in the Book of Genesis, the food of this tree gave everlasting life.

FOR EXPLORATION

1. Name the literary genre which best categorizes the selection from *A Progress to the Mines.*
2. Cite specific details from the selection that indicate the wealth, culture, and leisure of a gentleman planter.
3. America was at first mainly an agricultural storehouse for England. What evidence of change from this condition do you find in Byrd's report?
4. In *A Progress to the Mines* Byrd writes, ". . . I came to be instructed by so great a master in the mystery of making of iron." (*a*) What information on the industrial beginnings in the colonies do you gain from this selection? (*b*) How did Colonel Spotwood show himself to be proud of his standing in the iron industry? (*c*) What was his attitude in giving the information requested by Byrd?
5. The William Bradford and Anne Bradstreet selections give you some picture of life in the Massachusetts Bay Colony. How do their descriptions compare with Byrd's? How was life different? the same? Explain.

PRIVATE COLLECTION; COURTESY AMERICAN HERITAGE

William Byrd 1674/1744

William Byrd, although born in Virginia Colony, spent almost half his life in England. His father left him a large Virginia estate, near Williamsburg, on his death in 1704, and there Byrd set himself up as a member of the landed gentry devoted to civilized and gracious pursuits. His earlier education in England had given him a knowledge of Latin, Greek, and Hebrew, and he continued to read these languages daily to retain his fluency. His fame rested on a series of histories and diaries that give vivid and sometimes embarrassingly intimate glimpses into the personal, social, and public life of the time.

Jonathan Edwards

1703 / 1758

from

SINNERS IN THE
HANDS OF
AN ANGRY GOD

THE wrath of God is like great waters that are dammed for the present; they increase more and more and rise higher and higher, till an outlet is given; and the longer the stream is stopped, the more rapid and mighty is its course when once it is let loose. 'Tis true that judgment against your evil work has not been executed hitherto; the floods of God's vengeance have been withheld; but your guilt in the meantime is constantly increasing, and you are every day treasuring up more wrath; the waters are continually rising and waxing more and more mighty; and there is nothing but the mere pleasure of God that holds the waters back, that are unwilling to be stopped, and press hard to go forward. If God should only withdraw his hand from the floodgate it would immediately fly open, and the fiery floods of the fierceness and wrath of God would rush forth with inconceivable fury, and would come upon you with omnipotent power; and if your strength were ten thousand times greater than it is, yea, ten thousand times greater than the strength of the stoutest, sturdiest devil in hell, it would be nothing to withstand or endure it.

The bow of God's wrath is bent, and the arrow made ready on the string, and justice bends the arrow at your heart and strains the bow, and it is nothing but the mere pleasure of God, and that of an angry God, without any promise or obligation at all, that keeps the arrow one moment from being made drunk with your blood.

Thus are all you that never passed under a great change of heart by the mighty power of the Spirit of God upon your souls; all that were never born again and made new creatures, and raised from being dead in sin to a state of new and before al-together unexperienced light and life (however you may have reformed your life in many things, and may have had religious affections, and may keep up a form of religion in your families and closets and in the house of God, and may be strict in it), you are thus in the hands of an angry God; 'tis nothing but his mere pleasure that keeps you from being this moment swallowed up in everlasting destruction.

However unconvinced you may now be of the truth of what you hear, by and by you will be fully convinced of it. Those that are gone from being in the like circumstances with you, see that it was so with them; for destruction came suddenly upon most of them; when they expected nothing of it, and while they were saying, Peace and Safety. Now they see that those things that they depended on for peace and safety were nothing but thin air and empty shadows.

The God that holds you over the pit of hell much as one holds a spider or some loathsome insect over the fire, abhors you, and is dreadfully provoked; his wrath toward you burns like fire; he looks upon you as worthy of nothing else but to be cast into the fire; he is of purer eyes than to bear to have you in his sight; you are ten thousand times so abominable in his eyes as the most hateful and venomous serpent is in ours. You have offended him infinitely more than ever a stubborn rebel did his prince; and yet it is nothing but his hand that holds you from falling into the fire every moment. 'Tis ascribed to nothing else, that you did not go to hell the last night; that you were suffered to awake again in this world after you closed your eyes to sleep and there is no other reason to be given why you have not dropped into hell since you arose in the morning, but that God's hand has held you up. There is no other reason to be given why you have not gone to hell since you have sat here in the house of God, provoking his pure eyes by your sinful wicked manner of attending his solemn worship. Yea, there is nothing else that is to be given as a reason why you don't this very moment drop down into hell.

O sinner! Consider the fearful danger you are in. 'Tis a great furnace of wrath, a wide and bottomless pit, full of the fire of wrath, that you are held over in the hand of that God whose wrath is provoked and incensed as much against you as against many of the damned in hell. You hang by a slender thread, with the flames of divine wrath flashing about it, and ready every moment to singe it and burn it asunder; and you have no interest in any Mediator, and nothing to lay hold of to save yourself, nothing to keep off the flames of wrath, nothing of your own, nothing that you ever have done, nothing that you can do, to induce God to spare you one moment. . . .

DISCUSSION

During the seventeenth and eighteenth centuries, in America as well as in England, the **sermon** flourished as a popular literary genre. Though intended for oral delivery, the sermon, like its written counterpart, the **essay,** expresses a point of view which the author wishes to convey to his audience. Edwards chose for the subject of this famous "terror" sermon one which was still popular during the mid-eighteenth century in Puritan New England: the ultimate depravity of man and the unlimited power and beneficence of God. In order to convince his listeners, in this case his congregation, of the validity of his ideas, Edwards relied upon figures of speech, rhetorical devices such as: the **simile,** a comparison using the words "like" or "as"; the **metaphor,** a similar comparison without "like" or "as." A simile or a metaphor can become an **extended metaphor** when the original idea is developed further and further.

Though we tend no longer to think of the prose sermon as a literary form, it continues to survive. Most notable are the famous sermons of the late Dr. Martin Luther King, Jr.

FOR EXPLORATION

1. Edwards develops three extended metaphors to provide the image of an angry God and sinners headed for destruction. Identify the extended metaphors from the selection as well as the figures of speech from which they are developed.

2. Edwards' sermons were powerful to the congregations and readers of his time. (a) What can you deduce about the religious convictions of the average member of his congregation? (b) How effective do you think his sermons would be today?

3. Do you feel that Edwards enjoyed picturing a God of wrath? If so, why would he be less interested in depicting a God of love? Can you see any rhetorical advantages in either portrait? Explain.

4. Judging from your own experience, has the image of the churchman changed? Could a minister today judge a congregation in Edwards' terms? Why or why not?

Jonathan Edwards 1703/1758

Jonathan Edwards is probably the most eminent theologian that America has yet produced. He was born in Connecticut and educated at Yale, where he studied theology. His early career was spent as minister in the church at Northampton, Massachusetts, where he encouraged the Great Awakening, the first of a series of religious revivals in America that continue to this day. His congregation became uneasy when he began to place emphasis on a public account of religious experience, and dismissed him in 1750. He went then to an Indian mission village, Stockbridge, Massachusetts, where he served as minister from 1751 to 1757. He was then appointed president of the College of New Jersey (later, Princeton), but died of smallpox just three months after assuming the office. He published a long list of important religious works still read by students of religion and literature, among them *A Divine and Supernatural Light* (1734) and *Freedom of the Will* (1754).

YALE UNIVERSITY ART GALLERY, BEQUEST OF EUGENE PHELPS EDWARDS, 1938

SINNERS

In the Hands of an

Angry GOD.

A SERMON

Preached at *Enfield*, *July* 8th 1 7 4 1.

At a Time of great Awakenings; and attended with remarkable Impreffions on many of the Hearers.

By *Jonathan Edwards*, A.M.

Paftor of the Church of CHRIST in *Northampton*.

Amos ix. 2, 3. *Though they dig into Hell, thence ſhall mine Hand take them; though they climb up to Heaven, thence will I bring them down. And though they hide themſelves in the Top of Carmel, I will ſearch and take them out thence; and though they be hid from my Sight in the Bottom of the Sea, thence I will command the Serpent, and he ſhall bite them.*

BOSTON: Printed and Sold by S. KNEELAND and T. GREEN. in Queen-Street over againft the Prifon. 1 7 4 1.

Hell Fire.

BY PERMISSION OF THE OLD SOUTH ASSOCIATION IN BOSTON

Esther Edwards

1732/1755

". . . THE AWFUL SWEETNESS OF WALKING WITH GOD"

NORTHAMPTON, Massachusetts, *February 13, 1741.* This is my ninth birthday, and Mrs. Edwards, my mother, has had me stitch these sundry sheets of paper into a book to make me a journal.

January 9, 1742. Mrs. Edwards was 33 years old today. That seems very old. I wonder if I shall live to be thirty-three. [She died when she was 23.] Mrs. Edwards seemed very serious all the day long; as if she were inwardly praying, "Lord, so teach me to number my days that I may apply my heart unto wisdom." Indeed, this she said to us girls when we were trying to practice some birthday frolics on her. And when she came from her devotions her face actually shone, as though, like Moses, she had come down from the Mount. I do not think we girls ever will be so saintly as our mother is. At any rate, we do not begin so. I do not know as I want to be.

February 13. Have just come tripping upstairs from morning worship and the song of the service still follows me. I have been thinking what a singing family the Edwards family is. Mother's voice we have heard in psalms and hymns and spiritual songs ever since our early babyhood. She sang us on our pilgrim way when we were in our cradles. And to all the house her voice is always uplifting like the lark's, as though her soul were mounting up to heaven's shining gate on wings of song. If father ever gets low-spirited from his "humors," as he calls them, her voice is to him like medicine, as David's harp was to King Saul. And when she once begins, there is Sarah and Jerusha and myself, like the ascending heights of an organ, ready to unite in making a joyful noise to the Lord, all over the house, so that our home is more like an aviary than the dwelling of a Colonial parson.

My mother says my journal thus far is rather stilted and mature for me; though everything in the family is mature.

March 6. Have just been caring for my mocking-bird, who is now rewarding me with song. The cat was lurking in the hall and I have just driven her away with a broom with which I have been sweeping the living-room. Though down by the fireside, at twilight, she is my favorite too. And even father, sometimes, while with us after supper, seems to enjoy her purring as he strokes her in his lap. Though I doubt if she has much divinity about her unless it is in her sparks of electricity when she is rubbed the wrong way.

May 1. I have just come back from a wonderful ride with my honored father, Mr. Edwards, through the spring woods. He usually rides alone. But today he said he had something he wanted to show me. The forests between our house and the full-banked river were very beautiful. The wild cherry and the dogwood were in full bloom. The squirrels were leaping from tree to tree, and the birds were making a various melody. Though father is usually taciturn or preoccupied—my mother will call these large words—even when he takes one of us children with him, today he discoursed to me of the awful sweetness of walking with God in Nature. He seems to feel God in the woods, the sky, and the grand sweep of the river which winds so majestically through the woody silences here.

When we reached the "Indian's Well" I slid off and brought a birchbark cup of crystal water for father to drink. But not before I had given myself a great surprise. For, having put on my mother's hat in sport, the first reflection in the dark water seemed to be the face of my mother instead of my own!

June, 1743. My mother has just come into the house with a bunch of sweet peas and put them on the stand where my honored father is shaving, though his beard is very slight. We have abundance of flowers and a vegetable garden which is early and thrifty. My honored father, of course, has not time to give attention to the garden, and so Mrs. Edwards looks after everything there. Almost before the snow has left the hills, she has it plowed and spaded by Rose's husband, who does all the hard work there. She is our colored cook. We hire her services from one of the prominent people in Father's parish, who owns both her and her husband. That word "owns" sounds strange about people! □

From SMALL VOICES by Josef and Dorothy Berger. © Copyright 1966 by Josef and Dorothy Berger. Reprinted by permission of Paul S. Ericksson, Inc.

DISCUSSION

If one reads only the notorious sermon "Sinners in the Hands of an Angry God," he might well be tempted to view Jonathan Edwards as a stern, humorless man of dogmatic religious stature, while completely disregarding his compassion. When seen through the innocent, loving, and candid eyes of Esther Edwards, his daughter, we begin to perceive a fuller, more realistic portrait of the man.

FOR EXPLORATION

1. (*a*) What incidents in Esther Edwards' narrative contribute to a more rounded picture of her father? (*b*) What evidence is there in the narrative to support preconceptions you may have developed concerning Jonathan Edwards?

2. (*a*) What does Esther Edwards call her book? (*b*) Name the literary genre that best categorizes her "book."

3. In her February 13th entry, Esther Edwards made use of at least two familiar literary techniques, one of which is a figure of speech. Name these techniques and cite examples of their use from the narrative.

Esther Edwards

At the age of twenty Esther Edwards married a Presbyterian clergyman, Aaron Burr, one of the founders and later president of Princeton University. She had two children, a son and daughter; the son, named Aaron after his father, grew up to become the third Vice President of the United States.

BY PERMISSION OF THE OLD SOUTH ASSOCIATION IN BOSTON

Cotton Mather

1633/1728

The following text contains obsure, archaic, and variant spellings ("unperswadeably," "affayrs," "oxe," "extream," for example) as well as irregular use of capitals ("Depositions," "Touch," "Cattle," "River"). As you read, note how the American language has evolved during the last three hundred years.

from

THE WONDERS OF THE INVISIBLE WORLD (1693)

The trial of Elizabeth How, at the court of Oyer and Terminer, held by adjournment at Salem, June 30, 1692.

I. Elizabeth How pleading Not Guilty to the Indictment of Witchcrafts, then charged upon her, the Court, according to the usual proceeding of the Courts in England, in such Cases, began with hearing the Depositions of Several Afflicted People,[1] who were grievously Tortured by sensible and evident Witchcrafts, and all complained of the Prisoner, as the cause of their Trouble. It was also found that the Sufferers were not able to bear her Look, as likewise, that in their greatest Swoons, they distinguished her Touch from other peoples, being thereby raised out of them.

And there was other Testimony of people to whom the shape of this How gave trouble Nine or Ten years ago.

II. It has been a most usual thing for the Bewitched persons, at the same time that the Spectres representing the Witches Troubled them, to be visited with Apparitions of Ghosts, pretending to have bin Murdered by the Witches then represented.[2] And sometimes the confessions of the witches afterwards acknowledged those very Murders, which these Apparitions charged upon them; altho' they had never heard what informations had been given by the Sufferers.

There were such Apparitions of Ghosts testified by some of the present Sufferers, and the Ghosts affirmed that this How had Murdered them: which thing were Fear'd but not prov'd.

III. This How had made some Attempts of Joyning to the Church, at Ipswich, several years ago; but she was deny'd an Admission into that Holy Society, partly through a suspicion of witchcraft, then urged against her. And there now came in Testimony, of Preternatural Mischiefs, presently befalling some that had been Instrumental to Debar her from the Communion, whereupon she was Intruding.

IV. There was a particular Deposition of Joseph Safford, That his Wife had conceived an extream Aversion to this How, on the Reports of her Witchcrafts: but How one day, taking her by the hand, and saying, "I believe you are not Ignorant of the great Scandal that I ly under, by an evil Report Raised upon me," She immediately, unreasonably, and unperswadeably, even like one Enchanted, began to take this Womans part. How being soon after propounded, as desiring an Admission to the Table of the Lord, some of the pious Brethren were unsatisfy'd about her. The Elders appointed a Meeting to hear Matters objected against her; and no Arguments in the world could hinder this Goodwife Safford from going to the Lecture. She did indeed promise, with much ado, that she would not go to the Church-Meeting, yet she could not refrain going thither also. How's Affayrs there were so Canvased, that she came off rather Guilty than Cleared; nevertheless Goodwife Safford could not forbear taking her by the Hand, and saying, "Tho' you are Condemned before men, you are Justify'd before God." She was quickly taken in a very strange manner, Frantick, Raving, Raging and Crying out, "Goody How must come into the Church; she is a precious Saint; and tho' she be Condemned before Men, she is Justify'd before God." So she continued for the space of two or three Hours; and then fell into a Trance. But coming to her self, she cry'd out, "Ha! I was mistaken"; and afterwards again repeated, "Ha! I was mistaken!" Being asked by a

---

1. *the Depositions . . . People,* the testimony of several people who alleged themselves to be the victims of witchcraft.
2. *to be visited . . . represented,* the Afflicted People were visited not only by the spectres of witches, but also by ghosts who claimed they were murdered by the witches.

stander by, "Wherein?" She replyed, "I thought Goody How had been a Precious Saint of God, but now I see she is a Witch. She has Bewitched me, and my Child, and we shall never be well, till there be Testimony for her, that she may be taken into the Church." And How said afterwards, that she was very Sorry to see Safford at the Church-Meeting mentioned. Safford after this declared herself to be afflicted by the Shape of How; and from that Shape she endured many Miseries.

V. John How, Brother to the Husband of the prisoner testifyed, that he refusing to accompany the prisoner unto her Examination, as was by her desired, immediately some of his Cattle were Bewitched to Death, Leaping three or four foot high, turning about, Squeaking, Falling, and Dying, at once; and going to cut off an Ear, for an use that might as well perhaps have been Omitted, the Hand wherein he held his knife was taken very Numb, and so it remained, and full of Pain, for several Dayes; being not well at this very Time. And he suspected this prisoner for the Author of it.

VI. Nehemiah Abbot testify'd, that unusual and mischievous Accidents would befal his cattle, whenever he had any Difference with this Prisoner. Once, Particularly, she wished his Oxe Choaked; and within a Little while that Oxe was Choaked with a Turnip in his Throat. At another time, refusing to lend his horse, at the Request of her Daughter, the horse was in a Preternatural manner abused. And several other Odd Things of that kind were testify'd.

VII. There came in Testimony, that one goodwife Sherwin, upon some Difference with How, was Bewitched, and that she Dy'd, Charging this How of having an Hand in her Death. And that other People had their Barrels of Drink unaccountably mischieved, spoilt, and spilt, upon their Displeasing of her.

The things in themselves were Trivial; but there being such a Course of them, it made them the more to be considered. Among others, Martha Wood gave her Testimony, that a Little after her Father had been employ'd in gathering an Account of Howes Conversation, they once and again Lost Great Quantities of Drink out of their Vessels, in such a manner, as they could ascribe to nothing but Witchcraft. As also, that How giving her some Apples, when she had eaten of them she was taken with a very strange kind of a maze, insomuch that she knew not what she said or did.

VIII. There was Likewise a cluster of Depositions, that one Isaac Cummings refusing to lend his Mare unto the Husband of this How, the mare was within a Day or two taken in a strange condition. The Beast seemed much Abused; being Bruised, as if she had been Running over the Rocks, and marked where the Bridle went, as if burnt with a Red hot Bridle. Moreover, one using a Pipe of Tobacco for the Cure of the Beast, a blew Flame issued out of her, took hold of her Hair, and not only Spread and Burnt on her, but it also flew upwards towards the Roof of the Barn, and had like to have set the Barn on Fire. And the Mare dy'd very suddenly.

IX. Timothy Perley and his Wife Testify'd, not only that unaccountable Mischiefs befel their Cattle, upon their having of Differences with this Prisoner: but also, that they had a Daughter destroy'd by Witchcrafts; which Daughter still charged How as the cause of her Affliction; and it was noted, that she would be struck down, whenever How were spoken of. She was often endeavoured to be Thrown into the Fire, and into the Water, in her strange Fits: tho' her Father had Corrected her for Charging How with Bewitching her, yet (as was testify'd by others also) she said, she was sure of it and must dy standing to it. Accordingly she Charged How to the very Death; and said, Tho' How could Afflict and Torment her Body, yet she could not Hurt her Soul: and, That the Truth of this matter would appear, when she should be Dead and Gone.

X. Francis Lane testify'd, That being hired by the Husband of this How to get him a parcel of Posts and Rails, this Lane hired John Pearly to assist him. This Prisoner then told Lane, that she believed the Posts and Rails would not do, because John Perley helped him; but that if he had got them alone, without John Pearlies help, they might have done well enough. When James How came to receive his Posts and Rails of Lane, How taking them up by the ends, they, tho' good and sound, yet unaccountably broke off, so that Lane was forced to get Thirty or Forty more. And this Prisoner being informed of it, she said, she told him so before; because Pearly help'd about them.

XI. Afterwards there came in the Confessions of several other (penitent) Witches, which affirmed this How to be one of those, who with them had been baptized by the Devil in the River at Newbery-Falls: before which, he made them there kneel down by the Brink of the River and Worship him. □

DISCUSSION

"The Trial of Elizabeth How" from Cotton Mather's narrative, *The Wonders of the Invisible World*, introduces the unusual nonfictional genre of **court reporting.** Though not often included among the various categories of literature, such accounts can often be found in mystery or detective novels.

Mather's courtroom accounts come closest in both form and intention to modern journalism. Indeed, *The Wonders of the Invisible World* was read avidly in Mather's day much

as we today read newspaper reports, in order to follow the development of contemporary events.

There is a tendency today to view Cotton Mather as the arch-villain of the Salem witch trials, the man responsible for the senseless executions of those accused of witchcraft. In fact, Mather only wished the accused to repent before their Lord. Years later in his personal diary he was to express the fear that ". . . the Divine displeasure might overtake my family for my not appearing with Vigor to stop the proceedings of the judges when the Inexplicable Storm from the Invisible World assaulted the country."

FOR EXPLORATION

1. We speak of religious freedom as one of the inalienable rights of our society. Based upon your reading, was there separation of church and state in the Massachusetts Bay Colony during the seventeenth century? Explain.
2. Most complaints against Elizabeth How concerned the casting of spells against livestock and the spoiling of fer-

mented drink. *(a)* Why would these be likely charges in the struggling colony? *(b)* Why would these be considered serious crimes?
3. Try to find rational causes that would explain any of the charges brought against Elizabeth How; give at least two instances that would refute the testimony of her fellow colonists.

CREATIVE RESPONSE

1. Try describing the alleged ceremony in the river at Newberry Falls (XI). To help you get started, Nathaniel Hawthorne describes such a witch's sabbath in his short story "Young Goodman Brown."
2. Over the course of history large segments of society have succumbed to the influence of mass hysteria: the "Reign of Terror" during the French Revolution; the Salem witch

hunts; the Temperance movement following World War I; the McCarthy hearings of the early 1950's; the California Gold Rush of 1849; the Draft Riots of 1863; the rock-music festivals of the late 1960's; etc. In some instances, mass hysteria has had dire consequences, while on other occasions the results have been relatively harmless. Selecting one of the above examples or one of your own choice, write an essay wherein you argue the merits and/or liabilities of such behavior and attempt to explain its causes.

Cotton Mather 1663/1728

Cotton Mather came from a long and distinguished line of clergymen; his grandfather was John Mather, his father Increase Mather, both important colonial leaders and writers. Cotton Mather graduated from Harvard at the age of fourteen, and soon began his career as minister at the Old North Church of Boston, a position he held until his death. He married three times and fathered fifteen children, and

he preached and wrote without cease, publishing during his life more than 400 items. His masterpiece is *Magnalia Christi Americana* (A History of Christ's Church in America, 1702). But his most curious book is *The Wonders of the Invisible World* (1693), in which he makes a Biblical defense of the existence of witchcraft, and describes the workings of the Devil and his witches in New England during this time.

A COLONIAL BEST SELLER

The Whole Booke of Psalmes Faithfully Translated into English Metre came off the press of Stephan Daye in Cambridge, Massachusetts in 1640. A slender calf-bound volume with sturdy brass clasps, it was the first book to be printed in British America. We know it as the "Bay" Psalm Book because of its immediate adoption, as a hymnal, by the churches in Massachusetts Bay Colony.

We do not usually associate the Puritans with music, but the singing of the Psalms was an integral part of their worship and a matter of grave concern. The Bay Psalm Book was the colonial Puritan's contribution to the long history of English versions of the Psalms, or Psalters. Beginning with a few Psalms translated into prose (which could be chanted) and then into meter (which could be sung), the English, by 1562, had a complete Psalter of the one hundred fifty Psalms of the Old Testament together with sixty-five tunes. It was this edition which the Puritans carried with them to New England. However, like other aspects of religious worship which had offended them, the New England Puritans felt this Psalter needed to be "purified." To their way of thinking, the early translators had sacrificed the sense of the Biblical text in order to achieve rhyme or graceful expression. The New England Puritan wanted to sing a more literal translation—one which clearly respected the meaning of the Hebrew text. This demand for accuracy rather than elegance shaped the translation undertaken by three Puritan divines about 1636. The following lines from the Twenty-third Psalm illustrate how these men "respected rather a plain translation, than to smooth our verses with the sweetness of any paraphrase."

> The Lord to mee a shepheard is,
>   want therefore shall not I.
> Hee in the folds of tender-grasse,
>   doth cause mee downe to lie:
> To waters calme me gently leads
>   Restore my soule doth hee:
> he doth in paths of righteousness:
>   for his names sake leade mee.

The Bay Psalm Book, selling at twenty pence a copy, was a colonial best seller. It was revised and enlarged, went through fifty editions, and for over a century the New England Puritan carried it with him to worship. It even found adherents in England and Scotland. Only ten of the original seventeen hundred copies printed by Stephan Daye are known to be in existence. One sold for $151,000 in 1947. The Bay Psalm Book, once a commonplace of Puritan life, is today a collector's item.

Title page from the first edition of the "Bay" Psalm Book.

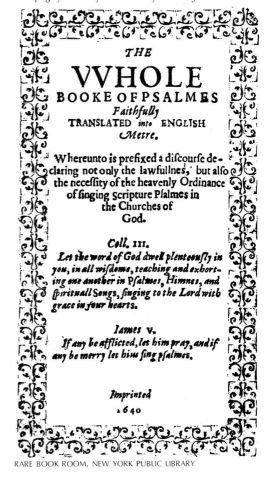

RARE BOOK ROOM, NEW YORK PUBLIC LIBRARY

Edward Taylor

c. 1645 / 1729

UPON A SPIDER

CATCHING A FLY

Thou sorrow, venom elf.
  Is this thy play,
To spin a web out of thyself
  To catch a fly?
5   For why?

I saw a pettish wasp
  Fall foul therein:
Whom yet thy whorl pins[1] did not clasp
  Lest he should fling
10   His sting.

But as afraid, remote
  Didst stand hereat,
And with thy little fingers stroke
  And gently tap
15   His back.

Thus gently him didst treat
  Lest he should pet,[2]
And in a froppish,[3] waspish heat
  Should greatly fret[4]
20   Thy net.

Whereas the silly fly,
  Caught by its leg,
Thou by the throat took'st hastily,
  And 'hind the head
25   Bite dead.

This goes to pot,[5] that not
  Nature doth call.[6]
Strive not above what strength hath got,
  Lest in the brawl
30   Thou fall.

This fray seems thus to us:
  Hell's Spider gets
His entrails spun to whip cords[7] thus,
  And wove to nets,
35   And sets.

To tangle Adam's race
  In's[8] stratagems
To their destructions, spoil'd, made base
  By venom things,
40   Damn'd sins.

But mighty, Gracious Lord,
  Communicate
Thy Grace to break the cord; afford[9]
  Us glory's gate
45   And state.

We'll nightingale sing like,
  When perched on high
In glory's cage, Thy glory, bright:
  Yea, thankfully,
50   For joy.

From THE POETICAL WORKS OF EDWARD TAYLOR, ed. Thomas H. Johnson (Princeton Paperback, 1966). Copyright Rockland 1939; Princeton University Press, 1943. Reprinted by permission of Princeton University Press.
1. *whorl pins*, the projecting pins of a whorl, or small flywheel, used to secure thread on a spindle. The poet uses this image metaphorically to suggest the motion of the spider's legs.
2. *pet*, to become peevish.
3. *froppish*, fretful, irritable.
4. *fret*, to fray, wear away.
5. *goes to pot. 1.v.*, *Colloq.* to go to ruin; *2.n.*, *Obs.* a deep pit, Hell; *3.v.*, *Colloq.* to secure or catch, to "bag."
6. *that not Nature doth call*, who does not depend upon Natural Reason, man's inherent capacity to know good from evil.
7. *whip cords*, sturdy cords made from animal entrails.
8. *In's*, in his.
9. *afford*, grant, provide.

UPON WHAT BASE?

Upon what base was fixed the lathe wherein
He turned this globe and rigolled it[1] so trim?
Who blew the bellows of His furnace vast?
Or held the mold wherein the world was cast?
Who laid its cornerstone? Or whose

5   command?
Where stand the pillars upon which it stands?
Who laced and filleted[2] the earth so fine
With rivers like green ribbons smaragdine?[3]
Who made the seas its selvage,[4] and its locks

10 Like a quilt ball within a silver box?[5]
Who spread its canopy? Or curtains spun?
Who in this bowling alley bowled the sun?

From THE POETICAL WORKS OF EDWARD TAYLOR, ed. Thomas H. Johnson (Princeton Paperback, 1966). Copyright Rockland 1939;
Princeton University Press, 1943. Reprinted by permission of Princeton University Press.
1. *rigolled* (rig'əld) *it*, shaped and grooved it so that its various
parts fitted snugly together.
2. *filleted*, edged.
3. *smaragdine* (smä rag'dīn), having the deep green color of
emeralds.
4. *Who made . . . selvage* (sel'vij), Who made the seas the edges
or borders of the earth?
5. *locks . . . box*, landlocked lakes or arms of the sea that look
like balls of quilting materials in a silver-colored sewing box.

DISCUSSION

Since our earliest writers, the Planters and Puritans, were
immigrants, they still bore the imprint of their homeland,
England. This fact is most evident in the poetry of Edward
Taylor. Taylor's poetic style sprung directly from the same
English literary tradition that nurtured such fine poets as
John Donne, John Milton, and Ben Jonson. Most typical
of this tradition was an emphasis upon the skillful and often
complicated use of language in order to convey weighty,
or metaphysical ideas. Taylor, like his fellow English poets,
made extensive use of **figurative language, punning, allusion,** and **analogy** for greater and more-precise expression.

Analogy is "a comparison of points of likeness between
two otherwise dissimilar things. An analogy uses the more
familiar to explain or enforce the less familiar."

FOR EXPLORATION

Upon a Spider Catching a Fly

1. With the aid of the appropriate footnote, identify the pun in the sixth stanza and explain the possible interpretations of that stanza as suggested by the various meanings.

2. *(a)* Who is "Hell's Spider" (line 32)? *(b)* What are "venom things" (line 39)? *(c)* What is "the cord" (line 43)?

3. *(a)* Explain the figure of speech used in the seventh stanza. *(b)* Explain the figure of speech used in the last stanza.

4. How is the poem an analogy? Explain.

Upon What Base?

1. Edward Taylor is known for his homely metaphors drawn from personal experience. *(a)* State the central image in "Upon What Base?" *(b)* To what kinds of earthly craftsmen does Taylor refer to reinforce his central image?

2. *(a)* In "Upon What Base?" what particular aspects of the beauty of the earth does Taylor select for comment in lines 7–11? *(b)* What in this poem might surprise the modern reader?

3. In what ways does reading Taylor's poetry increase your understanding of everyday life in colonial New England?

Edward Taylor c. 1645/1729

The most talented American poet of the early period, Edward Taylor was born in England and came to America in his early twenties. He attended Harvard, and later became pastor of the church at Westfield, Massachusetts. He married twice, and had a total of thirteen children. Taylor did not publish his poems during his lifetime, and probably very few people read them in manuscript. Indeed, his poems were generally forgotten until the twentieth century, when a few were placed in print in 1939. His poetic genius was then recognized, and his complete poems were published in 1960. He is the only American poet of the metaphysical school, comparable in some ways with John Donne and other British poets of the seventeenth century.

PLANTERS AND PURITANS

Then and Now

Every American grows up learning the myths of his country's past. These myths are etched deeply in the psyche and come to the surface constantly as vivid images. A national holiday like Thanksgiving evokes pictures of stiffly-starched and soberly prayerful pilgrims gathered around an abundant table of simple fare (including wild turkey) with romantically stalwart and friendly Indians hovering dimly in the background. Generations of schoolchildren have reenacted the rescue of the adventurer-explorer John Smith by the beautiful Indian princess Pocahontas, just at the moment her father's warriors were poised to beat out his brains. Ever since the famous witch trials of Puritan times which found the spirit of evil rampant in New England and the very Devil himself masterminding a plot to corrupt and capture the country, the practice of witchcraft (or some variation of awesome evildoing) has continued to fascinate Americans, and has inspired their pursuit of master villains who are somehow causing all the nation's problems and difficulties.

These common images and notions should recall to us how much we share in a common American heritage of myth and legend, but they should also recall the wide gap between myth and reality. We cannot say with certainty even now what the reality of the Puritan period was. But the broad outlines and some facts are clear enough. It was not until over a century after Columbus' discovery of America in 1492 that the English began to develop a growing interest in settling the country, and then two distinct lines of settlement began, creating a division that was to have immense consequences for subsequent history. To the South, beginning with the founding of Jamestown in Virginia in 1607, came the planters, drawn largely from the British landed aristocracy, who were interested in establishing tobacco plantations requiring a large labor force made up primarily of African slaves. To the North, beginning with the founding of Plymouth in Massachusetts in 1620, came the Pilgrims and Puritans, drawn mostly from the various protesting and Protestant groups that had broken away from the Church of England and were seeking a place where they might practice the religion of their choice and invention.

The seeds of the American Civil War (1861–1865) were sown in that long-ago division in the settlement of Massachusetts and Virginia. And those same seeds continue to flourish today, as seen in the large migrations of Blacks from the South to large northern urban centers like New York and Chicago. Foreigners visiting America tend to discover two countries today still—North and South. In the two there are different ways of speaking, different ways of thinking, different ways of living. Many of these differences can be traced back to the differences in origin between the Puritans and the planters.

A less visible, more subtle kind of inheritance from this early period is religious. The first Puritans were called by that name because they had attempted to "purify" or reform the Church of England by stripping away much of the ritual, ceremony, pomp, and paraphernalia of the traditional service, reducing it to its simplest Biblical terms. As they pared away what they considered the excesses of religion, the Puritans developed a lean, spare, somber form of religious worship, simple if not actually simplistic. In the Calvinistic tradition, they placed emphasis on the fate of "sinners in the hands of an angry God," and they spread the gloomy belief that men were fated from birth to be among the elect and saved, or among the damned and doomed. The religious convictions filtered through all facets of life, as the earliest settlers attempted to establish a theocracy with God as the head of state and the Bible as the law of the land. Ironically, many of those who came to America in search of religious freedom ended up on the side of religious authoritarianism and intolerance.

In spite of the gloom and doom implicit in the religious beliefs, there was a good deal of joy and fun in life then as now. But the fun and joy were no doubt qualified by a universal sense of guilt. To what extent America today remains a Puritan nation is debatable. But many observers of American culture profess to see remnants of the Puritan heritage in the persistence of a pervasive sense of guilt, in recurrent national flare-ups of self-righteous indignation, in the continuing pastime of debating with much heat and little light small points of religious doctrine, in a kind of didactic approach to life and the world. Even something like Calvinistic predestination may be found in a contemporary sense of doom springing from a conviction of psychological or social determinism—a sense that Fate has settled the end of man and his world.

The witch trials that took place in Salem, Massachusetts, in the early 1690's resulted in the execution (mainly by hanging) of some twenty individuals. This attempt to eradicate the evil of a community or country by identifying and eliminating certain individuals for collusion with the Devil (or for involvement in satanic and sinful plots) has fascinated the American imagination ever since. Indeed, the term "witch hunt" is commonly heard today applied not to the area of religion but to politics—any search for a scapegoat who can be blamed for all the ills of the society and whose elimination will eliminate the problems. In the early 1950's, Senator Joseph McCarthy conducted single-handedly such a witch hunt for, as he put it, pinkos, radicals, and communists, in and out of government. In the process, many innocent and talented people were permanently damaged in reputation and usefulness to the society. American playwright Arthur Miller set his play, *The Crucible*

(1953), back in the Puritan period at the time of the witch trials, but his audiences knew that his play was really about the McCarthy witch hunts of the 1950's. The success of *The Crucible* indicates how relevant the period of the Planters and Puritans continues for Americans today.

from

Act 3   THE CRUCIBLE

Arthur Miller

Setting: in 1692, in the Salem, Massachusetts meeting house

Deputy-Governor Danforth has come to investigate charges of witchcraft brought by psychologically twisted Abigail Williams and her submissive band of hysterical girls against innocent members of the community. In this climactic scene, one of Abigail's girls, Mary Warren, has confessed that their bewitched behavior has been all a pretense, but Abigail accuses her of assuming the shape of a menacing yellow bird and Mary is frightened into submission. Mercy Lewis and Susanna Walcott are among the followers of Abigail. John Proctor (and his wife) are among the accused. The Reverend John Hale remains skeptical that witchcraft has been practiced. Reverend Parris is among the large group of people who either believe in the signs and evidence of witchcraft, or find it politically wise to pretend such belief.

(ABIGAIL, *with a weird, wild, chilling cry, screams up to the ceiling.*)

ABIGAIL. You will not! Begone! Begone, I say!

DANFORTH. What is it, child? (*But* ABIGAIL, *pointing with fear, is now raising up her frightened eyes, her awed face, toward the ceiling—the* GIRLS *are doing the same—and now* HATHORNE, HALE, PUTNAM, CHEEVER, HERRICK, *and* DANFORTH *do the same.*) What's there? (*He lowers his eyes from the ceiling, and now he is frightened; there is real tension in his voice.*) Child! (*She is transfixed—with all the* GIRLS, *she is whimpering open-mouthed, agape at the ceiling.*) Girls! Why do you—?

MERCY LEWIS (*pointing*). It's on the beam! Behind the rafter!

DANFORTH (*looking up*). Where!

Excerpt from Act 3 from THE CRUCIBLE by Arthur Miller. Copyright © 1952, 1953 by Arthur Miller. Reprinted by permission of The Viking Press, Inc., and Martin Secker & Warburg Limited.

ABIGAIL. Why—? *(She gulps.)* Why do you come, yellow bird?

PROCTOR. Where's a bird? I see no bird!

ABIGAIL *(to the ceiling)*. My face? My face?

PROCTOR. Mr. Hale—

DANFORTH. Be quiet!

PROCTOR *(to HALE)*. Do you see a bird?

DANFORTH. Be quiet!!

ABIGAIL *(to the ceiling, in a genuine conversation with the "bird," as though trying to talk it out of attacking her)*. But God made my face; you cannot want to tear my face. Envy is a deadly sin, Mary.

MARY WARREN *(on her feet with a spring, and horrified, pleading)*. Abby!

ABIGAIL *(unperturbed, continuing to the "bird")*. Oh, Mary, this is a black art to change your shape. No, I cannot, I cannot stop my mouth; it's God's work I do.

MARY WARREN. Abby, I'm *here!*

PROCTOR *(frantically)*. They're pretending, Mr. Danforth!

ABIGAIL *(now she takes a backward step, as though in fear the bird will swoop down momentarily)*. Oh, please, Mary! Don't come down.

SUSANNA WALCOTT. Her claws, she's stretching her claws!

PROCTOR. Lies, lies.

ABIGAIL *(backing further, eyes still fixed above)*. Mary, please don't hurt me!

MARY WARREN *(to DANFORTH)*. I'm not hurting her!

DANFORTH *(to MARY WARREN)*. Why does she see this vision?

MARY WARREN. She sees nothin'!

ABIGAIL *(now staring full front as though hypnotized, and mimicking the exact tone of MARY WARREN's cry)*. She sees nothin'!

MARY WARREN *(pleading)*. Abby, you mustn't!

ABIGAIL AND ALL THE GIRLS *(all transfixed)*. Abby, you mustn't!

MARY WARREN *(to all the GIRLS)*. I'm here, I'm here!

GIRLS. I'm here, I'm here!

DANFORTH *(horrified)*. Mary Warren! Draw back your spirit out of them!

MARY WARREN. Mr. Danforth!

GIRLS *(cutting her off)*. Mr. Danforth!

DANFORTH. Have you compacted with the Devil? Have you?

MARY WARREN. Never, never!

GIRLS. Never, never!

RUBBING BY ANN PARKER/AVON NEAL

DANFORTH (*growing hysterical*). Why can they only repeat you?

PROCTOR. Give me a whip—I'll stop it!

MARY WARREN. They're sporting. They—!

GIRLS. They're sporting!

MARY WARREN (*turning on them all hysterically and stamping her feet*). Abby, stop it!

GIRLS (*stamping their feet*). Abby, stop it!

MARY WARREN. Stop it!

GIRLS. Stop it!

MARY WARREN (*screaming it out at the top of her lungs, and raising her fists*). Stop it!!

GIRLS (*raising their fists*). Stop it!!

(MARY WARREN, *utterly confounded, and becoming overwhelmed by* ABIGAIL'S—*and the* GIRLS'—*utter conviction, starts to whimper, hands half raised, powerless, and all the* GIRLS *begin whimpering exactly as she does.*)

DANFORTH. A little while ago you were afflicted. Now it seems you afflict others; where did you find this power?

MARY WARREN (*staring at* ABIGAIL). I—have no power.

GIRLS. I have no power.

PROCTOR. They're gulling you, Mister!

DANFORTH. Why did you turn about this past two weeks? You have seen the Devil, have you not?

HALE (*indicating* ABIGAIL *and the* GIRLS). You cannot believe them!

MARY WARREN. I—

PROCTOR (*sensing her weakening*). Mary, God damns all liars!

DANFORTH (*pounding it into her*). You have seen the Devil, you have made compact with Lucifer, have you not?

PROCTOR. God damns liars, Mary!

(MARY *utters something unintelligible, staring at* ABIGAIL, *who keeps watching the "bird" above.*)

DANFORTH. I cannot hear you. What do you say? (MARY *utters again unintelligibly.*) You will confess yourself or you will hang! (*He turns her roughly to face him.*) Do you know who I am? I say you will hang if you do not open with me!

PROCTOR. Mary, remember the angel Raphael—do that which is good and—

ABIGAIL (*pointing upward*). The wings! Her wings are spreading! Mary, please, don't, don't—!

HALE. I see nothing, Your Honor!

DANFORTH. Do you confess this power! (*He is an inch from her face.*) Speak!

ABIGAIL. She's going to come down! She's walking the beam!

DANFORTH. Will you speak!

MARY WARREN (*staring in horror*). I cannot!

GIRLS. I cannot!

PARRIS. Cast the Devil out! Look him in the face! Trample him! We'll save you, Mary, only stand fast against him and—

ABIGAIL (*looking up*). Look out! She's coming down! *She and all the* GIRLS *run to one wall, shielding their eyes. And now, as though cornered, they let out a gigantic scream, and* MARY, *as though infected, opens her mouth and screams with them. Gradually* ABIGAIL *and the* GIRLS *leave off, until only* MARY *is left there, staring up at the "bird," screaming madly. All watch her, horrified by this evident fit.* PROCTOR *strides to her.*

PROCTOR. Mary, tell the Governor what they— (*He has hardly got a word out, when, seeing him coming for her, she rushes out of his reach, screaming in horror.*)

MARY WARREN. Don't touch me—don't touch me! (*At which the* GIRLS *halt at the door.*)

PROCTOR (*astonished*). Mary!

MARY WARREN (*pointing at* PROCTOR). You're the Devil's man!

(*He is stopped in his tracks.*)

PARRIS. Praise God!

GIRLS. Praise God!

PROCTOR (*numbed*). Mary, how—?

MARY WARREN. I'll not hang with you! I love God, I love God.

DANFORTH (*to* MARY). He bid you do the Devil's work?

MARY WARREN (*hysterically, indicating* PROCTOR). He come at me by night and every day to sign, to sign, to—

DANFORTH. Sign what?

PARRIS. The Devil's book? He come with a book?

MARY WARREN (*hysterically, pointing at* PROCTOR, *fearful of him*). My name, he want my name. "I'll murder you," he says, "if my wife hangs! We must go and overthrow the court," he says!

(DANFORTH'S *head jerks toward* PROCTOR, *shock and horror in his face.*)

PROCTOR (*turning, appealing to* HALE). Mr. Hale!

MARY WARREN (*her sobs beginning*). He wake me every night, his eyes were like coals and his fingers claw my neck, and I sign, I sign . . .

HALE. Excellency, this child's gone wild!

PROCTOR (as DANFORTH'S *wide eyes pour on him*). Mary, Mary!

MARY WARREN (*screaming at him*). No, I love God; I go your way no more. I love God, I bless God. (*Sobbing, she rushes to* ABIGAIL.) Abby, Abby, I'll never hurt you more! (*They all watch, as* ABIGAIL, *out of her infinite charity, reaches out and draws the sobbing* MARY *to her, and then looks up to* DANFORTH.)

DANFORTH (*to* PROCTOR). What are you? (PROCTOR *is beyond speech in his anger.*) You are combined with anti-Christ, are you not? I have seen your power; you will not deny it! What say you, Mister?

HALE. Excellency—

DANFORTH. I will have nothing from you, Mr. Hale! (*To* PROCTOR) Will you confess yourself befouled with Hell, or do you keep that black allegiance yet? What say you?

PROCTOR (*his mind wild, breathless*). I say—I say— God is dead!

PARRIS. Hear it, hear it!

PROCTOR (*laughs insanely, then*). A fire, a fire is burning! I hear the boot of Lucifer, I see his filthy face! And it is my face, and yours, Danforth! For them that quail to bring men out of ignorance, as I have quailed, and as you quail now when you know in all your black hearts that this be fraud— God damns our kind especially, and we will burn, we will burn together.

DANFORTH. Marshal! Take him and Corey with him to the jail!

HALE (*starting across to the door*). I denounce these proceedings!

PROCTOR. You are pulling Heaven down and raising up a whore!

HALE. I denounce these proceedings, I quit this court! (*He slams the door to the outside behind him.*)

DANFORTH (*calling to him in a fury*). Mr. Hale! Mr. Hale!

THE CURTAIN FALLS

chapter two

FOUNDERS OF THE NATION

1756

TAPESTRY DONE IN 1756, SHOWING A WEDDING PARTY ARRIVING AT A CHURCH—COURTESY, AMERICAN ANTIQUARIAN SOCIETY

Hector St. John de Crèvecoeur

1735 / 1813

WHAT IS AN AMERICAN?

WHAT, then, is the American, this new man? He is neither an European nor the descendant of an European; hence that strange mixture of blood, which you will find in no other country. I could point out to you a family whose grandfather was an Englishman, whose wife was Dutch, whose son married a French woman, and whose present four sons have now four wives of different nations. *He* is an American, who, leaving behind him all his ancient prejudices and manners, receives new ones from the new mode of life he has embraced, the new government he obeys, and the new rank he holds. He becomes an American by being received in the broad lap of our great Alma Mater. Here individuals of all nations are melted into a new race of men, whose labours and posterity will one day cause great changes in the world. Americans are the western pilgrims who are carrying along with them that great mass of arts, sciences, vigour, and industry which began long since in the East; they will finish the great circle. The Americans were once scattered all over Europe; here they are incorporated into one of the finest systems of population which has ever appeared, and which will hereafter become distinct by the power of the different climates they inhabit. The American ought therefore to love this country much better than that wherein either he or his forefathers were born. Here the rewards of his industry follow with equal steps the progress of his labour; his labour is founded on the basis of nature, self-interest; can it want a stronger allurement? Wives and children, who before in vain demanded of him a morsel of bread, now, fat and frolicsome, gladly help their father to clear those fields whence exuberant crops are to arise to feed and to clothe them all, without any part being claimed, either by a despotic prince, a rich abbot, or a mighty lord. Here religion demands but little of him: a small voluntary salary to the minister and gratitude to God; can he refuse these? The American is a new man, who acts upon new principles; he must therefore entertain new ideas and form new opinions. From involuntary idleness, servile dependence, penury, and useless labour, he has passed to toils of a very different nature, rewarded by ample subsistence. This is an American.

British America is divided into many provinces, forming a large association scattered along a coast of 1,500 miles extent and about 200 wide. This society I would fain examine, at least such as it appears in the middle provinces; if it does not afford that variety of tinges and gradations which may be observed in Europe, we have colours peculiar to ourselves. For instance, it is natural to conceive that those who live near the sea must be very different from those who live in the woods; the intermediate space will afford a separate and distinct class.

Men are like plants; the goodness and flavour of the fruit proceeds from the peculiar soil and exposition in which they grow. We are nothing but what we derive from the air we breathe, the climate we inhabit, the government we obey, the system of religion we profess, and the nature of our employment. Here you will find but few crimes; these have acquired as yet no root among us. I wish I were able to trace all my ideas; if my ignorance prevents me from describing them properly, I hope I shall be able to delineate a few of the outlines; which is all I propose.

Those who live near the sea feed more on fish than on flesh and often encounter that boisterous element. This renders them more bold and enterprising; this leads them to neglect the confined occupations of the land. They see and converse with a

"What Is an American?" by Hector St. John de Crèvecoeur from LET-TERS FROM AN AMERICAN FARMER. The New American Library of World Literature, Inc.

variety of people; their intercourse with mankind becomes extensive. The sea inspires them with a love of traffic, a desire of transporting produce from one place to another, and leads them to a variety of resources which supply the place of labour. Those who inhabit the middle settlements, by far the most numerous, must be very different; the simple cultivation of the earth purifies them, but the indulgences of the government, the soft remonstrances of religion, the rank of independent freeholders, must necessarily inspire them with sentiments, very little known in Europe among a people of the same class. What do I say? Europe has no such class of men; the early knowledge they acquire, the early bargains they make, give them a great degree of sagacity. As freemen, they will be litigious; pride and obstinacy are often the cause of lawsuits; the nature of our laws and governments may be another. As citizens, it is easy to imagine that they will carefully read the newspapers, enter into every political disquisition, freely blame or censure governors and others. As farmers, they will be careful and anxious to get as much as they can, because what they get is their own. As northern men, they will love the cheerful cup. As Christians, religion curbs them not in their opinions; the general indulgence leaves every one to think for themselves in spiritual matters; the law inspects our actions; our thoughts are left to God. Industry, good living, selfishness, litigiousness, country politics, the pride of freemen, religious indifference, are their characteristics. If you recede still farther from the sea, you will come into more modern settlements; they exhibit the same strong lineaments, in a ruder appearance. Religion seems to have still less influence, and their manners are less improved.

Now we arrive near the great woods, near the last inhabited districts; there men seem to be placed still farther beyond the reach of government, which in some measure leaves them to themselves. How can it pervade every corner, as they were driven there by misfortunes, necessity of beginnings, desire of acquiring large tracks of land, idleness, frequent want of economy, ancient debts; the reunion of such people does not afford a very pleasing spectacle. When discord, want of unity and friendship, when either drunkenness or idleness prevail in such remote districts, contention, inactivity, and wretchedness must ensue. There are not the same remedies to these evils as in a long-established community. The few magistrates they have are in general little better than the rest; they are often in a perfect state of war; that of man against man, sometimes decided by blows, sometimes by means of the law; that of man against every wild inhabitant of these venerable woods, of which they are come to dispossess them. There men appear to be no better than carnivorous animals of a superior rank, living on the flesh of wild animals when they can catch them, and when they are not able, they subsist on grain. He who would wish to see America in its proper light and have a true idea of its feeble beginnings and barbarous rudiments must visit our extended line of frontiers, where the last settlers dwell and where he may see the first labours of settlement, the mode of clearing the earth, in all their different appearances, where men are wholly left dependent on their native tempers and on the spur of uncertain industry, which often fails when not sanctified by the efficacy of a few moral rules. There, remote from the power of example and check of shame, many families exhibit the most hideous parts of our society. They are a kind of forlorn hope, preceding by ten or twelve years the most respectable army of veterans which come after them. In that space, prosperity will polish some, vice and the law will drive off the rest, who, uniting again with others like themselves, will recede still farther, making room for more industrious people, who will finish their improvements convert the log-house into a convenient habitation, and rejoicing that the first heavy labours are finished, will change in a few years that hitherto barbarous country into a fine, fertile, well-regulated district. Such is our progress; such is the march of the Europeans toward the interior parts of this continent. In all societies there are off-casts; this impure part serves as our precursors or pioneers; my father himself was one of that class, but he came upon honest principles and was therefore one of the few who held fast; by good conduct and temperance, he transmitted to me his fair inheritance, when not above one in fourteen of his contemporaries had the same good fortune.

Forty years ago, this smiling country was thus inhabited; it is now purged, a general decency of manners prevails throughout, and such has been the fate of our best countries.

Exclusive of those general characteristics, each province has its own, founded on the government, climate, mode of husbandry, customs, and peculiarity of circumstances. Europeans submit insensibly to these great powers and become, in the course of a few generations, not only Americans in general, but either Pennsylvanians, Virginians, or provincials under some other name. Whoever traverses the continent must easily observe those strong differences, which will grow more evident in time. The inhabitants of Canada, Massachusetts, the middle provinces, the southern ones, will be as different as their climates; their only points of unity will be those of religion and language. ☐

DISCUSSION

Often nonfiction is thought of solely as the objective presentation of facts. Although there are indeed types of nonfiction that aim to present facts as objectively as possible (historical chronicles and news reports, for example), Crèvecoeur's *Letters from an American Farmer* is not of that genre. Crèvecoeur said, "Sentiment and feeling are the only guides I know."

Although Crèvecoeur combined many literary techniques in his writing, the section printed here might well be called an **essay,** a type of literature that expresses the author's personal feelings on a subject.

FOR EXPLORATION

1. What ways of life described in the essay are no longer part of present-day America?
2. Crèvecoeur's best-known theory is that of America's being a melting pot. Reread the first half of paragraph 1, page C 52. Has history proven the theory true? Give examples from contemporary life to prove your point.
3. In elaborating on the melting-pot idea, Crèvecoeur states that the American should love America more than he does the country of his forefathers. (a) With what reasons does he support his statement? (b) Do you think these reasons were true for the majority of American colonists? for the majority of Americans today?

4. (a) What adjectives might describe the author's attitude toward the frontiersman? (b) Do you find this attitude admirable? Why or why not?
5. What happens to the frontiersman when the "more respectable army of veterans" takes over the frontier?
6. In Crèvecoeur's time the possibility for westward expansion, for the continual opening of new frontiers, seemed limitless. What attitudes toward the land itself might be bred by such a belief?
7. At present, with most of the United States land settled, many consider the frontier a thing of the past while others see new, nongeographic frontiers yet to be conquered. What are some frontiers still open to man?

CREATIVE RESPONSE

Answer Crèvecoeur's question "What is an American?" in an essay incorporating your own "sentiment and feeling."

Hector St. John de Crèvecoeur
1735 / 1813

Born in France, Crèvecoeur was educated in England. At nineteen he sailed for Canada to become a mapmaker with the French army. Eventually he settled on a frontier farm in New York where he proved to be an excellent farmer, introducing to America the cultivation of alfalfa and a number of other crops. Despite his fondness for the American way of life, when the colonies revolted his sympathies lay with England. His unpopular position made life difficult, so he left for France to wait out the duration. Crèvecoeur returned to America only to discover his home had been burned during an Indian raid and his wife dead. He spent the next seven years as French consul, working to increase commerce between the two allies. In 1790 he took a leave of absence, sailed for Europe, and never returned.

Benjamin Franklin

1706/1790

from

THE AUTOBIOGRAPHY OF BENJAMIN FRANKLIN 1706 / 1730

From a child I was fond of reading, and all the little money that came into my hands was ever laid out in books. Pleased with the *Pilgrim's Progress,* my first collection was of John Bunyan's works in separate little volumes. I afterward sold them to enable me to buy R. Burton's *Historical Collections;* they were small chapmen's books, and cheap, forty or fifty in all. My father's little library consisted chiefly of books in polemic divinity, most of which I read, and have since often regretted that, at a time when I had such a thirst for knowledge, more proper books had not fallen in my way, since it was now resolved I should not be a clergyman. Plutarch's *Lives* there was in which I read abundantly, and I still think that time spent to great advantage. There was also a book of De Foe's, called an *Essay on Projects,* and another of Dr. Mather's, called *Essays to do Good,* which perhaps gave me a turn of thinking that had an influence on some of the principal future events of my life.

This bookish inclination at length determined my father to make me a printer, though he had already one son (James) of that profession. In 1717 my brother James returned from England with a press and letters to set up his business in Boston. I liked it much better than that of my father, but still had a hankering for the sea. To prevent the apprehended effect of such an inclination, my father was impatient to have me bound to my brother. I stood out some time, but at last was persuaded, and signed the indentures[1] when I was yet but twelve years old. I was to serve as an apprentice till I was twenty-one years of age, only I was to be allowed journeyman's wages during the last year. In a little time I made great proficiency in the business, and became a useful hand to my brother. I now had access to better books. An acquaintance with the apprentices of booksellers enabled me sometimes to borrow a small one, which I was careful to return soon and clean. Often I sat up in my room reading the greatest part of the night, when the book was borrowed in the evening and to be returned early in the morning, lest it should be missed or wanted.

And after some time an ingenious tradesman, Mr. Matthew Adams, who had a pretty collection of books, and who frequented our printing-house, took notice of me, invited me to his library, and very kindly lent me such books as I chose to read. I now took a fancy to poetry, and made some little pieces; my brother, thinking it might turn to account, encouraged me, and put me on composing occasional ballads. One was called *The Lighthouse Tragedy,* and contained an account of the drowning of Captain Worthilake, with his two daughters; the other was a sailor's song, on the taking of *Teach* (or Blackbeard) the pirate. They were wretched stuff, in the Grub-street-[2]ballad style; and when they were printed he sent me about the town to sell them. The first sold wonderfully; the event, being recent, having made a great noise. This flattered my vanity; but my father discouraged me by ridiculing my performances, and telling me verse-makers were generally beggars. So I escaped being a poet, most probably a very bad one; but as prose writing has been of great use to me in the course of my life, and was a principal means of my advancement, I shall tell you how, in such a situation, I acquired what little ability I have in that way.

There was another bookish lad in the town, John Collins by name, with whom I was intimately acquainted. We sometimes disputed, and very fond we were of argument, and very desirous of confuting one another, which disputatious turn, by the way, is apt to become a very bad habit, making people often extremely disagreeable in company by the contradiction that is necessary to bring it into practice; and thence, besides souring and spoiling the conversation, is productive of disgusts and, perhaps, enmities where you may have occasion for friendship. I had caught it by reading my father's books of dispute about religion. Persons of good sense, I have since observed, seldom fall into it, except law-

From AUTOBIOGRAPHY OF BENJAMIN FRANKLIN edited by John Bigelow. G. P. Putnam's Sons.
1. *indentures,* contracts requiring one person to serve another for a specified period, working without pay but given room, board, and a chance to learn a trade.
2. *Grub-street,* a street in London, home of impoverished and usually untalented writers.

yers, university men, and men of all sorts that have been bred at Edinborough.[3]

A question was once, somehow or other, started between Collins and me, of the propriety of educating the female sex in learning, and their abilities for study. He was of opinion that it was improper, and that they were naturally unequal to it. I took the contrary side, perhaps a little for dispute's sake. He was naturally more eloquent, had a ready plenty of words, and sometimes, as I thought, bore me down more by his fluency than by the strength of his reasons. As we parted without settling the point, and were not to see one another again for some time, I sat down to put my arguments in writing, which I copied fair and sent to him. He answered, and I replied. Three or four letters of a side had passed, when my father happened to find my papers and read them. Without entering into the discussion, he took occasion to talk to me about the manner of my writing; observed that, though I had the advantage of my antagonist in correct spelling and pointing (which I ow'd to the printing-house), I fell far short in elegance of expression, in method and in perspicuity, of which he convinced me by several instances. I saw the justice of his remarks, and thence grew more attentive to the manner in writing and determined to endeavor at improvement.

About this time I met with an odd volume of the *Spectator*.[4] It was the third. I had never before seen any of them. I bought it, read it over and over, and was much delighted with it. I thought the writing excellent, and wished, if possible, to imitate it. With this view I took some of the papers, and, making short hints of the sentiment in each sentence, laid them by a few days, and then, without looking at the book, try'd to compleat the papers again, by expressing each hinted sentiment at length, and as fully as it had been expressed before, in any suitable words that should come to hand. Then I compared my *Spectator* with the original, discovered some of my faults, and corrected them. But I found I wanted a stock of words, or a readiness in recollecting and using them, which I thought I should have acquired before that time if I had gone on making verses; since the continual occasion for words of the same import, but of different length, to suit the measure, or of different sound for the rhyme, would have laid me under a constant necessity of searching for variety, and also have tended to fix that variety in my mind, and make me master of it. Therefore I took

some of the tales and turned them into verse; and, after a time, when I had pretty well forgotten the prose, turned them back again. I also sometimes jumbled my collections of hints into confusion, and after some weeks endeavored to reduce them into the best order, before I began to form the full sentences and compleat the paper. This was to teach me method in the arrangement of thoughts. By comparing my work afterwards with the original, I discovered my faults and amended them; but I sometimes had the pleasure of fancying that, in certain particulars of small import, I had been lucky enough to improve the method or the language, and this encouraged me to think I might possibly in time come to be a tolerable English writer, of which I was extremely ambitious. My time for these exercises and for reading was at night, after work or before it began in the morning, or on Sundays, when I contrived to be in the printing-house alone, evading as much as I could the common attendance on public worship which my father used to exact of me when I was under his care, and which indeed I still thought a duty, though I could not, as it seemed to me, afford time to practise it.

When about 16 years of age I happened to meet with a book, written by one Tryon, recommending a vegetable diet. I determined to go into it. My brother, being yet unmarried, did not keep house, but boarded himself and his apprentices in another family. My refusing to eat flesh occasioned an inconveniency, and I was frequently chid for my singularity. I made myself acquainted with Tryon's manner of preparing some of his dishes, such as boiling potatoes or rice, making hasty pudding, and a few others, and then proposed to my brother, that if he would give me, weekly, half the money he paid for my board, I would board myself. He instantly agreed to it, and I presently found that I could save half what he paid me. This was an additional fund for buying books. But I had another advantage in it. My brother and the rest going from the printing-house to their meals, I remained there alone, and, despatching presently my light repast, which often was no more than a bisket or a slice of bread, a handfull of raisins, or a tart from the pastry-cook's, and a glass of water, had the rest of the time, till their

---

3. *Edinborough*, the University of Edinburgh in Scotland.
4. *Spectator*, a London newspaper published by Joseph Addison and Richard Steele in the early eighteenth century. The paper is famous for the perfection of its writing style.

return, for study, in which I made the greater progress, from that greater clearness of head and quicker apprehension which usually attend temperance in eating and drinking.

And now it was that, being on some occasion made asham'd of my ignorance in figures, which I had twice failed in learning when at school, I took Cocker's book of Arithmetick, and went through the whole by myself with great ease. I also read Seller's and Shermy's books of Navigation, and became acquainted with the little geometry they contain; but never proceeded far in that science. And I read about this time Locke *On Human Understanding,* and the *Art of Thinking,* by Messrs. du Port Royal.

While I was intent on improving my language, I met with an English grammar (I think it was Greenwood's), at the end of which there were two little sketches of the arts of rhetoric and logic, the latter finishing with a specimen of a dispute in the Socratic method,[5] and soon after I procur'd Xenophon's *Memorable Things of Socrates,* wherein there are many instances of the same method. I was charm'd with it, adopted it; dropt my abrupt contradiction and positive argumentation, and put on the humble inquirer and doubter. And being then, from reading Shaftesbury and Collins,[6] become a real doubter in many points of our religious doctrine, I found this method safest for myself, and very embarrassing to those against whom I used it; therefore I took a delight in it, practis'd it continually, and grew very artful and expert in drawing people, even of superior knowledge, into concessions, the consequences of which they did not foresee, entangling them in difficulties out of which they could not extricate themselves, and so obtaining victories that neither myself nor my cause always deserved. I continu'd this method some few years, but gradually left it, retaining only the habit of expressing myself in terms of modest diffidence, never using, when I advanced any thing that may possibly be disputed, the words *certainly, undoubtedly,* or any others that give the air of positiveness to an opinion, but rather say, I conceive or apprehend a thing to be so and so; it appears to me, or *I should think it so or so,* for such and such reasons; or *I imagine it to be so;* or *it is so, if I am not mistaken.* This habit, I believe, has been of great advantage to me when I have had occasion to inculcate my opinions, and persuade men into measures that I have been from time to time engag'd in promoting; and, as the chief ends of conversation are to *inform* or to be *informed,* to *please* or to *persuade,* I wish well-meaning, sensible men would not lessen their power of doing good by a positive, assuming manner, that seldom fails to disgust, tends to create opposition, and to defeat every one of those purposes for which speech was given to us,—to wit, giving or receiving information or pleasure. For, if you would inform, a positive and dogmatical manner in advancing your sentiments may provoke contradiction and prevent a candid attention. If you wish information and improvement from the knowledge of others, and yet at the same time express yourself as firmly fix'd in your present opinions, modest, sensible men, who do not love disputation, will probably leave you undisturbed in the possession of your error. And by such a manner, you can seldom hope to recommend yourself in *pleasing* your hearers, or to persuade those whose concurrence you desire. Pope[7] says, judiciously:

Men should be taught as if you taught them not,
And things unknown propos'd as things forgot;

farther recommending to us

To speak, tho' sure, with seeming diffidence.

And he might have coupled with this line that which he has coupled with another, I think, less properly:

For want of modesty is want of sense.

If you ask, Why less properly? I must repeat the lines:

Immodest words admit of no defense,
For want of modesty is want of sense.

Now, is not *want of sense* (where a man is so unfortunate as to want it) some apology for his *want of modesty?* and would not the lines stand more justly thus?

Immodest words admit *but* this defense,
That want of modesty is want of sense.

This, however, I should submit to better judgments.

---

5. *Socratic method,* use of a series of questions designed to make an opponent contradict himself in an argument.
6. *Shaftesbury and Collins,* Anthony Ashley Cooper, third earl of Shaftesbury (1671–1713) and Anthony Collins (1676–1729). Shaftesbury wrote of man's inherent goodness and ability to tell right from wrong. Collins urged man to question religious doctrine. The views of both men would have contradicted Puritan beliefs.
7. *Pope,* Alexander Pope, eighteenth-century British poet.

My brother had, in 1720 or 1721, begun to print a newspaper. It was the second that appeared in America, and was called the *New England Courant*.[8] The only one before it was the *Boston News-Letter*. I remember his being dissuaded by some of his friends from the undertaking, as not likely to succeed, one newspaper being, in their judgment, enough for America. At this time [1771] there are not less than five-and-twenty. He went on, however, with the undertaking, and after having worked in composing the types and printing off the sheets, I was employed to carry the papers thro' the streets to the customers.

He had some ingenious men among his friends, who amus'd themselves by writing little pieces for this paper, which gain'd it credit and made it more in demand, and these gentlemen often visited us. Hearing their conversations, and their accounts of the approbation their papers were received with, I was excited to try my hand among them; but, being still a boy, and suspecting that my brother would object to printing any thing of mine in his paper if he knew it to be mine, I contrived to disguise my hand, and, writing an anonymous paper, I put it in at night, under the door of the printing-house. It was found in the morning, and communicated to his writing friends when they call'd in as usual. They read it, commented on it in my hearing, and I had the exquisite pleasure of finding it met with their approbation, and that, in their different guesses at the author, none were named but men of some character among us for learning and ingenuity. I suppose now that I was rather lucky in my judges, and that perhaps they were not really so very good ones as I then esteem'd them.

Encourag'd, however, by this, I wrote and convey'd in the same way to the press several more papers, which were equally approv'd; and I kept my secret till my small fund of sense for such performances was pretty well exhausted, and then I discovered it, when I began to be considered a little more by my brother's acquaintance, and in a manner that did not quite please him, as he thought, probably with reason, that it tended to make me too vain. And, perhaps, this might be one occasion of the differences that we began to have about this time. Though a brother, he considered himself as my master, and me as his apprentice, and, accordingly, expected the same services from me as he would from another, while I thought he demean'd me too much in some

he requir'd of me, who from a brother expected more indulgence. Our disputes were often brought before our father, and I fancy I was either generally in the right, or else a better pleader, because the judgment was generally in my favor. But my brother was passionate, and had often beaten me, which I took extreamly amiss; and, thinking my apprenticeship very tedious, I was continually wishing for some opportunity of shortening it, which at length offered in a manner unexpected.[9]

One of the pieces in our newspaper on some political point, which I have now forgotten, gave offense to the Assembly. He was taken up, censur'd, and imprison'd for a month, by the Speaker's warrant, I suppose, because he would not discover his author. I too was taken up and examin'd before the council; but, tho' I did not give them any satisfaction, they content'd themselves with admonishing me, and dismissed me, considering me, perhaps, as an apprentice, who was bound to keep his master's secrets.

During my brother's confinement, which I resented a good deal, notwithstanding our private differences, I had the management of the paper; and I made bold to give our rulers some rubs in it, which my brother took very kindly, while others began to consider me in an unfavorable light, as a young genius that had a turn for libelling and satyr. My brother's discharge was accompany'd with an order of the House (a very odd one), that *"James Franklin should no longer print the paper called the New England Courant."*

There was a consultation held in our printing-house among his friends, what he should do in this case. Some proposed to evade the order by changing the name of the paper; but my brother, seeing inconveniences in that, it was finally concluded on as a better way, to let it be printed for the future under the name of BENJAMIN FRANKLIN; and to avoid the censure of the Assembly, that might fall on him as still printing it by his apprentice, the contrivance was that my old indenture should be return'd to me, with a full discharge on the back of it, to be shown on occasion, but to secure to him the benefit of my service, I was to sign new indentures

8. *second . . . Courant.* The *New England Courant* was actually the fourth newspaper published in America.
9. *Though a brother . . . unexpected.* Franklin himself noted: "I fancy his harsh and tyrannical treatment of me might be a means of impressing me with that aversion to arbitrary power that has stuck to me through my whole life."

for the remainder of the term, which were to be kept private. A very flimsy scheme it was; however, it was immediately executed, and the paper went on accordingly, under my name for several months. □

from

THE WAY TO WEALTH

It would be thought a hard government that should tax its people one-tenth part of their time, to be employed in its service. But idleness taxes many of us much more, if we reckon all that is spent in absolute sloth, or doing of nothing, with that which is spent in idle employments or amusements that amount to nothing. Sloth, by bringing on diseases, absolutely shortens life. *Sloth, like rust, consumes faster than labor wears; while the used key is always bright,* as Poor Richard says. *But dost thou love life, then do not squander time, for that's the stuff life is made of,* as Poor Richard says. How much more than is necessary do we spend in sleep, forgetting, that *The sleeping fox catches no poultry,* and that *There will be sleeping enough in the grave,* as Poor Richard says.

If time be of all things the most precious, *wasting time* must be, as Poor Richard says, *the greatest prodigality;* since, as he elsewhere tells us, *Lost time is never found again;* and what we call *time enough, always proves little enough.* Let us then be up and doing, and doing to the purpose; so by diligence we do more with less perplexity. *Sloth makes all things difficult, but industry all easy;* and *He that riseth late must trot all day, and shall scarce overtake his business at night;* while *Laziness travels so slowly, that Poverty soon overtakes him. Drive thy business, let not that drive thee;* and *Early to bed, and early to rise, makes a man healthy, wealthy, and wise,* as Poor Richard says.

So what signifies wishing and hoping for better times? We may make these times better, if we bestir ourselves. *Industry need not wish,* and *He that lives upon hope will die fasting. There are no gains without pains;* then *Help, hands, for I have no lands;* or, if I have, they are smartly taxed. *He that hath a trade hath an estate;* and *He that hath a calling hath an office of profit and honor,* as Poor Richard says; but then the trade must be worked at, and the calling well followed, or neither the estate nor the office will enable us to pay our taxes. If we are industrious, we shall never starve; for, *At the working-man's house hunger looks in, but dares not enter.* Nor will the bailiff or the constable enter, for *Industry pays debts, while despair increaseth them.* What though you have found no treasure, nor has any rich relation left you a legacy. *Diligence is the mother of good luck, and God gives all things to industry. Then plough deep while sluggards sleep, and you shall have corn to sell and to keep.* Work while it is called today, for you know not how much you may be hindered tomorrow. *One today is worth two tomorrows,* as Poor Richard says; and further, *Never leave that till tomorrow, which you can do today.* If you were a servant, would you not be ashamed that a good master should catch you idle? Are you then your own master? *Be ashamed to catch yourself idle,* when there is so much to be done for yourself, your family, your country, and your king. Handle your tools without mittens; remember, that *The cat in gloves catches no mice,* as Poor Richard says. It is true there is much to be done, and perhaps you are weak-handed; but stick to it steadily, and you will see great effects; for *Constant dropping wears away stones;* and *By diligence and patience the mouse ate in two the cable;* and *Little strokes fell great oaks.*

Methinks I hear some of you say, "Must a man afford himself no leisure?" I will tell thee, my friend, what Poor Richard says, *Employ thy time well, if thou meanest to gain leisure;* and, *Since thou art not sure of a minute, throw not away an hour.* Leisure is time for doing something useful; this leisure the diligent man will obtain, but the lazy man never; for *A life of leisure and a life of laziness are two things. Many, without labor, would live by their wits only, but they break for want of stock;* whereas industry gives comfort, and plenty, and respect. *Fly pleasures, and they will follow you. The diligent spinner has a large shift;* and *Now I have a sheep and a cow, everybody bids me good morrow;* all of which is well said by Poor Richard.

BENJAMIN FRANKLIN BY DAVID MARTIN—WHITE HOUSE COLLECTION

SPEECH IN THE CONVENTION, AT THE CONCLUSION
OF ITS DELIBERATIONS, SEPTEMBER 17, 1787

Mr. President,

I confess, that I do not entirely approve of this Constitution at present; but, Sir, I am not sure I shall never approve it; for, having lived long, I have experienced many instances of being obliged, by better information or fuller consideration, to change opinions even on important subjects, which I once thought right, but found to be otherwise. It is therefore that, the older I grow, the more apt am I to doubt my own judgment of others. Most men, indeed, as well as most sects in religion, think themselves in possession of all truth, and that wherever others differ from them it is so far error. Steele,[1] a Protestant, in a dedication, tells the Pope, that the only difference between our two churches in their opinions of the certainty of their doctrine, is, the Romish

---

1. *Steele.* The reference is probably to Richard Steele, the English essayist, who joined with Joseph Addison in writing the *Spectator.*

Church is *infallible*, and the Church of England is *never in the wrong*. But, though many private persons think almost as highly of their own infallibility as of that of their sect, few express it so naturally as a certain French lady, who, in a little dispute with her sister, said, "But I meet with nobody but myself that is always in the right." "*Je ne trouve que moi qui aie toujours raison.*"

In these sentiments, Sir, I agree to this Constitution, with all its faults—if they are such, because I think a general government necessary for us, and there is no *form* of government but what may be a blessing to the people, if well administered; and I believe, further, that this is likely to be well administered for a course of years, and can only end in despotism, as other forms have done before it, when the people shall become so corrupted as to need despotic government, being incapable of any other. I doubt, too, whether any other convention we can obtain, may be able to make a better constitution; for, when you assemble a number of men, to have the advantage of their joint wisdom, you inevitably assemble with those men all their prejudices, their passions, their errors of opinion, their local interests, and their selfish views. From such an assembly can a *perfect* production be expected? It therefore astonishes me, Sir, to find this system approaching so near to perfection as it does; and I think it will astonish our enemies, who are waiting with confidence to hear that our counsels are confounded like those of the builders of Babel,[2] and that our States are on the point of separation, only to meet hereafter for the purpose of cutting one another's throats. Thus I consent, Sir, to this Constitution, because I expect no better, and because I am not sure

that it is not the best. The opinions I have had of its *errors* I sacrifice to the public good. I have never whispered a syllable of them abroad. Within these walls they were born, and here they will die. If every one of us, in returning to our constituents, were to report the objections he has had to it, and endeavor to gain partisans in support of them, we might prevent its being generally received, and thereby lose all the salutary effects and great advantages resulting naturally in our favor among foreign nations, as well as among ourselves, from any real or apparent unanimity. Much of the strength and efficiency of any government, in procuring and securing happiness to the people, depends on *opinion*, on the general opinion of the goodness of that government, as well as of the wisdom and integrity of its governors. I hope, therefore, for our own sakes, as a part of the people, and for the sake of our posterity, that we shall act heartily and unanimously in recommending this Constitution, wherever our influence may extend, and turn our future thoughts and endeavors to the means of having it *well administered*.

On the whole, Sir, I cannot help expressing a wish, that every member of the convention who may still have objections to it, would with me on this occasion doubt a little of his own infallibility, and, to make *manifest* our *unanimity*, put his name to this instrument. ☐

---

2. *builders of Babel.* According to the Bible (Genesis 11:1−9), builders of the ancient city of Babylon decided to construct a tower that would reach to heaven. God punished them by changing their language into several different languages. Unable to understand one another, they had to leave the tower unfinished.

DISCUSSION

Franklin's **autobiography** (an account of a person's life or a part of his life, written by that person) is one of the most famous works of early American literature. Yet Franklin is equally well known for *Poor Richard's Almanack*, volumes of which were published between 1733 and 1758. The sayings of Poor Richard were very popular at the time they were written and Franklin later summed up their wisdom in *The Way to Wealth*. This work is full of the **epigrams** and **aphorisms** that made the *Almanack* a success. An **epigram** is a highly polished verse or saying ending with a witty turn. An **aphorism** is a short, pithy saying that differs from an epigram in that it is not necessarily witty.

FOR EXPLORATION

from *The Autobiography* . . .

1. The self-made man, the man who teaches himself what is necessary to gain his objectives and rises above humble origins with no help from others, has long been an American ideal. Franklin is considered a model of this ideal. Give specific examples of incidents in *The Autobiography* that demonstrate the qualities of the self-made man.
2. Many people find the self-made man unpleasant company, believing that his conversation is often limited to accounts of how hard he had to struggle and the relative ease of the lives of others. When reading from the *Autobiography*, did you find Franklin to be such unpleasant company? Point out passages in the text to support your answer.

from *The Way to Wealth*

Skim this selection, taking note of the epigrams and aphorisms. *(a)* Why might Franklin have chosen this particular way of giving advice to his readers? *(b)* What advantage does this form have over, for example, an essay on the evils of laziness?

"Speech in the Convention . . ."

1. As a group, the founders of the United States are often compared to present-day "radicals" who call for sweeping, immediate, and not necessarily peaceful change. Do you think that such a comparison applies specifically to Franklin? Support your answer by citing lines from the speech that show his view of the colonists' situation, his emotional state, his philosophy about government.
2. *(a)* Why does Franklin urge the delegates not to discuss their objections to the new constitution with the people they are representing? Do you agree with his reasoning? *(b)* Is such a suggestion truly *democratic*? Might such action at times be necessary? *(c)* Can you think of cases in which this idea might be abused?

WORDS

Franklin's Speech in the Convention fairly rolls with words derived from Latin. When, for example, he pleads for *unanimity* of action, he is asking that the delegates be of one mind (*unus animus*).

Show how the original meaning of each Latin word below has been retained in the sentences that follow it.

fallere, to deceive

1. Franklin asked the delegates to doubt a little of their own *infallibility*.

2. In thinking the colonists wouldn't fight, the British held a *fallacious* belief.

salus, good health

1. Franklin pointed out that a unanimous decision would have *salutary* effects.

2. The southern delegates enjoyed a *salubrious* climate.

efficere, to accomplish

1. Franklin declared that the *efficiency* of any government depended upon opinion.

2. The British believed in the *efficacy* of the redcoats.

integer, whole

1. Franklin relied upon the *integrity* of his fellow delegates.

2. Volunteer militia were *integrated* with professional soldiers in the Revolutionary army.

Benjamin Franklin 1706 / 1790

Benjamin Franklin was born the son of a Boston tallow-maker. He had little schooling and at the age of ten was apprenticed to his father. But the boy disliked the trade, and after considering and rejecting a number of other vocations, he became a printer's apprentice in his brother's shop. After working there for the five years covered in the autobiography excerpt, Franklin broke the secret papers of indenture and, at the age of seventeen, headed for Philadelphia to make his fortune. He experienced a number of hard, disappointing years but finally acquired his own printing shop. He married and settled down, worked to create an image of frugal industriousness, and cultivated friends who might prove good business contacts. He bought and revitalized the *Philadelphia Gazette*, forerunner to the *Saturday Evening Post*, and in 1730 began publishing *Poor Richard's Almanack*. He became active in community affairs and fathered an impressive list of ideas and institutions, among them the first circulating library in America, the University of Pennsylvania, and a hospital for the poor of Philadelphia.

The growth of his printing company and some wise investments enabled Franklin to retire when he was forty-four and devote his time to inventing and scientific experiments. His findings established him as the leading scientist of the Western Hemisphere and caused his election to the exclusive Royal Society.

It was only natural that a man of Franklin's talents should be sought out for public office. The Pennsylvania legislature sent him to London in 1757 to represent Pennsylvania in its disputes with the mother country. Between 1768 and 1770 three more of the colonies asked Franklin to represent them and he quickly came to be considered the chief spokesman for the colonies as a whole. By 1775 he had given up his once strong hope for reconciliation with England and returned to America where he was elected to the Second Continental Congress.

Later that year he was appointed commissioner to France and sailed for Paris in hopes of obtaining military assistance. His fame as a scientist and philosopher of the New World preceded him, and "Dr. Franklin," as he was called, was immensely popular with the French people. The French court discovered him to be a brilliant conversationalist with a worldly wisdom and a quick wit. It was primarily his popularity and skill which secured the much needed support of France and Spain, the decisive factor in the winning of the American Revolution. Franklin helped negotiate the Treaty of Paris (1783), by which England recognized American independence, and then returned to America in 1785. Despite the fact that he was then seventy-nine years old and in poor health, he went on to serve as president of the Commonwealth of Pennsylvania and then as a member of the Constitutional Convention. "Speech in the Convention, at the Conclusion of Its Deliberation" was delivered at the age of eighty-one, three years before his death.

Though Franklin did not consider himself a serious writer and never finished a single full-length book, he wrote clearly and persuasively, and was probably the finest pamphleteer of his era.

Thomas Paine

1737 / 1809

from

THE AMERICAN CRISIS

THESE are the times that try men's souls: The summer soldier and the sunshine patriot will in this crisis, shrink from the service of his country; but he that stands it NOW, deserves the love and thanks of man and woman. Tyranny, like hell, is not easily conquered; yet we have this consolation with us, that the harder the conflict, the more glorious the triumph. What we obtain too cheap, we esteem too lightly:—'Tis dearness only that gives everything its value. Heaven knows how to put a proper price upon its goods; and it would be strange indeed, if so celestial an article as FREEDOM should not be highly rated. Britain, with an army to enforce her tyranny, has declared that she has a right (*not only to*) TAX but "to BIND *us in* ALL CASES WHATSOEVER," and if being *bound in that manner,* is not slavery, then is there not such a thing as slavery upon earth. Even the expression is impious, for so unlimited a power can belong only to GOD. . . .

I have as little superstition in me as any man living, but my secret opinion has ever been, and still is, that God Almighty will not give up a people to military destruction, or leave them unsupportedly to perish, who have so earnestly and so repeatedly sought to avoid the calamities of war, by every decent method which wisdom could invent. Neither have I so much of the infidel in me, as to suppose that he has relinquished the government of the world, and given us up to the care of devils; and as I do not, I cannot see on what grounds the king of Britain can look up to Heaven for help against us: a common murderer, a highwayman, or a house-breaker, has as good a pretence as he. . . .

I once felt all that kind of anger, which a man ought to feel against the mean principles that are held by the tories: A noted one, who kept a tavern at Amboy, was standing at his door, with as pretty a child in his hand, about eight or nine years old, as I ever saw, and after speaking his mind as freely as he thought was prudent, finished with this un-fatherly expression, *"Well! give me peace in my day."* Not a man lives on the continent but fully believes that a separation must some time or other finally take place, and a generous parent should have said, *"If there must be trouble, let it be in my day, that my child may have peace,"* and this single reflection, well applied, is sufficient to awaken every man to duty. Not a place upon earth might be so happy as America. Her situation is remote from all the wrangling world, and she has nothing to do but to trade with them. A man can distinguish himself between temper and principle, and I am as confident, as I am that GOD governs the world, that America will never be happy till she gets clear of foreign dominion. Wars, without ceasing, will break out till that period arrives, and the continent must in the end be conqueror; for though the flame of liberty may sometimes cease to shine, the coal can never expire. . . .

The heart that feels not now is dead; the blood of his children will curse his cowardice, who shrinks back at a time when a little might have saved the whole, and made *them* happy. I love the man that can smile in trouble, that can gather strength from distress, and grow brave by reflection. 'Tis the business of little minds to shrink; but he whose heart is firm, and whose conscience approves his conduct, will pursue his principles unto death. My own line of reasoning is to myself as straight and clear as a ray of light. Not all the treasures of the world, so far as I believe, could have induced me to support an offensive war, for I think it murder; but if a thief breaks into my house, burns and destroys my property, and kills or threatens to kill me, or those that are in it, and to *"bind me in all cases whatsoever"* to his absolute will, am I to suffer it? What signifies it to me, whether he who does it is a king or a common man; my countryman or not my countryman; whether it be done by an individual villain, or an army of them? If we reason to the root of things we shall find no difference; neither can any just cause be assigned why we should punish in the one case and pardon in the other. ☐

DISCUSSION

When applied to writing, the term **tone** may be used two ways. First, it may serve to describe the writer's attitude toward both his subject and his **audience,** those people he hopes to reach through his writing. A writer's tone may be described as solemn, reasonable, persuasive, inflammatory, or any number of other adjectives and combinations of adjectives, depending upon his feelings about and knowledge of his subject and audience. (For example, "Her reasonable and persuasive tone convinced the other students to follow her; her essay also won top honors in the composition class.")

The term **tone** may also be used to describe the overall mood of the work itself. (For example, "The tone of his last novel was so negative and depressing that I had to force myself to finish reading it.")

FOR EXPLORATION

1. What adjectives might best describe Paine's tone in this selection? Find specific words and ideas in the essay to support your choices.

2. (a) Paine's audience was obviously the American colonist, but what particular type or group within the larger category was he trying to convince? (b) What was his attitude toward these people? What particular words and ideas in the essay support your answer?

3. Compare and contrast the tone of this selection with that of Franklin's speech before the convention, page C 60.

CREATIVE RESPONSE

Decide on one topic that is of interest to your class and on which everyone does not already have the same opinion; then divide the class into four groups. Each of you should now write an essay in which you try to persuade your audience that your opinion on the topic is the one that they should share and act upon. Each group will write for a different audience, following the guidelines in column b. Be prepared to read and discuss your essays in class.

Group I, audience of students who are in sympathy with your opinion but have not yet committed themselves to your cause.

Group II, audience of teachers and other adults who are in sympathy with your opinion but have not yet committed themselves to your cause.

Group III, audience of students who are either indifferent or opposed to your opinion.

Group IV, audience of teachers and other adults who are either indifferent or opposed to your opinion.

Thomas Paine   1737 / 1809

When Thomas Paine first came to America he was thirty-seven. He had lived an inconspicuous life, born into an English social structure which had no use for his talents. After having worked at jobs ranging from corset-maker to grocer, Paine was able to meet Benjamin Franklin in London. Franklin thought him an "ingenious, worthy young man," and in 1774 paid his passage to America and supplied him with a letter of recommendation. In America Paine quickly came into his own. He became a newspaper editor and strong proponent of separation from Britain. Paine's first pamphlet, *Common Sense,* appeared in January of 1776, at a time when most Americans still hoped the quarrel with England could be resolved amicably. Paine pointed out the advantage, necessity, and obligation of a break with Britain and urged "an open and determined DECLARATION FOR INDEPENDENCE." The pamphlet is said to have sold 500,000 copies, a remarkable figure for those days. Paine then enlisted in the Continental army in time for the retreat across New Jersey. Along the way the first installment of the *American Crisis* was written. Subsequent issues would appear irregularly throughout the war, especially at points when the cause seemed to falter. Paine gave unstintingly of himself throughout the Revolution and its end found him honored but poor. Pennsylvania gave him £500 in recognition of his efforts and New York awarded him a confiscated Loyalist farm.

He lived uneventfully for a number of years and then in 1787 left for England in order to construct there an iron bridge he had invented. Four years later while still in England, Paine replied to British condemnation of the French Revolution with an essay entitled *Rights of Man.* In it he not only maintained that government exists to guarantee the rights of the individual but suggested that the British monarchy be replaced with a republican form of government. Those Paine suggested replacing were predictably ungracious and Paine, who had fled for France, was tried in absentia for treason, and outlawed.

In France Paine was welcomed and honored until a change in French politics caused him to be arrested and imprisoned during the Terror of Robespierre. He was released a year later, having spent his imprisonment writing the first part of *The Age of Reason.* It was a work which affirmed Paine's belief in a God, but so dissected the Bible and criticized Christianity that when Paine later returned to America he found himself an outcast. Libeled and ostracized, he died impoverished at the age of seventy-two.

Phillis Wheatley

c. 1753 / 1784

TO S. M.,[1] A YOUNG AFRICAN PAINTER ON SEEING HIS WORKS

To show the lab'ring bosom's deep intent,
And thought in living characters to paint,
When first thy pencil did those beauties give,
And breathing figures learnt from thee to live,
5 How did those prospects give my soul delight,
A new creation rushing on my sight!
Still, wondrous youth! each noble path pursue;
On deathless glories fix thine ardent view:
Still may the painter's and the poet's fire,
10 To aid thy pencil and thy verse conspire!
And may the charms of each seraphic theme
Conduct thy footsteps to immortal fame!
High to the blissful wonders of the skies
Elate thy soul, and raise thy wishful eyes.
15 Thrice happy, when exalted to survey
That splendid city, crowned with endless day,
Whose twice six gates on radiant hinges ring:

Celestial Salem blooms in endless spring.
Calm and serene thy moments glide along,
20 And may the muse inspire each future song!
Still, with the sweets of contemplation blessed,
May peace with balmy wings your soul invest!
But when these shades of time are chased away,
And darkness ends in everlasting day,
25 On what seraphic pinions shall we move,
And view the landscapes in the realms above!
There shall thy tongue in heavenly murmurs flow,
And there my muse with heavenly transport glow;
No more to tell of Damon's[2] tender sighs,
30 Or rising radiance of Aurora's[3] eyes;
For nobler themes demand a nobler strain,
And purer language on the ethereal plain.
Cease, gentle Muse![4] the solemn gloom of night
Now seals the fair creation from my sight.

"To S. M., a Young African Painter on Seeing His Works" by Phillis Wheatley from EARLY NEGRO AMERICAN WRITERS edited by Benjamin Brawley. Published by The University of North Carolina Press.

1. S. M., Scipio Moorhead, a Black slave who lived and painted in colonial Boston.
2. Damon, a man in Roman legend who became a hostage and nearly lost his life for his friend Pythias.
3. Aurora, Roman goddess of dawn.
4. Muse, the spirit believed to inspire a poet at the time he creates a poem.

HIS EXCELLENCY GENERAL WASHINGTON

Celestial choir! enthron'd in realms of light,
Columbia's scenes of glorious toils I write.
While freedom's cause her anxious breast alarms,
She flashes dreadful in refulgent arms.
5 See mother earth her offspring's fate bemoan,
And nations gaze at scenes before unknown!
See the bright beams of heaven's revolving light
Involved in sorrows and the veil of night!
The goddess comes, she moves divinely fair,
10 Olive and laurel[1] binds her golden hair:
Wherever shines this native of the skies,
Unnumber'd charms and recent graces rise.
Muse! bow propitious while my pen relates
How pour her armies through a thousand gates;
As when Eolus[2] heaven's fair face deforms,
Enwrapped in tempest and a night of storms;
Astonish'd ocean feels the wild uproar,
The refluent surges beat the sounding shore,
Or thick as leaves in Autumn's golden reign,
20 Such, and so many, moves the warrior's train.
In bright array they seek the work of war,

Where high unfurl'd the ensign waves in air.
Shall I to Washington their praise recite?
Enough thou know'st them in the fields of fight.
25 Thee, first in place and honours,—we demand
The grace and glory of thy martial band.
Fam'd for thy valour, for thy virtues more,
Here every tongue thy guardian aid implore!
One century scarce performed its destin'd round,
30 When Gallic[3] powers Columbia's fury found;
And so may you, whoever dares disgrace
The land of freedom's heaven-defended race!
Fix'd are the eyes of nations on the scales,
For in their hopes Columbia's arm prevails.
35 Anon Britannia droops the pensive head,
While round increase the rising hills of dead.
Ah! cruel blindness to Columbia's state!
Lament thy thirst of boundless power too late.
Proceed, great chief, with virtue on thy side,
40 Thy every action let the goddess guide.
A crown, a mansion, and a throne that shine,
With gold unfading, *Washington*, be thine.

Phillis Wheatley c. 1753 / 1784

Phillis Wheatley was born in Africa and at the age of eight brought by slave ship to Boston. By the time she was thirteen she was writing poetry and translating Latin. On her arrival in America she was bought by John Wheatley, a prosperous tailor, who encouraged her studies. Without benefit of formal schooling, she quickly taught herself English and then went on to learn Latin. She was fond of classical literature and modeled her poetry after such contemporary English poets as Pope and Gray. Considered a member of the family and never treated as a slave, Wheatley was formally given her freedom when she was twenty. Concerned for her frail health, the Wheatleys at this time sent her to London with their son Nathanial, hoping the ocean air and change of climate would be beneficial. Miss Wheatley achieved immediate popularity in London social circles, but their stay was cut short by the serious illness of Mrs. Wheatley. Shortly after their return to Boston, Mrs. Wheatley died; the death of Mr. Wheatley followed soon after.

She married a few years later, but the marriage proved an unhappy one. Her overbearing husband was often disagreeable and she became estranged from her former friends; two of her three children died in early infancy. Isolated, poor, and too proud to let the surviving members of the Wheatley family know of her plight, she took on menial work despite her frail condition. She died alone and in poverty at the age of thirty-one. Her end coincided with the death of her third child and they were buried together in an unmarked grave.

"His Excellency General Washington" by Phillis Wheatley from EARLY NEGRO AMERICAN WRITERS edited by Benjamin Brawley. University of North Carolina Press.

1. *Olive and laurel.* The olive branch is a symbol of peace; a wreath of laurel symbolizes victory.
2. *Eolus*, probably Æolus, Greek god of the winds.
3. *Gallic*, French.

DISCUSSION

Phillis Wheatley's poetry, like the work of most early American writers, relies heavily on the example set by the masters of English literature. The poems printed here employ many of the techniques that British poets and readers alike at that time considered necessary to the writing of poetry: a strict pattern of rhyme and rhythm, allusions to figures in Greek and Roman mythology, and a formal and rather lofty tone.

The poems also make use of a number of figures of speech, among these **personification,** the treating of a thing or an abstraction as if it were a person.

FOR EXPLORATION

"To S. M., . . ."

1. While the title tells the reader who the poet is speaking to, the poem itself gives more specific reasons for Wheatley's praise of S. M. *(a)* What has he been able to do that makes her admire him? *(b)* What hopes does she have for his future?

2. Of what is the poet speaking when referring to "shades of time," "darkness," and "everlasting day"?

3. What fate does Wheatley envision for both herself and the painter? How is this role to differ from their present, earthly one?

"His Excellency, General Washington"

1. What purpose do the two opening lines serve?

2. Who is Columbia? What figure of speech is Wheatley using here?

3. Note that lines 2-22 serve to describe Columbia. *(a)* What impression do they give? *(b)* What specific words, phrases, and especially figures of speech create this impression?

4. Where in the poem is Washington first mentioned? How does the poet regard him?

5. *(a)* How does the poet view England? *(b)* How do other countries regard the struggle between England and the colonies? *(c)* What will be its outcome? Support your answers with lines from the poem.

6. The poet closes by combining the two subjects she has developed throughout: Columbia and Washington. What opinion of and hopes for the two does Wheatley voice?

CREATIVE RESPONSE

1. Historians have marveled at the fact that Phillis Wheatley, brought from Africa at the age of eight and nearly all her life a slave, was able to achieve such an advanced degree of scholarship and artistic expression. Her experience was certainly not typical of most African slaves in America, but neither was it typical of most women. (See selection from Franklin's autobiography, page C 56, column a, paragraph 1.)

Explore your own history texts and materials from school and public libraries for accounts of the status of slaves and that of women in colonial America. Report findings to the class. Those interested might trace each group's struggle for equality from colonial times to the present.

2. Some critics, while granting Phillis Wheatley's achievement a high degree of respect, voice the wish that she had used her talents to tell of the African's true lot in America or to teach her countrymen the worth and dignity of their African heritage. How would you defend the poet's work in the face of this argument?

Thomas Jefferson

1743 / 1826

THE DECLARATION OF INDEPENDENCE

WHEN, in the course of human events, it becomes necessary for one people to dissolve the political bands which have connected them with another, and to assume, among the Powers of the earth, the separate and equal station to which the Laws of Nature and of Nature's God entitle them, a decent respect to the opinions of mankind requires that they should declare the causes which impel them to the separation.

We hold these truths to be self-evident: that all men are created equal; that they are endowed by their Creator with certain inalienable Rights; that among these are Life, Liberty, and the pursuit of Happiness. That, to secure these Rights, Governments are instituted among Men, deriving their just powers from the consent of the governed—That, whenever any Form of Government becomes destructive of these ends, it is the Right of the People to alter or abolish it, and to institute new Government, laying its foundation on such Principles, and organizing its Powers in such form, as to them shall seem most likely to effect their Safety and Happiness. Prudence, indeed, will dictate that Governments long established should not be changed for light and transient causes; and, accordingly, all experience hath shown that mankind are more disposed to suffer, while evils are sufferable, than to right themselves by abolishing the forms to which they are accustomed. But, when a long train of abuses and usurpations, pursuing invariably the same Object, evinces a design to reduce them under absolute Despotism, it is their right, it is their duty, to throw off such Government, and to provide new Guards for their future security. Such has been the patient sufferance of these Colonies, and such is now the necessity which constrains them to alter their former Systems of Government. The history of the present King of Great Britain is a history of repeated injuries and usurpations, all having in direct object the establishment of an absolute Tyranny over these States. To prove this, let Facts be submitted to a candid world:

He has refused his Assent to Laws the most wholesome and necessary for the public good.

He has forbidden his Governors to pass Laws of immediate and pressing importance, unless suspended in their operation till his Assent should be obtained; and, when so suspended, he has utterly neglected to attend to them.

He has refused to pass other Laws for the accommodation of large districts of people, unless those people would relinquish the rights of Representation in the Legislature; a right inestimable to them, and formidable to tyrants only.

He has called together legislative bodies at places unusual, uncomfortable, and distant from the depository of their Public Records, for the sole purpose of fatiguing them into compliance with his measures.

He has dissolved Representative Houses repeatedly for opposing, with manly firmness, his invasions on the rights of the people.

He has refused for a long time after such dissolutions to cause others to be elected; whereby the Legislative Powers, incapable of Annihilation, have returned to the People at large for their exercise; the State remaining, in the meantime, exposed to all the dangers of invasions from without, and convulsions within.

He has endeavored to prevent the Population of these States; for that purpose obstructing the Laws for Naturalization of Foreigners; refusing to pass others to encourage their migrations hither, and raising the conditions of new Appropriations of Lands.

He has obstructed the Administration of Justice by refusing his Assent to Laws for establishing Judiciary Powers.

He has made Judges dependent on his Will alone for the tenure of their offices, and the amount and Payment of their salaries.

He has erected a multitude of New Offices, and sent hither swarms of Officers to harass our People and eat out their substance.

He has kept among us, in times of Peace, Standing Armies, without the Consent of our legislatures.

He has affected to render the Military independent of and superior to the Civil Power.

He has combined with others to subject us to a jurisdiction foreign to our constitution, and unacknowledged by our laws: giving his Assent to their Acts of pretended Legislation:

For quartering large bodies of armed troops among us;

For protecting them, by a mock Trial, from Punishment for any Murders which they should commit on the Inhabitants of these States;

For cutting off our Trade with all parts of the world;

For imposing Taxes on us without our Consent;

For depriving us, in many cases, of the benefits of Trial by Jury;

For transporting us beyond Seas to be tried for pretended offences;

For abolishing the free System of English Laws in a neighboring Province,[1] establishing therein an Arbitrary government, and enlarging its Boundaries, so as to render it at once an example and fit instrument for introducing the same absolute rule into these Colonies;

For taking away our Charters, abolishing our most valuable Laws, and altering, fundamentally, the Forms of our Governments;

For suspending our own Legislatures, and declaring themselves invested with Power to legislate for us in all cases whatsoever.

He has abdicated Government here by declaring us out of his Protection, and waging War against us.

He has plundered our seas, ravaged our Coasts, burnt our towns, and destroyed the Lives of our People.

He is, at this time, transporting large Armies of foreign Mercenaries to complete the works of death, desolation, and tyranny, already begun with circumstances of Cruelty and Perfidy scarcely paralleled in the most barbarous ages, and totally unworthy the Head of a civilized nation.

He has constrained our fellow Citizens, taken Captive on the high Seas, to bear Arms against their Country, to become the executioners of their friends and Brethren, or to fall themselves by their Hands.

He has excited domestic insurrections amongst us, and has endeavored to bring on the inhabitants of our frontiers the merciless Indian Savages, whose known rule of warfare is an undistinguished destruction of all ages, sexes, and conditions.

In every stage of these Oppressions, We have Petitioned for Redress, in the most humble terms: Our repeated Petitions have been answered only by repeated injury. A Prince, whose character is thus marked by every act which may define a Tyrant, is unfit to be the ruler of a free People.

Nor have We been wanting in attentions to our British brethren. We have warned them, from time to time, of attempts by their legislature to extend an unwarrantable jurisdiction over us. We have reminded them of the circumstances of our emigration and settlement here. We have appealed to their native justice and magnanimity, and we have conjured them, by the ties of our common kindred, to disavow these usurpations, which would inevitably interrupt our connections and correspondence. They, too, have been deaf to the voice of justice and of consanguinity. We must, therefore, acquiesce in the necessity which denounces our Separation, and hold them, as we hold the rest of mankind—Enemies in War—in Peace, Friends.

WE, THEREFORE, the REPRESENTATIVES of the UNITED STATES OF AMERICA, in GENERAL CONGRESS Assembled, appealing to the Supreme Judge of the world for the rectitude of our intentions, Do, in the Name and by the Authority of the good People of these Colonies, solemnly PUBLISH and DECLARE, That these United Colonies are, and of Right ought to be, FREE AND INDEPENDENT STATES; that they are Absolved from all Allegiance to the British Crown, and that all political connection between them and the State of Great Britain is, and ought to be, totally dissolved; and that, as FREE AND INDEPENDENT STATES, they have full Power to levy War, conclude Peace, contract Alliances, establish Commerce, and to do all other Acts and Things which INDEPENDENT STATES may of right do. And, for the support of this Declaration, with a firm reliance on the Protection of Divine Providence, we mutually pledge to each other our Lives, our Fortunes, and our Sacred Honor.

---

1. *a neighboring Province*, Quebec, which England had acquired as a result of the French and Indian War. According to the Quebec Act of 1774, French Civil Law was established, a royal governor was appointed, and the boundaries were enlarged to include much of the country between the Ohio and the Mississippi rivers.

1. What is the purpose of the first paragraph?
2. Reread the first sentence of paragraph 2. In listing what he believes to be man's "inalienable Rights," why does Jefferson say "the pursuit of Happiness" rather than merely "Happiness"?
3. According to paragraph 2, what is the purpose of government? Where does government get its power?
4. Under what circumstances may a government be changed or abolished? Whose job is it to do the changing or abolishing? Why?
5. Notice that the first half of paragraph 2 presents a general philosophy of the rights and responsibilities of both people and government. What is the purpose of the last half of the paragraph?
6. After listing the colonists grievances (paragraphs 3–29), Jefferson makes clear the fact that they have tried using peaceful means to draw the king's attention to their plight. What is the purpose of such a statement?
7. Jefferson describes the English people as "our British brethren," calling attention to their "magnanimity" and "native justice," noting the "common kindred" of them and the colonists. Considering the fact that he concludes this paragraph by saying that they have not heard the pleas of their colonial relatives and declaring the British people "Enemies in War—in Peace, Friends," what might be the reason for his initial praise?
8. What is the purpose of the last paragraph? Is its tone in keeping with that of the body of the Declaration? Why or why not?
9. Read aloud the last sentence of the Declaration. With what emotion does it leave the listener? What particular words, by both their sounds and meanings, contribute to the creation of this emotion?

CREATIVE RESPONSE

The Declaration of Independence states the colonists' belief that the power of government should lie with those who are governed. A movement voicing a similar idea presently exists in the United States. The more moderate supporters of this movement urge greater individual participation in the decision-making process, usually through voter-registration drives, education programs, and the supporting of "grass roots" candidates for political office. More radical elements within the movement urge a complete restructuring of the governmental system by any means necessary to return a more direct governing power to the citizens themselves.

In the 1960's and early 1970's, advocates of this idea coined slogans, created posters, wrote both fiction and nonfiction, composed songs, and used various other means to communicate their beliefs to the people of the country.

Assume that you are an advocate of American independence living in the colonies in 1776. Given the fact that at that time in history only certain media would be available to you, make a poster, write a ballad, essay, or dramatic sketch, or use any other means to express to your fellow colonists your belief in and support of the struggle for freedom from England.

Thomas Jefferson 1743 / 1826

In another age Thomas Jefferson would most likely never have been elected President. He lacked charisma, found political strife distasteful, was relatively free of personal ambition, and was ineffective in public speaking (John Adams described him as "the most silent man in Congress. . . . I never heard him utter three sentences together."). Yet he was the apostle of an ideal, and grew to be a symbol of it. And he was a brilliant man. When speaking at a dinner for Nobel prize-winners, John Kennedy described it as "the most extraordinary collection of talent, of human knowledge, that has ever been gathered together at the White House, with the possible exception of when Thomas Jefferson dined alone."

A Virginia planter and aristocrat, a graduate of William and Mary College, a lawyer by profession, Jefferson had little to gain and everything to lose by advocating rebellion against British rule. He served first in the Virginia House of Burgesses and was one of the Virginia representatives to the Second Continental Congress. At the Congress Jefferson was asked to replace a departing member of the declaration committee, and then reluctantly agreed to attempt a draft of the document. The resulting Declaration of Independence, though debated on and changed by Congress, was, more than most state papers, the work of a single man. It remains Jefferson's masterpiece.

He subsequently served as governor of Virginia, Franklin's successor as minister to France, secretary of state under Washington, Vice President in John Hamilton's administration, and finally as President from 1801 to 1809. When he died he was buried at his home at Monticello under an inscription of his own choosing: "Author of the Declaration of American Independence, of the Statute of Virginia for religious freedom, and Father of the University of Virginia."

"THE MANNER OF THEIR FISHING" C. 1585, WATERCOLOR BY JOHN WHITE—TRUSTEES OF THE BRITISH MUSEUM

The manner of their fishing.

Canooe.

William Bartram   1739 / 1823

from

TRAVELS THROUGH NORTH AND SOUTH CAROLINA, GEORGIA, EAST AND WEST FLORIDA

The White Trader of Spalding's Upper Store

On our arrival at the Upper Store,[1] we found it occupied by a white trader who had for a companion a very handsome Seminole young woman. Her father, who was a prince by the name of White Captain, was an old chief of the Seminoles, and with part of his family, to the number of ten or twelve, was encamped in an orange grove near the stores, having lately come in from a hunt.

This white trader, soon after our arrival, delivered up the goods and storehouses to my companion and joined his father-in-law's camp, and soon after went away into the forests on hunting and trading amongst the flying camps of Seminoles.

He is at this time unhappy in his connections with his beautiful savage. It is but a few years since he came here, I think from North Carolina, a stout, genteel, well-bred man, active and of a heroic and amiable disposition; and by his industry, honesty, and engaging manners had gained the affections of the Indians and soon made a little fortune by traffic with the Seminoles. When he unfortunately met with this little charmer, they were married in the Indian manner. He loves her sincerely, as she possesses every perfection in her person to render a man happy. Her features are beautiful and manners engaging. Innocence, modesty, and love appear to a stranger in every action and movement, and these powerful graces she has so artfully played upon her beguiled and vanquished lover and unhappy slave as to have already drained him of all his possessions, which she dishonestly distributes amongst her savage relations. He is now poor, emaciated, and half distracted, often threatening to shoot her and afterwards put an end to his own life; yet he has not resolution even to leave her, but now endeavors to drown and forget his sorrows in deep draughts of brandy. Her father condemns her dishonesty and cruel conduct.

These particulars were related to me by my old friend the trader, directly after a long conference which he had with the White Captain on the subject, his son-in-law being present. The scene was affecting; they both shed tears plentifully. My reasons for mentioning this affair, so foreign to my business, was to exhibit an instance of the power of beauty in a savage and her art and finesse in improving it to her private ends. It is, however, but doing justice to the virtue and moral conduct of the Seminoles, and American aborigines in general, to observe that the character of this woman is condemned and detested by her own people of both sexes. If her husband should turn her away, according to the customs and usages of these people, she would not get a husband again, as a divorce seldom takes place but in consequence of a deliberate, impartial trial and public condemnation, and then she would be looked upon as a harlot.

Such is the virtue of these untutored savages; but I am afraid this is a common-phrase epithet, having no meaning or at least improperly applied; for these people are both well tutored and civil. It is apparent to an impartial observer, who resides but a little time amongst them, that it is from the most delicate sense of the honor and reputation of their tribes and families that their laws and customs receive their force and energy. This is the divine principle which influences their moral conduct and solely preserves their constitution and civil government in that purity in which they are found to prevail amongst them. □

From JOHN AND WILLIAM BARTRAM'S AMERICA by William Bartram, edited by Helen Gere Cruickshank. Copyright 1957 by The Devin-Adair Company. Reprinted by permission of the publisher The Devin-Adair Company.

1. *Upper Store,* trading post located near the town of Astor near the upper end of Lake George in Florida.

OBSERVATIONS ON THE CREEK AND CHEROKEE INDIANS [1]

Philadelphia, Dec. 15, 1789

Thus you have, Sir,

My observations and conjectures on these matters, with all the truth and accuracy that my slender abilities will admit of, and without reserve. If they should not answer your wishes and expectations, I desire you will ascribe it to my misapprehension of the queries or lack of knowledge, etc., etc.

I doubt not but you will readily excuse bad writing, composition, and spelling. My weakness of sight, I hope, will plead for me, when I assure you I have been obliged to write the greater part of this with my eyes shut, and that with pain.

I do not mention this to claim any sort of obligation from you, Sir, for all that I know concerning these matters are due to you and to science.

I remain, Sir,

With every sentiment of respect and esteem, your obliged friend,

Wm. Bartram

IV. COMPARATIVE RELIGIOUS ADVANCEMENT

Query. Which of the tribes of Indians visited by you are the most polished in their religion, in their manners, in their language, in their government, etc., etc.?

Answer. If adopting or imitating the manners and customs of the white people is to be termed civilization, perhaps the Cherokees have made the greatest advance.

But I presume, if we are to form and establish our judgments from the opinions and rules laid down by the greatest doctors of morality, philosophers, and divines, either of the ancients or moderns, the Muscogulges must have approbation, and engage our esteem.

Their religion is, perhaps, as pure as that which was in the beginning revealed to the first families of mankind. They have no notion or conception of any other God but the Great Spirit on high, the giver and taker away of the breath of life; which is as much as to say that eternal Supreme Being who created and governs the universe. They worship none else.

They pay a kind of homage to the sun, moon, and planets, as the mediators or ministers of the Great Spirit in dispensing His attributes for their comfort and well-being in this life. They have some religious rites and forms, which are managed by their priests or doctors, who make the people believe, by their cunning and craft, that they have a supernatural spiritual communication with invisible spirits of good or evil, and that they have the power of good and evil. They make the people believe that, by conjuring, they can bring rain, fine weather, heat, cooling breezes, thunder and lightning, bring on or expel and cure sickness, etc., etc.

XII. FOOD AND MEANS OF SUBSISTENCE

Query. Does the food of the Indian appear to be principally animal or vegetable? What are the principal vegetables employed for food by them? What vegetables do they cultivate for food besides maize, different species of gourds, etc.? What are the principal vegetables of which they make their bread? Do you think the tribes you visited were acquainted with the use of salt before they became acquainted with the Europeans? If you think they were not, what substances did they employ as substitutes?

Answer. Their animal food consisted chiefly of venison, bear's flesh, turkeys, hares, wild fowl, and domestic poultry; and also of domestic kine, as beeves, goats, and swine—never horse's flesh, though they have horses in great plenty—neither do they eat the flesh of dogs, cats, or any such creatures as are usually rejected by white people.

Their vegetable food consists chiefly of corn (Zea), rice, Convolvulus batatas, or those nourishing roots usually called sweet or Spanish potatoes (but in the Creek confederacy they never plant or eat the Irish potato). All the species of the Phaseolus and Dolichos [2] in use among the whites are cultivated by the Creeks, Cherokees, etc. and make up a great part of their food. All the species of Cucurbita,

---

1. *Creek and Cherokee Indians.* The Muskhogean (or *Creek* as the English called them) lived in Alabama and Georgia. The Cherokee tribe lived in the southern Alleghenies.

2. *Phaseolus and Dolichos,* beans and peas.

squashes, pumpkins, watermelons, etc.; but of the cucumeres,[3] they cultivate none of the species as yet, neither do they cultivate our farinaceous grains, as wheat, barley, spelts, rye, buckwheat, etc. (not having got the use of the plough amongst them, though it has been introduced some years ago). The chiefs rejected it, alleging it would starve their old people who employed themselves in planting and selling their produce to traders, for their support and maintenance; seeing that by permitting the traders to use the plough, one or two persons could easily raise more grain than all the old people of the town could do by using the hoe. Turnips, parsnips, salads, etc., they have no knowledge of. Rice (Oryza) they plant in hills on high, dry ground, in their gardens; by this management a few grains in a hill (the hills about four feet apart) spread every way incredibly and seem more prolific than cultivated in water, as in the white settlements of Carolina; the heads or panicles are larger and heavier, and the grain is larger, firmer, or more farinaceous, much sweeter, and more nourishing. Each family raises enough of this excellent grain for its own use.

But, besides the cultivated fruits above recited, with peaches, oranges, plums (Chickasaw plums), figs, and some apples, they have in use a vast variety of wild or native vegetables, both fruit and roots, viz., Diospyros, Morus rubra, Gleditsia, Multiloba, S. triacanthus; all the species of Juglans and acorns, from which they extract a very sweet oil which enters into all their cooking, and several species of *palms*, which furnish them with a great variety of agreeable and nourishing food. Grapes, too, they have in great variety and abundance, which they feed on occasionally when ripe. They also prepare them for keeping and lay up for winter and spring time. A species of Smilax[4] (S. pseudochina) affords a delicious and nourishing food, which is prepared from its vast, tuberous roots.

They dig up these roots and, while yet fresh and full of juice, chop them in pieces and then macerate them well in wooden mortars. This substance they put in vessels nearly filled with clean water, when, being well mixed with paddles, whilst the fine particles are yet floating in the liquid, they decant it off into other vessels, leaving the farinaceous material at the bottom; this, being taken out and dried, is an impalpable powder of farina, of reddish color. This, when mixed with boiling water, becomes a beautiful jelly which, when sweetened with honey or sugar, affords a most nourishing food for children and aged people; or when mixed with fine corn flour and fried in fresh bear's grease, makes excellent fritters. . . .

---

3. *cucumeres*, cucumbers and gourds.
4. *Smilax*, long-stalked greenbriar.

DISCUSSION

Son of a famous naturalist and himself a trained scientist, William Bartram described his explorations in the new country in a way quite different from that of other early chroniclers. Bartram's purpose in making his five-year trip through what is now the southeastern United States was to gather data on both the inhabitants and the physical features of the area. His reports were originally written for scientists whose knowledge and training were similar to his own, but Bartram's accounts soon became popular with a much wider and more varied audience. Bartram possessed artistic as well as scientific abilities; the perception and skill of the poet and painter are apparent in the accounts, making them much more than the mere presentation of scientific data, and therefore of interest to those outside the scientific community.

Bartram's time saw the development of the romantic movement among writers and philosophers in England and Europe. One characteristic of this movement was a reverence for nature, a belief that through communion with wild and unspoiled land and primitive people, land and people untouched by civilization, man could gain inspiration and strength. This belief gave rise to the somewhat simplistic concept of the "noble savage," the inhabitant of the wilderness living in harmony with his surroundings, satisfying his simple, basic needs, not exposed to and therefore untainted by the corrupting influences of civilization. Bartram was familiar with the ideas of the early romantics; his accounts of life among the Indians show that he too held with the idea of the noble savage.

But Bartram's effect on the romantics was more far-reaching than was theirs on him. His accounts of a land both exotic and unspoiled influenced and often provided settings for works by such famous English romantic poets as William Wordsworth and Samuel Taylor Coleridge and for the French philosopher Jean Jacques Rousseau.

from *Travels . . .*

1. What is Bartram's purpose in relating the anecdote of the trader and the Seminole woman?
2. Describe the tone of this selection. What does it tell you about Bartram's attitude toward the Seminoles?

Observations on the Creek and Cherokee Indians

1. In what specific parts of this selection is Bartram's training as a scientist most apparent?
2. In light of the information about the romantics given in the Discussion, what particular information in this selection do you think would have been of special interest to them?
3. Contrast the tone of the two Bartram selections with that of the account by Captain John Smith (page 25 C). What factors might account for the difference between them?

William Bartram 1739 / 1823

William Bartram was the first real student of the American Indian. He was accepted as one of them, and the Seminoles called him Puc-puggy, the Flower Hunter. His career as naturalist and chronicler of his explorations was an extension of the efforts of his father, John Bartram, the pioneer American botanist. William had little formal education, but his youth on the family experimental farm in Pennsylvania, and his father's guidance, tutoring, and encouragement more than compensated. At the age of twenty-six he began accompanying his father on the elder botanist's expeditions. By 1773 William had begun his own explorations: sketching, recording his observations, and studying the people. His studies made him one of the foremost botanists of his day, and his descriptions of his travels were sources of inspiration for a generation of writers. He was a devout Quaker, a shy quiet man who never married.

DICTIONARY OF AMERICAN PORTRAITS

FOUNDERS OF THE NATION

Then and Now

Every country has its historical moments or figures that become focal points of national adulation and patriotic fervor, symbols of the people in their unity and solidarity. America's myths and symbols serving these purposes belong to the colonial period up to the Revolutionary War and the founding of the United States of America. Not only historical events but also their dates take on a special luster when they come to symbolize critical stages in the life cycle of a country: in 1773, the Boston Tea Party; 1774, the First Continental Congress; 1775, the midnight ride of Paul Revere; 1776, the Declaration of Independence; 1783, victory in the Revolutionary War; 1787, convention called for writing the Constitution of the United States; 1789, George Washington elected first President; 1796, John Adams becomes second President; 1800, Thomas Jefferson inaugurated as third President.

These are only a few of the events and people of the period that have assumed heroic proportions for later generations, often supported more by legend than by fact, and elevated to an almost sacred status in the psycho-religious life of the nation. When some part of this mythic history is detached from the dim mists of history and brought into the revealing light of the present, it can prove discomfiting and even disturbing. Every so often someone decides to test the political awareness of today by the standards followed by the founding fathers, and stands on street corners asking the citizens to sign the Declaration of Independence—without identifying it as such. The clear-cut right to make revolution against oppressive governments affirmed by the Declaration frightens many of today's Americans, and they refuse to subscribe to one of their country's founding documents. Many patriots proud of those ancestors who dressed up as Indians and boarded ships in Boston Harbor to dump tea overboard are the first to decry as unpatriotic those contemporaries who, dressed in various garbs (sometimes even Indian), take part in what they believe to be principled and morally symbolic acts such as sit-ins against racial discrimination.

But the colonial period has supplied America with more than its myths. It has also proved to be the period of origin of some of the most enduring aspects of the American Quest and the American Dream. Crèvecoeur asked, in *Letters from an American Farmer* (1782), "What then is the American, this new man?" Crèvecoeur attempted to answer the question himself, and invented the metaphor of the melting pot for his purposes. He could not have known that his question would continue to haunt Americans down into the twentieth century, and that, some two hundred years later, they would still be exploring and debating the morality of the melting pot. To what extent should minority groups attempt to keep their ethnic identity? To what extent should they let that identity be bubbled away in the American melting pot? But behind such questions is a subtler one that remains—is this American, indeed, a genuinely new man? Has the American experiment, American democracy, created detectable differences in its citizens? What are they? How do they affect behavior? We find ourselves today asking the same question that Crèvecoeur posed two centuries ago: "What then is the American, this new man?"

But the American quest for identity is closely linked to the American Dream. And each American has had to define that dream for himself. National heroes have made major contributions to that definition, and probably none more than Benjamin Franklin. Franklin lived the rags-to-riches myth of America and then described his formula for success in his *Autobiography*. He rose from a waif carrying a long loaf of bread under his arm in Philadelphia to become one of the shapers of the country's basic principles in U.S. founding documents. But probably the most popular legacy left by Franklin has been his series of aphorisms collected under the title, "The Way to Wealth." Rise early, work hard, keep clean—and become rich. This isn't, of course, what Franklin meant, but for many this has been inscribed as the recipe for the American Dream. And some Americans who have, to their surprise, found such a simplistic formula successful, have ended up asking themselves, "Is that all?" The American Dream remains to this day as undefined, unfulfilled, and elusive as it did when the settlers and founders first conceived it back at the beginning of the country's history.

Of all the dates and events that have established themselves in the American mythological past, none has been lodged more firmly than July 4, 1776, Independence Day. Long before they know what they are celebrating, young Americans gorge themselves at picnics, yawn at interminable patriotic speeches, and threaten themselves and others by carelessly shooting off fireworks—all in celebration of the Fourth. In many ways, the event deserves the celebration. The writing and signing of the Declaration of Independence by a small group of the representatives of the thirteen original colonies remains a remarkable event of history by any standards we might apply. There have been many attempts to explain, explore, or re-create the event, and one of the most interesting, charming, and even moving is a musical play by Peter Stone and Sherman Edwards, called simply *1776*. Based on the reading of Jefferson's original Declaration reprinted below, Scene 7 is especially dramatic.

In the scene, Jefferson has completed his assignment to write a draft of the Declaration, and the assembled Congress begins the task of revising the document in preparation for signing it. But final approval is in serious doubt because some members do not want to defy the mother country and actually declare independence; they still hope for possible reconciliation and do not want to take the irrevocable step that will brand them, in England's eyes, traitors. But the major issue that almost prevented the birth of the new country was that which divided the North and the South—slavery. Speculation as to the course of this country's history had Jefferson refused to allow the crucial changes demanded by some members of the Congress has long fascinated Americans. Would there have been an American Dream? What direction might that Dream have taken?

A DECLARATION BY THE REPRESENTATIVES OF THE UNITED STATES OF AMERICA, IN GENERAL CONGRESS ASSEMBLED[1]

July 4, 1776

When, in the course of human events, it becomes necessary for one people to dissolve the political bands which have connected them with another, and to assume among the powers of the earth the separate and equal station to which the laws of nature and of nature's God entitle them, a decent respect to the opinions of mankind requires that they should declare the causes which impel them to the separation.

We hold these truths to be self-evident; that all men are created equal; that they are endowed by their creator with [*inherent and*][2] inalienable rights; that among these are life, liberty, and the pursuit of happiness; that to secure these rights, governments are instituted among men, deriving their just powers from the consent of the governed; that whenever any form of government becomes destructive of these ends, it is the right of the people to alter or to abolish it, and to institute new government, laying its foundation on such principles, and organizing

---

1. *A Declaration . . . Assembled.* This was Jefferson's original title. The text parts which were stricken by the Congress are shown in italics within brackets. The insertions are reprinted as footnotes.
2. *certain*

its powers in such form, as to them shall seem most likely to effect their safety and happiness. Prudence, indeed, will dictate that governments long established should not be changed for light and transient causes; and accordingly all experience hath shown that mankind are more disposed to suffer while evils are sufferable, than to right themselves by abolishing the forms to which they are accustomed. But when a long train of abuses and usurpations [*begun at a distinguished period and*] pursuing invariably the same object, evinces a design to reduce them under absolute despotism, it is their right, it is their duty to throw off such government, and to provide new guards for their future security. Such has been the patient sufferance of these Colonies; and such is now the necessity which constrains them to [*expunge*]³ their former systems of government. The history of the present King of Great Britain is a history of [*unremitting*]⁴ injuries and usurpations, [*among which appears no solitary fact to contradict the uniform tenor of the rest, but all have*]⁵ in direct object the establishment of an absolute tyranny over these States. To prove this, let facts be submitted to a candid world [*for the truth of which we pledge a faith yet unsullied by falsehood*].

He has refused his assent to laws the most wholesome and necessary for the public good.

He has forbidden his governors to pass laws of immediate and pressing importance, unless suspended in their operation till his assent should be obtained; and, when so suspended, he has utterly neglected to attend to them.

He has refused to pass other laws for the accommodation of large districts of people, unless those people would relinquish the right of representation in the Legislature, a right inestimable to them, and formidable to tyrants only.

He has called together legislative bodies at places unusual, uncomfortable, and distant from the depository of their public records, for the sole purpose of fatiguing them into compliance with his measures.

He has dissolved representative houses repeatedly [*and continually*] for opposing with manly firmness his invasions on the rights of the people.

He has refused for a long time after such dissolutions to cause others to be elected, whereby the legislative powers, incapable of annihilation, have returned to the people at large for their exercise, the State remaining, in the meantime, exposed to all the dangers of invasion from without and convulsions within.

He has endeavored to prevent the population of these States; for that purpose obstructing the laws for naturalization of foreigners, refusing to pass others to encourage their migrations hither, and raising the conditions of new appropriations of lands.

He has [*suffered*]⁶ the administration of justice [*totally to cease in some of these States*]⁷ refusing his assent to laws for establishing judiciary powers.

He has made [*our*] judges dependent on his will alone for the tenure of their offices, and the amount and payment of their salaries.

He has erected a multitude of new offices, [*by a self-assumed power*] and sent hither swarms of new officers to harass our people and eat out their substance.

He has kept among us in times of peace standing armies [*and ships of war*] without the consent of our Legislatures.

He has affected to render the military independent of, and superior to, the civil power.

He has combined with others to subject us to a jurisdiction foreign to our constitutions and unacknowledged by our laws, giving his assent to their acts of pretended legislation for quartering large bodies of armed troops among us; for protecting them by a mock trial from punishment for any murders which they should commit on the inhabitants of these States; for cutting off our trade with all parts of the world; for imposing taxes on us without our consent; for depriving us [   ]⁸ of the benefits of trial by jury; for transporting us beyond seas to be tried for pretended offences; for abolishing the free system of English laws in a neighboring province, establishing therein an arbitrary government, and enlarging its boundaries, so as to render it at once an example and fit instrument for introducing the same absolute rule into these [*States*];⁹ for taking away our charters, abolishing our most valuable laws, and altering fundamentally the forms of our governments; for suspending our own Legislatures, and declaring themselves invested with power to legislate for us in all cases whatsoever.

---

3. *alter*
4. *repeated*
5. *all having*
6. *obstructed*
7. *by*
8. *in many cases*
9. *Colonies*

He has abdicated government here [*withdrawing his governors, and declaring us out of his allegiance and protection*].[10]

He has plundered our seas, ravaged our coasts, burnt our towns, and destroyed the lives of our people.

He is at this time transporting large armies of foreign mercenaries to complete the works of death, desolation, and tyranny already begun with circumstances of cruelty and perfidy [ ][11] unworthy the head of a civilized nation.

He has constrained our fellow-citizens taken captive on the high seas to bear arms against their country, to become the executioners of their friends and brethren, or to fall themselves by their hands.

He has [ ][12] endeavored to bring on the inhabitants of our frontiers the merciless Indian savages, whose known rule of warfare is an undistinguished destruction of all ages, sexes, and conditions [*of existence*].

[*He has incited treasonable insurrections of our fellow-citizens, with the allurements of forfeiture and confiscation of our property.*

He has waged cruel war against human nature itself, violating its most sacred rights of life and liberty in the persons of a distant people who never offended him, captivating and carrying them into slavery in another hemisphere, or to incur miserable death in their transportation thither. This piratical warfare, the opprobrium of INFIDEL *powers, is the warfare of the* CHRISTIAN *King of Great Britain. Determined to keep open a market where* MEN *should be bought and sold, he has prostituted his negative for suppressing every legislative attempt to prohibit or to restrain this execrable commerce. And that this assemblage of horrors might want no fact of distinguished die, he is now exciting those very people to rise in arms among us, and to purchase that liberty of which he has deprived them, by murdering the people on whom he also obtruded them: thus paying off former crimes committed against the* LIBERTIES *of one people with crimes which he urges them to commit against the* LIVES *of another.*]

In every stage of these oppressions we have petitioned for redress in the most humble terms: our repeated petitions have been answered only by repeated injuries.

A Prince whose character is thus marked by every act which may define a tyrant is unfit to be the ruler of a [ ][13] people [*who mean to be free. Future ages will scarcely believe that the hardiness of one man adventured, within the short compass of twelve years only, to lay a foundation so broad and so undisguised for tyranny over a people fostered and fixed in principles of freedom.*]

Nor have we been wanting in attentions to our British brethren. We have warned them from time to time of attempts by their legislature to extend [*a*][14] jurisdiction over [*these our States*].[15] We have reminded them of the circumstances of our emigration and settlement here, [*no one of which could warrant so strange a pretension: that these were effected at the expense of our own blood and treasure, unassisted by the wealth or the strength of Great Britain: that in constituting indeed our several forms of government we had adopted one common king, thereby laying a foundation for perpetual league and amity with them: but that submission to their parliament was no part of our Constitution, nor ever in idea, if history may be credited: and,*] we [ ][16] appealed to their native justice and magnanimity [*as well as to*][17] the ties of our common kindred to disavow these usurpations which [*were likely to*][18] interrupt our connection and correspondence. They too have been deaf to the voice of justice and of consanguinity, [*and when occasions have been given them, by the regular course of their laws, of removing from their councils the disturbers of our harmony, they have, by their free election, reestablished them in power. At this very time too, they are permitting their chief magistrate to send over not only soldiers of our common blood, but Scotch and foreign mercenaries to invade and destroy us. These facts have given the last stab to agonizing affection, and manly spirit bids us to renounce forever these unfeeling brethren. We must endeavor to forget our former love for them, and hold them as we hold the rest of mankind, enemies in war, in peace friends. We might have been a free and a great people together; but a communication of grandeur and of freedom, it seems, is below their dignity. Be it so, since they will have*]

---

10. *by declaring us out of his protection, and waging war against us*
11. *scarcely paralleled in the most barbarous ages, and totally*
12. *excited domestic insurrection among us, and has*
13. *free*
14. *an unwarrantable*
15. *us*
16. *have*
17. *and we have conjured them by*
18. *would inevitably*

it. *The road to happiness and to glory is open to us too. We will tread it apart from them, and]*[19] acquiesce in the necessity which denounces our [*eternal*] separation [   ]!*[20]

We therefore the representatives of the United States of America in General Congress assembled, [   ]*[21] do in the name, and by the authority of the good people of these [*States reject and renounce all allegiance and subjection to the kings of Great Britain and all others who may hereafter claim by, through, or under them; we utterly dissolve all political connection which may heretofore have subsisted between us and the people or parliament of Great Britain: and finally we do assert and declare these Colonies to be free and independent States,]*[22] and that as free and independent States, they have full power to levy war, conclude peace, contract alliances, establish commerce, and to do all other acts and things which independent States may of right do.

And for the support of this declaration, [   ]*[23] we mutually pledge to each other our lives, our fortunes, and our sacred honor.

---

19. *We must therefore*
20. *and hold them as we hold the rest of mankind, enemies in war, in peace friends*
21. *appealing to the supreme judge of the world for the rectitude of our intentions,*
22. *Colonies, solemnly publish and declare, that these united Colonies are, and of right ought to be, free and independent States; that they are absolved from all allegiance to the British crown, and that all political connection between them and the state of Great Britain is, and ought to be, totally dissolved;*
23. *with a firm reliance on the protection of divine providence,*

HISTORICAL SOCIETY OF PENNSYLVANIA

OVERLEAF: DETAIL FROM CASWELL QUILT—THE METROPOLITAN MUSEUM OF ART, GIFT OF KATHERINE KEYES, 1938, IN MEMORY OF HER FATHER, HOMER EATON KEYES.

THOMAS JEFFERSON   / **81** C

chapter three

EARLY
NATIONAL
PERIOD

Washington Irving

1783 / 1859

KNICKERBOCKER'S HISTORY OF NEW YORK

BOOK II
[ARRIVAL OF THE DUTCH]
CHAPTER II

Containing an account of a mighty Ark which floated, under the protection of St. Nicholas, from Holland to Gibbet Island—the descent of the strange Animals therefrom—a great victory, and a description of the ancient village of Communipaw.

The delectable accounts given by the great Hudson, and Master Juet, of the country they had discovered, excited not a little talk and speculation among the good people of Holland.—Letters patent were granted by government to an association of merchants, called the West-India company, for the exclusive trade on Hudson river, on which they erected a trading house called Fort Aurania, or Orange, at present the superb and hospitable city of Albany. But I forbear to dwell on the various commercial and colonizing enterprizes which took place; among which was that of Mynheer Adrian Block, who discovered and gave a name to Block Island, since famous for its cheese—and shall barely confine myself to that, which gave birth to this renowned city.

It was some three or four years after the return of the immortal Hendrick, that a crew of honest, well meaning, copper headed, low dutch colonists set sail from the city of Amsterdam, for the shores of America. It is an irreparable loss to history, and a great proof of the darkness of the age, and the lamentable neglect of the noble art of book-making, since so industriously cultivated by knowing sea-captains, and spruce super-cargoes, that an expedition so interesting and important in its results, should have been passed over in utter silence. To my great great grandfather am I again indebted, for the few facts, I am enabled to give concerning it —he having once more embarked for this country, with a full determination, as he said, of ending his days here—and of begetting a race of Knicker-

bockers, that should rise to be great men in the land.

The ship in which these illustrious adventurers set sail was called the *Goede Vrouw,* or Good Woman, in compliment to the wife of the President of the West India Company, who was allowed by every body (except her husband) to be a singularly sweet tempered lady, when not in liquor. It was in truth a gallant vessel, of the most approved dutch construction, and made by the ablest ship carpenters of Amsterdam, who it is well known, always model their ships after the fair forms of their country women. Accordingly it had one hundred feet in the keel, one hundred feet in the beam, and one hundred feet from the bottom of the stern post to the tafforel. Like the beauteous model, who was declared the greatest belle in Amsterdam, it was full in the bows, with a pair of enormous cat-heads, a copper bottom, and withal, a most prodigious poop!

The architect, who was somewhat of a religious man, far from decorating the ship with pagan idols, such as Jupiter, Neptune, or Hercules[1] (which hea-thenish abominations, I have no doubt, occasion the misfortunes and shipwrack of many a noble vessel) he I say, on the contrary, did laudibly erect for a head, a goodly image of St. Nicholas,[2] equipped with a low, broad brimmed hat, a huge pair of Flemish trunk hose, and a pipe that reached to the end of the bowsprit. Thus gallantly furnished, the staunch ship floated sideways, like a majestic goose, out of the harbour of the great city of Amsterdam, and all the bells, that were not otherwise engaged, rung a triple bob-major on the joyful occasion.

My great great grandfather remarks, that the voyage was uncommonly prosperous, for being under the especial care of the ever-revered St. Nicholas, the Goede Vrouw seemed to be endowed with qualities, unknown to common vessels. Thus she made as much lee-way as head-way, could get along very nearly as fast with the wind a-head, as when it was a-poop—and was particularly great in a calm; in consequence of which singular advan-

---

A HISTORY OF NEW YORK BY DIEDRICH KNICKERBOCKER by Washington Irving, edited by S. T. Williams and T. McDowell. Harcourt Brace Jovanovich, Inc.

1. *Jupiter, Neptune, or Hercules.* Jupiter was the chief Roman god, the Rain-god and Cloud-gatherer, lord of life and light; Neptune was Jupiter's brother and chief god of the sea; Hercules was a myth-ical Greek hero who possessed exceptional strength.
2. *St. Nicholas,* the patron saint of sailors.

tages, she made out to accomplish her voyage in a very few months, and came to anchor at the mouth of the Hudson, a little to the east of Gibbet Island.

Here lifting up their eyes, they beheld, on what is at present called the Jersey shore, a small Indian village, pleasantly embowered in a grove of spreading elms, and the natives all collected on the beach, gazing in stupid admiration at the Goede Vrouw. A boat was immediately dispatched to enter into a treaty with them, and approaching the shore, hailed them through a trumpet, in the most friendly terms; but so horribly confounded were these poor savages at the tremendous and uncouth sound of the low dutch language, that they one and all took to their heels, scampered over the Bergen hills, nor did they stop until they had buried themselves, head and ears, in the marshes, on the other side, where they all miserably perished to a man—and their bones being collected, and decently covered by the Tammany Society[3] of that day, formed that singular mound, called *Rattle-snake-hill,* which rises out of the centre of the salt marshes, a little to the east of the Newark Causeway.

Animated by this unlooked-for victory our valiant heroes sprang ashore in triumph, took possession of the soil as conquerors in the name of their High Mightinesses the lords states general, and marching fearlessly forward, carried the village of *Communi-*

paw by storm—having nobody to withstand them, but some half a score of old squaws, and poppooses, whom they tortured to death with low dutch. On looking about them they were so transported with the excellencies of the place, that they had very little doubt, the blessed St. Nicholas, had guided them thither, as the very spot whereon to settle their colony. The softness of the soil was wonderfully adapted to the driving of piles; the swamps and marshes around them afforded ample opportunities for the constructing of dykes and dams; the shallowness of the shore was peculiarly favourable to the building of docks—in a word, this spot abounded with all the singular inconveniences, and aquatic obstacles, necessary for the foundation of a great dutch city. On making a faithful report therefore, to the crew of the Goede Vrouw, they one and all determined that this was the destined end of their voyage. Accordingly they descended from the Goede Vrouw, men women and children, in goodly groups, as did the animals of yore from the ark, and formed themselves into a thriving settlement, which they called by the Indian name *Communipaw.* . . . □

---

3. *Tammany Society,* founded in 1789 in part as the common soldiers' opposition to the Society of Cincinnati which had been organized by some high-ranking officers and was believed to be an attempt at establishing a hereditary aristocracy within the army.

THE DEVIL AND TOM WALKER

A few miles from Boston in Massachusetts, there is a deep inlet, winding several miles into the interior of the country from Charles Bay, and terminating in a thickly wooded swamp or morass. On one side of this inlet is a beautiful dark grove; on the opposite side the land rises abruptly from the water's edge into a high ridge, on which grow a few scattered oaks of great age and immense size.

Under one of these gigantic trees, according to old stories, there was a great amount of treasure buried by Kidd the pirate. The inlet allowed a facility to bring the money in a boat secretly and at night to the very foot of the hill; the elevation of the place

permitted a good lookout to be kept that no one was at hand; while the remarkable trees formed good landmarks by which the place might easily be found again. The old stories add, moreover, that the devil presided at the hiding of the money, and took it under his guardianship; but this, it is well known, he always does with buried treasure, particularly when it has been ill-gotten. Be that as it may, Kidd never returned to recover his wealth, being shortly after seized at Boston, sent out to England, and there hanged for a pirate.

About the year 1727, just at the time that earthquakes were prevalent in New England, and shook many tall sinners down upon their knees, there lived near this place a meager, miserly fellow, of the name of Tom Walker. He had a wife as miserly as himself; they were so miserly that they even conspired to cheat each other. Whatever the woman could lay hands on, she hid away; a hen could not cackle but she was on the alert to secure the new-laid egg. Her husband was continually prying about to detect her secret hoards, and many and fierce were the conflicts that took place about what ought to have been common property.

They lived in a forlorn-looking house that stood alone, and had an air of starvation. A few straggling savin trees, emblems of sterility, grew near it; no smoke ever curled from its chimney; no traveler stopped at its door. A miserable horse, whose ribs were as articulate as the bars of a gridiron, stalked about a field, where a thin carpet of moss, scarcely covering the ragged beds of pudding stone, tantalized and balked his hunger; and sometimes he would lean his head over the fence, look piteously at the passer-by, and seem to petition deliverance from this land of famine.

The house and its inmates had altogether a bad name. Tom's wife was a tall termagant, fierce of temper, loud of tongue, and strong of arm. Her voice was often heard in wordy warfare with her husband; and his face sometimes showed signs that their conflicts were not confined to words. No one ventured, however, to interfere between them. The lonely wayfarer shrunk within himself at the horrid clamor and clapper-clawing,[1] eyed the den of discord askance; and hurried on his way, rejoicing, if a bachelor, in his celibacy.

One day that Tom Walker had been to a distant part of the neighborhood, he took what he considered a short cut homeward, through the swamp. Like most short cuts, it was an ill-chosen route. The swamp was thickly grown with great gloomy pines and hemlocks, some of them ninety feet high, which made it dark at noonday and a retreat for all the owls of the neighborhood. It was full of pits and quagmires, partly covered with weeds and mosses, where the green surface often betrayed the traveler into a gulf of black, smothering mud; there were also dark and stagnant pools, the abodes of the tadpole, the bull-frog, and the water snake, where the trunks of pines and hemlocks lay half-drowned, half-rotting, looking like alligators sleeping in the mire.

Tom had long been picking his way cautiously through this treacherous forest, stepping from tuft to tuft of rushes and roots, which afforded precarious footholds among deep sloughs; or pacing carefully,

like a cat, along the prostrate trunks of trees, startled now and then by the sudden screaming of the bittern, or the quacking of wild duck rising on the wing from some solitary pool. At length he arrived at a firm piece of ground, which ran out like a peninsula into the deep bosom of the swamp. It had been one of the strongholds of the Indians during their wars with the first colonists. Here they had thrown up a kind of fort, which they had looked upon as almost impregnable, and had used as a place of refuge for their squaws and children. Nothing remained of the old Indian fort but a few embankments, gradually sinking to the level of the surrounding earth and already overgrown in part by oaks and other forest trees, the foliage of which formed a contrast to the dark pines and hemlocks of the swamp.

It was late in the dusk of evening when Tom Walker reached the old fort, and he paused there awhile to rest himself. Anyone but he would have felt unwilling to linger in this lonely, melancholy place, for the common people had a bad opinion of it, from the stories handed down from the time of the Indian wars, when it was asserted that the savages held incantations here and made sacrifices to the evil spirit.

Tom Walker, however, was not a man to be troubled with any fears of the kind. He reposed himself for some time on the trunk of a fallen hemlock, listening to the boding cry of the tree toad, and delving with his walking staff into a mound of black mold at his feet. As he turned up the soil unconsciously, his staff struck against something hard. He raked it out of the vegetable mold, and lo! a cloven skull, with an Indian tomahawk buried deep in it, lay before him. The rust on the weapon showed the time that had elapsed since this deathblow had been given. It was a dreary memento of the fierce struggle that had taken place in this last foothold of the Indian warriors. "Humph!" said Tom Walker as he gave it a kick to shake the dirt from it.

"Let that skull alone!" said a gruff voice. Tom lifted up his eyes and beheld a great black man seated directly opposite him, on the stump of a tree. He was exceedingly surprised, having neither heard nor seen anyone approach; and he was still more perplexed on observing, as well as the gathering gloom would permit, that the stranger was neither

---

1. *clapper-clawing*, an argument accompanied by scratching and slapping.

Negro nor Indian. It is true he was dressed in a rude half-Indian garb, and had a red belt or sash swathed round his body; but his face was neither black nor copper color, but swarthy and dingy, and begrimed with soot, as if he had been accustomed to toil among fires and forges. He had a shock of coarse black hair that stood out from his head in all directions, and bore an ax on his shoulder.

He scowled for a moment at Tom with a pair of great red eyes.

"What are you doing on my grounds?" said the black man, with a hoarse, growling voice.

"Your grounds!" said Tom, with a sneer, "no more your grounds than mine; they belong to Deacon Peabody."

"Deacon Peabody be damned," said the stranger, "as I flatter myself he will be, if he does not look more to his own sins and less to those of his neighbors. Look yonder, and see how Deacon Peabody is faring."

Tom looked in the direction that the stranger pointed and beheld one of the great trees, fair and flourishing without, but rotten at the core, and saw that it had been nearly hewn through, so that the first high wind was likely to blow it down. On the bark of the tree was scored the name of Deacon Peabody, an eminent man who had waxed wealthy by driving shrewd bargains with the Indians. He now looked around, and found most of the tall trees marked with the name of some great man of the colony, and all more or less scored by the ax. The one on which he had been seated, and which had evidently just been hewn down, bore the name of Crowninshield; and he recollected a mighty rich man of that name, who made a vulgar display of wealth, which it was whispered he had acquired by buccaneering.

"He's just ready for burning!" said the black man, with a growl of triumph. "You see I am likely to have a good stock of firewood for winter."

"But what right have you," said Tom, "to cut down Deacon Peabody's timber?"

"The right of a prior claim," said the other. "This woodland belonged to me long before one of your white-faced race put foot upon the soil."

"And pray, who are you, if I may be so bold?" said Tom.

"Oh, I go by various names. I am the wild huntsman in some countries; the black miner in others. In this neighborhood I am known by the name of the black woodsman. I am he to whom the red men consecrated this spot, and in honor of whom they now and then roasted a white man, by way of sweet-smelling sacrifice. Since the red men have been exterminated by you white savages, I amuse myself by presiding at the persecutions of Quakers and Anabaptists;[2] I am the great patron and prompter of slave dealers, and the grand master of the Salem witches."[3]

"The upshot of all which is, that, if I mistake not," said Tom sturdily, "you are he commonly called Old Scratch."

"The same, at your service!" replied the black man, with a half-civil nod.

Such was the opening of this interview, according to the old story; though it has almost too familiar an air to be credited. One would think that to meet with such a singular personage, in this wild, lonely place, would have shaken any man's nerves; but Tom was a hard-minded fellow, not easily daunted, and he had lived so long with a termagant wife that he did not even fear the devil.

It is said that after this commencement they had a long and earnest conversation together, as Tom returned homeward. The black man told him of great sums of money buried by Kidd the pirate, under the oak trees on the high ridge, not far from the morass. All these were under his command, and protected by his power, so that none could find them but such as propitiated his favor. These he offered to place within Tom Walker's reach, having conceived an especial kindness for him; but they were to be had only on certain conditions. What these conditions were may be easily surmised, though Tom never disclosed them publicly. They must have been very hard, for he required time to think of them, and he was not a man to stick at trifles when money was in view.

When they had reached the edge of the swamp, the stranger paused. "What proof have I that all you have been telling me is true?" said Tom. "There's my signature," said the black man, pressing his finger on Tom's forehead. So saying, he turned off among the thickest of the swamp, and seemed, as Tom said, to go down, down, down, into the earth, until he totally disappeared.

---

2. *Anabaptists* (an'ə bap'tists), members of a Protestant sect which originated in Switzerland in the sixteenth century. Quakers and Anabaptists were persecuted in the Massachusetts colony.

3. *Salem witches*, women accused of witchcraft in the Salem witch trials of 1692.

When Tom reached home, he found the black print of a finger burned, as it were, into his forehead, which nothing could obliterate.

The first news his wife had to tell him was the sudden death of Absalom Crowninshield, the rich buccaneer. It was announced in the papers with the usual flourish that "A great man had fallen in Israel."[4]

Tom recollected the tree which his black friend had just hewn down and which was ready for burning. "Let the freebooter roast," said Tom; "who cares!" He now felt convinced that all he had heard and seen was no illusion.

He was not prone to let his wife into his confidence; but as this was an uneasy secret, he willingly shared it with her. All her avarice was awakened at the mention of hidden gold, and she urged her husband to comply with the black man's terms, and secure what would make them wealthy for life. However Tom might have felt disposed to sell himself to the devil, he was determined not to do so to oblige his wife; so he flatly refused, out of the mere spirit of contradiction. Many were the quarrels they had on the subject; but the more she talked, the more resolute was Tom not to be damned to please her.

At length she determined to drive the bargain on her own account, and if she succeeded, to keep all the gain to herself. Being of the same fearless temper as her husband, she set off for the old Indian fort toward the close of a summer's day. She was many hours absent. When she came back, she was reserved and sullen in her replies. She spoke something of a black man, whom she met about twilight hewing at the root of a tall tree. He was sulky, however, and would not come to terms; she was to go again with a propitiatory offering, but what it was she forbore to say.

The next evening she set off again for the swamp, with her apron heavily laden. Tom waited and waited for her, but in vain; midnight came, but she did not make her appearance; morning, noon, night returned, but still she did not come. Tom now grew uneasy for her safety, especially as he found she had carried off in her apron the silver tea pot and spoons, and every portable article of value. Another night elapsed, another morning came; but no wife. In a word, she was never heard of more.

What was her real fate nobody knows, in consequence of so many pretending to know. It is one of those facts which have become confounded by a variety of historians. Some asserted that she lost her way among the tangled mazes of the swamp, and sank into some pit or slough; others, more uncharitable, hinted that she had eloped with the household booty, and made off to some other province; while others surmised that the tempter had decoyed her into a dismal quagmire, on the top of which her hat was found lying. In confirmation of this, it was said a great black man, with an ax on his shoulder, was seen late that very evening coming out of the swamp, carrying a bundle tied in a check apron, with an air of surly triumph.

The most current and probable story, however, observes that Tom Walker grew so anxious about the fate of his wife and his property that he set out at length to seek them both at the Indian fort. During a long summer's afternoon he searched about the gloomy place, but no wife was to be seen. He called her name repeatedly, but she was nowhere to be heard. The bittern alone responded to his voice, as he flew screaming by; or the bullfrog croaked dolefully from a neighboring pool. At length, it is said, just in the brown hour of twilight, when the owls began to hoot, and the bats to flit about, his attention was attracted by the clamor of carrion crows hovering about a cypress tree. He looked up and beheld a bundle tied in a check apron and hanging in the branches of the tree, with a great vulture perched hard by, as if keeping watch upon it. He leaped with joy; for he recognized his wife's apron and supposed it to contain the household valuables.

"Let us get hold of the property," said he consolingly to himself, "and we will endeavor to do without the woman."

As he scrambled up the tree, the vulture spread its wide wings and sailed off screaming into the deep shadows of the forest. Tom seized the checked apron, but, woeful sight! found nothing but a heart and liver tied up in it!

Such, according to this most authentic old story, was all that was to be found of Tom's wife. She had probably attempted to deal with the black man as she had been accustomed to deal with her husband; but though a female scold is generally considered a match for the devil, yet in this instance she appears to have had the worst of it. She must have died game, however; for it is said Tom noticed many prints of

<hr>

4. *Israel*, Massachusetts. The Puritans of Massachusetts regarded their colony as the Promised Land (Israel).

cloven feet deeply stamped upon the tree, and found handfuls of hair that looked as if they had been plucked from the coarse black shock of the woodsman. Tom knew his wife's prowess by experience. He shrugged his shoulders as he looked at the signs of a fierce clapper-clawing. "Egad," said he to himself, "Old Scratch must have had a tough time of it!"

Tom consoled himself for the loss of his property with the loss of his wife, for he was a man of fortitude. He even felt something like gratitude toward the black woodsman, who, he considered, had done him a kindness. He sought, therefore, to cultivate a further acquaintance with him, but for some time without success; the old blacklegs played shy, for whatever people may think, he is not always to be had for calling for; he knows how to play his cards when pretty sure of his game.

At length, it is said, when delay had whetted Tom's eagerness to the quick, and prepared him to agree to anything rather than not gain the promised treasure, he met the black man one evening in his usual woodsman's dress, with his ax on his shoulder, sauntering along the swamp and humming a tune. He affected to receive Tom's advances with great indifference, made brief replies, and went on humming his tune.

By degrees, however, Tom brought him to business, and they began to haggle about the terms on which the former was to have the pirate's treasure. There was one condition which need not be mentioned, being generally understood in all cases where the devil grants favors; but there were others about which, though of less importance, he was inflexibly obstinate. He insisted that the money found through his means should be employed in his service. He proposed, therefore, that Tom should employ it in the black traffic; that is to say, that he should fit out a slave ship. This, however, Tom resolutely refused; he was bad enough in all conscience, but the devil himself could not tempt him to turn slave trader.

Finding Tom so squeamish on this point, he did not insist upon it, but proposed, instead, that he should turn usurer, the devil being extremely anxious for the increase of usurers, looking upon them as his peculiar people.

To this no objections were made, for it was just to Tom's taste.

"You shall open a broker's shop in Boston next month," said the black man.

"I'll do it tomorrow, if you wish," said Tom Walker.

"You shall lend money at two per cent a month."

"Egad, I'll charge four!" replied Tom Walker.

"You shall extort bonds, foreclose mortgages, drive the merchants to bankruptcy—"

"I'll drive them to the devil," cried Tom Walker.

"You are the usurer for my money!" said blacklegs with delight. "When will you want the rhino?"[5]

"This very night."

"Done!" said the devil.

"Done!" said Tom Walker. So they shook hands and struck a bargain.

A few days' time saw Tom Walker seated behind his desk in a counting house in Boston.

His reputation for a ready-moneyed man, who would lend money out for a good consideration, soon spread abroad. Everybody remembers the time of Governor Belcher,[6] when money was particularly scarce. It was a time of paper credit.[7] The country had been deluged with government bills, the famous Land Bank[8] had been established; there had been a rage for speculating; the people had run mad with schemes for new settlements, for building cities in the wilderness; land jobbers[9] went about with maps of grants, and townships, and El Dorados,[10] lying nobody knew where, but which everybody was ready to purchase. In a word, the great speculating fever which breaks out every now and then in the country had raged to an alarming degree, and everybody was dreaming of making sudden fortunes from nothing. As usual the fever had subsided; the dream had gone off, and the imaginary fortunes with it; the patients were left in doleful plight, and the whole country resounded with the consequent cry of "hard times."

At this propitious time of public distress did Tom Walker set up as usurer in Boston. His door was soon thronged by customers. The needy and adventurous,

---

5. *rhino* (rī′nō), money. [*Slang*]

6. *Governor Belcher,* Jonathan Belcher, who governed Massachusetts from 1730 to 1741.

7. *paper credit,* assets that existed on paper but were actually of no value.

8. *Land Bank,* a scheme to relieve the shortage of gold in Massachusetts by establishing a bank whose resources rested on real-estate mortgages.

9. *land jobbers,* men who bought tracts of undeveloped land as a speculation and sold them to others.

10. *El Dorado,* imaginary country abounding in gold searched for by Spaniards in the sixteenth century. The name now applies to any place where riches can be had easily and quickly.

the gambling speculator, the dreaming land jobber, the thriftless tradesman, the merchant with cracked credit—in short, everyone driven to raise money by desperate means and desperate sacrifices hurried to Tom Walker.

Thus Tom was the universal friend of the needy, and acted like a "friend in need"; that is to say, he always exacted good pay and good security. In proportion to the distress of the applicant was the hardness of his terms. He accumulated bonds and mortgages; gradually squeezed his customers closer and closer; and sent them at length, dry as a sponge, from his door.

In this way he made money hand over hand; became a rich and mighty man, and exalted his cocked hat upon 'Change.[11] He built himself, as usual, a vast house, out of ostentation; but left the greater part of it unfinished and unfurnished, out of parsimony. He even set up a carriage in the fullness of his vain-glory, though he nearly starved the horses which drew it; and as the ungreased wheels groaned and screeched on the axletrees, you would have thought you heard the souls of the poor debtors he was squeezing.

As Tom waxed old, however, he grew thoughtful. Having secured the good things of this world, he began to feel anxious about those of the next. He thought with regret on the bargain he had made with his black friend, and set his wits to work to cheat him out of the conditions. He became, therefore, all of a sudden, a violent churchgoer. He prayed loudly and strenuously, as if heaven were to be taken by force of lungs. Indeed, one might always tell when he had sinned most during the week by the clamor of his Sunday devotion. The quiet Christians who had been modestly and steadfastly traveling Zionward,[12] were struck with self-reproach at seeing themselves so suddenly outstripped in their career by this new-made convert. Tom was as rigid in religious as in money matters; he was a stern supervisor and censurer of his neighbors, and seemed to think every sin entered up to their account became a credit on his own side of the page. He even talked of the expediency of reviving the persecution of Quakers and Anabaptists. In a word, Tom's zeal became as notorious as his riches.

Still, in spite of all this strenuous attention to forms, Tom had a lurking dread that the devil, after all, would have his due. That he might not be taken unawares, therefore, it is said he always carried a small Bible in his coat pocket. He had also a great folio Bible on his counting-house desk, and would frequently be found reading it when people called on business; on such occasions he would lay his green spectacles in the book, to mark the place, while he turned round to drive some usurious bargain.

Some say that Tom grew a little crack-brained in his old days, and that, fancying his end approaching, he had his horse new shod, saddled and bridled, and buried with his feet uppermost; because he supposed that at the last day the world would be turned upside down in which case he should find his horse standing ready for mounting, and he was determined at the worst to give his old friend a run for it. This, however, is probably a mere old wives' fable. If he really did take such a precaution, it was totally superfluous; at least so says the authentic old legend, which closes his story in the following manner.

One hot summer afternoon in the dog days, just as a terrible black thundergust was coming up, Tom sat in his counting house in his white cap and India silk morning gown. He was on the point of foreclosing a mortgage, by which he would complete the ruin of an unlucky land speculator for whom he had professed the greatest friendship. The poor land jobber begged him to grant a few months' indulgence. Tom had grown testy and irritated, and refused another day.

"My family will be ruined and brought upon the parish,"[13] said the land jobber.

"Charity begins at home," replied Tom; "I must take care of myself in these hard times."

"You have made so much money out of me," said the speculator.

Tom lost his patience and his piety. "The devil take me," said he, "if I have made a farthing!"

Just then there were three loud knocks at the street door. He stepped out to see who was there. A black man was holding a black horse, which neighed and stamped with impatience.

"Tom, you're come for," said the black fellow, gruffly. Tom shrank back, but too late. He had left his little Bible at the bottom of his coat pocket, and

---

11. *'Change,* the Exchange, or the financial center of Boston, where merchants, traders, and brokers do business.
12. *Zionward,* toward heaven. Zion, originally the hill in Jerusalem on which the temple stood, is often used to typify heaven.
13. *brought upon the parish,* forced to depend upon public charity for support.

THE DEVIL AND TOM WALKER, 1856 BY JOHN QUIDOR—THE CLEVELAND MUSEUM OF ART, MR. AND MRS. WILLIAM H. MARLATT FUND

his big Bible on the desk buried under the mortgage he was about to foreclose; never was sinner taken more unawares. The black man whisked him like a child into the saddle, gave the horse the lash, and away he galloped, with Tom on his back, in the midst of the thunderstorm. The clerks stuck their pens behind their ears, and stared after him from the windows. Away went Tom Walker, dashing down the streets, his white cap bobbing up and down, his morning gown fluttering in the wind, and his steed striking fire out of the pavement at every bound. When the clerks turned to look for the black man, he had disappeared.

Tom Walker never returned to foreclose the mortgage. A countryman, who lived on the border of the swamp, reported that in the height of the thundergust he had heard a great clattering of hoofs and a howling along the road, and running to the window caught sight of a figure, such as I have described, on a horse that galloped like mad across the fields, over the hills, and down into the black hemlock swamp toward the old Indian fort; and that shortly after, a thunderbolt falling in that direction seemed to set the whole forest in a blaze.

The good people of Boston shook their heads and shrugged their shoulders, but had been so much accustomed to witches and goblins and tricks of the devil in all kinds of shapes, from the first settlement of the colony, that they were not so much horror-struck as might have been expected. Trustees were appointed to take charge of Tom's effects. There was nothing, however, to administer upon. On searching his coffers, all his bonds and mortgages were found reduced to cinders. In place of gold and silver, his iron chest was filled with chips and shavings; two skeletons lay in his stable instead of his half-starved horses, and the very next day his great house took fire and burned to the ground.

Such was the end of Tom Walker and his ill-gotten wealth. Let all griping money brokers lay this story to heart. The truth of it is not to be doubted. The very hole under the oak trees whence he dug Kidd's money is to be seen to this day; and the neighboring swamp and old Indian fort are often haunted on stormy nights by a figure on horseback, in morning gown and white cap, which is doubtless the troubled spirit of the usurer. In fact, the story has resolved itself into a proverb, and is the origin of that popular saying, so prevalent throughout New England, of "The Devil and Tom Walker." ☐

DISCUSSION

Satire, though practiced by American political writers during the founding of the nation, did not achieve literary prominence until publication of Washington Irving's *Knickerbocker's History of New York*. Irving, by blending eighteenth-century British satiric theory with native subjects and locales, helped create a truly American form of satire that has been emulated by authors and journalists ever since.

Satire is the name given to a "work or portion of a work that by witty techniques of various types makes its subject ridiculous." Though ridicule is the aim of satire, good satire—whether its subject be an individual, society, or humankind—implies a corrective for faults or **foibles.** Therefore, it is usually considered constructive.

Unlike novels, plays, and poetry, satire does not fall neatly into the categories of literary genre. It is best described as a **mode,** or way in which a genre is treated. In *Knickerbocker's History of New York*, for example, the genre is history while the mode is satire. Thus, we can speak of the work as **mock-history.** When an author intentionally satirizes an entire genre, as Irving does in his *History*, we say he is writing a **parody.**

Satire is achieved in many ways and through the use of various techniques. **Burlesque** ridicules mainly by exaggeration, often mocking its subject through the use of **caricature. Caricature** is usually a humorous attack on a characteristic or trait of the subject being satirized and follows the formula of exaggerating these selected features. Both of these elements can be found in Irving's description of the Dutch. The **stereotype** or "stock" character is also used in satire. Both Tom and his wife in "The Devil and Tom Walker" are stereotypic misers. **Hyperbole** is a figure of speech in which exaggeration of fact is used in order to produce a comic effect. An example from "The Devil and Tom Walker" is ". . . a female scold is generally considered a match for the devil."

FOR EXPLORATION

Knickerbocker's History of New York

1. What in the author's **argument** (the initial paragraph used to summarize the selection) alerts the reader that Irving is writing a burlesque?
2. What satiric technique does Irving employ in the description of the *Goed Vrouw*? Whom and what are ridiculed?
3. Twice in this selection Irving pokes fun at the Dutch language. Explain the satiric technique he uses.
4. Irving's description at the end of the selection of the newly founded settlement at Communipaw ridicules the Dutch's choice of such a place, yet it says something about human nature. What?
5. What is the *tone* of Irving's satire? Is it bitter or gentle? Explain.

The Devil and Tom Walker

1. The Woodsman tells Tom: "Since the red men have been exterminated by you white savages, I amuse myself by presiding at the persecutions of Quakers and Anabaptists. . . ." Compare the tone of this statement with that of *Knickerbocker's History of New York*.

2. What is the meaning of the Woodsman's scoring of trees? What do the trees symbolize?
3. Tom strongly objects to the Woodsman's suggestion that he become a slave trader but readily agrees to engage in usury. Does Irving imply that there are degrees of morality and sinfulness? Explain.
4. Irving describes land speculation as a "fever" and the speculators as "patients." What is he saying through these metaphors about the love of money?
5. As Tom ages he becomes "a violent churchgoer": "He was as rigid in religious as in money matters; he was a stern supervisor and censurer of his neighbors, and seemed to think every sin entered up to their account became a credit on his own side of the page." Is Tom's conversion genuine? Explain.
6. Is Irving satirizing an individual, society, or the whole of humankind? At what foibles does he level his attack?
7. Dramatic Irony is a literary device whereby a character inadvertently speaks the truth, foreshadowing tragic events of which he is unaware. Find the sentence in the conclusion of the tale where Tom makes an ironic statement.
8. Some tales about pacts with the devil end tragically for their heroes, illustrating the moral that one should never sell one's soul. Is "The Devil and Tom Walker" a tragedy? Explain. What, if any, is the moral of the tale?

WORDS

Washington Irving's humor is based partially on the use of many rather difficult words, like the adjectives from "The Devil and Tom Walker" in the first column below. Copy each of these adjectives on a sheet of paper. Then choose antonyms from the second column and write them after the correct adjectives.

parsimonious	simple
propitiatory	rare
ostentatious	squeamish
inflexible	begrimed
superfluous	pliant
ill-gotten	antagonistic
melancholy	false
authentic	generous
testy	necessary
prevalent	joyous
	patient
	honest
	expedient

SLEEPY HOLLOW RESTORATIONS

Washington Irving   1783 / 1859

Washington Irving is called the "Father of American literature." Many of those who followed would have better claim to greatness, but Irving was the first. Coming at a time when Europe doubted that anything of real literary merit could spring from such an uncultured wilderness, Irving provided America with a much longed-for measure of self-esteem.

Raised in New York City, Irving was the youngest of eleven children, a position which made him the favorite of his brothers and sisters. Thus, despite a strict Presbyterian father, Irving led a carefree, indulgent existence.

At the age of nineteen he began writing satirical society sketches which appeared first in a four-page daily paper put out by one of his brothers and then later in *Salmagundi*, a magazine published by Irving and an assortment of friends. As he was trying to finish his first full-length book, *Knickerbocker's History of New York*, Irving suffered a tragic loss in the death of his fiancée. Irving describes himself as nearly out of his mind for weeks after her death, but he returned to his writing and, almost as an anodyne, went on to complete the final chapters.

Though the book was immensely successful, Irving was still not committed to a career in writing. He spent six years dabbling in Washington society, editing a magazine, and acting as an aide-de-camp in the War of 1812. Finally he left New York for Liverpool, England, having been asked to put in order a branch of the hardware business owned by the five Irving brothers. Within a few years the business had collapsed and Irving was left with little alternative but to support himself through his writing. He stayed in England studying romantic histories and German folklore. The stories and articles he wrote appeared in installments between 1819 and 1820 and were subsequently published as *The Sketch Book*. With such stories as "Rip Van Winkle" and "The Legend of Sleepy Hollow," the book was proclaimed a masterpiece and Irving became famous.

With success and fortune Irving once again neglected his work. He published *Tales of a Traveller* in 1824, a collection of second-hand, poorly finished stories which damaged his image; his financial situation deteriorated; and his romantic life grew complicated.

His solution was an escape to Spain where he immersed himself in Spanish history and legend. He spent four diligent years writing the *History of the Life and Voyages of Christopher Columbus, Chronicle of the Conquest of Granada,* and *The Alhambra*. They were painstaking efforts which helped restore his previous reputation.

His return to New York was a triumphant one; he was honored and eulogized as the symbol of American literature. Yet his prime was past, and the words that followed were shadows of his earlier gift. He made a tour of the western plains and wrote a number of popular books on the frontier. With the exception of four successful years as minister to Spain, Irving lived the rest of his life at "Sunnyside," an estate along the Hudson not far from Tarryton and Sleepy Hollow. He died at the age of seventy-six, completing in his last year the fifth and final volume of a biography of Washington, the man for whom he had been named.

James Fenimore Cooper

1789 / 1851

from

THE DEERSLAYER

The events of The Deerslayer, *from which the following selection is taken, take place between 1740 and 1745. Natty Bumppo, at this time a young man, has been reared by the Delaware Indians. He therefore has been trained in the ways of the forest and of the Indians. His closest friend is a young Delaware chief, Chingachgook, who is engaged to an Indian girl named Hist. This girl has been stolen by the Hurons and adopted into their tribe. In attempting her rescue, Deerslayer has himself been captured by the Hurons.*

It was one of the common expedients of the savages, on such occasions, to put the nerves of their victims to the severest proofs. On the other hand, it was a matter of Indian pride to betray no yielding to terror or pain, but for the prisoner to provoke his enemies to such acts of violence as would soonest produce death. Many a warrior had been known to bring his own sufferings to a more speedy termination, by taunting reproaches and reviling language, when he found that his physical system was giving way under the agony of sufferings produced by a hellish ingenuity that might well eclipse all that has been said of the infernal devices of religious persecution. This happy expedient of taking refuge from the ferocity of his foes in their passions was denied Deerslayer, however, by his peculiar notions of the duty of a white man; and he had stoutly made up his mind to endure everything in preference to disgracing his color.

No sooner did the young men understand that they were at liberty to commence than some of the boldest and most forward among them sprang into the arena, tomahawk in hand. Here they prepared to throw that dangerous weapon, the object being to strike the tree as near as possible to the victim's head without absolutely hitting him. This was so hazardous an experiment that none but those who were known to be exceedingly expert with the weapon were allowed to enter the lists[1] at all, lest an early death might interfere with the expected entertainment. In the truest hands, it was seldom that the captive escaped injury in these trials; and it often happened that death followed even when the blow was not premeditated. In the particular case of our hero, Rivenoak[2] and the older warriors were apprehensive that the example of the Panther's fate[3] might prove a motive with some fiery spirit suddenly to sacrifice his conqueror, when the temptation of effecting it in precisely the same manner, and possibly with the identical weapon with which the warrior had fallen, offered. This circumstance, of itself, rendered the ordeal of the tomahawk doubly critical for the Deerslayer.

It would seem, however, that all who now entered what we shall call the lists were more disposed to exhibit their own dexterity than to resent the deaths of their comrades. Each prepared himself for the trial with the feelings of rivalry rather than with the desire for vengeance; and for the first few minutes the prisoner had little more connection with the result than grew out of the interest that necessarily attached itself to a living target. The young men were eager, instead of being fierce, and Rivenoak thought he still saw signs of being able to save the life of the captive when the vanity of the young men had been gratified, always admitting that it was not sacrificed to the delicate experiments that were about to be made.

The first youth who presented himself for the trial was called the Raven, having as yet had no opportunity of obtaining a more warlike sobriquet. He was remarkable for high pretension rather than for skill or exploits, and those who knew his character thought the captive in imminent danger when he took his stand and poised the tomahawk. Nevertheless, the young man was good-natured, and no thought was uppermost in his mind other than the desire to make a better cast than any of his fellows. Deerslayer got an inkling of this warrior's want of reputation by the injunctions that he had received

---

1. *enter the lists,* join in the contest. This is a phrase borrowed from the tournaments of the Middle Ages.
2. *Rivenoak* (riv′ən ōk′), a Huron chief who wanted Deerslayer to join his tribe.
3. *the Panther's fate.* Deerslayer had killed the Panther, a Huron warrior, with his tomahawk.

from the seniors, who, indeed, would have objected to his appearing in the arena at all but for an influence derived from his father, an aged warrior of great merit, who was then in the lodges of the tribe.[4] Still, our hero maintained an appearance of self-possession. He had made up his mind that his hour was come, and it would have been a mercy, instead of a calamity, to fall by the unsteadiness of the first hand that was raised against him.

After a suitable number of flourishes and gesticulations that promised much more than he could perform, the Raven let the tomahawk quit his hand. The weapon whirled through the air with the usual evolutions, cut a chip from the sapling to which the prisoner was bound, within a few inches of his cheek, and stuck in a large oak that grew several yards behind him. This was decidedly a bad effort, and a common sneer proclaimed as much, to the great mortification of the young man. On the other hand, there was a general but suppressed murmur of admiration at the steadiness with which the captive stood the trial. The head was the only part he could move, and this had been purposely left free, that the tormentors might have the amusement, and the tormented endure the shame, of dodging and otherwise attempting to avoid the blows. Deerslayer disappointed these hopes by a command of nerve that rendered his whole body as immovable as the tree to which he was bound. Nor did he even adopt the natural and usual expedient of shutting his eyes, the firmest and oldest warrior of the red men never having more disdainfully denied himself this advantage, under similar circumstances.

The Raven had no sooner made his unsuccessful and puerile effort than he was succeeded by Le Daim-Mose,[5] or the Moose, a middle-aged warrior, who was particularly skillful in the use of the tomahawk, and from whose attempt the spectators confidently looked for gratification. This man had none of the good nature of the Raven, but he would gladly have sacrificed the captive to his hatred of the palefaces generally, were it not for the greater interest he felt in his own success as one particularly skillful in the use of this weapon. He took his stand quietly but with an air of confidence, poised his little ax but a single instant, advanced a foot with a quick motion, and threw. Deerslayer saw the keen instrument whirling toward him, and believed all was over; still he was not touched. The tomahawk had actually bound the head of the captive to the tree by carrying before it some of his hair, having buried itself deep beneath the soft bark. A general yell expressed the delight of the spectators, and the Moose felt his heart soften a little toward the prisoner, whose steadiness of nerve alone enabled him to give this evidence of his consummate skill.

Le Daim-Mose was succeeded by the Bounding Boy, or Le Garçon qui Bondi,[6] who came leaping into the circle like a hound or a goat at play. This was one of those elastic youths whose muscles seemed always in motion, and who either affected or who from habit was actually unable to move in any other manner than by showing the antics just mentioned. Nevertheless he was both brave and skillful, and had gained the respect of his people by deeds in war as well as success in the hunts. A far nobler name would long since have fallen to his share had not a Frenchman of rank inadvertently given him this sobriquet, which he religiously preserved as coming from his great father who lived beyond the wide salt lake. The Bounding Boy skipped about in front of the captive, menacing him with his tomahawk, now on one side and now on another and then again in front, in the vain hope of being able to extort some sign of fear by this parade of danger. At length Deerslayer's patience became exhausted by all this mummery, and he spoke for the first time since the trial had actually commenced.

"Throw away, Huron!" he cried, "or your tomahawk will forget its arr'nd.[7] Why do you keep loping about like a fa'an[8] that's showing its dam how well it can skip, when you're a warrior grown, yourself, and a warrior grown defies you and all your silly antics? Throw, or the Huron gals will laugh in your face."

Although not intended to produce such an effect, the last words aroused the "Bounding" warrior to fury. The same nervous excitability which rendered him so active in his person made it difficult to repress his feelings, and the words were scarcely past the lips of the speaker than the tomahawk left the

---

4. *in the lodges of the tribe*, at home with the main body of Hurons. The Indians who were torturing Deerslayer belonged to a group who had come within the English boundaries for hunting and fishing.

5. *Le Daim-Mose*, (lə da/mōz/), a French name meaning "the moose deer." The Hurons made friends with the French, and many of them were called by names the French had given them.

6. *Le Garçon qui Bondi* (lə gar sōɴ/ kē bōɴ di/), French for "the boy who bounds."

7. *arr'nd*, errand.

8. *fa'an*, fawn.

hand of the Indian. Nor was it cast without good will, and a fierce determination to slay. Had the intention been less deadly, the danger might have been greater. The aim was uncertain, and the weapon glanced near the cheek of the captive, slightly cutting the shoulder in its evolutions. This was the first instance in which any other object than that of terrifying the prisoner and of displaying skill had been manifested; and the Bounding Boy was immediately led from the arena and was warmly rebuked for his intemperate haste, which had come so near defeating all the hopes of the band.

To this irritable person succeeded several other young warriors, who not only hurled the tomahawk but who cast the knife, a far more dangerous experiment, with reckless indifference; yet they always manifested a skill that prevented any injury to the captive. Several times Deerslayer was grazed, but in no instance did he receive what might be termed a wound. The unflinching firmness with which he faced his assailants, more especially in the sort of rally with which this trial terminated, excited a profound respect in the spectators; and when the chiefs announced that the prisoner had well withstood the trials of the knife and the tomahawk, there was not a single individual in the band who really felt any hostility toward him, with the exception of Sumach[9] and the Bounding Boy. These two discontented spirits got together, it is true, feeding each other's ire; but, as yet, their malignant feelings were confined very much to themselves, though there existed the danger that the others, ere long, could not fail to be excited by their own efforts into that demoniacal state which usually accompanied all similar scenes among the red men.

Rivenoak now told his people that the paleface had proved himself to be a man. He might live with the Delawares, but he had not been made woman with that tribe. He wished to know whether it was the desire of the Hurons to proceed any further. Even the gentlest of the females, however, had received too much satisfaction in the late trials to forego their expectations of a gratifying exhibition; and there was but one voice[10] in the request to proceed. The politic chief, who had some such desire to receive so celebrated a hunter into his tribe as a European minister had to devise a new and available means of taxation, sought every plausible means of arresting the trial in season; for he well knew if permitted to go far enough to arouse the

more ferocious passions of the tormentors, it would be as easy to dam the waters of the great lakes of his own region as to attempt to arrest them in their bloody career. He therefore called four or five of the best marksmen to him and bid them put the captive to the proof of the rifle, while, at the same time, he cautioned them touching the necessity of their maintaining their own credit by the closest attention to the manner of exhibiting their skill.

When Deerslayer saw the chosen warriors step into the circle with their arms prepared for service, he felt some such relief as the miserable sufferer who had long endured the agonies of disease feels at the certain approach of death. Any trifling variance in the aim of this formidable weapon would prove fatal, since, the head being the target, or rather the point it was desired to graze without injury, an inch or two of difference in the line of projection must at once determine the question of life or death.

In the torture by the rifle there was none of the latitude permitted that appeared in the case of even Gessler's apple,[11] a hair's-breadth being, in fact, the utmost limits that an expert marksman would allow himself on an occasion like this. Victims were frequently shot through the head by too eager or unskillful hands; and it often occurred that, exasperated by the fortitude and taunts of the prisoner, death was dealt intentionally in a moment of ungovernable irritation. All this Deerslayer well knew, for it was in relating the traditions of such scenes, as well as of the battles and victories of their people, that the old men beguiled the long winter evenings in their cabins. He now fully expected the end of his career, and experienced a sort of melancholy pleasure in the idea that he was to fall by a weapon as much beloved as the rifle. . . .

The warriors prepared to exhibit their skill, as there was a double object in view: that of putting the constancy of the captive to the proof, and that of showing how steady were the hands of the marksmen under circumstances of excitement. The distance was small, and, in one sense, safe. But in diminishing the distance taken by the tormentors, the trial to the nerves of the captive was essentially

9. *with the exception of Sumach* (sü′mak or shü′mak). Sumach was the sister of the Panther.
10. *there was but one voice*, all of the Hurons spoke together in agreement.
11. *in the case of even Gessler's apple.* According to legend, Gessler was the Austrian tyrant who forced William Tell to shoot the apple from the head of his little son.

increased. The face of Deerslayer, indeed, was just removed sufficiently from the ends of the guns to escape the effects of the flash, and his steady eye was enabled to look directly into their muzzles, as it might be, in anticipation of the fatal messenger that was to issue from each. The cunning Hurons well knew this fact; and scarce one leveled his piece without first causing it to point as near as possible at the forehead of the prisoner, in the hope that his fortitude would fail him, and that the band would enjoy the triumph of seeing a victim quail under their ingenious cruelty. Nevertheless, each of the competitors was still careful not to injure, the disgrace of striking prematurely being second only to that of failing altogether in attaining the object.

Shot after shot was made, all the bullets coming in close proximity to the Deerslayer's head, without touching it. Still, no one could detect even the twitching of a muscle on the part of the captive, or the slightest winking of an eye. This indomitable resolution, which so much exceeded everything of its kind that any present had before witnessed, might be referred to three distinct causes. The first was resignation to his fate, blended with natural steadiness of deportment, for our hero had calmly made up his mind that he must die, and preferred this mode to any other; the second was his great familiarity with this particular weapon, which deprived it of all the terror that is usually connected with the mere form of the danger; and the third was this familiarity carried out in practice, to a degree so nice as to enable the intended victim to tell, within an inch, the precise spot where each bullet must strike, for he calculated its range by looking in at the bore of the piece. So exact was Deerslayer's estimation of the line of fire that his pride finally got the better of his resignation, and, when five or six had discharged their bullets into the trees, he could not refrain from expressing his contempt.

"You may call this shooting, Mingos,"[12] he exclaimed, "but we've squaws among the Delawares, and I have known Dutch gals on the Mohawk, that could outdo your greatest indivors. Ondo these arms of mine; put a rifle into my hands; and I'll pin the thinnest war lock in your party to any tree you can show me, and this at a hundred yards—aye, or at two hundred, if the object can be seen—nineteen shots in twenty—or, for that matter, twenty in twenty, if the piece is creditable and trusty!"

A low, menacing murmur followed this cool taunt;

the ire of the warriors kindled at listening to such a reproach from one who so far disdained their efforts as to refuse even to wink when a rifle was discharged as near his face as could be done without burning it. Rivenoak perceived that the moment was critical; and, still retaining his hope of adopting so noted a hunter into his tribe, the politic old chief interposed in time, probably, to prevent an immediate resort to that portion of the torture which must necessarily have produced death, through extreme bodily suffering if in no other manner. Moving into the center of the irritated group, he addressed them with his usual wily logic and plausible manner, at once suppressing the fierce movement that had commenced.

"I see how it is," he said. "We have been like the palefaces when they fasten their doors at night, out of fear of the red man. They use so many bars that the fire comes and burns them before they can get out. We have bound the Deerslayer too tight; the thongs keep his limbs from shaking, and his eyes from shutting. Loosen him; let us see what his own body is really made of."

It is often the case when we are thwarted in a cherished scheme that any expedient, however unlikely to succeed, is gladly resorted to, in preference to a total abandonment of the project. So it was with the Hurons. The proposal of the chief found instant favor; and several hands were immediately at work cutting and tearing the ropes of bark from the body of our hero. In half a minute Deerslayer stood free from bonds. Some time was necessary that he should recover the use of his limbs, the circulation of the blood having been checked by the tightness of the ligatures; and this was accorded to him by the politic Rivenoak under the pretense that his body would be more likely to submit to apprehension if its true tone were restored, though really with a view to give time to the fierce passions which had been awakened in the bosoms of his young men to subside. This ruse succeeded; and Deerslayer, by rubbing his limbs, stamping his feet, and moving about, soon regained the circulation, recovering all his physical powers as if nothing had occurred to disturb them.

It is seldom men think of death in the pride of their health and strength. So it was with Deerslayer. Having been helplessly bound, and, as he had every

12. *Mingos* (min'gōz), a name scornfully applied by the Delawares to their enemies.

reason to suppose, so lately on the very verge of the other world, to find himself so unexpectedly liberated, in possession of his strength, and with a full command of limb, acted on him like a sudden restoration to life, reanimating hopes that he had once absolutely abandoned. From that instant all his plans changed. In this he simply obeyed a law of nature; for while we have wished to represent our hero as being resigned to his fate, it has been far from our intention to represent him as anxious to die. From the instant that his buoyancy of feeling revived, his thoughts were keenly bent on the various projects that presented themselves as modes of evading the designs of his enemies; and he again became the quick-witted, ingenious, and determined woodsman, alive to all his own powers and resources. The change was so great that his mind resumed its elasticity; and, no longer thinking of submission, it dwelt only on the devices of the sort of warfare in which he was engaged.

As soon as Deerslayer was released, the band divided itself in a circle around him in order to hedge him in; and the desire to break down his spirit grew in them, precisely as they saw proofs of the difficulty there would be in subduing it. The honor of the band was now involved in the issue; and even the female sex lost all its sympathy with suffering, in the desire to save the reputation of the tribe. The voices of the girls, soft and melodious as nature had made them, were heard mingling with the menaces of the men; and the wrongs of Sumach suddenly assumed the character of injuries inflicted on every Huron female. Yielding to this rising tumult the men drew back a little, signifying to the females that they left the captive, for a time, in their hands, it being a common practice on such occasions for the women to endeavor to throw the victim into a rage by their taunts and revilings, and then to turn him suddenly over to the men in a state of mind that was little favorable to resisting the agony of bodily suffering. Nor was this party without the proper instruments for effecting such a purpose. Sumach had a notoriety as a scold; and one or two crones had come out with the party, most probably as the conservators of its decency and moral discipline, such things occurring in savage as well as civilized life. It is unnecessary to repeat all that ferocity and ignorance could invent for such a purpose, the only difference between this outbreaking of feminine anger and a similar scene among ourselves consisting in the figures of speech and the epithets, the Huron women calling their prisoner by the names of the lower and least respected animals that were known to themselves.

But Deerslayer's mind was too much occupied to permit him to be disturbed by the abuse of excited hags; and their rage necessarily increasing with his indifference, as his indifference increased with their rage, the furies soon rendered themselves impotent by their own excesses. Perceiving that the attempt was a complete failure, the warriors interfered to put a stop to this scene, and this so much the more because preparations were now seriously making for the commencement of the real tortures, or that which would put the fortitude of the sufferer to the test of severe bodily pain. . . . Fragments of dried wood were rapidly collected near the sapling; the splinters which it was intended to thrust into the flesh of the victim, previously to lighting, were all collected; and the thongs were already produced to bind him to the tree. . . .

Suddenly a young Indian came bounding through the Huron ranks, leaping into the very center of the circle in a way to denote the utmost confidence or a temerity bordering on foolhardiness. Five or six sentinels were still watching the lake at different and distant points; and it was the first impression of Rivenoak that one of these had come in with tidings of import. Still, the movements of the stranger were so rapid, and his war dress, which scarcely left him more drapery than an antique statue, had so little distinguishing about it, that, at the first moment, it was impossible to ascertain whether he were friend or foe. Three leaps carried this warrior to the side of Deerslayer. Not till this was effected did the stranger bestow a glance on any other object; then he turned and showed the astonished Hurons the noble brow, fine person, and eagle eye of a young warrior in the paint and panoply of a Delaware. He had a rifle in each hand, the butts of both resting on the earth, while from one dangled its proper pouch and horn. This was Killdeer,[13] which even as he looked boldly and in defiance on the crowd around him, he suffered to fall back into the hands of the proper owner. The presence of two armed men, though it was in their midst, startled the Hurons. Their rifles were scattered about against the different trees and their only weapons were their knives and tomahawks. Still, they had too much self-

---

13. *Killdeer*, Deerslayer's rifle.

possession to betray fear. It was little likely that so small a force would assail so strong a band; and each man expected some extraordinary proposition to succeed so decisive a step. The stranger did not seem disposed to disappoint them; he prepared to speak.

"Hurons," he said, "this earth is very big. The great lakes are big, too; there is room beyond them for the Iroquois; there is room for the Delawares on this side. I am Chingachgook, the son of Uncas, the kinsman of Tamenund. That paleface is my friend. My heart was heavy when I missed him. Come, let us say farewell, and go on our path."

"Hurons, this is your mortal enemy, the Great Serpent[14] of them you hate!" cried Briarthorn.[15] "If he escape, blood will be in your moccasin prints from this spot to the Canadas. I am all Huron."[16]

As the last words were uttered, the traitor cast his knife at the naked breast of the Delaware. With a quick movement Chingachgook avoided the blow, the dangerous weapon burying its point in a pine. At the next instant a similar weapon glanced from the hand of the Serpent, and quivered in the recreant's heart. A minute had scarcely elapsed from the moment in which Chingachgook bounded into the circle, and that in which Briarthorn fell, like a dog, dead in his tracks. The rapidity of events prevented the Hurons from acting; but this catastrophe permitted no further delay. A common exclamation followed, and the whole party was in motion. At this instant a sound unusual to the woods was heard, and every Huron, male and female, paused to listen with ears erect and faces filled with expectation. The sound was regular and heavy, as if the earth were struck with beetles. Objects became visible among the trees of the background, and a body of troops was seen advancing with measured tread. They came upon the charge, the scarlet of the King's livery shining among the bright green foliage of the forest.

The scene that followed is not easily described. It was one in which wild confusion, despair, and frenzied efforts were so blended as to destroy the unity and distinctness of the action. A general yell burst from the enclosed Hurons; it was succeeded by the hearty cheers of England. Still, not a musket or rifle was fired, though that steady, measured tramp continued, and the bayonet was seen gleaming in advance of a line that counted nearly sixty men. The Hurons were taken at a fearful disadvantage. On three sides was the water, while their formidable and trained foes cut them off from flight on the fourth. Each warrior rushed for his arms, and then all on the point, man, woman, and child, eagerly sought cover. In this scene of confusion and dismay, however, nothing could surpass the discretion and coolness of Deerslayer. He threw himself on a flank of the retiring Hurons, who were inclining off toward the southern margin of the point, in the hope of escaping through the water. Deerslayer watched his opportunity, and finding two of his recent tormentors in range, his rifle first broke the silence of the terrific scene. The bullet brought down both at one discharge. This drew a general fire from the Hurons, and the rifle and war cry of the Serpent were heard in the clamor. Still the trained men returned no answering volley, if we except the short, prompt word of authority, and that heavy, measured, and menacing tread. Presently, however, the shrieks, groans, and denunciations that usually accompany the use of the bayonet followed. That terrible and deadly weapon was glutted in vengeance. The scene that succeeded was one of those of which so many have occurred in our own times, in which neither age nor sex forms an exemption to the lot of a savage warfare. □

---

14. *the Great Serpent*, Chingachgook.
15. *Briarthorn*, a Delaware warrior, traitor to his tribe, who had joined the Hurons.
16. *I am all Huron*. Briarthorn, the traitor, is asserting that he is more loyal than are the Hurons themselves.

DISCUSSION

The Deerslayer, from which this episode is taken, was the last and perhaps finest novel to compose James Fenimore Cooper's five-part adventure saga, *The Leatherstocking Tales*. Cooper's literary fame, in fact, is based—both at home and abroad—upon the reputation of these novels. As our first great novelist, Cooper developed not only a new literary mode for America, the **adventure tale,** but also one of the most memorable and often imitated heroes in our fiction, Natty Bumppo: frontiersman.

Many elements typical of both James Fenimore Cooper's plot method and characterization can be found in this selection. Because they have been imitated so often these elements may seem today to be almost cliché. One must remember that in Cooper's day they were indeed novel. These include: the brave, faultless hero; the loyal Indian companion; the encounter with physical danger; physical danger as a test of prowess; and, of course, the hair-breadth rescue.

FOR EXPLORATION

1. What popular form of T.V. and movie adventure does this excerpt from *The Deerslayer* most closely resemble?
2. Explain how Cooper arranged his plot in order to create suspense.
3. Contrasting Captain John Smith's escape (page 25 C) with that of Natty Bumppo, what characteristics enable each man to make his escape?
4. Contrasting William Bartram's description of Indian life (page 73 C) with that of Cooper, which, if either, do you find more realistic?
5. What heroic characteristics does Natty Bumppo possess? Are they believable? Explain.
6. In your opinion, are the events of the story realistic? Explain your answer.

CREATIVE RESPONSE

One critic has said that Cooper, or for that matter any author, could have only written stories that romanticize the Indian and frontier life long after they had actually ceased to exist. In a short essay defend or attack this statement on the basis of your readings on this subject.

WORDS

In *The Deerslayer* Cooper writes: "The first youth who presented himself for the trial was called the Raven, having as yet had no opportunity of obtaining a more warlike *sobriquet*." A sobriquet (sō′brə kā) is a secondary name which is so descriptive of a person (or a place or a thing) that it identifies him as effectively as his primary or proper name.

1. Referring to an unabridged dictionary, determine the origin of the word *sobriquet*. What was its original meaning?

2. List the various sobriquets which Cooper employs in the selection from *The Deerslayer*. In what ways are they effective?

Sobriquets are not confined to fiction. You frequently meet them in other context. For example, you may have a fanciful nickname or call a friend by his. The sportscaster you heard during the World Series may have called the baseball a "pill." You may have seen a cartoon picturing the United States as "Uncle Sam," a New Mexico license plate boasting the "Land of Enchantment," or a travel poster proclaiming Rome as the "Eternal City."

1. Substitute the primary name for each sobriquet listed below.

2. Select one sobriquet and explain its effectiveness.

paleface	Old Glory
Deerslayer	Bard of Avon
redcoat	iron horse
John Bull	Jolly Roger
alma mater	staff of life

James Fenimore Cooper   1789 / 1851

James Fenimore Cooper was a thirty-year-old gentleman-farmer who disliked even so much as writing a letter, when he suddenly turned novelist. While reading out loud to his wife from a tedious English novel, Cooper insisted he could write a better book himself. Within the year he had completed his first novel, but it seems doubtful he made good his boast. With genteel English characters and English settings of which he knew next to nothing, it would be difficult to find many duller novels. But Cooper quickly turned to more successful subjects. He began to write about the Revolutionary War, about the frontier he had known as a child, and about the sea where he had been an officer in the Navy. And despite the romantic excesses, the melodrama, the sometimes stilted dialogue, the occasional indifference to craft and detail, there was a vitality and energy to his narratives which made him a magnificent storyteller. Within a few years he was famous and by the end of his career had completed thirty-three novels as well as volumes of social comment, naval history, and travel description.

William Cullen Bryant

1794 / 1878

HYMN OF THE CITY

Not in the solitude
Alone may man commune with Heaven, or see,
   Only in savage wood
And sunny vale, the present Deity;
5   Or only hear his voice
Where the winds whisper and the waves rejoice.

Even here do I behold
Thy steps, Almighty!—here, amid the crowd,
   Through the great city rolled,
10 With everlasting murmur deep and loud—
   Choking the ways that wind
'Mong the proud piles, the work of human kind.

Thy golden sunshine comes
From the round heaven, and on their dwellings lies
15   And lights their inner homes;
For them thou fill'st with air the unbounded skies,
   And givest them the stores
Of ocean, and the harvests of its shores.

Thy Spirit is around,
20 Quickening the restless mass that sweeps along:
   And this eternal sound—
Voices and footfalls of the numberless throng—
   Like the resounding sea,
Or like the rainy tempest, speaks of thee.

25   And when the hour of rest
Comes, like a calm upon the mid-sea brine,
   Hushing its billowy breast—
The quiet of that moment too is thine;
   It breathes of Him who keeps
30 The vast and helpless city while it sleeps.

THANATOPSIS

The word thanatopsis *is a combination of Greek words meaning "a view of death." As you read, try to determine what attitude toward death Bryant is presenting.*

To him who in the love of Nature holds
Communion with her visible forms, she speaks
A various language; for his gayer hours
She has a voice of gladness, and a smile
5 And eloquence of beauty, and she glides
Into his darker musings with a mild
And healing sympathy that steals away
Their sharpness ere he is aware. When thoughts
Of the last bitter hour come like a blight
10 Over thy spirit, and sad images
Of the stern agony, and shroud, and pall,
And breathless darkness, and the narrow house[1]
Make thee to shudder and grow sick at heart—
Go forth, under the open sky, and list
15 To Nature's teachings, while from all around—
Earth and her waters, and the depths of air—
Comes a still voice—
                              Yet a few days, and thee
The all-beholding sun shall see no more
In all his course; nor yet in the cold ground,
20 Where thy pale form was laid with many tears,
Nor in the embrace of ocean shall exist
Thy image. Earth, that nourished thee, shall claim
Thy growth, to be resolved to earth again,
And, lost each human trace, surrendering up
25 Thine individual being, shalt thou go
To mix forever with the elements,
To be a brother to the insensible rock
And to the sluggish clod which the rude swain
Turns with his share and treads upon. The oak
30 Shall send his roots abroad and pierce thy mold.
Yet not to thine eternal resting place
Shalt thou retire alone; nor couldst thou wish
Couch more magnificent. Thou shalt lie down
With patriarchs of the infant world—with kings,
35 The powerful of the earth—the wise, the good,
Fair forms, and hoary seers of ages past,
All in one mighty sepulcher. The hills

---

1. *the narrow house,* the grave.

Rock-ribbed and ancient as the sun; the vales
Stretching in pensive quietness between;
40　The venerable woods; rivers that move
In majesty; and the complaining brooks
That make the meadows green; and, poured
　　　round all
Old Ocean's gray and melancholy waste—
Are but the solemn decorations all
45　Of the great tomb of man. The golden sun,
The planets, all the infinite host of heaven,
Are shining on the sad abodes of death
Through the still lapse of ages. All that tread
The globe are but a handful to the tribes
50　That slumber in its bosom. Take the wings
Of morning, pierce the Barcan wilderness,[2]
Or lose thyself in the continuous woods
Where rolls the Oregon,[3] and hears no sound
Save his own dashings—yet the dead are there;
55　And millions in those solitudes, since first
The flight of years began, have laid them down
In their last sleep—the dead reign there alone.
So shalt thou rest, and what if thou withdraw
In silence from the living, and no friend
60　Take note of thy departure? All that breathe
Will share thy destiny. The gay will laugh
When thou art gone, the solemn brood of care

Plod on, and each one as before will chase
His favorite phantom; yet all these shall leave
Their mirth and their employments, and shall
65　　come
And make their bed with thee. As the long train
Of ages glides away, the sons of men,
The youth in life's green spring, and he who goes
In the full strength of years, matron and maid,
70　The speechless babe, and the gray-headed man—
Shall one by one be gathered to thy side,
By those who in their turn shall follow them.
So live, that when thy summons comes to join
The innumerable caravan which moves
75　To that mysterious realm, where each shall take
His chamber in the silent halls of death,
Thou go not, like the quarry slave at night,
Scourged to his dungeon, but, sustained and
　　　soothed
By an unfaltering trust, approach thy grave
80　Like one who wraps the drapery of his couch
About him, and lies down to pleasant dreams.

2.　*Barcan wilderness*, the desert land of Cyrenaica (sir′ə na′əkə),
which was formerly the ancient kingdom of Barca, in northern Africa.
3.　*the Oregon*, the old name for the Columbia River, which flows
between the states of Oregon and Washington.

DISCUSSION

Though writers during the Early National Period displayed a more remarkable degree of independence from the main currents of European and English literature than did their predecessors, the influences of the Old World were nevertheless felt throughout a large portion of the nineteenth century. Such was the case in the poetry of William Cullen Bryant; the major influence upon his technique and ideology was **Romanticism.**

Briefly, some ideological concepts of **Romanticism** that are reflected in Bryant's poetry are: a belief in the mutability of the physical world, that it is subject to decline and decay; the belief that while everything changes and dies, God, the Absolute, remains immortal; and lastly, that this immutable Spirit reveals Himself through His greatest—though mutable—work, Nature.

Stylistically, Bryant also borrowed from the poets of the Romantic Movement. One finds in his poetry the same use of artificially lofty diction and syntax. Like other Romantic poets, Bryant was fond of using archaic syntax in order to convey a serious, philosophical tone. Thus, Bryant

used in his poetry such words as "thou," "thy," "shalt," "couldst," and "list" (for "listen"). Another interesting stylistic technique which is found again and again in poetry, is **inversion. Inversion,** or **anastrophe,** is the displacement of a word, phrase, or clause from its normal position in a sentence, either for emphasis or poetic effect. It is frequently used in poetry so as to maintain meter and/or rhyme scheme. An example of the simple inversion of a word, in this case the adjective, from Henry Wadsworth Longfellow's "Prelude to Evangeline" is, ". . . the forest primeval." Perhaps a more familiar example is one from Samuel Francis Smith's poem "America": ". . . Of thee I sing. . . ." Here, the prepositional phrase has been placed before the noun clause. A more complex example of inversion involving word, phrase, and clause displacements is found in Samuel Taylor Coleridge's poem "Kubla Khan":

"In Xanadu did Kubla Khan
A stately pleasure-dome decree. . ."

FOR EXPLORATION

Thanatopsis

1. The following quotations from "Thanatopsis" contain inversions. Without altering the meaning and using only Bryant's words, put both quotations in their "normal" order, eliminating all inversions. (a) "Yet a few days, and thee the all-beholding sun shall see no more in all his course. . . ." (b) "Yet not to thine eternal resting place shalt thou retire alone. . . ." (c) Cite an example of your own of the poet's use of inversion.
2. The best way to grasp the meaning of "Thanatopsis" as a whole is to consider first the ideas developed in its various parts. (a) *Lines 1–17:* What does the poet suggest that man do when he is oppressed by thoughts of death? (b) *Lines 17–57:* What comfort does Nature offer the man facing death? (c) *Lines 58–72:* Why is dying unmourned not important? (d) *Lines 73–81:* What is important?
3. (a) What is the "mighty sepulcher" to which the poet refers in *line 37?* (b) What is the "destiny" that the poet speaks of in *lines 60–61?*
4. What figure of speech does Bryant employ in the last two lines? What is he saying death is like?

5. When Bryant published his volume *Poems* (1821) he added to "Thanatopsis" *lines 1–17* (up to "Yet a few days. . .") and the last sixteen lines (beginning with "As the long train. . ."). (a) What function does the addition at the beginning of the poem serve? (b) What is the purpose of the last sixteen lines?
6. Do you find the ideas expressed in "Thanatopsis" consoling or disturbing? Explain your answer.

Hymn to the City

1. Where else, other than the solitude of Nature, does the poet feel the presence of God?
2. What aspects of Nature do both the solitude and the subject of the poem share?
3. Identify the similes used in the last two stanzas of the poem. Explain their meaning within the context of the poem.
4. Do you agree or not with the sentiments expressed in the poem? Explain.

CULVER PICTURES, INC.

William Cullen Bryant   1794 / 1878

Born in Massachusetts and raised amidst the still untouched beauty of the Hampshire Hills, William Cullen Bryant spent much of his youth walking the woods which would so dominate his poetry. A precocious child who could read at the age of sixteen months, he early wanted to be a poet and saw some of his verses printed in a local paper when he was ten. Bryant's finest poem "Thanatopsis" was written when he was but seventeen years old. Perhaps fearing that some of the more strictly religious members of his family would object to it, he hid it away in his desk.

Bryant was at this time apprenticed to the law; while he continued to write, he deposited his efforts in his desk and seemingly forgot about them. Bryant's father eventually discovered the cache and without mentioning his find took the poems to the *North American Review*, the editors of which initially assumed the verses to be a hoax since they felt there was no author on this side of the Atlantic capable of such quality. Once printed though, the poetry did not gain wide acceptance, and for a while it seemed Bryant was doomed to a law practice he disliked. But recognition slowly grew in literary circles, and he was eventually offered a number of editorial positions. He was finally made managing editor of the *Evening Post* when he was thirty-four. During his forty-nine years in control of the paper, Bryant was a vigorous Jacksonian Democrat and made the paper an early advocate of the abolitionist movement.

Edgar Allan Poe

1809 / 1849

THE BLACK CAT

FOR the most wild yet most homely narrative which I am about to pen, I neither expect nor solicit belief. Mad indeed would I be to expect it, in a case where my very senses reject their own evidence. Yet, mad am I not—and very surely do I not dream. But to-morrow I die, and to-day I would unburden my soul. My immediate purpose is to place before the world, plainly, succinctly, and without comment, a series of mere household events. In their consequences, these events have terrified—have tortured—have destroyed me. Yet I will not attempt to expound them. To me, they have presented little but horror—to many they will seem less terrible than *baroques*.[1] Hereafter, perhaps, some intellect may be found which will reduce my phantasm to the common-place—some intellect more calm, more logical, and far less excitable than my own, which will perceive, in the circumstances I detail with awe, nothing more than an ordinary succession of very natural causes and effects.

From my infancy I was noted for the docility and humanity of my disposition. My tenderness of heart was even so conspicuous as to make me the jest of my companions. I was especially fond of animals, and was indulged by my parents with a great variety of pets. With these I spent most of my time, and never was so happy as when feeding and caressing them. This peculiarity of character grew with my growth, and, in my manhood, I derived from it one of my principal sources of pleasure. To those who have cherished an affection for a faithful and sagacious dog, I need hardly be at the trouble of explaining the nature or the intensity of the grati-fication thus derivable. There is something in the unselfish and self-sacrificing love of a brute, which goes directly to the heart of him who has had frequent occasion to test the paltry friendship and gossamer fidelity of mere *Man*.

I married early, and was happy to find in my wife a disposition not uncongenial with my own. Ob-serving my partiality for domestic pets, she lost no opportunity of procuring those of the most agreeable kind. We had birds, gold-fish, a fine dog, rabbits, a small monkey, and a *cat*.

This latter was a remarkably large and beautiful animal, entirely black, and sagacious to an aston-ishing degree. In speaking of his intelligence, my wife, who at heart was not a little tinctured with superstition, made frequent allusion to the ancient popular notion, which regarded all black cats as witches in disguise. Not that she was ever *serious* upon this point—and I mention the matter at all for no better reason than that it happens, just now, to be remembered.

Pluto—this was the cat's name—was my favorite pet and playmate. I alone fed him, and he attended me wherever I went about the house. It was even with difficulty that I could prevent him from fol-lowing me through the streets.

Our friendship lasted, in this manner, for several years, during which my general temperament and character—through the instrumentality of the Fiend Intemperance—had (I blush to confess it) experi-enced a radical alteration for the worse. I grew, day by day, more moody, more irritable, more regardless of the feelings of others. I suffered myself to use intemperate language to my wife. At length, I even offered her personal violence. My pets, of course, were made to feel the change in my disposition. I not only neglected, but ill-used them. For Pluto, however, I still retained sufficient regard to restrain me from maltreating him, as I made no scruple of maltreating the rabbits, the monkey, or even the dog, when, by accident, or through affection, they came in my way. But my disease grew upon me—for what disease is like Alcohol!—and at length even Pluto, who was now becoming old, and consequently somewhat peevish—even Pluto began to experience the effects of my ill temper.

One night, returning home, much intoxicated, from one of my haunts about town, I fancied that the cat avoided my presence. I seized him; when, in his fright at my violence, he inflicted a slight wound upon my hand with his teeth. The fury of a demon instantly possessed me. I knew myself no longer. My original soul seemed, at once, to take its flight from

---

1. *baroques*, grotesque, fantastic tales.

my body; and a more than fiendish malevolence, gin-nurtured, thrilled every fibre of my frame. I took from my waistcoat-pocket a penknife, opened it, grasped the poor beast by the throat, and deliberately cut one of its eyes from the socket! I blush, I burn, I shudder, while I pen the damnable atrocity.

When reason returned with the morning—when I had slept off the fumes of the night's debauch —I experienced a sentiment half of horror, half of remorse, for the crime of which I had been guilty; but it was, at best, a feeble and equivocal feeling, and the soul remained untouched. I again plunged into excess, and soon drowned in wine all memory of the deed.

In the meantime the cat slowly recovered. The socket of the lost eye presented, it is true, a frightful appearance, but he no longer appeared to suffer any pain. He went about the house as usual, but, as might be expected, fled in extreme terror at my approach. I had so much of my old heart left, as to be at first grieved by this evident dislike on the part of a creature which had once so loved me. But this feeling soon gave place to irritation. And then came, as if to my final and irrevocable overthrow the spirit of PERVERSENESS. Of this spirit philosophy takes no account. Yet I am not more sure that my soul lives, than I am that perverseness is one of the primitive impulses of the human heart—one of the indivisible primary faculties, or sentiments, which give direction to the character of Man. Who has not, a hundred times, found himself committing a vile or a stupid action, for no other reason than because he knows he should *not*? Have we not a perpetual inclination, in the teeth of our best judgment, to violate that which is *Law*, merely because we understand it to be such? This spirit of perverseness, I say, came to my final overthrow. It was this unfathomable longing of the soul *to vex itself*—to offer violence to its own nature—to do wrong for the wrong's sake only—that urged me to continue and finally to consummate the injury I had inflicted upon the unoffending brute. One morning, in cold blood, I slipped a noose about its neck and hung it to the limb of a tree;—hung it with the tears streaming from my eyes, and with the bitterest remorse at my heart;—hung it *because* I knew that it had loved me, and *because* I felt it had given me no reason of offence;—hung it *because* I knew that in so doing I was committing a sin—a deadly sin that would so jeopardize my immortal soul as to place it—if such

a thing were possible—even beyond the reach of the infinite mercy of the Most Merciful and Most Terrible God.

On the night of the day on which this most cruel deed was done, I was aroused from sleep by the cry of fire. The curtains of my bed were in flames. The whole house was blazing. It was with great difficulty that my wife, a servant, and myself, made our escape from the conflagration. The destruction was complete. My entire worldly wealth was swallowed up, and I resigned myself thenceforward to despair.

I am above the weakness of seeking to establish a sequence of cause and effect, between the disaster and the atrocity. But I am detailing a chain of facts —and wish not to leave even a possible link imperfect. On the day succeeding the fire, I visited the ruins. The walls, with one exception, had fallen in. This exception was found in a compartment wall, not very thick, which stood about the middle of the house, and against which had rested the head of my bed. The plastering had here, in great measure, resisted the action of the fire—a fact which I attributed to its having been recently spread. About this wall a dense crowd were collected, and many persons seemed to be examining a particular portion of it with very minute and eager attention. The words "strange!" "singular!" and other similar expressions, excited my curiosity. I approached and saw, as if graven in *bas-relief*[2] upon the white surface, the figure of a gigantic *cat*. The impression was given with an accuracy truly marvelous. There was a rope about the animal's neck.

When I first beheld this apparition—for I could scarcely regard it as less—my wonder and my terror were extreme. But at length reflection came to my aid. The cat, I remembered, had been hung in a garden adjacent to the house. Upon the alarm of fire, this garden had been immediately filled by the crowd—by some one of whom the animal must have been cut from the tree and thrown, through an open window, into my chamber. This had probably been done with the view of arousing me from sleep. The falling of other walls had compressed the victim of my cruelty into the substance of the freshly-spread plaster; the lime of which, with the flames, and the *ammonia* from the carcass, had then accomplished the portraiture as I saw it.

---

2. *bas-relief*, a carving or scupture in which the figures project only slightly from the background.

Although I thus readily accounted to my reason, if not altogether to my conscience, for the startling fact just detailed, it did not the less fail to make a deep impression upon my fancy. For months I could not rid myself of the phantasm of the cat; and, during this period, there came back into my spirit a half-sentiment that seemed, but was not, remorse. I went so far as to regret the loss of the animal, and to look about me, among the vile haunts which I now habitually frequented, for another pet of the same species, and of somewhat similar appearance, with which to supply its place.

One night as I sat, half stupefied, in a den of more than infamy, my attention was suddenly drawn to some black object, reposing upon the head of one of the immense hogsheads of gin, or of rum, which constituted the chief furniture of the apartment. I had been looking steadily at the top of this hogshead for some minutes, and what now caused me surprise was the fact that I had not sooner perceived the object thereupon. I approached it, and touched it with my hand. It was a black cat—a very large one —fully as large as Pluto, and closely resembling him in every respect but one. Pluto had not a white hair upon any portion of his body; but this cat had a large, although indefinite splotch of white, covering nearly the whole region of the breast.

Upon my touching him, he immediately arose, purred loudly, rubbed against my hand, and appeared delighted with my notice. This, then, was the very creature of which I was in search. I at once offered to purchase it of the landlord; but this person made no claim to it—knew nothing of it —had never seen it before.

I continued my caresses, and when I prepared to go home, the animal evinced a disposition to accompany me. I permitted it to do so; occasionally stooping and patting it as I proceeded. When it reached the house it domesticated itself at once, and became immediately a great favorite with my wife.

For my own part, I soon found a dislike to it arising within me. This was just the reverse of what I had anticipated; but—I know not how or why it was—its evident fondness for myself rather disgusted and annoyed me. By slow degrees these feelings of disgust and annoyance rose into the bitterness of hatred. I avoided the creature; a certain sense of shame, and the remembrance of my former deed of cruelty, preventing me from physically abusing it.

I did not, for some weeks, strike, or otherwise violently ill use it; but gradually—very gradually —I came to look upon it with unutterable loathing, and to flee silently from its odious presence, as from the breath of a pestilence.

What added, no doubt, to my hatred of the beast, was the discovery, on the morning after I brought it home, that, like Pluto, it also had been deprived of one of its eyes. This circumstance, however, only endeared it to my wife, who, as I have already said, possessed, in a high degree, that humanity of feeling which had once been my distinguishing trait, and the source of many of my simplest and purest pleasures.

With my aversion to this cat, however, its partiality for myself seemed to increase. It followed my footsteps with a pertinacity which it would be difficult to make the reader comprehend. Whenever I sat, it would crouch beneath my chair, or spring upon my knees, covering me with its loathsome caresses. If I arose to walk it would get between my feet and thus nearly throw me down, or, fastening its long and sharp claws in my dress, clamber, in this manner, to my breast. At such times, although I longed to destroy it with a blow, I was yet withheld from so doing, partly by a memory of my former crime, but chiefly—let me confess it at once—by absolute *dread* of the beast.

This dread was not exactly a dread of physical evil—and yet I should be at a loss how otherwise to define it. I am almost ashamed to own—yes, even in this felon's cell, I am almost ashamed to own —that the terror and horror with which the animal inspired me, had been heightened by one of the merest chimeras it would be possible to conceive. My wife had called my attention, more than once, to the character of the mark of white hair, of which I have spoken, and which constituted the sole visible difference between the strange beast and the one I had destroyed. The reader will remember that this mark, although large, had been originally very indefinite; but, by slow degrees—degrees nearly imperceptible, and which for a long time my reason struggled to reject as fanciful—it had, at length, assumed a rigorous distinctness of outline. It was now the representation of an object that I shudder to name—and for this, above all, I loathed, and dreaded, and would have rid myself of the monster had I dared—it was now, I say, the image of a hideous—of a ghastly thing—of the GALLOWS!—oh, mournful and terrible engine of Horror and of Crime—of Agony and of Death!

And now was I indeed wretched beyond the wretchedness of mere Humanity. And *a brute beast*—whose fellow I had contemptuously destroyed—*a brute beast* to work out for *me*—for me, a man fashioned in the image of the High God—so much of insufferable woe! Alas! neither by day nor by night knew I the blessing of rest any more! During the former the creature left me no moment alone, and in the latter I started hourly from dreams of unutterable fear to find the hot breath of *the thing* upon my face, and its vast weight—an incarnate nightmare that I had no power to shake off—incumbent eternally upon my *heart!*

Beneath the pressure of torments such as these the feeble remnant of the good within me succumbed. Evil thoughts became my sole intimates—the darkest and most evil of thoughts. The moodiness of my usual temper increased to hatred of all things and of all mankind; while from the sudden, frequent, and ungovernable outbursts of a fury to which I now blindly abandoned myself, my uncomplaining wife, alas, was the most usual and the most patient of sufferers.

One day she accompanied me, upon some household errand, into the cellar of the old building which our poverty compelled us to inhabit. The cat followed me down the steep stairs, and, nearly throwing me headlong, exasperated me to madness. Uplifting an axe, and forgetting in my wrath the childish dread which had hitherto stayed my hand, I aimed a blow at the animal, which, of course, would have proved instantly fatal had it descended as I wished. But this blow was arrested by the hand of my wife. Goaded by the interference into a rage more than demoniacal, I withdrew my arm from her grasp and buried the axe in her brain. She fell dead upon the spot without a groan.

This hideous murder accomplished, I set myself forthwith, and with entire deliberation, to the task of concealing the body. I knew that I could not remove it from the house, either by day or by night, without the risk of being observed by the neighbors. Many projects entered my mind. At one period I thought of cutting the corpse into minute fragments, and destroying them by fire. At another, I resolved to dig a grave for it in the floor of the cellar. Again, I deliberated about casting it in the well in the yard—about packing it in a box, as if merchandise, with the usual arrangements, and so getting a porter to take it from the house. Finally I hit upon what I considered a far better expedient than either of these. I determined to wall it up in the cellar, as the monks of the Middle Ages are recorded to have walled up their victims.

For a purpose such as this the cellar was well adapted. Its walls were loosely constructed, and had lately been plastered throughout with a rough plaster, which the dampness of the atmosphere had prevented from hardening. Moreover, in one of the walls was a projection, caused by a false chimney, or fireplace, that had been filled up and made to resemble the rest of the cellar. I made no doubt that I could readily displace the bricks at this point, insert the corpse, and wall the whole up as before, so that no eye could detect any thing suspicious.

And in this calculation I was not deceived. By means of a crowbar I easily dislodged the bricks, and, having carefully deposited the body against the inner wall, I propped it in that position, while with little trouble I relaid the whole structure as it originally stood. Having procured mortar, sand, and hair, with every possible precaution, I prepared a plaster which could not be distinguished from the old, and with this I very carefully went over the new brick-work. When I had finished, I felt satisfied that all was right. The wall did not present the slightest appearance of having been disturbed. The rubbish on the floor was picked up with the minutest care. I looked around triumphantly, and said to myself: "Here at least, then, my labor has not been in vain."

My next step was to look for the beast which had been the cause of so much wretchedness; for I had, at length, firmly resolved to put it to death. Had I been able to meet with it at the moment, there could have been no doubt of its fate; but it appeared that the crafty animal had been alarmed at the violence of my previous anger, and forbore to present itself in my present mood. It is impossible to describe or to imagine the deep, the blissful sense of relief which the absence of the detested creature occasioned in my bosom. It did not make its appearance during the night; and thus for one night, at least, since its introduction into the house, I soundly and tranquilly slept; aye, *slept* even with the burden of murder upon my soul.

The second and the third day passed, and still my tormentor came not. Once again I breathed as a freeman. The monster, in terror, had fled the premises for ever! I should behold it no more! My happiness was supreme! The guilt of my dark deed disturbed me but little. Some few inquiries had been made, but these had been readily answered. Even a search had been instituted—but of course nothing was to be discovered. I looked upon my future felicity as secured.

Upon the fourth day of the assassination, a party of the police came, very unexpectedly, into the house, and proceeded again to make rigorous investigation of the premises. Secure, however, in the inscrutability of my place of concealment, I felt no embarrassment whatever. The officers bade me accompany them in their search. They left no nook or corner unexplored. At length, for the third or fourth time, they descended into the cellar. I quivered not in a muscle. My heart beat calmly as that of one who slumbers in innocence. I walked the cellar from end to end. I folded my arms upon my bosom, and roamed easily to and fro. The police were thoroughly satisfied and prepared to depart. The glee at my heart was too strong to be restrained. I burned to say if but one word, by way of triumph, and to render doubly sure their assurance of my guiltlessness.

"Gentlemen," I said at last, as the party ascended the steps, "I delight to have allayed your suspicions. I wish you all health and a little more courtesy. By the bye, gentlemen, this—this is a very well-constructed house," (in the rabid desire to say something easily, I scarcely knew what I uttered at all),—"I may say an *excellently* well-constructed house. These walls—are you going, gentlemen?—these walls are solidly put together"; and here, through the mere frenzy of bravado, I rapped heavily with a cane which I held in my hand, upon that very portion of the brickwork behind which stood the corpse of the wife of my bosom.

But may God shield and deliver me from the fangs of the Arch-Fiend! No sooner had the reverberation of my blows sunk into silence, than I was answered by a voice from within the tomb!—by a cry, at first muffled and broken, like the sobbing of a child, and then quickly swelling into one long, loud, and continuous scream, utterly anomalous and inhuman —a howl—a wailing shriek, half of horror and half of triumph, such as might have arisen only out of hell, conjointly from the throats of the damned in their agony and of the demons that exult in the damnation.

Of my own thoughts it is folly to speak. Swooning, I staggered to the opposite wall. For one instant the party on the stairs remained motionless, through extremity of terror and awe. In the next a dozen stout arms were toiling at the wall. It fell bodily. The corpse, already greatly decayed and clotted with gore, stood erect before the eyes of the spectators. Upon its head, with red extended mouth and solitary eye of fire, sat the hideous beast whose craft had seduced me into murder, and whose informing voice had consigned me to the hangman. I had walled the monster up within the tomb. □

THE CONSTRUCTION OF A TALE

A skillful literary artist has constructed a tale. If wise, he has not fashioned his thoughts to accommodate his incidents; but having conceived, with deliberate care, a certain unique or single *effect* to be wrought out, he then invents such incidents—he then combines such events as may best aid him in establishing this preconceived effect. If his very initial sentence tend not to the outbringing of this effect, then he has failed in his first step. In the whole composition there should be no word written, of which the tendency, direct or indirect, is not to the one preëstablished design. And by such means, with such care and skill, a picture is at length painted which leaves in the mind of him who contemplates it with a kindred art, a sense of the fullest satisfaction. The idea of the tale has been presented unblemished, because undisturbed; and this is an end unattainable by the novel. Undue brevity is just as exceptionable here as in the poem, but undue length is yet more to be avoided.

From Poe's review of Hawthorne's *Twice-Told Tales*, in *Graham's Magazine*, May 1842

THE FALL OF
THE HOUSE OF USHER

Son cœur est un luth suspendu;
Sitôt qu'on le touche il résonne.[1]

—*De Béranger*

DURING the whole of a dull, dark, and soundless day in the autumn of the year, when the clouds hung oppressively low in the heavens, I had been passing alone, on horseback, through a singularly dreary tract of country, and at length found myself, as the shades of the evening drew on, within view of the melancholy House of Usher. I know not how it was —but, with the first glimpse of the building, a sense of insufferable gloom pervaded my spirit. I say insufferable; for the feeling was unrelieved by any of that half-pleasurable, because poetic, sentiment with which the mind usually receives even the sternest natural images of the desolate or terrible. I looked upon the scene before me—upon the mere house, and the simple landscape features of the domain— upon the bleak walls—upon the vacant eye-like windows—upon a few rank sedges—and upon a few white trunks of decayed trees—with an utter depression of soul which I can compare to no earthly sensation more properly than to the after-dream of the reveller upon opium—the bitter lapse into everyday life—the hideous dropping off of the veil. There was an iciness, a sinking, a sickening of the heart —an unredeemed dreariness of thought which no goading of the imagination could torture into aught of the sublime. What was it—I paused to think— what was it that so unnerved me in the comtemplation of the House of Usher? It was a mystery all insoluble; nor could I grapple with the shadowy fancies that crowded upon me as I pondered. I was forced to fall back upon the unsatisfactory conclusion, that while, beyond doubt, there *are* combinations of very simple natural objects which have the power of thus affecting us, still the analysis of this power lies among considerations beyond our depth. It was possible, I reflected, that a mere different arrangement of the particulars of the scene, of the details of the picture, would be sufficient to modify, or perhaps to annihilate its capacity for sorrowful impression; and, acting upon this idea, I reined my horse to the precipitous brink of a black and lurid tarn that lay in unruffled lustre by the dwelling, and gazed down—but with a shudder even more thrilling than before—upon the remodelled and inverted images of the gray sedge, and the ghastly tree-stems, and the vacant and eye-like windows.

Nevertheless, in this mansion of gloom I now proposed to myself a sojourn of some weeks. Its proprietor, Roderick Usher, had been one of my boon companions in boyhood; but many years had elapsed since our last meeting. A letter, however, had lately reached me in a distant part of the country—a letter from him—which, in its wildly importunate nature, had admitted of no other than a personal reply. The MS.[2] gave evidence of nervous agitation. The writer spoke of acute bodily illness —of a mental disorder which oppressed him—and of an earnest desire to see me, as his best and indeed his only personal friend, with a view of attempting, by the cheerfulness of my society, some alleviation of his malady. It was the manner in which all this, and much more, was said—it was the apparent *heart* that went with his request—which allowed me no room for hesitation; and I accordingly obeyed forthwith what I still considered a very singular summons.

Although, as boys, we had been even intimate associates, yet I really knew little of my friend. His reserve had been always excessive and habitual. I was aware, however, that his very ancient family had been noted, time out of mind, for a peculiar sensibility of temperament, displaying itself, through long ages, in many works of exalted art, and manifested, of late, in repeated deeds of munificent yet unobtrusive charity, as well as in a passionate devotion to the intricacies, perhaps even more than to the orthodox and easily recognizable beauties, of musical science. I had learned, too, the very remarkable fact, that the stem of the Usher race, all time-honored as it was, had put forth, at no period, any enduring branch; in other words, that the entire family lay in the direct line of descent, and had

---

1. *Son . . . résonne*, from the poem "Le Refus" by Pierre de Béranger (1780–1857). "His heart is a suspended lute;/Touch it and the strings resound." [*French*]
2. *MS.*, an abbreviation for "manuscript."

always, with very trifling and very temporary variation, so lain. It was this deficiency, I considered, while running over in thought the perfect keeping of the character of the premises with the accredited character of the people, and while speculating upon the possible influence which the one, in the long lapse of centuries, might have exercised upon the other—it was this deficiency, perhaps, of collateral issue, and the consequent undeviating transmission, from sire to son, of the patrimony with the name, which had, at length, so identified the two as to merge the original title of the estate in the quaint and equivocal appellation of the "House of Usher" —an appellation which seemed to include, in the minds of the peasantry who used it, both the family and the family mansion.

I have said that the sole effect of my somewhat childish experiment—that of looking down within the tarn—had been to deepen the first singular impression. There can be no doubt that the consciousness of the rapid increase of my superstition—for why should I not so term it?—served mainly to accelerate the increase itself. Such, I have long known, is the paradoxical law of all sentiments having terror as a basis. And it might have been for this reason only, that, when I again uplifted my eyes to the house itself, from its image in the pool, there grew in my mind a strange fancy—a fancy so ridiculous, indeed, that I but mention it to show the vivid force of the sensations which oppressed me. I had so worked upon my imagination as really to believe that about the whole mansion and domain there hung an atmosphere peculiar to themselves and their immediate vicinity—an atmosphere which had no affinity with the air of heaven, but which had reeked up from the decayed trees, and the gray wall, and the silent tarn—a pestilent and mystic vapor, dull, sluggish, faintly discernible, and leaden-hued.

Shaking off from my spirit what *must* have been a dream, I scanned more narrowly the real aspect of the building. Its principal feature seemed to be that of an excessive antiquity. The discoloration of ages had been great. Minute fungi overspread the whole exterior, hanging in a fine tangled web-work from the eaves. Yet all this was apart from any extraordinary dilapidation. No portion of the masonry had fallen; and there appeared to be a wild inconsistency between its still perfect adaptation of parts, and the crumbling condition of the individual stones. In this there was much that reminded me of the specious totality of old wood-work which has rotted for long years in some neglected vault, with no disturbance from the breath of the external air. Beyond this indication of extensive decay, however, the fabric gave little token of instability. Perhaps the eye of a scrutinizing observer might have discovered a barely perceptible fissure, which, extending from the roof of the building in front, made its way down the wall in a zigzag direction, until it became lost in the sullen waters of the tarn.

Noticing these things, I rode over a short causeway to the house. A servant in waiting took my horse, and I entered the Gothic archway of the hall. A valet, of stealthy step, thence conducted me, in silence, through many dark and intricate passages in my progress to the *studio* of his master. Much that I encountered on the way contributed, I know not how, to heighten the vague sentiments of which I have already spoken. While the objects around me—while the carvings of the ceilings, the sombre tapestries of the walls, the ebon blackness of the floors, and the phantasmagoric armorial trophies which rattled as I strode, were but matters to which, or to such as which, I had been accustomed from my infancy—while I hesitated not to acknowledge how familiar was all this—I still wondered to find how unfamiliar were the fancies which ordinary images were stirring up. On one of the staircases, I met the physician of the family. His countenance, I thought, wore a mingled expression of low cunning and perplexity. He accosted me with trepidation and passed on. The valet now threw open a door and ushered me into the presence of his master.

The room in which I found myself was very large and lofty. The windows were long, narrow, and pointed, and at so vast a distance from the black oaken floor as to be altogether inaccessible from within. Feeble gleams of encrimsoned light made their way through the trellissed panes, and served to render sufficiently distinct the more prominent objects around; the eye, however, struggled in vain to reach the remoter angles of the chamber, or the recesses of the vaulted and fretted ceiling. Dark draperies hung upon the walls. The general furniture was profuse, comfortless, antique, and tattered. Many books and musical instruments lay scattered about, but failed to give any vitality to the scene. I felt that I breathed an atmosphere of sorrow. An air of stern, deep, and irredeemable gloom hung over and pervaded all.

Upon my entrance, Usher arose from a sofa on which he had been lying at full length, and greeted me with a vivacious warmth which had much in it, I at first thought, of an overdone cordiality—of the constrained effort of the *ennuyé*[3] man of the world. A glance, however, at his countenance convinced me of his perfect sincerity. We sat down; and for some moments, while he spoke not, I gazed upon him with a feeling half of pity, half of awe. Surely, man had never before so terribly altered, in so brief a period, as had Roderick Usher! It was with difficulty that I could bring myself to admit the identity of the wan being before me with the companion of my early boyhood. Yet the character of his face had been at all times remarkable. A cadaverousness of complexion; an eye large, liquid, and luminous beyond comparison; lips somewhat thin and very pallid, but of a surpassingly beautiful curve; a nose of a delicate Hebrew model, but with a breadth of nostril unusual in similar formations; a finely moulded chin, speaking, in its want of prominence, of a want of moral energy; hair of a more than web-like softness and tenuity;—these features, with an inordinate expansion above the regions of the temple, made up altogether a countenance not easily to be forgotten. And now in the mere exaggeration of the prevailing character of these features, and of the expression they were wont to convey, lay so much of change that I doubted to whom I spoke. The now ghastly pallor of the skin, and the now miraculous lustre of the eye, above all things startled and even awed me. The silken hair, too, had been suffered to grow all unheeded, and as, in its wild gossamer texture, it floated rather than fell about the face, I could not, even with effort, connect its Arabesque expression with any idea of simple humanity.

In the manner of my friend I was at once struck with an incoherence—an inconsistency; and I soon found this to arise from a series of feeble and futile struggles to overcome an habitual trepidancy—an excessive nervous agitation. For something of this nature I had indeed been prepared, no less by his letter, than by reminiscences of certain boyish traits, and by conclusions deduced from his peculiar physical confirmation and temperament. His action was alternately vivacious and sullen. His voice varied rapidly from a tremulous indecision (when the animal spirits seemed utterly in abeyance) to that species of energetic concision—that abrupt, weighty, unhurried, and hollow-sounding enunciation—that leaden, self-balanced, and perfectly modulated guttural utterance, which may be observed in the lost drunkard, or the irreclaimable eater of opium, during the periods of his most intense excitement.

It was thus that he spoke of the object of my visit, of his earnest desire to see me, and of the solace he expected me to afford him. He entered, at some length, into what he conceived to be the nature of his malady. It was, he said, a constitutional and a family evil, and one for which he despaired to find a remedy—a mere nervous affection, he immediately added, which would undoubtedly soon pass off. It displayed itself in a host of unnatural sensations. Some of these, as he detailed them, interested and bewildered me; although, perhaps, the terms and the general manner of their narration had their weight. He suffered much from a morbid acuteness of the senses; the most insipid food was alone endurable; he could wear only garments of certain texture; the odors of all flowers were oppressive; his eyes were tortured by even a faint light; and there were but peculiar sounds, and these from stringed instruments, which did not inspire him with horror.

To an anomalous species of terror I found him a bounden slave. "I shall perish," said he, "I *must* perish in this deplorable folly. Thus, thus, and not otherwise, shall I be lost. I dread the events of the future, not in themselves, but in their results. I shudder at the thought of any, even the most trivial, incident, which may operate upon this intolerable agitation of soul. I have, indeed, no abhorrence of danger, except in its absolute effect—in terror. In this unnerved, in this pitiable, condition I feel that the period will sooner or later arrive when I must abandon life and reason together, in some struggle with the grim phantasm, FEAR."

I learned, moreover, at intervals, and through broken and equivocal hints, another singular feature of his mental condition. He was enchained by certain superstitious impressions in regard to the dwelling which he tenanted, and whence, for many years, he had never ventured forth—in regard to an influence whose supposititious force was conveyed in terms too shadowy here to be re-stated—an influence which some peculiarities in the mere form and substance of his family mansion had, by dint of long sufferance, he said, obtained over his spirit —an effect which the *physique* of the gray walls and

---

3. *ennuyé*, bored. [*French*]

turrets, and of the dim tarn into which they all looked down, had, at length, brought about upon the *morale* of his existence.

He admitted, however, although with hesitation, that much of the peculiar gloom which thus afflicted him could be traced to a more natural and far more palpable origin—to the severe and long-continued illness—indeed to the evidently approaching dissolution—of a tenderly beloved sister, his sole companion for long years, his last and only relative on earth. "Her decease," he said, with a bitterness which I can never forget, "would leave him (him, the hopeless and the frail) the last of the ancient race of the Ushers." While he spoke, the lady Madeline (for so was she called) passed through a remote portion of the apartment, and, without having noticed my presence, disappeared. I regarded her with an utter astonishment not unmingled with dread; and yet I found it impossible to account for such feelings. A sensation of stupor oppressed me as my eyes followed her retreating steps. When a door, at length, closed upon her, my glance sought instinctively and eagerly the countenance of the brother; but he had buried his face in his hands, and I could only perceive that a far more than ordinary wanness had overspread the emaciated fingers through which trickled many passionate tears.

The disease of the lady Madeline had long baffled the skill of her physicians. A settled apathy, a gradual wasting away of the person, and frequent although transient affections of a partially cataleptical character were the unusual diagnosis. Hitherto she had steadily borne up against the pressure of her malady, and had not betaken herself finally to bed; but on the closing in of the evening of my arrival at the house, she succumbed (as her brother told me at night with inexpressible agitation) to the prostrating power of the destroyer; and I learned that the glimpse I had obtained of her person would thus probably be the last I should obtain—that the lady, at least while living, would be seen by me no more.

For several days ensuing, her name was unmentioned by either Usher or myself; and during this period I was busied in earnest endeavors to alleviate the melancholy of my friend. We painted and read together, or I listened, as if in a dream, to the wild improvisations of his speaking guitar. And thus, as a closer and still closer intimacy admitted me more unreservedly into the recesses of his spirit, the more bitterly did I perceive the futility of all attempt at cheering a mind from which darkness, as if an inherent positive quality, poured forth upon all objects of the moral and physical universe in one unceasing radiation of gloom.

I shall ever bear about me a memory of the many solemn hours I thus spent alone with the master of the House of Usher. Yet I should fail in any attempt to convey an idea of the exact character of the studies, or of the occupations, in which he involved me, or led me the way. An excited and highly distempered ideality[4] threw a sulphureous lustre over all. His long improvised dirges will ring forever in my ears. Among other things, I hold painfully in mind a certain singular perversion and amplification of the wild air of the last waltz of von Weber.[5] From the paintings over which his elaborate fancy brooded, and which grew, touch by touch, into vaguenesses at which I shuddered the more thrillingly, because I shuddered knowing not why—from these paintings (vivid as their images now are before me) I would in vain endeavor to educe more than a small portion which should lie within the compass of merely written words. By the utter simplicity, by the nakedness of his designs, he arrested and overawed attention. If ever mortal painted an idea, that mortal was Roderick Usher. For me at least, in the circumstances then surrounding me, there arose out of the pure abstractions which the hypochondriac contrived to throw upon his canvas, an intensity of intolerable awe, no shadow of which felt I ever yet in the contemplation of the certainly glowing yet too concrete reveries of Fuseli.[6]

One of the phantasmagoric conceptions of my friend, partaking not so rigidly of the spirit of abstraction, may be shadowed forth, although feebly, in words. A small picture presented the interior of an immensely long and rectangular vault or tunnel, with low walls, smooth, white, and without interruption or device. Certain accessory points of the design served well to convey the idea that this excavation lay at an exceeding depth below the surface of the earth. No outlet was observed in any portion of its vast extent, and no torch or other artificial source of light was discernible; yet a flood

---

4. *distempered ideality,* unbalanced or disturbed state of being.
5. *von Weber,* Carl Maria Friedrich Ernst von Weber (1786–1826), a German composer whose music concentrated on arousing romantic emotions.
6. *Fuseli,* Henry Fuseli (1741–1825), a Swiss-English painter also known as Johann Heinrich Fussli. The figures in his paintings are usually cast in poses suggesting violent activity.

of intense rays rolled throughout, and bathed the whole in a ghastly and inappropriate splendor.

I have just spoken of that morbid condition of the auditory nerve which rendered all music intolerable to the sufferer, with the exception of certain effects of stringed instruments. It was, perhaps, the narrow limits to which he thus confined himself upon the guitar which gave birth, in great measure, to the fantastic character of his performances. But the fervid *facility* of his *impromptus* could not be so accounted for. They must have been, and were, in the notes, as well as in the words of his wild fantasias (for he not unfrequently accompanied himself with rhymed verbal improvisations), the result of that intense mental collectedness and concentration to which I have previously alluded as observable only in particular moments of the highest artificial excitement. The words of one of these rhapsodies I have easily remembered. I was, perhaps, the more forcibly impressed with it as he gave it, because, in the under or mystic current of its meaning, I fancied that I perceived, and for the first time, a full consciousness on the part of Usher of the tottering of his lofty reason upon her throne. The verses, which were entitled "The Haunted Palace," ran very nearly, if not accurately, thus:—

I

In the greenest of our valleys,
  By good angels tenanted,
Once a fair and stately palace—
  Radiant palace—reared its head.
In the monarch Thought's dominion—
  It stood there!
Never seraph spread a pinion
  Over fabric half so fair.

II

Banners yellow, glorious, golden,
  On its roof did float and flow
(This—all this—was in the olden
  Time long ago);
And every gentle air that dallied,
  In that sweet day,
Along the ramparts plumed and pallid,
  A winged odor went away.

III

Wanderers in that happy valley
  Through two luminous windows saw
Spirits moving musically

To a lute's well-tunèd law;
Round about a throne, where sitting
  (Porphyrogene!)[7]
In state his glory well befitting,
  The ruler of the realm was seen.

IV

And all with pearl and ruby glowing
  Was the fair palace door,
Through which came flowing, flowing, flowing
  And sparkling evermore,
A troop of Echoes whose sweet duty
  Was but to sing,
In voices of surpassing beauty,
  The wit and wisdom of their king.

V

But evil things, in robes of sorrow,
  Assailed the monarch's high estate;
(Ah, let us mourn, for never morrow
  Shall dawn upon him, desolate!)
And, round about his home, the glory
  That blushed and bloomed
Is but a dim-remembered story
  Of the old time entombed.

VI

And travellers now within that valley,
  Through the red-litten windows see
Vast forms that move fantastically
  To a discordant melody;
While, like a rapid ghastly river,
  Through the pale door;
A hideous throng rush out forever,
  And laugh—but smile no more.

I well remember that suggestions arising from this ballad led us into a train of thought wherein there became manifest an opinion of Usher's which I mention not so much on account of its novelty (for other men have thought thus), as on account of the pertinacity with which he maintained it. This opinion, in its general form, was that of the sentience of all vegetable things. But, in his disordered fancy, the idea had assumed a more daring character, and trespassed, under certain conditions, upon the kingdom of inorganization. I lack words to express the full extent, or the earnest *abandon* of his per-

---

7. *Porphyrogene,* born of royalty.

suasion. The belief, however, was connected (as I have previously hinted) with the gray stones of the home of his forefathers. The conditions of the sentence had been here, he imagined, fulfilled in the method of collocation of these stones—in the order of their arrangement, as well as in that of the many *fungi* which overspread them, and of the decayed trees which stood around—above all, in the long undisturbed endurance of this arrangement, and in its reduplication in the still waters of the tarn. Its evidence—the evidence of the sentience—was to be seen, he said (and I here started as he spoke), in the gradual yet certain condensation of an atmosphere of their own about the waters and the walls. The result was discoverable, he added, in that silent yet importunate and terrible influence which for centuries had moulded the destinies of his family, and which made *him* what I now saw him—what he was. Such opinions need no comment, and I will make none.

Our books—the books which, for years, had formed no small portion of the mental existence of the invalid—were, as might be supposed, in strict keeping with this character of phantasm. We pored together over such works as the "Ververt et Chartreuse" of Gresset; the "Belphegor" of Machiavelli; the "Heaven and Hell" of Swedenborg; the "Subterranean Voyage of Nicholas Klimm" of Holberg; the "Chiromancy" of Robert Flud, of Jean D'Indaginé, and of Dela Chambre; the "Journey into the Blue Distance of Tieck"; and the "City of the Sun of Campanella." One favorite volume was a small octavo edition of the "Directorium Inquisitorium," by the Dominican Eymeric de Gironne; and there were passages in Pomponius Mela, about the old African Satyrs and Ægipans, over which Usher would sit dreaming for hours. His chief delight, however, was found in the perusal of an exceedingly rare and curious book in quarto Gothic—the manual of a forgotten church—the *Vigiliæ Mortuorum secundum Chorum Ecclesiæ Maguntinæ*.[8]

I could not help thinking of the wild ritual of this work, and of its probable influence upon the hypochondriac, when, one evening, having informed me abruptly that the lady Madeline was no more, he stated his intention of preserving her corpse for a fortnight (previously to its final interment), in one of the numerous vaults within the main walls of the building. The worldly reason, however, assigned for this singular proceeding, was one which I did not feel at liberty to dispute. The brother had been led to his resolution (so he told me) by consideration of the unusual character of the malady of the deceased, of certain obtrusive and eager inquiries on the part of her medical men, and of the remote and exposed situation of the burial-ground of the family. I will not deny that when I called to mind the sinister countenance of the person whom I met upon the staircase, on the day of my arrival at the house, I had no desire to oppose what I regarded as at best but a harmless, and by no means an unnatural, precaution.

At the request of Usher, I personally aided him in the arrangements for the temporary entombment. The body having been encoffined, we two alone bore it to its rest. The vault in which we placed it (and which had been so long unopened that our torches, half smothered in its oppressive atmosphere, gave us little opportunity for investigation) was small, damp, and entirely without means of admission for light; lying, at great depth, immediately beneath that portion of the building in which was my own sleeping apartment. It had been used, apparently, in remote feudal times, for the worst purposes of a donjon-keep,[9] and, in later days, as a place of deposit for powder, or some other highly combustible substance, as a portion of its floor, and the whole interior of a long archway through which we reached it, were carefully sheathed with copper. The door, of massive iron, had been, also, similarly protected. Its immense weight caused an unusually sharp, grating sound, as it moved upon its hinges.

Having deposited our mournful burden upon tressels within this region of horror, we partially turned aside the yet unscrewed lid of the coffin, and looked upon the face of the tenant. A striking similitude between the brother and sister now first arrested my attention; and Usher, divining, perhaps, my thoughts, murmured out some few words from which I learned that the deceased and himself had been twins, and that sympathies of a scarcely intelligible nature had always existed between them. Our glances, however, rested not long upon the dead—for we could not regard her unawed. The disease which had thus entombed the lady in the maturity of youth, had left, as usual in all maladies of a strictly cataleptical character, the mockery of a faint blush upon the

---

8. *Ververt et . . . Maguntinæ*, books of mysticism and magic.
9. *donjon-keep*, a massive chief tower in ancient castles.

bosom and the face, and that suspiciously lingering smile upon the lip which is so terrible in death. We replaced and screwed down the lid, and, having secured the door of iron, made our way, with toil, into the scarcely less gloomy apartments of the upper portion of the house.

And now, some days of bitter grief having elapsed, an observable change came over the features of the mental disorder of my friend. His ordinary manner had vanished. His ordinary occupations were neglected or forgotten. He roamed from chamber to chamber with hurried, unequal, and objectless step. The pallor of his countenance had assumed, if possible, a more ghastly hue—but the luminousness of his eye had utterly gone out. The once occasional huskiness of his tone was heard no more; and a tremulous quaver, as if of extreme terror, habitually characterized his utterance. There were times, indeed, when I thought his unceasingly agitated mind was laboring with some oppressive secret, to divulge which he struggled for the necessary courage. At times, again, I was obliged to resolve all into the mere inexplicable vagaries of madness. for I beheld him gazing upon vacancy for long hours, in an attitude of the profoundest attention, as if listening to some imaginary sound. It was no wonder that his condition terrified—that it infected me. I felt creeping upon me, by slow yet certain degrees, the wild influences of his own fantastic yet impressive superstitions.

It was, especially, upon retiring to bed late in the night of the seventh or eighth day after the placing of the lady Madeline within the donjon, that I experienced the full power of such feelings. Sleep came not near my couch—while the hours waned and waned away. I struggled to reason off the nervousness which had dominion over me. I endeavored to believe that much, if not all of what I felt, was due to the bewildering influence of the gloomy furniture of the room—of the dark and tattered draperies, which, tortured into motion by the breath of a rising tempest, swayed fitfully to and fro upon the walls, and rustled uneasily about the decorations of the bed. But my efforts were fruitless. An irrepressible tremor gradually pervaded my frame; and, at length, there sat upon my very heart an incubus of utterly causeless alarm. Shaking this off with a gasp and a struggle, I uplifted myself upon the pillows, and, peering earnestly within the intense darkness of the chamber, hearkened—I know not why, except that

an instinctive spirit prompted me—to certain low and indefinite sounds which came, through the pauses of the storm, at long intervals, I knew not whence. Overpowered by an intense sentiment of horror, unaccountable yet unendurable, I threw on my clothes with haste (for I felt that I should sleep no more during the night), and endeavored to arouse myself from the pitiable condition into which I had fallen, by pacing rapidly to and fro through the apartment.

I had taken but few turns in this manner, when a light step on an adjoining staircase arrested my attention. I presently recognized it as that of Usher. In an instant afterward he rapped, with a gentle touch, at my door, and entered, bearing a lamp. His countenance was, as usual, cadaverously wan—but, moreover, there was a species of mad hilarity in his eyes—an evidently restrained *hysteria* in his whole demeanor. His air appalled me—but any thing was preferable to the solitude which I had so long endured, and I even welcomed his presence as a relief.

"And you have not seen it?" he said abruptly, after having stared about him for some moments in silence—"you have not then seen it?—but, stay! you shall." Thus speaking, and having carefully shaded his lamp, he hurried to one of the casements, and threw it freely open to the storm.

The impetuous fury of the entering gust nearly lifted us from our feet. It was, indeed, a tempestuous yet sternly beautiful night, and one wildly singular in its terror and its beauty. A whirlwind had apparently collected its force in our vicinity; for there were frequent and violent alterations in the direction of the wind; and the exceeding density of the clouds (which hung so low as to press upon the turrets of the house) did not prevent our perceiving the life-like velocity with which they flew careering from all points against each other, without passing away into the distance. I say that even their exceeding density did not prevent our perceiving this—yet we had no glimpse of the moon or stars, nor was there any flashing forth of the lightning. But the under surfaces of the huge masses of agitated vapor, as well as all terrestrial objects immediately around us, were glowing in the unnatural light of a faintly luminous and distinctly visible gaseous exhalation which hung about and enshrouded the mansion.

"You must not—you shall not behold this!" said I, shuddering, to Usher, as I led him, with a gentle violence, from the window to a seat. "These appearances, which bewilder you, are merely electrical phenomena not uncommon—or it may be that they have their ghastly origin in the rank miasma of the tarn. Let us close this casement;—the air is chilling and dangerous to your frame. Here is one of your favorite romances. I will read, and you shall listen: —and so we will pass away this terrible night together."

The antique volume which I had taken up was the "Mad Trist" of Sir Launcelot Canning; but I had called it a favorite of Usher's more in sad jest than in earnest; for, in truth, there is little in its uncouth and unimaginative prolixity which could have had interest for the lofty and spiritual ideality of my friend. It was, however, the only book immediately at hand; and I indulged a vague hope that the excitement which now agitated the hypochondriac, might find relief (for the history of mental disorder is full of similar anomalies) even in the extremeness of the folly which I should read. Could I have judged, indeed, by the wild overstrained air of vivacity with which he hearkened, or apparently hearkened, to the words of the tale, I might well have congratulated myself upon the success of my design.

I had arrived at that well-known portion of the story where Ethelred, the hero of the Trist, having sought in vain for peaceable admission into the dwelling of the hermit, proceeds to make good an entrance by force. Here, it will be remembered, the words of the narrative run thus:

"And Ethelred, who was by nature of a doughty heart, and who was now mighty withal, on account of the powerfulness of the wine which he had drunken, waited no longer to hold parley with the hermit, who, in sooth, was of an obstinate and maliceful turn, but, feeling the rain upon his shoulders, and fearing the rising of the tempest, uplifted his mace outright, and, with blows, made quickly room in the plankings of the door for his gauntleted hand; and now pulling therewith sturdily, he so cracked and ripped, and tore all asunder, that the noise of the dry and hollow-sounding wood alarumed and reverberated throughout the forest."

At the termination of this sentence I started and, for a moment, paused; for it appeared to me (although I at once concluded that my excited fancy had deceived me)—it appeared to me that, from some very remote portion of the mansion, there came, indistinctly to my ears, what might have been, in its exact similarity of character, the echo

(but a stifled and dull one certainly) of the very cracking and ripping sound which Sir Launcelot had so particularly described. It was, beyond doubt, the coincidence alone which had arrested my attention; for, amid the rattling of the sashes of the casements, and the ordinary commingled noises of the still increasing storm, the sound, in itself, had nothing, surely, which should have interested or disturbed me. I continued the story:

"But the good champion Ethelred, now entering within the door, was sore enraged and amazed to perceive no signal of the maliceful hermit; but, in the stead thereof, a dragon of a scaly and prodigious demeanor and of a fiery tongue, which sate in guard before a palace of gold, with a floor of silver; and upon the wall there hung a shield of shining brass with this legend enwritten—

Who entereth herein, a conqueror hath bin;
Who slayeth the dragon, the shield he shall win.

And Ethelred uplifted his mace, and struck upon the head of the dragon, which fell before him, and gave up his pesty breath, with a shriek so horrid and harsh, and withal so piercing, that Ethelred had fain to close his ears with his hands against the dreadful noise of it, the like whereof was never before heard."

Here again I paused abruptly, and now with a feeling of wild amazement—for there could be no doubt whatever that, in this instance, I did actually hear (although from what direction it proceeded I found it impossible to say) a low and apparently distant, but harsh, protracted, and most unusual screaming or grating sound—the exact counterpart of what my fancy had already conjured up for the dragon's unnatural shriek as described by the romancer.

Oppressed, as I certainly was, upon the occurrence of this second and most extraordinary coincidence, by a thousand conflicting sensations, in which wonder and extreme terror were predominant, I still retained sufficient presence of mind to avoid exciting, by any observation, the sensitive nervousness of my companion. I was by no means certain that he had noticed the sounds in question; although, assuredly, a strange alteration had, during the last few minutes, taken place in his demeanor. From a position fronting my own, he had gradually brought round his chair, so as to sit with his face to the door of the chamber; and thus I could but partially perceive his features, although I saw that his lips trembled as if he were murmuring inaudibly. His head had dropped upon his breast—yet I knew that he was not asleep, from the wide and rigid opening of the eye as I caught a glance of it in profile. The motion of his body, too, was at variance with this idea—for he rocked from side to side with a gentle yet constant and uniform sway. Having rapidly taken notice of all this, I resumed the narrative of Sir Launcelot, which thus proceeded:

"And now, the champion, having escaped from the terrible fury of the dragon, bethinking himself of the brazen shield, and of the breaking up of the enchantment which was upon it, removed the carcass from out of the way before him, and approached valorously over the silver pavement of the castle to where the shield was upon the wall; which in sooth tarried not for his full coming, but fell down at his feet upon the silver floor, with a mighty great and terrible ringing sound."

No sooner had these syllables passed my lips, than—as if a shield of brass had indeed, at the moment, fallen heavily upon a floor of silver—I became aware of a distinct, hollow, metallic, and clangorous, yet apparently muffled, reverberation. Completely unnerved, I leaped to my feet; but the measured rocking movement of Usher was undisturbed. I rushed to the chair in which he sat. His eyes were bent fixedly before him, and throughout his whole countenance there reigned a stony rigidity. But, as I placed my hand upon his shoulder, there came a strong shudder over his whole person; a sickly smile quivered about his lips; and I saw that he spoke in a low, hurried, and gibbering murmur, as if unconscious of my presence. Bending closely over him, I at length drank in the hideous import of his words.

"Now hear it?—yes, I hear it, and *have* heard it. Long—long—long—many minutes, many hours, many days, have I heard it—yet I dared not—oh, pity me, miserable wretch that I am!—I dared not —I *dared* not speak! *We have put her living in the tomb!* Said I not that my senses were acute? I *now* tell you that I heard her first feeble movements in the hollow coffin. I heard them—many, many days ago—yet I dared not—*I dared not speak!* And now to-night—Ethelred—ha! ha!—the breaking of the hermit's door, and the death-cry of the dragon, and

the clangor of the shield—say, rather, the rending of her coffin, and the grating of the iron hinges of her prison, and her struggles within the coppered archway of the vault! Oh! whither shall I fly? Will she not be here anon? Is she not hurrying to upbraid me for my haste? Have I not heard her footstep on the stair? Do I not distinguish that heavy and horrible beating of her heart? Madman!"—here he sprang furiously to his feet, and shrieked out his syllables, as if in the effort he were giving up his soul—"*Madman! I tell you that she now stands without the door!*"

As if in the superhuman energy of his utterance there had been found the potency of a spell, the huge antique panels to which the speaker pointed threw slowly back, upon the instant, their ponderous and ebony jaws. It was the work of the rushing gust—but then without those doors there *did* stand the lofty and enshrouded figure of the lady Madeline of Usher. There was blood upon her white robes, and the evidence of some bitter struggle upon every portion of her emaciated frame. For a moment she remained trembling and reeling to and fro upon the threshold—then, with a low moaning cry, fell heavily inward upon the person of her brother, and in her violent and now final death-agonies, bore him to the floor a corpse, and a victim to the terrors he had anticipated.

From that chamber, and from that mansion, I fled aghast. The storm was still abroad in all its wrath as I found myself crossing the old causeway. Suddenly there shot along the path a wild light, and I turned to see whence a gleam so unusual could have issued; for the vast house and its shadows were alone behind me. The radiance was that of the full, setting, and blood-red moon, which now shone vividly through that once barely discernible fissure, of which I have before spoken as extending from the roof of the building, in a zigzag direction, to the base. While I gazed, this fissure rapidly widened—there came a fierce breath of the whirlwind—the entire orb of the satellite burst at once upon my sight—my brain reeled as I saw the mighty walls rushing asunder—there was a long tumultuous shouting sound like the voice of a thousand waters —and the deep and dank tarn at my feet closed sullenly and silently over the fragments of the *"House of Usher."* □

Poems by Poe

ANNABEL LEE

It was many and many a year ago,
  In a kingdom by the sea,
That a maiden there lived whom you may know
  By the name of Annabel Lee;
5 And this maiden she lived with no other thought
  Than to love and be loved by me.

I was a child and *she* was a child,
  In this kingdom by the sea,
But we loved with a love that was more than
    love—
10 I and my Annabel Lee;
With a love that the wingèd seraphs of heaven
  Coveted her and me.

And this was the reason that, long ago,
  In this kingdom by the sea,
15 A wind blew out of a cloud, chilling
  My beautiful Annabel Lee;
So that her highborn kinsmen came
  And bore her away from me,
To shut her up in a sepulcher
20 In this kingdom by the sea.

The angels, not half so happy in heaven,
  Went envying her and me—
Yes! that was the reason (as all men know,
  In this kingdom by the sea)
25 That the wind came out of the cloud by night,
  Chilling and killing my Annabel Lee.

But our love it was stronger by far than the love
  Of those who were older than we,
  Of many far wiser than we;
30 And neither the angels in heaven above,
  Nor the demons down under the sea,
Can ever dissever my soul from the soul
  Of the beautiful Annabel Lee;

For the moon never beams, without bringing me
    dreams
35 Of the beautiful Annabel Lee;
And the stars never rise, but I feel the bright eyes
  Of the beautiful Annabel Lee;
And so, all the night-tide, I lie down by the side
Of my darling—my darling—my life and my bride,
40 In the sepulcher there by the sea,
  In her tomb by the sounding sea.

TO HELEN

Helen, thy beauty is to me
Like those Nicean barks of yore,
That gently, o'er a perfumed sea,
The weary, wayworn wanderer bore
5 To his own native shore.

On desperate seas long wont to roam,
Thy hyacinth hair, thy classic face,
Thy Naiad[1] airs, have brought me home
  To the Glory that was Greece
10 And the grandeur that was Rome.

Lo! in yon brilliant window niche
How statuelike I see thee stand,
The agate lamp within thy hand!
Ah, Psyche,[2] from the regions which
15 Are Holy Land!

---

1. *Naiad*, a nymph believed to live in and give life to lakes, rivers, springs, and fountains.
2. *Psyche*, in Greek mythology, the personification of the soul. Cupid fell in love with her and visited her at night. He forbade her to seek to learn who he was, but because her sisters told her he was a monster, she brought a lamp to the bedside one night when he was asleep.

THE SLEEPER

At midnight, in the month of June,
I stand beneath the mystic moon.
An opiate vapor, dewy, dim,
Exhales from out her golden rim,
5 And, softly dripping, drop by drop,
Upon the quiet mountain top,
Steals drowsily and musically
Into the universal valley.
The rosemary nods upon the grave;
10 The lily lolls upon the wave;
Wrapping the fog about its breast,
The ruin moulders into rest;
Looking like Lethe,[1] see! the lake
A conscious slumber seems to take,
15 And would not, for the world, awake.
All Beauty sleeps!—and lo! where lies
(Her casement open to the skies)
Irene, with her Destinies!

Oh, lady bright! can it be right—
20 This window open to the night?
The wanton airs, from the tree-top,
Laughingly through the lattice drop—
The bodiless airs, a wizard rout,
Flit through thy chamber in and out,
25 And wave the curtain canopy
So fitfully—so carefully—
Above the closed and fringed lid
'Neath which thy slumb'ring soul lies hid,
That, o'er the floor and down the wall,
30 Like ghosts the shadows rise and fall!
Oh, lady dear, hast thou no fear?
Why and what art thou dreaming here?
Sure thou art come o'er far-off seas,
A wonder to these garden trees!
35 Strange is thy pallor! strange thy dress!
Strange, above all, thy length of tress,
And this all solemn silentness!

The lady sleeps! Oh, may her sleep,
Which is enduring, so be deep!
40 Heaven have her in its sacred keep!
This chamber changed for one more holy,
This bed for one more melancholy,
I pray to God that she may lie

Forever with unopened eye,
45 While the dim sheeted ghosts go by!
My love, she sleeps! Oh, may her sleep,
As it is lasting, so be deep!
Soft may the worms about her creep!
Far in the forest, dim and old,
50 For her may some tall vault unfold—
Some vault that oft hath flung its black
And winged panels fluttering back,
Triumphant, o'er the crested palls,
Of her grand family funerals—
55 Some sepulchre, remote, alone,
Against whose portal she hath thrown,
In childhood, many an idle stone—
Some tomb from out whose sounding door
She ne'er shall force an echo more,
60 Thrilling to think, poor child of sin!
It was the dead who groaned within.

THE LAKE—TO—

In spring of youth it was my lot
To haunt of the wide world a spot
The which I could not love the less—
So lovely was the loneliness
5 Of a wild lake, with black rock bound,
And the tall pines that towered around.

But when the Night had thrown her pall
Upon that spot, as upon all,
And the mystic wind went by
10 Murmuring in melody—
Then—ah! then I would awake
To the terror of the lone lake.

Yet that terror was not fright,
But a tremulous delight—
15 A feeling not the jewelled mine
Could teach or bribe me to define—
Nor Love—although the Love were thine.

Death was in that poisonous wave,
And in its gulf a fitting grave
20 For him who thence could solace bring
To his lone imagining—
Whose solitary soul could make
An Eden of that dim lake.

---

1. *Lethe*, in Greek mythology, a river in Hades whose waters cause the souls to forget their pasts.

DISCUSSION

A case could be made that the aesthetic influences operative upon Edgar Allan Poe were the same ones that influenced Irving, Cooper, Bryant, and many other writers of the early nineteenth century. One can find in Poe's works innumerable instances where the influence of Romanticism —with its philosophy of Idealism and quest for "supernal beauty"—is indeed present; one need only look at the poems. But as Poe himself once replied when criticized early in his career for imitating too closely the macabre gothicism of the German Romantics, the terror he really wished to evoke was "not of Germany but of the soul."

This is not to deny that Poe wrote **gothic tales,** what we today would call horror stories. Many of his stories certainly fall into this category. A **gothic tale** is a story of the ghastly and horrible, replete with old, decaying castles, rattling chains, ghosts, zombies, mutilations, premature entombments, crypts, and other effects that we usually attribute to the supernatural. Both tales included in this anthology, particularly "The Black Cat" and—to a lesser degree— "The Fall of the House of Usher," can be understood on one level as gothic tales. But Poe's statement does diminish the claims of several of his critics, that his works reflected the literary influences of the day. Poe's tales and poems were so unusual, so unlike those of his predecessors, both in this country and in Europe, that it would be difficult to credit any current vogue as his source of inspiration.

There is another aspect of Poe's tales that recent literary criticism has uncovered. Certain of his tales can be understood on another level, as pre-Freudian studies in abnormal psychology. Indeed, much of the terror evoked in even "The Black Cat" may be attributed to the mad, depraved narrator's internal state of mind. After a while, we too begin to see the events of the story from his paranoid viewpoint. He is obsessed with the cat, unnaturally frightened by it, and ultimately driven by these illogical fears to commit the sadistic acts that destroy both his wife and himself.

"The Fall of the House of Usher" can also be understood on this level. Edward H. Davidson in his book *Poe: A Critical Study* has offered the following explanation of the tale. He interprets the tale as a detailed, symbolic account of the derangement and dissipation of an individual's personality. The house itself is the symbolic embodiment of this individual. The fissure in the house, noted by the narrator at the beginning of the story, represents an irreconcilable fracture in the individual's personality. Madeline Usher represents the portion of personality that we call the senses: hearing, seeing, touching, tasting, and smelling. Roderick Usher represents the mind or intellect. Through the action of the story, we learn that the intellect is attempting to detach itself from its more physically oriented twin. This is symbolized by Roderick's aversion to his own senses (". . . the odors of all flowers were oppressive; his eyes were tortured by even a faint light. . . ," etc.) and by his premature entombment of his sister Madeline. Living without her, that is, without the senses, Roderick begins to suffer an ". . . intolerable agitation of the soul." When Madeline returns from the crypt at the end of the tale to claim the maddened Roderick for death, the allegory is complete: the mind can neither live nor die without its counterpart, the physical senses. Immediately thereafter the house, symbol of a now deranged individual, crumbles into the rank tarn, leaving the narrator running in terror for his own sanity.

We know from the facts of Poe's biography that he indeed suffered from the conflicts detailed in both of these stories: that he had a perverse capacity for self-sabotage; that he too was an unstable person. Though it can be a dangerous precedent to attempt to always connect a man's biography with his work, in the case of Poe there seems good reason. By and large, the great works that he produced had no definite artistic milieu from which to spring. Instead, they appear to be the nightmarish outcroppings of this maladjusted, tortured genius.

FOR EXPLORATION

The Black Cat

1. What does a "black cat" connote? What associations do you make when you think of this animal?

2. Where is the narrator as he relates his tale?

3. Poe constructed "The Black Cat" in such a way that the reasons behind the events of the tale remain somewhat ambiguous. Are the events of the story based—as the narrator suggests—upon ". . . an ordinary succession of very natural causes and effects," or are they indeed caused by the supernatural? Be sure in your explanation to account for the following incidents: (a) the apparition of the first cat upon the burned wall; (b) the appearance of the gallowslike pattern upon the chest of the second cat; and (c) the discovery of the second cat behind the cellar wall.

4. Does the hero undo himself or is he betrayed by his cat? Explain.

5. The narrator tells us that ". . . perverseness is one of the primitive impulses of the human heart." Explain the meaning of this statement in the context of the tale. Write a brief essay of two or three paragraphs in which you argue the veracity of this statement. Be sure to support your argument with examples from the story and/or your own experience.

1. Part of Poe's fame rests with his ability to create mood by the use of connotative language. *(a)* Examine carefully the opening paragraph of the story and cite at least ten such words that help create mood. *(b)* From this evidence, what type of mood did Poe wish to convey?

2. Describe Roderick Usher. From what malady does he suffer? What strange sensitivities does he manifest?

3. Find the narrator's description of Roderick's picture. What event does it foreshadow?

4. The narrator tells us that Roderick's poem, "The Haunted Palace," told him something of Roderick's ". . . lofty reason upon her throne." What happens to this faculty at the conclusion of the poem? What event in the story does it foreshadow?

5. *(a)* What reason does Roderick give for the immediate entombment of Madeline Usher? *(b)* What hint does Poe give the reader that Madeline may still be alive?

6. What purpose does the narrator's reading of the "Mad Trist" serve in the development of the tale? Is it effective?

7. Explain how Roderick Usher is a "victim to the terrors he had anticipated."

8. In the third paragraph of the tale, Poe identifies the Usher family with what edifice? How is this borne out in the conclusion of the tale?

Poems

The magic which Poe's poetry has exerted over several generations of readers lies principally in its matchless melody. Some of the devices which Poe used to haunt the ear and to create a mood appropriate to his theme will add to your appreciation.

Rhyme. The **end rhyme,** or rhyme at the end of a line, is only one of the rhyming devices Poe has used. Far more unusual and elaborate is his use of **internal rhyme** within the lines. Read the last stanza of "Annabel Lee" slowly. Notice that *beams* in line 34 rhymes with *dreams* at its end, that the word *rise* in line 36 rhymes with *eyes* at the end of the line, and that *night-tide* and *side* in line 38 rhyme with each other and with *bride* at the end of line 39.

Alliteration, the repetition of the initial sound of two or more closely related words or accented syllables, is frequently used by Poe. Again referring to the last stanza of "Annabel Lee," notice the alliterative effect of *sepulcher* and *sea* in line 40, and of *sounding* and *sea* in line 41.

Assonance, the resemblance in the sound of the vowel in two or more accented syllables, adds greatly to the musical effect of the poetry. The last stanza of "Annabel Lee" is an excellent example of how Poe mingles assonance and internal rhyme. The long *e* sound of the internally rhymed words *beams* and *dreams* (line 34) is repeated in *me* in the same line, in *Lee* (lines 35 and 37), in *feel* (line 36), and in *sea* (lines 40 and 41). Also, the long *i* sound of the internally rhymed words *rise* and *eyes* (line 36), *night-tide* and *side* (line 38), and *bride* (line 39) is repeated in *bright* (line 36), in *lie* (line 38), in *my* and *life* (line 39), and in *by* (lines 38, 40, and 41). Notice that the *o* sound in *moon* (line 34) is repeated in *tomb* (line 41) and is closely related to the *o* sound in *beautiful* (lines 35 and 37).

Repetition, the deliberate repeating of a word or phrase, is particularly striking in Poe's poetry. Notice, for example, how Poe has repeated in "Annabel Lee" the phrase, *kingdom by the sea* (lines 2, 8, 14, 20, and 24). Poe's use of *love* in slightly varied phrases (lines 6, 9, 11, and 27) also achieves a subtle effect of repetition.

Choose a stanza of "The Sleeper" or "To Helen" that you find exceptionally musical and prepare to read it aloud to the class. Be ready to point out whatever examples of rhyme, alliteration, assonance, or repetition it may contain. Would you agree that "To Helen" produces a more restrained effect than "Annabel Lee" and "The Sleeper"? Why?

Edgar Allan Poe 1809/1849

The persisting picture of Edgar Allan Poe is one of a romantic eccentric. In reality, he was more insecure than haunted, his life more destitute than mad.

Orphaned before he was three, Poe was taken into the home of John Allan, a wealthy Richmond, Virginia merchant. When Poe declined an interest in mercantiling and spoke of a literary career, Mr. Allan was contemptuous. After many violent quarrels Poe left home, resolved to live off his writing. But he never quite succeeded.

He married his cousin Virginia Clemm and also supported Virginia's mother. Meeting only limited success with his stories and poetry, Poe took on the editorship of a series of magazines. He worked diligently, vastly increasing circulation, yet he was not paid well. His editorial positions were followed and sometimes interrupted by unstable periods of the deepest despair.

An important force in the literary world for his critical writings, he was not well known otherwise until the publication of his poem "The Raven." But fame did little to alleviate his poverty. Two winters later Poe was ill, withdrawn, and unable to work. Virginia died of tuberculosis and with her death the instability which haunted Poe intensified. Though his last years were not without periods of achievement, his paranoia increased. He disappeared one day to be found later, battered and drunk. After four days of delirium he died.

EARLY NATIONAL PERIOD

Then and Now

The early national period of the new United States of America was a period of development, growth, experimentation, and search. Above all, it was a time of extension of the American nation and the American identity. Thomas Jefferson served as President of the young country during some of the most critical of these early years (1800–1808), and with one stroke of the pen increased the physical dimensions of the nation by about 140 percent in the Louisiana Purchase (1803). Out of this area, for which Jefferson paid Napoleon of France the sum of fifteen million dollars, a total of thirteen additional states of the Union were eventually carved—those lying all along the Mississippi basin.

In expanding the country to the west, Jefferson pointed the way of its growth, both physical and psychic. The knowledge that there was always some virgin land lying out West to explore and settle, especially if the going got too rough in the East, shaped the lives and dreams of countless generations of Americans. To be able to "light out" for the "territory" (as Huckleberry Finn suggests at the end of his *Adventures*) was to be able always to begin over again, to

follow failure with a new hope of success, to be astonishingly optimistic in the middle of incredible deprivation and hardship. That vast wilderness and frontier to the west, which was ultimately to be pushed to the waters of the Pacific, had much to do with determining the nature of the developing country and with forming the character of its people.

Also under Jefferson's administration, the famed Lewis and Clark expedition took place, in effect opening up for travel and settlement the far West. The expedition, led by Meriwether Lewis and William Clark, pushed its explorations all the way to the Pacific Ocean, receiving invaluable help in one critical segment of the journey from an Indian woman guide, Sacajawea (the Bird Woman). The expedition lasted from 1803 to 1806, and its conclusion marked the beginning of the great movement of the people west— trappers, traders, settlers on foot, by Conestoga wagon, on river barges and boats. At first a trickle, the movement became a flood and was to last through the nineteenth century and beyond. But in the 1890's, when the Census Bureau officially declared the frontier closed (because of the population density of the western states), the movement had finally ceased to have the force and meaning it once had had for the country.

As the nation grew in size and ambition, many observers worried about its spirit and soul, especially as tallied by its arts, including literature. An English critic, Sydney Smith, wrote in *The Edinburgh Review* in 1819: "In the four quarters of the globe, who reads an American book? or goes to an American play? or looks at an American picture?" The questions stung the national pride, and American writers fretted at the difficulties they confronted—and tried harder.

The efforts paid off, for during this period some American writers did begin to attract notice abroad, and their books drew attention and praise from important foreign literary figures. Although English literary models were still admired and followed (especially novelist Sir Walter Scott and poet William Wordsworth), the American writers turned to the American scene and civilization, and found their materials in the culture and history, the lore and landscape of their native land. Irving, Cooper, Bryant, and Poe all found audiences in foreign lands. Much of the interest, clearly, was in reading about life in a new, experimental country which appeared remote and exotic to most Europeans. But the American writers were praised by critics as well as by plain readers, and observers saw this recognition as a sign of the maturing of American culture.

One of the ironies of American literary history is that at least two of the writers of this period have had greater critical acclaim abroad than at home. Poe was early translated into French, and many important French poets praised and imitated him, and his critical reputation to this day is higher in France than in America (but, of course, Poe has always been popular and widely read in his own country). Cooper, too, has been highly praised abroad, not so much by critics, however, as by European youths whose ideas of America have been shaped by Cooper's novels about American frontiersmen and Indians. The Scandinavian countries have especially been fond of reading Cooper, particularly the Leatherstocking Tales (including *The Deerslayer*).

Perhaps one of the reasons Cooper's novels have not been as popular at home is that Americans already know the reality of their country remarkably well, and know that what they will find in Cooper will not be that reality or any other that bears much relationship to the past, but rather a myth largely of Cooper's and his countrymen's creation. It is difficult to say when the native disillusion with Cooper set in, but as far back as the late nineteenth century, Mark Twain wrote a critical piece on him that sums up fairly well—and with telling humor—a good many of his deficiencies. Twain took as his primary target Cooper's *Deerslayer*.

from

Fenimore Cooper's

LITERARY OFFENSES

Samuel Clemens

The Pathfinder and *The Deerslayer* stand at the head of Cooper's novels as artistic creations. There are others of his works which contain parts as perfect as are to be found in these, and scenes even more thrilling. Not one can be compared with either of them as a finished whole.

The defects in both of these tales are comparatively slight. They were pure works of art.—*Prof. Lounsbury.*

The five tales reveal an extraordinary fulness of invention.

. . . One of the very greatest characters in fiction, Natty Bumppo. . . .

The craft of the woodsman, the tricks of the trapper, all the delicate art of the forest, were familiar to Cooper from his youth up.—*Prof. Brander Matthews.*

Cooper is the greatest artist in the domain of romantic fiction yet produced by America.—*Wilkie Collins.*

It seems to me that it was far from right for the Professor of English Literature in Yale, the Professor of English Literature in Columbia, and Wilkie Collins to deliver opinions on Cooper's literature without having read some of it. It would have been much more decorous to keep silent and let persons talk who have read Cooper.

Cooper's art has some defects. In one place in *Deerslayer,* and in the restricted space of two-thirds of a page, Cooper has scored 114 offenses against literary art out of a possible 115. It breaks the record.

There are nineteen rules governing literary art in the domain of romantic fiction—some say twenty-two. In *Deerslayer* Cooper violated eighteen of them. These eighteen require:

1. That a tale shall accomplish something and arrive somewhere. But the *Deerslayer* tale accomplishes nothing and arrives in the air.

2. They require that the episodes of a tale shall

From SELECTED SHORTER WRITINGS OF MARK TWAIN, edited by Walter Blair. Copyright 1895, 1897 by North American Review.

be necessary parts of the tale, and shall help to develop it. But as the *Deerslayer* tale is not a tale, and accomplishes nothing and arrives nowhere, the episodes have no rightful place in the work, since there was nothing for them to develop.

3. They require that the personages in a tale shall be alive, except in the case of corpses, and that always the reader shall be able to tell the corpses from the others. But this detail has often been overlooked in the *Deerslayer* tale.

4. They require that the personages in a tale, both dead and alive, shall exhibit a sufficient excuse for being there. But this detail also has been overlooked in the *Deerslayer* tale.

5. They require that when the personages of a tale deal in conversation, the talk shall sound like human talk, and be talk such as human beings would be likely to talk in the given circumstances, and have a discoverable meaning, also a discoverable purpose, and a show of relevancy, and remain in the neighborhood of the subject in hand, and be interesting to the reader, and help out the tale, and stop when the people cannot think of anything more to say. But this requirement has been ignored from the beginning of the *Deerslayer* tale to the end of it.

6. They require that when the author describes the character of a personage in his tale, the conduct and conversation of that personage shall justify said description. But this law gets little or no attention in the *Deerslayer* tale, as Natty Bumppo's case will amply prove.

7. They require that when a personage talks like an illustrated, gilt-edged, tree-calf, hand-tooled, seven-dollar Friendship's Offering in the beginning of a paragraph, he shall not talk like a negro minstrel in the end of it. But this rule is flung down and danced upon in the *Deerslayer* tale.

8. They require that crass stupidities shall not be played upon the reader as "the craft of the woodsman, the delicate art of the forest," by either the author or the people in the tale. But this rule is persistently violated in the *Deerslayer* tale.

9. They require that the personages of a tale shall confine themselves to possibilities and let miracles alone; or, if they venture a miracle, the author must so plausibly set it forth as to make it look possible and reasonable. But these rules are not respected in the *Deerslayer* tale.

10. They require that the author shall make the reader feel a deep interest in the personages of his tale and in their fate; and that he shall make the reader love the good people in the tale and hate the bad ones. But the reader of the *Deerslayer* tale dislikes the good people in it, is indifferent to the others, and wishes they would all get drowned together.

11. They require that the characters in a tale shall be so clearly defined that the reader can tell beforehand what each will do in a given emergency. But in the *Deerslayer* tale this rule is vacated.

In addition to these large rules there are some little ones. These require that the author shall

12. *Say* what he is proposing to say, not merely come near it.

13. Use the right word, not its second cousin.

14. Eschew surplusage.

15. Not omit necessary details.

16. Avoid slovenliness of form.

17. Use good grammar.

18. Employ a simple and straightforward style.

Even these seven are coldly and persistently violated in the *Deerslayer* tale.

Cooper's gift in the way of invention was not a rich endowment; but such as it was he liked to work it, he was pleased with the effects, and indeed he did some quite sweet things with it. In his little box of stage-properties he kept six or eight cunning devices, tricks, artifices for his savages and woodsmen to deceive and circumvent each other with, and he was never so happy as when he was working these innocent things and seeing them go. A favorite one was to make a moccasined person tread in the tracks of the moccasined enemy, and thus hide his own trail. Cooper wore out barrels and barrels of moccasins in working that trick. Another stage-property that he pulled out of his box pretty frequently was his broken twig. He prized his broken twig above all the rest of his effects, and worked it the hardest. It is a restful chapter in any book of his when somebody doesn't step on a dry twig and alarm all the reds and whites for two hundred yards around. Every time a Cooper person is in peril, and absolute silence is worth four dollars a minute, he is sure to step on a dry twig. There may be a hundred handier things to step on, but that wouldn't satisfy Cooper. Cooper requires him to turn out and find a dry twig; and if he can't do it, go and borrow one. In fact, the Leather Stocking Series ought to have been called the Broken Twig Series. . . .

RENAISSANCE

MEDITATION BY THE SEA ABOUT 1855, ANONYMOUS—M. AND M. KAROLIK COLLECTION, COURTESY, THE MUSEUM OF FINE ARTS, BOSTON

TRANSCENDENTALISM

Though closely related to the English and European Romantic movement (see *Discussion:* Bartram, page 75C; Bryant, page 103C) of the late eighteenth and early nineteenth centuries, the philosophy called *Transcendentalism* that gained a large following in New England during the early 1830's was not merely an American restatement of Romantic ideas. Rather, it was the combining of these ideas with existing elements of American belief. The result was a philosophical movement in many ways similar to that which had occurred in England and Germany, but at the same time different. The Romantic movement, in holding with the individual worth and goodness of humanity, glorifying the pleasures of communion with nature, condemning society for its distracting and corrupting materialism, and urging individual freedom of expression—freedom from the rules and constraints of earlier philosophies and theologies— appealed to a country beginning to chafe at the restrictions of an already declining Puritanism.

The term *Transcendentalism* is not itself an invention of the New England Transcendentalists; the German philosopher Immanuel Kant (1724–1804) had used it in his writing. To its New England advocates the term came to embody the central idea of their philosophy: that there is some knowledge of reality, or truth, that man grasps not through logic or the laws of science but through the intuition of his divine intellect. Because of this inherent, extra-intellectual ability, the Transcendentalists believed that each person should follow the sway of his own beliefs and ideas, however divergent from the social norm they might be. They believed that the individual's intuitive response to any given situation would be the right thing for him to do. Closely related to this idea is that of the integrity of the individual, the belief that each person is inherently good, capable of making his own decisions, and worthy of the respect of every other human being. These ideas found a sympathetic response among a people who had long held in high regard the democratic and individualistic principles of the early settler, statesman, and citizen.

Inevitably, these ideas were to clash with the doctrines of organized religion. An earlier group of New England intellectuals broke away from Puritanism and founded the Unitarian Church during the late eighteenth century. Their split with the established church was in a large part due to the intellectual and commercial trends of the age. In a day when commerce and science had become predominant, where material comfort and social mobility were becoming increasingly accessible to more and more people, the old religion—Puritanism—must have indeed seemed irrelevant. By the 1830's the Unitarians, yesterday's rebels, had become Boston's establishment, dominating the city's intellectual centers, both the church and Harvard University.

Ironically, Emerson as well as many other early Transcendentalists began their careers as divinity students, studying at the latter institution for the Unitarian ministry. Many of these people were, in fact, the children of influential members of the Unitarian church. The former rebels, Boston's economic, social, political, and cultural elite, found themselves—by the early 1830's—embroiled in yet another intellectual insurrection, though this time it was they who were under attack.

Transcendentalists like Emerson did not limit their attacks solely to questions of theology, but went beyond church issues to the very fabric of society itself. To them, sterility in religion had its analogues in both public and private life. They believed that rationalism, the philosophy from which modern science had sprung, denied the profound sense of mystery that these thinkers found in both nature and humanity. They felt that current thought had reduced God to a watchmaker who once having built and wound the Universe now sat back and detachedly observed. The individual in this scheme was likewise reduced, as Thoreau said, "to a cog" or wheel in this universal machine. Social conformity, materialism, and what they believed to be a lack of moral commitment angered these young men and women. In addition to their writings, their beliefs found expression in various movements: feminism, abolitionism, utopianism and communalism, and even the beginnings of labor unionism.

In their opposition to the rationalistic tendencies of their age, the Transcendentalists adopted a type of philosophy best termed *Idealism*. Actually, Transcendentalism incorporates elements from many philosophies and religions; Neo-Platonism, Puritan mysticism, Hinduism, Pantheism, and European Romanticism, to name but a few. Unlike the rationalists, idealists believe that material objects do not have a real existence of their own. Rather, these objects are diffused parts or aspects of God, the Over-Soul. Material objects therefore mirror or reflect an ideal world. Thus, by contemplating objects in nature, the individual can transcend this world and discover union with God and the Ideal. The key innate quality used by the individual to achieve this state of union is his intuition. Intuition is granted every soul at birth. Tangential to this belief is reincarnation, for at death Idealists believe that the individual's soul returns to its source, God, where it may be again dispatched to this world as another life.

Transcendentalism greatly influenced the course of American literature, affecting the writings of both those who adhered to its principles and those who reacted against them.

Ralph Waldo Emerson

1803/1882

Speak your latent conviction, and it shall be the universal sense.

Society everywhere is in conspiracy against the manhood of every one of its members.

Nothing is at last sacred but the integrity of your own mind.

My life is for itself and not for a spectacle.

A foolish consistency is the hobgoblin of little minds,   Adored by little statesmen and philosophers and divines.

An institution is the lengthened shadow of one man.

Life only avails, not the having lived.

Insist on yourself; never imitate.

The civilized man has built a coach, but has lost the use of his feet.

FABLE

The mountain and the squirrel
Had a quarrel,
And the former called the latter "Little Prig;"
Bun replied,
5   "You are doubtless very big;
But all sorts of things and weather
Must be taken in together,
To make up a year
And a sphere.
10   And I think it no disgrace
To occupy my place.
If I'm not so large as you,
You are not so small as I,
And not half so spry.
15   I'll not deny you make
A very pretty squirrel track;
Talents differ; all is well and wisely put;
If I cannot carry forests on my back,
Neither can you crack a nut."

from "NATURE"

I BECOME A TRANSPARENT EYEBALL

*Crossing a bare common, in snow puddles, at twilight, under a clouded sky,
  without having in my thoughts any occurrence of special good fortune, I have
  enjoyed a perfect exhilaration.
I am glad to the brink of fear.
In the woods, too, a man casts off his years, as the snake his slough, and at
  what period soever of life is always a child.
In the woods is perpetual youth.
Within these plantations of God, a decorum and sanctity reign, a perennial
  festival is dressed, and the guest sees not how he should tire of them
  in a thousand years.
In the woods, we return to reason and faith.
There I feel that nothing can befall me in life,—no disgrace, no calamity
  (leaving me my eyes), which nature cannot repair.
Standing on the bare ground,—my head bathed by the blithe air and uplifted
  into infinite space,—all mean egotism vanishes.*

*I become a transparent eyeball;
  I am nothing;
    I see all;
        the currents of the Universal Being circulate through me;
          I am part or parcel of God.*

*The name of the nearest friend sounds then foreign and accidental: to be
  brothers, to be acquaintances, master or servant, is then a trifle and a
  disturbance.
I am the lover of uncontained and immortal beauty.
In the wilderness, I find something more dear and connate than in streets
  or villages.
In the tranquil landscape, and especially in the distant line of the horizon,
  man beholds somewhat as beautiful as his own nature.*

from "SELF - RELIANCE"

NATIONAL PORTRAIT GALLERY

A NONCONFORMIST

WHOSO would be a man, must be a nonconformist. He who would gather immortal palms must not be hindered by the name of goodness, but must explore if it be goodness. Nothing is at last sacred but the integrity of your own mind. Absolve you to yourself, and you shall have the suffrage of the world. I remember an answer which when quite young I was prompted to make to a valued adviser who was wont to importune me with the dear old doctrines of the church. On my saying, "What have I to do with the sacredness of traditions, if I live wholly from within?" my friend suggested,—"But these impulses may be from below, not from above." I replied, "They do not seem to me to be such; but if I am the Devil's child, I will live then from the Devil." No law can be sacred to me but that of my nature. Good and bad are but names very readily transferable to that or this; the only right is what is after my constitution; the only wrong what is against it. A man is to carry himself in the presence of all opposition as if every thing were titular and ephemeral but he. I am ashamed to think how easily we capitulate to badges and names, to large societies and dead institutions. Every decent and well-spoken individual affects and sways me more than is right. I ought to go upright and vital, and speak the rude truth in all ways. If malice and vanity wear the coat of philanthropy, shall that pass? If an angry bigot assumes this bountiful cause of Abolition, and comes to me with his last news from Barbadoes,[1] why should I not say to him, "Go love thy infant; love thy wood-chopper; be good-natured and modest; have that grace; and never varnish your hard, un-charitable ambition with this incredible tenderness for black folk a thousand miles off. Thy love afar is spite at home." Rough and graceless would be such greeting, but truth is handsomer than the affectation of love. Your goodness must have some edge to it,—else it is none. The doctrine of hatred must be preached, as the counteraction of the doctrine of love, when that pules and whines. I shun father and mother and wife and brother when my genius calls me. I would write on the lintels of the door-post, *Whim.* I hope it is somewhat better than whim at last, but we cannot spend the day in explanation. Expect me not to show cause why I seek or why I exclude company. Then again, do not tell me, as a good man did today, of my obligation to put all poor men in good situations. Are they *my* poor? I tell thee, thou foolish philanthropist, that I grudge the dollar, the dime, the cent I give to such men as do not belong to me and to whom I do not belong. There is a class of persons to whom by all spiritual affinity I am bought and sold; for them I will go to prison if need be; but your miscellaneous popular charities; the education at college of fools; the building of meeting-houses to the vain end to which many now stand; alms to sots, and the thousand-fold Relief Societies;—though I confess with shame I sometimes succumb and give the dollar, it is a wicked dollar, which by and by I shall have the manhood to withhold. ☐

---

1. *Barbadoes.* Slaves had arrived in America from Barbadoes in the West Indies where they had been brought from Africa. The British abolished slavery in the West Indies in 1833.

TRAVELING

It is for want of self-culture that the superstition of Traveling, whose idols are Italy, England, Egypt, retains its fascination for all educated Americans. They who made England, Italy, or Greece venerable in the imagination, did so by sticking fast where they were, like an axis of the earth. In manly hours we feel that duty is our place. The soul is no traveler; the wise man stays at home, and when his necessities, his duties, on any occasion call him from his house, or into foreign lands, he is at home still and shall make men sensible by the expression of his countenance that he goes, the missionary of wisdom and virtue, and visits cities and men like a sovereign and not like an interloper or a valet.

I have no churlish objection to the circumnavigation of the globe for the purposes of art, of study, and benevolence, so that the man is first domesticated, or does not go abroad with the hope of finding somewhat greater than he knows. He who travels to be amused, or to get somewhat which he does not carry, travels away from himself, and grows old even in youth among old things. In Thebes, in Palmyra,[1] his will and mind have become old and dilapidated as they. He carries ruins to ruins.

Traveling is a fool's paradise. Our first journeys discover to us the indifference of places. At home I dream that at Naples, at Rome, I can be intoxicated with beauty and lose my sadness. I pack my trunk, embrace my friends, embark on the sea and at last wake up in Naples, and there beside me is the stern fact, the sad self, unrelenting, identical, that I fled from. I seek the Vatican and the palaces. I affect to be intoxicated with sights and suggestions, but I am not intoxicated. My giant goes with me wherever I go. □

---

1. *Thebes . . . Palmyra*, ancient cities. Thebes was the capital of ancient Egypt. Palmyra, in Syria, was known as the city of Tadmor in the Bible and was said to have been founded by Solomon.

RELIANCE ON PROPERTY

And so the reliance on Property, including the reliance on governments which protect it, is the want of self-reliance. Men have looked away from themselves and at things so long that they have come to esteem the religious, learned and civil institutions as guards of property, and they deprecate assaults on these, because they feel them to be assaults on property. They measure their esteem of each other by what each has, and not by what each is. But a cultivated man becomes ashamed of his property, out of new respect for his nature. Especially he hates what he has if he see that it is accidental,—came to him by inheritance, or gift, or crime; then he feels that it is not having; it does not belong to him, has no root in him and merely lies there because no revolution or no robber takes it away. But that which a man is, does always by necessity acquire; and what the man acquires, is living property, which does not wait the beck of rulers, or mobs, or revolutions, or fire, or storm, or bankruptcies, but perpetually renews itself wherever the man breathes. "Thy lot or portion of life," said the Caliph Ali,[1] "is seeking after thee; therefore be at rest from seeking after it." Our dependence on these foreign goods leads us to our slavish respect for numbers. The political parties meet in numerous conventions; the greater the concourse and with each new uproar of announcement, The delegation from Essex! The Democrats from New Hampshire! The Whigs of Maine! the young patriot feels himself stronger than before by a new thousand of eyes and arms. In like manner the reformers summon conventions and vote and resolve in multitude. Not so, O friends! will the God deign to enter

---

1. *Caliph Ali*, the fourth successor of Mohammed as civil and spiritual leader of the Moslems. A collection of his sayings had been translated into English in 1832.

and inhabit you, but by a method precisely the reverse. It is only as a man puts off all foreign support and stands alone that I see him to be strong and to prevail. He is weaker by every recruit to his banner. Is not a man better than a town? Ask nothing of men, and, in the endless mutation, thou only firm column must presently appear the upholder of all that surrounds thee. He who knows that power is inborn, that he is weak because he has looked for good out of him and elsewhere, and, so perceiving, throws himself unhesitatingly on his thought, instantly rights himself, stands in the erect position, commands his limbs, works miracles; just as a man who stands on his feet is stronger than a man who stands on his head. □

from
"THE AMERICAN SCHOLAR"

MAN THINKING

IT is one of those fables which out of an unknown antiquity convey an unlooked-for wisdom, that the gods, in the beginning, divided Man into men, that he might be more helpful to himself; just as the hand was divided into fingers, the better to answer its end.

The old fable covers a doctrine ever new and sublime; that there is One Man,—present to all particular men only partially, or through one faculty; and that you must take the whole society to find the whole man. Man is not a farmer, or a professor, or an engineer, but he is all. Man is priest, and scholar, and statesman, and producer, and soldier. In the *divided* or social state these functions are parcelled out to individuals, each of whom aims to do his stint of the joint work, whilst each other performs his. The fable implies that the individual, to possess himself, must sometimes return from his own labor to embrace all the other laborers. But, unfortunately, this original unit, this fountain of power, has been so distributed to multitudes, has been so minutely subdivided and peddled out, that it is spilled into drops, and cannot be gathered. The state of society is one in which the members have suffered amputation from the trunk, and strut about so many walking monsters,—a good finger, a neck, a stomach, an elbow, but never a man.

Man is thus metamorphosed into a thing, into many things. The planter, who is Man sent out into the field to gather food, is seldom cheered by any idea of the true dignity of his ministry. He sees his bushel and his cart, and nothing beyond, and sinks into the farmer, instead of Man on the farm. The tradesman scarcely ever gives an ideal worth to his work, but is ridden by the routine of his craft, and the soul is subject to dollars. The priest becomes a form; the attorney a statute-book; the mechanic a machine; the sailor a rope of the ship.

In this distribution of functions the scholar is the delegated intellect. In the right state he is *Man Thinking*. In the degenerate state, when the victim of society, he tends to become a mere thinker, or still worse, the parrot of other men's thinking.

In this view of him, as Man Thinking, the theory of his office is contained. Him Nature solicits with all her placid, all her monitory pictures; him the past instructs; him the future invites. Is not indeed every man a student, and do not all things exist for the student's behoof? And, finally, is not the true scholar the only true master? □

from "THE POET"

THE SUBLIME VISION

IT is a secret which every intellectual man quickly learns, that beyond the energy of his possessed and conscious intellect he is capable of a new energy (as of an intellect doubled on itself), by abandonment to the nature of things; that beside his privacy of power as an individual man, there is a great public power on which he can draw, by unlocking, at all risks, his human doors, and suffering the ethereal tides to roll and circulate through him; then he is caught up into the life of the Universe, his speech is thunder, his thought is law, and his words are universally intelligible as the plants and animals. The poet knows that he speaks adequately then only when he speaks somewhat wildly, or "with the flower of the mind"; not with the intellect used as an organ, but with the intellect released from all service and suffered to take its direction from its celestial life; or as the ancients were wont to express themselves, not with intellect alone but with the intellect inebriated by nectar. As the traveler who has lost his way throws his reins on his horse's neck and trusts to the instinct of the animal to find his road, so must we do with the divine animal who carries us through this world. For if in any manner we can stimulate this instinct, new passages are opened for us into nature; the mind flows into and through things hardest and highest, and the metamorphosis is possible.

This is the reason why bards love wine, mead, narcotics, coffee, tea, opium, the fumes of sandalwood and tobacco, or whatever other procurers of animal exhilaration. All men avail themselves of such means as they can, to add this extraordinary power to their normal powers; and to this end they prize conversation, music, pictures, sculpture, dancing, theaters, traveling, war, mobs, fires, gaming, politics, or love, or science, or animal intoxication,—which are several coarser or finer *quasi*-mechanical substitutes for the true nectar, which is the ravishment of the intellect by coming nearer to the fact. These are auxiliaries to the centrifugal tendency of a man, to his passage out into free space, and they help him to escape the custody of that body in which he is pent up, and of that jail-yard of individual relations in which he is enclosed. Hence a great number of such as were professionally expressers of Beauty, as painters, poets, musicians and actors, have been more than others wont to lead a life of pleasure and indulgence; all but the few who received the true nectar; and, as it was a spurious mode of attaining freedom, as it was an emancipation not into the heavens but into the freedom of baser places, they were punished for that advantage they won, by a dissipation and deterioration. But never can any advantage be taken of nature by a trick. The spirit of the world, the great calm presence of the Creator, comes not forth to the sorceries of opium or of wine. The sublime vision comes to the pure and simple soul in a clean and chaste body. That is not an inspiration, which we owe to narcotics, but some counterfeit excitement and fury. Milton[1] says that the lyric poet may drink wine and live generously, but the epic poet, he who shall sing of the gods and their descent unto men, must drink water out of a wooden bowl. For poetry is not "Devil's wine," but God's wine. It is with this as it is with toys. We fill the hands and nurseries of our children with all manner of dolls, drums and horses; withdrawing their eyes from the plain face and sufficing objects of nature, the sun and moon, the animals, the water and stones, which should be their toys. So the poet's habit of living should be set on a key so low that the common influences should delight him. His cheerfulness should be the gift of the sunlight; the air should suffice for his inspiration, and he should be tipsy with water. That spirit which suffices quiet hearts, which seems to come forth to such from every dry knoll of sere grass, from every pine stump and half-imbedded stone on which the dull March sun shines, comes forth to the poor and hungry, and such as are of simple taste. If thou fill thy brain with Boston and New York, with fashion and covetousness, and wilt stimulate thy jaded senses with wine and French coffee, thou shalt find no radiance of wisdom in the lonely waste of the pine woods. □

1. *Milton,* John Milton (1608–1674), English poet.

EACH AND ALL

Little thinks, in the field, yon red-cloaked clown,[1]
Of thee from the hill-top looking down;
The heifer that lows in the upland farm,
Far-heard, lows not thine ear to charm;
The sexton, tolling the bell at noon,
Dreams not that great Napoleon
Stops his horse, and lists with delight,
Whilst his files sweep round yon Alpine height;
Nor knowest thou what argument
Thy life to thy neighbor's creed has lent.
All are needed by each one;
Nothing is fair or good alone.

I thought the sparrow's note from heaven,
Singing at dawn on the alder bough;
I brought him home, in his nest, at even;[2]
He sings the song, but it cheers not now,
For I did not bring home the river and sky;
He sang to my ear, they sang to my eye.

The delicate shells lay on the shore;
The bubbles of the latest wave
Fresh pearls to their enamel gave,
And the bellowing of the savage sea
Greeted their safe escape to me.
I wiped away the weeds and foam,
I fetched my sea-born treasures home;
But the poor, unsightly, noisome things
Had left their beauty on the shore
With the sun and the sand and the wild uproar.

The lover watched his graceful maid,
As 'mid the virgin train she strayed,
Nor knew her beauty's best attire
Was woven still by the snow-white choir.
At last she came to his hermitage,
Like the bird from the woodlands to the cage—
The gay enchantment was undone;
A gentle wife, but fairy none.

Then I said, "I covet Truth;
Beauty is unripe childhood's cheat—
I leave it behind with the games of youth."
As I spoke, beneath my feet
The ground-pine curled its pretty wreath,
Running over the club-moss burrs;
I inhaled the violet's breath;
Around me stood the oaks and firs;

Pine cones and acorns lay on the ground;
Over me soared the eternal sky,
Full of light and deity;
Again I saw, again I heard,
The rolling river, the morning bird;—
Beauty through my senses stole,
I yielded myself to the perfect whole.

BRAHMA[1]

If the red slayer think he slays,
    Or if the slain think he is slain,
They know not well the subtle ways
    I keep, and pass, and turn again.

Far or forgot to me is near;
    Shadow and sunlight are the same;
The vanished gods to me appear;
    And one to me are shame and fame.

They reckon ill who leave me out;
    When me they fly, I am the wings;
I am the doubter and the doubt,
    And I the hymn the Brahmin[2] sings.

The strong gods pine for my abode,
    And pine in vain the sacred Seven;[3]
But thou, meek lover of the good!
    Find me, and turn thy back on heaven.

EACH AND ALL 1. *clown*, a rustic or yokel.
2. *at even*, at evening time.
BRAHMA 1. *Brahma*, according to Hindu belief, the supreme soul of the universe. Brahma is illimitable, timeless, formless.
2. *Brahmin*, a member of the highest, priestly caste in the Hindu religion.
3. *sacred Seven*, the seven most revered saints in the Brahmin's religion.

DAYS

Daughters of Time, the hypocritic Days,
Muffled and dumb like barefoot dervishes,
And marching single in an endless file,
Bring diadems and fagots in their hands.
5 To each they offer gifts after his will,
Bread, kingdoms, stars, and sky that holds them all.

I, in my pleached garden, watched the pomp,
Forgot my morning wishes, hastily
Took a few herbs and apples, and the Day
10 Turned and departed silent. I, too late,
Under her solemn fillet saw the scorn.

TERMINUS[1]

It is time to be old,
To take in sail:—
The god of bounds,
Who sets to seas a shore,
5 Came to me in his fatal rounds,
And said: 'No more!
No farther shoot
Thy broad ambitious branches, and thy root.
Fancy departs: no more invent;
10 Contract thy firmament
To compass of a tent.
There's not enough for this and that,
Make thy option which of two;
Economize the failing river,
15 Not the less revere the Giver,
Leave the many and hold the few.
Timely wise accept the terms,
Soften the fall with wary foot;
A little while
20 Still plan and smile,
And,—fault of novel germs,—

Mature the unfallen fruit.
Curse, if thou wilt, thy sires,
Bad husbands of their fires,
25 Who, when they gave thee breath,
Failed to bequeath
The needful sinew stark as once,
The Baresark marrow to thy bones,
But left a legacy of ebbing veins,
30 Inconstant heat and nerveless reins,—
Amid the Muses, left thee deaf and dumb,
Amid the gladiators, halt and numb.'

As the bird trims her to the gale,
I trim myself to the storm of time,
35 I man the rudder, reef the sail,
Obey the voice at eve obeyed at prime:
'Lowly faithful, banish fear,
Right onward drive unharmed;
The port, well worth the cruise, is near,
40 And every wave is charmed.'

TERMINUS **1.** *Terminus*, in Roman mythology, the guardian of boundaries.

DISCUSSION

Fable

A **fable** is a short tale meant to teach a lesson; the lesson is usually summarized in the **moral** (the inner meaning or teaching of the fable). Fables need not be written in verse, and although the characters in most fables are talking animals they are not invariably so. Sometimes the characters are humans and sometimes inanimate objects.

FOR EXPLORATION

1. Which lines in the poem state the moral of this fable? If one were to adopt the sentiment expressed in the moral as his own philosophy, what would be his attitude toward both others and the world around him? If he were to attempt to adhere to this philosophy in his daily life, with what practices and institutions in present-day society might he clash?
2. What characteristics does the fable form have in common with the aphorisms and epigrams of Franklin's *The Way to Wealth*, page 59C?

CREATIVE RESPONSE

Those interested in the fable might read the works of Aesop and Jean de La Fontaine, then write an original fable to present to the class for discussion.

DISCUSSION

selections from the essays

Throughout his life Emerson recorded his daily thoughts and experiences in a series of notebooks. He referred to these journals when preparing a lecture or writing a poem or essay, often incorporating whole passages from them into the new text. The first selection, though part of the essay "Nature," was originally a journal entry. The other selections also contain many ideas first recorded in the notebooks.

FOR EXPLORATION

I Become a Transparent Eyeball

1. The first sentence in the selection gives the background or the circumstances under which the author becomes "glad to the brink of fear." Given the information in the first sentence, is it possible to state any logical reasons for his overwhelming exhilaration?

2. According to Emerson, where is one most likely to undergo the experience being described? Why?
3. What particular human quality must one relinquish before achieving the state of being a "transparent eyeball"? What aids a person in reaching this state?

A Nonconformist

1. *(a)* Against what established ideas and institutions does Emerson rebel? What are his reasons for refusing to conform to each? *(b)* In each case, do you agree or disagree with Emerson? Why? *(c)* If you do agree, do you think it is possible to apply his ideas to your own life? Why or why not?

Traveling

1. Emerson objects to man's traveling in hopes of ". . . finding somewhat which he does not carry." To what is Emerson referring? Support your answer.
2. What is the "giant" of the last line? Why does traveling not rid the traveler of it? How could the traveler rid himself of the giant?

Reliance on Property

1. *(a)* According to Emerson, man's reliance on and interest in the amassing of property is done at the expense of what? Support your answer with lines from the selection. *(b)* Do you agree with Emerson? Does his idea hold true today? Give reasons for your answer.
2. Explain the analogy in the last sentence. (*i.e.*, Speaking literally, what is the "man who stands on his feet" doing differently from the "man who stands on his head"?)

Man Thinking

1. What truth about man is the fable discussed in the first two paragraphs designed to illustrate?
2. According to Emerson, how has the fable's original idea been perverted?
3. What is the difference between "a mere thinker" and "Man Thinking"?

The Sublime Vision

1. Reread the first paragraph of the selection. In what

ways is the state that the poet must try to achieve similar to that described in "I Become a Transparent Eyeball"?
2. To what use do some poets put the various stimulants listed in paragraph 2? Do these stimulants produce the desired effect? If so, what is the effect? If not, what effect *is* produced? Cite lines from the text to prove your answer.
3. What is the purpose of the comments on children's toys (column b, lines 20–25)?
4. Reread the selection from column b, line 26, to the end. According to these lines, what provides the only true poetic inspiration?

CREATIVE RESPONSE

1. The desire to alter in some way or to go beyond the usual boundaries of consciousness is not limited to the Transcendentalist. Currently, various groups advocate what they feel to be the means of achieving this end. Exercise, special diet, drugs, meditation, chanting, and countless other practices are considered by their practitioners to be the one true way to reach the goal.

Working singly or in groups, use your libraries to explore the philosophy behind any of these schools of thought. Set aside a day to report findings and answer questions from the class. In your discussion, pay special attention to how the various philosophies are similar and how they differ—not only from each other but from Transcendentalism as well.
2. Prepare several questions that you would like to ask Emerson if Emerson were to be propelled into this century to talk about the application of his philosophy to contemporary life. Questions might cover such areas as our use of both legal and illegal drugs, foreign and domestic policy, cultural and recreational activities, the educational system. At the next class meeting each student should take a turn at being Emerson and answering one or two of the collected questions.

DISCUSSION

the poetry of Emerson

When reading these poems you undoubtedly noticed the presence of many of the ideas that characterize the Transcendentalist. Emerson's poetry, like his prose, is concerned with the discussion and expansion of his philosophy.

In discussing Emerson's poetry, pay special attention to the **speaker** in each poem. In some cases, the poet may choose to speak in his own voice, viewing the material with his own eyes. At other times he may find it more effective to create a character and speak through that character, describing events from the viewpoint of the character rather than from his own. Knowing who is speaking in a poem provides a valuable key to the understanding of the poem.

FOR EXPLORATION

Each and All

1. In the first stanza, the speaker lists four occasions when someone or something unwittingly gives pleasure or sustenance to another. What are these?
2. How do the last two lines of the first stanza relate to the ideas expressed in stanzas two, three, and four as well as those in stanza one?
3. What do the bird of the second stanza, the shells of the third, and the maiden of the fourth stanza all have in common?
4. What has led the speaker to the conclusion he expresses in the first three lines of the last stanza?
5. What effect does the sudden perception described in lines 40–51 have on the poet? What does this perception do to the conclusion discussed in question 4?
6. What comprises the "perfect whole" of the last line?
7. In what ways are the ideas in this poem similar to those of "I Become a Transparent Eyeball" and "The Sublime Vision"? In each case, what has triggered the heightening of the consciousness?
8. Given the information contained in the poem, who do you think is speaking?

Brahma

1. Who is the speaker, the *I* in the poem?
2. What image does the term "red slayer" evoke?
3. A number of apparent contradictions can be found in the poem; name several of these.
4. Is it possible to explain logically a statement like that in line 6: "Shadow and sunlight are the same"?
5. In what sense might one slay and yet not slay? be slain and yet not be slain? (In answering this question, consider the lines from the New Testament: "He who loses his life shall find it.")

Days

1. Is the speaker in this poem the same as that of "Brahma"? How do you know?
2. What poetic device has Emerson used throughout the poem? Cite lines to prove your answer.
3. What image is created through the use of the following: "muffled and dumb," "barefoot dervishes," "pomp," and "solemn fillet"?
4. The speaker calls the Days "hypocritic" and later

describes their marching in a single, "endless file." From the speaker's viewpoint, in what sense might they be called hypocritic?

5. According to line 4, what do the Days carry? What relationship, if any, exists between the two things?

6. What "gifts" do the days offer? Can you see any sort of progression in the list of gifts?

7. Where in the list of gifts would "a few herbs and apples" fall? What might the speaker's "morning wishes" have been?

8. Why is the Day scornful? At whom is the scorn directed?

Terminus

1. At what time in the speaker's life is the poem set?

2. What advice does the god of boundaries give the speaker? Cite lines from the poem to prove your answer.

3. What is the tone of the poem? What does it tell you about the speaker's outlook?

CREATIVE RESPONSE

Beginning in 1836, advocates of Transcendentalism began to hold informal meetings at Emerson's home in Concord. The group, which came to be called the Transcendental Club, attracted a varied and—in the opinion of the movement's critics—bizarre membership. While the extreme individualism inherent in Transcendentalism did indeed attract a heterogeneous following, many of the club's members were intelligent, creative, and far ahead of their time.

Interested students might report on the following Transcendentalists and their activities:

—Bronson Alcott and free schools
—the Brook Farm experiment in communal living
—*The Dial*
—Margaret Fuller, Elizabeth Peabody, and feminism in the Transcendentalist movement.

THE CONCORD FREE PUBLIC LIBRARY

Ralph Waldo Emerson   1803 / 1882

Emerson was the progeny of a long line of ministers. After graduating from Harvard and teaching for several years, he entered Harvard Divinity School. When in 1829 he married and was assigned the pastorate of the Second Church of Boston, he appeared settled and contented. But in 1831 his wife died; a year later he resigned his ministry because he did not hold with some forms of the worship. He went abroad; there, through his association with Carlyle, Wordsworth, and Coleridge, he became intimate with the transcendental thought.

Within a few years of his return to America he remarried and settled in Concord. With a firmer, clearer understanding of his own philosophy, he began to lecture. Though in most ways a private, introspective man, he enjoyed the response of a live audience and for a number of years subjected himself to real hardship on tours into rural midwest areas to spread his idealism. "In all my lectures," Emerson wrote, "I have taught one doctrine, namely, the infinitude of the private man."

Henry David Thoreau

1817/1862

My life has been the poem I would have writ,
But I could not both live and utter it. (1849)

from

WALDEN

WHY I WENT TO THE WOODS

I went to the woods because I wished to live deliberately, to front only the essential facts of life, and see if I could not learn what it had to teach, and not, when I came to die, discover that I had not lived. I did not wish to live what was not life, living is so dear; nor did I wish to practice resignation, unless it was quite necessary. I wanted to live deep and suck out all the marrow of life, to live so sturdily and Spartanlike as to put to rout all that was not life, to cut a broad swath and shave close, to drive life into a corner, and reduce it to its lowest terms, and, if it proved to be mean, why then to get the whole and genuine meanness of it, and publish its meanness to the world; or if it were sublime, to know it by experience, and be able to give a true account of it in my next excursion.[1] For most men, it appears to me, are in a strange uncertainty about it, whether it is of the devil or of God, and have *somewhat hastily* concluded that it is the chief end of man here to "glorify God and enjoy Him forever."[2]

Still we live meanly, like ants, though the fable tells us that we were long ago changed into men;[3] like pygmies we fight with cranes;[4] it is error upon error, and clout upon clout, and our best virtue has for its occasion a superfluous and evitable wretchedness. Our life is frittered away by detail. An honest man has hardly need to count more than his ten fin-

gers or in extreme cases he may add his ten toes, and lump the rest.

Simplicity, simplicity, simplicity! I say, let your affairs be as two or three, and not a hundred or a thousand; instead of a million count half a dozen, and keep your accounts on your thumbnail. In the midst of this chopping sea of civilized life, such are the clouds and storms and quicksands and thousand-and-one items to be allowed for, that a man has to live, if he would not founder and go to the bottom and not make his port at all, by dead reckoning,[5] and he must be a great calculator indeed who succeeds. Simplify, simplify. Instead of three meals a day, if it be necessary eat but one; instead of a hundred dishes, five; and reduce other things in proportion. Our life is like a German Confederacy, made up of petty states,[6] with its boundary forever fluctuating, so that even a German cannot tell you how it is bounded at any moment. The nation itself, with all its so-called internal improvements, which, by the way, are all external and superficial, is just such an unwieldy and overgrown establishment, cluttered with furniture and tripped up by its own traps, ruined by luxury and heedless expense, by want of calculation and a worthy aim, as the million households in the land; and the only cure for it as for them is in a rigid economy, a stern and more than Spartan simplicity of life and elevation of purpose. It lives too fast. Men think that it is essential that the *Nation* have commerce, and export ice, and talk through a telegraph, and ride thirty

---

1. *my next excursion*, my next or future life.
2. *"glorify God and enjoy Him forever,"* the answer in the Westminster Catechism of the Presbyterian Church to the question, "What is the chief end of man?"
3. *ants . . . men.* According to Greek legend, the Myrmidons, the followers of Achilles, were ants changed into men.
4. *like pygmies we fight with cranes.* Homer and other ancient writers believed that the pygmies, dwarf inhabitants of Africa, carried on warfare with the cranes.
5. *dead reckoning,* calculation of a ship's position by using a compass and studying the record of the voyage, and without using observations of the sun and stars.
6. *a German Confederacy, made up of petty states.* At the time Thoreau wrote *Walden*, Germany as a nation did not exist. Until the rise of Napoleon at the end of the eighteenth century, there had been a German emperor, but he was a mere figurehead; in each of the several hundred German states the real ruler was its prince or duke. At the Congress of Vienna (1814–1815), which met to reorganize Europe after Napoleon's defeat at the Battle of Waterloo, the German states were reduced in number from several hundred to thirty-eight and a loose German Confederation was formed. However, the real power remained with the heads of the states rather than in the confederation. In 1871 Bismarck, a statesman from Prussia, the strongest of the German states, welded Germany into an empire.

miles an hour, without a doubt, whether *they* do or not; but whether we should live like baboons or like men is a little uncertain. If we do not get out sleepers, and forge rails, and devote days and nights to the work, but go to tinkering upon our *lives* to improve them, who will build railroads? And if railroads are not built, how shall we get to heaven in season? But if we stay at home and mind our business, who will want railroads? We do not ride on the railroad; it rides upon us. □

THE BATTLE OF THE ANTS

ONE day when I went out to my woodpile, or rather my pile of stumps, I observed two large ants, the one red, the other much larger, nearly half an inch long, and black, fiercely contending with one another. Having once got hold, they never let go, but struggled and wrestled and rolled on the chips incessantly. Looking farther, I was surprised to find the chips were covered with such combatants—that it was not a *duellum*, but a *bellum*,[1] a war between two races of ants, the red always pitted against the black, and frequently two red ones to one black. The legions of these Myrmidons[2] covered all the hills and vales in my woodyard, and the ground was already strewn with the dead and dying, both red and black. It was the only battle which I have ever witnessed, the only battlefield I ever trod while the battle was raging; internecine war; the red republicans on the one hand, and the black imperialists[3] on the other. On every side they were engaged in deadly combat, yet without any noise that I could hear, and human soldiers never fought so resolutely.

I watched a couple that were fast locked in each other's embraces, in a little sunny valley amid the chips, now at noonday prepared to fight till the sun went down, or life went out. The smaller red champion had fastened himself like a vise to his adversary's front, and through all the tumblings on that field never for an instant ceased to gnaw at one of his feelers near the root, having already caused the other to go by the board; while the stronger black one dashed him from side to side, and, as I saw on looking nearer, had already divested him of several of his members. They fought with more pertinacity than bulldogs. Neither manifested the least disposition to retreat. It was evident that their battle cry was "Conquer or die."

In the meanwhile there came along a single red ant on the hillside of this valley, evidently full of excitement, who either had dispatched his foe or had not yet taken part in the battle (probably the latter, for he had lost none of his limbs); whose mother had charged him to return with his shield or upon it.[4] Or perchance he was some Achilles, who had nourished his wrath apart, and had now come to avenge or rescue his Patroclus.[5] He saw this unequal combat from afar. He drew near with rapid pace till he stood on his guard within half an inch of the combatants; then, watching his opportunity, he sprang upon the black warrior, and commenced his operations near the root of his right foreleg, leaving the foe to select among his own members.

And so there were three united for life, as if a new kind of attraction had been invented which put all other locks and cements to shame. I should not have wondered by this time to find that they had their re-

---

1. *not a* duellum (dü el′əm) *but a* bellum (bel′əm), not merely a duel between two contestants but a war between two armies.
2. *Myrmidons* (mér′mi donz), warriors of ancient Thessaly, according to Greek legend.
3. *red republicans . . . black imperialists.* At the time this selection was published in 1854, Europe had recently undergone several revolutions in which the people of a number of countries had rebelled against their rulers.
4. *whose mother . . . with his shield or upon it.* According to tales of ancient Greece this was the command given by Spartan mothers to their sons when the sons went off to war. It means: Die rather than surrender.
5. *Achilles* (ə kil′ēz) . . . *Patroclus* (pə trō′kləs). Because of a quarrel with Agamemnon (ag′ə mem′non), the Greek commander in chief in the Trojan War, Achilles sulked in his tent. But when he heard that his friend Patroclus had been killed, he hurried into the battle to avenge him.

spective musical bands stationed on some eminent chip, and playing their national airs the while, to excite the slow and cheer the dying combatants. I was myself excited somewhat even as if they had been men. The more you think of it, the less the difference. And certainly there is not the fight recorded in Concord history,[6] at least, if in the history of America, that will bear a moment's comparison with this, whether for the numbers engaged in it, or for the patriotism and heroism displayed. For numbers and for carnage it was an Austerlitz[7] or Dresden.[8] Concord Fight! Two killed on the patriots' side,[9] and Luther Blanchard wounded! Why, here every ant was a Buttrick[10]—"Fire, for God's sake fire!"—and thousands shared the fate of Davis and Hosmer. There was not one hireling there. I have no doubt that it was a principle they fought for, as much as our ancestors, and not to avoid a threepenny tax on their tea;[11] and the results of this battle will be as important and memorable to those whom it concerns as those of the battle of Bunker Hill, at least.

I took up the chip on which the three I have particularly described were struggling, carried it into my house, and placed it under a tumbler on my window sill, in order to see the issue. Holding a microscope to the first-mentioned red ant, I saw that, though he was assiduously gnawing at the near foreleg of his enemy, having severed his remaining feeler, his own breast was all torn away, exposing what vitals he had there to the jaws of the black warrior, whose breastplate was apparently too thick for him to pierce; and the dark carbuncles of the sufferer's eyes shone with ferocity such as war only could excite. They struggled half an hour longer under the tumbler, and when I looked again the black soldier had severed the heads of his foes from their

bodies, and the still living heads were hanging on either side of him like ghastly trophies at his saddlebow, still apparently as firmly fastened as ever, and he was endeavoring with feeble struggles, being without feelers and with only the remnant of a leg, and I know not how many other wounds, to divest himself of them; which after half an hour more he accomplished.

I raised the glass, and he went off over the window sill in that crippled state. Whether he finally survived that combat, and spent the remainder of his days in some Hôtel des Invalides,[12] I do not know; but I thought that his industry would not be worth much thereafter. I never learned which party was victorious, nor the cause of the war; but I felt for the rest of that day as if I had had my feelings excited and harrowed by witnessing the struggle, the ferocity and carnage, of a human battle before my door. □

---

6. *the fight recorded in Concord history*, the second battle of the Revolutionary War, on April 19, 1775.
7. *Austerlitz* (ôs/tər lits), battle fought in old Austria (now Czechoslovakia) during the Napoleonic Wars. Here in 1805 Napoleon defeated the Russians and Austrians. Many thousands were killed.
8. *Dresden*, the last of Napoleon's great victories, in which he defeated the Russian, Austrian, and Prussian forces in 1813. Dresden is in Germany.
9. *Two killed on the patriots' side*. Thoreau is writing of the mid-morning fight at the North Bridge when the militia advanced and attacked the British on guard there. Two Americans, Captain Isaac Davis and a man named Hosmer (both mentioned below), were killed.
10. *Buttrick*, the major in command of the Concord militia in the fight at the North Bridge.
11. *a threepenny tax on their tea*, a reference to the Boston Tea Party and the colonists' objections to taxation without representation.
12. *Hôtel des Invalides* (ō tel/ dā zäN vä lēd/), a beautiful monument in Paris founded by Louis XIV as a residence for old and wounded veterans of the French armies.

WHY I LEFT THE WOODS

I left the woods for as good a reason as I went there. Perhaps it seemed to me that I had several more lives to live, and could not spare any more time for that one. It is remarkable how easily and insensibly we fall into a particular route, and make a beaten track for ourselves. I had not lived there a week before my feet wore a path from my door to the pondside; and though it is five or six years since I trod it, it is still quite distinct. It is true, I fear, that others may have fallen into it, and so helped to keep it open. The surface of the earth is soft and impressible by the feet of men; and so with the paths which the mind travels. How worn and dusty, then, must be the highways of the world, how deep the ruts of tradition and conformity! I did not wish to take a cabin passage, but rather to go before the mast and on the deck of the world, for there I could best see the moonlight amid the mountains. I do not wish to go below now.

I learned this, at least, by my experiment: that if one advances confidently in the direction of his dreams, and endeavors to live the life which he has imagined, he will meet with a success unexpected in common hours. He will put some things behind, will pass an invisible boundary; new, universal, and more liberal laws will begin to establish themselves around and within him; or the old laws be expanded, and interpreted in his favor in a more liberal sense, and he will live with the license of a higher order of beings. In proportion as he simplifies his life, the laws of the universe will appear less complex, and solitude will not be solitude, nor poverty poverty, nor weakness weakness. If you have built castles in the air, your work need not be lost; that is where they should be. Now put the foundations under them. . . .

Why should we be in such desperate haste to succeed and in such desperate enterprises? If a man does not keep pace with his companions, perhaps it is because he hears a different drummer. Let him step to the music which he hears, however measured or far away. It is not important that he should mature as soon as an apple tree or an oak. Shall he turn his spring into summer? If the condition of things which we were made for is not yet, what were any reality which we can substitute? We will not be shipwrecked on a vain reality. Shall we with pains erect a heaven of blue glass over ourselves, though when it is done we shall be sure to gaze still at the true ethereal heaven far above, as if the former were not?

There was an artist in the city of Kouroo who was disposed to strive after perfection. One day it came into his mind to make a staff. Having considered that in an imperfect work time is an ingredient, but into a perfect work time does not enter, he said to himself, It shall be perfect in all respects, though I should do nothing else in my life. He proceeded instantly to the forest for wood, being resolved that it should not be made of unsuitable material; and as he searched for and rejected stick after stick, his friends gradually deserted him, for they grew old in their works and died, but he grew not older by a moment. His singleness of purpose and resolution, and his elevated piety, endowed him, without his knowledge, with perennial youth. As he made no compromise with Time, Time kept out of his way, and only sighed at a distance because he could not overcome him. Before he had found a stick in all respects suitable the city of Kouroo was a hoary ruin, and he sat on one of its mounds to peel the stick. Before he had given it the proper shape the dynasty of the Candahars[1] was at an end, and with the point of the stick he wrote the name of the last of that race in the sand, and then resumed his work. By the time he had smoothed and polished the staff Kalpa was no longer the pole-star; and ere he had put on the ferule and the head adorned with precious stones, Brahma had awoke and slumbered many times.[2] But why do I stay to mention these things? When the finishing stroke was put to his work, it suddenly expanded before the eyes of the astonished artist into the fairest of all the creations of Brahma. He had made a new system in making a staff, a world with full and fair proportions; in which, though the old cities and dynasties had passed away, fairer and more glorious ones had taken their places. And now he saw by the heap of shavings still fresh at his feet, that, for him and his work, the former lapse of time had been an illusion, and that no more time had elapsed than is required for a single scintillation from the brain of Brahma to fall on and inflame the tinder of a mortal brain. The

---

1. *Candahars,* Kandahar, an Afghanistan city long ruled by Darius I, king of the Achaemenid dynasty of Persia, and taken by Alexander in 329 B.C.

2. *Kalpa . . . many times.* According to Hindu belief, Brahma is the creator of the world which endures for 2,160,000,000 years and then is destroyed, only to be recreated by him after a like duration. Each 4,320,000,000-year period of this sort constitutes a day and a night of Brahma, or a Kalpa.

material was pure, and his art was pure; how could the result be other than wonderful?

No face which we can give to a matter will stead us so well at last as the truth. This alone wears well. For the most part, we are not where we are, but in a false position. Through an infirmity of our natures, we suppose a case, and put ourselves into it, and hence are in two cases at the same time, and it is doubly difficult to get out. In sane moments we regard only the facts, the case that is. Say what you have to say, not what you ought. Any truth is better than make-believe. Tom Hyde, the tinker, standing on the gallows, was asked if he had anything to say. "Tell the tailors," said he, "to remember to make a knot in their thread before they take the first stitch." His companion's prayer is forgotten.

However mean your life is, meet it and live it; do not shun it and call it hard names. It is not so bad as you are. It looks poorest when you are richest. The fault-finder will find faults even in paradise. Love your life, poor as it is. You may perhaps have some pleasant, thrilling, glorious hours, even in a poorhouse. The setting sun is reflected from the windows of the alms-house as brightly as from the rich man's abode; the snow melts before its door as early in the spring. I do not see but a quiet mind may live as contentedly there, and have as cheering thoughts, as in a palace. The town's poor seem to me often to live the most independent lives of any. Maybe they are simply great enough to receive without misgiving. Most think that they are above being supported by the town; but it oftener happens that they are not above supporting themselves by dishonest means, which should be more disreputable. Cultivate poverty like a garden herb, like sage. Do not trouble yourself much to get new things, whether clothes or friends. Turn the old; return to them. Things do not change; we change. Sell your clothes and keep your thoughts. God will see that you do not want society. If I were confined to a corner of a garret all my days, like a spider, the world would be just as large to me while I had my thoughts about me. The philosopher said: "From an army of three divisions one can take away its general, and put it in disorder; from the man the most abject and vulgar one cannot take away his thought." Do not seek so anxiously to be developed, to subject yourself to many influences to be played on; it is all dissipation. Humility like darkness reveals the heavenly lights. The shadows of poverty and meanness gather around us, "and lo! creation

widens to our view."[3] We are often reminded that if there were bestowed on us the wealth of Crœsus,[4] our aims must still be the same, and our means essentially the same. Moreover, if you are restricted in your range by poverty, if you cannot buy books and newspapers, for instance, you are but confined to the most significant and vital experiences; you are compelled to deal with the material which yields the most sugar and the most starch. It is life near the bone where it is sweetest. You are defended from being a trifler. No man loses ever on a lower level by magnanimity on a higher. Superfluous wealth can buy superfluities only. Money is not required to buy one necessary of the soul. . . .

Rather than love, than money, than fame, give me truth: I sat at a table where were rich food and wine in abundance, an obsequious attendance, but sincerity and truth were not; and I went away hungry from the inhospitable board. The hospitality was as cold as the ices. I thought that there was no need of ice to freeze them. They talked to me of the age of the wine and the fame of the vintage; but I thought of an older, a newer, and purer wine, of a more glorious vintage, which they had not got, and could not buy. The style, the house and grounds and "entertainment" pass for nothing with me. I called on the king, but he made me wait in his hall, and conducted like a man incapacitated for hospitality. There was a man in my neighborhood who lived in a hollow tree. His manners were truly regal. I should have done better had I called on him. . . .

There is an incessant influx of novelty into the world, and yet we tolerate incredible dullness. I need only suggest what kind of sermons are still listened to in the most enlightened countries. There are such words as joy and sorrow, but they are only the burden of a psalm, sung with a nasal twang, while we believe in the ordinary and mean. We think that we can change our clothes only. It is said that the British Empire is very large and respectable, and that the United States are a first-rate power. We do not believe that a tide rises and falls behind every man which can float the British Empire like a chip, if he should ever harbor it in his mind. Who knows what sort of seventeen-year locust will next come out of the ground? The government of the world I live in

---

3. "*and lo . . . view,*" a slight misquotation from "Night," a sonnet by Joseph Blanco White (1775–1841).
4. *Crœsus* (krē′sus), a king of Lydia in the 6th century B.C. renowned for his vast wealth.

was not framed, like that of Britain, in after-dinner conversations over the wine.

The life in us is like the water in the river. It may rise this year higher than man has ever known it, and flood the parched uplands; even this may be the eventful year, which will drown out all our muskrats. It was not always dry land where we dwell. I see far inland the banks which the stream anciently washed, before science began to record its freshets. Everyone has heard the story which has gone the rounds of New England, of a strong and beautiful bug which came out of the dry leaf of an old table of apple-tree wood, which had stood in a farmer's kitchen for sixty years, first in Connecticut, and afterward in Massachusetts,—from an egg deposited in the living tree many years earlier still, as appeared by counting the annual layers beyond it; which was heard gnawing out for several weeks, hatched perchance by the heat of an urn. Who does not feel his faith in a resurrec-

tion and immortality strengthened by hearing of this? Who knows what beautiful and winged life, whose egg has been buried for ages under many concentric layers of woodenness in the dead dry life of society, deposited at first in the alburnum of the green and living tree, which has been gradually converted into the semblance of its well-seasoned tomb,—heard perchance gnawing out now for years by the astonished family of man, as they sat round the festive board,—may unexpectedly come forth from amidst society's most trival and handselled furniture, to enjoy its perfect summer life at last!

I do not say that John or Jonathan will realize all this; but such is the character of that morrow which mere lapse of time can never make to dawn. The light which puts out our eyes is darkness to us. Only that day dawns to which we are awake. There is more day to dawn. The sun is but a morning star. □

from

CIVIL DISOBEDIENCE

I heartily accept the motto,—"That government is best which governs least"; and I should like to see it acted up to more rapidly and systematically. Carried out, it finally amounts to this, which also I believe,—"That government is best which governs not at all" and when men are prepared for it, that will be the kind of government which they will have. Government is at best but an expedient; but most governments are usually, and all governments are sometimes, inexpedient. The objections which have been brought against a standing army, and they are many and weighty, and deserve to prevail, may also at last be brought against a standing government. The standing army is only an arm of the standing government. The government itself, which is only the mode which the people have chosen to execute their will, is equally liable to be abused and perverted before the people can act through it. Witness the present

Mexican war, the work of comparatively a few individuals using the standing government as their tool;[1] for, in the outset, the people would not have consented to this measure.

This American government,—what is it but a tradition, though a recent one, endeavoring to transmit itself unimpaired to posterity, but each instant losing some of its integrity? It has not the vitality and force of a single living man; for a single man can bend it to his will. It is a sort of wooden gun to the people themselves. But it is not the less necessary for this; for the people must have some complicated machinery or other, and hear its din, to satisfy that idea of government which they have. Governments show thus how successfully men can be imposed on, even impose on themselves, for their own advantage. It is excel-

---

1. *Mexican war . . . tool.* The Mexican War (1846–1848) ended with the United States acquiring nearly all the territory now comprising New Mexico, Colorado, Utah, Nevada, Arizona, and California. Northern reformers believed the war resulted primarily from the desire of southern politicians and northern cotton merchants to extend slave territory.

lent, we must all allow. Yet this government never of itself furthered any enterprise, but by the alacrity with which it got out of its way. *It* does not keep the country free. *It* does not settle the West. *It* does not educate. The character inherent in the American people has done all that has been accomplished; and it would have done somewhat more, if the government had not sometimes got in its way. For government is an expedient by which men would fain succeed in letting one another alone; and, as has been said, when it is most expedient, the governed are most let alone by it. Trade and commerce, if they were not made of India-rubber, would never manage to bounce over the obstacles which legislators are continually putting in their way; and, if one were to judge these men wholly by the effects of their actions and not partly by their intentions, they would deserve to be classed and punished with those mischievous persons who put obstructions on the railroads.

But, to speak practically and as a citizen, unlike those who call themselves no-government men, I ask for, not at once no government, but *at once* a better government. Let every man make known what kind of government would command his respect, and that will be one step toward obtaining it.

After all, the practical reason why, when the power is once in the hands of the people, a majority are permitted, and for a long period continue, to rule is not because they are most likely to be in the right, nor because this seems fairest to the minority, but because they are physically the strongest. But a government in which the majority rule in all cases cannot be based on justice, even as far as men understand it. Can there not be a government in which majorities do not virtually decide right and wrong, but conscience?—in which majorities decide only those questions to which the rule of expediency is applicable? Must the citizen ever for a moment, or in the least degree, resign his conscience to the legislator? Why has every man a conscience, then? I think that we should be men first, and subjects afterward. It is not desirable to cultivate a respect for the law, so much as for the right. The only obligation which I have a right to assume is to do at any time what I think right. It is truly enough said that a corporation has no conscience; but a corporation of conscientious men is a corporation *with* a conscience. Law never made men a whit more just; and, by means of their respect for it, even the well-disposed

are daily made the agents of injustice. A common and natural result of an undue respect for law is, that you may see a file of soldiers, colonel, captain, corporal, privates, powder-monkeys, and all, marching in admirable order over hill and dale to the wars, against their wills, ay, against their common sense and consciences, which makes it very steep marching indeed, and produces a palpitation of the heart. They have no doubt that it is a damnable business in which they are concerned; they are all peaceably inclined. Now, what are they? Men at all? or small movable forts and magazines, at the service of some unscrupulous man in power? Visit the Navy-Yard, and behold a marine, such a man as an American government can make, or such as it can make a man with its black arts,—a mere shadow and reminiscence of humanity, a man laid out alive and standing, and already, as one may say, buried under arms with funeral accompaniments, though it may be

Not a drum was heard, not a funeral note,
  As his corse to the rampart we hurried;
Not a soldier discharged his farewell shot
  O'er the grave where our hero we buried.[2]

The mass of men serve the state thus, not as men mainly, but as machines, with their bodies. They are the standing army, and the militia, jailers, constables, posse comitatus, etc. In most cases there is no free exercise whatever of the judgment or of the moral sense; but they put themselves on a level with wood and earth and stones; and wooden men can perhaps be manufactured that will serve the purpose as well. Such command no more respect than men of straw or a lump of dirt. They have the same sort of worth only as horses and dogs. Yet such as these even are commonly esteemed good citizens. Others—as most legislators, politicians, lawyers, ministers, and officeholders—serve the state chiefly with their heads; and, as they rarely make any moral distinctions, they are as likely to serve the Devil, without *intending* it, as God. A very few, as heroes, patriots, martyrs, reformers in the great sense, and *men*, serve the state with their consciences also, and so necessarily resist it for the most part; and they are commonly treated as enemies by it. A wise man will only be useful as a man, and will not submit to be "clay," and "stop a

---

2. *"Not a drum . . . buried,"* the opening lines of "Burial of Sir John Moore at Coruna" by Charles Wolfe (1791–1823), an Irish clergyman.

hole to keep the wind away,"[3] but leave that office to his dust at least:

> I am too high-born to be propertied,
> To be a secondary at control,
> Or useful serving-man and instrument
> To any sovereign state throughout the world.[4]

He who gives himself entirely to his fellow-men appears to them useless and selfish; but he who gives himself partially to them is pronounced a benefactor and philanthropist.

How does it become a man to behave toward this American government today? I answer, that he cannot without disgrace be associated with it.[5] I cannot for an instant recognize that political organization as *my* government which is the *slave's* government also.

All men recognize the right of revolution; that is, the right to refuse allegiance to, and to resist, the government, when its tyranny or its inefficiency are great and unendurable. But almost all say that such is not the case now. But such was the case, they think, in the Revolution of '75. If one were to tell me that this was a bad government because it taxed certain foreign commodities brought to its ports, it is most probable that I should not make an ado about it, for I can do without them. All machines have their friction; and possibly this does enough good to counterbalance the evil. At any rate, it is a great evil to make a stir about it. But when the friction comes to have its machine, and oppression and robbery are organized, I say, let us not have such a machine any longer. In other words, when a sixth of the population of a nation which has undertaken to be the refuge of liberty are slaves, and a whole country is unjustly overrun and conquered by a foreign army, and subjected to military law, I think that it is not too soon for honest men to rebel and revolutionize. What makes this duty the more urgent is the fact that the country so overrun is not our own, but ours is the invading army.

Paley, a common authority with many on moral questions, in his chapter on the "Duty of Submission to Civil Government,"[6] resolves all civil obligation into expediency; and he proceeds to say, "that so long as the interest of the whole society requires it, that is, so long as the established government cannot be resisted or changed without public inconveniency, it is the will of God that the established gov-

ernment be obeyed, and no longer. . . . This principle being admitted, the justice of every particular case of resistance is reduced to a computation of the quantity of the danger and grievance on the one side, and of the probability and expense of redressing it on the other." Of this, he says, every man shall judge for himself. But Paley appears never to have contemplated those cases to which the rule of expediency does not apply, in which a people, as well as an individual, must do justice, cost what it may. If I have unjustly wrested a plank from a drowning man, I must restore it to him though I drown myself. This, according to Paley, would be inconvenient. But he that would save his life, in such a case, shall lose it.[7] This people must cease to hold slaves, and to make war on Mexico, though it cost them their existence as a people. . . .

Practically speaking, the opponents to a reform in Massachusetts are not a hundred thousand politicians at the South, but a hundred thousand merchants and farmers here, who are more interested in commerce and agriculture than they are in humanity, and are not prepared to do justice to the slave and to Mexico, *cost what it may.* I quarrel not with far-off foes, but with those who, near at home, co-operate with, and do the bidding of, those far away, and without whom the latter would be harmless. We are accustomed to say, that the mass of men are unprepared; but improvement is slow, because the few are not materially wiser or better than the many. It is not so important that many should be as good as you, as that there be some absolute goodness somewhere; for that will leaven the whole lump.[8] There are thousands who are *in opinion* opposed to slavery and to the war, who yet in effect do nothing to put an end to them; who, esteeming themselves children of Washington and Franklin, sit down with their hands in their pockets, and say that they know not what to do, and do nothing; who even postpone the question of

---

3. *"clay . . . away,"* by William Shakespeare, from *Hamlet*, Act v, scene 1. The original lines read, "Imperious Cæsar, dead and turn'd to clay,/ Might stop a hole to keep the wind away."
4. *"I am . . . world,"* by William Shakespeare, from *King John*, Act v, scene 1, lines 79–82.
5. *How does . . . with it.* Many believed President Polk's administration (1845–1849) was strengthening slavery through fugitive-slave laws and the Mexican War.
6. *Paley . . . Government,* a reference to *Principles of Moral and Political Philosophy* by William Paley (1743–1805), a British thinker.
7. *But he . . . lose it,* a loose reference to Luke 9:24.
8. *that will leaven the whole lump,* a loose reference to I Corinthians 5:6.

freedom to the question of free-trade, and quietly read the prices-current along with the latest advices from Mexico, after dinner, and, it may be, fall asleep over them both. What is the price-current of an honest man and patriot to-day? They hesitate, and they regret, and sometimes they petition; but they do nothing in earnest and with effect. They will wait, well disposed, for others to remedy the evil, that they may no longer have it to regret. At most, they give only a cheap vote, and a feeble countenance and God-speed, to the right, as it goes by them. There are nine hundred and ninety-nine patrons of virtue to one virtuous man. But it is easier to deal with the real possessor of a thing than with the temporary guardian of it. . . .

It is not a man's duty, as a matter of course, to devote himself to the eradication of any, even the most enormous wrong; he may still properly have other concerns to engage him; but it is his duty, at least, to wash his hands of it, and, if he gives it no thought longer, not to give it practically his support. If I devote myself to other pursuits and contemplations, I must first see, at least, that I do not pursue them sitting upon another man's shoulders. I must get off him first, that he may pursue his contemplations too. See what gross inconsistency is tolerated. I have heard some of my townsmen say, "I should like to have them order me out to help put down an insurrection of the slaves, or to march to Mexico;—see if I would go"; and yet these very men have each, directly by their allegiance, and so indirectly, at least, by their money, furnished a substitute. The soldier is applauded who refuses to serve in an unjust war by those who do not refuse to sustain the unjust government which makes the war; is applauded by those whose own act and authority he disregards and sets at naught; as if the state were penitent to that degree that it hired one to scourge it while it sinned, but not to that degree that it left off sinning for a moment. Thus, under the name of Order and Civil Government, we are all made at last to pay homage to and support our own meanness. After the first blush of sin comes its indifference; and from immoral it becomes, as it were, *un*moral, and not quite unnecessary to that life which we have made. . . .

If the injustice is part of the necessary friction of the machine of government, let it go, let it go: perchance it will wear smooth,—certainly the machine will wear out. If the injustice has a spring, or a pulley, or a rope, or a crank, exclusively for itself, then per-haps you may consider whether the remedy will not be worse than the evil; but if it is of such a nature that it requires you to be the agent of injustice to another, then, I say, break the law. Let your life be a counter friction to stop the machine. What I have to do is to see, at any rate, that I do not lend myself to the wrong which I condemn.

As for adopting the ways which the state has provided for remedying the evil, I know not of such ways. They take too much time, and a man's life will be gone. I have other affairs to attend to. I came into this world, not chiefly to make this a good place to live in, but to live in it, be it good or bad. A man has not everything to do, but something; and because he cannot do *everything*, it is not necessary that he should do *something* wrong. It is not my business to be petitioning the Governor or the Legislature any more than it is theirs to petition me; and if they should not hear my petition, what should I do then? But in this case the state has provided no way: its very Constitution is the evil. This may seem to be harsh and stubborn and unconciliatory; but it is to treat with the utmost kindness and consideration the only spirit that can appreciate or deserves it. So is all change for the better, like birth and death, which convulse the body.

I do not hesitate to say, that those who call themselves Abolitionists should at once effectually withdraw their support, both in person and property, from the government of Massachusetts, and not wait till they constitute a majority of one, before they suffer the right to prevail through them. I think that it is enough if they have God on their side, without waiting for that other one. Moreover, any man more right than his neighbors constitutes a majority of one already.

I meet this American government, or its representative, the state government, directly, and face to face, once a year—no more—in the person of its tax-gatherer; this is the only mode in which a man situated as I am necessarily meets it; and it then says distinctly, Recognize me; and the simplest, the most effectual, and, in the present posture of affairs, the indispensablest mode of treating with it on this head, of expressing your little satisfaction with and love for it is to deny it then. My civil neighbor, the tax-gatherer, is the very man I have to deal with,—for it is, after all, with men and not with parchment that I quarrel,—and he has voluntarily chosen to be an agent of the government. How shall he ever know well what he is and does as an officer of the government, or as a man, until he is obliged to consider whether he shall treat me, his neighbor, for whom he has respect, as a neighbor and well-disposed man, or as a maniac and disturber of the peace, and see if he can get over this obstruction to his neighborliness without a ruder and more impetuous thought or speech corresponding with his action. I know this well, that if one thousand, if one hundred, if ten men whom I could name,—if ten *honest* men only,—ay, if *one* HONEST man, in this State of Massachusetts, *ceasing to hold slaves*, were actually to withdraw from this copartnership, and be locked up in the county jail therefore, it would be the abolition of slavery in America. For it matters not how small the beginning may seem to be: what is once well done is done forever. . . .

Under a government which imprisons any unjustly, the true place for a just man is also a prison. The proper place today, the only place which Massachusetts has provided for her freer and less desponding spirits, is in her prisons, to be put out and locked out of the State by her own act, as they have already put themselves out by their principles. It is there that the fugitive slave, and the Mexican prisoner on parole, and the Indian come to plead the wrongs of his race should find them; on that separate, but more free and honorable ground, where the State places those who are not *with* her, but *against* her,—the only house in a slave State in which a free man can abide with honor. If any think that their influence would be lost there, and their voices no longer afflict the ear of the State, that they would not be as an enemy within its walls, they do not know by how much truth is stronger than error, nor how much more eloquently and effectively he can combat injustice who has experienced a little in his own person. Cast your whole vote, not a strip of paper merely, but your whole influence. A minority is powerless while it conforms to the majority; it is not even a minority then; but it is irresistible when it clogs by its whole weight. If the alternative is to keep all just men in prison, or give up war and slavery, the State will not hesitate which to choose. If a thousand men were not to pay their tax-bills this year, that would not be a violent and bloody measure, as it would be to pay them, and enable the State to commit violence and shed innocent blood. This is, in fact, the definition of a peaceable revolution, if any such is possible. If the tax-gatherer, or any other public officer, asks me,

as one has done, "But what shall I do?" my answer is, "If you really wish to do anything, resign your office." When the subject has refused allegiance, and the officer has resigned his office, then the revolution is accomplished. But even suppose blood should flow. Is there not a sort of blood shed when the conscience is wounded? Through this wound a man's real manhood and immortality flow out, and he bleeds to an everlasting death. I see this blood flowing now.

I have contemplated the imprisonment of the offender, rather than the seizure of his goods,—though both will serve the same purpose,—because they who assert the purest right, and consequently are most dangerous to a corrupt State, commonly have not spent much time in accumulating property. To such the State renders comparatively small service, and a slight tax is wont to appear exorbitant, particularly if they are obliged to earn it by special labor with their hands. If there were one who lived wholly without the use of money, the State itself would hesitate to demand it of him. But the rich man—not to make any invidious comparison—is always sold to the institution which makes him rich. Absolutely speaking, the more money, the less virtue; for money comes between a man and his objects, and obtains them for him; and it was certainly no great virtue to obtain it. It puts to rest many questions which he would otherwise be taxed to answer; while the only new question which it puts is the hard but superfluous one, how to spend it. Thus his moral ground is taken from under his feet. The opportunities of living are diminished in proportion as what are called the "means" are increased. The best thing a man can do for his culture when he is rich is to endeavor to carry out those schemes which he entertained when he was poor. Christ answered the Herodians[9] according to their condition. "Show me the tribute-money," said he;—and one took a penny out of his pocket;— if you use money which has the image of Cæsar on it, and which he has made current and valuable, that is, *if you are men of the State*, and gladly enjoy the advantages of Cæsar's government, then pay him back some of his own when he demands it. "Render therefore to Cæsar that which is Cæsar's, and to God those things which are God's,"—leaving them no

---

9. *Herodians*, members of a political party of biblical times who were partisans of Herod the Great, king of Judea, and who opposed Jesus.

wiser than before as to which was which; for they did not wish to know. . . .

I have paid no poll-tax for six years. I was put into a jail once on this account, for one night; and, as I stood considering the walls of solid stone, two or three feet thick, the door of wood and iron, a foot thick, and the iron grating which strained the light, I could not help being struck with the foolishness of that institution which treated me as if I were mere flesh and blood and bones, to be locked up. I wondered that it should have concluded at length that this was the best use it could put me to, and had never thought to avail itself of my services in some way. I saw that, if there was a wall of stone between me and my townsmen, there was a still more difficult one to climb or break through before they could get to be as free as I was. I did not for a moment feel confined, and the walls seemed a great waste of stone and mortar. I felt as if I alone of all my townsmen had paid my tax. They plainly did not know how to treat me, but behaved like persons who are underbred. In every threat and in every compliment there was a blunder; for they thought that my chief desire was to stand the other side of that stone wall. I could not but smile to see how industriously they locked the door on my meditations, which followed them out again without let or hindrance, and *they* were really all that was dangerous. As they could not reach me, they had resolved to punish my body; just as boys, if they cannot come at some person against whom they have a spite, will abuse his dog. I saw that the State was half-witted, that it was timid as a lone woman with her silver spoons, and that it did not know its friends from its foes, and I lost all my remaining respect for it, and pitied it. . . .

When I came out of prison,—for some one interfered, and paid that tax,[10]—I did not perceive that great changes had taken place on the common, such as he observed who went in a youth and emerged a tottering and gray-headed man; and yet a change had to my eyes come over the scene,—the town, and State, and country,—greater than any that mere time could effect. I saw yet more distinctly the State in which I lived. I saw to what extent the people among whom I lived could be trusted as good neighbors and friends; that their friendship was for summer weather only; that they did not greatly propose to do right; that they were a distinct race from me by their prejudices and superstitions, as the Chinamen and Malays are; that in their sacrifices to humanity they

ran no risks, not even to their property; that after all they were not so noble but they treated the thief as he had treated them, and hoped, by a certain outward observance and a few prayers, and by walking in a particular straight though useless path from time to time, to save their souls. This may be to judge my neighbors harshly; for I believe that many of them are not aware that they have such an institution as the jail in their village. . . .

If others pay the tax which is demanded of me, from a sympathy with the State, they do but what they have already done in their own case, or rather they abet injustice to a greater extent than the State requires. If they pay the tax from a mistaken interest in the individual taxed, to save his property, or prevent his going to jail, it is because they have not considered wisely how far they let their private feelings interfere with the public good. . . .

I do not wish to quarrel with any man or nation. I do not wish to split hairs, to make fine distinctions, or set myself up as better than my neighbors. I seek rather, I may say, even an excuse for conforming to the laws of the land. I am but too ready to conform to them. Indeed, I have reason to suspect myself on this head; and each year, as the tax-gatherer comes round, I find myself disposed to review the acts and position of the general and State governments, and the spirit of the people, to discover a pretext for conformity.

We must affect our country as our parents,
And if at any time we alienate
Our love or industry from doing it honor,
We must respect effects and teach the soul
Matter of conscience and religion
And not desire of rule or benefit.

I believe that the State will soon be able to take all my work of this sort out of my hands, and then I shall be no better a patriot than my fellow-countrymen. Seen from a lower point of view, the Constitution, with all its faults, is very good; the law and the courts are very respectable; even this State and this American government are, in many respects, very admirable, and rare things, to be thankful for, such as a great many have described them; but seen from a

10. *some one . . . tax.* According to legend, Ralph Waldo Emerson (see selections beginning on page 129C) paid the tax, but according to family reminiscence the tax was paid by his Aunt Maria.

point of view a little higher, they are what I have described them; seen from a higher still, and the highest, who shall say what they are, or that they are worth looking at or thinking of at all? . . .

They who know of no purer sources of truth, who have traced up its stream no higher, stand, and wisely stand, by the Bible and the Constitution, and drink at it there with reverence and humility; but they who behold where it comes trickling into this lake or that pool, gird up their loins once more, and continue their pilgrimage toward its fountain-head. . . .

The authority of government, even such as I am willing to submit to,—for I will cheerfully obey those who know and can do better than I, and in many things even those who neither know nor can do so well,—is still an impure one: to be strictly just, it must have the sanction and consent of the governed. It can have no pure right over my person and property but what I conceded to it. The progress from an absolute to a limited monarchy, from a limited monarchy to a democracy, is a progress toward a true respect for the individual. Even the Chinese philosopher was wise enough to regard the individual as the basis of the empire. Is a democracy, such as we know it, the last improvement possible in government? Is it not possible to take a step further towards recognizing and organizing the rights of man? There will never be a really free and enlightened State until the State comes to recognize the individual as a higher and independent power, from which all its own power and authority are derived, and treats him accordingly. I please myself with imagining a State at last which can afford to be just to all men, and to treat the individual with respect as a neighbor; which even would not think it inconsistent with its own repose if a few were to live aloof from it, not meddling with it, nor embraced by it, who fulfilled all the duties of neighbors and fellow-men. A State which bore this kind of fruit, and suffered it to drop off as fast as it ripened, would prepare the way for a still more perfect and glorious State, which also I have imagined, but not yet anywhere seen. □

FOR EXPLORATION

selections from Walden

1. How might a person "live what was not life"?
2. Reread the paragraph beginning "Simplicity, simplicity, simplicity. . ." (page C 140, column b, paragraph 1). Are the ideas in it applicable to contemporary life? Do you think it possible or desirable today to "keep your accounts on your thumbnail"? Why or why not?
3. What is the tone of "The Battle of the Ants"? How does this tone differ from that of the other two selections from *Walden?* Support your answer.
4. Compare and contrast Thoreau's reason for going to the woods and his reason for leaving them. Give lines from the text to prove any points you make.
5. According to Emerson's philosophy, is Thoreau standing on his head or on his feet?
6. At present, many people are attempting to imitate Thoreau's Walden experiment, leaving society and living close to nature, attempting to survive on the essentials rather than spend their lives in the acquisition of material things. However, several contemporary social critics have recently written of the violence done to Thoreau's philosophy by many of his latter-day followers. Given the fact that it is not only impossible but also unfair to lump together all those experimenting with alternative life-styles, what basic differences can you see between Thoreau's philosophy and that of many of those who currently profess to be living according to his ideas?

from Civil Disobedience

1. What similarities, if any, exist between Thoreau's attitude toward government and Emerson's philosophy in "A Nonconformist" (page 131C)? Support your answer with lines from both essays.
2. Thoreau presents his reader with two major justifications for civil disobedience, one fairly theoretical, the other personal. What are these justifications? Support your answer with lines from the text.
3. In your opinion, have conditions changed much since the time Thoreau wrote his essay? (One way to approach this question is to see which, if any, of the points he makes might be applied to current conditions.)

CREATIVE RESPONSE

Choose any one of the quotations below as the topic for a personal essay. In writing your essay, keep in mind Thoreau's technique of using specific, concrete examples to make abstract philosophical points both clear and interesting.

"Rather than love, than money, than fame, give me truth."

"Our life is frittered away by detail."

"We do not ride on the railroad; it rides upon us."

"If a man does not keep pace with his companions, perhaps it is because he hears a different drummer."

"There is an incessant influx of novelty into the world, and yet we tolerate incredible dullness."

"He who gives himself entirely to his fellow men appears to them useless and selfish; but he who gives himself partially to them is pronounced a benefactor and philanthropist."

"Under a government which imprisons any unjustly, the true place for a just man is also a prison."

WORDS

Since Thoreau often uses a common word in an unusual sense, we are likely to miss his meaning. Examine the sentence on page 141 C in which he tells us that the three battling ants were "united for life, as if a new kind of *attraction* had been invented which put all other locks and cements to shame." Obviously, Thoreau is not using *attraction* in its usual sense of "that which allures." Turn to a dictionary and select the definition that does fit the context. Then reword the sentence, without using the word *attraction*, in such a way as to make it clear. Explain, too, why the following words are particularly appropriate in the sentence: *united, locks,* and *cement.*

THE THOREAU SOCIETY AND

THE CONCORD FREE PUBLIC LIBRARY,

CONCORD, MASS.

Henry David Thoreau   1817 / 1862

Though generally liked by most of the Concord townspeople, Thoreau was considered a bit of an eccentric. A Harvard graduate, he nonetheless spent his life walking the woods, making pencils in the family business, working occasionally as a handyman, and seeming to cherish idleness. In the eyes of his contemporaries, Henry David Thoreau had not amounted to much.

While the world expected one definition of success, Thoreau lived another; and his writing won for itself a permanence and influence that that of his contemporaries did not. Perhaps the core which gave Thoreau's thoughts their resilience was the integrity of his life. For Thoreau acted out the dictates of his conscience with a determination unsettling to more cautious lives. While Emerson and most others were holding themselves aloof from the slavery problem, Thoreau was helping runaway slaves escape to Canada. When others advised caution, Thoreau became the first American to speak in defense of John Brown. It is said when Emerson visited Thoreau on his day in jail and asked, "Henry, why are you here?" Thoreau answered, "Waldo, why are you *not* here?"

Thoreau was raised in Concord and lived most of his life there, extolling its virtues and proclaiming it a microcosm of the world. Drawn to Emerson's ideas, he joined that household for a time as combination caretaker and intellectual companion. Thoreau was strongly influenced by the older man, and Emerson saw in his protégé the next great champion of transcendentalism. Yet, as the years passed the friendship between Thoreau and Emerson waned. With different values and expectations each was disappointed in the other.

At the age of twenty-eight Thoreau began his stay at Walden Pond. The hut he built there is sometimes referred to as a hermitage; more accurately it was a retreat which allowed him the time for introspection, nature study, and writing. He left Walden a more mature man, firm in his beliefs, and carrying with him the basis of the two books he would publish in his lifetime. His journals would result in *Walden*. And he had completed the rough draft of his first book: *A Week on the Concord and Merrimack Rivers.*

Thoreau died from tuberculosis at the age of forty-four. A few hours before his death an aunt asked if he had "made his peace with God." Thoreau replied, "I have never quarreled with Him."

THE FACTORY GIRLS OF LOWELL

LOWELL, Massachusetts, close to Thoreau's beloved Concord, mushroomed in his lifetime from a sleepy country village into one of the major cotton-manufacturing centers of New England. The Concord and Merrimack rivers, where Thoreau fished and boated and which he knew so intimately, furnished the power that drove the looms and spinning machines. Although Thoreau feared the industrialization he saw around him, for a while at least, Lowell was an industrial Utopia. Prominent visitors such as Andrew Jackson, Charles Dickens, and Davy Crockett came to admire the new factories and the good working conditions; they left praising the remarkable factory girls of Lowell.

In mid-nineteenth century it was unusual to find women working in factories. Married ladies and young girls alike were expected to busy themselves in the home, within their family circle. But because women were familiar with keeping bobbin and loom threads unbroken and unsnarled, the mill owners of Lowell had sought out local farm girls for their factories. The mill owners had their hands full persuading them to come. No God-fearing Yankee farmer was willing to send his daughter, young and respectable as she was, away from home and family. It was unheard of! Faced with such dour reluctance, the mill owners had no choice but to provide the moral atmosphere and protection young ladies required. They did so by building company-owned boarding houses where the girls could live under the chaperoning eye of a stern matron.

Then the girls flocked to Lowell from the country. They were capable and literate young women trained for the arduous and varied tasks of farmlife. For the princely sum of $3.50 a week, they watched the bobbins, tended the looms, and often packed the finished product. They remained in Lowell long enough to bank a suitable dowry and then returned home to the farm and marriage.

Working the same twelve-hour day they had been accustomed to on the farm, these country girls still had the energy to pursue a variety of intellectual interests. In full-skirted dresses, with parasols over their arms, they crowded the lecture halls to hear men like Emerson speak; they listened to church sermons with equal enthusiasm. Their reading was extensive for they shared books with one another—often smuggling copies into the factory, to their overseers' dismay.

The most remarkable thing about the factory girls, however, was their writing. The light verse, original stories, and moral essays, which they wrote for their church literary circles, eventually were collected and published in their own periodical, the *Lowell Offering*. Written and edited by the factory girls, and financed by the mill owners, four issues of the *Offering* appeared in 1840 and in 1841, and several more issues after 1842. The *Lowell Offering*, it is true, was the work of amateur writers; but if its literary quality was not of the highest caliber, neither can it be dismissed as inferior.

When all the industrial abuses Thoreau feared came into being, the country girls left Lowell. We remember them today for their short-lived *Offering*, which shows us dramatically that the New England factory worker shared the same literary interests as his better known American contemporaries did.

CULVER PICTURES, INC.

CHURCH BELLS RINGING, RAINY WINTER NIGHT, 1917 BY CHARLES E. BURCHFIELD—THE CLEVELAND MUSEUM OF ART, GIFT OF MRS. LOUISE M. DUNN IN MEMORY OF HENRY G. KELLER

Nathaniel Hawthorne

1804 / 1864

THE
BIRTHMARK

IN the latter part of the last century there lived a man of science, an eminent proficient in every branch of natural philosophy, who not long before our story opens had made experience of a spiritual affinity more attractive than any chemical one. He had left his laboratory to the care of an assistant, cleared his fine countenance from the furnace smoke, washed the stain of acids from his fingers, and persuaded a beautiful woman to become his wife. In those days when the comparatively recent discovery of electricity and other kindred mysteries of Nature seemed to open paths into the region of miracle, it was not unusual for the love of science to rival the love of woman in its depth and absorbing energy. The higher intellect, the imagination, the spirit, and even the heart might all find their congenial aliment in pursuits which, as some of their ardent votaries believed, would ascend from one step of powerful intelligence to another, until the philosopher should lay his hand on the secret of creative force and perhaps make new worlds for himself. We know not whether Aylmer possessed this degree of faith in man's ultimate control over Nature. He had devoted himself, however, too unreservedly to scientific studies ever to be weaned from them by any second passion. His love for his young wife might prove the stronger of the two; but it could only be by intertwining itself with his love of science, and uniting the strength of the latter to his own.

Such a union accordingly took place, and was attended with truly remarkable consequences and a deeply impressive moral. One day, very soon after their marriage, Aylmer sat gazing at his wife with a trouble in his countenance that grew stronger until he spoke.

"Georgiana," said he, "has it never occurred to you that the mark upon your cheek might be removed?"

"No, indeed," said she, smiling; but perceiving the seriousness of his manner, she blushed deeply. "To tell you the truth it has been so often called a charm that I was simple enough to imagine it might be so."

"Ah, upon another face perhaps it might," replied her husband; "but never on yours. No, dearest Georgiana, you came so nearly perfect from the hand of Nature that this slightest possible defect, which we hesitate whether to term a defect or a beauty, shocks me, as being the visible mark of earthly imperfection."

"Shocks you, my husband!" cried Georgiana, deeply hurt; at first reddening with momentary anger, but then bursting into tears. "Then why did you take me from my mother's side? You cannot love what shocks you!"

To explain this conversation it must be mentioned that in the centre of Georgiana's left cheek there was a singular mark, deeply interwoven, as it were, with the texture and substance of her face. In the usual state of her complexion—a healthy though delicate bloom—the mark wore a tint of deeper crimson, which imperfectly defined its shape amid the surrounding rosiness. When she blushed it gradually became more indistinct, and finally vanished amid the triumphant rush of blood that bathed the whole cheek with its brilliant glow. But if any shifting motion caused her to turn pale there was the mark again, a crimson stain upon the snow, in what Aylmer sometimes deemed an almost fearful distinctness. Its shape bore not a little similarity to the human hand, though of the smallest pygmy size. Georgiana's lovers were wont to say that some fairy at her birth hour had laid her tiny hand upon the infant's cheek, and left this impress there in token of the magic endowments that were to give her such sway over all hearts. Many a desperate swain would have risked life for the privilege of pressing his lips to the mysterious hand. It must not be concealed, however, that the impression wrought by this fairy sign manual varied exceedingly, according to the difference of temperament in the beholders. Some fastidious persons—but they were exclusively of her own sex—affirmed that the bloody hand, as they chose to call it, quite destroyed the effect of Georgiana's beauty, and rendered her countenance even hideous. But it would be as reasonable to say that one of those small blue stains which sometimes occur in the purest statuary marble would convert the Eve of Powers[1] to a monster. Masculine observers, if the birthmark did not heighten their admiration, contented themselves with wishing it away, that the world might possess one living specimen of ideal loveliness without the semblance of a flaw. After his marriage,—for he thought little or nothing of the matter before,—Aylmer discovered that this was the case with himself.

Had she been less beautiful,—if Envy's self could have found aught else to sneer at,—he might have felt his affection heightened by the prettiness of this mimic hand, now vaguely portrayed, now lost, now stealing forth again and glimmering to and fro with every pulse of emotion that throbbed within her heart; but seeing her otherwise so perfect, he found this one defect grow more and more intolerable with every moment of their united lives. It was the fatal flaw of humanity which Nature, in one shape or another, stamps ineffaceably on all her productions, either to imply that they are temporary and finite, or that their perfection must be wrought by toil and pain. The crimson hand expressed the ineludible grip in which mortality clutches the highest and purest of earthly mould, degrading them into kindred with the lowest, and even with the very brutes, like whom their visible frames return to dust. In this manner, selecting it as the symbol of his wife's liability to sin, sorrow, decay, and death, Aylmer's sombre imagination was not long in rendering the birthmark a frightful object, causing him more trouble and horror than ever Georgiana's beauty, whether of soul or sense, had given him delight.

At all the seasons which should have been their happiest, he invariably and without intending it, nay, in spite of a purpose to the contrary, reverted to this one disastrous topic. Trifling as it at first appeared, it so connected itself with innumerable trains of thought and modes of feeling that it became the central point of all. With the morning twilight Aylmer opened his eyes upon his wife's face and recognized the symbol of imperfection; and when they sat together at the evening hearth his eyes wandered stealthily to her cheek, and beheld, flickering with the blaze of the wood fire, the spectral hand that wrote mortality where he would fain have worshipped. Georgiana soon learned to shudder at his gaze. It needed but a glance with the peculiar expression that his face often wore to change the roses of her cheek into a deathlike paleness, amid which the crimson hand was brought strongly out, like a bas-relief of ruby on the whitest marble.

Late one night when the lights were growing dim, so as hardly to betray the stain on the poor wife's cheek, she herself, for the first time, voluntarily took up the subject.

"Do you remember, my dear Aylmer," said she, with a feeble attempt at a smile, "have you any recollection of a dream last night about this odious hand?"

"None! none whatever!" replied Aylmer, starting; but then he added, in a dry, cold tone, affected for the sake of concealing the real depth of his emotion, "I might well dream of it; for before I fell asleep it had taken a pretty firm hold of my fancy."

"And you did dream of it?" continued Georgiana, hastily; for she dreaded lest a gush of tears should interrupt what she had to say. "A terrible dream! I wonder that you can forget it. Is it possible to forget this one expression?—'It is in her heart now; we must have it out!' Reflect, my husband; for by all means I would have you recall that dream."

The mind is in a sad state when Sleep, the all-involving, cannot confine her spectres within the dim region of her sway, but suffers them to break forth, affrighting this actual life with secrets that perchance belong to a deeper one. Aylmer now remembered his dream. He had fancied himself with his servant Aminadab, attempting an operation for the removal of the birthmark; but the deeper went the knife, the deeper sank the hand, until at length its tiny grasp appeared to have caught hold of Georgiana's heart; whence, however, her husband was inexorably resolved to cut or wrench it away.

When the dream had shaped itself perfectly in his memory, Aylmer sat in his wife's presence with a guilty feeling. Truth often finds its way to the mind close muffled in robes of sleep, and then speaks with uncompromising directness of matters in regard to which we practise an unconscious self-deception during our waking moments. Until now he had not been aware of the tyrannizing influence acquired by one idea over his mind, and of the lengths which he might find in his heart to go for the sake of giving himself peace.

"Aylmer," resumed Georgiana, solemnly, "I know not what may be the cost to both of us to rid me of

1. *Eve of Powers*, a statue of Eve produced by the American sculptor, Hiram Powers (1805–1873).

this fatal birthmark. Perhaps its removal may cause cureless deformity; or it may be the stain goes as deep as life itself. Again: do we know that there is a possibility, on any terms, of unclasping the firm gripe of this little hand which was laid upon me before I came into the world?"

"Dearest Georgiana, I have spent much thought upon the subject," hastily interrupted Aylmer. "I am convinced of the perfect practicability of its removal."

"If there be the remotest possibility of it," continued Georgiana, "let the attempt be made at whatever risk. Danger is nothing to me; for life, while this hateful mark makes me the object of your horror and disgust,—life is a burden which I would fling down with joy. Either remove this dreadful hand, or take my wretched life! You have deep science. All the world bears witness of it. You have achieved great wonders. Cannot you remove this little, little mark, which I cover with the tips of two small fingers? Is this beyond your power, for the sake of your own peace, and to save your poor wife from madness?"

"Noblest, dearest, tenderest wife," cried Aylmer, rapturously, "doubt not my power. I have already given this matter the deepest thought—thought which might almost have enlightened me to create a being less perfect than yourself. Georgiana, you have led me deeper than ever into the heart of science. I feel myself fully competent to render this dear cheek as faultless as its fellow; and then, most beloved, what will be my triumph when I shall have corrected what Nature left imperfect in her fairest work! Even Pygmalion,[2] when his sculptured woman assumed life, felt not greater ecstasy than mine will be."

"It is resolved, then," said Georgiana, faintly smiling. "And, Aylmer, spare me not, though you should find the birthmark take refuge in my heart at last."

Her husband tenderly kissed her cheek—her right cheek—not that which bore the impress of the crimson hand.

The next day Aylmer apprised his wife of a plan that he had formed whereby he might have opportunity for the intense thought and constant watchfulness which the proposed operation would require; while Georgiana, likewise, would enjoy the perfect repose essential to its success. They were to seclude themselves in the extensive apartments occupied by Aylmer as a laboratory, and where, during his toil-

some youth, he had made discoveries in the elemental powers of Nature that had roused the admiration of all the learned societies in Europe. Seated calmly in this laboratory, the pale philosopher had investigated the secrets of the highest cloud region and of the profoundest mines; he had satisfied himself of the causes that kindled and kept alive the fires of the volcano; and had explained the mystery of fountains, and how it is that they gush forth, some so bright and pure, and others with such rich medicinal virtues, from the dark bosom of the earth. Here, took, at an earlier period, he had studied the wonders of the human frame, and attempted to fathom the very process by which Nature assimilates all her precious influences from earth and air, and from the spiritual world, to create and foster man, her masterpiece. The latter pursuit, however, Aylmer had long laid aside in unwilling recognition of the truth—against which all seekers sooner or later stumble—that our great creative Mother, while she amuses us with apparently working in the broadest sunshine, is yet severely careful to keep her own secrets, and, in spite of her pretended openness, shows us nothing but results. She permits us, indeed, to mar, but seldom to mend, and, like a jealous patentee, on no account to make. Now, however, Aylmer resumed these half-forgotten investigations; not, of course, with such hopes or wishes as first suggested them; but because they involved much physiological truth and lay in the path of his proposed scheme for the treatment of Georgiana.

As he led her over the threshold of the laboratory, Georgiana was cold and tremulous. Aylmer looked cheerfully into her face, with intent to reassure her, but was so startled with the intense glow of the birthmark upon the whiteness of her cheek that he could not restrain a strong convulsive shudder. His wife fainted.

"Aminadab! Aminadab!" shouted Aylmer, stamping violently on the floor.

Forthwith there issued from an inner apartment a man of low stature, but bulky frame, with shaggy hair hanging about his visage, which was grimed with the vapors of the furnace. This personage had been Aylmer's underworker during his whole scientific career, and was admirably fitted for that office by his great mechanical readiness, and the skill with

2. *Pygmalion*, in Greek mythology, a sculptor of Cyprus who made an ivory statue of a maiden which he fell in love with and which Venus, the goddess of love, brought to life.

which, while incapable of comprehending a single principle, he executed all the details of his master's experiments. With his vast strength, his shaggy hair, his smoky aspect, and the indescribable earthiness that incrusted him, he seemed to represent man's physical nature; while Aylmer's slender figure, and pale, intellectual face, were no less apt a type of the spiritual element.

"Throw open the door of the boudoir, Aminadab," said Aylmer, "and burn a pastil."

"Yes, master," answered Aminadab, looking intently at the lifeless form of Georgiana; and then he muttered to himself, "If she were my wife, I'd never part with that birthmark."

When Georgiana recovered consciousness she found herself breathing an atmosphere of penetrating fragrance, the gentle potency of which had recalled her from her deathlike faintness. The scene around her looked like enchantment. Aylmer had converted those smoky, dingy, sombre rooms, where he had spent his brightest years in recondite pursuits, into a series of beautiful apartments not unfit to be the secluded abode of a lovely woman. The walls were hung with gorgeous curtains, which imparted the combination of grandeur and grace that no other species of adornment can achieve; and as they fell from the ceiling to the floor, their rich and ponderous folds, concealing all angles and straight lines, appeared to shut in the scene from infinite space. For aught Georgiana knew, it might be a pavilion among the clouds. And Aylmer, excluding the sunshine, which would have interfered with his chemical processes, had supplied its place with perfumed lamps, emitting flames of various hue, but all uniting in a soft, impurpled radiance. He now knelt by his wife's side, watching her earnestly, but without alarm; for he was confident in his science, and felt that he could draw a magic circle round her within which no evil might intrude.

"Where am I? Ah, I remember," said Georgiana, faintly; and she placed her hand over her cheek to hide the terrible mark from her husband's eyes.

"Fear not, dearest!" exclaimed he. "Do not shrink from me! Believe me, Georgiana, I even rejoice in this single imperfection, since it will be such a rapture to remove it."

"Oh, spare me!" sadly replied his wife. "Pray do not look at it again. I never can forget that convulsive shudder."

In order to soothe Georgiana, and, as it were, to release her mind from the burden of actual things, Aylmer now put in practice some of the light and playful secrets which science had taught him among its profounder lore. Airy figures, absolutely bodiless ideas, and forms of unsubstantial beauty came and danced before her, imprinting their momentary footsteps on beams of light. Though she had some indistinct idea of the method of these optical phenomena, still the illusion was almost perfect enough to warrant the belief that her husband possessed sway over the spiritual world. Then again, when she felt a wish to look forth from her seclusion, immediately, as if her thoughts were answered, the procession of external existence flitted across a screen. The scenery and the figures of actual life were perfectly represented, but with that bewitching, yet indescribable difference which always makes a picture, an image, or a shadow so much more attractive than the original. When wearied of this, Aylmer bade her cast her eyes upon a vessel containing a quantity of earth. She did so, with little interest at first; but was soon startled to perceive the germ of a plant shooting upward from the soil. Then came the slender stalk; the leaves gradually unfolded themselves; and amid them was a perfect and lovely flower.

"It is magical!" cried Georgiana. "I dare not touch it."

"Nay, pluck it," answered Aylmer,—"pluck it, and inhale its brief perfume while you may. The flower will wither in a few moments and leave nothing save its brown seed vessels; but thence may be perpetuated a race as ephemeral as itself."

But Georgiana had no sooner touched the flower than the whole plant suffered a blight, its leaves turning coal-black as if by the agency of fire.

"There was too powerful a stimulus," said Aylmer, thoughtfully.

To make up for this abortive experiment, he proposed to take her portrait by a scientific process of his own invention. It was to be effected by rays of light striking upon a polished plate of metal. Georgiana assented; but, on looking at the result, was affrighted to find the features of the portrait blurred and indefinable; while the minute figure of a hand appeared where the cheek should have been. Aylmer snatched the metallic plate and threw it into a jar of corrosive acid.

Soon, however, he forgot these mortifying failures. In the intervals of study and chemical experiment he came to her flushed and exhausted, but seemed invigorated by her presence, and spoke in glowing language of the resources of his art. He gave a history of the long dynasty of the alchemists, who spent so many ages in quest of the universal solvent by which the golden principle might be elicited from all things vile and base. Aylmer appeared to believe that, by the plainest scientific logic, it was altogether within the limits of possibility to discover this long-sought medium; "but," he added, "a philosopher who should go deep enough to acquire the power would attain too lofty a wisdom to stoop to the exercise of it." Not less singular were his opinions in regard to the elixir vitæ.[3] He more than intimated that it was at his option to concoct a liquid that should prolong life for years, perhaps interminably; but that it would produce a discord in Nature which all the world, and chiefly the quaffer of the immortal nostrum, would find cause to curse.

"Aylmer, are you in earnest?" asked Georgiana, looking at him with amazement and fear. "It is terrible to possess such power, or even to dream of possessing it."

"Oh, do not tremble, my love," said her husband. "I would not wrong either you or myself by working such inharmonious effects upon our lives; but I would have you consider how trifling, in comparison, is the skill requisite to remove this little hand."

At the mention of the birthmark, Georgiana, as usual, shrank as if a redhot iron had touched her cheek.

Again Aylmer applied himself to his labors. She could hear his voice in the distant furnace room giving directions to Aminadab, whose harsh, uncouth, misshapen tones were audible in response, more like the grunt or growl of a brute than human speech. After hours of absence, Aylmer reappeared and proposed that she should now examine his cabinet of chemical products and natural treasures of the earth. Among the former he showed her a small vial, in which, he remarked, was contained a gentle yet most powerful fragrance, capable of impregnating all the breezes that blow across a kingdom. They were of inestimable value, the contents of that little vial; and, as he said so, he threw some of the perfume into the air and filled the room with piercing and invigorating delight.

"And what is this?" asked Georgiana, pointing to a small crystal globe containing a gold-colored liquid. "It is so beautiful to the eye that I could imagine it the elixir of life."

"In one sense it is," replied Aylmer; "or, rather, the elixir of immortality. It is the most precious poison that ever was concocted in this world. By its aid I could apportion the lifetime of any mortal at whom you might point your finger. The strength of the dose would determine whether he were to linger out years, or drop dead in the midst of a breath. No king on his guarded throne could keep his life if I, in my private station, should deem that the welfare of millions justified me in depriving him of it."

"Why do you keep such a terrific drug?" inquired Georgiana in horror.

"Do not mistrust me, dearest," said her husband, smiling; "its virtuous potency is yet greater than its harmful one. But see! here is a powerful cosmetic. With a few drops of this in a vase of water, freckles may be washed away as easily as the hands are cleansed. A stronger infusion would take the blood out of the cheek, and leave the rosiest beauty a pale ghost."

"Is it with this lotion that you intend to bathe my cheek?" asked Georgiana, anxiously.

"Oh, no," hastily replied her husband; "this is merely superficial. Your case demands a remedy that shall go deeper."

In his interviews with Georgiana, Aylmer generally made minute inquiries as to her sensations and whether the confinement of the rooms and the temperature of the atmosphere agreed with her. These questions had such a particular drift that Georgiana began to conjecture that she was already subjected to certain physical influences, either breathed in with the fragrant air or taken with her food. She fancied likewise, but it might be altogether fancy, that there was a stirring up of her system—a strange, indefinite sensation creeping through her veins, and tingling, half painfully, half pleasurably, at her heart. Still, whenever she dared to look into the mirror, there she beheld herself pale as a white rose and with the crimson birthmark stamped upon her cheek. Not even Aylmer now hated it so much as she.

To dispel the tedium of the hours which her husband found it necessary to devote to the processes of combination and analysis, Georgiana turned over the volumes of his scientific library. In many dark

---

3. *elixir vitæ* (ə lik′sər vī′tē), elixir of life, a substance capable of prolonging life indefinitely.

old tomes she met with chapters full of romance and poetry. They were the works of the philosophers of the middle ages, such as Albertus Magnus, Cornelius Agrippa, Paracelsus, and the famous friar who created the prophetic Brazen Head. All these antique naturalists stood in advance of their centuries, yet were imbued with some of their credulity, and therefore were believed, and perhaps imagined themselves to have acquired from the investigation of Nature a power above Nature, and from physics a sway over the spiritual world. Hardly less curious and imaginative were the early volumes of the Transactions of the Royal Society, in which the members, knowing little of the limits of natural possibility, were continually recording wonders or proposing methods whereby wonders might be wrought.

But to Georgiana the most engrossing volume was a large folio from her husband's own hand, in which he had recorded every experiment of his scientific career, its original aim, the methods adopted for its development, and its final success or failure, with the circumstances to which either event was attributable. The book, in truth, was both the history and emblem of his ardent, ambitious, imaginative, yet practical and laborious life. He handled physical details as if there were nothing beyond them; yet spiritualized them all, and redeemed himself from materialism by his strong and eager aspiration towards the infinite. In his grasp the veriest clod of earth assumed a soul. Georgiana, as she read, reverenced Aylmer and loved him more profoundly than ever, but with a less entire dependence on his judgment than heretofore. Much as he had accomplished, she could not but observe that his most splendid successes were almost invariably failures, if compared with the ideal at which he aimed. His brightest diamonds were the merest pebbles, and felt to be so by himself, in comparison with the inestimable gems which lay hidden beyond his reach. The volume, rich with achievements that had won renown for its author, was yet as melancholy a record as ever mortal hand had penned. It was the sad confession and continual exemplification of the shortcomings of the composite man, the spirit burdened with clay and working in matter, and of the despair that assails the higher nature at finding itself so miserably thwarted by the earthly part. Perhaps every man of genius in whatever sphere might recognize the image of his own experience in Aylmer's journal.

So deeply did these reflections affect Georgiana that she laid her face upon the open volume and burst into tears. In this situation she was found by her husband.

"It is dangerous to read in a sorcerer's books," said he, with a smile, though his countenance was uneasy and displeased. "Georgiana, there are pages in that volume which I can scarcely glance over and keep my senses. Take heed lest it prove as detrimental to you."

"It has made me worship you more than ever," said she.

"Ah, wait for this one success," rejoined he, "then worship me if you will. I shall deem myself hardly unworthy of it. But come, I have sought you for the luxury of your voice. Sing to me, dearest."

So she poured out the liquid music of her voice to quench the thirst of his spirit. He then took his leave with a boyish exuberance of gayety, assuring her that her seclusion would endure but a little longer, and that the result was already certain. Scarcely had he departed when Georgiana felt irresistibly impelled to follow him. She had forgotten to inform Aylmer of a symptom which for two or three hours past had begun to excite her attention. It was a sensation in the fatal birthmark, not painful, but which induced a restlessness throughout her system. Hastening after her husband, she intruded for the first time into the laboratory.

The first thing that struck her eye was the furnace, that hot and feverish worker, with the intense glow of its fire, which by the quantities of soot clustered above it seemed to have been burning for ages. There was a distilling apparatus in full operation. Around the room were retorts, tubes, cylinders, crucibles, and other apparatus of chemical research. An electrical machine stood ready for immediate use. The atmosphere felt oppressively close, and was tainted with gaseous odors which had been tormented forth by the processes of science. The severe and homely simplicity of the apartment, with its naked walls and brick pavement, looked strange, accustomed as Georgiana had become to the fantastic elegance of her boudoir. But what chiefly, indeed almost solely, drew her attention, was the aspect of Aylmer himself.

He was pale as death, anxious and absorbed, and hung over the furnace as it if depended upon his utmost watchfulness whether the liquid which it was distilling should be the draught of immortal happiness or misery. How different from the sanguine and joyous mien that he had assumed for Georgiana's encouragement!

"Carefully now, Aminadab; carefully, thou human machine; carefully, thou man of clay!" muttered Aylmer, more to himself than his assistant. "Now, if there be a thought too much or too little, it is all over."

"Ho! ho!" mumbled Aminadab. "Look, master! look!"

Aylmer raised his eyes hastily, and at first reddened, then grew paler than ever, on beholding Georgiana. He rushed towards her and seized her arm with a gripe that left the print of his fingers upon it.

"Why do you come hither? Have you no trust in your husband?" cried he, impetuously. "Would you throw the blight of that fatal birthmark over my labors? It is not well done. Go, prying woman, go!"

"Nay, Aylmer," said Georgiana with the firmness of which she possessed no stinted endowment, "it is not you that have a right to complain. You mistrust your wife; you have concealed the anxiety with which you watch the development of this experiment. Think not so unworthily of me, my husband. Tell me all the risk we run, and fear not that I shall shrink; for my share in it is far less than your own."

"No, no, Georgiana!" said Aylmer, impatiently; "it must not be."

"I submit," replied she calmly. "And, Aylmer, I shall quaff whatever draught you bring me; but it will be on the same principle that would induce me to take a dose of poison if offered by your hand."

"My noble wife," said Aylmer, deeply moved, "I knew not the height and depth of your nature until now. Nothing shall be concealed. Know, then, that this crimson hand, superficial as it seems, has clutched its grasp into your being with a strength of which I had no previous conception. I have already administered agents powerful enough to do aught except to change your entire physical system. Only one thing remains to be tried. If that fail us we are ruined."

"Why did you hesitate to tell me this?" asked she.

"Because, Georgiana," said Aylmer, in a low voice, "there is danger."

"Danger? There is but one danger—that this horrible stigma shall be left upon my cheek!" cried

Georgiana. "Remove it, remove it, whatever be the cost, or we shall both go mad!"

"Heaven knows your words are too true," said Aylmer, sadly. "And now, dearest, return to your boudoir. In a little while all will be tested."

He conducted her back and took leave of her with a solemn tenderness which spoke far more than his words how much was now at stake. After his departure Georgiana became rapt in musings. She considered the character of Aylmer, and did it completer justice than at any previous moment. Her heart exulted, while it trembled, at his honorable love—so pure and lofty that it would accept nothing less than perfection nor miserably make itself contented with an earthlier nature than he had dreamed of. She felt how much more precious was such a sentiment than that meaner kind which would have borne with the imperfection for her sake, and have been guilty of treason to holy love by degrading its perfect idea to the level of the actual; and with her whole spirit she prayed that, for a single moment, she might satisfy his highest and deepest conception. Longer than one moment she well knew it could not be; for his spirit was ever on the march, ever ascending, and each instant required something that was beyond the scope of the instant before.

The sound of her husband's footsteps aroused her. He bore a crystal goblet containing a liquor colorless as water, but bright enough to be the draught of immortality. Aylmer was pale; but it seemed rather the consequence of a highly-wrought state of mind and tension of spirit than of fear or doubt.

"The concoction of the draught has been perfect," said he, in answer to Georgiana's look. "Unless all my science have deceived me, it cannot fail."

"Save on your account, my dearest Aylmer," observed his wife, "I might wish to put off this birthmark of mortality by relinquishing mortality itself in preference to any other mode. Life is but a sad possession to those who have attained precisely the degree of moral advancement at which I stand. Were I weaker and blinder it might be happiness. Were I stronger, it might be endured hopefully. But, being what I find myself, methinks I am of all mortals the most fit to die."

"You are fit for heaven without tasting death!" replied her husband. "But why do we speak of dying? The draught cannot fail. Behold its effect upon this plant."

On the window seat there stood a geranium diseased with yellow blotches, which had overspread all its leaves. Aylmer poured a small quantity of the liquid upon the soil in which it grew. In a little time, when the roots of the plant had taken up the moisture, the unsightly blotches began to be extinguished in a living verdure.

"There needed no proof," said Georgiana, quietly. "Give me the goblet. I joyfully stake all upon your word."

"Drink, then, thou lofty creature!" exclaimed Aylmer, with fervid admiration. "There is no taint of imperfection on thy spirit. Thy sensible frame, too, shall soon be all perfect."

She quaffed the liquid and returned the goblet to his hand.

"It is grateful," said she with a placid smile. "Methinks it is like water from a heavenly fountain; for it contains I know not what of unobtrusive fragrance and deliciousness. It allays a feverish thirst that had parched me for many days. Now, dearest, let me sleep. My earthly senses are closing over my spirit like the leaves around the heart of a rose at sunset."

She spoke the last words with a gentle reluctance, as if it required almost more energy than she could command to pronounce the faint and lingering syllables. Scarcely had they loitered through her lips ere she was lost in slumber. Aylmer sat by her side, watching her aspect with the emotions proper to a man the whole value of whose existence was involved in the process now to be tested. Mingled with this mood, however, was the philosophic investigation characteristic of the man of science. Not the minutest symptom escaped him. A heightened flush of the cheek, a slight irregularity of breath, a quiver of the eyelid, a hardly perceptible tremor through the frame,—such were the details which, as the moments passed, he wrote down in his folio volume. Intense thought had set its stamp upon every previous page of that volume, but the thoughts of years were all concentrated upon the last.

While thus employed, he failed not to gaze often at the fatal hand, and not without a shudder. Yet once, by a strange and unaccountable impulse, he pressed it with his lips. His spirit recoiled, however, in the very act; and Georgiana, out of the midst of her deep sleep, moved uneasily and murmured as if in remonstrance. Again Aylmer resumed his watch. Nor was it without avail. The crimson hand, which at first had been strongly visible upon the marble paleness of Georgiana's cheek, now grew more faintly outlined. She remained not less pale than ever; but the birthmark, with every breath that came and went, lost somewhat of its former distinctness. Its presence had been awful; its departure was more awful still. Watch the stain of the rainbow fading out of the sky, and you will know how that mysterious symbol passed away.

"By Heaven! it is well-nigh gone!" said Aylmer to himself, in almost irrepressible ecstasy. "I can scarcely trace it now. Success! success! And now it is like the faintest rose color. The lightest flush of blood across her cheek would overcome it. But she is so pale!"

He drew aside the window curtain and suffered the light of natural day to fall into the room and rest upon her cheek. At the same time he heard a gross, hoarse chuckle, which he had long known as his servant Aminadab's expression of delight.

"Ah, clod! ah, earthly mass!" cried Aylmer, laughing in a sort of frenzy, "you have served me well! Matter and spirit—earth and heaven—have both done their part in this! Laugh, thing of the senses! You have earned the right to laugh."

These exclamations broke Georgiana's sleep. She slowly unclosed her eyes and gazed into the mirror which her husband had arranged for that purpose. A faint smile flitted over her lips when she recognized how barely perceptible was now that crimson hand which had once blazed forth with such disastrous brilliancy as to scare away all their happiness. But then her eyes sought Aylmer's face with a trouble and anxiety that he could by no means account for.

"My poor Aylmer!" murmured she.

"Poor? Nay, richest, happiest, most favored!" exclaimed he. "My peerless bride, it is successful! You are perfect!"

"My poor Aylmer," she repeated, with a more than human tenderness, "you have aimed loftily; you have done nobly. Do not repent that with so high and pure a feeling, you have rejected the best the earth could offer. Aylmer, dearest Aylmer, I am dying!"

Alas! it was too true! The fatal hand had grappled with the mystery of life, and was the bond by which an angelic spirit kept itself in union with a mortal frame. As the last crimson tint of the birthmark—that sole token of human imperfection—faded from her cheek, the parting breath of the now perfect woman passed into the atmosphere, and her soul, lingering a moment near her husband, took its heavenward flight. Then a hoarse, chuckling laugh was heard again! Thus ever does the gross fatality of earth exult in its invariable triumph over the immortal essence which, in this dim sphere of half development, demands the completeness of a higher state. Yet, had Aylmer reached a profounder wisdom, he need not thus have flung away the happiness which would have woven his mortal life of the selfsame texture with the celestial. The momentary circumstance was too strong for him; he failed to look beyond the shadowy scope of time, and, living once for all in eternity, to find the perfect future in the present. □

DISCUSSION

Hawthorne was acquainted with the leading Transcendentalists of his time, often meeting with Emerson and his group to discuss the philosophy. He spent several months at Brook Farm, the experiment in communal living founded by a number of these Transcendentalists. Hawthorne married Sophia Peabody, an ardent advocate of Transcendentalism, yet he himself never fully adopted the philosophy.

Although he did hold with many of the Transcendentalist beliefs, Hawthorne's main interests lay in the United States Puritan past and the effects of that past on man and his problems. Hawthorne's ancestors had numbered among the first settlers of New England, and one had been a judge at the Salem witch trials. Hawthorne became steeped in colonial history and used this knowledge to good effect in his writing, especially in what is considered his greatest novel, *The Scarlet Letter.*

In *The Scarlet Letter,* as in much of his other writing, he fused historical fact with imaginative detail to create an **allegory** or a narrative in which characters, action, and sometimes setting represent abstract concepts or moral qualities.

FOR EXPLORATION

1. Describe the tone of the story. What particular words and situations contribute to this tone?

2. In the first paragraph of the story, Aylmer is introduced as a man with a consuming love for science. How, then, will his love for Georgiana fit into his life? Give lines from the paragraph to prove your answer.

3. What is Georgiana's reaction when she discovers that Aylmer has always fallen short of the goals he set for himself? How does her feeling about his failure differ from his attitude toward her birthmark?

4. What basic difference is there between Aylmer's philosophy and that of the Transcendentalists?

5. Why do Aylmer's attempts to perfect Georgiana fail?

6. Do you find Georgiana's attitude and behavior throughout the story admirable? Why or why not?

7. If this story were viewed as an allegory, what concept or moral quality might be represented by Aylmer? by Georgiana? by Aminadab?

Nathaniel Hawthorne 1804/1864

Born in Salem, Massachusetts, Nathaniel Hawthorne was the son of a shipmaster who died when the boy was four. Brought up in a restrained household where his mother took all her meals in her room, he acquired what he called the "cursed habits" of solitude. After attending Bowdoin College he returned home and in that unsociable setting found himself slipping into seclusion. He would later romanticize this period as the "twelve dark years."

Though he eventually left the aloof family household, he remained a reserved and distant man. Both Melville and Emerson were to discover how difficult it was to establish a close friendship with him, and neither succeeded entirely.

While not widely recognized, he was always moderately successful and there were men of his own time, such as Melville, who realized the importance of his work. Hawthorne's interest in the Puritan ethic resulted in *Twice-Told Tales* (1837) and *Mosses from an Old Manse* (1846), the latter containing "The Birthmark." The novels, *The Scarlet Letter* and *The House of the Seven Gables,* both romances concerned with the decadence of Puritanism, followed. He was to write much more before the decline of his creative powers. He has been recognized as a classic interpreter of the spiritual history of New England and, like Poe, a leader in the development of the American short story.

Herman Melville

1819 / 1891

from
A PASSAGE TO
THE ENCHANTED ISLES:
LAS ENCANTADAS

SKETCH NINTH

HOOD'S ISLE AND THE HERMIT OBERLUS

"That darkesome glen they enter, where they find
That cursed man low sitting on the ground,
Musing full sadly in his sullein mind;
His griesly lockes long grouen and unbound,
Disordered hong about his shoulders round,
And hid his face, through which his hollow eyne
Lookt deadly dull, and stared as astound;
His raw-bone cheekes, through penurie and pine,
Were shronke into the jawes, as he did never dine.
His garments nought but many ragged clouts,
With thornes together pind and patched reads,
The which his naked sides he wrapt abouts."

Southeast of Crossman's Isle lies Hood's Isle, or McCain's Beclouded Isle; and upon its south side is a vitreous cove with a wide strand of dark pounded black lava, called Black Beach, or Oberlus's Landing. It might fitly have been styled Charon's.[1]

It received its name from a wild white creature who spent many years here; in the person of a European bringing into this savage region qualities more diabolical than are to be found among any of the surrounding cannibals.

About half a century ago, Oberlus deserted at the above-named island, then, as now, a solitude. He built himself a den of lava and clinkers, about a mile from the Landing, subsequently called after him, in a vale, or expanded gulch, containing here and there among the rocks about two acres of soil capable of rude cultivation; the only place on the isle not too blasted for that purpose. Here he succeeded in raising a sort of degenerate potatoes and pumpkins, which from time to time he exchanged with needy whalemen passing, for spirits or dollars.

His appearance, from all accounts, was that of the victim of some malignant sorceress; he seemed to have drunk of Circe's cup;[2] beast-like; rags insufficient to hid his nakedness; his befreckled skin blistered by continual exposure to the sun; nose flat; countenance contorted, heavy, earthy; hair and beard unshorn, profuse, and of fiery red. He struck strangers much as if he were a volcanic creature thrown up by the same convulsion which exploded into sight the isle. All bepatched and coiled asleep in his lonely lava den among the mountains, he looked, they say, as a heaped drift of withered leaves, torn from autumn trees, and so left in some hidden nook by the whirling halt for an instant of a fierce night-wind, which then ruthlessly sweeps on, somewhere else to repeat the capricious act. It is also reported to have been the strangest sight, this same Oberlus, of a sultry, cloudy morning, hidden under his shocking old black tarpaulin hat, hoeing potatoes among the lava. So warped and crooked was his strange nature, that the very handle of his hoe seemed gradually to have shrunk and twisted in his grasp, being a wretched bent stick, elbowed more like a savage's war-sickle than a civilized hoe-handle. It was his mysterious custom upon a first encounter with a stranger ever to present his back; possibly, because that was his better side, since it revealed the least. If the encounter chanced in his garden, as it sometimes did— the new-landed strangers going from the sea-side straight through the gorge, to hunt up the queer green-grocer reported doing business here—Oberlus for a time hoed on, unmindful of all greeting, jovial or bland; as the curious stranger would turn to face him, the recluse, hoe in hand, as diligently would avert himself; bowed over, and sullenly revolving round his murphy hill. Thus far for hoeing. When planting, his whole aspect and all his gestures were so malevolently and uselessly sinister and secret, that

From PIAZZA TALES by Herman Melville, edited by Egbert S. Oliver. Published by Hendricks House, Inc.

1. *Charon,* in Greek mythology, an aged boatman who ferries the souls of the dead across the river Styx to the entrance to the underworld.
2. *he seemed to have drunk of Circe's cup.* In Greek mythology, Circe is a beautiful witch who turns men into beasts.

he seemed rather in act of dropping poison into wells than potatoes into soil. But among his lesser and more harmless marvels was an idea he ever had, that his visitors came equally as well led by longings to behold the mighty hermit Oberlus in his royal state of solitude, as simply to obtain potatoes, or find whatever company might be upon a barren isle. It seems incredible that such a being should possess such vanity; a misanthrope be conceited; but he really had his notion; and upon the strength of it, often gave himself amusing airs to captains. But after all, this is somewhat of a piece with the well-known eccentricity of some convicts, proud of that very hatefulness which makes them notorious. At other times, another unaccountable whim would seize him, and he would long dodge advancing strangers round the clinkered corners of his hut; sometimes like a stealthy bear, he would slink through the withered thickets up the mountains, and refuse to see the human face.

Except his occasional visitors from the sea, for a long period, the only companions of Oberlus were the crawling tortoises; and he seemed more than degraded to their level, having no desires for a time beyond theirs, unless it were for the stupor brought on by drunkenness. But sufficiently debased as he appeared, there yet lurked in him, only awaiting occasion for discovery, a still further proneness. Indeed, the sole superiority of Oberlus over the tortoises was his possession of a larger capacity of degradation; and along with that, something like an intelligent will to it. Moreover, what is about to be revealed, perhaps will show, that selfish ambition, or the love of rule for its own sake, far from being the peculiar infirmity of noble minds, is shared by beings which have no mind at all. No creatures are so selfishly tyrannical as some brutes; as any one who has observed the tenants of the pasture must occasionally have observed.

"This island's mine by Sycorax[3] my mother," said Oberlus to himself, glaring round upon his haggard solitude. By some means, barter or theft—for in those days ships at intervals still kept touching at his Landing—he obtained an old musket, with a few charges of powder and ball. Possessed of arms, he was stimulated to enterprise, as a tiger that first feels the coming of its claws. The long habit of sole dominion over every object round him, his almost unbroken solitude, his never encountering humanity except on terms of misanthropic independence, or mercantile craftiness, and even such encounters being comparatively but rare; all this must have gradually nourished in him a vast idea of his own importance, together with a pure animal sort of scorn for all the rest of the universe.

The unfortunate Creole, who enjoyed his brief term of royalty at Charles's Isle was perhaps in some degree influenced by not unworthy motives; such as prompt other adventurous spirits to lead colonists into distant regions and assume political preëminence over them. His summary execution of many of his Peruvians is quite pardonable, considering the desperate characters he had to deal with; while his offering canine battle to the banded rebels seems under the circumstances altogether just. But for this King Oberlus and what shortly follows, no shade of palliation can be given. He acted out of mere delight in tyranny and cruelty, by virtue of a quality in him inherited from Sycorax his mother. Armed now with that shocking blunderbuss, strong in the thought of being master of that horrid isle, he panted for a chance to prove his potency upon the first specimen of humanity which should fall unbefriended into his hands.

Nor was he long without it. One day he spied a boat upon the beach, with one man, a Negro, standing by it. Some distance off was a ship, and Oberlus immediately knew how matters stood. The vessel had put in for wood, and the boat's crew had gone into the thickets for it. From a convenient spot he kept watch of the boat, till presently a straggling company appeared loaded with billets. Throwing these on the beach, they again went into the thickets, while the Negro proceeded to load the boat.

Oberlus now makes all haste and accosts the Negro, who, aghast at seeing any living being inhabiting such a solitude, and especially so horrific a one, immediately falls into a panic, not at all lessened by the ursine suavity of Oberlus, who begs the favor of assisting him in his labors. The Negro stands with several billets on his shoulder, in act of shouldering others; and Oberlus, with a short cord concealed in his bosom, kindly proceeds to lift those other billets to their place. In so doing, he persists in keeping behind the Negro, who, rightly suspicious of this, in vain dodges about to gain the front of Oberlus; but Oberlus dodges also; till at last, weary of this bootless attempt at treachery, or fearful of being sur-

---

3. *Sycorax.* In William Shakespeare's *The Tempest,* Sycorax is the mother of Caliban, a savage and deformed slave.

prised by the remainder of the party, Oberlus runs off a little space to a bush, and fetching his blunderbuss, savagely commands the Negro to desist work and follow him. He refuses. Whereupon, presenting his piece, Oberlus snaps at him. Luckily the blunderbuss misses fire; but by this time, frightened out of his wits, the Negro, upon a second intrepid summons, drops his billets, surrenders at discretion, and follows on. By a narrow defile familiar to him, Oberlus speedily removes out of sight of the water.

On their way up the mountains, he exultingly informs the Negro, that henceforth he is to work for him, and be his slave, and that his treatment would entirely depend on his future conduct. But Oberlus, deceived by the first impulsive cowardice of the black, in an evil moment slackens his vigilance. Passing through a narrow way, and perceiving his leader quite off his guard, the Negro, a powerful fellow, suddenly grasps him in his arms, throws him down, wrests his musketoon from him, ties his hands with the monster's own cord, shoulders him, and returns with him down to the boat. When the rest of the party arrive, Oberlus is carried on board the ship. This proved an Englishman, and a smuggler; a sort of craft not apt to be over-charitable. Oberlus is severely whipped, then handcuffed, taken ashore, and compelled to make known his habitation and produce his property. His potatoes, pumpkins, and tortoises, with a pile of dollars he had hoarded from his mercantile operations were secured on the spot. But while the too vindictive smugglers were busy destroying his hut and garden, Oberlus makes his escape into the mountains, and conceals himself there in impenetrable recesses, only known to himself, till the ship sails, when he ventures back, and by means of an old file which he sticks into a tree, contrives to free himself from his handcuffs.

Brooding among the ruins of his hut, and the desolate clinkers and extinct volcanoes of this outcast isle, the insulted misanthrope now meditates a signal revenge upon humanity, but conceals his purposes. Vessels still touch the Landing at times; and by-and-by Oberlus is enabled to supply them with some vegetables.

Warned by his former failure in kidnapping strangers, he now pursues a quite different plan. When seamen come ashore, he makes up to them like a free-and-easy comrade, invites them to his hut, and with whatever affability his red-haired grimness may assume, entreats them to drink his liquor and be merry. But his guests need little pressing; and so, soon as rendered insensible, are tied hand and foot, and pitched among the clinkers, are there concealed till the ship departs, when, finding themselves entirely dependent upon Oberlus, alarmed at his changed demeanor, his savage threats, and above all, that shocking blunderbuss, they willingly enlist under him, becoming his humble slaves, and Oberlus the most incredible of tyrants. So much so, that two or three perish beneath his initiating process. He sets the remainder—four of them—to breaking the caked soil; transporting upon their backs loads of loamy earth, scooped up in moist clefts among the mountains; keeps them on the roughest fare; presents his piece at the slightest hint of insurrection; and in all respects converts them into reptiles at his feet—plebeian garter-snakes to this Lord Anaconda.

At last, Oberlus contrives to stock his arsenal with four rusty cutlasses, and an added supply of powder and ball intended for his blunderbuss. Remitting in good part the labor of his slaves, he now approves himself a man, or rather devil, of great abilities in the way of cajoling or coercing others into acquiescence with his own ulterior designs, however at first abhorrent to them. But indeed, prepared for almost any eventual evil by their previous lawless life, as a sort of ranging Cow-Boys of the sea, which had dissolved within them the whole moral man, so that they were ready to concrete in the first offered mould of baseness now; rotted down from manhood by their hopeless misery on the isle; wonted to cringe in all things to their lord, himself the worst of slaves; these wretches were now become wholly corrupted to his hands. He used them as creatures of an inferior race; in short, he gaffles his four animals, and makes murderers of them; out of cowards fitly manufacturing bravos.

Now, sword or dagger, human arms are but artificial claws and fangs, tied on like false spurs to the fighting cock. So, we repeat, Oberlus, czar of the isle, gaffles his four subjects; that is, with intent of glory, puts four rusty cutlasses into their hands. Like any other autocrat, he had a noble army now.

It might be thought a servile war would hereupon ensue. Arms in the hands of trodden slaves? how indiscreet of Emperor Oberlus! Nay, they had but cutlasses—sad old scythes enough—he a blunderbuss, which by its blind scatterings of all sort of boulders, clinkers, and other scoria would annihilate all four mutineers, like four pigeons at one shot. Besides, at first he did not sleep in his accustomed hut; every lurid sunset, for a time, he might have been seen wending his way among the riven mountains, there to secrete himself till dawn in some sulphurous pitfall, undiscoverable to his gang; but finding this at last too troublesome, he now each evening tied his slaves hand and foot, hid the cutlasses, and thrusting them into his barracks, shut to the door, and lying down before it, beneath a rude shed lately added, slept out the night, blunderbuss in hand.

It is supposed that not content with daily parading over a cindery solitude at the head his fine army, Oberlus now meditated the most active mischief; his probable object being to surprise some passing ship touching at his dominions, massacre the crew, and run away with her to parts unknown. While these plans were simmering in his head, two ships touch in company at the isle, on the opposite side to his; when his designs undergo a sudden change.

The ships are in want of vegetables, which Oberlus promises in great abundance, provided they send their boats round to his landing, so that the crews may bring the vegetables from his garden; informing the two captains, at the same time, that his rascals—slaves and soldiers—had become so abominably lazy and good-for-nothing of late, that he could not make them work by ordinary inducements, and did not have the heart to be severe with them.

The arrangement was agreed to, and the boats were sent and hauled upon the beach. The crews went to the lava hut; but to their surprise nobody was there. After waiting till their patience was exhausted, they returned to the shore, when lo, some stranger—not the Good Samaritan either—seems to have very recently passed that way. Three of the boats were broken in a thousand pieces, and the fourth was missing. By hard toil over the mountains and through the clinkers, some of the strangers succeeded in returning to that side of the isle where the ships lay, when fresh boats are sent to the relief of the rest of the hapless party.

However amazed at the treachery of Oberlus, the two captains, afraid of new and still more mysterious atrocities—and indeed, half imputing such strange events to the enchantments associated with these isles—perceive no security but in instant flight; leaving Oberlus and his army in quiet possession of the stolen boat.

On the eve of sailing they put a letter in a keg, giving the Pacific Ocean intelligence of the affair, and moored the keg in the bay. Some time subsequent, the keg was opened by another captain chancing to anchor there, but not until after he had dispatched a boat round to Oberlus's Landing. As may be readily surmised, he felt no little inquietude till the boat's return; when another letter was handed him, giving Oberlus's version of the affair. This precious document had been found pinned half-mildewed to the clinker wall of the sulphurous and deserted hut. It ran as follows: showing that Oberlus was at least an accomplished writer, and no mere boor; and what is more, was capable of the most tristful eloquence.

"Sir: I am the most unfortunate ill-treated gentleman that lives. I am a patriot, exiled from my country by the cruel hand of tyranny.

"Banished to these Enchanted Isles, I have again and again besought captains of ships to sell me a boat, but always have been refused, though I offered the handsomest prices in Mexican dollars. At length an opportunity presented of possessing myself of one, and I did not let it slip.

"I have been long endeavoring, by hard labor and much solitary suffering, to accumulate something to make myself comfortable in a virtuous though unhappy old age; but at various times have been robbed and beaten by men professing to be Christians.

"To-day I sail from the Enchanted group in the good boat Charity bound to the Feejee Isles.[4]

"FATHERLESS OBERLUS.

"P.S.—Behind the clinkers, nigh the oven, you will find the old fowl. Do not kill it; be patient; I leave it setting; if it shall have any chicks, I hereby bequeath them to you, whoever you may be. But don't count your chicks before they are hatched."

The fowl proved a starveling rooster, reduced to a sitting posture by sheer debility.

Oberlus declares that he was bound to the Feejee Isles; but this was only to throw pursuers on a false scent. For, after a long time, he arrived, alone in his open boat, at Guayaquil.[5] As his miscreants were never again beheld on Hood's Isle, it is supposed, either that they perished for want of water on the passage to Guayaquil, or, what is quite as probable, were thrown overboard by Oberlus, when he found the water growing scarce.

---

4. *Feejee Isles* (Fiji Islands), an island group in the southwest Pacific Ocean.
5. *Guayaquil* (gwī′ ä kēl′), the seaport of Guayas province in southwest Ecuador.

From Guayaquil Oberlus proceeded to Payta;[6] and there, with that nameless witchery peculiar to some of the ugliest animals, wound himself into the affections of a tawny damsel; prevailing upon her to accompany him back to his Enchanted Isle; which doubtless he painted as a Paradise of flowers, not a Tartarus[7] of clinkers.

But unfortunately for the colonization of Hood's Isle with a choice variety of animated nature, the extraordinary and devilish aspect of Oberlus made him to be regarded in Payta as a highly suspicious character. So that being found concealed one night, with matches in his pocket, under the hull of a small vessel just ready to be launched, he was seized and thrown into jail.

The jails in most South American towns are generally of the least wholesome sort. Built of huge cakes of sun-burnt brick, and containing but one room, without windows or yard, and but one door heavily grated with wooden bars, they present both within and without the grimmest aspect. As public edifices they conspicuously stand upon the hot and dusty Plaza, offering to view, through the gratings, their villainous and hopeless inmates, burrowing in all sorts of tragic squalor. And here for a long time, Oberlus was seen; the central figure of a mongrel and assassin band; a creature whom it is religion to detest, since it is philanthropy to hate a misanthrope.

Note.—They who may be disposed to question the possibility of the character above depicted, are referred to the 2d vol. of Porter's Voyage into the Pacific, where they will recognize many sentences, for expedition's sake derived verbatim from thence, and incorporated here; the main difference—save a few passing reflections—between the two accounts being, that the present writer has added to Porter's facts accessory ones picked up in the Pacific from reliable sources; and where facts conflict, has naturally preferred his own authorities to Porter's. As, for instance, *his* authorities place Oberlus on Hood's Isle: Porter's, on Charles's Isle. The letter found in the hut is also somewhat different; for while at the Encantadas he was informed that, not only did it evince a certain clerkliness, but was full of the strangest satiric effrontery which does not adequately appear in Porter's version. I accordingly altered it to suit the general character of its author.

---

6. *Payta* (Paita) (pī′ tä), a seaport town in northwest Peru.
7. *Tartarus*, in Greek mythology, the deepest region of the underworld.

POEMS OF MELVILLE

SHILOH

A Requiem
(April, 1862)

Skimming lightly, wheeling still,
   The swallows fly low
Over the field in clouded days,
   The forest-field of Shiloh[1]—
5 Over the field where April rain
Solaced the parched ones stretched in pain
   Through the pause of night
That followed the Sunday fight
   Around the church of Shiloh—
10 The church so lone, the log-built one,

That echoed to many a parting groan
   And natural prayer
Of dying foemen mingled there—
Foemen at morn, but friends at eve—
15 Fame or country least their care:
(What like a bullet can undeceive!)
   But now they lie low,
While over them the swallows skim,
   And all is hushed at Shiloh.

---

1. *Shiloh.* A costly but indecisive battle between the Federal army and the Confederates took place at Shiloh, Tennessee.

STONEWALL JACKSON

Mortally wounded at Chancellorsville

May, 1863

The Man who fiercest charged in fight,
　Whose sword and prayer were long—
　　Stonewall!
Even him who stoutly stood for Wrong,
5　How can we praise? Yet coming days
　Shall not forget him with this song.

Dead is the Man whose Cause is dead,
　Vainly he died and set his seal—
　　Stonewall!
10　Earnest in error, as we feel;
True to the thing he deemed was due,
　True as John Brown or steel.

Relentlessly he routed us;
　But *we* relent, for he is low—
15　　Stonewall!
Justly his fame we outlaw; so
We drop a tear on the bold Virginian's bier,
　Because no wreath we owe.

THE PORTENT　(1859)

Hanging from the beam,
　Slowly swaying (such the law),
Gaunt the shadow on your green,
　Shenandoah!
5　The cut is on the crown
　(Lo, John Brown),
And the stabs shall heal no more.

Hidden in the cap
　Is the anguish none can draw;
10　So your future veils its face,
　Shenandoah!
But the streaming beard is shown
　(Weird John Brown),
The meteor of the war.

DISCUSSION

Though not always essential or even desirable, historical background can sometimes serve to make a work of literature more easily understood and appreciated. Such is the case with the Melville selections printed here. Although each is able to stand on its own without any background information, some knowledge of the places Melville described and of the time he wrote is helpful in discussing the selections:

Las Encantadas or the Enchanted Isles, known also as the Galápagos, is a group of Pacific islands located on the equator about 650 miles west of Ecuador. Barren, rocky, and desolate, the islands are named for the giant tortoises (galápagos) found there, the oldest living creatures on earth.

The three poems pertain to events relating to slavery and the Civil War. "The Portent" tells of the death of John Brown, an ardent abolitionist who in 1859 attacked the government arsenal at Harpers Ferry, Virginia, in hopes of seizing arms to use in a slave uprising. Brown's group was defeated; Brown himself was wounded, captured, and brought to trial before his wounds had healed. He was found guilty of treason and hanged.

Traditional belief held that meteors and comets portended civil strife. In 1859 a meteor shower was visible throughout a large part of the United States. Many people thought it foretold a major conflict.

FOR EXPLORATION

A Passage to the Enchanted Isles: Las Encantadas

Compare and contrast Melville's description of Oberlus with the Romantic idea of the noble savage and the Transcendental view of the individual's relationship to nature.

Shiloh

1. What is a requiem?
2. Listen to the poem read aloud. What is its tone?
3. What is the deception alluded to in line 16? How does a bullet clear up the deception? What is the irony of the situation?

Stonewall Jackson

What is Melville's attitude toward Stonewall Jackson? What are the reasons for this attitude? Support your answer with lines from the poem.

The Portent

1. What event is described in the first stanza?
2. Who or what is the speaker addressing as "Shenandoah"?
3. Read the first stanza aloud. What effect does line 6 have on the poem's tone?
4. What is the "cap" of line 8?
5. What two things are being compared in lines 8–11?
6. Discuss the aptness of the use of "streaming" in line 12.
7. In what way might John Brown be considered a "meteor of the war"?
8. Reread the poem. What is its effect? How does the line "(Weird John Brown)" contribute to this effect?

CREATIVE RESPONSE

Melville was not alone in his fascination with the Encantadas. Charles Darwin stopped there in 1835 on his famous voyage in the *Beagle*. His study of the islands' life forms was instrumental in developing his theory of evolution. Many accounts of this voyage have been written. One of special appeal to the layman is Alan Moorehead's *Darwin and the Beagle* which interested students might read and report on to the class.

CULVER PICTURES, INC.

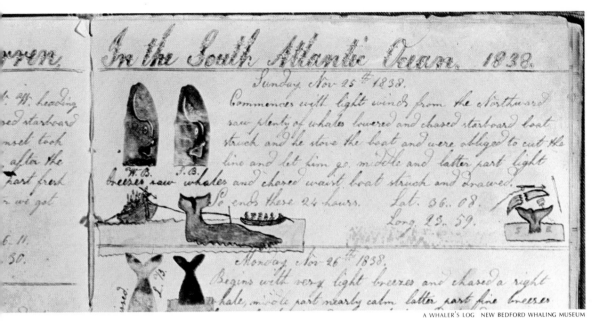

A WHALER'S LOG   NEW BEDFORD WHALING MUSEUM

Herman Melville   1819 / 1891

Herman Melville was born into a distinguished but financially unstable New York family; his youth was one of genteel pretense. When his father died in 1832 Melville left school to take on a series of jobs, finally shipping as cabin boy to Liverpool. This voyage, to be described in *Redburn* (1849), was the beginning of many remarkable experiences which would become the foundation for his novels. He next sailed for the South Seas on a whaler, the voyage which would later provide the background for *Moby Dick* (1851). He jumped ship at the Marquesas Islands, and as related in *Typee* (1846), took refuge among the cannibalistic Typees. He lived with them a short while and then left on a passing Australian whaler which dropped him off in Tahiti. His stay in Tahiti resulted in *Omoo* (1847). He then enlisted as an ordinary seaman on the frigate *United States* until the ship's eventual return to Boston. His account of cruelty and tyranny in *White Jacket* (1850) added fuel to a movement which would shortly result in the abolishment of flogging on ships of the U.S. Navy.

The colorful descriptions of Melville's experiences in *Typee* and *Omoo* won the interest of a curious and fascinated public. He was widely read and became known as the man who had lived amongst cannibals. But with succeeding works Melville's craft became deeper and more demanding. A public which preferred simple adventure had little use for meaning and allegory. As the brilliance of his writing increased his popularity diminished. His criticism of missionaries in *Omoo* had further set segments of the public against him. Thus when his masterpiece *Moby Dick* was published just five years after his initial success, it was ignored, and remained largely unread for over seventy years.

After the exhaustive effort of *Moby Dick* and the disappointment of its reception, Melville's productivity decreased sharply. He supported himself in his later years as a customs inspector and died forgotten at the age of seventy-two.

Some of the subsequent histories of American literature did not even mention his name. Barrett Wendall's *Literary History of America* published in 1900 reads, "Herman Melville, with his books about the South Seas, which Robert Louis Stevenson is said to have declared the best ever written, and with his novels of maritime adventure, began a career of literary promise, which never came to fruition." Melville was finally rediscovered in the 1920's and today *Moby Dick* is considered the greatest American novel ever written.

Perhaps the best available characterization of Melville is to be found in the journals of his friend Hawthorne. Describing a meeting in England Hawthorne writes, "We took a pretty long walk together, and sat down in a hollow among the sand hills (sheltering ourselves from the high, cool wind) and smoked a cigar. Melville, as he always does, began to reason of Providence and futurity, and of everything that lies beyond human ken, and informed me that he had 'pretty much made up his mind to be annihilated'; but still he does not seem to rest in that anticipation; and, I think, will never rest until he gets hold of a definite belief. It is strange how he persists—and has persisted ever since I knew him, and probably long before—in wandering to-and-fro over these deserts, as dismal and monotonous as the sand hills amid which we were sitting. He can neither believe, nor be comfortable in his unbelief; and he is too honest and courageous not to try to do one or the other . . . he has a very high and noble nature. . . ."

JASPER JOHNS "MAP," 1961, COLLECTION THE MUSEUM OF MODERN ART, NEW YORK, GIFT OF MR. AND MRS. ROBERT C. SCULL

RENAISSANCE

Then and Now

Many critics of American culture have noted with some wonder and interest the sudden flowering, at about the middle of the nineteenth century, of American literature. It is, indeed, possible to discover a five-year period, 1850–1855, which is crowded with American classics: 1850: Emerson's *Representative Men*, Hawthorne's *The Scarlet Letter;* 1851: Melville's *Moby Dick*, Hawthorne's *The House of the Seven Gables;* 1852: Harriet Beecher Stowe's *Uncle Tom's Cabin*, Hawthorne's *The Blithedale Romance*, Melville's *Pierre;* 1854: Thoreau's *Walden;* 1855: Walt Whitman's *Leaves of Grass*, Melville's *Benito Cereno*, Henry Wadsworth Longfellow's *Hiawatha*.

There is, of course, something quite artificial in limiting observation to one-half of a single decade, and, moreover, the works listed above that appeared from 1850–1855 are not all of the same level of achievement. Nevertheless, the phenomenon is startling. The readers alive during that five-year period witnessed the publication of most of the nineteenth century's classic American writers, and were privileged to read for the first time a number of books that were to establish themselves firmly not only as American but as world classics.

A number of critics have attempted to explain this phenomenon in book-length studies, and the titles they have invented suggest the ways they have looked at this remarkably creative period: Lewis Mumford, *The Golden Day* (1926); Van Wyck Brooks, *The Flowering of New England;* F. O. Matthiessen, *American Renaissance* (1941). Whatever name is applied to the period and to its high achievement, the facts themselves remain something of a puzzle and an enigma. Why was it that a country that had produced some very fine but no indisputably great writers should suddenly and without warning give voice to a number of authors who would enter and help redirect the stream of world literature? Emerson, Thoreau, Hawthorne, and Melville were writers of this stature.

Obviously no single answer can be given to such a complex question. But no one can doubt that a number of factors contributed to the American Renaissance. Of no small importance was the disappearance of some of the earlier distractions and difficulties that stood in the way of the development of a native culture. By the middle of the nineteenth century it was no longer necessary for Americans to remain so totally preoccupied with the simple business of survival in a wilderness or frontier. They had more time both to write and to read books. There was, moreover, a restlessness and ferment in the country that contributed to the clash and sharpening of ideas. Religious debate had been carried on from the moment of the first settlement in the 1600's, and that debate had continued with an infinite variety of philosophical ramifications down into the nineteenth century. Political experimentation and debate were deeply ingrained in the American character from the beginning, and as new states joined the Union and new territories opened up for settlement, the new possibilities excited the American imagination. The issue of slavery aroused fierce emotions and endless argument in the "land of the free."

No one of these factors can be said to be the principal one in making the American Renaissance, but they all contributed. There were, however, other elements. Who can say what produces genius? Genius is genius, and is in some sense its own cause. And the writers of this period were writers, in some meaning of the word, of genius. Moreover, they appeared at a moment in history when the country was in search of its identity (as distinct from its European origins) and was open to writers who might help in the search.

Emerson has been called the fountainhead of American literature, not only because his essays and poems have had wide influence beyond his own time and place, but also because he provided a title and a date with which to celebrate the beginning of American cultural independence. The title is "The American Scholar," and the date is 1837, when Emerson delivered his address before the Phi Beta Kappa Society at Harvard. In that famous speech, Emerson announced: "Our day of dependence, our long apprenticeship to the learning of other lands, draws to a close." And he told his countrymen: "We will walk on our own feet; we will work with our own hands; we will speak our own minds." Emerson's remarks, said Oliver Wendell Holmes, constituted "our intellectual Declaration of Independence." Emerson's "The American Scholar" proved to be both a declaration and a prophecy, and the prophecy saw its fulfillment in the American Renaissance.

Like all classics, the classic American books continue to have a vitality and relevance long after the death of their authors. No single work better exemplifies this fact than Thoreau's *Civil Disobedience*. When Thoreau went to jail for refusing to pay his taxes in protest over a war which he felt unjust, he set a pattern of behavior that has been studied and followed many times since. Many national and world leaders since Thoreau have paid tribute to him and his book as important in their education and as demonstrating a way to muster moral force in confronting superior physical force and possible violence. Here are some of the testimonials:

A LEGACY OF CREATIVE PROTEST

The Rev. Martin Luther King, Jr.

DURING my early college days I read Thoreau's essay on civil disobedience for the first time. Fascinated by the idea of refusing to cooperate with an evil system, I was so deeply moved that I re-read the work several times. I became convinced then that non-cooperation with evil is as much a moral obligation as is cooperation with good. No other person has been more eloquent and passionate in getting this idea across than Henry David Thoreau. As a result of his writings and personal witness we are the heirs of a legacy of creative protest. It goes without saying that the teachings of Thoreau are alive today, indeed, they are more alive today than ever before. Whether expressed in a sit-in at lunch counters, a freedom ride into Mississippi, a peaceful protest in Albany, Georgia, a bus boycott in Montgomery, Alabama, it is an outgrowth of Thoreau's insistence that evil must be resisted and no moral man can patiently adjust to injustice.

"A Legacy of Creative Protest" by Martin Luther King, Jr. from THOREAU IN OUR SEASON, edited by John H. Hicks. Copyright © 1962, 1966 by The University of Massachusetts Press. Reprinted by permission.

from

HOMAGE TO GANDHI

Webb Miller

. . . As an admirer of Thoreau, I thought I detected similarities in Gandhi's ideas and Thoreau's philosophy. The first question I put to him was: "Did you ever read an American named Henry D. Thoreau?" His eyes brightened and he chuckled.

"Why, of course I read Thoreau. I read *Walden* first in Johannesburg in South Africa in 1906 and his ideas influenced me greatly. I adopted some of them and recommended the study of Thoreau to all my friends who were helping me in the cause of Indian independence. Why, I actually took the name of my movement from Thoreau's essay, 'On the Duty of Civil Disobedience,' written about eighty years ago. Until I read that essay I never found a suitable English translation for my Indian word, *Satyagraha.* You remember that Thoreau invented and practiced the idea of civil disobedience in Concord, Massachusetts, by refusing to pay his poll tax as a protest against the United States government. He went to jail, too. There is no doubt that Thoreau's ideas greatly influenced my movement in India."

I think I was perhaps the first to discover the curious fact that the wizened Hindu mystic adopted from the hermit philosopher of Concord the strange political concept of nonviolent civil disobedience which deeply influenced the teeming millions in India; that the example of the gentle visionary of Walden Pond inspired millions to defy without arms the power of the world's greatest empire; that the ideas of the sensitive man in Concord who detested violence and bloodshed had after eighty-one years resulted in hundreds of deaths, the injury of ten thousand, and imprisonment of perhaps a hundred thousand in India, on the other side of the world.

When Thoreau wrote the essay, "On the Duty of Civil Disobedience," in 1849 he was thinking of Negro slavery and the Mexican war of 1848. He was making a one-man rebellion against the American government because he disagreed with its policies on these questions. He conceived the idea of manifesting his rebellion against the national government by refusing to pay his poll tax, and went to jail. This was the genesis of the concept which Gandhi used in his rebellion against the British government for not granting self-government in India. There can be little doubt that the inspiration of Thoreau had much to do with India's attainment of a wide measure of autonomy and self-government from Britain in the Government of India Act of 1935, which Gandhi's civil-disobedience campaign hastened. When I stood beside Thoreau's grave in the mellow sunlight of a May afternoon several years later, I wondered what Thoreau would think if he could know that his ideas and one night in jail in Concord had indirectly influenced the current of history and the lives of 350,000,000 Indians three generations later.

From long reading of Thoreau I am convinced that his philosophical conceptions emanated largely from Indian literature. In *Walden* he repeatedly mentions the Vedas[1] and other Hindu literature and once says: "I . . . who loved so well the philosophy of India. . . ." It would seem that Gandhi received back from America what was fundamentally the philosophy of India after it had been distilled and crystallized in the mind of Thoreau. This perhaps explains why the Hindu mentality so readily accepted his ideas. . . .

From *"Homage to Gandhi"* from I FOUND NO PEACE by Webb Miller. Copyright 1936 by Webb Miller. Reprinted by permission of Simon and Schuster, Inc.
1. *the Vedas,* the more than one hundred existing books that make up the most ancient sacred literature of the Hindus.

MAN'S DUTY AS MAN

Martin Buber

Es sind nun nahezu sechzig Jahre her, dass ich Thoreaus Traktat über den "bürgerlichen Ungehorsam" kennen lernte. Ich las ihn mit dem starken Gefühl: Das ist etwas, was mich unmittelbar angeht. Erst sehr viel später aber habe ich verstanden, woher jenes Gefühl kam. Es war das Konkrete, Persönliche, das "Jetzt und Hier" an der Schrift, was ihr mein Herz gewann. Thoreau formulierte nicht einen allgemeinen Grundsatz als solchen; er beschrieb und begründete seine Haltung in einer bestimmten historisch-biographischen Situation. Er sprach seinen Leser im Bereiche dieser ihnen gemeinsamen Situation so an, dass der Leser nicht bloss erfuhr, warum Thoreau damals so handelte, wie er handelte, sondern—wofern dieser Leser nur redlich und unbefangen war—auch, dass er selber, der Leser, gegebenenfalls eben solcherweise handeln musste, wenn es ihm ernstlich darum zu tun war, seine menschliche Existenz zu verwirklichen.

Es geht hier nicht einfach um einen der vielen Einzelfälle in dem Kampf einer machtlosen Wahrheit gegen eine wahrheitsfeindlich gewordene Macht. Es geht um die ganz konkrete Aufzeigung des Punktes, an dem je und je dieser Kampf zur Pflicht des Menschen *als Mensch* wird. Indem Thoreau von seiner geschichtlichen Situation so konkret spricht, wie er es tut, sagt er das für alle Menschengeschichte Gültige auf die richtige Weise aus.

JERUSALEM, OCTOBER 15, 1962

It is now nearly sixty years since I first got to know Thoreau's essay "Civil Disobedience." I read it with the strong feeling that here was something that concerned me directly. Not till very much later, however, did I understand the origin of this feeling. It was the concrete, the personal element, the "here and now" of this work that won me over. Thoreau did not put forth a general proposition as such; he described and established his attitude in a specific historical-biographic situation. He addressed his reader within the very sphere of this situation common to both of them in such a way that the reader not only discovered why Thoreau acted as he did at that time but also that the reader—assuming him of course to be honest and dispassionate—would have to act in just such a way whenever the proper occasion arose, provided he was seriously engaged in fulfilling his existence as a human person.

The question here is not just about one of the numerous individual cases in the struggle between a truth powerless to act and a power that has become the enemy of truth. It is really a question of the absolutely concrete demonstration of the point at which this struggle at any moment becomes man's duty *as man*. By speaking as concretely as he does about his own historical situation, Thoreau expresses exactly that which is valid for all human history.

(Translated by the author)

"Man's Duty as Man" by Martin Buber from THOREAU IN OUR SEASON, edited by John H. Hicks. Copyright © 1962, 1966 by The University of Massachusetts Press. Reprinted by permission.

OVERLEAF: JOHN BROWN GOING TO HIS HANGING, 1942 BY HORACE PIPPIN —COURTESY OF THE PENNSYLVANIA ACADEMY OF THE FINE ARTS

END OF
AN ERA

THE FIRESIDE POETS

Henry Wadsworth Longfellow   1807/1882

DIVINA COMMEDIA

In July of 1861 Longfellow's second wife met with a fatal household accident. A match ignited her dress, and despite Longfellow's desperate attempt to extinguish the flames, she died the next day. Longfellow, overcome by the tragedy, sought solace for his grief in work. The difficult task he set for himself was the translation into English of the Divina Commedia *(di vē'nä kōm mä'dyä), or* Divine Comedy, *by Dante Alighieri (dän'tä ä'li gyär'i), one of the greatest of Italian poets. This epic poem consists of three parts,* which describe Dante's imaginary journey to Hell, Purgatory, and Paradise. In his translation, Longfellow prefaced each part with two sonnets. In these sonnets the cathedral represents Dante's epic, a majestic "edifice" of poetry. Although Longfellow's purpose apparently is to describe the cathedral, he is actually commenting both on Dante's poem and the comfort it offered him in his grief. Sonnets One and Two, which follow, prefaced "Inferno," the first part of the Divine Comedy.*

One

Oft have I seen at some cathedral door
    A laborer, pausing in the dust and heat,
    Lay down his burden, and with reverent feet
    Enter, and cross himself, and on the floor
5 Kneel to repeat his paternoster[1] o'er;
    Far off the noises of the world retreat;
    The loud vociferations of the street
    Become an undistinguishable roar.
So, as I enter here from day to day,
10 And leave my burden at this minster gate,[2]
    Kneeling in prayer, and not ashamed to pray,
The tumult of the time disconsolate
    To inarticulate murmurs dies away,
    While the eternal ages watch and wait.

Two

How strange the sculptures that adorn these towers!
    This crowd of statues, in whose folded sleeves
    Birds build their nests; while canopied with leaves
    Parvis[1] and portal bloom like trellised bowers,
5 And the vast minster seems a cross of flowers![2]
    But fiends and dragons on the gargoyled eaves
    Watch the dead Christ between the living thieves,
    And, underneath, the traitor Judas lowers!
Ah! from what agonies of heart and brain,
10 What exultations trampling on despair,
    What tenderness, what tears, what hate of wrong,
What passionate outcry of a soul in pain,
    Uprose this poem of the earth and air,
    This medieval miracle of song!

ONE. **1.** *paternoster* (pat′ər nos′tər), the Lord's Prayer, so called because the opening words are "Pater Noster" in Latin.
2. *minster gate,* the cathedral door.

TWO. **1.** *Parvis,* church porch.
2. *the vast minster . . . cross of flowers.* Most European cathedrals were built in the shape of a cross. To the poet, the carved and ornamental cathedral seen from above suggests a cross of flowers.

NATURE

As a fond mother, when the day is o'er,
   Leads by the hand her little child to bed,
   Half willing, half reluctant to be led,
   And leave his broken playthings on the floor,
5 Still gazing at them through the open door,
   Nor wholly reassured and comforted
   By promises of others in their stead,
   Which, though more splendid, may not please
      him more;
So Nature deals with us, and takes away
10   Our playthings one by one, and by the hand
   Leads us to rest so gently, that we go
Scarce knowing if we wish to go or stay,
   Being too full of sleep to understand
   How far the unknown transcends the what
      we know.

MEZZO CAMMIN[1]

Half of my life is gone, and I have let
   The years slip from me and have not fulfilled
   The aspiration of my youth, to build
   Some tower of song with lofty parapet.
5 Not indolence, nor pleasure, nor the fret
   Of restless passions that would not be stilled,
   But sorrow, and a care that almost killed,
   Kept me from what I may accomplish yet;
Though, half-way up the hill, I see the Past
10   Lying beneath me with its sounds and sights,—
   A city in the twilight dim and vast,
With smoking roofs, soft bells, and gleaming
      lights,—
   And hear above me on the autumnal blast
   The cataract of Death far thundering from
      the heights.

---

1. *Mezzo Cammin*, halfway up the road. [*Italian*] Dante uses this phrase in *Divina Commedia* to signify the middle of his life, a period of lost ideals, moral disillusionment, and wasted efforts.

THE SONNET

Among the major New England poets, the one most influenced by European verse patterns was Longfellow. One of the verse forms which challenged his poetic ability, as it had challenged poets before him, was the sonnet.

A sonnet is a lyric poem of fourteen lines written in iambic pentameter, a meter with five accents in each line. Originated by Italian poets during the thirteenth century, it reached perfection a century later in the work of Petrarch (pē' trärk), and came to be known as the Petrarchan or Italian sonnet. The fourteen lines of the Italian sonnet impose a rigid rhyme scheme: the first eight lines, called the *octave*, rhyme *abbaabba* and present the poet's subject; the concluding six lines, or *sestet*, rhyme *cdecde* and indicate the significance of the facts set forth, or resolve the problem posed, in the octave.

When English poets of the sixteenth century discovered Petrarch, they were challenged by the demands the Italian sonnet made upon a poet's artistry. In experimenting with the verse form they often altered its original rhyme scheme—the most notable variation being the English sonnet which rhymes *abab/cdcd/efef/gg*.

Thus, when he attempted the sonnet, Longfellow had both the Italian and the English tradition to draw upon. It is typical of his interest in Old World literature that he chose the older Italian form, and a tribute to his artistry that he mastered its difficult discipline.

Oliver Wendell Holmes   1809/1894

THE CHAMBERED NAUTILUS

This poem was first published in The Autocrat of the Breakfast-Table, *a volume of Addisonian essays describing imaginary table-talk at a Boston boarding house. The conversations express Holmes' philosophy and his concept of the New England character. The volume contains a number of the author's poems. In introducing this poem, Holmes wrote: "I will read you a few lines . . . suggested by . . . one of those chambered shells to which is given the name of pearly nautilus. . . . The name [*nautilus from the Greek naus, "ship"*] shows that it has long been compared to a ship." In describing the shell itself Holmes wrote of "the series of enlarging compartments successively dwelt in by the animal that inhabits the shell, which is built in a widening spiral." From this "widening spiral" the poet draws his lesson.*

This is the ship of pearl, which, poets feign,
    Sails the unshadowed main—
    The venturous bark that flings
On the sweet summer wind its purpled wings
5 In gulfs enchanted, where the Siren sings,[1]
    And coral reefs lie bare,
Where the cold sea-maids[2] rise to sun their streaming
    hair.

Its webs of living gauze[3] no more unfurl;
    Wrecked is the ship of pearl!
10   And every chambered cell,
Where its dim dreaming life was wont to dwell,
As the frail tenant shaped his growing shell,
    Before thee lies revealed—
Its irised[4] ceiling rent, its sunless crypt unsealed!

15 Year after year beheld the silent toil
    That spread his lustrous coil;
    Still, as the spiral grew,
He left the past year's dwelling for the new,
Stole with soft step its shining archway through,
20   Built up its idle door,
Stretched in his last-found home, and knew the old
    no more.

Thanks for the heavenly message brought by thee,
    Child of the wandering sea,
    Cast from her lap, forlorn!
25 From thy dead lips a clearer note is born
Than ever Triton[5] blew from wreathèd horn!
    While on mine ear it rings,
Through the deep caves of thought I hear a voice
    that sings:

Build thee more stately mansions, O my soul,
30   As the swift seasons roll!
    Leave thy low-vaulted past!
Let each new temple, nobler than the last,
Shut thee from heaven with a dome more vast,
    Till thou at length art free,
35 Leaving thine outgrown shell by life's unresting sea!

1. *the Siren sings.* In Greek mythology, the sirens were nymphs who by their sweet singing lured sailors to destruction.
2. *sea-maids,* mermaids.
3. *webs of living gauze,* tentacles.
4. *irised,* containing the colors of the rainbow.
5. *Triton,* in Greek mythology, the son of Poseidon, god of the sea. His conch shell horn makes the roaring of the ocean.

THE LAST LEAF

This poem was suggested to Holmes by the sight of the aged Major Thomas Melville, Herman Melville's grandfather. This "venerable relic of the Revolution," as Holmes called him, had been one of the "Indians" who participated in the Boston Tea Party (1774).

I saw him once before,
As he passed by the door,
   And again
The pavement stones resound,
5 As he totters o'er the ground
   With his cane.

They say that in his prime,
Ere the pruning-knife of Time
   Cut him down,
10 Not a better man was found
By the Crier on his round
   Through the town.

But now he walks the streets,
And he looks at all he meets
15   Sad and wan,
And he shakes his feeble head,
That it seems as if he said,
   "They are gone."

The mossy marbles rest
20 On the lips that he has pressed
   In their bloom,
And the names he loved to hear
Have been carved for many a year
   On the tomb.

25 My grandmamma has said—
Poor old lady, she is dead
   Long ago—
That he had a Roman nose,
And his cheek was like a rose
30   In the snow.

But now his nose is thin,
And it rests upon his chin
   Life a staff,
And a crook is in his back,
35 And a melancholy crack
   In his laugh.

I know it is a sin
For me to sit and grin
   At him here;
40 But the old three-cornered hat,
And the breeches, and all that,
   Are so queer!

And if I should live to be
The last leaf upon the tree
45   In the spring,
Let them smile, as I do now,
At the old forsaken bough
   Where I cling.

James Russell Lowell   1819/1891

THE BIGLOW PAPERS

No. III

Guvener B. is a sensible man;
   He stays to his home an' looks arter his folks;
He draws his furrer ez straight ez he can,
   An' into nobody's tater-patch pokes;
5   But John P.
       Robinson he
   Sez he wunt vote for Guvener B.

My! aint it terrible? Wut shall we du?
   We can't never choose him o' course,—thet' s flat;
10 Guess we shall hev to come round, (don't you?)
   An' go in fer thunder an' guns, an' all that;
       Fer John P.
       Robinson he
   Sez he wunt vote fer Guvener B.

15 Gineral C. is a dreffle smart man:
   He 's ben on all sides thet give places or pelf;
But consistency still wuz a part of his plan,—
   He 's ben true to *one* party,—an' thet is himself;—
       So John P.
20   Robinson he
   Sez he shall vote fer Gineral C.

Gineral C. he goes in fer the war;[1]
   He don't vally principle more 'n an old cud;
Wut did God make us raytional creeturs fer,
25   But glory an' gunpowder, plunder an' blood?
       So John P.
       Robinson he
   Sez he shall vote fer Gineral C.

We were gittin' on nicely up here to our village,
30   With good old idees o' wut 's right an' wut aint,
We kind o' thought Christ went agin war an' pillage,
   An' thet eppyletts worn't the best mark of a saint;
       But John P.
       Robinson he
35   Sez this kind o' thing 's an exploded idee.

The side of our country must ollers be took,
   An' Presidunt Polk,[2] you know, *he* is our country.
An' the angel thet writes all our sins in a book
   Puts the *debit* to him, an' to us the *per contry;*
40   An' John P.
       Robinson he
   Sez this is his view o' the thing to a T.

Parson Wilbur he calls all these argimunts lies;
   Sez they 're nothin' on airth but jest *fee, faw, fum;*
45 An' thet all this big talk of our destinies
   Is half on it ign'ance, an' t' other half rum;
       But John P.
       Robinson he
   Sez it aint no sech thing; an', of course, so
   must we.

50 Parson Wilbur sez *he* never heerd in his life
   Thet th' Apostles rigged out in their swaller-tail
   coats,
An' marched round in front of a drum an' a fife,
   To git some on 'em office, an' some on 'em votes;
       But John P.
55   Robinson he
   Sez they didn't know everythin' down in Judee.

Wal, it's a marcy we've gut folks to tell us
   The rights an' the wrongs o' these matters, I vow,—
God sends country lawyers, an' other wise fellers,
60   To start the world's team wen it gits in a slough;
       Fer John P.
       Robinson he
   Sez the world 'll go right, ef he hollers out Gee![3]

---

1. *the war,* the Mexican War (1846–1848). Northern reformers
were opposed to the war, which they believed was being fought to
extend slave territory.
2. *Presidunt Polk.* The administration of President James Knox
Polk (1845–1849) was often blamed for the Mexican War.
3. *Gee,* the command to horses directing them to turn to the right.

John Greenleaf Whittier 1807/1892

ICHABOD

In 1850, the Senate of the United States was debating whether slavery should be permitted in the new territories acquired as a result of the Mexican War. Northern abolitionists expected Daniel Webster, the Massachusetts senator and the most famous orator of his day, to take a strong antislavery position. In his speech on March 7, however, Webster supported compromist proposals which extended slavery into these new territories. Webster's speech was a bitter disappointment to the abolitionists, particularly to Whittier, who admired Webster greatly. In protest, Whittier wrote "Ichabod." The poem takes its title from the Bible (I Samuel 4:21): "And she named the child Ichabod, saying, the glory is departed from Israel."

So fallen! so lost! the light withdrawn
    Which once he wore!
The glory from his gray hairs gone
    Forevermore!

5 Revile him not—the Tempter hath
    A snare for all;
And pitying tears, not scorn and wrath,
    Befit his fall!

Oh, dumb be passion's stormy rage,
10   When he who might
Have lighted up and led his age,
    Falls back in night.

Scorn! would the angels laugh, to mark
    A bright soul driven,
15 Fiend-goaded, down the endless dark,
    From hope and heaven!

Let not the land once proud of him
    Insult him now,

Nor brand with deeper shame his dim,
20   Dishonored brow.

But let its humbled sons, instead,
    From sea to lake,
A long lament, as for the dead,
    In sadness make.

25 Of all we loved and honored, naught
    Save power remains—
A fallen angel's pride of thought,
    Still strong in chains.

All else is gone; from those great eyes
30   The soul has fled:
When faith is lost, when honor dies,
    The man is dead!

Then, pay the reverence of old days
    To his dead fame;
35 Walk backward, with averted gaze,
    And hide the shame!

TELLING THE BEES

This poem, written in 1858 before Whittier had ended his career as an abolitionist, is based upon a superstition which he thus explained: "A remarkable custom, brought from the Old Country, formerly prevailed in the rural districts of New England. On the death of a member of the family, the bees were at once informed of the event, and their hives dressed in mourning. This ceremonial was supposed to prevent the swarms from leaving their hives and seeking a new home." In this poem the ballad stanzas, the evocation of the scene, the use of a tradition are typical of Whittier at his best.

Here is the place; right over the hill
    Runs the path I took;
You can see the gap in the old wall still,
And the stepping-stones in the shallow brook.

5 There is the house, with the gate red-barred,
    And the poplars tall;
And the barn's brown length, and the cattle-yard,
    And the white horns tossing above the wall.

There are the beehives ranged in the sun;
10   And down by the brink
Of the brook are her poor flowers, weed-o'errun,
    Pansy and daffodil, rose and pink.

A year has gone, as the tortoise goes,
    Heavy and slow;
15 And the same rose blows, and the same sun glows,
    And the same brook sings of a year ago.

There's the same sweet clover-smell in the breeze;
    And the June sun warm
Tangles his wings of fire in the trees,
20   Setting, as then, over Fernside farm.

I mind me how with a lover's care
    From my Sunday coat
I brushed off the burs, and smoothed my hair,
    And cooled at the brookside my brow and throat.

25 Since we parted, a month had passed—
    To love, a year;
Down through the beeches I looked at last
    On the little red gate and the well-sweep near.

I can see it all now—the slantwise rain
30   Of light through the leaves,
The sundown's blaze on her windowpane,
    The bloom of her roses under the eaves.

Just the same as a month before—
    The house and the trees,
35 The barn's brown gable, the vine by the door—
    Nothing changed but the hives of bees.

Before them, under the garden wall,
    Forward and back,
Went drearily singing the chore-girl small,
40   Draping each hive with a shred of black.

Trembling, I listened: the summer sun
    Had the chill of snow;
For I knew she was telling the bees of one
    Gone on the journey we all must go!

45 Then I said to myself, "My Mary weeps
    For the dead today:
Haply her blind old grandsire sleeps
    The fret and the pain of his age away."

But her dog whined low; on the doorway sill,
50   With his cane to his chin,
The old man sat; and the chore-girl still
    Sung to the bees stealing out and in.

And the song she was singing ever since
    In my ear sounds on:—
55 "Stay at home, pretty bees, fly not hence!
    Mistress Mary is dead and gone!"

HENRY WADSWORTH LONGFELLOW

FOR EXPLORATION

DIVINA COMMEDIA

One

1. What situation does the octave (see article, page 179 C) describe? What is the tone of this description? What particular words and phrases contribute to this tone?

2. What is the purpose of the word *so* at the beginning of the sestet? In what way is the speaker like the workman?

3. Read the last three lines aloud. With what emotion do they leave the listener?

Two

2. What is the cause of the "agonies of the heart and brain" (line 9)? What is the result of these agonies?

3. Note that the sestet is an exclamation, an outpouring of wonder and awe. What has aroused this feeling in the speaker?

Nature

1. What two situations are being compared? What is such a comparison called? What purpose does it serve?

2. What are the "playthings" of line 10? What does the use of this particular word tell you about the speaker's view of life?

3. If one were not "too full of sleep to understand/How far the unknown transcends the what / we know," would his attitude toward death be as acquiescent and untroubled as is the speaker's? Defend your answer.

Mezzo Cammin

1. What was the speaker's youthful aspiration? Why has he been unable to fulfill it? Has he completely abandoned his efforts to do so? Prove your answers with lines from the poem.

2. What effect does the word *though* in line 9 have on the tone of the poem?

3. Reread the description of the past as the speaker sees it from his vantage point "halfway up the hill" (lines 9–12). What temptation might be inherent in viewing one's past in such a way?

4. Contrast the last two lines of the poem with lines 9–12. What particular words in the final lines create the contrast between the speaker's past and his future?

OLIVER WENDELL HOLMES

FOR EXPLORATION

The Chambered Nautilus

1. Reread the first three stanzas. What is the poet describing? What has happened to this object?

2. In stanza 4, to what does the author address his thanks? Why does he feel the need to give thanks?

3. What is the tone of the last stanza? With what emotion does it leave the reader? Support your answer with lines from the text.

4. What lesson might a writer with a less optimistic outlook have derived from viewing the broken shell?

The Last Leaf

In what basic way does this poem about old age differ from Emerson's "Terminus" (page C 136)? What effect does this difference have on the tone of each poem? Cite lines from both poems to support your answer.

JAMES RUSSELL LOWELL

FOR EXPLORATION

The Biglow Papers

No. III

1. Briefly describe the characters of Guvener B., John P. Robinson, Gineral C., and Parson Wilbur. What is the speaker's attitude toward each? Defend your answers by citing lines from the poem.

2. Does the speaker truly think that "it's a marcy we've gut folks to tell us / The rights an' wrongs o' these matters . . . ?" If he does, why does he? If you don't think his tone is serious, how would you describe it? Support your answer.

3. Political comment of the kind found in this poem often does not age well; once the issues it is concerned with become history, the writing itself loses any appeal and significance other than the historical. Do you find this to be the case with "The Biglow Papers, No. III?" If not, what elements in it make the poem of interest to the modern student? Does it contain any ideas or comments that might apply to current situations or public figures?

JOHN GREENLEAF WHITTIER

FOR EXPLORATION

Ichabod

1. What adjectives might describe Whittier's attitude toward Webster and what he has done? Support your answer.
2. Given the situation (see headnote, page 183 C), do you find Whittier's attitude justifiable? admirable? Why or why not?

Telling the Bees

1. Reread the first three stanzas, paying particular attention to the imagery. What change in tone is created by the last two lines of stanza three? What particular words bring about this change?
2. How much time has elapsed since the speaker last saw the farm? From his point of view, what irony is contained in the fact that ". . . the same rose blows, and the same sun glows,/and the same brook sings . . ."?
3. Reread the entire poem. Are you able to see, feel, and smell the place being described? Are you able to share the speaker's various emotions? If so, what has the poet done to enable you to experience the poem in this way? Support your answer.

Henry Wadsworth Longfellow
1807 / 1882

Longfellow was born in Portland, Maine, and educated at Bowdoin College. After his graduation he was offered a professorship of modern languages there on condition of further study. He studied and traveled abroad for three years, visiting France, Spain, Italy, and Germany.

He remained at Bowdoin for six years, dividing his time between teaching and writing. On the strength of his work there he was offered a professorship at Harvard, again with a provision of a leave of absence to continue his studies abroad. During this second trip, lasting nearly two years, his first wife died and he met the woman who, after a long courtship, was to become his second wife.

He taught at Harvard for nearly twenty years, years of great creative activity. He communicated his enthusiasm about European people and their literature to readers outside his classes by writing travel books in which he distilled the essence of his foreign experiences. He also made translations of the works of European writers which embodied the emotions of the originals and echoed their music. This practice in translation aided him greatly in perfecting his poetic technique. His first book of original poems, *Voices of the Night* (1839), showed this skill in

PORTRAIT OF LONGFELLOW PAINTED BY HIS SON ERNEST IN 1876
LONGFELLOW HOUSE TRUST

deceptively simple verses which gained him a national reputation. He finally resigned his professorship in favor of James Russell Lowell in 1854 in order to devote his attention exclusively to writing.

In January 1840, he wrote a friend that in his ballad, "The Wreck of the Hesperus," he had naturalized a form which had long flourished abroad. Longfellow's adaptation of the ballad to American materials illustrates his chief literary achievement, which was the introduction of foreign themes and poetic forms into American literature. *Evangeline* (1847), *The Song of Hiawatha* (1855), and *The Courtship of Miles Standish* (1858), were long narrative poems in the manner of similar European poems but treating American legends. *The Golden Legend* (1851) a cycle of religious mystery plays, embodies themes and forms of medieval European literature. *Tales of a Wayside Inn* (1863) collected a series of stories, most of them of American origin, in a poem constructed in the manner of Chaucer's *Canterbury Tales.*

Oliver Wendell Holmes   1809 / 1894

Holmes was born in Cambridge and educated at Harvard. He began to study law, but abandoned this for medicine after a year. Since the best training in medicine was then offered abroad, Holmes studied in Edinburgh, then Paris, before returning home to receive his M.D. from the Harvard Medical School in 1836, the same year in which he published *Poems*, his first volume. After practicing a very short time he taught medicine at Dartmouth for two years. He returned to practice in Boston after his marriage in 1840, but again abandoned it in favor of a professorship of anatomy and physiology at Harvard, where he remained until his retirement in 1882.

In both his poetry and prose Holmes strove for the light informal tone, the charm and the humor, of eighteenth-century literature. Many of his verses were "occasional"; that is, they were composed for reading aloud on certain festive occasions—at a college class reunion, on an anniversary, at a celebration—and are some of the most graceful and witty examples of this type of writing ever composed.

The same sprightliness, vigor, wisdom, and charm that are displayed in the poems are apparent also in Holmes' essays, which began appearing serially in the *Atlantic Monthly* after it was founded by Holmes and a group of friends in 1857. The first collection of these essays, which are in the form of conversations among a group of people gather around a boarding-house table, appeared in 1858 as *The Autocrat of the Breakfast-Table*. It was followed by *The Professor at the Breakfast-Table* (1860), *The Poet at the Breakfast-Table* (1872), and *Over the Teacups* (1891).

James Russell Lowell   1819 / 1891

Lowell was born in Cambridge and educated at Harvard, graduating from the College in 1838 and the Law School in 1840. However, within two years he had abandoned the practice of law for literature. During the next few years he contributed fervent editorials and poems championing numerous social causes to various periodicals. In 1846, having already established a considerable reputation as a writer, he wrote a very popular series of poems strongly opposing the war with Mexico. These poems—*The Biglow Papers*—written in Yankee dialect, successfully combined rustic humor and serious satiric intent. They were combined in book form in 1848. During the Civil War, Lowell revived his rustic oracle for a second series of *Biglow Papers*, which appeared in the *Atlantic Monthly* between 1862 and 1866. In 1848, the same year which saw the appearance of the first series of *Biglow Papers*, Lowell also published *A Fable for Critics*, a humorous commentary on the leading literary figures of his day, and *The Vision of Sir Launfal*, an Arthurian romance.

In 1855, when Longfellow retired from his professorship at Harvard, Lowell succeeded him, teaching there until 1876. In 1857 Lowell helped found the *Atlantic Monthly* and edited it until 1861. Lowell was also appointed to diplomatic posts, serving as ambassador to Spain from 1880 to 1885. During the last six years of his life, Lowell lived quietly in Cambridge, leaving his home only for two brief trips abroad.

John Greenleaf Whittier   1807 / 1892

Whittier was born and reared on a farm in the township of Haverhill, Massachusetts. He had almost no formal education and even his reading was limited to the few devotional books that his Quaker parents had in their home. However, at an early age he did encounter the works of another rural poet, Robert Burns (1759–1796), which exerted a great influence over him.

When he was nineteen, one of Whittier's poems was published by the abolitionist William Lloyd Garrison in a paper which he edited. This was the beginning of a lifelong association between the two men, and marked the start of Whittier's career both as a writer and as a reformer. Under Garrison's influence, Whittier returned to school, spending two terms at the Haverhill Academy. After this he taught school and held various types of editorial positions while continuing to write poems and articles in support of the abolitionist cause.

For the next twenty-five years, the bulk of his energies was devoted to the antislavery movement. In 1840 he moved from Haverhill a short distance away to Amesbury, where he was to remain for the rest of his life. During these years he matured as a poet, but it was not until the publication of his masterpiece, *Snow-Bound*, which appeared in 1866, that he achieved a national reputation as a poet.

CRISIS WITHIN

SPIRITUALS

Spirituals were the religious folk songs of the American Negro slave.

Although some spirituals are exuberant, most express the slave's misery in bondage and his yearning for freedom. They are generally told in terms borrowed from the Old Testament tales of the captivity of the Israelites, a captivity seen by the slaves to be analagous to their own.

SWING LOW, SWEET CHARIOT

Swing low, sweet chariot,
Comin' for to carry me home.

I looked over Jordan and what did I see,
Comin' for to carry me home?
A band of angels comin' aftah me,
Comin' for to carry me home.

5 If you git there before I do,
Comin' for to carry me home,
Tell all my frien's I'm a-comin', too,
Comin' for to carry me home.

The brightes' day that ever I saw,
10 Comin' for to carry me home,
When Jesus washed my sins away,
Comin' for to carry me home.

I'm sometimes up an' sometimes down,
Comin' for to carry me home,
15 But still my soul feel heavenly-boun',
Comin' for to carry me home.

DEEP RIVER

Deep river, my home is over Jordan.
Deep river, Lord, I want to cross over into
  Campground.
Oh, chillun, oh, don't you want to go
To that gospel feast, that promised land,
5 That land where all is peace?
Walk into heaven and take my seat
And cast my crown at Jesus' feet. Lord,
Deep river, my home is over Jordan.
Deep river, Lord, I want to cross over into
  Campground.

GO DOWN, MOSES

When Israel was in Egypt's land,
  Let my people go!
Oppress'd so hard dey could not stand,
  Let my people go!

Chorus
5 Go down, Moses,
  Way down in Egypt's land.
Tell ole Pha-raoh,
  Let my people go!

Thus say de Lord, bold Moses said,
10 Let my people go!
If not I'll smite your first-born dead,
  Let my people go!

Chorus
Go down, Moses,
  Way down in Egypt's land.
15 Tell ole Pha-raoh,
  Let my people go!

No more shall dey in bondage toil,
  Let my people go!
Let dem come out wid Egypt's spoil,
20 Let my people go!

Chorus
Go down, Moses,
  Way down in Egypt's land.
Tell ole Pha-raoh,
  Let my people go!

James W. C. Pennington

1809/1870

ESCAPE: A SLAVE NARRATIVE

IT was the Sabbath; the holy day which God in his infinite wisdom gave for the rest of both man and beast. In the state of Maryland, the slaves generally have the Sabbath, except in those districts where the evil weed, tobacco, is cultivated; and then, when it is the season for setting the plant, they are liable to be robbed of this only rest.

It was in the month of November, somewhat past the middle of the month. It was a bright day, and all was quiet. Most of the slaves were resting about their quarters; others had leave to visit their friends on other plantations, and were absent. The evening previous I had arranged my little bundle of clothing, and had secreted it at some distance from the house. I had spent most of the forenoon in my workshop, engaged in deep and solemn thought.

It is impossible for me now to recollect all the perplexing thoughts that passed through my mind during that forenoon; it was a day of heartaching to me. But I distinctly remember the two great difficulties that stood in the way of my flight: I had a father and mother whom I dearly loved,—I had also six sisters and four brothers on the plantation. The question was, shall I hide my purpose from them? moreover, how will my flight affect them when I am gone? Will they not be suspected? Will not the whole family be sold off as a disaffected family, as is generally the case when one of its members flies? But a still more trying question was, how can I expect to succeed, I have no knowledge of distance or direction—I know that Pennsylvania is a free state, but I know not where its soil begins, or where that of Maryland ends? Indeed, at this time there was no safety in Pennsylvania, New Jersey, or New York, for a fugitive, except in lurking-places, or under the care of judicious friends, who could be entrusted not only with liberty, but also with life itself.

With such difficulties before my mind, the day had rapidly worn away; and it was just past noon. One of my perplexing questions I had settled—I had re- solved to let no one into my secret; but the other difficulty was now to be met. It was to be met without the least knowledge of its magnitude, except by imagination. Yet of one thing there could be no mistake, that the consequences of a failure would be most serious. Within my recollection no one had attempted to escape from my master; but I had many cases in my mind's eye, of slaves of other planters who had failed, and who had been made examples of the most cruel treatment, by flogging and selling to the far South, where they were never to see their friends more. I was not without serious apprehension that such would be my fate. The bare possibility was impressively solemn; but the hour was now come, and the man must act and be free, or remain a slave for ever. How the impression came to be upon my mind I cannot tell; but there was a strange and horrifying belief, that if I did not meet the crisis that day, I should be self-doomed—that my ear would be nailed to the door-post for ever. The emotions of that moment I cannot fully depict. Hope, fear, dread, terror, love, sorrow, and deep melancholy were mingled in my mind together; my mental state was one of most painful distraction. When I looked at my numerous family—a beloved father and mother, eleven brothers and sisters, etc.; but when I looked at slavery as such; when I looked at it in its mildest form, with all its annoyances; and above all, when I remembered that one of the chief annoyances of slavery, in the most mild form, is the liability of being at any moment sold into the worst form, it seemed that no consideration, not even that of life itself, could tempt me to give up the thought of flight. And then when I considered the difficulties of the way—the reward that would be offered—the human bloodhounds that would be set upon my track—the weariness—the hunger—the gloomy thought, of not only losing all one's friends in one day, but of having to seek and to make new friends in a strange world. But, as I have said, the hour was come, and the man must act, or for ever be a slave.

It was now two o'clock. I stepped into the quarter; there was a strange and melancholy silence mingled with the destitution that was apparent in every part of the house. The only morsel I could see in the shape of food, was a piece of Indian-flour bread, it might be half-a-pound in weight. This I placed in my pocket, and giving a last look at the aspect of the house, and at a few small children who were playing at the door, I sallied forth thoughtfully and melancholy, and after crossing the barn-yard, a few moments' walk brought me to a small cave, near the mouth of which lay a pile of stones, and into which I had deposited my clothes. From this, my course lay through thick and heavy woods and back lands to ——town, where my brother lived. This town was six miles distance. It was now near three o'clock, but my object was neither to be seen on the road, or to approach the town by daylight, as I was well-known there, and as any intelligence of my having been seen there would at once put the pursuers on my track. This first six miles of my flight, I not only travelled very slowly, therefore, so as to avoid carrying any daylight to this town; but during this walk another very perplexing question was agitating my mind. Shall I call on my brother as I pass through, and shew him what I am about! My brother was older than I, we were much attached; I had been in the habit of looking to him for counsel.

I entered the town about dark, resolved, all things in view, *not* to shew myself to my brother. Having passed through the town without being recognised, I now found myself under cover of night, a solitary wanderer from home and friends; my only guide was the *north star*, by this I knew my general course northward, but at what point I should strike Penn., or when and where I should find a friend I knew not. Another feeling now occupied my mind,—I felt like a mariner who has gotten his ship outside of the harbour and has spread his sails to the breeze. The cargo is on board—the ship is cleared—and the voyage I must make; besides, this being my first night, almost everything will depend upon my clearing the coast before the day dawns. In order to do this my flight must be rapid. I therefore set forth in sorrowful earnest, only now and then I was cheered by the *wild* hope, that I should somewhere and at some time be free.

The night was fine for the season, and passed on with little interruption for want of strength, until, about three o'clock in the morning, I began to feel the chilling effects of the dew.

At this moment, gloom and melancholy again spread through my whole soul. The prospect of utter destitution which threatened me was more than I could bear, and my heart began to melt. What substance is there in a piece of dry Indian-bread? What nourishment is there in it to warm the nerves of one already chilled to the heart? Will this afford a sufficient sustenance after the toil of the night? But while these thoughts were agitating my mind, the day dawned upon me, in the midst of an open extent of country, where the only shelter I could find, without risking my travel by daylight, was a corn shock, but a few hundred yards from the road, and here I must pass my first day out. The day was an unhappy one; my hiding-place was extremely precarious. I had to sit in a squatting position the whole day, without the least chance to rest. But, besides this, my scanty pittance did not afford me that nourishment which my hard night's travel needed. Night came again to my relief, and I sallied forth to pursue my journey. By this time, not a crumb of my crust remained, and I was hungry and began to feel the desperation of distress.

As I travelled I felt my strength failing and my spirits wavered; my mind was in a deep and melancholy dream. It was cloudy; I could not see my star, and had serious misgivings about my course.

In this way the night passed away, and just at the dawn of day I found a few sour apples, and took my shelter under the arch of a small bridge that crossed the road. Here I passed the second day in ambush.

This day would have been more pleasant than the previous, but the sour apples, and a draught of cold water, had produced any thing but a favourable effect; indeed, I suffered most of the day with severe symptoms of cramp. The day passed away again without any further incident, and as I set out at nightfall I felt quite satisfied that I could not pass another twenty-four hours without nourishment. I made but little progress during the night, and often sat down, and slept frequently fifteen or twenty minutes. At the dawn of the third day I continued my travel. As I had found my way to a public turnpike road during the night, I came very early in the morning to a toll-gate, where the only person I saw, was a lad about twelve years of age. I inquired of him where the road led to. He informed me it led to Baltimore. I asked him the distance, he said it was eighteen miles.

This intelligence was perfectly astounding to me. My master lived eighty miles from Baltimore. I was now sixty-two miles from home. That distance in the right direction, would have placed me several miles across Mason and Dixon's line,[1] but I was evidently yet in the state of Maryland.

---

1. *Mason and Dixon's line,* the southern boundary line of Pennsylvania which was laid out by Charles Mason and Jeremiah Dixon, two English astronomers. The line became part of the boundary between the free and slave states.

I ventured to ask the lad at the gate another question—Which is the best way to Philadelphia? Said he, you can take a road which turns off about half-a-mile below this, and goes to Getsburgh, or you can go on to Baltimore and take the packet.

I made no reply, but my thought was, that I was as near Baltimore and Baltimore-packets as would answer my purpose.

In a few moments I came to the road to which the lad had referred, and felt some relief when I had gotten out of that great public highway, "The National Turnpike," which I found it to be.

When I had walked a mile on this road, and when it had now gotten to be about nine o'clock, I met a young man with a load of hay. He drew up his horses, and addressed me in a very kind tone, when the following dialogue took place between us.

"Are you travelling any distance, my friend?"

"I am on my way to Philadelphia."

"Are you free?"

"Yes, sir."

"I suppose, then, you are provided with free papers?"

"No, sir. I have no papers."

"Well, my friend, you should not travel on this road: you will be taken up before you have gone three miles. There are men living on this road who are constantly on the look-out for your people; and it is seldom that one escapes them who attempts to pass by day."

He then very kindly gave me advice where to turn off the road at a certain point, and how to find my way to a certain house, where I would meet with an old gentleman who would further advise me whether I had better remain till night, or go on.

I left this interesting young man; and such was my surprise and chagrin at the thought of having so widely missed my way, and my alarm at being in such a dangerous position, that in ten minutes I had so far forgotten his directions as to deem it unwise to attempt to follow them, lest I should miss my way, and get into evil hands.

I, however, left the road, and went into a small piece of wood, but not finding a sufficient hiding-place, and it being a busy part of the day, when persons were at work about the fields, I thought I should excite less suspicion by keeping in the road, so I returned to the road; but the events of the next few moments proved that I committed a serious mistake.

I went about a mile, making in all two miles from

the spot where I met my young friend, and about five miles from the toll-gate to which I have referred, and I found myself at the twenty-four miles' stone from Baltimore. It was now about ten o'clock in the forenoon; my strength was greatly exhausted by reason of the want of suitable food; but the excitement that was then going on in my mind, left me little time to think of my *need* of food. Under ordinary circumstances as a traveller, I should have been glad to see the "Tavern," which was near the mile-stone; but as the case stood with me, I deemed it a dangerous place to pass, much less to stop at. I was therefore passing it as quietly and as rapidly as possible, when from the lot just opposite the house, or sign-post, I heard a coarse stern voice cry, "Halloo!"

I turned my face to the left, the direction from which the voice came, and observed that it proceeded from a man who was digging potatoes. I answered him politely; when the following occurred:—

"Who do *you* belong to?"

"I am free, sir."

"Have you got papers?"

"No, sir."

"Well, you must stop here."

By this time he had got astride the fence, making his way into the road. I said,

"My business is onward, sir, and I do not wish to stop."

"I will see then if you don't stop, you black rascal."

He was now in the middle of the road, making after me in a brisk walk.

I saw that a crisis was at hand; I had no weapons of any kind, not even a pocket-knife; but I asked myself, shall I surrender without a struggle. The instinctive answer was, "No." What will you do? continue to walk; if he runs after you, run; get him as far from the house as you can, then turn suddenly and smite him on the knee with a stone; that will render him, at least, unable to pursue you.

This was a desperate scheme, but I could think of no other, and my habits as a blacksmith had given my eye and hand such mechanical skill, that I felt quite sure that if I could only get a stone in my hand, and have time to wield it, I should not miss his knee-pan.

He began to breathe short. He was evidently vexed because I did not halt, and I felt more and more provoked at the idea of being thus pursued by a man to whom I had not done the least injury. I had just began to glance my eye about for a stone to grasp, when he made a tiger-like leap at me. This of course brought us to running. At this moment he yelled out "Jake Shouster!" and at the next moment the door of a small house standing to the left was opened, and out jumped a shoemaker girded up in his leather apron, with his knife in hand. He sprang forward and seized me by the collar, while the other seized my arms behind. I was now in the grasp of two men, either of whom were larger bodied than myself, and one of whom was armed with a dangerous weapon.

Standing in the door of the shoemaker's shop, was a third man; and in the potato lot I had passed, was still a fourth man. Thus surrounded by superior physical force, the fortune of the day it seemed to me was gone.

My heart melted away, I sunk resistlessly into the hands of my captors, who dragged me immediately into the tavern which was near. I ask my reader to go in with me, and see how the case goes.

A few moments after I was taken into the bar-room, the news having gone as by electricity, the house and yard were crowded with gossipers, who had left their business to come and see "the runaway nigger." This hastily assembled congregation consisted of men, women, and children, each one had a look to give at, and a word to say about the "nigger."

But among the whole, there stood one whose name I have never known, but who evidently wore the garb of a man whose profession bound him to speak for the dumb, but he, standing head and shoulders above all that were round about, spoke the first hard sentence against me. Said he, "That fellow is a runaway I know; put him in jail a few days, and you will soon hear where he came from." And then fixing a fiend-like gaze upon me, he continued, "if I lived on this road, *you* fellows would not find such clear running as you do, I'd trap more of you."

But now comes the pinch of the case, the case of conscience to me even at this moment. Emboldened by the cruel speech just recited, my captors enclosed me, and said, "Come now, this matter may easily be settled without you going to jail; who do you belong to, and where did you come from?"

The facts here demanded were in my breast. I knew according to the law of slavery, who I belonged to and where I came from, and I must now do one of three things—I must refuse to speak at all, or I must communicate the fact, or I must tell an untruth. How

would an untutored slave, who had never heard of such a writer as Archdeacon Paley,[2] be likely to act in such a dilemma? The first point decided was, the facts in this case are my private property. These men have no more right to them than a highway robber has to my purse. What will be the consequence if I put them in possession of the facts. In forty-eight hours, I shall have received perhaps one hundred lashes, and be on my way to the Louisiana cotton-fields. Of what service will it be to them. They will get a paltry sum of two hundred dollars. Is not my liberty worth more to me than two hundred dollars are to them?

I resolved, therefore, to insist that I was free. This not being satisfactory without other evidence, they tied my hands and set out, and went to a magistrate who lived about half a mile distant. It so happened, that when we arrived at his house he was not at home. This was to them a disappointment, but to me it was a relief; but I soon learned by their conversation, that there was still another magistrate in the neighbourhood, and that they would go to him. In about twenty minutes, and after climbing fences and jumping ditches, we, captors and captive, stood before his door, but it was after the same manner as before—he was not at home. By this time the day had worn away to one or two o'clock, and my captors evidently began to feel somewhat impatient of the loss of time. We were about a mile and a quarter from the tavern. As we set out on our return, they began to parley. Finding it was difficult for me to get over fences with my hands tied, they untied me, and said, "Now John," that being the name they had given me, "if you have run away from any one, it would be much better for you to tell us!" but I continued to affirm that I was free. I knew, however, that my situation was very critical, owing to the shortness of the distance I must be from home: my advertisement might overtake me at any moment.

On our way back to the tavern, we passed through a small skirt of wood, where I resolved to make an effort to escape again. One of my captors was walking on either side of me; I made a sudden turn, with my left arm sweeping the legs of one of my captors from under him; I left him nearly standing on his head, and took to my heels. As soon as they could recover they both took after me. We had to mount a fence. This I did most successfully, and making

2. *Archdeacon Paley,* William Paley (1743–1805), an English theologian and moralist.

across an open field towards another wood; one of my captors being a long-legged man, was in advance of the other, and consequently nearing me. We had a hill to rise, and during the ascent he gained on me. Once more I thought of self-defence. I am trying to escape peaceably, but this man is determined that I shall not.

My case was now desperate; and I took this desperate thought: "I will run him a little farther from his coadjutor; I will then suddenly catch a stone, and wound him in the breast." This was my fixed purpose, and I had arrived near the point on the top of the hill, where I expected to do the act, when to my surprise and dismay, I saw the other side of the hill was not only all ploughed up, but we came suddenly upon a man ploughing, who as suddenly left his plough and cut off my flight, by seizing me by the collar, when at the same moment my pursuer seized my arms behind. Here I was again in a sad fix. By this time the other pursuer had come up; I was most savagely thrown down on the ploughed ground with my face downward, the ploughman placed his knee upon my shoulders, one of my captors put his upon my legs, while the other tied my arms behind me. I was then dragged up and marched off with kicks, punches and imprecations.

We got to the tavern at three o'clock. Here they again cooled down, and made an appeal to me to make a disclosure. I saw that my attempt to escape strengthened their belief that I was a fugitive. I said to them, "If you will not put me in jail, I will now tell you where I am from." They promised. "Well," said I, "a few weeks ago, I was sold from the eastern shore to a slave-trader, who had a large gang, and set out for Georgia, but when he got to a town in Virginia, he was taken sick, and died with the small-pox. Several of his gang also died with it, so that the people in the town became alarmed, and did not wish the gang to remain among them. No one claimed us, or wished to have anything to do with us; I left the rest, and thought I would go somewhere and get work."

When I said this, it was evidently believed by those who were present, and notwithstanding the unkind feeling that had existed, there was a murmur of approbation. At the same time I perceived that a panic began to seize some, at the idea that I was one of a small-pox gang. Several who had clustered near me, moved off to a respectful distance. One or two left the bar-room, and murmured, "better let the small-pox nigger go."

I was then asked what was the name of the slave-trader. Without premeditation, I said, "John Henderson."

"John Henderson," said one of my captors, "I knew him; I took up a yaller boy for him about two years ago, and got fifty dollars. He passed out with a gang about that time, and the boy ran away from him at Frederickstown. What kind of a man was he?"

At a venture, I gave a description of him. "Yes," said he, "that is the man." By this time all the gossippers had cleared the coast; our friend, "Jake Shouster," had also gone back to his bench to finish his custom work, after having "lost nearly the whole day, trotting about with a nigger tied," as I heard his wife say as she called him home to his dinner. I was now left alone with the man who first called to me in the morning. In a sober manner, he made this proposal to me: "John, I have a brother living in Risterstown, four miles off, who keeps a tavern; I think you had better go and live with him, till we see what will turn up. He wants an ostler." I at once assented to this. "Well," said he, "take something to eat, and I will go with you."

Although I had so completely frustrated their designs for the moment, I knew that it would by no means answer for me to go into that town, where there were prisons, handbills, newspapers, and travellers. My intention was, to start with him, but not to enter the town alive.

I sat down to eat; it was Wednesday, four o'clock, and this was the first regular meal I had since Sunday morning. This over, we set out, and to my surprise, he proposed to walk. We had gone about a mile and a-half, and we were approaching a wood through which the road passed with a bend. I fixed upon that as the spot where I would either free myself from this man, or die in his arms. I had resolved upon a plan of operation—it was this: to stop short, face about, and commence action; and neither ask or give quarters, until I was free or dead!

We had got within six rods of the spot, when a gentleman turned the corner, meeting us on horseback. He came up, and entered into conversation with my captor, both of them speaking in Dutch, so that I knew not what they said. After a few moments, this gentleman addressed himself to me in English, and I then learned that he was one of the magistrates on whom we had called in the morning; I felt that another crisis was at hand. Using his saddle as his bench, he put on an extremely stern and magisterial-like face, holding up his horse not unlike a field-marshal in the act of reviewing troops, and carried me through a most rigid examination in reference to the statement I had made. I repeated carefully all I had said; at the close, he said, "Well, you had better stay among us a few months, until we see what is to be done with you." It was then agreed that we should go back to the tavern, and there settle upon some further plan. When we arrived at the tavern, the magistrate alighted from his horse, and went into the bar-room. He took another close glance at me, and went over some points of the former examination. He seemed quite satisfied of the correctness of my statement, and made the following proposition: that I should go and live with him for a short time, stating that he had a few acres of corn and potatoes to get in, and that he would give me twenty-five cents per day. I most cheerfully assented to this proposal. It was also agreed that I should remain at the tavern with my captor that night, and that he would accompany me in the morning. This part of the arrangement I did not like, but of course I could not say so. Things being thus arranged, the magistrate mounted his horse, and went on his way home.

It had been cloudy and rainy during the afternoon, but the western sky having partially cleared at this moment, I perceived that it was near the setting of the sun.

My captor had left his hired man most of the day to dig potatoes alone; but the waggon being now loaded, it being time to convey the potatoes into the barn, and the horses being all ready for that purpose, he was obliged to go into the potato field and give assistance.

I should say here, that his wife had been driven away by the small-pox panic about three o'clock, and had not yet returned; this left no one in the house, but a boy, about nine years of age.

As he went out, he spoke to the boy in Dutch, which I supposed, from the little fellow's conduct, to be instructions to watch me closely, which he certainly did.

The potato lot was across the public road, directly in front of the house; at the back of the house, and about 300 yards distant, there was a thick wood. The circumstances of the case would not allow me to think for one moment of remaining there for the night—the time had come for another effort—but there were two serious difficulties. One was, that I must either deceive or dispatch this boy who is watching me with intense vigilance. I am glad to say, that the latter did not for a moment seriously enter my mind. To deceive him effectually, I left my coat and went to the back door, from which my course would be direct to the wood. When I got to the door, I found that the barn, to which the waggon must soon come, lay just to the right, and overlooking the path I must take to the wood. In front of me lay a garden surrounded by a picket fence, to the left of me was a small gate, and that by passing through that gate would throw me into an open field, and give me clear running to the wood; but on looking through the gate, I saw that my captor, being with the team, would see me if I attempted to start before he moved from the position he then occupied. To add to my difficulty the horses had baulked; while waiting for the decisive moment, the boy came to the door and asked me why I did not come in. I told him I felt unwell, and wished him to be so kind as to hand me a glass of water; expecting while he was gone to get it, the team would clear, so that I could start. While he was gone, another attempt was made to start the team but failed; he came with the water and I quickly used it up by gargling my throat and by drinking a part. I asked him to serve me by giving me another glass: he gave me a look of close scrutiny, but went in for the water. I heard him fill the glass, and start to return with it; when the hind end of the waggon cleared the corner of the house, which stood in a range with the fence along which I was to pass in getting to the wood. As I passed out the gate, I "squared my main-yard,"[3] and laid my course up the line of fence, I cast a last glance over my right shoulder, and saw the boy just perch his head above the garden picket to look after me; I heard at the same time great confusion with the team, the rain having made the ground slippery, and the horses having to cross the road with a slant and rise to get into the barn, it required great effort after they started to prevent their baulking. I felt some assurance that although the boy might give the alarm, my captor could not leave the team until it was in the barn. I heard the horses' feet on the barn-floor, just as I leaped the fence, and darted into the wood.

The sun was now quite down behind the western horizon, and just at this time a heavy dark curtain of

---

3. *I "squared my main-yard."* In nautical terms, the main-yard is the mast on which the mainsail is extended. Pennington is saying that he faced squarely the direction in which he intended to run.

clouds was let down, which seemed to usher in haste the night shade. I have never before or since seen anything which seemed to me to compare in sublimity with the spreading of the night shades at the close of that day. My reflections upon the events of that day, and upon the close of it, since I became acquainted with the Bible, have frequently brought to my mind that beautiful passage in the Book of Job, "He holdeth back the face of His throne, and spreadeth a cloud before it."

Before I proceed to the critical events and final deliverance of the next chapter, I cannot forbear to pause a moment here for reflection. The reader may well imagine how the events of the past day affected my mind. You have seen what was done to me; you have heard what was said to me—you have also seen what I have done, and heard what I have said. If you ask me whether I had expected before I left home, to gain my liberty by shedding men's blood, or breaking their limbs? I answer, No! and as evidence of this, I had provided no weapon whatever; not so much as a penknife—it never once entered my mind. I cannot say that I expected to have the ill fortune of meeting with any human being who would attempt to impede my flight.

If you ask me if I expected when I left home to gain my liberty by fabrications and untruths? I answer, No! my parents, slaves as they were, had always taught me, when they could, that "truth may be blamed but cannot be ashamed"; so far as their example was concerned, I had no habits of untruth. I was arrested, and the demand made upon me, "Who do you belong to?" Knowing the fatal use these men would make of *my* truth, I at once concluded that they had no more right to it than a highwayman has to a traveller's purse.

If you ask me whether I now really believe that I gained my liberty by those lies? I answer, No! I now believe that I should be free, had I told the truth; but, at that moment, I could not see any other way to baffle my enemies, and escape their clutches.

The history of that day has never ceased to inspire me with a deeper hatred of slavery; I never recur to it but with the most intense horror at a system which can put a man not only in peril of liberty, limb, and life itself, but which may even send him in haste to the bar of God with a lie upon his lips.

Whatever my readers may think, therefore, of the history of events of the day, do not admire in it the fabrications; but *see* in it the impediments that often fall into the pathway of the flying bondman. *See* how human bloodhounds gratuitously chase, catch, and tempt him to shed blood and lie; how when he would do good, evil is thrust upon him.

Almost immediately on entering the wood, I not only found myself embosomed in the darkness of the night, but I also found myself entangled in a thick forest of undergrowth, which had been quite thoroughly wetted by the afternoon rain.

I penetrated through the wood, thick and thin, and more or less wet, to the distance I should think of three miles. By this time my clothes were all thoroughly soaked through, and I felt once more a gloom and wretchedness; the recollection of which makes me shudder at this distant day. My young friends in this highly favoured Christian country, surrounded with all the comforts of home and parental care, visited by pastors and Sabbath-school teachers, think of the dreary condition of the blacksmith boy in the dark wood that night; and then consider that thousands of his brethren have had to undergo much greater hardships in their flight from slavery.

I was now out of the hands of those who had so cruelly teased me during the day; but a number of fearful thoughts rushed into my mind to alarm me. It was dark and cloudy, so that I could not see the *north star*. How do I know what ravenous beasts are in this wood? How do I know what precipices may be within its bounds? I cannot rest in this wood tomorrow, for it will be searched by those men from whom I have escaped; but how shall I regain the road? How shall I know when I am on the right road again?

These are some of the thoughts that filled my mind with gloom and alarm.

At a venture I struck an angle northward in search of the road. After several hours of zigzag and laborious travel, dragging through briars, thorns and running vines, I emerged from the wood and found myself wading marshy ground and over ditches.

I can form no correct idea of the distance I travelled, but I came to a road, I should think about three o'clock in the morning. It so happened that I came out near where there was a fork in the road of three prongs.

Now arose a serious query—Which is the right prong for me? I was reminded by the circumstance of a superstitious proverb among the slaves, that "the left-hand turning was unlucky," but as I had never been in the habit of placing faith in this or any similar superstition, I am not aware that it had the least weight upon my mind, as I had the same difficulty with reference to the right-hand turning. After a few moments parley with myself, I took the central prong of the road and pushed on with all my speed.

It had not cleared off, but a fresh wind had sprung up; it was chilly and searching. This with my wet clothing made me very uncomfortable; my nerves began to quiver before the searching wind. The barking of mastiffs, the crowing of fowls, and the distant rattling of market waggons, warned me that the day was approaching.

My British reader[4] must remember that in the region where I was, we know nothing of the long hours of twilight you enjoy here. With us the day is measured more by the immediate presence of the sun, and the night by the prevalence of actual darkness.

The day dawned upon me when I was near a small house and barn, situated close to the road-side. The barn was too near the road, and too small to afford secure shelter for the day; but as I cast my eye around by the dim light, I could see no wood, and no larger barn. It seemed to be an open country to a wide extent. The sun was travelling so rapidly from his eastern chamber, that ten or fifteen minutes would spread broad daylight over my track. Whether *my* deed was evil, *you* may judge, but I freely confess that I did *then* prefer darkness rather than light; I therefore took to the mow of the little barn at a great risk, as the events of the day will shew. It so happened that the barn was filled with corn fodder, newly cured and lately got in. You are aware that however quietly one may crawl into such a bed, he is compelled to make much more noise than if it were a feather-bed; and also considerably more than if it were hay or straw. Besides inflicting upon my own excited imagination the belief that I made noise enough to be heard by the inmates of the house who were likely to be rising at the time, I had the misfortune to attract the notice of a little house-dog, such as we call in that part of the world a "fice," on account of its being not only the smallest species of the canine race, but also, because it is the most saucy, noisy, and teasing of all dogs. This little creature commenced a fierce barking. I had at once great fears that the mischievous little thing would betray me; I fully apprehended that as soon as the man of the house arose, he would come and make search in the barn. It now being entirely daylight, it was too late to retreat from this shelter, even if I could have

found another; I, therefore, bedded myself down into the fodder as best I could, and entered upon the annoyances of the day, with the frail hope to sustain my mind.

It was Thursday morning; the clouds that had veiled the sky during the latter part of the previous day and the previous night were gone. It was not until about an hour after the sun rose that I heard any out-door movements about the house. As soon as I heard those movements, I was satisfied there was but one man about the house, and that he was preparing to go some distance to work for the day. This was fortunate for me; the busy movements about the yard, and especially the active preparations in the house for breakfast, silenced my unwelcome little annoyer, the fice, until after the man had gone, when he commenced afresh, and continued with occasional intermissions through the day. He made regular sallies from the house to the barn, and after smelling about, would fly back to the house, barking furiously; thus he strove most skilfully throughout the entire day to raise an alarm. There seemed to be no one about the house but one or two small children and the mother, after the man was gone. About ten o'clock my attention was gravely directed to another trial; how could I pass the day without food. The reader will remember it is Thursday, and the only regular meal I have taken since Sunday, was yesterday in the midst of great agitation, about four o'clock; that since that I have performed my arduous night's travel. At one moment, I had nearly concluded to go and present myself at the door, and ask the woman of the house to have compassion and give me food; but then I feared the consequences might be fatal, and I resolved to suffer the day out. The wind sprang up fresh and cool; the barn being small and the crevices large, my wet clothes were dried by it, and chilled me through and through.

I cannot now, with pen or tongue, give a correct idea of the feeling of wretchedness I experienced; every nerve in my system quivered, so that not a particle of my flesh was at rest. In this way I passed the day till about the middle of the afternoon, when there seemed to be an unusual stir about the public road, which passed close by the barn. Men seemed to be passing in parties on horseback, and talking anxiously. From a word which I now and then over-

---

4. *My British reader.* This narrative was first published in England, where James Pennington had fled to raise money to buy his freedom.

heard, I had not a shadow of doubt that they were in search of me. One I heard say, "I ought to catch such a fellow, the only liberty he should have for one fortnight, would be ten feet of rope." Another I heard say, "I reckon he is in that wood now." Another said, "Who would have thought that rascal was so 'cute?" All this while the little fice was mingling his voice with those of the horsemen, and the noise of the horses' feet. I listened and trembled.

Just before the setting of the sun, the labouring man of the house returned, and commenced his evening duties about the house and barn; chopping wood, getting up his cow, feeding his pigs, etc., attended by the little brute, who continued barking at short intervals. He came several times into the barn below. While matters were passing thus, I heard the approach of horses again, and as they came up nearer, I was led to believe that all I had heard pass were returning in one party. They passed the barn and halted at the house, when I recognized the voice of my old captor; addressing the labourer, he asked, "Have you seen a runaway nigger pass here today?"

LABOURER.—"No; I have not been at home since early this morning. Where did he come from?"

CAPTOR.—"I caught him down below here yesterday morning. I had him all day, and just at night he fooled me and got away. A party of us have been after him all day; we have been up to the line, but can't hear or see any thing of him. I heard this morning where he came from. He is a blacksmith, and a stiff reward is out for him—two hundred dollars."

LABOURER.—"He is worth looking for."

CAPTOR.—"I reckon so. If I get my clutches on him again, I'll mosey him down to —— before I eat or sleep."

Reader, you may if you can, imagine what the state of my mind was at this moment. I shall make no attempt to describe it to you; to my great relief, however, the party rode off, and the labourer after finishing his work went into the house. Hope seemed now to dawn for me once more; darkness was rapidly approaching, but the moments of twilight seemed much longer than they did the evening before. At length the sable covering had spread itself over the earth. About eight o'clock I ventured to descend from the mow of the barn into the road. The little dog the while began a furious fit of barking, so much so, that I was sure that with what his master had learned about me, he could not fail to believe I was about his premises. I quickly crossed the road, and got into an open field opposite. After stepping lightly about two hundred yards, I halted, and on listening, I heard the door open. Feeling about on the ground, I picked up two stones, and one in each hand I made off as fast as I could, but I heard nothing more that indicated pursuit, and after going some distance I discharged my encumbrance, as from the reduced state of my bodily strength, I could not afford to carry ballast.

This incident had the effect to start me under great disadvantage to make a good night's journey, as it threw me at once off the road, and compelled me to encounter at once the tedious and laborious task of beating my way across marshy fields, and to drag through woods and thickets where there were no paths.

After several hours I found my way back to the road, but the hope of making any thing like clever speed was out of the question. All I could do was to keep my legs in motion, and this I continued to do with the utmost difficulty. The latter part of the night I suffered extremely from cold. There came a heavy frost; I expected at every moment to fall on the road and perish. I came to a corn-field covered with heavy shocks of Indian corn that had been cut; I went into this and got an ear, and then crept into one of the shocks; ate as much of it as I could, and thought I would rest a little and start again, but weary nature could not sustain the operation of grinding hard corn for its own nourishment, and I sunk to sleep.

When I awoke, the sun was shining around; I started with alarm, but it was too late to think of seeking any other shelter; I therefore nestled myself down, and concealed myself as best I could from the light of day. After recovering a little from my fright, I commenced again eating my whole corn. Grain by grain I worked away at it; when my jaws grew tired, as they often did, I would rest, and then begin afresh. Thus, although I began an early breakfast, I was nearly the whole of the forenoon before I had done.

Nothing of importance occurred during the day, until about the middle of the afternoon, when I was thrown into a panic by the appearance of a party of gunners, who passed near me with their dogs. After shooting one or two birds, however, and passing within a few rods of my frail covering, they went on, and left me once more in hope. Friday night came without any other incident worth naming. As I sallied out, I felt evident benefit from the ear of corn I had nibbled away. My strength was considerably renewed; though I was far from being nourished, I felt that my life was at least safe from death by hunger. Thus encouraged, I set out with better speed than I had made since Sunday and Monday night. I had a presentiment, too, that I must be near free soil. I had not yet the least idea where I should find a home or a friend, still my spirits were so highly elated, that I took the whole of the road to myself; I ran, hopped, skipped, jumped, clapped my hands, and talked to myself. But to the old slaveholder I had left, I said, "Ah! ah! old fellow, I told you I'd fix you."

After an hour or two of such freaks of joy, a gloom would come over me in connexion with these questions, "But where are you going? What are you going to do? What will you do with freedom without father, mother, sisters, and brothers? What will you say when you are asked where you were born? You know nothing of the world; how will you explain the fact of your ignorance?"

These questions made me feel deeply the magnitude of the difficulties yet before me.

Saturday morning dawned upon me; and although my strength seemed yet considerably fresh, I began to feel a hunger somewhat more destructive and pinching, if possible, than I had before. I resolved, at all risk, to continue my travel by day-light, and to ask information of the first person I met.

The events of the next chapter will shew what fortune followed this resolve.

The resolution of which I informed the reader at the close of the last chapter, being put into practice, I continued my flight on the public road; and a little after the sun rose, I came in sight of a toll-gate again. For a moment all the events which followed my passing a toll-gate on Wednesday morning, came fresh to my recollection, and produced some hesitation; but at all events, said I, I will try again.

On arriving at the gate, I found it attended by an elderly woman, whom I afterwards learned was a widow, and an excellent Christian woman. I asked her if I was in Pennsylvania. On being informed that I was, I asked her if she knew where I could get employ? She said she did not; but advised me to go to W. W., a Quaker, who lived about three miles from her, whom I would find to take an interest in me. She gave me directions which way to take; I thanked her, and bade her good morning, and was very careful to follow her directions.

In about half an hour I stood trembling at the door of W. W. After knocking, the door opened upon a comfortably spread table; the sight of which seemed at once to increase my hunger sevenfold. Not daring to enter, I said I had been sent to him in search of employ. "Well," said he, "Come in and take thy breakfast, and get warm, and we will talk about it; thee must be cold without any coat." "*Come in and take thy breakfast, and get warm!*" These words spoken by a stranger, but with such an air of simple sincerity and fatherly kindness, made an overwhelming impression upon my mind. They made me feel, spite of all my fear and timidity, that I had, in the providence of God, found a friend and a home. He at once gained my confidence; and I felt that I might confide to him a fact which I had, as yet, confided to no one.

From that day to this, whenever I discover the least disposition in my heart to disregard the wretched condition of any poor or distressed persons with whom I meet, I call to mind these words—"*Come in and take thy breakfast, and get warm.*" They invariably remind me of what I was at that time; my condition was as wretched as that of any human being can possibly be, with the exception of the loss of health or reason. I had but four pieces of clothing about my person, having left all the rest in the hands of my captors. I was a starving fugitive, without home or friends—a reward offered for my person in the public papers—pursued by cruel man-hunters, and no claim upon him to whose door I went. Had he turned me away, I must have perished. Nay, he took me in, and gave me of his food, and shared with me his own garments. Such treatment I had never before received at the hands of any white man. ☐

1. What mental conflicts did Pennington have to resolve before he could make a definite and final decision to run away? How did he resolve these conflicts?
2. What particular aspect of Pennington's philosophy allowed him to view his owner, his pursuers, and his captors with the degree of charity that he did? What irony is contained in this situation?
3. What is the tone of this selection? Support your answer.

CREATIVE RESPONSE

The Pennington narrative is only one of a number of writings by those who experienced slavery. Collections with contents ranging from accounts of the passage from Africa to the escape and subsequent activities of former slaves are now available. Interested students may want to check school and public libraries for such works and present reports and bibliographies to the class.

James W. C. Pennington   1809 / 1870

Pennington was born a slave in Maryland. He was trained as a blacksmith and continued in that trade until, at twenty-one, he escaped from his master and fled to Pennsylvania where he was taken in by a Quaker family. He spent six months there, receiving his first education. He then moved to Long Island, found work, and continued his education, attending school at night. He became a teacher and a minister and was active in the antislavery movement, attending meetings and writing in support of abolition. After the passage of the Fugitive Slave Law in 1850, fearing recapture, he went abroad until friends had successfully negotiated with his former master to secure his freedom. His account of his early life, *The Fugitive Blacksmith*, was published in 1850.

TO BE SOLD on board the Ship *Bance-Island*, on tuesday the 6th of *May* next, at *Ashley-Ferry*; a choice cargo of about 250 fine healthy NEGROES, just arrived from the Windward & Rice Coast. —The utmost care has already been taken, and shall be continued, to keep them free from the least danger of being infected with the SMALL-POX, no boat having been on board, and all other communication with people from *Charles-Town* prevented.

Austin, Laurens, & Appleby.

N. B. Full one Half of the above Negroes have had the SMALL-POX in their own Country.

ADVERTISEMENT OF A CARGO OF SLAVES ABOARD A SHIP ANCHORED OFF CHARLESTON, DURING A PLAGUE OF SMALLPOX

YOUNG SLAVES TAKEN FROM A SLAVER BY THE BRITISH SHIP "UNDINE"—LIBRARY OF CONGRESS

Frederick Douglass

c. 1817/1895

from
WHAT THE BLACK
MAN WANTS

(Delivered at the Annual Meeting of the Massachusetts Anti-Slavery Society in Boston, 1865)

. . . I have had but one idea for the last three years to present to the American people, and the phraseology in which I clothe it is the old abolition phraseology. I am for the "immediate, unconditional, and universal" enfranchisement of the black man, in every state in the Union. Without this, his liberty is a mockery; without this, you might as well almost retain the old name of slavery for his condition; for, in fact, if he is not the slave of the individual master, he is the slave of society, and holds his liberty as a privilege, not as a right. He is at the mercy of the mob, and has no means of protecting himself.

It may be objected, however, that this pressing of the Negro's right to suffrage is premature. Let us have slavery abolished, it may be said, let us have labor organized, and then, in the natural course of events, the right of suffrage will be extended to the Negro. I do not agree with this. The constitution of the human mind is such, that if it once disregards the conviction forced upon it by a revelation of truth, it requires the exercise of a higher power to produce the same conviction afterward. The American people are now in tears. The Shenandoah has run blood,[1] the best blood of the North. All around Richmond, the blood of New England and of the North has been shed, of your sons, your brothers, and your fathers. We all feel, in the existence of this rebellion, that judgments terrible, widespread, far-reaching, overwhelming, are abroad in the land; and we feel, in view of these judgments, just now, a disposition to learn righteousness. This is the hour. Our streets are in mourning, tears are falling at every fireside, and under the chastisement of this rebellion we have almost come up to the point of conceding this great, this all-important right of suffrage. I fear that if we

fail to do it now, if Abolitionists fail to press it now, we may not see, for centuries to come, the same disposition that exists at this moment. Hence, I say, now is the time to press this right.

It may be asked, "Why do you want it? Some men have got along very well without it. Women have not this right." Shall we justify one wrong by another? That is a sufficient answer. Shall we at this moment justify the deprivation of the Negro of the right to vote, because some one else is deprived of that privilege? I hold that women, as well as men, have the right to vote, and my heart and my voice go with the movement to extend suffrage to woman; but that question rests upon another basis than that on which our right rests. We may be asked, I say, why we want it. I will tell you why we want it. We want it because it is our right, first of all. No class of men can, without insulting their own nature, be content with any deprivations of their rights. We want it, again, as a means for educating our race. Men are so constituted that they derive their conviction of their own possibilities largely from the estimate formed of them by others. If nothing is expected of a people, that people will find it difficult to contradict that expectation. By depriving us of suffrage, you affirm our incapacity to form an intelligent judgment respecting public men and public measures; you declare before the world that we are unfit to exercise the elective franchise, and by this means lead us to undervalue ourselves, to put a low estimate upon ourselves, and to feel that we have no possibilities like other men. Again, I want the elective franchise, for one, as a colored man, because ours is a peculiar government, based upon a peculiar idea, and that idea is universal suffrage. If I were in a monarchical government, or an autocratic or aristocratic government, where the few bore rule and the many were subject, there would be no special stigma resting upon me, because I did not exercise the elective franchise. It would do me no great violence. Mingling with the mass, I should partake of the strength of the mass, and I should have the same incentives to endeavor with the mass of my fellow men; it would be no particular burden, no particular deprivation; but here, where universal suffrage is the rule, where that is the fundamental idea of the government, to

---

1. *The Shenandoah has run blood.* Harpers Ferry, West Virginia, is situated on the Shenandoah River. In 1859 John Brown led a raid on the arsenal at Harpers Ferry in an attempt to gain arms for a slave uprising.

rule us out is to make us an exception, to brand us with the stigma of inferiority, and to invite to our heads the missiles of those about us; therefore, I want the franchise for the black man. . . .

I ask my friends who are apologizing for not insisting upon this right, where can the black man look in this country for the assertion of this right, if he may not look to the Massachusetts Anti-Slavery Society? Where under the whole heavens can he look for sympathy in asserting this right, if he may not look to this platform? Have you lifted us up to a certain height to see that we are men, and then are any disposed to leave us there, without seeing that we are put in possession of all our rights? We look naturally to this platform for the assertion of all our rights, and for this one especially. I understand the anti-slavery societies of this country to be based on two principles—first, the freedom of the blacks of this country; and, second, the elevation of them. Let me not be misunderstood here. I am not asking for sympathy at the hands of Abolitionists, sympathy at the hands of any. I think the American people are disposed often to be generous rather than just. I look over this country at the present time, and I see educational societies, sanitary commissions, freedmen's associations and the like,—all very good: but in regard to the colored people there is always more that is benevolent, I perceive, than just, manifested towards us. What I ask for the Negro is not benevolence, not pity, not sympathy, but simple justice. The American people have always been anxious to know what they shall do with us. . . .

Everybody has asked the question, and they learned to ask it early of the Abolitionists, "What shall we do with the Negro?" I have had but one answer from the beginning. Do nothing with us! Your doing with us has already played the mischief with us. Do nothing with us! If the apples will not remain on the tree of their own strength, if they are worm-eaten at the core, if they are early ripe and disposed to fall, let them fall! I am not for tying or fastening them on the tree in any way, except by nature's plan, and if they will not stay there, let them fall. And if the Negro can not stand on his own legs, let him fall also. All I ask is, give him a chance to stand on his own legs! Let him alone! If you see him on his way to school, let him alone,—don't disturb him. If you see him going to the dinner table at a hotel, let him go! If you see him going to the ballot-box, let him alone,—don't disturb him! If you see him going into a workshop, just let him alone,—your interference is doing him a positive injury. . . . Let him fall if he can not stand alone! If the Negro can not live by the line of eternal justice, . . . the fault will not be yours; it will be his who made the Negro, and established that line for his government. Let him live or die by that. If you will only untie his hands, and give him a chance, I think he will live. . . . ☐

FOR EXPLORATION

1. What is Douglass' purpose in speaking to his audience as he does? Of what does he hope to convince them?
2. Notice the date of the address. Why is Douglass afraid that the society will not sustain its zeal in working for Black sufferage? Support your answer with passages from the text.
3. One rhetorical technique often used by those who hope to convince is that of anticipating and stating the arguments that one's opponent is likely to give, and answering these arguments even before the opponent has had a chance to voice them. Douglass makes use of this technique at least three times in his address. What are

these arguments? How does Douglass refute them? Support your answers with passages from the text.
4. Douglass states that the ". . . American people are disposed often to be generous rather than just." What is the difference between generosity and justice? Which quality do you find the more admirable? Do you agree with the statement in its historical context? Do you think it is true of the people of the United States today?
5. Reread the last two paragraphs of the address; contrast their tone with that of Pennington's narrative. Support any points you make.

Douglass says that "If nothing is expected of a people, that people will find it difficult to contradict that expectation." Write a personal essay in which you attempt to either prove or disprove this statement, supporting with specific examples any points you make. Note that the statement might apply to an individual, a social grouping (such as high-school students), or ethnic and nationality groups.

Frederick Douglass 1817? / 1895

Douglass was born a slave in Maryland. During his childhood he spent some time in a Baltimore home as a house servant, where he was taught to read and write. An unsuccessful attempt to escape from slavery resulted in his arrest. His master secured his release and for a time he was apprenticed to a ship caulker. His next attempt was successful and he reached New York City in September 1838, where he married. He and his wife moved to New Bedford, where he found employment as a laborer.

Upon reading William Lloyd Garrison's abolitionist newspaper *The Liberator,* Douglass discovered the anti-slavery movement, and became active in it. In 1845 he published *Narrative of the Life of Frederick Douglass.* Following this he spent two years abroad, visiting England and Ireland. This trip had a great impact on the development of his thought. He now saw that emancipation was but a necessary first step in the black man's struggle for complete independence.

When he returned to the United States in 1847, Douglass purchased his freedom and established an independent black newspaper, the *North Star,* which he issued for the next seventeen years. He was briefly associated with John Brown, and after Brown's raid on the arsenal at Harper's Ferry, an attempt was made to arrest Douglass as a co-conspirator, but he fled, first to Canada, then to England again, where he remained for six months.

During the Civil War, Douglass helped organize regiments of black soldiers for the Union Army. After the war, during Reconstruction, he worked for suffrage and civil rights for the former slaves. He held a number of official positions with the government in later years, finally being appointed United States Minister to Haiti.

LIBRARY OF CONGRESS

SINGERS IN BLUE AND GRAY

Huddled around campfires or marching into battle, soldiers in Blue and Gray sang to lift their spirits or their courage. Just as the soldiers of the Revolution had treasured "Yankee Doodle," the soldier-singers of the War Between the States favored certain unforgettable tunes.

The Union man probably volunteered for service to the stirring strains of "The Battle Cry of Freedom," while the Confederate heard his call to arms in "The Bonnie Blue Flag." Once in uniform, the fighting man had little recreation; singing was the one way he could relieve the interminable drills and marches, the waiting to fight and the fear of fighting. On a day of high spirits, the tune of "Goober Peas" might float above a Southern encampment or "Grafted into the Army" might ring out in Union trenches. A soldier's longing for the girl back home was echoed in "Aura Lea" and "Lorena." The soldier-singers of the Civil War paid scant attention to the origin of the songs they sang; Southerners, for example, sang "My Darling Nellie Gray" without changing the abolitionist lyrics. As the war went on and on, Yankee and Confederate alike poured their weariness and homesickness into the sentimental ballads "Tenting on the Old Camp Ground" and "Just Before the Battle, Mother."

The two great marching songs of the Civil War, "Dixie" and "The Battle Hymn of the Republic," have interesting histories. "Dixie" was first sung on Broadway by Bryant's Minstrels in 1859. The nonsense words and lively tune made it immediately popular all over the country.

I wish I was in de land ob cotton,
Old times dar am not forgotten;
　　Look away! Look away! Look away! Dixie Land!
In Dixie Land whar I was born in,
Early on one frosty mornin',
　　Look away! Look away! Look away! Dixie Land!

Chorus
Den I wish I was in Dixie! Hooray! Hooray!
In Dixie's Land we'll take our stand, to lib an'
　　die in Dixie.
Away! away! away down South in Dixie.
Away! away! away down South in Dixie.

The song was introduced to the South in a New Orleans production of *Pocahontas* just before the war began. Confederate regiments in Louisiana took it up; soon it was widely used in the Southern armies. Several literary "improvements" of "Dixie" were written, but the original song by Northern-born and pro-Union Daniel Decatur Emmett became, ironically, the rallying song of the Confederacy.

The martial and resounding lyrics of "The Battle Hymn of the Republic" were written by a well-known reform leader of the time, Julia Ward Howe. On a visit to a Union camp near Washington, D.C., Mrs. Howe had heard the soldiers singing the popular "John Brown's Body," a doggerel song which had fitted its words to an old Southern revival hymn. Inspired by the music and the scene, Mrs. Howe returned home to compose fresh lyrics for the old hymn. Her version was first published in the *Atlantic Monthly* in February 1862. "The Battle Hymn of the Republic" quickly became the great marching song of the North.

Mine eyes have seen the glory of the coming of
　　the Lord:
He is trampling out the vintage where the grapes
　　of wrath are stored:
He hath loosed the fateful lightning of His
　　terrible swift sword;
　　His truth is marching on.

Chorus
Glory! glory! Hallelujah!
Glory! glory! Hallelujah!
Glory! glory! Hallelujah!
　　His truth is marching on!

LIBRARY OF CONGRESS

Henry Timrod

1828/1867

CHARLESTON

Calm as that second summer which precedes
   The first fall of the snow,
In the broad sunlight of heroic deeds,
   The City bides the foe.

5 As yet, behind their ramparts stern and proud,
   Her bolted thunders sleep—
Dark Sumter,[1] like a battlemented cloud,
   Looms o'er the solemn deep.

No Calpe[2] frowns from lofty cliff or scar
10   To guard the holy strand;
But Moultrie[3] holds in leash her dogs of war
   Above the level sand.

And down the dunes a thousand guns lie couched,
   Unseen, beside the flood—
15 Like tigers in some Orient jungle crouched
   That wait and watch for blood.

Meanwhile, through streets still echoing with trade,
   Walk grave and thoughtful men,
Whose hands may one day wield the patriot's blade
20   As lightly as the pen.

And maidens, with such eyes as would grow dim
   Over a bleeding hound,
Seem each one to have caught the strength of him
   Whose sword she sadly bound.

25 Thus girt without and garrisoned at home,
   Day patient following day,
Old Charleston looks from roof, and spire, and dome,
   Across her tranquil bay.

Ships, through a hundred foes, from Saxon lands
30   And spicy Indian ports,
Bring Saxon steel and iron to her hands,
   And Summer to her courts.

But still, along yon dim Atlantic line,
   The only hostile smoke
35 Creeps like a harmless mist above the brine,
   From some frail, floating oak.

Shall the Spring dawn, and she still clad in smiles,
   And with an unscathed brow,
Rest in the strong arms of her palm-crowned isles,
40   As fair and free as now?

We know not; in the temple of the Fates
   God has inscribed her doom;
And, all untroubled in her faith, she waits
   The triumph or the tomb.

ODE

Sleep sweetly in your humble graves,
   Sleep, martyrs of a fallen cause;
Though yet no marble column craves
   The pilgrim here to pause.

5 In seeds of laurel in the earth,
   The blossom of your fame is blown,
And somewhere, waiting for its birth,
   The shaft is in the stone!

Meanwhile, behalf the tardy years
10   Which keep in trust your storied tombs,
Behold! your sisters bring their tears,
   And these memorial blooms.

Small tributes! but your shades will smile
   More proudly on these wreaths today,
15 Than when some cannon-molded pile
   Shall overlook this bay.

Stoop, angels, hither from the skies!
   There is no holier spot of ground
Than where defeated valor lies,
20   By mourning beauty crowned!

CHARLESTON. **1.** *Sumter*, Fort Sumter, located in Charleston harbor.
The capture of this fort by Confederate forces on April 12, 1861,
marked the opening of the Civil War.
2. *Calpe*, the Rock of Gibraltar.
3. *Moultrie*. Colonel William Moultrie (1731–1805) defeated a
British fleet on June 28, 1776, from a half-finished fort on Sullivan's
Island in Charleston harbor.

FOR EXPLORATION

Charleston

1. Who is the "foe" of line 4?
2. What is the Rock of Gibralter a symbol of? What is the effect of the poet's contrasting Charleston with Gibralter and other fortresses?
3. Reread stanzas 5 and 6. How would you characterize the picture of southern men and women given by these lines?
4. What term is more commonly applied to the ships that Timrod praises in stanza 8?

Ode

1. An **ode** is a serious **lyric** poem written in celebration or commemoration of a special occasion. Who and what is being celebrated in this poem?
2. Given the tone of this poem and the time at which it was written, what emotion did it probably arouse in those who then heard it?

Henry Timrod   1828 / 1867

Timrod was born in Charleston, South Carolina, and at eighteen entered Franklin College (later the University of Georgia). Ill-health and insufficient means forced him to withdraw after two years. Upon returning to Charleston, he began to read law in the office of a local lawyer, but abandoned this after a short time. He continued his studies on his own with the hope of qualifying for a professorship, but, when he was unable to secure such a post, took a job as a tutor on a plantation. He continued tutoring for ten years, meanwhile writing verses which were published in periodicals. In 1860 he published a volume of poems which was favorably received, but the beginning of the Civil War put an end to his hopes of gaining a large audience for his work. He spent a short time in the Confederate Army but was discharged because of his health. He became the editor of a paper in Columbia, South Carolina, but lost his livelihood when the city was burned. The remainder of his life was a continuing struggle with poverty and ill-health. It was not until some years after his death that, through the efforts of a group of friends and admirers, he achieved a reputation as a poet.

DICTIONARY OF AMERICAN PORTRAITS

Abraham Lincoln

1809/1865

SECOND INAUGURAL ADDRESS, MARCH 4, 1865

FELLOW Countrymen: At this second appearing to take the oath of the presidential office, there is less occasion for an extended address than there was at the first. Then a statement, somewhat in detail, of a course to be pursued, seemed fitting and proper. Now, at the expiration of four years, during which public declarations have been constantly called forth on every point and phase of the great contest which still absorbs the attention and engrosses the energies of the nation, little that is new could be presented. The progress of our arms, upon which all else chiefly depends, is as well known to the public as to myself; and it is, I trust, reasonably satisfactory and encouraging to all. With high hope for the future, no prediction in regard to it is ventured.

On the occasion corresponding to this four years ago, all thoughts were anxiously directed to an impending civil war. All dreaded it—all sought to avert it. While the inaugural address was being delivered from this place, devoted altogether to saving the Union without war, insurgent agents were in the city seeking to destroy it without war—seeking to dissolve the Union, and divide effects, by negotiation. Both parties deprecated war; but one of them would make war rather than let the nation survive; and the other would accept war rather than let it perish. And the war came.

One eighth of the whole population were colored slaves, not distributed generally over the Union, but localized in the southern part of it. These slaves constituted a peculiar and powerful interest. All knew that this interest was, somehow, the cause of the war. To strengthen, perpetuate, and extend this interest was the object for which the insurgents would rend the Union, even by war; while the government claimed no right to do more than to restrict the territorial enlargement of it.

Neither party expected for the war the magnitude or the duration which it has already attained. Neither anticipated that the cause of the conflict might cease with, or even before, the conflict itself should cease. Each looked for an easier triumph and a result less fundamental and astounding. Both read the same Bible, and pray to the same God; and each invokes His aid against the other. It may seem strange that any man should dare to ask a just God's assistance in wringing their bread from the sweat of other men's faces; but let us judge not, that we be not judged.[1] The prayers of both could not be answered—that of neither has been answered fully.

The Almighty has His own purposes. "Woe unto the world because of offenses! for it must needs be that offenses come; but woe to that man by whom the offense cometh."[2] If we shall suppose that American slavery is one of those offenses which in the providence of God, must needs come, but which, having continued through His appointed time, He now wills to remove, and that He gives to both North and South this terrible war, as the woe due to those by whom the offense came, shall we discern therein any departure from those divine attributes which the believers in a living God always ascribe to Him? Fondly do we hope—fervently do we pray—that this mighty scourge of war may speedily pass away. Yet, if God wills that it continue until all the wealth piled by the bondman's two hundred and fifty years of unrequited toil shall be sunk, and until every drop of blood drawn with the lash shall be paid by another drawn with the sword, as was said three thousand years ago, so still it must be said, "The judgments of the Lord are true and righteous altogether."[3]

With malice toward none; with charity for all; with firmness in the right, as God gives us to see the right, let us strive on to finish the work we are in; to bind up the nation's wounds; to care for him who shall have borne the battle, and for his widow and his orphan—to do all which may achieve and cherish a just and lasting peace among ourselves, and with all nations. □

---

1. *judge not . . . judged.* Matthew 7:1.
2. *"Woe unto the world . . . the offense cometh."* Matthew 18:7.
3. *"The judgments . . . righteous altogether."* Psalms 19:9.

FOR EXPLORATION

1. According to Lincoln, what was the purpose of the North in entering and fighting the war?
2. Judging from this address, what was Lincoln's own attitude toward slavery?
3. How did Lincoln feel about the preservation of the Union?
4. How are the quotations from the Bible useful in developing the point made in the final paragraph?
5. Do you agree with those who regard this address as a piece of great literature? In answering, consider such points as word choice, word order, variation in sentence structure, use of figures of speech, creation of the tone.

CREATIVE RESPONSE

Compare and contrast Lincoln's tone in this selection with that of the three preceding writers (Pennington, Douglass, and Timrod). Then divide the class into four groups. Each group should assume responsibility for defending the position of one of the four writers. In an open discussion, members of the four groups should discuss their view of the conflict that is threatening to destroy the nation. Keep in mind that group members should stay "in character." (For example, it is highly unlikely that anyone defending Lincoln's position would direct a ranting, abusive tirade at members of the other groups no matter how much he might disagree with them.)

WORDS

The adjective *inaugural* is formed from the verb *inaugurate,* which has a very interesting history. Look up its origin in an unabridged dictionary and be prepared to explain how it came to have its present meaning.

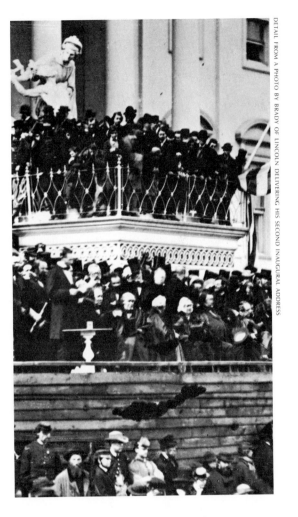

DETAIL FROM A PHOTO BY BRADY OF LINCOLN DELIVERING HIS SECOND INAUGURAL ADDRESS

Abraham Lincoln   1809 / 1865

So remote was Lincoln from the traditional man of past ages that James Russell Lowell described him as "the first American." A hundred years later he still remains "the first American," without any doubt the foremost figure in the national mythology. Homely, largely self-educated, faced with the greatest crisis that his country had yet had to meet, Lincoln was hated as well as loved, and he suffered patiently through setback after setback before the Union he loved was finally saved. Then he died at the hands of an assassin, calling forth national mourning.

Sidney Lanier
1842/1881

THE CLOUD

Sail on, sail on, fair cousin Cloud;
Oh, loiter hither from the sea.
   Still-eyed and shadow-brow'd,
Steal off from yon far-drifting crowd,
5 And come and brood upon the marsh with me.

Yon laboring low horizon-smoke,
Yon stringent sail, toil not for thee
   Nor me: did heaven's stroke
The whole deep with drown'd commerce choke,
10 No pitiless tease of risk or bottomry

Would to thy rainy office close
Thy will, or lock mine eyes from tears
   Part wept for traders'-woes,
Part for that ventures mean as those
15 In issue bind such sovereign hopes and fears.

Stern Cloud, thy downward countenance stares
Blank on the blank-faced marsh, and thou
   Mindest of dark affairs;
Thy substance seems a warp of cares;
20 Like late wounds run the wrinkles on thy brow.

Well may'st thou pause, and gloom, and stare,
A visible conscience; I arraign
   Thee, criminal Cloud, of rare
Contempts on Mercy, Right, and Prayer,
25 Of murders, arsons, thefts, of nameless stain.

Yet though life's logic grow as gray
As thou, my soul's not in eclipse.
   Cold Cloud, but yesterday
Thy lightning slew a child at play,
30 And then a priest with prayers upon his lips

For his enemies, and then a bright
Lady that did but ope the door
   Upon the stormy night
To let a begger in,—strange spite,—
35 And then thy sulky rain refused to pour

Till thy quick torch a barn had burned
Where twelve months' store of victual lay
   A widow's sons had earned,
Which done, thy floods of rain returned,—
40 The river raped their little herd away.

"The Cloud" by Sidney Lanier from THE CENTENNIAL EDITION OF THE WORKS OF SIDNEY LANIER, Vol. I, edited by Charles R. Anderson. Reprinted by permission of The Johns Hopkins Press.

What myriad righteous errands high
Thy flames *might* run on! In that hour
    Thou slewest the child, oh why
Not rather slay Calamity,
45 Breeder of Pain and Doubt, infernal Power?

Or why not plunge thy blades about
Some maggot politician throng
    Swarming to parcel out
The body of a land, and rout
50 The maw-conventicle,[1] and ungorge Wrong?

    What the cloud doeth,
    The Lord knoweth,
    The cloud knoweth not.
    What the artist doeth,
55   *The Lord knoweth;*
    Knoweth the artist not?

Well-answered! O dear artists, ye
—Whether in forms of curve or hue
    Or tone, your gospels be—
60 Say wrong, *This work is not of me,*
But God: it is not true, it is not true.

Awful is Art, because 'tis free.
The artist trembles o'er his plan,
    Where men his Self must see.
65 Who made a song or picture, he
Did it, and not another, God nor man.

My Lord is large, my Lord is strong:
Giving, He gave: my me is mine.
    How poor, how strange, how wrong,
70 To dream He wrote the little song
I made to Him with love's unforced design!

Oh, not as clouds dim laws have plann'd
To strike down Good and fight for Ill,
    Oh, not as harps that stand
75 In the wind[2] and sound the wind's command:
Each artist—gift of terror!—owns his will.

For thee, Cloud,—if thou spend thine all
Upon the South's o'er-brimming sea
    That needs thee not; or crawl
80 To the dry provinces, and fall
Till every convert clod shall give to thee

Green worship; if thou grow or fade,
Bring mad delight or misery,
    Fly east or west, be made
85 Snow, hail, rain, wind, grass, rose, light, shade;—
What is it all to thee? There is no thee.

Pass, kinsman Cloud, now fair and mild:
Discharge the will that's not thine own.
    I work in freedom wild,
90 But work, as plays a little child,
Sure of the Father, Self, and Love, alone.

---

1. *maw-conventicle,* an unlawful, evil secret meeting.
2. *harps that stand in the wind.* The reference is to Aeolian harps, harps or lyres whose strings are sounded by the wind, thus producing unusual tones.

THE RAVEN DAYS

Our hearths are gone out, and our hearts are broken,
    And but the ghosts of homes to us remain,
And ghostly eyes and hollow sighs give token
    From friend to friend of an unspoken pain.

5 O, Raven Days, dark Raven Days of sorrow,
    Bring to us, in your whetted ivory beaks,
Some sign out of the far land of To-morrow,
    Some strip of sea-green dawn, some orange streaks.

Ye float in dusky files, forever croaking—
10   Ye chill our manhood with your dreary shade.
Pale, in the dark, not even God invoking,
    We lie in chains, too weak to be afraid.

O Raven Days, dark Raven Days of sorrow,
    Will ever any warm light come again?
15 Will ever the lit mountains of To-morrow
    Begin to gleam across the mournful plain?

"The Raven Days" by Sidney Lanier from THE CENTENNIAL EDITION OF THE WORKS OF SIDNEY LANIER, Vol. I, edited by Charles R. Anderson. Reprinted by permission of The Johns Hopkins Press.

DISCUSSION

Lanier, a poetic innovator, rebelled against what he called the "prim smugness and cleanshaven propriety" of conventional verse forms. As he explained in *The Science of English Verse*, he—like Poe—regarded poetry as "in all respects a phenomenon of sound" and held that "the main distinction between music and verse is . . . the difference between the scale of tones used in music and the scales of tones used by the human speaking voice." In analyzing the rhythms of poetry, accordingly, Lanier used musical nota-tions; and, wrote his most individual poems with the melodies, cadences, and overall patterns of musical composition in mind. His lyrics foreshadow much of today's poetry also in the rhythmical variations they employ: the shifting line lengths and rhythms used in imitation of musical instruments—violin, flute, oboe, horns, etc. In many ways Lanier's innovations parallel those of both Whitman and Dickinson.

FOR EXPLORATION

The Cloud

1. When an author (or poet) invests natural or inanimate objects with living or human qualities he is said to have committed the **pathetic fallacy.** (eg., "The trees groaned"). *(a)* Cite an example of the pathetic fallacy from the first stanza of the poem "The Cloud." *(b)* What natural object does Lanier invest with living qualities? *(c)* How does the poet develop the pathetic fallacy in the succeeding forty lines? Explain.

2. Give the line from the refrain of the poem (lines 51–56) that negates the idea of the pathetic fallacy.

3. What do you suppose is the poet's answer to the question posed in line 56? Explain.

4. Explicate lines 62–64. What does the poet mean when he says: "The artist trembles o'er his plan/ Where men his Self must see"?

5. What is the poet asserting in line 68: " . . . my me is mine"? How does this assertion relate to the rest of the stanza? Explain.

6. A **conceit** is an elaborate, surprising, and often outlandish figure of speech comparing two very dissimilar things. Conceits are frequently metaphors, similes, or analogies. Explain Lanier's conceit comparing the artist with an Aeolian harp (lines 74–75). Does the poet believe that the artist is like an Aeolian harp? Explain.

7. The poet again invokes the pathetic fallacy near the conclusion of the poem. Cite an example of this from the third and second to last stanzas of the poem. Cite the line from the second to last stanza that illustrates Lanier's knowledge that the pathetic fallacy is indeed fallacious.

8. Identify and explain the poet's simile for the artist in the last stanza. How does this notion relate to Lanier's previous ideas about the artist's "freedom"? Explain.

The Raven Days

1. Does the poem "The Raven Days" express personal or communal loss? Give evidence from the poem in support of your answer.

2. What do you think the poem "The Raven Days" is really about? (Hint: If you are not sure, see Lanier's biography.)

3. How is the raven, symbol of death and destruction, an appropriate conceit for the period the poet is lamenting? Explain.

BETTMANN ARCHIVES, INC.

Sidney Lanier 1842 / 1881

Lanier was born in Macon, Georgia, and educated at Oglethorpe University. After graduation he enlisted in the Confederate Army and served for the duration of the war. The last five months of the war he was imprisoned in a Federal camp where, as a result of exposure, his health was impaired for the rest of his life.

After the war, while teaching school and working as a hotel clerk, Lanier found time to revive an earlier interest in writing. He published a novel, *Tiger-Lilies,* in 1867. But he decided he had a greater enthusiasm for poetry than for fiction, and he worked hard to perfect his skill. Lanier was a musician as well as a poet. A flutist of great ability, he was a member of the Peabody Symphony Orchestra in Baltimore in the 1870's. During these same years he was a lecturer in literature at Johns Hopkins University.

Lanier worked very hard at the writing of poetry, but it was not until several of his poems were published in a periodical in 1875 that he achieved recognition. However, *Poems,* a volume which was published in 1877, was not well received and his hope that his work at Johns Hopkins would result in a professorship was unrealized. The last few years of his life were spent in preparing his lectures and in writing some of his finest poetry.

END OF AN ERA

Then and Now

From the beginning of the settlement of America, when John Smith established his colony in Virginia, and when William Bradford brought the *Mayflower* to Massachusetts, the seeds of controversy and conflict were sown. As the South developed an agrarian economy that grew dependent on slavery for labor, so the North developed an economy of crafts, shopkeeping, business, and industry that used the labor of free men. The controversy flared up briefly in the founding of the country, in the composition of those key documents that formed the basis of government. In the writing of the Declaration of Independence, a compromise—a silent assent to slavery—kept the document from being discarded before it could be proclaimed. And the Constitution itself represented a compromise on the issue. Thus the country came into existence without resolution of one of the gravest issues that divided the people ideologically.

It is difficult to look back from our vantage point in the latter half of the twentieth century without feeling genuine regret that the issue had not been earlier resolved. Not only did postponement of dealing with the issue lead to a devastating civil war which exhausted both South and North for a long period of time, but it also bestowed on the present time (and deep into the future) a heritage of bitterness and a host of problems. What we cannot realize, perhaps, is that however sordid the earlier compromises on the issue appear, the alternative might well have been simply giving up the dream of creating a new country. In any event, the issue of slavery is the one issue that almost succeeded in dissolving the Union.

Throughout the first half of the nineteenth century, tension on the issue grew as the abolitionists of the North confronted the slaveholders of the South in the political arena. The slaves themselves made contributions to the controversy. In 1831, for example, a Virginia slave by the name of Nat Turner led an insurrection that resulted in the death of over fifty whites; Turner and some sixteen of his followers were hanged, but the case was kept alive by the publication of Nat Turner's *Confessions* in 1831 (and in our own time by William Styron's novel, *The Confessions of Nat Turner*, 1967). Slave narratives appeared depicting the grim life of slavery, one of the most celebrated being *Narrative of the Life of Frederick Douglass, An American Slave, Written by Himself*, published in 1845.

Congressional acts frequently enflamed the controversy, and often inspired outright defiance. The Fugitive Slave Law of 1850 compelled the return of runaway slaves to their owners. Many Northerners, including Emerson and Thoreau, swore that they would not uphold it. Indeed, abolitionists and others in the North participated in setting up stations along an "underground railroad" to assist the slaves to escape from the South into the North and up to Canada. Violence flared up in Boston when an angry mob attempted to rescue a runaway slave from the police, necessitating the intervention of United States troops.

A recurring issue in Congress was whether new states, as they entered the Union, would be slave or free. It was agreed that the issue in Kansas would be decided by popular vote in 1855. John Brown was deeply involved in the violence that flared up over the debate. Senator Charles Sumner, a leading abolitionist from Massachusetts, gave a speech, "The Crime Against Kansas," in the Senate and was severely caned on the Senate floor by a Southerner, suffering injuries from which he never fully recovered.

In 1857, the Supreme Court made the famous Dred Scott decision, which further increased tensions. Dred Scott was a slave who had been taken by his owner into a free state and then brought back to the slave state. The slave sued for his freedom, but the Supreme Court denied his petition on grounds that he was not a citizen of the United States and therefore did not have the right to use the U.S. court system. Abraham Lincoln in Illinois (in his debates with Stephen A. Douglas) attacked the Supreme Court's position.

· The story of the Civil War is almost as familiar to us now as the story of the Revolutionary War. In the latter the nation was born, and in the Civil War it survived its severest test and came of age. The events of the period and their dates have been lifted from history and mythologized: In 1861, the secession of southern states and the firing on Fort Sumter to begin the conflict; in 1863 the "Emancipation Proclamation" freeing the slaves and Abraham Lincoln's "Gettysburg Address;" in 1864, Sherman's March to the Sea; in 1865, the surrender of Lee to Grant at Appomattox on April 9, and the assassination of Abraham Lincoln on April 14. These are only a few of the events of the time that still seem to fascinate Americans, as they go back over their past again and again in search of the origins of feelings and attitudes that continue to shape their lives.

There is no more fascinating individual who is an important part of that past than John Brown. He first walked into history when he moved with his five sons to Kansas, intent on rooting out pro-slavery sentiment. He was involved there in the killing of five pro-slavery neighbors. In 1859 he moved to Harpers Ferry, Virginia, where he planned and executed an attack on the U.S. armory, which he and his band of twenty-one men occupied briefly. His scheme was to establish a base for freeing large numbers of slaves and organizing a large Black army. He and his group were attacked by a force of Marines under the command of Robert E. Lee; many of Brown's followers were killed and Brown was captured, and, after a hasty trial, sentenced to be hanged. On the morning of his hanging, John Brown said: "I, John Brown, am now quite certain that the crimes of this guilty land will never be purged away but with blood." He was, of course, proved right.

John Brown has been described as both a hero and a madman, in history, poetry, fiction, and drama. The following scene comes from a play by Barrie Stavis, *Harpers Ferry*. In it, John Brown attempts to recruit the famed ex-slave and newspaper editor, Frederick Douglass, for his "army."

from

HARPERS FERRY

Barrie Stavis
Act 2, Scene 3

JOHN BROWN. We must find a man—one single man. He must be an escaped slave, a man of judgment and bravery, a powerful orator. A Negro whose heroic deeds are known even to the most benighted slave in the darkest corner of slavery. I cannot go to the slaves—I am a prisoner of my white skin. But this Negro—when he says to the slave, "Rise up, take this weapon," there will be no hesitation.

KAGI. Frederick Douglass!

STEVENS. Douglass—yes!

JOHN BROWN. Frederick Douglass.

KAGI. You do not have the right even to ask him to join us. His newspaper reaches thousands of people.

JOHN BROWN. Is the editing of an anti-slavery paper more important than the firing of a rifle and the freeing of an army of slaves? He will have to suspend his work for a short period of time.

KAGI. Frederick Douglass' life is too valuable to risk in this venture.

JOHN BROWN. Are you saying our lives are less valuable than his?

KAGI. Yes! Our lives are less valuable than his.

JOHN BROWN (*brushing aside their objections*). In the final balance, our lives will be measured by what

From HARPERS FERRY by Barrie Stavis. Copyright 1960, 1967 by Barrie Stavis. Reprinted by permission of A. S. Barnes & Company, Inc.

we accomplish. I am asking him to meet me in secret near the abandoned quarry outside of Chambersburg. Kagi, you will go with me. I know Frederick Douglass will join us. (*The lights fade on this area and come up on the playing area of the abandoned quarry near Chambersburg. The quarry, filled with water, has become a pool.* JOHN BROWN *and* KAGI *move into the quarry area as* FREDERICK DOUGLASS *and* SHIELDS GREEN *come in from the other side.* DOUGLASS *is a Mulatto,* GREEN *is a full-blooded Negro.* JOHN BROWN *and* DOUGLASS *occupy center of area.* KAGI *and* GREEN *are out of the major focus of scene until indicated, watching the two principals intently. There is scarcely any pause between* JOHN BROWN'S *last speech and the following.*) A year ago I could talk about Harpers Ferry only in general terms. But now with the information gathered by Cook, I am positive the attack can succeed.

DOUGLASS. Nothing you have said has changed my mind. Harpers Ferry is a steel trap. One jaw of the trap is the bridge over the Potomac River, the other jaw is the bridge over the Shenandoah.

JOHN BROWN. Listen to me. Listen to me. At the Potomac Bridge there is only one watchman. We overpower him and enter Harpers Ferry. Then a few of our men will capture the Arsenal and the Armory— (*holds up a restraining hand as* DOUGLASS *attempts to interject*) It sounds more grand than it is; there is but a single watchman at the Armory gate. I will have control of Harpers Ferry for thirty hours, during which time the slaves will rise up in numbers and join our banner. These are the hours, Frederick, when God and I have crucial need for you.

DOUGLASS. Soft, soft, my friend. We haven't yet come to the moment of my participation.

JOHN BROWN. Before the town is able to organize a defense, we will march across the Shenandoah Bridge and then set fire to it. And the host will be covenanted on the other side of the burning bridge—the bridge behind us, the mountain range before us. (*Again he holds up his hand to forestall* DOUGLASS) A short, hard climb of several miles and we are safe in the mountain ranges—safe in the Alleghenies.

DOUGLASS. Again, you are already up in the mountains.

JOHN BROWN. Once there, no force can dislodge us. Two dozen men can hold back a thousand. We will swoop down on the flat plateau lands, gather up our slaves and retreat back into the mountains. (DOUGLASS *impatiently tries to interrupt.* JOHN BROWN *holds up a hand to cut him off.*) It is an Army I am talking about, an Army in continuous operation recruiting its further soldiers from the ranks of the slaves it has liberated. (DOUGLASS *tries to interrupt; again* JOHN BROWN *pushes on.*) We will destroy the money value of slave property— for no master will know when a piece of his human property worth fifteen hundred dollars will disappear in the night to join us in the mountains. I begin at the outside rim of the slave states, Virginia; as I push deeper, I force a continual shrinking up of the slave area. . . . All this is possible to attain. Is it not worth a great risk?

DOUGLASS (*quiet and deliberate*). How many men have you at the present moment?

JOHN BROWN. At this moment my Army consists of seventeen men.

DOUGLASS. And how many more men can you expect by the night of the attack?

JOHN BROWN. Perhaps ten—perhaps five.

DOUGLASS. So—your maximum force will be about twenty-five men? And with this band you plan to—

JOHN BROWN. Army—not band.

DOUGLASS. And with this band you—

JOHN BROWN. Army. Not band. We are a legal body with a military organization.

DOUGLASS. Call it "Army" if you insist. But the enemy you fight will consider you nothing more than a rebel band.

JOHN BROWN. Not so many years ago my grandfather, Captain John Brown, by name, as I am named, fought against King George and the English. They who fought in the Revolutionary War were also called rebels. But it is victory or defeat which determines whether they be heroes or traitors. I expect finally to win this great campaign, therefore call it "Army"—an Army in the mountain wilderness.

DOUGLASS. Again you are in that mountain wilderness! But I see you trapped in Harpers Ferry. The raid will fail. There will be no army in the mountains. There will only be the desolate fact of twenty-odd men carrying out a doomed raid on a Southern town, trapped, captured, tried, found guilty, hanged.

JOHN BROWN. What are you saying to me, Frederick Douglass?

DOUGLASS. I am pleading with you not to go on this raid. I am saying to you further, if you insist on going, I will not join you.

JOHN BROWN. Frederick—Frederick—do not say this to me.

(Two rifle shots are heard in rapid succession. JOHN BROWN and KAGI seize their rifles. DOUGLASS and GREEN take out their revolvers. All stand motionless. The following speeches are whispered.)

KAGI. Slave catchers. *(KAGI listens intently.)* One set of footsteps. One man.

DOUGLASS. Into the underbrush. *(He motions to GREEN. They go quickly.)*

JOHN BROWN *(sits at edge of pool, rifle by his side. Gets his fishing rod, a sturdy six-foot pole from edge of pool, takes a worm from a packet and baits his hook. To KAGI).* Sit there. Read your book. Have your rifle ready.

KAGI *(does so).* Why bother with a worm?

JOHN BROWN. It would offend my sense of completion if the worm were omitted. . . . Do I look like a farmer spending a quiet hour?

KAGI. Exactly. But, please, don't flick your wrist so energetically. There are no fish in the quarry. *(A DEER-HUNTER with a rifle enters rapidly. He is surprised to stumble on them.)*

THE DEER-HUNTER. Hello! I had no idea—

JOHN BROWN. I give you the blessings of the day, young man.

THE DEER-HUNTER. Thank you, old farmer. I am trailing a deer which I just shot. Did you hear any plunging in the thicket?

KAGI *(rising, looks off).* There! We heard something over there.

THE DEER-HUNTER *(starts off, then turns and looks at JOHN BROWN intently).* Any fish in that quarry?

JOHN BROWN. First time we've been here. *(The DEER-HUNTER goes. JOHN BROWN continues fishing. KAGI looks after the DEER-HUNTER, indicates that all is safe. DOUGLASS and GREEN return.)*

DOUGLASS *(studies JOHN BROWN in silence for a moment before beginning).* It is your thought that the slaves will rise up and flock to your banner if you have a strong, persuasive Negro voice to assure them it's no betrayal?

JOHN BROWN. That is so.

DOUGLASS. And you plan to incorporate these newly arisen slaves into your Army?

JOHN BROWN. Yes.

DOUGLASS. You are in error. The Canadians are the bravest and most experienced of my people. To escape, a slave had to dare bullet and blood-hound, swamp and mountain. Many failed. In Canada, they have been trained in the uses of the rifle and the pistol. Yes. The Canadians could have been incorporated into your Army in a single day. Not so the slaves from this area. Some will make capable soldiers; others will not. *(JOHN BROWN makes as if to interject. DOUGLASS prevents him.)* Second, there is the question of training. It is a crime punishable by death for a slave to *hold* a rifle in his hand. It will take weeks, months, before they can learn to shoot. Yet when you strike Harpers Ferry your Army must be ready. The one thing you do not have is the six months' time necessary to train your Army.

JOHN BROWN *(takes the sturdy six-foot fishing pole, and forcefully tears the line off it. Then he takes from his pocket a black steel object, which proves to be the blade of a pike. He fits blade onto shaft and holds it aloft).* Here is my solution to that problem.

DOUGLASS. What is it?

JOHN BROWN. A pike.

DOUGLASS. A pike?

JOHN BROWN. For hundreds of years, in Europe, the pike has been the weapon of the foot soldier. Until they learn how to use a rifle, these newly freed soldiers will use the pike.

DOUGLASS. A pike!

JOHN BROWN *(thrusts blade hard at DOUGLASS' body, stopping short an inch away from DOUGLASS' chest).* Would you like to be at the sharp end of this weapon with a determined man behind it? I have a thousand of them, the blades and the poles, waiting for a thousand slaves to rise up and take them in their hands.

DOUGLASS. A pike! The rifle has changed the techniques of warfare. Fighting is no longer hand-to-hand combat.

JOHN BROWN. I foresee much close-quarter fighting. Besides, the pikes are an in-between measure until each man learns the rifle. Go on to your next point.

DOUGLASS. But you haven't answered the original point, namely, that newly arisen slaves who have never held a rifle in their hands cannot be substituted for bold, strong, well-trained Canadians.

JOHN BROWN. Go on to your next point.

DOUGLASS. It is your expectation that a multitude of

slaves will arise when they hear of your raid on Harpers Ferry?

JOHN BROWN. It is.

DOUGLASS. False. There is no heavy Negro population here. This is farming country—farming country. There are a few slaves on one farm, several on another. It is only in the deeper South, on the large plantations, that there are heavy concentrations of slaves—fifty—a hundred on a plantation. But not in Virginia. *(JOHN BROWN tries to interrupt. DOUGLASS cuts him off.)* I give you the reality of the situation; accept it as such. . . . And why attack the Federal Government Armory and Arsenal? Surely you realize that by attacking the Federal Government, it has no choice but to crush you.

JOHN BROWN. God is with us. Who can prevail against us?

DOUGLASS. The Federal Government. Or, do you think it will stand by idly even though you have captured its buildings, seized its weapons, made prisoner its employees?

JOHN BROWN. I chose Harpers Ferry precisely because it has the Armory and the Arsenal. I am pitting my morality against that of the Government of the United States. It is both right and necessary for a man who believes that his government is committing a crime against God and against the least and the last and the lowliest of this land, to rise up and match his morality against that of his government. I believe in the ultimate goodness of the people of this land. Once we are in the mountains, my Army with its pikes will place this question of slavery squarely before them. They will be faced with it in their waking and their sleeping—and oh, the discomfort of squirming away from commitment—until one day squirming is no longer possible. When that time comes, the people will decide with me and with my Army. Is all this not worth a great risk?

DOUGLASS. My reason and my understanding tell me that you will fail, that Harpers Ferry will end in that final desolate fact of capture and death. But how I pray that I am wrong. If only I am wrong!

JOHN BROWN. Come with me, Frederick. I will defend you with my life.

DOUGLASS. I do not ask you to defend me with your life. I am ready to give my life when necessary. But I am not ready to throw my life away. I have work to do and I have a responsibility toward it.

KAGI. Let me ask you a question. Would you join us in the raid if you thought it would be successful?

DOUGLASS. No. I still would not go. The tools to him who can use them. Raiding is not my work.

KAGI. But what if, by joining us, the scales will be turned, the weight and balance of the situation changed sufficiently to bring about success?

DOUGLASS. I have a responsibility to the work I do. To let myself be deflected would be doing a disservice to the cause for which we both do battle. . . . It would be easier for me to say, "Yes. I will go with you to Harpers Ferry." But "No" it is. I have a different path to travel.

JOHN BROWN. Then two men, both dedicated to the same cause, at the self-same moment, can take totally opposite courses of action and yet each be correct and justified?

DOUGLASS *(nods slowly and soberly)*. Totally opposite courses of action, yet each justified.

JOHN BROWN. Then—it is right for you not to go. Go back to Rochester and your paper. As for me—it is my task to strike at Harpers Ferry. My entire life has been shaping to this final expression of my love of God and the need to see all the children of the human family equal in freedom.

DOUGLASS. I plead with you, do not go—but I know you will. *(He clasps JOHN BROWN.)*

JOHN BROWN. You say goodbye to me as though for the last time.

DOUGLASS. It is. It is the last time. *(He turns and silently shakes hands with KAGI. Then he motions to GREEN to go.)*

GREEN *(to JOHN BROWN)*. Will it do good, the raid, even if it fails?

JOHN BROWN. If we win, we will win greatly. But even if we fail at Harpers Ferry, we will still win.

(GREEN turns to DOUGLASS for confirmation.)

DOUGLASS. It will do good.

GREEN. Even if it fails?

DOUGLASS. Even if it fails.

GREEN. I go then with the old man. *(JOHN BROWN puts his rifle in GREEN's hands. JOHN BROWN and DOUGLASS turn away from each other and go off a few steps in opposite directions. Then suddenly and rapidly, they turn back and go into each other's arms, clasping one another. They kiss the other's cheek. There is a quick moment of silent grief. DOUGLASS starts off. JOHN BROWN calls out after him.)*

JOHN BROWN. Go your way, Frederick Douglass, go

your way. My way is to Harpers Ferry. *(The lights fade on this area and come up on the area of the Kennedy Farmhouse as* JOHN BROWN, KAGI, *and* GREEN *move into the Farmhouse area. All the men are present in the Farmhouse including* COOK; *they are armed. Each man wears a long gray scarf around his neck. They are the scarves which* MARTHA *has been knitting.* MARY *and* MARTHA[1] *are not present. There is scarcely any pause between* JOHN BROWN'S *last speech and this one.)* Men, take up your arms. We march down on Harpers Ferry.

KAGI. Attention! Form a column of twos. *(The men form in twos.)* Gentlemen, the Commander-in-Chief of the Provisional Army—Captain John Brown.

JOHN BROWN. From the Table of Organization, you know each company in our Army consists of 72 soldiers. *(With an edge of irony and wit.)* But some of you who have been appointed captains do not have a single soldier under your command for the reason that at this moment your company consists of yourself alone. *(Most serious.)* But our Army will grow. And who will be able to stand up against our Army in the mountains? . . . Take out your maps. *(Each of the men takes a map from his pocket.)* We move on Harpers Ferry two at a time. Captains Tidd and Cook, you two will lead the Army, fifty yards ahead of the column. If you meet anyone, detain him in loud conversation, so the rest of the Army can get off the road and hide in the brush. When you get to the spot I have marked on your maps, cut the telegraph wires.

(To all.) The moment the wires are cut, the plan goes into operation. You all have your instructions. Follow them without fail. *(There is a short pause. Gravely.)* Captain Watson Brown and Private Taylor, your task is especially important. As quickly as you can after we enter Harpers Ferry, take control of the bridge over the Shenandoah River. Keep control of it. At all costs, keep control. It is our path into the mountains. *(Giving a carpet-bag to* OWEN.) Captain Owen Brown, you and Private Barclay Coppoc are to remain here on guard. Tomorrow morning I will send wagon and men to load our belongings. The instant the house is cleared, join us at Harpers Ferry. Be sure this bag goes with you. It contains my papers and documents. *(To all.)* Remember and remember again—no noise. If a man resists, use knife or sword. No shot is to be fired except in extreme emergency. Knife or sword, but no bullet. *(After a brief silence,* JOHN BROWN *raises his free hand in benediction.)* May the Angels of the Lord enfold and protect you. *(Pause. . . . then.)* Captain Kagi, arrange the line-up for the march.

KAGI. Soldiers, file outside.

JOHN BROWN *(only he and the two men who are the rear guard, remain.* JOHN BROWN, *rifle in the crook of his arm, stands erect).* Lord, God of Justice and Wrath, I have heard the weeping in Egypt. I go to my work. *(He goes. From far off the roll of a drum is heard. The lights dim rapidly. Blackout.)*

END OF ACT ONE

1. *Mary and Martha,* wife and daughter of John Brown.

chapter six

THE MODERN TEMPER

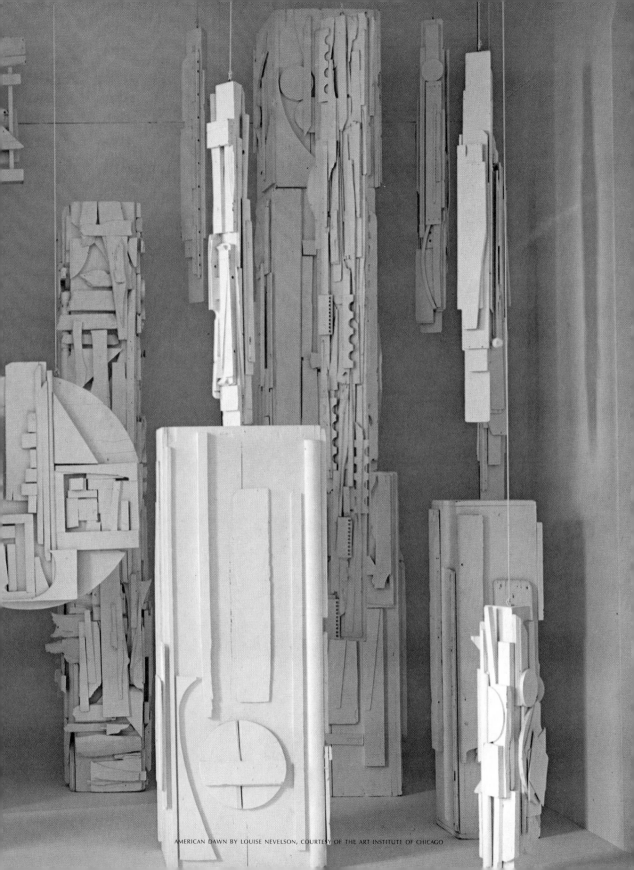

AMERICAN DAWN BY LOUISE NEVELSON, COURTESY OF THE ART INSTITUTE OF CHICAGO

Samuel Clemens

1835 / 1910

THE CELEBRATED
JUMPING FROG
OF CALAVERAS COUNTY

In compliance with the request of a friend of mine, who wrote me from the East, I called on good-natured, garrulous old Simon Wheeler, and inquired after my friend's friend, Leonidas W. Smiley, as requested to do, and I hereunto append the result. I have a lurking suspicion that *Leonidas W.* Smiley is a myth; that my friend never knew such a personage; and that he only conjectured that if I asked old Wheeler about him, it would remind him of his infamous *Jim* Smiley, and he would go to work and bore me to death with some exasperating reminiscence of him as long and as tedious as it should be useless to me. If that was the design, it succeeded.

I found Simon Wheeler dozing comfortably by the barroom stove of the dilapidated tavern in the decayed mining camp of Angel's, and I noticed that he was fat and baldheaded, and had an expression of winning gentleness and simplicity upon his tranquil countenance. He roused up, and gave me good day. I told him a friend of mine had commissioned me to make some inquiries about a cherished companion of his boyhood named *Leonidas W.* Smiley—*Rev. Leonidas W.* Smiley, a young minister of the Gospel, who he had heard was at one time a resident of Angel's Camp. I added that if Mr. Wheeler could tell me anything about this Rev. Leonidas W. Smiley, I would feel under many obligations to him.

Simon Wheeler backed me into a corner and blockaded me there with his chair, and then sat down and reeled off the monotonous narrative which follows this paragraph. He never smiled, he never frowned, he never changed his voice from the gentle-flowing key to which he tuned his initial sentence, he never betrayed the slightest suspicion of enthusiasm; but all through the interminable narrative there ran a vein of impressive earnestness and sincerity which showed me plainly that, so far from his imagining that there was anything ridiculous or funny about his story, he regarded it as a really important matter, and admired its two heroes as men of transcendent genius in finesse. I let him go on in his own way, and never interrupted him once.

"Rev. Leonidas W. H'm, Reverend Le—well, there was a feller here once by the name of *Jim* Smiley, in the winter of '49—or maybe it was the spring of '50—I don't recollect exactly, somehow, though what makes me think it was one or the other is because I remember the big flume wasn't finished when he first came to the camp. But anyway, he was the curiousest man about always betting on anything that turned up you ever see, if he could get anybody to bet on the other side; and if he couldn't, he'd change sides. Any way that suited the other man would suit *him*—any way just so's he got a bet, *he* was satisfied. But still he was lucky, uncommon lucky; he most always come out winner. He was always ready and laying for a chance; there couldn't be no solit'ry thing mentioned but that feller'd offer to bet on it, and take any side you please, as I was just telling you. If there was a horse race, you'd find him flush or you'd find him busted at the end of it; if there was a dog fight, he'd bet on it; if there was a cat fight, he'd bet on it; if there was a chicken fight, he'd bet on it. Why, if there was two birds setting on a fence, he would bet you which one would fly first; or if there was a camp meeting, he would be there reg'lar to bet on Parson Walker, which he judged to be the best exhorter about there, and so he was too, and a good man. If he even see a straddlebug start to go anywheres, he would bet you how long it would take him to get wherever he was going to, and if you took him up, he would foller that straddlebug to Mexico but what he would find out where he was bound for and how long he was on the road.

"Lots of the boys here has seen Smiley, and can tell you about him. Why, it never made no difference to *him*—he'd bet on *anything*—the dangdest feller. Parson Walker's wife laid very sick once, for a good while, and it seemed as if they warn't going to save her; but one morning he come in, and Smiley asked how she was, and he said she was considerable better—thank the Lord for His inf'nite mercy—and coming on so smart that with the blessing of Prov'dence she'd get well yet; and Smiley, before he thought, says, 'Well, I'll resk two-and-a-half that she don't anyway.'

"Thish-yer Smiley had a mare—the boys called her the fifteen-minute nag, but that was only in fun, you know, because of course she was faster than that—and he used to win money on that horse, for all she was so slow and always had the asthma, or the distemper, or the consumption, or something of that kind. They used to give her two or three hundred yards' start, and then pass her under way; but always at the fag end of the race she'd get excited and desperate-like, and come cavorting and straddling up, and scattering her legs around limber, sometimes in the air, and sometimes out to one side among the fences, and kicking up m-o-r-e dust and raising m-o-r-e racket with her coughing and sneezing and blowing her nose—and *always* fetch up at the stand just about a neck ahead, as near as you could cipher it down.

"And he had a little small bull pup, that to look at him you'd think he wan't worth a cent but to set around and look ornery and lay for a chance to steal something. But as soon as money was up on him he was a different dog; his under jaw'd begin to stick out like the fo'castle of a steamboat, and his teeth would uncover and shine like the furnaces. And a dog might tackle him and bullyrag him, and bite him, and throw him over his shoulder two or three times, and Andrew Jackson—which was the name of the pup—Andrew Jackson would never let on but what *he* was satisfied, and hadn't expected nothing else—and the bets being doubled and doubled on the other side all the time, till the money was all up; and then all of a sudden he would grab that other dog jest by the j'int of his hind leg and freeze to it—not chaw, you understand, but only just grip and hang on till they throwed up the sponge, if it was a year.

"Smiley always come out winner on that pup, till he harnessed a dog once that didn't have no hind legs, because they'd been sawed off by a circular saw, and when the thing had gone along far enough, and the money was all up, and he come to make a snatch for his pet holt, he saw in a minute how he'd been imposed on, and how the other dog had him in the door,[1] so to speak, and he 'peared surprised, and then he looked sorter discouraged-like, and didn't try no more to win the fight, and so

he got shucked out[2] bad. He give Smiley a look, as much as to say his heart was broke, and it was *his* fault, for putting up a dog that hadn't no hind legs for him to take holt of, which was his main dependence in a fight, and then he limped off a piece and laid down and died. It was a good pup, was that Andrew Jackson, and would have made a name for hisself if he'd lived, for the stuff was in him and he had genius—I know it, because he hadn't had no opportunities to speak of, and it don't stand to reason that a dog could make such a fight as he could under them circumstances if he hadn't no talent. It always makes me feel sorry when I think of that last fight of his'n, and the way it turned out.

"Well, thish-yer Smiley had rat terriers, and chicken cocks, and tomcats and all them kind of things, till you couldn't rest, and you couldn't fetch nothing for him to bet on but he'd match you. He ketched a frog one day, and took him home, and said he calk'lated to edercate him; and so he never done nothing for three months but set in his back yard and learn that frog to jump. And you bet he *did* learn him, too. He'd give him a little punch behind, and the next minute you'd see that frog whirling in the air like a doughnut—see him turn one summer-set, or maybe a couple, if he got a good start, and come down flat-footed and all right, like a cat. He got him up so in the matter of catching flies, and kep' him in practice so constant, that he'd nail a fly every time as far as he could see him.

"Smiley said all a frog wanted was education, and he could do 'most anything—and I believe him. Why, I've seen him set Dan'l Webster down here on this floor—Dan'l Webster was the name of the frog—and sing out, 'Flies, Dan'l, flies!' and quicker'n you could wink he'd spring straight up and snake a fly off'n the counter there, and flop down on the floor ag'in as solid as a gob of mud, and fall to scratching the side of his head with his hind foot as indifferent as if he hadn't no idea he'd been doin' any more'n any frog might do. You never see a frog so modest and straightfor'ard as he was, for all he was so gifted. And when it come to fair and square jumping on a dead level, he could get over more ground at one straddle than any animal of his breed you ever see. Jumping on a dead

---

1. *had him in the door*, had him at a disadvantage.
2. *shucked out*, beaten.

level was his strong suit, you understand; and when it come to that, Smiley would ante up money on him as long as he had a red.[3] Smiley was monstrous proud of his frog, and well he might be, for fellers that had traveled and been everywheres all said he laid over any frog that ever *they* see.

"Well, Smiley kept the beast in a little lattice box, and he used to fetch him downtown sometimes and lay for a bet. One day a feller—a stranger in the camp, he was—come across him with his box, and says:

"'What might it be that you've got in the box?'

"And Smiley says, sorter indifferent-like, 'It might be a parrot, or it might be a canary, maybe, but it ain't—it's only just a frog.'

"And the feller took it, and looked at it careful, and turned it round this way and that, and says, 'H'm—so 'tis. Well, what's *he* good for?'

"'Well,' Smiley says, easy and careless, 'he's good enough for *one* thing, I should judge—he can outjump ary frog in Calaveras County.'

"The feller took the box again, and took another long, particular look, and give it back to Smiley, and says, very deliberate, 'Well, I don't see no p'ints about that frog that's any better'n any other frog.'

"'Maybe you don't,' Smiley says. 'Maybe you understand frogs and maybe you don't understand 'em; maybe you've had experience, and maybe you ain't only a amature, as it were. Anyways, I've got *my* opinion, and I'll resk forty dollars that he can outjump any frog in Calaveras County.'

"And the feller studied a minute, and then says, kinder sad-like, 'Well, I'm only a stranger here, and I ain't got no frog; but if I had a frog, I'd bet you.'

"And then Smiley says, 'That's all right—that's all right—if you'll hold my box a minute, I'll go and get you a frog.' And so the feller took the box, and put up his forty dollars along with Smiley's, and set down to wait.

"So he set there a good while thinking and thinking to himself, and then he got the frog out and prized his mouth open and took a teaspoon and filled him full of quail shot—filled him pretty near up to his chin—and set him on the floor.

"Smiley he went to the swamp and slopped around in the mud for a long time, and finally he ketched a frog, and fetched him in, and give him to this feller, and says:

"'Now, if you're ready, set him alongside of

Dan'l, with his forepaws just even with Dan'l's, and I'll give the word.' Then he says, 'One—two—three—jump!' and him and the feller touched up the frogs from behind, and the new frog hopped off, but Dan'l give a heave and hysted up his shoulders—so—like a Frenchman, but it wan't no use—he couldn't budge; he was planted as solid as an anvil, and he couldn't no more stir than if he was anchored out. Smiley was a good deal surprised, and he was disgusted too, but he didn't have no idea what the matter was, of course.

"The feller took the money and started away; and when he was going out at the door, he sorter jerked his thumb over his shoulder—this way—at Dan'l, and says again, very deliberate, 'Well, *I* don't see no p'ints about that frog that's any better'n any other frog.'

"Smiley he stood scratching his head and looking down at Dan'l a long time, and at last he says, 'I do wonder what in the nation that frog throw'd off for—I wonder if there ain't something the matter with him—he 'pears to look mighty baggy, somehow.' And he ketched Dan'l by the nap of the neck, and lifted him up, and says, 'Why blame my cats if he don't weigh five pound!' and turned him upside down, and he belched out a double handful of shot. And then Smiley see how it was, and he was the maddest man—he set the frog down and took out after that feller, but he never ketched him. And—"

[Here Simon Wheeler heard his name called from the front yard, and got up to see what was wanted.] And turning to me as he moved away, he said: "Just set where you are, stranger, and rest easy—I ain't going to be gone a second."

But, by your leave, I did not think that a continuation of the history of the enterprising vagabond *Jim* Smiley would be likely to afford me much information concerning the Rev. *Leonidas W.* Smiley, and so I started away.

At the door I met the sociable Wheeler returning, and he buttonholed me and recommenced:

"Well, thish-yer Smiley had a yaller one-eyed cow that didn't have no tail, only just a short stump like a bannanner, and—"

However, lacking both time and inclination, I did not wait to hear about the afflicted cow, but took my leave. □

---

3. *a red*, a red cent, or any money at all.

CARTOON SHOWING TWAIN RIDING TO FAME,
AND FORTUNE ON HIS "JUMPING FROG"

CULVER PICTURES, INC.

from

LIFE ON THE MISSISSIPPI

When I was a boy, there was but one permanent ambition among my comrades in our village on the west bank of the Mississippi River. That was, to be a steamboatman. We had transient ambitions of other sorts, but they were only transient. When a circus came and went, it left us all burning to become clowns; the first Negro minstrel show that ever came to our section left us all suffering to try that kind of life; now and then we had a hope that if we lived and were good, God would permit us to be pirates. These ambitions faded out, each in its turn; but the ambition to be a steamboatman always remained.

Once a day a cheap, gaudy packet arrived upward from St. Louis, and another downward from Keokuk.[1] Before these events, the day was glorious with expectancy; after them, the day was a dead and empty thing. Not only the boys, but the whole village, felt this. After all these years I can picture that old time to myself now, just as it was then: the white town drowsing in the sunshine of a summer's morning; the streets empty, or pretty nearly so; one or two clerks sitting in front of the Water Street stores, with their splint-bottomed chairs[2] tilted back against the walls, chins on breasts, hats slouched over their faces, asleep—with shingle-shavings enough around to show what broke them down; a sow and a litter of pigs loafing along the sidewalk, doing a good business in watermelon rinds and seeds; two or three lonely little freight piles scattered about the levee; a pile of skids on the slope of the stone-paved wharf, and the fragrant town drunkard asleep in the shadow of them; two or three wood flats[3] at the head of the wharf, but nobody to listen to the peaceful lapping of the wavelets against them; the great Mississippi, the majestic, the magnificent Mississippi, rolling its mile-wide tide along, shining in the sun; the dense forest away on the other side; the point above the town, and the point below, bounding the river-glimpse and turning it into a sort of sea, and withal a very still and brilliant and lonely one. Presently a film of dark smoke appears above one of those remote points: instantly a Negro drayman, famous for his quick eye and prodigious voice, lifts up the cry, "S-t-e-a-m-boat a-comin'!" and the scene changes! The town drunkard stirs, the clerks wake up, a furious clatter of drays follows, every house and store pours out a human contribution, and all in a twinkling the dead town is alive and moving. Drays, carts, men, boys, all go hurrying from many quarters to a common center, the wharf. Assembled there, the people fasten their eyes upon the coming boat as upon a wonder they are seeing for the first time. And the boat *is* rather a handsome sight, too. She is long and sharp and trim and pretty; she has two tall, fancy-topped chimneys, with a gilded device of some kind swung between them; a fanciful pilot house, all glass and gingerbread,

---

1. *Keokuk* (kē′ə kuk), a Mississippi River town in the southeastern corner of Iowa, about fifty miles above Hannibal.
2. *splint-bottomed chairs*, chairs with seats woven of thin strips (splints) of wood.
3. *wood flats*, small flat-bottomed boats.

perched on top of the texas deck[4] behind them; the paddle boxes[5] are gorgeous with a picture or with gilded rays above the boat's name; the boiler deck, the hurricane deck,[6] and the texas deck are fenced and ornamented with clean white railings; there is a flag gallantly flying from the jack staff;[7] the furnace doors are open and the fires glaring bravely; the upper decks are black with passengers; the captain stands by the big bell, calm, imposing, the envy of all; great volumes of the blackest smoke are rolling and tumbling out of the chimneys—a husbanded grandeur created with a bit of pitch pine just before arriving at a town; the crew are grouped on the forecastle; the broad stage[8] is run far out over the port bow, and a deck hand stands picturesquely on the end of it with a coil of rope in his hand; the pent steam is screaming through the gauge cocks; the captain lifts his hand, a bell rings, the wheels stop; then they turn back, churning the water to foam, and the steamer is at rest. Then such a scramble as there is to get aboard, and to get ashore, and to take in freight and to discharge freight, all at one and the same time; and such a yelling and cursing as the mates facilitate it all with! Ten minutes later the steamer is under way again, with no flag on the jack staff and no black smoke issuing from the chimneys. After ten more minutes the town is dead again, and the town drunkard asleep by the skids once more.

My father was a justice of the peace, and I supposed he possessed the power of life and death over all men, and could hang anybody that offended him. This was distinction enough for me as a general thing; but the desire to be a steamboatman kept intruding, nevertheless. I first wanted to be a cabin boy, so that I could come out with a white apron on and shake a tablecloth over the side, where all my old comrades could see me; later I thought I would rather be the deck hand who stood on the end of the stage-plank with the coil of rope in his hand, because he was particularly conspicuous. But these were only daydreams—they were too heavenly to be contemplated as real possibilities.

By and by one of our boys went away. He was not heard of for a long time. At last he turned up as apprentice engineer or "striker" on a steamboat. This thing shook the bottom out of all my Sunday-school teachings. That boy had been notoriously worldly, and I just the reverse; yet he was exalted to this eminence, and I left in obscurity and misery. There was nothing generous about this fellow in

his greatness. He would always manage to have a rusty bolt to scrub while his boat tarried at our town, and he would sit on the inside guard[9] and scrub it, where we all could see him and envy him and loathe him. And whenever his boat was laid up he would come home and swell around the town in his blackest and greasiest clothes, so that nobody could help remembering that he was a steamboatman; and he used all sorts of steamboat technicalities in his talk, as if he were so used to them that he forgot common people could not understand them. He would speak of the "labboard"[10] side of a horse in an easy, natural way that would make one wish he was dead. And he was always talking about "St. Looy" like an old citizen; he would refer casually to occasions when he was "coming down Fourth Street," or when he was "passing by the Planter's House," or when there was a fire and he took a turn on the brakes of "the old Big Missouri"; and then he would go on and lie about how many towns the size of ours were burned down there that day. Two or three of the boys had long been persons of consideration among us because they had been to St. Louis once and had a vague general knowledge of its wonders, but the day of their glory was over now. They lapsed into a humble silence, and learned to disappear when the ruthless cub engineer approached. This fellow had money, too, and hair oil. Also an ignorant silver watch and a showy brass watch chain. He wore a leather belt and used no suspenders. If ever a youth was cordially admired and hated by his comrades, this one was. No girl could withstand his charms. He "cut out" every boy in the village. When his boat blew up at last, it diffused a tranquil contentment among us such as we had not known for months. But when he came home the next week, alive, renowned, and appeared in church all battered up and bandaged, a shining hero, stared at

---

4. *texas deck.* The texas is a range of staterooms adjacent to the pilot house reserved for officers. The texas deck adjoins these living quarters.

5. *paddle boxes,* the wooden coverings built over the upper part of the paddle wheels which propelled the steamer.

6. *the boiler deck, the hurricane deck.* The boiler deck is that part of the upper deck immediately over the boilers; the hurricane deck is the topmost deck.

7. *jack staff,* a short pole erected at the front of the vessel.

8. *forecastle . . . stage.* The forecastle is an upper deck at the forward part of the ship; the stage is a stage-plank or gangplank.

9. *inside guard,* part of the steamboat's deck which curves out over the paddle wheel.

10. *"labboard,"* larboard, the left or port side of a ship.

and wondered over by everybody, it seemed to us that the partiality of Providence for an undeserving reptile had reached a point where it was open to criticism.

This creature's career could produce but one result, and it speedily followed. Boy after boy managed to get on the river. The minister's son became an engineer. The doctor's and the postmaster's sons became mud clerks;[11] the wholesale liquor dealer's son became a barkeeper on a boat; four sons of the chief merchant, and two sons of the county judge, became pilots. Pilot was the grandest position of all. The pilot, even in those days of trivial wages, had a princely salary—from a hundred and fifty to two hundred and fifty dollars a month, and no board to pay. Two months of his wages would pay a preacher's salary for a year. Now some of us were left disconsolate. We could not get on the river —at least our parents would not let us.

So, by and by, I ran away. I said I would never come home again till I was a pilot and could come in glory. But somehow I could not manage it. I went meekly aboard a few of the boats that lay packed together like sardines at the long St. Louis wharf, and humbly inquired for the pilots, but got only a cold shoulder and short words from mates and clerks. I had to make the best of this sort of treatment for the time being, but I had comforting daydreams of a future when I should be a great and honored pilot, with plenty of money, and could kill some of these mates and clerks and pay for them.

---

11. *mud clerks*, second clerks, so called because it was their duty to go ashore at unimportant stops, often mere mudbanks, to receive or check off freight.

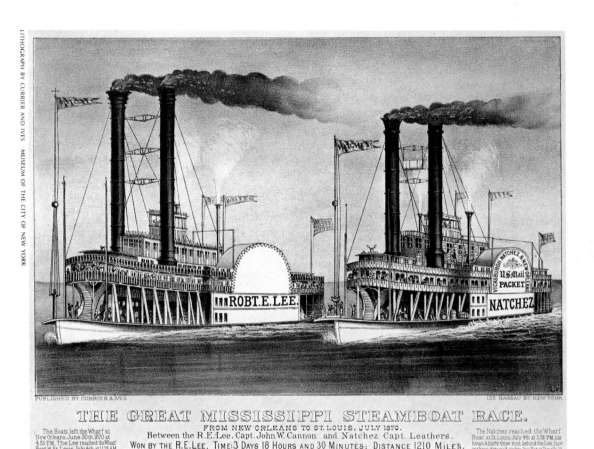

LITHOGRAPH BY CURRIER AND IVES   MUSEUM OF THE CITY OF NEW YORK

PUBLISHED BY CURRIER & IVES   125 NASSAU ST NEW YORK

THE GREAT MISSISSIPPI STEAMBOAT RACE.

FROM NEW ORLEANS TO ST. LOUIS, JULY 1870.

Between the R.E.Lee. Capt. John W. Cannon and Natchez Capt. Leathers.

WON BY THE R.E.LEE. TIME: 3 DAYS 18 HOURS AND 30 MINUTES; DISTANCE 1210 MILES.

The Boats left the Wharf at New Orleans, June 30th 1870 at 4.55 P.M. The Lee reached the Wharf Boat at St Louis July 4th at 11.25 A.M.

The Natchez reached the Wharf Boat at St Louis July 4th at 5.58 P.M. six hours & thirty three min. behind the Lee, having been detained six hrs at Devils Id.

THE PRIVATE HISTORY OF
A CAMPAIGN THAT FAILED

YOU have heard from a great many people who did something in the war, is it not fair and right that you listen a little moment to one who started out to do something in it, but didn't? Thousands entered the war, got just a taste of it, and then stepped out again permanently. These, by their very numbers, are respectable and are therefore entitled to a sort of a voice—not a loud one but a modest one, not a boastful one but an apologetic one. They ought not to be allowed much space among better people—people who did something. I grant that, but they ought at least to be allowed to state why they didn't do anything and also to explain the process by which they didn't do anything. Surely this kind of light must have a sort of value.

Out West there was a good deal of confusion in men's minds during the first months of the great trouble—a good deal of unsettledness, of leaning first this way, then that, then the other way. It was hard for us to get our bearings. I call to mind an instance of this. I was piloting on the Mississippi when the news came that South Carolina had gone out of the Union on the 20th of December, 1860. My pilot mate was a New Yorker. He was strong for the Union; so was I. But he would not listen to me with any patience; my loyalty was smirched, to his eye, because my father had owned slaves. I said in palliation of this dark fact that I had heard my father say, some years before he died, that slavery was a great wrong and that he would free the solitary Negro he then owned if he could think it right to give away the property of the family when he was so straitened in means. My mate retorted that a mere impulse was nothing—anybody could pretend to a good impulse, and went on decrying my Unionism and libeling my ancestry. A month later the secession atmosphere had considerably thickened on the Lower Mississippi and I became a rebel; so did he. We were together in New Orleans the 26th of January, when Louisiana went out of the Union. He did his full share of the rebel shouting but was bitterly opposed to letting me do mine. He said that I came of bad stock—of a father who had been willing to set slaves free. In the following summer he was piloting a Federal gunboat and shouting for the Union again and I was in the Confederate army. I held his note for some borrowed money. He was one of the most upright men I ever knew but he repudiated that note without hesitation because I was a rebel and the son of a man who owned slaves.

In that summer of 1861 the first wash of the wave of war broke upon the shores of Missouri. Our state was invaded by the Union forces. They took possession of St. Louis, Jefferson Barracks, and some other points. The Governor, Claib Jackson, issued his proclamation calling out fifty thousand militia to repel the invader.

I was visiting in the small town where my boyhood had been spent, Hannibal, Marion County. Several of us got together in a secret place by night and formed ourselves into a military company. One Tom Lyman, a young fellow of a good deal of spirit but of no military experience, was made captain; I was made second lieutenant. We had no first lieutenant; I do not know why; it was long ago. There were fifteen of us. By the advice of an innocent connected with the organization we called ourselves the Marion Rangers. I do not remember that any one found fault with the name. I did not; I thought it sounded quite well. The young fellow who proposed this title was perhaps a fair sample of the kind of stuff we were made of. He was young, ignorant, good-natured, well-meaning, trivial, full of romance, and given to reading chivalric novels and singing forlorn love-ditties. He had some pathetic little nickel-plated aristocratic instincts and detested his name, which was Dunlap; detested it partly because it was nearly as common in that region as Smith but mainly because it had a plebeian sound to his ear. So he tried to ennoble it by writing it in this way: *d'Unlap.* That contented his eye but left his ear unsatisfied, for people gave the new name the same old pronunciation—emphasis on the front end of it. He then did the bravest thing that can be imagined, a thing to make one shiver when one remembers how the world is given to resenting shams and affectations, he began to write his name so: *d'Un Lap.* And he waited patiently through the long storm of mud that was flung at this work of art and he had his reward at last, for he lived to see that name accepted and the emphasis put where he wanted it

"The Private History of a Campaign that Failed" from THE AMERICAN CLAIMANT by Mark Twain. By permission of Harper & Row, Publishers, Inc.

by people who had known him all his life, and to whom the tribe of Dunlaps had been as familiar as the rain and the sunshine for forty years. So sure of victory at last is the courage that can wait. He said he had found by consulting some ancient French chronicles that the name was rightly and originally written d'Un Lap, and said that if it were translated into English it would mean Peterson: *Lap*, Latin or Greek, he said, for stone or rock, same as the French *pierre*, that is to say, Peter: *d'*, of or from; *un*, a or one; hence, d'Un Lap, of or from a stone or a Peter; that is to say, one who is the son of a stone, the son of a Peter—Peterson. Our militia company were not learned and the explanation confused them; so they called him Peterson Dunlap. He proved useful to us in his way; he named our camps for us and he generally struck a name that was "no slouch," as the boys said.

That is one sample of us. Another was Ed Stevens, son of the town jeweler, trim-built, handsome, graceful, neat as a cat; bright, educated, but given over entirely to fun. There was nothing serious in life to him. As far as he was concerned, this military expedition of ours was simply a holiday. I should say that about half of us looked upon it in the same way; not consciously, perhaps, but unconsciously. We did not think; we were not capable of it. As for myself, I was full of unreasoning joy to be done with turning out of bed at midnight and four in the morning for a while, grateful to have a change, new scenes, new occupations, a new interest. In my thoughts that was as far as I went; I did not go into the details; as a rule one doesn't at twenty-four.

Another sample was Smith, the blacksmith's apprentice. This vast donkey had some pluck, of a slow and sluggish nature, but a soft heart; at one time he would knock a horse down for some impropriety and at another he would get homesick and cry. However, he had one ultimate credit to his account which some of us hadn't; he stuck to the war and was killed in battle at last.

Jo Bowers, another sample, was a huge, good-natured, flax-headed lubber, lazy, sentimental, full of harmless brag, a grumbler by nature; an experienced, industrious, ambitious, and often quite picturesque liar and yet not a successful one, for he had had no intelligent training but was allowed to come up just any way. This life was serious enough to him, and seldom satisfactory. But he was a good fellow, anyway, and the boys all liked

him. He was made orderly sergeant; Stevens was made corporal.

These samples will answer—and they are quite fair ones. Well, this herd of cattle started for the war. What could you expect of them? They did as well as they knew how but, really, what was justly to be expected of them? Nothing, I should say. That is what they did.

We waited for a dark night, for caution and secrecy were necessary; then toward midnight we stole in couples and from various directions to the Griffith place, beyond the town; from that point we set out together on foot. Hannibal lies at the extreme southeastern corner of Marion County, on the Mississippi River; our objective point was the hamlet of New London, ten miles away, in Ralls County.

The first hour was all fun, all idle nonsense and laughter. But that could not be kept up. The steady trudging came to be like work, the play had somehow oozed out of it, the stillness of the woods and the somberness of the night began to throw a depressing influence over the spirits of the boys, and presently the talking died out and each person shut himself up in his own thoughts. During the last half of the second hour nobody said a word.

Now we approached a log farm-house where, according to report, there was a guard of five Union soldiers. Lyman called a halt and there, in the deep gloom of the overhanging branches, he began to whisper a plan of assault upon that house, which made the gloom more depressing that it was before. It was a crucial moment; we realized with a cold suddenness that here was no jest—we were standing face to face with actual war. We were equal to the occasion. In our response there was no hesitation, no indecision: we said that if Lyman wanted to meddle with those soldiers, he could go ahead and do it, but if he waited for us to follow him, he would wait a long time.

Lyman urged, pleaded, tried to shame us, but it had no effect. Our course was plain, our minds were made up: we would flank the farm-house—go out around. And that was what we did.

We struck into the woods and entered upon a rough time, stumbling over roots, getting tangled in vines and torn by briers. At last we reached an open place in a safe region and sat down, blown and hot, to cool off and nurse our scratches and bruises. Lyman was annoyed but the rest of us were cheerful; we had flanked the farm-house, we had made our first military movement and it was a success; we had nothing to fret about, we were feeling just the other way. Horse-play and laughing began again; the expedition was become a holiday frolic once more.

Then we had two more hours of dull trudging and ultimate silence and depression; then about dawn we straggled into New London, soiled, heel-blistered, fagged with our little march, and all of us except Stevens in a sour and raspy humor and privately down on the war. We stacked our shabby old shotguns in Colonel Ralls's barn and then went in a body and breakfasted with that veteran of the Mexican War. Afterward he took us to a distant meadow, and there in the shade of a tree we listened to an old-fashioned speech from him, full of gunpowder and glory, full of that adjective-piling, mixed metaphor and windy declamation which were regarded as eloquence in that ancient time and that remote region; and then he swore us on the Bible to be faithful to the State of Missouri and drive all invaders from her soil, no matter whence they might come or under what flag they might march. This mixed us considerably and we could not make out just what service we were embarked in, but Colonel Ralls, the practised politician and phrase-juggler, was not similarly in doubt; he knew quite clearly that he had invested us in the cause of the Southern Confederacy. He closed the solemnities by belting around me the sword which his neighbor, Colonel Brown, had worn at Buena Vista and Molino del Rey;[1] and he accompanied this act with another impressive blast.

Then we formed in line of battle and marched four miles to a shady and pleasant piece of woods on the border of the far-reaching expanses of a flowery prairie. It was an enchanting region for war —our kind of war.

We pierced the forest about half a mile and took up a strong position, with some low, rocky, and wooded hills behind us and a purling, limpid creek in front. Straightway half the command were in swimming and the other half fishing. The ass with the French name gave this position a romantic title but it was too long, so the boys shortened and simplified it to Camp Ralls.

We occupied an old maple-sugar camp, whose half-rotted troughs were still propped against the trees. A long corn-crib served for sleeping-quarters for the battalion. On our left, half a mile away, were Mason's farm and house, and he was a friend to the cause. Shortly after noon the farmers began to arrive from several directions with mules and horses for our use, and these they lent us for as long as the war might last, which they judged would be about three months. The animals were of all sizes, all colors, and all breeds. They were mainly young and frisky, and nobody in the command could stay on them long at a time, for we were town boys and ignorant of horsemanship. The creature that fell to my share was a very small mule, and yet so quick and active that it could throw me without difficulty, and it did this whenever I got on it. Then it would bray—stretching its neck out, laying its ears back, and spreading its jaws till you could see down to its works. It was a disagreeable animal in every way. If I took it by the bridle and tried to lead it off the grounds, it would sit down and brace back and no one could budge it. However, I was not entirely destitute of military resources and I did presently manage to spoil this game, for I had seen many a steamboat aground in my time and knew a trick or two which even a grounded mule would be obliged to respect. There was a well by the corn-crib; so I substituted thirty fathom of rope for the bridle, and fetched him home with the windlass.

I will anticipate here sufficiently to say that we did learn to ride after some days' practice, but never well. We could not learn to like our animals; they were not choice ones and most of them had annoying peculiarities of one kind or another. Stevens's horse would carry him, when he was not noticing, under the huge excrescences which form on the trunks of oak-trees, and wipe him out of the saddle; in this way Stevens got several bad hurts. Sergeant Bowers's horse was very large and tall, with slim, long legs, and looked like a railroad bridge. His size enabled him to reach all about, and as far as he wanted to, with his head; so he was always biting Bowers's legs. On the march, in the sun, Bowers slept a good deal, and as soon as the horse recognized that he was asleep he would reach around and bite him on the leg. His legs were black and blue with bites. This was the only thing that could ever make him swear but this always did; whenever his horse bit him he always swore, and of course Stevens, who laughed at everything, laughed at this and would even get into such convulsions over it as to lose his balance and fall off his horse; and

---

1. *Buena Vista and Molino del Rey*, sites of two 1847 battles of the Mexican War.

then Bowers, already irritated by the pain of the horse-bite, would resent the laughter with hard language, and there would be a quarrel; so that horse made no end of trouble and bad blood in the command.

However, I will get back to where I was—our first afternoon in the sugar-camp. The sugar-troughs came very handy as horse-troughs and we had plenty of corn to fill them with. I ordered Sergeant Bowers to feed my mule, but he said that if I reckoned he went to war to be a dry-nurse to a mule it wouldn't take me very long to find out my mistake. I believed that this was insubordination but I was full of uncertainties about everything military, and so I let the thing pass and went and ordered Smith, the blacksmith's apprentice, to feed the mule; but he merely gave me a large, cold, sarcastic grin, such as an ostensibly seven-year-old horse gives you when you lift his lip and find he is fourteen, and turned his back on me. I then went to the captain and asked if it were not right and proper and military for me to have an orderly. He said it was but as there was only one orderly in the corps, it was but right that he himself should have Bowers on his staff. Bowers said he wouldn't serve on anybody's staff, and if anybody thought he could make him, let him try it. So, of course, the thing had to be dropped; there was no other way.

Next, nobody would cook; it was considered a degradation; so we had no dinner. We lazied the rest of the pleasant afternoon away, some dozing under the trees, some smoking cob-pipes and talking sweethearts and war, some playing games. By late supper-time all hands were famished and to meet the difficulty all hands turned to on an equal footing, and gathered wood, built fires, and cooked the meal. Afterward everything was smooth for a while; then trouble broke out between the corporal and the sergeant, each claiming to rank the other. Nobody knew which was the higher office; so Lyman had to settle the matter by making the rank of both officers equal. The commander of an ignorant crew like that has many troubles and vexations which probably do not occur in the regular army at all. However, with the song-singing and yarn-spinning around the camp-fire, everything presently became serene again, and by and by we raked the corn down level in one end of the crib and all went to bed on it, tying a horse to the door, so that he would neigh if any one tried to get in.

We had some horsemanship drill every forenoon; then, afternoons, we rode off here and there in squads a few miles and visited the farmers' girls, and had a youthful good time and got an honest good dinner or supper, and then home again to camp, happy and content.

For a time life was idly delicious, it was perfect; there was nothing to mar it. Then came some farmers with an alarm one day. They said it was rumored that the enemy were advancing in our direction from over Hyde's prairie. The result was a sharp stir among us, and general consternation. It was a rude awakening from our pleasant trance. The rumor was but a rumor—nothing definite about it; so in the confusion we did not know which way to retreat. Lyman was for not retreating at all in these uncertain circumstances, but he found that if he tried to maintain that attitude he would fare badly, for the command were in no humor to put up with insubordination. So he yielded the point and called a council of war, to consist of himself and the three other officers; but the privates made such a fuss about being left out that we had to allow them to remain, for they were already present and doing the most of the talking too. The question was, which way to retreat; but all were so flurried that nobody seemed to have even a guess to offer. Except Lyman. He explained in a few calm words that, inasmuch as the enemy were approaching from over Hyde's prairie, our course was simple: all we had to do was not to retreat *toward* him; any other direction would answer our needs perfectly. Everybody saw in a moment how true this was, and how wise, so Lyman got a great many compliments. It was now decided that we should fall back on Mason's farm.

It was after dark by this time and as we could not know how soon the enemy might arrive, it did not seem best to try to take the horses and things with us; so we only took the guns and ammunition, and started at once. The route was very rough and hilly and rocky, and presently the night grew very black and rain began to fall; so we had a troublesome time of it, struggling and stumbling along in the dark, and soon some person slipped and fell, and then the next person behind stumbled over him and fell, and so did the rest, one after the other; and then Bowers came, with the keg of powder in his arms, while the command were all mixed together, arms and legs, on the muddy slope, and so he fell, of course, with the keg, and this started the whole detachment down the hill in a body, and they landed in the brook at the bottom in a pile, and each that was undermost pulling the hair and scratching and biting those that were on top of him, and those that were being scratched and bitten scratching and biting the rest in their turn, and all saying they would die before they would ever go to war again if they ever got out of this brook this time and the invader might rot for all they cared, and the country along with him—and all such talk as that, which was dismal to hear and take part in, in such smothered, low voices, and such a grisly dark place and so wet, and the enemy, maybe, coming any moment.

The keg of powder was lost, and the guns too; so the growling and complaining continued straight along while the brigade pawed around the pasty hillside and slopped around in the brook hunting for these things; consequently we lost considerable time at this, and then we heard a sound and held our breath and listened, and it seemed to be the enemy coming, though it could have been a cow, for it had a cough like a cow; but we did not wait but left a couple of guns behind and struck out for Mason's again as briskly as we could scramble along in the dark. But we got lost presently among the rugged little ravines and wasted a deal of time finding the way again, so it was after nine when we reached Mason's stile at last; and then before we could open our mouths to give the countersign several dogs came bounding over the fence with great riot and noise, and each of them took a soldier by the slack of his trousers and began to back away with him. We could not shoot the dogs without endangering the persons they were attached to; so we had to look on helpless at what was perhaps the most mortifying spectacle of the Civil War. There was light enough and to spare, for the Masons had now run out on the porch with candles in their hands. The old man and his son came and undid the dogs without difficulty, all but Bowers's; but they couldn't undo his dog, they didn't know his combination; he was of the bull kind and seemed to be set with a Yale time-lock, but they got him loose at last with some scalding water, of which Bowers got his share and returned thanks. Peterson Dunlap afterward made up a fine name for this engagement, and also for the night march which preceded it, but both have long ago faded out of my memory.

We now went into the house and they began to ask us a world of questions, whereby it presently came out that we did not know anything concerning who or what we were running from; so the old gentleman made himself very frank and said we were a curious breed of soldiers and guessed we could be depended on to end up the war in time, because no government could stand the expense of the shoe-leather we should cost it trying to follow us around. "Marion *Rangers!* good name, b'gosh!" said he. And wanted to know why we hadn't had a picket-guard at the place where the road entered the prairie, and why we hadn't sent out a scouting party to spy out the enemy and bring us an account of his strength, and so on, before jumping up and stampeding out of a strong position upon a mere vague rumor—and so on, and so forth, till he made us all feel shabbier than the dogs had done, not half so enthusiastically welcome. So we went to bed shamed and low-spirited, except Stevens. Soon Stevens began to devise a garment for Bowers which could be made to automatically display his battle-scars to the grateful or conceal them from the envious, according to his occasions, but Bowers was in no humor for this, so there was a fight and when it was over Stevens had some battle-scars of his own to think about.

Then we got a little sleep. But after all we had gone through, our activities were not over for the night, for about two o'clock in the morning we heard a shout of warning from down the lane, accompanied by a chorus from all the dogs, and in a moment everybody was up and flying around to find out what the alarm was about. The alarmist was a horseman who gave notice that a detachment of Union soldiers was on its way from Hannibal with orders to capture and hang any bands like ours which it would find, and said we had no time to lose. Farmer Mason was in a flurry this time himself. He hurried us out of the house with all haste, and sent one of his Negroes with us to show us where to hide ourselves and our telltale guns among the ravines half a mile away. It was raining heavily.

We struck down the lane, then across some rocky pasture-land which offered good advantages for stumbling; consequently we were down in the mud most of the time, and every time a man went down he blackguarded the war and the people that started it and everybody connected with it, and gave himself the master dose of all for being so foolish as to go into it. At last we reached the wooded mouth of a ravine, and there we huddled ourselves under the streaming trees and sent the Negro back home. It was a dismal and heart-breaking time. We were like to be drowned with the rain, deafened with the howling wind and the booming thunder, and blinded by the lightning. It was indeed a wild night. The drenching we were getting was misery enough, but a deeper misery still was the reflection that the halter might end us before we were a day older. A death of this shameful sort had not occurred to us as being among the possibilities of war. It took the romance all out of the campaign and turned our dreams of glory into a repulsive nightmare. As for doubting that so barbarous an order had been given, not one of us did that.

The long night wore itself out at last, and then the Negro came to us with the news that the alarm had manifestly been a false one and that breakfast would soon be ready. Straightway we were light-hearted again, and the world was bright and life as full of hope and promise as ever—for we were young then. How long ago that was! Twenty-four years.

The mongrel child of philology named the night's refuge Camp Devastation and no soul objected. The Masons gave us a Missouri country breakfast in Missourian abundance, and we needed it: hot biscuits, hot "wheat bread," prettily criss-crossed in a lattice pattern on top, hot corn-pone, fried chicken, bacon, coffee, eggs, milk, buttermilk, etc., and the world may be confidently challenged to furnish the equal of such a breakfast, as it is cooked in the South.

We stayed several days at Mason's, and after all these years the memory of the dullness and still-ness and lifelessness of that slumberous farm-house still oppresses my spirit as with a sense of the presence of death and mourning. There was nothing to do, nothing to think about; there was no interest in life. The male part of the household were away in the fields all day, the women were busy and out of our sight; there was no sound but the plaintive wailing of a spinning-wheel, forever moaning out from some distant room, the most lonesome sound in nature, a sound steeped and sodden with home-sickness and the emptiness of life. The family went to bed about dark every night, and as we were not invited to intrude any new customs we naturally fol-lowed theirs. Those nights were a hundred years long to youths accustomed to being up till twelve. We lay awake and miserable till that hour every time, and

grew old and decrepit waiting through the still eternities for the clock-strikes. This was no place for town boys. So at last it was with something very like joy that we received news that the enemy were on our track again. With a new birth of the old warrior spirit we sprang to our places in line of battle and fell back on Camp Ralls.

Captain Lyman had taken a hint from Mason's talk, and he now gave orders that our camp should be guarded against surprise by the posting of pickets. I was ordered to place a picket at the forks of the road in Hyde's prairie. Night shut down black and threatening. I told Sergeant Bowers to go out to that place and stay till midnight and, just as I was expecting, he said he wouldn't do it. I tried to get others to go but all refused. Some excused them-selves on account of the weather, but the rest were frank enough to say they wouldn't go in any kind of weather. This kind of thing sounds odd now, and impossible, but there was no surprise in it at the time. On the contrary, it seemed a perfectly natural thing to do. There were scores of little camps scattered over Missouri where the same thing was happening. These camps were composed of young men who had been born and reared to a sturdy independence, and who did not know what it meant to be ordered around by Tom, Dick, and Harry, whom they had known familiarly all their lives in the village or on the farm. It is quite within the probabilities that this same thing was happening all over the South. James Redpath recognized the justice of this assumption and furnished the follow-ing instance in support of it. During a short stay in East Tennessee he was in a citizen colonel's tent one day talking, when a big private appeared at the door and, without salute or other circumlocu-tion, said to the colonel:

"Say, Jim, I'm a-goin' home for a few days."

"What for?"

"Well, I hain't b'en there for a right smart while and I'd like to see how things is comin' on."

"How long are you going to be gone?"

"'Bout two weeks."

"Well, don't be gone longer than that, and get back sooner if you can."

That was all, and the citizen officer resumed his conversation where the private had broken it off. This was in the first months of the war, of course. The camps in our part of Missouri were under Briga-dier-General Thomas H. Harris. He was a townsman of ours, a first-rate fellow and well liked, but we had all familiarly known him as the sole and modest-salaried operator in our telegraph-office, where he had to send about one despatch a week in ordinary times and two when there was a rush of business; consequently, when he appeared in our midst one day on the wing, and delivered a military command of some sort in a large military fashion, nobody was surprised at the response which he got from the assembled soldiery:

"Oh, now, what'll you take to *don't*, Tom Harris?"

It was quite the natural thing. One might justly imagine that we were hopeless material for war. And so we seemed in our ignorant state, but there were those among us who afterward learned the grim trade, learned to obey like machines, became valuable soldiers; fought all through the war, and came out at the end with excellent records. One of the very boys who refused to go out on picket duty that night and called me an ass for thinking he would expose himself to danger in such a foolhardy way, had become distinguished for intrepidity before he was a year older.

I did secure my picket that night, not by authority but by diplomacy. I got Bowers to go by agreeing to exchange ranks with him for the time being, and go along and stand the watch with him as his subordinate. We stayed out there a couple of dreary hours in the pitchy darkness and the rain, with nothing to modify the dreariness but Bowers's monotonous growlings at the war and the weather; then we began to nod and presently found it next to impossible to stay in the saddle, so we gave up the tedious job and went back to the camp without waiting for the relief guard. We rode into camp without interruption or objection from anybody and the enemy could have done the same, for there were no sentries. Everybody was asleep; at midnight there was nobody to send out another picket, so none was sent. We never tried to establish a watch at night again, as far as I remember, but we generally kept a picket out in the daytime.

In that camp the whole command slept on the corn in the big corn-crib and there was usually a general row before morning, for the place was full of rats and they would scramble over the boys' bodies and faces, annoying and irritating everybody, and now and then they would bite some one's toe, and the person who owned the toe would start up and magnify his English and begin to throw corn in

the dark. The ears were half as heavy as bricks and when they struck they hurt. The persons struck would respond and inside of five minutes every man would be locked in a death-grip with his neighbor. There was a grievous deal of blood shed in the corn-crib but this was all that was spilt while I was in the war. No, that is not quite true. But for one circumstance it would have been all. I will come to that now.

Our scares were frequent. Every few days rumors would come that the enemy were approaching. In these cases we always fell back on some other camp of ours; we never stayed where we were. But the rumors always turned out to be false, so at last even we began to grow indifferent to them. One night a Negro was sent to our corn-crib with the same old warning, the enemy was hovering in our neighborhood. We all said let him hover. We resolved to stay still and be comfortable. It was a fine warlike resolution, and no doubt we all felt the stir of it in our veins—for a moment. We had been having a very jolly time, that was full of horse-play and school-boy hilarity, but that cooled down now and presently the fast-waning fire of forced jokes and forced laughs died out altogether and the company became silent. Silent and nervous. And soon uneasy—worried—apprehensive. We had said we would stay and we were committed. We could have been persuaded to go but there was nobody brave enough to suggest it. An almost noiseless movement presently began in the dark by a general but unvoiced impulse. When the movement was completed each man knew that he was not the only person who had crept to the front wall and had his eye at a crack between the logs. No, we were all there, all there with our hearts in our throats and staring out toward the sugar-troughs where the forest footpath came through. It was late and there was a deep woodsy stillness everywhere. There was a veiled moonlight, which was only just strong enough to enable us to mark the general shape of objects. Presently a muffled sound caught our ears and we recognized it as the hoof-beats of a horse or horses. And right away a figure appeared in the forest path; it could have been made of smoke, its mass had so little sharpness of outline. It was a man on horseback and it seemed to me that there were others behind him. I got hold of a gun in the dark, and pushed it through a crack between the logs, hardly knowing what I was doing, I was so dazed with fright. Somebody said "Fire!" I pulled the trigger. I seemed to see a hundred flashes and hear a hundred reports; then I saw the man fall down out of the saddle. My first feeling was of surprised gratification; my first impulse was an apprentice-sportsman's impulse to run and pick up his game. Somebody said, hardly audibly, "Good—we've got him!—wait for the rest." But the rest did not come. We waited—listened—still no more came. There was not a sound, not the whisper of a leaf; just perfect stillness, an uncanny kind of stillness which was all the more uncanny on account of the damp, earthy, late-night smells now rising and pervading it. Then, wondering, we crept stealthily out and approached the man. When we got to him the moon revealed him distinctly. He was lying on his back with his arms abroad, his mouth was open and his chest heaving with long gasps, and his white shirt-front was all splashed with blood. The thought shot through me that I was a murderer, that I had killed a man, a man who had never done me any harm. That was the coldest sensation that ever went through my marrow. I was down by him in a moment, helplessly stroking his forehead, and I would have given anything then—my own life freely—to make him again what he had been five minutes before. And all the boys seemed to be feeling in the same way; they hung over him, full of pitying interest, and tried all they could to help him and said all sorts of regretful things. They had forgotten all about the enemy, they thought only of this one forlorn unit of the foe. Once my imagination persuaded me that the dying man gave me a reproachful look out of his shadowy eyes, and it seemed to me that I could rather he had stabbed me than done that. He muttered and mumbled like a dreamer in his sleep about his wife and his child, and I thought with a new despair, "This thing that I have done does not end with him; it falls upon *them* too, and they never did me any harm, any more than he."

In a little while the man was dead. He was killed in war, killed in fair and legitimate war, killed in battle, as you may say, and yet he was as sincerely mourned by the opposing force as if he had been their brother. The boys stood there a half-hour sorrowing over him and recalling the details of the tragedy, and wondering who he might be and if he were a spy, and saying that if it were to do over again they would not hurt him unless he attacked them first. It soon came out that mine was not the only shot fired; there were five others, a division of the guilt which was a great relief to me since it in some degree lightened and diminished the burden I was carrying. There were six shots fired at once but I was not in my right mind at the time, and my heated imagination had magnified my one shot into a volley.

The man was not in uniform and was not armed. He was a stranger in the country, that was all we ever found out about him. The thought of him got to preying upon me every night; I could not get rid of it. I could not drive it away, the taking of that unoffending life seemed such a wanton thing. And it seemed an epitome of war, that all war must be just that the killing of strangers against whom you feel no personal animosity, strangers whom in other circumstances you would help if you found them in trouble, and who would help you if you needed it. My campaign was spoiled. It seemed to me that I was not rightly equipped for this awful business, that war was intended for men and I for a child's nurse. I resolved to retire from this avocation of sham soldiership while I could save some remnant of my self-respect. These morbid thoughts clung to me against reason, for at bottom I did not believe I had touched that man. The law of probabilities decreed me guiltless of his blood for in all my small experience with guns I had never hit anything I had tried to hit and I knew I had done my best to hit him. Yet there was no solace in the thought. Against a diseased imagination demonstration goes for nothing.

The rest of my war experience was of a piece with what I have already told of it. We kept monotonously falling back upon one camp or another and eating up the farmers and their families. They ought to have shot us; on the contrary, they were as hospitably kind and courteous to us as if we had deserved it. In one of these camps we found Ab Grimes, an Upper Mississippi pilot who afterward became famous as a dare-devil rebel spy, whose career bristled with desperate adventures. The look and style of his comrades suggested that they had not come into the war to play and their deeds made good the conjecture later. They were fine horsemen and good revolver shots, but their favorite. arm was the lasso. Each had one at his pommel and could snatch a man out of the saddle with it every time, on a full gallop, at any reasonable distance.

In another camp the chief was a fierce and profane old blacksmith of sixty and he had furnished his twenty recruits with gigantic home-made bowie-knives, to be swung with two hands like the *machetes* of the Isthmus.[2] It was a grisly spectacle to see that earnest band practising their murderous cuts and slashes under the eye of that remorseless old fanatic.

The last camp which we fell back upon was in a hollow near the village of Florida were I was born, in Monroe County. Here we were warned one day that a Union colonel was sweeping down on us with a whole regiment at his heel. This looked decidedly serious. Our boys went apart and consulted; then we went back and told the other companies present that the war was a disappointment to us and we were going to disband. They were getting ready themselves to fall back on some place or other, and we were only waiting for General Tom Harris, who was expected to arrive at any moment, so they tried to persuade us to wait a little while but the majority of us said no, we were accustomed to falling back and didn't need any of Tom Harris's help, we could get along perfectly well without him and save time, too. So about half of our fifteen, including myself, mounted and left on the instant; the others yielded to persuasion and stayed—stayed through the war.

An hour later we met General Harris on the road, with two or three people in his company, his staff probably, but we could not tell; none of them were in uniform; uniforms had not come into vogue among us yet. Harris ordered us back but we told him there was a Union colonel coming with a whole regiment in his wake and it looked as if there was going to be a disturbance, so we had concluded to go home. He raged a little but it was of no use, our minds were made up. We had done our share, had killed one man, exterminated one army, such as it was; let him go and kill the rest and that would end the war. I did not see that brisk young general again until last year; then he was wearing white hair and whiskers.

In time I came to know that Union colonel whose coming frightened me out of the war and crippled the Southern cause to that extent—General Grant. I came within a few hours of seeing him when he was as unknown as I was myself; at a time when anybody could have said, "Grant?—Ulysses S. Grant? I do not remember hearing the name before." It seems difficult to realize that there was once a time when such a remark could be rationally made but there *was*, and I was within a few miles of the place and the occasion too, though proceeding in the other direction.

The thoughtful will not throw this war paper of mine lightly aside as being valueless. It has this value: it is a not unfair picture of what went on in many and many a militia camp in the first months of the rebellion, when the green recruits were without discipline, without the steadying and heartening influence of trained leaders, when all their circumstances were new and strange and charged with exaggerated terrors, and before the invaluable experience of actual collision in the field had turned them from rabbits into soldiers. If this side of the picture of that early day has not before been put into history, then history has been to that degree incomplete, for it had and has its rightful place there. There was more Bull Run[3] material scattered through the early camps of this country than exhibited itself at Bull Run. And yet it learned its trade presently and helped to fight the great battles later. I could have become a soldier myself if I had waited. I had got part of it learned, I knew more about retreating than the man that invented retreating. □

---

2. *the Isthmus*, the Isthmus of Panama.
3. *Bull Run*, a battle fought July 21, 1861, in which the Confederates defeated the Federals and which transformed what began as a rebellion into a civil war.

THE WAR PRAYER

IT was a time of great and exalting excitement. The country was up in arms, the war was on, in every breast burned the holy fire of patriotism; the drums were beating, the bands playing, the toy pistols popping, the bunched firecrackers hissing and spluttering; on every hand and far down the receding and fading spread of roofs and balconies a fluttering wilderness of flags flashed in the sun; daily the young volunteers marched down the wide avenue gay and fine in their new uniforms, the proud fathers and mothers and sisters and sweethearts cheering them with voices choked with happy emotion as they swung by; nightly the packed mass meetings listened, panting, to patriot oratory which stirred the deepest deeps of their hearts and which they interrupted at briefest intervals with cyclones of applause, the tears running down their cheeks the while; in the churches the pastors preached devotion to flag and country and invoked the God of Battles, beseeching His aid in our good cause in outpouring of fervid eloquence which moved every listener. It was indeed a glad and gracious time, and the half-dozen rash spirits that ventured to disapprove of the war and cast a doubt upon its righteousness straightway got such a stern and angry warning that for their personal safety's sake they quickly shrank out of sight and offended no more in that way.

Sunday morning came—next day the battalions would leave for the front; the church was filled; the volunteers were there, their young faces alight with martial dreams—visions of the stern advance, the gathering momentum, the rushing charge, the flashing sabers, the flight of the foe, the tumult, the enveloping smoke, the fierce pursuit, the surrender!— then home from the war, bronzed heroes, welcomed, adored, submerged in golden seas of glory! With the volunteers sat their dear ones, proud, happy, and envied by the neighbors and friends who had no sons and brothers to send forth to the field of honor, there to win for the flag or, failing, die the noblest of noble deaths. The service proceeded; a war chapter from the Old Testament was read; the first prayer was said; it was followed by an organ burst that shook the building, and with one impulse the house rose, with glowing eyes and beating hearts, and poured out that tremendous invocation—

"God the all-terrible! Thou who ordainest,
Thunder thy clarion and lightning thy sword!"

Then came the "long" prayer. None could remember the like of it for passionate pleading and moving and beautiful language. The burden of its supplication was that an ever-merciful and benignant Father of us all would watch over our noble young soldiers and aid, comfort, and encourage them in their patriotic work; bless them, shield them in the day of battle and the hour of peril, bear them in His mighty hand, make them strong and confident, invincible in the bloody onset; help them to crush the foe, grant to them and to their flag and country imperishable honor and glory—

An aged stranger entered and moved with slow and noiseless step up the main aisle, his eyes fixed upon the minister, his long body clothed in a robe that reached to his feet, his head bare, his white hair descending in a frothy cataract to his shoulders, his seamy face unnaturally pale, pale even to ghastliness. With all eyes following him and wondering, he made his silent way; without pausing, he ascended to the preacher's side and stood there, waiting. With shut lids the preacher, unconscious of his presence, continued his moving prayer, and at last finished it with the words, uttered in fervent appeal, "Bless our arms, grant us the victory, O Lord our God, Father and Protector of our land and flag!"

The stranger touched his arm, motioned him to step aside—which the startled minister did—and took his place. During some moments he surveyed the spell-bound audience with solemn eyes in which burned an uncanny light; then in a deep voice he said:

"I come from the Throne—bearing a message from Almighty God!" The words smote the house with a shock; if the stranger perceived it he gave no attention. "He has heard the prayer of His servant your shepherd and will grant it if such shall be your desire after I, His messenger, shall have explained to you its import—that is to say, its full import. For it is like unto many of the prayers of men, in that it asks for more than he who utters it is aware of— except he pause and think.

"God's servant and yours has prayed his prayer.

"The War Prayer" from EUROPE AND ELSEWHERE by Mark Twain. Copyright, 1923, renewed 1951 by The Mark Twain Company. By permission of Harper & Row, Publishers, Inc.

Has he paused and taken thought? Is it one prayer? No, it is two—one uttered, the other not. Both have reached the ear of Him Who heareth all supplications, the spoken and the unspoken. Ponder this—keep it in mind. If you would beseech a blessing upon yourself, beware! lest without intent you invoke a curse upon a neighbor at the same time. If you pray for the blessing of rain upon your crop which needs it, by that act you are possibly praying for a curse upon some neighbor's crop which may not need rain and can be injured by it.

"You have heard your servant's prayer—the uttered part of it. I am commissioned of God to put into words the other part of it—that part which the pastor, and also you in your hearts, fervently prayed silently. And ignorantly and unthinkingly? God grant that it was so! You heard these words: 'Grant us the victory, O Lord our God!' That is sufficient. The *whole* of the uttered prayer is compact into those pregnant words. Elaborations were not necessary. When you have prayed for victory you have prayed for many unmentioned results which follow victory —*must* follow it, cannot help but follow it. Upon the listening spirit of God the Father fell also the unspoken part of the prayer. He commandeth me to put it into words. Listen!

"O Lord our Father, our young patriots, idols of our hearts, go forth to battle—be Thou near them!

With them, in spirit, we also go forth from the sweet peace of our beloved firesides to smite the foe. O Lord our God, help us to tear their soldiers to bloody shreds with our shells; help us to cover their smiling fields with the pale forms of their patriot dead; help us to drown the thunder of the guns with the shrieks of their wounded, writhing in pain; help us to lay waste their humble homes with a hurricane of fire; help us to wring the hearts of their unoffending widows with unavailing grief; help us to turn them out roofless with their little children to wander unfriended the wastes of their desolated land in rags and hunger and thirst, sports of the sun flames of summer and the icy winds of winter, broken in spirit, worn with travail, imploring Thee for the refuge of the grave and denied it—for our sakes who adore Thee, Lord, blast their hopes, blight their lives, protract their bitter pilgrimage, make heavy their steps, water their way with their tears, stain the white snow with the blood of their wounded feet! We ask it, in the spirit of love, of Him Who is the Source of Love, and Who is the ever-faithful refuge and friend of all that are sore beset and seek His aid with humble and contrite hearts. Amen.

(*After a pause*) "Ye have prayed it; if ye still desire it, speak! The messenger of the Most High waits."

It was believed afterward that the man was a lunatic, because there was no sense in what he said. □

DISCUSSION

The Celebrated Jumping Frog of Calaveras County

"The Celebrated Jumping Frog" is an example of a truly native genre, the **tall tale.** Originally an oral tradition that included tales of such American folk heros as Paul Bunyan, John Henry, and Mike Fink—the Mississippi Riverman, the tall tale eventually found its way into the American literary tradition after the Civil War. It is said that the tales originated as mutual entertainment during the long, lonely, frontier nights. Each "yarn-spinner," through obvious exaggeration and, more often, outright lies, would try to top the last outrageously fictitious tale. Clemens has preserved for us in "The Celebrated Jumping Frog" not only the tall tale but also the colorful yarn-spinner, a character who has long since disappeared from American life.

FOR EXPLORATION

1. To capture the flavor of the oral yarn in writing, it is necessary for an author to make it possible for his reader to see the narrator as well as hear him speak. (*a*) What parts of "The Celebrated Jumping Frog" are devoted to acquainting the reader with Simon Wheeler, the narrator of the yarn? (*b*) What kinds of information does Clemens give about Wheeler? (*c*) How does this information add to the humor of the story? (*d*) Discuss why Clemens uses peculiar sentence patterns, intentional misspellings, and grammatical errors in the yarn itself. (*e*) Why does he italicize certain words? Explain.

2. (*a*) Cite two particularly comic passages in Wheeler's monologue and explain why they are humorous. (*b*) Explain why "The Celebrated Jumping Frog" was probably much funnier to readers a hundred years ago than it is to us today.

3. An old tradition of literature involves the classic situation of "the trickster tricked." Relate Smiley to this convention.

DISCUSSION

from Life on the Mississippi
and The Private History of a Campaign That Failed

Memoirs constitute a genre of literature seldom discussed and generally dismissed as minor history or biography. But because memoirs are written as firsthand, if limited, history, they may, in fact, be a more accurate and honest portrayal of life as it actually was than history written from hindsight or secondhand. Certainly real, live, people emerge from both Clemens' *Life on the Mississippi* and "The Private History of a Campaign That Failed"; and this is one of the main functions of literature.

FOR EXPLORATION

Life on the Mississippi

1. In the selection from *Life on the Mississippi* Clemens mentions three transient or passing ambitions of the boys of Hannibal. *(a)* What were these transient ambitions? *(b)* What was Clemens' purpose in mentioning them?
2. Paragraph two is a very long one, but it is not difficult to follow if you notice Clemens' careful arrangement of his materials. *(a)* What simple fact does he state in the first sentence? *(b)* In the second sentence what contrast does he suggest that he will illustrate? *(c)* Where does he begin and end the "before" picture? *(d)* The "after" picture? *(e)* What does he place between these contrasting pictures? *(f)* Cite some of the details that are most helpful to you in sensing the mood of each section of the paragraph.
3. In what ways does Clemens introduce humor into the story of the local boy who became an apprentice engineer?
4. How does one go about choosing his life's work? Do you think Clemens' description of the process accurate? Explain.

The Private History of a Campaign That Failed

1. In the introductory and concluding paragraphs of these memoirs, Clemens speaks of the importance of personal history. Discuss the validity of his remarks.
2. In "The Private History of a Campaign That Failed" a number of incidental character sketches emerge from the narrative. Relate what you have learned about the physical characteristics, mannerisms, and background of two of the following volunteers: Dunlap, Stevens, Smith, and Bowers.
3. How does the forming of the militia compare with America's present attitudes toward the glories of warfare? What factors have contributed to our present attitudes about war? Explain.

4. What incident brings home the reality of warfare to the volunteers? How does Clemens make this event significant to the reader?
5. Comment in a short essay of two or three paragraphs upon the ideas expressed in the following quotation from "The Private History":

> ". . . the taking of that unoffending life seemed such a wanton thing. And it seemed an epitome of war, that all war must be just that, the killing of strangers against whom you feel no personal animosity, strangers whom in other circumstances you would help if you found them in trouble, and who would help you if you needed it."

CREATIVE RESPONSE

War as Clemens viewed it was a bumbling, desperate endeavor with most of the time filled with tedious waiting or endless retreats. Interview a returned veteran and find out if his experiences were similar to Clemens'. Write an account of the interview and compare your findings with those of other members of your class. Stephen Crane's *The Red Badge of Courage* is another interesting account of a young man's experiences with warfare. Compare Crane's hero's experiences with those of Clemens. How do they differ? How are they similar?

DISCUSSION

The War Prayer

"The War Prayer" contains the familiar tone and devices of **parable.** A **parable** is a story or anecdote that answers a moral question, usually illustrating an ethical lesson. The most well known parables among Americans appear in the New Testament.

FOR EXPLORATION

1. Was the aged stranger mad or was he an emissary of God? Explain.
2. Comment on the stranger's contention that prayers for victory are double-edged. Do you agree or disagree? Explain.
3. Discuss the effect of the third-to-last paragraph in which the stranger implores God's aid. What elements of the prayer expose man's hypocrisy?
4. Does God choose sides? Defend your answer in an essay of no more than three paragraphs using evidence from "The War Prayer" and/or your own observations.

On a sheet of paper answer each of the following questions. Be ready to explain why you decided as you did. Use a dictionary if necessary.

1. If the drayman on the steamboat called out in a *prodigious* voice, did he (a) speak clearly, (b) call out loudly, or (c) swear?

2. If the steamboat was *husbanding* its pitch pine, was it (a) using it sparingly, (b) wasting it, or (c) using it to make a grand effect?

3. When the "striker" used steamboat *technicalities* in his talk, was he (a) swearing in the fashion of rivermen, (b) using terms that applied especially to steamboats, or (c) bragging about his adventures?

4. If old Simon Wheeler was a *garrulous* man, was he (a) reticent, (b) enthusiastic, or (c) talkative?

5. As a genius in *finesse*, did Jim Smiley have (a) a talent for losing wagers, (b) a skill in handling delicate situations, or (c) a tendency to cheat?

Samuel Langhorne Clemens
1835 / 1910

Samuel Clemens was raised in the Mississippi River town of Hannibal, Missouri; many of the adventures of Tom Sawyer can be traced back to his own childhood. His father died when Sam was twelve and Clemens left school to help support the family. He was apprenticed as a printer's devil and for a number of years worked on his brother's paper. In his early twenties Clemens was able to apprentice himself to a steamboat pilot on the Mississippi. After a year and a half he graduated to licensed pilot and the next few years were perhaps the happiest of his life. They ended when the Civil War put a stop to traffic on the Mississippi.

Torn between regional loyalties and his opposition to slavery, Clemens was uncertain in his allegiance. An abortive attempt at soldiering for the Confederacy convinced him he should avoid the conflict and so he left with his brother for Nevada. After unsuccessfully trying his hand at prospecting, Clemens became a journalist under the pseudonym of Mark Twain, a depth measurement in river navigation. He was a reporter and correspondent in Virginia City and then in California where in 1865 he wrote "The Celebrated Jumping Frog of Calaveras County." It appeared in a New York magazine and was quickly picked up and printed by newspapers across the nation.

Capitalizing on the success of the story, Clemens sailed to New York and in 1867 a collection of sketches headed by the "Jumping Frog" story was published. That same year he joined a group of tourists sailing for the Mediterranean and the Holy Land. His humorous accounts of the Americans taking in the wonders of the Old World were collected and released as *The Innocents Abroad*. It sold prodigiously and Clemens was very quickly becoming both renowned and rich.

At the age of thirty-five Clemens married and settled down. He lived in Hartford, New York, for the next seventeen years and while there produced his finest writing; *The Adventures of Tom Sawyer* (1876), *A Tramp Abroad* (1880), *The Prince and the Pauper* (1882), *Life on the Mississippi* (1883), *The Adventures of Huckleberry Finn* (1884), and *A Connecticut Yankee at King Arthur's Court* (1889) are all of this period. He spent his royalty money carelessly, living sumptuously and investing in speculative schemes which invariably fell through. Hundreds of thousands of dollars were spent supporting an inventor in his unfruitful efforts at building a typesetting machine. Clemens further invested in his own publishing firm which eventually collapsed. He finally faced bankruptcy, but instead of filing such papers, insisted he would pay all his creditors in full and set off on an around-the-world lecture tour to raise the money.

Life was especially hard on him in the final years; his wife and two of his three daughters died. His long-standing feud with the more brutal capacities of human nature left him bitter and disillusioned. In 1899 he wrote William Dean Howells, "I have been reading the morning paper. I do it every morning—well knowing that I shall find in it the usual depravities and basenesses and hypocrisies and cruelties that make up civilization, and cause me to put in the rest of the day pleading for the damnation of the human race." Clemens seems to have experienced a combination of despair, pity, and resignation. He once said, "Everything human is pathetic. The secret source of humor itself is not joy but sorrow. There is no humor in heaven."

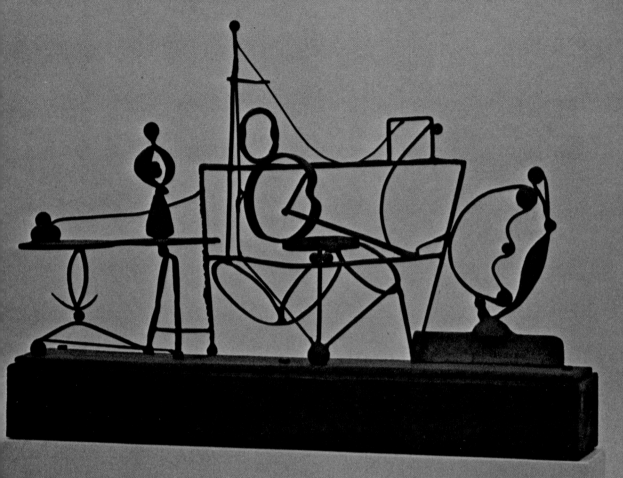

DAVID SMITH "INTERIOR," 1937—COLLECTION OF DR. AND MRS. IRVING R. JUSTER

Walt Whitman

1819 / 1892

I HEAR AMERICA SINGING

I hear America singing, the varied carols I hear,
Those of mechanics, each one singing his as it should be blithe and strong,
The carpenter singing his as he measures his plank or beam,
The mason singing his as he makes ready for work, or leaves off work,
5   The boatman singing what belongs to him in his boat, the deckhand singing on the steamboat deck,
The shoemaker singing as he sits on his bench, the hatter singing as he stands,
The wood-cutter's song, the ploughboy's on his way in the morning, or at noon intermission or at sundown,
The delicious singing of the mother, or of the young wife at work, or of the girl sewing or washing,
Each singing what belongs to him or her and to none else,
10   The day what belongs to the day—at night the party of young fellows, robust, friendly,
Singing with open mouths their strong melodious songs.

THERE WAS A CHILD WENT FORTH

There was a child went forth every day,
And the first object he look'd upon, that object he became,
And that object became part of him for the day or a certain part of the day,
Or for many years or stretching cycles of years.

5 The early lilacs became part of this child,
And grass and white and red morning-glories, and white and red clover, and the song of the phœbe-bird,
And the Third-month lambs and the sow's pink-faint litter, and the mare's foal and the cow's calf,
And the noisy brood of the barnyard or by the mire of the pond-side,
And the fish suspending themselves so curiously below there, and the beautiful curious liquid,
10 And the water-plants with their graceful flat heads, all became part of him.

The field-sprouts of Fourth-month and Fifth-month became part of him,
Winter-grain sprouts and those of the light-yellow corn, and the esculent roots of the garden,
And the apple-trees cover'd with blossoms and the fruit afterward, and woodberries, and the commonest
  weeds by the road,
And the old drunkard staggering home from the outhouse of the tavern whence he had lately risen,
15 And the schoolmistress that pass'd on her way to the school,
And the friendly boys that pass'd, and the quarrelsome boys,
And the tidy and fresh-cheek'd girls, and the barefoot Negro boy and girl,
And all the changes of city and country wherever he went.

His own parents, he that had father'd him and she that had conceiv'd him in her womb and birth'd him,
20 They gave this child more of themselves than that,
They gave him afterward every day, they became part of him.

The mother at home quietly placing the dishes on the supper-table,
The mother with mild words, clean her cap and gown, a wholesome odor falling off her person and clothes
  as she walks by,
The father, strong, self-sufficient, manly, mean, anger'd, unjust,
25 The blow, the quick loud word, the tight bargain, the crafty lure,
The family usages, the language, the company, the furniture, the yearning and swelling heart,
Affection that will not be gainsay'd, the sense of what is real, the thought if after all it should prove unreal,
The doubts of day-time and the doubts of night-time, the curious whether and how,
Whether that which appears so is so, or is it all flashes and specks?
30 Men and women crowding fast in the streets, if they are not flashes and specks what are they?
The streets themselves and the facades of houses, and goods in the windows,
Vehicles, teams, the heavy-plank'd wharves, the huge crossing at the ferries,
The village on the highland seen from afar at sunset, the river between,
Shadows, aureola and mist, the light falling on roofs and gables of white or brown two miles off,
35 The schooner near by sleepily dropping down the tide, the little boat slack-tow'd astern,
The hurrying tumbling waves, quick-broken crests, slapping,
The strata of color'd clouds, the long bar of maroon-tint away solitary by itself, the spread of purity it lies
  motionless in,
The horizon's edge, the flying sea-crow, the fragrance of salt marsh and shore mud,
These became part of that child who went forth every day, and who now goes, and will always go forth
  every day.

CROSSING BROOKLYN FERRY

1

Flood-tide below me! I see you face to face!
Clouds of the west—sun there half an hour high—I see you also face to face.

Crowds of men and women attired in the usual costumes, how curious you are to me!
On the ferry-boats the hundreds and hundreds that cross, returning home, are more curious to me than you
    suppose,
And you that shall cross from shore to shore years hence are more to me, and more in my meditations, than
    you might suppose.

2

The impalpable sustenance of me from all things at all hours of the day,
The simple, compact, well-join'd scheme, myself disintegrated, every one disintegrated yet part of the
    scheme,
The similitudes of the past and those of the future,
The glories strung like beads on my smallest sights and hearings, on the walk in the street and the passage
    over the river,
10 The current rushing so swiftly and swimming with me far away,
The others that are to follow me, the ties between me and them,
The certainty of others, the life, love, sight, hearing of others.

Others will enter the gates of the ferry and cross from shore to shore,
Others will watch the run of the flood-tide,
Others will see the shipping of Manhattan north and west, and the heights of Brooklyn to the south and east,
Others will see the islands large and small;
Fifty years hence, others will see them as they cross, the sun half an hour high,
A hundred years hence, or ever so many hundred years hence, others will see them,
Will enjoy the sunset, the pouring-in of the flood-tide, the falling-back to the sea of the ebb-tide.

3

20 It avails not, time nor place—distance avails not,
I am with you, you men and women of a generation, or ever so many generations hence,
Just as you feel when you look on the river and sky, so I felt,
Just as any of you is one of a living crowd, I was one of a crowd,
Just as you are refresh'd by the gladness of the river and the bright flow, I was refresh'd,
Just as you stand and lean on the rail, yet hurry with the swift current, I stood yet was hurried,
Just as you look on the numberless masts of ships and the thick-stemm'd pipes of steamboats, I look'd.

I too many and many a time cross'd the river of old,
Watched the Twelfth-month sea-gulls, saw them high in the air floating with motionless wings, oscillating
    their bodies,
Saw how the glistening yellow lit up parts of their bodies and left the rest in strong shadow,
30 Saw the slow-wheeling circles and the gradual edging toward the south,
Saw the reflection of the summer sky in the water,
Had my eyes dazzled by the shimmering track of beams,
Look'd at the fine centrifugal spokes of light round the shape of my head in the sunlit water,
Look'd on the haze on the hills southward and south—westward,

Look'd on the vapor as it flew in fleeces tinged with violet,
Look'd toward the lower bay to notice the vessels arriving,
Saw their approach, saw aboard those that were near me,
Saw the white sails of schooners and sloops, saw the ships at anchor,
The sailors at work in the rigging or out astride the spars,
40 The round masts, the swinging motion of the hulls, the slender serpentine pennants,
The large and small steamers in motion, the pilots in their pilot-houses,
The white wake left by the passage, the quick tremulous whirl of the wheels,
The flags of all nations, the falling of them at sunset,
The scallop-edged waves in the twilight, the ladled cups, the frolicsome crests and glistening,
The stretch afar growing dimmer and dimmer, the gray walls of the granite storehouses by the docks,
On the river the shadowy group, the big steam-tug closely flank'd on each side by the barges, the hay-boat,
    the belated lighter,
On the neighboring shore the fires from the foundry chimneys burning high and glaringly into the night,
Casting their flicker of black contrasted with wild red and yellow light over the tops of houses, and down
    into the clefts of streets.

4

These and all else were to me the same as they are to you,
50 I loved well those cities, loved well the stately and rapid river,
The men and women I saw were all near to me,
Others the same—others who look back on me because I look'd forward to them,
(The time will come, though I stop here to-day and to-night.)

5

What is it then between us?
What is the count of the scores or hundreds of years between us?

Whatever it is, it avails not—distance avails not, and place avails not,
I too lived, Brooklyn of ample hills was mine,
I too walk'd the streets of Manhattan island, and bathed in the waters around it,
I too felt the curious abrupt questionings stir within me.
60 In the day among crowds of people sometimes they came upon me,
In my walks home late at night or as I lay in my bed they came upon me,
I too had been struck from the float forever held in solution,
I too had receiv'd identity by my body,
That I was I knew was of my body, and what I should be I knew I should be of my body.

6

It is not upon you alone the dark patches fall,
The dark threw its patches down upon me also,
The best I had done seem'd to me blank and suspicious,
My great thoughts as I supposed them, were they not in reality meagre?
Nor is it you alone who know what it is to be evil,
70 I am he who knew what it was to be evil,
I too knitted the old knot of contrariety,
Blabb'd, blush'd, resented, lied, stole, grudg'd,
Had guile, anger, lust, hot wishes I dared not speak,
Was wayward, vain, greedy, shallow, sly, cowardly, malignant,
The wolf, the snake, the hog, not wanting in me,

The cheating look, the frivolous word, the adulterous wish, not wanting,
Refusals, hates, postponements, meanness, laziness, none of these wanting,
Was one with the rest, the days and haps of the rest,
Was call'd by my nighest name by clear loud voices of young men as they saw me approaching or passing,
Felt their arms on my neck as I stood, or the negligent leaning of their flesh against me as I sat,
Saw many I loved in the street or ferry-boat or public assembly, yet never told them a word,
Lived the same life with the rest, the same old laughing, gnawing, sleeping,
Play'd the part that still looks back on the actor or actress,
The same old role, the role that is what we make it, as great as we like,
Or as small as we like, or both great and small.

7

Closer yet I approach you,
What thought you have of me now, I had as much of you—I laid in my stores in advance,
I consider'd long and seriously of you before you were born.

Who was to know what should come home to me?
Who knows but I am enjoying this?
Who knows, for all the distance, but I am as good as looking at you now, for all you cannot see me?

8

Ah, what can ever be more stately and admirable to me than mast-hemm'd Manhattan?
River and sunset and scallop-edg'd waves of flood-tide?
The sea-gulls oscillating their bodies, the hay-boat in the twilight, and the belated lighter?
What gods can exceed these that clasp me by the hand, and with voices I love call me promptly and loudly
    by my nighest name as I approach?
What is more subtle than this which ties me to the woman or man that looks in my face?
Which fuses me into you now, and pours my meaning into you?

We understand then do we not?
What I promis'd without mentioning it, have you not accepted?
What the study could not teach—what the preaching could not accomplish is accomplish'd, is it not?

9

Flow on, river! flow with the flood-tide, and ebb with the ebb-tide!
Frolic on, crested and scallop-edg'd waves!
Gorgeous clouds of the sunset! drench with your splendor me, or the men and women generations after me!
Cross from shore to shore, countless crowds of passengers!
Stand up, tall masts of Mannahatta! stand up, beautiful hills of Brooklyn!
Throb, baffled and curious brain! throw out questions and answers!
Suspend here and everywhere, eternal float of solution!
Gaze, loving and thirsting eyes, in the house or street or public assembly!
Sound out, voices of young men! loudly and musically call me by my nighest name!
Live, old life! play the part that looks back on the actor or actress!
Play the old role, the role that is great or small according as one makes it!
Consider, you who peruse me, whether I may not in unknown ways be looking upon you;
Be firm, rail over the river, to support those who lean idly, yet haste with the hasting current;
Fly on, sea-birds! Fly sideways, or wheel in large circles high in the air;
Receive the summer sky, you water, and faithfully hold it till all downcast eyes have time to take it from you!
Diverge, fine spokes of light, from the shape of my head, or any one's head, in the sunlit water!

Come on, ships from the lower bay! pass up or down, white-sail'd schooners, sloops, lighters!
Flaunt away, flags of all nations! be duly lower'd at sunset!
Burn high your fires, foundry chimneys! cast black shadows at nightfall! cast red and yellow light over the
    tops of the houses!
120 Appearances, now or henceforth, indicate what you are,
You necessary film, continue to envelop the soul,
About my body for me, and your body for you, be hung our divinest aromas,
Thrive, cities—bring your freight, bring your shows, ample and sufficient rivers,
Expand, being than which none else is perhaps more spiritual,
Keep your places, objects than which none else is more lasting.

You have waited, you always wait, you dumb, beautiful ministers,
We receive you with free sense at last, and are insatiate henceforward,
Not you any more shall be able to foil us, or withhold yourselves from us,
We use you, and do not cast you aside—we plant you permanently within us,
130 We fathom you not—we love you—there is perfection in you also,
You furnish your parts toward eternity,
Great or small, you furnish your parts toward the soul.

SPARKLES FROM THE WHEEL

Where the city's ceaseless crowd moves on the livelong day,
Withdrawn I join a group of children watching, I pause aside with them.

By the curb toward the edge of the flagging,
A knife-grinder works at his wheel sharpening a great knife,
5 Bending over he carefully holds it to the stone, by foot and knee,
With measur'd tread he turns rapidly, as he presses with light but firm hand,
Forth issue then in copious golden jets,
Sparkles from the wheel.

The scene and all its belongings, how they seize and affect me,
10 The sad sharp-chinn'd old man with worn clothes and broad shoulder-band of leather,
Myself effusing and fluid, a phantom curiously floating, now here absorb'd and arrested,
The group, (an unminded point set in a vast surrounding),
The attentive, quiet children, the loud, proud, restive base of the streets,
The low hoarse purr of the whirling stone, the light-press'd blade,
15 Diffusing, dropping, sideways-darting, in tiny showers of gold,
Sparkles from the wheel.

CAVALRY CROSSING A FORD

A line in long array where they wind betwixt green islands,
They take a serpentine course, their arms flash in the sun—hark to the musical clank,
Behold the silvery river, in it the splashing horses loitering stop to drink,
Behold the brown-faced men, each group, each person a picture, the negligent rest on the saddles,
5 Some emerge on the opposite bank, others are just entering the ford—while,
Scarlet and blue and snowy white,
The guidon flags flutter gaily in the wind.

BIVOUAC ON A MOUNTAIN SIDE

I see before me now a traveling army halting,
Below a fertile valley spread, with barns and the orchards of summer,
Behind, the terraced sides of a mountain, abrupt, in places rising high,
Broken, with rocks, with clinging cedars, with tall shapes dingily seen,
5 The numerous camp-fires scatter'd near and far, some away up on the mountain,
The shadowy forms of men and horses, looming, large-sized, flickering,
And over all the sky—the sky! far, far out of reach, studded, breaking out, the eternal stars.

TO THE EAST AND TO THE WEST

To the East and to the West,
To the man of the Seaside State and of Pennsylvania,
To the Kanadian of the north, to the Southerner I love,
These with perfect trust to depict you as myself, the germs are in all men,
5 I believe the main purport of these States is to found a superb friendship, exalté, previously unknown,
Because I perceive it waits, and has been always waiting, latent in all men.

A NOISELESS PATIENT SPIDER

A noiseless patient spider,
I mark'd where on a little promontory it stood isolated,
Mark'd how to explore the vacant vast surrounding,
It launch'd forth filament, filament, filament, out of itself,
5 Ever unreeling them, ever tirelessly speeding them.

And you O my soul where you stand,
Surrounded, detached, in measureless oceans of space,
Ceaselessly musing, venturing, throwing, seeking the spheres to connect them,
Till the bridge you will need be form'd, till the ductile anchor hold,
10 Till the gossamer thread you fling catch somewhere, O my soul.

I Hear America Singing

FOR EXPLORATION

1. In general, most poetry written prior to Whitman's day dealt with idealized characters or extraordinary heroes. What class of people did Whitman choose to portray?
2. Why is " . . . each person singing what belongs to him or her and to none else . . . " (line 9)? Explain.

There Was a Child Went Forth

DISCUSSION

Instead of using conventional rhymes and meters to give structure to his poems, Whitman relied, in part, upon the careful patterning of **imagery.** An **image** is a word or phrase that appeals to the senses—sight, smell, sound, touch, or taste—in such a manner as to suggest objects or their characteristics. A basic element of both prose and poetry, images usually serve to create "pictures" or concrete sensations similar to memory in the reader's mind.

FOR EXPLORATION

1. Each of the following groups of lines present an image pattern: lines 1–13; 14–17; 19–26; 30–34; and 35–38. (*a*) Classify the imagery in each by subject matter. (*b*) Do the "pictures" form a progressive pattern? If so, how? (*c*) Does the imagery unify the poem? Explain.
2. Explicate lines 19–21. How did the child's parents become "part of him"?
3. What natural phenomenon is the poet describing through the use of imagery in line 37?
4. How long a period of time does the poem encompass?

CREATIVE RESPONSE

After rereading the poem write a short essay of two or three paragraphs discussing the significance of the ideas presented in lines 2–4. Include, if you wish, examples from your own experiences in support of your views.

Crossing Brooklyn Ferry

DISCUSSION

Like a great deal of Whitman's poetry, "Crossing Brooklyn Ferry" is **lyrical.** Unlike the sonnet and other strictly defined poetic forms, the term **lyrical** has come to mean a mode of expression or general way of treating a subject. While a **narrative poem** tells a story, a **lyric poem** is more subjective, relying more on the imaginative and ecstatic to express personal emotions, attitudes, or thoughts. Whitman has taken a seemingly simple subject, the daily ferry-boat excursion at sunset from Manhattan to Brooklyn, and used it as the starting point for a lyrical meditation on the diversity, continuity, and unity of all time, all life, and all objects.

Central to Whitman's theme is the identity and place of the individual within the scheme of things. Regarding what he called the mystery of individuality, Whitman once wrote in his journal: "I cannot understand the mystery but I am always conscious of myself as two—as my soul and I; and I reckon it is the same with all men and women." [To be] ". . . struck from the *float* [i.e., life's ongoing succession of changes] forever held in solution . . . " (line 62) is to acknowledge this mystery. It is to experience the strange stirrings of "otherness," to experience what it truly is to be an individual, separate yet a part of the world.

FOR EXPLORATION

1. Whom is the poet addressing in line 5 of the first section? Whom is he addressing throughout the poem?
2. Explicate line 20: "It avails not, time nor place—distance avails not. . . ." (*a*) When this line is echoed later in the poem it is in answer to what question? (*b*) Does this statement remind you of any other philosophy that you have studied? If so, which one?
3. What does the poet mean in line 52 when he says: " . . . others . . . look back on me because I look'd forward to them . . . "? What is meant by "back" and "forward"? Who are the "others"?
4. (*a*) What is meant by "dark patches" (line 65, section 6)? (*b*) What is "the same old role" (line 84, section 6)? Why is it as great or small as we make it (lines 84–5, section 6)?

5. Who are the "gods" the poet refers to in line 95, section 8? Why does the poet call them gods? Are they "real" gods?
6. What is Whitman doing with imagery in section 9? What impact does this technique have on the reader?
7. What are the "dumb, beautiful ministers" (line 126, section 9)? How do we "use" them (line 129)?
8. Gay Wilson Allen, a noted Whitman critic and biographer, has said that, by analogy, the poem itself becomes a ferry between the poet and the reader. What does the poem cross, if not an actual river? Do you agree or disagree with this statement? Explain.

CREATIVE RESPONSE

In a short essay of two or three paragraphs, answer the poet's query of lines 98–100.

Shorter Poems

FOR EXPLORATION

1. A **vignette** is a brief literary description or sketch. Writers achieve this desired "picture" or scene through the careful composition of images. Which of the shorter poems would you term vignettes? Which would you term lyrical? Which poem combines the vignette with lyrical elements?
2. The term **onomatopoeia** refers to the use of words in such a way that the sound of the words imitates the sound of the thing spoken about; for example, "the buzzing bee." Give an example of onomatopoeia from the last stanza of "Sparkles from the Wheel" and explain how it contributes to the "picture" the poet wished to present.
3. At one time during his life Whitman was a journalist. What journalistic elements do you find in "Cavalry Crossing a Ford" and "Bivouac on a Mountain Side"? How might journalistic training enhance a writer's abilities?
4. Do Whitman's war poems communicate more or less to you about the Civil War than the Mathew Brady photograph on page C 204? Explain.
5. Whitman has been called a prophet by many admirers of his verse. Assuming that this is so, what is the prophecy of "To the East and to the West"? Has it come true? Explain.
6. (a) What is the "filament" (line 4) in "A Noiseless Patient Spider"? (b) Give the name of the literary technique used by the poet to compare the spider and the soul, and likewise, the first and last stanzas. (c) What is Whitman saying about the individual and his relationship to the world? Explain.

CREATIVE RESPONSE

Recalling that vignettes are composed of carefully selected images, write a sketch of your own based on some scene that you have observed. Whether you decide to write in prose or poetry, remember that the best descriptions conjure clear "pictures" in the reader's mind.

RARE BOOK ROOM, NEW YORK PUBLIC LIBRARY

Walt Whitman   1819 / 1892

On May 31, 1819, Walter Whitman, Jr. was born—of native Dutch-English stock—on a farm at West Hills, Long Island. Though a contemporary of Bryant, Poe, Emerson, Thoreau, Whittier, Lowell, and Longfellow, there is sufficient reason for considering Whitman our first modern poet. Unlike these other writers and poets, each of whom enjoyed in their youth at least some degree of material comfort as well as formal education, Whitman's family was poor and his education ceased early in his teens, when it was necessary for him to seek employment to help support his growing family. During these early years he was apprenticed as a printer's assistant and also taught at various country public schools that dotted the farm communities and towns of then rural Long Island.

When Whitman was four his father gave up farming to become a carpenter and moved the family to the growing village of Brooklyn, also on Long Island. A disgruntled failure most of his life, the older Whitman had hoped to succeed at house building in the rapidly expanding community. A stubborn individualist who entertained an interest in the radical political theories of the day, he may have been a significant influence in the development of his son's democratic and egalitarian ideals. Surely Walter Sr.'s personal friendship with Elias Hicks, the radical Quaker evangelist, as well as his knowledge of the ideas of other religious and political dissidents probably helped shape many of the beliefs that his poet-son was later to voice. The intellectual and spiritual climate of Long Island in many ways paralleled that of Boston, when the Transcendental movement began. Hicks, for example, advocated an individualist religion where each member had spiritual access to his Maker, thus communing with and receiving inspiration directly from God. For a long time the island had been a refuge for those who could no longer comfortably live in either the pietistic, theocratic towns of Connecticut nor the established, aristocratic Hudson River Valley. Whitman, much later in life, once remarked of his early friendships with the local merchants, sailors, farmers, and fishermen that these were ". . . my best experiences and deepest lessons in human nature."

As Whitman grew older, he felt the pull of the growing city, New York, and was attracted to the endless bustle and variety of its life. Between 1839 and 1848 he found employment with a number of Manhattan and Brooklyn newspapers as an editor-reporter. During this phase of his life, he came to know the theaters, concert halls, opera houses, pubs, ferries, morgues, political rallies, and street-life of the city. He was particularly fond of riding the horse-drawn omnibuses and ferries, chatting and loafing all the while with their colorful drivers and pilots. Though he was surely unaware of it at the time, he was gathering much of the material that would later appear in his poetry. Indeed, the detached observations of the reporter seem to emerge in the crisp images of his greatest poem, "Song of Myself":

"The suicide sprawls on the bloody floor of the bedroom,
I witness the corpse with its dabbed hair, I note where
the pistol has fallen."

After a short stint of three months on the New Orleans Crescent in 1848, Whitman gave up newspaper work and returned home. His visit to New Orleans fired his imagination for he had seen a good deal of the young nation: the deep South, the Mississippi Valley, the Great Lakes, the Ohio Valley, and the farms and cities of the East. We know very little about Whitman during the years 1848 to 1854. He worked at carpentry with his father and brothers and apparently frequented the public libraries, absorbing most of the world's classics and current works. His brother George gives us some hints of Walt's activities: "He made a living . . . wrote a little, worked a little, loafed a little. He had an idea that money was of no consequence." Sometime during 1854 he underwent a great deal of internal turmoil, perhaps brought on by his father's paralysis and subsequent invalidism. Perhaps all the varied pictures of life that he had been absorbing were seeking expression. By early July of 1855, within days of his father's death, he published a thin volume of twelve long, untitled poems with a lengthy prose preface.

Public success was long in coming. Few people read either the first or second edition of Leaves of Grass. Many of those who had read his poetry rejected it as crude or gross. Whittier reportedly threw his copy into a fire. Bryant, whom Whitman befriended while they were both newspapermen in Brooklyn, ceased to associate with the younger poet. Even young Henry James wrote a scathing review of his poems. Though the book was a financial failure, there were influential readers and critics who were receptive to Whitman's revolutionary verse: Emerson, Thoreau, Abe Lincoln, and the English poets Dante Gabriel Rossetti and A. C. Swinburne. Whitman found, however, that he had to return to newspaper work in order to support himself, saving poetry for his spare hours. The period 1855 to 1865 marks his years of greatest poetic achievement.

Whitman was in his forties when the Civil War broke out and therefore too old to enlist as a soldier. Also, the need to provide financial support for his widowed mother probably ended any ideas he might have had about joining. Nevertheless, he went first to Virginia and then to Washington to care for his brother George who had been wounded at Fredericksburg. He witnessed much of the carnage of those early battles and wrote a number of poems based on his observations which were included in later editions of Leaves of Grass. He remained in Washington throughout the war years, working as a male nurse in Union hospitals. He even stayed after the war working in veterans' hospitals and subsisting on minor appointments that he received from the government, until 1873 when he suffered a paralytic stroke.

He left Washington for Camden, New Jersey, where he resided during the final years of his life. There he supervised the publication of more editions of Leaves of Grass, always including both new poems as well as revisions of older poems. One edition, the last, he approved from his death-bed. But his later works lacked the vigor, the brutal force, of his earliest poems. They were more pensive and serene. His thoughts on humanity and life led him to develop new themes: the brotherhood of all peoples and the peace and beauty of death. Death became for Whitman the greatest "democrat" of all for it was an experience that all people, rich and poor, saints and sinners, must share. He became convinced that "the untold want by life and land ne'er granted" could be satisfied only when the voyager reached the land of death. The only true life, he said in his last poems, must be that which follows death:

"I bequeath myself to the dirt to grow from the grass
I love,
If you want me again look for me under your boot soles."

The end came March 26, 1892. During his last years, Whitman began to win solid recognition. A number of the leading literary men of England praised and published his work, and more and more Americans came to admire it. After his death, his reputation continued to grow, and today he is classed among the greatest of American poets.

Ambrose Bierce

1842 / 1913

AN OCCURRENCE
AT OWL CREEK BRIDGE

A man stood upon a railroad bridge in northern Alabama, looking down into the swift water twenty feet below. The man's hands were behind his back, the wrists bound with a cord. A rope closely encircled his neck. It was attached to a stout crosstimber above his head and the slack fell to the level of his knees. Some loose boards laid upon the sleepers supporting the metals of the railway supplied a footing for him and his executioners—two private soldiers of the Federal army, directed by a sergeant who in civil life may have been a deputy sheriff. At a short remove upon the same temporary platform was an officer in the uniform of his rank, armed. He was a captain. A sentinel at each end of the bridge stood with his rifle in the position known as "support," that is to say, vertical in front of the left shoulder, the hammer resting on the forearm thrown straight across the chest—a formal and unnatural position, enforcing an erect carriage of the body. It did not appear to be the duty of these two men to know what was occurring at the centre of the bridge; they merely blockaded the two ends of the foot planking that traversed it.

Beyond one of the sentinels nobody was in sight; the railroad ran straight away into a forest for a hundred yards, then, curving, was lost to view. Doubtless there was an outpost farther along. The other bank of the stream was open ground—a gentle acclivity topped with a stockade of vertical tree trunks, loop-holed for rifles, with a single embrasure through which protruded the muzzle of a brass cannon commanding the bridge. Midway of the slope between bridge and fort were the spectators—a single company of infantry in line, at "parade rest," the butts of the rifles on the ground, the barrels inclining slightly backward against the right shoulder, the hands crossed upon the stock. A lieutenant stood at the right of the line, the point of his sword upon the ground, his left hand resting upon his right. Excepting the group of four at the centre of the bridge, not a man moved. The company faced the bridge, staring stonily, motionless. The sentinels, facing the banks of the stream, might have been statues to adorn the bridge. The captain stood with folded arms, silent, observing the work of his subordinates, but making no sign. Death is a dignitary who when he comes announced is to be received with formal manifestations of respect, even by those most familiar with him. In the code of military etiquette silence and fixity are forms of deference.

The man who was engaged in being hanged was apparently about thirty-five years of age. He was a civilian, if one might judge from his habit, which was that of a planter. His features were good— a straight nose, firm mouth, broad forehead, from which his long, dark hair was combed straight back, falling behind his ears to the collar of his well-fitting frock coat. He wore a mustache and pointed beard, but no whiskers; his eyes were large and dark gray, and had a kindly expression which one would hardly have expected in one whose neck was in the hemp. Evidently this was no vulgar assassin. The liberal military code makes provision for hanging many kinds of persons, and gentlemen are not excluded.

The preparations being complete, the two private soldiers stepped aside and each drew away the plank upon which he had been standing. The sergeant turned to the captain, saluted and placed himself immediately behind that officer, who in turn moved apart one pace. These movements left the condemned man and the sergeant standing on the two ends of the same plank, which spanned three of the cross-ties of the bridge. The end upon which the civilian stood almost, but not quite, reached a fourth. This plank had been held in place by the weight of the captain; it was now held by that of the sergeant. At a signal from the former the latter would step aside, the plank would tilt and the condemned man go down between two ties. The arrangement commended itself to his judgment as simple and effective. His face had not been covered nor his eyes bandaged. He looked a moment at his "unsteadfast footing," then let his gaze wander to the swirling water of the stream racing madly beneath his feet.

"An Occurrence at Owl Creek Bridge" from GHOST AND HORROR STORIES OF AMBROSE BIERCE. Published by the Neale Publishing Co., 1909, 1912.

A piece of dancing driftwood caught his attenion and his eyes followed it down the current. How slowly it appeared to move! What a sluggish stream!

He closed his eyes in order to fix his last thoughts upon his wife and children. The water, touched to gold by the early sun, the brooding mists under the banks at some distance down the stream, the fort, the soldiers, the piece of drift—all had distracted him. And now he became conscious of a new disturbance. Striking through the thought of his dear ones was a sound which he could neither ignore nor understand, a sharp, distinct, metallic percussion like the stroke of a blacksmith's hammer upon the anvil; it had the same ringing quality. He wondered what it was, and whether immeasurably distant or nearby—it seemed both. Its recurrence was regular, but as slow as the tolling of a death knell. He awaited each stroke with impatience and—he knew not why—apprehension. The intervals of silence grew progressively longer; the delays became maddening. With their greater infrequency the sounds increased in strength and sharpness. They hurt his ear like the thrust of a knife; he feared he would shriek. What he heard was the ticking of his watch.

He unclosed his eyes and saw again the water below him. "If I could free my hands," he thought, "I might throw off the noose and spring into the stream. By diving I could evade the bullets and, swimming vigorously, reach the bank, take to the woods and get away home. My home, thank God, is as yet outside their lines; my wife and little ones are still beyond the invader's farthest advance."

As these thoughts, which have here to be set down in words, were flashed into the doomed man's brain rather than evolved from it the captain nodded to the sergeant. The sergeant stepped aside.

II

Peyton Farquhar was a well-to-do planter, of an old and highly respected Alabama family. Being a slave owner and like other slave owners a politician he was naturally an original secessionist and ardently devoted to the Southern cause. Circumstances of an imperious nature, which it is unnecessary to relate here, had prevented him from taking service with the gallant army that had fought the disastrous campaigns ending with the fall of Corinth, and he chafed under the inglorious restraint, longing for the release of his energies, the larger life of the soldier,

the opportunity for distinction. That opportunity, he felt, would come, as it comes to all in war time. Meanwhile he did what he could. No service was too humble for him to perform in aid of the South, no adventure too perilous for him to undertake if consistent with the character of a civilian who was at heart a soldier, and who in good faith and without too much qualification assented to at least a part of the frankly villainous dictum that all is fair in love and war.

One evening while Farquhar and his wife were sitting on a rustic bench near the entrance to his grounds, a gray-clad soldier[1] rode up to the gate and asked for a drink of water. Mrs. Farquhar was only too happy to serve him with her own white hands. While she was fetching the water her husband approached the dusty horseman and inquired eagerly for news from the front.

"The Yanks are repairing the railroads," said the man, "and are getting ready for another advance. They have reached the Owl Creek bridge, put it in order and built a stockade on the north bank. The commandant has issued an order, which is posted everywhere, declaring that any civilian caught interfering with the railroad, its bridges, tunnels or trains will be summarily hanged. I saw the order."

"How far is it to the Owl Creek bridge?" Farquhar asked.

"About thirty miles."

"Is there no force on this side the creek?"

"Only a picket post half a mile out, on the railroad, and a single sentinel at this end of the bridge."

"Suppose a man—a civilian and student of hanging—should elude the picket post and perhaps get the better of the sentinel," said Farquhar, smiling, "what could he accomplish?"

The soldier reflected. "I was there a month ago," he replied. "I observed that the flood of last winter had lodged a great quantity of driftwood against the wooden pier at this end of the bridge. It is now dry and would burn like tow."

The lady had now brought the water, which the soldier drank. He thanked her ceremoniously, bowed to her husband and rode away. An hour later, after nightfall, he repassed the plantation, going northward in the direction from which he had come. He was a Federal scout.

---

1. *a gray-clad soldier.* Confederate soldiers wore gray uniforms.

III

As Peyton Farquhar fell straight downward through the bridge he lost consciousness and was as one already dead. From this state he was awakened—ages later, it seemed to him—by the pain of a sharp pressure upon his throat, followed by a sense of suffocation. Keen, poignant agonies seemed to shoot from his neck downward through every fibre of his body and limbs. These pains appeared to flash along well-defined lines of ramification and to beat with an inconceivably rapid periodicity. They seemed like streams of pulsating fire heating him to an intolerable temperature. As to his head, he was conscious of nothing but a feeling of fulness—of congestion. These sensations were unaccompanied by thought. The intellectual part of his nature was already effaced; he had power only to feel, and feeling was torment. He was conscious of motion. Encompassed in a luminous cloud, of which he was now merely the fiery heart, without material substance, he swung through unthinkable arcs of oscillation, like a vast pendulum. Then all at once, with terrible suddenness, the light about him shot upward with the noise of a loud plash; a frightful roaring was in his ears, and all was cold and dark. The power of thought was restored; he knew that the rope had broken and he had fallen into the stream. There was no additional strangulation; the noose about his neck was already suffocating him and kept the water from his lungs. To die of hanging at the bottom of a river!—the idea seemed to him ludicrous. He opened his eyes in the darkness and saw above him a gleam of light, but how distant, how inaccessible! He was still sinking for the light became fainter and fainter until it was a mere glimmer. Then it began to grow and brighten, and he knew that he was rising toward the surface—knew it with reluctance, for he was now very comfortable. "To be hanged and drowned," he thought, "that is not so bad; but I do not wish to be shot. No; I will not be shot; that is not fair."

He was not conscious of an effort, but a sharp pain in his wrist apprised him that he was trying to free his hands. He gave the struggle his attention, as an idler might observe the feat of a juggler, without interest in the outcome. What splendid effort!—what magnificent, what superhuman strength! Ah, that was a fine endeavor! Bravo! The cord fell away; his arms parted and floated upward, the hands dimly seen on each side in the growing light. He watched them with a new interest as first one and then the other pounced upon the noose at his neck. They tore it away and thrust it fiercely aside, its undulations resembling those of a water-snake. "Put it back, put it back!" He thought he shouted these words to his hands, for the undoing of the noose had been succeeded by the direst pang that he had yet experienced. His neck ached horribly; his brain was on fire; his heart, which had been fluttering faintly, gave a great leap, trying to force itself out at his mouth. His whole body was racked and wrenched with an insupportable anguish! But his disobedient hands gave no heed to the command. They beat the water vigorously with quick, downward strokes, forcing him to the surface. He felt his head emerge; his eyes were blinded by the sunlight; his chest expanded convulsively, and with a supreme and crowning agony his lungs engulfed a great draught of air, which instantly he expelled in a shriek!

He was now in full possession of his physical senses. They were, indeed, preternaturally keen and alert. Something in the awful disturbance of his organic system had so exalted and refined them that they made record of things never before perceived. He felt the ripples upon his face and heard their separate sounds as they struck. He looked at the forest on the bank of the stream, saw the individual trees, the leaves and the veining of each leaf—saw the very insects upon them: the locusts, the brilliant-bodied flies, the gray spiders stretching their webs from twig to twig. He noted the prismatic colors in all the dewdrops upon a million blades of grass. The humming of the gnats that danced above the eddies of the stream, the beating of the dragon-flies' wings, the strokes of the water-spiders' legs, like oars which had lifted their boat—all these made audible music. A fish slid along beneath his eyes and he heard the rush of its body parting the water.

He had come to the surface facing down the stream; in a moment the visible world seemed to wheel slowly round, himself the pivotal point, and he saw the bridge, the fort, the soldiers upon the bridge, the captain, the sergeant, the two privates, his executioners. They were in silhouette against the blue sky. They shouted and gesticulated, pointing at him. The captain had drawn his pistol, but did not fire; the others were unarmed. Their movements were grotesque and horrible, their forms gigantic.

Suddenly he heard a sharp report and something struck the water smartly within a few inches of his head, spattering his face with spray. He heard a second report, and saw one of the sentinels with his rifle at his shoulder, a light cloud of blue smoke rising from the muzzle. The man in the water saw the eye of the man on the bridge gazing into his own through the sights of the rifle. He observed that it was a gray eye and remembered having read that gray eyes were keenest, and that all famous marksmen had them. Nevertheless, this one had missed.

A counter-swirl had caught Farquhar and turned him half round; he was again looking into the forest on the bank opposite the fort. The sound of a clear, high voice in a monotonous singsong now rang out behind him and came across the water with a distinctness that pierced and subdued all other sounds, even the beating of the ripples in his ears. Although no soldier, he had frequented camps enough to know the dread significance of that deliberate, drawling, aspirated chant; the lieutenant on shore was taking a part in the morning's work. How coldly and pitilessly—with what an even, calm intonation, presaging, and enforcing tranquillity in the men—with what accurately measured intervals fell those cruel words:

"Attention, company! . . . Shoulder arms! . . . Ready! . . . Aim! . . . Fire!"

Farquhar dived—dived as deeply as he could. The water roared in his ears like the voice of Niagara, yet he heard the dulled thunder of the volley and, rising again toward the surface, met shining bits of metal, singularly flattened, oscillating slowly downward. Some of them touched him on the face and hands, then fell away, continuing their descent. One lodged between his collar and neck; it was uncomfortably warm and he snatched it out.

As he rose to the surface, gasping for breath, he saw that he had been a long time under water; he was perceptibly farther down stream—nearer to safety. The soldiers had almost finished reloading; the metal ramrods flashed all at once in the sunshine as they were drawn from the barrels, turned in the air, and thrust into their sockets. The two sentinels fired again, independently and ineffectually.

The hunted man saw all this over his shoulder; he was now swimming vigorously with the current.

His brain was as energetic as his arms and legs; he thought with the rapidity of lightning.

"The officer," he reasoned, "will not make that martinet's error a second time. It is as easy to dodge a volley as a single shot. He has probably already given the command to fire at will. God help me, I cannot dodge them all!"

An appalling plash within two yards of him was followed by a loud, rushing sound, *diminuendo*,[2] which seemed to travel back through the air to the fort and died in an explosion which stirred the very river to its deeps! A rising sheet of water curved over him, fell down upon him, blinded him, strangled him! The cannon had taken a hand in the game. As he shook his head free from the commotion of the smitten water he heard the deflected shot humming through the air ahead, and in an instant it was cracking and smashing the branches in the forest beyond.

"They will not do that again," he thought; "the next time they will use a charge of grape. I must keep my eye upon the gun; the smoke will apprise me—the report arrives too late; it lags behind the missile. That is a good gun."

Suddenly he felt himself whirled round and round—spinning like a top. The water, the banks, the forests, the now distant bridge, fort and men—all were commingled and blurred. Objects were represented by their colors only; circular horizontal streaks of color—that was all he saw. He had been caught in a vortex and was being whirled on with a velocity of advance and gyration that made him giddy and sick. In a few moments he was flung upon the gravel at the foot of the left bank of the stream —the southern bank—and behind a projecting point which concealed him from his enemies. The sudden arrest of his motion, the abrasion of one of his hands on the gravel, restored him, and he wept with delight. He dug his fingers into the sand, threw it over himself in handfuls and audibly blessed it. It looked like diamonds, rubies, emeralds; he could think of nothing beautiful which it did not resemble. The trees upon the bank were giant garden plants; he noted a definite order in their arrangement, inhaled the fragrance of their blooms. A strange, roseate light shone through the spaces among their trunks and the wind made in their

---

2. *diminuendo*, with gradually diminishing volume, a term used in music.

branches the music of æolian harps.[3] He had no wish to perfect his escape—was content to remain in that enchanting spot until retaken.

A whiz and rattle of grapeshot among the branches high above his head roused him from his dream. The baffled cannoneer had fired him a random farewell. He sprang to his feet, rushed up the sloping bank, and plunged into the forest.

All that day he traveled, laying his course by the rounding sun. The forest seemed interminable; nowhere did he discover a break in it, not even a woodman's road. He had not known that he lived in so wild a region. There was something uncanny in the revelation.

By nightfall he was fatigued, footsore, famishing. The thought of his wife and children urged him on. At last he found a road which led him in what he knew to be the right direction. It was as wide and straight as a city street, yet it seemed untraveled. No fields bordered it, no dwelling anywhere. Not so much as the barking of a dog suggested human habitation. The black bodies of the trees formed a straight wall on both sides, terminating on the horizon in a point, like a diagram in a lesson in perspective. Overhead, as he looked up through this rift in the wood, shone great golden stars looking unfamiliar and grouped in strange constellations. He was sure they were arranged in some order which had a secret and malign significance. The wood on either side was full of singular noises, among which —once, twice, and again—he distinctly heard whispers in an unknown tongue.

His neck was in pain and lifting his hand to it he found it horribly swollen. He knew that it had a circle of black where the rope had bruised it. His eyes felt congested; he could no longer close them. His tongue was swollen with thirst; he relieved its fever by thrusting it forward from between his teeth into the cold air. How softly the turf had carpeted the untraveled avenue—he could no longer feel the roadway beneath his feet!

Doubtless, despite his suffering, he had fallen asleep while walking, for now he sees another scene—perhaps he has merely recovered from a delirium. He stands at the gate of his own home. All is as he left it, and all bright and beautiful in the morning sunshine. He must have traveled the entire night. As he pushes open the gate and passes up the wide white walk, he sees a flutter of female garments; his wife, looking fresh and cool and sweet, steps down from the veranda to meet him. At the bottom of the steps she stands waiting, with a smile of ineffable joy, an attitude of matchless grace and dignity. Ah, how beautiful she is! He springs forward with extended arms. As he is about to clasp her he feels a stunning blow upon the back of the neck; a blinding white light blazes all about him with a sound like the shock of a cannon—then all is darkness and silence!

Peyton Farquhar was dead; his body, with a broken neck, swung gently from side to side beneath the timbers of the Owl Creek bridge. ☐

---

3. *æolian harps*, musical instruments consisting of a box across which strings are stretched. They are placed at open windows where the wind can produce harmonic, sweet tones.

DISCUSSION

Ambrose Bierce, like Poe, wrote many tales of the uncanny and supernatural. In "An Occurrence at Owl Creek Bridge" he has created a dimension in which reality is heightened, time is rearranged, and the dream life of the imagination is woven inextricably into physical events. Colors, sounds, and sensations come to life with extraordinary vividness. These effects are often called **magic realism** by literary critics. In this imaginary realm events are depicted as if the reader were seeing reality through a kaleidoscope.

FOR EXPLORATION

1. (a) Cite paragraphs where sight and sound explode into new brilliance. (b) Cite paragraphs where time is rearranged.
2. Discuss the problem of "real" reality in this story. What actually occurred? Did Peyton Farquhar escape or did he only imagine it; or did the Union officer imagine that Peyton was hanged? Explain.
3. How does the title contribute to the ambiguity of the tale's conclusion? Explain.
4. Assuming that Peyton is hanged at the end of the tale, what hints does the author give the reader that this is only a desperate dream?
5. How does the tale illustrate our attachment to life? Explain.

Ambrose Bierce 1842/1914?

DICTIONARY OF AMERICAN PORTRAITS

Raised on an Ohio farm, Ambrose Bierce was the youngest of a large, poor, pious family. He was later reluctant to talk about his beginnings and is said to have despised his relatives. At fifteen he left home and spent two years as a printer's devil. There followed a year at the Kentucky Military Institute, the only schooling he would receive, and then the Civil War broke out. He enlisted as a drummer boy, fought bravely in some of the most difficult fighting of the war, and was repeatedly promoted. At war's end he was awarded the brevit title of Major.

Living in San Francisco afterwards, Bierce began writing short satiric pieces for one of the weeklies, was given his own column, and soon thereafter was made editor of the paper. It was a period of fiery personal journalism for which Bierce's vitriolic wit was ideally suited. Bierce was married in 1871, and a few months later he and his wife sailed for England. He stayed there four years, working on the staff of *Fun* magazine, a comfortable member of a group of literary cronies. But his wife grew tired of England and returned to California. From there she announced the impending arrival of their third child and Bierce was soon sailing for San Francisco. For the next ten years he wrote his famous "Prattler" column for the *Argonaut*. The column was bought in 1887 by William Randolph Hearst and placed on the editorial page of the Sunday *Examiner*.

By this time Bierce's merciless wit had made him the dictator of literary tastes for the west coast. His reign was an uneven one, his literary tastes at times less than ideal. He was capable of championing the mediocre and attacking the genuine for emotional personal reasons. Though no doubt talented and popular in his journalism, he fell short of greatness. His work lacked an underlying compassion necessary if one's satire is to be more than momentarily entertaining.

His fiction, on the other hand, seems to have won for itself a small but lasting place. He wrote haunting, climactic stories, often with strange psychological twists, a few of which have emerged with time as classics.

Bierce spent a number of his later years in Washington, D.C., fighting the battles of and reporting for the Hearst newspapers. In 1913 at the age of seventy-one he seemed perhaps weary of it all. He left for Mexico to cover the revolution there and disappeared from sight. Upon leaving he wrote a friend, "Goodbye, if you hear of my being stood up against a Mexican stone wall and shot to rags please know that I think it a pretty good way to depart this life. It beats old age, disease, or falling down the cellar stairs. To be a Gringo in Mexico—ah, that is euthanasia!"

Folk Songs of the West

As the pioneers and frontiersmen explored and settled the West, their thoughts, feelings, and experiences found expression in ballad-like song of which the following are typical.

SHENANDOAH

Oh, Missouri, she's a mighty river,
   Away you rolling river.
The Red-skins' camp lies on its borders,
   Ah-ha, I'm bound away 'cross the wide Missouri.

The white man loved the Indian maiden,
   Away you rolling river.
With notions sweet his canoe was laden.
   Ah-ha, I'm bound away 'cross the wide Missouri.

"O Shenandoah, I love your daughter,
   Away you rolling river.
I'll take her 'cross yon rolling water."
   Ah-ha, I'm bound away 'cross the wide Missouri.

The chief disdained the trader's dollars:
   Away you rolling river.
"My daughter never you shall follow."
   Ah-ha, I'm bound away 'cross the wide Missouri.

At last there came a Yankee skipper,
   Away you rolling river.
He winked his eye, and he tipped his flipper.
   Ah-ha, I'm bound away 'cross the wide Missouri.

He sold the chief that fire-water,
   Away you rolling river.
And 'cross the river he stole his daughter,
   Ah-ha, I'm bound away 'cross the wide Missouri.

"O Shenandoah, I long to hear you,
   Away you rolling river.
Across that wide and rolling river."
   Ah-ha, I'm bound away 'cross the wide Missouri.

THE WAGONER'S LAD

"My horses ain't hungry, they won't eat your hay,
It's farewell dear Polly, I'm riding away:
Your parents despise me 'cause I'm over poor;
They say I ain't fittin' to enter your door!

"I'm just a poor cowboy, I don't own no herd;
I ain't got much money, but give you my word,
I'm handy at roping up poor loneful strays,
An' we'll sure be rich 'fore the end of our days!

"Dear Polly, you promised to be my own wife,
You vowed for to wed me and share all through life,
So mind your words, Polly, I've not long to stay:
Please pack up your duds and we'll ride far away!"

"You know I'm your Polly, your sweet loving dear;
'Cause my kin despise you, don't you have a fear.
Just calm down your feelings and raise up your head;
I know you're the fittin' man for me to wed!

"Yes, Tom, I'll go with you, though you're poor,
   I'm told,
But it's love I'm wanting, not silver or gold—
Tie on my belongings, we'll ride till we come
To some far-off cabin, and there make our home!

"I mourn for to leave maw, she treats me so fine,
But I've given my promise to you, cowboy mine!
So I'll bid good-bye to my parents this day,
Then we'll mount our ponies and lope far away!

"Far over the mountains we'll come to a rest
In a pretty valley, and build us a nest:
We'll raise a big herd, and a fine family,
And live out our lives there, Tom, all happily!"

"Shenandoah" by W. B. Whall from SEA SONGS AND SHANTIES. Reprinted by permission of Brown, Son & Ferguson, Ltd.

Melody: William A. Owens, Texas Folk Songs (Austin: Texas Folklore Society, 1950) reproduced by permission.

Emily Dickinson
1830 / 1886

441

This is my letter to the World
That never wrote to Me—
The simple News that Nature told—
With tender Majesty

5 Her Message is committed
To Hands I cannot see—
For love of Her—Sweet—countrymen—
Judge tenderly—of Me

In reading Emily Dickinson, you may need, in your imagination, to punctuate her poems with conventional punctuation. Her first editors, back in the 1890's, changed the poems to conform to readers' expectations, as in the following:

This is my letter to the world,
    That never wrote to me,—
The simple news that Nature told,
    With tender majesty.

5 Her message is committed
    To hands I cannot see;
For love of her, sweet countrymen,
    Judge tenderly of me!

During her lifetime, Emily Dickinson published only seven out of the 1,775 poems that she wrote. The complete body of her poetry was not finally published until 1955, and the editors this time preserved her unconventional language, syntax, and punctuation. Since she had not given her poems titles, her editors gave them numbers—approximately in the order in which they were written. Her favorite mark was the dash, and she seems to have used it mainly to indicate simply a pause—for meaning or emphasis—in the reading.

LIFE

108

Surgeons must be very careful
When they take the knife!
Underneath their fine incisions
Stirs the Culprit—*Life!*

435

Much Madness is divinest Sense—
To a discerning Eye—
Much Sense—the starkest Madness—
'Tis the Majority
5 In this, as All, prevail—
Assent—and you are sane—
Demur—you're straightway dangerous—
And handled with a Chain—

952

A Man may make a Remark—
In itself—a quiet thing
That may furnish the Fuse unto a Spark
In dormant nature—lain—

5 Let us deport—with skill—
Let us discourse—with care—
Powder exists in Charcoal—
Before it exists in Fire.

1287

In this short Life
That only lasts an hour
How much—how little—is
Within our power

1455

Opinion is a flitting thing,
But Truth, outlasts the Sun—
If then we cannot own them both—
Possess the oldest one—

Reprinted by permission of the publishers and the Trustees of Amherst College from Thomas H. Johnson, Editor, THE POEMS OF EMILY DICKINSON, Cambridge, Mass.: The Belknap Press of Harvard University Press, Copyright, 1951, 1955, by The President and Fellows of Harvard College.

NATURE

214

I taste a liquor never brewed—
From Tankards scooped in Pearl—
Not all the Vats upon the Rhine
Yield such an Alcohol!

5 Inebriate of Air—am I—
And Debauchee of Dew—
Reeling—thro endless summer days—
From inns of Molten Blue—

When "Landlords" turn the drunken Bee
10 Out of the Foxglove's door—
When Butterflies—renounce their "drams"—
I shall but drink the more!

Till Seraphs swing their snowy Hats—
And Saints—to windows run—
15 To see the little Tippler
Leaning against the—Sun—

In reviewing Emily Dickinson's poems when they first
appeared in 1892, Thomas Bailey Aldrich regretted her
lack of "metrical training," and revised the first stanza of
this poem to suit his and perhaps his audience's taste:

I taste a liquor never brewed
In vats upon the Rhine;
No tankard ever held a draught
Of alcohol like mine.

986

A narrow Fellow in the Grass
Occasionally rides—
You may have met Him—did you not
His notice sudden is—

5 The Grass divides as with a Comb—
A spotted shaft is seen—
And then it closes at your feet
And opens further on—

He likes a Boggy Acre
10 A Floor too cool for Corn—
Yet when a Boy, and Barefoot—
I more than once at Noon
Have passed, I thought, a Whip lash

Unbraiding in the Sun
15 When stooping to secure it
It wrinkled, and was gone—

Several of Nature's People
I know, and they know me—
I feel for them a transport
20 Of cordiality—

But never met this Fellow
Attended, or alone
Without a tighter breathing
And Zero at the Bone—

1079

The Sun went down—no Man looked on—
The Earth and I, alone,
Were present at the Majesty—
He triumphed, and went on—

5 The Sun went up—no Man looked on—
The Earth and I and One
A nameless Bird—a Stranger
Were Witness for the Crown—

1755

To make a prairie it takes a clover and one bee,
One clover, and a bee,
And revery.
The revery alone will do,
If bees are few.

Reprinted by permission of the publishers and the Trustees of
Amherst College from Thomas H. Johnson, Editor, THE POEMS OF
EMILY DICKINSON, Cambridge, Mass.: The Belknap Press of Har-
vard University Press, Copyright, 1951, 1955, by The President and
Fellows of Harvard College.

LOVE

511

If you were coming in the Fall,
I'd brush the Summer by
With half a smile, and half a spurn,
As Housewives do, a Fly.

5 If I could see you in a year,
I'd wind the months in balls—
And put them each in separate Drawers,
For fear the numbers fuse—

If only Centuries, delayed,
10 I'd count them on my Hand,
Subtracting, till my fingers dropped
Into Van Dieman's Land.[1]

If certain, when this life was out—
That yours and mine, should be
15 I'd toss it yonder, like a Rind,
And take Eternity—

But, now, uncertain of the length
Of this, that is between,
It goads me, like the Goblin Bee—
20 That will not state—its sting.

568

We learned the Whole of Love—
The Alphabet—the Words—
A Chapter—then the mighty Book—
Then—Revelation closed—

5 But in Each Other's eyes
An Ignorance beheld—
Diviner than the Childhood's
And each to each, a Child—

Attempted to expound
10 What Neither—understood—
Alas, that Wisdom is so large—
and Truth—so manifold!

664

Of all the Souls that stand create—
I have elected—One—
When Sense from Spirit—files away—
And Subterfuge—is done—
5 When that which is—and that which was—

Apart—intrinsic—stand—
And this brief Drama in the flesh—
Is shifted—like a Sand—
When Figures show their royal Front—
10 And Mists—are carved away,
Behold the Atom—I preferred—
To all the lists of Clay!

ANGUISH

77

I never hear the word "escape"
Without a quicker blood,
A sudden expectation,
A flying attitude!

5 I never hear of prisons broad
By soldiers battered down,
But I tug childish at my bars
Only to fail again!

280

I felt a Funeral, in my Brain,
And Mourners to and fro
Kept treading—treading—till it seemed
That Sense was breaking through—

5 And when they all were seated,
A Service, like a Drum—
Kept beating—beating—till I thought
My Mind was going numb—

And then I heard them lift a Box
10 And creak across my Soul
With those same Boots of Lead, again,
Then Space—began to toll,

As all the Heavens were a Bell,
And Being, but an Ear,

Reprinted by permission of the publishers and the Trustees of Amherst College from Thomas H. Johnson, Editor, THE POEMS OF EMILY DICKINSON, Cambridge, Mass.: The Belknap Press of Harvard University Press, Copyright, 1951, 1955, by The President and Fellows of Harvard College.

1. *Van Dieman's Land*, Tasmania, an island off the southern coast of Australia.

15 And I, and Silence, some strange Race
Wrecked, solitary, here—

And then a Plank in Reason, broke,
And I dropped down, and down—
And hit a World, at every plunge,
20 And Finished knowing—then—

609

I Years had been from Home
And now before the Door
I dared not enter, lest a Face
I never saw before

5 Stare stolid into mine
And ask my Business there—
"My Business but a Life I left
Was such remaining there?"

I leaned upon the Awe—
10 I lingered with Before—
The Second like an Ocean rolled
And broke against my ear—

I laughed a crumbling Laugh
That I could fear a Door
15 Who Consternation compassed
And never winced before.[1]

I fitted to the Latch
My Hand, with trembling care
Lest back the awful Door should spring
20 And leave me in the Floor—

Then moved my Fingers off
As cautiously as Glass
And held my ears, and like a Thief
Fled gasping from the House—

1233

Had I not seen the Sun
I could have borne the shade
But Light a newer Wilderness
My Wilderness has made—

501

This World is not Conclusion.
A Species stands beyond—
Invisible, as Music—
But positive, as Sound—
5 It beckons, and it baffles—
Philosophy—don't know—
And through a Riddle, at the last—
Sagacity, must go—
To guess it, puzzles scholars—
10 To gain it, Men have borne
Contempt of Generations
And Crucifixion, shown—
Faith slips—and laughs, and rallies—
Blushes, if any see—
15 Plucks at a twig of Evidence—
And asks a Vane, the way—
Much Gesture, from the Pulpit—
Strong Hallelujahs roll—
Narcotics cannot still the Tooth
20 That nibbles at the soul—

Reprinted by permission of the publishers and the Trustees of Amherst College from Thomas H. Johnson, Editor, THE POEMS OF EMILY DICKINSON, Cambridge, Mass.: The Belknap Press of Harvard University Press, Copyright, 1951, 1955, by The President and Fellows of Harvard College.

1. *That I . . . before.* That I, who had encompassed consternation and never winced before, could fear a door.

DEATH

465

I heard a Fly buzz—when I died—
The Stillness in the Room
Was like the Stillness in the Air—
Between the Heaves of Storm—

5 The Eyes around—had wrung them dry—
And Breaths were gathering firm
For that last Onset—when the King
Be witnessed—in the Room—

I willed my Keepsakes—Signed away
10 What portion of me be
Assignable—and then it was
There interposed a Fly—

With Blue—uncertain stumbling Buzz—
Between the light—and me—
15 And then the Windows failed—and then
I could not see to see—

When this poem was first published in the 1890's shortly
after Emily Dickinson's death, her editors revised and
regularized it:

I heard a fly buzz when I died;
 The stillness round my form
Was like the stillness in the air
 Between the heaves of storm.

5 The eyes beside had wrung them dry,
 And breaths were gathering sure
For that last onset, when the king
 Be witnessed in his power.

I willed my keepsakes, signed away
10 What portion of me I
Could make assignable,—and then
 There interposed a fly,

With blue, uncertain, stumbling buzz,
 Between the light and me;
15 And then the windows failed, and then
 I could not see to see.

712

Because I could not stop for Death—
He kindly stopped for me—
The Carriage held but just Ourselves—
And Immortality.

5 We slowly drove—He knew no haste
And I had put away
My labor and my leisure too,
For His Civility—

We passed the School, where Children strove
10 At Recess—in the Ring—
We passed the Fields of Gazing Grain—
We passed the Setting Sun—

Or rather—He passed Us—
The Dews drew quivering and chill—
15 For only Gossamer, my Gown—
My Tippet—only Tulle—

We paused before a House that seemed
A Swelling of the Ground—
The Roof was scarcely visible—
20 The Cornice—in the Ground—

Since then—'tis Centuries—and yet
Feels shorter than the Day
I first surmised the Horses' Heads
Were toward Eternity—

1445

Death is the supple Suitor
That wins at last—
It is a stealthy Wooing
Conducted first
5 By pallid innuendoes
And dim approach
But brave at last with Bugles
And a bisected Coach
It bears away in triumph
10 To Troth unknown
And Kindred as responsive
As Porcelain.

Reprinted by permission of the publishers and the Trustees of Amherst College from Thomas H. Johnson, Editor, THE POEMS OF
EMILY DICKINSON, Cambridge, Mass.: The Belknap Press of Harvard University Press, Copyright, 1951, 1955, by The President and
Fellows of Harvard College.

FOR EXPLORATION

Life

1. In Poem 108, why is life the "Culprit"?
2. In Poem 435, how can "Madness" ever be "divinest Sense"?

Nature

1. In Poem 214, which version of the first stanza, Emily Dickinson's or that of Thomas Bailey Aldrich, seems to you best? Why?
2. Explore the different attitudes toward nature expressed in Poems 214 and 986.

Love

1. Discuss the progression of images in Poem 511.
2. Explain the central metaphor of Poem 568.
3. What is the "Subterfuge" referred to in Poem 664, line 4?

Anguish

1. Explain the reference to "an Ear" in Poem 280, stanza 4.
2. What is the encounter feared in Poem 609? Explain.

3. At the end of Poem 501, what is the "Tooth" that "nibbles at the soul"?

Death

1. Discuss the two versions of Poem 465, and explain which you think is best.
2. (a) What are the differences in attitude toward death found in Poems 465, 712, and 1445? (b) Relate the different images in the poems to the different attitudes.

AMHERST COLLEGE

Emily Dickinson 1830 / 1886

Emily Dickinson and her poetry never fully belonged to their own time. Neither conformed to popular expectations, and each was unique.

Dickinson lived all her life in Amherst, Massachusetts. In her youth she was a vivacious and fun-loving girl. But the society in which she grew up was very strict, with precise specifications as to the proper manners and beliefs for young women. It was a world where fun itself was officially frowned upon, where intellectual curiosity and agility were deemed most unladylike. Though an innately religious person, Dickinson did not accept the Calvinist views of the New England church; and her attendance at Mount Holyoke Female Seminary, which she had excitedly anticipated, was marred by daily sessions with the school's headmistress who worked tirelessly for her conversion. But while an apparently shy girl, Dickinson had about her a firmness which would not relent and after a year's struggle she was removed from the school.

In her mid-twenties Dickinson gradually withdrew from public life and lived thereafter in almost total seclusion from all but the immediate members of her family.

Her poetry writing began in earnest in the late fall of 1861. The most direct influence on her style seems to have come from some of Emerson's poetry, a book of which was given to her when she was nineteen. Dickinson also took to heart Emerson's admonition for self reliance, a prerequisite to her unconventional life and poetry. Nevertheless she at times wished for critical appraisal. Reading an article of advice to beginning writers by Thomas Wentworth Higginson, Dickinson mailed four of her poems to the dashing abolitionist and asked, "Are you too deeply occupied to say if my verse is alive?" Though he never realized the true importance of her work, he found himself intrigued and went on to encourage her.

There are indications that Dickinson realized the quality and possible importance of her work. Yet she had no wish for recognition in her own time and despite the urging of friends declined to publish, saying her "barefoot rank" was better. She lived out her life in seclusion, her privacy a complex preference which had stiffened into habit. She seemed contented with the company of her family, with her large Newfoundland dog, with nature, and with her poetry.

STEPHEN CRANE'S OWN STORY

He Tells How the Commodore Was Wrecked and How He Escaped.

Tried to Tow Their Companions Who Were on the Raft—— Last Dash for the Shore Through the Surf.

Copyright 1897, by The Press Company, Limited

JACKSONVILLE, Fla., Jan 6—It was the afternoon of New Year's. The Commodore lay at her dock in Jacksonville and three long blasts of her whistle, which even to this time impressed me with their sadness. Somehow, they sounded as a . . .

On Monday, January 4, 1897, readers of The New York Press awoke to the following headlines:

Commodore's Wrecked Seamen Struggle for Life in Heavy Surf
STEPHEN CRANE, NOVELIST, SWIMS ASHORE
Young New York Writer Astonishes the Sea Dogs by His Courage in the Face of Death.

Stephen Crane, correspondent and novelist, had left for an assignment in Cuba aboard the filibuster boat Commodore. The boat, laden with arms and ammunition destined for Cuban revolutionaries, met with disaster and swamped along the coast of Florida. The following story, based upon the experiences of Crane, the Captain, and two other castaways in a ten-foot dinghy, bears the stamp of the experienced reporter, for it is scrupulously faithful to the facts and the order of their occurrence. Yet the story which emerged is, at the same time, as different from truth as art must always be from life. Crane did not merely want to "tell the story as it happened." Perhaps this accounts for his failure to become a successful newspaperman. He wanted instead to make a statement about the interrelationships between life and death, Nature and the individual. One of Crane's finest successes in this latter venture—the writing of fiction—is "The Open Boat."

Stephen Crane

1871 / 1900

THE OPEN BOAT

A Tale Intended to be after the Fact:
Being the Experience of Four Men
from the Sunk Steamer Commodore

I

NONE of them knew the colour of the sky. Their eyes glanced level, and were fastened upon the waves that swept toward them. These waves were of the hue of slate, save for the tops, which were of foaming white, and all of the men knew the colours of the sea. The horizon narrowed and widened, and dipped and rose, and at all times its edge was jagged with waves that seemed thrust up in points like rocks.

Many a man ought to have a bathtub larger than the boat which here rode upon the sea. These waves were most wrongfully and barbarously abrupt and tall, and each froth-top was a problem in small-boat navigation.

The cook squatted in the bottom, and looked with both eyes at the six inches of gunwale which separated him from the ocean. His sleeves were rolled over his fat forearms, and the two flaps of his unbuttoned vest dangled as he bent to bail out the boat. Often he said, "Gawd! that was a narrow clip." As he remarked it he invariably gazed eastward over the broken sea.

The oiler, steering with one of the two oars in the boat, sometimes raised himself suddenly to keep clear of water that swirled in over the stern. It was a thin little oar, and it seemed often ready to snap.

The correspondent, pulling at the other oar, watched the waves and wondered why he was there.

The injured captain, lying in the bow, was at this time buried in that profound dejection and indifference which comes, temporarily at least, to even the bravest and most enduring when, willy-nilly, the firm fails, the army loses, the ship goes down. The mind of the master of a vessel is rooted deep in the timbers of her, though he command for a day or a decade; and this captain had on him the stern impression of a scene in the greys of dawn of seven turned faces, and later a stump of a topmast with a white ball on it, that slashed to and fro at the waves, went low and lower, and down. Thereafter there was something strange in his voice. Although steady, it was deep with mourning, and of a quality beyond oration or tears.

"Keep 'er a little more south, Billie," said he.

"A little more south, sir," said the oiler in the stern.

A seat in his boat was not unlike a seat upon a bucking broncho, and by the same token a broncho is not much smaller. The craft pranced and reared and plunged like an animal. As each wave came, and she rose for it, she seemed like a horse making at a fence outrageously high. The manner of her scramble over these walls of water is a mystic thing, and, moreover, at the top of them were ordinarily these problems in white water, the foam racing down from the summit of each wave requiring a new leap, and a leap from the air. Then, after scornfully bumping a crest, she would slide and race and splash down a long incline, and arrive bobbing and nodding in front of the next menace.

A singular disadvantage of the sea lies in the fact that after successfully surmounting one wave you discover that there is another behind it just as important and just as nervously anxious to do something effective in the way of swamping boats. In a ten-foot dinghy one can get an idea of the resources of the sea in the line of waves that is not probable to the average experience which is never at sea in a dinghy. As each slaty wall of water approached, it shut all else from the view of the men in the boat, and it was not difficult to imagine that this particular wave was the final outburst of the ocean, the last effort of the grim water. There was a terrible grace in the move of the waves, and they came in silence, save for the snarling of the crests.

In the wan light the faces of the men must have been grey. Their eyes must have glinted in strange ways as they gazed steadily astern. Viewed from a balcony, the whole thing would doubtless have been weirdly picturesque. But the men in the boat had no time to see it, and if they had had leisure, there were other things to occupy their minds. The sun swung steadily up the sky, and they knew it was

"*The Open Boat*" by Stephen Crane from STEPHEN CRANE: AN OMNIBUS. Copyright 1958. Reprinted by permission of Alfred A. Knopf, Inc.

broad day because the colour of the sea changed from slate to emerald green streaked with amber lights, and the foam was like tumbling snow. The process of the breaking day was unknown to them. They were aware only of this effect upon the colour of the waves that rolled toward them.

In disjointed sentences the cook and the correspondent argued as to the difference between a life-saving station and a house of refuge. The cook had said: "There's a house of refuge just north of the Mosquito Inlet Light, and as soon as they see us they'll come off in their boat and pick us up."

"As soon as who see us?" said the correspondent.

"The crew," said the cook.

"Houses of refuge don't have crews," said the correspondent. "As I understand them, they are only places where clothes and grub are stored for the benefit of shipwrecked people. They don't carry crews."

"Oh, yes, they do," said the cook.

"No, they don't," said the correspondent.

"Well, we're not there yet, anyhow," said the oiler, in the stern.

"Well," said the cook, "perhaps it's not a house of refuge that I'm thinking of as being near Mosquito Inlet Light; perhaps it's a life-saving station."

"We're not there yet," said the oiler in the stern.

II

As the boat bounced from the top of each wave the wind tore through the hair of the hatless men, and as the craft plopped her stern down again the spray slashed past them. The crest of each of these waves was a hill, from the top of which the men surveyed for a moment a broad tumultuous expanse, shining and wind-riven. It was probably splendid, it was probably glorious, this play of the free sea, wild with lights of emerald and white and amber.

"Bully good thing it's an on-shore wind," said the cook. "If not, where would we be? Wouldn't have a show."

"That's right," said the correspondent.

The busy oiler nodded his assent.

Then the captain, in the bow, chuckled in a way that expressed humour, contempt, tragedy, all in one. "Do you think we've got much of a show now, boys?" said he.

Whereupon the three were silent, save for a trifle of hemming and hawing. To express any particular optimism at this time they felt to be childish and stupid, but they all doubtless possessed this sense of the situation in their minds. A young man thinks doggedly at such times. On the other hand, the ethics of their condition was decidedly against any open suggestion of hopelessness. So they were silent.

"Oh, well," said the captain, soothing his children, "we'll get ashore all right."

But there was that in his tone which made them think; so the oiler quoth, "Yes! if this wind holds."

The cook was bailing. "Yes! if we don't catch hell in the surf."

Canton-flannel gulls flew near and far. Sometimes they sat down on the sea, near patches of brown seaweed that rolled over the waves with a movement like carpets on a line in a gale. The birds sat comfortably in groups, and they were envied by some in the dinghy, for the wrath of the sea was no more to them than it was to a covey of prairie chickens a thousand miles inland. Often they came very close and stared at the men with black bead-like eyes. At these times they were uncanny and sinister in their unblinking scrutiny, and the men hooted angrily at them, telling them to be gone. One came, and evidently decided to alight on the top of the captain's head. The bird flew parallel to the boat and did not circle, but made short sidelong jumps in the air in chicken-fashion. His black eyes were wistfully fixed upon the captain's head. "Ugly brute," said the oiler to the bird. "You look as if you were made with a jackknife." The cook and the correspondent swore darkly at the creature. The captain naturally wished to knock it away with the end of the heavy painter, but he did not dare do it, because anything resembling an emphatic gesture would have capsized this freighted boat; and so, with his open hand, the captain gently and carefully waved the gull away. After it had been discouraged from the pursuit the captain breathed easier on account of his hair, and others breathed easier because the bird struck their minds at this time as being somehow gruesome and ominous.

In the meantime the oiler and the correspondent rowed. And also they rowed. They sat together in the same seat, and each rowed an oar. Then the oiler took both oars; then the correspondent took both oars; then the oiler; then the correspondent. They rowed and they rowed. The very ticklish part of the business was when the time came for the reclining one in the stern to take his turn at the oars. By the very last star of truth, it is easier to steal eggs from under a hen than it was to change seats in the dinghy. First the man in the stern slid his hand along the thwart and moved with care, as if he were of Sèvres.[1] Then the man in the rowing-seat slid his hand along the other thwart. It was all done with the most extraordinary care. As the two sidled past each other, the whole party kept watchful eyes on the coming wave, and the captain cried: "Look out, now! Steady, there!"

The brown mats of seaweed that appeared from time to time were like islands, bits of earth. They were travelling, apparently, neither one way nor the other. They were, to all intents, stationary. They informed the men in the boat that it was making progress slowly toward the land.

The captain, rearing cautiously in the bow after the dinghy soared on a great swell, said that he had seen the lighthouse at Mosquito Inlet. Presently the cook remarked that he had seen it. The correspondent was at the oars then, and for some reason he too wished to look at the lighthouse; but his back was toward the far shore, and the waves were important, and for some time he could not seize an opportunity to turn his head. But at last there came a wave more gentle than the others, and when at the crest of it he swiftly scoured the western horizon.

"See it?" said the captain.

"No," said the correspondent, slowly; "I didn't see anything."

"Look again," said the captain. He pointed. "It's exactly in that direction."

At the top of another wave the correspondent did as he was bid, and this time his eyes chanced on a small, still thing on the edge of the swaying horizon. It was precisely like the point of a pin. It took an anxious eye to find a lighthouse so tiny.

"Think we'll make it, Captain?"

"If this wind holds and the boat don't swamp, we can't do much else," said the captain.

The little boat, lifted by each towering sea and splashed viciously by the crests, made progress that in the absence of seaweed was not apparent to those in her. She seemed just a wee thing wallowing, miraculously top up, at the mercy of five oceans. Occasionally a great spread of water, like white flames, swarmed into her.

"Bail her, cook," said the captain, serenely.

"All right, Captain," said the cheerful cook.

III

It would be difficult to describe the subtle brotherhood of men that was here established on the seas. No one said that it was so. No one mentioned it. But it dwelt in the boat, and each man felt it warm him. They were a captain, an oiler, a cook, and a correspondent, and they were friends—friends in a more curiously iron-bound degree than may be common. The hurt captain, lying against the water-jar in the bow, spoke always in a low voice and calmly; but he could never command a more ready and swiftly obedient crew than the motley three of the dinghy. It was more than a mere recognition of what was best for the common safety. There was surely in it a quality that was personal and heart-felt. And after this devotion to the commander of the boat, there was this comradeship, that the correspondent, for instance, who had been taught to be cynical of men, knew even at the time was the best experience of his life. But no one said that it was so. No one mentioned it.

"I wish we had a sail," remarked the captain. "We might try my overcoat on the end of an oar, and give you two boys a chance to rest." So the cook and the correspondent held the mast and spread wide the overcoat; the oiler steered; and the little boat made good way with her new rig. Sometimes the oiler had to scull sharply to keep a sea from breaking into the boat, but otherwise sailing was a success.

Meanwhile the lighthouse had been growing slowly larger. It had now almost assumed colour, and appeared like a little grey shadow on the sky. The man at the oars could not be prevented from turning his head rather often to try for a glimpse of this little grey shadow.

At last, from the top of each wave, the men in the tossing boat could see land. Even as the lighthouse was an upright shadow on the sky, this land seemed but a long black shadow on the sea. It certainly was thinner than paper. "We must be about opposite New Smyrna,"[2] said the cook, who had coasted this shore often in schooners. "Captain, by the way, I believe they abandoned that life-saving station there about a year ago."

---

1. *Sèvres*, a famous French manufactory of porcelain and a museum of ceramics.
2. *New Smyrna* (New Smyrna Beach), a city on the eastern coast of Florida, 15 miles south of Daytona Beach.

"Did they?" said the captain.

The wind slowly died away. The cook and the correspondent were not now obliged to slave in order to hold high the oar. But the waves continued their old impetuous swooping at the dinghy, and the little craft, no longer under way, struggled woundily over them. The oiler or the correspondent took the oars again.

Shipwrecks are apropos of nothing. If men could only train for them and have them occur when the men had reached pink condition, there would be less drowning at sea. Of the four in the dinghy none had slept any time worth mentioning for two days and two nights previous to embarking in the dinghy, and in the excitement of clambering about the deck of a foundering ship they had also forgotten to eat heartily.

For these reasons, and for others, neither the oiler nor the correspondent was fond of rowing at this time. The correspondent wondered ingenuously how in the name of all that was sane could there be people who thought it amusing to row a boat. It was not an amusement; it was a diabolical punishment, and even a genius of mental aberrations could never conclude that it was anything but a horror to the muscles and a crime against the back. He mentioned to the boat in general how the amusement of rowing struck him, and the weary-faced oiler smiled in full sympathy. Previously to the foundering, by the way, the oiler had worked a double watch in the engine-room of the ship.

"Take her easy now, boys," said the captain. "Don't spend yourselves. If we have to run a surf you'll need all your strength, because we'll sure have to swim for it. Take your time."

Slowly the land arose from the sea. From a black line it became a line of black and a line of white—trees and sand. Finally the captain said that he could make out a house on the shore. "That's the house of refuge, sure," said the cook. "They'll see us before long, and come out after us."

The distant lighthouse reared high. "The keeper ought to be able to make us out now, if he's looking through a glass," said the captain. "He'll notify the life-saving people."

"None of those other boats could have got ashore to give word of this wreck," said the oiler, in a low voice, "else the life-boat would be out hunting us."

Slowly and beautifully the land loomed out of the sea. The wind came again. It had veered from the north-east to the south-east. Finally a new sound struck the ears of the men in the boat. It was the low thunder of the surf on the shore. "We'll never be able to make the lighthouse now," said the captain. "Swing her head a little more north, Billie."

"A little more north, sir," said the oiler.

Whereupon the little boat turned her nose once more down the wind, and all but the oarsman watched the shore grow. Under the influence of this expansion doubt and direful apprehension were leaving the minds of the men. The management of the boat was still most absorbing, but it could not prevent a quiet cheerfulness. In an hour, perhaps, they would be ashore.

Their backbones had become thoroughly used to balancing in the boat, and they now rode this wild colt of a dinghy like circus men. The correspondent thought that he had been drenched to the skin, but happening to feel in the top pocket of his coat, he found therein eight cigars. Four of them were soaked with sea-water; four were perfectly scatheless. After a search, somebody produced three dry matches; and thereupon the four waifs rode impudently in their little boat and, with an assurance of an impending rescue shining in their eyes, puffed at the big cigars, and judged well and ill of all men. Everybody took a drink of water.

IV

"Cook," remarked the captain, "there don't seem to be any signs of life about your house of refuge."

"No," replied the cook. "Funny they don't see us!"

A broad stretch of lowly coast lay before the eyes of the men. It was of low dunes topped with dark vegetation. The roar of the surf was plain, and sometimes they could see the white lip of a wave as it spun up the beach. A tiny house was blocked out black upon the sky. Southward, the slim lighthouse lifted its little grey length.

Tide, wind, and waves were swinging the dinghy northward. "Funny they don't see us," said the men.

The surf's roar was here dulled, but its tone was nevertheless thunderous and mighty. As the boat swam over the great rollers the men sat listening to this roar. "We'll swamp sure," said everybody.

It is fair to say here that there was not a life-saving station within twenty miles in either direction; but the men did not know this fact, and in consequence they made dark and opprobrious remarks concerning the eyesight of the nation's life-savers. Four scowling men sat in the dinghy and surpassed records in the invention of epithets.

"Funny they don't see us."

The light-heartedness of a former time had completely faded. To their sharpened minds it was easy to conjure pictures of all kinds of incompetency and blindness and, indeed, cowardice. There was the shore of the populous land, and it was bitter and bitter to them that from it came no sign.

"Well," said the captain, ultimately, "I suppose we'll have to make a try for ourselves. If we stay out here too long, we'll none of us have strength left to swim after the boat swamps."

And so the oiler, who was at the oars, turned the boat straight for the shore. There was a sudden tightening of muscles. There was some thinking.

"If we don't all get ashore," said the captain—"if we don't all get ashore, I suppose you fellows know where to send news of my finish?"

They then briefly exchanged some addresses and admonitions. As for the reflections of the men, there was a great deal of rage in them. Perchance they might be formulated thus: "If I am going to be drowned—if I am going to be drowned—if I am going to be drowned, why, in the name of the seven mad gods who rule the sea, was I allowed to come thus far and contemplate sand and trees? Was I brought here merely to have my nose dragged away as I was about to nibble the sacred cheese of life? It is preposterous. If this old ninny-woman, Fate, cannot do better than this, she should be deprived of the management of men's fortunes. She is an old hen who knows not her intention. If she has decided to drown me, why did she not do it in the beginning and save me all this trouble? The whole affair is absurd.—But no; she cannot mean to drown me. She dare not drown me. She cannot drown me. Not after all this work." Afterward the man might have had an impulse to shake his fist at the clouds. "Just you drown me now, and then hear what I call you!"

The billows that came at this time were more formidable. They seemed always just about to break and roll over the little boat in a turmoil of foam. There was a preparatory and long growl in the speech of them. No mind unused to the sea would have concluded that the dinghy could ascend these sheer heights in time. The shore was still afar. The

oiler was a wily surfman. "Boys," he said swiftly, "she won't live three minutes more, and we're too far out to swim. Shall I take her to sea again, Captain?"

"Yes; go ahead!" said the captain.

This oiler, by a series of quick miracles and fast and steady oarsmanship, turned the boat in the middle of the surf and took her safely to sea again.

There was a considerable silence as the boat bumped over the furrowed sea to deeper water. Then somebody in gloom spoke: "Well, anyhow, they must have seen us from the shore by now."

The gulls went in slanting flight up the wind toward the grey, desolate east. A squall, marked by dingy clouds and clouds brick-red like smoke from a burning building, appeared from the south-east.

"What do you think of those life-saving people? Ain't they peaches?"

"Funny they haven't seen us."

"Maybe they think we're out here for sport! Maybe they think we're fishin'. Maybe they think we're damned fools."

It was a long afternoon. A changed tide tried to force them southward, but wind and wave said northward. Far ahead, where coast-line, sea, and sky formed their mighty angle, there were little dots which seemed to indicate a city on the shore.

"St. Augustine?"[3]

The captain shook his head. "Too near Mosquito Inlet."

And the oiler rowed, and then the correspondent rowed; then the oiler rowed. It was a weary business. The human back can become the seat of more aches and pains than are registered in books for the composite anatomy of a regiment. It is a limited area, but it can become the theatre of innumerable muscular conflicts, tangles, wrenches, knots, and other comforts.

"Did you ever like to row, Billie?" asked the correspondent.

"No," said the oiler; "hang it!"

When one exchanged the rowing-seat for a place in the bottom of the boat, he suffered a bodily depression that caused him to be careless of everything save an obligation to wiggle one finger. There was cold sea-water swashing to and fro in the boat, and he lay in it. His head, pillowed on a thwart,

---

3. *St. Augustine*, a city in northeastern Florida, on the Atlantic coast, about 65 miles north of New Smyrna Beach.

was within an inch of the swirl of a wave-crest, and sometimes a particularly obstreperous sea came inboard and drenched him once more. But these matters did not annoy him. It is almost certain that if the boat had capsized he would have tumbled comfortably out upon the ocean as if he felt sure that it was a great soft mattress.

"Look! There's a man on the shore!"

"Where?"

"There! See 'im? See 'im?"

"Yes, sure! He's walking along."

"Now he's stopped. Look! He's facing us!"

"He's waving at us!"

"So he is! By thunder!"

"Ah, now we're all right! Now we're all right! There'll be a boat out here for us in half an hour."

"He's going on. He's running. He's going up to that house there."

The remote beach seemed lower than the sea, and it required a searching glance to discern the little black figure. The captain saw a floating stick, and they rowed to it. A bath towel was by some weird chance in the boat, and, tying this on the stick, the captain waved it. The oarsman did not dare turn his head, so he was obliged to ask questions.

"What's he doing now?"

"He's standing still again. He's looking, I think.— There he goes again—toward the house.—Now he's stopped again."

"Is he waving at us?"

"No, not now; he was, though."

"Look! There comes another man!"

"He's running."

"Look at him go, would you!"

"Why, he's on a bicycle. Now he's met the other man. They're both waving at us. Look!"

"There comes something up the beach."

"What the devil is that thing?"

"Why, it looks like a boat."

"Why, certainly, it's a boat."

"No; it's on wheels."

"Yes, so it is. Well, that must be the life-boat. They drag them along shore on a wagon."

"That's the life-boat, sure."

"No, by God, it's—it's an omnibus."

"I tell you it's a life-boat."

"It is not! It's an omnibus. I can see it plain. See? One of these big hotel omnibuses."

"By thunder, you're right. It's an omnibus, sure as fate. What do you suppose they are doing with

an omnibus? Maybe they are going around collecting the life-crew, hey?"

"That's it, likely. Look! There's a fellow waving a little black flag. He's standing on the steps of the omnibus. There come those other two fellows. Now they're all talking together. Look at the fellow with the flag. Maybe he ain't waving it!"

"That ain't a flag, is it? That's his coat. Why, certainly, that's his coat."

"So it is; it's his coat. He's taken it off and is waving it around his head. But would you look at him swing it!"

"Oh, say, there isn't any life-saving station there. That's just a winter-resort hotel omnibus that has brought over some of the boarders to see us drown."

"What's that idiot with the coat mean? What's he signalling, anyhow?"

"It looks as if he were trying to tell us to go north. There must be a life-saving station up there."

"No; he thinks we're fishing. Just giving us a merry hand. See? Ah, there, Willie!"

"Well, I wish I could make something out of those signals. What do you suppose he means?"

"He don't mean anything; he's just playing."

"Well, if he'd just signal us to try the surf again, or to go to sea and wait, or go north, or go south, or go to hell, there would be some reason in it. But look at him! He just stands there and keeps his coat revolving like a wheel. The ass!"

"There come more people."

"Now there's quite a mob. Look! Isn't that a boat?"

"Where? Oh, I see where you mean. No, that's no boat."

"That fellow is still waving his coat."

"He must think we like to see him do that. Why don't he quit it? It don't mean anything."

"I don't know. I think he is trying to make us go north. It must be that there's a life-saving station there somewhere."

"Say, he ain't tired yet. Look at 'im wave!"

"Wonder how long he can keep that up. He's been revolving his coat ever since he caught sight of us. He's an idiot. Why aren't they getting men to bring a boat out? A fishing-boat—one of those big yawls—could come out here all right. Why don't he do something?"

"Oh, it's all right now."

"They'll have a boat out here for us in less than no time, now that they've seen us."

A faint yellow tone came into the sky over the

low land. The shadows on the sea slowly deepened. The wind bore coldness with it, and the men began to shiver.

"Holy smoke!" said one, allowing his voice to express his impious mood, "if we keep on monkeying out here! If we've got to flounder out here all night!"

"Oh, we'll never have to stay here all night! Don't you worry. They've seen us now, and it won't be long before they'll come chasing out after us."

The shore grew dusky. The man waving a coat blended gradually into this gloom, and it swallowed in the same manner the omnibus and the group of people. The spray, when it dashed uproariously over the side, made the voyagers shrink and swear like men who were being branded.

"I'd like to catch the chump who waved the coat. I feel like socking him one, just for luck."

"Why? What did he do?"

"Oh, nothing, but then he seemed so damned cheerful."

In the meantime the oiler rowed, and then the correspondent rowed, and then the oiler rowed. Grey-faced and bowed forward, they mechanically, turn by turn, plied the leaden oars. The form of the lighthouse had vanished from the southern horizon, but finally a pale star appeared, just lifting from the sea. The streaked saffron in the west passed before the all-merging darkness, and the sea to the east was black. The land had vanished, and was expressed only by the low and drear thunder of the surf.

"If I am going to be drowned—if I am going to be drowned—if I am going to be drowned, why, in the name of the seven mad gods who rule the sea, was I allowed to come thus far and contemplate sand and trees? Was I brought here merely to have my nose dragged away as I was about to nibble the sacred cheese of life?"

The patient captain, drooped over the water-jar, was sometimes obliged to speak to the oarsman.

"Keep her head up! Keep her head up!"

"Keep her head up, sir." The voices were weary and low.

This was surely a quiet evening. All save the oarsman lay heavily and listlessly in the boat's bottom. As for him, his eyes were just capable of noting the tall black waves that swept forward in a most sinister silence, save for an occasional subdued growl of a crest.

The cook's head was on a thwart, and he looked without interest at the water under his nose. He was deep in other scenes. Finally he spoke. "Billie," he murmured, dreamfully, "what kind of pie do you like best?"

V

"Pie!" said the oiler and the correspondent, agitatedly. "Don't talk about those things, blast you!"

"Well," said the cook, "I was just thinking about ham sandwiches and—"

A night on the sea in an open boat is a long night. As darkness settled finally, the shine of the light, lifting from the sea in the south, changed to full gold. On the northern horizon a new light appeared, a small bluish gleam on the edge of the waters. These two lights were the furniture of the world. Otherwise there was nothing but waves.

Two men huddled in the stern, and distances were so magnificent in the dinghy that the rower was enabled to keep his feet partly warm by thrusting them under his companions. Their legs indeed extended far under the rowing-seat until they touched the feet of the captain forward. Sometimes, despite the efforts of the tired oarsman, a wave came piling into the boat, an icy wave of the night, and the chilling water soaked them anew. They would twist their bodies for a moment and groan, and sleep the dead sleep once more, while the water in the boat gurgled about them as the craft rocked.

The plan of the oiler and the correspondent was for one to row until he lost the ability, and then arouse the other from his sea-water couch in the bottom of the boat.

The oiler plied the oars until his head drooped forward and the overpowering sleep blinded him; and he rowed yet afterward. Then he touched a man in the bottom of the boat, and called his name. "Will you spell me for a little while?" he said, meekly.

"Sure, Billie," said the correspondent, awaking and dragging himself to a sitting position. They exchanged places carefully, and the oiler, cuddling down in the sea-water at the cook's side, seemed to go to sleep instantly.

The particular violence of the sea had ceased. The waves came without snarling. The obligation of the man at the oars was to keep the boat headed so that the tilt of the rollers would not capsize her, and to preserve her from filling when the crests rushed past. The black waves were silent and hard to be seen in the darkness. Often one was almost upon the boat before the oarsman was aware.

In a low voice the correspondent addressed the captain. He was not sure that the captain was awake, although this iron man seemed to be always awake. "Captain, shall I keep her making for that light north, sir?"

The same steady voice answered him. "Yes. Keep it about two points[4] off the port bow."

The cook had tied a life-belt around himself in order to get even the warmth which this clumsy cork contrivance could donate, and he seemed almost stove-like when a rower, whose teeth invariably chattered wildly as soon as he ceased his labour, dropped down to sleep.

The correspondent, as he rowed, looked down at the two men sleeping underfoot. The cook's arm was around the oiler's shoulders, and, with their fragmentary clothing and haggard faces, they were the babes of the sea—a grotesque rendering of the old babes in the wood.

Later he must have grown stupid at his work, for suddenly there was a growling of water, and a crest came with a roar and a swash into the boat, and it was a wonder that it did not set the cook afloat in his life-belt. The cook continued to sleep, but the oiler sat up, blinking his eyes and shaking with the new cold.

"Oh, I'm awful sorry, Billie," said the correspondent, contritely.

"That's all right, old boy," said the oiler, and lay down again and was asleep.

Presently it seemed that even the captain dozed, and the correspondent thought that he was the one man afloat on all the oceans. The wind had a voice as it came over the waves, and it was sadder than the end.

There was a long, loud swishing astern of the boat, and a gleaming trail of phosphorescence, like blue flame, was furrowed on the black waters. It might have been made by a monstrous knife.

Then there came a stillness, while the correspondent breathed with open mouth and looked at the sea.

Suddenly there was another swish and another long flash of bluish light, and this time it was alongside the boat, and might almost been reached with an oar. The correspondent saw an enormous fin speed like a shadow through the water, hurling the crystalline spray and leaving the long glowing trail.

The correspondent looked over his shoulder at the captain. His face was hidden, and he seemed to be asleep. He looked at the babes of the sea. They certainly were asleep. So, being bereft of sympathy, he leaned a little way to one side and swore softly into the sea.

But the thing did not then leave the vicinity of the boat. Ahead or astern, on one side or the other, at intervals long or short, fled the long sparkling streak, and there was to be heard the *whirroo* of the dark fin. The speed and power of the thing was greatly to be admired. It cut the water like a gigantic and keen projectile.

The presence of this biding thing did not affect the man with the same horror that it would if he had been a picnicker. He simply looked at the sea dully and swore in an undertone.

Nevertheless, it is true that he did not wish to be alone with the thing. He wished one of his companions to awake by chance and keep him company with it. But the captain hung motionless over the water-jar, and the oiler and the cook in the bottom of the boat were plunged in slumber.

VI

"If I am going to be drowned—if I am going to be drowned—if I am going to be drowned, why, in the name of the seven mad gods who rule the sea, was I allowed to come thus far and contemplate sand and trees?"

During this dismal night, it may be remarked that a man would conclude that it was really the intention of the seven mad gods to drown him, despite the abominable injustice of it. For it was certainly an abominable injustice to drown a man who had worked so hard, so hard. The man felt it would be a crime most unnatural. Other people had drowned at sea since galleys swarmed with painted sails, but still—

When it occurs to a man that nature does not regard him as important, and that she feels she would not maim the universe by disposing of him, he at

---

4. *two points*, two compass points or 22.5° to the left.

first wishes to throw bricks at the temple, and he hates deeply the fact that there are no bricks and no temples. Any visible expression of nature would surely be pelleted with his jeers.

Then, if there be no tangible thing to hoot, he feels, perhaps, the desire to confront a personification and indulge in pleas, bowed to one knee, and with hands supplicant, saying, "Yes, but I love myself."

A high cold star on a winter's night is the word he feels that she says to him. Thereafter he knows the pathos of his situation.

The men in the dinghy had not discussed these matters, but each had, no doubt, reflected upon them in silence and according to his mind. There was seldom any expression upon their faces save the general one of complete weariness. Speech was devoted to the business of the boat.

To chime the notes of his emotion, a verse mysteriously entered the correspondent's head. He had even forgotten that he had forgotten this verse, but it suddenly was in his mind.

A soldier of the Legion[5] lay dying in Algiers;
There was lack of woman's nursing, there was dearth
of woman's tears;
But a comrade stood beside him, and he took that
comrade's hand,
And he said, "I never more shall see my own, my
native land."

In his childhood the correspondent had been made acquainted with the fact that a soldier of the Legion lay dying in Algiers, but he had never regarded the fact as important. Myriads of his schoolfellows had informed him of the soldier's plight, but the dinning had naturally ended by making him perfectly indifferent. He had never considered it his affair that a soldier of the Legion lay dying in Algiers, nor had it appeared to him as a matter for sorrow. It was less to him than the breaking of a pencil's point.

Now, however, it quaintly came to him as a human, living thing. It was no longer merely a picture of a few throes in the breast of a poet, meanwhile drinking tea and warming his feet at the grate; it was an actuality—stern, mournful, and fine.

The correspondent plainly saw the soldier. He lay on the sand with his feet out straight and still. While his pale left hand was upon his chest in an attempt to thwart the going of his life, the blood came between his fingers. In the far Algerian distance, a city of low square forms was set against a sky that was faint with the last sunset hues. The correspondent, plying the oars and dreaming of the slow and slower movements of the lips of the soldier, was moved by a profound and perfectly impersonal comprehension. He was sorry for the soldier of the Legion who lay dying in Algiers.

The thing which had followed the boat and waited had evidently grown bored at the delay. There was no longer to be heard the slash of the cutwater, and there was no longer the flame of the long trail. The light in the north still glimmered, but it was apparently no nearer to the boat. Sometimes the boom of the surf rang in the correspondent's ears, and he turned the craft seaward then and rowed harder. Southward, some one had evidently built a watch-fire on the beach. It was too low and too far to be seen, but it made a shimmering, roseate reflection upon the bluff in back of it, and this could be discerned from the boat. The wind came stronger, and sometimes a wave suddenly raged out like a mountain cat, and there was to be seen the sheen and sparkle of a broken crest.

The captain, in the bow, moved on his water-jar and sat erect. "Pretty long night," he observed to the correspondent. He looked at the shore. "Those life-saving people take their time."

"Did you see that shark playing around?"

"Yes, I saw him. He was a big fellow, all right."

"Wish I had known you were awake."

Later the correspondent spoke into the bottom of the boat. "Billie!" There was a slow and gradual disentanglement. "Billie, will you spell me?"

"Sure," said the oiler.

As soon as the correspondent touched the cold, comfortable sea-water in the bottom of the boat and had huddled close to the cook's life-belt he was deep in sleep, despite the fact that his teeth played all the popular airs. This sleep was so good to him that it was but a moment before he heard a voice call his name in a tone that demonstrated the last stages of exhaustion. "Will you spell me?"

"Sure, Billie."

The light in the north had mysteriously vanished, but the correspondent took his course from the wide-awake captain.

---

5. *the Legion*, the French Foreign Legion.

Later in the night they took the boat farther out to sea, and the captain directed the cook to take one oar at the stern and keep the boat facing the seas. He was to call out if he should hear the thunder of the surf. This plan enabled the oiler and the correspondent to get respite together. "We'll give those boys a chance to get into shape again," said the captain. They curled down and, after a few preliminary chatterings and trembles, slept once more the dead sleep. Neither knew they had bequeathed to the cook the company of another shark, or perhaps the same shark.

As the boat caroused on the waves, spray occasionally bumped over the side and gave them a fresh soaking, but this had no power to break their repose. The ominous slash of the wind and the water affected them as it would have affected mummies.

"Boys," said the cook, with the notes of every reluctance in his voice, "she's drifted in pretty close. I guess one of you had better take her to sea again." The correspondent, aroused, heard the crash of the toppled crests.

As he was rowing, the captain gave him some whisky-and-water, and this steadied the chills out of him. "If I ever get ashore and anybody shows me even a photograph of an oar—"

At last there was a short conversation.

"Billie!—Billie, will you spell me?"

"Sure," said the oiler.

VII

When the correspondent again opened his eyes, the sea and the sky were each of the grey hue of the dawning. Later, carmine and gold was painted upon the waters. The morning appeared finally, in its splendour, with a sky of pure blue, and the sunlight flamed on the tips of the waves.

On the distant dunes were set many little black cottages, and a tall white windmill reared above them. No man, nor dog, nor bicycle appeared on the beach. The cottages might have formed a deserted village.

The voyagers scanned the shore. A conference was held in the boat. "Well," said the captain, "if no help is coming, we might better try a run through the surf right away. If we stay out here much longer we will be too weak to do anything for ourselves at all." The others silently acquiesced in this reasoning. The boat was headed for the beach. The correspondent wondered if none ever ascended the tall wind-tower, and if then they never looked seaward. This tower was a giant, standing with its back to the plight of the ants. It represented in a degree, to the correspondent, the serenity of nature amid the struggles of the individual—nature in the wind, and nature in the vision of men. She did not seem cruel to him then, nor beneficent, nor treacherous, nor wise. But she was indifferent, flatly indifferent. It is, perhaps, plausible that a man in this situation, impressed with the unconcern of the universe, should see the innumerable flaws of his life, and have them taste wickedly in his mind, and wish for another chance. A distinction between right and wrong seems absurdly clear to him, then, in this new ignorance of the grave-edge, and he understands that if he were given another opportunity he would mend his conduct and his words, and be better and brighter during an introduction or at a tea.

"Now, boys," said the captain, "she is going to swamp sure. All we can do is to work her in as far as possible, and then when she swamps, pile out and scramble for the beach. Keep cool now, and don't jump until she swamps sure."

The oiler took the oars. Over his shoulders he scanned the surf. "Captain," he said, "I think I'd better bring her about and keep her head-on to the seas and back her in."

"All right, Billie," said the captain. "Back her in." The oiler swung the boat then, and, seated in the stern, the cook and the correspondent were obliged to look over their shoulders to contemplate the lonely and indifferent shore.

The monstrous inshore rollers heaved the boat high until the men were again enabled to see the white sheets of water scudding up the slanted beach. "We won't get in very close," said the captain. Each time a man could wrest his attention from the rollers, he turned his glance toward the shore, and in the expression of the eyes during this contemplation there was a singular quality. The correspondent, observing the others, knew that they were not afraid, but the full meaning of their glances was shrouded.

As for himself, he was too tired to grapple fundamentally with the fact. He tried to coerce his mind into thinking of it, but the mind was dominated at this time by the muscles, and the muscles said they did not care. It merely occurred to him that if he should drown it would be a shame.

There were no hurried words, no pallor, no plain agitation. The men simply looked at the shore. "Now, remember to get well clear of the boat when you jump," said the captain.

Seaward the crest of a roller suddenly fell with a thunderous crash, and the long white comber came roaring down upon the boat.

"Steady now," said the captain. The men were silent. They turned their eyes from the shore to the comber and waited. The boat slid up the incline, leaped at the furious top, bounced over it, and swung down the long back of the wave. Some water had been shipped, and the cook bailed it out.

But the next crest crashed also. The tumbling, boiling flood of white water caught the boat and whirled it almost perpendicular. Water swarmed in from all sides. The correspondent had his hands on the gunwale at this time, and when the water entered at that place he swiftly withdrew his fingers, as if he objected to wetting them.

The little boat, drunken with this weight of water, reeled and snuggled deeper into the sea.

"Bail her out, cook! Bail her out!" said the captain.

"All right, Captain," said the cook.

"Now, boys, the next one will do for us sure," said the oiler. "Mind to jump clear of the boat."

The third wave moved forward, huge, furious, implacable. It fairly swallowed the dinghy, and almost simultaneously the men tumbled into the sea. A piece of life-belt had lain in the bottom of the boat, and as the correspondent went overboard he held this to his chest with his left hand.

The January water was icy, and he reflected immediately that it was colder than he had expected to find it off the coast of Florida. This appeared to his dazed mind as a fact important enough to be noted at the time. The coldness of the water was sad; it was tragic. This fact was somehow mixed and confused with his opinion of his own situation, so that it seemed almost a proper reason for tears. The water was cold.

When he came to the surface he was conscious of little but the noisy water. Afterward he saw his companions in the sea. The oiler was ahead in the race. He was swimming strongly and rapidly. Off to the correspondent's left, the cook's great white and corked back bulged out of the water; and in the rear the captain was hanging with his one good hand to the keel of the overturned dinghy.

There is a certain immovable quality to a shore, and the correspondent wondered at it amid the confusion of the sea.

It seemed also very attractive; but the correspondent knew that it was a long journey, and he paddled leisurely. The piece of life-preserver lay under him, and sometimes he whirled down the incline of a wave as if he were on a hand-sled.

But finally he arrived at a place in the sea where travel was beset with difficulty. He did not pause swimming to inquire what manner of current had caught him, but there his progress ceased. The shore was set before him like a bit of scenery on a stage, and he looked at it and understood with his eyes each detail of it.

As the cook passed, much farther to the left, the captain was calling to him, "Turn over on your back, cook! Turn over on your back and use the oar."

"All right, sir." The cook turned on his back, and, paddling with an oar, went ahead as if he were a canoe.

Presently the boat also passed to the left of the correspondent, with the captain clinging with one hand to the keel. He would have appeared like a man raising himself to look over a board fence if it were not for the extraordinary gymnastics of the boat. The correspondent marvelled that the captain could still hold to it.

They passed on nearer to shore—the oiler, the cook, the captain—and following them went the water-jar, bouncing gaily over the seas.

The correspondent remained in the grip of this strange new enemy—a current. The shore, with its white slope of sand and its green bluff topped with little silent cottages, was spread like a picture before him. It was very near to him then, but he was impressed as one who, in a gallery, looks at a scene from Brittany or Algiers.

He thought: "I am going to drown? Can it be possible? Can it be possible? Can it be possible?" Perhaps an individual must consider his own death to be the final phenomenon of nature.

But later a wave perhaps whirled him out of this small deadly current, for he found suddenly that he could again make progress toward the shore. Later still he was aware that the captain, clinging with one hand to the keel of the dinghy, had his face turned away from the shore and toward him, and was calling his name. "Come to the boat! Come to the boat!"

In his struggle to reach the captain and the boat,

he reflected that when one gets properly wearied drowning must really be a comfortable arrangement —a cessation of hostilities accompanied by a large degree of relief; and he was glad of it, for the main thing in his mind for some moments had been horror of the temporary agony. He did not wish to be hurt.

Presently he saw a man running along the shore. He was undressing with most remarkable speed. Coat, trousers, shirt, everything flew magically off him.

"Come to the boat!" called the captain.

"All right, Captain." As the correspondent paddled, he saw the captain let himself down to bottom and leave the boat. Then the correspondent performed his one little marvel of the voyage. A large wave caught him and flung him with ease and supreme speed completely over the boat and far beyond it. It struck him even then as an event in gymnastics and a true miracle of the sea. An overturned boat in the surf is not a plaything to a swimming man.

The correspondent arrived in water that reached only to his waist, but his condition did not enable him to stand for more than a moment. Each wave knocked him into a heap, and the undertow pulled at him.

Then he saw the man who had been running and undressing, and undressing and running, come bounding into the water. He dragged ashore the cook, and then waded toward the captain; but the captain waved him away and sent him to the correspondent. He was naked—naked as a tree in winter; but a halo was about his head, and he shone like a saint. He gave a strong pull, and a long drag, and a bully heave at the correspondent's hand. The correspondent, schooled in the minor formulæ, said, "Thanks, old man." But suddenly the man cried, "What's that?" He pointed a swift finger. The correspondent said, "Go."

In the shallows, face downward, lay the oiler. His forehead touched sand that was periodically, between each wave, clear of the sea.

The correspondent did not know all that transpired afterward. When he achieved safe ground he fell, striking the sand with each particular part of his body. It was as if he had dropped from a roof, but the thud was grateful to him.

It seemed that instantly the beach was populated with men with blankets, clothes, and flasks, and women with coffee-pots and all the remedies sacred to their minds. The welcome of the land to the men from the sea was warm and generous; but a still and dripping shape was carried slowly up the beach, and the land's welcome for it could only be the different and sinister hospitality of the grave.

When it came night, the white waves paced to and fro in the moonlight, and the wind brought the sound of the great sea's voice to the men on the shore, and they felt that they could then be interpreters. ☐

A MAN ADRIFT ON A SLIM SPAR

A man adrift on a slim spar
A horizon smaller than the rim of a bottle
Tented waves rearing lashy dark points
The near whine of froth in circles.
5   God is cold.

The incessant raise and swing of the sea
And growl after growl of crest
The sinkings, green, seething, endless
The upheaval half-completed.
10   God is cold.

The seas are in the hollow of The Hand;
Oceans may be turned to a spray
Raining down through the stars
Because of a gesture of pity toward a babe.
15 Oceans may become grey ashes,
Die with a long moan and a roar
Amid the tumult of the fishes
And the cries of the ships,
Because The Hand beckons the mice.

"A Man Adrift on a Slim Spar" by Stephen Crane from THE COLLECTED POEMS OF STEPHEN CRANE. Published 1930 by Alfred A. Knopf, Inc.

20 A horizon smaller than a doomed assassin's cap,
Inky, surging tumults
A reeling, drunken sky and no sky
A pale hand sliding from a polished spar.
                                    God is cold.

25 The puff of a coat imprisoning air:
A face kissing the water-death
A weary slow sway of a lost hand
And the sea, the moving sea, the sea.
                                    God is cold.

THE LIVID LIGHTNINGS
FLASHED IN THE CLOUDS

The livid lightnings flashed in the clouds;
The leaden thunders crashed.
A worshipper raised his arm.
"Hearken! Hearken! The voice of God!"
5 "Not so," said a man.
"The voice of God whispers in the heart
So softly
That the soul pauses,
Making no noise,
10 And strives for these melodies,
Distant, sighing, like faintest breath,
And all the being is still to hear."

THE WAYFARER

The wayfarer
Perceiving the pathway to truth
Was struck with astonishment.
It was thickly grown with weeds.
5 "Ha," he said,
"I see that none has passed here
In a long time."
Later he saw that each weed
Was a singular knife.
10 "Well," he mumbled at last,
"Doubtless there are other roads."

A NEWSPAPER IS A
COLLECTION OF HALF-INJUSTICES

A newspaper is a collection of half-injustices
Which, bawled by boys from mile to mile,
Spreads its curious opinion
To a million merciful and sneering men,
5 While families cuddle the joys of the fireside
When spurred by tale of dire lone agony.
A newspaper is a court
Where every one is kindly and unfairly tried
By a squalor of honest men.
10 A newspaper is a market
Where wisdom sells its freedom
And melons are crowned by the crowd.
A newspaper is a game
Where his error scores the player victory
15 While another's skill wins death.
A newspaper is a symbol;
It is fetless life's chronicle,
A collection of loud tales
Concentrating eternal stupidities,
20 That in remote ages lived unhaltered,
Roaming through a fenceless world.

"The Livid Lightnings Flashed in the Clouds," "The Wayfarer," and
"A Newspaper Is a Collection of Half-Injustices" by Stephen Crane
from THE POEMS OF STEPHEN CRANE, ed. Joseph Katz.

DISCUSSION

The Open Boat

The stories and novels of Stephen Crane truly mark the complete development of the "modern temper." While elements of Romanticism and Transcendentalism may be found in the poetry of Dickinson and Whitman, and a nostalgic sense of the past and its ideals is present in Clemens' prose, Crane's works are wholly modern in both philosophy and technique.

Crane has been called a Naturalist by many critics. This designation, though admittedly broad, best describes the literary attitudes that arose in the wake of various scientific and social discoveries. Darwin, Freud, and Marx had revolutionized the natural and social sciences. While working in different fields, each of these men expounded— to some degree—the deterministic factors of biology, psychology, and economics. Inherent in their thinking was a decided bias for causality, or the understanding of phenomenon through the studying of cause and effect relationships. Influenced by this type of thinking, naturalist writers depicted events as rigidly determined by the forces of heredity and environment, and tended to describe the world as a bleak and hopeless place. In temperament, the movement was in direct opposition to Romanticism. While Romanticism (and also Transcendentalism) maintained a holy and mystical presence in nature, **Naturalism** stressed the discoverable, deterministic laws of nature. If God exists in the Naturalist writer's world, He is, like nature, cold and indifferent to the plight of the individual.

While Naturalism best describes Crane's philosophy, **Impressionism** and **Symbolism** are the literary techniques that he most often used. Symbolism is the use, in literature, of objects or events to represent something other and beyond themselves, frequently abstract ideas and concepts. A symbol—often an image, metaphor, or simile—suggests referents beyond the actual sensation or figure of speech. The last sentence of the fourth paragraph on page 265C from "The Open Boat" carries symbolic connotations: "It was a thin little oar, and it seemed often ready to snap." This image, other than describing an oar, also suggests the vulnerability of the castaways and their dinghy at the hands of nature, in this case the sea. (Crane makes much use of symbols in his poetry as well as his prose.)

Crane also made use of impressionistic techniques, more often for the overall organization of his material rather than the actual construction of sentences, paragraphs, etc. Impressionism is a mode of writing derived from the painting techniques of the French artists Monet, Degas, Manet, and Renoir. It is a highly personal method in that the author's temperament, or point-of-view, is the basis for organization as well as the selection of details. Rather than present a cold, photographic representation of fact, the author tries to depict an object or event (such as thirty hours in a dinghy) as it personally affected him. Often this means selecting significant details and discarding others so as to suggest the author's impression of the experience. The whole of "The Open Boat" is, in a sense, impressionistic because Crane, the writer, clearly interpreted and selected the facts that Crane, the correspondent, had gathered. In this way Crane utilized impressionistic as well as symbolistic technique in order to express his naturalistic philosophy.

FOR EXPLORATION

The Open Boat
1. What is the significance of the opening sentence? Is it possible that "none of them [would know] the colour of the sky"? Explain.
2. (*a*) Why do the sea gulls seem ". . . somehow gruesome and ominous . . . ," ". . . uncanny and sinister in their unblinking scrutiny . . ."? (*b*) How do they illustrate the precarious situation of the castaways?
3. (*a*) Describe the attitude of the castaways at the conclusion of section III (page C 268). (*b*) Contrast their attitude at the end of this section with their feelings later in section IV. (*c*) What effect does this contrast have on the reader?
4. On page 271 C, section IV, Crane introduces a **refrain** or recurrent statement that appears again later in the story.

Identify this refrain. Metaphorically, what are men and women to ". . . the seven mad gods who rule the sea . . ."?
5. One of the literary techniques used by Crane is the **pathetic fallacy.** (*a*) Cite one or two examples of the pathetic fallacy from the story. (*b*) How is Crane's use of the pathetic fallacy "impressionistic"? Explain. (*c*) How is Crane's use of this technique different from Lanier's in the poem "The Cloud" (pages C 212–213 C)?
6. In Section VI, pages C 272–273 C, the correspondent ponders nature and its relationship to the individual. Contrast Crane's understanding of this question with that of the Transcendentalists.

7. "This tower was a giant, standing with its back to the plight of the ants. It represented in a degree, to the correspondent, the serenity of nature amid the struggles of the individual—nature in the wind, and nature in the vision of men. She did not seem cruel to him then, nor beneficent, nor treacherous, nor wise. But she was indifferent, flatly indifferent." (a) What metaphor does Crane use in this passage to describe humanity? (b) Write a short essay of no more than three paragraphs in which you attack or defend the ideas expressed regarding the human condition.
8. Irony is a term used to describe any situation where two meanings or interpretations are at odds. In **verbal irony** the actual meaning of a statement is different, often opposite, from what the statement literally says. **Irony of situation** refers to an occurrence which is contrary to what is expected or appropriate. (a) Explain why the oiler's death is ironic. Cite examples in support of your answer. (b) What type of irony does Crane use in the death of the oiler, verbal irony or irony of situation?
9. Explain why the description, near the conclusion of the story, of the water-jar, ". . . bouncing gaily over the seas" is symbolic.
10. What is the meaning of the last sentence of the story? Why would the survivors become "interpreters"? What would they interpret? For whom?

FOR EXPLORATION

Poetry
1. (a) Whose "Hand" does the poet refer to in line 11 of "A Man Adrift on a Slim Spar"? (b) Cite examples of the pathetic fallacy from this poem. (c) Give two metaphors for humanity that appear in both "The Open Boat" and this poem. (d) How is the poem "A Man Adrift on a Slim Spar" imagistic?
2. A critic has said that while Crane's story "The Open Boat" is an impressionistic abstraction of an actual incident, the poem "A Man Adrift on a Slim Spar" is, in truth, an abstraction of the story. In a short essay, compare and contrast Crane's view of the human condition as seen in these two separate works. Is the critic correct? Explain.
3. Compare the religious attitudes of the worshiper in "The Livid Lightnings Flashed in the Clouds" with those of the correspondent (quoted above in question 7). How do these attitudes relate to Crane's use of the pathetic fallacy?
4. Explain the use of analogy in the poem "The Wayfarer." What is the poet saying about "the pathway to truth"?
5. In "A Newspaper Is a Collection of Half-Injustices," what does Crane believe a newspaper symbolizes? Do you agree or disagree with the poet's evaluation? Explain.

Stephen Crane   1871 / 1900

Stephen Crane was twenty-eight when he died of tuberculosis, his health never fully restored after his ordeal in the dinghy of the sunk *Commodore*. But in the few years available to him he wrote two exceptional novels, some intriguing poetry, and a number of excellent short stories (William Dean Howells once called "The Open Boat" the finest short story in English.) Crane attended college for two semesters, in his final semester spending more time on newspaper reporting and baseball than on his studies. The next five years he lived in New York at the old Art Students League on East Twenty-third Street. He was often hungry and ill. What little money he had came from occasional free-lance newspaper work. His beat was the Bowery saloons and the slums that surrounded him.

He brought the grim realities around him alive in his first book *Maggie: A Girl of the Streets* (1893), the first American naturalist novel. The story it told was so harsh and sordid that he was unable to find a publisher. Crane borrowed $700 and printed it himself. He was able to sell only a limited number of copies and the rest sat in his room. When coal ran low the books were used to keep the fire going.

Two years later Crane published his major achievement *The Red Badge of Courage*, a remarkably real war story considering that the author had never experienced combat. The book sold in enormous quantity. And, though it earned Crane less than $100, it made him a celebrity. He was offered work as a correspondent, took a trip out west, and then, due to the subject of his celebrated novel, seemed a logical choice for war correspondent. He was on his way to cover insurrectionist activity in Cuba when the *Commodore* sank. He later covered the Greco-Turkish war and the Spanish-American war in Cuba for the American newspaper publisher, William Randolph Hearst. He lived his last years in England, the subject of malicious and false gossip at home.

Edith Wharton

1862 / 1937

A JOURNEY

As she lay in her berth, staring at the shadows overhead, the rush of the wheels was in her brain, driving her deeper and deeper into circles of wakeful lucidity. The sleeping car had sunk into its night silence. Through the wet windowpane she watched the sudden lights, the long stretches of hurrying blackness. Now and then she turned her head and looked through the opening in the hangings at her husband's curtains across the aisle. . . .

She wondered restlessly if he wanted anything and if she could hear him if he called. His voice had grown very weak within the last months and it irritated him when she did not hear. This irritability, this increasing childish petulance seemed to give expression to their imperceptible estrangement. Like two faces looking at one another through a sheet of glass they were close together, almost touching, but they could not hear or feel each other: the conductivity between them was broken. She, at least, had this sense of separation, and she fancied sometimes that she saw it reflected in the look with which he supplemented his failing words. Doubtless the fault was hers. She was too impenetrably healthy to be touched by the irrelevancies of disease. Her self-reproachful tenderness was tinged with the sense of his irrationality: she had a vague feeling that there was a purpose in his helpless tyrannies. The suddenness of the change had found her so unprepared. A year ago their pulses had beat to one robust measure; both had the same prodigal confidence in an exhaustless future. Now their energies no longer kept step: hers still bounded ahead of life, pre-empting unclaimed regions of hope and activity, while his lagged behind, vainly struggling to overtake her.

When they married, she had such arrears of living to make up: her days had been as bare as the whitewashed schoolroom where she forced innutritious facts upon reluctant children. His coming had broken in on the slumber of circumstance, widening the present till it became the encloser of remotest chances. But imperceptibly the horizon narrowed. Life had a grudge against her: she was never to be allowed to spread her wings.

At first the doctors had said that six weeks of mild air would set him right; but when he came back this assurance was explained as having of course included a winter in a dry climate. They gave up their pretty house, storing the wedding presents and new furniture, and went to Colorado. She had hated it there from the first. Nobody knew her or cared about her; there was no one to wonder at the good match she had made, or to envy her the new dresses and the visiting cards which were still a surprise to her. And he kept growing worse. She felt herself beset with difficulties too evasive to be fought by so direct a temperament. She still loved him, of course; but he was gradually, undefinably ceasing to be himself. The man she had married had been strong, active, gently masterful: the male whose pleasure it is to clear a way through the material obstructions of life; but now it was she who was the protector, he who must be shielded from importunities and given his drops or his beef juice though the skies were falling. The routine of the sickroom bewildered her; this punctual administering of medicine seemed as idle as some uncomprehended religious mummery.

There were moments, indeed, when warm gushes of pity swept away her instinctive resentment of his condition, when she still found his old self in his eyes as they groped for each other through the dense medium of his weakness. But these moments had grown rare. Sometimes he frightened her: his sunken expressionless face seemed that of a stranger; his voice was weak and hoarse; his thin-lipped smile a mere muscular contraction. Her hand avoided his damp soft skin, which had lost the familiar roughness of health: she caught herself furtively watching him as she might have watched a strange animal. It frightened her to feel that this was the man she loved; there were hours when to tell him what she suffered seemed the one escape from her fears. But in general she judged herself more leniently, reflecting that she had perhaps been too long alone with him, and that she would feel differently when they were at home again, surrounded by her robust and buoyant family. How she had rejoiced when the doctors at last gave their consent to his going home! She knew, of course,

"A Journey" is reprinted by permission of Charles Scribner's Sons from THE GREATER INCLINATION by Edith Wharton (1899).

what the decision meant; they both knew. It meant that he was to die; but they dressed the truth in hopeful euphemisms, and at times, in the joy of preparation, she really forgot the purpose of their journey, and slipped into an eager allusion to next year's plans.

At last the day of leaving came. She had a dreadful fear that they would never get away; that somehow at the last moment he would fail her; that the doctors held one of their accustomed treacheries in reserve; but nothing happened. They drove to the station, he was installed in a seat with a rug over his knees and a cushion at his back, and she hung out of the window waving unregretful farewells to the acquaintances she had really never liked till then.

The first twenty-four hours had passed off well. He revived a little and it amused him to look out of the window and to observe the humors of the car. The second day he began to grow weary and to chafe under the dispassionate stare of the freckled child with the lump of chewing gum. She had to explain to the child's mother that her husband was too ill to be disturbed: a statement received by that lady with a resentment visibly supported by the maternal sentiment of the whole car. . . .

That night he slept badly and the next morning his temperature frightened her: she was sure he was growing worse. The day passed slowly, punctuated by the small irritations of travel. Watching his tired face, she traced in its contractions every rattle and jolt of the train, till her own body vibrated with sympathetic fatigue. She felt the others observing him too, and hovered restlessly between him and the line of interrogative eyes. The freckled child hung about him like a fly; offers of candy and picture books failed to dislodge her: she twisted one leg around the other and watched him imperturbably. The porter, as he passed, lingered with vague proffers of help, probably inspired by philanthropic passengers swelling with the sense that "something ought to be done"; and one nervous man in a skull cap was audibly concerned as to the possible effect on his wife's health.

The hours dragged on in a dreary inoccupation. Towards dusk she sat down beside him and he laid his hand on hers. The touch startled her. He seemed to be calling her from far off. She looked at him helplessly and his smile went through her like a physical pang.

"Are you very tired?" she asked.

"No, not very."

"We'll be there soon now."

"Yes, very soon."

"This time tomorrow—"

He nodded and they sat silent. When she had put him to bed and crawled into her own berth she tried to cheer herself with the thought that in less than twenty-four hours they would be in New York. Her people would all be at the station to meet her—she pictured their round unanxious faces pressing through the crowd. She only hoped they would not tell him too loudly that he was looking splendidly and would be all right in no time: the subtler sympathies developed by long contact with suffering were making her aware of a certain coarseness of texture in the family sensibilities.

Suddenly she thought she heard him call. She parted the curtains and listened. No, it was only a man snoring at the other end of the car. His snores had a greasy sound, as though they passed through tallow. She lay down and tried to sleep. . . . Had she not heard him move? She started up trembling. . . . The silence frightened her more than any sound. He might not be able to make her hear—he might be calling her now. . . . What made her think of such things? It was merely the familiar tendency of an overtired mind to fasten itself on the most intolerable chance within the range of its forebodings. . . . Putting her head out, she listened: but she could not distinguish his breathing from that of the other pairs of lungs about her. She longed to get up and look at him, but she knew the impulse was a mere vent for her restlessness, and the fear of disturbing him restrained her. . . . The regular movement of his curtain reassured her, she knew not why; she remembered that he had wished her a cheerful good night; and the sheer inability to endure her fears a moment longer made her put them from her with an effort of her whole sound-tired body. She turned on her side and slept.

She sat up stiffly, staring out at the dawn. The train was rushing through a region of bare hillocks huddled against a lifeless sky. It looked like the first day of creation. The air of the car was close, and she pushed up her window to let in the keen wind. Then she looked at her watch: it was seven o'clock, and soon the people about her would be stirring. She slipped into her clothes, smoothed her disheveled hair and crept to the dressing room. When she had washed her face and adjusted her dress she felt more hopeful. It was always a struggle for her not to be cheerful in the morning. Her cheeks burned deliciously under the coarse towel and the wet hair about her temples broke into strong upward tendrils. Every inch of her was full of life and elasticity. And in ten hours they would be at home!

She stepped to her husband's berth: it was time for him to take his early glass of milk. The window shade was down, and in the dusk of the curtained enclosure she could just see that he lay sideways, with his face away from her. She leaned over him and drew up the shade. As she did so she touched one of his hands. It felt cold. . . .

She bent closer, laying her hand on his arm and calling him by name. He did not move. She spoke again more loudly; she grasped his shoulder and gently shook it. He lay motionless. She caught hold of his hand again: it slipped from her limply, like a dead thing. A dead thing?

Her breath caught. She must see his face. She leaned forward, and hurriedly, shrinkingly, with a sickening reluctance of the flesh, laid her hands on his shoulders and turned him over. His head fell back; his face looked small and smooth; he gazed at her with steady eyes.

She remained motionless for a long time, holding him thus; and they looked at each other. Suddenly she shrank back: the longing to scream, to call out, to fly from him, had almost overpowered her. But a strong hand arrested her. Good God! If it were known that he was dead they would be put off the train at the next station—

In a terrifying flash of remembrance there arose before her a scene she had once witnessed in traveling, when a husband and wife, whose child had died in the train, had been thrust out at some chance station. She saw them standing on the platform with the child's body between them; she had never forgotten the dazed look with which they followed the receding train. And this was what would happen to her. Within the next hour she might find herself on the platform of some strange station, alone with her husband's body. . . . Anything but that! It was too horrible— She quivered like a creature at bay.

As she cowered there, she felt the train moving more slowly. It was coming then—they were approaching a station! She saw again the husband and wife standing on the lonely platform; and with a violent gesture she drew down the shade to hide her husband's face.

Feeling dizzy, she sank down on the edge of the berth, keeping away from his outstretched body, and pulling the curtains close, so that he and she were shut into a kind of sepulchral twilight. She tried to think. At all costs she must conceal the fact that he was dead. But how? Her mind refused to act: she could not plan, combine. She could think of no way but to sit there, clutching the curtains, all day long. . . .

She heard the porter making up her bed; people were beginning to move about the car; the dressing-room door was being opened and shut. She tried to rouse herself. At length with a supreme effort she rose to her feet, stepping into the aisle of the car and drawing the curtains tight behind her. She noticed that they still parted slightly with the motion of the car, and finding a pin in her dress she fastened them together. Now she was safe. She looked round and saw the porter. She fancied he was watching her.

"Ain't he awake yet?" he inquired.

"No," she faltered.

"I got his milk all ready when he wants it. You know you told me to have it for him by seven."

She nodded silently and crept into her seat.

At half-past eight the train reached Buffalo. By this time the other passengers were dressed and the berths had been folded back for the day. The porter, moving to and fro under his burden of sheets and pillows, glanced at her as he passed. At length he said: "Ain't he going to get up? You know we're ordered to make up the berths as early as we can."

She turned cold with fear. They were just entering the station.

"Oh, not yet," she stammered. "Not till he's had his milk. Won't you get it, please?"

"All right. Soon as we start again."

When the train moved on he reappeared with the milk. She took it from him and sat vaguely looking at it: her brain moved slowly from one idea to another, as though they were steppingstones set far apart across a whirling flood. At length she became aware that the porter still hovered expectantly.

"Will I give it to him?" he suggested.

"Oh, no," she cried, rising. "He—he's asleep yet, I think—"

She waited till the porter had passed on; then she unpinned the curtains and slipped behind them. In the semiobscurity her husband's face stared up at her like a marble mask with agate eyes. The eyes were dreadful. She put out her hand and drew down the lids. Then she remembered the glass of milk in her other hand: what was she to do with it? She thought of raising the window and throwing it out; but to do so she would have to lean across his body and bring her face close to his. She decided to drink the milk.

She returned to her seat with the empty glass and after a while the porter came back to get it.

"When'll I fold up his bed?" he asked.

"Oh, not now—not yet; he's ill—he's very ill. Can't you let him stay as he is? The doctor wants him to lie down as much as possible."

He scratched his head. "Well, if he's *really* sick—"

He took the empty glass and walked away, explaining to the passengers that the party behind the curtains was too sick to get up just yet.

She found herself the center of sympathetic eyes. A motherly woman with an intimate smile sat down beside her.

"I'm real sorry to hear your husband's sick. I've had a remarkable amount of sickness in my family and maybe I could assist you. Can I take a look at him?"

"Oh, no—no, please! He mustn't be disturbed."

The lady accepted the rebuff indulgently.

"Well, it's just as you say, of course, but you don't look to me as if you'd had much experience in sickness and I'd have been glad to assist you. What do you generally do when your husband's taken this way?"

"I—I let him sleep."

"Too much sleep ain't any too healthful either. Don't you give him any medicine?"

"Y—yes."

"Don't you wake him to take it?"

"Yes."

"When does he take the next dose?"

"Not for—two hours—"

The lady looked disappointed. "Well, if I was you I'd try giving it oftener. That's what I do with my folks."

After that many faces seemed to press upon her. The passengers were on their way to the dining car, and she was conscious that as they passed down the aisle they glanced curiously at the closed curtains. One lantern-jawed man with prominent eyes stood still and tried to shoot his projecting glance through the division between the folds. The freckled child, returning from breakfast, waylaid the passers with a buttery clutch, saying in a loud whisper, "He's sick";

and once the conductor came by, asking for tickets. She shrank into her corner and looked out of the window at the flying trees and houses, meaningless hieroglyphs of an endlessly unrolled papyrus.

Now and then the train stopped, and the newcomers on entering the car stared in turn at the closed curtains. More and more people seemed to pass—their faces began to blend fantastically with the images surging in her brain. . . .

Later in the day a fat man detached himself from the mist of faces. He had a creased stomach and soft pale lips. As he pressed himself into the seat facing her she noticed that he was dressed in black broadcloth, with a soiled white tie.

"Husband's pretty bad this morning, is he?"

"Yes."

"Dear, dear! Now that's terribly distressing, ain't it?" An apostolic smile revealed his gold-filled teeth. "Of course you know there's no sech thing as sickness. Ain't that a lovely thought? Death itself is but a deloosion of our grosser senses. On'y lay yourself open to the influx of the sperrit, submit yourself passively to the action of the divine force, and disease and dissolution will cease to exist for you. If you could indooce your husband to read this little pamphlet—"

The faces about her again grew indistinct. She had a vague recollection of hearing the motherly lady and the parent of the freckled child ardently disputing the relative advantages of trying several medicines at once, or of taking each in turn; the motherly lady maintaining that the competitive system saved time; the other objecting that you couldn't tell which remedy had effected the cure; their voices went on and on, like bell buoys droning through a fog. . . . The porter came up now and then with questions that she did not understand, but somehow she must have answered since he went away again without repeating them; every two hours the motherly lady reminded her that her husband ought to have his drops; people left the car and others replaced them. . . .

Her head was spinning and she tried to steady herself by clutching at her thoughts as they swept by, but they slipped away from her like bushes on the side of a sheer precipice down which she seemed to be falling. Suddenly her mind grew clear again and she found herself vividly picturing what would happen when the train reached New York. She shuddered as it occurred to her that he would be quite cold and that someone might perceive he had been dead since morning.

She thought hurriedly: "If they see I am not surprised they will suspect something. They will ask questions, and if I tell them the truth they won't believe me—no one would believe me! It will be terrible"—and she kept repeating to herself—"I must pretend I don't know. I must pretend I don't know. When they open the curtains I must go up to him quite naturally—and then I must scream!" She had an idea that the scream would be very hard to do.

Gradually new thoughts crowded upon her, vivid and urgent: she tried to separate and restrain them, but they beset her clamorously, like her school children at the end of a hot day, when she was too tired to silence them. Her head grew confused, and she felt a sick fear of forgetting her part, of betraying herself by some unguarded word or look.

"I must pretend I don't know," she went on murmuring. The words had lost their significance, but she repeated them mechanically, as though they had been a magic formula, until suddenly she heard herself saying: "I can't remember, I can't remember!"

Her voice sounded very loud, and she looked about her in terror; but no one seemed to notice that she had spoken.

As she glanced down the car her eye caught the curtains of her husband's berth, and she began to examine the monotonous arabesques woven through their heavy folds. The pattern was intricate and difficult to trace; she gazed fixedly at the curtains and as she did so the thick stuff grew transparent and through it she saw her husband's face—his dead face. She struggled to avert her look, but her eyes refused to move and her head seemed to be held in a vice. At last, with an effort that left her weak and shaking, she turned away; but it was of no use; close in front of her, small and smooth, was her husband's face. It seemed to be suspended in the air between her and the false braids of the woman who sat in front of her. With an uncontrollable gesture she stretched out her hand to push the face away, and suddenly she felt the touch of his smooth skin. She repressed a cry and half started from her seat. The woman with the false braids looked around, and feeling that she must justify her movement in some way she rose and lifted her traveling bag from the opposite seat. She unlocked the bag and looked into it; but the first object her hand met was a small flask of her husband's, thrust there at the last moment, in the haste

of departure. She locked the bag and closed her eyes . . . his face was there again, hanging between her eyeballs and lids like a waxen mask against a red curtain. . . .

She roused herself with a shiver. Had she fainted or slept? Hours seemed to have elapsed; but it was still broad day, and the people about her were sitting in the same attitudes as before.

A sudden sense of hunger made her aware that she had eaten nothing since morning. The thought of food filled her with disgust, but she dreaded a return of faintness, and remembering that she had some biscuits in her bag she took one out and ate it. The dry crumbs choked her, and she hastily swallowed a little brandy from her husband's flask. The burning sensation in her throat acted as a counter-irritant, momentarily relieving the dull ache of her nerves. Then she felt a gently-stealing warmth, as though a soft air fanned her, and the swarming fears relaxed their clutch, receding through the stillness that enclosed her, a stillness soothing as the spacious quietude of a summer day. She slept.

Through her sleep she felt the impetuous rush of the train. It seemed to be life itself that was sweeping her on with headlong inexorable force—sweeping her into darkness and terror, and the awe of unknown days.—Now all at once everything was still—not a sound, not a pulsation. . . . She was dead in her turn, and lay beside him with smooth upstaring face. How quiet it was!—and yet she heard feet coming, the feet of the men who were to carry them away. . . . She could feel too—she felt a sudden prolonged vibration, a series of hard shocks, and then another plunge into darkness: the darkness of death this time—a black whirlwind on which they were both spinning like leaves, in wild uncoiling spirals, with millions and millions of the dead. . . .

She sprang up in terror. Her sleep must have lasted a long time, for the winter day had paled and the lights had been lit. The car was in confusion, and as she regained her self-possession she saw that the passengers were gathering up their wraps and bags. The woman with the false braids had brought from the dressing room a sickly ivy plant in a bottle, and the Christian Scientist was reversing his cuffs. The porter passed down the aisle with his impartial brush. An impersonal figure with a gold-banded cap asked for her husband's ticket. A voice shouted "Baiggage *ex*press!" and she heard the clicking of metal as the passengers handed over their checks.

Presently her window was blocked by an expanse of sooty wall, and the train passed into the Harlem tunnel. The journey was over; in a few minutes she would see her family pushing their joyous way through the throng at the station. Her heart dilated. The worst terror was past. . . .

"We'd better get him up now, hadn't we?" asked the porter, touching her arm.

He had her husband's hat in his hand and was meditatively revolving it under his brush.

She looked at the hat and tried to speak; but suddenly the car grew dark. She flung up her arms, struggling to catch at something, and fell face downward, striking her head against the dead man's berth.

☐

DISCUSSION

A Journey

Edith Wharton's short stories and novels belong to a literary movement called **Realism** that began with Clemens shortly after the end of the Civil War. From roughly 1865–1900—the period of rapid growth, industrialization, and human displacement—this movement was the dominant literary force in America, including such noted writers as Henry James and W. D. Howells.

Howells defined **Realism** as "the truthful treatment of material," or **verisimiltude.** Though this element has always been present to some degree in all American literature from the time of the "planters and Puritans" to the present, it becomes initially apparent in the poetry of Whitman and the works of the generation that followed him. In its broadest sense, **Realism** is the faithful representation in literature of the actual events of life.

Realism arose out of a protest against Romanticism. Its proponents felt that romantic fiction was too idealized, too symmetrical, and therefore, unlike real life. Shunning the cataclysmically tragic and overly heroic events of life that attracted Romantic and Naturalist writers alike, the Realists chose instead to portray the more commonplace. Unlike the Romanticist and Naturalist who seek either physical laws or ideal laws, respectively, in nature or human actions, the Realist is very much concerned with the immediate ethical consequences of everyday life as well as the effects of his art on his audience. Where Crane wished to depict the individual pitched against indifferent nature under circumstances of great stress, Wharton preferred to represent the equally desperate inner conflicts of a woman in a personally tragic yet not unusual situation.

Thus, the Realist writer's usual subject matter is the smaller catastrophes of the bourgeoisie, their themes tending to deal more with peoples' manners and mores. Wharton and James strove through their works to objectively imitate, as closely as possible, the plotless actualities of real life. At Realism's most developed stage, as in Edith Wharton's "A Journey," the writer explores the psychology of the individual, discovering and rendering for the reader his innermost thoughts, anxieties, and dilemmas.

FOR EXPLORATION

1. (*a*) How much time actually elapses in the story? (*b*) Does it seem longer than it really is? Why?
2. The story contains very little action. What then is most of the narrative given to? How is this "realistic"?
3. (*a*) What is the woman's greatest fear throughout the story? Why? (*b*) What is her greatest wish? Why? (*c*) Does this attitude seem callous to you? (*d*) Is it realistic?
4. (*a*) Having kept her composure throughout the entire journey, why does the woman finally collapse? (*b*) What in the porter's actions seems to cause her collapse? Why?
5. List some of the characteristics of Realism that are present in the story.

CREATIVE RESPONSE

Wharton, in many ways, was one of the first women to receive acclaim as well as success as a writer. Discuss in class why it took so long for women to receive recognition as writers and poets. What factors might have contributed to this situation? What social realities made Wharton's success possible while hindering the aspirations of other women who wrote? How has the status of the woman writer changed in the last hundred years? How has it not changed?

EDITH WHARTON 1862 / 1937

Edith Wharton was born into a New York family of wealth and distinction. She was educated by private tutors, spent much of her youth traveling between New York and Europe, and eventually settled in France.

Although her first writings were poems, she finally turned to short stories and novels. She sometimes wrote stories of the supernatural, but she was primarily known as a social satirist who wrote about the New York leisure class. Particularly in her short stories one can see the economy, the symmetry of structure, and the polished subtlety of style that the author commanded.

THE MODERN TEMPER

Then and Now

The Civil War saved the Union from splitting asunder, freed the slaves, and impoverished the South. It is often forgotten how close to defeat the North was on several occasions, and how near to a stunning victory the South. It was, therefore, with a great sigh of relief that the end was welcomed. But there was a feeling also that the nation had passed a critical test, that it had been tried and tested, and had in the process proved its maturity. It was as though the country were an innocent, adolescent youth who, in the war, had demonstrated his manhood, lost his innocence, and attained the wisdom of searing experience. James Russell Lowell expressed something of this feeling in his "Ode Recited at the Harvard Commemoration," written for the war dead:

> Who now shall sneer?
> Who dare again to say we trace
> Our lines to a plebeian race?

In effect, these lines say to Europe: "We have proved ourselves at last."

Lincoln's assassination only a few days after the end of the war plunged the country into a time of both grief and tension. Lincoln had indicated that he would be conciliatory to the defeated South. His death inspired to action those who were vindictive and wanted to grind the South down in revenge for its rebellion. The era of Reconstruction in the South, the era of carpetbaggers (Northerners who went south to exploit) and scalawags (native Southerners who joined in the exploitation), lasted until 1877, when the federal troops were withdrawn and the area reverted to local control and rule. By this time the nation's attention was directed to other matters.

Most important of these no doubt was the explosive growth of business and industry. Symbolic of this growth was the development of the railroads during this period. The thirty-five thousand miles of railroad tracks of 1865 had increased to about two hundred thousand miles by the end of the century. But perhaps more important than quantity of track was the area of the country that it rescued from wilderness. In 1869 the Union Pacific Railroad which, in effect, linked America from the Atlantic to the Pacific oceans, was completed. Walt Whitman was moved to celebrate this event (together with the completion of the Suez Canal and the trans-Atlantic cable,

making three engineering feats that "rounded the globe") in a poem, "Passage to India." He saw the railroad symbolically, as—

> Bridging the three or four thousand miles of land travel,
> Tying the Eastern to the Western sea,
> The road between Europe and Asia.

In brief, the "one world" that we now confront daily was born in this period of frantic building and expansion.

In "Passage to India" Whitman called for a spiritual achievement to parallel the amazing engineering achievements of the age, and he had good reason. The period was a time of great plunder and exploitation, of greedy materialism and political corruption, of financial piracy and labor strife. In short, it was a time of great vitality and extremes. Great fortunes were accumulated and some people went hungry in the growing cities. Immigrants from Europe poured into the country in search of fortune, and found themselves doing the hard labor of building a country out of wilderness.

In a sense, the Civil War and its aftermath gave birth to modern America and to modern literature. Such writers as Walt Whitman, Mark Twain, and Emily Dickinson found the subjects and materials for their works in their own experience and in their own back yards. Walt Whitman proclaimed himself the "poet of America" and conspicuously included "these states" in his poems. Mark Twain found the locale of his greatest works, *Tom Sawyer* and *Huckleberry Finn*, in the area of middle America where he grew up as a boy—Hannibal, Missouri, and the Mississippi River. Emily Dickinson discovered the substance for her fragile poems in the garden next to her house in Amherst and in her living room and kitchen. Each of these writers appeared not so much concerned with concluding and extending something out of the past as with finding and beginning something new for the future. With them we have the origins of the modern literary period that reaches into our own time.

The modern temper of Twain, Whitman, and Dickinson is to be found not only in their substance but in their literary forms and in their astonishing use of language. Twain brought a dimension and kind of humor to the novel that it had not embraced before, Whitman developed and extended the possibilities of free verse, and Emily Dickinson adopted slant rhymes and bizarre syntactical patterns that were new to poetry. But perhaps the greatest innovation these writers made was in language and style. Each in his own way brought the American language—the language of the farms and streets, the language of steamboatmen and Westerners, the language of the New England household and kitchen—into the novels, poems, and essays that Americans were going to read. The language was simple and direct, sometimes slangy, generally native, different in ways both conspicuous and subtle from the "literary" and British language that previous American writers had often used.

The impact of the writers of this period on modern literature is incalculable. A few examples will suggest something of its nature. Ernest Hemingway, who single-handedly set the pattern for the modern prose style, claimed that all modern American literature came from Twain and *Huckleberry Finn*. The English poet W. H. Auden is said to have read Emily Dickinson and then decided to become a poet—and her influence is seen in his poetry. As for Whitman—see the testimony below from Amy Lowell's "Walt Whitman and the New Poetry."

from

WALT WHITMAN AND THE NEW POETRY

Amy Lowell

. . . the moderns, even the modern practitioners of "cadenced verse," with the possible exception of Carl Sandburg, owe very little of their form to Whitman. What they do owe is an attitude, to determine which we must first consider what was this vision of the world that Whitman had. It is not difficult to find out. The whole of *Leaves of Grass* shouts it to us, and he has also explained it in page after page of prose. He hands it to us like a nut wrapped in a shell. The shell is his speech—the nut? Well, as I have said, I doubt whether he himself had ever really seen it. Here is his brief, final summary:

"As long as the States continue to absorb and be dominated by the poetry of the Old World, and remain unsupplied with autochthonous[1] song, to express, vitalize and give color to and define their material and political success, and minister to them distinctively, so long will they stop short of first-class Nationality and remain defective."

Walt Whitman proposed to give them this au-

tochthonous song. He would make a poetry of America, he would make it of the lives of the great even strata of work-people. He would include all activities, all trades, he would be the voice of the whole continent from coast to coast, he would be North, and South, and Middle, he would laud his country and believe in her; nothing should be beneath him, nothing above. It was a magnificent aim, and in great part he did exactly what he set out to do.

He saw that science had changed the face of the world; he knew that we must adjust. He believed in the poet's mission of seer. It was the poet who must proclaim not only the moment, but its future. He had read the words of a French critic who said that "owing to the special tendency to science and its all-devouring force, poetry would cease to be read in fifty years." He took up the challenge, and set himself to the task of refutation. He saw himself as America. In a curious, detached kind of way, he lifted himself, for purposes of expression into the rôle of American superman. He took himself, and what he knew of America, and deified them into an ideal.

From "Walt Whitman and the New Poetry" by Amy Lowell from POETRY AND POETS. Copyright 1930 (pp. 73, 74, 75 and 79–81). Copyright renewed 1958 by Harvey H. Bundy and G. d'Andelot Berlin. Reprinted by permission of the publisher, Houghton Mifflin Company.

1. *autochthonous* (ô tok′thə nəs), indigenous, native.

It was a great and noble thing to have someone sing for America, America as a base, a homeland, not as a colony. The other poets of Whitman's day read far too much like colonials; only Lowell touched a native savour; the others, for all their Water-Fowls and Barbara Frietchies and Paul Reveres[2] were (in a literary sense) directly sprung from British loins. We needed Whitman's message; we need it to-day. We need it as he meant it, rather than as he said it; much of it is in our blood, un-noticed but invigorating. . . .

And this prophet—Whitman is called the voice of his period, but here is a forward gaze which is almost uncanny:

I see not America only, not only Liberty's nation but
    other nations preparing,
I see tremendous entrances and exits, new combina-
    tions, the solidarity of races. . . .
I see men marching and countermarching by swift
    millions,
I see frontiers and boundaries of old aristocracies
    broken,
I see the landmarks of European kings removed,
I see this day the People beginning their landmarks.

The extreme left wing of poetry might take those lines as a battle slogan were they unrelated to their whole. But the people in Whitman's eyes was no rapacious plunderer; it was a good quiet village folk, well able, because slow to conclude yet firm in con-clusion, to govern itself. The poem goes on:

I see Freedom, completely arm'd and victorious and
    very haughty, with Law on one side and Peace
    on the other.

Law and Peace, but Whitman was no pacifist. Try as our literary aliens may to force him into the rôle of tutelary god to the conscientious objector, he resists. We should all know that he resisted, that he was bone and sinew of resistance in what he believed a righteous cause, if we read him instead of books about him. *Drum-Taps* is scarcely the volume of a pacifist. And this man knew war. He followed the armies; in the hospital tents—the terrible hospitals of those days with practically no anæsthetics and no antiseptics at all—he saw suffering with naked eyes. He walked battlefields in the red sunsets of days of conflict:

Look down, fair moon, and bathe this scene,
Pour softly down night's nimbus floods on faces
    ghastly, swollen, purple,
On the dead on their backs with arms tossed wide,
Pour down your unstinted nimbus, sacred moon.

. . .

The modern poet is bitter. He has lost his old vision in the reek of war. He is not sad and merciful, he hates—hates the waste and useless horror of war. The setting-back of the clock of civilization is always in his consciousness. It is so with all the sincere writers of the present day. This consciousness of waste is minimized to Whitman by his far-seeing outlook of a present necessity. Besides, once more I reiterate that he was a man of his time. Not yet the day when dreamers dared proclaim their hope a possible reality. We are more self-conscious to-day. It may be a gain; it may be a loss; but it is a fact. Besides, not in all the ranks of modern poetry has there yet appeared a seer.

Was Whitman's vision a true one? This America which he so loved, has she that within her through which she can rise victorious above all catastrophes? It is all in his poem "Thou Mother with thy Equal Brood":

In many a smiling mask death shall approach beguil-
    ing thee, thou in disease shalt swelter,
The livid cancer spread its hideous claws, clinging
    upon thy breasts, seeking to strike deep within,
Consumption of the worst, moral consumption, shall
    rouge thy face with hectic,
But thou shalt face thy fortunes, thy diseases, and
    surmount them all.

He could write so because it was only a vision. In security he could gaze clear-eyed at chaos, for the future has its perspective as well as the past. Do not expect such utterance from modern poets. The disease is here; haply we may preserve our sanity. To keep on going, to see beauty still beyond the red night, that is the awful task before our poets to-day.

. . .   1930

---

2. *Water-Fowls . . . Paul Reveres.* The references are to poems by William Cullen Bryant, John Greenleaf Whittier, and Henry Wads-worth Longfellow, respectively.

THE
TWENTIETH
CENTURY

chapter seven

THE NEW
SHORT STORY

SINJERLI-VARIATION IV, 1968 BY FRANK STELLA—COLLECTION OF MR. AND MRS. BURTON TREMAINE, MERIDEN, CONN.

Theodore Dreiser

MC EWEN OF THE SHINING SLAVE MAKERS

IT was a hot day in August. The parching rays of a summer sun had faded the once sappy green leaves of the trees to a dull and dusty hue. The grass, still good to look upon in shady places, spread sere and dry where the light had fallen unbroken. The roads were hot with thick dust, and wherever a stone path led, it reflected heat to weary body and soul.

Robert McEwen had taken a seat under a fine old beech tree whose broad arms cast a welcome shade. He had come here out of the toil of the busy streets.

For a time he gave himself over to blank contemplation of the broad park and the occasional carriages that jingled by. Presently his meditation was broken by an ant on his trousers, which he flipped away with his finger. This awoke him to the thought that there might be more upon him. He stood up, shaking and brushing himself. Then he noticed an ant running along the walk in front of him. He stamped on it.

"I guess that will do for you," he said, half aloud, and sat down again.

Now only did he really notice the walk. It was wide and hard and hot. Many ants were hurrying about, and now he saw that they were black. At last, one more active than the others fixed his eye. He followed it with his glance for more than a score of feet.

This particular ant was progressing urgently, now to the right, now to the left, stopping here and there, but never for more than a second. Its energy, the zig-zag course it pursued, the frequency with which it halted to examine something, enlisted his interest. As he gazed, the path grew in imagination until it assumed immense proportions.

Suddenly he bestirred himself, took a single glance and then jumped, rubbing his eyes. He was in an unknown world, strange in every detail. The branched and many-limbed trees had disappeared. A forest of immense flat swords of green swayed in the air above him. The ground between lacked its carpet of green and was roughly strewn with immense boulders of clay. The air was strong with an odor which seemed strange and yet familiar. Only the hot sun streaming down and a sky of faultless blue betokened a familiar world. In regard to himself McEwen felt peculiar and yet familiar. What was it that made these surroundings and himself seem odd and yet usual? He could not tell. His three pairs of limbs and his vigorous mandibles seemed natural enough. The fact that he sensed rather than saw things was natural and yet odd. Forthwith moved by a sense of duty, necessity, and a kind of tribal obligation which he more felt than understood, he set out in search of food and prey and presently came to a broad plain, so wide that his eye could scarce command more than what seemed an immediate portion of it. He halted and breathed with a feeling of relief. Just then a voice startled him.

"Anything to eat hereabout?" questioned the new-comer in a friendly and yet self-interested tone.

McEwen drew back.

"I do not know," he said, "I have just—"

"Terrible," said the stranger, not waiting to hear his answer. "It looks like famine. You know the Sanguineæ have gone to war."

"No," answered McEwen mechanically.

"Yes," said the other, "they raided the Fuscæ yesterday. They'll be down on us next."

With that the stranger made off. McEwen was about to exclaim at the use of the word *us* when a ravenous craving for food, brought now forcibly to his mind by the words of the other, made him start in haste after him.

Then came another who bespoke him in passing.

"I haven't found a thing to-day, and I've been all the way to the Pratensis region. I didn't dare go any further without having some others with me. They're hungry, too, up there, though they've just made a raid. You heard the Sanguineæ went to war, didn't you?"

"Yes, he told me," said McEwen, indicating the retreating figure of the stranger.

"Oh, Ermi. Yes, he's been over in their territory. Well, I'll be going now."

"McEwen of the Shining Slave Makers" by Theodore Dreiser from THE BEST SHORT STORIES OF THEODORE DREISER with an introduction by James T. Farrell. Reprinted by permission of Harold J. Dies, trustee of The Dreiser Trust.

McEwen hastened after Ermi at a good pace, and soon overtook him. The latter had stopped and was gathering in his mandibles a jagged crumb, almost as large as himself.

"Oh!" exclaimed McEwen eagerly, "where did you get that?"

"Here," said Ermi.

"Will you give me a little?"

"I will not," said the other, and a light came in his eye that was almost evil.

"All right," said McEwen, made bold by hunger and yet cautious by danger, "which way would you advise me to look?"

"Wherever you please," said Ermi, "why ask me? You are not new at seeking," and strode off.

"The forest was better than this," thought McEwen; "there I would not die of the heat, anyhow, and I might find food. Here is nothing," and he turned and glanced about for a sight of the jungle whence he had come.

Far to the left and rear of him he saw it, those great up-standing swords. As he gazed, revolving in his troubled mind whether he should return or not, he saw another like himself hurrying toward him out of the distance.

He eagerly hailed the newcomer, who was yet a long way off.

"What is it?" asked the other, coming up rapidly.

"Do you know where I can get something to eat?"

"Is that why you called me?" he answered, eyeing him angrily. "Do you ask in time of famine? Certainly not. If I had anything for myself, I would not be out here. Go and hunt for it like the rest of us. Why should you be asking?"

"I have been hunting," cried McEwen, his anger rising. "I have searched here until I am almost starved."

"No worse off than any of us, are you?" said the other. "Look at me. Do you suppose I am feasting?"

He went off in high dudgeon, and McEwen gazed after him in astonishment. The indifference and sufficiency were at once surprising and yet familiar. Later he found himself falling rapidly into helpless lassitude from both hunger and heat, when a voice, as of one in pain, hailed him.

"Ho!" it cried.

"Hello!" he answered.

"Come, come!" was the feeble reply.

McEwen started forward at once. When he was still many times his own length away he recognized the voice as that of his testy friend of a little while before, but now sadly changed. He was stretched upon the earth, working his mandibles feebly.

"What is it?" asked McEwen solicitously. "What ails you? How did this happen?"

"I don't know," said the other. "I was passing along here when that struck me," indicating a huge boulder. "I am done for, though. You may as well have this food now, since you are one of us. The tribe can use what you do not eat," he sighed.

"Oh, nothing of the sort," said McEwen solicitously, the while he viewed the crushed limbs and side of the sufferer. "You'll be all right. Why do you speak of death? Just tell me where to take you, or whom to go for."

"No," said the other, "it would be no use. You see how it is. They could do nothing for me. I did not want your aid. I merely wanted you to have this food here. I shall not want it now."

"Don't say that," returned McEwen. "You mustn't talk about dying. There must be something I can do. Tell me. I don't want your food."

"No, there isn't anything you could do. There isn't any cure, you know that. Report, when you return, how I was killed. Just leave me now and take that with you. They need it, if you do not."

McEwen viewed him silently. This reference to a colony or tribe or home seemed to clarify many things for him. He remembered now apparently the long road he had come, the immense galleries of the colony to which he belonged under the earth, the passages by which he had made his way in and out, the powerful and revered ant mother, various larvæ to be fed and eggs to be tended. To be sure. That was it. He was a part of this immense colony or group. The heat must have affected his sensory powers. He must gather food and return there—kill spiders, beetles, grubs, and bring them back to help provision the colony. That was it. Only there were so few to be found here, for some reason.

The sufferer closed his eyes in evident pain, and trembled convulsively. Then he fell back and died.

McEwen gazed upon the now fast stiffening body, with all but indifference, and wondered. The spectacle seemed so familiar as to be all but commonplace. Apparently he had seen so many die that way. Had he not, in times past, reported the deaths of hundreds?

"Is he dead?" asked a voice at his side.

"Yes," said McEwen, scarcely bringing himself out

of his meditation sufficiently to observe the new-comer.

"Well, then, he will not need this, I guess," said the other, and he seized upon the huge lump with his mandibles, but McEwen was on the alert and savage into the bargain, on the instant. He, too, gripped his mandibles upon it.

"I was called by him to have this, before he died," he shouted "and I propose to have it. Let go."

"That I will not," said the other with great vigor and energy. "I'll have some of it at least," and, giving a mighty wrench, which sent both himself and McEwen sprawling, he tore off a goodly portion of it and ran, gaining his feet so quickly that he was a good length off before McEwen arose. The latter was too hungry, however, to linger in useless rage, and now fell to and ate before any other should disturb him. Then, feeling partially satisfied, he stretched himself languorously and continued more at his leisure. After a time he shook himself out of his torpor which had seized on him with his eating, and made off for the distant jungle, in which direction, as he now felt, lay the colony home.

He was in one of the darkest and thickest portions of the route thither when there was borne to him from afar the sound of feet in marching time, and a murmuring as of distant voices. He stopped and listened. Presently the sounds grew louder and more individual. He could now tell that a great company was nearing him. The narrow path which he followed was clear for some distance, and open to observation. Not knowing what creatures he was about to meet, he stepped out of it into a thicket at one side and took up a position behind a great boulder. The tramp of many feet was now so close as to bode contact and discovery, and he saw, through the interstices of green stalks, a strange column filing along the path he had left. They were no other than a company of red warriors—slave makers[1] like himself, only of a different species, the fierce Sanguineæ that Ermi had spoken of as having gone to war.

To war they certainly had been, and no doubt were going again. Nearly every warrior carried with him some mark of plunder or of death. Many bore in their mandibles dead bodies of the enemy or their larvæ captured from a Fuscan colony. Others bore upon their legs the severed heads of the poor blacks who had been slain in the defense of their home, and whose jaws still clung to their foes, fixed in the rigor of death. Still others dragged the bodies of their victims, and shouted as they went, making the long, lonely path to ring with uncanny sounds as they disappeared in the distance.

McEwen came furtively out after a time and looked after them. He had gotten far to the left of the warriors and somewhat to the front of them, and was just about to leave the shadow of one clump of bushes to hurry to a neighboring stone, when there filed out from the very shelter upon which he had his eye fixed, the figure of one whom he immediately recognized as Ermi. The latter seemed to await a favorable opportunity when he should not be observed, and then started running. McEwen followed. In the distance could be seen a group of the Sanguineæ, who had evidently paused for something, moving about in great excitement, in groups of two or three, gesticulating and talking. Some of those not otherwise engaged displayed a sensibility of danger or a lust of war by working their jaws and sawing at heavy stones with their mandibles. Presently one gazed in the direction of Ermi, and shouted to the others.

Immediately four warriors set out in pursuit. McEwen hastened after Ermi, to see what would become of him. Discreetly hidden himself, he could do this with considerable equanimity. As he approached, he saw Ermi moving backward and forward, endeavoring to close the entrance to a cave in which he had now taken refuge. Apparently that warrior had become aware that no time was to be lost, since he also could see the pursuing Sanguineæ. With a swiftness born of daring and a keen realization of danger, he arranged a large boulder at the very edge of the portal as a key, and then others in such position that when the first should topple in the others would follow. Then he crawled deftly inside the portal, and pulling the keystone, toppled the whole mass in after him.

This was hardly done when the Sanguineæ were upon him. They were four cruel, murderous fighters, deeply scarred. One, called by the others Og, had a black's head at his thigh. One of his temples bore a scar, and the tip of his left antenna was broken. He was a keen old warrior, however, and scented the prey at once.

"Hi, you!" he shouted to the others. "Here's the place."

Just then another drew near to the portal which

---

1. *slave makers.* The chief purpose of ant warfare is to make slaves of other species.

Ermi had barricaded. He looked at it closely, walked about several times, sounded with his antennæ and then listened. There was no answer.

"Hist!" he exclaimed to the others.

Now they came up. They also looked, but so well had Ermi done his work that they were puzzled.

"I'm not sure," said Og, "it looks to me more like an abandoned cave than an entrance."

"Tear it open, anyway," advocated Ponan, the second of the quartette, speaking for the first time. "There may be no other exit."

"Aha!" cried Og. "Good! We will see anyhow."

"Come on!" yelled Maru, a third, seizing the largest boulder. "Mandibles to!"

"Out with him!" cried Om, jumping eagerly to work. "We will have him out in a jiffy!"

It was not an easy task, as the boulders were heavy and deep, but they tore them out. Later they dragged forth Ermi, who, finding himself captured, seized the head of Maru with his mandibles. Og, on the other hand, seized one of Ermi's legs in his powerful jaws. The others also had taken hold. The antennæ of all were thrown back, and the entire mass went pushing and shoving, turning and tumbling in a whirl.

McEwen gazed, excited and sympathetic. At first he thought to avoid it all, having a horror of death, but a moment later decided to come to his friend's rescue, a feeling of tribal relationship which was overwhelming coming over him. Springing forward, he clambered upon the back of Og, at whose neck he began to saw with his powerful teeth. Og, realizing a new adversary, released his hold upon Ermi's limb and endeavored to shake off his new enemy. McEwen held tight, however. The others, however, too excited to observe the newcomer, still struggled to destroy Ermi. The latter had stuck steadily to his labor of killing Maru, and now, when Og's hold was loosened, he gave a powerful crush and Maru breathed his last. This advantaged him little, however, for both Ponan and Om were attacking his sides.

"Take that!" shouted Om, throwing himself violently upon Ermi and turning him over. "Saw off his head, Ponan."

Ponan released his hold and sprang for Ermi's head. There was a kicking and crushing of jaws, and Ponan secured his grip.

"Kill him!" yelled Om. "Come, Og! Come!"

At this very moment Og's severed head fell to the ground, and McEwen leaping from his back, sprang to the aid of Ermi.

"Come!" he shouted at Ponan, who was sawing at Ermi's head. "It's two to two now," and McEwen gave such a wrench to Ponan's side that he writhed in pain, and released his hold on Ermi.

But recovering himself he leaped upon McEwen, and bore him down, sprawling.

The fight was now more desperate than ever. The combatants rolled and tossed. McEwen's right antenna was broken by his fall, and one of his legs was injured. He could seem to get no hold upon his adversary, whom he now felt to be working toward his neck.

"Let go!" he yelled, gnashing at him with his mandibles, but Ponan only tightened his murderous jaws.

Better fortune was now with Ermi, however, who was a more experienced fighter. Getting a grip upon Om's body, he hurled him to the ground and left him stunned and senseless.

Seeing McEwen's predicament, he now sprang to his aid. The latter was being sadly worsted and but for the generous aid of Ermi, would have been killed. The latter struck Ponan a terrific blow with his head and having stunned him, dragged him off. The two, though much injured, now seized upon the unfortunate Sanguinea and tore him in two, and would have done as much for Om, had they not discovered that that bedraggled warrior had recovered sufficiently to crawl away and hide.

McEwen and Ermi now drew near to each other in warm admiration.

"Come with me," said Ermi. "They are all about here now and that coward who escaped will have them upon us. There is a corridor into our home from here, only I was not able to reach it before they caught me. Help me barricade this entrance."

Together they built up the stones more effectually than before, and then entered, toppling the mass in behind them. With considerable labor, they built up another barricade below.

"You watch a moment, now," said Ermi to McEwen, and then hurried down a long passage through which he soon returned bringing with him a sentinel, who took up guard duty at the point where the fight had occurred. "He will stay here and give the alarm in case another attack is made," he commented.

"Come now," he added, touching McEwen affectionately with his antennæ. Leading the way, Ermi took him along a long winding corridor with which, somehow, he seemed to be familiar, and through various secret passages into the colony house.

"You see," he said to McEwen familiarly, as they went, "they could not have gotten in here, even if they had killed me, without knowing the way. Our passageways are too intricate. But it is as well to keep a picket there, now that they are about. Where have you been? You do not belong to our colony, do you?"

McEwen related his experiences since their meeting in the desert, without explaining where he came from. He knew that he was a member of some other colony of this same tribe without being sure of which one. A strange feeling of wandering confusion possessed him, as though he had been injured in some way, somewhere, and was lost for the moment.

"Well, you might as well stay with us, now," said Ermi. "Are you hungry?"

"Very," said McEwen.

"Then we will eat at once."

McEwen now gazed upon a domed chamber of vast proportions, with which, also, he seemed familiar, an old inhabitant of one such, no less. It had several doors that opened out into galleries, and corridors leading to other chambers and store rooms, a home for thousands.

Many members of this allied family now hurried to meet them, all genially enough.

"You have had an encounter with them?" asked several at once.

"Nothing to speak of," said Ermi, who, fighter that he was, had also a touch of vanity. "Look after my friend here, who has saved my life."

"Not I!" cried McEwen warmly.

They could not explain, however, before they were seized by their admirers and carried into a chamber where none of the din of preparation penetrated, and where was a carpet of soft grass threads upon which they might lie.

Injured though they were, neither could endure lying still for long, and were soon poking about, though unable to do anything. McEwen was privileged to idle and listlessly watch an attack on one portal of the cave which lasted an entire day, resulting in failure for the invaders. It was a rather broken affair, the principal excitement occurring about the barricaded portals and secret exits at the end of the long corridors, where McEwen often found himself in the way. The story of his prowess had been well told by Ermi, and he was a friend and hero

whom many served. A sort of ambulance service was established which not only looked to the bringing in of the injured, but also to the removal of the dead. A graveyard was prepared just outside one of the secret entrances, far from the scene of the siege, and here the dead were laid in orderly rows.

The siege having ended temporarily the same day it began, the household resumed its old order. Those who had remained within went forth for forage. The care of the communal young, which had been somewhat interrupted, was now resumed. Larvæ and chrysalis, which had been left almost unattended in the vast nurseries, were moved to and fro between the rooms where the broken sunlight warmed, and the shadow gave them rest.

"There is war ahead," said Ermi to McEwen one day not long after this. "These Sanguineæ will never let us alone until we give them battle. We shall have to stir up the whole race of Shining Slave Makers and fight all the Sanguineæ before we have peace again."

"Good," said McEwen. "I am ready."

"So am I," answered Ermi, "but it is no light matter. They are our ancient enemy and as powerful as we. If we meet again you will see war that is war."

Not long after this McEwen and Ermi, foraging together, encountered a Sanguinea, who fought with them and was slain. Numerous Lucidi, of which tribe he found himself to be a member, left the community of a morning to labor and were never heard of again. Encounters between parties of both camps were frequent, and orderly living ceased.

At last the entire community was in a ferment, and a council was called. It was held in the main saloon of the formicary, a vast chamber whose hollowed dome rose like the open sky above them. The queen of the community was present, and all the chief warriors, including Ermi and McEwen. Loud talking and fierce comment were indulged in to no point, until Yumi, long a light in the councils of the Lucidi, spoke. He was short and sharp of speech.

"We must go to war," he said. "Our old enemies will give us no peace. Send couriers to all the colonies of the Shining Slave Makers. We will meet the Red Slave Makers as we did before."

"Ah," said an old Lucidi, who stood at McEwen's side, "that was a great battle. You don't remember. You were too young. There were thousands and thousands in that. I could not walk for the dead."

"Are we to have another such?" asked McEwen.

"If the rest of us come. We are a great people. The Shining Slave Makers are numberless."

Just then another voice spoke, and Ermi listened.

"Let us send for them to come here. When the Sanguineæ again lay siege let us pour out and destroy them. Let none escape."

"Let us first send couriers and hear what our people say," broke in Ermi loudly. "The Sanguineæ are a vast people also. We must have numbers. It must be a decisive battle."

"Ay, ay," answered many. "Send the couriers!"

Forthwith messengers were dispatched to all parts, calling the hordes of the Shining Slave Makers to war. In due course they returned, bringing information that they were coming. Their colonies also had been attacked. Later the warriors of the allied tribes began to put in an appearance.

It was a gathering of legions. The paths in the forests about resounded with their halloos. With the arrival of the first cohorts of these friendly colonies, there was a minor encounter with an irritant host of the Sanguineæ foraging hereabout, who were driven back and destroyed. Later there were many minor encounters and deaths before the hosts were fully assembled, but the end was not yet. All knew that. The Sanguineæ had fled, but not in cowardice. They would return.

The one problem with this vast host, now that it was assembled, was food. Eventually they expected to discover this in the sacked homes of the Sanguineæ, but temporarily other provision must be made. The entire region had to be scoured. Colonies of Fuscæ and Schauffusi living in nearby territory were attacked and destroyed. Their storehouses were ransacked and the contents distributed. Every form of life was attacked and still there was not enough.

Both McEwen and Ermi, now inseparable, joined in one of these raids. It was upon a colony of Fuscæ, who had their home in a neighboring forest. The company went singing on their way until within a short distance of the colony, when they became silent.

"Let us not lose track of one another," said McEwen.

"No," said Ermi, "but they are nothing. We will take all they possess without a struggle. See them running."

As he said this, he motioned in the direction of several Fuscæ that were fleeing toward their portals in terror. The Lucidi set up a shout, and darted after, plunging into the open gates, striking and slaying as they went. In a few minutes those first in came out again carrying their booty. Others were singly engaged in fiercest battle with large groups of the weaker Fuscæ. Only a few of the latter were inclined to fight. They seemed for the most part dazed by their misfortunes. Numbers hung from the topmost blades of the towering sword-trees, and the broad, floor-like leaves of the massive weeds, about their caves where they had taken refuge, holding in their jaws baby larvæ and cocoons rescued from the invaders, with which they had hurriedly fled to these nearest elevated objects.

Singly, McEwen pursued a dozen, and reveled in the sport of killing them. He tumbled them with rushes of his body, crushed them with his mandibles, and poisoned them with his formic sting.[2]

"Do you need help?" called Ermi once, who was always near and shouting.

"Yes," called McEwen scornfully, "bring me more of them."

Soon the deadly work was over and the two comrades, gathering a mass of food, joined the returning band, singing as they went.

"To-morrow," said Ermi, as they went along, "we will meet the Sanguineæ. It is agreed. The leaders are conferring now."

McEwen did not learn where these latter were, but somehow he was pleased. An insane lust of combat was now upon him.

"They will not be four to two this time," he laughed exultingly.

"No, and we will not be barricading against them, either," laughed Ermi, the lust of war simmering in his veins.

As they came near their camp, however, they found a large number of the assembled companies already in motion. Thousands upon thousands of those who had arrived were already assembled in one group or another and were prepared for action. There were cries and sounds of fighting, and long lines of Lucidi hurrying hither and thither.

"What's the matter?" asked Ermi excitedly.

"The Sanguineæ," was the answer. "They are returning."

Instantly McEwen became sober. Ermi turned to him affectionately.

---

2. *formic sting.* Ants produce formic acid which they inject into their enemies from a sting at the tip of their abdomens.

"Now," he said solemnly, "courage. We're in for it."

A tremendous hubbub followed. Already vast legions of the Lucidi were bearing away to the east. McEwen and Ermi, not being able to find their own, fell in with a strange company.

"Order!" shouted a voice in their ears. "Fall in line. We are called."

The twain mechanically obeyed, and dropped behind a regular line. Soon they were winding along with other long lines of warriors through the tall sword trees, and in a little while reached a huge, smooth, open plain where already the actual fighting had begun. Thousands were here, apparently hundreds of thousands. There was little order, and scarcely any was needed apparently, since all contacts were individual or between small groups. It all depended now on numbers, and the results of the contests between individuals, or at the most, these small groups. Ermi, McEwen, and several other Lucidi were about to seize upon one Sanguinea, who was approaching them, when an amazing rush of the latter broke them, and McEwen found himself separated from Ermi with a red demon snapping at his throat. Dazed by the shock and clamor, he almost fell a prey to this first charge. A moment later, however, his courage and daring returned. With a furious bound, he recovered himself and forced himself upon his adversary, snapping his jaws in his neck.

"Take that!" he said to the tumbling carcass.

He had no sooner ended one foe, however, than another clutched him. They were on every hand, hard, merciless fighters like himself and Ermi who rushed and tore and sawed with amazing force. McEwen faced his newest adversary swiftly. While the latter was seeking for McEwen's head and antennæ with his mandibles, the former with a quick snap seized his foe by the neck. Turning up his abdomen, he ejected formic acid into the throat of the other. That finished him.

Meanwhile the battle continued on every hand with the same mad vehemence. Already the dead clogged the ground. Here, single combatants struggled—there, whole lines moved and swayed in deadly combat. Ever and anon new lines were formed, and strange hosts of friends or enemies came up, falling upon the combatants of both sides with murderous enthusiasm. McEwen, in a strange daze and lust of death, seemed to think nothing of it. He was alone now—lost in a tossing sea of war, and

terror seemed to have forsaken him. It was wonderful, he thought, mysterious—

As enemy after enemy assailed him, he fought them as he best knew, an old method to him, apparently, and as they died, he wished them to die—broken, poisoned, sawed in two. He began to count and exult in the numbers he had slain. It was at last as though he were dreaming, and all around was a vain, dark, surging mass of enemies.

Finally, four of the Sanguineæ seized upon him in a group, and he went down before them, almost helpless. Swiftly they tore at his head and body, endeavoring to dispose of him quickly. One seized a leg, another an antenna. A third jumped and sawed at his neck. Still he did not care. It was all war, and he would struggle to the last shred of his strength, eagerly, enthusiastically. At last he seemed to lose consciousness.

When he opened his eyes again, Ermi was beside him.

"Well?" said Ermi.

"Well?" answered McEwen.

"You were about done for, then."

"Was I?" he answered. "How are things going?"

"I cannot tell yet," said Ermi. "All I know is that you were faring badly when I came up. Two of them were dead, but the other two were killing you."

"You should have left me to them," said McEwen, noticing now for the first time Ermi's wounds. "It does not matter so much—one Lucidi more or less—what of it? But you have been injured."

"I—oh, nothing. You are the one to complain. I fear you are badly injured."

"Oh, I," returned McEwen heavily, feeling at last the weight of death upon him, "I am done for. I cannot live. I felt myself dying some time ago."

He closed his eyes and trembled. In another moment—

II

McEwen opened his eyes. Strangely enough he was looking out upon jingling carriages and loitering passersby in the great city park. It was all so strange, by comparison with that which he had so recently seen, the tall buildings in the distance, instead of the sword trees, the trees, the flowers. He jumped to his feet in astonishment, then sank back again in equal amaze, a passerby eyeing him curiously the while.

"I have been asleep," he said in a troubled way. "I have been dreaming. And what a dream!"

He shut his eyes again, wishing, for some strange reason—charm, sympathy, strangeness—to regain the lost scene. An odd longing filled his heart, a sense of comradeship lost, of some friend he knew missing. When he opened his eyes again he seemed to realize something more of what had been happening but it was fading, fading.

At his feet lay the plain and the ants with whom he had recently been—or so he thought. Yes, there, only a few feet away in the parched grass, was an arid spot, over-run with insects. He gazed upon it, in amazement, searching for the details of a lost world. Now, as he saw, coming closer, a giant battle was in progress, such a one, for instance, as that in which he had been engaged in his dream. The ground was strewn with dead ants. Thousands upon thousands were sawing and striking at each other quite in the manner in which he had dreamed. What was this?—a revelation of the spirit and significance of a lesser life or of his own—or what? And what was life if the strange passions, moods and necessities which conditioned him here could condition those there on so minute a plane?

"Why, I was there," he said dazedly and a little dreamfully, "a little while ago. I died there—or as well as died there—in my dream. At least I woke out of it into this or sank from that into this."

Stooping closer he could see where lines were drawn, how in places the forces raged in confusion, and the field was cluttered with the dead. At one moment an odd mad enthusiasm such as he had experienced in his dream-world lay hold of him, and he looked for the advantage of the Shining Slave Makers—the blacks—as he thought of the two warring hosts as against the reds. But finding it not, the mood passed, and he stood gazing, lost in wonder. What a strange world! he thought. What worlds within worlds, all apparently full of necessity, contention, binding emotions and unities—and all with sorrow, their sorrow—a vague, sad something out of far-off things which had been there, and was here in this strong bright city day, had been there and would be here until this odd, strange thing called *life* had ended. □

DISCUSSION

Theodore Dreiser's short story is not a conventional realistic tale but more of a **fantasy** (an account of impossible or fantastic happenings) and is related to the **fairy tale** (children's stories involving supernatural beings such as giants or witches) and the **fable** (a brief, moral tale about human-like animals). Dreiser clearly wants to entertain the reader, but he also wants to convey a serious theme concerning war.

FOR EXPLORATION

1. When do you discover that the main narrative of the story is a dream? Reread the opening paragraphs to find out what hints are given that McEwen is going to sleep and that what happens in the ant-world is a dream.

2. In the major battle in the war of the ants, we read that an "insane lust of combat" seizes McEwen, and that the "lust of war" simmers in Ermi's veins. (a) How has Dreiser prepared us for these feelings in the ants? (b) Discuss the ways in which Dreiser, here and elsewhere in the story, seems to be presenting a view of man and his wars.

3. On the opening of Part II, the perspective suddenly shifts back to the "real" world; discuss the ways in which Dreiser shocks the reader into realization that the narrative in which he is caught up is a dream.

4. In Part II, Dreiser writes: "What was this?—a revelation of the spirit and significance of a lesser life or of his own—or what? And what was life if the strange passions, moods and necessities which conditioned him here could condition those there on so minute a plane?" How would you answer these questions? Discuss.

CREATIVE RESPONSE

1. Write an account of a dream in which you turn into a nonhuman creature and enter a strange world which may or may not have some resemblances to the human world.
2. Read Franz Kafka's *Metamorphosis*, in which the protagonist turns into a giant insect. Make a comparison of the Dreiser and Kafka stories as to their technique, their effect, or their serious purpose.

HISTORICAL PICTURES SERVICE, CHICAGO

Theodore Dreiser   1871 / 1945

The twelfth of thirteen children, Theodore Dreiser was born in Terre Haute, Indiana. He grew up in poverty. His father was a religious zealot who moved the family from one Indiana town to another, each change a doomed effort at economic betterment. Frequently the children were ostracized, in part perhaps because of their father's fanatical religious beliefs, but more certainly simply because of their extreme poverty. Dreiser worked at any number of jobs in his youth. He at one time collected bills for an easy-payment furniture company; at other various moments he washed dishes, shoveled coal, drove for a laundry, clerked in a stockroom, and helped in a real estate office. A kindly woman made it possible for him to attend Indiana University, but he left after a year feeling that his studies "did not concern ordinary life at all." On his own in Chicago, Dreiser began working as a newspaper reporter. Eight years later he published the naturalistic novel *Sister Carrie* (1900).

It was the story of a young girl who escapes from poverty through a romantic liaison with a well-to-do gentleman. Though an honest, compassionate story in which the sexual aspects were not treated salaciously, it did not follow the prescribed formula, sin was not followed by swift and righteous punishment. The book was suppressed.

It seemed Dreiser would either have to change his style or risk the possibility of laboring over works which might never be read. He chose not to change. In order to support himself he continued his newspaper work until 1905 and then edited a series of magazines. In 1911 Dreiser published *Jennie Gerhart,* a novel with the same objectionable story pattern as his earlier work. But this time the book reached the public, setting off a heated controversy which lasted for over a decade. When *Sister Carrie* was given a third and at last public printing a year later, the outcry increased. The books were vehemently attacked, described as "immoral," and some attempts made to ban or block their sale. Nevertheless, Dreiser continued to write as a naturalist and there were those who came to his defense. His most omnipotent champion was H. L. Mencken of the satiric wit. (See selection page M 120.) Together they eventually made acceptable the honesty and realism of the great novelists of this century

The proof of their success came in 1925 with the publication of Dreiser's *An American Tragedy.* Though its naturalism was as uncompromising as that of his earlier works, there were fewer voices raised against it and the book was an immediate popular success. Dreiser was no different; it was America that had changed.

Sherwood Anderson

BROTHER DEATH

THERE were the two oak stumps, knee high to a not-too-tall man and cut quite squarely across. They became to the two children objects of wonder. They had seen the two trees cut but had run away just as the trees fell. They hadn't thought of the two stumps, to be left standing there; hadn't even looked at them. Afterwards Ted said to his sister Mary, speaking of the stumps: "I wonder if they bled, like legs, when a surgeon cuts a man's leg off." He had been hearing war stories. A man came to the farm one day to visit one of the farm-hands, a man who had been in the World War[1] and lost an arm. He stood in one of the barns talking. When Ted said that, Mary spoke up at once. She hadn't been lucky enough to be at the barn when the one-armed man was there talking, and was jealous. "Why not a woman or a girl's leg?" she said, but Ted said the idea was silly. "Women and girls don't get their legs and arms cut off," he declared. "Why not? I'd just like to know why not?" Mary kept saying.

It would have been something if they had stayed, that day the trees were cut. "We might have gone and touched the places," Ted said. He meant the stumps. Would they have been warm? Would they have bled? They did go and touch the places afterwards, but it was a cold day and the stumps were cold. Ted stuck to his point that only men's arms and legs were cut off, but Mary thought of automobile accidents. "You can't think just of wars. There might be an automobile accident," she declared, but Ted wouldn't be convinced.

They were both children, but something had made them both in an odd way old. Mary was fourteen and Ted eleven, but Ted wasn't strong and that rather evened things up. They were the children of a well-to-do Virginia farmer named John Grey in the Blue Ridge country in Southwestern Virginia. There was a wide valley called the "Rich Valley" with a railroad and a small river running through it and high mountains in sight, to the north and south. Ted had some kind of a heart disease, a lesion, something of the sort, the result of a severe attack of diphtheria when he was a child of eight. He was thin and not strong but curiously alive. The doctor said he might die at any moment, might just drop down dead. The fact had drawn him peculiarly close to his sister Mary. It had awakened a strong and determined maternalism in her.

The whole family, the neighbors on neighboring farms in the valley, and even the other children at the schoolhouse where they went to school recognized something as existing between the two children. "Look at them going along there," people said. "They do seem to have good times together, but they are so serious. For such young children they are too serious. Still, I suppose, under the circumstances, it's natural." Of course, everyone knew about Ted. It had done something to Mary. At fourteen she was both a child and a grown woman. The woman side of her kept popping out at unexpected moments.

She had sensed something concerning her brother Ted. It was because he was as he was, having that

"Brother Death" by Sherwood Anderson from DEATH IN THE WOODS AND OTHER STORIES. Copyright 1933 by Sherwood Anderson. Renewed. Reprinted by permission of Harold Ober Associates Incorporated.
1. *the World War*, World War I (1914–1919).

kind of a heart, a heart likely at any moment to stop beating, leaving him dead, cut down like a young tree. The others in the Grey family, that is to say, the older ones, the mother and father and an older brother, Don, who was eighteen now, recognized something as belonging to the two children, being, as it were, between them, but the recognition wasn't very definite. People in your own family are likely at any moment to do strange, sometimes hurtful things to you. You have to watch them. Ted and Mary had both found that out.

The brother Don was like the father, already at eighteen almost a grown man. He was that sort, the kind people speak of, saying: "He's a good man. He'll make a good solid dependable man." The father, when he was a young man, never drank, never went chasing the girls, was never wild. There had been enough wild young ones in the Rich Valley when he was a lad. Some of them had inherited big farms and had lost them, gambling, drinking, fooling with fast horses and chasing after the women. It had been almost a Virginia tradition, but John Grey was a land man. All the Greys were. There were other large cattle farms owned by Greys up and down the valley.

John Grey, everyone said, was a natural cattle man. He knew beef cattle, of the big so-called export type, how to pick and feed them to make beef. He knew how and where to get the right kind of young stock to turn into his fields. It was the blue-grass country. Big beef cattle went directly off the pastures to market. The Grey farm contained over twelve hundred acres, most of it in blue-grass.

The father was a land man, land hungry. He had begun, as a cattle farmer, with a small place, inherited from his father, some two hundred acres, lying next to what was then the big Aspinwahl place and, after he began, he never stopped getting more land. He kept cutting in on the Aspinwahls who were a rather horsey, fast lot. They thought of themselves as Virginia aristocrats, having, as they weren't so modest about pointing out, a family going back and back, family tradition, guests always being entertained, fast horses kept, money being bet on fast horses. John Grey getting their land, now twenty acres, then thirty, then fifty, until at last he got the old Aspinwahl house, with one of the Aspinwahl girls, not a young one, not one of the best-looking ones, as wife. The Aspinwahl place was down, by that time, to less than a hundred acres, but he went on, year after year, always being careful and shrewd, making every penny count, never wasting a cent, adding and adding to what was now the Grey place. The former Aspinwahl house was a large old brick house with fireplaces in all the rooms and was very comfortable.

People wondered why Louise Aspinwahl had married John Grey, but when they were wondering they smiled. The Aspinwahl girls were all well educated, had all been away to college, but Louise wasn't so pretty. She got nicer after marriage, suddenly almost beautiful. The Aspinwahls were, as everyone knew, naturally sensitive, really first class but the men couldn't hang onto land and the Greys could. In all that section of Virginia, people gave John Grey credit for being what he was. They respected him. "He's on the level," they said, "as honest as a horse. He has cattle sense, that's it." He could run his big hand down over the flank of a steer and say, almost to the pound, what he would weigh on the scales or he could look at a calf or a yearling and say, "He'll do," and he would do. A steer is a steer. He isn't supposed to do anything but make beef.

There was Don, the oldest son of the Grey family. He was so evidently destined to be a Grey, to be another like his father. He had long been a star in the 4H Club of the Virginia county and, even as a lad of nine and ten, had won prizes at steer judging. At twelve he had produced, no one helping him, doing all the work himself, more bushels of corn on an acre of land than any other boy in the State.

It was all a little amazing, even a bit queer to Mary Grey, being as she was a girl peculiarly conscious, so old and young, so aware. There was Don, the older brother, big and strong of body, like the father, and there was the younger brother Ted. Ordinarily, in the ordinary course of life, she being what she was—female—it would have been quite natural and right for her to have given her young girl's admiration to Don but she didn't. For some reason, Don barely existed for her. He was outside, not in it, while for her Ted, the seemingly weak one of the family, was everything.

Still there Don was, so big of body, so quiet, so apparently sure of himself. The father had begun, as a young cattle man, with the two hundred acres, and now he had the twelve hundred. What would Don Grey do when he started? Already he knew, although he didn't say anything, that he wanted to start. He wanted to run things, be his own boss. His father had offered to send him away to college, to an agricultural college, but he wouldn't go. "No. I can learn more here," he said.

Already there was a contest, always kept under the surface, between the father and son. It concerned ways of doing things, decisions to be made. As yet the son always surrendered.

It is like that in a family, little isolated groups formed within the larger group, jealousies, concealed hatreds, silent battles secretly going on—among the Greys, Mary and Ted, Don and his father, the mother and the two younger children, Gladys, a girl child of six now, who adored her brother Don, and Harry, a boy child of two.

As for Mary and Ted, they lived within their own world, but their own world had not been established without a struggle. The point was that Ted, having the heart that might at any moment stop beating, was always being treated tenderly by the others. Only Mary understood that—how it infuriated and hurt him.

"No, Ted, I wouldn't do that."

"Now, Ted, do be careful."

Sometimes Ted went white and trembling with anger, Don, the father, the mother, all keeping at him like that. It didn't matter what he wanted to do, learn to drive one of the two family cars, climb a tree to find a bird's nest, run a race with Mary. Naturally, being on a farm, he wanted to try his hand at breaking a colt, beginning with him, getting a saddle on, having it out with him. "No, Ted. You can't." He had learned to swear, picking it up from the farmhands and from the boys at the country school. "Hell!" he said to Mary. Only Mary understood how he felt, and she had not put the matter very definitely into words, not even to herself. It was one of the things that made her old when she was so young. It made her stand aside from the others of the family, aroused in her a curious determination. "They shall not." She caught herself saying the words to herself. "They shall not."

"If he is to have but a few years of life, they shall not spoil what he is to have. Why should they make him die, over and over, day after day?" The thoughts in her mind did not become so definite. She had resentment against the others. She was like a soldier, standing guard over Ted.

The two children drew more and more away, into their own world and only once did what Mary felt come to the surface. That was with the mother.

It was on an early Summer day and Ted and Mary were playing in the rain. They were on a side porch of the house, where the water came pouring down from the eaves. At a corner of the porch there was a great stream, and first Ted and then Mary dashed through it, returning to the porch with clothes soaked and water running in streams from soaked hair. There was something joyous, the feel of the cold water on the body, under clothes, and they were shrieking with laughter when the mother came to the door. She looked at Ted. There was fear and anxiety in her voice. "Oh, Ted, you know you mustn't, you mustn't." Just that. All the rest implied. Nothing said to Mary. There it was. "Oh, Ted, you mustn't. You mustn't run hard, climb trees, ride horses. The least shock to you may do it." It was the old story again, and, of course, Ted understood. He went white and trembled. Why couldn't the rest understand that was a hundred times worse for him? On that day, without answering his mother, he ran off the porch and through the rain toward the barns. He wanted to go hide himself from everyone. Mary knew how he felt.

She got suddenly very old and very angry. The mother and daughter stood looking at each other, the woman nearing fifty and the child of fourteen. It was getting everything in the family reversed. Mary felt that but felt she had to do something. "You should have more sense, Mother," she said seriously. She also had gone white. Her lips trembled. "You mustn't do it any more. Don't you ever do it again."

"What, child?" There was astonishment and half anger in the mother's voice.

"Always making him think of it," Mary said. She wanted to cry but didn't.

The mother understood. There was a queer tense moment before Mary also walked off, toward the barns, in the rain. It wasn't all so clear. The mother wanted to fly at the child, perhaps shake her for daring to be so impudent. A child like that to decide things—to dare to reprove her mother. There was so much implied—even that Ted be allowed to die, quickly, suddenly, rather than that death, danger of sudden death, be brought again and again to his attention. There were values in life, implied by a child's words: "Life, what is it worth? Is death the most terrible thing?" The mother turned and went silently into the house while Mary, going to the barns, presently found Ted. He was in an empty horse stall, standing with his back to the wall, staring. There were no explanations. "Well," Ted said presently, and, "Come on, Ted," Mary replied. It was necessary to do something even perhaps more risky than playing in the rain. The rain was already passing. "Let's take off our shoes," Mary said. Going barefoot was one of the things forbidden Ted. They took their shoes off and, leaving them in the barn, went into an orchard. There was a small creek below the orchard, a creek that went down to the river and now it would be in flood. They went into it and once Mary got swept off her feet so that Ted had to pull her out. She spoke then. "I told Mother," she said, looking serious.

"What?" Ted said. "Gee, I guess maybe I saved you from drowning," he added.

"Sure you did," said Mary. "I told her to let you alone." She grew suddenly fierce. "They've all got to—they've got to let you alone," she said.

There was a bond. Ted did his share. He was imaginative and could think of plenty of risky things to do. Perhaps the mother spoke to the father and to Don, the older brother. There was a new inclination in the family to keep hands off the pair, and the fact seemed to give the two children new room in life. Something seemed to open out. There was a little inner world created, always, every day, being re-created, and in it there was a kind of new security. It seemed to the two children—they could not have put their feelings into words—that, being in their own created world, feeling a security there, they could suddenly look out at the outside world, and see, in a new way, what was going on out there in the world that belonged also to others.

It was a world to be thought about, looked at, a world of drama too, the drama of human relations, outside their own world, in a family, on a farm, in a farmhouse. . . . On a farm, calves and yearling steers arriving to be fattened, great heavy steers going off to market, colts being broken to work or to saddle, lambs born in the late Winter. The human side of life was more difficult, to a child often incomprehensible, but after the speech to the mother, on the porch of the house that day when it rained, it seemed to Mary almost as though she and Ted had set up a new family. Everything about the farm, the house and the barns got nicer. There was a new freedom. The two children walked along a country road, returning to the farm from school in the late afternoon. There were other children in the road but they managed to fall behind or they got ahead. There were plans made. "I'm going to be a nurse when I grow up," Mary said. She may have remembered dimly the woman nurse, from the county-seat town, who had come to stay in the house when Ted was so ill. Ted said that as soon as he could—it would be when he was younger yet than Don was now—he intended to leave and go out West . . . far out, he said. He wanted to be a cowboy or a bronco-buster or something, and that failing, he thought he would be a railroad engineer. The railroad that went down through the Rich Valley crossed a corner of the Grey farm, and, from the road in the afternoon, they could sometimes see trains, quite far away, the smoke rolling up. There was a faint rumbling noise, and on clear days they could see the flying piston rods of the engines.

As for the two stumps in the field near the house, they were what was left of two oak trees. The children had known the trees. They were cut one day in the early Fall.

There was a back porch to the Grey house—the house that had once been the seat of the Aspinwahl family—and from the porch steps a path led down to a stone spring house. A spring came out of the ground just there, and there was a tiny stream that went along the edge of a field, past two large barns and out across a meadow to a creek—called a "branch" in Virginia, and the two trees stood close together beyond the spring house and the fence.

They were lusty trees, their roots down in the rich, always damp soil, and one of them had a great limb that came down near the ground, so that Ted and Mary could climb into it and out another limb into its brother tree, and in the Fall, when other trees, at the front and side of the house, had shed their leaves, blood-red leaves still clung to the two oaks. They were like dry blood on gray days, but on other days, when the sun came out, the trees flamed against the distant hills. The leaves clung, whispering and talking when the wind blew, so that the trees themselves seemed carrying on a conversation.

John Grey had decided he would have the trees cut. At first it was not a very definite decision. "I think I'll have them cut," he announced.

"But why?" his wife asked. The trees meant a good deal to her. They had been planted, just in that spot, by her grandfather, she said, having in mind just a certain effect. "You see how, in the Fall, when you stand on the back porch, they are so nice against the hills." She spoke of the trees, already quite large, having been brought from a distant woods. Her mother had often spoken of it. The man, her grandfather, had a special feeling for trees. "An Aspinwahl would do that," John Grey said. "There is enough yard, here about the house, and enough trees. They do not shade the house or the yard. An Aspinwahl would go to all that trouble for trees and then plant them where grass might be growing." He had suddenly determined, a half-formed determination in him suddenly hardening. He had perhaps heard too much of the Aspinwahls and their ways. The conversation regarding the trees took place at the table, at the noon hour, and Mary and Ted heard it all.

It began at the table and was carried on afterwards out of doors, in the yard back of the house. The wife had followed her husband out. He always left the table suddenly and silently, getting quickly up and going out heavily, shutting doors with a bang as he went. "Don't, John," the wife said, standing on the porch and calling to her husband. It was a cold day but the sun was out and the trees were like great bonfires against gray distant fields and hills. The older son of the family, young Don, the one so physically like the father and apparently so like him in every other way, had come out of the house with the mother, followed by the two children, Ted and Mary, and at first Don said nothing, but, when the father did not answer the mother's protest but started toward the barn, he also spoke. What he said was obviously the determining thing, hardening the father.

To the two other children—they had walked a little aside and stood together watching and listening—there was something. There was their own child's world. "Let us alone and we'll let you alone." It wasn't as definite as that. Most of the definite thoughts about what happened in the yard that afternoon came to Mary Grey long afterwards, when she was a grown woman. At the moment there was merely a sudden sharpening of the feeling of isolation, a wall between herself and Ted and the others. The father, even then perhaps, seen in a new light, Don and the mother seen in a new light.

There was something, a driving destructive thing in life, in all relationships between people. All of this felt dimly that day—she always believed both by herself and Ted—but only thought out long afterwards, after Ted was dead. There was the farm her father had won from the Aspinwahls—greater persistence, greater shrewdness. In a family, little re-

marks dropped from time to time, an impression slowly built up. The father, John Grey, was a successful man. He had acquired. He owned. He was the commander, the one having the power to do his will. And the power had run out and covered, not only other human lives, impulses in others, wishes, hungers in others . . . he himself might not have, might not even understand . . . but it went far beyond that. It was, curiously, the power also of life and death. Did Mary Grey think such thoughts at that moment? . . . She couldn't have. . . . Still there was her own peculiar situation, her relationship with her brother Ted, who was to die.

Ownership that gave curious rights, dominances—fathers over children, men and women over lands, houses, factories in cities, fields. "I will have the trees in that orchard cut. They produce apples but not of the right sort. There is no money in apples of that sort any more."

"But, Sir . . . you see . . . look . . . the trees there against that hill, against the sky."

"Nonsense. Sentimentality."

Confusion.

It would have been such nonsense to think of the father of Mary Grey as a man without feeling. He had struggled hard all his life, perhaps, as a young man, gone without things wanted, deeply hungered for. Someone has to manage things in this life. Possessions mean power, the right to say "Do this" or "Do that." If you struggle long and hard for a thing it becomes infinitely sweet to you.

Was there a kind of hatred between the father and the older son of the Grey family? "You are one also who has this thing—the impulse to power, so like my own. Now you are young and I am growing old." Admiration mixed with fear. If you would retain power it will not do to admit fear.

The young Don was so curiously like the father. There were the same lines about the jaws, the same eyes. They were both heavy men. Already the young man walked like the father, slammed doors as did the father. There was the same curious lack of delicacy of thought and touch—the heaviness that plows through, gets things done. When John Grey had married Louise Aspinwahl he was already a mature man, on his way to success. Such men do not marry young and recklessly. Now he was nearly sixty and there was the son—so like himself, having the same kind of strength.

Both land lovers, possession lovers. "It is my farm,

my house, my horses, cattle, sheep." Soon now, another ten years, fifteen at the most, and the father would be ready for death. "See, already my hand slips a little. All of this to go out of my grasp." He, John Grey, had not got all of these possessions so easily. It had taken much patience, much persistence. No one but himself would ever quite know. Five, ten, fifteen years of work and saving, getting the Aspinwahl farm piece by piece. "The fools!" They had liked to think of themselves as aristocrats, throwing the land away, now twenty acres, now thirty, now fifty.

Raising horses that could never plow an acre of land.

And they had robbed the land too, had never put anything back, doing nothing to enrich it, build it up. Such a one thinking: "I'm an Aspinwahl, a gentleman. I do not soil my hands at the plow."

"Fools who do not know the meaning of land owned, possessions, money—responsibility. It is they who are second-rate men."

He had got an Aspinwahl for a wife and, as it had turned out, she was the best, the smartest and in the end, the best-looking one of the lot.

And now there was his son, standing at the moment near the mother. They had both come down off the porch. It would be natural and right for this one—he being what he already was, what he would become—for him, in his turn, to come into possession, to take command.

There would be, of course, the rights of the other children. If you have the stuff in you (John Grey felt that his son Don had) there is a way to manage. You buy the others out, make arrangements. There was Ted—he wouldn't be alive—and Mary and the two younger children. "The better for you if you have to struggle."

All of this, the implication of the moment of sudden struggle between a father and son, coming slowly afterwards to the man's daughter, as yet little more than a child. Does the drama take place when the seed is put into the ground or afterwards when the plant has pushed out of the ground and the bud breaks open, or still later, when the fruit ripens? There were the Greys with their ability—slow, saving, able, determined, patient. Why had they superseded the Aspinwahls in the Rich Valley? Aspinwahl blood also in the two children, Mary and Ted.

There was an Aspinwahl man—called "Uncle Fred," a brother to Louise Grey—who came some-

times to the farm. He was a rather striking-looking, tall old man with a gray Vandyke beard and a mustache, somewhat shabbily dressed but always with an indefinable air of class. He came from the county-seat town, where he lived now with a daughter who had married a merchant, a polite courtly old man who always froze into a queer silence in the presence of the sister's husband.

The son Don was standing near the mother on the day in the Fall, and the two children, Mary and Ted, stood apart.

"Don't, John," Louise Grey said again. The father, who had started toward the barns, stopped.

"Well, I guess I will."

"No, you won't," said young Don, speaking suddenly. There was a queer fixed look in his eyes. It had flashed into life—something that was between the two men: "I possess" . . . "I will possess." The father wheeled and looked sharply at the son and then ignored him.

For a moment the mother continued pleading.

"But why, why?"

"They make too much shade. The grass does not grow."

"But there is so much grass, so many acres of grass."

John Grey was answering his wife, but now again he looked at his son. There were unspoken words flying back and forth.

"I possess. I am in command here. What do you mean by telling me that I won't?"

"Ha! So! You possess now but soon I will possess."

"I'll see you in hell first."

"You fool! Not yet! Not yet!"

None of the words, set down above, was spoken at the moment, and afterwards the daughter Mary never did remember the exact words that had passed between the two men. There was a sudden quick flash of determination in Don—even perhaps sudden determination to stand by the mother—even perhaps something else—a feeling in the young Don out of the Aspinwahl blood in him—for the moment tree love superseding grass love—grass that would fatten steers. . . .

Winner of 4H Club prizes, champion young corn-raiser, judge of steers, land lover, possession lover.

"You won't," Don said again.

"Won't what?"

"Won't cut those trees."

The father said nothing more at the moment but

walked away from the little group toward the barns. The sun was still shining brightly. There was a sharp cold little wind. The two trees were like bonfires lighted against distant hills.

It was the noon hour and there were two men, both young, employees on the farm, who lived in a small tenant house beyond the barns. One of them, a man with a harelip, was married and the other, a rather handsome silent young man, boarded with him. They had just come from the midday meal and were going toward one of the barns. It was the beginning of the Fall corn-cutting time and they would be going together to a distant field to cut corn.

The father went to the barn and returned with the two men. They brought axes and a long cross-cut saw. "I want you to cut those two trees." There was something, a blind, even stupid determination in the man, John Grey. And at that moment his wife, the mother of his children . . . There was no way any of the children could ever know how many moments of the sort she had been through. She had married John Grey. He was her man.

"If you do, Father . . ." Don Grey said coldly.

"Do as I tell you! Cut those two trees!" This addressed to the two workmen. The one who had a harelip laughed. His laughter was like the bray of a donkey.

"Don't," said Louise Grey, but she was not addressing her husband this time. She stepped to her son and put a hand on his arm.

"Don't."

"*Don't cross him. Don't cross my man.*" Could a child like Mary Grey comprehend? It takes time to understand things that happen in life. Life unfolds slowly to the mind. Mary was standing with Ted, whose young face was white and tense. Death at his elbow. At any moment. At any moment.

"*I have been through this a hundred times. This is the way this man I married has succeeded. Nothing stops him. I married him; I have had my children by him.*

"*We women choose to submit.*

"*This is my affair, more than yours, Don, my son.*"

A woman hanging onto her things—the family, created about her.

The son not seeing things with her eyes. He shook off his mother's hand, lying on his arm. Louise Grey was younger than her husband, but, if he was now nearing sixty, she was drawing near fifty. At the moment she looked very delicate and fragile. There was

something, at the moment, in her bearing . . . Was there, after all, something in blood, the Aspinwahl blood?

In a dim way perhaps, at the moment the child Mary did comprehend. Women and their men. For her then, at that time, there was but one male, the child Ted. Afterwards she remembered how he looked at that moment, the curiously serious old look on his young face. There was even, she thought later, a kind of contempt for both the father and brother, as though he might have been saying to himself—he couldn't really have been saying it—he was too young: "*Well, we'll see. This is something. These foolish ones—my father and my brother. I myself haven't long to live. I'll see what I can, while I do live.*"

The brother Don stepped over near to where his father stood.

"If you do, Father . . ." he said again.

"Well?"

"I'll walk off this farm and I'll never come back."

"All right. Go then."

The father began directing the two men who had begun cutting the trees, each man taking a tree. The young man with the harelip kept laughing, the laughter like the bray of a donkey. "Stop that," the father said sharply, and the sound ceased abruptly. The son Don walked away, going rather aimlessly toward the barn. He approached one of the barns and then stopped. The mother, white now, half ran into the house.

The son returned toward the house, passing the two younger children without looking at them, but did not enter. The father did not look at him. He went hesitatingly along a path at the front of the house and through a gate and into a road. The road ran for several miles down through the valley and then, turning, went over a mountain to the county-seat town.

As it happened, only Mary saw the son Don when he returned to the farm. There were three or four tense days. Perhaps, all the time, the mother and son had been secretly in touch. There was a telephone in the house. The father stayed all day in the fields, and when he was in the house was silent.

Mary was in one of the barns on the day when Don came back and when the father and son met. It was an odd meeting.

The son came, Mary always afterwards thought, rather sheepishly. The father came out of a horse's stall. He had been throwing corn to work horses. Neither the father nor the son saw Mary. There was a car parked in the barn and she had crawled into the driver's seat, her hands on the steering wheel, pretending she was driving.

"Well," the father said. If he felt triumphant, he did not show his feeling.

"Well," said the son, "I have come back."

"Yes, I see," the father said. "They are cutting corn." He walked toward the barn door and then stopped. "It will be yours soon now," he said. "You can be boss then."

He said no more and both men went away, the father toward the distant fields and the son toward the house. Mary was afterwards quite sure that nothing more was ever said.

What had the father meant?

"When it is yours you can be the boss." It was too much for the child. Knowledge comes slowly. It meant:

"You will be in command, and for you, in your turn, it will be necessary to assert.

"Such men as we are cannot fool with delicate stuff. Some men are meant to command and others must obey. You can make them obey in your turn.

"There is a kind of death.

"Something in you must die before you can possess and command."

There was, so obviously, more than one kind of death. For Don Grey one kind and for the younger brother Ted, soon now perhaps, another.

Mary ran out of the barn that day, wanting eagerly to get out into the light, and afterwards, for a long time, she did not try to think her way through what had happened. She and her brother Ted did, however, afterwards, before he died, discuss quite often the two trees. They went on a cold day and put their fingers on the stumps, but the stumps were cold. Ted kept asserting that only men get their legs and arms cut off, and she protested. They continued doing things that had been forbidden Ted to do, but no one protested, and, a year or two later, when he died, he died during the night in his bed.

But while he lived, there was always, Mary afterwards thought, a curious sense of freedom, something that belonged to him that made it good, a great happiness, to be with him. It was, she finally thought, because having to die his kind of death, he never had to make the surrender his brother had made—to be sure of possessions, success, his time to command—would never have to face the more subtle and terrible death that had come to his older brother. □

DISCUSSION

In "Brother Death," Anderson often uses a **foil** for a character—another character that represents an opposing nature or belief. For example, the two brothers, Ted and Don, are so unlike each other as to be, in effect, opposites in their view of life, possessions, and death. Another example is the two hired men who finally cut down the tree—one married and harelipped, the other single and handsome, one silent, the other noisy and laughing.

FOR EXPLORATION

1. Discuss the mother and father of the story as foils for each other. What are their differences, and what are the sources of their differences?

2. (a) Why does the story begin with Ted and Mary observing the two trees already cut, with only the stumps remaining? (b) Wouldn't Anderson have been able to create more suspense if he had not revealed that the trees had actually been cut until the end of the story? (c) How important to Anderson's purposes is the suspense? Discuss.

3. (a) Discuss the ways in which Anderson develops the reader's concern for the trees, especially in the paragraph beginning: "They were lusty trees, their roots down in the rich, always damp soil. . . ." (b) What do the trees appear to symbolize?

4. What various meanings can you discover for the title of the story, "Brother Death"? See, especially, the last three paragraphs of the story.

CREATIVE RESPONSE

1. "There was something, a driving destructive thing in life, in all relationships between people." Thus begins a paragraph in the last half of "Brother Death." In a short essay, show how this sentence relates to the action of the story.

2. Have you ever observed, in your own experience, this "destructive thing in life" in your relationships with people? Write a short account in which you tell how you made a discovery of it.

BROWN BROTHERS

Sherwood Anderson   1876 / 1941

Sherwood Anderson grew up in Clyde, Ohio, working at odd jobs ranging from errand boy to stable groom. His father, a wandering house painter and harness maker, never made much money but was a very entertaining story-teller and amateur actor. From him, and from a literary idol, Mark Twain, young Anderson learned to use the rhythms of the oral story, an ability that later enabled him to achieve in his writings a deceptively unstudied air of reminiscence and improvisation.

At the age of fourteen Anderson quit school. For over twenty years he worked at various jobs both in Clyde and in Chicago, served in the Spanish-American War, returned to school, became a writer of advertising copy, and finally established a manufacturing company specializing in roof paint. He was thirty-six years old when, married and the father of three children, he suddenly left his factory and departed for Chicago, determined to devote his life to writing.

For a time he once again wrote advertising copy to support himself. Then in 1919 he published his first volume of short stories, *Winesburg, Ohio*. The book marked a radical change not only in the content but also in the form of the American short story. Since Anderson felt that "the true history of life" was "the history of moments" and not a charted plan, events in his stories often are not arranged in well-defined and completed patterns. Rather they seem to be the recording of events in the frustrated lives of undistinguished people in small-town America. With the additional publication of two other collections of short narratives, *The Triumph of the Egg* (1921) and *Horses and Men* (1923), Anderson became one of the important innovators in American literature.

Beginning in 1921 Anderson spent three restless years in part searching for a conducive atmosphere for his writing. After traveling in Europe, he lived for a time in New York, for a time in New Orleans where he met and encouraged William Faulkner. He finally settled in Marion, Virginia; bought the two town newspapers, one Republican and the other Democrat; and proceeded to act as managing editor for both of them. To the surprise of those who thought the move a momentary whim, Anderson lived there the rest of his life. The quality of his writing from this time on was not as brilliant as in the beginning, but one of his less impressive novels was something of a best seller, a condition which had not existed with his earlier, more important works. Anderson died at the age of sixty-four on his way to South America on an unofficial good-will trip.

Katherine Anne Porter

THE JILTING OF
GRANNY WEATHERALL

SHE flicked her wrist neatly out of Doctor Harry's pudgy careful fingers and pulled the sheet up to her chin. The brat ought to be in knee breeches. Doctoring around the country with spectacles on his nose! "Get along now, take your schoolbooks and go. There's nothing wrong with me."

Doctor Harry spread a warm paw like a cushion on her forehead where the forked green vein danced and made her eyelids twitch. "Now, now, be a good girl, and we'll have you up in no time."

"That's no way to speak to a woman nearly eighty years old just because she's down. I'd have you respect your elders, young man."

"Well, Missy, excuse me." Doctor Harry patted her cheek. "But I've got to warn you, haven't I? You're a marvel, but you must be careful or you're going to be good and sorry."

"Don't tell me what I'm going to be. I'm on my feet now, morally speaking. It's Cornelia. I had to go to bed to get rid of her."

Her bones felt loose, and floated around in her skin, and Doctor Harry floated like a balloon around the foot of the bed. He floated and pulled down his waistcoat and swung his glasses on a cord. "Well, stay where you are, it certainly can't hurt you."

"Get along and doctor your sick," said Granny Weatherall. "Leave a well woman alone. I'll call for you when I want you. . . . Where were you forty years ago when I pulled through milkleg and double pneumonia? You weren't even born. Don't let Cornelia lead you on," she shouted, because Doctor Harry appeared to float up to the ceiling and out. "I pay my own bills, and I don't throw my money away on nonsense!"

She meant to wave goodby, but it was too much trouble. Her eyes closed of themselves, it was like a dark curtain drawn around the bed. The pillow rose and floated under her, pleasant as a hammock in a light wind. She listened to the leaves rustling outside the window. No, somebody was swishing newspapers; no, Cornelia and Doctor Harry were whispering together. She leaped broad awake, thinking they whispered in her ear.

"She was never like this, *never* like this!" "Well, what can we expect?" "Yes, eighty years old. . . ."

Well, and what if she was? She still had ears. It was like Cornelia to whisper around doors. She always kept things secret in such a public way. She was always being tactful and kind. Cornelia was dutiful; that was the trouble with her. Dutiful and good: "So good and dutiful," said Granny, "that I'd like to spank her." She saw herself spanking Cornelia and making a fine job of it.

"What'd you say, Mother?"

Granny felt her face tying up in hard knots.

"Can't a body think, I'd like to know?"

"I thought you might want something."

"I do. I want a lot of things. First off, go away and don't whisper."

She lay and drowsed, hoping in her sleep that the children would keep out and let her rest a minute. It had been a long day. Not that she was tired. It was always pleasant to snatch a minute now and then. There was always so much to be done, let me see: tomorrow.

Tomorrow was far away and there was nothing to trouble about. Things were finished somehow when the time came; thank God there was always a little margin over for peace: then a person could spread out the plan of life and tuck in the edges orderly. It was good to have everything clean and folded away, with the hair brushes and tonic bottles sitting straight on the white embroidered linen: the day started without fuss and the pantry shelves laid out with rows of jelly glasses and brown jugs and white stone-china jars with blue whirligigs and words painted on them: coffee, tea, sugar, ginger, cinnamon, allspice: and the bronze clock with the lion on top nicely dusted off. The dust that lion could collect in twenty-four hours! The box in the attic with all those letters tied up, well, she'd have to go through that tomorrow. All those letters—George's letters and John's letters and her letters to them both—lying around for the children to find afterward made her uneasy. Yes, that would be tomorrow's business. No use to let them know how silly she had been once.

Copyright, 1930, 1958, by Katherine Anne Porter. Reprinted from her volume FLOWERING JUDAS AND OTHER STORIES by permission of Harcourt Brace Jovanovich, Inc. and Jonathan Cape Ltd.

While she was rummaging around she found death in her mind and it felt clammy and unfamiliar. She had spent so much time preparing for death there was no need for bringing it up again. Let it take care of itself now. When she was sixty she had felt very old, finished, and went around making farewell trips to see her children and grandchildren, with a secret in her mind: This is the very last of your mother, children! Then she made her will and came down with a long fever. That was all just a notion like a lot of other things, but it was lucky too, for she had once and for all got over the idea of dying for a long time. Now she couldn't be worried. She hoped she had better sense now. Her father had lived to be one hundred and two years old and had drunk a noggin of strong hot toddy on his last birthday. He told the reporters it was his daily habit, and he owed his long life to that. He had made quite a scandal and was very pleased about it. She believed she'd just plague Cornelia a little.

"Cornelia! Cornelia!" No footsteps, but a sudden hand on her cheek. "Bless you, where have you been?"

"Here, Mother."

"Well, Cornelia, I want a noggin of hot toddy."

"Are you cold, darling?"

"I'm chilly, Cornelia. Lying in bed stops the circulation. I must have told you that a thousand times."

Well, she could just hear Cornelia telling her husband that Mother was getting a little childish and they'd have to humor her. The thing that most annoyed her was that Cornelia thought she was deaf, dumb, and blind. Little hasty glances and tiny gestures tossed around her and over her head saying, "Don't cross her, let her have her way, she's eighty years old," and she sitting there as if she lived in a thin glass cage. Sometimes Granny almost made up her mind to pack up and move back to her own house where nobody could remind her every minute that she was old. Wait, wait, Cornelia, till your own children whisper behind your back!

In her day she had kept a better house and had got more work done. She wasn't too old yet for Lydia to be driving eighty miles for advice when one of the children jumped the track, and Jimmy still dropped in and talked things over: "Now, Mammy, you've a good business head, I want to know what you think of this? . . ." Old. Cornelia couldn't change the furniture around without asking. Little things, little things! They had been so sweet when they were little. Granny wished the old days were back again with the children young and everything to be done over. It had been a hard pull, but not too much for her. When she thought of all the food she had cooked, and all the clothes she had cut and sewed, and all the gardens she had made—well, the children showed it. There they were, made out of her, and they couldn't get away from that. Sometimes she wanted to see John again and point to them and say, Well, I didn't do so badly, did I? But that would have to wait. That was for tomorrow. She used to think of him as a man, but now all the children were older than their father, and he would be a child beside her if she saw him now. It seemed strange and there was something wrong in the idea. Why, he couldn't possibly recognize her. She had fenced in a hundred acres once, digging the postholes herself and clamping the wires with just a Negro boy to help. That changed a woman. John would be looking for a young woman with the peaked Spanish comb in her hair and the painted fan. Digging postholes changed a woman. Riding country roads in the winter when women had their babies was another thing: sitting up nights with sick horses and sick Negroes and sick children and hardly ever losing one. John, I hardly ever lost one of them! John would see that in a minute, that would be something he could understand, she wouldn't have to explain anything!

It made her feel like rolling up her sleeves and putting the whole place to rights again. No matter if Cornelia was determined to be everywhere at once, there were a great many things left undone on this place. She would start tomorrow and do them. It was good to be strong enough for everything, even if all you made melted and changed and slipped under your hands, so that by the time you finished you almost forgot what you were working for. What was it I set out to do? she asked herself intently, but she could not remember. A fog rose over the valley, she saw it marching across the creek swallowing the trees and moving up the hill like an army of ghosts. Soon it would be at the near edge of the orchard, and then it was time to go in and light the lamps. Come in, children, don't stay out in the night air.

Lighting the lamps had been beautiful. The children huddled up to her and breathed like little calves waiting at the bars in the twilight. Their eyes followed the match and watched the flame rise and settle in a blue curve, then they moved away from her. The lamp was lit, they didn't have to be scared and hang on to mother any more. Never, never, never more. God, for all my life I thank Thee. Without Thee, my God, I could never have done it. Hail, Mary, full of grace.[1]

I want you to pick all the fruit this year and see that nothing is wasted. There's always someone who can use it. Don't let good things rot for want of using. You waste life when you waste good food. Don't let things get lost. It's bitter to lose things. Now, don't let me get to thinking, not when I am tired and taking a little nap before supper. . . .

The pillow rose about her shoulders and pressed against her heart and the memory was being squeezed out of it: oh, push down the pillow, somebody: it would smother her if she tried to hold it. Such a fresh breeze blowing and such a green day with no threats in it. But he had not come, just the same. What does a woman do when she has put on the white veil and set out the white cake for a man and he doesn't come? She tried to remember. No, I swear he never harmed me but in that. He never harmed me but in that . . . and what if he did? There was the day, the day, but a whirl of dark smoke rose and covered it, crept up and over into the bright field where everything was planted so carefully in orderly rows. That was hell, she knew hell when she saw it. For sixty years she had prayed against remembering him and against losing her soul in the deep pit of hell, and now the two things were mingled in one and the thought of him was a smoky cloud from hell that moved and crept in her head when she had just got rid of Doctor Harry and was trying to rest a minute. Wounded vanity, Ellen, said a sharp voice in the top of her mind. Don't let your wounded vanity get the upper hand of you. Plenty of girls get jilted. You were jilted, weren't you? Then stand up to it. Her eyelids wavered and let in streamers of blue-gray light like tissue paper over her eyes. She must get up and pull the shades down or she'd never sleep. She was in bed again and the shades were not down. How could that happen? Better turn over, hide from the light, sleeping in the light gave you nightmares. "Mother, how do you feel now?" and a stinging wetness on her forehead. But I don't like having my face washed in cold water!

Hapsy? George? Lydia? Jimmy? No, Cornelia, and her features were swollen and full of little puddles. "They're coming, darling, they'll all be here soon." Go wash your face, child, you look funny.

Instead of obeying, Cornelia knelt down and put her head on the pillow. She seemed to be talking but there was no sound. "Well, are you tongue-tied? Whose birthday is it? Are you going to give a party?"

Cornelia's mouth moved urgently in strange shapes. "Don't do that, you bother me, daughter."

"Oh, no, Mother. Oh, no. . . ."

Nonsense. It was strange about children. They disputed your every word. "No what, Cornelia?"

"Here's Doctor Harry."

"I won't see that boy again. He just left five minutes ago."

"That was this morning, Mother. It's night now. Here's the nurse."

"This is Doctor Harry, Mrs. Weatherall. I never saw you look so young and happy!"

"Ah, I'll never be young again—but I'd be happy if they'd let me lie in peace and get rested."

She thought she spoke up loudly, but no one answered. A warm weight on her forehead, a warm bracelet on her wrist, and a breeze went on whispering, trying to tell her something. A shuffle of leaves in the everlasting hand of God, He blew on them and they danced and rattled. "Mother, don't mind, we're going to give you a little hypodermic." "Look here, daughter, how do ants get in this bed? I saw sugar ants yesterday." Did you send for Hapsy too?

It was Hapsy she really wanted. She had to go a long way back through a great many rooms to find Hapsy standing with a baby on her arm. She seemed to herself to be Hapsy also, and the baby on Hapsy's arm was Hapsy and himself and herself, all at once, and there was no surprise in the meeting. Then Hapsy melted from within and turned flimsy as gray gauze and the baby was a gauzy shadow, and Hapsy came up close and said, "I thought you'd never come," and looked at her very searchingly and said, "You haven't changed a bit!" They leaned forward to kiss, when Cornelia began whispering from a long way off, "Oh, is there anything you want to tell me? Is there anything I can do for you?"

Yes, she had changed her mind after sixty years and she would like to see George. I want you to find George. Find him and be sure to tell him I forgot him. I want him to know I had my husband just the same and my children and my house like any other wom-

---

1. *Hail, Mary, full of grace.* The opening line of a Catholic prayer.

an. A good house too and a good husband that I loved and fine children out of him. Better than I hoped for even. Tell him I was given back everything he took away and more. Oh, no, oh, God, no, there was something else besides the house and the man and the children. Oh, surely they were not all? What was it? Something not given back. . . . Her breath crowded down under her ribs and grew into a monstrous frightening shape with cutting edges; it bored up into her head, and the agony was unbelievable: Yes, John, get the Doctor now, no more talk, my time has come.

When this one was born it should be the last. The last. It should have been born first, for it was the one she had truly wanted. Everything came in good time. Nothing left out, left over. She was strong, in three days she would be as well as ever. Better. A woman needed milk in her to have her full health.

"Mother, do you hear me?"

"I've been telling you—"

"Mother, Father Connolly's here."

"I went to Holy Communion only last week. Tell him I'm not so sinful as all that."

"Father just wants to speak to you."

He could speak as much as he pleased. It was like him to drop in and inquire about her soul as if it were a teething baby, and then stay on for a cup of tea and a round of cards and gossip. He always had a funny story of some sort, usually about an Irishman who made his little mistakes and confessed them, and the point lay in some absurd thing he would blurt out in the confessional showing his struggles between native piety and original sin. Granny felt easy about her soul. Cornelia, where are your manners? Give Father Connolly a chair. She had her secret comfortable understanding with a few favorite saints who cleared a straight road to God for her. All as surely signed and sealed as the papers for the new Forty Acres. Forever . . . heirs and assigns forever. Since the day the wedding cake was not cut, but thrown out and wasted. The whole bottom dropped out of the world, and there she was blind and sweating with nothing under her feet and the walls falling away. His hand had caught her under the breast, she had not fallen, there was the freshly polished floor with the green rug on it, just as before. He had cursed like a sailor's parrot and said, "I'll kill him for you." Don't lay a hand on him, for my sake leave something to God. "Now, Ellen, you must believe what I tell you. . . ."

So there was nothing, nothing to worry about any more, except sometimes in the night one of the children screamed in a nightmare, and they both hustled out shaking and hunting for the matches and calling, "There, wait a minute, here we are!" John, get the doctor now, Hapsy's time has come. But there was Hapsy standing by the bed in a white cap. "Cornelia, tell Hapsy to take off her cap. I can't see her plain."

Her eyes opened very wide and the room stood out like a picture she had seen somewhere. Dark colors with the shadows rising toward the ceiling in long angles. The tall black dresser gleamed with nothing on it but John's picture, enlarged from a little one, with John's eyes very black when they should have been blue. You never saw him, so how do you know how he looked? But the man insisted the copy was perfect, it was very rich and handsome. For a picture, yes, but it's not my husband. The table by the bed had a linen cover and a candle and a crucifix. The light was blue from Cornelia's silk lampshades. No sort of light at all, just frippery. You had to live forty years with kerosene lamps to appreciate honest electricity. She felt very strong and she saw Doctor Harry with a rosy nimbus around him.

"You look like a saint, Doctor Harry, and I vow that's as near as you'll ever come to it."

"She's saying something."

"I heard you, Cornelia. What's all this carrying-on?"

"Father Connolly's saying—"

Cornelia's voice staggered and bumped like a cart in a bad road. It rounded corners and turned back again and arrived nowhere. Granny stepped up in the cart very lightly and reached for the reins, but a man sat beside her and she knew him by his hands, driving the cart. She did not look in his face, for she knew without seeing, but looked instead down the road where the trees leaned over and bowed to each other and a thousand birds were singing a Mass. She felt like singing too, but she put her hand in the bosom of her dress and pulled out a rosary, and Father Connolly murmured Latin in a very solemn voice and tickled her feet.[2] My God, will you stop that nonsense? I'm a married woman. What if he did run away and leave me to face the priest by myself? I found another a whole world better. I wouldn't

---

2. *Father Connolly . . . feet.* The priest is administering the sacrament for the dying, which includes anointing the hands and feet.

have exchanged my husband for anybody except St. Michael himself, and you may tell him that for me with a thank you in the bargain.

Light flashed on her closed eyelids, and a deep roaring shook her. Cornelia, is that lightning? I hear thunder. There's going to be a storm. Close all the windows. Call the children in. . . . "Mother, here we are, all of us." "Is that you, Hapsy?" "Oh, no, I'm Lydia. We drove as fast as we could." Their faces drifted above her, drifted away. The rosary fell out of her hands and Lydia put it back. Jimmy tried to help, their hands fumbled together, and Granny closed two fingers around Jimmy's thumb. Beads wouldn't do, it must be something alive. She was so amazed her thoughts ran round and round. So, my dear Lord, this is my death and I wasn't even thinking about it. My children have come to see me die. But I can't, it's not time. Oh, I always hated surprises. I wanted to give Cornelia the amethyst set— Cornelia, you're to have the amethyst set, but Hapsy's to wear it when she wants, and, Doctor Harry, do shut up. Nobody sent for you. Oh, my dear Lord, do wait a minute. I meant to do something about the Forty Acres, Jimmy doesn't need it and Lydia will later on, with that worthless husband of hers. I meant to finish the altar cloth and send six bottles of wine to Sister Borgia for her dyspepsia.

I want to send six bottles of wine to Sister Borgia, Father Connolly, now don't let me forget.

Cornelia's voice made short turns and tilted over and crashed. "Oh, Mother, oh, Mother, oh, Mother. . . ."

"I'm not going, Cornelia. I'm taken by surprise. I can't go."

You'll see Hapsy again. What about her? "I thought you'd never come." Granny made a long journey outward, looking for Hapsy. What if I don't find her? What then? Her heart sank down and down, there was no bottom to death, she couldn't come to the end of it. The blue light from Cornelia's lampshade drew into a tiny point in the center of her brain, it flickered and winked like an eye, quietly it fluttered and dwindled. Granny lay curled down within herself, amazed and watchful, staring at the point of light that was herself; her body was now only a deeper mass of shadow in an endless darkness and this darkness would curl around the light and swallow it up. God, give a sign!

For the second time there was no sign. Again no bridegroom and the priest in the house. She could not remember any other sorrow because this grief wiped them all away. Oh, no, there's nothing more cruel than this—I'll never forgive it. She stretched herself with a deep breath and blew out the light. □

DISCUSSION

In "The Jilting of Granny Weatherall," time is a fluid medium. One time period flows gently into another, as the mind is moved by chance memories, recurring phrases or images. It is thus that our minds work. Re-creation of this mind-flow is, in fiction, called the **stream of consciousness.** Thoughts and images and ideas and memories flow through the mind as in a river that is flooding and carrying with it all the debris it encounters. For another example of this fictional method or technique, see Ambrose Bierce, "An Occurrence at Owl Creek Bridge" (page 251 C).

FOR EXPLORATION

1. (a) Describe what happens in the sickroom while Granny is reliving the past. (b) How much time do these actual events cover? (c) How is the seemingly random order in which past events come into Granny's mind related to happenings in the sickroom? (d) To what situations in the past do Granny's thoughts keep returning? Why?

2. (a) Tell in detail the story of the jilting mentioned in the title. (b) What significance do you find in Miss Porter's choice of a surname for Granny? (c) How long ago did the jilting occur? (d) What is Granny's attitude toward it? (e) Why does the author reveal the facts about the jilting as she does instead of giving the information straightforwardly and then ending her story?

3. In "The Jilting of Granny Weatherall," the style of writing suggests the vagueness and confusion as well as the moments of clarity that characterize Granny. Thus passages like ". . . Doctor Harry floated like a balloon around the foot of the bed" alternate with sharp images like ". . . white stone-china jars with blue whirligigs and words painted on them . . . ." (*a*) Cite passages in which the manner of writing reflects Granny's state of mind. (*b*) Do most of the clearly visualized scenes relate to the present or the past? Explain why this is so.

CREATIVE RESPONSE

One of the hardest things in the world to do is to observe your own mind at work or play. Try to catch your self off-guard to see how your mind really moves from one idea or image to another. What set it in motion? What changed the direction? Write an account of spying on your own mind.

Katherine Anne Porter   1890 /

In 1941 while living in Baton Rouge, Louisiana, Katherine Anne Porter was asked for a biographical sketch and responded in part as follows: "I was born at Indian Creek, Texas, brought up in Texas and Louisiana, and educated in small Southern convent schools. I was precocious, nervous, rebellious, unteachable, and made life very uncomfortable for myself and I suppose for those around me. As soon as I learned to form letters on paper, at about three years, I began to write stories, and this has been the basic and absorbing occupation, the intact line of my life which directs my actions, determines my point of view, and profoundly affects my character and personality, my social beliefs and economic status, and the kind of friendships I form. I did not choose this vocation, and if I had any say in the matter, I would not have chosen it. I made no attempt to publish anything until I was thirty, but I have written and destroyed manuscripts quite literally by the trunkful. I spent fifteen years wandering about, weighted horribly with masses of paper and little else. Yet for this vocation I was and am willing to live and die, and I consider very few other things of the slightest importance. . . .

"My reading until my twenty-fifth year was a grand sweep of all English and translated classics from the beginning up to about 1800. Then I began with the newcomers, and found new incitements. Wherever I have lived I have done book reviewing, political articles, hack writing of all kinds,

editing, rewriting other people's manuscripts, by way of earning a living—and a sorry living it was, too. Without the help of devoted friends I should have perished many times over. . . ." There are aspects of her life she does not touch upon. At the age of twenty-one she was working for a newspaper in Chicago; she later played bit parts in motion pictures, and still later went to Mexico to study Aztec and Mayan art where she became involved in the Obregon Revolution.

Porter's first published volume was *Flowering Judas and Other Stories*, which appeared in 1930. The stories, "The Jilting of Granny Weatherall" among them, were delicate and precise, sensitive and subtle. The years of preparation had paid off in a technical mastery of the art of writing which was impeccable. The important place Porter has won for herself among contemporary American writers is based on a comparatively small total output. A slow writer, she has produced only a few books in the more than forty years since *Flowering Judas* was first published. Furthermore, some of her works have experienced substantial delays in publication because of the exacting care which goes into her writing. Her first and only novel *Ship of Fools* was begun in 1940 and did not reach completion until 1962. She calls it the "hardest thing I ever did in my life." A biography of Cotton Mather begun in 1927 is still not finished.

In 1966 Porter won both the National Book Award and the Pulitzer Prize for *The Collected Stories of Katherine Anne Porter.*

VOGUE COVER OF FLAPPER—COPYRIGHT (C) 1927, 1955 BY THE CONDE NAST PUBLICATIONS INC.

Francis Scott Fitzgerald

BERNICE
BOBS HER HAIR

AFTER dark on Saturday night one could stand on the first tee of the golf course and see the country-club windows as a yellow expanse over a very black and wavy ocean. The waves of this ocean, so to speak, were the heads of many curious caddies, a few of the more ingenious chauffeurs, the golf professional's deaf sister—and there were usually several stray, diffident waves who might have rolled inside had they so desired. This was the gallery.

The balcony was inside. It consisted of the circle of wicker chairs that lined the wall of the combination clubroom and ballroom. At these Saturday night dances it was largely feminine; a great babble of middle-aged ladies with sharp eyes and icy hearts behind lorgnettes and large bosoms. The main function of the balcony was critical. It occasionally showed grudging admiration, but never approval, for it is well known among ladies over thirty-five that when the younger set dance in the summertime it is with the very worst intentions in the world, and if they are not bombarded with stony eyes stray couples will dance weird barbaric interludes in the corners, and the more popular, more dangerous girls will sometimes be kissed in the parked limousines of unsuspecting dowagers.

But, after all, this critical circle is not close enough to the stage to see the actors' faces and catch the subtler by-play. It can only frown and lean, ask questions and make satisfactory deductions from its set of postulates, such as the one which states that every young man with a large income leads the life of a hunted partridge. It never really appreciates the drama of the shifting, semicruel world of adolescence. No; boxes, orchestra-circle, principals, and chorus are represented by the medley of faces and voices that sway to the plaintive African rhythm of Dyer's dance orchestra.

From sixteen-year-old Otis Ormonde, who has two more years at Hill School, to G. Reece Stoddard, over whose bureau at home hangs a Harvard law diploma; from little Madeleine Hogue, whose hair still feels strange and uncomfortable on top of her head, to Bessie MacRae, who has been the life of the party a little too long—more than ten years—the medley is not only the center of the stage but contains the only people capable of getting an unobstructed view of it.

With a flourish and a bang the music stops. The couples exchange artificial, effortless smiles, facetiously repeat "*la-de-da-da*-dum-*dum*," and then the clatter of young feminine voices soars over the burst of clapping.

A few disappointed stags caught in midfloor as they had been about to cut in subsided listlessly back to the walls, because this was not like the riotous Christmas dances—these summer hops were considered just pleasantly warm and exciting, where even the younger marrieds rose and performed ancient waltzes and terrifying fox trots to the tolerant amusement of their younger brothers and sisters.

Warren McIntyre, who casually attended Yale, being one of the unfortunate stags, felt in his dinner-coat pocket for a cigarette and strolled out onto the wide, semidark veranda, where couples were scattered at tables, filling the lantern-hung night with vague words and hazy laughter. He nodded here and there at the less absorbed and as he passed each couple some half-forgotten fragment of a story played in his mind, for it was not a large city and every one was Who's Who to every one else's past. There, for example, were Jim Strain and Ethel Demorest, who had been privately engaged for three years. Every one knew that as soon as Jim managed to hold a job for more than two months she would marry him. Yet how bored they both looked, and how wearily Ethel regarded Jim sometimes, as if she wondered why she had trained the vines of her affection on such a wind-shaken poplar.

Warren was nineteen and rather pitying with those of his friends who hadn't gone East to college. But, like most boys, he bragged tremendously about the girls of his city when he was away from it. There was Genevieve Ormonde, who regularly made the rounds of dances, house parties, and football games at Princeton, Yale, Williams, and Cornell; there was black-eyed Roberta Dillon, who was quite as famous

"Bernice Bobs Her Hair" (Copyright 1920 The Curtis Publishing Company; renewal copyright 1948) is reprinted by permission of Charles Scribner's Sons and the Bodley Head, from FLAPPERS AND PHILOSOPHERS by F. Scott Fitzgerald. (British Source: The Bodley Head Scott Fitzgerald Volume 5).

to her own generation as Hiram Johnson or Ty Cobb[1]; and, of course, there was Marjorie Harvey, who besides having a fairylike face and a dazzling, bewildering tongue was already justly celebrated for having turned five cart wheels in succession during the past pump-and-slipper dance at New Haven.

Warren, who had grown up across the street from Marjorie, had long been "crazy about her." Sometimes she seemed to reciprocate his feeling with a faint gratitude, but she had tried him by her infallible test and informed him gravely that she did not love him. Her test was that when she was away from him she forgot him and had affairs with other boys. Warren found this discouraging, especially as Marjorie had been making little trips all summer, and for the first two or three days after each arrival home he saw great heaps of mail on the Harveys' hall table addressed to her in various masculine handwritings. To make matters worse, all during the month of August she had been visited by her cousin Bernice from Eau Claire, and it seemed impossible to see her alone. It was always necessary to hunt round and find someone to take care of Bernice. As August waned this was becoming more and more difficult.

Much as Warren worshiped Marjorie, he had to admit that Cousin Bernice was sorta hopeless. She was pretty, with dark hair and high color, but she was no fun on a party. Every Saturday night he danced a long arduous duty dance with her to please Marjorie, but he had never been anything but bored in her company.

"Warren"—a soft voice at his elbow broke in upon his thoughts, and he turned to see Marjorie, flushed and radiant as usual. She laid a hand on his shoulder and a glow settled almost imperceptibly over him.

"Warren," she whispered, "do something for me—dance with Bernice. She's been stuck with little Otis Ormonde for almost an hour."

Warren's glow faded.

"Why—sure," he answered half-heartedly.

"You don't mind, do you? I'll see that you don't get stuck."

"'Sall right."

Marjorie smiled—that smile that was thanks enough.

"You're an angel, and I'm obliged loads."

With a sigh the angel glanced round the veranda, but Bernice and Otis were not in sight. He wandered back inside, and there in front of the women's dressing room he found Otis in the center of a group of young men who were convulsed with laughter. Otis was brandishing a piece of timber he had picked up, and discoursing volubly.

"She's gone in to fix her hair," he announced wildly. "I'm waiting to dance another hour with her."

Their laughter was renewed.

"Why don't some of you cut in?" cried Otis resentfully. "She likes more variety."

"Why, Otis," suggested a friend, "you've just barely got used to her."

"Why the two-by-four, Otis?" inquired Warren, smiling.

"The two-by-four? Oh, this? This is a club. When she comes out I'll hit her on the head and knock her in again."

Warren collapsed on a settee and howled with glee.

"Never mind, Otis," he articulated finally. "I'm relieving you this time."

Otis simulated a sudden fainting attack and handed the stick to Warren.

"If you need it, old man," he said hoarsely.

No matter how beautiful or brilliant a girl may be, the reputation of not being frequently cut in on makes her position at a dance unfortunate. Perhaps boys prefer her company to that of the butterflies with whom they dance a dozen times an evening, but youth in this jazz-nourished generation is temperamentally restless, and the idea of fox-trotting more than one full fox trot with the same girl is distasteful, not to say odious. When it comes to several dances and the intermissions between, she can be quite sure that a young man, once relieved, will never tread on her wayward toes again.

Warren danced the next full dance with Bernice, and finally, thankful for the intermission, he led her to a table on the veranda. There was a moment's silence while she did unimpressive things with her fan.

"It's hotter here than in Eau Claire," she said.

Warren stifled a sigh and nodded. It might be for all he knew or cared. He wondered idly whether she was a poor conversationalist because she got no attention or got no attention because she was a poor conversationalist.

1. *Hiram Johnson or Ty Cobb,* a politician and a baseball player whose reputations reached legendary proportions during the twenties.

"You going to be here much longer?" he asked, and then turned rather red. She might suspect his reasons for asking.

"Another week," she answered, and stared at him as if to lunge at his next remark when it left his lips.

Warren fidgeted. Then with a sudden charitable impulse he decided to try part of his line on her. He turned and looked at her eyes.

"You've got an awfully kissable mouth," he began quietly.

This was a remark that he sometimes made to girls at college proms when they were talking in just such half dark as this. Bernice distinctly jumped. She turned an ungraceful red and became clumsy with her fan. No one had ever made such a remark to her before.

"Fresh!"—the word had slipped out before she realized it, and she bit her lip. Too late she decided to be amused, and offered him a flustered smile.

Warren was annoyed. Though not accustomed to have that remark taken seriously, still it usually provoked a laugh or a paragraph of sentimental banter. And he hated to be called fresh, except in a joking way. His charitable impulse died and he switched the topic.

"Jim Strain and Ethel Demorest sitting out as usual," he commented.

This was more in Bernice's line, but a faint regret mingled with her relief as the subject changed. Men did not talk to her about kissable mouths, but she knew that they talked in some such way to other girls.

"Oh, yes," she said, and laughed. "I hear they've been mooning round for years without a red penny. Isn't it silly?"

Warren's disgust increased. Jim Strain was a close friend of his brother's, and anyway he considered it bad form to sneer at people for not having money. But Bernice had had no intention of sneering. She was merely nervous.

When Marjorie and Bernice reached home at half after midnight they said good night at the top of the stairs. Though cousins, they were not intimates. As a matter of fact Marjorie had no female intimates —she considered girls stupid. Bernice on the contrary all through this parent-arranged visit had rather longed to exchange those confidences flavored with giggles and tears that she considered an indispensable factor in all feminine intercourse. But in this respect she found Marjorie rather cold; felt somehow the same difficulty in talking to her that she had in talking to men. Marjorie never giggled, was never frightened, seldom embarrassed, and in fact had very few of the qualities which Bernice considered appropriately and blessedly feminine.

As Bernice busied herself with toothbrush and paste this night she wondered for the hundredth time why she never had any attention when she was away from home. That her family were the wealthiest in Eau Claire, that her mother entertained tremendously, gave little dinners for her daughter before all dances and bought her a car of her own to drive round in, never occurred to her as factors in her home-town social success. Like most girls she had been brought up on the warm milk prepared by Annie Fellows Johnston[2] and on novels in which the female was beloved because of certain mysterious womanly qualities, always mentioned but never displayed.

Bernice felt a vague pain that she was not at present engaged in being popular. She did not know that had it not been for Marjorie's campaigning she would have danced the entire evening with one man; but she knew that even in Eau Claire other girls with less position and less pulchritude were given a much bigger rush. She attributed this to something subtly unscrupulous in those girls. It had never worried her, and if it had her mother would have assured her that the other girls cheapened themselves and that men really respected girls like Bernice.

She turned out the light in her bathroom, and on an impulse decided to go in and chat for a moment with her Aunt Josephine, whose light was still on. Her soft slippers bore her noiselessly down the carpeted hall, but hearing voices inside she stopped near the partly opened door. Then she caught her own name, and without any definite intention of eavesdropping lingered—and the thread of the conversation going on inside pierced her consciousness sharply as if it had been drawn through with a needle.

"She's absolutely hopeless!" It was Marjorie's voice. "Oh, I know what you're going to say! So many people have told you how pretty and sweet she is, and how she can cook! What of it? She has a bum time. Men don't like her."

2. *Annie Fellows Johnston* (1863–1931), creator of *The Little Colonel* stories, a series of children's books whose heroine lived in a world where simple virtues were glorified and good intentions prevailed.

"What's a little cheap popularity?"

Mrs. Harvey sounded annoyed.

"It's everything when you're eighteen," said Marjorie emphatically. "I've done my best. I've been polite and I've made men dance with her, but they just won't stand being bored. When I think of that gorgeous coloring wasted on such a ninny, and think what Martha Carey could do with it—oh!"

"There's no courtesy these days."

Mrs. Harvey's voice implied that modern situations were too much for her. When she was a girl all young ladies who belonged to nice families had glorious times.

"Well," said Marjorie, "no girl can permanently bolster up a lame-duck visitor, because these days it's every girl for herself. I've even tried to drop her hints about clothes and things, and she's been furious—given me the funniest looks. She's sensitive enough to know she's not getting away with much, but I'll bet she consoles herself by thinking that she's very virtuous and that I'm too gay and fickle and will come to a bad end. All unpopular girls think that way. Sour grapes! Sarah Hopkins refers to Genevieve and Roberta and me as gardenia girls! I'll bet she'd give ten years of her life and her European education to be a gardenia girl and have three or four men in love with her and be cut in on every few feet at dances."

"It seems to me," interrupted Mrs. Harvey rather wearily, "that you ought to be able to do something for Bernice. I know she's not very vivacious."

Marjorie groaned.

"Vivacious! Good grief! I've never heard her say anything to a boy except that it's hot or the floor's crowded or that she's going to school in New York next year. Sometimes she asks them what kind of car they have and tells them the kind she has. Thrilling!"

There was a short silence, and then Mrs. Harvey took up her refrain:

"All I know is that other girls not half so sweet and attractive get partners. Martha Carey, for instance, is stout and loud, and her mother is distinctly common. Roberta Dillon is so thin this year that she looks as though Arizona were the place for her. She's dancing herself to death."

"But, Mother," objected Marjorie impatiently, "Martha is cheerful and awfully witty and an awfully slick girl, and Roberta's a marvelous dancer. She's been popular for ages!"

Mrs. Harvey yawned.

"I think it's that crazy Indian blood in Bernice," continued Marjorie. "Maybe she's a reversion to type. Indian women all just sat round and never said anything."

"Go to bed, you silly child," laughed Mrs. Harvey. "I wouldn't have told you that if I'd thought you were going to remember it. And I think most of your ideas are perfectly idiotic," she finished sleepily.

There was another silence, while Marjorie considered whether or not convincing her mother was worth the trouble. People over forty can seldom be permanently convinced of anything. At eighteen our convictions are hills from which we look; at forty-five they are caves in which we hide.

Having decided this, Marjorie said good night. When she came out into the hall it was quite empty.

While Marjorie was breakfasting late next day Bernice came into the room with a rather formal good morning, sat down opposite, stared intently over, and slightly moistened her lips.

"What's on your mind?" inquired Marjorie, rather puzzled.

Bernice paused before she threw her hand grenade.

"I heard what you said about me to your mother last night."

Marjorie was startled, but she showed only a faintly heightened color and her voice was quite even when she spoke.

"Where were you?"

"In the hall. I didn't mean to listen—at first."

After an involuntary look of contempt Marjorie dropped her eyes and became very interested in balancing a stray corn flake on her finger.

"I guess I'd better go back to Eau Claire—if I'm such a nuisance." Bernice's lower lip was trembling violently and she continued on a wavering note: "I've tried to be nice, and—and I've been first neglected and then insulted. No one ever visited me and got such treatment."

Marjorie was silent.

"But I'm in the way, I see. I'm a drag on you. Your friends don't like me." She paused, and then remembered another one of her grievances. "Of course I was furious last week when you tried to hint to me that that dress was unbecoming. Don't you think I know how to dress myself?"

"No," murmured Marjorie less than half-aloud.

"What?"

"I didn't hint anything," said Marjorie succinctly.

"I said, as I remember, that it was better to wear a becoming dress three times straight than to alternate it with two frights."

"Do you think that was a very nice thing to say?"

"I wasn't trying to be nice." Then after a pause: "When do you want to go?"

Bernice drew in her breath sharply.

"Oh!" It was a little half-cry.

Marjorie looked up in surprise.

"Didn't you say you were going?"

"Yes, but—"

"Oh, you were only bluffing!"

They stared at each other across the breakfast table for a moment. Misty waves were passing before Bernice's eyes, while Marjorie's face wore that rather hard expression that she used when slightly intoxicated undergraduates were making love to her.

"So you were bluffing," she repeated as if it were what she might have expected.

Bernice admitted it by bursting into tears. Marjorie's eyes showed boredom.

"You're my cousin," sobbed Bernice. "I'm v-v-visiting you. I was to stay a month, and if I go home my mother will know and she'll wah-wonder—"

Marjorie waited until the shower of broken words collapsed into little sniffles.

"I'll give you my month's allowance," she said coldly, "and you can spend this last week anywhere you want. There's a very nice hotel—"

Bernice's sobs rose to a flute note, and rising of a sudden she fled from the room.

An hour later, while Marjorie was in the library absorbed in composing one of those non-committal, marvelously elusive letters that only a young girl can write, Bernice reappeared, very red-eyed and consciously calm. She cast no glance at Marjorie but took a book at random from the shelf and sat down as if to read. Marjorie seemed absorbed in her letter and continued writing. When the clock showed noon Bernice closed her book with a snap.

"I suppose I'd better get my railroad ticket."

This was not the beginning of the speech she had rehearsed upstairs, but as Marjorie was not getting her cues—wasn't urging her to be reasonable; it's all a mistake—it was the best opening she could muster.

"Just wait till I finish this letter," said Marjorie without looking round. "I want to get it off in the next mail."

After another minute, during which her pen scratched busily, she turned round and relaxed with an air of "at your service." Again Bernice had to speak.

"Do you want me to go home?"

"Well," said Marjorie, considering, "I suppose if you're not having a good time you'd better go. No use being miserable."

"Don't you think common kindness—"

"Oh, please don't quote *Little Women*!" cried Marjorie impatiently, "That's out of style."

"You think so?"

"Heavens, yes! What modern girl could live like those inane females?"

"They were the models for our mothers."

Marjorie laughed.

"Yes, they were—not! Besides, our mothers were all very well in their way, but they know very little about their daughters' problems."

Bernice drew herself up.

"Please don't talk about my mother."

Marjorie laughed.

"I don't think I mentioned her."

Bernice felt that she was being led away from her subject.

"Do you think you've treated me very well?"

"I've done my best. You're rather hard material to work with."

The lids of Bernice's eyes reddened.

"I think you're hard and selfish, and you haven't a feminine quality in you."

"Oh, my Lord!" cried Marjorie in desperation. "You little nut! Girls like you are responsible for all the tiresome colorless marriages; all those ghastly inefficiencies that pass as feminine qualities. What a blow it must be when a man with imagination marries the beautiful bundle of clothes that he's been building ideals round, and finds that she's just a weak, whining, cowardly mass of affectations!"

Bernice's mouth had slipped half open.

"The womanly woman!" continued Marjorie. "Her whole early life is occupied in whining criticisms of girls like me who really do have a good time."

Bernice's jaw descended farther as Marjorie's voice rose.

"There's some excuse for an ugly girl whining. If I'd been irretrievably ugly I'd never have forgiven my parents for bringing me into the world. But you're starting life without any handicap—" Marjorie's little fist clenched. "If you expect me to weep with you you'll be disappointed. Go or stay, just as you like." And picking up her letters she left the room.

Bernice claimed a headache and failed to appear at luncheon. They had a matinee date for the afternoon, but the headache persisting, Marjorie made explanations to a not very downcast boy. But when she returned late in the afternoon she found Bernice with a strangely set face waiting for her in her bedroom.

"I've decided," began Bernice without preliminaries, "that maybe you're right about things—possibly not. But if you'll tell me why your friends aren't—aren't interested in me I'll see if I can do what you want me to."

Marjorie was at the mirror shaking down her hair.

"Do you mean it?"

"Yes."

"Without reservations? Will you do exactly what I say?"

"Well, I—"

"Well nothing! Will you do exactly as I say?"

"If they're sensible things."

"They're not! You're no case for sensible things."

"Are you going to make—to recommend—"

"Yes, everything. If I tell you to take boxing lessons you'll have to do it. Write home and tell your mother you're going to stay another two weeks."

"If you'll tell me—"

"All right—I'll just give you a few examples now. First, you have no ease of manner. Why? Because you're never sure about your personal appearance. When a girl feels that she's perfectly groomed and dressed she can forget that part of her. That's charm. The more parts of yourself you can afford to forget the more charm you have."

"Don't I look all right?"

"No; for instance, you never take care of your eyebrows. They're black and lustrous, but by leaving them straggly they're a blemish. They'd be beautiful if you'd take care of them in one-tenth the time you take doing nothing. You're going to brush them so that they'll grow straight."

Bernice raised the brows in question.

"Do you mean to say that men notice eyebrows?"

"Yes—subconsciously. And when you go home you ought to have your teeth straightened a little. It's almost imperceptible, still—"

"But I thought," interrupted Bernice in bewilderment, "that you despised little dainty feminine things like that."

"I hate dainty minds," answered Marjorie. "But a girl has to be dainty in person. If she looks like a million dollars she can talk about Russia, ping-pong, or the League of Nations and get away with it."

"What else?"

"Oh, I'm just beginning! There's your dancing."

"Don't I dance all right?"

"No, you don't—you lean on a man; yes, you do—ever so slightly. I noticed it when we were dancing together yesterday. And you dance standing up straight instead of bending over a little. Probably some old lady on the side line once told you that you looked so dignified that way. But except with a very small girl it's much harder on the man, and he's the one that counts."

"Go on." Bernice's brain was reeling.

"Well, you've got to learn to be nice to men who are sad birds. You look as if you'd been insulted whenever you're thrown with any except the most popular boys. Why, Bernice, I'm cut in on every few feet—and who does most of it? Why, those very sad birds. No girl can afford to neglect them. They're the big part of any crowd. Young boys too shy to talk are the very best conversational practice. Clumsy boys are the best dancing practice. If you can follow them and yet look graceful you can follow a baby tank across a barb-wire skyscraper."

Bernice sighed profoundly, but Marjorie was not through.

"If you go to a dance and really amuse, say, three sad birds that dance with you; if you talk so well to them that they forget they're stuck with you, you've done something. They'll come back next time, and gradually so many sad birds will dance with you that the attractive boys will see there's no danger of being stuck—then they'll dance with you."

"Yes," agreed Bernice faintly. "I think I begin to see."

"And finally," concluded Marjorie, "poise and charm will just come. You'll wake up some morning knowing you've attained it, and men will know it too."

Bernice rose.

"It's been awfully kind of you—but nobody's ever talked to me like this before, and I feel sort of startled."

Marjorie made no answer but gazed pensively at her own image in the mirror.

"You're a peach to help me," continued Bernice.

Still Marjorie did not answer, and Bernice thought she had seemed too grateful.

"I know you don't like sentiment," she said timidly.

Marjorie turned to her quickly.

"Oh, I wasn't thinking about that. I was considering whether we hadn't better bob your hair."

Bernice collapsed backward upon the bed.

On the following Wednesday evening there was a dinner-dance at the country club. When the guests strolled in, Bernice found her place card with a slight feeling of irritation. Though at her right sat G. Reece Stoddard, a most desirable and distinguished young bachelor, the all-important left held only Charley Paulson. Charley lacked height, beauty, and social shrewdness, and in her new enlightenment Bernice decided that his only qualification to be her partner was that he had never been stuck with her. But this feeling of irritation left with the last of the soup plates, and Marjorie's specific instruction came to her. Swallowing her pride she turned to Charley Paulson and plunged.

"Do you think I ought to bob my hair, Mr. Charley Paulson?"

Charley looked up in surprise.

"Why?"

"Because I'm considering it. It's such a sure and easy way of attracting attention."

Charley smiled pleasantly. He could not know this had been rehearsed. He replied that he didn't know much about bobbed hair. But Bernice was there to tell him.

"I want to be a society vampire, you see," she announced coolly, and went on to inform him that bobbed hair was the necessary prelude. She added that she wanted to ask his advice, because she had heard he was so critical about girls.

Charley, who knew as much about the psychology of women as he did of the mental states of Buddhist contemplatives, felt vaguely flattered.

"So I've decided," she continued, her voice rising slightly, "that early next week I'm going down to the Sevier Hotel barbershop, sit in the first chair, and get my hair bobbed." She faltered, noticing that the people near her had paused in their conversation and were listening; but after a confused second Marjorie's coaching told, and she finished her paragraph to the vicinity at large. "Of course I'm charging admission, but if you'll all come down and encourage me I'll issue passes for the inside seats."

There was a ripple of appreciative laughter, and under cover of it G. Reece Stoddard leaned over quickly and said close to her ear: "I'll take a box right now."

She met his eyes and smiled as if he had said something surpassingly brilliant.

"Do you believe in bobbed hair?" asked G. Reece in the same undertone.

"I think it's unmoral," affirmed Bernice gravely. "But, of course, you've either got to amuse people or feed 'em or shock 'em." Marjorie had culled this from Oscar Wilde.[3] It was greeted with a ripple of laughter from the men and a series of quick, intent looks from the girls. And then as though she had said nothing of wit or moment Bernice turned again to Charley and spoke confidentially in his ear.

"I want to ask you your opinion of several people. I imagine you're a wonderful judge of character."

Charley thrilled faintly—paid her a subtle compliment by overturning her water.

Two hours later, while Warren McIntyre was standing passively in the stag line abstracted, watching the dancers and wondering whither and with whom Marjorie had disappeared, an unrelated perception began to creep slowly upon him—a perception that Bernice, cousin to Marjorie, had been cut in on several times in the past five minutes. He closed his eyes, opened them, and looked again. Several minutes back she had been dancing with a visiting boy, a matter easily accounted for; a visiting boy would know no better. But now she was dancing with someone else, and there was Charley Paulson headed for her with enthusiastic determination in his eye. Funny—Charley seldom danced with more than three girls an evening.

Warren was distinctly surprised when—the exchange having been effected—the man relieved proved to be none other than G. Reece Stoddard himself. And G. Reece seemed not at all jubilant at being relieved. Next time Bernice danced near, Warren regarded her intently. Yes, she was pretty, distinctly pretty; and tonight her face seemed really vivacious. She had that look that no woman, however histrionically proficient, can successfully counterfeit—she looked as if she were having a good time. He liked the way she had her hair arranged, wondered if it was brilliantine that made it glisten so. And that dress was becoming—a dark red that set off her

---

3. *Oscar Wilde* (1854–1900), Irish poet and dramatist known for his wit.

shadowy eyes and high coloring. He remembered that he had thought her pretty when she first came to town, before he had realized that she was dull. Too bad she was dull—dull girls unbearable—certainly pretty though.

His thoughts zigzagged back to Marjorie. This disappearance would be like other disappearances. When she reappeared he would demand where she had been—would be told emphatically that it was none of his business. What a pity she was so sure of him! She basked in the knowledge that no other girl in town interested him; she defied him to fall in love with Genevieve or Roberta.

Warren sighed. The way to Marjorie's affections was a labyrinth indeed. He looked up. Bernice was again dancing with the visiting boy. Half unconsciously he took a step out from the stag line in her direction, and hesitated. Then he said to himself that it was charity. He walked toward her—collided suddenly with G. Reece Stoddard.

"Pardon me," said Warren.

But G. Reece had not stopped to apologize. He had again cut in on Bernice.

That night at one o'clock Marjorie, with one hand on the electric-light switch in the hall, turned to take a last look at Bernice's sparkling eyes.

"So it worked?"

"Oh, Marjorie, yes!" cried Bernice.

"I saw you were having a gay time."

"I did! The only trouble was that about midnight I ran short of talk. I had to repeat myself—with different men of course. I hope they won't compare notes."

"Men don't," said Marjorie, yawning, "and it wouldn't matter if they did—they'd think you were even trickier."

She snapped out the light, and as they started up the stairs Bernice grasped the banister thankfully. For the first time in her life she had been danced tired.

"You see," said Marjorie at the top of the stairs, "one man sees another man cut in and he thinks there must be something there. Well, we'll fix up some new stuff tomorrow. Good night."

"Good night."

As Bernice took down her hair she passed the evening before her in review. She had followed instructions exactly. Even when Charley Paulson cut in

for the eighth time she had simulated delight and had apparently been both interested and flattered. She had not talked about the weather or Eau Claire or automobiles or her school, but had confined her conversation to me, you, and us.

But a few minutes before she fell asleep a rebellious thought was churning drowsily in her brain —after all, it was she who had done it. Marjorie, to be sure, had given her her conversation, but then Marjorie got much of her conversation out of things she read. Bernice had bought the red dress, though she had never valued it highly before Marjorie dug it out of her trunk—and her own voice had said the words, her own lips had smiled, her own feet had danced. Marjorie—nice girl—vain, though—nice evening—nice boys—like Warren—Warren—Warren—what's-his-name—Warren—

She fell asleep.

To Bernice the next week was a revelation. With the feeling that people really enjoyed looking at her and listening to her came the foundation of self-confidence. Of course there were numerous mistakes at first. She did not know, for instance, that Draycott Deyo was studying for the ministry; she was unaware that he had cut in on her because he thought she was a quiet, reserved girl. Had she known these things she would not have treated him to the line which began "Hello, Shell Shock!" and continued with the bathtub story—"It takes a frightful lot of energy to fix my hair in the summer—there's so much of it—so I always fix it first and powder my face and put on my hat; then I get into the bathtub, and dress afterward. Don't you think that's the best plan?"

Though Draycott Deyo was in the throes of difficulties concerning baptisms by immersion and might possibly have seen a connection, it must be admitted that he did not. He considered feminine bathing an immoral subject, and gave her some of his ideas on the depravity of modern society.

But to offset that unfortunate occurrence Bernice had several signal successes to her credit. Little Otis Ormonde pleaded off from a trip East and elected instead to follow her with a puppylike devotion, to the amusement of his crowd and to the irritation of G. Reece Stoddard, several of whose afternoon calls Otis completely ruined by the disgusting tenderness of the glances he bent on Bernice.

He even told her the story of the two-by-four and the dressing room to show her how frightfully mistaken he and everyone else had been in their first judgment of her. Bernice laughed off that incident with a slight sinking sensation.

Of all Bernice's conversation perhaps the best known and most universally approved was the line about the bobbing of her hair.

"Oh, Bernice, when you goin' to get the hair bobbed?"

"Day after tomorrow maybe," she would reply, laughing. "Will you come and see me? Because I'm counting on you, you know."

"Will we? You know! But you better hurry up."

Bernice, whose tonsorial intentions were strictly dishonorable, would laugh again.

"Pretty soon now. You'd be surprised."

But perhaps the most significant symbol of her success was the gray car of the hypercritical Warren McIntyre, parked daily in front of the Harvey house. At first the parlor maid was distinctly startled when he asked for Bernice instead of Marjorie; after a week of it she told the cook that Miss Bernice had gotta holda Miss Marjorie's best fella.

And Miss Bernice had. Perhaps it began with Warren's desire to rouse jealousy in Marjorie; perhaps it was the familiar though unrecognized strain of Marjorie in Bernice's conversation; perhaps it was both of these and something of sincere attraction besides. But somehow the collective mind of the younger set knew within a week that Marjorie's most reliable beau had made an amazing face-about and was giving an indisputable rush to Marjorie's guest. The question of the moment was how Marjorie would take it. Warren called Bernice on the phone twice a day, sent her notes, and they were frequently seen together in his roadster, obviously engrossed in one of these tense, significant conversations as to whether or not he was sincere.

Marjorie on being twitted only laughed. She said she was mighty glad that Warren had at last found someone who appreciated him. So the younger set laughed, too, and guessed that Marjorie didn't care and let it go at that.

One afternoon when there were only three days left of her visit Bernice was waiting in the hall for Warren, with whom she was going to a bridge party. She was in rather a blissful mood, and when Marjorie —also bound for the party—appeared beside her and began casually to adjust her hat in the mirror,

Bernice was utterly unprepared for anything in the nature of a clash. Marjorie did her work very coldly and succinctly in three sentences.

"You may as well get Warren out of your head," she said coldly.

"What?" Bernice was utterly astounded.

"You may as well stop making a fool of yourself over Warren McIntyre. He doesn't care a snap of his fingers about you."

For a tense moment they regarded each other— Marjorie scornful, aloof; Bernice astounded, half-angry, half-afraid. Then two cars drove up in front of the house and there was a riotous honking. Both of them gasped faintly, turned, and side by side hurried out.

All through the bridge party Bernice strove in vain to master a rising uneasiness. She had offended Marjorie, the sphinx of sphinxes. With the most wholesome and innocent intentions in the world she had stolen Marjorie's property. She felt suddenly and horribly guilty. After the bridge game, when they sat in an informal circle and the conversation became general, the storm gradually broke. Little Otis Ormonde inadvertently precipitated it.

"When you going back to kindergarten, Otis?" someone had asked.

"Me? Day Bernice gets her hair bobbed."

"Then your education's over," said Marjorie quickly. "That's only a bluff of hers. I should think you'd have realized."

"That a fact?" demanded Otis, giving Bernice a reproachful glance.

Bernice's ears burned as she tried to think up an effectual comeback. In the face of this direct attack her imagination was paralyzed.

"There's a lot of bluffs in the world," continued Marjorie quite pleasantly. "I should think you'd be young enough to know that, Otis."

"Well," said Otis, "Maybe so. But gee! With a line like Bernice's—"

"Really?" yawned Marjorie. "What's her latest bon mot?"

No one seemed to know. In fact, Bernice, having trifled with her muse's beau, had said nothing memorable of late.

"Was that really all a line?" asked Roberta curiously.

Bernice hesitated. She felt that wit in some form was demanded of her, but under her cousin's suddenly frigid eyes she was completely incapacitated.

"I don't know," she stalled.

"Splush!" said Marjorie. "Admit it!"

Bernice saw that Warren's eyes had left a ukulele he had been tinkering with and were fixed on her questioningly.

"Oh, I don't know!" she repeated steadily. Her cheeks were glowing.

"Splush!" remarked Marjorie again.

"Come through, Bernice," urged Otis. "Tell her where to get off."

Bernice looked round again—she seemed unable to get away from Warren's eyes.

"I like bobbed hair," she said hurriedly, as if he had asked her a question, "and I intend to bob mine."

"When?" demanded Marjorie.

"Any time."

"No time like the present," suggested Roberta.

Otis jumped to his feet.

"Good stuff!" he cried. "We'll have a summer bobbing party. Sevier Hotel barbershop, I think you said."

In an instant all were on their feet. Bernice's heart throbbed violently.

"What?" she gasped.

Out of the group came Marjorie's voice, very clear and contemptuous.

"Don't worry—she'll back out!"

"Come on, Bernice!" cried Otis, starting toward the door.

Four eyes—Warren's and Marjorie's—stared at her, challenged her, defied her. For another second she wavered wildly.

"All right," she said swiftly, "I don't care if I do."

An eternity of minutes later, riding downtown through the late afternoon beside Warren, the others following in Roberta's car close behind, Bernice had all the sensations of Marie Antoinette bound for the guillotine in a tumbrel.

Vaguely she wondered why she did not cry out that it was all a mistake. It was all she could do to keep from clutching her hair with both hands to protect it from the suddenly hostile world. Yet she did neither. Even the thought of her mother was no deterrent now. This was the test supreme of her sportsmanship, her right to walk unchallenged in the starry heaven of popular girls.

Warren was moodily silent, and when they came to the hotel he drew up at the curb and nodded to Bernice to precede him out. Roberta's car emptied a laughing crowd into the shop, which presented two bold plate-glass windows to the street.

Bernice stood on the curb and looked at the sign, Sevier Barbershop. It was a guillotine indeed, and the hangman was the first barber, who, attired in a white coat and smoking a cigarette, leaned nonchalantly against the first chair. He must have heard of her; he must have been waiting all week, smoking eternal cigarettes beside that portentous, too-often-mentioned first chair. Would they blindfold her? No, but they would tie a white cloth round her neck lest any of her blood—nonsense—hair—would get on her clothes.

"All right, Bernice," said Warren quickly.

With her chin in the air she crossed the sidewalk, pushed open the swinging screen door, and giving not a glance to the uproarious, riotous row that occupied the waiting bench, went up to the first barber.

"I want you to bob my hair."

The first barber's mouth slid somewhat open. His cigarette dropped to the floor.

"Huh?"

"My hair—bob it!"

Refusing further preliminaries, Bernice took her seat on high. A man in the chair next to her turned on his side and gave her a glance, half lather, half amazement. One barber started and spoiled little Willy Schuneman's monthly haircut. Mr. O'Reilly in the last chair grunted and swore musically in ancient Gaelic as a razor bit into his cheek. Two bootblacks became wide-eyed and rushed for her feet. No, Bernice didn't care for a shine.

Outside a passer-by stopped and stared; a couple joined him; half a dozen small boys' noses sprang into life, flattened against the glass; and snatches of conversation borne on the summer breeze drifted in through the screen door.

"Lookada long hair on a kid!"

"Where'd yuh get 'at stuff? 'At's a bearded lady he just finished shavin'."

But Bernice saw nothing, heard nothing. Her only living sense told her that this man in the white coat had removed one tortoise-shell comb and then another; that his fingers were fumbling clumsily with unfamiliar hairpins; that this hair, this wonderful hair of hers, was going—she would never again feel its long voluptuous pull as it hung in a dark-brown glory down her back. For a second she was near breaking down, and then the picture before her swam mechanically into her vision—Marjorie's mouth curling in a faint ironic smile as if to say: "Give up and get down! You tried to buck me and I called your bluff. You see you haven't got a prayer."

And some last energy rose up in Bernice, for she clinched her hands under the white cloth, and there was a curious narrowing of her eyes that Marjorie remarked on to someone long afterward.

Twenty minutes later the barber swung her round to face the mirror, and she flinched at the full extent of the damage that had been wrought. Her hair was not curly, and now it lay in lank lifeless blocks on both sides of her suddenly pale face. It was ugly as sin—she had known it would be ugly as sin. Her face's chief charm had been a Madonna-like simplicity. Now that was gone and she was—well, frightfully mediocre—not stagey; only ridiculous, like a Greenwich Villager who had left her spectacles at home.

As she climbed down from the chair she tried to smile—failed miserably. She saw two of the girls exchange glances; noticed Marjorie's mouth curved in attenuated mockery—and that Warren's eyes were suddenly very cold.

"You see"—her words fell into an awkward pause —"I've done it."

"Yes, you've—done it," admitted Warren.

"Do you like it?"

There was a half-hearted "Sure" from two or three voices, another awkward pause, and then Marjorie turned swiftly and with serpentlike intensity to Warren.

"Would you mind running me down to the cleaners?" she asked. "I've simply got to get a dress there before supper. Roberta's driving right home and she can take the others."

Warren stared abstractedly at some infinite speck out the window. Then for an instant his eyes rested coldly on Bernice before they turned to Marjorie.

"Be glad to," he said slowly.

Bernice did not fully realize the outrageous trap that had been set for her until she met her aunt's amazed glance just before dinner.

"Why, Bernice!"

"I've bobbed it, Aunt Josephine."

"Why, child!"

"Do you like it?"

"Why, Ber-nice!"

"I suppose I've shocked you."

"No, but what'll Mrs. Deyo think tomorrow night? Bernice, you should have waited until after the Deyos' dance—you should have waited if you wanted to do that."

"It was sudden, Aunt Josephine. Anyway, why does it matter to Mrs. Deyo particularly?"

"Why, child," cried Mrs. Harvey, "in her paper on 'The Foibles of the Younger Generation' that she read at the last meeting of the Thursday Club she devoted fifteen minutes to bobbed hair. It's her pet abomination. And the dance is for you and Marjorie!"

"I'm sorry."

"Oh, Bernice, what'll your mother say? She'll think I let you do it."

"I'm sorry."

Dinner was an agony. She had made a hasty attempt with a curling iron, and burned her finger and much hair. She could see that her aunt was both worried and grieved, and her uncle kept saying, "Well, I'll be darned!" over and over in a hurt and faintly hostile tone. And Marjorie sat very quietly, entrenched behind a faint smile, a faintly mocking smile.

Somehow she got through the evening. Three boys called; Marjorie disappeared with one of them, and Bernice made a listless unsuccessful attempt to entertain the two others—sighed thankfully as she climbed the stairs to her room at half past ten. What a day!

When she had undressed for the night the door opened and Marjorie came in.

"Bernice," she said, "I'm awfully sorry about the Deyo dance. I'll give you my word of honor I'd forgotten all about it."

"'Sall right," said Bernice shortly. Standing before the mirror she passed her comb slowly through her short hair.

"I'll take you downtown tomorrow," continued Marjorie, "and the hairdresser'll fix it so you'll look slick. I didn't imagine you'd go through with it. I'm really mighty sorry."

"Oh, 'sall right!"

"Still it's your last night, so I suppose it won't matter much."

Then Bernice winced as Marjorie tossed her own hair over her shoulders and began to twist it slowly into two long blonde braids until in her cream-colored negligee she looked like a delicate painting of some Saxon princess. Fascinated, Bernice watched the braids grow. Heavy and luxurious they were, moving under the supple fingers like restive snakes—and to Bernice remained this relic and the curling iron and a tomorrow full of eyes. She could see G. Reece Stoddard, who liked her, assuming his Harvard manner and telling his dinner partner that Bernice shouldn't have been allowed to go to the movies so much; she could see Draycott Deyo exchanging glances with his mother and then being conscientiously charitable to her. But then perhaps by tomorrow Mrs. Deyo would have heard the news; would send round an icy little note requesting that she fail to appear—and behind her back they would all laugh and know that Marjorie had made a fool of her; that her chance at beauty had been sacrificed to the jealous whim of a selfish girl. She sat down suddenly before the mirror, biting the inside of her cheek.

"I like it," she said with an effort. "I think it'll be becoming."

Marjorie smiled.

"It looks all right. For heaven's sake, don't let it worry you!"

"I won't."

"Good night, Bernice."

But as the door closed something snapped within Bernice. She sprang dynamically to her feet, clenching her hands, then swiftly and noiselessly crossed over to her bed and from underneath it dragged out her suitcase. Into it she tossed toilet articles and a change of clothing. Then she turned to her trunk and quickly dumped in two drawerfuls of lingerie and summer dresses. She moved quietly, but with deadly efficiency, and in three-quarters of an hour her trunk was locked and strapped and she was fully dressed in a becoming new traveling suit that Marjorie had helped her pick out.

Sitting down at her desk she wrote a short note to Mrs. Harvey, in which she briefly outlined her reasons for going. She sealed it, addressed it, and laid it on her pillow. She glanced at her watch. The train left at one, and she knew that if she walked down to the Marborough Hotel two blocks away she could easily get a taxicab.

Suddenly she drew in her breath sharply and an expression flashed into her eyes that a practiced character reader might have connected vaguely with the set look she had worn in the barber's chair—somehow a development of it. It was quite a new look for Bernice—and it carried consequences.

She went stealthily to the bureau, picked up an article that lay there, and turning out all the lights stood quietly until her eyes became accustomed to the darkness. Softly she pushed open the door to Marjorie's room. She heard the quiet, even breathing of an untroubled conscience asleep.

She was by the bedside now, very deliberate and calm. She acted swiftly. Bending over she found one of the braids of Marjorie's hair, followed it up with her hand to the point nearest the head, and then holding it a little slack so that the sleeper would feel no pull, she reached down with the shears and severed it. With the pigtail in her hand she held her breath. Marjorie had muttered something in her sleep. Bernice deftly amputated the other braid, paused for an instant, and then flitted swiftly and silently back to her own room.

Downstairs she opened the big front door, closed it carefully behind her, and feeling oddly happy and exuberant stepped off the porch into the moonlight, swinging her heavy grip like a shopping bag. After a minute's brisk walk she discovered that her left hand still held the two blonde braids. She laughed unexpectedly—had to shut her mouth hard to keep from emitting an absolute peal. She was passing Warren's house now, and on the impulse she set down her baggage, and swinging the braids like pieces of rope flung them at the wooden porch, where they landed with a slight thud. She laughed again, no longer restraining herself.

"Huh!" she giggled wildly. "Scalp the selfish thing!"

Then picking up her suitcase she set off at a half-run down the moonlit street.   ☐

DISCUSSION

The world of "Bernice Bobs Her Hair" is the post–World War I world of the Roaring Twenties, a time that appears now as a time of youth and gayety. Its world was the country club, house parties, affluence, bobbed hair, of flappers in short long-waisted dresses, pleated skirts and sweaters, of "vampires," of "bathtub gin" and "home brew" (ways of combating Prohibition). It was a world in which one went to all-night dances, or took the new portable Victrola out into the country and danced on the "hard road" (paved highways)—and there was so little traffic that one could *do* it. Its world was that of a permissive society, its motto (not universally accepted) that "youth must have its fling." It was the age of the "Lost Generation" (a name that Ernest Hemingway borrowed from Gertrude Stein to use as an epigraph in his novel, *The Sun Also Rises*).

FOR EXPLORATION

1. (*a*) Reread the first six paragraphs of "Bernice Bobs Her Hair," noting the careful attention Fitzgerald gives to the development of setting. Why is a clear knowledge of the setting important to an understanding of the characters and action? (*b*) Characterize the tone established in these paragraphs and discuss the way the author creates it.

2. (*a*) Examine the differences between the temperaments, minds, and moral dispositions of Bernice and Marjorie. (*b*) What characteristics do the girls share? (*c*) Is Marjorie's attitude toward her cousin cold and hard, or is it simply realistic? Explain.

3. (*a*) What parts do the young men who appear in the story play? (*b*) Do any of them emerge as true individuals, or do they seem to be stereotypes? Justify your stand. (*c*) What might have been Fitzgerald's purpose in portraying them as he did?

4. (*a*) What attitude does Fitzgerald have toward the characters who populate this story? (*b*) Does he pass any moral judgments upon them? Explain. (*c*) With whom does he seem more sympathetic—Marjorie or Bernice?

5. During the course of the story, the hair bob develops a symbolic significance. (*a*) What does it symbolize to Bernice before she has her hair cut? (*b*) How does its meaning alter for her during and after the cut? (*c*) What does the hair symbolize to Marjorie? (*d*) Does it have the symbolic significance for Marjorie's friends? (*e*) Of what is it a symbol to the adults who either appear or are mentioned in the story?

6. (*a*) Did you expect the story to end as it did, or did the ending come as a surprise to you? (*b*) Does Fitzgerald give any prior indication of what Bernice's final action will be, or is the ending a mere trick one?

7. Those critics who demand that all good fiction have depth often characterize Fitzgerald as a writer who "speaks well but says nothing." (*a*) Does "Bernice Bobs Her Hair" serve any function other than pure entertainment? Explain. (*b*) Could the story be classified as one which wraps "shallow ideas" in "glittering phrases"? Justify your answer.

CREATIVE RESPONSE

1. Marjorie considers that "People over forty can seldom be permanently convinced of anything." Consider your own experience and write an essay confirming or revising or contradicting this statement.

2. Is Fitzgerald's "jazz-nourished generation" much different from the present-day "rock-nourished" generation? Write an account of your generation comparing it with the generation described in "Bernice Bobs Her Hair."

WORDS

"What's her latest bon mot?" Marjorie asks facetiously when Otis refers to Bernice's abilities as a conversationalist. The literal translation of the French phrase *bon mot* is "good word." However, the phrase has been adopted into English usage and has come to mean "witty remark" or "clever saying."

Listed below are some French expressions which appear frequently in both English and American writings. After each expression, translations of the individual words making up the expression are given. Look up each expression in a dictionary and explain how the current English meaning is related to the original meaning of the individual French words. Then write nine sentences in each of which you use one of these phrases. (Be sure you know how to pronounce the expressions.)

1. beau monde (*beau*, beautiful; *monde*, world)
2. bête noire (*bête*, beast; *noire*, black)
3. bon vivant (*bon*, good; *vivant*, living)
4. coup d'état (*coup*, blow; *état*, state)
5. esprit de corps (*esprit*, spirit; *corps*, corps)
6. faux pas (*faux*, false; *pas*, step)
7. hors d'oeuvre (*hors*, without; *oeuvre*, work)
8. noblesse oblige (*noblesse*, nobility; *oblige*, obligates)
9. savoir-faire (*savoir*, knowing; *faire*, to do)

IVAN MASSAR FROM BLACK STAR

Francis Scott Fitzgerald   1896 / 1940

F. Scott Fitzgerald was born into a prosperous family of St. Paul, Minnesota. After a few years in the schools of St. Paul, he was at a fairly early age sent to a private school in New Jersey and from there on to four years at Princeton University. Shortly after America's entrance into World War I he left college without completing his degree and joined the army, serving as an aide-de-camp until demobilized in 1919. Living in New York City after the war, Fitzgerald wished to become a newspaper reporter. But he was turned down by seven different publications and instead ended up writing streetcar advertising slogans for an advertisement agency. He left the position three months later when the sale of a short story provided the encouragement he needed to return to St. Paul and begin work on a novel. It was finished in 1920 (the same year he married Zelda Sayre, also a writer). The novel was *This Side of Paradise,* which within weeks of its publication made Fitzgerald a national celebrity. The rest of his life was marked by a struggle between the temptations of wealth and fame and a desire to do the best work of which he was capable. Often he gave in to the temptations. He and Zelda spent much time with just the sort of people Fitzgerald criticized in his writings. The couple's exploits in New York, their unorthodox life in France, their personal problems—which somehow always became public—were a constant source of food for a sensation-hungry world press. And often Fitzgerald's work paralleled his life: much of his writing consists of little more than shallow ideas dressed in glittering phrases. But when Fitzgerald was at his best, he was exceedingly good. *The Great Gatsby,* which appeared in 1925, is not only a brilliant comment on the twenties, but also an ironic treatment of the American success myth.

When the 1930's ushered in the depression, the American attitude changed; but Fitzgerald continued to write in the vein that had brought him fame. In 1934 he published *Tender Is the Night,* a moving and well-written novel about Americans in Europe. Its sophisticated, decadent characters failed to arouse the interest of people overwhelmed by the problems of the depression, and the book sold poorly. No longer the idol of the American reading public, beset by personal and financial worries, Fitzgerald accepted work as a Hollywood screen writer. The commercial demands of the film colony only compounded his problems, and his years in Hollywood were tormented ones. Alcohol became his means of escape from a world he no longer understood. During his last years he tried to write, but the work he produced was at its best lacking in restraint and at its worst chaotic. Fitzgerald died of a heart attack in 1940, feeling that he, like so many of the young men he had created, was a failure.

William Faulkner

THE BEAR

HE was ten. But it had already begun, long before that day when at last he wrote his age in two figures and he saw for the first time the camp where his father and Major de Spain and old General Compson and the others spent two weeks each November and two weeks again each June. He had already inherited then, without ever having seen it, the tremendous bear with one trap-ruined foot which, in an area almost a hundred miles deep, had earned for itself a name, a definite designation like a living man.

He had listened to it for years: the long legend of corncribs rifled, of shoats and grown pigs and even calves carried bodily into the woods and devoured, of traps and deadfalls overthrown and dogs mangled and slain, and shotgun and even rifle charges delivered at point-blank range and with no more effect than so many peas blown through a tube by a boy— a corridor of wreckage and destruction beginning back before he was born, through which sped, not fast but rather with the ruthless and irresistible deliberation of a locomotive, the shaggy tremendous shape.

It ran in his knowledge before ever he saw it. It looked and towered in his dreams before he even saw the unaxed woods where it left its crooked print, shaggy, huge, red-eyed, not malevolent but just big —too big for the dogs which tried to bay it, for the horses which tried to ride it down, for the men and the bullets they fired into it, too big for the very country which was its constricting scope. He seemed to see it entire with a child's complete divination before he ever laid eyes on either—the doomed wilderness whose edges were being constantly and punily gnawed at by men with axes and plows who feared it because it was wilderness, men myriad and nameless even to one another in the land where the old bear had earned a name, through which ran not even a mortal animal but an anachronism, indomitable and invincible, out of an old dead time, a phantom, epitome and apotheosis of the old wild life at which the puny humans swarmed and hacked in a fury of abhorrence and fear, like pygmies about the ankles of a drowsing elephant: the old bear solitary, indomitable and alone, widowered, childless, and absolved of mortality—old Priam[1] reft of his old wife and having outlived all his sons.

Until he was ten, each November he would watch the wagon containing the dogs and the bedding and food and guns and his father and Tennie's Jim, the Negro, and Sam Fathers, the Indian, son of a slave woman and a Chickasaw chief, depart on the road to town, to Jefferson where Major de Spain and the others would join them. To the boy, at seven, eight, and nine, they were not going into the Big Bottom to hunt bear and deer, but to keep yearly rendezvous with the bear which they did not even intend to kill. Two weeks later they would return, with no trophy, no head and skin. He had not expected it. He had not even been afraid it would be in the wagon. He believed that even after he was ten and his father would let him go too, for those two weeks in November, he would merely make another one, along with his father and Major de Spain and General Compson and the others, the dogs which feared to bay at it and the rifles and shotguns which failed even to bleed it, in the yearly pageant of the old bear's furious immortality.

Then he heard the dogs. It was in the second week of his first time in the camp. He stood with Sam Fathers against a big oak beside the faint crossing where they had stood each dawn for nine days now, hearing the dogs. He had heard them once before, one morning last week—a murmur, sourceless, echoing through the wet woods, swelling presently into separate voices which he could recognize and call by name. He had raised and cocked the gun as Sam told him and stood motionless again while the uproar, the invisible course, swept up and past and faded; it seemed to him that he could actually see the deer, the buck, blond, smoke-colored, elongated with speed, fleeing, vanishing, the woods, the gray solitude, still ringing even when the cries of the dogs had died away.

"Now let the hammers down," Sam said.

"You knew they were not coming here too," he said.

"Yes," Sam said. "I want you to learn how to do when you didn't shoot. It's after the chance for the

---

Copyright 1942 and renewed 1970 by Estelle Faulkner and Jill Faulkner Summers. An expanded version of this story appears in GO DOWN MOSES, by William Faulkner. Reprinted by permission of Random House, Inc. the author's Literary Estate and Chatto and Windus Ltd.
1. *Priam* (prī′əm), the last king of Troy. His wife and sons were killed by the Greeks during the Trojan War.

bear or the deer has done already come and gone that men and dogs get killed."

"Anyway," he said, "it was just a deer."

Then on the tenth morning he heard the dogs again. And he readied the too-long, too-heavy gun as Sam had taught him, before Sam even spoke. But this time it was no deer, no ringing chorus of dogs running strong on a free scent, but a moiling yapping an octave too high, with something more than indecision and even abjectness in it, not even moving very fast, taking a long time to pass completely out of hearing, leaving them somewhere in the air that echo, thin, slightly hysterical, abject, almost grieving, with no sense of a fleeing, unseen, smoke-colored, grass-eating shape ahead of it, and Sam, who had taught him first of all to cock the gun and take position where he could see everywhere and then never move again, had himself moved up beside him; he could hear Sam breathing at his shoulder and he could see the arched curve of the old man's inhaling nostrils.

"Hah," Sam said. "Not even running. Walking."

"Old Ben!" the boy said. "But up here!" he cried. "Way up here!"

"He do it every year," Sam said. "Once. Maybe to see who in camp this time, if he can shoot or not. Whether we got the dog yet that can bay and hold him. He'll take them to the river, then he'll send them back home. We may as well go back, too; see how they look when they come back to camp."

When they reached the camp the hounds were already there, ten of them crouching back under the kitchen, the boy and Sam squatting to peer back into the obscurity where they huddled, quiet, the eyes luminous, glowing at them and vanishing, and no sound, only that effluvium of something more than dog, stronger than dog and not just animal, just beast, because still there had been nothing in front of that abject and almost painful yapping save the solitude, the wilderness, so that when the eleventh hound came in at noon and with all others watching—even old Uncle Ash, who called himself first a cook— Sam daubed the tattered ear and the raked shoulder with turpentine and axle grease, to the boy it was still no living creature, but the wilderness which, leaning for the moment down, had patted lightly once the hound's temerity.

"Just like a man," Sam said. "Just like folks. Put off as long as she could having to be brave, knowing all the time that sooner or later she would have to be brave to keep on living with herself, and knowing all the time beforehand what was going to happen to her when she done it."

That afternoon, himself on the one-eyed wagon mule which did not mind the smell of blood nor, as they told him, of bear, and with Sam on the other one, they rode for more than three hours through the rapid, shortening winter day. They followed no path, no trail even that he could see; almost at once they were in a country which he had never seen before. Then he knew why Sam had made him ride the mule which would not spook. The sound one stopped short and tried to whirl and bolt even as Sam got down, blowing its breath, jerking and wrenching at the rein, while Sam held it, coaxing it forward with his voice, since he could not risk tying it, drawing it forward while the boy got down from the marred one.

Then, standing beside Sam in the gloom of the dying afternoon, he looked down at the rotted overturned log, gutted and scored with claw marks, and in the wet earth beside it, the print of the enormous warped two-toed foot. He knew now what he had smelled when he peered under the kitchen where the dogs huddled. He realized for the first time that the bear which had run in his listening and loomed in his dreams since before he could remember to the contrary, and which, therefore, must have existed in the listening and dreams of his father and Major de Spain and even old General Compson, too, before they began to remember in their turn, was a mortal animal, and that if they had departed for the camp each November without any actual hope of bringing its trophy back, it was not because it could not be slain, but because so far they had had no actual hope to.

"Tomorrow," he said.

"We'll try tomorrow," Sam said. "We ain't got the dog yet."

"We've got eleven. They ran him this morning."

"It won't need but one," Sam said. "He ain't here. Maybe he ain't nowhere. The only other way will be for him to run by accident over somebody that has a gun."

"That wouldn't be me," the boy said. "It will be Walter or Major or—"

"It might," Sam said. "You watch close in the morning. Because he's smart. That's how come he has lived this long. If he gets hemmed up and has to pick out somebody to run over, he will pick out you."

"How?" the boy said. "How will he know—" He ceased. "You mean he already knows me, that I ain't never been here before, ain't had time to find out yet whether I—" He ceased again, looking at Sam, the old man whose face revealed nothing until it smiled. He said humbly, not even amazed, "It was me he was watching. I don't reckon he did need to come but once."

The next morning they left the camp three hours before daylight. They rode this time because it was too far to walk, even the dogs in the wagon; again the first gray light found him in a place which he had never seen before, where Sam had placed him and told him to stay and then departed. With the gun which was too big for him, which did not even belong to him, but to Major de Spain, and which he had fired only once—at a stump on the first day, to learn the recoil and how to reload it—he stood against a gum tree beside a little bayou whose black still water crept without movement out of a cane-brake and crossed a small clearing and into cane again, where, invisible, a bird—the big woodpecker called Lord-to-God by Negroes—clattered at a dead limb.

It was a stand like any other, dissimilar only in incidentals to the one where he had stood each morning for ten days; a territory new to him, yet no less familiar than that other one which, after almost two weeks, he had come to believe he knew a little —the same solitude, the same loneliness through which human beings had merely passed without altering it, leaving no mark, no scar, which looked exactly as it must have looked when the first ancestor of Sam Fathers' Chickasaw predecessors crept into it and looked about, club or stone ax or bone arrow drawn and poised; different only because, squatting at the edge of the kitchen, he smelled the hounds huddled and cringing beneath it and saw the raked ear and shoulder of the one who, Sam said, had had to be brave once in order to live with herself, and saw yesterday in the earth beside the gutted log the print of the living foot.

He heard no dogs at all. He never did hear them. He only heard the drumming of the woodpecker stop short off and knew that the bear was looking at him. He never saw it. He did not know whether it was in front of him or behind him. He did not move, holding the useless gun, which he had not even had warning to cock and which even now he did not cock, tasting in his saliva that taint as of brass which

he knew now because he had smelled it when he peered under the kitchen at the huddled dogs.

Then it was gone. As abruptly as it had ceased, the woodpecker's dry, monotonous clatter set up again, and after a while he even believed he could hear the dogs—a murmur, scarce a sound even, which he had probably been hearing for some time before he even remarked it, drifting into hearing and then out again, dying away. They came nowhere near him. If it was a bear they ran, it was another bear. It was Sam himself who came out of the cane and crossed the bayou, followed by the injured bitch of yesterday. She was almost at heel, like a bird dog, making no sound. She came and crouched against his leg, trembling, staring off into the cane.

"I didn't see him," he said. "I didn't, Sam!"

"I know it," Sam said. "He done the looking. You didn't hear him neither, did you?"

"No," the boy said. "I—"

"He's smart," Sam said. "Too smart." He looked down at the hound, trembling faintly and steadily against the boy's knee. From the raked shoulder a few drops of fresh blood oozed and clung. "Too big. We ain't got the dog yet. But maybe someday. Maybe not next time. But someday."

So I must see him, he thought. *I must look at him.* Otherwise, it seemed to him that it would go on like this forever, as it had gone on with his father and Major de Spain, who was older than his father, and even with old General Compson, who had been old enough to be a brigade commander in 1865. Otherwise, it would go on so forever, next time and next time, after and after and after. It seemed to him that he could never see the two of them, himself and the bear, shadowy in the limbo from which time emerged, becoming time; the old bear absolved of mortality and himself partaking, sharing a little of it, enough of it. And he knew now what he had smelled in the huddled dogs and tasted in his saliva. He recognized fear. *So I will have to see him*, he thought, without dread or even hope. *I will have to look at him.*

It was in June of the next year. He was eleven. They were in camp again, celebrating Major de Spain's and General Compson's birthdays. Although the one had been born in September and the other in the depth of winter and in another decade, they had met for two weeks to fish and shoot squirrels and turkey and run coons and wildcats with the dogs at night. That is, he and Boon Hoggenback and the Negroes fished and shot squirrels and ran the coons and cats, because the proved hunters, not only Major de Spain and old General Compson, who spent those two weeks sitting in a rocking chair before a tremendous iron pot of Brunswick stew, stirring and tasting, with old Ash to quarrel with about how he was making it and Tennie's Jim to pour whiskey from the demijohn into the tin dipper from which he drank, but even the boy's father and Walter Ewell, who were still young enough, scorned such, other than shooting the wild gobblers with pistols for wagers on their marksmanship.

Or, that is, his father and the others believed he was hunting squirrels. Until the third day, he thought that Sam Fathers believed that too. Each morning he would leave the camp right after breakfast. He had his own gun now, a Christmas present. He went back to the tree beside the bayou where he had stood that morning. Using the compass which old General Compson had given him, he ranged from that point; he was teaching himself to be a better-than-fair woodsman without knowing he was doing it. On the second day he even found the gutted log where he had first seen the crooked print. It was almost completely crumbled now, healing with unbelievable speed, a passionate and almost visible relinquishment, back into the earth from which the tree had grown.

He ranged the summer woods now, green with gloom; if anything, actually dimmer than in November's gray dissolution, where, even at noon, the sun fell only in intermittent dappling upon the earth, which never completely dried out and which crawled with snakes—moccasins and water snakes and rattlers, themselves the color of the dappling gloom, so that he would not always see them until they moved, returning later and later, first day, second day, passing in the twilight of the third evening the little log pen enclosing the log stable where Sam was putting up the horses for the night.

"You ain't looked right yet," Sam said.

He stopped. For a moment he didn't answer. Then he said peacefully, in a peaceful rushing burst as when a boy's miniature dam in a little brook gives way, "All right. But how? I went to the bayou. I even found that log again. I—"

"I reckon that was all right. Likely he's been watching you. You never saw his foot?"

"I," the boy said—"I didn't—I never thought—"

"It's the gun," Sam said. He stood beside the fence, motionless—the old man, the Indian, in the battered faded overalls and the five-cent straw hat which in the Negro's race had been the badge of his enslavement and was now the regalia of his freedom. The camp—the clearing, the house, the barn and its tiny lot with which Major de Spain in his turn had scratched punily and evanescently at the wilderness —faded in the dusk, back into the immemorial darkness of the woods. *The gun*, the boy thought. *The gun.*

"Be scared," Sam said. "You can't help that. But don't be afraid. Ain't nothing in the woods going to hurt you unless you corner it, or it smells that you are afraid. A bear or a deer, too, has got to be scared of a coward the same as a brave man has got to be."

The gun, the boy thought.

"You will have to choose," Sam said.

He left the camp before daylight, long before Uncle Ash would wake in his quilts on the kitchen floor and start the fire for breakfast. He had only the compass and a stick for snakes. He could go almost a mile before he would begin to need the compass. He sat on a log, the invisible compass in his invisible hand, while the secret night sounds, fallen still at his movements, scurried again and then ceased for good, and the owls ceased and gave over to the waking of day birds, and he could see the compass. Then he went fast yet still quietly; he was becoming better and better as a woodsman, still without having yet realized it.

He jumped a doe and a fawn at sunrise, walked them out of the bed, close enough to see them—the crash of undergrowth, the white scut, the fawn scudding behind her faster than he had believed it could run. He was hunting right, upwind, as Sam had taught him; not that it mattered now. He had left the gun; of his own will and relinquishment he had accepted not a gambit, not a choice, but a condition in which not only the bear's heretofore inviolable anonymity but all the old rules and balances of hunter and hunted had been abrogated. He would not even be afraid, not even in the moment when the fear would take him completely—blood, skin, bowels, bones, memory from the long time before it became his memory—all save that thin, clear, immortal lucidity which alone differed him from this bear and from all the other bear and deer he would ever kill in the humility and pride of his skill and endurance, to which Sam had spoken when he leaned in the twilight on the lot fence yesterday.

By noon he was far beyond the little bayou, farther into the new and alien country than he had ever been. He was traveling now not only by the old, heavy, biscuit-thick silver watch which had belonged to his grandfather. When he stopped at last, it was for the first time since he had risen from the log at dawn when he could see the compass. It was far enough. He had left the camp nine hours ago; nine hours from now, dark would have already been an hour old. But he didn't think that. He thought, *All right. Yes. But what?* and stood for a moment, alien and small in the green and topless solitude, answering his own question before it had formed and ceased. It was the watch, the compass, the stick— the three lifeless mechanicals with which for nine hours he had fended the wilderness off; he hung the watch and compass carefully on a bush and leaned the stick beside them and relinquished completely to it.

He had not been going very fast for the last two or three hours. He went no faster now, since distance would not matter even if he could have gone fast. And he was trying to keep a bearing on the tree where he had left the compass, trying to complete a circle which would bring him back to it or at least intersect itself, since direction would not matter now either. But the tree was not there, and he did as Sam had schooled him—made the next circle in the opposite direction, so that the two patterns would bisect somewhere, but crossing no print of his own feet, finding the tree at last, but in the wrong place— no bush, no compass, no watch—and the tree not even the tree, because there was a down log beside it and he did what Sam Fathers had told him was the next thing and the last.

As he sat down on the log he saw the crooked print—the warped, tremendous, two-toed indentation which, even as he watched it, filled with water. As he looked up, the wilderness coalesced, solidified—the glade, the tree he sought, the bush, the watch and the compass glinting where a ray of sunlight touched them. Then he saw the bear. It did not emerge, appear; it was just there, immobile, solid, fixed in the hot dappling of the green and windless noon, not as big as he had dreamed it, but as big as he had expected it, bigger, dimensionless against the dappled obscurity, looking at him where he sat quietly on the log and looked back at it.

Then it moved. It made no sound. It did not hurry. It crossed the glade, walking for an instant into the full glare of the sun; when it reached the other side it stopped again and looked back at him across one shoulder while his quiet breathing inhaled and exhaled three times.

Then it was gone. It didn't walk into the woods, the undergrowth. It faded, sank back into the wilderness as he had watched a fish, a huge old bass, sink and vanish into the dark depths of its pool without even any movement of its fins.

He thought, *It will be next fall.* But it was not next fall, nor the next nor the next. He was fourteen then. He had killed his buck, and Sam Fathers had marked his face with the hot blood, and in the next year he killed a bear. But even before that accolade he had become as competent in the woods as many grown men with the same experience; by his fourteenth year he was a better woodsman than most grown men with more. There was no territory within thirty miles of the camp that he did not know—bayou, ridge, brake, landmark, tree, and path. He could have led anyone to any point in it without deviation, and brought them out again. He knew the game trails that even Sam Fathers did not know; in his thirteenth year he found a buck's bedding place, and unbeknown to his father he borrowed Walter Ewell's rifle and lay in wait at dawn and killed the buck when it walked back to the bed, as Sam had told him how the old Chickasaw fathers did.

But not the old bear, although by now he knew its footprints better than he did his own, and not only the crooked one. He could see any one of the three sound ones and distinguish it from any other, and not only by its size. There were other bears within these thirty miles which left tracks almost as large, but this was more than that. If Sam Fathers had been his mentor and the backyard rabbits and squirrels at home his kindergarten, then the wilderness the old bear ran was his college, the old male bear itself, so long unwifed and childless as to have become its own ungendered progenitor, was his alma mater. But he never saw it.

He could find the crooked print now almost whenever he liked, fifteen or ten or five miles, or sometimes nearer the camp than that. Twice while on stand during the three years he heard the dogs strike its trail by accident; on the second time they jumped it seemingly, the voices high, abject, almost human in hysteria, as on that first morning two years ago. But not the bear itself. He would remember that noon three years ago, the glade, himself and the bear fixed during that moment in the windless and dappled blaze, and it would seem to him that it had never happened, that he had dreamed that too. But it had happened. They had looked at each other, they had emerged from the wilderness old as earth, synchronized to the instant by something more than the blood that moved the flesh and bones which bore them, and touched, pledged something, affirmed something more lasting than the frail web of bones and flesh which any accident could obliterate.

Then he saw it again. Because of the very fact that he thought of nothing else, he had forgotten to look for it. He was still-hunting with Walter Ewell's rifle. He saw it cross the end of a long blowdown, a corridor where a tornado had swept, rushing through rather than over the tangle of trunks and branches as a locomotive would have, faster than he had ever believed it could move, almost as fast as a deer even, because a deer would have spent most of that time in the air, faster than he could bring the rifle sights with it. And now he knew what had been wrong during all the three years. He sat on a log, shaking and trembling as if he had never seen the woods before nor anything that ran them, wondering with incredulous amazement how he could have forgotten the very thing which Sam Fathers had told him and which the bear itself had proved the next day and had now returned after three years to reaffirm.

And now he knew what Sam Fathers had meant about the right dog, a dog in which size would mean less than nothing. So when he returned alone in April—school was out then, so that the sons of farmers could help with the land's planting, and at last his father had granted him permission, on his promise to be back in four days—he had the dog. It was his own, a mongrel of the sort called by Negroes a fyce, a ratter, itself not much bigger than a rat and possessing that bravery which had long since stopped being courage and had become foolhardiness.

It did not take four days. Alone again, he found the trail on the first morning. It was not a stalk; it was an ambush. He timed the meeting almost as if it were an appointment with a human being. Himself holding the fyce muffled in a feed sack and Sam Fathers with two of the hounds on a piece of a plowline rope, they lay downwind of the trail at dawn of the second morning. They were so close that the bear turned without even running, as if in surprised amazement at the shrill and frantic uproar of the released fyce, turning at bay against the trunk of a tree, on its hind feet; it seemed to the boy that it would never stop rising, taller and taller, and even the two hounds seemed to take a desperate and despairing courage from the fyce, following it as it went in.

Then he realized that the fyce was actually not going to stop. He flung, threw the gun away, and ran; when he overtook and grasped the frantically pinwheeling little dog, it seemed to him that he was directly under the bear.

He could smell it, strong and hot and rank. Sprawling, he looked up to where it loomed and towered over him like a cloudburst and colored like a thunderclap, quite familiar, peacefully and even lucidly familiar, until he remembered: This was the way he had used to dream about it. Then it was gone. He didn't see it go. He knelt, holding the frantic fyce with both hands, hearing the abashed wailing of the hounds drawing farther and farther away, until Sam came up. He carried the gun. He laid it down quietly beside the boy and stood looking down at him.

"You've done seed him twice now with a gun in your hands," he said. "This time you couldn't have missed him."

The boy rose. He still held the fyce. Even in his arms and clear of the ground, it yapped frantically, straining and surging after the fading uproar of the two hounds like a tangle of wire springs. He was panting a little, but he was neither shaking nor trembling now.

"Neither could you!" he said. "You had the gun! Neither did you!"

"And you didn't shoot," his father said. "How close were you?"

"I don't know, sir," he said. "There was a big wood tick inside his right hind leg. I saw that. But I didn't have the gun then."

"But you didn't shoot when you had the gun," his father said. "Why?"

But he didn't answer, and his father didn't wait for him to, rising and crossing the room, across the pelt of the bear which the boy had killed two years ago and the larger one which his father had killed before he was born, to the bookcase beneath the mounted head of the boy's first buck. It was the room which his father called the office, from which all the plantation business was transacted; in it for the fourteen years of his life he had heard the best of all talking. Major de Spain would be there and some-times old General Compson, and Walter Ewell and Boon Hoggenback and Sam Fathers and Tennie's Jim, too, were hunters, knew the woods and what ran them.

He would hear it, not talking himself but listening —the wilderness, the big woods, bigger and older than any recorded document of white man fatuous enough to believe he had bought any fragment of it or Indian ruthless enough to pretend that any frag-ment of it had been his to convey. It was of the men, not white nor black nor red, but men, hunters with the will and hardihood to endure and the humility and skill to survive, and the dogs and the bear and deer juxtaposed and reliefed against it, ordered and compelled by and within the wilderness in the an-cient and unremitting contest by the ancient and im-mitigable rules which voided all regrets and brooked no quarter, the voices quiet and weighty and de-liberate for retrospection and recollection and exact remembering, while he squatted in the blazing fire-light as Tennie's Jim squatted, who stirred only to put more wood on the fire and to pass the bottle from one glass to another. Because the bottle was always present, so that after a while it seemed to him that those fierce instants of heart and brain and courage and wiliness and speed were concentrated and distilled into that brown liquor which not women, not boys and children, but only hunters drank, drinking not of the blood they had spilled but some condensation of the wild immortal spirit, drinking it moderately, humbly even, not with the pagan's base hope of acquiring the virtues of cun-ning and strength and speed, but in salute to them.

His father returned with the book and sat down again and opened it. "Listen," he said. He read the five stanzas aloud, his voice quiet and deliberate in the room where there was no fire now because it was already spring. Then he looked up. The boy watched him. "All right," his father said. "Listen." He read again, but only the second stanza this time, to the end of it, the last two lines, and closed the book and put it on the table beside him. "She cannot fade, though thou hast not thy bliss, for ever wilt thou love, and she be fair,"[2] he said.

"He's talking about a girl," the boy said.

"He had to talk about something," his father said. Then he said, "He was talking about truth. Truth doesn't change. Truth is one thing. It covers all things which touch the heart—honor and pride and pity and justice and courage and love. Do you see now?"

He didn't know. Somehow it was simpler than that. There was an old bear, fierce and ruthless, not merely just to stay alive, but with the fierce pride of liberty and freedom, proud enough of the liberty and freedom to see it threatened without fear or even alarm; nay, who at times even seemed de-liberately to put that freedom and liberty in jeopardy in order to savor them, to remind his old strong bones and flesh to keep supple and quick to defend and preserve them. There was an old man, son of a Negro slave and an Indian king, inheritor on the one side of the long chronicle of a people who had learned humility through suffering, and pride through the endurance which survived the suffering and in-justice, and on the other side, the chronicle of a people even longer in the land than the first, yet who no longer existed in the land at all save in the sol-itary brotherhood of an old Negro's alien blood and the wild and invincible spirit of an old bear. There was a boy who wished to learn humility and pride in order to become skillful and worthy in the woods, who suddenly found himself becoming so skillful so rapidly that he feared he would never become worthy because he had not learned humility and pride, although he had tried to, until one day and as suddenly he discovered that an old man who could not have defined either had led him, as though by the hand, to that point where an old bear and a little mongrel of a dog showed him that, by possess-ing one thing other, he would possess them both.

And a little dog, nameless and mongrel and many-fathered, grown, yet weighing less than six pounds, saying as if to itself, "I can't be dangerous, because there's nothing much smaller than I am; I can't be fierce, because they would call it just noise; I can't be humble, because I'm already too close to the ground to genuflect; I can't be proud, because I wouldn't be near enough to it for anyone to know who was casting the shadow, and I don't even know that I'm not going to heaven, because they have al-ready decided that I don't possess an immortal soul. So all I can be is brave. But it's all right. I can be that, even if they still call it just noise."

That was all. It was simple, much simpler than somebody talking in a book about a youth and a

---

2. "She cannot . . . be fair," the last two lines of "Ode on a Grecian Urn," a poem by John Keats (1795–1821).

girl he would never need to grieve over, because he could never approach any nearer her and would never have to get any farther away. He had heard about a bear, and finally got big enough to trail it, and he trailed it four years and at last met it with a gun in his hands and he didn't shoot. Because a little dog—But he could have shot long before the little dog covered the twenty yards to where the bear waited, and Sam Fathers could have shot at any time during that interminable minute while Old Ben stood on his hind feet over them. He stopped. His father was watching him gravely across the spring-rife twilight of the room; when he spoke, his words were as quiet as the twilight, too, not loud, because they did not need to be because they would last. "Courage, and honor, and pride," his father said, "and pity, and love of justice and of liberty. They all touch the heart, and what the heart holds to becomes truth, as far as we know the truth. Do you see now?"

Sam, and Old Ben, and Nip, he thought. And himself too. He had been all right too. His father had said so. "Yes, sir," he said. □

DISCUSSION

"The Bear" might be called a **Bildungsroman**—a German term which means a story about growing up, not just physically but spiritually and emotionally, becoming aware of what it is to be an adult. Such growth comes from the education bestowed by experience of deep and lasting meaning. For another example of this kind of fiction, see John Steinbeck's "Flight" (page M 56).

FOR EXPLORATION

1. The first part of the story, up to the time the boy goes to hunt the bear (page 43 M, column b, paragraph 2) may be regarded as the introduction or *exposition*. (*a*) What has the boy learned about the bear? (*b*) The boy regards the bear as "not even a mortal animal but an anachronism, indomitable and invincible, out of an old dead time, a phantom, epitome and apotheosis of the old wild life." Interpret this statement and explain what this view of the bear tells the reader about the boy. (*c*) In what way does the exposition establish the tone of the story?

2. On his initial trip to the swamp the boy has his first experience with the bear (page M 44, column a, paragraph 2 to page 45 M, column b, paragraph 5). (*a*) How does he know the dogs are on the bear's trail? (*b*) Reread Sam Fathers' comment about the dog whose shoulder is raked by the bear (page M 44, column a, paragraph 7). What does it mean? (*c*) What does the boy learn from seeing the print of the bear's warped foot? (*d*) Why does Sam believe the bear can't be caught? (*e*) How does the boy discover on the next morning's hunt that the unseen bear is looking at him? (*f*) When does he realize what the effluvium under the porch where the dogs are huddled as well as the "taint as of brass" in his saliva is?

3. When the boy is eleven he visits the swamp again (page 45 M, column b, paragraph 7 to page 47 M, column b, paragraph 1). (*a*) How does he pass the time that the men think he is squirrel hunting? (*b*) What choice concerning the gun does Sam put up to him? (*c*) What does he find it necessary to do before he finally sees the bear? (*d*) What is the significance of his *quiet* inhaling and exhaling three times when he sees the bear?

4. The boy is fourteen when he has his next face-to-face meeting with Old Ben (page 47 M, column b, paragraph 2 to page M 48, column b, paragraph 5). (*a*) Give examples of his progress as a woodsman in the intervening years. (*b*) What does he remember after he has seen the bear "cross the end of a long blowdown"? (*c*) What does his dog do when they meet the bear? (*d*) What does he do?

5. In the concluding section of the story (page M 48, column b, paragraph 6) the boy and his father discuss his adventure. (*a*) Why does his father read Keats' "Ode on a Grecian Urn" to him, emphasizing certain lines (page 49 M, column a, paragraph 2)? (*b*) How does the boy explain his failure to shoot the bear? (*c*) What is the purpose of this last section of the story?

6. The theme of the story is the way a child gradually attains maturity. (*a*) What part does Sam Fathers play in the boy's progress toward maturity? (*b*) What part does the bear play? (*c*) What is the father's role?

7. Beginning with mention of the hound whose shoulder is raked by the bear (page M 44, column a, paragraph 7), references to the meaning of bravery recur throughout the story. (*a*) Locate and explain the meaning of several of these

references. (*b*) What seems to be Faulkner's conception of bravery? (*c*) How is the concept of bravery related to the theme of the story?

8. (*a*) What is the narrative point of view in "The Bear"? (*b*) How does it serve as a unifying influence?

9. Faulkner gives a detailed description of the woods in which the boy hunts. (*a*) How does he convey that the woods are wild, dense, and vast? (*b*) Why is it important to the story that these woods be more than a tamed forest preserve?

10. At the conclusion of the story the boy sees that Sam Fathers, the bear, and the fyce embody certain concepts which he has begun to understand. What concept does each of these represent?

CREATIVE RESPONSE

1. Write a short essay in which you explain how "humility" and "pride" may be justified, in the story or from your own experience, as compatible with each other.

2. Have you witnessed or been part of an experience that

seemed to move someone markedly from the status of childhood to the status of adulthood? Write an account of someone "growing up" through coming to know or becoming aware of something not understood before.

William Faulkner   1897 / 1962

Faulkner was born in New Albany, Mississippi, but his family soon moved to Oxford, Mississippi, where he spent the rest of his life.

During World War I, he enlisted in the Canadian Air Force. The war ended before he saw any action. Returning to Mississippi, he enrolled at the University under a special program, but left before graduating.

By this time, he had become interested in poetry and spent a good deal of time both reading and writing. In 1924 his first book of poetry, *The Marble Faun*, was published with the help of a friend. In the same year, Faulkner went to New Orleans where he met Sherwood Anderson. It was Anderson who convinced him to try writing stories and novels. With Anderson's aid, Faulkner's first novel, *Soldiers' Pay*, was published. After his novel dealing with the war, Anderson advised Faulkner to write about what he knew best. With this advice in mind, Faulkner changed his subject-matter and embarked on a successful career.

Although Faulkner's writing is not autobiographical, many of his characters and most of his settings are drawn from his own life. For example, in the woods outside Oxford, Mississippi, there did live an enormous bear which no one was able to kill.

Faulkner's writing is known for its inventiveness. He was preoccupied with form and experimented with different means of bringing reality to his works. He was mostly concerned with psychological action and used free association of images to facilitate this psychological approach. Because of his complex style, Faulkner's works were not popularly read until he was awarded the 1949 Nobel Prize in literature.

BERN KEATING FROM BLACK STAR

Ernest Hemingway

IN ANOTHER COUNTRY

IN the fall the war[1] was always there, but we did not go to it any more. It was cold in the fall in Milan and the dark came very early. Then the electric lights came on, and it was pleasant along the streets looking in the windows. There was much game hanging outside the shops, and the snow powdered in the fur of the foxes and the wind blew their tails. The deer hung stiff and heavy and empty, and small birds blew in the wind and the wind turned their feathers. It was a cold fall and the wind came down from the mountains.

We were all at the hospital every afternoon, and there were different ways of walking across the town through the dusk to the hospital. Two of the ways were alongside canals, but they were long. Always, though, you crossed a bridge across a canal to enter the hospital. There was a choice of three bridges. On one of them a woman sold roasted chestnuts. It was warm, standing in front of her charcoal fire, and the chestnuts were warm afterward in your pocket. The hospital was very old and very beautiful, and you entered through a gate and walked across a courtyard and out a gate on the other side. There were usually funerals starting from the courtyard. Beyond the old hospital were the new brick pavilions, and there we met every afternoon and were all very polite and interested in what was the matter, and sat in the machines that were to make so much difference.

The doctor came up to the machine where I was sitting and said: "What did you like best to do before the war? Did you practice a sport?"

I said: "Yes, football."

"Good," he said. "You will be able to play football again better than ever."

My knee did not bend and the leg dropped straight from the knee to the ankle without a calf, and the machine was to bend the knee and make it move as in riding a tricycle. But it did not bend yet, and instead the machine lurched when it came to the bending part. The doctor said: "That will all pass. You are a fortunate young man. You will play football again like a champion."

In the next machine was a major who had a little hand like a baby's. He winked at me when the doctor examined his hand, which was between two leather straps that bounced up and down and flapped the stiff fingers, and said: "And will I too play football, captain-doctor?" He had been a very great fencer, and before the war the greatest fencer in Italy.

The doctor went to his office in the back room and brought a photograph which showed a hand that had been withered almost as small as the major's, before it had taken a machine course, and after was a little larger. The major held the photograph with his good hand and looked at it very carefully. "A wound?" he asked.

"An industrial accident," the doctor said.

"Very interesting, very interesting," the major said, and handed it back to the doctor.

"You have confidence?"

"No," said the major.

There were three boys who came each day who were about the same age I was. They were all three from Milan, and one of them was to be a lawyer, and one was to be a painter, and one had intended to be a soldier, and after we were finished with the machines, sometimes we walked back together to the Café Cova, which was next door to the Scala.[2] We walked the short way through the communist quarter because we were four together. The people hated us because we were officers, and from a wine-shop some one called out, "A basso gli ufficiali!"[3] as we passed. Another boy who walked with us sometimes and made us five wore a black silk handkerchief across his face because he had no nose then and his face was to be rebuilt. He had gone out to the front from the military academy and been wounded within an hour after he had gone into the front line for the first time. They rebuilt his face, but he came from a very old family and they could never get the nose exactly right. He went to South America and worked in a bank. But this was a long time ago, and

"In Another Country" (Copyright 1927 Charles Scribner's Sons; renewal copyright 1955) is reprinted by permission of Charles Scribner's Sons and Jonathan Cape Limited from MEN WITHOUT WOMEN by Ernest Hemingway (British Title: THE FIRST FORTY-NINE STORIES).
1. *the war*, World War I (1914–1919).
2. *the Scala*, La Scala, Milan's world-famous opera house.
3. *"A basso gli ufficiali!"* Down with the officers! [*Italian*]

then we did not any of us know how it was going to be afterward. We only knew then that there was always the war, but that we were not going to it any more.

We all had the same medals, except the boy with the black silk bandage across his face, and he had not been at the front long enough to get any medals. The tall boy with a very pale face who was to be a lawyer had been a lieutenant of Arditi[4] and had three medals of the sort we each had only one of. He had lived a very long time with death and was a little detached. We were all a little detached, and there was nothing that held us together except that we met every afternoon at the hospital. Although, as we walked to the Cova through the tough part of town, walking in the dark, with light and singing coming out of the wineshops, and sometimes having to walk into the street when the men and women would crowd together on the sidewalk so that we would have had to jostle them to get by, we felt held together by there being something that had happened that they, the people who disliked us, did not understand.

We ourselves all understood the Cova, where it was rich and warm and not too brightly lighted, and noisy and smoky at certain hours, and there were always girls at the tables and the illustrated papers on a rack on the wall. The girls at the Cova were very patriotic, and I found that the most patriotic people in Italy were the café girls—and I believe they are still patriotic.

The boys at first were very polite about my medals and asked me what I had done to get them. I showed them the papers, which were written in very beautiful language and full of *fratellanza* and *abnegazione*,[5] but which really said, with the adjective removed, that I had been given the medals because I was an American. After that their manner changed a little toward me, although I was their friend against outsiders. I was a friend, but I was never really one of them after they had read the citations, because it had been different with them and they had done very different things to get their medals. I had been wounded, it was true; but we all knew that being wounded, after all, was really an accident. I was never ashamed of the ribbons, though, and sometimes, after the cocktail hour, I would imagine myself having done all the things they had done to get their medals; but walking home at night through the empty streets with the cold wind and all the shops closed, trying to keep near the street lights, I knew that I would never have done such things, and I was very much afraid to die, and often lay in bed at night by myself, afraid to die and wondering how I would be when I went back to the front again.

The three with the medals were like hunting hawks; and I was not a hawk, although I might seem a hawk to those who had never hunted; they, the three, knew better and so we drifted apart. But I stayed good friends with the boy who had been wounded his first day at the front, because he would never know now how he would have turned out; so he could never be accepted either, and I liked him because I thought perhaps he would not have turned out to be a hawk either.

The major, who had been the great fencer, did not believe in bravery, and spent much time while we sat in the machines correcting my grammar. He had complimented me on how I spoke Italian, and we talked together very easily. One day I had said that Italian seemed such an easy language to me that I could not take a great interest in it; everything was so easy to say. "Ah, yes," the major said. "Why, then, do you not take up the use of grammar?" So we took up the use of grammar, and soon Italian was such a difficult language that I was afraid to talk to him until I had the grammar straight in my mind.

The major came very regularly to the hospital. I do not think he ever missed a day, although I am sure he did not believe in the machines. There was a time when none of us believed in the machines, and one day the major said it was all nonsense. The machines were new then and it was we who were to prove them. It was an idiotic idea, he said, "a theory, like another." I had not learned my grammar, and he said I was a stupid impossible disgrace, and he was a fool to have bothered with me. He was a small man and he sat straight up in his chair with his right hand thrust into the machine and looked straight ahead at the wall while the straps thumped up and down with his fingers in them.

"What will you do when the war is over if it is over?" he asked me. "Speak grammatically!"

"I will go to the States."

"Are you married?"

---

4. *a lieutenant of Arditi*, a lieutenant in a picked group of volunteers which served as storm troops of the Italian infantry.
5. *fratellanza* (frä tel län′zä) *and abnegazione* (äb′ nä gä tzyō′ne), brotherhood and self-denial. [*Italian*]

"No, but I hope to be."

"The more of a fool you are," he said. He seemed very angry. "A man must not marry."

"Why, Signor Maggiore?" [6]

"Don't call me 'Signor Maggiore.'"

"Why must not a man marry?"

"He cannot marry. He cannot marry," he said angrily. "If he is to lose everything, he should not place himself in a position to lose that. He should not place himself in a position to lose. He should find things he cannot lose."

He spoke very angrily and bitterly, and looked straight ahead while he talked.

"But why should he necessarily lose it?"

"He'll lose it," the major said. He was looking at the wall. Then he looked down at the machine and jerked his little hand out from between the straps and slapped it hard against his thigh. "He'll lose it," he almost shouted. "Don't argue with me!" Then he called to the attendant who ran the machines. "Come and turn this damned thing off."

He went back into the other room for the light treatment and the massage. Then I heard him ask the doctor if he might use his telephone and he shut the door. When he came back into the room, I was sitting in another machine. He was wearing his cape and had his cap on, and he came directly toward my machine and put his arm on my shoulder.

"I am so sorry," he said, and patted me on the shoulder with his good hand. "I would not be rude. My wife has just died. You must forgive me."

"Oh—" I said, feeling sick for him. "I am *so* sorry."

He stood there biting his lower lip. "It is very difficult," he said. "I cannot resign myself."

He looked straight past me and out through the window. Then he began to cry. "I am utterly unable to resign myself," he said, and choked. And then crying, his head up looking at nothing, carrying himself straight and soldierly, with tears on both his cheeks and biting his lips, he walked past the machines and out the door.

The doctor told me that the major's wife, who was very young and whom he had not married until he was definitely invalided out of the war, had died of pneumonia. She had been sick only a few days. No one expected her to die. The major did not come to the hospital for three days. Then he came at the usual hour, wearing a black band on the sleeve of his uniform. When he came back, there were large framed photographs around the wall, of all sorts of wounds before and after they had been cured by the machines. In front of the machine the major used were three photographs of hands like his that were completely restored. I do not know where the doctor got them. I always understood we were the first to use the machines. The photographs did not make much difference to the major because he only looked out of the window. □

---

6. *Signor Maggiore* (sē′nyōr mäj jô′re), Mr. Major. In Italy it is a sign of respect to prefix an officer's rank with *Signor*.

DISCUSSION

"In Another Country" is an excellent example of Ernest Hemingway's sparse, compressed literary style. His terse style influenced several generations of writers, not only in America but around the world. He once explained the style to an interviewer: "I always try to write on the principle of the iceberg. There is seven-eighths of it underwater for every part that shows. Anything you know you can eliminate and it only strengthens your iceberg. It is the part that doesn't show. If a writer omits something because he does not know it then there is a hole in the story."

FOR EXPLORATION

1. A critic has pointed out that the opening paragraph offers a number of symbolic details which stand for the "'other countries' which the lonely characters portrayed in the story sense but do not enter." These countries are: "the country of battle from which [the characters'] wounds have removed them; that of peace which [the characters] glimpse through lighted windows from darkened streets; the country of nature symbolized by the game; and the country, finally,

of death—connoted by the cold, the dark, and by the wind which blows from the mountains." How is the exclusion of the soldiers from these "countries" important in this story?

2. Not only are the soldiers, as a group, shut off from other groups; as individuals, they are separated from one another. (*a*) How do they happen to be separated? (*b*) Have their war experiences had anything to do with their loneliness? Explain.

3. (*a*) Judging from your knowledge of the characters in Hemingway's stories, to what extent is the narrator typical of the characters Hemingway admires? (*b*) Are the other characters typical?

4. (*a*) How does the major differ from the other invalids? (*b*) Why does his wife's illness cause him to quarrel with the narrator?

5. Reread the passage in which the narrator describes the major's lack of confidence (page M 52, column b, paragraphs 1–6) and that in which he describes the major's grief (page 53 M, column b, paragraph 3 to page M 54, column b, paragraph 3). (*a*) Explain "the sequence of motion and fact" in each passage—in other words, what happens? (*b*) Characterize the diction and sentence structure in each passage, paying particular attention to the dialogue. (*c*) What emotional effect does each passage create? (*d*) Relate these incidents to this statement by Philip Young in *Ernest Hemingway:* "It is the major's pain that the story is about; the hero's wounds have been established, and there are now two casualties."

CREATIVE RESPONSE

1. Write a short essay comparing the picture of war presented in Hemingway's story with the picture in Ambrose Bierce's "An Occurrence at Owl Creek Bridge" (page 251 C).

2. Try your hand at using the Hemingway style in describing, mainly by understatement, a situation or scene that is highly charged emotionally. Work out the full details in your mind, but put on paper only the few details that will evoke or suggest the others. Don't be surprised if you find it more difficult to write sparingly than to write copiously.

UPI

Ernest Hemingway   1899 / 1961

Ernest Hemingway grew up in Oak Park, Illinois, where he won a considerable reputation as a high-school football player and boxer. During vacations, he hunted with his father, a physician, in northern Michigan. After graduation from high school, he worked as a newspaper reporter in Kansas City, where his interest in boxing and his skill as a sparring partner acquainted him with prizefighters and gunmen. Before the United States entered World War I, he served in a French ambulance unit; later he was seriously wounded while fighting in the Italian infantry. After the Armistice, Hemingway went to Paris. Here he worked as a correspondent for American newspapers and became identified with the "lost" generation. In 1924 his first volume of short stories, *In Our Time*, was published, and two years later *The Sun Also Rises*, his first successful novel, appeared.

As Hemingway's reputation as an artist grew, his activities and interests made him something of a celebrity. His fishing, boxing, hunting in Africa, and interest in the bullfights made him familiar to millions who had never read his books. He was further known as a war correspondent. What is possibly Hemingway's finest novel, *For Whom the Bell Tolls* (1940), grew out of his experiences in the Spanish Civil War. He was a supporter of the Loyalists, personally purchased ambulances for them, and made repeated trips there as a correspondent. When America entered World War II he spent two years on antisubmarine patrol duty in the Caribbean and then joined the American forces in Europe, ostensibly as a reporter. But in a sense Hemingway enjoyed the war and was much too involved in the conflict to do much reporting. By the time of the assault on Paris he was running his own private army of French irregulars.

Afterwards Hemingway lived on his estate in Cuba until the Castro revolution. His last publication was *The Old Man and the Sea* which was awarded the 1953 Pulitzer Prize. The following year he received the Nobel Prize for literature. He died from a gunshot wound while cleaning one of his weapons. Some friends believe he may have taken his own life.

John Steinbeck[1]

FLIGHT

ABOUT fifteen miles below Monterey, on the wild coast, the Torres family had their farm, a few sloping acres above a cliff that dropped to the brown reefs and to the hissing white waters of the ocean. Behind the farm the stone mountains stood up against the sky. The farm buildings huddled like little clinging aphids on the mountain skirts, crouched low to the ground as though the wind might blow them into the sea. The little shack, the rattling, rotting barn were gray-bitten with sea salt, beaten by the damp wind until they had taken on the color of the granite hills. Two horses, a red cow and a red calf, half a dozen pigs and a flock of lean, multi-colored chickens stocked the place. A little corn was raised on the sterile slope, and it grew short and thick under the wind, and all the cobs formed on the landward sides of the stalks.

Mama Torres, a lean, dry woman with ancient eyes, had ruled the farm for ten years, ever since her husband tripped over a stone in the field one day and fell full length on a rattlesnake. When one is bitten on the chest there is not much that can be done.

Mama Torres had three children, two undersized black ones of twelve and fourteen, Emilio and Rosy, whom Mama kept fishing on the rocks below the farm when the sea was kind and when the truant officer was in some distant part of Monterey County. And there was Pepé, the tall smiling son of nineteen, a gentle, affectionate boy, but very lazy. Pepé had a tall head, pointed at the top, and from its peak coarse black hair grew down like a thatch all around. Over his smiling little eyes Mama cut a straight bang so he could see. Pepé had sharp Indian cheekbones and an eagle nose, but his mouth was as sweet and shapely as a girl's mouth, and his chin was fragile and chiseled. He was loose and gangling, all legs and feet and wrists, and he was very lazy. Mama thought him fine and brave, but she never told him so. She said, "Some lazy cow must have got into thy father's family, else how could I have a son like thee." And she said, "When I carried thee, a sneaking lazy coyote came out of the brush and looked at me one day. That must have made thee so."

Pepé smiled sheepishly and stabbed at the ground with his knife to keep the blade sharp and free from rust. It was his inheritance, that knife, his father's knife. The long heavy blade folded back into the black handle. There was a button on the handle. When Pepé pressed the button, the blade leaped out ready for use. The knife was with Pepé always, for it had been his father's knife.

One sunny morning when the sea below the cliff was glinting and blue and the white surf creamed on the reef, when even the stone mountains looked kindly, Mama Torres called out the door of the shack, "Pepé, I have a labor for thee."

There was no answer. Mama listened. From behind the barn she heard a burst of laughter. She lifted her full long skirt and walked in the direction of the noise.

Pepé was sitting on the ground with his back against a box. His white teeth glistened. On either side of him stood the two black ones, tense and expectant. Fifteen feet away a redwood post was set in the ground. Pepé's right hand lay limply in his lap and in the palm the big black knife rested. The blade was closed back into the handle. Pepé looked smiling at the sky.

Suddenly Emilio cried, "Ya!"

Pepé's wrist flicked like the head of a snake. The blade seemed to fly open in mid-air, and with a thump the point dug into the redwood post, and the black handle quivered. The three burst into excited laughter. Rosy ran to the post and pulled out the knife and brought it back to Pepé. He closed the blade and settled the knife carefully in his listless palm again. He grinned self-consciously at the sky.

"Ya!"

The heavy knife lanced out and sunk into the post again. Mama moved forward like a ship and scattered the play.

"*Flight*" from THE LONG VALLEY by John Steinbeck. Copyright 1938, © renewed 1966 by John Steinbeck. Reprinted by permission of The Viking Press, Inc. and McIntosh & Otis, Inc.

1. For biography see page 79 A.

"All day you do foolish things with the knife, like a toy-baby," she stormed. "Get up on thy huge feet that eat up shoes. Get up!" She took him by one loose shoulder and hoisted at him. Pepé grinned sheepishly and came half-heartedly to his feet. "Look!" Mama cried. "Big lazy, you must catch the horse and put on him thy father's saddle. You must ride to Monterey. The medicine bottle is empty. There is no salt. Go thou now, Peanut! Catch the horse."

A revolution took place in the relaxed figure of Pepé. "To Monterey, me? Alone? Si, Mama."

She scowled at him. "Do not think, big sheep, that you will buy candy. No, I will give you only enough for the medicine and the salt."

Pepé smiled. "Mama, you will put the hatband on the hat?"

She relented then. "Yes, Pepé. You may wear the hatband."

His voice grew insinuating, "And the green handkerchief, Mama?"

"Yes, if you go quickly and return with no trouble, the silk green handkerchief will go. If you make sure to take off the handkerchief when you eat so no spot may fall on it. . . ."

"Si, Mama. I will be careful. I am a man."

"Thou? A man? Thou art a peanut."

He went into the rickety barn and brought out a rope, and he walked agilely enough up the hill to catch the horse.

When he was ready and mounted before the door, mounted on his father's saddle that was so old that the oaken frame showed through torn leather in many places, then Mama brought out the round black hat with the tooled leather band, and she reached up and knotted the green silk handkerchief about his neck. Pepé's blue denim coat was much darker than his jeans, for it had been washed much less often.

Mama handed up the big medicine bottle and the silver coins. "That for the medicine," she said, "and that for the salt. That for a candle to burn for the papa. That for *dulces*[2] for the little ones. Our friend Mrs. Rodriguez will give you dinner and maybe a bed for the night. When you go to the church say only ten Paternosters and only twenty-five Ave Marias.[3] Oh! I know, big coyote. You would sit there flapping your mouth over Aves all day while you looked at the candles and the holy pictures. That is not good devotion to stare at the pretty things."

The black hat, covering the high pointed head and black thatched hair of Pepé, gave him dignity and age. He sat the rangy horse well. Mama thought how handsome he was, dark and lean and tall. "I would not send thee now alone, thou little one, except for the medicine," she said softly. "It is not good to have no medicine, for who knows when the toothache will come, or the sadness of the stomach. These things are."

"Adios, Mama," Pepé cried. "I will come back soon. You may send me often alone. I am a man."

"Thou art a foolish chicken."

He straightened his shoulders, flipped the reins against the horse's shoulder and rode away. He turned once and saw that they still watched him, Emilio and Rosy and Mama. Pepé grinned with pride and gladness and lifted the tough buckskin horse to a trot.

When he had dropped out of sight over a little dip in the road, Mama turned to the black ones, but she spoke to herself. "He is nearly a man now," she said. "It will be a nice thing to have a man in the house again." Her eyes sharpened on the children. "Go to the rocks now. The tide is going out. There will be abalones to be found." She put the iron hooks into their hands and saw them down the steep trail to the reefs. She brought the smooth stone *metate*[4] to the doorway and sat grinding her corn to flour and looking occasionally at the road over which Pepé had gone. The noonday came and then the afternoon, when the little ones beat the abalones on a rock to make them tender and Mama patted the tortillas to make them thin. They ate their dinner as the red sun was plunging down toward the ocean. They sat on the doorsteps and watched the big white moon come over the mountain tops.

Mama said, "He is now at the house of our friend Mrs. Rodriguez. She will give him nice things to eat and maybe a present."

Emilio said, "Some day I too will ride to Monterey for medicine. Did Pepé come to be a man today?"

Mama said wisely, "A boy gets to be a man when a man is needed. Remember this thing. I have known boys forty years old because there was no need for a man."

Soon afterwards they retired, Mama in her big

---

2. *dulces*, sweets. [*Spanish*]
3. *Paternosters . . . Ave Marias*, Our Fathers and Hail Marys, prayers.
4. *metate*, a stone used for grinding cereal seeds.

oak bed on one side of the room, Emilio and Rosy in their boxes full of straw and sheepskins on the other side of the room.

The moon went over the sky and the surf roared on the rocks. The roosters crowed the first call. The surf subsided to a whispering surge against the reef. The moon dropped toward the sea. The roosters crowed again.

The moon was near down to the water when Pepé rode on a winded horse to his home flat. His dog bounced out and circled the horse yelping with pleasure. Pepé slid off the saddle to the ground. The weathered little shack was silver in the moonlight and the square shadow of it was black to the north and east. Against the east the piling mountains were misty with light; their tops melted into the sky.

Pepé walked wearily up the three steps and into the house. It was dark inside. There was a rustle in the corner.

Mama cried out from her bed. "Who comes? Pepé, is it thou?"

"*Si*, Mama."

"Did you get the medicine?"

"*Si*, Mama."

"Well, go to sleep, then. I thought you would be sleeping at the house of Mrs. Rodriguez." Pepé stood silently in the dark room. "Why do you stand there, Pepé? Did you drink wine?"

"*Si*, Mama."

"Well, go to bed then and sleep out the wine."

His voice was tired and patient, but very firm. "Light the candle, Mama. I must go away into the mountains."

"What is this, Pepé? You are crazy." Mama struck a sulphur match and held the little blue burr until the flame spread up the stick. She set light to the candle on the floor beside her bed. "Now, Pepé, what is this you say?" She looked anxiously into his face.

He was changed. The fragile quality seemed to have gone from his chin. His mouth was less full than it had been, the lines of the lips were straighter, but in his eyes the greatest change had taken place. There was no laughter in them any more nor any bashfulness. They were sharp and bright and purposeful.

He told her in a tired monotone, told her everything just as it had happened. A few people came into the kitchen of Mrs. Rodriguez. There was wine to drink. Pepé drank wine. The little quarrel—the

man started toward Pepé and then the knife—it went almost by itself. It flew, it darted before Pepé knew it. As he talked, Mama's face grew stern, and it seemed to grow more lean. Pepé finished. "I am a man now, Mama. The man said names to me I could not allow."

Mama nodded. "Yes, thou art a man, my poor little Pepé. Thou art a man. I have seen it coming on thee. I have watched you throwing the knife into the post, and I have been afraid." For a moment her face had softened, but now it grew stern again. "Come! We must get you ready. Go. Awaken Emilio and Rosy. Go quickly."

Pepé stepped over to the corner where his brother and sister slept among the sheepskins. He leaned down and shook them gently. "Come, Rosy! Come, Emilio! The mama says you must arise."

The little black ones sat up and rubbed their eyes in the candlelight. Mama was out of bed now, her long black skirt over her nightgown. "Emilio," she cried. "Go up and catch the other horse for Pepé. Quickly now! Quickly." Emilio put his legs in his overalls and stumbled sleepily out the door.

"You heard no one behind you on the road?" Mama demanded.

"No, Mama. I listened carefully. No one was on the road."

Mama darted like a bird about the room. From a nail on the wall she took a canvas water bag and threw it on the floor. She stripped a blanket from her bed and rolled it into a tight tube and tied the ends with string. From a box beside the stove she lifted a flour sack half full of black stringy jerky. "Your father's black coat, Pepé. Here, put it on."

Pepé stood in the middle of the floor watching her activity. She reached behind the door and brought out the rifle, a long 38–56, worn shiny the whole length of the barrel. Pepé took it from her and held it in the crook of his elbow. Mama brought a little leather bag and counted the cartridges into his hand. "Only ten left," she warned. "You must not waste them."

Emilio put his head in the door. "'*Qui 'st 'l caballo,*[5] Mama."

"Put on the saddle from the other horse. Tie on the blanket. Here, tie the jerky to the saddle horn."

Still Pepé stood silently watching his mother's frantic activity. His chin looked hard, and his sweet

---

5. *Qui 'st 'l caballo.* Here is the horse. [*Spanish*]

mouth was drawn and thin. His little eyes followed Mama about the room almost suspiciously.

Rosy asked softly, "Where goes Pepé?"

Mama's eyes were fierce. "Pepé goes on a journey. Pepé is a man now. He has a man's thing to do."

Pepé straightened his shoulders. His mouth changed until he looked very much like Mama.

At last the preparation was finished. The loaded horse stood outside the door. The water bag dripped a line of moisture down the bay shoulder.

The moonlight was being thinned by the dawn and the big white moon was near down to the sea. The family stood by the shack. Mama confronted Pepé. "Look, my son! Do not stop until it is dark again. Do not sleep even though you are tired. Take care of the horse in order that he may not stop of weariness. Remember to be careful with the bullets— there are only ten. Do not fill thy stomach with jerky or it will make thee sick. Eat a little jerky and fill thy stomach with grass. When thou comest to the high mountains, if thou seest any of the dark watching men, go not near to them nor try to speak to them. And forget not thy prayers." She put her lean hands on Pepé's shoulders, stood on her toes and kissed him formally on both cheeks, and Pepé kissed her on both cheeks. Then he went to Emilio and Rosy and kissed both of their cheeks.

Pepé turned back to Mama. He seemed to look for a little softness, a little weakness in her. His eyes were searching, but Mama's face remained fierce. "Go now," she said. "Do not wait to be caught like a chicken."

Pepé pulled himself into the saddle. "I am a man," he said.

It was the first dawn when he rode up the hill toward the little canyon which let a trail into the mountains. Moonlight and daylight fought with each other, and the two warring qualities made it difficult to see. Before Pepé had gone a hundred yards, the outlines of his figure were misty; and long before he entered the canyon, he had become a gray, indefinite shadow.

Mama stood stiffly in front of her doorstep, and on either side of her stood Emilio and Rosy. They cast furtive glances at Mama now and then.

When the gray shape of Pepé melted into the hillside and disappeared, Mama relaxed. She began the high, whining keen of the death wail. "Our beautiful —our brave," she cried. "Our protector, our son is gone." Emilio and Rosy moaned beside her. "Our beautiful—our brave, he is gone." It was the formal wail. It rose to a high piercing whine and subsided to a moan. Mama raised it three times and then she turned and went into the house and shut the door.

Emilio and Rosy stood wondering in the dawn. They heard Mama whimpering in the house. They went out to sit on the cliff above the ocean. They touched shoulders. "When did Pepé come to be a man?" Emilio asked.

"Last night," said Rosy. "Last night in Monterey." The ocean clouds turned red with the sun that was behind the mountains.

"We will have no breakfast," said Emilio. "Mama will not want to cook." Rosy did not answer him. "Where is Pepé gone?" he asked.

Rosy looked around at him. She drew her knowledge from the quiet air. "He has gone on a journey. He will never come back."

"Is he dead? Do you think he is dead?"

Rosy looked back at the ocean again. A little steamer, drawing a line of smoke, sat on the edge of the horizon. "He is not dead," Rosy explained. "Not yet."

Pepé rested the big rifle across the saddle in front of him. He let the horse walk up the hill and he didn't look back. The stony slope took on a coat of short brush so that Pepé found the entrance to a trail and entered it.

When he came to the canyon opening, he swung once in his saddle and looked back, but the houses were swallowed in the misty light. Pepé jerked forward again. The high shoulder of the canyon closed in on him. His horse stretched out its neck and sighed and settled to the trail.

It was a well-worn path, dark soft leaf-mold earth strewn with broken pieces of sandstone. The trail rounded the shoulder of the canyon and dropped steeply into the bed of the stream. In the shallows the water ran smoothly, glinting in the first morning sun. Small round stones on the bottom were as brown as rust with sun moss. In the sand along the edges of the stream the tall, rich wild mint grew, while in the water itself the cress, old and tough, had gone to heavy seed.

The path went into the stream and emerged on the other side. The horse sloshed into the water and stopped. Pepé dropped his bridle and let the beast drink of the running water.

Soon the canyon sides became steep and the first

giant sentinel redwoods guarded the trail, great round red trunks bearing foliage as green and lacy as ferns. Once Pepé was among the trees, the sun was lost. A perfumed and purple light lay in the pale green of the underbrush. Gooseberry bushes and blackberries and tall ferns lined the stream, and overhead the branches of the redwoods met and cut off the sky.

Pepé drank from the water bag, and he reached into the flour sack and brought out a black string of jerky. His white teeth gnawed at the string until the tough meat parted. He chewed slowly and drank occasionally from the water bag. His little eyes were slumberous and tired, but the muscles of his face were hard set. The earth of the trail was black now. It gave up a hollow sound under the walking hoof-beats.

The stream fell more sharply. Little waterfalls splashed on the stones. Five-fingered ferns hung over the water and dripped spray from their fingertips. Pepé rode half over in his saddle, dangling one leg loosely. He picked a bay leaf from a tree beside the way and put it into his mouth for a moment to flavor the dry jerky. He held the gun loosely across the pommel.

Suddenly he squared in his saddle, swung the horse from the trail and kicked it hurriedly up behind a big redwood tree. He pulled up the reins tight against the bit to keep the horse from whinnying. His face was intent and his nostrils quivered a little.

A hollow pounding came down the trail, and a horseman rode by, a fat man with red cheeks and a white stubble beard. His horse put down its head and blubbered at the trail when it came to the place where Pepé had turned off. "Hold up!" said the man and he pulled up his horse's head.

When the last sound of the hoofs died away, Pepé came back into the trail again. He did not relax in the saddle any more. He lifted the big rifle and swung the lever to throw a shell into the chamber, and then he let down the hammer to half cock.

The trail grew very steep. Now the redwood trees were smaller and their tops were dead, bitten dead where the wind reached them. The horse plodded on; the sun went slowly overhead and started down toward the afternoon.

Where the stream came out of a side canyon, the trail left it. Pepé dismounted and watered his horse and filled up his water bag. As soon as the trail had parted from the stream, the trees were gone and only the thick brittle sage and manzanita and chaparral edged the trail. And the soft black earth was gone, too, leaving only the light tan broken rock for the trail bed. Lizards scampered away into the brush as the horse rattled over the little stones.

Pepé turned in his saddle and looked back. He was in the open now: he could be seen from a distance. As he ascended the trail the country grew more rough and terrible and dry. The way wound about the bases of great square rocks. Little gray rabbits skittered in the brush. A bird made a monotonous high creaking. Eastward the bare rock mountaintops were pale and powder-dry under the dropping sun. The horse plodded up and up the trail toward a little V in the ridge which was the pass.

Pepé looked suspiciously back every minute or so, and his eyes sought the tops of the ridges ahead. Once, on a white barren spur, he saw a black figure for a moment, but he looked quickly away, for it was one of the dark watchers. No one knew who the watchers were, nor where they lived, but it was better to ignore them and never to show interest in them. They did not bother one who stayed on the trail and minded his own business.

The air was parched and full of light dust blown by the breeze from the eroding mountains. Pepé drank sparingly from his bag and corked it tightly and hung it on the horn again. The trail moved up the dry shale hillside, avoiding rocks, dropping under clefts, climbing in and out of old water scars. When he arrived at the little pass he stopped and looked back for a long time. No dark watchers were to be seen now. The trail behind was empty. Only the high tops of the redwoods indicated where the stream flowed.

Pepé rode on through the pass. His little eyes were nearly closed with weariness, but his face was stern, relentless and manly. The high mountain wind coasted sighing through the pass and whistled on the edges of the big blocks of broken granite. In the air, a red-tailed hawk sailed over close to the ridge and screamed angrily. Pepé went slowly through the broken jagged pass and looked down on the other side.

The trail dropped quickly, staggering among broken rock. At the bottom of the slope there was a dark crease, thick with brush, and on the other side of the crease a little flat, in which a grove of oak trees grew. A scar of green grass cut across the flat.

And behind the flat another mountain rose, desolate with dead rocks and starving little black bushes. Pepé drank from the bag again for the air was so dry that it encrusted his nostrils and burned his lips. He put the horse down the trail. The hooves slipped and struggled on the steep way, starting little stones that rolled off into the brush. The sun was gone behind the westward mountain now, but still it glowed brilliantly on the oaks and on the grassy flat. The rocks and the hillsides still sent up waves of the heat they had gathered from the day's sun.

Pepé looked up to the top of the next dry withered ridge. He saw a dark form against the sky, a man's figure standing on top of a rock, and he glanced away quickly not to appear curious. When a moment later he looked up again, the figure was gone.

Downward the trail was quickly covered. Sometimes the horse floundered for footing, sometimes set his feet and slid a little way. They came at last to the bottom where the dark chaparral was higher than Pepé's head. He held up his rifle on one side and his arm on the other to shield his face from the sharp brittle fingers of the brush.

Up and out of the crease he rode, and up a little cliff. The grassy flat was before him, and the round comfortable oaks. For a moment he studied the trail down which he had come, but there was no movement and no sound from it. Finally he rode out over the flat, to the green streak, and at the upper end of the damp he found a little spring welling out of the earth and dropping into a dug basin before it seeped out over the flat.

Pepé filled his bag first, and then he let the thirsty horse drink out of the pool. He led the horse to the clump of oaks, and in the middle of the grove, fairly protected from sight on all sides, he took off the saddle and the bridle and laid them on the ground. The horse stretched his jaws sideways and yawned. Pepé knotted the lead rope about the horse's neck and tied him to a sapling among the oaks, where he could graze in a fairly large circle.

When the horse was gnawing hungrily at the dry grass, Pepé went to the saddle and took a black string of jerky from the sack and strolled to an oak tree on the edge of the grove, from under which he could watch the trail. He sat down in the crisp dry oak leaves and automatically felt for his big black knife to cut the jerky, but he had no knife. He leaned back on his elbow and gnawed at the tough strong meat. His face was blank, but it was a man's face.

The bright evening light washed the eastern ridge, but the valley was darkening. Doves flew down from the hills to the spring, and the quail came running out of the brush and joined them, calling clearly to one another.

Out of the corner of his eye Pepé saw a shadow grow out of the bushy crease. He turned his head slowly. A big spotted wildcat was creeping toward the spring, belly to the ground, moving like thought.

Pepé cocked his rifle and edged the muzzle slowly around. Then he looked apprehensively up the trail and dropped the hammer again. From the ground beside him he picked an oak twig and threw it toward the spring. The quail flew up with a roar and the doves whistled away. The big cat stood up: for a long moment he looked at Pepé with cold yellow eyes, and then fearlessly walked back into the gulch.

The dusk gathered quickly in the deep valley. Pepé muttered his prayers, put his head down on his arm and went instantly to sleep.

The moon came up and filled the valley with cold blue light, and the wind swept rustling down from the peaks. The owls worked up and down the slopes looking for rabbits. Down in the brush of the gulch a coyote gabbled. The oak trees whispered softly in the night breeze.

Pepé started up, listening. His horse had whinnied. The moon was just slipping behind the western ridge, leaving the valley in darkness behind it. Pepé sat tensely gripping his rifle. From far up the trail he heard an answering whinny and the crash of shod hooves on the broken rock. He jumped to his feet, ran to his horse and led it under the trees. He threw on the saddle and cinched it tight for the steep trail, caught the unwilling head and forced the bit into the mouth. He felt the saddle to make sure the water bag and the sack of jerky were there. Then he mounted and turned up the hill.

It was velvet dark. The horse found the entrance to the trail where it left the flat, and started up, stumbling and slipping on the rocks. Pepé's hand rose up to his head. His hat was gone. He had left it under the oak tree.

The horse had struggled far up the trail when the first change of dawn came into the air, a steel grayness as light mixed thoroughly with dark. Gradually the sharp snaggled edge of the ridge stood out above them, rotten granite tortured and eaten by the winds of time. Pepé had dropped his reins on the horn, leaving direction to the horse. The brush grabbed at his legs in the dark until one knee of his jeans was ripped.

Gradually the light flowed down over the ridge. The starved brush and rocks stood out in the half light, strange and lonely in high perspective. Then there came warmth into the light. Pepé drew up and looked back, but he could see nothing in the darker valley below. The sky turned blue over the coming sun. In the waste of the mountain-side, the poor dry brush grew only three feet high. Here and there, big outcroppings of unrotted granite stood up like moldering houses. Pepé relaxed a little. He drank from his water bag and bit off a piece of jerky. A single eagle flew over, high in the light.

Without warning Pepé's horse screamed and fell on its side. He was almost down before the rifle crash echoed up from the valley. From a hole behind the struggling shoulder, a stream of bright crimson blood pumped and stopped and pumped and stopped. The hooves threshed on the ground. Pepé lay half stunned beside the horse. He looked slowly down the hill. A piece of sage clipped off beside his head and another crash echoed up from side to side of the canyon. Pepé flung himself frantically behind a bush.

He crawled up the hill on his knees and on one hand. His right hand held the rifle up off the ground and pushed it ahead of him. He moved with the instinctive care of an animal. Rapidly he wormed his way toward one of the big outcroppings of granite on the hill above him. Where the brush was high he doubled up and ran, but where the cover was slight he wriggled forward on his stomach, pushing the rifle ahead of him. In the last little distance there was no cover at all. Pepé poised and then he darted across the space and flashed around the corner of the rock.

He leaned panting against the stone. When his breath came easier he moved along behind the big rock until he came to a narrow split that offered a thin section of vision down the hill. Pepé lay on his stomach and pushed the rifle barrel through the slit and waited.

The sun reddened the western ridges now. Already the buzzards were settling down toward the place where the horse lay. A small brown bird scratched in the dead sage leaves directly in front of the rifle muzzle. The coasting eagle flew back toward the rising sun.

Pepé saw a little movement in the brush far below.

His grip tightened on the gun. A little brown doe stepped daintily out on the trail and crossed it and disappeared into the brush again. For a long time Pepé waited. Far below he could see the little flat and the oak trees and the slash of green. Suddenly his eyes flashed back at the trail again. A quarter of a mile down there had been a quick movement in the chaparral. The rifle swung over. The front sight nestled in the V of the rear sight. Pepé studied for a moment and then raised the rear sight a notch. The little movement in the brush came again. The sight settled on it. Pepé squeezed the trigger. The explosion crashed down the mountain and up the other side, and came rattling back. The whole side of the slope grew still. No more movement. And then a white streak cut into the granite of the slit and a bullet whined away and a crash sounded up from below. Pepé felt a sharp pain in his right hand. A sliver of granite was sticking out from between his first and second knuckles and the point protruded from his palm. Carefully he pulled out the sliver of stone. The wound bled evenly and gently. No vein nor artery was cut.

Pepé looked into a little dusty cave in the rock and gathered a handful of spider web, and he pressed the mass into the cut, plastering the soft web into the blood. The flow stopped almost at once.

The rifle was on the ground. Pepé picked it up, levered a new shell into the chamber. And then he slid into the brush on his stomach. Far to the right he crawled, and then up the hill, moving slowly and carefully, crawling to cover and resting and then crawling again.

In the mountains the sun is high in its arc before it penetrates the gorges. The hot face looked over the hill and brought instant heat with it. The white light beat on the rocks and reflected from them and rose up quivering from the earth again, and the rocks and bushes seemed to quiver behind the air.

Pepé crawled in the general direction of the ridge peak, zig-zagging for cover. The deep cut between his knuckles began to throb. He crawled close to a rattlesnake before he saw it, and when it raised its dry head and made a soft beginning whirr, he backed up and took another way. The quick gray lizards flashed in front of him, raising a tiny line of dust. He found another mass of spider web and pressed it against his throbbing hand.

Pepé was pushing the rifle with his left hand now. Little drops of sweat ran to the ends of his coarse black hair and rolled down his cheeks. His lips and tongue were growing thick and heavy. His lips writhed to draw saliva into his mouth. His little dark eyes were uneasy and suspicious. Once when a gray lizard paused in front of him on the parched ground and turned its head sideways he crushed it flat with a stone.

When the sun slid past noon he had not gone a mile. He crawled exhaustedly a last hundred yards to a patch of high sharp manzanita, crawled desperately, and when the patch was reached he wriggled in among the tough gnarly trunks and dropped his head on his left arm. There was little shade in the meager brush, but there was cover and safety. Pepé went to sleep as he lay and the sun beat on his back. A few little birds hopped close to him and peered and hopped away. Pepé squirmed in his sleep and he raised and dropped his wounded hand again and again.

The sun went down behind the peaks and the cool evening came, and then the dark. A coyote yelled from the hillside, Pepé started awake and looked about with misty eyes. His hand was swollen and heavy; a little thread of pain ran up the inside of his arm and settled in a pocket in his armpit. He peered about and then stood up, for the mountains were black and the moon had not yet risen. Pepé stood up in the dark. The coat of his father pressed on his arm. His tongue was swollen until it nearly filled his mouth. He wriggled out of the coat and dropped it in the brush, and then he struggled up the hill, falling over rocks and tearing his way through the brush. The rifle knocked against stones as he went. Little dry avalanches of gravel and shattered stone went whispering down the hill behind him.

After a while the old moon came up and showed the jagged ridge top ahead of him. By moonlight Pepé traveled more easily. He bent forward so that his throbbing arm hung away from his body. The journey uphill was made in dashes and rests, a frantic rush up a few yards and then a rest. The wind coasted down the slope rattling the dry stems of the bushes.

The moon was at meridian when Pepé came at last to the sharp backbone of the ridge top. On the last hundred yards of the rise no soil had clung under the wearing winds. The way was on solid rock. He clambered to the top and looked down on the other side. There was a draw like the last below him, misty with moonlight, brushed with dry struggling sage

and chaparral. On the other side the hill rose up sharply and at the top the jagged rotten teeth of the mountain showed against the sky. At the bottom of the cut the brush was thick and dark.

Pepé stumbled down the hill. His throat was almost closed with thirst. At first he tried to run, but immediately he fell and rolled. After that he went more carefully. The moon was just disappearing behind the mountains when he came to the bottom. He crawled into the heavy brush feeling with his fingers for water. There was no water in the bed of the stream, only damp earth. Pepé laid his gun down and scooped up a handful of mud and put it in his mouth, and then he spluttered and scraped the earth from his tongue with his finger, for the mud drew at his mouth like a poultice. He dug a hole in the stream bed with his fingers, dug a little basin to catch water; but before it was very deep his head fell forward on .the damp ground and he slept.

The dawn came and the heat of the day fell on the earth, and still Pepé slept. Late in the afternoon his head jerked up. He looked slowly around. His eyes were slits of wariness. Twenty feet away in the heavy brush a big tawny mountain lion stood looking at him. Its long thick tail waved gracefully, its ears erect with interest, not laid back dangerously. The lion squatted down on its stomach and watched him.

Pepé looked at the hole he had dug in the earth. A half inch of muddy water had collected in the bottom. He tore the sleeve from his hurt arm, with his teeth ripped out a little square, soaked it in the water and put it in his mouth. Over and over he filled the cloth and sucked it.

Still the lion sat and watched him. The evening came down but there was no movement on the hills. No birds visited the dry bottom of the cut. Pepé looked occasionally at the lion. The eyes of the yellow beast drooped as though he were about to sleep. He yawned and his long thin red tongue curled out. Suddenly his head jerked around and his nostrils quivered. His big tail lashed. He stood up and slunk like a tawny shadow into the thick brush.

A moment later Pepé heard the sound, the faint far crash of horses' hooves on gravel. And he heard something else, a high whining yelp of a dog.

Pepé took his rifle in his left hand and he glided into the brush almost as quietly as the lion had. In the darkening evening he crouched up the hill toward the next ridge. Only when the dark came did he stand up. His energy was short. Once it was dark he fell over the rocks and slipped to his knees on the steep slope, but he moved on and on up the hill, climbing and scrabbling over the broken hillside.

When he was far up toward the top, he lay down and slept for a little while. The withered moon, shining on his face, awakened him. He stood up and moved up the hill. Fifty yards away he stopped and turned back, for he had forgotten his rifle. He walked heavily down and poked about in the brush, but he could not find his gun. At last he lay down to rest. The pocket of pain in his armpit had grown more sharp. His arm seemed to swell out and fall with every heartbeat. There was no position lying down where the heavy arm did not press against his armpit.

With the effort of a hurt beast, Pepé got up and moved again toward the top of the ridge. He held his swollen arm away from his body with his left hand. Up the steep hill he dragged himself, a few steps and a rest, and a few more steps. At last he was nearing the top. The moon showed the uneven sharp back of it against the sky.

Pepé's brain spun in a big spiral up and away from him. He slumped to the ground and lay still. The rock ridge top was only a hundred feet above him.

The moon moved over the sky. Pepé half turned on his back. His tongue tried to make words, but only a thick hissing came from between his lips.

When the dawn came, Pepé pulled himself up. His eyes were sane again. He drew his great puffed arm in front of him and looked at the angry wound. The black line ran up from his wrist to his armpit. Automatically he reached in his pocket for the big black knife, but it was not there. His eyes searched the ground. He picked up a sharp blade of stone and scraped at the wound, sawed at the proud flesh and then squeezed the green juice out in big drops. Instantly he threw back his head and whined like a dog. His whole right side shuddered at the pain, but the pain cleared his head.

In the gray light he struggled up the last slope to the ridge and crawled over and lay down behind a line of rocks. Below him lay a deep canyon exactly like the last, waterless and desolate. There was no flat, no oak trees, not even heavy brush in the bottom of it. And on the other side a sharp ridge stood up, thinly brushed with starving sage, littered with broken granite. Strewn over the hill there were giant outcroppings, and on the top the granite teeth stood out against the sky.

The new day was light now. The flame of sun came over the ridge and fell on Pepé where he lay on the ground. His coarse black hair was littered with twigs and bits of spider web. His eyes had retreated back into his head. Between his lips the tip of his black tongue showed.

He sat up and dragged his great arm into his lap and nursed it, rocking his body and moaning in his throat. He threw back his head and looked up into the pale sky. A big black bird circled nearly out of sight, and far to the left another was sailing near.

He lifted his head to listen, for a familiar sound had come to him from the valley he had climbed out of; it was the crying yelp of hounds, excited and feverish, on a trail.

Pepé bowed his head quickly. He tried to speak rapid words but only a thick hiss came from his lips. He drew a shaky cross on his breast with his left hand. It was a long struggle to get to his feet. He crawled slowly and mechanically to the top of a big rock on the ridge peak. Once there, he arose slowly, swaying to his feet, and stood erect. Far below he could see the dark brush where he had slept. He braced his feet and stood there, black against the morning sky.

There came a ripping sound at his feet. A piece of stone flew up and a bullet droned off into the next gorge. The hollow crash echoed up from below. Pepé looked down for a moment and then pulled himself straight again.

His body jarred back. His left hand fluttered helplessly toward his breast. The second crash sounded from below. Pepé swung forward and toppled from the rock. His body struck and rolled over and over, starting a little avalanche. And when at last he stopped against a bush, the avalanche slid slowly down and covered up his head. □

DISCUSSION

Comparing two similar works is a good way to study literature. Each of the works studied becomes richer, as we find common or different attitudes invoked and emotions aroused. Faulkner's "The Bear" (page 43 M) and Steinbeck's "Flight" encourage comparison, though one ends in life and wisdom, and the other in courage and death, though the former is in the Deep South and the latter on the Pacific Coast. Both have to do with discovering what it is to be a man.

FOR EXPLORATION

1. Near the beginning of the story, Pepé demonstrates his skill at throwing his knife for his brother and sister. Why is this incident portrayed so vividly?

2. Mama Torres tells Pepé, when he says that he is a man, "Thou art a peanut." Later, when he leaves on his important errand, she tells her other children, "He is nearly a man now." And when Pepé returns and prepares to flee, she says, "Yes, thou art a man." Discuss the reasons for her changing attitude.

3. During Pepé's flight, are you told by Steinbeck what his thinking and feelings are, or are you kept outside his mind and emotions and left in the position of an exterior observer? Discuss and explain the effect of Steinbeck's technique.

4. Pepé's pursuers remain nameless, faceless, and invisible. Why are we never allowed to observe them?

5. Explain Pepé's behavior described in the last three paragraphs of the story: he stands in clear view of the pursuers giving them ample opportunity to aim their rifles and kill him.

CREATIVE RESPONSE

1. Animal imagery plays an important part in "Flight." Animals appear in the very first paragraph, and Mama Torres calls Pepé a "lazy coyote" and a "foolish chicken." As Pepé scrambles in flight up the mountain, he is kept company by birds, lizards, snakes, and other animals. Reread the story carefully, examining Steinbeck's use of animal imagery, and write an essay exploring the particular effects he achieves through its use.

2. The "crime" that Pepé commits is not presented dramatically in the story, but is simply related by Pepé to his mother: "He told her in a tired monotone, told her everything just as it had happened. A few people came into the kitchen of Mrs. Rodriguez. There was wine to drink. Pepé drank wine. The little quarrel—the man started toward Pepé and then the knife—it went almost by itself. It flew, it darted before Pepé knew it." Imagine what the quarrel might have been, imagine the other characters present and involved, and re-create the scene of this important event. Dramatize it on paper or improvise the drama with fellow students for a class production.

Richard Wright

THE MAN WHO SAW
THE FLOOD

When the flood waters recede,
the poor folk along the river
start from scratch.

AT last the flood waters had receded. A black father, a black mother, and a black child tramped through muddy fields, leading a tired cow by a thin bit of rope. They stopped on a hilltop and shifted the bundles on their shoulders. As far as they could see the ground was covered with flood silt. The little girl lifted a skinny finger and pointed to a mud-caked cabin.

"Look, Pa! Ain tha our home?"

The man, round-shouldered, clad in blue, ragged overalls, looked with bewildered eyes. Without moving a muscle, scarcely moving his lips, he said: "Yeah."

For five minutes they did not speak or move. The flood waters had been more than eight feet high here. Every tree, blade of grass, and stray stick had its flood mark; caky, yellow mud. It clung to the ground, cracking thinly here and there in spider web fashion. Over the stark fields came a gusty spring wind. The sky was high, blue, full of white clouds and sunshine. Over all hung a first-day strangeness.

"The henhouse is gone," sighed the woman.

"N the pigpen," sighed the man.

They spoke without bitterness.

"Ah reckon them chickens is all done drowned."

"Yeah."

"Miz Flora's house is gone, too," said the little girl.

They looked at a clump of trees where their neighbor's house had stood.

"Lawd!"

"Yuh reckon anybody knows where they is?"

"Hard t tell."

The man walked down the slope and stood uncertainly.

"There wuz a road erlong here somewheres," he said.

But there was no road now. Just a wide sweep of yellow, scalloped silt.

"Look, Tom!" called the woman. "Here's a piece of our gate!"

The gatepost was half buried in the ground. A rusty hinge stood stiff, like a lonely finger. Tom pried it loose and caught it firmly in his hand. There was nothing particular he wanted to do with it; he just stood holding it firmly. Finally he dropped it, looked up, and said:

"C mon. Les go down n see whut we kin do."

Because it sat in a slight depression, the ground about the cabin was soft and slimy.

"Gimme tha bag o lime, May," he said.

With his shoes sucking in mud, he went slowly around the cabin, spreading the white lime with thick fingers. When he reached the front again he had a little left; he shook the bag out on the porch. The fine grains of floating lime flickered in the sunlight.

"Tha oughta hep some," he said.

"Now, yuh be careful, Sal!" said May. "Don yuh go n fall down in all this mud, yuh hear?"

"Yessum."

The steps were gone. Tom lifted May and Sally to the porch. They stood a moment looking at the half-opened door. He had shut it when he left, but somehow it seemed natural that he should find it open. The planks in the porch floor were swollen and warped. The cabin had two colors; near the bottom it was a solid yellow; at the top it was the familiar gray. It looked weird, as though its ghost were standing beside it.

The cow lowed.

"Tie Pat t the pos on the en of the porch, May."

May tied the rope slowly, listlessly. When they attempted to open the front door, it would not budge. It was not until Tom placed his shoulder against it and gave it a stout shove that it scraped back jerkily. The front room was dark and silent. The

"The Man Who Saw the Flood" by Richard Wright from EIGHT MEN. Copyright 1937 by Weekly Masses Co., Inc. Reprinted by permission of Paul R. Reynolds, Inc.

damp smell of flood silt came fresh and sharp to their nostrils. Only one-half of the upper window was clear, and through it fell a rectangle of dingy light. The floors swam in ooze. Like a mute warning, a wavering flood mark went high around the walls of the room. A dresser sat cater-cornered, its drawers and sides bulging like a bloated corpse. The bed, with the mattress still on it, was like a giant casket forged of mud. Two smashed chairs lay in a corner, as though huddled together for protection.

"Les see the kitchen," said Tom.

The stovepipe was gone. But the stove stood in the same place.

"The stove's still good. We kin clean it."

"Yeah."

"But where's the table?"

"Lawd knows."

"It must've washed erway wid the rest of the stuff, Ah reckon."

They opened the back door and looked out. They missed the barn, the henhouse, and the pigpen.

"Tom, yuh bettah try tha ol pump n see ef eny watah's there."

The pump was stiff. Tom threw his weight on the handle and carried it up and down. No water came. He pumped on. There was a dry hollow cough. Then yellow water trickled. He caught his breath and kept pumping. The water flowed white.

"Thank Gawd! We's got some watah."

"Yuh bettah boil it fo yuh use it," he said.

"Yeah. Ah know."

"Look, Pa! Here's yo ax," called Sally.

Tom took the ax from her. "Yeah. Ah'll need this."

"N here's somethin else," called Sally, digging spoons out of the mud.

"Waal, Ahma git a bucket n start cleanin," said May. "Ain no use in waitin, cause we's gotta sleep on them floors tonight."

When she was filling the bucket from the pump, Tom called from around the cabin. "May, look! Ah done foun mah plow!" Proudly he dragged the silt-caked plow to the pump. "Ah'll wash it n it'll be awright."

"Ahm hongry," said Sally.

"Now, yuh jus wait! Yuh et this mawnin," said May. She turned to Tom. "Now, whutcha gonna do, Tom?"

He stood looking at the mud-filled fields.

"Yuh goin back t Burgess?"

"Ah reckon Ah have to."

"Whut else kin yuh do?"

"Nothin," he said. "Lawd, but Ah sho hate t start all over wid tha white man. Ah'd leave here ef Ah could. Ah owes im nigh eight hundred dollahs. N we needs a hoss, grub, seed, n a lot mo other things. Ef we keeps on like this tha white man'll own us body n soul."

"But, Tom, there ain nothin else t do," she said. "Ef we try t run erway they'll put us in jail."

"It coulda been worse," she said.

Sally came running from the kitchen. "Pa!"

"Hunh?"

"There's a shelf in the kitchen the flood didn git!"

"Where?"

"Right up over the stove."

"But, chile, ain nothin up there," said May.

"But there's somethin on it," said Sally.

"C mon. Les see."

High and dry, untouched by the flood-water, was a box of matches. And beside it a half-full sack of Bull Durham tobacco. He took a match from the box and scratched it on his overalls. It burned to his fingers before he dropped it.

"May!"

"Hunh?"

"Look! Here's ma bacco n some matches!"

She stared unbelievingly. "Lawd!" she breathed.

Tom rolled a cigarette clumsily.

May washed the stove, gathered some sticks, and after some difficulty, made a fire. The kitchen stove smoked, and their eyes smarted. May put water on to heat and went into the front room. It was getting dark. From the bundles they took a kerosene lamp and lit it. Outside Pat lowed longingly into the thickening gloam and tinkled her cowbell.

"Tha old cow's hongry," said May.

"Ah reckon Ah'll have t be gittin erlong t Burgess."

They stood on the front porch.

"Yuh bettah git on, Tom, fo it gits too dark."

"Yeah."

The wind had stopped blowing. In the east a cluster of stars hung.

"Yuh goin, Tom?"

"Ah reckon Ah have t."

"Ma, Ah'm hongry," said Sally.

"Wait erwhile, honey. Ma knows yuh's hongry."

Tom threw his cigarette away and sighed.

"Look! Here comes somebody!"

"Thas Mistah Burgess now!"

A mud-caked buggy rolled up. The shaggy horse

was splattered all over. Burgess leaned his white face out of the buggy and spat.

"Well, I see you're back."

"Yessuh."

"How things look?"

"They don look so good, Mistah."

"What seems to be the trouble?"

"Waal. Ah ain got no hoss, no grub, nothin. The only thing Ah got is tha ol cow there . . ."

"You owe eight hundred dollahs down at the store, Tom."

"Yessuh, Ah know. But, Mistah Burgess, can't yuh knock somethin off tha, seein as how Ahm down n out now?"

"You ate that grub, and I got to pay for it, Tom."

"Yessuh, Ah know."

"It's going to be a little tough, Tom. But you got to go through with it. Two of the boys tried to run away this morning and dodge their debts, and I had to have the sheriff pick em up. I wasn't looking for no trouble out of you, Tom . . . The rest of the families are going back."

Leaning out of the buggy, Burgess waited. In the surrounding stillness the cowbell tinkled again. Tom stood with his back against a post.

"Yuh got t go on, Tom. We ain't got nothin here," said May.

Tom looked at Burgess.

"Mistah Burgess, Ah don wanna make no trouble. But this is jus *too* hard. Ahm worse off now than befo. Ah got to start from scratch."

"Get in the buggy and come with me. I'll stake you with grub. We can talk over how you can pay it back." Tom said nothing. He rested his back against the post and looked at the mud-filled fields.

"Well," asked Burgess. "You coming?" Tom said nothing. He got slowly to the ground and pulled himself into the buggy. May watched them drive off.

"Hurry back, Tom!"

"Awright."

"Ma, tell Pa t bring me some 'lasses," begged Sally.

"Oh, Tom!"

Tom's head came out of the side of the buggy.

"Hunh?"

"Bring some 'lasses!"

"*Hunh?*"

"Bring some 'lasses for Sal!"

"Awright!"

She watched the buggy disappear over the crest of the muddy hill. Then she sighed, caught Sally's hand, and turned back into the cabin. ☐

DISCUSSION

There are two markedly different styles in "The Man Who Saw the Flood": the style of the narrator, which is quite conventional and familiar; and the language used by the characters, which is the **dialect** of southern Blacks (which can, of course, be heard in the north also). Spelling is used to suggest the pronunciation of actual speech. Wright uses the dialect to make his characters more vivid and more appealingly human.

FOR EXPLORATION

1. Compare the language of the black family with the language of Mr. Burgess at the end of the story. Discuss the ways in which Wright uses language to differentiate his characters.

2. Explain the way in which Mr. Burgess keeps the black sharecropper family in bondage.

3. Is Tom near the point of rebellion near the end of the story? Why doesn't he rebel?

4. What is the effect of the story's conclusion with Tom promising to bring back "lasses" for Sally? Explain.

5. Discuss the title of the story, "The Man Who Saw the Flood."

CREATIVE RESPONSE

Go through the story with some care, noting the objects which the family seems most interested in finding. From these and other clues in the story, reconstruct the kind of life the family must have had before the flood and write an account of that life.

WIDE WORLD PHOTOS

Richard Wright   1908 / 1960

Richard Wright was born on a plantation near Natchez, Mississippi. He grew up, by his own description, unruly and unwanted. Wright was five years old when his father deserted the family. Within another five years his mother had succumbed to complete paralysis and he was passed from relative to relative until at the age of fifteen Wright struck out on his own. He worked in Memphis, Tennessee, at various unskilled jobs and then during the depression bummed all over the country, ending up in Chicago. There he became active in the labor movement and in 1936 joined the Communist Party.

Wright's literary interests were first awakened reading H. L. Mencken while a Memphis postal clerk. When he reached Chicago he was able to join a WPA Writer's Project and by 1938 had published *Uncle Tom's Children,* a collection of four stories, one of which had already won the annual *Story* magazine award. He followed this with *Native Son* (1940), a best seller about a young black man executed for murder. It was a major breakthrough in that it achieved the kind of recognition and popularity which black literature had hitherto been denied. His next important work was the autobiographical *Black Boy* (1945), a novel which confirmed Wright's position among America's leading writers. Wright had in the meantime broken with the Communist Party and would in a later essay, *The God That Failed* (1950), describe his disenchantment.

After World War II Wright expatriated to France, living and writing in Paris until his death at the age of fifty-two. "The Man Who Saw the Flood" is taken from *Eight Men,* published posthumously in 1961.

Eudora Welty

A WORN PATH

I T was December—a bright frozen day in the early morning. Far out in the country there was an old Negro woman with her head tied in a red rag, coming along a path through the pinewoods. Her name was Phoenix Jackson. She was very old and small and she walked slowly in the dark pine shadows, moving a little from side to side in her steps, with the balanced heaviness and lightness of a pendulum in a grandfather clock. She carried a thin, small cane made from an umbrella, and with this she kept tapping the frozen earth in front of her. This made a grave and persistent noise in the still air, that seemed meditative like the chirping of a solitary little bird.

She wore a dark striped dress reaching down to her shoe tops, and an equally long apron of bleached sugar sacks, with a full pocket: all neat and tidy, but every time she took a step she might have fallen over her shoelaces, which dragged from her unlaced shoes. She looked straight ahead. Her eyes were blue with age. Her skin had a pattern all its own of numberless branching wrinkles and as though a whole little tree stood in the middle of her forehead, but a golden color ran underneath, and the two knobs of her cheeks were illumined by a yellow burning under the dark. Under the red rag her hair came down on her neck in the frailest of ringlets, still black, and with an odor like copper.

Now and then there was a quivering in the thicket. Old Phoenix said, "Out of my way, all you foxes, owls, beetles, jack rabbits, coons and wild animals! . . . Keep out from under these feet, little bob-whites. . . . Keep the big wild hogs out of my path. Don't let none of those come running my direction. I got a long way." Under her small black-freckled hand her cane, limber as a buggy whip, would switch at the brush as if to rouse up any hiding things.

On she went. The woods were deep and still. The sun made the pine needles almost too bright to look at, up where the wind rocked. The cones dropped as light as feathers. Down in the hollow was the mourning dove—it was not too late for him.

The path ran up a hill. "Seem like there is chains about my feet, time I get this far," she said, in the voice of argument old people keep to use with themselves. "Something always take a hold of me on this hill—pleads I should stay."

After she got to the top she turned and gave a full, severe look behind her where she had come. "Up through pines," she said at length. "Now down through oaks."

Her eyes opened their widest, and she started down gently. But before she got to the bottom of the hill a bush caught her dress.

Her fingers were busy and intent, but her skirts were full and long, so that before she could pull them free in one place they were caught in another. It was not possible to allow the dress to tear. "I in the thorny bush," she said. "Thorns, you doing your appointed work. Never want to let folks pass, no sir. Old eyes thought you was a pretty little *green* bush."

Finally, trembling all over, she stood free, and after a moment dared to stoop for her cane.

"Sun so high!" she cried, leaning back and looking, while the thick tears went over her eyes. "The time getting all gone here."

At the foot of this hill was a place where a log was laid across the creek.

"Now comes the trial," said Phoenix.

Putting her right foot out, she mounted the log and shut her eyes. Lifting her skirt, leveling her cane fiercely before her, like a festival figure in some parade, she began to march across. Then she opened her eyes and she was safe on the other side.

"I wasn't as old as I thought," she said.

But she sat down to rest. She spread her skirts on the bank around her and folded her hands over her knees. Up above her was a tree in a pearly cloud of mistletoe. She did not dare to close her eyes, and when a little boy brought her a plate with a slice of marble-cake on it she spoke to him. "That would be acceptable," she said. But when she went to take it there was just her own hand in the air.

So she left that tree, and had to go through a barbed-wire fence. There she had to creep and

Copyright 1941, renewed 1969 by Eudora Welty. Reprinted from her volume, A CURTAIN OF GREEN AND OTHER STORIES, by permission of Harcourt Brace Jovanovich, Inc., and Russell & Volkening, Inc.

crawl, spreading her knees and stretching her fingers like a baby trying to climb the steps. But she talked loudly to herself: she could not let her dress be torn now, so late in the day, and she could not pay for having her arm or her leg sawed off if she got caught fast where she was.

At last she was safe through the fence and risen up out in the clearing. Big dead trees, like black men with one arm, were standing in the purple stalks of the withered cotton field. There sat a buzzard.

"Who you watching?"

In the furrow she made her way along.

"Glad this not the season for bulls," she said, looking sideways, "and the good Lord made his snakes to curl up and sleep in the winter. A pleasure I don't see no two-headed snake coming around that tree, where it come once. It took a while to get by him, back in the summer."

She passed through the old cotton and went into a field of dead corn. It whispered and shook and was taller than her head. "Through the maze now," she said, for there was no path.

Then there was something tall, black, and skinny there, moving before her.

At first she took it for a man. It could have been a man dancing in the field. But she stood still and listened, and it did not make a sound. It was as silent as a ghost.

"Ghost," she said sharply, "who be you the ghost of? For I have heard of nary death close by."

But there was no answer—only the ragged dancing in the wind.

She shut her eyes, reached out her hand, and touched a sleeve. She found a coat and inside that an emptiness, cold as ice.

"You scarecrow," she said. Her face lighted. "I ought to be shut up for good," she said with laughter. "My senses is gone. I too old. I the oldest people I ever know. Dance, old scarecrow," she said, "while I dancing with you."

She kicked her foot over the furrow, and with mouth drawn down, shook her head once or twice in a little strutting way. Some husks blew down and whirled in streamers about her skirts.

Then she went on, parting her way from side to side with the cane, through the whispering field. At last she came to the end, to a wagon track where the silver grass blew between the red ruts. The quail were walking around like pullets, seeming all dainty and unseen.

"Walk pretty," she said. "This the easy place. This the easy going."

She followed the track, swaying through the quiet bare fields, through the little strings of trees silver in their dead leaves, past cabins silver from weather, with the doors and windows boarded shut, all like old women under a spell sitting there. "I walking in their sleep," she said, nodding her head vigorously.

In a ravine she went where a spring was silently flowing through a hollow log. Old Phoenix bent and drank. "Sweet-gum makes the water sweet," she said, and drank more. "Nobody know who made this well, for it was here when I was born."

The track crossed a swampy part where the moss hung as white as lace from every limb. "Sleep on, alligators, and blow your bubbles." Then the track went into the road.

Deep, deep the road went down between the high green-colored banks. Overhead the live-oaks met, and it was as dark as a cave.

A black dog with a lolling tongue came up out of the weeds by the ditch. She was meditating, and not ready, and when he came at her she only hit him a little with her cane. Over she went in the ditch, like a little puff of milkweed.

Down there, her senses drifted away. A dream visited her, and she reached her hand up, but nothing reached down and gave her a pull. So she lay there and presently went to talking. "Old woman," she said to herself, "that black dog come up out of the weeds to stall your off, and now there he sitting on his fine tail, smiling at you."

A white man finally came along and found her—a hunter, a young man, with his dog on a chain.

"Well, Granny!" he laughed. "What are you doing there?"

"Lying on my back like a June-bug waiting to be turned over, mister," she said, reaching up her hand.

He lifted her up, gave her a swing in the air, and set her down. "Anything broken, Granny?"

"No sir, them old dead weeds is springy enough," said Phoenix, when she had got her breath. "I thank you for your trouble."

"Where do you live, Granny?" he asked, while the two dogs were growling at each other.

"Away back yonder, sir, behind the ridge. You can't even see it from here."

"On your way home?"

"No sir, I going to town."

"Why, that's too far! That's as far as I walk when I come out myself, and I get something for my trouble." He patted the stuffed bag he carried, and there hung down a little closed claw. It was one of the bob-whites, with its beak hooked bitterly to show it was dead. "Now you go on home, Granny!"

"I bound to go to town, mister," said Phoenix. "The time come around."

He gave another laugh, filling the whole landscape. "I know you old colored people! Wouldn't miss going to town to see Santa Claus!"

But something held old Phoenix very still. The deep lines in her face went into a fierce and different radiation. Without warning, she had seen with her own eyes a flashing nickel fall out of the man's pocket onto the ground.

"How old are you, Granny?" he was saying.

"There is no telling, mister," she said, "no telling."

Then she gave a little cry and clapped her hands and said, "Git on away from here, dog! Look! Look at that dog!" She laughed as if in admiration. "He ain't scared of nobody. He a big black dog." She whispered, "Sic him!"

"Watch me get rid of that cur," said the man. "Sic him, Pete! Sic him!"

Phoenix heard the dogs fighting, and heard the man running and throwing sticks. She even heard a gunshot. But she was slowly bending forward by that time, further and further forward, the lids stretched down over her eyes, as if she were doing this in her sleep. Her chin was lowered almost to her knees. The yellow palm of her hand came out from the fold of her apron. Her fingers slid down and along the ground under the piece of money with the grace and care they would have in lifting an egg from under a setting hen. Then she slowly straightened up, she stood erect, and the nickel was in her apron pocket. A bird flew by. Her lips moved. "God watching me the whole time. I come to stealing."

The man came back, and his own dog panted about them. "Well, I scared him off that time," he said, and then he laughed and lifted his gun and pointed it at Phoenix.

She stood straight and faced him.

"Doesn't the gun scare you?" he said, still pointing it.

"No, sir, I seen plenty go off closer by, in my day, and for less than what I done," she said, holding utterly still.

He smiled, and shouldered the gun. "Well, Granny," he said, "you must be a hundred years old, and scared of nothing. I'd give you a dime if I had any money with me. But you take my advice and stay home, and nothing will happen to you."

"I bound to go on my way, mister," said Phoenix. She inclined her head in the red rag. Then they went in different directions, but she could hear the gun shooting again and again over the hill.

She walked on. The shadows hung from the oak trees to the road like curtains. Then she smelled wood-smoke, and smelled the river, and she saw a steeple and the cabins on their steep steps. Dozens of little black children whirled around her. There ahead was Natchez shining. Bells were ringing. She walked on.

In the paved city it was Christmas time. There were red and green electric lights strung and criss-crossed everywhere, and all turned on in the daytime. Old Phoenix would have been lost if she had not distrusted her eyesight and depended on her feet to know where to take her.

She paused quietly on the sidewalk where people were passing by. A lady came along in the crowd, carrying an armful of red-, green- and silver-wrapped presents; she gave off perfume like the red roses in hot summer, and Phoenix stopped her.

"Please, missy, will you lace up my shoe?" She held up her foot.

"What do you want, Grandma?"

"See my shoe," said Phoenix. "Do all right for out in the country, but wouldn't look right to go in a big building."

"Stand still then, Grandma," said the lady. She put her packages down on the sidewalk beside her and laced and tied both shoes tightly.

"Can't lace 'em with a cane," said Phoenix. "Thank you, missy. I doesn't mind asking a nice lady to tie up my shoe, when I gets out on the street."

Moving slowly and from side to side, she went into the big building, and into a tower of steps, where she walked up and around and around until her feet knew to stop.

She entered a door, and there she saw nailed up on the wall the document that had been stamped with the gold seal and framed in the gold frame, which matched the dream that was hung up in her head.

"Here I be," she said. There was a fixed and ceremonial stiffness over her body.

"A charity case, I suppose," said an attendant who sat at the desk before her.

But Phoenix only looked above her head. There was sweat on her face, the wrinkles in her skin shone like a bright net.

"Speak up, Grandma," the woman said. "What's your name? We must have your history, you know. Have you been here before? What seems to be the trouble with you?"

Old Phoenix only gave a twitch to her face as if a fly were bothering her.

"Are you deaf?" cried the attendant.

But then the nurse came in.

"Oh, that's just old Aunt Phoenix," she said. "She doesn't come for herself—she has a little grandson. She makes these trips just as regular as clockwork. She lives away back off the Old Natchez Trace." She bent down. "Well, Aunt Phoenix, why don't you just take a seat? We won't keep you standing after your long trip." She pointed.

The old woman sat down, bolt upright in the chair.

"Now, how is the boy?" asked the nurse.

Old Phoenix did not speak.

"I said, how is the boy?"

But Phoenix only waited and stared straight ahead, her face very solemn and withdrawn into rigidity.

"Is his throat any better?" asked the nurse. "Aunt Phoenix, don't you hear me? Is your grandson's throat any better since the last time you came for the medicine?"

With her hands on her knees, the old woman waited, silent, erect and motionless, just as if she were in armor.

"You mustn't take up our time this way, Aunt Phoenix," the nurse said. "Tell us quickly about your grandson, and get it over. He isn't dead, is he?"

At last there came a flicker and then a flame of comprehension across her face, and she spoke.

"My grandson. It was my memory had left me. There I sat and forgot why I made my long trip."

"Forgot?" The nurse frowned. "After you came so far?"

Then Phoenix was like an old woman begging a dignified forgiveness for waking up frightened in the night. "I never did go to school, I was too old at the Surrender,"[1] she said in a soft voice. "I'm an old woman without an education. It was my memory fail me. My little grandson, he is just the same, and I forgot it in the coming."

"Throat never heals, does it?" said the nurse, speaking in a loud, sure voice to old Phoenix. By now she had a card with something written on it, a little list. "Yes. Swallowed lye. When was it?—January—two-three years ago—"

Phoenix spoke unasked now. "No, missy, he not dead, he just the same. Every little while his throat begin to close up again, and he not able to swallow. He not get his breath. He not able to help himself. So the time come around, and I go on another trip for the soothing medicine."

"All right. The doctor said as long as you came to get it, you could have it," said the nurse. "But it's an obstinate case."

"My little grandson, he sit up there in the house all wrapped up, waiting by himself," Phoenix went on. "We is the only two left in the world. He suffer and it don't seem to put him back at all. He got a sweet look. He going to last. He wear a little patch quilt and peep out holding his mouth open like a little bird. I remembers so plain now. I not going to forget him again, no, the whole enduring time. I could tell him from all the others in creation."

"All right." The nurse was trying to hush her now. She brought her a bottle of medicine. "Charity," she said, making a check mark in a book.

Old Phoenix held the bottle close to her eyes, and then carefully put it into her pocket.

"I thank you," she said.

"It's Christmas time, Grandma," said the attendant. "Could I give you a few pennies out of my purse?"

"Five pennies is a nickel," said Phoenix stiffly.

"Here's a nickel," said the attendant.

Phoenix rose carefully and held out her hand. She received the nickel and then fished the other nickel out of her pocket and laid it beside the new one. She stared at her palm closely, with her head on one side.

Then she gave a tap with her cane on the floor.

"This is what come to me to do," she said. "I going to the store and buy my child a little windmill they sells, made out of paper. He going to find it hard to believe there such a thing in the world. I'll march myself back where he waiting, holding it straight up in this hand."

She lifted her free hand, gave a little nod, turned around, and walked out of the doctor's office. Then her slow step began on the stairs, going down. □

----

1. *the Surrender*, the Surrender of the Confederate Army to the Union Army at Appomattox on April 9, 1865.

DISCUSSION

"A Worn Path" might be described as **local color** fiction—
fiction that identifies closely with one area of the country
by presenting its people, dialect, folklore, climate, vegetation, manners, customs, and dress in vivid detail. But Eudora
Welty is interested in something more than dramatizing
regional differences and eccentricities. "A Worn Path" is
not only local but also universal in the glimpse it gives into
the heart of a deeply human human being.

FOR EXPLORATION

1. As we accompany ancient Phoenix Jackson on her solitary trek across the countryside and encounter with her
the obstacles in her path and listen to her talking with the
world, what kind of person do we discover her to be?
2. What is the meaning of the title, "A Worn Path"?
3. What traits of character does Phoenix exhibit in her
encounter with the white man, who helps her out of the
ditch into which she has fallen?
4. Why does Eudora Welty withhold the purpose of Phoenix's visit until near the end?
5. Discuss the effect of the conclusion of the story, in which
Phoenix announces her intention to buy her grandchild a
paper windmill. What does this reveal about their lives?

CREATIVE RESPONSE

1. Describe Phoenix Jackson's return journey from the
town to her house, carrying the paper windmill, and encountering on the way back the white man who has by
now missed the nickel that he lost out of his pocket.
2. Write a final scene in which Phoenix Jackson enters her
cabin and presents the paper windmill to her grandson.

CULVER PICTURES, INC.

Eudora Welty   1909 /

Eudora Welty was born in Jackson, Mississippi, and has
spent most of her life in her native state. She attended the
University of Wisconsin, then went to New York where she
studied journalism at Columbia University and wrote
publicity, society news, and radio scripts. After returning
to Mississippi, she settled down to a career of writing, with
gardening, painting, and photography as avocations. Her
first volume of short stories, *A Curtain of Green*, was published in 1941. The title story won the O. Henry Memorial
Award for that year. Since then she has published several
other volumes of short stories and a number of novels, her
most recent being *Losing Battles* (1970).

Welty lives quietly and alone in her home of forty years.
She treasures her privacy and not long ago commented,
"Writing fiction is an interior affair. Novels and stories
always will be put down little by little out of personal
feeling and personal beliefs arrived at alone and at firsthand
over a period of time as time is needed. To go outside and
beat the drum is only to interrupt, interrupt . . . Fiction has,
and must keep, a private address. For life is lived in a
private place; where it means anything is inside the mind
and heart."

Prudencio de Pereda

CONQUISTADOR

I thought, when I was young, that you worked according to your nationality. We were Spanish, and my father, grandfather, and uncles were all in the cigar business. There was a definite rule about this, I believed—a *law*. I thought so particularly during those times when I listened to my father and the other men of our family talk business, and heard them complain bitterly about the cigar business and about what a dishonorable trade it was, and how they were cursed the moment they took it up.

This used to surprise me—especially in regard to my father, because on the rare visits to his store it had seemed like a wonderful place. It had a broad, rich-looking, nickel-plated counter, neatly stacked with bright-colored boxes of cigars, and with shining hookahs and lighters along its top. The floor was white tile, and the inside wall of the store was a great mirror. The customers I'd seen had been well-dressed men with booming voices, rich gold chains around their full stomachs, and canes and gloves in their hands. There had been an air of wealth and strength in that store as I remembered it.

Still my father was one of the most vehement in his denunciations of the cigar business. "Let them raise the blood to my face in shame," he once said, in his correct, intense Spanish, "if I permit any of my sons to go into this business. Yes. Let them do that!" I admired my father for his feelings, but felt that he was just talking, that my three brothers and I were all fated for the cigar business, just as my father and uncles had been. Indeed, even at this time, my older brother, who was only ten but figured himself a wise American, had already begun to do some special errands for my father. He would not only deliver boxes of cigars to the hotels in the neighborhood of my father's store in the Borough Hall section of Brooklyn, but would even take the elevated and go over the river and into the city to make deliveries.

When I begged him to tell me about this, he acted very casual and unafraid, and when, out of my genuine concern for him, I asked, "Aren't you going to be an aviator any more?" he said, "Sure! What's the matter with you? What d'you think I'm saving my money for?" I pitied him all the more, and worried myself inside for him. He was doomed—just as my father and uncles had been doomed. He would never be an aviator; nor would I ever be a bullfighter—and poor Justo would never have his big shoeshine parlor, or have his twin, Bifanio, as a sweeper. Bifanio hadn't made up his mind, yet, as to what he wanted to be, but the twins always did things together.

My older brother would never take me with him when he went on his errands. I was too young—though I was only two years younger than he. After we came home from school, he would put on his Sunday suit and new shoes and go down to my father's store on the trolley. I often wept as I pleaded with him to take me—just once, just this once! I didn't want to get into the cigar business, and was afraid of the city, but I would have risked anything to be allowed to ride on an elevated train.

My brother never relented, and my first experience in the cigar business came through an accident and without his help. It was something bigger than he'd ever done, and I should have felt boastful; instead, it filled me with terror and shame, and, at once, I understood the feelings of my father and the other men of our family.

How it happened was natural enough. Mother was making another try to have a girl, "a little sister," as she explained formally to us, and we three younger boys were farmed out. My older brother, Joe, stayed at home because he could do errands, make phone calls, and generally help around the house, and besides, as he explained to me, he was old enough to understand things. I didn't feel too bad, because I was going to Grandmother's and not to an aunt's, as the twins had. Going to Grandmother's had some responsibility, for there were always errands to be done and I would often have to act as translator. My grandmother spoke only about ten words of English, and my grandfather just a few more.

On the third day of my stay there—it was the Fourth of July—Grandfather had announced early that he wouldn't "go out" today. "Going out" meant going to work. My grandfather was in the most stigmatized form of the cigar business—he was a *teveriano* or "junk dealer," one of those itinerant

---

"*Conquistador*" by Prudencio de Pereda from WINDMILLS IN BROOKLYN, Atheneum, copyright © 1960. Reprinted by permission of the author.

salesmen who were scorned by the rest of the trade because they dealt completely in lies: in false labels, false representation, and false merchandise—very cheap cigars for which they secured exorbitant prices—and so brought still more disgrace to the Spaniards who had enough as it was by merely being in the legitimate cigar business.

I had heard all this at home—listening eagerly because the *teveriano* was certainly the most interesting of all the cigar men—but I'd never been able to connect the fabulous stories of *teverianos* with my mild, sad grandfather. For one thing, he was always very poor.

Grandmother didn't turn to look at him as she answered: "Do you observe American holidays, now?" She had a great dislike for everything American. She had been a great lady in Spain.

"One has to dance to the song they play," Grandfather said, shrugging his shoulders.

"And one has to pay the rent they ask!" Grandmother said this very sharply. I knew I should have left the room then, but I felt too sorry for my grandfather. He was growing very red. "We're at the fourth, now," Grandmother said. "That's five days late."

"Well?" Grandmother said, turning.

"I know that. I'm in accord with you. But not in front of the boy, please! Not in front of the boy, woman!"

"The boy knows it!"

"But not from me!" Grandfather stood up suddenly and came over to me. His hands were trembling. He took my arm and led me into the front parlor. He stood me by the window and sat down in the big chair. "Watch the celebrations!" he said. "Watch the celebrations!" I stared fixedly out the open window, knowing there weren't going to be any celebrations around here, but not wanting to tell my grandfather.

We stayed there only a short time, because the bell rang in a few moments—I couldn't see who it was—and quick, happy steps came up the stairs and we heard Agapito's voice greeting my grandmother. He called her "Dona," the most respectful title in Spanish, but he was laughing and warm as he talked.

Just as Grandfather was not, Agapito was the perfect example of the *teveriano*. He was still a very young man and had only been in America a short time, but he was easily the most famous—as well as the most criticized—of the salesmen. He was dressed that day as I imagined a *teveriano* would dress: a fine white linen suit, brown patent-leather shoes with button tops, a bright polka-dot bow tie, and a Panama straw with a multicolored band. When he came smiling into the front room, I thought he looked like the perfect man of the world, and he seemed to fill the room with brightness. He was very respectful to my grandfather, as he'd been to Grandmother, and when he suggested that they go out for a little bit, he said it in a quiet, serious voice. "We'll take the boy with us, yes?" he said, patting my shoulder and smiling at me. Agapito had neat white teeth and a small black mustache. He had a dark Spanish skin, and I thought he was very handsome. I'd always liked him, in spite of the stories I'd heard about him.

Grandfather answered Agapito's suggestion to go out by quietly shrugging his shoulders, but when Agapito suggested that they take me, his face took on the dark, stubborn look again.

"Yes, take the boy!" my grandmother called from the kitchen. "He hasn't been out. He may see some things. Holiday things." My grandfather shrugged his shoulders again.

We took a trolley—an open summer trolley—and we stayed on till the end of the line, and I saw that we'd come to the dock section. We could see the colored stacks of the big liners tied up at the piers. The big street was empty and quiet and that made the wonderful ships seem more intimate in the sun. Agapito kept pointing out things to me, but Grandfather walked along very quietly. He was dressed in his best black suit, with a black derby hat, and his face looked very worried. His black, drooping mustache made his face look very sad.

When we'd gone a few blocks, we turned into a side street and went into a small cigar store. I saw that this was Miguelin's. I knew Miguelin from seeing him at home and at the Spanish dances. He was a little, gray old man, and his store was dusty and old. He wrapped up seven new boxes of cigars for us, not wrapping them in brown paper but just with a heavy string so that you could see it was cigars and all the beautiful labels showed. Agapito gave him fourteen dollars. I counted them—and figured out that meant two dollars per box. Grandfather wanted to pay, but Agapito stopped him and made him put his wallet away. Agapito seemed to have charge of everything—he'd paid our fares on the trolley, too —and he would bend over and talk to Grandfather in a low voice while he patted him on the shoulder. I felt happy about this. I wanted my grandfather to lose his worry.

When we left Miguelin's, we turned to the big street again, and walked back the way we'd come. We walked very slowly, and Agapito kept talking to Grandfather and looking into each saloon that we passed. The saloons were the only places that were open today and there weren't many men in any of them. We were coming to a big one on the opposite corner, when Agapito said to my grandfather: "This one! This one seems good." The saloon had a big, bright shiny front and had a big hotel upstairs. I read the name "Monaghan" on the big sign over the swinging doors. As we crossed, Agapito took my hand firmly, and as we went in, I saw that the saloon was big and shiny and clean. It reminded me of my father's store. There was a big counter on one side with a great mirror on the wall and another counter on the other side with trays of food filling it all along. The tile floor was very clean and had no sawdust on it, and there was a big back room with tables that had white tablecloths.

Agapito stood inside the doorway, smiling and looking around as if he liked the place. Then he led us over to the big counter with the mirror. We found a place easily because there were only a few men standing there, and Agapito placed the cigar boxes on the counter and nodded and smiled to the man behind the counter. He pointed to my grandfather and then to himself and said "Whiskey!" very plainly. He pronounced it "vhiskey." He patted me on the head, and smiled at the man again, and said, "Ginger ale!" He pronounced this well, except that he said "al" instead of "ale."

There was another man behind the counter, standing farther back. He had his jacket off and his sleeves rolled up, but he didn't have an apron on. He was a big man with a red face and he was smoking a big cigar. He had a gold chain across his vest and two big rings on his right hand, and he looked like one of my father's rich customers. When I stared at him, he winked at me and laughed. He'd been watching Agapito and my grandfather who were leaning on the big counter with their feet on the brass rail. Agapito had been talking in Spanish and laughing as he and my grandfather drank their whiskey.

The big man walked up to them slowly and patted the cigar boxes. Agapito turned his head up suddenly, in surprise, and then smiled at the big man and bowed to him.

"Havanas?" the big man said. He had a strong deep voice.

Agapito nodded quickly. "Yes! I am from Havana. I am from Havana."

"I mean the cigars," the big man said, laughing. He had brown teeth, but a nice face.

"Oh! Also, also!" Agapito said. He laughed and kept nodding his head. "From Havana, also. For my friend! I bring them." He pointed outside. "The ship! You understand? From Havana to Spain. I bring them to friend here. I stop off." He spoke in short spurts, but he pronounced very clearly. He stopped smiling and became very serious as he pulled one of the boxes out of the bundle, opened it with his little gold knife and picked out two cigars carefully. He handed them over to the big man and nodded vigorously when the big man seemed to hesitate.

"For Fourth of July!" Agapito said. He smiled again. "Happy Fourth of July!" He nodded and pressed the cigars into the man's hand.

The big man smelled the cigars and nodded to him. "Good flavor," he said. He turned and said something to the man in the apron and this man took the bottle and poured more whiskey into Agapito's and my grandfather's glasses. Agapito raised his glass to him, and then my grandfather did.

The big man kept smelling the cigars and then he patted the boxes again. "What would they cost?— How much?" he said, when Agapito looked puzzled. Agapito spread his hands. "For a friend," he said. "You understand. No. . . ." He made the motion with his hands again.

"Customs?" the big man said.

"Customs!" Agapito nodded quickly and smiled. He rubbed his hands. "No customs! Customs."

"Well, how much? How much, anyway?" The big man patted the boxes.

Agapito held a finger up, and turned to my grandfather. "This one seems to have money," he said in Spanish. "This one can pay."

"Take care, hombre," my grandfather said.

"No, don't disquiet yourself, Don Jose. I know what I'm doing." Agapito patted Grandfather's arm, turned to the big man and smiled. "My friend, here. He remember. He remember everything." He ran his finger up and down the boxes. "All the boxes. Seven! Sixty dollars. Cost for my friend."

Sixty dollars! This was a shock to me—if a man buys seven boxes of cigars for fourteen dollars, two dollars per box, and sells them for—sixty dollars! I understood why the big man made such a face and then laughed. I hadn't minded all the lies that Agapito had told because I knew that *teverianos* worked like that, but when he asked his high, high figure, I got shocked and embarrassed—and then, very frightened for us. The glass felt heavy in my hand, and I held my head down because I knew that I was blushing.

I'd heard that *teverianos* asked robber prices, but I never thought that Agapito would take the chance today, when he had my grandfather and me with him. He was going to get us into trouble. He was making us take a chance—because he wanted to. And we were all going to get into trouble.

The big man said something to Agapito and Agapito said, "Well—you know, sir. Havanas!"

I didn't hear the big man answer but then Agapito said very brightly, "You interested? You interested in cigars?" I hated his accent, now. His lying.

"I was looking for ten boxes. I could use ten boxes," the big man said slowly.

Agapito was talking in Spanish, then. He must have been talking to my grandfather. "You stay here," he said, still speaking respectfully. "I will run to Miguelin's and get three more boxes. I will run fast. You stay here. This is a good thing."

"Yes, hombre, it is," I heard my grandfather say. "Let him take these seven boxes and let us be through here. Let it stay a good thing."

"There is no danger," Agapito said quickly.

"If there is, entrust it to me," my grandfather said sternly and I looked up suddenly to see that his face had taken on the stubborn look again. "I wasn't thinking of that. I was thinking that we have a good thing. Let us take it, and be gone."

"I don't work like that," Agapito said. "You know that, Don José," he said more softly.

"Then, as you wish."

"You will stay?"

"As you wish!"

I watched, in rage but fascinated, as Agapito turned back to smile at the big man who was leaning on the counter with his old cigar in his mouth. Agapito brought his hands together. "We fix it,"

he said, and nodded. "Three more boxes, I will bring from the boat. For ten boxes"—he ran his fingers up and down the seven on the counter and held up three fingers—"ten boxes—for eighty dollars—for you!" He pointed at the big man.

The big man stared at Agapito for a moment, and then nodded and said, "Okay. Eighty dollars." What a fool this one is, too, I thought. His face looked stupid to me, now.

"You give me fifty dollars, now," Agapito said. He smiled. "I give money to guard—small money. You understand? My friend wait here, I come back. With three more."

Did Grandfather understand that? Did Grandfather know what Agapito was saying? I stared at his face, but couldn't see anything. I was weak with fright and fear, but I didn't dare say a word. The big man had taken out his wallet without hesitation and given Agapito five new bills—tens they must have been. Agapito smiled and nodded as he put them in his wallet quickly. He patted Grandfather on the arm, saying, "Don't worry yourself. I'll be back immediately," and then patted me on the head—I couldn't duck fast enough—and went out into the street.

I stared at the floor. I wouldn't look at my grandfather. I'd finished the ginger ale, but I wouldn't go over to put the glass on the counter. I heard the big man say something to Grandfather that Grandfather didn't answer. "No speak English, eh?" the big man said, and laughed. He took up the bundle of cigars and moved down to the end of the counter—where I could see him by just lifting my eyes a little—and he began to open every box.

I had to look at my grandfather, then. Did he see what danger we were in? He was staring at the mirror. His hands were steady, but he was sweating. I glared at him, at first, but then wanted to cry. I went up and put the glass by his side and he looked down at me and then turned to stare up at the big man as he was opening each box. Then, he turned back, finished his drink in one slug and turned to me. His back was to the big man and he put his hand on my shoulder. I could smell the whiskey on his breath as he bent down. "Get thee out of here," he said. "Act as if thou art going out calmly." My grandfather always used the familiar "thee" with us, and his voice was calm and easy now but I could see that he was sweating badly. His hand felt very tight on my shoulder. "Get thyself to the trolley station. Stand by the trees there and wait for me. No matter how long, I will come. Do nothing but wait for me. I will escape this in some way. I will get out, and get to thee. I will escape this and get to thee. In whatever way, I will.

"Without crying, thee!" he said. "Without crying!" I hadn't started to cry yet, but my lip had begun to tremble. I bit my lip and started to shake my head even before he'd finished. "And think well of me," he was saying. "Think well of me. I did not want this situation for thee. Thou wilt not? Thou wilt not do it?"

"No. I stay. I stay here with you." His face had the stubborn look again and he pushed my shoulder but held his grip tightly on it. He glared at me, but I kept shaking my head. "Stay, then!" he said. "Stay!" He dropped his hand from my shoulder but reached to take my hand and then turned to lean on the bar again, holding my hand. A moment later, when he poured more whiskey into his glass, he did it with his left hand, but poured it very neatly. He lifted the glass in his left hand, and began to sip the whiskey slowly.

Grandfather had been a waiter in Spain. He was very proud of that. He'd been a waiter at the best hotel in Tangier just before he'd come to the United States, and a prince, a duke, and two princesses had been among his patrons. My mother was born in Tangier, and, though she couldn't remember anything of her part in the life there, she told us many stories about it. The three years spent in Tangier had been the happiest time in the life of her family.

My grandmother's brother had come to the United States some years before and made an immediate success as a *teveriano*. He wrote glowing letters to my grandmother, telling her of the wonderful opportunities in the trade and urging her to make José, my grandfather, see reason and come to America. Does he want to be a waiter all his life? the brother would ask. He'd felt very bad when she'd married a waiter. He was her only brother and they were very close.

Grandfather was content. He didn't want to leave. The letters got more boastful, and then pleading. Finally, my granduncle sent enough money to pay first-class passage for all three and the pressure was too much for my grandfather. He consented, and he came to the United States with his family—to a tenement district in Hoboken, New Jersey. They moved to Brooklyn shortly after, when my aunt was born,

but to a tenement district again, and they had never lived better than that. Grandfather—as Mother would say, in ending these stories—was just not a good salesman.

I was thinking these things as I gripped Grandfather's hand and stared up at him, and the anger that I'd felt before turned to pity. I love you, I thought. Once, I pulled his arm and said, "We could go to the bathroom—first me, then you—sneak out that way." He glared down at me with a stubborn look. "No. In no such manner. When we go, we go through the front door. We are men." He turned to stare at the mirror, but then turned quickly back to me. "Dost thou have to go to the toilet? Truly?"

I shook my head.

"Good!" he said, and turned to the mirror.

I thought we stood like that for a long time—it seemed like a long, long time to me—but Agapito said later that he'd only been gone sixteen minutes, that he'd counted them. Agapito's face was sweating when he came back, and his Panama was pushed back on his head, but he was smiling and looked very happy, and his clothes were still very neat. "I run! I run!" he said to the big man. "To ship. To ship and back!" He'd put the new boxes on the counter and was opening each one with his penknife and holding the open box up to the big man. The boxes looked very new and I thought that one of the labels looked wet. Surely, the big man would see, now. He would see the truth, now, I thought. And it would serve Agapito right. He'd be in it, now. Grandfather and I could run. We'd get away. Agapito was the one they'd hold.

The big man smelled every box and even touched the wet wrapper, but he nodded seriously and then stupidly took out his wallet and gave Agapito three more ten dollar bills. The man with the apron had filled Agapito's glass again and Agapito held out one of the bills to him, but he shook his head. Then, Agapito put the bills in his wallet and picked out a one-dollar bill that he folded and handed to the man in the apron. "For you," he said. "For you." He smiled and nodded. Then, he held up the whiskey, smiled and nodded again, and drank it in one gulp.

I had been tugging at Grandfather's hand, wanting to start, wanting us to go, but Grandfather held his tight grip and waited until Agapito had shaken hands with both men, and then he himself nodded to them, and we all turned towards the door.

We walked very slowly as we went outside and crossed the street. Grandfather wanted to walk fast, but Agapito was holding his arm and walking very slowly. "Don't worry yourself," he said, after a moment. "We'll turn down the first street. For now, we walk slowly—very slowly, and with dignity."

We turned down the first street, walked down that block, and then turned in the direction of the trolleys. As soon as we'd made this last turn, Agapito stopped and took out his wallet. He handed Grandfather three ten-dollar bills. Grandfather pushed them back. "Hombre!" he said, "don't embarrass me."

"Please!" Agapito said. "This is your share."

"It's too much."

"It's half. We were equally involved." Agapito pressed the bills into Grandfather's hand. "Equally!" he said, letting go.

Grandfather put the bills in his little black purse. "I'm very appreciative. Very!" he said.

"For nothing!" Agapito said. "For nothing!" As we walked, now, he was smiling and happy again. He took off his hat and rubbed his face with a big silk handkerchief. "One has to see these things, Don Jose. One has to see them. To believe them, one has to see them. Havanas!" he shook his head and laughed. "And you mustn't feel that we cheat them!" he said, when Grandfather didn't answer. "This one buys them as Havanas. He gives them out as Havanas—probably at some festival—and those who take them, take them as Havanas, and smoke them. No matter how bad the cigars, for them they are Havanas. Yes, Don Jose. We sell Havanas—they buy Havanas!"

On the trolley, after he'd paid our fares, Agapito slipped a half dollar into the conductor's pocket. "For Fourth of July!" he said. The conductor blushed, and nodded. Later, Agapito stood up and took off his hat. "Life for the United States of America!" he called out. "Happy Fourth of July to everybody!" The two people who were sitting up at the front end of the trolley smiled and shook their heads. They thought he was drunk.

Agapito left, soon after we got home. Then, Grandmother went out. "I'll get some ham," she said. "We'll eat well, tonight." Grandfather and I were in the front room, and she'd come to the door. "The delicatessen has good ham."

Grandfather nodded. "We're most fortunate," he said, without looking up. "Most fortunate."

Grandmother turned back and stared at him with a cold face. She was dressed in her black skirt and black silk waist, and she looked like the pictures of the Queen Mother in the Spanish magazines we had, except that Grandmother was much more beautiful. "Yes," she said, in a calm voice. "Most fortunate. You, in particular! You needn't go out for some days, now. Perhaps grow a beard, here."

Grandfather got very red, but didn't look up. He shrugged his shoulders as Grandmother turned and went out. After a moment, he reached over to me and pulled me to the side of the chair. He kept his arm around me and patted my head. "Thou!" he said. He looked straight at me. "Thou must forget what thou heardst today, what thou sawst. All of it! Forget especially what thy grandmother said. She is a fine woman. Nothing of today was like her. It is I who am weak. The fault is mine. Thou wilt understand this some day. Thou wilt, yes. What thou must remember is this"—he pressed my shoulder—"that thou must be strong. Remember that! Let no woman—whether she be thy mother who is my own flesh, or the woman thou wilt marry—let none of them press thee or influence thee in choosing thy profession. Thou, thou alone, must move through the world to make thy money, thou alone must suffer—so thou must choose. And hold to that!

"Thou art the bullfighter, no?"

"Or one who guides an elevated train," I said. "One of those."

"Good. Thou might change, but whatever thou shouldst choose—hold to it. Grip it well."

I nodded.

"Doest thou know what she referred to in that of the beard?" he said, in a softer voice.

"No, Grandfather," I lied.

"Well, it was this: I had a fine beard when I was a waiter in Tangier. It was a full, well-cut beard and I was a fine figure with it. One afternoon, the major-domo—he who was chief of all our waiters—the major-domo, Don Felix, came to me and said, 'Jose, you must shave that beard. Too many patrons are coming in and talking to you and treating you as the major-domo. I regret this, but you must shave it, because there is only one major-domo here, and it is me. No one else can look like a major-domo. No one else will.'

"I went home to thy grandmother and told her this, and she said, 'Yes. The man has reason. You must shave your beard.' I had thought that she would have objections, that she would show anger. I had thought that she loved the beard as I did—it was a fine beard. But she did not—or, if she did, she would not let it stand before Don Felix's objection.

"So, I cut it off!" my grandfather said. He brushed his hand under his chin. "That was a mistake. I should have held to my first thought. I should have defended myself. I should have left my place and sought another job in Tangier—or Gibraltar or La Linea where there are fine hotels. *I* was doing the waiting, and *I* should have thought of *myself*." He stopped and stared at me. "Thou seest?" he said. "Stop thou at the first mistake. Stop there."

I nodded, and he pressed my shoulder again and then reached over and lifted me on to his lap. He cradled my head on his shoulder and rocked slowly back and forth. "We must gladden ourselves," he said, "before she comes. We must gladden ourselves and be smiling. This is difficult for her, too. Difficult. We must gladden ourselves, now. Yes! We must gladden ourselves for her."

I was nodding my head to say, Yes, when my forehead felt something wet and I looked up and saw that the tears were falling down his cheeks.

THE END

DISCUSSION

America has been called the melting pot of nations because of the many different immigrant groups that have come to this country and been "melted down" into the general mixture known as American. Frequently forgotten has been the pain and anguish and loss in the melting process. "Conquistador" is a poignant story describing something of that pain and loss. As such writers as Prudencio de Pereda (see also Américo Parédes' "The Hammon and the Beans," page M 100) search through their varied heritages, salvaging what elements of a disappearing culture they can, the "melting-pot" metaphor seems less applicable and perhaps less desirable than it once did. Perhaps it would be better to adopt the metaphor of the "mosaic," which suggests that each immigrant group might take pride in preserving its own cultural identity even at the same time that it fits into the patchwork pattern of America.

FOR EXPLORATION

1. *Conquistador* is the term applied to the conquerors of Mexico. What is its meaning as the title of this story?
2. Compare and contrast the characters of the grandfather and Agapito.
3. When Agapito exclaims (near the end), "And you mustn't feel that we cheat them," what does he mean? Is he sincere or hypocritical?
4. Explain the relevance of the story of the beard the grandfather tells at the end of the story.
5. What does the boy-narrator of the story learn from the experience?

CREATIVE RESPONSE

In "Conquistador," as the narrator and the grandfather wait for Agapito to run and pick up the three extra boxes of cigars, the saloon keepers begin to open the seven boxes that they have just agreed to buy. What if they had discovered that they were being tricked into buying cheap cigars disguised as expensive cigars (as the boy fears they will so discover)? What happens? Write the scene portraying the reaction of the boy and his grandfather.

Prudencio de Pereda   1912 /

Born and raised in Brooklyn, Prudencio de Pereda grew up as part of the Spanish community described in "Conquistador." He decided to become a writer at the age of six, wrote his first short story the following year, and in his junior year in high school wrote "The Spaniard" which was printed in *Story* magazine. During the depression he worked as an interpreter, tutor, translator, and post-office employee. Beginning in 1937 his works began appearing in such collections as *O'Henry Memorial Award Prize* *Stories* and *O'Brien's Best American Short Stories*. In the meantime the Spanish Civil War had begun and De Pereda spent a number of years working with Hemingway on the commentary of two films dealing with the conflict. In 1955 he completed his graduate studies in Library Science and since then has worked as a librarian. One of his latest novels, *Windmills in Brooklyn* (1960), continues the narrative begun in "Conquistador."

Carson McCullers

THE HAUNTED BOY

HUGH looked for his mother at the corner, but she was not in the yard. Sometimes she would be out fooling with the border of spring flowers—the candytuft, the sweet William, the lobelias (she had taught him the names)—but today the green front lawn with the borders of many-colored flowers was empty under the frail sunshine of the mid-April afternoon. Hugh raced up the sidewalk, and John followed him. They finished the front steps with two bounds, and the door slammed after them.

"Mamma!" Hugh called.

It was then, in the unanswering silence as they stood in the empty, wax-floored hall, that Hugh felt there was something wrong. There was no fire in the grate of the sitting room, and since he was used to the flicker of firelight during the cold months, the room on this first warm day seemed strangely naked and cheerless. Hugh shivered. He was glad John was there. The sun shone on a red piece in the flowered rug. Red-bright, red-dark, red-dead—Hugh sickened with a sudden chill remembrance of "the other time." The red darkened to a dizzy black.

"What's the matter, Brown?" John asked. "You look so white."

Hugh shook himself and put his hand to his forehead. "Nothing. Let's go back to the kitchen."

"I can't stay but just a minute," John said. "I'm obligated to sell those tickets. I have to eat and run."

The kitchen, with the fresh checked towels and clean pans, was now the best room in the house. And on the enameled table there was a lemon pie that she had made. Assured by the everyday kitchen and the pie, Hugh stepped back into the hall and raised his face again to call upstairs.

"Mother! Oh, Mamma!"

Again there was no answer.

"My mother made this pie," he said. Quickly, he found a knife and cut into the pie—to dispel the gathering sense of dread.

"Think you ought to cut it, Brown?"

"Sure thing, Laney."

They called each other by their last names this spring, unless they happened to forget. To Hugh it seemed sporty and grown and somehow grand. Hugh liked John better than any other boy at school. John was two years older than Hugh, and compared to him the other boys seemed like a silly crowd of punks. John was the best student in the sophomore class, brainy but not the least bit a teacher's pet, and he was the best athlete too. Hugh was a freshman and didn't have so many friends that first year of high school—he had somehow cut himself off, because he was so afraid.

"Mamma always has me something nice for after school." Hugh put a big piece of pie on a saucer for John—for Laney.

"This pie is certainly super."

"The crust is made of crunched-up graham crackers instead of regular pie dough," Hugh said, "because pie dough is a lot of trouble. We think this graham-cracker pastry is just as good. Naturally, my mother can make regular pie dough if she wants to."

Hugh could not keep still; he walked up and down the kitchen, eating the pie wedge he carried on the palm of his hand. His brown hair was mussed with nervous rakings, and his gentle gold-brown eyes were haunted with pained perplexity. John, who remained seated at the table, sensed Hugh's uneasiness and wrapped one gangling leg around the other.

"I'm really obligated to sell those Glee Club tickets."

"Don't go. You have the whole afternoon." He was afraid of the empty house. He needed John, he needed someone; most of all he needed to hear his mother's voice and know she was in the house with him. "Maybe Mamma is taking a bath," he said. "I'll holler again."

The answer to his third call too was silence.

"I guess your mother must have gone to the movie or gone shopping or something."

"No," Hugh said. "She would have left a note. She always does when she's gone when I come home from school."

"We haven't looked for a note," John said. "May-

"The Haunted Boy" from THE COLLECTED SHORT STORIES and THE BALLAD OF THE SAD CAFÉ by Carson McCullers. Copyright 1936, 1955 by Carson McCullers. Reprinted by permission of the publisher, Houghton Mifflin Company and Floria Lasky as the Executor of the Estate of Carson McCullers.

be she left it under the door mat or somewhere in the living room."

Hugh was inconsolable. "No. She would have left it right under this pie. She knows I always run first to the kitchen."

"Maybe she had a phone call or thought of something she suddenly wanted to do."

"She *might* have," he said. "I remember she said to Daddy that one of these days she was going to buy herself some new clothes." This flash of hope did not survive its expression. He pushed his hair back and started from the room. "I guess I'd better go upstairs. I ought to go upstairs while you are here."

He stood with his arm around the newel post; the smell of varnished stairs, the sight of the closed white bathroom door at the top revived again "the other time." He clung to the newel post, and his feet would not move to climb the stairs. The red turned again to whirling, sick dark. Hugh sat down. *Stick your head between your legs,* he ordered, remembering Scout first aid.

"Hugh," John called. "Hugh!"

The dizziness clearing, Hugh accepted a fresh chagrin—Laney was calling him by his ordinary first name; he thought he was a sissy about his mother, unworthy of being called by his last name in the grand, sporty way they used before. The dizziness cleared when he returned to the kitchen.

"Brown," said John, and the chagrin disappeared. "Does this establishment have anything pertaining to a cow? A white, fluid liquid. In French they call it *lait.* Here we call it plain old milk."

The stupidity of shock lightened. "Oh, Laney, I am a dope! Please excuse me. I clean forgot." Hugh fetched the milk from the refrigerator and found two glasses. "I didn't think. My mind was on something else."

"I know," John said. After a moment he asked in a calm voice, looking steadily at Hugh's eyes: "Why are you so worried about your mother? Is she sick, Hugh?"

Hugh knew now that the first name was not a slight; it was because John was talking too serious to be sporty. He liked John better than any friend he had ever had. He felt more natural sitting across the kitchen table from John, somehow safer. As he looked into John's gray, peaceful eyes, the balm of affection soothed the dread.

John asked again, still steadily: "Hugh, is your mother sick?"

Hugh could have answered no other boy. He had talked with no one about his mother, except his father, and even those intimacies had been rare, oblique. They could approach the subject only when they were occupied with something else, doing carpentry work or the two times they hunted in the woods together—or when they were cooking supper or washing dishes.

"She's not exactly sick," he said, "but Daddy and I have been worried about her. At least, we used to be worried for a while."

John asked: "Is it a kind of heart trouble?"

Hugh's voice was strained. "Did you hear about that fight I had with that slob Clem Roberts? I scraped his slob face on the gravel walk and nearly killed him sure enough. He's still got scars or at least he did have a bandage on for two days. I had to stay in school every afternoon for a week. But I nearly killed him. I would have if Mr. Paxton hadn't come along and dragged me off."

"I heard about it."

"You know why I wanted to kill him?"

For a moment John's eyes flickered away.

Hugh tensed himself; his raw boy hands clutched the table edge; he took a deep, hoarse breath. "That slob was telling everybody that my mother was in Milledgeville. He was spreading it around that my mother was crazy."

"The dirty bastard."

Hugh said in a clear, defeated voice, "My mother *was* in Milledgeville. But that doesn't mean that she was crazy," he added quickly. "In that big State hospital, there are buildings for people who are crazy, and there are other buildings, for people who are just sick. Mamma was sick for a while. Daddy and me discussed it and decided that the hospital in Milledgeville was the place where there were the best doctors and she would get the best care. But she was the furtherest from crazy than anybody in the world. You know Mamma, John." He said again, "I ought to go upstairs."

John said: "I have always thought that your mother is one of the nicest ladies in this town."

"You see, Mamma had a peculiar thing happen, and afterward she was blue."

Confession, the first deep-rooted words, opened the festered secrecy of the boy's heart, and he continued more rapidly, urgent and finding unforeseen relief.

"Last year my mother thought she was going to

have a little baby. She talked it over with Daddy and me," he said proudly. "We wanted a girl. I was going to choose the name. We were so tickled. I hunted up all my old toys—my electric train and the tracks . . . I was going to name her Crystal—how does the name strike you for a girl? It reminds me of something bright and dainty."

"Was the little baby born dead?"

Even with John, Hugh's ears turned hot; his cold hands touched them. "No, it was what they call a tumor. That's what happened to my mother. They had to operate at the hospital here." He was embarrassed and his voice was very low. "Then she had something called change of life." The words were terrible to Hugh. "And afterward she was blue. Daddy said it was a shock to her nervous system. It's something that happens to ladies; she was just blue and run-down."

Although there was no red, no red in the kitchen anywhere, Hugh was approaching "the other time."

"One day, she just sort of gave up—one day last fall." Hugh's eyes were wide open and glaring: again he climbed the stairs and opened the bathroom door—he put his hand to his eyes to shut out the memory. "She tried to—hurt herself. I found her when I came in from school."

John reached out and carefully stroked Hugh's sweatered arm.

"Don't worry. A lot of people have to go to hospitals because they are run-down and blue. Could happen to anybody."

"We had to put her in the hospital—the best hospital." The recollection of those long, long months was stained with a dull loneliness, as cruel in its lasting unappeasement as "the other time"—how long had it lasted? In the hospital Mamma could walk around and she always had on shoes.

John said carefully: "This pie is certainly super."

"My mother is a super cook. She cooks things like meat pie and salmon loaf—as well as steaks and hot dogs."

"I hate to eat and run," John said.

Hugh was so frightened of being left alone that he felt the alarm in his own loud heart.

"Don't go," he urged. "Let's talk for a little while."

"Talk about what?"

Hugh could not tell him. Not even John Laney. He could tell no one of the empty house and the horror of the time before. "Do you ever cry?" he asked John. "I don't."

"I do sometimes," John admitted.

"I wish I had known you better when Mother was away. Daddy and me used to go hunting nearly every Saturday. We *lived* on quail and dove. I bet you would have liked that." He added in a lower tone, "On Sunday we went to the hospital."

John said: "It's a kind of a delicate proposition selling those tickets. A lot of people don't enjoy the High School Glee Club operettas. Unless they know someone in it personally, they'd rather stay home with a good TV show. A lot of people buy tickets on the basis of being public-spirited."

"We're going to get a television set real soon."

"I couldn't exist without television," John said.

Hugh's voice was apologetic. "Daddy wants to clean up the hospital bills first because as everybody knows sickness is a very expensive proposition. Then we'll get TV."

John lifted his milk glass. "Skoal," he said. "That's a Swedish word you say before you drink. A good-luck word."

"You know so many foreign words and languages."

"Not so many," John said truthfully. "Just 'kaput' and 'adios' and 'skoal' and stuff we learn in French class. That's not much."

"That's *beaucoup*," said Hugh, and he felt witty and pleased with himself.

Suddenly the stored tension burst into physical activity. Hugh grabbed the basketball out on the porch and rushed into the back yard. He dribbled the ball several times and aimed at the goal his father had put up on his last birthday. When he missed he bounced the ball to John, who had come after him. It was good to be outdoors and the relief of natural play brought Hugh the first line of a poem. "My heart is like a basketball." Usually when a poem came to him he would lie sprawled on the living room floor, studying to hunt rhymes, his tongue working on the side of his mouth. His mother would call him Shelley-Poe when she stepped over him, and sometimes she would put her foot lightly on his behind. His mother always liked his poems; today the second line came quickly, like magic. He said it out loud to John: " 'My heart is like a basketball, bouncing with glee down the hall.' How do you like that for the start of a poem?"

"Sounds kind of crazy to me," John said. Then he corrected himself hastily. "I mean it sounds—odd. Odd, I meant."

Hugh realized why John had changed the word,

and the elation of play and poems left him instantly. He caught the ball and stood with it cradled in his arms. The afternoon was golden and the wisteria vine on the porch was in full, unshattered bloom. The wisteria was like lavender waterfalls. The fresh breeze smelled of sun-warmed flowers. The sunlit sky was blue and cloudless. It was the first warm day of spring.

"I have to shove off," John said.

"No!" Hugh's voice was desperate. "Don't you want another piece of pie? I never heard of anybody eating just one piece of pie."

He steered John into the house and this time he called only out of habit because he always called on coming in. "Mother!" He was cold after the bright, sunny outdoors. He was cold not only because of the weather but because he was so scared.

"My mother has been home a month and every afternoon she's always here when I come home from school. Always, always."

They stood in the kitchen looking at the lemon pie. And to Hugh the cut pie looked somehow—odd. As they stood motionless in the kitchen the silence was creepy and odd too.

"Doesn't this house seem quiet to you?"

"It's because you don't have television. We put on our TV at seven o'clock and it stays on all day and night until we go to bed. Whether anybody's in the living room or not. There're plays and skits and gags going on continually."

"We have a radio, of course, and a vic."

"But that's not the company of a good TV. You won't know when your mother is in the house or not when you get TV."

Hugh didn't answer. Their footsteps sounded hollow in the hall. He felt sick as he stood on the first step with his arm around the newel post. "If you could just come upstairs for a minute—"

John's voice was suddenly impatient and loud. "How many times have I told you I'm obligated to sell those tickets. You have to be public-spirited about things like Glee Clubs."

"Just for a second—I have something important to show you upstairs."

John did not ask what it was and Hugh sought desperately to name something important enough to get John upstairs. He said finally: "I'm assembling a hi-fi machine. You have to know a lot about electronics—my father is helping me."

But even when he spoke he knew John did not for a second believe the lie. Who would buy a hi-fi when they didn't have television? He hated John, as you hate people you have to need so badly. He had to say something more and he straightened his shoulders.

"I just want you to know how much I value your friendship. During these past months I had somehow cut myself off from people."

"That's O.K., Brown. You oughtn't to be so sensitive because your mother was—where she was."

John had his hand on the door and Hugh was trembling. "I thought if you could come up for just a minute—"

John looked at him with anxious, puzzled eyes. Then he asked slowly: "Is there something you are scared of upstairs?"

Hugh wanted to tell him everything. But he could not tell what his mother had done that September afternoon. It was too terrible and—odd. It was like something a *patient* would do, and not like his mother at all. Although his eyes were wild with terror and his body trembled he said: "I'm not scared."

"Well, so long. I'm sorry I have to go—but to be obligated is to be obligated."

John closed the front door, and he was alone in the empty house. Nothing could save him now. Even if a whole crowd of boys were listening to TV in the living room, laughing at funny gags and jokes, it would still not help him. He had to go upstairs and find her. He sought courage from the last thing John had said, and repeated the words aloud: "To be obligated is to be obligated." But the words did not give him any of John's thoughtlessness and courage; they were creepy and strange in the silence.

He turned slowly to go upstairs. His heart was not like a basketball but like a fast, jazz drum, beating faster and faster as he climbed the stairs. His feet dragged as though he waded through knee-deep water and he held on to the banisters. The house looked odd, crazy. As he looked down at the ground-floor table with the vase of fresh spring flowers that too looked somehow peculiar. There was a mirror on the second floor and his own face startled him, so crazy did it seem to him. The initial of his high school sweater was backward and wrong in the reflection and his mouth was open like an asylum idiot. He shut his mouth and he looked better. Still the objects he saw—the table downstairs, the sofa upstairs— looked somehow cracked or jarred because of the dread in him, although they were the familiar things of everyday. He fastened his eyes on the closed door at the right of the stairs and the fast, jazz drum beat faster.

He opened the bathroom door and for a moment the dread that had haunted him all that afternoon made him see again the room as he had seen it "the other time." His mother lay on the floor and there was blood everywhere. His mother lay there dead and there was blood everywhere, on her slashed wrist, and a pool of blood had trickled to the bathtub and lay dammed there. Hugh touched the doorframe and steadied himself. Then the room settled and he realized this was not "the other time." The April sunlight brightened the clean white tiles. There was only bathroom brightness and the sunny window. He went to the bedroom and saw the empty bed with the rose-colored spread. The lady things were on the dresser. The room was as it always looked and nothing had happened . . . nothing had happened and he flung himself on the quilted rose bed and cried from relief and a strained, bleak tired-ness that had lasted so long. The sobs jerked his whole body and quieted his jazz, fast heart.

Hugh had not cried all those months. He had not cried at "the other time," when he found his mother alone in that empty house with blood everywhere. He had not cried but he made a Scout mistake. He had first lifted his mother's heavy, bloody body before he tried to bandage her. He had not cried when he called his father. He had not cried those few days when they were deciding what to do. He hadn't even cried when the doctor suggested Mill-edgeville, or when he and his father took her to the hospital in the car—although his father cried on the way home. He had not cried at the meals they made —steak every night for a whole month so that they felt steak was running out of their eyes, their ears; then they had switched to hot dogs, and ate them until hot dogs ran out of their ears, their eyes. They got in ruts of food and were messy about the kitchen, so that it was never nice except the Saturday the cleaning woman came. He did not cry those lone-some afternoons after he had the fight with Clem Roberts and felt the other boys were thinking queer things of his mother. He stayed at home in the messy kitchen, eating fig newtons or chocolate bars. Or he went to see a neighbor's television—Miss Richards, an old maid who saw old-maid shows. He had not cried when his father drank too much so that it took

his appetite and Hugh had to eat alone. He had not even cried on those long, waiting Sundays when they went to Milledgeville and he twice saw a lady on a porch without any shoes on and talking to her-self. A lady who was a patient and who struck at him with a horror he could not name. He did not cry when at first his mother would say: *Don't punish me by making me stay here. Let me go home.* He had not cried at the terrible words that haunted him—"change of life"—"crazy"—"Milledgeville" —he could not cry all during those long months strained with dullness and want and dread.

He still sobbed on the rose bedspread which was soft and cool against his wet cheeks. He was sobbing so loud that he did not hear the front door open, did not even hear his mother call or the footsteps on the stairs. He still sobbed when his mother touched him and burrowed his face hard in the spread. He even stiffened his legs and kicked his feet.

"Why, Loveyboy," his mother said, calling him a long-ago child name. "What's happened?"

He sobbed even louder, although his mother tried to turn his face to her. He wanted her to worry. He did not turn around until she had finally left the bed, and then he looked at her. She had on a different dress—blue silk it looked like in the pale spring light.

"Darling, what's happened?"

The terror of the afternoon was over, but he could not tell it to his mother. He could not tell her what he had feared, or explain the horror of things that were never there at all—but had once been there.

"Why did you do it?"

"The first warm day I just suddenly decided to buy myself some new clothes."

But he was not talking about clothes; he was think-ing about "the other time" and the grudge that had started when he saw the blood and horror and felt *why did she do this to me.* He thought of the grudge against the mother he loved the most in the world. All those last, sad months the anger had bounced against the love with guilt between.

"I bought two dresses and two petticoats. How do you like them?"

"I hate them!" Hugh said angrily. "Your slip is showing."

She turned around twice and the petticoat showed terribly. "It's supposed to show, goofy. It's the style."

"I still don't like it."

"I ate a sandwich at the tearoom with two cups of cocoa and then went to Mendel's. There were so many pretty things I couldn't seem to get away. I bought these two dresses and look, Hugh! The shoes!''

His mother went to the bed and switched on the light so he could see. The shoes were flat-heeled and *blue*—with diamond sparkles on the toes. He did not know how to criticize. ''They look more like evening shoes than things you wear on the street.''

''I have never owned any colored shoes before. I couldn't resist them.''

His mother sort of danced over toward the window, making the petticoat twirl under the new dress. Hugh had stopped crying now, but he was still angry.

''I don't like it because it makes you look like you're trying to seem young, and I bet you are forty years old.''

His mother stopped dancing and stood still at the window. Her face was suddenly quiet and sad. ''I'll be forty-three years old in June.''

He had hurt her and suddenly the anger vanished and there was only love. ''Mamma, I shouldn't have said that.''

''I realized when I was shopping that I hadn't been in a store for more than a year. Imagine!''

Hugh could not stand the sad quietness and the mother he loved so much. He could not stand his love or his mother's prettiness. He wiped the tears on the sleeve of his sweater and got up from the bed. ''I have never seen you so pretty, or a dress and slip so pretty.'' He crouched down before his mother and touched the bright shoes. ''The shoes are really super.''

''I thought the minute I laid eyes on them that you would like them.'' She pulled Hugh up and kissed him on the cheek. ''Now I've got lipstick on you.''

Hugh quoted a witty remark he had heard before as he scrubbed off the lipstick. ''It only shows I'm popular.''

''Hugh, why were you crying when I came in? Did something at school upset you?''

''It was only that when I came in and found you gone and no note or anything—''

''I forgot all about a note.''

''And all afternoon I felt—John Laney came in but he had to go sell Glee Club tickets. All afternoon I felt—''

''What? What was the matter?''

But he could not tell the mother he loved about the terror and the cause. He said at last: ''All afternoon I felt—odd.''

Afterward when his father came home he called Hugh to come out into the back yard with him. His father had a worried look—as though he spied a valuable tool Hugh had left outside. But there was no tool and the basketball was put back in its place on the back porch.

''Son,'' his father said, ''there's something I want to tell you.''

''Yes, sir?''

''Your mother said that you had been crying this afternoon.'' His father did not wait for him to explain. ''I just want us to have a close understanding with each other. Is there anything about school—or girls—or something that puzzles you? Why were you crying?''

Hugh looked back at the afternoon and already it was far away, distant as a peculiar view seen at the wrong end of a telescope.

''I don't know,'' he said. ''I guess maybe I was somehow nervous.''

His father put his arm around his shoulder. ''Nobody can be nervous before they are sixteen years old. You have a long way to go.''

''I know.''

''I have never seen your mother look so well. She looks so gay and pretty, better than she's looked in years. Don't you realize that?''

''The slip—the petticoat is supposed to show. It's a new style.''

''Soon it will be summer,'' his father said. ''And we'll go on picnics—the three of us.'' The words brought an instant vision of glare on the yellow creek and the summer-leaved, adventurous woods. His father added: ''I came out here to tell you something else.''

''Yes, sir?''

''I just want you to know that I realize how fine you were all that bad time. How fine, how damn fine.''

His father was using a swear word as if he were talking to a grown man. His father was not a person to hand out compliments—always he was strict with report cards and tools left around. His father never praised him or used grown words or anything. Hugh felt his face grow hot and he touched it with his cold hands.

''I just wanted to tell you that, Son.'' He shook Hugh by the shoulder. ''You'll be taller than your old man in a year or so.'' Quickly his father went into the house, leaving Hugh to the sweet and unaccustomed aftermath of praise.

Hugh stood in the darkening yard after the sunset colors faded in the west and the wisteria was dark purple. The kitchen light was on and he saw his mother fixing dinner. He knew that something was finished; the terror was far from him now, also the anger that had bounced with love, the dread and guilt. Although he felt he would never cry again—or at least not until he was sixteen—in the brightness of his tears glistened the safe, lighted kitchen, now that he was no longer a haunted boy, now that he was glad somehow, and not afraid. □

DISCUSSION

"The Haunted Boy" builds suspense until it becomes almost unbearable, as we hang back with Hugh from going upstairs to open the closed bathroom door to discover what lies behind it. We feel with Hugh his dread of discovering there a repetition of what he found on one previous occasion. That "other time" seems to fuse with the present time, and when Hugh finally, and all alone, does open the door, he sees there the blood and body he had seen before, his imagination is so vivid and his expectation so great. But finally the "other time" disappears, and the door opens on nothing more than tiles bright with sunshine. This intense psychological experience brings the release of pent-up tears, as the world falls back into its accustomed place.

FOR EXPLORATION

1. Explain the title, "The Haunted Boy."
2. (a) What devices does Hugh use to keep John around? (b) Why doesn't Hugh tell John that he is afraid and that he needs his help?
3. Why not open the story with an account of the "other time" when Hugh actually did find his mother in the bathroom after her attempted suicide?
4. What is the effect of the mother, on her appearance, talking about her shopping expedition and her purchases of new clothes?
5. The story concludes with the father having a private talk with Hugh. Explore the effect of this talk on Hugh and the significance of this conversation as a conclusion to the story.

CREATIVE RESPONSE

1. Write an account of the fight that Hugh had with that "slob Clem Roberts" because Roberts was spreading the rumor that Hugh's mother was crazy.
2. Try your own hand at building suspense in a story, following the pattern Carson McCullers used in this account.

WIDE WORLD PHOTOS

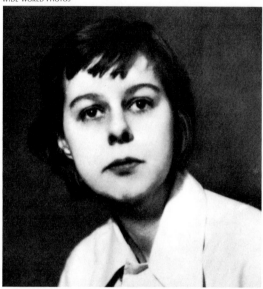

Carson Smith McCullers 1917 / 1967

Born in Columbus, Georgia, Carson McCullers was sixteen when she finished high school and began writing. She also at that time had hopes of becoming a concert pianist; and two years later she left for New York expecting to attend classes at both Columbia University and the Juilliard Foundation. But on her second day in the city she lost all her tuition money on the subway. She took on a series of part-time jobs and tried to attend classes at night, but her heart wasn't in it. She was fired from her jobs and did little studying. The spring found her hanging around the piers, planning voyages to other lands. But she continued writing and the following year two of her stories were published. With renewed determination she spent two years writing in North Carolina, and by the time she was twenty-two could boast a major success, *The Heart Is a Lonely Hunter* (1940).

Her total life's output was small, with many years between publications, but her works were consistently valuable, unique, and compassionate. *The Ballad of the Sad Café* (1951) is considered her finest effort.

Donald Barthelme

THE JOKER'S GREATEST TRIUMPH

FREDRIC went over to his friend Bruce Wayne's house about every Tuesday night. Bruce would be typically sitting in his study drinking a glass of something. Fredric would come in and sit down and look around the study in which there were many trophies of past exploits.

"Well Fredric what have you been doing? Anything?"

"No Bruce things have been just sort of rocking along."

"Well this is Tuesday night and usually there's some action on Tuesday night."

"I know Bruce or otherwise I wouldn't pick Tuesday night to come over."

"You want me to turn on the radio Fredric? Usually there's something interesting on the radio or maybe you'd like a little music from my hi-fi?"

Bruce Wayne's radio was a special short-wave model with many extra features. When Bruce turned it on there was a squealing noise and then they were listening to Tokyo or somewhere. Above the radio on the wall hung a trophy from an exploit: a long African spear with a spearhead made of tin.

"Tell me Bruce what is it you're drinking there?" Fredric asked.

"I'm sorry Fredric it's tomato juice. Can I get you a glass?"

"Does it have anything in it or is it just plain tomato juice?"

"It's tomato juice with a little vodka."

"Yes I wouldn't mind a glass," Fredric said. "Not too heavy on the vodka please."

While Bruce went out to the kitchen to make the drink Fredric got up and went over to examine the African spear more closely. It was he saw tipped with a rusty darkish substance, probably some rare exotic poison he thought.

"What is this stuff on the end of this African spear?" he asked when Bruce came back into the room.

"I must have left the other bottle of vodka in the Batmobile," Bruce said. "Oh that's curare, deadliest of the South American poisons," he affirmed. "It attacks the motor nerves. Be careful there and don't scratch yourself."

"That's okay I'll just drink this tomato juice straight," Fredric said settling himself in his chair and looking out of the window. "Oh-oh there's the bat symbol spotlighted against the sky. This must mean a call from Commissioner Gordon at headquarters."

Bruce looked out of the window. A long beam of yellowish light culminating in a perfect bat symbol lanced the evening sky.

"I told you Tuesday night was usually a good night," Bruce Wayne said. He put his vodka-and-tomato-juice down on the piano. "Hold on a minute while I change will you?"

"Sure, take your time," Fredric said. "By the way is Robin still at Andover?"

"Yes," Bruce said. "He'll be home for Thanksgiving, I think. He's having a little trouble with his French."

"Well I didn't mean to interrupt you," Fredric said. "Go ahead and change. I'll just look at this magazine."

After Bruce had changed they both went out to the garage where the Batmobile and the Batplane waited.

Batman was humming a tune which Fredric recognized as being the "Warsaw Concerto." "Which one shall we take?" he said. "It's always hard to decide on a vague and indeterminate kind of assignment like this."

"Let's flip," Fredric suggested.

"Do you have a quarter?" Batman asked.

"No but I have a dime. That should be okay," Fredric said. They flipped, heads for the Batmobile, tails for the Batplane. The coin came up heads.

"Well," Batman said as they climbed into the comfortable Batmobile, "at least you can have some vodka now. It's under the seat."

"I hate to drink it straight," Fredric said.

"Press that button there on the dashboard," Batman said. Fredric pressed the button and a panel on

"The Joker's Greatest Triumph" from COME BACK, DR. CALIGARI by Donald Barthelme. Copyright © 1961, 1964 by Donald Barthelme. Reprinted by permission of Little, Brown and Co. and The Sterling Lord Agency, Inc.

the dashboard slid back to reveal a little bar, with ice, glasses, water, soda, quinine, lemons, limes etc.

"Thanks," Fredric said. "Can I mix you one?"

"Not while I'm working," Batman said. "Is there enough quinine water? I forgot to get some when I went to the liquor store last night."

"Plenty," Fredric said. He enjoyed his vodka tonic as Batman wheeled the great Batmobile expertly through the dark streets of Gotham City.

In Commissioner Gordon's office at Police Headquarters the Commissioner said: "Glad you finally got here Batman. Who is this with you?"

"This is my friend Fredric Brown," Batman said. "Fredric, Commissioner Gordon." The two men shook hands and Batman said: "Now Commissioner, what is this all about?"

"This!" Commissioner Gordon said. He placed a small ship model on the desk before him. "The package came by messenger, addressed to you, Batman! I'm afraid your old enemy, The Joker, is on the loose again!"

Batman hummed a peculiar melody which Fredric recognized as the "Cornish Rhapsody" which is on the other side of the "Warsaw Concerto."

"Hmmmmm!" Batman said. "This sounds to me like another one of The Joker's challenges to a duel of wits!"

"Flying Dutchman!" Fredric exclaimed, reading the name painted on the bow of the model ship. "The name of a famous old ghost vessel? What can it mean!"

"A cleverly disguised clue!" Batman said. "'The Flying Dutchman' meant here is probably the Dutch jewel merchant Hendrik van Voort who is flying to Gotham City tonight with a delivery of precious gems!"

"Good thinking Batman!" Commissioner Gordon said. "I probably never would have figured it out in a thousand years!"

"Well we'll have to hurry to get out to the airport!" Batman said. "What's the best way to get there from here Commissioner?"

"Well if I were you I'd go out 34th Street until you hit the War Memorial, then take a right on Memorial Drive until it connects with Gotham Parkway! After you're on the Parkway it's clear sailing!" he indicated.

"Wait a minute!" Batman said. "Wouldn't it be quicker to get on the Dugan Expressway where it comes in there at 11th Street and then take the North Loop out to the Richardson Freeway? Don't you think that would save time?"

"Well I come to work that way!" the Commissioner said. "But they're putting in another two lanes on the North Loop, so that you have to detour down Strand, then cut over to 99th to get back on the Expressway! Takes you about two miles out of your way!" he said.

"Okay!" Batman said, "we'll go out 34th! Thanks Commissioner and don't worry about anything! Come on Fredric!"

"Oh by the way," Commissioner Gordon said. "How's Robin doing at Exeter?"

"It's not Exeter it's Andover," Batman said. "He's doing very well. Having a little trouble with his French."

"I had a little trouble with it myself," the Commissioner said jovially. "*Où est mon livre?*"[1]

"*Où est ton livre?*" Batman said.

"*Où est son livre?*" the Commissioner said pointing at Fredric.

"*Tout cela s'est passé en dix-neuf cent vingt-quatre,*"[2] Fredric said.

"Well we'd better creep Commissioner," Batman said. "The Joker as you know is a pretty slippery customer. Come on Fredric."

"Glad to have met you Commissioner," Fredric said.

"Me too," the Commissioner said, shaking Fredric's hand. "This is a fine-appearing young man Batman. Where did you find him?"

"He's just a friend," Batman said smiling under his mask. "We get together usually on Tuesday nights and have a few."

"What do you do Fredric? I mean how do you make your living?"

"I sell *Grit*, a newspaper which has most of its circulation concentrated in rural areas," Fredric said. "However I sell it right here in Gotham City. Many of today's leaders sold *Grit* during their boyhoods."

"Okay," said Commissioner Gordon, ushering them out of his office. "Good luck. *Téléphonez-moi un de ces jours.*"[3]

---

1. *Où est mon livre?* Where is my book? *Où est ton livre?* Where is your book? *Où est son livre?* Where is his book? [*French*]
2. *Tout cela s'est passé en dix-neuf cent vingt-quatre.* All that became passé in 1924. [*French*]
3. *Téléphonez-moi un de ces jours.* Call me one of these days. [*French*]

"Righto," Batman said, and they hurried down the street to the Batmobile, which was parked in a truck zone.

"Can we stop for a minute on the way?" Fredric asked. "I'm out of cigarettes."

"There are some Viceroys in the glove compartment," Batman said pushing a button. A panel on the dashboard slid back to reveal a fresh carton of Viceroys.

"I usually prefer Kents," Fredric said, "but Viceroys are tasty too."

"They're all about the same I find," Batman said. "Most of the alleged differences in cigarettes are just advertising as far as I'm concerned."

"I wouldn't be surprised if you were right about that," Fredric said. The Batmobile sped down the dark streets of Gotham City toward Gotham Airport.

"Turn on the radio," Batman suggested. "Maybe we can catch the news or something."

Fredric turned on the radio but there was nothing unusual on it.

At Gotham Airport the jewel merchant Hendrik van Voort was just dismounting from his KLM jet when the Batmobile wheeled onto the landing strip, waved through the gates by respectful airport police in gray uniforms.

"Well everything seems to be okay," Batman said. "There's the armored car waiting to take Mr. van Voort to his destination."

"That's a new kind of armored car isn't it?" Fredric asked.

Without a word Batman leaped through the open door of the armored car and grappled with the shadowy figure inside.

HA HA HA HA HA HA HA HA HA HA HA HA HA HA HA HA HA HA HA!

"That's The Joker's laugh!" Fredric reflected. "The man inside the armored car must be the grinning clown of crime himself!"

"Batman! I thought that clue I sent you would leave you *completely at sea!*"

"No, Joker! I'm afraid this leaves your plans *up in the air!*"

"But not for long Batman! I'm going to bring you *down to earth!*"

With a swift movement, The Joker crashed the armored car into the side of the Terminal Building!

CRASH!

"Great Scott!" Fredric said to himself. "Batman is stunned! He's helpless!"

"You foiled my plans Batman," The Joker said, "but before the police get here, I'm going to lift that mask of yours and find out who you *really are!* HA HA HA HA HA HA HA HA HA HA HA HA HA HA HA HA HA HA HA HA HA HA HA!"

Fredric watched, horror-stricken. "Great Scott! The Joker has unmasked Batman! Now he knows that Batman is really *Bruce Wayne!*"

At this moment Robin, who was supposed to be at Andover, many miles away, landed the Batplane on the airstrip and came racing toward the wrecked armored car! But The Joker, alerted, grasped a cable lowered by a hovering helicopter and was quickly lifted skyward! Robin paused at the armored car and put the mask back on Batman's face!

"Hello Robin!" Fredric called. "I thought you were at Andover!"

"I was but I got a sudden feeling Batman needed me so I flew here in the Batplane," Robin said. "How've you been?"

"Fine," Fredric said. "But we left the Batplane in the garage, back at the Bat-Cave. I don't understand."

"We have two of everything," Robin explained. "Although it's not generally known."

With Fredric's aid Robin carried the stunned Batman to the waiting Batmobile. "You drive the Batmobile back to the Bat-Cave and I'll follow in the Batplane," Robin said. "All right?"

"Check," Fredric said. "Don't you think we ought to give him a little brandy or something?"

"That's a good idea," Robin said. "Press that button there on the dashboard. That's the brandy button."

Fredric pressed the button and a panel slid back, revealing a bottle of B & B and the appropriate number of glasses.

"This is pretty tasty," Fredric said, tasting the B & B. "How much is it a fifth?"

"Around eight dollars," Robin said. "There, that seems to be restoring him to his senses."

"Great Scott," Batman said, "what happened?"

"The Joker crashed the armored car and you were stunned," Fredric explained.

"Hi Robin what are you doing here? I thought you were up at school," Batman said.

"I was," Robin said. "Are you okay now? Can you drive home okay?"

"I think so," Batman said. "What happened to The Joker?"

"He got away," Fredric said, "but not before lifting your mask while you lay stunned in the wreckage of the wrecked armored car.''

"Yes Batman," Robin said seriously, "I think he learned your real identity."

"Great Scott!" Batman said. "If he reveals it to the whole world it will mean the end of my career as a crime-fighter! Well, it's a problem."

They drove seriously back to the Bat-Cave, thinking about the problem. Later, in Bruce Wayne's study, Bruce Wayne, Fredric, and Robin, who was now dressed in the conservative Andover clothes of Dick Grayson, Bruce Wayne's ward, mulled the whole thing over between them.

"What makes The Joker tick I wonder?" Fredric said. "I mean what are his real motivations?"

"Consider him at any level of conduct," Bruce said slowly, "in the home, on the street, in interpersonal relations, in jail—always there is an extraordinary contradiction. He is dirty and compulsively neat, aloof and desperately gregarious, enthusiastic and sullen, generous and stingy, a snappy dresser and a scarecrow, a gentleman and a boor, given to extremes of happiness and despair, singularly well able to apply himself and capable of frittering away a lifetime in trivial pursuits, decorous and unseemly, kind and cruel, tolerant yet open to the most outrageous varieties of bigotry, a great friend and an implacable enemy, a lover and an abominator of women, sweet-spoken and foul-mouthed, a rake and a puritan, swelling with hubris and haunted by inferiority, outcast and social climber, felon and phi-

lanthropist, barbarian and patron of the arts, enamored of novelty and solidly conservative, philosopher and fool, Republican and Democrat, large of soul and unbearably petty, distant and brimming with friendly impulses, an inveterate liar and astonishingly strict with petty cash, adventurous and timid, imaginative and stolid, malignly destructive and a planter of trees on Arbor Day—I tell you frankly, the man is a mess."

"That's extremely well said Bruce," Fredric stated. "I think you've given really a very thoughtful analysis."

"I was paraphrasing what Mark Schorer said about Sinclair Lewis,"[4] Bruce replied.

"Well it's very brilliant just the same," Fredric noted. "I guess I'd better go home now."

"We could all use a little sleep," Bruce Wayne said. "By the way Fredric how are the *Grit* sales coming along? Are you getting many subscriptions?"

"Yes quite a few Bruce," Fredric said. "I've been doing particularly well in the wealthier sections of Gotham City although the strength of *Grit* is usually found in rural areas. By the way Dick if you want to borrow my language records to help you with your French you can come by Saturday."

"Thanks Fredric I'll do that," Dick said.

"Okay Bruce," Fredric said, "I'll see you next Tuesday night probably unless something comes up."

---

4. *Mark Schorer . . . Sinclair Lewis.* In 1961 Mark Schorer published a biography of the American writer Sinclair Lewis entitled *Sinclair Lewis: An American Life.*

DISCUSSION

"The Joker's Greatest Triumph" is a **parody,** a spoof, a take-off on a familiar story and style. The target is "Batman," the well-known comic strip and one-time TV series. Because Batman is something of a superhuman creature, the parody has many aspects of the **mock-heroic,** emphasizing the excesses of the too-heroic hero, the physically impressive creature (such as Odysseus, Beowulf, or Paul Bunyan) who bashes his way through every obstacle, always on the side of right and virtue.

FOR EXPLORATION

1. Discuss the ways the following aspects or details are used to poke fun at the original Batman stories. (And then find other examples.)

    a. Bruce drinking tomato juice with vodka.

    b. Bruce-Batman humming the "Warsaw Concerto."

    c. The elaborate bar in the batmobile.

    d. The "Flying Dutchman" as a clue to the Joker's intention.

    e. The discussion as to which route to take to the airport in pursuit of the Joker.

2. When Batman captures the Joker, they exchange a few remarks. Examine the puns printed in italics and discuss their effect.

3. In a long speech near the end of the story, Bruce-Batman analyzes the motivation of the Joker, and concludes—"the man is a mess." Examine and discuss this speech, particularly its effect as parody and humor.

CREATIVE RESPONSE

Batman is a part of America's "popular culture." Find a similar figure, perhaps from the comic strips or TV programs, and try your hand writing a parody patterned after Barthelme's. Tarzan? Little Orphan Annie? Dick Tracy?

JILL KREMENTZ

Donald Barthelme 1931 /

Within four years of his first collection of short stories published in 1964, Donald Barthelme was being described as "probably the most perversely gifted writer in the U.S." Born in Philadelphia, he was raised and educated in Houston, Texas. Barthelme has worked as a newspaper reporter, university public relations man, magazine editor, and curator of a modern art galley. He presently resides in New York City, works in the mornings, often walks about the Village in the afternoon, and has a social life which has been described as "incredibly commonplace." His short stories, which appear most frequently in the *New Yorker*, are regularly collected and released in book form. He has also published a novel *Snow White* (1967) which received substantial critical acclaim.

John Updike

THE FAMILY MEADOW

THE family always reconvenes in the meadow. For generations it has been traditional, this particular New Jersey meadow, with its great walnut tree making shade for the tables and its slow little creek where the children can push themselves about in a rowboat and nibble watercress and pretend to fish. Early this morning, Uncle Jesse came down from the stone house that his father's father's brother had built and drove the stakes, with their carefully tied rag flags, that would tell the cars where to park. The air was still, inert with the postdawn laziness that foretells the effort of a hot day, and between blows of his hammer Jesse heard the breakfast dishes clinking beneath the kitchen window and the younger collie barking behind the house. A mild man, Jesse moved scrupulously, mildly through the wet grass that he had scythed yesterday. The legs of his gray workman's pants slowly grew soaked with dew and milkweed spittle. When the stakes were planted, he walked out the lane with the REUNION signs, past the houses. He avoided looking at the houses, as if glancing into their wide dead windows would wake them.

By nine o'clock Henry has come up from Camden with a carful—Eva, Mary, Fritz, Fred, the twins, and, incredibly, Aunt Eula. It is incredible she is still alive, after seven strokes. Her shrivelled head munches irritably and her arms twitch, trying to shake off assistance, as if she intends to dance. They settle her in an aluminum chair beneath the walnut tree. She faces the creek, and the helpless waggle of her old skull seems to establish itself in sympathy with the oscillating shimmer of the sunlight on the slow water. The men, working in silent pairs whose unison is as profound as blood, carry down the tables from the barn, where they are stacked from one year to the next. In truth, it has been three summers since the last reunion, and it was feared that there might never be another. Aunt Jocelyn, her gray hair done up in braids, comes out of her kitchen to say hello on the dirt drive. Behind her lingers her granddaughter, Karen, in white Levis and bare feet, with something shadowy and doubtful about her dark eyes, as if she had been intensely watching television. The girl's father—not here; he is working in Philadelphia—is Italian, and as she matures an alien beauty estranges her, so that during her annual visits to her grandparents' place, which when she was a child had seemed to her a green island, it is now she herself, at thirteen, who seems the island. She feels surrounded by the past, cut off from the images—a luncheonette, a civic swimming pool, an auditorium festooned with crêpe paper—that represent life to her, the present, her youth. The air around her feels brown, as in old photographs. These men greeting her seem to have stepped from an album. The men, remembering their original prejudice against her mother's marrying a Catholic, are especially cordial to her, so jovially attentive that Jocelyn suddenly puts her arm around the girl, expressing a strange multitude of things; that she loves her, that she is one of them, that she needs to be shielded, suddenly, from the pronged kidding of men.

By ten-thirty Horace's crowd has come down from Trenton, and the Oranges clan is arriving, in several cars. The first car says it dropped Cousin Claude in downtown Burlington because he was sure that the second car, which had faded out of sight behind them, needed to be told the way. The second car, with a whoop of hilarity, says it took the bypass and never saw him. He arrives in a third car, driven by Jimmy and Ethel Thompson from Morristown, who say they saw this forlorn figure standing along Route 130 trying to thumb a ride and as they were passing him Ethel cried, "Why, I think that's Claude!" Zealous and reckless, a true believer in good deeds, Claude is always getting into scrapes like this, and enjoying it. He stands surrounded by laughing women, a typical man of this family, tall, with a tribal boyishness, a stubborn refusal to look his age, to lose his hair. Though his face is pitted and gouged by melancholy, Claude looks closer to forty than the sixty he is, and, though he works in Newark, he still speaks with the rural softness and slide of middle New Jersey. He has the gift—the privilege—of mak-

Copyright © 1965 by John Updike. Reprinted from THE MUSIC SCHOOL, by John Updike, by permission of Alfred A. Knopf, Inc. and Andre Deutsch. Originally appeared in *The New Yorker*.

ing these women laugh; the women uniformly run to fat and their laughter has a sameness, a quality both naïve and merciless, as if laughter meant too much to them. Jimmy and Ethel Thompson, whose name is not the family name, stand off to one side, in the unscythed grass, a fragile elderly couple whose links to the family have all died away but who have come because they received a mimeographed postcard inviting them. They are like those isolated corners of interjections and foreign syllables in a poorly planned crossword puzzle.

The twins bring down from the barn the horseshoes and the quoits. Uncle Jesse drives the stakes and pegs in the places that, after three summers, still show as spots of depressed sparseness in the grass. The sun, reaching toward noon, domineers over the meadow; the shade of the walnut tree grows smaller and more noticeably cool. By noon, all have arrived, including the Dodge station wagon from central Pennsylvania, the young pregnant Wilmington cousin who married an airline pilot, and the White Plains people, who climb from their car looking like clowns, wearing red-striped shorts and rhinestone-studded sunglasses. Handshakes are exchanged that feel to one man like a knobbed woodcarving and to the other like a cow's slippery, unresisting teat. Women kiss, kiss stickily, with little overlapping patches of adhesive cheek and clicking conflicts of spectacle rims, under the white unslanting sun. The very insects shrink toward the shade. The eating begins. Clams steam, corn steams, salad wilts, butter runs, hot dogs turn, torn chicken shines in the savage light. Iced tea, brewed in forty-quart milk cans, chuckles when sloshed. Paper plates buckle on broad laps. Plastic butter knives, asked to cut cold ham, refuse. Children underfoot in the pleased frenzy eat only potato chips. Somehow, as the first wave of appetite subsides, the long tables turn musical, and a murmur rises to the blank sky, a cackle rendered harmonious by a remote singleness of ancestor; a kind of fabric is woven and hung, a tapestry of the family fortunes, the threads of which include milkmen, ministers, mailmen, bankruptcy, death by war, death by automobile, insanity—a strangely prevalent thread, the thread of insanity. Never far from a farm or the memory of a farm, the family has hovered in honorable obscurity, between poverty and wealth, between jail and high office. Real-estate dealers, schoolteachers, veterinarians are its noblemen; butchers, electricians, door-to-door salesmen its yeomen. Protestant, teetotalling, and undaring, ironically virtuous and mildly proud, it has added to America's statistics without altering their meaning. Whence, then, this strange joy?

Watermelons smelling of childhood cellars are produced and massively sliced. The sun passes noon and the shadows relax in the intimate grass of this antique meadow. To the music of reminiscence is added the rhythmic chunking of thrown quoits. They are held curiously, between a straight thumb and four fingers curled as a unit, close to the chest, and thrown with a soft constrained motion that implies realms of unused strength. The twins and the children, as if superstitiously, have yielded the game to the older men, Fritz and Ed, Fred and Jesse, who, in pairs, after due estimation and measurement of the fall, pick up their four quoits, clink them together to clean them, and alternately send them back through the air on a high arc, floating with a spin-held slant like that of gyroscopes. The other pair measures, decides, and stoops. When they tap their quoits together, decades fall away. Even their competitive crowing has something measured about it, something patient, like the studied way their shirtsleeves are rolled up above their elbows. The backs of their shirts are ageless. Generations have sweated in just this style, under the arms, across the shoulder blades, and wherever the suspenders rub. The younger men and the teen-age girls play a softball game along the base paths that Jesse has scythed. The children discover the rowboat and, using the oars as poles, bump from bank to bank. When they dip their hands into the calm brown water, where no fish lives, a mother watching from beneath the walnut tree shrieks, "Keep your hands inside the boat! Uncle Jesse says the creek's polluted!"

And there is a stagnant fragrance the lengthening afternoon strains from the happy meadow. Aunt Eula nods herself asleep, and her false teeth slip down, so her face seems mummified and the children giggle in terror. Flies, an exploding population, discover the remains of the picnic and skate giddily on its odors. The softball game grows boring, except to the airline pilot, a rather fancy gloveman excited by the admiration of Cousin Karen in her tight white Levis. The Pennsylvania and New York people begin to pack their cars. The time has come for the photograph. Their history is kept by these photographs of timeless people in changing costumes standing linked and flushed in a moment of mid-summer heat. All line up, from resurrected Aunt Eula, twitching and snapping like a mud turtle, to the unborn baby in the belly of the Delaware cousin. To get them all in, Jesse has to squat, but in doing so he brings the houses into his viewfinder. He does not want them in the picture, he does not want them there at all. They surround his meadow on three sides, raw ranch shacks built from one bastard design but painted in a patchwork of pastel shades.

Their back yards, each nurturing an aluminum clothes tree, come right to the far bank of the creek, polluting it, and though a tall link fence holds back the children who have gathered in these yards to watch the picnic as if it were a circus or a zoo, the stare of the houses—mismatched kitchen windows squinting above the gaping cement mouth of a garage—cannot be held back. Not only do they stare, they speak, so that Jesse can hear them even at night. *Sell*, they say. *Sell*. □

DISCUSSION

Not much happens in "The Family Meadow"—just a big family reunion which brings together a large number of slightly related people who eat too much and play a few games on a hot summer day. The question is, how is Updike able to make this interesting and significant? The answer lies in his style and his theme. By ingenious selection of detail and use of metaphor, Updike paints an extremely vivid picture. And at the same time, he invests a simple, ordinary situation with elements that suggest the universal modern situation or dilemma—the sense of irretrievable loss that haunts us all, the pangs of anguish that come to us in the middle of the night.

FOR EXPLORATION

1. Updike's style has been a matter of controversy among critics ever since he began to publish his fiction. One critic said that his sentences seemed to stand up and take little bows. Analyze the effect, in their context, of the following sentences—and then find others that strike you as unusually interesting:

a. Paragraph 2: "Her shrivelled head munches irritably and her arms twitch, trying to shake off assistance, as if she intends to dance."

b. Paragraph 2: "The air around her feels brown, as in old photographs. These men greeting her seem to have stepped from an album."

c. Paragraph 3: "[The couple standing to one side] are like those isolated corners of interjections and foreign syllables in a poorly planned crossword puzzle."

d. Paragraph 4: "Plastic butter knives, asked to cut cold ham, refuse."

e. Paragraph 6: "Flies, an exploding population, discover the remains of the picnic and skate giddily on its odors."

2. At the heart of "The Family Meadow" is a contrast between the old times and ways, and modern times. Discuss the ways in which the last sentences of the last two paragraphs deepen and extend the meaning of a story about a family reunion:

a. "Keep your hands inside the boat! Uncle Jesse says the creek's polluted!"

b. ". . . the stare of the houses—mismatched kitchen windows squinting above the gaping cement mouth of a garage—cannot be held back. Not only do they stare, they speak, so that Jesse can hear them even at night. *Sell*, they say. *Sell*."

CREATIVE RESPONSE

1. In paragraph 2 of "The Family Meadow," the young girl Karen, "in white levis and bare feet," appears "cut off from images—a luncheonette, a civic swimming pool, an auditorium festooned with crepe paper—that represent life to her, the present, her youth." Write an account of the family reunion from Karen's point of view.

2. Try writing an essay which evokes or denies the nostalgia of such an event as a family reunion. See how many sensory details you can crowd in, as Updike does—the feel of the weather, the sensations of the family meal, the characters briefly but tellingly represented.

JILL KREMENTZ

John Updike   1932 /

John Updike was born and raised in Shillington, Pennsylvania. He was an only child who enjoyed reading and was skilled at drawing. Updike attended Harvard University and after graduating in 1954 spent a year at the Ruskin School of Drawing and Fine Art in Oxford, England. He then gave up the idea of being a professional artist and decided to write for a living. Returning to America he joined the staff of the *New Yorker*. He left two years later but still contributes stories and poems. Updike has to date published five highly acclaimed novels; *The Centaur* (1963) won the National Book Award. He lives now with his wife and four children in Ipswich, Massachusetts.

Américo Parédes

THE HAMMON
AND THE BEANS

ONCE we lived in one of my grandfather's houses near Fort Jones. It was just a block from the parade grounds, a big frame house painted a dirty yellow. My mother hated it, especially because of the pigeons that cooed all day about the eaves. They had fleas, she said. But it was a quiet neighborhood at least, too far from the center of town for automobiles and too near for musical, night-roaming drunks.

At this time Jonesville-on-the-Grande was not the thriving little city that it is today. We told off our days by the routine on the post. At six sharp the flag was raised on the parade grounds to the cackling of the bugles,[1] and a field piece thundered out a salute. The sound of the shot bounced away through the morning mist until its echoes worked their way into every corner of town. Jonesville-on-the-Grande woke to the cannon's roar, as if to battle, and the day began.

At eight the whistle from the post laundry sent us children off to school. The whole town stopped for lunch with the noon whistle, and after lunch everybody went back to work when the post laundry said that it was one o'clock, except for those who could afford to be old-fashioned and took the siesta. The post was the town's clock, you might have said, or like some insistent elder person who was always there to tell you it was time.

At six the flag came down, and we went to watch through the high wire fence that divided the post from the town. Sometimes we joined in the ceremony,[2] standing at salute until the sound of the cannon made us jump. That must have been when we had just studied about George Washington in school, or recited "The Song of Marion's Men" about Marion the Fox and the British cavalry that chased him up and down the broad Santee.[3] But at other times we stuck out our tongues and jeered at the soldiers.

Perhaps the night before we had hung at the edges of a group of old men and listened to tales about Aniceto Pizaña and the "border troubles," as the local paper still called them when it referred to them gingerly in passing.

It was because of the border troubles, ten years or so before, that the soldiers had come back to old Fort Jones. But we did not hate them for that; we admired them even, at least sometimes. But when we were thinking about the border troubles instead of Marion the Fox we hooted them and the flag they were lowering, which for the moment was theirs alone, just as we would have jeered an opposing ball team, in a friendly sort of way. On these occasions even Chonita would join in the mockery, though she usually ran home at the stroke of six. But whether we taunted or saluted, the distant men in khaki uniforms went about their motions without noticing us at all.

The last word from the post came in the night when a distant bugle blew. At nine it was all right because all the lights were on. But sometimes I heard it at eleven[4] when everything was dark and still, and it made me feel that I was all alone in the world. I would even doubt that I was me, and that put me in such a fright that I felt like yelling out just to make sure I was really there. But next morning the sun shone and life began all over again, with its whistles and cannon shots and bugles blowing. And so we lived, we and the post, side by side with the wire fence in between.

The wandering soldiers whom the bugle called home at night did not wander in our neighborhood, and none of us ever went into Fort Jones. None except Chonita. Every evening when the flag came down she would leave off playing and go down towards what was known as the "lower" gate of the post, the one that opened not on Main Street but

---

"The Hammon and the Beans" by Américo Parédes from THE TEXAS OBSERVER, (April 18, 1963). Reprinted by permission.

1. *six . . . bugles*, "reveille," a signal to awaken the soldiers in the morning.

2. *the flag came down . . . ceremony*, "retreat," the ceremony at which the national flag on a military post is lowered at sunset.

3. *Marion the Fox . . . Santee*. During the Revolutionary War, General Francis Marion (1732–1795) organized a band of guerrilla volunteers which became famous for its successful exploits against the British. Marion was nicknamed "the Swamp Fox" for skillfully eluding the British by following swamp paths. The Santee is a river in South Carolina which figured in Marion's operations.

4. *At nine . . . at eleven*. At nine in the evening "tattoo" is sounded to summon the soldiers to their quarters; "taps" is the signal sounding "lights out" at eleven. It is also sounded at the burial of a military person.

against the poorest part of town. She went into the grounds and to the mess halls and pressed her nose against the screens and watched the soldiers eat. They sat at long tables calling to each other through food-stuffed mouths.

"Hey bud, pass the coffee!"

"Give me the ham!"

"Yeah, give me the beans!"

After the soldiers were through the cooks came out and scolded Chonita, and then they gave her packages with things to eat.

Chonita's mother did our washing, in gratefulness —as my mother put it—for the use of a vacant lot of my grandfather's which was a couple of blocks down the street. On the lot was an old one-room shack which had been a shed long ago, and this Chonita's father had patched up with flattened-out pieces of tin. He was a laborer. Ever since the end of the border troubles there had been a development boom in the Valley, and Chonita's father was getting his share of the good times. Clearing brush and building irrigation ditches he sometimes pulled down as much as six dollars a week. He drank a good deal of it up, it was true. But corn was just a few cents a bushel in those days. He was the breadwinner, you might say, while Chonita furnished the luxuries.

Chonita was a poet too. I had just moved into the neighborhood when a boy came up to me and said, "Come on! Let's go hear Chonita make a speech."

She was already on top of the alley fence when we got there, a scrawny little girl of about nine, her bare dirty feet clinging to the fence almost like hands. A dozen other kids were there below her, waiting. Some were boys I knew at school; five or six were her younger brothers and sisters.

"Speech! Speech!" they all cried. "Let Chonita make a speech! Talk in English, Chonita!"

They were grinning and nudging each other except for her brothers and sisters, who looked up at her with proud serious faces. She gazed out beyond us all with a grand, distant air and then she spoke.

"Give me the hammon and the beans!" she yelled. "Give me the hammon and the beans!"

She leaped off the fence and everybody cheered and told her how good it was and how she could talk English better than the teachers at the grammar school.

I thought it was a pretty poor joke. Every evening almost, they would make her get up on the fence and yell, "Give me the hammon and the beans!" And everybody would cheer and make her think she was talking English. As for me, I would wait there until she got it over with so we could play at something else. I wondered how long it would be before they got tired of it all. I never did find out because just about that time I got the chills and fever, and when I got up and around Chonita wasn't there anymore.

In later years I thought of her a lot, especially during the thirties when I was growing up. Those years would have been just made for her. Many's the time I have seen her in my mind's eyes, in the picket lines[5] demanding not bread, not cake, but the hammon and the beans. But it didn't work out that way.

One night Doctor Zapata came into our kitchen through the back door. He set his bag on the table and said to my father, who had opened the door for him, "Well, she is dead."

My father flinched. "What was it?" he asked.

The doctor had gone to the window and he stood with his back to us, looking out toward the light of Fort Jones. "Pneumonia, flu, malnutrition, worms, the evil eye," he said without turning around. "What the hell difference does it make?"

"I wish I had known how sick she was," my father said in a very mild tone. "Not that it's really my affair, but I wish I had."

The doctor snorted and shook his head.

My mother came in and I asked her who was dead. She told me. It made me feel strange but I did not cry. My mother put her arm around my shoulders. "She is in Heaven now," she said. "She is happy."

I shrugged her arm away and sat down in one of the kitchen chairs.

"They're like animals," the doctor was saying. He turned round suddenly and his eyes glistened in the light. "Do you know what that brute of a father was doing when I left? He was laughing! Drinking and laughing with his friends."

"There's no telling what the poor man feels," my mother said.

My father made a deprecatory gesture. "It wasn't his daughter anyway."

"No?" the doctor said. He sounded interested.

"This is the woman's second husband," my father explained. "First one died before the girl was born, shot and hanged from a mesquite limb. He was

---

5. *the thirties . . . picket lines.* During the economic depression of the 1930's people showed their protest against situations and conditions by forming picket lines.

working too close to the tracks the day the Olmito train was derailed.''

"You know what?'' the doctor said. "In classical times they did things better. Take Troy,[6] for instance. After they stormed the city they grabbed the babies by the heels and dashed them against the wall. That was more humane.''

My father smiled. "You sound very radical. You sound just like your relative down there in Morelos.''

"No relative of mine,'' the doctor said. "I'm a conservative, the son of a conservative, and you know that I wouldn't be here except for that little detail.''

"Habit,'' my father said. "Pure habit, pure tradition. You're a radical at heart.''

"It depends on how you define radicalism,'' the doctor answered. "People tend to use words too loosely. A dentist could be called a radical, I suppose. He pulls up things by the roots.''

My father chuckled.

"Any bandit in Mexico nowadays can give himself a political label,'' the doctor went on, "and that makes him respectable. He's a leader of the people.''

"Take Villa,[7] now—'' my father began.

"Villa was a different type of man,'' the doctor broke in.

"I don't see any difference.''

The doctor came over to the table and sat down. "Now look at it this way,'' he began, his finger in front of my father's face. My father threw back his head and laughed.

"You'd better go to bed and rest,'' my mother told me. "You're not completely well, you know.''

So I went to bed, but I didn't go to sleep, not right away. I lay there for a long time while behind my darkened eyelids Emiliano Zapata's[8] cavalry charged down to the broad Santee, where there were grave men with hoary hair. I was still awake at eleven when the cold voice of the bugle went gliding in and out of the dark like something that couldn't find its way back to wherever it had been. I thought of Chonita in Heaven, and I saw her in her torn and dirty dress, with a pair of bright wings attached, flying round and round like a butterfly shouting, "Give me the hammon and the beans!''

Then I cried. And whether it was the bugle, or whether it was Chonita or what, to this day I do not know. But cry I did, and I felt much better after that. □

---

6. *Troy*, ancient city in northwestern Asia Minor, the scene, in Greek legend, of the Trojan War.
7. *Villa*, Francisco Villa (1877–1923), called *Pancho Villa*, Mexican revolutionary leader.
8. *Emiliano Zapata* (1877?–1919), Mexican revolutionist, guerrilla leader and agrarian reformer.

DISCUSSION

During the late nineteenth and early twentieth century, much American fiction was local-color fiction, devoted to a particular region of the country. Since World War II, emphasis seems to have shifted from region to ethnic groups, and American literature has been enriched by writers of various ethnic groups—Jewish, black, Chicano, Indian, and others—writing out of their personal experience about their people and culture. "The Hammon and the Beans'' is such a work.

FOR EXPLORATION

1. "The Hammon and the Beans" is a story about the relationship of Jonesville-on-the-Grande and an Army post. In paragraph three, we are told that "the post was the town's clock." Explain what this means, and explore the effect on the town of the post functioning as clock.
2. *(a)* What was the attitude of the soldiers toward Chonita? *(b)* What was the status of her family in the community? Discuss.

3. We are told "Chonita was a poet too." Discuss the possible meanings.
4. *(a)* Discuss the effect of Chonita's death on the doctor and the narrator's family. *(b)* Why does the narrator wait to cry until late at night, after he has gone to bed?

CREATIVE RESPONSE

1. The doctor says: "A dentist could be called a radical, I suppose. He pulls up things by the roots." Explore the meaning of this definition, and reread the discussion between the father and the doctor about conservatism and radicalism. Explain the terms as they use them, show why they disagree, and compose your own definition of the terms.

2. "The Hammon and the Beans" describes the narrator's delayed emotional reaction to an event. Recall an experience of your own in which you did not react emotionally until some time after an important event. Explore the reasons.

Américo Parédes   1915 /

Américo Parédes grew up in Brownsville, Texas, attended Brownsville Junior College, and then after a period in the Far East returned to receive his A.B. from the University of Texas in 1951. Five years later he completed his Ph.D. degree, the dissertation for which was a study of the regional folk legend concerning Gregorio Cortez, later depicted in Parédes' novel *With His Pistol in His Hand* (1958).

He is now a member of the English faculty at the University of Texas. In his free time he is a guitarist and collector of folk songs.

COURTESY OF THE UNIVERSITY OF TEXAS PRESS

ARTICLE
AND ESSAY

GAMMA KSI BY MORRIS LOUIS—ANDRE EMMERICH GALLERY

E. B. White

WALDEN

Miss Nims, take a letter to Henry David Thoreau. Dear Henry: I thought of you the other afternoon as I was approaching Concord doing fifty on Route 62. That is a high speed at which to hold a philosopher in one's mind, but in this century we are a nimble bunch.

On one of the lawns in the outskirts of the village a woman was cutting the grass with a motorized lawn mower. What made me think of you was that the machine had rather got away from her, although she was game enough, and in the brief glimpse I had of the scene it appeared to me that the lawn was mowing the lady.[1] She kept a tight grip on the handles, which throbbed violently with every explosion of the one-cylinder motor, and as she sheered around bushes and lurched along at a reluctant trot behind her impetuous servant, she looked like a puppy who had grabbed something that was too much for him. Concord hasn't changed much, Henry; the farm implements and the animals still have the upper hand.

I may as well admit that I was journeying to Concord with the deliberate intention of visiting your woods; for although I have never knelt at the grave of a philosopher nor placed wreaths on moldy poets, and have often gone a mile out of my way to avoid some place of historical interest, I have always wanted to see Walden Pond. The account which you left of your sojourn there is, you will be amused to learn, a document of increasing penitence; each year it seems to gain a little headway, as the world loses ground. We may all be transcendental yet, whether we like it nor not. As our common complexities increase, any tale of individual simplicity (and yours is the best written and the cockiest) acquires a new fascination; as our goods accumulate, but not our well-being, your report of an existence without material adornment takes on a certain awkward credibility.

My purpose in going to Walden Pond, like yours, was not to live cheaply or to live dearly there, but to transact some private business with the fewest obstacles. Approaching Concord, doing forty, doing forty-five, doing fifty, the steering wheel held snug in my palms, the highway held grimly in my vision, the crown of the road now serving me (on the right-hand curves), now defeating me (on the left-hand curves), I began to rouse myself from the stupefaction which a day's motor journey induces. It was a delicious evening, Henry, when the whole body is one sense, and imbibes delight through every pore, if I may coin a phrase. Fields were richly brown where the harrow, drawn by the stripped Ford, had lately sunk its teeth; pastures were green; and overhead the sky had that same everlasting great look which you will find on Page 144 of the Oxford pocket edition.[2] I could feel the road entering me, through tire, wheel, spring, and cushion; shall I not have intelligence with earth too? Am I not partly leaves and vegetable mold myself?—a man of infinite horsepower, yet partly leaves.

Stay with me on 62 and it will take you into Concord. As I say, it was a delicious evening. The snake had come forth to die in a bloody S on the highway, the wheel upon its head, its bowels flat now and exposed. The turtle had come up too to cross the road and die in the attempt, its hard shell smashed under the rubber blow, its intestinal yearning (for the other side of the road) forever squashed. There was a sign by the wayside which announced that the road had a "cotton surface." You wouldn't know what that is, but neither, for that matter, did I. There is a cryptic ingredient in many of our modern improvements—we are awed and pleased without knowing quite what we are enjoying. It is something to be traveling on a road with a cotton surface.

The civilization round Concord today is an odd

"Walden"—June, 1939—in ONE MAN'S MEAT by E. B. White. Copyright, 1939, 1967, by E. B. White. Reprinted by permission of Harper & Row, Publishers, Inc.
1. *it appeared . . . the lady.* White is echoing Thoreau's own words (see "Why I Went to the Woods," page C 140) to make a satiric reference to modern man.
2. *the Oxford pocket edition,* an edition of *Walden* published by the Oxford Press.

distillation of city, village, farm, and manor. The houses, yards, fields look not quite suburban, not quite rural. Under the bronze beech and the blue spruce of the departed baron grazes the milch goat of the heirs. Under the porte-cochere stands the reconditioned station wagon; under the grape arbor sit the puppies for sale. (But why do men degenerate ever? What makes families run out?)

It was June and everywhere June was publishing her immemorial stanza; in the lilacs, in the syringa, in the freshly edged paths and the sweetness of moist beloved gardens, and the little wire wickets that preserve the tulips' front. Farmers were already moving the fruits of their toil into their yards, arranging the rhubarb, the asparagus, the strictly fresh eggs on the painted stands under the little shed roofs with the patent shingles. And though it was almost a hundred years since you had taken your ax and started cutting out your home on Walden Pond, I was interested to observe that the philosophical spirit was still alive in Massachusetts; in the center of a vacant lot some boys were assembling the framework of a rude shelter, their whole mind and skill concentrated in the rather inauspicious helter-skeleton of studs and rafters. They too were escaping from town, to live naturally, in a rich blend of savagery and philosophy.

That evening, after supper at the inn, I strolled out into the twilight to dream my shapeless transcendental dreams and see that the car was locked up for the night (first open the right front door, then reach over, straining, and pull up the handles of the left rear and the left front till you hear the click, then the handle of the right rear, then shut the right front but open it again, remembering that the key is still in the ignition switch, remove the key, shut the right front again with a bang, push the tiny keyhole cover to one side, insert key, turn, and withdraw). It is what we all do, Henry. It is called locking the car. It is said to confuse thieves and keep them from making off with the lap robe. Four doors to lock behind one robe. The driver himself never uses a lap robe, the free movement of his legs being vital to the operation of the vehicle; so that when he locks the car it is a pure and unselfish act. I have in my life gained very little essential heat from lap robes, yet I have ever been at pains to lock them up.

The evening was full of sounds, some of which would have stirred your memory. The robins still love the elms of New England villages at sundown. There is enough of the thrush in them to make song

inevitable at the end of day, and enough of the tramp to make them hang round the dwellings of men. A robin, like many another American, dearly loves a white house with green blinds. Concord is still full of them.

Your fellow townsmen were stirring abroad—not many afoot, most of them in their cars; and the sound which they made in Concord at evening was a rustling and a whispering. The sound lacks steadfastness and is wholly unlike that of a train. A train, as you know who lived so near the Fitchburg line, whistles once or twice sadly and is gone, trailing a memory in smoke soothing to ear and mind. Automobiles, skirting a village green, are like flies that have gained the inner ear—they buzz, cease, pause, start, shift, stop, halt, brake, and the whole effect is a nervous polytone curiously disturbing.

As I wandered along, the toc toc of Ping-pong balls drifted from an attic window. In front of the Reuben Brown house a Buick was drawn up. At the wheel, motionless, his hat upon his head, a man sat, listening to "Amos and Andy"[3] on the radio (it is a drama of many scenes and without an end). The deep voice of Andrew Brown, emerging from the car, although it originated more than two hundred miles away, was unstrained by distance. When you used to sit on the shore of your pond on Sunday morning, listening to the church bells of Acton and Concord, you were aware of the excellent filter of the intervening atmosphere. Science has attended to that, and sound now maintains its intensity without regard for distance. Properly sponsored, it goes on forever.

A fire engine, out for a trial spin, roared past Emerson's house, hot with readiness for public duty. Over the barn roofs the martins dipped and chittered. A swarthy daughter of an asparagus grower, in culottes, shirt, and bandanna, pedaled past on her bicycle. It was indeed a delicious evening, and I returned to the inn (I believe it was your house once) to rock with the old ladies on the concrete veranda.

Next morning early I started afoot for Walden, out Main Street and down Thoreau, past the depot and the Minuteman Chevrolet Company. The morning was fresh and in a beanfield along the way I flushed an agriculturalist, quietly studying his beans. Thoreau Street soon joined Number 126, an artery of the State. We number our highways nowadays, our

---

3. "Amos and Andy," a popular radio show of the 1940's, relating the comedy antics of two black men. Andy's full name was Andrew Brown.

speed being so great we can remember little of their quality or character and are lucky to remember their number. (Men have an indistinct notion that if they keep up this activity long enough all will at length ride somewhere, in next to no time.) Your pond is on 126.

I knew I must be nearing your woodland retreat when the Golden Pheasant lunchroom came into view—Sealtest ice cream, toasted sandwiches, hot frankfurters, waffles, tonics, and lunches. Were I the proprietor, I should add rice, Indian meal, and molasses—just for old time's sake. The Pheasant, incidentally, is for sale: a chance for some nature lover who wishes to set himself up beside a pond in the Concord atmosphere and live deliberately, fronting only the essential facts of life[4] on Number 126. Beyond the Pheasant was a place called Walden Breezes, an oasis whose porch pillars were made of old green shutters sawed into lengths. On the porch was a distorting mirror, to give the traveler a comical image of himself, who had miraculously learned to gaze in an ordinary glass without smiling. Behind the Breezes, in a sun-parched clearing, dwelt your philosophical descendants in their trailers, each trailer the size of your hut, but all grouped together for the sake of congeniality. Trailer people leave the city, as you did, to discover solitude and in any weather, at any hour of the day or night, to improve the nick of time; but they soon collect in villages and get bogged deeper in the mud than ever. The camp behind Walden Breezes was just rousing itself to the morning. The ground was packed hard under the heel, and the sun came through the clearing to bake the soil and enlarge the wry smell of cramped housekeeping. Cushman's bakery truck had stopped to deliver an early basket of rolls. A camp dog, seeing me in the road, barked petulantly. A man emerged from one of the trailers and set forth with a bucket to draw water from some forest tap.

Leaving the highway I turned off into the woods toward the pond, which was apparent through the foliage. The floor of the forest was strewn with dried old oak leaves and *Transcripts*.[5] From beneath the flattened popcorn wrapper (*granum explosum*) peeped the frail violet. I followed a footpath and descended to the water's edge. The pond lay clear and blue in the morning light, as you have seen it so many times. In the shallows a man's water-logged shirt undulated gently. A few flies came out to greet me and convoy me to your cove, past the No Bathing

signs on which the fellows and the girls had scrawled their names. I felt strangely excited suddenly to be snooping around your premises, tiptoeing along watchfully, as though not to tread by mistake upon the intervening century. Before I got to the cove I heard something which seemed to me quite wonderful: I heard your frog, a full, clear *troonk*, guiding me, still hoarse and solemn, bridging the years as the robins had bridged them in the sweetness of the village evening. But he soon quit, and I came on a couple of young boys throwing stones at him.

Your frontyard is marked by a bronze tablet set in stone. Four small granite posts, a few feet away, show where the house was. On top of the tablet was a pair of faded blue bathing trunks with a white stripe. Back of it is a pile of stones, a sort of cairn, left by your visitors as a tribute I suppose. It is a rather ugly little heap of stones, Henry. In fact the hillside itself seems faded, browbeaten; a few tall skinny pines, bare of lower limbs, a smattering of young maples in suitable green, some birches and oaks, and a number of trees felled by the last big wind. It was from the bole of one of these fallen pines, torn up by the roots, that I extracted the stone which I added to the cairn—sentimental act in which I was interrupted by a small terrier from a nearby picnic group, who confronted me and wanted to know about the stone.

I sat down for a while on one of the posts of your house to listen to the bluebottles and the dragonflies. The invaded glade sprawled shabby and mean at my feet, but the flies were tuned to the old vibration. There were remains of a fire in your ruins, but I doubt that it was yours; also two beer bottles trodden into the soil had become part of earth. A young oak had taken root in your house, and two or three ferns, unrolling like the ticklers at a banquet. The only other furnishings were a DuBarry pattern sheet, a page torn from a picture magazine, and some crusts in wax paper.

Before I quit I walked clear round the pond and found the place where you used to sit on the northeast side to get the sun in the fall, and the beach where you got sand for scrubbing your floor. On the eastern side of the pond, where the highway borders it, the State has built dressing rooms for swimmers, a float with diving towers, drinking fountains of porcelain, and rowboats for hire. The pond is in fact a

---

4. *live deliberately . . . of life*, another echo of Thoreau's words.
5. *Transcripts*, *The Boston Evening Transcript*, which ceased publication in 1941.

State Preserve, and carries a twenty-dollar fine for picking wild flowers, a decree signed in all solemnity by your fellow citizens Walter C. Wardwell, Erson B. Barlow, and Nathaniel I. Bowditch. There was a smell of creosote where they had been building a wide wooden stairway to the road and the parking area. Swimmers and boaters were arriving; bodies plunged vigorously into the water and emerged wet and beautiful in the bright air. As I left, a boatload of town boys were splashing about in midpond, kidding and fooling, the young fellows singing at the tops of their lungs in a wild chorus:

Amer-ica, Amer-ica, God shed his grace on thee,
And crown thy good with brotherhood
From sea to shi-ning sea!

I walked back to town along the railroad, following your custom. The rails were expanding noisily in the hot sun, and on the slope of the roadbed the wild grape and the blackberry sent up their creepers to the track.

The expense of my brief sojourn in Concord was:

Canvas shoes	$1.95
Baseball bat	.25 ⎱ gifts to take
Left-handed	
fielder's glove	1.25 ⎰ back to a boy
Hotel and meals	4.25
In all	$7.70

As you see, this amount was almost what you spent for food for eight months.[6] I cannot defend the shoes or the expenditure for shelter and food: they reveal a meanness and grossness in my nature which you would find contemptible. The baseball equipment, however, is the kind of impediment with which you were never on even terms. You must remember that the house where you practiced the sort of economy which I respect was haunted only by mice and squirrels. You never had to cope with a shortstop. □

---

6. *As you see . . . months.* In Thoreau's account of his stay at Walden Pond, he listed all his expenses for the eight months. Food cost him $8.74.

JAMES COYNE FROM BLACK STAR

Holden Caulfield, teen-age hero of Salinger's *Catcher in the Rye,* has an imagination game he likes to play: selecting a favorite historical character and giving him a phone call.

Such is E. B. White's device here, a letter that gives him a wonderful vehicle for comparisons between idealistic America and the commercialized country of today.

FOR EXPLORATION

1. Find topics that White discusses that might be difficult for Thoreau to understand.
2. (*a*) What specific examples of a desecrated environment does White mention? (*b*) How do you think Thoreau would react to what has happened to his former backwoods utopia?
3. White develops the theme of the complexities of modern life through such examples as the necessity of locking a car and the difficulties of managing a power mower. Can

you think of other pertinent examples to illustrate Thoreau's claim that material possessions are more a curse than a blessing?
4. Is White satirizing the realities of modern life or the idealism of Thoreau's philosophy? Or both? Explain.
5. (*a*) What ironies are implicit in White's list of expenditures at the end of the essay? (*b*) Can you find other parallels between the essay and Thoreau's report of his days in the woods (pages C 140–C 152)?

CREATIVE RESPONSE

Select another essayist from this anthology (Clemens' comments on steamboating, on pages 225 C–227 C, for example), and write that author about how his subject would be viewed today. What tone would you adopt? What contrasts would you emphasize?

WORDS

An author with as individual and distinctive a style as E. B. White will frequently make word choices that are surprising and delightful. Below you will find a number of the sentences that White used in "Walden" with some word or phrase left out of each. (1) Complete each sentence using the word or phrase you might have expected to follow in that context before you read the essay. (2) Look again at the sentence quoted to find how White actually completed it. (3) Explain how White's "surprise ending" helped him accomplish his purpose.

(*a*) The account which you left of your sojourn there is, you will be amused to learn, a document of increasing _____. (page M 106, column a, paragraph 3)

(*b*) . . . as our goods accumulate but not our well-being, your report of an existence without material adornment takes on _____. (page M 106, column a, paragraph 3)

(*c*) That evening, after supper at the inn, I strolled out into the twilight to dream my shapeless transcendental dreams and see _____. (page 107 M, column a, paragraph 2)

(*d*) The floor of the forest was strewn with dried old oak leaves and _____. (page M 108, column a, paragraph 2)

E. B. White   1899 /

After he had graduated from Cornell University, E. B. White adventured for a while in the West, but returned to his native state to work for two unsatisfying years as a production assistant and copywriter for an advertising agency in New York. During this time, however, he was sending contributions to *The New Yorker.* Through these he earned an editorial post in "The Talk of the Town" department where he wrote "Notes and Comment" for many years. In the earlier days he also reported and wrote many of the "Talk" stories that follow this editorial page. Since it is this department that really sets the tone for the entire magazine, the style of *The New Yorker* became identified with that of E. B. White. Actually his style is inimitable.

Many people believe that White is the best of modern American essayists, and some have tried to describe his unique gift. *Time* magazine has said that his style is "a sort of precocious offhand humming." As is evident in the accompanying essay, this seemingly offhand grace serves to heighten the brilliant precision of his insights.

In 1971 he was honored with the National Book Committee's Medal for Literature.

George Santayana

WAR

To fight is a radical instinct; if men have nothing else to fight over, they will fight over words, fancies, or women, or they will fight because they dislike each other's looks, or because they have met walking in opposite directions. To knock a thing down, especially if it is cocked at an arrogant angle, is a deep delight to the blood. To fight for a reason and in a calculating spirit is something your true warrior despises; even a coward might screw his courage up to such a reasonable conflict. The joy and glory of fighting lie in its pure spontaneity and consequent generosity; you are not fighting for gain, but for sport and for victory. Victory, no doubt, has its fruits for the victor. If fighting were not a possible means of livelihood, the bellicose instinct could never have established itself in any long-lived race. A few men can live on plunder, just as there is room in the world for some beasts of prey; other men are reduced to living on industry, just as there are diligent bees, ants, and herbivorous kine. But victory need have no good fruits for the people whose army is victorious. That it sometimes does so is an ulterior and blessed circumstance hardly to be reckoned upon.

Since barbarism has its pleasures it naturally has its apologists. There are panegyrists of war who say that without a periodical bleeding a race decays and loses its manhood. Experience is directly opposed to this shameless assertion. It is war that wastes a nation's wealth, chokes its industries, kills its flower, narrows its sympathies, condemns it to be governed by adventurers, and leaves the puny, deformed, and unmanly to breed the next generation. Internecine war, foreign and civil, brought about the greatest set-back which the life of reason has ever suffered; it exterminated the Greek and Italian aristocracies. Instead of being descended from heroes, modern nations are descended from slaves; and it is not their bodies only that show it. After a long peace, if the conditions of life are propitious, we observe a peo-ple's energies bursting their barriers; they become aggressive on the strength they have stored up in their remote and unchecked development. It is the unmutilated race, fresh from the struggle with nature (in which the best survive, while in war it is often the best that perish), that descends victoriously into the arena of nations and conquers disciplined armies at the first blow, becomes the military aristocracy of the next epoch, and is itself ultimately sapped and decimated by luxury and battle and merged at last into the ignoble conglomerate beneath. Then, perhaps, in some other virgin country a genuine humanity is again found, capable of victory because unbled by war. To call war the soil of courage and virtue is like calling debauchery the soil of love.

Blind courage is an animal virtue indispensable in a world full of dangers and evils where a certain insensibility and dash are requisite to skirt the precipice without vertigo. Such animal courage seems therefore beautiful rather than desperate or cruel, and being the lowest and most instinctive of virtues it is the one most widely and sincerely admired. In the form of steadiness under risks rationally taken, and perseverance so long as there is a chance of success, courage is a true virtue; but it ceases to be one when the love of danger, a useful passion when danger is unavoidable, begins to lead men into evils which it was unnecessary to face. Bravado, provocativeness, and a gambler's instinct, with a love of hitting hard for the sake of exercise, is a temper which ought already to be counted among the vices rather than the virtues of man. To delight in war is a merit in the soldier, a dangerous quality in the captain, and a positive crime in the statesman.

The panegyrist of war places himself on the lowest level on which a moralist or patriot can stand, and shows as great a want of refined feeling as of right reason. For the glories of war are all blood-stained, delirious, and infected with crime; the combative instinct is a savage prompting by which one man's good is found in another's evil. The existence of such a contradiction in the moral world is the original sin of nature, whence flows every other wrong. He

Reprinted from LITTLE ESSAYS DRAWN FROM THE WRITINGS OF GEORGE SANTAYANA edited by Logan Pearsall Smith. Reprinted by permission of Constable and Company, Ltd. and the Executors of the Smith Estate. Copyright 1920 by Constable and Company, Ltd.

is a willing accomplice of that perversity in things who delights in another's discomfiture or in his own, and craves the blind tension of plunging into danger without reason, or the idiot's pleasure in facing a pure chance. To find joy in another's trouble is, as man is constituted, not unnatural, though it is wicked; and to find joy in one's own trouble, though it be madness, is not yet impossible for man. These are the chaotic depths of that dreaming nature out of which humanity has to grow. ☐

FOR EXPLORATION

1. (*a*) How did you read this essay? Did the way you read it have anything to do with its style? Its thought? Both? (*b*) Look up the definitions of *epigram* and *aphorism* and locate examples of each in this essay. How do the characteristics of these devices contribute to the style or "feel" of the essay?
2. (*a*) Explain Santayana's attitude toward courage, mentioning the conditions under which he regards it (*1*) as a virtue, (*2*) as a vice. (*b*) Santayana writes: "To delight in war is a merit in the soldier, a dangerous quality in the captain, and a positive crime in the statesman." How is this statement related to his views on courage?
3. This essay was written about the time of World War I. (*a*) How has the "art of war" changed since then? (*b*) Partly as a result of these changes there is very little written today about the "glories" of war. Do you think that man has grown out of his craving for the excitement of war? Explain.
4. Santayana tells us what war does to society. What evidence do you find to support his contention in the short story "In Another Country" (pages M 52–M 54)?

CREATIVE RESPONSE

Write a short essay supporting or denying Santayana's claim that "Instead of being descended from hereos, modern nations are descended from slaves; and it is not only their bodies that show it."

George Santayana   1863 / 1952

George Santayana (sän′tə yä′nə) moved to Boston from his birthplace in Madrid, Spain, at the age of eight. After studying at Harvard and the University of Berlin, he returned to the Boston area to begin a distinguished teaching career as one of Harvard's most eminent professors of philosophy. Santayana was never a highly technical philosopher, and the style of his two most important works, *The Life of Reason* and *The Sense of Beauty*, makes them good reading for the layman. His artistic genius was remarkably demonstrated when his only novel, *The Last Puritan*, finished in 1935 when he was over seventy years old, became a best seller.

Although Santayana's main concerns in his philosophy were beauty and reason, he never had any illusions about the brutal aspects of human nature. In later years his horror of the incredible stupidity of war deepened. After extensive travel in Europe between the wars, he gained asylum at a convent in Rome at the outbreak of World War II. When in 1944 he was found still at the convent by the advancing Allied armies, he told reporters, "I shall never leave here. . . . There has been so much killing and so much suffering in the world's history. In solitude it is possible to love mankind; in the world, there can be nothing but secret or open war."[1]

In the essay "War," written early in this century, Santayana was less fatalistic and more detached. Nonetheless, while he believed then that mankind could improve, he indicated clearly that man's indulgence in war was positive evidence of how far he had to grow.

---

1. *Time*, June 26, 1944, p. 42.

Art Buchwald

THE FEMININE MISTAQUE

*In this humorous article,
which sex is* really *being
put down?*

UNLIKE most American husbands, I am very concerned about the problems of the modern American Woman and her struggle for fulfillment. My bible has been *The Feminine Mystique,*[1] and no one admires Betty Friedan, the author, more than I do.

Therefore, the other night when I came home from work and found my wife scrubbing the floor, I said to her, "Do you know who you are?"

"I'm sorry," she said blankly. "What did you say?"

"Do you know who you are? Do you have any identity besides being a wife, a mother and a servant?"

"I don't think so," she replied. "Don't step over there. I just mopped it."

"Aren't you concerned that you've traded in your brains for a broom? Can you stand there and tell me that you are contented, happy and satisfied with your lot?"

"Would you rinse out this pail for me?" she said. "I want to know one thing. Are you trying to start a fight with me, are you trying out a new article idea on me, or are you trying to cover up something that you've done?"

"I'm not doing any of them. But I happened to have read *The Feminine Mystique,* and it occurs to me you should want more out of life than this drab existence that you're leading now."

"I'm baking some homemade bread," she said. "I hope the kids like it."

"Answer my question."

"Well, if you must know, I would really like to be a mailman, but I'm afraid to take the civil-service exam."

"That's right, make fun of me. All over America there are millions of unhappy, unfulfilled women who are searching for a place in the sun, who are nothing but sex objects to their husbands, and you stand there making bread and then tell me you're satisfied."

"I didn't say I was satisfied," she said, "but I figure I've got a pretty good deal and I don't want to louse it up."

"You know why you don't want to louse it up?" I said to her as she set the table for dinner. "Because you're dominated by me. I've denied you your birthright and destroyed you as an individual."

"Maybe I could join a sit-in at the White House."

"That's not what I'm talking about. By being a mother and a wife you are suffering from a problem that has no name. You are lavishing love and affection on me and the children, and this is causing havoc to your id."

"Now don't start knocking my id," she said, draining the spaghetti into a pan. "I know I look out for you and I take care of the children and I keep the house clean and I entertain well—but nobody's perfect."

She then asked me to make her a drink.

"Ah-hah," I said. "Do you know there are a million known alcoholic housewives in this country and there are another million who are on tranquilizers? Why is that?"

"I have no idea."

"Because they are unfulfilled. They are searching for something they'll never find in their homes."

"Maybe I'll go out and have an affair."

"You don't have to go that far," I told her.

"How far do you want me to go?"

"Outside this house is a whole new world. Go out and embrace it. Find the *real* you."

"I will if you go find the children. Dinner is ready."

Later that night, as she was putting up her hair, I noticed she yawned.

"Why did you yawn?" I asked her.

"I'm tired."

"No you're not, you're suffering from housewives'

Copyright © 1965 Downe Publishing, Inc. Reprinted by Special Permission of the *Ladies' Home Journal* and the author.

1. *The Feminine Mystique,* a book by Betty Friedan, published in 1963, which explains that society has convinced women that the only honorable job for them is that of wife and mother, making it most difficult for them to pursue careers if they want to and causing many frustrations. The publication of this book is often cited as the beginning of the Women's Liberation Movement.

fatigue," I said triumphantly. "Betty Friedan calls it 'the illness that has no name.' No doctor can get at its cause or cure. You are slowly dying of boredom. Every intelligent, able-bodied woman who has no goal, no ambition to make her stretch and grow, is committing a kind of suicide. Do you think I want to live with that on my conscience the rest of my life?"

"Do you mean to say, every time I yawn, you feel guilty?"

"Something like that," I admitted.

"OK, if you want me to take my rightful place in society, I will."

A few nights later I came home from work, and found the front door wide open, the kids in the kitchen eating corn flakes, the dog tearing up the rug and the television set going full blast.

"Where's your mother?" I asked.

"She said to tell you she got a job with Sears, Roebuck and she has to work until nine tonight," my 10-year-old said as she took a swing at her brother.

It took me 20 minutes to get her on the phone. "You come home right away," I shouted. "Do you realize what is going on around here?"

"I'll be home at nine. I've finally found myself. The real me."

"Where?"

"Between the pot-holder counter and ladies' pajamas. Now I know what it is to be fulfilled."

I walked into the kitchen, and my son said, "You want puffed wheat or corn flakes?"

"Corn flakes," I said sadly. "Go easy on the milk."

□

Arthur Buchwald   1925 /

Art Buchwald was born in Mount Vernon, New York. Just sixteen when World War II began, he quit high school to join the Marines. After serving in the Pacific, Buchwald attended the University of Southern California for three years, editing the college humor magazine and almost failing an English course in humor. He left in 1948 without finishing his degree requirements when a $250 veteran's bonus was enough for a one-way airline ticket to Paris. He began there as a correspondent and was soon writing a thrice-weekly column syndicated through the Paris edition of the *New York Herald Tribune* and translated into nearly a dozen foreign languages. He lived in Paris with his wife Anne McGarry, onetime fashion coordinator for Neiman-Marcus, and three children until 1962 when he moved his beat to Washington, D.C.

FOR EXPLORATION

1. Would you say that this piece is a satire in the sense that it has a serious purpose (to correct a social abuse, for instance) or is its purpose merely to have a bit of fun?
2. How is the wife portrayed here? The husband? Who is the more idealistic, who the more realistic? Are their roles stereotyped? Interchangeable?
3. What irony is there in the wife's comment "I finally found myself"?
4. A reader of this piece commented: "I don't feel that Buchwald gives a fair portrait of the married woman's role and responsibilities or a fair representation of the vocational choices open to her. The whole article is demeaning." Agree or disagree.

Edna St. Vincent Millay[1]

FEAR

Nicola Sacco (1891–1927) and Bartolomeo Van-zetti (1888–1927) were charged with the robbery (on April 15, 1920) of a Massachusetts shoe com-pany's payroll and the killing of the paymaster and his guard. At their trial both men had witnesses to prove they were not at the scene of the crime but their testimony was discredited by state witnesses.

Although much of the evidence against Sacco and Vanzetti was later refuted, prejudice against them was strong because they had been draft dodgers, anarchists, and labor agitators. And in spite of being exonerated of the crime by a condemned criminal who admitted he had been a member of a gang re-sponsible for the killings, an investigating com-mittee appointed by the governor of Massachusetts upheld the death sentences; Sacco and Vanzetti were executed.

The case inspired many literary works, among them the following essay. Edna St. Vincent Millay also wrote a poem, which has become famous, on the case: "Justice Denied in Massachusetts" (page M 216).

THERE are two names you would not have me mention, for you are sick of the sound of them. All men must die, you say, and these men have died, and would that their names might die with them; would that their names were as names written in the sand, you say, to be dissipated by the next incoming tide! For you long to return to your gracious world of a year ago, where people had pretty manners and did not raise their voices; where people whom you knew, whom you had entertained in your houses, did not shout and weep and walk the streets vulgarly carrying banners, because two quite inconsequential people, two men who could not even speak good English, were about to be put forever out of mis-chief's way. *Do* let us forget, you say; after all, what *does* it matter?

You are right; it does not matter very much. In a world more beautiful than this it would have mat-tered more. On the surface of a Christianity already so spotted and defaced by the crimes of the Church this stain does not show very dark. In a freedom al-ready so riddled and gashed by the crimes of the state this ugly rent is with difficulty to be distin-guished at all.

And you are right; it is well to forget that men die. So far we have devised no way to defeat death, or to outwit him, or to buy him over. At any moment the cloud may split above us and the golden spear of death leap at the heart; at any moment the earth crack and the hand of death reach up from the abyss to grasp our ankles; at any moment the wind rise and sweep the roofs from our houses, making one dust of our ceilings and ourselves. And if not, we shall die soon, anyhow. It is well to forget that this is so.

But that man before his time, wantonly and with-out sorrow, is thrust from the light of the sun into the darkness of the grave by his brother's blindness or fear it is well to remember, at least until it has been shown to the satisfaction of all that this too is beyond our power to change.

Two months ago, in Massachusetts, these men whom I do not name were efficiently despatched out of the sunlight into the darkness of the grave. The executions of the death sentence upon them went forward without interference; there were no violent demonstrations. Whatever of agitation there was has steadily decreased since that night. Today things are very quiet. From time to time some small newspaper remarks editorially that the hysteria which swept the country has abated, and congratulates its readers upon having escaped disintegration. Aside from this there is little comment. The general opinion is that the affair has pretty well blown over. And the world sleeps easy on this pillow.

Yet if all is quiet today, it is more for this reason than for any other; that though you sit in the same

---

"Fear" by Edna St. Vincent Millay. Copyright 1927, 1955 by Edna St. Vincent Millay and Norma Millay Ellis.
1. For biography see page 219 M.

room with a man you cannot hear his thoughts. And the tumult is in the mind; the shouting and rioting are in the thinking mind. Nothing has abated; nothing has changed; nothing is forgotten. It is as if the two months which have elapsed were but the drawing of a breath. In very truth, for those who sat in silence on that night of the 22d of August, waiting for news from the prison, and in silence when the news came, it is still the night of the 22d of August, for there has been no dawn.

I do not call these men by name, for I know how nervous and irritable you become at the sight of these names on the printed page; how your cheek flushes and you cluck with exasperation; how you turn to your family with words on your tongue which in former days you would not have used at all—"vipers, vermin, filth." This is because you were just dozing off nicely again after the shocking uproar of two months ago, and do not wish to be disturbed. You are as cross as an old dog asleep on the hearth if I shake you and try to get you out into the rainy wind. This is because what you most want out of life is not to be disturbed. You wish to lie peacefully asleep for a few years yet, and then to lie peacefully dead.

If you should rouse yourself for a moment and look about you at the world, you would be troubled, I think, and feel less peaceful and secure, seeing how it is possible for a man as innocent as yourself of any crime to be cast into prison and be killed. For whether or not these men whom I do not name were guilty of the crime of murder, it was not for murder that they died. The crime for which they died was the crime of breathing upon the frosty window and looking out.

"These Anarchists!" you say; "shall I never hear the last of them?"

Indeed, I fear it will be some time before you hear the last of them. I do not mean by this what you think I mean. I do not mean that plotting mischief is afoot, that thousands of people hitherto gentle and retired are now grimly engaged in fashioning engines of death to plant beneath the State House floor. This is not what I mean, although you will say it is what I meant.

It is of your children I was thinking, your young sons and daughters, your grandsons and granddaughters, these young people with whom you have already so much difficulty, because, as you say, they have so few illusions. How often already have they not stood looking at you coldly while with warm cheek and faltering accent you presented your pretty concepts: duty, honor, courage, purity, sacrifice—those fragile dolls of yours, that are always dressed for summer, no matter what the sky?

Your children heard you discussing the case in question. "Anarchists, murderers, Anarchists, Anarchists." This was your discussion of the case. They looked at you, yawned, and left the room.

Their minds are dark to you. But they are busy. Out of your sight they read, they ponder, they work things out. In your presence they often sit in a not too respectful silence, interrupting suddenly your placid remarks by their brisk utterance of some untidy truth never mentioned in your house before.

They are frankly occupied chiefly with the real business of life, which, as everybody knows, is having your own way, and getting as much as possible for as little as possible. It is you who have taught them this angular truth; you have failed only in that you have not been able to impart to them as well the ruffles and passementerie with which you are accustomed to adorn it. They were just beginning to look about them at life when war broke out and surrounded them with death. They know how important it is to have a good time while you can; in the next war it is they who will be taken.

As for their illusions, well, they have seen you at war, and they are beginning to understand why you went to war; they have seen you engaged in many another dubious and embarrassing activity; and now they have seen this. They who have been chidden time and again for having so little softness in them see now their parents, for all their gentle voices and courteous ways, more hard, more unscrupulous, more relentless, than themselves in their most iron moods. It is from these children, I fear, that you are likely to hear again on the subject, though not in so many words.

But, you say, what we did was done for the good of the country, to protect its honor, its institutions, the glory of its flag.

What is this honor, that a breath can tarnish? This glory, that a whisper can bring it low? What are these noble institutions, that a wind from any quarter can set to trembling like towers of jelly?

You do not know exactly what they are. For you do not live with them. They are not trees to shade you, water to quench your thirst. They are golden coins, hidden under the mattress in a very soiled wallet.

The only pleasure they afford you is the rapturous dread lest some one may be taking them away. And some one is taking them away. But not the one you think.

Unkindness, hypocrisy, and greed—these are the forces that shall bring us low and enslave our children. Yet we quarter their troops in our houses without a murmur. We show them where the treasure is hid. But they know it already.

This is the way you look at it: These men were Anarchists, and they are well out of the way; you are fortunate to have escaped destruction at their hands; they were probably murderers; but, in any case, they are well out of the way. It was that word Anarchist which brought them to the chair; that word, and your ignorance of its meaning.

For you do not at all know what an Anarchist is. And all through this trial in which the word Anarchist has played such an important part you have not even looked up the word in the dictionary, your position being that, in the first place, you know quite well enough, and, in the second place, you would think shame to know.

An Anarchist, you insist, is a man who makes bombs and puts them under the State House, and that is that. On the contrary, that is by no means that. The person you have in mind is not an Anarchist, he is a bomber. You will find him everywhere—among Anarchists, among Fascists, among dry-law enforcers, among Modernists, among Fundamentalists, and freely distributed throughout the Ku Klux Klan. He is that person who, when he does not like a thing, lynches it, tars and feathers it, lays a curse upon it, or puts a bomb under it. His name is legion, and you will find him in every party.

An Anarchist, according to the dictionary, is a person who believes that human beings are naturally good, and that if left to themselves they would, by mutual agreement, govern themselves much better and much more peaceably than they are being governed now by a government based on violence. An interesting theory. Nonsense, of course, because man is not naturally good; man is naturally cruel, selfish, and vain, and what he would be if left to his own devices it is horrible to contemplate. Still, it is an interesting concept, very idealistic, very pretty.

Of those who hold with the theory of Anarchism, the dictionary further tells us, there is one group whose members "occasionally resort to an act of violence against representatives of oppression to express a protest against, or to draw public attention to, existing social wrongs." (It is in this group that your bombers are happy and at home.) But "generally speaking," says the dictionary, "Anarchism repudiates violent methods, and hopes for a gradual evolution towards its goal."

Ah, you will say, but these men belonged to the violent group!

Their history would indicate otherwise. Up to the time of their detention for the crime for which they were later sentenced to die no slightest act of violence had ever been attributed to either of them. There are those who would have given much to be able to bring to light against them such an act of violence, and were unable to do so; it is to the counsel for the prosecution that I refer. "Throughout the entire trial" (I quote the uncontested statement of one who was in a position to know the facts)—"not one word of testimony was introduced against their character for honesty, peace, and good order."

I am going into this in some detail because I find it interesting. You, I fear, find it not only uninteresting, but vaguely and uncomfortably obscene. Yet, after all, you have very plentifully had your say on the subject—that action of yours, you know, that spoke so much louder than any words.

These men were castaways upon our shore, and we, an ignorant and savage tribe, have put them to death because their speech and their manners were different from our own, and because to the untutored mind that which is strange is in its infancy ludicrous, but in its prime evil, dangerous, and to be done away with.

These men were put to death because they made you nervous; and your children know it. The minds of your children are like clear pools, reflecting faithfully whatever passes on the bank; whereas in the pool of your own mind, whenever an alien image bends above, a fish of terror leaps to meet it, shattering its reflection.

I am free to say these things because I am not an Anarchist, although you will say that I am. It is unreasonable to you that a person should go to any trouble in behalf of another person unless the two are members of the same family, or of the same fraternity, or, at the remotest, of the same political party. As regards yourself and the man who lives next door to you, you wish him well, but not so very well. Even if he is a member of the same church as yourself, you do not wish him so inordinately well.

Whereas if he does not belong to the same church as yourself, and if, in addition, he does things a little out of the ordinary, such as walk in the street without a hat, you do not wish him well at all. In any case, as regards your neighbor and yourself, although you have no desire to see his house burn down or his children killed in a motor accident, a most modest worldly success will do very well for him, as far as you are concerned. For these and other reasons sufficiently naïve and self-revealing, you take it as a matter of course that, of the many persons involved in the recent agitation in Boston, those who were not in the thing for what they could get out of it were revolutionists of the most flagrant dye. It is impossible for you to conceive that men could weep in public and women permit themselves to be thrown in jail because (as it seemed to them) the blue hem of Justice was being dragged in the mire. In the world in which you live Justice is a woman of stone above a court-house door.

As I said before, I am not sufficiently idealistic to share the political opinions of these men with whose fate I am concerned. It is impossible for me to be an Anarchist, for I do not believe in the essential goodness of man; man is quite patently, to my sight, the worm of the Moody and Sankey[2] hymns. Except for this fact, I should of course think twice before writing as I do. For, although I was born in this country, and am possessed of that simple right of the citizen to hold any opinions he may choose and to express any opinions he may hold, yet to avail one's self of this right and express opinions contrary to the opinions of the majority may become, as we have lately seen, a folly punishable by the extreme correction. For surely you are not still insisting that these two poor wretches were put to death solely for the crime of murder? You and I both know that we must be careful, not only what we do, but also what we say, and even what we think, if we would not have one day our sleep brutally broken in upon and ourselves rudely forced to enter a place where we do not at all wish to go. And surely you will not deny that, if you would remain undisturbed, it is more important to be on the side of the established order of things than to be innocent of even the grossest crime?

As I said before, I dare say these things because I am not an Anarchist; but I dare say them for another reason, too: because my personal physical freedom, my power to go in and out when I choose, my personal life even, is no longer quite as important to me as it once was. Death even, that outrageous intrusion, appears to me at moments, and more especially when I think of what happened in Boston two months ago, death appears to me somewhat as a darkened room, in which one might rest one's battered temples out of the world's way, leaving the sweeping of the crossings to those who still think it important that the crossings be swept. As if indeed it mattered the least bit in the world whether the crossings be clean or foul, when of all the people passing to and fro there in the course of an eight-hour day not one out of ten thousand has a spark of true courage in his heart, or any love at all, beyond the love of a cat for the fire, for any earthly creature other than himself. The world, the physical world, and that once was all in all to me, has at moments such as these no road through a wood, no stretch of shore, that can bring me comfort. The beauty of these things can no longer at such moments make up to me at all for the ugliness of man, his cruelty, his greed, his lying face.

---

2. *Moody and Sankey.* Evangelist Dwight L. Moody and composer Ira D. Sankey wrote gospel hymns and conducted several evangelical crusades together.

FOR EXPLORATION

1. Why has this essay been titled "Fear"?

2. Does this essay gain or lose force because it glosses over details of the case it refers to? Why?

3. What type of person, what style of living, does this essay attack? From the issues raised in this essay, and from what you know of its historical background, is such an attack justified in your opinion?

4. To what audience is this essay addressed? What type of person might be expected to be most sympathetic to its point of view?

5. Millay argues that the word "Anarchist" was widely misused, its meaning completely distorted. Can you think of any words, likewise misapplied and emotionally loaded, in use today? How do such terms affect our thinking?

6. What is the tone of the last sentence? Has this tone been sustained throughout the whole essay? Or do other tones intrude?

7. "Mankind cannot bear too much reality." Discuss the essay in terms of this statement.

CREATIVE RESPONSE

Millay's essay was written in response to a social and human issue over which there had been much sharply divided opinion, and toward which many had grown quite apathetic. Pick one issue which you think has been neglected recently by the public, and revive argument about it with an imaginative opponent. What responses must you anticipate from him? How would you handle the response: "I don't want to hear any more about it—I'm sick and tired of the whole subject"? When thinking about your presentation, consider whether you want to use highly emotional language to make your point or whether calm argumentation would be better suited to your purpose. Which approach has Millay used?

MILLAY PROTESTING THE EXECUTION OF
SACCO AND VANZETTI IN 1927—UPI

H. L. Mencken

from

THE AMERICAN LANGUAGE

THE HALLMARKS OF AMERICAN

THE characters chiefly noted in American English by all who have discussed it are, first, its general uniformity throughout the country; second, its impatient disregard for grammatical, syntactical and phonological rule and precedent; and third, its large capacity (distinctly greater than that of the English of present-day England) for taking in new words and phrases from outside sources, and for manufacturing them of its own materials.

The first of these characters has struck every observer, native and foreign. In place of the discordant local dialects of all the other major countries, including England, we have a general *Volkssprache*[1] for the whole nation, and if it is conditioned at all it is only by minor differences in pronunciation and vocabulary, and by the linguistic struggles of various groups of newcomers. No other country can show such linguistic solidarity, nor any approach to it—not even Canada, for there a large minority of the population resists speaking English altogether. The Little Russian of the Ukraine is unintelligible to the citizen of Moscow; the Northern Italian can scarcely follow a conversation in Sicilian; the Low German from Hamburg is a foreigner in Munich; the Breton flounders in Gascony. Even in the United Kingdom there are wide divergences.[2] "When we remember," says the New International Encyclopedia, "that the dialects of the counties in England have marked differences—so marked, indeed, that it may be doubted whether a Lancashire miner and a Lincolnshire farmer could understand each other—we may well be proud that our vast country has, strictly speaking, only one language." There are some regional peculiarities in pronunciation and intonation, and they will be examined in some detail in Chapter VII, but when it comes to the words they habitually use and the way they use them all Americans, even the less tutored, follow pretty much the same line. A Boston taxi-driver could go to work in Chicago or San Francisco without running any risk of misunderstanding his new fares. Once he had flattened his *a*'s a bit and picked up a few dozen localisms, he would be, to all linguistic intents and purposes, fully naturalized.

Of the intrinsic differences that separate American from English the chief have their roots in the obvious disparity between the environment and traditions of the American people since the Seventeenth Century and those of the English. The latter have lived under a relatively stable social order, and it has impressed upon their souls their characteristic respect for what is customary and of good report. Until the World War brought chaos to most of their institutions, their whole lives were regulated, perhaps more than those of any other people save the Spaniards, by a regard for precedent. The Americans, though partly of the same blood, have felt no such restraint, and acquired no such habit of conformity. On the contrary, they have plunged to the other extreme, for the conditions of life in their country have put a high value upon the precisely opposite qualities of curiosity and daring, and so they have acquired that character of restlessness, that impatience of forms, that disdain of the dead hand, which now broadly marks them. From the first, says a literary historian, they have been "less phlegmatic, less conservative than the English. There were climatic influences, it may be; there was surely a spirit of intensity everywhere that made for short effort."[3] Thus, in the arts, and thus in business, in politics, in daily intercourse, in habits of mind and speech. The American is not, of course, lacking in

From "The Hallmarks of American," in THE AMERICAN LANGUAGE, 4th Edition by H. L. Mencken. Copyright 1936 and renewed 1964 by August Mencken and Mercantile Safe Deposit and Trust Co. Reprinted by permission of Alfred A. Knopf, Inc.

1. *Volkssprache*, common language. [*German*]
2. *Even in . . . divergences.* W. W. Skeat distinguishes 9 principal dialects in Scotland, 3 in Ireland, and 30 in England and Wales. See his *English Dialects From the Eighth Century to the Present Day;* Cambridge, 1911, p. 107 ff. [*Mencken's note*]
3. *"less phlegmatic . . . effort."* F. L. Pattee: *A History of American Literature Since 1870;* New York, 1916. See also *The American Novel*, by Carl Van Doren; New York, 1921. [*Mencken's note*]

a capacity for discipline; he has it highly developed; he submits to leadership readily, and even to tyranny. But, by a curious twist, it is not the leadership that is old and decorous that commonly fetches him, but the leadership that is new and extravagant. He will resist dictation out of the past, but he will follow a new messiah with almost Russian willingness, and into the wildest vagaries of economics, religion, morals and speech. A new fallacy in politics spreads faster in the United States than anywhere else on earth, and so does a new fashion in hats, or a new revelation of God, or a new means of killing time, or a new shibboleth, or metaphor, or piece of slang. Thus the American, on his linguistic side, likes to make his language as he goes along, and not all the hard work of the schoolmarm can hold the business back. A novelty loses nothing by the fact that it is a novelty; it rather gains something, and particularly if it meets the national fancy for the terse, the vivid, and, above all, the bold and imaginative. The characteristic American habit of reducing complex concepts to the starkest abbreviations was already noticeable in colonial times, and such highly typical Americanisms as *O.K.*, *N.G.*, and *P.D.Q.*,[4] have been traced back to the early days of the Republic. Nor are the influences that shaped these tendencies invisible today, for institution-making is yet going on, and so is language-making. In so modest an operation as that which has evolved *bunco* from *buncombe* and *bunk* from *bunco* there is evidence of a phenomenon which the philologian recognizes as belonging to the most lusty stages of speech.

But of more importance than the sheer inventions, if only because much more numerous, are the extensions of the vocabulary, both absolutely and in ready workableness, by the devices of rhetoric. The American, from the beginning, has been the most ardent of recorded rhetoricians. His politics bristles with pungent epithets; his whole history has been bedizened with tall talk; his fundamental institutions rest far more upon brilliant phrases than upon logical ideas. And in small things as in large he exercises continually an incomparable capacity for projecting hidden and often fantastic relationships into arresting parts of speech. Such a term as *rubberneck* is almost a complete treatise on American psychology; it reveals the national habit of mind more clearly than any labored inquiry could ever reveal it. It has in it precisely the boldness and contempt for ordered

forms that are so characteristically American, and it has too the grotesque humor of the country, and the delight in devastating opprobriums, and the acute feeling for the succinct and savory. The same qualities are in *rough-house, water-wagon, has-been, lame-duck, speed-cop* and a thousand other such racy substantives, and in all the great stock of native verbs and adjectives. There is indeed, but a shadowy boundary in these new coinages between the various parts of speech. *Corral,* borrowed from the Spanish, immediately becomes a verb and the father of an adjective. *Bust,* carved out of *burst,* erects itself into a noun. *Bum,* coming by way of an earlier *bummer* from the German, becomes noun, adjective, verb and adverb. Verbs are fashioned out of substantives by the simple process of prefixing the preposition: *to engineer, to stump, to hog, to style, to author.* Others grow out of an intermediate adjective, as *to boom.* Others are made by torturing nouns with harsh affixes, as *to burglarize* and *to itemize,* or by groping for the root, as *to resurrect* and *to jell.* Yet others are changed from intransitive to transitive; a sleeping-car *sleeps* thirty passengers. So with the adjectives. They are made of substantives unchanged: *codfish, jitney.* Or by bold combinations: *down-and-out, up-state, flat-footed.* Or by shading down suffixes to a barbaric simplicity: *scary, classy, tasty.* Or by working over adverbs until they tremble on the brink between adverb and adjective: *right, sure* and *near* are examples.

All these processes, of course, are also to be observed in the history of the English of England; at the time of its sturdiest growth they were in the most active possible being. They are, indeed, common to all tongues; "the essence of language," says Dr. Jespersen,[5] "is activity." But if you will put the English of today beside the American of today you will see at once how much more forcibly they are in operation in the latter than in the former. The standard Southern dialect of English has been arrested in its growth by its purists and grammarians, and burdened with irrational affectations by fashionable pretension. It shows no living change since the reign of Samuel Johnson.[6] Its tendency is to combat all that expansive gusto which made for its pliancy and

---

4. *O.K., N.G., and P.D.Q.,* okay, no good, and pretty damn quick.
5. *Dr. Jespersen,* Jens Otto Harry Jespersen (1860–1943), a Danish philologist who invented an international language, Novial.
6. *Samuel Johnson* (1709–1784), an English lexicographer who completed compiling a dictionary in 1755.

resilience in the days of Shakespeare.[7] In place of the old loose-footedness there is set up a preciosity which, in one direction, takes the form of clumsy artificialities in the spoken language, and in another shows itself in the even clumsier Johnsonese of so much current English writing—the Jargon denounced by Sir Arthur Quiller-Couch in his Cambridge lectures. This "infirmity of speech" Quiller-Couch finds "in parliamentary debates and in the newspapers; . . . it has become the medium through which Boards of Government, County Councils, Syndicates, Committees, Commercial Firms, express the processes as well as the conclusions of their thought, and so voice the reason of their being." Distinct from journalese, the two yet overlap, "and have a knack of assimilating each other's vices."[8]

American, despite the gallant efforts of the pedagogues, has so far escaped any such suffocating formalization. We, too, of course, have our occasional practitioners of the authentic English Jargon, but in the main our faults lie in precisely the opposite direction. That is to say, we incline toward a directness of statement which, at its greatest, lacks restraint and urbanity altogether, and toward a hospitality which often admits novelties for the mere sake of their novelty, and is quite uncritical of the difference between a genuine improvement in succinctness and clarity, and mere extravagant raciness. "The tendency," says one English observer, "is . . . to consider the speech of any man, as any man himself, as good as any other."[9] The Americans, adds a Scots professor, "are determined to hack their way through the language, as their ancestors through forests, regardless of the valuable growths that may be sacrificed in blazing the trail."[10] But this Scot dismisses the English neologisms of the day, when ranged beside the American stock, as "dwiny, feeble stuff"; "it is to America," he admits, "that we must chiefly look in future for the replenishment and freshening of our language. . . ."

Let American confront a novel problem alongside English, and immediately its superior imaginativeness and resourcefulness become obvious. *Movie* is better than *cinema;* and the English begin to admit the fact by adopting the word; it is not only better American, it is better English. *Bill-board* is better than *hoarding. Office-holder* is more honest, more picturesque, more thoroughly Anglo-Saxon than *public-servant. Stem-winder* somehow has more life

in it, more fancy and vividness, than the literal *keyless-watch.* Turn to the terminology of *railroading* (itself, by the way, an Americanism): its creation fell upon the two peoples equally, but they tackled the job independently. The English, seeking a figure to denominate the wedge-shaped fender in front of a locomotive, called it a *plough;* the Americans, characteristically, gave it the far more pungent name of *cow-catcher.* So with the casting which guides the wheels from one rail to another. The English called it a *crossing-plate;* the Americans, more responsive to the suggestion in its shape, called it a *frog.* American is full of what Bret Harte[11] called the "saber-cuts of Saxon"; it meets Montaigne's[12] ideal of "a succulent and nervous speech, short and compact, not as much delicated and combed out as vehement and brusque, rather arbitrary than monotonous, not pedantic but soldierly, as Suetonius[13] called Cæsar's Latin." One pictures the common materials of English dumped into a pot, exotic flavorings added, and the bubblings assiduously and expectantly skimmed. What is old

---

7. *Its tendency . . . Shakespeare.* Rather curiously, the two authorities who were most influential, during the nineteenth century, in keeping it to a rigid pattern were both Americans. They were Lindley Murray (1745–1826) and Joseph E. Worcester (1784–1865). Murray, a Pennsylvanian, went to England after the Revolution, and in 1795 published his *Grammar of the English Language.* It had an extraordinary sale in England, and was accepted as the court of last resort in usage down to quite recent times. Worcester's *Universal and Critical Dictionary of the English Language,* 1846, divided the honors of authority in England with B. H. Smart's *Dictionary,* published during the same year. It was extensively pirated. Thus, says Thomas R. Lounsbury (*The Standard of Pronunciation in English,* New York, 1904, p. 220), "the Londoner frequently got his pure London pronunciation from a citizen of this country who was never outside of New England for more than a few months of his life." Worcester was also accepted at Harvard and at the University of Virginia, but elsewhere in the United States Webster prevailed. [*Mencken's note*]
8. *This "infirmity . . . vices."* See the chapter, "Interlude on Jargon," in Quiller-Couch's *On the Art of Writing;* New York, 1916. Appropriately enough, large parts of the learned critic's book are written in the very Jargon he attacks. See also Ch. VI of *Growth and Structure of the English Language,* by O. Jespersen, 3rd ed., rev.; Leipzig, 1919, especially p. 143ff. See also "Official English," in *English,* March, 1919, p. 7; April, p. 45, and August, p. 135, and "The Decay of Syntax," in the *London Times Literary Supplement,* May 8, 1919, p. 1. [*Mencken's note*]
9. *"The tendency . . . other."* Alexander Francis: *Americans: An Impression;* New York, 1900. [*Mencken's note*]
10. *The Americans . . . trail. Breaking Priscian's Head,* by J. Y. T. Greig; London, 1929. [*Mencken's note*]
11. *Bret Harte* (1836–1902), an American writer, especially of short stories.
12. *Montaigne,* Michel Eyquem de Montaigne (1533–1592), a French philosopher and essayist.
13. *Suetonius* (70 A.D.?–140 A.D.), a Roman historian and biographer. His most widely read work is *The Lives of the Caesars.*

and respected is already in decay the moment it comes into contact with what is new and vivid. "When we Americans are through with the English language," says Mr. Dooley,[14] "it will look as if it had been run over by a musical comedy. . . ." □

14. *Mr. Dooley*, Finley Peter Dunne (1867–1936). As Mr. Dooley he was known as the exponent of American-Irish humorous satire on current personages and events.

FOR EXPLORATION

1. (*a*) Why does Britain not have "one common" language? (*b*) Can you think of any regional variations in terminology (pertaining to items of food or drink, for instance) that demonstrate language diversity in the United States?
2. Why are the British less flexible than Americans in creating new terms, according to Mencken? Can you think of any recent examples of British slang (from rock music or fashions) that might indicate increased flexibility in Britain?
3. Would you describe American English as still vigorous and active today? What areas of the language seem to be changing the fastest? What contributions have various ethnic groups made?

CREATIVE RESPONSE

Choose a dozen popular or current terms you use ("freak-out," "sit-in," "bird-brain," "gross," for example), and compare them with their standard synonyms. Discuss why they may well be more descriptive, more picturesque, and have more impact than the standard words.

Henry Louis Mencken   1880 / 1956

H. L. Mencken was born in Baltimore and lived there all his life. At the age of nineteen, without having attended college, he joined the staff of the Baltimore *Morning Herald* and within a few years had risen to the rank of editor. When the paper closed in 1906 he moved to the Baltimore *Sun*, an association which would last for thirty-five years. His weekly newspaper column, syndicated across the country, and his editorship of the *American Mercury* magazine (1924–1933) made Mencken enormously influential. He attacked Puritanism, prohibition, academicism, and "public agencies, all of which are muddle-headed and most of which are corrupt." And he did it with an ingenious and derisive wit. He was irascible, irreverent, outrageous, and mischievous.

A master of the language, Mencken also made a passionate study of it. *The American Language*, published in 1919 with two additional supplements in the 1940's, while full of the humor, bias, feuding, and festivity that is Mencken, is above all a scholarly and far-reaching work, the finest ever done on the subject.

With time, the cigar chomping lambaster of America's most cherished institutions found that many of his battles had been won and some of the others no longer mattered. His virulent opposition to Roosevelt's New Deal decreased his popularity and his influence gradually faded. In 1941 he gave up his regular column in the Baltimore *Sun* and two years later published the last of three autobiographical reminiscences: *Happy Days: 1880–1892* (1940), *Newspaper Days: 1889–1906* (1941), and *Heathen Days: 1890–1936* (1943).

After a cerebral thrombosis in 1948 he lived the remaining eight years as an invalid in his Baltimore home.

Archibald MacLeish[1]
ARS POETICA

A poem should be palpable and mute
As a globed fruit

Dumb
As old medallions to the thumb

5 Silent as the sleeve-worn stone
Of casement ledges where the moss has grown—

A poem should be wordless
As the flight of birds

A poem should be motionless in time
10 As the moon climbs

Leaving, as the moon releases
Twig by twig the night-entangled trees,

Leaving, as the moon behind the winter leaves,
Memory by memory the mind—

15 A poem should be motionless in time
As the moon climbs

A poem should be equal to:
Not true

For all the history of grief
20 An empty doorway and a maple leaf

For love
The leaning grasses and two lights above the sea—

A poem should not mean
But be

From COLLECTED POEMS OF ARCHIBALD MACLEISH 1917–1952, Houghton Mifflin Company.
1. For biography, see page 233 M.

Donald Stauffer

MACLEISH'S "ARS POETICA"

However we may interpret its significance, Mr. MacLeish has unmistakably given us his first demand in five overlapping adjectives: a poem should be palpable, mute, dumb, silent, and wordless. There can be no doubt that in these lines Mr. MacLeish has wished to give a general statement of the necessary qualities, or quality, of a poem. But immediately these ideas—and a quality must necessarily be an idea abstracted from some thing or some things more complex—are illustrated concretely, in images that might have been drawn from Keats or Tennyson or Rossetti,[1] and we have in the first section a globed fruit, old medallions, stone, and birds in flight. This tendency to think of the idea, or the quality, in concrete terms is carried even further by the modifying adjectives and phrases that will compel a more vivid realization of the object imagined as so very quiet. A poem is as silent as a stone. Such a comparison might be overlooked because we have heard the phrase "still as a stone" so

Reprinted from THE NATURE OF POETRY by Donald Stauffer. By permission of W. W. Norton & Company, Inc. Copyright 1946 by W. W. Norton & Company, Inc.
1. *Keats or Tennyson or Rossetti*, English poets; John Keats (1795–1821), Alfred Lord Tennyson (1809–1892), and Dante Gabriel Rossetti (1828–1882).

often. Therefore, to rouse our attention, the poem is as silent as a particular worn.stone; and to make us believe that it is worn the coined adjective "sleeve-worn" (akin to "thread-bare"? worn by sleeves resting upon it? worn out at elbow and cuff, like a sleeve?) turns us to yet another image from concrete experience. And then the sleeve-worn stone is particularized and modified by a tangible ledge, which in turn is modified by a tangible casement, and the whole is modified by an arresting specific detail, designed to catch or convince our imagination: "where the moss has grown."

The other sections develop in like fashion, but in place of the four similitudes of the first section, the second section repeats the same image—that a poem in some way is like the moon—four times. Here again the particular interpretation may vary from reader to reader, although most would probably feel that a poem wakens in the reader's consciousness memory after memory, complex, minute, and exact, just as moonlight, against the motionless, durable, illimitable night, etches out twigs and leaves and innumerable silhouettes. But all readers would agree that the writer is saying a poem is timeless, although even this idea is seemingly given more tangible form by translating it from time to space— "*motionless* in time." Particularly interesting is the device of suggesting timelessness through repetition rather than through change of images. In this section the final pair of lines mirrors the first, so that we are meant to feel, in the changeless concrete image of the moon, that time has not elapsed, or that if it has, it has made no difference, for the end and the beginning are the same.

The third section continues the minuet between meaning and its concrete embodiment. The first and fourth pairs of lines are direct statements, and as such, considered purely by themselves rather than in the light of the whole, are not poetic because they defy this very law of concreteness that the poem is designed to proclaim. Most readers would agree that they present the argument that a poem does not state its meaning directly, syllogistically, logically, rationally; its meaning rather exists in the recognition of unstated, sometimes unformulated, equivalences between its concrete symbols and what they symbolize. In this last section of the poem, the two middle pairs of lines are excellent illustrations of the doctrine of concreteness which Mr. MacLeish has so unconcretely expounded in the first pair and the last. Within a poem we come upon an empty doorway and a maple leaf; in the crucible of our imagination these objects assume a general significance and become "all the history of grief." Similarly the leaning grasses and two lights above the sea become in our minds the symbols of love. This is the way poetry works. The significance of a poem to any individual reader need be no less sharp than the significance of a mathematical proposition, though within limits this significance may vary from reader to reader as the mathematical proposition cannot do. But the *technique* of expressing significance in poetry demands sharp, specific *detail*. The concrete symbols, the things of this world as we know it— these are the invariable stuff of poetry, as, to the same extent, they need be of no other form of verbal communication. Poetry must operate through such concrete symbols. □

FOR EXPLORATION

MacLeish gives us a serious poem, and Stauffer gives us a serious bit of literary criticism. In what ways does the criticism contribute to your enjoyment or understanding of the poem? Do you feel the criticism detracts from your enjoyment of the poem in any way? How?

Donald Alfred Stauffer   1902 / 1952

Donald Stauffer was an educator, critic, novelist, and poet. After being valedictorian of Princeton's Class of '23, he went on to receive a Rhodes scholarship, a Guggenheim fellowship, and, in 1928, his Ph.D. Stauffer then joined the English department at Princeton University and eventually rose to its chairmanship. His teaching was interrupted for three years during World War II when he served in the South Pacific with air combat intelligence. He died of a heart attack while teaching in England as the Eastman Professor from the United States to Oxford University.

Theodore Spencer

HOW TO CRITICIZE A POEM

1.

I propose to examine the following poem:

Thirty days hath September,
April, June, and November:
All the rest have thirty-one,
Excepting February alone,
Which has only eight and a score
Till leap-year gives it one day more.

2.

The previous critics who have studied this poem, Coleridge[1] among them, have failed to explain what we may describe as its fundamental *dynamic*.[2] This I now propose to do. The first thing to observe is the order in which the names (or verbal constructs) of the months are presented. According to the prose meaning—what I shall henceforth call the prose-demand—"September" should not precede, it should follow "April," as a glance at the calendar will show. Indeed "September" should follow not only "April," it should also follow "June" if the prose-demand is to be properly satisfied. The prose order of the first two lines should therefore read: "Thirty days hath April, June, September, and November." That is the only sequence consonant with prose logic.

3.

Why then, we ask ourselves, did the poet violate what educated readers know to be the facts? Was he ignorant of the calendar, believing that September preceded April in the progress of the seasons? It is difficult to imagine that such was the case. We must find another explanation. It is here that the principle of dynamic analysis comes to our aid.

4.

Dynamic analysis proves that the most successful poetry achieves its effect by producing an *expectation* in the reader's mind before his sensibility is fully prepared to receive the full impact of the poem. The reader makes a *proto-response* which preconditions him to the total response toward which his fully equilibrized organs of apperception subconsciously tend. It is this proto-response which the poet has here so sensitively manipulated. The ordinary reader, trained only to prose-demands, expects the usual order of the months. But the poet's sensibility knows that poetic truth is more immediately effective than the truth of literal chronology. He does not *state* the inevitable sequence; he *prepares* us for it. In his profound analysis of the two varieties of mensual time, he puts the *gentlest* month first. (Notice how the harsh sound of "pt" in "September" is softened by the "e" sound on either side of it.) It is the month in which vegetation first begins to fade, but which does not as yet give us a sense of tragic fatality.

5.

Hence the poet prepares us, dynamically, for what is to follow. By beginning his list of the months *in medias res*,[3] he is enabled to return later to the beginning of the series of contrasts which is the subject of his poem. The analogy to the "Oedipus Rex" of Euripides and the "Iliad" of Dante[4] at once becomes clear. Recent criticism has only too often failed to observe that these works also illustrate the dynamic method by beginning in the middle of things. It is a striking fact, hitherto (I believe) unnoticed, that a Latin poem called the "Aeneid"[5] does much the

---

"How To Criticize a Poem" by Theodore Spencer from THE NEW REPUBLIC (December 6, 1943).
1. *Coleridge*, Samuel Taylor Coleridge (1772–1834), an English poet.
2. *dynamic*, that which causes the effect of movement or progression in a work.
3. *in medias res*, in the middle, without the formality of an introduction. [*Latin*]
4. the "Oedipus Rex" . . . Dante. Oedipus Rex is a Greek tragic drama by Sophocles, not Euripides, which related the tale of a man who unknowingly marries his mother. "The Illiad" is an epic poem by Homer, not Dante, which tells of the Trojan War.
5. the "Aeneid," an epic poem that recounts the wanderings of Aeneas and his companions through Carthage, Sicily, and Italy after the fall of Troy, and the wars preceding the founding of Rome.

same thing. We expect the author of that poem to begin with the departure of his hero from Troy, just as we expect the author of our poem to begin with "April." But in neither case is our expectation fulfilled. Cato,[6] the author of the "Aeneid," creates dynamic suspense by beginning with Aeneas in Carthage; our anonymous poet treats his readers' sensibilities in a similar fashion by beginning with "September," and then *going back* to "April" and "June."

6.

But the sensibility of the poet does not stop at this point. Having described what is true of *four* months, he disposes of *seven* more with masterly economy. In a series of pungent constructs his sensibility sums up their inexorable limitations: they *All* (the capitalization should be noted) "have thirty-one." The poet's sensibility communicates a feeling to the sensibility of the reader so that the sensibility of both, with reference to their previous but independent sensibilities, is fused into that momentary communion of sensibility which is the final sensibility that poetry can give both to the sensibility of the poet and the sensibility of the reader. The texture and structure of the poem have erupted into a major reaction. The ambiguity of equilibrium is achieved.

7.

Against these two groups of spatial, temporal and numerical measurements—one consisting of four months, the other of seven—the tragic individual, the sole exception, "February," is dramatically placed. February is "alone," is cut off from communion with his fellows. The tragic note is struck the moment "February" is mentioned. For the initial sound of the word "excepting" is "X," and as that sound strikes the sensibility of the reader's ear a number of associations subconsciously accumulate. We think of the spot, the murderous and lonely spot, which "X" has so frequently marked; we remember the examinations of our childhood where the wrong answers were implacably signaled with "X"; we think of ex-kings and exile, of lonely crossroads and executions, of the inexorable anonymity of those who cannot sign their names. . . .

8.

And yet the poet gives us one ray of hope, though it eventually proves to be illusory. The lonely "February" (notice how the "alone" in line four is echoed by the "only" in line five), the solitary and maladjusted individual who is obviously the hero and crucial figure of the poem, is not condemned to the routine which his fellows, in their different ways, must forever obey. Like Hamlet, he has a capacity for change. He is a symbol of individualism, and the rhythm of the lines which are devoted to him signalizes a gayety, however desperate, which immediately wins our sympathy and reverberates profoundly in our sensibility.

9.

But (and this is the illusion to which I have previously referred) in spite of all his variety, his capacity for change, "February" cannot quite accomplish (and in this his tragedy consists) the *quantitative* value of the society in which circumstances have put him. No matter how often he may alternate from twenty-eight to twenty-nine (the poet, with his exquisite sensibility, does not actually *mention* those humiliating numbers), he can never achieve the bourgeois, if anonymous, security of "thirty-one," nor equal the more modest and aristocratic assurance of "thirty." Decade after decade, century after century, millennium after millennium, he is eternally frustrated. The only symbol of change in a changeless society, he is continually beaten down. Once every four years he tries to rise, to achieve the high, if delusive, level of his dreams. But he fails. He is always one day short, and the three years before the recurrence of his next effort are a sad interval in which the remembrance of previous disappointment melts into the futility of hope, only to sink back once more into the frustration of despair. Like Tantalus[7] he is forever stretched upon a wheel.

10.

So far I have been concerned chiefly with the

6. *Cato.* The "Aeneid" was written by Vergil, not Cato.
7. *Tantalus.* According to Greek mythology he was punished in the lower world by being placed in the midst of a lake whose waters reached to his chin but receded whenever he tried to quench his thirst. Over his head hung branches laden with fruit which receded when he tried to grasp them.

dynamic *analysis* of the poem. Further study should reveal the *synthesis* which can be made on the basis of the analysis which my thesis has tentatively attempted to bring to an emphasis. This, perhaps, the reader with a proper sensibility can achieve for himself. ☐

FOR EXPLORATION

Unlike Stauffer's serious criticism (pages M 124–125 M), Spencer's piece is a **parody. Parody** is a species of humor whose aim is to deflate excessiveness or pretentiousness by the simple procedure of imitating the form, but filling that form with utter nonsense which sounds like the real thing. Find the most completely nonsensical (but seemingly profound) statement that Spencer makes, and analyze how it illustrates excessiveness, how it is ridiculous. Have you read any critical article lately that you could likewise deflate? Try your hand at parodying a work of your choice.

CREATIVE RESPONSE

Find a collection of parodies in your library, and select from it those pieces which you find funniest. Consider what makes them pleasing: (1) Must you be familiar with the work parodied to enjoy the parody? (2) Is a parody of a really excellent work of art or criticism possible? (3) Would a parody of a work which you really admire or like offend you? (4) Why are some parodies failures?

Theodore Spencer   1902 / 1949

A poet whose work was lyric and metaphysical, Theodore Spencer was also a critic and teacher. He graduated from Princeton University in the same class as Donald Stauffer and went on to earn his Ph.D. at Harvard. Most of his adult life was spent teaching at Harvard and in 1946 he was designated the Boyleston Professor of Rhetoric and Oratory. While his primary field of study was Elizabethan literature, he was also an authority on the contemporary novel and modern poetry. Like Stauffer he died in middle age of a heart attack.

BIOGRAPHY

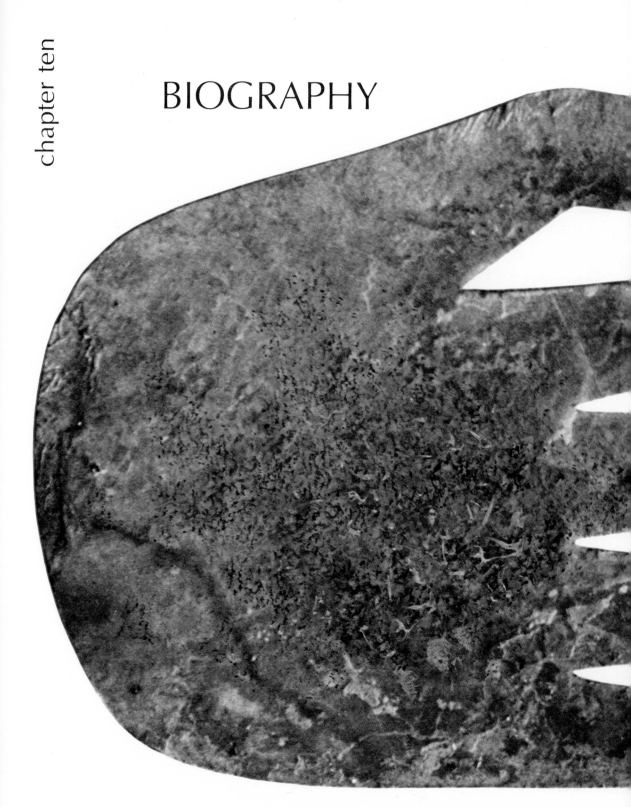

PREHISTORIC MARBLE HAND—COURTESY OF THE FIELD MUSEUM OF NATURAL HISTORY, CHICAGO

James Baldwin

from

NOTES OF A NATIVE SON

AUTOBIOGRAPHICAL NOTES

I was born in Harlem thirty-one years ago. I began plotting novels at about the time I learned to read. The story of my childhood is the usual bleak fantasy, and we can dismiss it with the restrained observation that I certainly would not consider living it again. In those days my mother was given to the exasperating and mysterious habit of having babies. As they were born, I took them over with one hand and held a book with the other. The children probably suffered, though they have since been kind enough to deny it, and in this way I read *Uncle Tom's Cabin* and *A Tale of Two Cities* over and over and over again; in this way, in fact, I read just about everything I could get my hands on—except the Bible, probably because it was the only book I was encouraged to read. I must also confess that I wrote —a great deal—and my first professional triumph, in any case, the first effort of mine to be seen in print, occurred at the age of twelve or thereabouts, when a short story I had written about the Spanish revolution won some sort of prize in an extremely short-lived church newspaper. I remember the story was censored by the lady editor, though I don't remember why, and I was outraged.

Also wrote plays, and songs, for one of which I received a letter of congratulations from Mayor La Guardia,[1] and poetry, about which the less said, the better. My mother was delighted by all these goings-on, but my father wasn't; he wanted me to be a preacher. When I was fourteen I became a preacher, and when I was seventeen I stopped. Very shortly thereafter I left home. For God knows how long I struggled with the world of commerce and industry— I guess they would say they struggled with *me*—and when I was about twenty-one I had enough done of a novel to get a Saxton Fellowship. When I was twenty-two the fellowship was over, the novel turned out to be unsalable, and I started waiting on tables in a Village restaurant and writing book reviews—mostly, as it turned out, about the Negro problem, concerning which the color of my skin made me automatically an expert. Did another book, in company with photographer Theodore Pelatowski, about the storefront churches in Harlem. This book met exactly the same fate as my first—fellowship, but no sale. (It was a Rosenwald Fellowship.) By the time I was twenty-four I had decided to stop reviewing books about the Negro problem—which, by this time, was only slightly less horrible in print than it was in life— and I packed my bags and went to France, where I finished, God knows how, *Go Tell It on the Mountain*.[2]

Any writer, I suppose, feels that the world into which he was born is nothing less than a conspiracy against the cultivation of his talent—which attitude certainly has a great deal to support it. On the other hand, it is only because the world looks on his talent with such a frightening indifference that the artist is compelled to make his talent important. So that any writer, looking back over even so short a span of time as I am here forced to assess, finds that the things which hurt him and the things which helped him cannot be divorced from each other; he could be helped in a certain way only because he was hurt in a certain way; and his help is simply to be enabled to move from one conundrum to the next—one is tempted to say that he moves from one disaster to the next. When one begins looking for influences one finds them by the score. I haven't thought much about my own, not enough anyway; I hazard that the King James Bible, the rhetoric of the store-front church, something ironic and violent and perpetually understated in Negro speech—and something of Dickens' love for bravura—have something to do with me today; but I wouldn't stake my life on it. Likewise, innumerable people have helped me in many ways; but finally, I suppose, the most difficult (and most rewarding) thing in my life has been the fact that I was born a Negro and was forced, therefore, to effect some kind of truce with this reality. (Truce, by the way, is the best one can hope for.)

From NOTES OF A NATIVE SON by James Baldwin. Copyright © 1955 by James Baldwin. Reprinted by permission of Beacon Press and Michael Joseph Ltd.
1. *Mayor La Guardia.* Fiorello La Guardia (1882–1947) was mayor of New York from 1934 to 1945.
2. *Go Tell It on the Mountain*, a novel published in 1953 dealing with Negro life in the United States. With it Baldwin's reputation was established.

One of the difficulties about being a Negro writer (and this is not special pleading, since I don't mean to suggest that he has it worse than anybody else) is that the Negro problem is written about so widely. The bookshelves groan under the weight of information, and everyone therefore considers himself informed. And this information, furthermore, operates usually (generally, popularly) to reinforce traditional attitudes. Of traditional attitudes there are only two— For or Against—and I, personally, find it difficult to say which attitude has caused me the most pain. I am speaking as a writer; from a social point of view I am perfectly aware that the change from ill-will to good-will, however motivated, however imperfect, however expressed, is better than no change at all.

But it is part of the business of the writer—as I see it—to examine attitudes, to go beneath the surface, to tap the source. From this point of view the Negro problem is nearly inaccessible. It is not only written about so widely; it is written about so badly. It is quite possible to say that the price a Negro pays for becoming articulate is to find himself, at length, with nothing to be articulate about. ("You taught me language," says Caliban to Prospero,[3] "and my profit on't is I know how to curse.") Consider: the tremendous social activity that this problem generates imposes on whites and Negroes alike the necessity of looking forward, of working to bring about a better day. This is fine, it keeps the waters troubled; it is all, indeed, that has made possible the Negro's progress. Nevertheless, social affairs are not generally speaking the writer's prime concern, whether they ought to be or not; it is absolutely necessary that he establish between himself and these affairs a distance which will allow, at least, for clarity, so that before he can look forward in any meaningful sense, he must first be allowed to take a long look back. In the context of the Negro problem neither whites nor blacks, for excellent reasons of their own, have the faintest desire to look back; but I think that the past is all that makes the present coherent, and further, that the past will remain horrible for exactly as long as we refuse to assess it honestly.

I know, in any case, that the most crucial time in my own development came when I was forced to recognize that I was a kind of bastard of the West; when I followed the line of my past I did not find myself in Europe but in Africa. And this meant that in some subtle way, in a really profound way, I brought to Shakespeare, Bach, Rembrandt, to the stones of Paris, to the cathedral at Chartres, and to the Empire State Building, a special attitude. These were not really my creations, they did not contain my history; I might search in them in vain forever for any reflection of myself. I was an interloper; this was not my heritage. At the same time I had no other heritage which I could possibly hope to use—I had certainly been unfitted for the jungle or the tribe. I would have to appropriate these white centuries, I would have to make them mine—I would have to accept my special attitude, my special place in this scheme—otherwise I would have no place in *any* scheme. What was the most difficult was the fact that I was forced to admit something I had always hidden from myself, which the American Negro has had to hide from himself as the price of his public progress; that I hated and feared white people. This did not mean that I loved black people; on the contrary, I despised them, possibly because they failed to produce Rembrandt. In effect, I hated and feared the world. And this meant, not only that I thus gave the world an altogether murderous power over me, but also that in such a self-destroying limbo I could never hope to write.

One writes out of one thing only—one's own experience. Everything depends on how relentlessly one forces from this experience the last drop, sweet or bitter, it can possibly give. This is the only real concern of the artist, to recreate out of the disorder of life that order which is art. The difficulty then, for me, of being a Negro writer was the fact that I was, in effect, prohibited from examining my own experience too closely by the tremendous demands and the very real dangers of my social situation.

I don't think the dilemma outlined above is uncommon. I do think, since writers work in the disastrously explicit medium of language, that it goes a little way towards explaining why, out of the enormous resources of Negro speech and life, and despite the example of Negro music, prose written by Negroes has been generally speaking so pallid and so harsh. I have not written about being a Negro at such length because I expect that to be my only subject, but only because it was the gate I had to unlock before I could hope to write about anything else. I don't think that the Negro problem in America can be even discussed coherently without bearing

---

3. *Caliban . . . Prospero.* In William Shakespeare's *Tempest,* Caliban is a deformed slave of Prospero, the rightful Duke of Milan, who was deposed by his brother and the King of Naples.

in mind its context; its context being the history, traditions, customs, the moral assumptions and preoccupations of the country; in short, the general social fabric. Appearances to the contrary, no one in America escapes its effects and everyone in America bears some responsibility for it. I believe this the more firmly because it is the overwhelming tendency to speak of this problem as though it were a thing apart. But in the work of Faulkner, in the general attitude and certain specific passages in Robert Penn Warren, and, most significantly, in the advent of Ralph Ellison,[4] one sees the beginnings—at least—of a more genuinely penetrating search. Mr. Ellison, by the way, is the first Negro novelist I have ever read to utilize in language, and brilliantly, some of the ambiguity and irony of Negro life.

About my interests: I don't know if I have any, unless the morbid desire to own a sixteen-millimeter camera and make experimental movies can be so classified. Otherwise, I love to eat and drink—it's my melancholy conviction that I've scarcely ever had enough to eat (this is because it's *impossible* to eat enough if you're worried about the next meal)— and I love to argue with people who do not disagree with me too profoundly, and I love to laugh. I do *not* like bohemia, or bohemians, I do not like people whose principal aim is pleasure, and I do not like people who are *earnest* about anything. I don't like people who like me because I'm a Negro; neither do I like people who find in the same accident grounds for contempt. I love America more than any other country in the world, and, exactly for this reason, I insist on the right to criticize her perpetually. I think all theories are suspect, that the finest principles may have to be modified, or may even be pulverized by the demands of life, and that one must find, therefore, one's own moral center and move through the world hoping that this center will guide one aright. I consider that I have many responsibilities, but none greater than this: to last, as Hemingway[5] says, and get my work done.

I want to be an honest man and a good writer. □

---

4. *Faulkner . . . Robert Penn Warren . . . Ralph Ellison.* William Faulkner (1897–1962), Robert Penn Warren (1905–   ), and Ralph Ellison (1914–   ) are American writers whose subject matter deals with the American Negro. Of the three, only Ralph Ellison is himself Black.
5. *Hemingway,* Ernest Hemingway (1899–1961), an American novelist and short-story writer.

WIDE WORLD PHOTOS

FOR EXPLORATION

1. Writers have remarked, time and again, that serious writing is the hardest work on earth. (*a*) What aspects of this autobiography bear out this observation? (*b*) From your own experience, would you agree or disagree? Why?
2. (*a*) What attitude does Baldwin take toward his early attempts at writing? (*b*) How is his attitude toward his role as a mature writer different? (*c*) What impression do you get of the man who wrote these statements?
3. What parts of this piece would you cite to emphasize its honesty and directness?
4. Compare Baldwin's report on the dilemmas of his racial identity with Countee Cullen's description of his in "Heritage" (pages M 206–207 M). (*a*) What similarities do you find? Are there any significant differences in point of view? (*b*) Which piece has the stronger resolution?

CREATIVE RESPONSE

In the next-to-final paragraph, Baldwin writes a *credo*, a statement of his beliefs. Try writing your own credo, following Baldwin's concise and direct manner.

James Baldwin   1924 /

James Baldwin was born in New York City and raised in Harlem. The son of a clergyman, he spent three years while still in high school as a Baptist preacher before a major reexamination of his beliefs caused him to leave the church. After graduation he moved from one odd job to another. He wrote in his free time, but his first novel, completed at the age of twenty-two, was a failure. Two years later, seeking a more relaxed racial climate where he might come to grips with himself as an individual rather than an abstraction, Baldwin left for Europe. He lived for ten years in Paris and while there produced *Go Tell It on the Mountain* (1953), *Giovanni's Room* (1956), and *Notes of a Native Son* (1955), a collection of essays from which "Autobiographical Notes" is taken. The success of these works quickly established Baldwin as one of America's finest new writers.

He has, since those years in France, lived in America, for a time in Istanbul, and now once again in Paris. His writing has, if anything, improved and branched out to include plays, the most notable being *Blues for Mr. Charlie* produced in 1964. In 1962 he published what many consider his finest novel to date, *Another Country*. But despite the popularity of his fiction, it seems increasingly likely that he will be remembered first for the brilliance of his essays. *The Fire Next Time* (1963) is a widely recognized masterpiece.

John Dos Passos

ARCHITECT

A muggy day in late spring in eighteen eighty-seven a tall youngster of eighteen with fine eyes and a handsome arrogant way of carrying his head arrived in Chicago with seven dollars left in his pocket from buying his ticket from Madison with some cash he'd got by pawning Plutarch's *Lives*, a Gibbon's *Decline and Fall of the Roman Empire* and an old furcollared coat.

Before leaving home to make himself a career in an architect's office (there was no architecture course at Wisconsin to clutter his mind with stale Beaux Arts drawings); the youngster had seen the dome of the new State Capitol in Madison collapse on account of bad rubblework in the piers, some thieving contractors' skimping materials to save the politicians their rakeoff, and perhaps a trifling but deadly error in the architect's plans;

he never forgot the roar of burst masonry, the flying plaster, the soaring dustcloud, the mashed bodies of the dead and dying being carried out, set faces livid with plasterdust.

Walking round downtown Chicago, crossing and recrossing the bridges over the Chicago River in the jingle and clatter of traffic, the rattle of vans and loaded wagons and the stamping of big drayhorses and the hooting of towboats with barges and the rumbling whistle of lakesteamers waiting for the draw,

he thought of the great continent stretching a thousand miles east and south and north, three thousand miles west, and everywhere, at mineheads, on the shores of newlydredged harbors, along watercourses, at the intersections of railroads, sprouting

shacks roundhouses tipples grainelevators stores warehouses tenements, great houses for the wealthy set in broad treeshaded lawns, domed statehouses on hills, hotels churches operahouses auditoriums.

He walked with long eager steps

towards the untrammeled future opening in every direction for a young man who'd keep his hands to his work and his wits sharp to invent.

The same day he landed a job in an architect's office.

Frank Lloyd Wright was the grandson of a Welsh hatter and preacher who'd settled in a rich Wisconsin valley, Spring Valley, and raised a big family of farmers and preachers and schoolteachers there. Wright's father was a preacher too, a restless illadjusted Newenglander who studied medicine, preached in a Baptist church in Weymouth, Massachusetts, and then as a Unitarian in the middle west, taught music, read Sanskrit and finally walked out on his family.

Young Wright was born on his grandfather's farm, went to school in Weymouth and Madison, worked summers on a farm of his uncle's in Wisconsin.

His training in architecture was the reading of Viollet le Duc, the apostle of the thirteenth century and of the pure structural mathematics of gothic stonemasonry, and the seven years he worked with Louis Sullivan in the office of Adler and Sullivan in Chicago. (It was Louis Sullivan who, after Richardson,[1] invented whatever was invented in nineteenth-century architecture in America).

When Frank Lloyd Wright left Sullivan he had already launched a distinctive style, prairie architecture. In Oak Park he built broad suburban dwellings for rich men that were the first buildings to break the hold on American builders' minds of centuries of pastward routine, of the wornout capital and plinth and pediment dragged through the centuries from the Acropolis,[2] and the jaded traditional stencils of Roman masonry, the halfobliterated Palladian[3] copybooks.

Frank Lloyd Wright was cutting out a new avenue that led towards the swift constructions in glassbricks and steel

foreshadowed today.

Delightedly he reached out for the new materials, steel in tension, glass, concrete, the million new metals and alloys.

The son and grandson of preachers, he became a preacher in blueprints,

---

"Architect" by John Dos Passos from THE BIG MONEY. Copyright by H. Marston Smith and Elizabeth H. Dos Passos, co-executors of the estate of John R. Dos Passos. Reprinted by permission.
1. *Richardson*, Henry Hobson Richardson (1838–1886), an American architect who won several competitions for the designing of churches in Massachusetts.
2. *the Acropolis*, a small plateau in the heart of Athens where the Greeks created the most beautiful temples and statues in the ancient world.
3. *Palladian*, relating to the classic style in architecture based on the works of the Italian architect Anrea Palladio (1518–1580).

ONE OF FRANK LLOYD WRIGHT'S MOST CONTROVERSIAL BUILDINGS—THE SOLOMON R. GUGGENHEIM MUSEUM, NEW YORK—COMPLETED IN 1959. PHOTO BY BOB AMFT projecting constructions in the American future instead of the European past.

Inventor of plans,

plotter of tomorrow's girderwork phrases,

he preaches to the young men coming of age in the time of oppression, cooped up by the plasterboard partitions of finance routine, their lives and plans made poor by feudal levies of parasite money standing astride every process to shake down progress for the cutting of coupons:

The properly citified citizen has become a broker, dealing chiefly in human frailties or the ideas and inventions of others, a puller of levers, a presser of buttons of vicarious power, his by way of machine craft . . . and over beside him and beneath him, even in his heart as he sleeps, is the taximeter of rent, in some form to goad this anxious consumer's unceasing struggle for or against more or less merciful or merciless money increment.

To the young men who spend their days and nights drafting the plans for new *rented aggregates of rented cells upended on hard pavements,*

he preaches

the horizons

of his boyhood,

a future that is not the rise of a few points in a hundred selected stocks, or an increase in carloadings, or a multiplication of credit in the bank or a rise in the rate on callmoney,

but a new clean construction, from the ground up, based on uses and needs,

towards the American future instead of towards the painsmeared past of Europe and Asia. Usonia he calls the broad teeming band of this new nation across the enormous continent between Atlantic and Pacific. He preaches a project for Usonia:

It is easy to realize how the complexity of crude utilitarian construction in the mechanical infancy of our growth, like the crude scaffolding for some noble building, did violence to the landscape. . . . The crude purpose of pioneering days has been accomplished. The scaffolding may be taken down and the true work, the culture of a civilization, may appear.

Like the life of many a preacher, prophet, exhorter, Frank Lloyd Wright's life has been stormy. He has raised children, had rows with wives, overstepped boundaries, got into difficulties with the law, divorce-courts, bankruptcy, always the yellow press yapping at his heels, his misfortunes yelled out in headlines in the evening papers: affairs with women, the nightmare horror of the burning of his house in Wisconsin.

By a curious irony

the building that is most completely his is the Imperial Hotel in Tokyo that was one of the few structures to come unharmed through the earthquake of 1923 (the day the cable came telling him that the building had stood saving so many hundreds of lives he writes was one of his happiest days)

and it was reading in German that most Americans first learned of his work.

His life has been full of arrogant projects unaccomplished. (How often does the preacher hear his voice echo back hollow from the empty hall, the draftsman watch the dust fuzz over the carefully-contrived plans, the architect see the rolledup blueprints curl yellowing and brittle in the filingcabinet.)

Twice he's rebuilt the house where he works in his grandfather's valley in Wisconsin after fires and disasters that would have smashed most men forever.

He works in Wisconsin,

an erect spare whitehaired man, his sons are architects, apprentices from all over the world come to work with him,

drafting the new city (he calls it Broadacre City).

Near and Far are beaten (to imagine the new city you must blot out every ingrained habit of the past, build a nation from the ground up with the new tools). For the architect there are only uses:

the incredible multiplication of functions, strength and tension in metal,

the dynamo, the electric coil, radio, the photoelectric cell, the internalcombustion motor,

glass

concrete;

and needs. (Tell us, doctors of philosophy, what are the needs of a man. At least a man needs to be notjailed notafraid nothungry notcold not without love, not a worker for a power he has never seen

that cares nothing for the uses and needs of a man or a woman or a child.)

Building a building is building the lives of the workers and dwellers in the building.

The buildings determine civilization as the cells in the honeycomb the functions of bees.

Perhaps in spite of himself the arrogant draftsman,

the dilettante in concrete, the bohemian artist for wealthy ladies desiring to pay for prominence with the startling elaboration of their homes has been forced by the logic of uses and needs, by the lifelong struggle against the dragging undertow of money in mortmain,

to draft plans that demand for their fulfillment a new life;

only in freedom can we build the Usonian city. His plans are coming to life. His blueprints, as once Walt Whitman's words, stir the young men:—

Frank Lloyd Wright,
patriarch of the new building,
not without honor except in his own country.

□

FOR EXPLORATION

1. How did the architectural disaster in Madison influence Wright's choice of career?

2. Dos Passos quotes Frank Lloyd Wright's philosophy on two occasions (the passages in italics). (*a*) What problems concerning the conditions of modern living do these passages raise? (*b*) How does Wright see improved buildings as helping to solve these problems? (*c*) In your opinion have architectural developments over the past few years followed Wright's advice?

3. What is "Usonia"? How does this term reflect Wright's ideals for America and her people?

4. It has been said that Dos Passos' style did in prose what E. E. Cummings' did in poetry. Read the Cummings poem, "Chanson Innocente" (pages M 228/229 M), and identify the stylistic devices they have in common. What special effects are achieved by these devices?

CREATIVE RESPONSE

Locate source books on the history of modern architecture and on Frank Lloyd Wright's buildings. Study whatever descriptions, pictures, or plans of his work you can find, and then design your own single unit dwelling (a house, say, for the average family), keeping in mind the human needs this building must satisfy. What modern materials would you use? What would be the approximate cost involved for materials? How much land would the building need for the right "feel"? How would it "fit" the land? How would it reflect your ideals? Draw sketches and plans in as much detail as time will allow.

COURTESY OF THE AUTHOR'S ESTATE

PHILIPPE HALSMAN

John Roderigo Dos Passos   1896 / 1970

John Dos Passos was born in Chicago, educated abroad and in the United States. After graduating from Harvard he went to Spain to study architecture but soon entered World War I, first with the French ambulance service, later with the U.S. medical corps. After the conflict he traveled as a newspaper correspondent in Spain, Mexico, New York, and the Near East. He increasingly devoted time to his writing and after a number of less important novels, in 1925 published *Manhattan Transfer* depicting the complex life of modern New York City. With this success and such later works as the *U.S.A.* trilogy he influenced a whole generation of young writers.

Dos Passos in his youth was an advocate of the political left. He actively supported labor unions and in 1927 was twice arrested for demonstrating against the Sacco-Vanzetti trial. Over the years he grew disillusioned with the abuses of bureaucracy and his thinking gradually changed to that of a conservative.

Lorraine Hansberry

from

TO BE YOUNG, GIFTED AND BLACK

CHICAGO: SOUTHSIDE SUMMERS

1.

For some time now—I think since I was a child—I have been possessed of the desire to put down the stuff of my life. That is a commonplace impulse, apparently, among persons of massive self-interest; sooner or later we all do it. And, I am quite certain, there is only one internal quarrel: how much of the truth to tell? How much, how much, how much! It *is* brutal, in sober uncompromising moments, to reflect on the comedy of concern we all enact when it comes to our precious images!

Even so, when such vanity as propels the writing of such memoirs is examined, certainly one would wish at least to have some boast of social service-ability on one's side. I shall set down in these pages what shall seem to me to be the truth of my life and essences . . . which are to be found, first of all, on the Southside of Chicago, where I was born. . . .

2.

All travelers to my city should ride the elevated trains that race along the back ways of Chicago. The lives you can look into!

I think you could find the tempo of my people on their back porches. The honesty of their living is there in the shabbiness. Scrubbed porches that sag and look their danger. Dirty gray wood steps. And always a line of white and pink clothes scrubbed so well, waving in the dirty wind of the city.

My people are poor. And they are tired. And they are determined to live.

Our Southside is a place apart: each piece of our living is a protest.

3.

I was born May 19, 1930, the last of four children.

Of love and my parents there is little to be written: their relationship to their children was utilitarian. We were fed and housed and dressed and outfitted with more cash than our associates and that was all. We were also vaguely taught certain vague absolutes: that we were better than no one but infinitely superior to everyone; that we were the products of the proudest and most mistreated of the races of man; that there was nothing enormously difficult about life; that one *succeeded* as a matter of course.

Life was not a struggle—it was something that one *did.* One won an argument because, if facts gave out, one invented them—with color! The only sinful people in the world were dull people. And, above all, there were two things which were never to be betrayed: the family and the race. But of love, there was nothing ever said.

If we were sick, we were sternly, impersonally and carefully nursed and doctored back to health. Fevers, toothaches were attended to with urgency and importance; one always felt *important* in my family. Mother came with a tray to your room with the soup and Vick's salve or gave the enemas in a steaming bathroom. But we were not fondled, any of us—head held to breast, fingers about that head—until we were grown, all of us, and my father died.

At his funeral I at last, in my memory, saw my mother hold her sons that way, and for the first time in her life my sister held me in her arms I think. We were not a loving people: we were passionate in our hostilities and affinities, but the caress embarrassed us.

We have changed little. . . .

4.

Seven years separated the nearest of my brothers and sisters and myself; I wear, I am sure, the ear-marks of that familial station to this day. Little has been written or thought to my knowledge about children who occupy that place: the last born sep-

From the book TO BE YOUNG, GIFTED AND BLACK: Lorraine Hansberry in Her Own Words, adapted by Robert Nemiroff. © 1969 by Robert Nemiroff and Robert Nemiroff as Executor of the Estate of Lorraine Hansberry. Published by Prentice-Hall, Inc., Englewood Cliffs, New Jersey. Reprinted by permission of Prentice-Hall, Inc. and William Morris Agency, Inc.

arated by an uncommon length of time from the next youngest. I suspect we are probably a race apart.

The last born is an object toy which comes in years when brothers and sisters who are seven, ten, twelve years older are old enough to appreciate it rather than poke out its eyes. They do not mind diapering you the first two years, but by the time you are five you are a pest that has to be attended to in the washroom, taken to the movies and "sat with" at night. You are not a person—you are a nuisance who is not particular fun any more. Consequently, you swiftly learn to play alone. . . .

5.

My childhood Southside summers were the ordinary city kind, full of the street games which other rememberers have turned into fine ballets these days, and rhymes that anticipated what some people insist on calling modern poetry:

Oh, Mary Mack, Mack, Mack
With the silver buttons, buttons, buttons
All down her back, back, back.
She asked her mother, mother, mother
For fifteen cents, cents, cents
To see the elephant, elephant, elephant
Jump the fence, fence, fence.
Well, he jumped so high, high, high
'Til he touched the sky, sky, sky
And he didn't come back, back, back
'Til the Fourth of Ju—ly, ly, ly!

I remember skinny little Southside bodies by the fives and tens of us panting the delicious hours away:
"May I?"
And the voice of authority: "Yes, you may—you may take one giant step."
One drew in all one's breath and tightened one's fist and pulled the small body against the heavens, stretching, straining all the muscles in the legs to make—one giant step.
It is a long time. One forgets the reason for the game. (For children's games are always explicit in their reasons for being. To play is to win something. Or not to be "it." Or to be high pointer, or outdoer or, sometimes—just *the winner*. But after a time one forgets.)

Why was it important to take a small step, a teeny step, or the most desired of all—one GIANT step?
A giant step *to where?*

6.

Evenings were spent mainly on the back porches where screen doors slammed in the darkness with those really very special summertime sounds. And, sometimes, when Chicago nights got too steamy, the whole family got into the car and went to the park and slept out in the open on blankets. Those were, of course, the best times of all because the grownups were invariably reminded of having been children in the South and told the best stories then. And it was also cool and sweet to be on the grass and there was usually the scent of freshly cut lemons or melons in the air. Daddy would lie on his back, as fathers must, and explain about how men thought the stars above us came to be and how far away they were.
I never did learn to believe that anything could be as far away as *that*. Especially the stars. . . .

7.

The man that I remember was an educated soul, though I think now, looking back, that it was as much a matter of the physical bearing of my father as his command of information and of thought that left that impression upon me. I know nothing of the "assurance of kings" and will not use that metaphor on account of it. Suffice it to say that my father's enduring image in my mind is that of a man whom kings might have imitated and properly created their own flattering descriptions of. A man who always seemed to be doing something brilliant and/or unusual to such an extent that to be doing something brilliant and/or unusual was the way I assumed fathers behaved.
He digested the laws of the State of Illinois and put them into little booklets. He invented complicated pumps and railroad devices. He could talk at length on American history and private enterprise (to which he utterly subscribed). And he carried his head in such a way that I was quite certain that there was nothing he was afraid of. Even writing this, how profoundly it shocks my inner senses to

realize suddenly that *my father*, like all men, must have known *fear.* . . .

8.

April 23, 1964

To the Editor,
The New York Times:

With reference to civil disobedience and the Congress of Racial Equality stall-in:
. . . My father was typical of a generation of Negroes who believed that the "American way" could successfully be made to work to democratize the United States. Thus, twenty-five years ago, he spent a small personal fortune, his considerable talents, and many years of his life fighting, in association with NAACP[1] attorneys, Chicago's "restrictive covenants" in one of this nation's ugliest ghettoes.

That fight also required that our family occupy the disputed property in a hellishly hostile "white neighborhood" in which, literally, howling mobs surrounded our house. One of their missiles almost took the life of the then eight-year-old signer of this letter. My memories of this "correct" way of fighting white supremacy in America include being spat at, cursed and pummeled in the daily trek to and from school. And I also remember my desperate and courageous mother, patrolling our house all night with a loaded German luger, doggedly guarding her four children, while my father fought the respectable part of the battle in the Washington court.

The fact that my father and the NAACP "won" a Supreme Court decision, in a now famous case which bears his name in the lawbooks, is—ironically—the sort of "progress" our satisfied friends allude to when they presume to deride the more radical

means of struggle. The cost, in emotional turmoil, time and money, which led to my father's early death as a permanently embittered exile in a foreign country when he saw that after such sacrificial efforts the Negroes of Chicago were as ghetto-locked as ever, does not seem to figure in their calculations.

That is the reality that I am faced with when I now read that some Negroes my own age and younger say that we must now lie down in the streets, tie up traffic, do whatever we can—take to the hills with guns if necessary—and fight back. Fatuous people remark these days on our "bitterness." Why, of course we are bitter. The entire situation suggests that the nation be reminded of the too little noted final lines of Langston Hughes' mighty poem:[2]

What happens to a dream deferred?
Does it dry up
Like a raisin in the sun?
Or fester like a sore—
And then run?
Does it stink like rotten meat?
Or crust and sugar over—
Like a syrupy sweet?

Maybe it just sags
Like a heavy load.

Or does it explode?

Sincerely,

Copyright 1951 by Langston Hughes. Reprinted from THE PANTHER AND THE LASH, by Langston Hughes, by permission of Alfred A. Knopf, Inc. and Harold Ober Associates, Incorporated.

1. *NAACP*, National Association for the Advancement of Colored People.
2. *Langston Hughes' mighty poem*, "Harlem," later published under the title "Dream Deferred."

FOR EXPLORATION

1. (*a*) What details in this autobiographical statement support the concluding letter of protest? (*b*) What details suggest that, despite difficulties, the writer's childhood was a happy one?

2. (*a*) Lorraine Hansberry states that in her family "nothing was ever said" of love. Do the relationships between her and her family, as described here, suggest that the family was unloving? Why or why not? (*b*) What was the writer's position in her family? Did this give her more or less responsibility and independence, bring her more or less attention than the other children?

3. Jean Jacques Rousseau, an eighteenth-century French philosopher, once said, "I may not be better than anybody, but at least I am different." What parallel feeling is expressed in this essay? Do you find any different emphasis here? Have you ever had similar feelings in regard to yourself or your family? Discuss.

4. (*a*) What feelings does the Langston Hughes poem reveal? How is the tone of the poem related to the tone of the letter? (*b*) The last two sections of this piece each end with a significant word, "fear" and "explode." Relate these words to the major details of Hansberry's personal history, and explain how the one condition might lead to the other.

CREATIVE RESPONSE

Identify yourself as a member of an oppressed group (ethnic, male or female, student or working man, young or aged, etc.) and write a personal history that would support your cause. You will find that, like Hansberry, you will have to be uncompromisingly honest about yourself and others.

Lorraine Hansberry   1930 / 1965

Lorraine Hansberry was twenty-one when she wrote the following note: "And so the sun will pass away—die away. Tones of blue—of deep quiet—lovely blue—float down and all the people's voices seem to grow quiet—quiet.

"And I remember all the twilights I have ever known—they float across my eyes.

"I think of forests and picnics—of being very warm in something cotton. Of smelling the earth—and loving life.

"Long live good life! And beauty . . . and love!"

Seven years later her first play, *A Raisin in the Sun,* opened on Broadway. Two months later she became the youngest American playwright, the fifth woman, and the only black writer ever to win the New York Drama Critics' Circle Award for the Best Play of the Year.

Six years later, at the age of thirty-four, she died of cancer.

The Sign in Sidney Brustein's Window is the only other of her plays to reach the stage while she lived. But she left behind three file cabinets of stage plays, screenplays, fiction, poetry, essays, speeches, memoirs, journals, and correspondence. Her husband, Robert Nemiroff, and others have been editing the papers. They include *Les Blancs,* a play Mr. Nemiroff feels may prove her most lasting accomplishment, and the autobiographical pieces which formed the basis for the play and novel of *To Be Young Gifted and Black.*

One of her last notes read, "If anything should happen—before 'tis done—may I trust that all commas and periods will be placed and someone will complete my thoughts—

"This last should be the least difficult—since there are so many who think as I do—"

Edgar Lee Masters

DREISER AT SPOON RIVER

Along with H. L. Mencken and Sinclair Lewis,[1] Edgar Lee Masters was a major force in the New Realism which broke through the genteel literary tradition that dominated American letters at the turn of the century. In Spoon River Anthology *(published anonymously in 1915) Masters had created his images of bitterness and frustration in a collection of epitaphs describing the secret lives of dead citizens. He made literary history in the poetic treatment of small-town America, adhering to the natural rhythms and colloquial form of spoken language.*

One of the poems in Spoon River Anthology *(Macmillan, 1915), describing Dreiser,[2] was called "Theodore the Poet":*

As a boy, Theodore, you sat for long hours
On the shore of the turbid Spoon
With deep-set eye staring at the door of the crawfish's
    burrow,
Waiting for him to appear, pushing ahead,
First his waving antennae, like straw of hay,
And soon his body, colored like soap-stone,
Gemmed with eyes of jet.
And you wondered in a trance of thought
What he knew, what he desired, and why he lived
    at all.
But later your vision watched for men and women
Hiding in burrows of fate amid great cities,
Looking for the souls of them to come out,
So that you could see
How they lived, and for what,
And why they kept crawling so busily
Along the sandy way where water fails
As the summer wanes.

Another portrait of his friend appeared in our May 1939 issue. It arrived at Esquire *with the following reassurance:*

The enclosed piece, "John Armstrong Entertains Dreiser at Spoon River," is a good thing to prove to the authorities that Esquire *is following an impeccable course. It is good history and all true.*

Yours,
E. L. Masters

ONE time when Dreiser was in Chicago gathering material for a novel, our talks day by day ranged the country, and it came about that I told him of the fiddler John Armstrong, who was famous in central Illinois for his stories and his fiddling, and as the son of Hannah Armstrong, Lincoln's friend and landlady. Armstrong lived in the village of Oakford, about eight miles north of New Salem Hill, where Lincoln was postmaster in his young manhood; he had lived near Oakford all his sixty-seven years. At this time I had never seen Armstrong; I had often planned to visit him. I wanted to hear him play the fiddle and to tell stories about Menard County and New Salem, about his people and the country of Lincoln's day. Some of these racy stories had been passed on to me by people who had come in contact with Armstrong. But that was not like hearing him tell them and interlard his words with oaths. So I had been informed; and somewhat to my surprise Dreiser became greatly interested in Armstrong, and when I told him that I had to be in Springfield the next day, only twenty miles from Oakford, and thought of going on to pay the long deferred visit to Armstrong, Dreiser said that he would go too, if he could manage his engagements. The result was that I went to Springfield, and there awaited a telegram from Dreiser, while I attended to some business in the Illinois capital.

John Armstrong belonged to the Lincoln history; not only was he the son of that Hannah Armstrong who had boarded Lincoln in his New Salem days but his father was that Jack Armstrong who was the wrestler, who had wrestled with Lincoln. His brother was that Duff Armstrong who had been defended by

"Dreiser at Spoon River" by Edgar Lee Masters from ESQUIRE. Copyright 1939. Permission granted by Mrs. Ellen C. Masters.
1. *H. L. Mencken and Sinclair Lewis.* See pages M 120 and A 66. For Masters' biography, see page 191 M.
2. *Dreiser.* See page M 4.

Lincoln, using an almanac to prove that the witnesses had misstated the facts when they testified that the moon was at the meridian at the moment that Duff Armstrong struck his victim Metzger with a neck yoke and produced his death. If the moon was not at the meridian, but was setting, the witnesses could not have seen the blow struck, or with what it was struck. That was the point of the almanac, which proved that the moon was setting.

After John's father died one summer of what John called "the lung fever," his words for pneumonia, long after Lincoln left New Salem Village for Springfield, John with his mother Hannah lived in various parts of the county of Menard in which Oakford is situated. Sometimes he lived with his mother and Duff in what is called Sandridge Precinct, and then near the Sangamon River, just across from Mason County. Here there were camp meetings and rowdy dances where the fiddlers came and the platform dancers performed under the spell of many drinks. It was at a camp meeting that Duff Armstrong killed Metzger. John told me that at this camp meeting "they would sit around where there was preachin' for a while, and then they'd go and get some drinks."

John grew up hearing his mother tell of New Salem and the days when she darned Lincoln's socks. He became saturated with the stories and the flavor of this countryside, with all that his mother told him of the horse racing, foot racing and horseshoe pitching, and loafing in Berry's Store, where Lincoln sat around telling anecdotes—all there at New Salem twenty years before John was born. At last, a good while after Lincoln's death, Hannah died, and John married a daughter of "Fiddler" Jones,[3] and carried on the art of the country fiddler. For many years by the time of my visit with Dreiser to see him at Oakford he had lived there, where he ran a grain elevator, and kept open house to his friends, where his wife Aunt Caroline delighted guests with her bountiful table, and where John entertained them with fiddling and storytelling. He was supposed to have many souvenirs of the Lincoln days; but in point of fact, as it turned out, he had nothing but a picture of his mother and one of Duff, a picture of some of the jurymen who tried Duff, and a book containing Lincoln's autograph. But John as the survivor of a time that was passed was of far greater interest than such things as these. I wanted to see him in order to know just what kind of people it was that Lincoln had lived with in his youth; and above that to hear

John talk and play the fiddle. Finally when I was ready to leave for Springfield, Dreiser could not accompany me. He said, however, that he would telegraph me the next day, if he could come then.

When I got to Springfield I told my father about Dreiser. As he did not read novels to any extent, but only law books and the like, he did not know Dreiser's work. He tried to get me to set off that very afternoon for Oakford, saying that John might die any time, and I would miss the chance of seeing him. Why wait for Dreiser? As a New York novelist Dreiser would not be interested in John, and would not appreciate him. What would he care for John's fiddling? However, I did not go to Oakford that afternoon. And the next morning a telegram came from Dreiser saying that he would be down from Chicago on the afternoon train. My father prepared to go with us. He telephoned John, who sent back a hearty welcome to all of us, saying that his wife would have the best dinner ready that she could prepare, and that he would meet us at the depot.

That afternoon my father got engaged in business so that he could not go. I went down to the station to meet Dreiser, from which also our train for Oakford departed. I was as surprised to see Dreiser get off the train, as I was to get his telegram. But there he was laughing and repeating some of the jokes of Armstrong that I had told him. He was in lively spirits. We boarded the Oakford train and soon were on our way. Dreiser looked out of the window studying the country. It was not greatly different from the Indiana landscape with which he was identified as a boy and young man. But at the edge of Springfield there were a lot of Italians repairing the track. He commented on their sturdiness and vitality. When we passed through the first little village and saw the typical American idlers standing by the station to watch the train arrive he contrasted their listless behavior with the spirited manner of the Italians we had seen. I pointed out to him places identified with my boyhood; the blacksmith shop at Cantrall where I had almost burned my fingers off; the Chautauqua Grounds near Petersburg which had been established in memory of Lincoln, and near at hand the place in the Sangamon River where I was nearly drowned. There was nothing there but the bend; for long before the water mill which succeeded the mill of Lincoln's day at New Salem, had vanished, and

3. "Fiddler" Jones, one of the Spoon River residents whose epitaph is related in *Spoon River Anthology*.

even the dam was all but obliterated. At Petersburg, twenty miles from Springfield, the train stopped long enough for me to tell him about various houses and buildings; the Old Menard House where Lincoln used to stop when he came to Petersburg to court; various buildings of local note about the square; the little brick station, no longer used, standing back from the track which was used when I was a boy in Petersburg, and from which I left when we moved from Petersburg to Lewistown, fifty miles north. When we left Petersburg we came to the farm country with which I was familiar, and to the hamlet of Atterberry, where the store still stood that was there when I was a boy, and was still managed by the man who had run it all these intervening years. A few miles beyond we came to Oakford, sighting first the grain elevator which John Armstrong owned and conducted; for he was a man of means, and had led a thrifty and industrious life, along with fiddling and hunting.

John was standing on the station platform. I knew him by the pictures of him that I had seen. He was glancing about with wildbird eyes for someone that looked like his idea of me. But I knew him at once and went to him, introducing Dreiser, who turned his eyes upon John and bored him through with scrutinizing penetration. John was not conscious of Dreiser's stare, nor did he seem to betray any curiosity in Dreiser, though Dreiser's coat with its fur collar, and his city apparel and city manner might well have caused a countryman to look the newcomer over. For himself John was freshly shaved, he had on clean linen and a good four-in-hand, his shoes were polished, he looked eminently respectable. I might have supposed that he had dressed for us, but it turned out that John was always careful of his appearance. His mother, Hannah, though a pioneer woman, had a certain breeding; and according to my grandmother, who knew and loved her for years, she was a woman of excellent character. John had derived from his home environment under her an understanding of good habits of life, of a kind of homely etiquette, of the ways of hospitality. As a liver and a hunter, as a man who had gone about his own country for years meeting all sorts of men in that locality John would have been at ease with anyone. He took Dreiser for just another man, one perhaps of a new type, but no matter for that. So we stood momentarily on the platform of the station, where Dreiser's great height contrasted with John's low stature. John said, "They say you're a writin' feller." And when Dreiser laughed and admitted that he was, John remarked, "Wal, by God, that was what I was told. Come on now boys we'll go to the house. Aunt Caroline has dinner about ready, and I've got some fine whisky for you. A feller over in the 'Burg giv' it to me."

Oakford was a village of just a few houses and about one hundred people. We passed up a street where there were two stores on one side and some houses on the other. "You remember Oakford, don't you, Lee?" John asked me. When I said I did, he went on, "Do you remember when Porky Jim Thomas run a sample room[4] right thar?" John pointed to one of the stores which had become a drug store. With this Dreiser exploded with laughter. To which John paid no attention. "Where is Porky Jim?" I inquired. "Wal," replied John, "I don't know exactly where he is at. He died about ten years ago. We buried him here in Oakford. We'll go and look at his grave tomorrow." Though I knew why the man was called Porky Jim I asked John for Dreiser's benefit where he got such a name. "Why, Cy Skaggs giv' him that name. You see runnin' that sample room he got as big around as a barl, and as purple in the face as a gobbler. He drank a quart of whisky a day, by God, and said that no man could be healthy without it. Cy Skaggs called him that, and it stuck."

Dreiser stopped to laugh which John seemed to take as a matter of course. He and I paused waiting for Dreiser, while John went on telling me about the last days of Porky Jim. "He had the dropsy, the doctors called it, and almost bust. They had to tap him; and a man told me they took off ten gallons of water. Once we had a hoss race here. One of the Atterberrys was raisin' quarter hosses. Porky Jim was thar takin' bets. He could hardly get around. 'Pears to me that's the last time I saw Porky before he got down at home." By this time Dreiser having laughed himself out came up to where we were standing, and on we went to John's house, which was only two blocks from the station.

John's house was a cottage of one story, but it was freshly painted and in good repair. His yard was large and surrounded by a picket fence. There were lilac bushes and other flowering growths on the lawn. At one side was a large vegetable garden where the stalks of last summer's corn stood, blasted and shak-

---

4. *a sample room,* where samples are displayed for the inspection of buyers for retail stores.

ing in the February wind. A brick walk led from the gate to the front door. From the chimney a cloud of soft coal smoke was pouring. John opened the door, held it ajar for us to enter, and we came in and set our handbags down and began to take in the room. It was small with a low ceiling. On the wall were black crayons of relatives; in the corner was an organ; in the center a soft-coal base burner with windows of isinglass through which the flames of a hot fire were flickering. On the floor was a rag carpet of many hues, and in a good state. John went on into the dining room, which we could see into. There a long table was already set, and from the kitchen beyond we could hear the steps of John's wife, Aunt Caroline, and her daughter, and the sizzling of food in the skillet. Dreiser looked at me and was still laughing. We stood there, thinking that John had gone out only for a moment. That proved to be true. He returned bearing the promised whisky, and we drank together. John was chuckling and talking and swearing with no stay. In a moment Aunt Caroline and her daughter came in. I shook hands with them as Aunt Caroline said, "I've knowed your pap since he was fifteen years old. He was at a dance about then where my brother fiddled. I knew your grandpap and your grandma, but I never knowed you before. They say you live in Chicago."

Meantime Dreiser stood unintroduced. "This here, Caroline, is a writin' feller from New York. By God, I've forgot your name." Dreiser told him in a quiet voice as his eyes flamed with mirth. "Yes," said John, "Dresser. Why, Caroline, you remember them Dressers that lived over thar by Salt Creek, just east of Dutchland. They was Dutch. Ain't you Dutch?" Dreiser replied that he was of German parentage. "I thought so," observed John.

Aunt Caroline and her daughter now disappeared to the kitchen and we sat down by the fire while John talked a stream, telling about various things that had happened in the neighborhood, about the horse races, the odd characters of the past. He was running over with stories. Dreiser sat there and laughed quietly to himself. John seemed to be oblivious of everything but the stories that he was telling. He kept punctuating his remarks with "by Gods," and laughing heartily at his own humor. Finally Dreiser asked him, "Did you know Lincoln?" "Well, I kain't say that I knowed him," John replied. "I seed him onct that I remember well. You see when Duff was tried— thar's his picture on the wall—I was only nine years

old. And my mother, that's Aunt Hannah as they called her, took me to Beardstown whar they had Duff in jail. That's when I seed Linkern." "What did he look like?" asked Dreiser, growing more interested. "Wal, by God, that's hard to answer. He looked like one of these here cranes you see along the Sangamon River—tall, you know, and thin. He didn't have no beard, that I remember. I know damn well he didn't have no beard, because my mother said so many times." "Did you see him sitting down as well as standing?" John looked at Dreiser sharply, seeing that the questions were growing acute. "You ain't no lawyer, are you, Dresser?" asked John. Dreiser answered that he wasn't a lawyer. "By God you sound like it," remarked John. "You sound like old Breese Johnson that used to be over at the 'Burg forty years ago." "I wanted to know how Lincoln looked when he was sitting down," Dreiser explained. "Wal, I expect he looked like one of these here grasshoppers with their jints stickin' up when they squat. You see Linkern had awful long legs. My mother said so. Over at Havaner thar was a man named Colonel Prickett. He told me that he seed Linkern on the platform thar onct, and that his knees stuck up half way to his waist." This was the tenor of the talk as Aunt Caroline entered to announce that dinner was ready.

"I expect you boys want to wash," John observed. He opened doors off the living room where we had been sitting and showed us into our separate rooms. There we found bowls and pitchers of water, and fresh towels. We also saw the very comfortable beds built up with feather ticks, and log-house quilts which Aunt Caroline had spread for us with hospitable care. We came back into the living room, though John had been standing as we washed near our doors in order to finish one of his stories. He was swearing and talking in the husky amusing voice that was his. All the while Dreiser was smiling or chuckling, or looking about with his penetrating eyes, as if he felt that he had never seen anyone like John, or any house just like this cottage was. John now took us into the dining room, and then as suddenly left us as he passed into the kitchen, remarking, "By God, I believe I'll wash myself." We could see him as he hid his face in his hands, and exploded the water about his face from a tin basin.

We sat down to a table of fried chicken, boiled ham and boiled beef; to potatoes, cabbage, rutabagas, carrots and onions; to hot biscuits and corn bread; to wild honey and every variety of preserves and canned berries; to pickles made of tomatoes, watermelon rinds, cucumbers; to blackberry pie and many kinds of cake; to milk and excellent cream; to coffee that was better than one usually finds in country households. John did not wait for us to begin. He started at once to feed, eating heartily, talking without remission, while Dreiser sat there silently partaking of the fare, rather delicately, not saying much, but laughing to himself at times at John's stories. His mood seemed to be one of respect for the household, of appreciation of the hospitality which was so generous, of comprehending interest in John as a veritable character. He really noted everything; even though at times seeming to be far away. Long after he referred to this visit, and repeated some of John's picturesque vernacular, showing that it had fastened itself in his memory.

An evening then followed in which Dreiser laughed and rocked; or sat with his head against the back of the chair, folding his handkerchief into squares, or leaning forward to ask John something, or to hear him better. At times he howled with delight. Aunt Caroline and her daughter washed the dishes, and came in the living room after the fun had started. Neither said anything; while Aunt Caroline was knitting and looking down at her work in respectful silence to John. He was going on as before, growing more animated, and piling one anecdote upon another, and calling the character he was portraying, or telling about nicknames that were in themselves as funny as the comedies he sketched. By seven o'clock the hour seemed late, for it was winter and darkness by then had long come upon the prairies, and the woods which skirted the Sangamon River two miles away, and the hills just near Oakford. And such silence without, save for the wind!

"The storm without might rair and rustle" we "did na mind the storm a whistle," there comfortably grouped about the coal stove watching the flames flicker against the isinglass doors. Aunt Caroline sat attentive upon her knitting, the daughter looked down demurely, somewhat abashed by John's guests; Dreiser folded his handkerchief, and John went on telling about quarter horses, camp meetings, dances, fiddler contests in which he had figured. Sometimes as many as fifty fiddlers came together at Havana, or one of the near-by towns, there in some hall to strive for a set of harness, a whip, a five-dollar gold piece as the prize for the best fiddling. And John

had often won the prize. "By God, I won 'er this time," was his comment.

Perhaps John would have talked on until sleep vanquished him, if I had not said that we wanted to hear him play the fiddle. He made no excuses, he just got up and got his fiddle. He asked his daughter to play the organ for him and to give him the key. The daughter arose without a word, with no expression on her face, just arose like a wraith and sat down at the organ and gave John the key. Then John tuned the fiddle, and sat back and began to tell stories again, rather he began to preface the playing of each piece with words concerning its origin and where it got its name, and where he heard it first. Nearly every tune was associated with something that had happened at a dance, at the county fair, at a camp meeting, a party, or a festival of some sort. For years he had attended these things which were a continuation of the New Salem events, of dances at the Rutledge Tavern, of horse races, on the prairie west of New Salem. Thus if he had lived at New Salem when Lincoln did we should not have had a truer re-creation of those days.

John played such pieces as *Rocky Road to Jordan, Way up Tar Creek, Foggy Mountain Top, Hell among the Yearlins, Little Drops of Brandy, The Wind that Shakes the Barley, Good Mornin' Uncle Johnny, I've Fetched Your Wagon Home,* as well as the more familiar pieces like *Zip Coon, Turkey in the Straw.* Sometimes he sang words as he played, like this:

"There was a woman in our town,
    In our town did dwell,
She loved her husband dear-i-lee,
    But another man twict as well."

He played a piece which he called *Toor-a Loor,* and another called *The Speckled Hen,* and another which he called *Chaw Roast Beef.* He sang and played *Swingin' in the Lane.* He played and sang *The Missouri Harmony:*

"When in death I shall calm recline
    O bear my heart to my mistress dear,
Tell her it lived on smiles and wine
    Of brightest hue while it languished here.
Bid her not shed one tear of sorrow
    To sully a heart so brilliant and light.
But balmy drops of the red grape borrow
    To bathe the relict from morn till night."

Concerning this, John said by way of preface before beginning, "This here is *The Missouri Harmony*. Linkern used to sing it, but he couldn't carry no tune. That's what my mother told me. But he'd try at it."

Between playing he was piling up anecdotes about "One Eyed" Clemons, "Corky Bill" Atterberry, "Quarter Hoss" Sam Lounsbury, "Snaggle Tooth" Engle, "Slicky Bill" Greene. Dreiser sat there convulsed with laughter, just quietly folding his handkerchief.

John played a piece which he called *Pete McCue's Straw Stack*, and he told us before playing it, "This here is called *Pete McCue's Straw Stack* named after old Peter McCue, who lived down by Tar Creek. They had a dance thar one time and the boys tied their horses close to a straw stack, and when they came out the hosses had et all the straw. They had been playing this piece that night, but after that they called it *Pete McCue's Straw Stack*. I forget what they called it before this."

Resting at times from the fiddle, John held the instrument against his arm and talked, telling us what platform dancing was, and about the famous platform dancers that he had known, one of whom growing excited with drink and music, had looked about the room and called out, "Clar the cheers out. I'm goin' to take off my shoes and come down on her." He did so and his feet went through the puncheon floor and that resulted in renaming the dance music. After that it was called *Skinnin' Your Shins* for the dancer had skinned his shins pretty badly. And John told about a noted strong man of Oakford who had whipped a savage bulldog with his own hands, and about Clay Bailey, who had entered the circus ring and taken an escaped leopard by the tail and dragged it back to its cage. "He couldn't have a-done that withouten he was drunk. The likker made him powerful strong and keerless." Aunt Caroline didn't bat an eye as John told these marvels. The daughter still sat at the organ waiting for John to name the next piece. Dreiser was red in the face from suppressed laughter.

John was as good a fiddler as I had ever heard; but he protested that he was a poor performer compared to his wife's brother, who had gone from Oakford years before, and had died in Iowa. "As fur as that's concerned," John confessed, "Fiddler Bill Watkins could beat me all holler, and he warn't a patchin to my wife's brother. He used to play for all the dances here and up Tar Creek—and fight! Why, by God,

onct over near the Lattimore, just this side of Dutchland, they was havin' a dance, and some fellers from Mason County was thar and had cum over to break it up. 'Fiddler Bill' jest laid down his fiddle, stepped from the platform, and whooped the whole lot. Now you see my Pap was Jack Armstrong, a powerful man he was in the arms and back; and the truth is Linkern never throwed him. It was a tie. My mother told me so a hundred times before she died."

"How big was your father?" I asked John. "Why he warn't so big," John replied. "He was short like I am, but husky, big chest, and weighed about one hundred eighty. He never was throwed, is what they tell me."

Dreiser by this time had looked at all the pictures on the wall. In an interval of fiddling he asked John about Duff Armstrong, whose picture hung near the entrance door. It was the face of a hard man, with wild eyes, rather cruel on the whole. John saw Dreiser looking at the picture and remarked, "You can believe Duff was a fightin' man. It was a fight that got him into the court at Beardstown where Linkern defended him with the almanac."

"How about that almanac?" asked Dreiser. "You were not at the trial, I have heard."

"No, I warn't," John admitted; "but I was down one time to Beardstown with my mother when Duff was thar in jail, before the trial."

"What did your mother say was done? She was present at the trial, wasn't she?"

"Yes, she was thar. She said Linkern handed a almanac to the judge which showed that the witnesses had lied about the moon."

"Yes, I know all about that," Dreiser interjected. "But do you know where he got the almanac? Did you ever hear that Lincoln had it printed for this case?"

"Yes, by God, I heard that," replied John with spirit; "but it ain't true. He got that almanac at the drug store. He went up and handed the almanac to the judge, and the judge seed that the moon was settin' and not at the meridian as the witnesses said. So how could they see Duff hit that feller with a neck yoke, because the moon was bright?"

"Yes, yes," said Dreiser, folding his handkerchief and leaning back, as if he had satisfied himself that John did not have anything of importance to reveal upon this subject.

"There's lots of stories about that almanac," said John. "Why one time over at Springfield I seed a affidavit that said that Linkern didn't change the almanac. And right on the wall thar is a picture of one of the jurymen that tried Duff. He was a smart man, and no one could play any trick on him."

Dreiser was now rocking and singing *Turkey in the Straw* to himself. "Came to the River and couldn't get across. Paid five dollars for an old blind hoss—Turkey in the straw, Turkey in the hay . . . etc."

I thought I'd suggest an idea, so I said, "John, here's something that hasn't been talked about much. That almanac was not legal evidence, and the judge was either fooled or else he admitted it in evidence, knowing it was illegal.

"It has turned out that an astronomical survey made at Harvard, I believe it was, showed that the moon was just where the almanac put it that night. But an Ayers or Sarsaparilla almanac would prove the state of the weather, or the position of the moon just as much as a Montgomery Ward catalogue would prove what their prices were; that is, if you just put the catalogue in evidence without someone from the store to swear that those prices were correct."

"Is that so?" said John in great surprise. "Wal, by God, Linkern got it in evidence."

"Yes, those were the good old days. No one thought of bringing an astronomer into court to testify where the moon was on a certain night at a certain hour and minute. An almanac was believed in. But here's something else; even if the moon was setting and not at the meridian the witnesses might have seen your brother strike that man Metzger with the neck yoke. What happened was that the evidence of these witnesses was clouded by the almanac. They said the moon was at the meridian, and the almanac showed it was setting. But, what of it? Your brother hit the man, didn't he?"

"You bet he did," was John's quick reply. "And I'll tell you why, by God. You see my brother and this man was here in Oakford before that. Duff was asleep on a barl; and this man come up and cotched him while he was asleep, and pulled him off the barl. So they fit right then and thar. There was bad blood betwixt them. And that night when Duff used the neck yoke there was a general fight with several in it; and this here Metzger was hit with a slung shot by somebody, and Duff hit him with a neck yoke. But what Duff did didn't kill him. It was the slung shot. A doctor got on the witness stand and

swore that it was the slung shot that cracked his skull. Besides all that, the evidence showed that Metzger ridin' home that night fell off his hoss several times. So how could you say that ary blow at the fight killed him? He might have cracked his head fallin' off his hoss; for as fur as that's concerned he rode home after bein' hit with the slung shot and the neck yoke. And Linkern's speech which made my mother cry, and everybody in the court room, freed Duff right thar."

"According to this, the position of the moon had as much to do with the case as the astrology of the Babylonians," I said.

"Is that so?" said John mildly. "Maybe you're right."

Dreiser began to sing:

"The prettiest girl that ever I saw
Was sucking cider through a straw.

"Play *Turkey in the Straw* again, John," he requested. And John played it with more spirit than ever, if that had been possible, keeping time with a loud thud of his foot. When he was not fiddling, his daughter sat patiently at the organ waiting for John to give the signal to play. She was not saying a word. His manner of starting off would be something like this: "This here is called *Hell Amongst the Yearlins*. I don't ricollect what it was furst called; but they had a dance over at Ben Sutton's onct, and while they was a dancin' the cattle broke into his corn. So ever since they have called it *Hell Amongst the Yearlins*."

It was evident by this time that John thought he had met a strange man in the person of Dreiser. John perhaps could not see whether Dreiser was interested in his exhibition or not. He was perhaps puzzled to know in just what mood Dreiser was laughing.

"The most curious man I ever seed," he said later. "When he looks at you with his good eye he seems to know a plenty. When his cockeye[5] turns up he looks like one of the Spilly boys. That good eye of his bores you right through. He asks questions as good as a lawyer."

The almanac case did not exhaust the subject of Duff. There was the matter of Duff's war record, and his discharge from the army by grace of Lincoln,

---

5. *his cockeye.* Dreiser did not have normal muscle control of his right eye.

specially exercised, at the instance of Hannah, whose journey to Washington to intercede for her son is in all the books about Lincoln.[6] Duff had died many years before, thus leaving a world that had puzzled him, and made wastage of him. "Duff kept a-drinkin'," was John's comment. "He got so anybody could whoop him. He went around showin' his discharge from the army and pickin' up money for drinks on it." John laid the fiddle aside by this time. He brought forth some of his souvenirs; little things that belonged to his mother; a book containing Lincoln's autograph; and a very good picture of his mother when she was probably toward seventy. It was the face of a dignified pioneer woman, not without a certain charm. He then told us that she had died in Iowa, far from the scenes of her interesting life.

The evening ended at ten, and we went to bed. The partition between my room and Dreiser's was thin. Sometime after lights were out, and John had attended to the stove for the night and retired, I heard Dreiser laughing. "What is the matter, Dreiser?" I called out.

"I was thinking that we were going to see the grave of Porky Jim in the morning. My God, how funny!"

There was a breakfast of ham and eggs, and cakes, and corn bread, and all the preserves of the night before. We had about an hour, before the train left for Springfield, to see the little cemetery on a rise of ground east of the railroad tracks. We wandered around as I read the names of men and women whom I had known as a boy when I drove about the country or went to Concord Church with my grandparents. Dreiser was walking with John. I paused before a stone on which was carved the name of James Thomas; and it meant nothing to me. I remembered no James Thomas. "Who was James Thomas, John?" I asked as he came closer to me.

"Why, by God, that's Porky Jim," said John with a chuckle.

"Porky Jim," laughed Dreiser. "Oh me, oh me!"

Standing here we could see the heavy woods about four miles north along the banks of the Sangamon River. The Spoon River was at least twenty miles farther north. We had said goodbye to Aunt Caroline and her daughter when we left the house. Now at the train we parted from John, who laughed as he said, "Come again, boys."

Much later than this I was in Springfield. John's daughter came to see me to ask me to go to Oakford to console her father. She said he was not well. By this time John was quite old. It was very difficult for me to take the time to go to Oakford; but the daughter was so urgent that I did so. She said that her father would be badly hurt if I did not pay him a visit.

After a trip on the train and some motoring I arrived. John was visibly ill, and in a quietude. He didn't want to fiddle for me; but after I had begged him to do so, he got his daughter to the organ and began to play. It was slack playing at first, then he did better. Darkness was coming early. It was four o'clock, and I had to go. He followed me to the door with a sort of melancholy air. He was going to Texas the next week for the winter.

"I'll see you in the spring, John, when I come."

"No," he said, in a matter of fact way, "you won't see me no more. I won't be here in the spring." Immediately after this correct prophecy concerning himself he suddenly brightened. "What's become of that feller that was here with you?"

"Oh," I replied, "he has published a book that everyone is talking about," referring to *An American Tragedy*.[7]

"Is that so?" said John. "Wal, he left something here, and I allus wanted to send it to him, and didn't know where he was."

"What was it?"

"Why, them things, drawers and a shirt that he slept here in."

"You mean pajamas?"

"Is that what you call 'em? Pajamas, eh?"

"Don't mind about sending them," I said, as I hurried down the walk to the car.

John died in January of 1926, two months after this farewell. Aunt Caroline lingered along till 1935. Thus ended the saga of the Armstrong family, which began with Aunt Hannah, who cooked and darned for Lincoln. □

---

6. *his discharge . . . Lincoln.* The same episode is related in Hannah Armstrong's epitaph in *Spoon River Anthology.* See page M 190.

7. *An American Tragedy,* a novel written by Dreiser in 1925 which tells the tragedy caused by a young man being tempted by his desire for luxury and wealth. The novel was meant as an indictment against the American economic system which Dreiser believed was the cause of the main character's downfall.

FOR EXPLORATION

1. (*a*) In the letter introducing this piece, Masters states that it is "good history." Would you agree or disagree? (*b*) Would you call this piece biography, autobiography, folklore, legend, character sketch, or a combination of some or all of these? Cite those sections which apply to each category.

2. Which one character dominates this report? What aspects of his character make him more vivid than the others?

3. (*a*) How do you explain Dreiser's actions? Is he laughing at John Armstrong or with him? Do you think he understands John and is sympathetic to his background? (*b*) How does John treat Dreiser? In what ways is he affected by Dreiser's behavior? (*c*) What does the incident of the pajamas say about the differences between the two men? (*d*) How might Dreiser's actions be related to the poem which introduces this piece?

4. (*a*) What impression did you get of the community from which Lincoln came? (*b*) Would you accept John Armstrong as an authority? Why or why not?

CREATIVE RESPONSE

Collect some of the nicknames created during frontier days, and noted here by Armstrong. What do they tell us about frontier life? Was it event- or people-oriented? Does it show affection and a sense of humor? How do they compare with nicknames you now use among your friends and acquaintances? How does their picturesqueness agree with what Mencken says of "The American Language" (pages M 120–123 M)?

HISTORICAL PICTURES SERVICE, CHICAGO

Jesse Stuart

COUNTRY SCHOOLTEACHER

WHEN I had first come to Winston, I wondered what my pupils did for recreation. I wondered what I would do for recreation. I had thought reading was about the only kind of recreation. It didn't take me long to learn differently. One evening in September I was invited to Bill Madden's home. He was one of my pupils. His father had invited six or seven of the local musicians in to play for us. We sat in the yard where the grass was dying and the peach-tree leaves had turned golden and the moon was high in the sky above us. We listened to this local band play with their banjos, fiddles, guitar, mandolin, and accordion from seven until eleven. They never played the same tune twice, and often when they played a fast breakdown, one of the listeners would dance. I had never heard old-time music sound as beautiful as this, in the moonlight of the mild September evening.

There was hardly a family in this big vicinity who didn't have a musician. This was part of their recreation. People had learned to play musical instruments to furnish their own music just as they had learned to plant, cultivate, and harvest crops for their food supply. They depended upon themselves.

I went with my pupils, their parents, and neighbors to cornhuskings, apple-peelings, bean-stringings,[1] square dances, and to the belling of the bride[2] when there was a wedding. Often we rode mules many miles through darkness or moonlight to these community events. . . . This was the most democratic recreation I had ever seen.

Not one of my pupils had ever seen a stage play. If one had ever seen a movie, I'd never heard of it. They didn't have to leave landlocked Winston to find recreation. They had it at home. They created it just as they created most of their necessities of life. As the autumn days wore on they popped corn over the blazing wood fires and made molasses-and-popcorn balls. There was somewhere to go every night. I couldn't accept all the invitations. Each pupil invited me to his home to spend the night. This was an old custom, for in the past years the teacher had boarded with his pupils, since his salary wasn't enough to enable him to pay his board and have anything left.

When the hunting season came, I hunted quail with my pupils. I hunted rabbits with them in the Tiber[3] weed fields. My pupils were good marksmen. But I gave them a few surprises at some of the shots I made. I had never told them about my years of hunting experience. I went to the autumn-coloring hills to hunt possums. And I taught them—as I had tried to teach them high-school subjects—a little about possum hunting: that on the still and misty, warm nights when not a leaf stirred was the time to catch possums and coons. When I learned more about the terrain of the east and west walls,[4] where the persimmons and papaws grew, I showed them where to find the possums. They—as I had once done—hunted for animal pelts, shipped them, and bought books and clothes with the money. I showed them how to take better care of their pelts. . . .

When the leaves changed color in the valley and the sun was bright as a brush-pile flame, I went on long hikes with my pupils. We'd take a hike to the autumn-colored hills soon as the school day was over. We'd take food to cook over an open fire on the summit of one of the walls that enclosed the valley. Sometimes the girls would go with us. . . .

Down in the valley we could see every splash of color. Green leaves were there still, for the Tiber mists had protected them against the biting frost. There were blood-red shoe-make[5] leaves, golden sycamore and poplar leaves, slate-colored water-birch leaves, and the dull- and bright-gold willow leaves. And down in the valley the corn shocks stood like wigwams in an Indian village. We could see the bright knee-high corn stubble glittering in the autumn sun. We could see the brown meadow stubble, too, where the hay had been mown and piled in high mounds with poles through the center.

Reprinted by permission of Charles Scribner's Sons and Jesse Stuart from THE THREAD THAT RUNS SO TRUE, pages 78–82, by Jesse Stuart Copyright 1949 Jesse Stuart.
1. *cornhuskings, apple-peelings, bean-stringings,* social gatherings at which the neighbors came together to help one another get their crops ready for winter use.
2. *the belling of the bride,* a noisy serenade for a newly married couple.
3. *the Tiber,* the river that flows through the valley.
4. *walls,* the hills that enclose the valley in which Winston is situated.
5. *shoe-make,* sumac.

Often I walked alone beside the Tiber in autumn. For there was a somberness that put me in a mood that was akin to poetry. I'd watch the big sycamore leaves zigzag from the interlocking branches above to the clear blue Tiber water and drift away like tiny golden ships. I'd find the farewell-to-summer[6] in bloom along this river. Then a great idea occurred to me. It wasn't about poetry. It was about schools.

I thought if every teacher in every school in America—rural, village, city, township, church, public, or private—could inspire his pupils with all the power he had, if he could teach them as they had never been taught before to live, to work, to play, and to share, if he could put ambition into their brains and hearts, that would be a great way to make a generation of the greatest citizenry America had ever had. All of this had to begin with the little unit. Each teacher had to do his share. Each teacher was responsible for the destiny of America, because the pupils came under his influence. The teacher held the destiny of a great country in his hand as no member of any other profession could hold it. All other professions stemmed from the products of his profession. . . .

When I told my pupils about a scholastic contest with Landsburgh High School, I watched their expressions. They were willing and ready for the challenge. The competitive spirit was in them.

"We must review everything we have covered in our textbooks," I told them. "We must cover more territory in our textbooks too. Hold up your right hands if you are willing!"

Every pupil raised his hand.

Right then we started to work. In addition to regular assignments, my pupils began reviewing all of the old assignments. . . .

Despite the challenge ahead and all the reviewing and study we planned to do, we never stopped play. The Tiber River was frozen over. The ring of skates and merry laughter broke the stillness of the winter nights. We skated on the white winding ribbon of ice beneath the high, cold winter moon. . . .

Over the weekends we'd go to Tiber, where we'd cut holes in the ice and gig fish. The boys and I would rabbit-hunt up and down the Tiber Valley in the old stubble fields now covered with snow and swept by wind. . . . When we hunted, the girls didn't go with us, but when we skated, fished, and rode sleighs, they went along. There was a long gentle slope not far from the schoolhouse, we found ideal for our sleighs. It was almost a mile to the end of our sleigh run. We went over the river bank and downstream for many yards on the Tiber ice. We rode sleighs during the noon hour, before and after school.

On winter days when the snow had melted, leaving the dark earth a sea of sloppy mud, we designed floor games for our little one-room school. They were simple games such as throwing bolts in small boxes. And we played darts. We also played a game called "fox and goose." We made our fox-and-goose boards and we played with white, yellow, and red grains of corn. We had to make our own recreation. I never saw a distracted look on a pupil's face. I never heard one complain that the short, dark winter days were boresome because there wasn't anything to do. I think each pupil silently prayed for the days to be longer. We were a united little group. We were small, but we were powerful. We played hard, and we studied hard. We studied and played while the December days passed.

That day in early January, we dismissed school. . . . This was the big day for us. It was too bad that another blizzard had swept our rugged land and that a stinging wind was smiting the valleys and the hills. But this didn't stop the boys and me from going. Leona Maddox, my best Latin pupil, couldn't go along. Her father, Alex Maddox, wouldn't let her ride a mule seventeen miles to Landsburgh to compete in a contest on a day like this. I couldn't persuade him to let her go.

On that cold blizzardy morning, Budge Waters[7] rode his mule to school very early and built a fire in the potbellied stove. When the rest of us arrived on our mules at approximately seven o'clock, Budge had the schoolroom warm. We tied our mules to the fence, stood before the fire, and warmed ourselves before we started on our journey. Then we unhitched our mules from the fence and climbed into the saddles. Little clouds of frozen snow in powdery puffs arose from the mules' hoofs as six pupils and their teacher rode down the road.

Though the force of wind in the Tiber Valley was powerful, it was at our backs. The wind was strong enough to give our mules more momentum. We made good time until we left the valley and climbed the big hill. Here, we faced the wind. It was a whip-

---

6. *farewell-to-summer*, a late blooming aster.
7. *Budge Waters*, a brilliant boy, the best student in the school.

ping wind—stinging, biting wind on this mountain—that made the water run from our eyes and our mules' eyes, but for us there was no turning back. We were going to Landsburgh High School. That was that. We were determined to meet this big school—big to us, for they outnumbered us twenty-six to one. Soon we were down in Hinton Valley. Then we rode to the top of the Raccoon Hill. . . .

"Mr. Stuart, I have been thinking," Budge Waters said, as we rode along together, "if you can sleep in a fodder shock when it's twelve degrees below zero, we can take this contest from Landsburgh High School! I've not forgotten how you walked seventeen miles to carry us books.[8] All of your pupils remember. We'll never let you down!"

Budge Waters thought of this because we were riding down the mountain where I had slept that night. Then we rode down into the Raccoon Valley, and Billie Leonard, only thirteen years old, complained of numbness in his hands, feet, and lips. He said he felt as if he was going to sleep. . . . We stopped at a home, tied our mules to the fence, and went in and asked to warm. Bert Patton, a stranger to us, piled more wood on the open fire until we were as warm as when we had left the schoolhouse. We told him who we were and where we were going.

"On a day like this!" he said, shaking his head sadly.

We climbed into the saddles again. We were over halfway now. The second hitch would put us at Landsburgh High School. We had valley all the way to Landsburgh, with walls of rugged hills on each side for windbreaks.

At eleven o'clock we rode across the Landsburgh High School yard, and hitched our mules to the fence around the athletic field. There were faces against the windowpanes watching us. Then we walked inside the high school, where Principal Ernest Charters met and welcomed us. He told us that he was surprised we had come on a day like this and that we had been able to arrive so soon.

In the principal's office my pupils and I huddled around the gas stove while we heard much laughter in the high-school corridors. The Landsburgh High School pupils thought we were a strange-looking lot. Many came inside their principal's office to take a look at us. We were regarded with curiosity, strangeness, and wonder. Never before had these pupils seen seven mules hitched to their school-yard fence. Never before had they competed scholastically with so few in number—competitors who had reached them by muleback. The Landsburgh High School principal didn't feel about the contest the way we felt. To him, this was just a "setup" to test his pupils for the district contest which would soon be held. He told me this when he went after the sealed envelopes that held the questions. We warmed before the gas stove while he made arrangements for the contest.

"These questions were made out by the state department of education," he said when he returned. "I don't know how hard they are."

My pupils stood silently by the stove and looked at each other. We were asked to go to one of the largest classrooms. A Landsburgh High School teacher had charge of giving the tests. When the Landsburgh High School pupils came through the door to compete against my pupils, we knew why Principal Charters had selected this large classroom. My pupils looked at each other, then at their competitors.

I entered redheaded Jesse Jarvis to compete with ten of their plane-geometry pupils. I entered Billie Leonard against twenty-one of their selected algebra pupils.

"Budge, you'll have to represent us in grammar, English literature, and history," I said. "And I believe I'll put you in civil government. Is that all right?"

"Yes," he agreed. Budge had never had a course in civil government. All he knew about it was what he had read in connection with history.

"Robert Batson, you enter in history and grammar.

"Robin Baylor, you enter in algebra.

"Snookie Baylor, you enter in algebra and plane geometry.

"Sorry, Mr. Charters," I said, "we don't have anyone to enter in Latin. My best Latin pupil, Leona Maddox, couldn't make this trip."

After the contest had begun, I left the room. Miss Bertha Madden was in charge. I took our mules to Walter Scott's barn on the east end of Landsburgh, where I fed and watered them.

With the exception of an interval when the contestants ate a quick lunch, the contest lasted until

---

8. *I've not forgotten . . . books.* Mr. Stuart had set out on foot to walk the seventeen miles to Landsburgh to bring back books for his pupils. On the way he lost the trail in a blinding snowstorm and had to spend the night out.

2:30 P.M. I had one pupil, Budge Waters, in four contests. I had planned to enter him in two. Just as soon as Budge had finished with civil government, we started grading the papers. All the pupils were requested to leave the room.

We graded the papers with keys. Mr. Charters, Miss Madden, and two other teachers and I did the grading. Mr. Charters read the answers on the keys, and we checked the answers. Once or twice we stopped long enough to discuss what stiff questions these were. We wondered how far we would have gotten if we—all of us, college graduates—had taken the same test. One of the teachers asked me, while we graded these papers, if Budge Waters had ever seen these questions.

When we were through grading the papers, Mr. Charters called the contestants into the classroom.

"I want to read you the scores of this contest," he said. His voice was nervous.

"Budge Waters, winner in English literature.

"Budge Waters, winner in grammar.

"Budge Waters, winner in history with almost a perfect score.

"Budge Waters, winner in civil government.

"Why didn't you bring just this one boy?" Principal Charters asked me.

"Because I've got other good pupils," I quickly retorted.

"Billie Leonard, winner in algebra, with plenty of points to spare.

"Jesse Jarvis, second in plane geometry.

"Snookie Baylor and Robin Baylor tied for second place in algebra.

"Congratulations," said Principal Charters, "to your pupils and to you, on your success. It looks as though Winston High will represent this county in the district scholastic contest. I've never heard of such a remarkable thing."

When we left the Landsburgh High School we heard defeated pupils crying because "a little mudhole in the road like Winston beat us."

In a few minutes our mule cavalcade passed the Landsburgh High School. Faces were against the windowpanes and many pupils waved jubilantly to us as we rode by, our coattails riding the wind behind our saddles, and the ends of our scarfs bright banners on the wind. We rode victoriously down the main street of Landsburgh on our way home.   □

FOR EXPLORATION

1. Does Stuart's report present an idealized or realistic portrayal of education in rural areas, in your opinion?
2. (*a*) Describe Stuart's view of the role of the teacher in our society. (*b*) Is such a role possible in the school systems of today? Is it desirable?
3. To what cause do you attribute the unusual success of the Winston pupils in the contest?
4. (*a*) What was the first reaction of the Landsburgh students to those from Winston? Why did they react in this way? (*b*) Why were some of the Landsburgh students particularly unhappy about their defeat? (*c*) Why was it that many of the Landsburgh students "waved jubilantly" to the group from Winston?
5. How might Stuart have used this incident to support his argument for raising the standards of educational opportunity in rural areas to match those in the towns and cities?

Jesse Stuart   1907 /

Jesse Stuart's grandparents had moved to W-Hollow, an isolated valley in the Kentucky mountains, because of a deadly feud with a rival clan in eastern Kentucky. The world into which Jesse was born in 1907, as he was to discover before many years had passed, was still one in which rivals in love and politics were apt to settle their differences with fists or firearms. Being tall and powerfully built, Jesse accepted this code readily.

Because his family was very poor and Jesse was needed on the farm, he had not had much schooling, nor had he had much use for schools, before he quit going altogether at the age of fifteen. Then one day, working on a construction gang at the nearby town of Greenup, he noticed well-dressed youngsters going to the large high school there. He gave up his job on the spot, took the exams, and enrolled. (He was later to return to this school, after working his way through a few years of college, as its principal.) Interested in poetry and inspired by Robert Burns, the Scottish poet, he began to write, and, encouraged by his teachers, he continued. In 1934 his first book of poems, *Man with a Bull-Tongue Plow*, was published and widely acclaimed. While he was laying the foundations for his writing career, Jesse Stuart was fighting the county politicians to bring greater educational opportunity to the rural schoolchildren. He was finally forced out of his position in the schools, and nearly killed in the bargain, but not before he had well begun a crusade that eventually succeeded and won him great admiration in Kentucky. In 1939 Jesse Stuart bought three hundred acres of land in W-Hollow and settled down there to write the poetry and books which have made him famous. *The Thread That Runs So True*, from which the accompanying selection is drawn, is the account of his life as a schoolteacher in the Kentucky mountain country.

COURTESY OF THE AUTHOR

POETRY:
DEVELOPMENTS AND
DEPARTURES

T. S. Eliot

THE LOVE SONG OF J. ALFRED PRUFROCK

S'io credesse che mia risposta fosse
A persona che mai tornasse al mondo,
Questa fiamma staria senza piu scosse.
Ma perciocche giammai di questo fondo
Non torno vivo alcun, s'i'odo il vero,
Senza tema d'infamia ti rispondo.[1]

Let us go then, you and I,
When the evening is spread out against the sky
Like a patient etherised upon a table;
Let us go, through certain half-deserted streets,
5 The muttering retreats
Of restless nights in one-night cheap hotels
And sawdust restaurants with oyster-shells:
Streets that follow like a tedious argument
Of insidious intent
10 To lead you to an overwhelming question. . .
Oh, do not ask, "What is it?"
Let us go and make our visit.

   In the room the women come and go
Talking of Michelangelo.

   The yellow fog that rubs its back upon the win-
15   dow-panes,
The yellow smoke that rubs its muzzle on the win-
         dow-panes
Licked its tongue into the corners of the evening,
Lingered upon the pools that stand in drains,
Let fall upon its back the soot that falls from chim-
         neys,
20 Slipped by the terrace, made a sudden leap,
And seeing that it was a soft October night,
Curled once about the house, and fell asleep.

   And indeed there will be time
For the yellow smoke that slides along the street,
25 Rubbing its back upon the window-panes;
There will be time, there will be time
To prepare a face to meet the faces that you meet;
There will be time to murder and create,
And time for all the works and days of hands
30 That lift and drop a question on your plate;
Time for you and time for me,
And time yet for a hundred indecisions,
And for a hundred visions and revisions,
Before the taking of a toast and tea.

35   In the room the women come and go
Talking of Michelangelo.

   And indeed there will be time
To wonder, "Do I dare?" and, "Do I dare?"
Time to turn back and descend the stair,
40 With a bald spot in the middle of my hair—
[They will say: "How his hair is growing thin!"]
My morning coat, my collar mounting firmly to
         the chin,
My necktie rich and modest, but asserted by a sim-
         ple pin—
[They will say: "But how his arms and legs are
         thin!"]
45 Do I dare
Disturb the universe?
In a minute there is time
For decisions and revisions which a minute will
         reverse.

"The Love Song of J. Alfred Prufrock" from COLLECTED POEMS 1909–1962 by T. S. Eliot, copyright, 1936, by Harcourt Brace Jovanovich, Inc., copyright, © 1963, 1964, by T. S. Eliot. Reprinted by permission of Harcourt Brace Jovanovich, Inc., and Faber and Faber Limited.

1. *S'io credesse . . . ti rispondo.* If I believed my answer were being made to one who could ever return to the world, this flame would gleam no more; but since, if what I hear is true, never from this abyss [hell] did living man return, I answer thee without fear of infamy. (Dante. *Inferno* XXVII, 61–66)

For I have known them all already, known them
    all:—
50 Have known the evenings, morning, afternoons,
I have measured out my life with coffee spoons;
I know the voices dying with a dying fall
Beneath the music from a farther room.
    So how should I presume?

    And I have known the eyes already, known
55   them all—
The eyes that fix you in a formulated phrase,
And when I am formulated, sprawling on a pin,
When I am pinned and wriggling on the wall,
Then how should I begin
60 To spit out all the butt-ends of my days and ways?
    And how should I presume?

    And I have known the arms already, known them
    all—
Arms that are braceleted and white and bare
[But in the lamplight, downed with light brown
    hair!]
65 Is it perfume from a dress
That makes me so digress?
Arms that lie along a table, or wrap about a shawl.
    And should I then presume?
    And how should I begin?
    . . . . .
70 Shall I say, I have gone at dusk through narrow streets
And watched the smoke that rises from the pipes
Of lonely men in shirt-sleeves, leaning out of win-
    dows? . . .

    I should have been a pair of ragged claws
Scuttling across the floors of silent seas.
    . . . . .
And the afternoon, the evening, sleeps so peace-
75   fully!
Smoothed by long fingers,

Asleep . . . tired . . . or it malingers,
Stretched on the floor, here beside you and me.
Should I, after tea and cakes and ices,
80 Have the strength to force the moment to its crisis?
But though I have wept and fasted, wept and prayed,
Though I have seen my head [grown slightly bald]
    brought in upon a platter,
I am no prophet—and here's no great matter;
I have seen the moment of my greatness flicker,
And I have seen the eternal Footman hold my coat,
85   and snicker,
And in short, I was afraid.

    And would it have been worth it, after all,
After the cups, the marmalade, the tea,
Among the porcelain, among some talk of you and
    me,
90 Would it have been worth while,
To have bitten off the matter with a smile,
To have squeezed the universe into a ball
To roll it toward some overwhelming question,
To say: "I am Lazarus, come from the dead,
95 Come back to tell you all, I shall tell you all"—
If one, settling a pillow by her head,
    Should say: "That is not what I meant at all.
    That is not it, at all."

    And would it have been worth it, after all,
100 Would it have been worth while,
After the sunsets and the dooryards and the sprin-
    kled streets,
After the novels, after the teacups, after the skirts
    that trail along the floor—
And this, and so much more?—
It is impossible to say just what I mean!
But as if a magic lantern threw the nerves in patterns
105   on a screen:

contd.

T. S. Eliot

Would it have been worth while
If one, settling a pillow or throwing off a shawl,
And turning toward the window, should say:
        "That is not it at all,
110 That is not what I meant, at all."

                . . . . .

No! I am not Prince Hamlet,[2] nor was meant to be;
Am an attendant lord, one that will do
To swell a progress, start a scene or two,
Advise the prince; no doubt, an easy tool,
115 Deferential, glad to be of use,
Politic, cautious, and meticulous;
Full of high sentence, but a bit obtuse;
At times, indeed, almost ridiculous—
Almost, at times, the Fool.

120   I grow old . . . I grow old . . .
I shall wear the bottoms of my trousers rolled.

Shall I part my hair behind? Do I dare to eat a
        peach?
I shall wear white flannel trousers, and walk upon
        the beach.
I have heard the mermaids singing, each to each.

125   I do not think that they will sing to me.

I have seen them riding seaward on the waves
Combing the white hair of the waves blown back
When the wind blows the water white and black.

We have lingered in the chambers of the sea
130 By sea-girls wreathed with seaweed red and brown
Till human voices wake us, and we drown.

---

2. *Prince Hamlet,* the hero of William Shakespeare's play *Hamlet,*
who set out to prove that his mother and uncle had murdered his
father.

FOR EXPLORATION

1. The words in the epigraph to the poem are spoken by Guido da Montefeltro whom Dante encounters in his imaginary journey through hell. Guido is wrapped in flames, suffering eternal torment for his sins on earth; and he confesses his sins as an evil counselor to Dante on the assumption that Dante, like himself, is a prisoner in hell and will not return to the realm of the living. (a) In what sense can you interpret Prufrock's Song as the confession of a soul in torment? What kinds of torment might he be suffering? (b) Guido was a worldly man of action (although a sinner). How does Prufrock compare with him? Does Prufrock's confession concern things he has done or things he has failed to do? (c) In what sense could you say that Prufrock, although still alive, is already "dead"?

2. (a) Who, specifically, are the "you" and "I" of the opening line of the poem? (b) Using imagery from the poem, describe what you think is Prufrock's physical appearance. What significance do his statements in lines 51 and 121 have in terms of his condition?

3. Of what does Prufrock seem most afraid?

4. Prufrock imagines himself in various guises. What overtones of meaning do the following phrases have in reference to his life? (a) "I am pinned and wriggling on the wall." (b) "I should have been a pair of ragged claws . . . ." (c) "I am no prophet . . . ." (d) "I am Lazarus, come from the dead . . . ." (e) "I am not Prince Hamlet, nor was meant to be,/Am an attendant lord . . . ." (Reread these in the context of the poem, before answering.)

5. The poem opens with a series of startling similes and metaphors. How are the evening and the fog presented? What do these metaphors and other elements of the scene say about life as it is viewed through Prufrock's eyes?

6. What kind of "overwhelming question" is Prufrock trying to ask?

7. (a) Why does Prufrock long for the song of the mermaids in the last lines of the poem? What might the mermaids' singing represent? Why does he despair of hearing their song again? (b) What is your interpretation of the paradoxical last line? What kinds of voices has Prufrock usually heard, as reported in the poem? What do these voices speak of in contrast to the mermaids' singing?

T. S. Eliot   1888 / 1965

Thomas Stearns Eliot was born in St. Louis, Missouri. He was educated at Harvard University where he received a master's degree in philosophy in 1910, the same year in which he began writing "The Love Song of J. Alfred Prufrock." He finished the poem the following year during a visit to Germany, but it wasn't published until 1915, with the help of Ezra Pound. Eliot returned to Harvard to teach for a few years, but in 1914 he went back to Germany. World War I broke out and Eliot could not return to America. He went to England to work, married, and became a British subject in 1926.

Eliot's poems made a strong impact on the literary intellectuals of his age. Through his poems and his discussions of technique, he did much to win acceptance of "difficult" modern poetry. In describing Eliot's poetry, one critic has noted that he "employs a complex verse, combining trivial and tawdry pictures with traditionally poetic subject-matter, linking the banalities of conversation to rich rhetoric and interrupting the present with flash-backs of the past." In recognition of his enormous contribution to modern poetry, T. S. Eliot was awarded the Nobel prize for literature in 1948.

PICTORIAL PARADE INC.

Ezra Pound

IN A STATION OF THE METRO

The apparition of these faces in the crowd;
Petals on a wet, black bough.

PORTRAIT D'UNE FEMME

Your mind and you are our Sargasso Sea,[1]
London has swept about you this score years
And bright ships left you this or that in fee:
Ideas, old gossip, oddments of all things,
5 Strange spars of knowledge and dimmed wares of price.
Great minds have sought you—lacking someone else.
You have been second always. Tragical?
No. You preferred it to the usual thing:
One dull man, dulling and uxorious,
10 One average mind—with one thought less, each year.
Oh, you are patient, I have seen you sit
Hours, where something might have floated up.
And now you pay one. Yes, you richly pay.
You are a person of some interest, one comes to you
15 And takes strange gain away:

Trophies fished up; some curious suggestion;
Fact that leads nowhere; and a tale or two,
Pregnant with mandrakes, or with something else
That might prove useful and yet never proves,
20 That never fits a corner or shows use,
Or finds its hour upon the loom of days:
The tarnished, gaudy, wonderful old work;
Idols and ambergris and rare inlays,
These are your riches, your great store; and yet
25 For all this sea-hoard of deciduous things,
Strange woods half sodden, and new brighter stuff:
In the slow float of different light and deep,
No! there is nothing! In the whole and all,
Nothing that's quite your own.
            Yet this is you.

"In a Station of the Metro" and "Portrait d'une Femme" by Ezra
Pound, PERSONAE (British title: COLLECTED SHORTER POEMS). Copyright
1926 by Ezra Pound. Reprinted by permission of New Directions
Publishing Corporation and Faber and Faber Limited.
PORTRAIT D'UNE FEMME **1.** *Sargasso Sea*, a large tract of compara-
tively still water in the North Atlantic Ocean.

EPITAPHS

Fu I

Fu I[1] loved the high cloud and the hill,
Alas, he died of alcohol.

Li Po

And Li Po[2] also died drunk.
He tried to embrace a moon
In the Yellow River.

"Epitaphs" (Fu I, Li Po) by Ezra Pound, PERSONAE (British title: COLLECTED SHORTER POEMS.) Copyright 1926 by Ezra Pound. Reprinted by permission of New Directions Publishing Corporation, and Faber and Faber Limited.

1. *Fu I.* Pound is probably referring to Tu Fu (712–770), a Chinese poet especially admired for his beautiful lyrics which were often descriptive of nature. His greatness was second only to that of Li Po, who was his sometime drinking companion.

2. *Li Po* (c.710–c.762), the greatest Chinese poet, who is said to have drowned from a boat in an effort while drunk to embrace the reflected moon.

FOR EXPLORATION

Portrait D'une Femme

1. Read this poem as a puzzle. Pound's title, which translates "Portrait of a Lady," is partly misleading: the "lady" is an extended metaphor (conceit) for something quite other than a person. The key to the poem lies primarily in lines 1–2 and 14–26. If the poem still leaves you puzzled after you have read it closely for clues, try to answer these questions: (*a*) What might "bright ships" sail on? (*b*) What carries with it a "sea hoard" of strange and useless objects? (*c*) What clue would the location of London provide?

2. Once you have the key to the poem, explain the metaphorical application of "lady" to the thing central to the poem. How is the implied comparison appropriate? In what sense has this "lady" been "second always" in the minds of men who have visited her?

Epitaphs

What two different states of intoxication do these poems deal with?

Ezra Pound   1885 /

Ezra Pound, one of the creators of the Imagist Movement in poetry, was born in Hailey, Idaho. After completing his education, he taught at Wabash College in Indiana but soon traveled to Europe where he lived as an expatriot until the end of World War II. By 1912 he was already an established poet with seven published volumes that combine the command of older tradition with impressive originality.

Pound became a good friend of T. S. Eliot's, and the two became early leaders in restoring to poetry the use of literary reference as an imaginative instrument. To read much of their poetry demands a knowledge of the classics. There are three qualities that predominate in Pound's work: a sensual presentation of particulars, an attempt to do away with cluttered exposition, and a mastery of verbal sound.

During World War II Pound was attracted to Mussolini's speeches and went to Italy to live where he made broadcasts directed at the American troops. In 1945 he was arrested by the United States government because of these broadcasts but was found unfit to stand trial for treason and was committed to St. Elizabeth's Hospital in Washington, D.C. When he was released in 1958, he returned to Italy where he now lives.

Hilda Doolittle (H. D.)

PALLAS[1]

They said:
she is high and far and blind
in her high pride,
but now that my head is bowed
5 in sorrow, I find
she is most kind.

We have taken life, they said,
blithely, not groped in a mist
for things that are not—
10 are, if you will, but bloodless—
why ask happiness of the dead?
and my heart bled.

Ah, could they know
how violets throw strange fire,
15 red and purple and gold,
how they glow
gold and purple and red
where her feet tread.

"*Pallas*" from H. D. SELECTED POEMS. Copyright © 1957 by Norman
Holmes Pearson. Reprinted by permission of Grove Press, Inc.
1. *Pallas*. In Greek mythology Pallas Athena is the goddess of the
city, the protector of civilized life, and the embodiment of wisdom,
reason, and purity.

FOR EXPLORATION

Pallas

1. Pallas Athena was the Greek goddess of, among other things, wisdom and war. It is, perhaps, the combination of these two elements that makes her incomprehensible to the "they" in the poem, and which endears her to the poem's speakers. Explore the ways in which "they" misunderstand and scorn Pallas, especially as indicated in the second stanza.

2. The speaker says that Pallas is "most kind." Relate this remark to the last stanza of the poem.

HEAT

O wind, rend open the heat,
cut apart the heat,
rend it to tatters.

Fruit cannot drop
5 through this thick air—
fruit cannot fall into heat
that presses up and blunts
the points of pears
and rounds the grapes.

10 Cut the heat—
plough through it,
turning it on either side
of your path.

"*Heat*" from H. D. SELECTED POEMS. Copyright © 1957 by Norman
Holmes Pearson. Reprinted by permission of Grove Press, Inc.

Heat

1. What qualities is heat given in this poem?
2. What imagery conveys this impression?

CREATIVE RESPONSE

Try to convey your own impression of an unbearably hot
day in a written form as compressed as this poem. What
sensations would you choose to emphasize? What two or
three images would you choose as most fitting?

Hilda Doolittle   1886 / 1961

Moved by the need for greater clarity and precision in
poetry, Hilda Doolittle, writing under the pseudonym H. D.,
became one of the first American imagist poets. Doolittle
was born in Bethlehem, Pennsylvania, and grew up in
Philadelphia. When she attended Bryn Mawr College, she
became good friends with Ezra Pound and Marianne
Moore. Like T. S. Eliot's, Doolittle's poetry was greatly
influenced by the work and encouragement of Ezra Pound.
It was Pound who described her poetry so perfectly when
he said, "Objective—no slither; direct—no excessive use of
adjectives, no metaphors that won't permit examination.
It's straight talk, straight as the Greek!"

William Carlos Williams

SPRING AND ALL

By the road to the contagious hospital
under the surge of the blue
mottled clouds driven from the
northeast—a cold wind. Beyond, the
5 waste of broad, muddy fields
brown with dried weeds, standing and fallen

patches of standing water
the scattering of tall trees

All along the road the reddish
10 purplish, forked, upstanding, twiggy
stuff of bushes and small trees
with dead, brown leaves under them
leafless vines—

Lifeless in appearance, sluggish
15 dazed spring approaches—

They enter the new world naked,
cold, uncertain of all
save that they enter. All about them
the cold, familiar wind—
20 Now the grass, tomorrow
the stiff curl of wild carrot leaf
One by one objects are defined—
It quickens: clarity, outline of leaf

But now the stark dignity of
25 entrance—Still, the profound change
has come upon them: rooted they
grip down and begin to awaken

William Carlos Williams, COLLECTED EARLIER POEMS. Copyright 1938 by William Carlos Williams. Reprinted by permission of New Directions Publishing Corporation and Laurence Pollinger Limited.

William Carlos Williams   1883 / 1963

Although for many years Dr. Williams spent much of his time seeing patients and delivering babies in and around Rutherford, New Jersey, he found time to write more than thirty-seven volumes of prose and poetry.

For Dr. Williams the everyday event had beauty, interest, and significance. His poetry deals with such common things as spring, plums, a wheelbarrow—in short, what one might see daily, yet not notice. His writing reflects the physician's experience of seeing people under all conditions of life—from when they are being born to the moment of their death. Such observation has given insight and substance to his poetry and stories. Two collections of his poetry are *Collected Later Poems* (1950) and *Collected Earlier Poems* (1951).

THE BOTTICELLIAN[1] TREES

The alphabet of
the trees

is fading in the
song of the leaves

5   the crossing
bars of the thin

letters that spelled
winter

and the cold
10 have been illumined

with
pointed green

by the rain and sun—
The strict simple

15 principles of
straight branches

are being modified
by pinched out

ifs of color, devout
20 conditions

the smiles of love—

. . . . .

until the stript
sentences

move as a woman's
25 limbs under cloth

and praise from secrecy
with hot ardor

love's ascendancy
in summer—

30 In summer the song
sings itself

above the muffled words—

William Carlos Williams, COLLECTED EARLIER POEMS. Copyright 1938 by William Carlos Williams. Reprinted by permission of New Directions Publishing Corporation and Laurence Pollinger Limited.
1. *Botticellian*, Sandro Botticelli (1445–1510), Italian painter, supreme master of linear motion.

FOR EXPLORATION

Spring and All

1. How does the description of spring given in this poem differ from conventional descriptions? What aspects of the spring does the poem emphasize?
2. How might the "contagious hospital" be related to the imagery and the theme of the poem?
3. Does the poem suggest that the beginning of life is an easy process? Why or why not?

The Botticellian Trees

1. What type of natural progression is described in this poem? How is this progression paralleled in language?
2. Could this be a poem about writing poetry? Explain.
3. What ideas are blended in the last three lines?

by Robert Hayden

The New Poetry Movement

Much that has occurred in contemporary American poetry can be seen as the culmination of tendencies originating in the nineteenth century with Walt Whitman, Emily Dickinson, and, to some extent, Stephen Crane. These poets are now generally considered to have been innovators, forerunners of modernism. And during the 1920's literary rebels eagerly claimed them as spiritual ancestors whose work had helped prepare the way for the New Poetry movement.

Known also as the Poetry Revival, the New Poetry Movement began in London as an international phenomenon before the First World War. Ezra Pound, the brilliant expatriate American poet, encouraged poets to break with the past in order to achieve greater freedom of expression. Pound's theories led to the concept of Imagism, which owed something to French Symbolism as well as to oriental and ancient Greek poetry. In the group of young poets attracted to the ideals of Imagism were the Americans John Gould Fletcher, Amy Lowell, Hilda Doolittle (who became well known as H. D.) and her English husband, Richard Aldington.

The Imagists (they sometimes referred to themselves rather artily as *Les Imagistes*) received attention for several years as a distinct group and had some influence on Carl Sandburg, Wallace Stevens, and Marianne Moore. Ezra Pound was their acknowledged leader, editing *Des Imagistes (Some Imagist Poets)* in 1914 and publishing essays and manifestoes. He defined the principles of Imagism as precision of diction and image, freedom in the choice of subjects, and a controlled freedom of rhythm based on musical cadence and not on traditional meters—free verse, in other words, which gave to the New Poetry Movement the alternate name of the Free Verse Revolt.

The revolt against poetic conventions had started early in the twentieth century. Two great poets, Edwin Arlington Robinson and Robert Frost, had already produced fresh and original work by the end of the first decade. Ignored at first, they later emerged as luminaries of the Poetry Revival. But in 1912, Harriet Monroe published the first number of *Poetry: A Magazine of Verse* in Chicago. This magazine was of strategic importance, providing a medium for the work of poets here and abroad, disseminating the new poetic theories, and bringing them into focus and to the attention of the public.

The New Poetry Movement, somewhat tentative during the war years, gained momentum in the 1920's. Now popularly referred to as the "Jazz Age," this was a period of drastic social change, a time of experimentation in life-styles as well as in the arts. The "modern mode" in literature was firmly established during the decade. Changes in moral outlook transformed poetic vision and technique. Poets sought to free their art from the gentility and didacticism of the previous generation. Freudian psychology, the changing status of women, the development of science and technology—all suggested new possibilities for poetry. Religious skepticism, growing since the last century, and the moral disillusionment caused by the war were recurrent themes in the new poetry.

WORLD WIDE PHOTOS

DOOLITTLE

COURTESY OF OCTOBER HOUSE, INC.

HAYDEN

UNDERWOOD AND UNDERWOOD

BENET

VIKING PRESS, PHOTO: GEORGE PLATT-LYNES

MOORE

POUND

WIDE WORLD PHOTOS

ROBINSON

BORIS DE RACHEWILTZ,
COURTESY OF NEW DIRECTIONS
PUBLISHING CORP.

American poets were frequently critics of society. Edna St. Vincent Millay, for example, in "Justice Denied in Massachusetts" protested what she and many of her contemporaries believed to be a miscarriage of justice in the execution of the philosophical anarchists, Sacco and Vanzetti. James Weldon Johnson, Claude McKay, and Countee Cullen spoke out in eloquent, often passionate, lyrics against racial injustice. Sandburg, Robinson, and Vachel Lindsay, among others, expressed their distrust of American materialism. The spiritual emptiness of an industrialized civilization, the sense of alienation and futility experienced by many individuals in the modern world were the central themes of T. S. Eliot's "The Love Song of J. Alfred Prufrock" and "The Waste Land."

But if poets were critics of twentieth-century life, they were also explorers engaged in exciting voyages of discovery. They turned to the American past for subjects and made use of indigenous folk materials. Some looked for a genuine "American rhythm," seeking it in jazz and spirituals, in the poetry and song of the American Indian. Folk heroes and legendary figures were celebrated in ballads and other forms of narrative poetry—Abe Lincoln, John Brown, Paul Bunyan, John Henry, Johnny Appleseed, etc. Poems derived from history and myth quite often blended psychological realism with romantic elements. A notable example was *John Brown's Body* (1926), Stephen Vincent Benét's book-length poem about the Civil War. Robinson, Frost, Sandburg, Edgar Lee Masters, and Lindsay, whose careers had started before the twenties, continued to write what may be called "poetry in the American grain."

Robert Frost

MENDING WALL

Something there is that doesn't love a wall,
That sends the frozen-ground-swell under it
And spills the upper boulders in the sun,
And makes gaps even two can pass abreast.
5 The work of hunters is another thing:
I have come after them and made repair
Where they have left not one stone on a stone,
But they would have the rabbit out of hiding,
To please the yelping dogs. The gaps I mean,
10 No one has seen them made or heard them made,
But at spring mending-time we find them there.
I let my neighbor know beyond the hill;
And on a day we meet to walk the line
And set the wall between us once again.
15 We keep the wall between us as we go.
To each the boulders that have fallen to each.
And some are loaves and some so nearly balls
We have to use a spell to make them balance:
"Stay where you are until our backs are turned!"
20 We wear our fingers rough with handling them.
Oh, just another kind of outdoor game,
One on a side. It comes to little more:
There where it is we do not need the wall:
He is all pine and I am apple orchard.
25 My apple trees will never get across
And eat the cones under his pines, I tell him.
He only says, "Good fences make good neighbors."
Spring is the mischief in me, and I wonder
If I could put a notion in his head:
30 "Why do they make good neighbors? Isn't it
Where there are cows? But here there are no cows.
Before I built a wall I'd ask to know
What I was walling in or walling out,
And to whom I was like to give offense.
35 Something there is that doesn't love a wall,
That wants it down." I could say "Elves" to him,
But it's not elves exactly, and I'd rather
He said it for himself. I see him there,
Bringing a stone grasped firmly by the top
40 In each hand, like an old-stone savage armed.
He moves in darkness as it seems to me,
Not of woods only and the shade of trees.
He will not go behind his father's saying,
And he likes having thought of it so well
He says again, "Good fences make good neigh-
45   bors."

From THE POETRY OF ROBERT FROST edited by Edward Connery Lathem. Copyright 1916, 1923, 1930, 1939, © 1969 by Holt, Rinehart and Winston, Inc. Copyright 1942, 1944, 1951, © 1958 by Robert Frost. Copyright © 1967, 1970 by Lesley Frost Ballantine. Reprinted by permission of Holt, Rinehart and Winston, Inc. and Jonathan Cape Ltd.

"OUT, OUT—"

The buzz saw snarled and rattled in the yard
And made dust and dropped stove-length sticks of
    wood,
Sweet-scented stuff when the breeze drew across it.
And from there those that lifted eyes could count
5 Five mountain ranges one behind the other
Under the sunset far into Vermont.
And the saw snarled and rattled, snarled and
    rattled,
As it ran light, or had to bear a load.
And nothing happened: day was all but done.
10 Call it a day, I wish they might have said
To please the boy by giving him the half hour
That a boy counts so much when saved from work.
His sister stood beside them in her apron
To tell them "Supper." At the word, the saw,
15 As if to prove saws knew what supper meant,
Leaped out at the boy's hand, or seemed to leap—

He must have given the hand. However it was,
Neither refused the meeting. But the hand!
The boy's first outcry was a rueful laugh,
20 As he swung toward them holding up the hand,
Half in appeal, but half as if to keep
The life from spilling. Then the boy saw all—
Since he was old enough to know, big boy
Doing a man's work, though a child at heart—
25 He saw all spoiled. "Don't let him cut my hand off—
The doctor, when he comes. Don't let him, sister!"
So. But the hand was gone already.
The doctor put him in the dark of ether.
He lay and puffed his lips out with his breath.
30 And then—the watcher at his pulse took fright.
No one believed. They listened at his heart.
Little—less—nothing!—and that ended it.
No more to build on there. And they, since they
Were not the one dead, turned to their affairs.

STOPPING BY WOODS
ON A SNOWY EVENING

Whose woods these are I think I know.
His house is in the village though;
He will not see me stopping here
To watch his woods fill up with snow.

5 My little horse must think it queer
To stop without a farmhouse near
Between the woods and frozen lake
The darkest evening of the year.

He gives his harness bells a shake
10 To ask if there is some mistake.
The only other sound's the sweep
Of easy wind and downy flake.

The woods are lovely, dark, and deep,
But I have promises to keep,
15 And miles to go before I sleep,
And miles to go before I sleep.

"Out, Out—" and "Stopping by Woods on a Snowy Evening"
from THE POETRY OF ROBERT FROST edited by Edward Connery
Lathem. Copyright 1916, 1923, 1930, 1939, © 1969 by Holt,
Rinehart and Winston, Inc. Copyright 1942, 1944, 1951, © 1958
by Robert Frost. Copyright © 1967, 1970 by Lesley Frost Ballantine. Reprinted by permission of Holt, Rinehart and Winston, Inc.
and Jonathan Cape Ltd.

Robert Frost

BIRCHES

When I see birches bend to left and right
Across the lines of straighter darker trees,
I like to think some boy's been swinging them.
But swinging doesn't bend them down to stay
5 As ice storms do. Often you must have seen them
Loaded with ice a sunny winter morning
After a rain. They click upon themselves
As the breeze rises, and turn many-colored
As the stir cracks and crazes their enamel.
10 Soon the sun's warmth makes them shed crystal shells
Shattering and avalanching on the snow crust—
Such heaps of broken glass to sweep away
You'd think the inner dome of heaven had fallen.
They are dragged to the withered bracken by the load,
15 And they seem not to break; though once they are bowed
So low for long, they never right themselves:
You may see their trunks arching in the woods
Years afterwards, trailing their leaves on the ground
Like girls on hands and knees that throw their hair
20 Before them over their heads to dry in the sun.
But I was going to say when Truth broke in
With all her matter of fact about the ice storm,
I should prefer to have some boy bend them
As he went out and in to fetch the cows—
25 Some boy too far from town to learn baseball,
Whose only play was what he found himself,
Summer or winter, and could play alone.
One by one he subdued his father's trees
By riding them down over and over again
30 Until he took the stiffness out of them,
And not one but hung limp, not one was left
For him to conquer. He learned all there was
To learn about not launching out too soon
And so not carrying the tree away
35 Clear to the ground. He always kept his poise
To the top branches, climbing carefully
With the same pains you use to fill a cup
Up to the brim, and even above the brim.
Then he flung outward, feet first, with a swish,

From THE POETRY OF ROBERT FROST edited by Edward Connery
Lathem. Copyright 1916, 1923, 1930, 1939, © 1969 by Holt,
Rinehart and Winston, Inc. Copyright 1942, 1944, 1951, © 1958
by Robert Frost, Copyright © 1967, 1970 by Lesley Frost Ballantine. Reprinted by permission of Holt, Rinehart and Winston, Inc.
and Jonathan Cape Ltd.

40 Kicking his way down through the air to the ground.
So was I once myself a swinger of birches.
And so I dream of going back to be.
It's when I'm weary of considerations,
And life is too much like a pathless wood
45 Where your face burns and tickles with the cobwebs
Broken across it, and one eye is weeping
From a twig's having lashed across it open.
I'd like to get away from earth awhile
And then come back to it and begin over.
50 May no fate willfully misunderstand me
And half grant what I wish and snatch me away
Not to return. Earth's the right place for love:
I don't know where it's likely to go better.
I'd like to go by climbing a birch tree,
55 And climb black branches up a snow-white trunk
Toward heaven, till the tree could bear no more,
But dipped its top and set me down again.
That would be good both going and coming back.
One could do worse than be a swinger of birches.

THE DEATH OF THE HIRED MAN

Mary sat musing on the lamp-flame at the table,
Waiting for Warren. When she heard his step,
She ran on tiptoe down the darkened passage
To meet him in the doorway with the news
5 And put him on his guard. "Silas is back."
She pushed him outward with her through the door
And shut it after her. "Be kind," she said.
She took the market things from Warren's arms
And set them on the porch, then drew him down
10 To sit beside her on the wooden steps.

"When was I ever anything but kind to him?
But I'll not have the fellow back," he said.
"I told him so last haying, didn't I?
If he left then, I said, that ended it.
15 What good is he? Who else will harbor him

At his age for the little he can do?
What help he is there's no depending on.
Off he goes always when I need him most.
He thinks he ought to earn a little pay,
20 Enough at least to buy tobacco with,
So he won't have to beg and be beholden.
'All right,' I say, 'I can't afford to pay
Any fixed wages, though I wish I could.'
'Someone else can.' 'Then someone else will have to.'
25 I shouldn't mind his bettering himself
If that was what it was. You can be certain,
When he begins like that, there's someone at him
Trying to coax him off with pocket money—
In haying time, when any help is scarce.
30 In winter he comes back to us. I'm done."

"The Death of the Hired Man" from THE POETRY OF ROBERT FROST edited by Edward Connery Lathem. Copyright 1930, 1939, © 1969 by Holt, Rinehart and Winston, Inc. Copyright © 1958 by Robert Frost. Copyright © 1967 by Lesley Frost Ballantine. Reprinted by permission of Holt, Rinehart and Winston, Inc., the Estate of Robert Frost, and Jonathan Cape Ltd.

Robert Frost

"Sh! not so loud: he'll hear you," Mary said.

"I want him to: he'll have to soon or late."

"He's worn out. He's asleep beside the stove.
When I came up from Rowe's I found him here,
35 Huddled against the barn door fast asleep,
A miserable sight, and frightening, too—
You needn't smile—I didn't recognize him—
I wasn't looking for him—and he's changed.
Wait till you see."

       "Where did you say he'd been?"

40 "He didn't say. I dragged him to the house,
And gave him tea and tried to make him smoke.
I tried to make him talk about his travels.
Nothing would do: he just kept nodding off."

"What did he say? Did he say anything?"

"But little."

45   "Anything? Mary, confess
He said he'd come to ditch the meadow for me."

"Warren!"

     "But did he? I just want to know."

"Of course he did. What would you have him say?
Surely you wouldn't grudge the poor old man
50 Some humble way to save his self-respect.
He added, if you really care to know,
He meant to clear the upper pasture, too.
That sounds like something you have heard before?
Warren, I wish you could have heard the way
55 He jumbled everything. I stopped to look
Two or three times—he made me feel so queer—

To see if he was talking in his sleep.
He ran on Harold Wilson—you remember—
The boy you had in haying four years since.
60 He's finished school, and teaching in his college.
Silas declares you'll have to get him back.
He says they two will make a team for work:
Between them they will lay this farm as smooth!
The way he mixed that in with other things.
65 He thinks young Wilson a likely lad, though daft
On education—you know how they fought
All through July under the blazing sun,
Silas up on the cart to build the load,
Harold along beside to pitch it on."

70 "Yes, I took care to keep well out of earshot."

"Well, those days trouble Silas like a dream.
You wouldn't think they would. How some things
    linger!
Harold's young college-boy's assurance piqued
    him.
After so many years he still keeps finding
75 Good arguments he sees he might have used.
I sympathize. I know just how it feels
To think of the right thing to say too late.
Harold's associated in his mind with Latin.
He asked me what I thought of Harold's saying
80 He studied Latin, like the violin,
Because he liked it—that an argument!
He said he couldn't make the boy believe
He could find water with a hazel prong—
Which showed how much good school had ever
    done him.
85 He wanted to go over that. But most of all
He thinks if he could have another chance
To teach him how to build a load of hay——"

"I know, that's Silas' one accomplishment.
He bundles every forkful in its place,
90 And tags and numbers it for future reference,
So he can find and easily dislodge it
In the unloading. Silas does that well.
He takes it out in bunches like big birds' nests.
You never see him standing on the hay
95 He's trying to lift, straining to lift himself.''

"He thinks if he could teach him that, he'd be
Some good perhaps to someone in the world.
He hates to see a boy the fool of books.
Poor Silas, so concerned for other folk,
100 And nothing to look backward to with pride,
And nothing to look forward to with hope,
So now and never any different.''

Part of a moon was falling down the west,
Dragging the whole sky with it to the hills.
105 Its light poured softly in her lap. She saw it
And spread her apron to it. She put out her hand
Among the harplike morning-glory strings,
Taut with the dew from garden bed to eaves,
As if she played unheard some tenderness
110 That wrought on him beside her in the night.
"Warren," she said, "he has come home to die:
You needn't be afraid he'll leave you this time.''

"Home," he mocked gently.

                "Yes, what else but home?
It all depends on what you mean by home.
115 Of course he's nothing to us, any more
Than was the hound that came a stranger to us
Out of the woods, worn out upon the trail.''

"Home is the place where, when you have to go
        there,
They have to take you in.''

                "I should have called it
120 Something you somehow haven't to deserve.''

Warren leaned out and took a step or two,
Picked up a little stick, and brought it back
And broke it in his hand and tossed it by.
"Silas has better claim on us you think
125 Than on his brother? Thirteen little miles
As the road winds would bring him to his door.
Silas has walked that far no doubt today.
Why doesn't he go there? His brother's rich,
A somebody—director in the bank.''

"He never told us that.''

130   "We know it, though.''

"I think his brother ought to help, of course.
I'll see to that if there is need. He ought of right
To take him in, and might be willing to—
He may be better than appearances.
135 But have some pity on Silas. Do you think
If he had any pride in claiming kin
Or anything he looked for from his brother,
He'd keep so still about him all this time?''

"I wonder what's between them.''

                "I can tell you.
140 Silas is what he is—we wouldn't mind him—
But just the kind that kinsfolk can't abide.
He never did a thing so very bad.
He don't know why he isn't quite as good
As anybody. Worthless though he is,
145 He won't be made ashamed to please his brother.''

"I can't think Si ever hurt anyone.''

"No, but he hurt my heart the way he lay
And rolled his old head on that sharp-edged chair-
        back.

                    contd.

He wouldn't let me put him on the lounge.
150 You must go in and see what you can do.
I made the bed up for him there tonight.
You'll be surprised at him—how much he's broken.
His working days are done; I'm sure of it."

"I'd not be in a hurry to say that."

155 "I haven't been. Go, look, see for youself.
But, Warren, please remember how it is:
He's come to help you ditch the meadow.
He has a plan. You mustn't laugh at him.
He may not speak of it, and then he may.
160 I'll sit and see if that small sailing cloud
Will hit or miss the moon."

                              It hit the moon.
Then there were three there, making a dim row,
The moon, the little silver cloud, and she.

Warren returned—too soon, it seemed to her—
165 Slipped to her side, caught up her hand and waited.

"Warren?" she questioned.

                    "Dead," was all he answered.

PHOTO BY KEN HEYMAN FROM RAPHO-GUILLUMETTE

Robert Frost   1874 / 1963

A man who lived most of his life with great simplicity in New England where nine generations of his ancestors had lived before him, Robert Frost, more than most poets, was a nationally known figure. Four times winner of the Pulitzer Prize in Poetry, he did much to win acceptance for modern poetry.

Much of Frost's poetry seems to grow naturally from the changing seasons, the wooded mountains, and the rugged farms north of Boston. But although Frost often uses this New England setting, he is not primarily either a nature poet or a local colorist. His setting is usually merely background for the New Englander himself. His basic interest is man; the drama of the human situation is the hard core of his poetry.

Like the New Englanders he writes about—and like most modern poets—Frost leaves much unsaid. His apparently simple poems often turn out to be rich in hidden meanings. A fine storyteller, he often gives only the facts of an episode and leaves it to the reader to discover the significance.

Part of Frost's popularity with the general reader has no doubt stemmed from the fact that his poetry looks and sounds "like poetry." Readers respond favorably to the familiar iambic pentameter lines he often uses or to other traditional verse forms and stanza patterns. Only on careful reading is the subtly changed rhythm apparent, or the fact that every word carries a particular weight of meaning. Frost once said that art should "clean" life and "strip it to form." There is nothing superfluous in the poetry of Robert Frost.

FOR EXPLORATION

Mending Wall

1. (*a*) How does the speaker characterize his neighbor? (*b*) How does each differ on the subject of the necessity of walls?

2. What meanings does the word "wall" acquire beyond an actual physical wall? Could you describe the neighbor as "walled in"? In what sense?

3. What role do natural forces play? Are they for or against walls?

"Out, Out—"

1. What kind of effect do the last two lines have on you? What do they hint about the boy's family? About the type of life he may have led?

2. What is unusual about the way the word "supper" is used?

3. This poem achieves its striking effects by focusing on certain details, and omitting a great many which would normally occur in a factual report. What details give the accident and the boy's reaction such vividness? What kinds of detail has Frost left out which give the incident such impact?

Stopping by Woods

1. What kind of impression does the sound of the words and the rhyme of this poem convey?

2. (*a*) What overtones do you catch in the last two lines of the poem? (*b*) Critics have commented that this is a poem about death. Would you agree or disagree? Why?

Birches

1. (*a*) What images, metaphors, and language effects are employed to describe the effect of ice storms on the birches?

(*b*) What effect does a boy's swinging on birches have, by way of contrast?

2. (*a*) According to Frost, swinging on birches is a very precise art. Describe it in detail. (*b*) What does the metaphor used to describe climbing birches to the highest possible point suggest about the satisfactions to be gained from such undertakings?

3. (*a*) What symbolic implications does swinging on birches acquire in the last third of the poem? What kind of balance does "both going and coming back" suggest? (*b*) Which realm—the ideal or real, heaven or earth—has the stronger attraction? Why? What are the drawbacks of each?

The Death of the Hired Man

1. (*a*) What kind of dramatic situation does this poem open with? Specifically, what has occurred between Silas and Warren? (*b*) What impression of Warren's character do you get from the opening dialogue? (*c*) Does Warren's attitude toward Silas change as the action progresses?

2. Why does Silas make Mary feel "so queer"? In what ways has Silas changed from what he once was?

3. (*a*) What type of man is Silas? What is his one accomplishment? (*b*) What aspect of his character does his criticism of Harold reflect?

4. (*a*) What does Mary mean in line 120? (*b*) Why, do you suppose, did Silas not try to return to his brother's home? (*c*) In what sense is this a poem about human allegiances, about people who are or are not "deserving"?

5. What in your opinion are the chief elements of Mary's compassion for Silas?

Edwin Arlington Robinson

MINIVER CHEEVY

Miniver Cheevy, child of scorn,
    Grew lean while he assailed the seasons;
He wept that he was ever born,
    And he had reasons.

5 Miniver loved the days of old
    When swords were bright and steeds were prancing;
The vision of a warrior bold
    Would set him dancing.

Miniver sighed for what was not,
10   And dreamed, and rested from his labors;
He dreamed of Thebes and Camelot,
    And Priam's neighbors.[1]

Miniver mourned the ripe renown
    That made so many a name so fragrant;
15 He mourned Romance, now on the town,[2]
    And Art, a vagrant.

Miniver loved the Medici,[3]
    Albeit he had never seen one;
He would have sinned incessantly
20   Could he have been one.

Miniver cursed the commonplace
    And eyed a khaki suit with loathing;
He missed the medieval grace
    Of iron clothing.

25 Miniver scorned the gold he sought,
    But sore annoyed was he without it;
Miniver thought, and thought, and thought,
    And thought about it.

Miniver Cheevy, born too late,
30   Scratched his head and kept on thinking;
Miniver coughed, and called it fate,
    And kept on drinking.

RICHARD CORY

Whenever Richard Cory went downtown,
    We people on the pavement looked at him:
He was a gentleman from sole to crown,
    Clean-favored, and imperially slim.

5 And he was always quietly arrayed,
    And he was always human when he talked;
But still he fluttered pulses when he said,
    "Good morning," and he glittered when he
        walked.

And he was rich—yes, richer than a king—
10   And admirably schooled in every grace:
In fine, we thought that he was everything
    To make us wish that we were in his place.

So on we worked, and waited for the light,
    And went without the meat, and cursed the
        bread;
15 And Richard Cory, one calm summer night,
    Went home and put a bullet through his head.

"*Miniver Cheevy*" (Copyright 1907 Charles Scribner's Sons; renewal copyright 1935) is reprinted by permission of Charles Scribner's Sons from THE TOWN DOWN THE RIVER by Edwin Arlington Robinson.

"*Richard Cory*" is reprinted by permission of Charles Scribner's Sons from THE CHILDREN OF THE NIGHT by Edwin Arlington Robinson (1897).

1. *Thebes . . . neighbors.* Thebes was the capital of ancient Egypt during its period of greatness. Camelot was the legendary site of King Arthur's palace. Priam was the last king of Troy; his neighbors were the Greeks, who conquered Troy in the Trojan War.
2. *on the town,* living on charity, a pauper.
3. *the Medici* (med′ə chē), the ruling family of Florence, Italy, during the fifteenth and sixteenth centuries, who were notable both for their generous patronage of art and for their lavish living and wicked lives.

CASSANDRA[1]

I heard one who said: "Verily,
    What word have I for children here?
Your Dollar is your only Word
    The wrath of it your only fear.

5 "You build it altars tall enough
    To make you see, but you are blind;
You cannot leave it long enough
    To look before you or behind.

 "When Reason beckons you to pause,
10   You laugh and say that you know best;
But what it is you know, you keep
    As dark as ingots in a chest.

 "You laugh and answer, 'We are young;
    O leave us now, and let us grow.'—
15 Not asking how much more of this
    Will Time endure or Fate bestow.

 "Because a few complacent years
    Have made your peril of your pride,
Think you that you are to go on
20   Forever pampered and untried?

 "What lost eclipse of history,
    What bivouac of the marching stars,
Has given the sign for you to see
    Millenniums and last great wars?

25 "What unrecorded overthrow
    Of all the world has ever known,
Or ever been, has made itself
    So plain to you, and you alone?

 "Your Dollar, Dove and Eagle make
30   A Trinity that even you
Rate higher than you rate yourselves;
    It pays, it flatters, and it's new.

 "And though your very flesh and blood
    Be what your Eagle eats and drinks,
35 You'll praise him for the best of birds,
    Not knowing what the Eagle thinks.

 "The power is yours, but not the sight;
    You see not upon what you tread;
You have the ages for your guide,
40   But not the wisdom to be led.

 "Think you to tread forever down
    The merciless old verities?
And are you never to have eyes
    To see the world for what it is?

45 "Are you to pay for what you have
    With all you are?"—No other word
We caught, but with a laughing crowd
    Moved on. None heeded, and few heard.

"Cassandra." Reprinted with permission of The Macmillan Company from COLLECTED POEMS by Edwin Arlington Robinson. Copyright 1916 by Edwin Arlington Robinson, renewed 1944 by Ruth Nivison.
1. *Cassandra*. Apollo gave her the gift of prophecy, but afterwards, when he became angry with her, he decreed that no one should believe her prophecies.

Miniver Cheevy

1. (*a*) How is Miniver not "a man of his time"? (*b*) Would he have been happy in the other times of which he dreams? Why or why not?

2. (*a*) What attitude does the speaker take toward Miniver in the last two stanzas? (*b*) Is there any ambivalence in Miniver's actions as described here?

Richard Cory

1. (*a*) What contrast between Richard Cory and the rest of the people is built up in the first two stanzas? In what ways does he stand out? (*b*) Is Cory portrayed sympathetically? Does he have the sympathy of the people who know him?

2. (*a*) What possible motive might Cory have had for killing himself? (*b*) Do you find any indication of this in the poem? Where?

Cassandra

1. What implications does the title have for the poem? Where in the poem do these implications become most evident?

2. Trace the use of imagery of blindness and worship in this poem. What kind of commentary on the people addressed do these provide?

3. Paraphrase lines 21–28. How are these lines related to the "merciless old verities" referred to in the next-to-last stanza?

Edwin Arlington Robinson 1869 / 1935

During the 1920's Edwin Arlington Robinson was generally regarded as America's greatest living poet. Three times during that decade he was awarded the Pulitzer Prize.

Robinson spent his youth in Gardiner, Maine. Financial difficulties subsequent to his father's death brought an end to his schooling after two years at Harvard. He returned to Gardiner and devoted his time to writing poetry. When he moved to New York in 1897 he led a hermitlike existence, taking jobs only to enable him to live and spending his greatest efforts on poetry. In 1916 *The Man Against the Sky* brought him sudden fame.

"Miniver Cheevy," "Richard Cory," and others of Robinson's best-known poems are part of the "Tilbury" portraits and grew out of his New England experiences. This Tilbury Town gallery is composed largely of "cheated dreamers" and "bewildered mediocrities," most of whom manage in one way or another to withdraw from hard reality. But Robinson's pessimism is always tempered by wit and imagination, often by flashes of wry humor. His thorough mastery of intricate and varied poetic forms and his fine feeling for the subtler meanings of words give his poems a distinctive flavor.

Carl Sandburg

GONE

Everybody loved Chick Lorimer in our town.
           Far off
      Everybody loved her.
So we all love a wild girl keeping a hold
5   On a dream she wants.
Nobody knows now where Chick Lorimer went.
Nobody knows why she packed her trunk . . . a few old things
And is gone,
        Gone with her little chin
10   Thrust ahead of her
        And her soft hair blowing careless
        From under a wide hat,
Dancer, singer, a laughing passionate lover.

Were there ten men or a hundred hunting Chick?
15 Were there five men or fifty with aching hearts?
      Everybody loved Chick Lorimer.
        Nobody knows where she's gone.

"Gone" from CHICAGO POEMS by Carl Sandburg, copyright, 1916, by
Holt, Rinehart and Winston, Inc.; copyright, 1944, by Carl Sandburg.
Reprinted by permission of Harcourt Brace Jovanovich, Inc.

Carl Sandburg

COOL TOMBS

When Abraham Lincoln was shoveled into the tombs, he forgot the
copperheads[1] and the assassin . . . in the dust, in the cool tombs.

And Ulysses Grant lost all thought of con men and Wall Street, cash
and Collateral turned ashes . . . in the dust, in the cool tombs.

Pocahontas' body, lovely as a poplar, sweet as a red haw in November or a pawpaw in May, did she wonder? does she remember?
. . . in the dust, in the cool tombs?

Take any streetful of people buying clothes and groceries, cheering
a hero or throwing confetti and blowing tin horns . . . tell me if
the lovers are losers . . . tell me if any get more than the lovers . . .
in the dust . . . in the cool tombs.

From CORNHUSKERS by Carl Sandburg. Copyright 1918 by Holt,
Rinehart and Winston, Inc. Copyright 1946 by Carl Sandburg. Re-
printed by permission of Holt, Rinehart and Winston, Inc. and
Laurence Pollinger Limited.
1. *copperheads*, people in the North who sympathized with the
South during the Civil War.

CHICAGO

Hog Butcher for the World,
Tool Maker, Stacker of Wheat,
Player with Railroads and the Nation's Freight Handler;
Stormy, husky, brawling,
5   City of the Big Shoulders:

They tell me you are wicked and I believe them, for I have seen your painted women
    under the gas lamps luring the farm boys.
And they tell me you are crooked and I answer: Yes, it is true I have seen the gunman
    kill and go free to kill again.
And they tell me you are brutal and my reply is: On the faces of women and children
    I have seen the marks of wanton hunger.
And having answered so I turn once more to those who sneer at this my city, and I
    give them back the sneer and say to them:
Come and show me another city with lifted head singing so proud to be alive and
10   coarse and strong and cunning.
Flinging magnetic curses amid the toil of piling job on job, here is a tall bold slugger
    set vivid against the little soft cities;
Fierce as a dog with tongue lapping for action, cunning as a savage pitted against the
    wilderness,
        Bareheaded,
        Shoveling,
15   Wrecking,
        Planning,
        Building, breaking, rebuilding,
Under the smoke, dust all over his mouth, laughing with white teeth,
Under the terrible burden of destiny laughing as a young man laughs,
20 Laughing even as an ignorant fighter laughs who has never lost a battle,
Bragging and laughing that under his wrist is the pulse, and under his ribs the heart
    of the people,
        Laughing!
Laughing the stormy, husky, brawling laughter of Youth, half-naked, sweating, proud
    to be Hog Butcher, Tool Maker, Stacker of Wheat, Player with Railroads and
    Freight Handler to the Nation.

From CHICAGO POEMS by Carl Sandburg. Copyright 1916 by Holt, Rinehart and Winston, Inc. Copyright 1944 by Carl Sandburg. Reprinted by permission of Holt, Rinehart and Winston, Inc. and Laurence Pollinger Limited.

Carl Sandburg

from

"FOUR PRELUDES ON PLAYTHINGS OF THE WIND"

"The past is a bucket of ashes."

It has happened before.
Strong men put up a city and got
          a nation together,
And paid singers to sing and women
5   to warble: We are the greatest city,
         the greatest nation,
         nothing like us ever was.

And while the singers sang
and the strong men listened
10 and paid the singers well
and felt good about it all,
         there were rats and lizards who listened
         . . . and the only listeners left now
         . . . are . . . the rats . . . and the lizards.

15 And there are black crows
crying, "Caw, caw,"
bringing mud and sticks
building a nest
over the words carved
20 on the doors where the panels were cedar
and the strips on the panels were gold
and the golden girls came singing:
         We are the greatest city,
         the greatest nation:
25   nothing like us ever was.

The only singers now are crows crying, "Caw, caw,"
And the sheets of rain whine in the wind and doorways.
And the only listeners now are . . . the rats . . . and the lizards.

From *"Four Preludes on Playthings of the Wind"* in SMOKE AND
STEEL by Carl Sandburg, copyright 1920 by Harcourt Brace Jovanovich, Inc., renewed, 1948 by Carl Sandburg. Reprinted by permission of the publishers.

FOR EXPLORATION

Gone

1. What impression do you get of Chick Lorimer? Does anything in the poem hint at why she left town?
2. What is meant by the statement "Far off/Everybody loved her"? How is this related to the questions at the end of the poem?

Cool Tombs

1. (*a*) What does the poem emphasize about the lives of Lincoln and Grant? (*b*) What in Pocahontas' life is emphasized, by contrast? (*c*) How does the language used to describe Grant and Lincoln, differ from that used to present Pocahontas?
2. How do you interpret the last four phrases of the poem? Are the lovers losers, as well?

Chicago

1. (*a*) What impressions of the city does this poem emphasize? What images convey these impressions? (*b*) What is the tone of the poem?
2. When "Chicago" was first published before World War I it created quite a sensation. What might have made the poem exciting at that time? Is the poem's idea, tone, and statement equally appropriate today? Why or why not?

from *Four Preludes*

1. How is the subtitle appropriate to the poem?
2. What contrast does the poem develop? How does the imagery in the poem support this?
3. What is ironic in the actions of the crows?

BROWN BROTHERS

Carl Sandburg 1878 / 1967

The genius of Carl Sandburg is shown in several areas. He was a greatly admired poet. He wrote delightful stories for children. His multivolumed biography of Lincoln placed him high among modern writers of biography. He received two Pulitzer Prizes, one for his *Complete Poems* (1951) and the other for *Abraham Lincoln: The War Years* (1939). He was a noted collector of folklore, and did much to popularize music of this type by singing folk songs and accompanying himself on the guitar.

Sandburg was born in Galesburg, Illinois, of Swedish immigrant parents. It was not until he was thirty-eight years old and had tried his hand at many different occupations that fame came to him with the publication of *Chicago Poems* (1916). Written in a free-verse style reminiscent of Walt Whitman, these poems, like those he wrote later, speak in the bold and often earthy idiom of the people. Sensitive to injustice and hypocrisy, fearful of the effect of industrialization on man, Sandburg found hope for the future in the common people.

Edgar Lee Masters

The following Edgar Lee Masters' poems are from Spoon River Anthology, *which was first published in 1915. The* Anthology *is made up of a series of epitaphs which the dead of a small Illinois community speak from their graves. Masters' purpose is to expose, often in ironic terms, the frailties, eccentricities, and failures of humans. Most of the speakers are embittered by life, but some, like Lucinda Matlock, speak with courage and optimism.*

LUCINDA MATLOCK

I went to dances at Chandlerville,
And played snap-out at Winchester.
One time we changed partners,
Driving home in the moonlight of middle June,
5 And then I found Davis.
We were married and lived together for seventy
     years,
Enjoying, working, raising the twelve children,
Eight of whom we lost
Ere I had reached the age of sixty.
10 I spun, I wove, I kept the house, I nursed the sick,
I made the garden, and for holiday
Rambled over the fields where sang the larks,
And by Spoon River gathering many a shell,
And many a flower and medicinal weed—
Shouting to the wooded hills, singing to the green
15   valleys.
At ninety-six I had lived enough, that is all,
And passed to a sweet repose.
What is this I hear of sorrow and weariness,
Anger, discontent, and drooping hopes?
20 Degenerate sons and daughters,
Life is too strong for you—
It takes life to love Life.

RICHARD BONE

When I first came to Spoon River
I did not know whether what they told me
Was true or false.
They would bring me the epitaph
5 And stand around the shop while I worked
And say "He was so kind," "He was wonderful,"
"She was the sweetest woman," "He was a
    consistent Christian."
And I chiseled for them whatever they wished,
10 All in ignorance of its truth.
But later, as I lived among the people here,
I knew how near to the life
Were the epitaphs that were ordered for them as they
    died.
15 But still I chiseled whatever they paid me to chisel
And made myself party to the false chronicles
Of the stones,
Even as the historian does who writes
Without knowing the truth,
Or because he is influenced to hide it.

MRS. CHARLES BLISS

Reverend Wiley advised me not to divorce him
For the sake of the children,
And Judge Somers advised him the same.
So we stuck to the end of the path.
5 But two of the children thought he was right,
And two of the children thought I was right.
And the two who sided with him blamed me,
And the two who sided with me blamed him,

"Lucinda Matlock, "Richard Bone," and "Mrs. Charles Bliss." Permission granted by Ellen C. Masters, SPOON RIVER ANTHOLOGY, Copyright © 1915, 1916, 1942 and 1949 by Edgar Lee Masters.

JOHN M. CHURCH

And they grieved for the one they sided with.
10 And all were torn with the guilt of judging,
And tortured in soul because they could not admire
Equally him and me.
Now every gardener knows that plants grown in
     cellars
Or under stones are twisted and yellow and weak.
15 And no mother would let her baby suck
Diseased milk from her breast.
Yet preachers and judges advise the raising of souls
Where there is no sunlight, but only twilight,
No warmth, but only dampness and cold—
20 Preachers and judges!

I was attorney for the "Q"
And the Indemnity Company which insured
The owners of the mine.
I pulled the wires with judge and jury,
5 And the upper courts, to beat the claims
Of the crippled, the widow and orphan,
And made a fortune thereat.
The bar association sang my praises
In a high-flown resolution.
10 And the floral tributes were many—
But the rats devoured my heart
And a snake made a nest in my skull!

GRANT WOOD "STONE CITY, IOWA," 1930—COLLECTION OF THE
JOSLYN ART MUSEUM, OMAHA, NEBRASKA

"John M. Church." Permission granted by Ellen C. Masters, SPOON
RIVER ANTHOLOGY, Copyright © 1915, 1916, 1942 and 1949 by
Edgar Lee Masters.

HANNAH ARMSTRONG

I wrote him a letter asking him for old times' sake
To discharge my sick boy from the army;
But maybe he couldn't read it.
Then I went to town and had James Garber,
5 Who wrote beautifully, write him a letter;
But maybe that was lost in the mails.
So I traveled all the way to Washington.
I was more than an hour finding the White House.
And when I found it they turned me away,
10 Hiding their smiles. Then I thought:
"Oh, well, he ain't the same as when I boarded him
And he and my husband worked together
And all of us called him Abe, there in Menard."
As a last attempt I turned to a guard and said:
15 "Please say it's old Aunt Hannah Armstrong
From Illinois, come to see him about her sick boy
In the army."
Well, just in a moment they let me in!
And when he saw me he broke in a laugh,
20 And dropped his business as president,
And wrote in his own hand Doug's discharge,
Talking the while of the early days,
And telling stories.

THE VILLAGE ATHEIST

Ye young debaters over the doctrine
Of the soul's immortality,
I who lie here was the village atheist,
Talkative, contentious, versed in the arguments
5 Of the infidels.
But through a long sickness
Coughing myself to death
I read the *Upanishads*[1] and the poetry of Jesus.
And they lighted a torch of hope and intuition.
10 And desire which the Shadow,
Leading me swiftly through the caverns of darkness,
Could not extinguish.
Listen to me, ye who live in the senses
And think through the senses only:
15 Immortality is not a gift,
Immortality is an achievement;
And only those who strive mightily
Shall possess it.

"Hannah Armstrong," and *"The Village Athiest."* Permission granted by Ellen C. Masters, SPOON RIVER ANTHOLOGY, Copyright © 1915, 1916, 1942 and 1949 by Edgar Lee Masters.
1. *the Upanishads,* ancient Indian treatises inquiring into the nature of the Divine Principle and the means of salvation. The fundamental doctrine of these treatises is the identification of the individual soul or self with the universal Self.

FOR EXPLORATION

Richard Bone
What does Bone mean in lines 10–11?

Lucinda Matlock

1. (*a*) How do the last five lines in particular characterize the speaker? (*b*) What sorrows or discontents has she suffered?
2. Do you think her sons and daughters are "degenerate" as she says, or is her use of this term indicative of a certain heartless toughness in her character? Defend your view.

John M. Church

How are the animals mentioned in the last two lines emblematic of Church's character?

Mrs. Charles Bliss

1. Do you find any irony in the speaker's married name? What?
2. What metaphor most powerfully describes the children's condition? What does it imply about their future? What does it imply about the relationship between Mr. and Mrs. Bliss?
3. How would you read the last line aloud to emphasize Mrs. Bliss' attitude toward preachers and judges?

Hannah Armstrong

1. Is President Lincoln presented in a sympathetic light in this poem? Why or why not?
2. Does the way in which Hannah is treated by the guards suggest what might have happened to her letters? How?
3. What one word would you use to describe Hannah's character?

The Village Atheist

In the last lines of the poem the speaker says that "only those who strive mightily" shall possess immortality. What effort has he made?

Edgar Lee Masters   1868 / 1950

As a young boy Masters began writing poems and stories, and during his brief sojourn at Knox College and his work in his father's law office, this remained an important interest. In 1891 he was admitted to the bar. The following year he went to Chicago where he became a highly respected lawyer. With the publication of *Spoon River Anthology* in 1915 his fame as a poet overshadowed his reputation as a lawyer. A few years later he abandoned law to devote all his time to writing and in 1924 published *The New Spoon River*.

Since their publication, the Spoon River epitaphs have appealed to thousands of readers. In addition to their subject matter, which readers have found as interesting and easy to understand as fiction, the simplicity of the conversational language and the free-verse form have made the poems popular. Even the most pessimistic epitaph is sharp and clear in language, and some of the verses sparkle with a sense of humor and a keen appreciation of beauty.

Masters continued to write poetry and biographies until his death. Although his later works were interesting and readable, he never again achieved the brilliance of the Spoon River poems.

Vachel Lindsay

GENERAL WILLIAM BOOTH ENTERS INTO HEAVEN

To be sung to the tune of THE BLOOD OF THE LAMB[1] with indicated instruments.

I

[*Bass drum beaten loudly.*]
Booth[2] led boldly with his big bass drum—
(Are you washed in the blood of the Lamb?)
The saints smiled gravely, and they said: "He's
    come."
(Are you washed in the blood of the Lamb?)
5 Walking lepers followed, rank on rank,
Lurching bravos from the ditches dank,
Drabs from the alleyways and drug fiends pale—
Minds still passion-ridden, soul-powers frail—
Vermin-eaten saints with moldy breath,
10 Unwashed legions with the ways of death—
(Are you washed in the blood of the Lamb?)

[*Banjos.*]
Every slum had sent its half-a-score
The round world over. (Booth had groaned for
    more.)
Every banner that the wide world flies
15 Bloomed with glory and transcendent dyes.
Big-voiced lasses made their banjos bang!
Tranced, fanatical, they shrieked and sang—
"Are you washed in the blood of the Lamb?"
Hallelujah! It was queer to see
20 Bull-necked convicts with that land make free!
Loons with bazoos blowed a blare, blare, blare
On, on, upward through the golden air.
(Are you washed in the blood of the Lamb?)

II

[*Bass drum slower and softer.*]
Booth died blind, and still by faith he trod,
25 Eyes still dazzled by the ways of God.
Booth led boldly and he looked the chief—
Eagle countenance in sharp relief,
Beard a-flying, air of high command
Unabated in that holy land.

[*Sweet flute music.*]
30 Jesus came from out the courthouse door,
Stretched His hands above the passing poor.
Booth saw not, but led his queer ones there
Round and round the mighty courthouse square.
Yet in an instant all that blear review.
35 Marched on spotless, clad in raiment new.
The lame were straightened, withered limbs
    uncurled,
And blind eyes opened on a new, sweet world.

[*Bass drum louder.*]
Drabs and vixens in a flash made whole!
Gone was the weasel-head, the snout, the jowl!
40 Sages and sibyls now, and athletes clean,
Rulers of empires, and of forests green!

"*General William Booth Enters Into Heaven.*" Reprinted with the permission of The Macmillan Company from COLLECTED POEMS by Vachel Lindsay. Copyright 1913 by the Macmillan Company.
1. *The Blood of the Lamb*, a hymn much used in the Salvation Army. The refrain, "Are you washed in the blood of the Lamb?" calls on the sinner to repent and receive Christ's forgiveness.
2. *Booth*, "General" William Booth (1829–1912), English preacher and founder of the Salvation Army, which strives to bring the comforts of religion to the poor and degraded.

[Grand chorus of all instruments. Tambourines to the foreground.]
The hosts were sandaled and their wings were fire!
(Are you washed in the blood of the Lamb?)
But their noise played havoc with the angel choir.
45 (Are you washed in the blood of the Lamb?)
Oh, shout Salvation! it was good to see
Kings and princes by the Lamb set free.
The banjos rattled and the tambourines
Jing-jing-jingled in the hands of queens!

[Reverently sung, no instruments.]
50 And when Booth halted by the curb for prayer
He saw his Master through the flag-filled air.
Christ came gently with a robe and crown
For Booth the soldier, while the throng knelt down.
He saw King Jesus. They were face to face,
55 And he knelt a-weeping in that holy place.
(Are you washed in the blood of the Lamb?)

FOR EXPLORATION

1. (*a*) In what kind of place does Booth's entry into heaven take place? Is it what you might expect? (*b*) Why is the military element in the poem appropriate? How does the rhythm reinforce this element?
2. The poem is flavored at many points by vivid revivalist language. What type of contrast or transformation does it emphasize?

CREATIVE RESPONSE

Devise a dramatic reading of the poem using the instrumentation suggested in the poem, or musical accompaniment of your own. Does the poem become more powerful and striking when performed?

Vachel Lindsay   1879 / 1931

The agricultural Middle West, with its strong belief in democracy and its equally strong religious beliefs, profoundly influenced the poetry of Vachel Lindsay. He was raised in Springfield, Illinois, a town rich in memories of Abraham Lincoln. After attending Hiram College in Ohio, he studied at the Art Institute of Chicago and at the New York School of Art. Believing that art and literature were necessary for all people, he began tramping across the country, a preacher in hobo garb. Often in exchange for a meal and a night's lodging he recited verses. In his poems he used the rhythms of the pulpit, of Fourth of July oratory, and of jazz to bring his Gospel of Beauty to people who would not listen to conventional poetry. It was while he was on a walking trip from Illinois to New Mexico in 1912 that he composed "General William Booth Enters into Heaven." Published in *Poetry*, this poem brought Lindsay fame.

The content of Lindsay's poetry was strongly influenced by the democratic ideas of Lincoln, Andrew Jackson, and Walt Whitman. From Edgar Allan Poe he learned how to vary his rhythms and to use words to create various kinds of musical effects. He saw the artistry of folk songs and caught their rhythms. All these elements he combined in what he called "the higher vaudeville"—a new kind of poetry direct in its approach, democratic in its outlook, startling in its pulsating, syncopated chants, and enlivened by humor and sharp imagery.

Stephen Vincent Benét

"JOHN BROWN LIES DEAD IN HIS GRAVE . . ."

John Brown[1] lies dead in his grave and does not stir,
It is nearly three years since he died and he does not stir,
There is no sound in his bones but the sound of armies
And that is an old sound.

5 He walks, you will say, he walks in front of the armies,
A straggler met him, going along to Manassas,[2]
With his gun on his shoulder, his phantom-sons at heel,
His eyes like misty coals.

A dead man saw him striding at Seven Pines,[3]
10 The bullets whistling through him like a torn flag,
A madman saw him whetting a sword on a Bible,
A cloud above Malvern Hill.[4]

But these are all lies. He slumbers. He does not stir.
The spring rains and the winter snows on his slumber
15 And the bones of his flesh breed armies and yet more armies
But he himself does not stir.

It will take more than cannon to shake his fortress,
His song is alive and throbs in the tramp of the columns,
His song is smoke blown out of the mouth of a cannon,
20 But his song and he are two.

from JOHN
BROWN'S BODY,
BOOK IV

From JOHN BROWN'S BODY by Stephen Vincent Benet, Holt, Rinehart and Winston, Inc. Copyright, 1927, 1928, by Stephen Vincent Benet. Copyright renewed, 1955, 1956, by Rosemary Carr-Benet. Reprinted by permission of Brandt & Brandt.
1. *John Brown* (1800–1859), American abolitionist who was hanged for leading a raid on the arsenal at Harpers Ferry in an attempt to gain arms for a slave uprising.
2. *Manassas,* a town in Virginia near where the battles of Bull Run were fought. The Confederates called these the battles of Manassas.
3. *Seven Pines,* a Civil War battle fought in 1862 near Richmond, Virginia.
4. *Malvern Hill,* an elevated plateau near Richmond, Virginia. A Civil War battle was fought here in 1862.

"YOU TOOK A CARRIAGE TO THAT BATTLEFIELD"

You took a carriage to that battlefield.[1]
Now, I suppose, you take a motor-bus,
But then, it was a carriage—and you ate
Fried chicken out of wrappings of waxed paper,
5 While the slow guide buzzed on about the war
And the enormous, curdled summer clouds
Piled up like giant cream puffs in the blue.
The carriage smelt of axle-grease and leather
And the old horse nodded a sleepy head
10 Adorned with a straw hat. His ears stuck through it.
It was the middle of hay-fever summer
And it was hot. And you could stand and look
All the way down from Cemetery Ridge,[2]
Much as it was, except for monuments
15 And startling groups of monumental men
Bursting in bronze and marble from the ground,
And all the curious names upon the gravestones. . . .

So peaceable it was, so calm and hot,
So tidy and great-skied.
                  No men had fought
20 There but enormous, monumental men
Who bled neat streams of uncorrupting bronze,
Even at the Round Tops,[3] even by Pickett's boulder,[4]
Where the bronze, open book could still be read
By visitors and sparrows and the wind:

contd.

from JOHN
BROWN'S BODY,
BOOK VII

From JOHN BROWN'S BODY by Stephen Vincent Benet. Holt, Rinehart and Winston, Inc. Copyright, 1927, 1928, by Stephen Vincent Benet. Copyright renewed, 1955, 1956, by Rosemary Carr Benet. Reprinted by permission of Brandt & Brandt.
1. *that battlefield,* Gettysburg, Pennsylvania. The battle that took place there in July 1863 is considered the turning point of the Civil War.
2. *Cemetery Ridge,* a battle site along Culp's hill at Gettysburg. Here the North found the South in a weak position and were able to attack.
3. *Round Tops.* Little Round Top and (Big) Round Top were hills at Gettysburg where there was desperate fighting.
4. *Pickett's boulder,* marks the site of "Pickett's Charge" at Gettysburg. The Confederates attempted an attack on Union troops but were disastrously defeated.

25 And the wind came, the wind moved in the grass,
   Saying . . . while the long light . . . and all so calm . . .

         "Pickett came
         And the South came
         And the end came,
30   And the grass comes
         And the wind blows
         On the bronze book
         On the bronze men
         On the grown grass,
35   And the wind says
         'Long ago
         Long
         Ago.'"

   Then it was time to buy a paperweight
40 With flags upon it in decalcomania
   And hope you wouldn't break it, driving home.

Stephen Vincent Benét   1898 / 1943

Born in Bethlehem, Pennsylvania, Stephen Vincent Benét was descended from three generations of professional soldiers. When Stephen was a boy, his father, an Army colonel, had argued for hours with him about the tactics used in the Civil War and introduced him to some good histories of that war.

Benét began to write while he was at preparatory school. His first book of poetry was published in 1915, the year he entered Yale. Due to the interest established during his childhood, Benét for many years wished to write a long poem about the Civil War, but the necessity of supporting a family made this impossible. In 1926 the problem was solved when he received a Guggenheim Fellowship. He took his family to Paris where the cost of living was lower and the atmosphere more conducive to writing. In 1928 he finished the 350-page narrative poem, which he had entitled *John Brown's Body*, and returned home.

The publication of *John Brown's Body* established Benét securely as a writer on the American past. The narrative poem became a popular best seller and won a Pulitzer Prize, an indication of its popular appeal as well as of its literary merit.

FOR EXPLORATION

John Brown . . .

1. (*a*) What does the last line mean? (*b*) How does John Brown's song manifest itself? (*c*) In what sense might his song be more powerful than the man's physical presence?
2. To what does line 17 apply?

You Took a Carriage . . .

1. What contrast is implied in: (*a*) The imagery of the sleepy summer day? (*b*) The neat array of "monumental men" in bronze? (*c*) The tourists' interests?
2. Do you find any similarities between the ways war monuments are presented in this poem and in Robert Lowell's "For the Union Dead" (pages M 252–253 M)? Explain.

Luís Muñoz Marín

PAMPHLET

I have broken the rainbow
against my heart
as one breaks a useless sword against a knee.
I have blown the clouds of rose colour and blood colour
5 beyond the farthest horizons.
I have drowned my dreams
in order to glut the dreams that sleep for me in the veins
of men who sweated and wept and raged
to season my coffee . . .

10 The dream that sleeps in breasts stifled by tuberculosis
        (A little air, a little sunshine!);
the dream that dreams in stomachs strangled by hunger
        (A bit of bread, a bit of white bread!);
the dream of bare feet

15   (Fewer stones on the road, Lord, fewer broken bottles!);
the dream of calloused hands
        (Moss . . . clean cambric . . . things smooth, soft, soothing!);
The dream of trampled hearts
        (Love . . . Life . . . Life! . . .)

20 I am the pamphleteer of God,
God's agitator,
and I go with the mob of stars and hungry men
toward the great dawn . . .

"*Pamphlet*" by Luis Munoz Marin, translated by Muna Lee de Munoz Marin from Dudley Fitts, AN ANTHOLOGY OF CONTEMPORARY LATIN AMERICAN POETRY. Copyright 1942 by New Directions Publishing Corporation. Reprinted by permission of New Directions Publishing Corporation.

Luís Muñoz Marín   1898 /

It was Luís Muñoz Marín's father who negotiated the Pact of Sagasta in 1896 with Spain which gained political identity for Puerto Rico. And in 1949 Luís Muñoz Marín became the first native Puerto Rican to be elected governor of the island. Although most of his life has been devoted to politics, Muñoz Marín is still known as "El Vate," The Bard.

Muñoz Marín spent a good deal of time in the United States in his youth. It is here that he met his wife and in the 1920's formed a literary group with Marya Zaturenska, Horace Gregory, Sara Teasdale, and Vachel Lindsay.

FOR EXPLORATION

1. What might the rainbow in the opening lines represent? How is it related to a "useless sword"? To the speaker's statement that he has "drowned his dreams"?
2. What does the poem "agitate" for? What in the poem supports your view?
3. What social contrast is latent in lines 8–9?

Paul Laurence Dunbar

ROBERT GOULD SHAW[1]

Why was it that the thunder voice of Fate
    Should call thee, studious, from the classic groves,
    Where calm-eyed Pallas[2] with still footstep roves,
And charge thee seek the turmoil of the state?
5 What bade thee hear the voice and rise elate,
    Leave home and kindred and thy spicy loaves,
    To lead th' unlettered and despised droves
To manhood's home and thunder at the gate?

Far better the slow blaze of Learning's light,
10   The cool and quiet of her dearer fane,
Than this hot terror of a hopeless fight,
    This cold endurance of the final pain,—
Since thou and those who with thee died for right
    Have died, the Present teaches, but in vain!

"Robert Gould Shaw" by Paul Laurence Dunbar. Reprinted by permission of Dodd, Mead & Company, Inc. from THE COMPLETE POEMS OF PAUL LAURENCE DUNBAR.
1. *Robert Gould Shaw* (1837–1863), an American Union officer in the Civil War who was colonel of the first regiment of Negro troops from a free state mustered into the United States Army. He died in battle.
2. *Pallas.* In Greek mythology Pallas Athena is the goddess of the city, the protector of civilized life, and the embodiment of wisdom, reason, and purity.

FOR EXPLORATION

Robert Gould Shaw

1. What is the argument of this sonnet? Is it still valid?
2. Compare the portrait of Shaw given here with that given in Robert Lowell's "For the Union Dead" (page M 252). Are both poems in agreement that Shaw died "in vain"?

THE POET

He sang of life, serenely sweet,
   With, now and then, a deeper note.
   From some high peak, nigh yet remote,
He voiced the world's absorbing beat.

5 He sang of love when earth was young,
   And Love, itself, was in his lays.
   But ah, the world, it turned to praise
A jingle in a broken tongue.

TO A CAPTIOUS CRITIC

Dear critic, who my lightness so deplores,
Would I might study to be prince of bores,
Right wisely would I rule that dull estate—
But, sir, I may not, till you abdicate.

"The Poet" and *"To a Captious Critic"* by Paul Laurence Dunbar. Reprinted by permission of Dodd, Mead, & Company, Inc. from THE COMPLETE POEMS OF PAUL LAURENCE DUNBAR.

Paul Laurence Dunbar   1872 / 1906

The son of former slaves who escaped by way of the Underground Railroad, Paul Laurence Dunbar could not afford to go to college. After graduating from high school in Dayton, Ohio, he went to work as an elevator operator. He was holding this job when his first book of poetry, *Oak and Ivy*, was published in 1893. The book made little impression, but his second collection, *Majors and Minors* (1895), came to the attention of William Dean Howells, who persuaded Dunbar to combine the best poetry from both books into one volume. The result was *Lyrics of a Lowly Life* (1896), which made Dunbar a national literary figure. This was the first time in 125 years—since Phillis Wheatley (see page C 66)—that a Black had received such wide recognition. Although his life was short, Dunbar published six collections of poetry, four collections of short stories, and four novels. His *Complete Poems* was published in 1913 and heralded the new era in literature for Black Americans.

The Poet / To a Captious Critic

Dunbar is noted for his highly skilled use of dialect and Negro themes. And unlike the works of many later Black writers, Dunbar's poetry lacked bitterness. You may wish to research some of Dunbar's dialect poetry and then discuss these two short poems: "The Poet" and "To a Captious Critic." Is Dunbar speaking of his own work? If you agree that he is, how does he seem to feel toward it?

James Weldon Johnson

THE CREATION

And God stepped out on space,
And he looked around and said:
I'm lonely—
I'll make me a world.

5 And as far as the eye of God could see
Darkness covered everything,
Blacker than a hundred midnights
Down in a cypress swamp.

Then God smiled,
10 And the light broke,
And the darkness rolled up on one side,
And the light stood shining on the other,
And God said: That's good!

Then God reached out and took the light in his
     hands,
15 And God rolled the light around in his hands
Until he made the sun;
And he set that sun a-blazing in the heavens.
And the light that was left from making the sun
God gathered it up in a shining ball
20 And flung it against the darkness,
Spangling the night with the moon and stars.
Then down between
The darkness and the light
He hurled the world;
25 And God said: That's good!

Then God himself stepped down—
And the sun was on his right hand,
And the moon was on his left;
The stars were clustered about his head,
30 And the earth was under his feet.
And God walked, and where he trod
His footsteps hollowed the valleys out
And bulged the mountains up.

Then he stopped and looked and saw
35 That the earth was hot and barren.
So God stepped over to the edge of the world
And he spat out the seven seas—
He batted his eyes, and the lightnings flashed—
He clapped his hands, and the thunders rolled—
40 And the waters above the earth came down,
The cooling waters came down.

Then the green grass sprouted,
And the little red flowers blossomed,
The pine tree pointed his finger to the sky,
45 And the oak spread out his arms,
The lakes cuddled down in the hollows of the
          ground,
And the rivers ran down to the sea;
And God smiled again,
And the rainbow appeared,
50 And curled itself around his shoulder.

Then God raised his arm and he waved his hand
Over the sea and over the land,
And he said: Bring forth! Bring forth!
And quicker than God could drop his hand,
55 Fishes and fowls
And beasts and birds
Swam the rivers and the seas,
Roamed the forests and the woods,
And split the air with their wings.
60 And God said: That's good!

Then God walked around,
And God looked around
On all that he had made.
He looked at his sun,
65 And he looked at his moon,
And he looked at his little stars;
He looked on his world
With all its living things,
And God said: I'm lonely still.

From GOD'S TROMBONES by James Weldon Johnson. Copyright
1927 by The Viking Press, Inc., renewed 1955 by Grace Nail Johnson. Reprinted by permission of The Viking Press, Inc.

70 Then God sat down—
On the side of a hill where he could think;
By a deep, wide river he sat down;
With his head in his hands,
God thought and thought,
75 Till he thought: I'll make me a man!

Up from the bed of the river
God scooped the clay;
And by the bank of the river
He kneeled him down;
80 And there the great God Almighty
Who lit the sun and fixed it in the sky,
Who flung the stars to the most far corner of the
    night,
Who rounded the earth in the middle of his hand;
This Great God
85 Like a mammy bending over her baby,
Kneeled down in the dust
Toiling over a lump of clay
Till he shaped it in his own image;

Then into it he blew the breath of life,
90 And man became a living soul.
Amen. Amen.

FOR EXPLORATION

1. "God made man in His own image, but man also makes
God in his own image." (a) What does this statement mean?
(b) Cite specific lines from "The Creation" that bear out
the statement.
2. (a) Cite images that the preacher uses to bring God
close to the everyday experience of the congregation.
(b) Which lines in their rhythm and phraseology are most
like Biblical language?
3. Describe the tone of the poem.

James Weldon Johnson   1871 / 1938

Although he will be longest remembered as a poet and
essayist, James Weldon Johnson was successful in many
fields. He taught school in his home town, Jacksonville,
Florida, while studying law, and after being admitted to
the Florida bar in 1897, he went to New York where he
prospered as a writer of songs and light opera. Later he was
equally successful as United States consul in Venezuela and
Nicaragua. As Johnson became older, the flair for rhythm
and the feeling for words that had made him a successful
song writer found different channels. He edited books of
Negro poetry and spirituals, and in 1927 he published
God's Trombones, his finest poetic achievement. In the
last years of his life, without ceasing to write, he turned
again to teaching.

From boyhood Johnson had been fascinated by the old-
time Negro preachers who translated Biblical events into
simple, understandable stories. Believing that their people
would find comfort in a God whose characteristics were
like those of men, the preachers pictured a gentle Father
Who experienced loneliness and worried over His children.
In these poetic retellings even the landscape of the Old
Testament came to resemble the familiar rural South. It
was such memories along with Johnson's own talent for
rhythm and expression that went into *God's Trombones*, a
series of seven Negro sermons in verse in which the phraseology of the Bible is beautifully fused with the primitive
poetry of an old-time preacher. "The Creation" is from
God's Trombones.

by Robert Hayden

The Harlem Renaissance

It was Vachel Lindsay who helped the Afro-American poet Langston Hughes gain early recognition. Hughes was a busboy at the Washington hotel where Lindsay stayed during one of his "vaudeville" tours, and Hughes ventured to show the famous poet a few of his poems. Lindsay was so enthusiastic that he included some of them in a public reading and afterwards told newspaper reporters about his discovery of a talented young black poet. Hughes subsequently became a leading figure in the Harlem Renaissance and, eventually, one of America's best-known poets.

The Harlem Renaissance, known also as the New Negro movement and the Negro Renaissance, was an important cultural manifestation of the mid-twenties. With Harlem as its center, the Renaissance was an upsurge of new racial attitudes and ideals on the part of Afro-Americans and an artistic and political awakening. It was partly inspired by the iconoclastic spirit of the times. The Harlem writers and artists were, like their white counterparts, in quest of new images, forms, techniques. They too were skeptical and disillusioned. What chiefly differentiated them, however, was their view of artistic endeavor as an extension of the struggle against oppression.

Besides Langston Hughes, the poets who achieved recognition during the Renaissance were Claude McKay, Countee Cullen (whose first book *Color* [1925] was published while he was still in college), Jean Toomer, and Arna Bontemps. James Weldon Johnson was a distinguished older poet associated with the New Negro movement and, together with its chief spokesman, Alain Locke, was honored as a mentor. Writing in both free and conventional verse, the Harlem poets expressed racial bitterness and racial pride more boldly than their predecessors had ever done. They affirmed their African heritage in poems often filled with exotic imagery, celebrating the "primitive" forces pulsing under the black man's veneer of civilization. This tendency to emphasize the primitive and exotic provoked the charge that the New Negroes replaced old stereotypes with new ones equally objectionable. Countee Cullen's "Heritage," which appeared in his second volume, *Copper Sun* (1927) was one of the best of these atavistic poems, although the Africa it describes is literary and romanticized.

Jazz rhythms, images from big-city life (Harlem's in particular), and themes from history and folklore were

HUGHES

JOHNSON

LINDSAY

CULLEN—HISTORICAL PICTURES

DUNBAR

found in the works of the Renaissance poets, several of whom were also novelists. Claude McKay's *Home to Harlem* (1922) contained poems that expressed something of the bittersweet quality of life in that city within a city. Jean Toomer's *Cane* (1923) was a volume of poems, sketches, and stories garnered from his experiences in the South and from his impressions of Afro-American life in the North. Blues and jazz suggested motifs and verse patterns for Langston Hughes' first book, *The Weary Blues* (1926). Arna Bontemps, who did not publish a book of his poetry during the Renaissance, contributed reflective personal lyrics and poems evoking a sense of the Negro past to *The Crisis* and *Opportunity*, magazines that encouraged the Harlem writers by publishing their writing and awarding various prizes.

The New Negro movement had some effect upon writers outside of the Harlem group, stimulating interest in Afro-American life and problems. Carl Van Vechten and Eugene O'Neill were among those who used material from this source. The movement had run its course by 1930.

Langston Hughes

**THEME
FOR ENGLISH B**

The instructor said,

*Go home and write
a page tonight.
And let that page come out of you—*
5 *Then, it will be true.*

I wonder if it's that simple?
I am twenty-two, colored, born in Winston-Salem.
I went to school there, then Durham, then here
to this college on the hill above Harlem.
10 I am the only colored student in my class.
The steps from the hill lead down into Harlem,
through a park, then I cross St. Nicholas,
Eighth Avenue, Seventh, and I come to the Y,
the Harlem Branch Y, where I take the elevator
15 up to my room, sit down, and write this page:

It's not easy to know what is true for you or me
at twenty-two, my age. But I guess I'm what
I feel and see and hear, Harlem, I hear you:
hear you, hear me—we two—you, me, talk on this page.
20 (I hear New York, too.) Me—who?
Well, I like to eat, sleep, drink, and be in love.
I like to work, read, learn, and understand life.
I like a pipe for a Christmas present,
or records—Bessie, bop, or Bach.[1]
25 I guess being colored doesn't make me *not* like
the same things other folks like who are other races.
So will my page be colored that I write?
Being me, it will not be white.
But it will be
30 a part of you, instructor.
You are white—
yet a part of me, as I am a part of you.

That's American.
Sometimes perhaps you don't want to be a part of me.
35 Nor do I often want to be a part of you.
But we are, that's true!
As I learn from you,
I guess you learn from me—
although you're older—and white—
40 and somewhat more free.

This is my page for English B.

"Theme for English B" from MONTAGE OF A DREAM DEFERRED by Langston Hughes. Copyright 1951 by Langston Hughes. Reprinted by permission of Harold Ober Associates Incorporated.
1. *Bessie . . . Bach,* Bessie Smith (1894–1937), a black blues singer; Johann Sebastian Bach (1685–1750), a German organist and composer of church, vocal, and instrumental music.

AS I GREW OLDER

It was a long time ago.
I have almost forgotten my dream.
But it was there then,
In front of me,
5 Bright like a sun—
My dream.

And then the wall rose,
Rose slowly,
Slowly,
10 Between me and my dream.
Rose slowly, slowly,
Dimming,
Hiding,
The light of my dream.
15 Rose until it touched the sky—
The wall.

Shadow.
I am black.

I lie down in the shadow.
20 No longer the light of my dream before me,
Above me.
Only the thick wall.
Only the shadow.
My hands!
25 My dark hands!
Break through the wall!
Find my dream!
Help me to shatter this darkness,
To smash this night,
30 To break this shadow
Into a thousand lights of sun,
Into a thousand whirling dreams
Of sun!

Copyright 1926 and renewed 1954 by Langston Hughes. Reprinted from SELECTED POEMS OF LANGSTON HUGHES, by permission of Alfred A. Knopf, Inc.

FOR EXPLORATION

Theme for English B

1. How does the poem follow the instructor's directions to the letter?
2. Do you find this poem particularly direct and honest? Why or why not? Explain your response in terms of the language and imagery of the poem.
3. How does the speaker feel his world differs from his instructor's? In what ways does he feel they are the same?

As I Grew Older

What is the "wall" that shuts the speaker off from the "light" of his dream?

CREATIVE RESPONSE

Can you think of any similar realization that took place as you grew up which shut out one of your dreams? How would you express this? Would you prefer the indirections of poetry to a direct, confessional diary entry, for instance? Discuss the possibilities for expression of a deeply personal theme. What would be most satisfying to you as creator? What would communicate most effectively to others?

Langston Hughes   1902 / 1967

Langston Hughes has been the poet laureate of the Black people for over twenty-five years.

He was born in Joplin, Missouri, and began writing poetry as a student at Central High School in Cleveland, Ohio. By the time he had graduated from Lincoln University in Pennsylvania in 1929 he was supporting himself with his writing. After the publication of his first book, *Weary Blues,* in 1926, he began traveling across the country giving public readings of his poetry, which were well received. But he always returned to New York City, to his home in Harlem, where he helped young writers who sought his advice.

In addition to poetry, Hughes has also written novels, newspaper columns, children's books, song lyrics, and the story of the NAACP.

Countee Cullen

HERITAGE *(For Harold Jackman)*

What is Africa to me:
Copper sun or scarlet sea,
Jungle star or jungle track,
Strong bronzed men, or regal black
Women from whose loins I sprang
When the Birds of Eden sang?
One three centuries removed
From the scenes his fathers loved,
Spicy grove, cinnamon tree,
10 *What is Africa to me?*

So I lie, who all day long
Want no sound except the song
Sung by wild barbaric birds
Goading massive jungle herds,
Juggernauts of flesh that pass
Trampling tall defiant grass
Where young forest lovers lie,
Plighting troth beneath the sky.
So I lie, who always hear,
20 Though I cram against my ear
Both my thumbs, and keep them there,
Great drums throbbing through the air.
So I lie, whose fount of pride,
Dear distress, and joy allied,
Is my somber flesh and skin,
With the dark blood dammed within
Like great pulsing tides of wine
That, I fear, must burst the fine
Channels of the chafing net
30 Where they surge and foam and fret.

Africa? A book one thumbs
Listlessly, till slumber comes.
Unremembered are her bats
Circling through the night, her cats
Crouching in the river reeds,
Stalking gentle flesh that feeds
By the river brink; no more
Does the bugle-throated roar
Cry that monarch claws have leapt
40 From the scabbards where they slept.
Silver snakes that once a year
Doff the lovely coats you wear,
Seek no covert in your fear
Lest a mortal eye should see;
What's your nakedness to me?
Here no leprous flowers rear
Fierce corollas in the air;
Here no bodies sleek and wet,
Dripping mingled rain and sweat,
50 Tread the savage measures of
Jungle boys and girls in love.
What is last year's snow to me,
Last year's anything? The tree
Budding yearly must forget
How its past arose or set—
Bough and blossom, flower, fruit,
Even what shy bird with mute
Wonder at her travail there,
Meekly labored in its hair.
60 *One three centuries removed*
From the scenes his fathers loved,
Spicy grove, cinnamon tree,
What is Africa to me?

So I lie, who find no peace
Night or day, no slight release
From the unremittant beat
Made by cruel padded feet

"Heritage" from ON THESE I STAND by Countee Cullen. Copyright, 1925 by Harper & Row, Publishers, Inc., renewed 1953 by Ida M. Cullen. Reprinted by permission of Harper & Row, Publishers, Inc.

Walking through my body's street.
Up and down they go, and back,
70 Treading out a jungle track.
So I lie, who never quite
Safely sleep from rain at night—
I can never rest at all
When the rain begins to fall;
Like a soul gone mad with pain
I must match its weird refrain;
Ever must I twist and squirm,
Writhing like a baited worm,
While its primal measures drip
80 Through my body, crying, "Strip!
Doff this new exuberance.
Come and dance the Lover's Dance!"
In an old remembered way
Rain works on me night and day.
Quaint, outlandish heathen gods
Black men fashion out of rods,
Clay, and brittle bits of stone,
In a likeness like their own,
My conversion came high-priced;
90 I belong to Jesus Christ,
Preacher of humility;
Heathen gods are naught to me.

Father, Son, and Holy Ghost,
So I make an idle boast;
Jesus of the twice-turned cheek,
Lamb of God, although I speak
With my mouth thus, in my heart

Do I play a double part.
Ever at Thy glowing altar
100 Must my heart grow sick and falter,
Wishing He I served were black,
Thinking then it would not lack
Precedent of pain to guide it,
Let who would or might deride it;
Surely then this flesh would know
Yours had borne a kindred woe.
Lord, I fashion dark gods, too,
Daring even to give You
Dark despairing features where,
110 Crowned with dark rebellious hair,
Patience wavers just so much as
Mortal grief compels, while touches
Quick and hot, of anger, rise
To smitten cheek and weary eyes.
Lord, forgive me if my need
Sometimes shapes a human creed.
All day long and all night through,
One thing only must I do:
Quench my pride and cool my blood,
120 *Lest I perish in the flood.*
Lest a hidden ember set
Timber that I thought was wet
Burning like the dryest flax,
Melting like the merest wax,
Lest the grave restore its dead.
Not yet has my heart or head
In the least way realized
They and I are civilized.

Countee Cullen   1903 / 1946

The influence of the English romantic poets of the nine-teenth century and of Edwin Arlington Robinson may be found in the lyrics of Countee Cullen. An adopted son of a Methodist minister, Cullen grew up in New York City, attended New York University, and received a master's degree in English literature from Harvard University. For a time he edited *Opportunity: Journal of Negro Life*, but his major occupation, in addition to writing poetry, was teaching French.

"Most things I write I do for the sheer joy of the music in them," he once said when talking about how he wrote poetry. In his lyrics he combines an understanding of the joys and sorrows of the Negro race with a thoughtful probing of the attitudes of men in relation to one another. Cullen collected what he considered to be the best verse written by Black poets and put them in an anthology which he titled *Caroling Dusk*. His ability and careful judgment made the book a notable addition to the few collections of this type that had preceded his.

Countee Cullen

ANY HUMAN TO ANOTHER

The ills I sorrow at
Not me alone
Like an arrow,
Pierce to the marrow,
5 Through the fat
And past the bone.

Your grief and mine
Must intertwine
Like sea and river,
10 Be fused and mingle,
Diverse yet single,
Forever and forever.

Let no man be so proud
And confident,
15 To think he is allowed
A little tent
Pitched in a meadow
Of sun and shadow
All his little own.

20 Joy may be shy, unique,
Friendly to a few,
Sorrow never scorned to speak
To any who
Were false or true.

25 Your every grief
Like a blade
Shining and unsheathed
Must strike me down.
Of bitter aloes wreathed,
30 My sorrow must be laid
On your head like a crown.

"Any Human to Another" from ON THESE I STAND by Countee Cullen. Copyright 1935 by Harper & Row, Publishers, Inc., renewed, 1963 by Ida M. Cullen. Reprinted by permission of Harper & Row, Publishers, Inc.

FOR EXPLORATION

Heritage

1. The speaker states, "in my heart/ Do I play a double part." In what ways, both social and religious, does the poem illustrate this "double" heritage? Is it a dilemma for the speaker?
2. Which part of the speaker's heritage seems the stronger or more insistent? What indications of this do you find in the poem?
3. (a) The speaker claims to be "removed" from Africa. To what extent is this true? (b) What do the figures of the "budding tree" and the "baited worm" convey about the speaker's condition?

Any Human to Another

1. What various images does the poet use to convey the idea or feeling of grief?
2. The ancient Greeks and Romans crowned victors with wreaths of laurel. From early times the word *aloes* has been used to symbolize grief or bitterness. (Aloes is a bitter drug made from the leaves of the aloe.) Using this information, explain the last three lines of "Any Human to Another."
3. Four centuries ago the English poet John Donne wrote: ". . . No man is an island, entire of itself; every man is a piece of the continent, a part of the main; if a clod be washed away by the sea, Europe is the less, as well as if a promontory were, as well as if a manor of thy friends or of thine own were; any man's death diminishes me, because I am involved in mankind . . . ."

Relate this statement to the theme of "Any Human to Another."

Claude McKay

THE TROPICS IN NEW YORK

Bananas ripe and green, and ginger-root,
  Cocoa in pods and alligator pears,
And tangerines and mangoes and grape fruit,
  Fit for the highest prize at parish fairs,

5 Set in the window, bringing memories
  Of fruit-trees laden by low-singing rills,
And dewy dawns, and mystical blue skies
  In benediction over nun-like hills.

My eyes grew dim, and I could no more gaze;
10 A wave of longing through my body swept,
And, hungry for the old, familiar ways,
  I turned aside and bowed my head and wept.

IF WE MUST DIE

If we must die, let it not be like hogs
Hunted and penned in an inglorious spot,
While round us bark the mad and hungry dogs,
Making their mock at our accursed lot.
5 If we must die, O let us nobly die,
So that our precious blood may not be shed
In vain; then even the monsters we defy
Shall be constrained to honor us though dead!
O kinsmen! we must meet the common foe!
10 Though far outnumbered let us show us brave,
And for their thousand blows deal one deathblow!
What though before us lies the open grave?
Like men we'll face the murderous, cowardly pack,
Pressed to the wall, dying, but fighting back!

"The Tropics in New York" and *"If We Must Die"* from SELECTED POEMS OF CLAUDE MCKAY, copyright 1953 by Bookman Associates. Reprinted by permission of Twayne Publishers, Inc.

FOR EXPLORATION

The Tropics in New York

1. For what is the speaker "hungry"? Why is the use of this word doubly appropriate here?
2. What mood pervades the speaker's memories? Why does he turn aside and weep?
3. Compare this poem to Countee Cullen's "Heritage" (page M 206). (*a*) What similarities do you find? What differences? (*b*) Which seems to give the most idealized picture of a homeland? Which seems the most honest statement? Why?

If We Must Die

Read the questions listed under Creative Response to Millay's "Justice Denied in Massachusetts" (page M 216), and discuss this poem in terms of them.

Claude McKay   1890 / 1948

Claude McKay began his writing career early. His first two collections of poems, reflecting his Jamaican background, were published just after he turned twenty. Shortly after their publication McKay came to the United States to study agriculture first at the Tuskegee Institute in Alabama and then at Kansas State University. But he soon discovered that he preferred writing and moved to New York. He settled in Harlem and began publishing his poems in small literary magazines. In 1922 his most important collection, *Harlem Shadows*, was published. In it, he achieved in his poetry poignant lyricism as well as effective protest.

Although McKay was primarily a poet, he was also a novelist and short-story writer. In all his writing he is noted for his portrayal of Negro life in the United States. Although his subjects may vary, the theme of protest is consistent. McKay insists that Blacks acknowledge their common suffering and assert themselves to relieve that suffering.

Marianne Moore

WHAT ARE YEARS?

What is our innocence,
what is our guilt? All are
   naked, none is safe. And whence
is courage: the unanswered question,
5 the resolute doubt,—
  dumbly calling, deafly listening—that
in misfortune, even death,
       encourages others
       and in its defeat, stirs

10   the soul to be strong? He
sees deep and is glad, who
   accedes to mortality
and in his imprisonment rises
upon himself as

15 the sea in a chasm, struggling to be
free and unable to be
     in its surrendering
     finds its continuing.

So he who strongly feels,
20 behaves. The very bird,
   grown taller as he sings, steels
his form straight up. Though he is captive,
his mighty singing
says, satisfaction is a lowly
25 thing, how pure a thing is joy.
     This is mortality,
     this is eternity.

"*What are Years?*" Reprinted with permission of The Macmillan Company and Faber and Faber Limited from COLLECTED POEMS (British Title: THE COMPLETE POEMS OF MARIANNE MOORE.) Copyright 1941 by Marianne Moore, renewed 1969 by Marianne Moore.

Marianne Moore   1887 / 1972

Marianne Moore was born just outside of St. Louis. After completing her education, but before turning to a full-time career as a writer, she taught at the U.S. Indian School in Carlisle, Pennsylvania, and then moved to New York where she worked as a private tutor, secretary, and assistant at the New York Public Library.

Moore's poetry is highly colored, moralistic, symbolic, and truthful. Most of her poems develop from her observation of animals. From the animals, she moves toward important truths. To her they are interesting beasts, but they also carry unique messages. She has a strong visual sense that adds to her poems; she sees things clearly and truthfully and doesn't fake anything.

Among the many prizes she has won, her *Collected Works* (1952) was awarded all three of the major American prizes for poetry: the Pulitzer Prize, the National Book Award, and the Bollingen Prize. Her *Complete Poems* was published in 1967.

FOR EXPLORATION

What Are Years?

This poem evolves from a series of paradoxes. Identify them and comment on the poem in terms of them. In what sense can they be said to be true?

POETRY

I, too, dislike it: there are things that are important beyond all this fiddle.
　　Reading it, however, with a perfect contempt for it, one discovers in
　　it after all, a place for the genuine.
　　　　Hands that can grasp, eyes
5　　　　that can dilate, hair that can rise
　　　　　if it must, these things are important not because a

high-sounding interpretation can be put upon them but because they are
　　useful. When they become so derivative as to become unintelligible,
　　the same thing may be said for all of us, that we
10　　do not admire what
　　we cannot understand: the bat
　　　holding on upside down or in quest of something to

eat, elephants pushing, a wild horse taking a roll, a tireless wolf under
　　a tree, the immovable critic twitching his skin like a horse that feels a flea, the base-
15　ball fan, the statistician—
　　　nor is it valid
　　　　to discriminate against 'business documents and

school-books'; all these phenomena are important. One must make a distinction
　　however: when dragged into prominence by half poets, the result is not poetry,
20　nor till the poets among us can be
　　　'literalists of
　　　the imagination'—above
　　　　insolence and triviality and can present

for inspection, 'imaginary gardens with real toads in them,' shall we have
25　it. In the meantime, if you demand on the one hand,
　　　the raw material of poetry in
　　　all its rawness and
　　　that which is on the other hand
　　　　genuine, you are interested in poetry.

Poetry

1. (a) According to this poem, on what does the "useful-ness" of poetry depend? (b) Need we always instantly like a poem for it to have a genuine effect upon us? (c) Is poetry, in Moore's view, more important than life? Would you argue with her view? Why or why not?
2. (a) What is it that "half poets" do that makes poetry less effective? (b) In your opinion are there any poems which you have recently read that demonstrate this?
3. (a) In what sense can modern poems be described as "imaginary gardens with real toads in them"? What com-prises the "rawness" of modern poetry? (b) Choose one poem in this unit to illustrate your response.

"*Poetry.*" Reprinted with permission of The Macmillan Company and Faber and Faber Limited from COLLECTED POEMS (British Title: THE COMPLETE POEMS OF MARIANNE MOORE). Copyright 1935 by Marianne Moore, renewed 1963 by Marianne Moore and T. S. Eliot.

MARK TOBEY "ABOVE THE EARTH," 1953. THE ART INSTITUTE OF CHICAGO, GIFT OF MR. AND MRS. SIGMUND KUNSTADTER

John Crowe Ransom

JANET WAKING

Beautifully Janet slept
Till it was deeply morning. She woke then
And thought about her dainty-feathered hen,
To see how it had kept.

5 One kiss she gave her mother.
Only a small one gave she to her daddy
Who would have kissed each curl of his shining
      baby;
No kiss at all for her brother.

"Old Chucky, old Chucky!" she cried,
10 Running across the world upon the grass
To Chucky's house, and listening. But alas,
Her Chucky had died.

It was a transmogrifying bee
Came droning down on Chucky's old bald head
15 And sat and put the poison. It scarcely bled,
But how exceedingly

And purply did the knot
Swell with the venom and communicate
Its rigor! Now the poor comb stood up straight
20 But Chucky did not.

So there was Janet
Kneeling on the wet grass, crying her brown hen
(Translated far beyond the daughters of men)
To rise and walk upon it.

25 And weeping fast as she had breath
Janet implored us, "Wake her from her sleep!"
And would not be instructed in how deep
Was the forgetful kingdom of death.

Copyright 1927 by Alfred A. Knopf, Inc. and renewed 1955 by
John Crowe Ransom. Reprinted from SELECTED POEMS, by John
Crowe Ransom, by permission of Alfred A. Knopf, Inc. and Laurence
Pollinger Limited.

FOR EXPLORATION

1. Why does the title include the word "waking"? What
pun is there on the word "wake" (as noun and verb)?
2. Why might Janet refuse to be "instructed"?
3. Do you detect any difference in attitude between the
speaker and Janet toward Chuckey's death? What words
or phrases support your opinion?

John Crowe Ransom 1888 /

John Crowe Ransom is noted as poet, literary critic, and
teacher. While teaching at Vanderbilt University in Nashville, Tennessee, he and seven other southern writers
formed "The Fugitive Group," which supported the "new
poetry" and published poems and critical essays in their
periodical, *The Fugitive*. In 1937 Ransom went to Kenyon
College, Ohio, where he founded the *Kenyon Review*.

His poems are notable for their gentle irony and lack of
sentimentality. The scene is often a domestic one. Unlike
some other modern poets, such as Cummings, Ransom
often works within regular rhythms, rhyme schemes, and
stanza forms. He has published several volumes of poetry,
including *Chills and Fever* (1924) and *Selected Poems* (1945
and 1963).

Elinor Wylie

PURITAN SONNET

Down to the Puritan marrow of my bones
There's something in this richness that I hate.
I love the look, austere, immaculate,
Of landscapes drawn in pearly monotones.
5 There's something in my very blood that owns
Bare hills, cold silver on a sky of slate,
A thread of water, churned to milky spate
Streaming through slanted pastures fenced with
      stones.

I love those skies, thin blue or snowy gray.
Those fields sparse-planted, rendering meager
10   sheaves;
That spring, briefer than apple-blossom's breath,
Summer, so much too beautiful to stay,
Swift autumn, like a bonfire of leaves,
And sleepy winter, like the sleep of death.

From "*Wild Peaches.*" Copyright 1921 and renewed 1949 by
William Rose Benét. Reprinted from COLLECTED POEMS OF ELINOR
WYLIE, by permission of Alfred A. Knopf, Inc.

FOR EXPLORATION

Puritan Sonnet

1. What images in the poem illustrate the speaker's love
of austerity?
2. Can you give any significance to the fact that the sonnet
ends with the word "death"? Which season of the year does
the speaker prefer? What characteristics of each of the other
seasons does she emphasize?
3. Discuss this sonnet in terms of the statement: "love of
austerity is simply another form of luxuriance."

THE PURITAN'S BALLAD

My love came up from Barnegat,[1]
  The sea was in his eyes;
He trod as softly as a cat
  And told me terrible lies.

5 His hair was yellow as new-cut pine
  In shavings curled and feathered;
I thought how silver it would shine
  By cruel winters weathered.

But he was in his twentieth year,
10 This time I'm speaking of;
We were head over heels in love with fear
  And half a-feared of love.

His feet were used to treading a gale
  And balancing thereon;
15 His face was brown as a foreign sail
  Threadbare against the sun.

His arms were thick as hickory logs
  Whittled to little wrists;
Strong as the teeth of terrier dogs
20 Were the fingers of his fists.

Within his arms I feared to sink
  Where lions shook their manes,
And dragons drawn in azure ink
  Leapt quickened by his veins.

25 Dreadful his strength and length of limb
  As the sea to foundering ships;
I dipped my hands in love for him
  No deeper than their tips.

But our palms were welded by a flame
30 The moment we came to part,
And on his knuckles I read my name
  Enscrolled within a heart.

Copyright 1928 and renewed 1956 by Edwina C. Rubenstein.
Reprinted from COLLECTED POEMS OF ELINOR WYLIE, by permission of
Alfred A. Knopf, Inc.
1. *Barnegat*, a town in eastern New Jersey.

FOR EXPLORATION

The Puritan's Ballad

1. (*a*) In what ways is the lover of the Puritan girl quite her
opposite in appearance and actions? (*b*) What are the girl's
expectations? Why is she attracted to him?
2. How might this explain the speaker's comment in lines
11–12?

CREATIVE RESPONSE

The last stanza of the poem, while it affirms the love that
has grown between the couple, does not indicate any conclusion to their relationship. You are left on your own to
speculate. Using the rhyme and verse form of the poem,
write your own conclusion. Do you think a happy or a
tragic ending is implied? Or would you have the ballad
end in a parting of their ways?

Elinor Wylie   1885 / 1928

Born into a wealthy and cultured family, Elinor Wylie
spent much of her childhood in Washington, D.C., where
her father served as Assistant Attorney-General under
Theodore Roosevelt. When she was eighteen, her grandfather took her to London and Paris for a season of parties and travel.

In the United States she made her home in New York
City, where she became acquainted with most of the prominent writers of that time. Her poetry was delicate, finely
wrought, painstakingly intelligent. She revised continually
until her poetry was as perfect as she could make it.

Edna St. Vincent Millay

JUSTICE DENIED IN MASSACHUSETTS[1]

Let us abandon then our gardens and go home
And sit in the sitting-room.
Shall the larkspur blossom or the corn grow under
    this cloud?
Sour to the fruitful seed
5 Is the cold earth under this cloud,
Fostering quack and weed, we have marched upon
    but cannot conquer;
We have bent the blades of our hoes against the
    stalks of them.

Let us go home, and sit in the sitting-room.
Not in our day
10 Shall the cloud go over and the sun rise as before,
Beneficent upon us
Out of the glittering bay,
And the warm winds be blown inward from the
    sea
Moving the blades of corn
15 With a peaceful sound.
Forlorn, forlorn,
Stands the blue hay-rack by the empty mow.
And the petals drop to the ground,

Leaving the tree unfruited.
The sun that warmed our stooping backs and
20   withered the weed uprooted—
We shall not feel it again.
We shall die in darkness, and be buried in the rain.

What from the splendid dead
We have inherited—
25 Furrows sweet to the grain, and the weed subdued—
See now the slug and the mildew plunder.
Evil does overwhelm
The larkspur and the corn;
We have seen them go under.

30 Let us sit here, sit still,
Here in the sitting-room until we die;
At the step of Death on the walk, rise and go;
Leaving to our children's children this beautiful
    doorway,
And this elm,
35 And a blighted earth to till
With a broken hoe.

"Justice Denied in Massachusetts" from COLLECTED POEMS, Harper & Row. Copyright 1921, 1928, 1931, 1948, 1954, © 1955, © 1958 by Edna St. Vincent Millay and Norma Millay Ellis.
1. See headnote page 115 M.

THE RETURN

Earth does not understand her child,
    Who from the loud gregarious town
Returns, depleted and defiled,
    To the still woods, to fling him down.

5 Earth can not count the sons she bore:
    The wounded lynx, the wounded man
Come trailing blood unto her door;
    She shelters both as best she can.

But she is early up and out,
10   To trim the year or strip its bones;
She has no time to stand about
    Talking of him in undertones

Who has no aim but to forget,
    Be left in peace, be lying thus
15 For days, for years, for centuries yet,
    Unshaven and anonymous;

Who, marked for failure, dulled by grief,
    Has traded in his wife and friend
For this warm ledge, this alder leaf:
20   Comfort that does not comprehend.

XLVII

Well, I have lost you; and I lost you fairly;
In my own way, and with my full consent.
Say what you will, kings in a tumbrel rarely
Went to their deaths more proud than this one went.
5 Some nights of apprehension and hot weeping
I will confess; but that's permitted me;
Day dried my eyes; I was not one for keeping
Rubbed in a cage a wing that would be free.
If I had loved you less or played you slyly
10 I might have held you for a summer more,
But at the cost of words I value highly,
And no such summer as the one before.
Should I outlive this anguish—and men do—
I shall have only good to say of you.

"The Return" from COLLECTED POEMS, Harper & Row. Copyright
1934, 1962 by Edna St. Vincent Millay and Norma Millay Ellis.
"Well, I have lost you fairly . . . ," from COLLECTED POEMS, HARPER
& ROW. Copyright 1921, 1928, 1931, 1948, 1954, © 1955, ©
1958 by Edna St. Vincent Millay and Norma Millay Ellis.

Edna St. Vincent Millay

CLXX

Read history: so learn your place in Time;
And go to sleep: all this was done before;
We do it better, fouling every shore;
We disinfect, we do not probe, the crime.
5 Our engines plunge into the seas, they climb
Above our atmosphere: we grow not more
Profound as we approach the ocean's floor;
Our flight is lofty, it is not sublime.
Yet long ago this Earth by struggling men
10 Was scuffed, was scraped by mouths that bubbled mud;
And will be so again, and yet again;
Until we trace our poison to its bud
And root, and there uproot it: until then,
Earth will be warmed each winter by man's blood.

"Read history; so you learn your place in Time . . ." from COL-
LECTED POEMS, Harper & Row. Copyright 1921, 1928, 1931, 1948,
1954 © 1955, © 1958 by Edna St. Vincent Millay and Norma
Millay Ellis.

FOR EXPLORATION

Justice Denied in Massachusetts

1. What is the overall tone of the poem?
2. In what ways do the forces of nature echo the injustice of man? How do these formal personifications underscore the tone of the poem?
3. What instances of hyperbole (exaggerated language) do you find in the poem? Do they successfully underscore the the seriousness of the theme? Why or why not?
4. What might the broken hoe symbolize? How is it related to what we have inherited from the "splendid dead"?

CREATIVE RESPONSE

The response to injustice or the voicing of social grievances has taken many forms, from artistic creation to outright, violent reprisal. In what ways might an artistic response such as this poem, be more forceful than direct action? What are the elements of good protest art in your opinion? Consider protest poetry that you have read in this unit, or songs, poems that you have read or heard recently (as well as expressions of grievance in other media) in arguing for or against. Perhaps these further questions will help clarify issues:

   1. Is the poem of protest more effective if its statement of grievance is direct, or indirect?
   2. Is such a poem helped or hindered by the use of florid

or exaggerated figures of speech, heavy use of emotive language, or overgeneralizations?

3. Should protest art solicit direct action from the reader or viewer, or should it seek to bring home to him a contemplative but vivid realization of the situation and its implications for him?

4. What forms other than the written can protest art take? Examples? Would you consider any of the other forms more persuasive than the written? Why?

5. On the basis of the emotional appeals they make, can you make any tentative guidelines for distinguishing between "good" protest art, and that which is propagandistic or "bad"?

FOR EXPLORATION

The Return

1. Does nature, as presented in this poem, take any special notice of man's return? Is this an indication that nature is "uncaring" toward all life? Explain.

2. In general, Romantic poetry, particularly in the last century, tended to present nature as a source of consolation and strength for man weary of the urban world. Would you call this poem anti-Romantic? Why?

XLVII

1. (a) What human situation does this sonnet deal with? (b) What is the speaker's attitude toward it? What metaphor conveys this attitude most powerfully?

2. What impression of the speaker's character does this sonnet convey?

CLXX

1. (a) Explain the irony in the words "we do it better." In what ways does the poem illustrate this irony?

2. Is there any hint in the poem that technological improvements will provide a solution?

CREATIVE RESPONSE

A favorite ending to medieval moral tales was the Latin maxim, *radix malorum est cupiditas*—"the root of all evil is greed." This theme has in fact been voiced repeatedly, throughout history, in the literature of Europe and America. Given the frequent recurrence of this theme, is "greed" a part of the human condition which has not and cannot be altered? If so, what consequences are likely for humanity? If not, how can it possibly be "uprooted"?

Edna St. Vincent Millay   1892 / 1950

Edna St. Vincent Millay was born in Maine. Even before the time she entered Vassar College, she had been contributing poetry to *St. Nicholas* magazine for several years. At nineteen she wrote "Renascence," a long lyric whose quiet melodic beginning is followed by an ecstatic affirmation of life.

Moving to Greenwich Village in New York City, Millay was recognized in the 1920's as the poetic voice of "flaming youth." For a few years the young and optimistic outlook she had voiced in "Renascence" was submerged; instead she expressed the cynicism and disillusionment of the "lost generation." In 1923 she was awarded the Pulitzer Prize for *The Harp-Weaver and Other Poems.*

For the last twenty-five years of her life Millay spent most of her time at Steepletop Farm in northern New York. Her poetry no longer possessed the serene optimism of "Renascence," nor was it the flippant, satiric verse of her Greenwich Village days. The lyrics and sonnets of this period are more subdued and less self-conscious than her earlier work. Showing genuine poetic power, they bear the mark of a striking and intense personality.

by Robert Hayden

Soapboxes on Parnassus

By the 1930's the ideals of the New Poetry had been accepted and no longer seemed radical or even controversial. Free verse was the preferred technique of many poets, and although Imagism as a distinct movement no longer existed, it was still a minor influence. Significant work in traditional forms continued, of course. Robinson published philosophical lyrics and narrative poems written in flexible yet definite metrical patterns. Robert Frost pursued what he called his "lover's quarrel with the world" in verse forms that were conventional, though the poet's vision and tone were highly individual. Personal and metaphysical poetry employing meter and rhyme often achieved notable distinction through the artistry of Edna St. Vincent Millay, Countee Cullen, Paul Engle, and Elinor Wylie.

The twentieth century is often described as an era of rapid, almost breathless change. Fashions in the arts change not by the generation but by the decade, though, inevitably, much is carried over from one period to the next, as a constant among the variables. Yet each decade has its own imprimatur, its own special focus. During the thirties, social consciousness and political awareness gave special impetus to American poetry.

Marxist radicalism, the labor struggle, the depression, and the menace of fascism determined the form and content of much of the literature of the period. Left-wing critics defined the role of the poet as that of propagandist, spokesman for a cause: the poet was to be a voice for the inarticulate masses, championing the oppressed victims of an unjust social order. The poetry written from this point of view was usually of negligible literary value, not because of its content primarily, but because it was more rhetorical and programmatic than imaginative. The question whether a valid distinction between art and propaganda could really be made was hotly debated in these years, and remains a controversial question today.

A great deal of socially conscious verse has lost its patina, retaining only a certain period interest, if any. There are, however, some exceptions. Much of the poetry of Archibald MacLeish and Kenneth Fearing was written out of a deep concern over injustice and human exploitation, and has not entirely lost its vitality and relevance. Langston Hughes, Margaret Walker, Frank Marshall Davis, and Richard Wright wrote perceptively about the Afro-American condition.

PICTORIAL PARADE INC.

MARÍN

PICTORIAL PARADE INC.

WYLIE

NEW YORK TIMES

MACLEISH

VASSAR COLLEGE LIBRARY

MILLAY

JILL KREMENTZ

AUDEN

Carl Sandburg's *The People, Yes* (1936) was evidence of the continuing interest in the folk culture shared by a number of artists during the period. The songs, oral literature, and customs of unsophisticated people not only suggested themes for poems, but were also regarded as indications of basic strengths and virtues necessary for fundamental social change.

Undoubtedly, the best political poetry of the thirties was written by W. H. Auden, the English poet who eventually became an American citizen. Auden revealed his left-wing sympathies in poems that were technically brilliant and intellectually complex reflections on the dilemmas of modern society. Auden was wry, mocking, satiric. His command of technique, the range of his diction and imagery, his ability to use every poetic device available marked him from the outset as a major poet. Other poets learned from him, and he attracted followers who imitated his style. By the end of the thirties, Auden had turned away from Marxism, having come to regard it as a threat to individual freedom.

W. H. Auden

THE UNKNOWN CITIZEN

(To JS/07/M/378 This Marble Monument Is Erected by the State)

He was found by the Bureau of Statistics to be
One against whom there was no official complaint,
And all the reports on his conduct agree
That, in the modern sense of an old-fashioned word, he was a saint,
5 For in everything he did he served the Greater Community.
Except for the War till the day he retired
He worked in a factory and never got fired,
But satisfied his employers, Fudge Motors Inc.
Yet he wasn't a scab or odd in his views,
10 For his Union reports that he paid his dues,
(Our report on his Union shows it was sound)
And our Social Psychology workers found
That he was popular with his mates and liked a drink.
The Press are convinced he bought a paper every day
15 And that his reactions to advertisements were normal in every way.
Policies taken out in his name prove that he was fully insured,
And his Health-card shows he was once in hospital but left it cured.
Both Producers Research and High-Grade Living declare
He was fully sensible to the advantages of the Instalment Plan
20 And had everything necessary to the Modern Man,
A phonograph, a radio, a car, and a frigidaire.
Our researchers into Public Opinion are content
That he held the proper opinions for the time of year;
When there was peace, he was for peace; when there was war, he went.
25 He was married and added five children to the population,
Which our Eugenist says was the right number for a parent of his generation,
And our teachers report that he never interfered with their education.
Was he free? Was he happy? The question is absurd:
Had anything been wrong, we should certainly have heard.

FOR EXPLORATION

The Unknown Citizen

1. What is the significance of the fact that the subject of this poem has no name, only a number?
2. How might he be said to have lived the "perfect" life? How is such "perfection" defined? How does this definition reflect on the society in which the subject lives?
3. How would you answer the questions in the next-to-last line of the poem—"Was he free? Was he happy?" Why does the speaker state that these questions are absurd?

Copyright 1940 and renewed 1968 by W. H. Auden. Reprinted from COLLECTED SHORTER POEMS 1927–1957, by W. H. Auden, by permission of Random House, Inc. and Faber and Faber, Ltd.

W. H. Auden   1907 /

When a young Englishman, Wystan Hugh Auden, began writing, the new poetry had already emerged from the pens of its first innovators. The more important of these men, T. S. Eliot, William Butler Yeats, and Ezra Pound, had achieved eminence and were in their writing prime when Auden used to meet with his fellow poets to discuss what

O WHAT IS THAT SOUND

O what is that sound which so thrills the ear
    Down in the valley drumming, drumming?
Only the scarlet soldiers, dear,
    The soldiers coming.

5 O what is that light I see flashing so clear
    Over the distance brightly, brightly?
Only the sun on their weapons, dear,
    As they step lightly.

O what are they doing with all that gear,
10   What are they doing this morning, this morning?
Only their usual manoeuvres, dear,
    Or perhaps a warning.

O why have they left the road down there,
    Why are they suddenly wheeling, wheeling?
15 Perhaps a change in their orders, dear.
    Why are you kneeling?

O haven't they stopped for the doctor's care,
    Haven't they reined their horses, their horses?
Why, they are none of them wounded, dear,
20   None of these forces.

O is it the parson they want, with white hair,
    Is it the parson, is it, is it?
No, they are passing his gateway, dear,
    Without a visit.

25 O it must be the farmer who lives so near.
    It must be the farmer so cunning, so cunning?
They have passed the farmyard already, dear,
    And now they are running.

O where are you going? Stay with me here!
30   Were the vows you swore deceiving, deceiving?
No, I promised to love you, dear,
    But I must be leaving.

O it's broken the lock and splintered the door,
    O it's the gate where they're turning, turning;
35 Their boots are heavy on the floor
    And their eyes are burning.

Copyright 1937 and renewed 1965 by W. H. Auden. Reprinted from COLLECTED SHORTER POEMS 1927–1957, by W. H. Auden, by permission of Random House, Inc. and Faber and Faber Ltd.

direction their lives and their thinking were taking. His own cynicism, his wit and originality, and revolutionary times made some of the early poetry that Auden wrote an uneven mixture of expression and ideas. Nonetheless, his poetry was outstanding enough even then to be awarded the King's Poetry Medal in 1937.

In 1938 Auden left England for the United States. Since he had always been in rebellion against the age and traditions of his native land, the openness and lack of tradition in this new country appealed to him. He became a citizen in 1946. His poetry began to lose some of its personal references and obscurities, yet retained its former deft wit and brilliance. In 1948 he won a Pulitzer Prize for his book *The Age of Anxiety;* he won the National Book Award for his volume of poetry *The Shield of Achilles* in 1956; and he was awarded the National Medal for Literature in 1967.

O What Is That Sound

1. (a) What did the first few stanzas lead you to expect? Were these expectations borne out by the ending? (b) How does the portrayal of the soldiers change as the poem progresses?

2. The ballad form (used in this poem) usually gives only a fragment of a highly dramatic situation. Describe as completely as you can the situation behind this poem, in terms of the following questions: (a) How does the woman initially view the soldiers? Her beloved? (b) What do the man's questions about the movements of the soldiers reveal about his state of mind? Is the woman aware of his feelings? (c) What has the man sworn? Why did he not ask her to flee with him? (d) Is there any indication in the last stanza that the woman's sympathies have switched from her beloved to the soldiers who are pursuing him? Where?

Allen Tate

THE WOLVES

There are wolves in the next room waiting
With heads bent low, thrust out, breathing
At nothing in the dark; between them and me
A white door patched with light from the hall
5 Where it seems never (so still is the house)
A man has walked from the front door to the stair.
It has all been forever. Beasts claw the floor.
I have brooded on angels and archfiends
But no man has ever sat where the next room's
10 Crowded with wolves, and for the honor of man
I affirm that never have I before. Now while
I have looked for the evening star at a cold window
And whistled when Arcturus spilt his light,
I've heard the wolves scuffle, and said: So this

15 Is man; so—what better conclusion is there—
The day will not follow night, and the heart
Of man has a little dignity, but less patience
Than a wolf's, and a duller sense that cannot
Smell its own mortality. (This and other
20 Meditations will be suited to other times
After dog silence howls his epitaph.)
Now remember courage, go to the door,
Open it and see whether coiled on the bed
Or cringing by the wall, a savage beast
25 Maybe with golden hair, with deep eyes
Like a bearded spider on a sunlit floor
Will snarl—and man can never be alone.

Allen Tate. *"The Wolves"* reprinted from THE SWIMMERS AND OTHER
SELECTED POEMS © 1970 by permission of The Swallow Press, Chicago, and Oxford University Press.
1. *Arcturus*, a giant fixed star just behind the Dipper.

FOR EXPLORATION

A reader of this poem commented that "the wolves in this
poem are as real as a nightmare that men can never escape.
Strangely, they always seem to be on the other side of a
closed door, and although one hears them, one never sees
them exactly. They cannot be shot, or run away from, or
walled out, as other predators." Does this reflect your
reaction to the poem? Why or why not?

Allen Tate   1899 /

Allen Tate was born in Winchester, Kentucky, and was
educated at Georgetown Preparatory School in Washington, D.C., and Vanderbilt University in Nashville, Tennessee. He has spent most of his life teaching poetry at various
universities.

Tate began his career as a poet early and achieved
renown before he was twenty-five. His career became a
search for a way of broadening modern poetry. He attempted to create a vision that exceeded mere feeling while
still containing feeling. In 1956 he was awarded the Bollingen Prize for Poetry.

DONG KINGMAN "THE EL AND SNOW," WHITNEY MUSEUM OF AMERICAN ART, NEW YORK

Kenneth Fearing

AMERICAN RHAPSODY (4)

First you bite your fingernails. And then you comb your hair again. And
    then you wait. And wait.
(They say, you know, that first you lie: And then you steal, they say. And
    then, they say, you kill.)

Then the doorbell rings. Then Peg drops in. And Bill. And Jane. And Doc.
And first you talk, and smoke, and hear the news and have a drink. Then
    you walk down the stairs.
And you dine, then, and go to a show after that, perhaps, and after that a
    night spot, and after that come home again, and climb the stairs
5   again, and again go to bed.

But first Peg argues, and Doc replies. First you dance the same dance
    and you drink the same drink you always drank before.

contd.

"American Rhapsody (4)" by Kenneth Fearing from COLLECTED
POEMS. Copyright 1940. Reprinted by permission of Ira Koenig,
Executor of The Estate of Kenneth F. Fearing.

And the piano builds a roof of notes above the world.
And the trumpet weaves a dome of music through space. And the drum
    makes a ceiling over space and time and night.
And then the table-wit. And then the check. Then home again to bed.
10 But first, the stairs.

And do you now, baby, as you climb the stairs, do you still feel as you felt
    back there?
Do you feel again as you felt this morning? And the night before? And then
    the night before that?

(They say, you know, that first you hear voices. And then you have visions,
    they say. Then, they say, you kick and scream and rave.)

Or do you feel: What is one more night in a lifetime of nights?
What is one more death, or friendship, or divorce out of two, or three? Or
15   four? Or five?
One more face among so many, many faces, one more life among so many
    million lives?
But first, baby, as you climb and count the stairs (and they total the same)
    did you, sometime or somewhere, have a different idea?
Is this, baby, what you were born to feel, and do, and be?

Kenneth Fearing   1902 / 1961

Kenneth Fearing, journalist, poet, novelist, was born in Chicago, Illinois. After graduating from the University of Wisconsin he returned to Chicago as a reporter for the Chicago City News Bureau. At the same time, he was writing poetry, and his first book was published in 1929. The publication of this book marks the beginning of Proletarian poetry as an American literary movement. In his poems, Fearing satirized the stupidity of contemporary middle-class society. More than any of his contemporaries, he succeeded in giving a sharp edge to his unflattering appraisal of the standards by which most Americans live.

FOR EXPLORATION

1. "Rhapsody" can mean a highly emotional, rapturous, or ecstatic utterance. Given this meaning, how is this poem or the people it portrays rhapsodic? Or is the title ironic? What actions in the poem, and what aspects of its diction, support your view?

2. Compare the view of life revealed in this poem with life as seen through Prufrock's eyes in T. S. Eliot's poem (pages M 160–M 162). What similarities do you find, if any?

E. E. Cummings

PITY THIS BUSY MONSTER, MANUNKIND

pity this busy monster,manunkind,

not. Progress is a comfortable disease:
your victim(death and life safely beyond)

plays with the bigness of his littleness
5 —electrons deify one razorblade
into a mountainrange; lenses extend

unwish through curving wherewhen till unwish
returns on its unself.
                          A world of made
10 is not a world of born—pity poor flesh

and trees,poor stars and stones,but never this
fine specimen of hypermagical

ultraomnipotence. We doctors know

a hopeless case if—listen:there's a hell
15 of a good universe next door;let's go

"Pity this busy monster, manunkind" by E. E. Cummings. Copyright, 1944, by E. E. Cummings. Reprinted from his volume, POEMS 1923– 1954, by permission of Harcourt Brace Jovanovich, Inc. and Granada Publishing Limited.

E. E. Cummings

CHANSON INNOCENTE[1]

in Just-
spring   when the world is mud-
luscious the little
lame balloonman

5 whistles   far   and wee

and eddieandbill come
running from marbles and
piracies and it's
spring

10 when the world is puddle-wonderful

the queer
old balloonman whistles
far   and   wee
and bettyandisbel come dancing

15 from hop-scotch and jump-rope and

it's
spring
and
        the

20   goat-footed

balloonMan   whistles
far
and
wee

Copyright, 1923, 1951, by E. E. Cummings. Reprinted from his volume, POEMS 1923–1954, by permission of Harcourt Brace Jovanovich, Inc. and MacGibbon & Kee.
1. *Chansom Innocente,* Innocent Song. [*French*]

MARION MOREHOUSE

FOR EXPLORATION

Pity this Busy Monster, Manunkind

1. (*a*) What tone does the phrase "busy monster" give the poem? (*b*) What kind of ambiguity does the placement of the word "not" at the beginning of the second line (after a space between lines) create?
2. (*a*) What in the poem comprises the "world of made"? What comprises the "world of born"? (*b*) To which realm does mankind give his primary allegiance?
3. How do the words "hypermagical ultraomnipotence" (as followed by the doctor's interrupted diagnosis) further indicate the poem's tone?
4. Do you feel that the whimsical ending is more appropriate than a serious indictment? Why?

Chanson Innocente

1. What words or phrases do you find most striking in this vision of spring? What specific sense impressions do they convey?
2. What might the "little lame balloonman" represent? Can you think of any reason why he is described as "goat-footed"?
3. Does the language in this poem at any point reflect the way children speak? How so?
4. In what ways does Cummings' view of spring in this poem differ from Williams' in "Spring and All"?

E. E. Cummings   1894 / 1962

A few years ago a student wrote to Edward Estlin Cummings (or e. e. cummings, as he signed his poems) requesting information. The student received a reply addressed and written in bold crayon colors. This unconventional mode of writing is indicative of the poet's impulse to experiment; it suggests also his sense of fun.

Cummings was reared according to a rather traditional New England pattern, ending with study at Harvard. During World War I, he served in the ambulance corps in France. After the war, unsettled and disillusioned, he went to Paris, like many other American writers and artists in the 1920's. Later he returned to America to live in Greenwich Village, New York, and to write and paint.

Cummings experimented with a problem poets have been trying to resolve since writing first began, the task of representing sounds on paper. He tried old methods and created new ones. He worked with rhymes, assonance, alliteration. He broke compound words into parts and put explanatory words or phrases between the parts. He ran words together to increase the tempo, or separated them, putting one to a line to express slow movement. Through his experiments he created some of the most delightful lyrics in contemporary poetry.

Robinson Jeffers

SHINE, PERISHING REPUBLIC

While this America settles in the mold of its vulgarity,
    heavily thickening to empire,
And protest, only a bubble in the molten mass, pops
    and sighs out, and the mass hardens,

I sadly smiling remember that the flower fades to
    make fruit, the fruit rots to make earth.
Out of the mother; and through the spring exultances,
    ripeness and decadence; and home to the
    mother.

You making haste haste on decay: not blameworthy;
5   life is good, be it stubbornly long or suddenly
A mortal splendor: meteors are not needed less than
    mountains: shine, perishing republic.

But for my children, I would have them keep their
    distance from the thickening center;
    corruption
Never has been compulsory, when the cities lie at
    the monster's feet there are left the moun-
    tains.

And boys, be in nothing so moderate as in love of
    man, a clever servant, insufferable master.
There is the trap that catches noblest spirits, that
10   caught—they say—God, when he walked on
    earth.

Copyright 1925 and renewed 1953 by Robinson Jeffers. Reprinted
from SELECTED POETRY OF ROBINSON JEFFERS, by permission of
Random House, Inc.

Robinson Jeffers   1887 / 1962

Although John Robinson Jeffers was born in Pittsburgh
and was educated in Europe, most of his life and poetry
were shaped by California. His family moved there when he
was sixteen, and that is where he went to college, receiving
his bachelor's degree at the age of eighteen. He then studied
medicine for three years and forestry for one year, but he
admitted, "I wasn't deeply interested in anything but
poetry." When he married, he and his wife wandered to
Carmel, California. They knew they had found the place
where they wanted to settle, so Jeffers built a house, with
his own hands, on the top of a hill, where they lived out
their lives and where he did all his writing.

Jeffers' feeling that poetry must become realistic led to
his writing narrative poems and drawing his subjects from
contemporary life. His style is something between blank
verse and free verse through which he reproduces colloquial speech without weakening the formal control of
the line. In his poems, Jeffers often expresses an aversion
for humans and society. He believes that humans are of
trifling importance, a species here today, gone tomorrow.

FOR EXPLORATION

Shine, Perishing Republic

1. With what specific phenomenon does the poem identify
the "thickening" of America? What other metaphors
support this?
2. Is the decay of the country viewed positively, neutrally,
or negatively? Does the poem place blame for this decay?
Explain.
3. What is meant by the admonition: "be in nothing so
moderate as in love of man"? How is such love, when
immoderate, a "trap"?
4. Would you say that this poem is more pessimistic than
Cummings' "Pity this Busy Monster Manunkind" (page
227 M)? Than Edna St. Vincent Millay's sonnet CLXX (page
M 218)?

BOATS IN A FOG

Sports and gallantries, the stage, the arts, the antics of dancers,
The exuberant voices of music,
Have charm for children but lack nobility; it is bitter earnestness
That makes beauty; the mind
5 Knows, grown adult.
               A sudden fog-drift muffled the ocean,
A throbbing of engines moved in it,
At length, a stone's throw out, between the rocks and the vapor,
One by one moved shadows
10 Out of the mystery, shadows, fishing-boats, trailing each other
Following the cliff for guidance,
Holding a difficult path between the peril of the sea-fog
And the foam on the shore granite.
One by one, trailing their leader, six crept by me,
15 Out of the vapor and into it,
The throb of their engines subdued by the fog, patient and cautious,
Coasting all round the peninsula
Back to the buoys in Monterey harbor. A flight of pelicans
Is nothing lovelier to look at;
20 The flight of the planets is nothing nobler; all the arts lose virtue
Against the essential reality
Of creatures going about their business among the equally
Earnest elements of nature.

Copyright 1925 and renewed 1953 by Robinson Jeffers. Reprinted from SELECTED POETRY OF ROBINSON JEFFERS, by permission of Random House, Inc.

FOR EXPLORATION

Boats in a Fog

1. In what ways might the central metaphor of boats in a fog reflect on human life?
2. Why is the procession of boats described as something equally as lovely as "the flight of pelicans" or the "flight of the planets"? What quality do all three share? In what significant way is the boats' journey different?

Richard Eberhart

THE HORSE CHESTNUT TREE

Boys in sporadic but tenacious droves
Come with sticks, as certainly as Autumn,
To assault the great horse chestnut tree.

There is a law governs their lawlessness.
5 Desire is in them for a shining amulet
And the best are those that are highest up.

They will not pick them easily from the ground.
With shrill arms they fling to the higher branches,
To hurry the work of nature for their pleasure.

10 I have seen them trooping down the street
Their pockets stuffed with chestnuts shucked,
        unshucked.
It is only evening keeps them from their wish.

Sometimes I run out in a kind of rage
To chase the boys away; I catch an arm,
15 Maybe, and laugh to think of being the lawgiver.

I was once such a young sprout myself
And fingered in my pocket the prize and trophy.
But still I moralize upon the day.

And see that we, outlaws on God's property,
20 Fling out imagination beyond the skies
Wishing a tangible good from the unknown.

And likewise death will drive us from the scene
With the great flowering world unbroken yet,
Which we held in idea, a little handful.

"The Horse Chestnut Tree" by Richard Eberhart from COLLECTED POEMS 1930–1960. Copyright © 1960 by Richard Eberhart. Reprinted by permission of Oxford University Press, Inc. and Chatto and Windus Ltd.

Richard Eberhart   1904 /

Richard Eberhart has been poet, teacher, and vice-president of a floor-polish manufacturing firm. After receiving degrees from Dartmouth College and Cambridge University, Eberhart became tutor to the son of King Prajahhipoh of Siam. During World War II he was a lieutenant commander in the Navy. Commenting on his varied career he has said that a poet has to be at least two persons: he must have enough energy to live in two worlds—the present world which he doesn't believe in, and the world of becoming which he makes real through his poetry.

In 1962 Eberhart received the Bollingen Prize for poetry, and in 1966 he was awarded a Pulitzer Prize. Although like Carl Sandburg and Vachel Lindsay he grew up in the Midwest, his poems do not suggest as theirs do the rhythms of Midwestern speech. The strength of his poetry lies in its honesty, its individualism, and in its directness. A thoughtful man, he writes simply of subjects that men of all ages have pondered: man's place in the universe, his destiny, and death.

FOR EXPLORATION

How are the boys' flinging sticks at the highest branches of the chestnut tree a metaphor for man's situation on earth? Explain the analogy in as much detail as the poem allows.

Archibald MacLeish

THE END OF THE WORLD

Quite unexpectedly as Vasserot
The armless ambidextrian was lighting
A match between his great and second toe
And Ralph the lion was engaged in biting
5 The neck of Madame Sossman while the drum
Pointed, and Teeny was about to cough
In waltz-time swinging Jocko by the thumb—
Quite unexpectedly the top blew off:

And there, there overhead, there, there, hung over
10 Those thousands of white faces, those dazed eyes,
There in the starless dark, the poise, the hover,
There with vast wings across the canceled skies,
There in the sudden blackness, the black pall
Of nothing, nothing, nothing—nothing at all.

"The End of the World" by Archibald MacLeish from COLLECTED POEMS. Copyright, 1952, by Archibald MacLeish. Reprinted by permission of the publisher, Houghton Mifflin Company.

Archibald MacLeish   1892 /

Archibald MacLeish was born in Glencoe, Illinois, and was educated at Yale and Harvard. He established himself in a prosperous law practice, but gave it up because he "never could believe in it." In 1923 he left for Paris with his wife and children. The opportunity to discuss theory with contemporary writers and to write his own poetry made him say that he dated the beginning of his life from that year. He stayed in France until 1928.

After he had returned to the United States, he traveled in Mexico, following the route of Cortez. The result was the narrative poem *Conquistador,* which won the Pulitzer Prize in 1933. During World War II as Director of the Office of Facts and Figures, he was responsible for wartime propaganda. He has been Librarian of Congress, and has also been active in the organization of UNESCO.

Although he won a Pulitzer Prize for a narrative poem, critics consider his lyric poetry his best. In 1953 he was awarded both the National Book Award and a second Pulitzer Prize for his *Collected Poems 1917–1952.* And in 1959 he won a third Pulitzer Prize, this time for drama, for his verse play, *J.B.*

FOR EXPLORATION

1. What is unusual about the characters and actions presented in the octet of this sonnet? What kind of world do they imply?
2. Is the announcement of the end of the world (in the last line of the octet) dramatic? Explain.
3. What contrast is set up in the sestet? How does the use of language convey this in particular?

Margaret Walker

IOWA FARMER

I talked to a farmer one day in Iowa.
We looked out far over acres of wheat.
He spoke with pride and yet not boastfully;
he had no need to fumble for his words.
5 He knew his land and there was love for home
within the soft serene eyes of his son.
His ugly house was clean against the storm;
there was no hunger deep within the heart
nor burning riveted within the bone,
10 but here they ate a satisfying bread.
Yet in the Middle West where wheat was plentiful;
where grain grew golden under sunny skies
and cattle fattened through the summer heat
I could remember more familiar sights.

CHILDHOOD

When I was a child I knew red miners
dressed raggedly and wearing carbide lamps.
I saw them come down red hills to their camps
dyed with red dust from old Ishkooda mines.
5 Night after night I met them on the roads,
or on the streets in town I caught their glance;
the swing of dinner buckets in their hands,
and grumbling undermining all their words.

I also lived in low cotton country
10 where moonlight hovered over ripe haystacks,
or stumps of trees, and croppers' rotting shacks
with famine, terror, flood, and plague near by;
where sentiment and hatred still held sway
and only bitter land was washed away.

"Iowa Farmer" and *"Childhood"* from FOR MY PEOPLE by Margret Walker. Copyright 1942 by Yale University Press and reprinted with their permission.

Margaret Walker   1915 /

Margaret Walker, the daughter of a Methodist minister, was born and raised in Birmingham, Alabama. She experienced a great deal of anguish as a Negro in the South and was confused by the prejudice she found there. When she left Birmingham to attend Northwestern University, she looked forward to the freer conditions in the North that she had heard so much about. But she was surprised to find that life was little better for a Black in the North than it was in the South. Her poetry is shaped by these experiences of unanticipated prejudice in college and the memories of her personal anguish in the South. After receiving her degree from Northwestern, she went to the State University of Iowa to work on her master's degree. Instead of the normal dissertation, she wrote a collection of poems in order to receive the degree.

In 1942 Walker gained sudden prominence when her first book, *For My People*, appeared as a result of her winning the Yale University Younger Poets Competition; she was the first Black poet to win. The poems in this collection are divided into three groups: first there are the public poems in which she speaks directly for the Black people, then there are the folk ballads written in the Black dialect, and finally there are the personal sonnets.

FOR EXPLORATION

1. What in the farmer's outlook on life does the speaker emphasize?

2. How does "Childhood" (and the biographical sketch of the poet explain the last line of "Iowa Farmer"? What has the poet experienced that the farmer never has?

Theodore Roethke

NIGHT JOURNEY

Now as the train bears west,
Its rhythm rocks the earth,
And from my Pullman berth
I stare into the night
5 While others take their rest.
Bridges of iron lace,
A suddenness of trees,
A lap of mountain mist
All cross my line of sight,
10 Then a bleak wasted place,
And a lake below my knees.
Full on my neck I feel
The straining at a curve;
My muscles move with steel,

15 I wake in every nerve.
I watch a beacon swing
From dark to blazing bright;
We thunder through ravines
And gullies washed with light.
20 Beyond the mountain pass
Mist deepens on the pane;
We rush into a rain
That rattles double glass.
Wheels shake the roadbed stone,
25 The pistons jerk and shove,
I stay up half the night
To see the land I love.

"Night Journey," copyright 1940 by Theodore Roethke from COL-LECTED POEMS OF THEODORE ROETHKE. Reprinted by permission of Doubleday & Company, Inc., and Faber and Faber Limited.

Theodore Roethke 1908/1963

Theodore Roethke (reth′kē) grew up in Saginaw, Michigan. In his spare time he worked in his father's greenhouse, and the liking for plants and flowers which he then developed crops up now and again in his poetry. Roethke left Saginaw to attend the University of Michigan and later Harvard.

Like many contemporary poets, Roethke taught literature at several colleges while continuing to write poetry of his own.

Roethke was highly praised by contemporary critics, some of them considering him one of the three or four best poets writing in the United States at mid-century. An extremely skillful technician, he manipulates rhyme and rhythm with such competence that the reader often senses the meaning of a poem emotionally before he has grasped it intellectually. In 1954 Roethke won a Pulitzer Prize for his volume of poems, *The Waking.*

FOR EXPLORATION

Discuss the ways this poem presents the sensations of night journey by train through its use of (a) rhythm, (b) imagery, and (c) figurative language.

Gwendolyn Brooks[1]

THE EXPLORER

Somehow to find a still spot in the noise
Was the frayed inner want, the winding, the frayed
      hope
Whose tatters he kept hunting through the din.
A velvet peace somewhere.
5 A room of wily hush somewhere within.

So tipping down the scrambled halls he set
Vague hands on throbbing knobs. There were
      behind
Only spiraling, high human voices,
The scream of nervous affairs,
10 Wee griefs,
Grand griefs. And choices.

He feared most of all the choices, that cried to be
      taken.

There were no bourns.
There were no quiet rooms.

"The Explorer" from THE BEAN-EATERS by Gwendolyn Brooks.
Copyright © 1959 by Gwendolyn Brooks. Reprinted by permission
of Harper & Row, Publishers, Inc.
1. For biography see page 49 A.

FOR EXPLORATION

The Explorer
In what ways could this poem be about a search for inner
peace? What things in the situation presented in the poem
thwart this search?

CREATIVE RESPONSE

Write a free-verse poem about the world as a crowded
apartment, and yourself as one of the inhabitants. What
one thing would you most long for?

MEDGAR EVERS[1]

The man whose height his fear improved he
arranged to fear no further. The raw
intoxicated time was time for better birth

                                    or

a final death
Old styles, old tempos, all the engagement of
the day—the sedate, the regulated fray—
the antique light the Moral rose, old gusts.
tight whistlings from the past, the mothballs
in the Love at last our man forswore.
Medgar Evers annoyed confetti and assorted
brands of businessmen's eyes.
The shows came down: to maxims and surprise.
And palsy.
Roaring no rapt arise-ye to the dead he
Leaned across tomorrow. People said that
he was holding clean globes in his hands.

Copyright *Chicago Magazine* 1964, New Chicago Foundation. Reprinted by permission of *Chicago Magazine*.

1. *Medgar Evers* (1925–1963), Mississippi state field secretary for the National Association for the Advancement of Colored People (N.A.A.C.P.) who was shot and killed by a white man due to his role in the civil rights movement.

FOR EXPLORATION

Medgar Evers

1. (*a*) What action is described in the first five lines? (*b*) What is meant by the phrase "whose height his fear improved"?

2. Lines 6–14 consist largely of metaphors that present certain aspects of racial relations which Evers rejected. What are the suggestions carried by the following phrases or metaphors: (*a*) "the sedate, the regulated fray"; (*b*) "tight whistlings from the past"; (*c*) "mothballs in the Love" and "the shows came down"?

3. (*a*) What might the phrases "Medgar Evers annoyed confetti" and "the shows came down" mean? (*b*) What does the phrase "he/Leaned across tomorrow" suggest? (*c*) What do the "clean globes" which Evers holds in his hands suggest to you?

Howard Nemerov

THE VACUUM

The house is so quiet now
The vacuum cleaner sulks in the corner closet,
Its bag limp as a stopped lung, its mouth
Grinning into the floor, maybe at my
5 Slovenly life, my dog-dead youth.

I've lived this way long enough,
But when my old woman died her soul
Went into that vacuum cleaner, and I can't bear
To see the bag swell like a belly, eating the dust
10 And the woolen mice, and begin to howl

Because there is old filth everywhere
She used to crawl, in the corner and under the
      stair.
I know now how life is cheap as dirt,
And still the hungry, angry heart
15 Hangs on and howls, biting at air.

The Vacuum from THE NEXT ROOM OF THE DREAM. Copyright © by Howard Nemerov, 1962. Reprinted by permission of Margot Johnson Agency.

Howard Nemerov 1920 /

The prize-winning poet, novelist, and short-story writer, Howard Nemerov, was born and raised in New York City and was educated at Harvard. After serving in the Royal Canadian Air Force and the United States Army Air Corps during World War II, he returned to New York and wrote his first book of poetry. Since then, he has taught at several colleges, been Consultant in Poetry to the Library of Congress, and is now Professor of English at Washington University in St. Louis.

Nemerov's writings are praised for their originality, wit, insight into the human condition, rhythm, imagery, and diction. The three main influences upon his writing are his childhood in the city, the violence he experienced during the war, and the world of nature. Many of his poems are analogies between elements in nature and characteristics of man. These analogies give his poetry a thoughtful quality rather than a felt lyric intensity.

FOR EXPLORATION

1. (a) Who is the speaker? What has happened to him?
(b) What does the vacuum cleaner represent to him? Why might the poet have chosen a vacuum cleaner as appropriate to express this?
2. (a) What kinds of word play do you detect in the poem?
(b) Is this poem entirely serious? Explain.

James Wright

MUTTERINGS OVER THE CRIB OF A DEAF CHILD

"How will he hear the bell at school
Arrange the broken afternoon,
And know how to run across the cool
Grasses where the starlings cry,
5 Or understand the day is gone?"

Well, someone lifting curious brows
Will take the measure of the clock.
And he will see the birchen boughs
Outside sagging dark from the sky,
10 And the shade crawling upon the rock.

"And how will he know to rise at morning?
His mother has other sons to waken,
She has the stove she must build to burning
Before the coals of the nighttime die;
15 And he never stirs when he is shaken."

I take it the air affects the skin,
And you remember, when you were young,
Sometimes you could feel the dawn begin,
And the fire would call you, by and by,
20 Out of the bed and bring you along.

"Well, good enough. To serve his needs
All kinds of arrangements can be made.
But what will you do if his finger bleeds?
Or a bobwhite whistles invisibly
25 And flutes like an angel off in the shade?"

He will learn pain. And, as for the bird,
It is always darkening when that comes out.
I will putter as though I had not heard,
And lift him into my arms and sing
30 Whether he hears my song or not.

"*Mutterings over the Crib of a Deaf Child.*" Copyright © 1957 by James Wright. Reprinted from COLLECTED POEMS, by James Wright, by permission of Wesleyan University Press and the author.

FOR EXPLORATION

1. (a) In what ways will the deaf child be sensitive to things we normally are not? (b) In what ways will he react like the rest of us?
2. The first, third, and fifth stanzas raise problems the deaf child will have to face. Which of these is insoluble?
3. What is the tone of the last two lines? What do they imply about the speaker's attitude toward the child?
4. It has often been said that poems are made out of the arguments we carry on with ourselves. Interpret the poem in terms of this statement.

James Wright   1927 /

James Wright was born in Martins Ferry, Ohio. After graduating from Kenyon College, he spent a year in Vienna on a Fulbright scholarship. He received his M.A. and Ph.D. degrees from the University of Washington and now teaches at Hunter College in New York.

Wright's poetry has been published in magazines in both the United States and Europe, and he has won several awards, among them the Robert Frost Poetry Prize and the Yale Younger Poets Award. In fact, Wright's first book of poetry was published by Yale as the first of its series of volumes by promising new poets.

Critics have compared Wright's poetry to that of Robinson and Frost. Like these older poets, he most often uses both rhyme and conventional meter. He is like them also in the compassion with which he views humanity and in the simple language in which he states his ideas.

Richard Wilbur

POTATO

for André du Bouchet
An underground grower, blind and a common brown;
Got a misshapen look, it's nudged where it could;
Simple as soil yet crowded as earth with all.

Cut open raw, it loosens a cool clean stench,
Mineral acid seeping from pores of prest meal;
It is like breaching a strangely refreshing tomb:

Therein the taste of first stones, the hands of dead slaves,
Waters men drank in the earliest frightful woods,
Flint-chips, and peat, and the cinders of buried camps.

Scrubbed under faucet water the planet skin
Polishes yellow, but tears to the plain insides;
Parching, the white's blue-hearted like hungry hands.

All of the cold dark kitchens, and war-frozen grey
Evening at window; I remember so many
Peeling potatoes quietly into chipt pails.

'It was potatoes saved us, they kept us alive.'
Then they had something to say akin to praise
For the mean earth-apples, too common to cherish or steal.

Times being hard, the Sikh and the Senegalese,
Hobo and Okie,[1] the body of Jesus the Jew,
Vestigial virtues, are eaten; we shall survive.

"Potato" from THE BEAUTIFUL CHANGES, (British Title: POEMS 1943–
1956). Copyright, 1947 by Richard Wilbur. Reprinted by permission
of Harcourt Brace Jovanovich, Inc., and Faber and Faber Limited.
1. *Sikh . . . Senegalese, Hobo and Okie,* uprooted or homeless
groups of people in India, Africa and America respectively.

What has not lost its savour shall hold us up,
And we are praising what saves us, what fills the need.
(Soon there'll be packets again, with Algerian fruits.)

Oh, it will not bear polish, the ancient potato,
Needn't be nourished by Caesars, will blow anywhere,
Hidden by nature, counted-on, stubborn and blind.

You may have noticed the bush that it pushes to air,
Comical-delicate, sometimes with second-rate flowers
Awkward and milky and beautiful only to hunger.

Richard Wilbur   1921 /

Richard Wilbur was born into a family which encouraged his early attempts at versifying. During his boyhood in a rural corner of New Jersey he developed the liking for the outdoor world which is apparent in much of his poetry. While he was a student at Amherst, he widened his knowledge of the United States by spending his summers bumming across country on freight cars. He served in the infantry during World War II, then took an M.A. degree at Harvard.

It was not until he had seen active service during the war that Wilbur began to work seriously at his poetry, trying through poetry to bring order into his disordered world. His first book of poems, *The Beautiful Changes* (1947), showed qualities that are apparent to a greater extent in his later poetry—a strong lyric note, mastery of form, and fusion of form and idea. Because he believes in the disciplines of meter, rhyme, and other formal devices, he attempts to reconcile these adjuncts of traditional poetry with the modern modes of thought and expression. It is this tendency in his poetry that has caused him to be called "a New Formalist."

FOR EXPLORATION

1. What does the poet find unusual about so common a thing as a potato? Which of its qualities does he emphasize? Is his description idealized in any way?

2. The potato is described as "simple as soil." In what sense is it linked to the soil that nurtured it? What metaphor emphasizes this link?

3. What are the implications of the line, "What has not lost its savour shall hold us up"? How might this apply to things other than food items?

CREATIVE RESPONSE

In whatever medium seems most appropriate to you (anything from the written word to "found art") find and represent the simple essence of something commonly overlooked or taken for granted. See if you can catch its "savour," and communicate it to others without explanation.

by Robert Hayden

Journey and Return

Like Auden, other poets also underwent a change of heart, caught up in the moral crises brought on by the Second World War. The bitter moral implications of war gave focus and intensity to the poetry of Marianne Moore, Gwendolyn Brooks, Karl Shapiro, Randall Jarrell, and Richard Eberhart. None of these poets harbored any romantic illusions about the glories of war. Together with other poets of the period they gave their readers, in precise and unsentimental language and striking imagery, an idea of the enormities of global conflict and the human suffering and debasement it caused.

During the war years and after, poetry tended to grow more subjective and metaphysical. Since many poets made use of private references closed to the general reader, poetry also became more obscure, and was often criticized as being too "intellectual," and sometimes derided as poetry written only for professional critics. Of course, some poets did try to conform to the principles of the New Criticism formulated by John Crowe Ransom, Allen Tate, Cleanth Brooks, and Robert Penn Warren, all of whom (with the exception of Brooks) were well-known southern poets. The New Critics emphasized the importance of formal structure, were partial to metaphysical verse, and frowned on social statement as inimical to the spirit of poetry.

Nevertheless, the poetry of T. S. Eliot, Robert Lowell, and W. H. Auden reflected the spiritual crisis of the forties. Tightly packed and often strenuously intellectual, their poetry involved complicated metrical and stanzaic patterns, and formed part of the revival of interest in form. In general the influence of the New Criticism produced poetry of elegant phrasing, carefully wrought images and textures,

and a respect for meticulous craftsmanship which characterized the earlier work of Richard Wilbur, Karl Shapiro, Randall Jarrell, John Ciardi, and Gwendolyn Brooks. Theodore Roethke was, in a sense, "wilder" than any of these poets, cultivating the irrational and surrealistic in free-form lyrics, voicing the terrors and beauties of existence and the natural world of growing things. Yet he was an accomplished writer of strictly patterned poems as well.

In the 1950's a negative reaction to formalism became apparent. The theories of the New Critics were challenged as irrelevant. The supremacy of Auden and Eliot was challenged by poets who took as their guides Ezra Pound and William Carlos Williams. Ezra Pound's poetry seemed to a new generation of poets the greatest work of the century. Pound's admirers were loud in their praise of him as the "originator" of modern poetry, but not everyone was prepared to go that far or to ignore the fact that Pound sometimes used his poetry as a vehicle for reactionary ideas. Although a controversial figure, Pound has been—as critic, poet, translator, polemicist—one of the major influences on twentieth-century literature. William Carlos Williams, physician and poet, was Pound's friend during his lifetime but did not share his views. Influenced in the early years of his career by Imagism, Williams subsequently wrote free-verse lyrics in what he thought of as an "American rhythm." Avoiding meter, he took the cadences of native speech as the basis for his rhythms. Everyday experiences, familiar objects, seemingly trivial actions or events, fleeting moments of recognition or awareness are among the typical materials he developed into poems with precision and, for the most part, without moralizing.

Williams and Pound, together with Walt Whitman, of

COURTESY OF THE AUTHOR

CIARDI

ROLLIE MCKENNA

WILBUR

IMOGEN CUNNINGHAM

ROETHKE

ROLLIE MCKENNA

RANSOM

HERB WEITMAN—WASHINGTON UNIVERSITY, ST. LOUIS

VAN DUYN

ROLLIE MCKENNA

WILLIAMS

course, were lauded by the emergent "Beat" poets of the mid 1950's as the natural enemies of formalist theory and practice. However, in their eagerness to rid poetry of artiness and elitism many Beat poets emphasized "communication" and "self-expression" at the expense of craftsmanship, and wrote poems which were banal, imprecise, and pretentious. With the Beat poets, figurative language fell into disfavor, and came to be regarded as a literary "cop-out," an evasion of reality.

The Beat phenomenon, centered for a while in New York's Greenwich Village and the North Beach area of San Francisco, signified a withdrawal from society by those who were contemptuous of its materialism and conformity. To be "beat" was to be tired of, worn out by, a corrupt world. It also connoted the rebelling individual's quest for "beatitude"—a beatific state induced by voluntary privation, anarchistic individualism, rock music, esoteric religious cults, drugs, sex.

Allen Ginsberg's "Howl" (1956), the central poem of the Beat movement, cries out against the destruction of "the best minds of my generation," yet concludes with the affirmation that life, however sordid and vicious, is holy. Among other "beats" who earned popular recognition was Lawrence Ferlinghetti, writer of poems that blend fantasy, wit, and whimsy into an oblique commentary on the condition of modern man. Beat poetry waned in the sixties, and many of its energies poured into the main stream of American poetry. Robert Creeley and Denise Levertov, for example, absorbed the Beat vitality and won reputations as influential *avant garde* poets writing in the traditions of Pound and Williams.

Randall Jarrell[1]

THE MACHINE-GUN

The broken blood, the hunting flame,
The pierced mask and the flowering shell
Are not placated—nor the face
That smouldered where the searchlights fell;

Our times lie in the welded hands,
Our fortune in the rubber face—
On the gunner's tripod, black with oil,
Spits and gapes the pythoness.

Reprinted with the permission of Farrar, Straus & Giroux, Inc. from
"The Machine-Gun" by Randall Jarrell from THE COMPLETE POEMS.
Copyright © 1968, 1969, by Mrs. Randall Jarrell.
1. For biography see page 65 A.
2. *tripod . . . the pythoness.* The priestess of Apollo at Delphi,
called the *Pythoness,* gave her oracles while seated upon the
sacred tripod.

FOR EXPLORATION

1. (*a*) What do the phrases "welded hands" and "rubber
face" suggest about our "times," our "fortune"? What
could each of these things be, literally? (*b*) How are they
related to the other images in the poem?

2. Jarrell compares the machine gun to a prophetess. Why
would the machine gun be a fitting agent of prophecy
about the modern world?

Robert Hayden

THE NIGHT-BLOOMING CEREUS

And so for nights
we waited, hoping to see
the heavy bud
    break into flower.

5   On its neck-like tube
hooking down from the edge
of the leaf-branch
    nearly to the floor,

the bud packed
10 tight with its miracle swayed
stiffly on breaths
    of air, moved

as though impelled
by stirrings within itself.
15 It repelled as much
    as it fascinated me

sometimes—snake,
eyeless bird head,
beak that would gape
20 with grotesque life-squawk.

But you, my dear,
conceded less to the bizarre
than to the imminence
    of bloom. Yet we agreed

25   we ought
to celebrate the blossom,
paint ourselves, dance
    in honor of

archaic mysteries
30 when it appeared. Meanwhile
we waited, aware
    of rigorous design.

Backster's
polygraph,[1] I thought,
35 would have shown
    (as clearly as it had

a philodendron's
fear) tribal sentience
in the cactus, focused
40   energy of will.

That belling of
tropic perfume—that
signalling
    not meant for us;

45   the darkness
cloyed with summoning
fragrance. We dropped
    trivial tasks

and marvelling
50 beheld at last the achieved
flower. Its moonlight
    petals were

still unfold-
ing, the spike fringe of the outer
55 perianth recessing
    as we watched.

Lunar presence,
foredoomed, already dying,
it charged the room
60   with plangency

older than human
cries, ancient as prayers
invoking Osiris, Krishna,
    Tézcatlipóca.[2]

65   We spoke
in whispers when
we spoke
    at all. . . .

"The Night-Blooming Cereus" from THE NIGHT-BLOOMING CEREUS
by Robert Hayden. Reprinted by permission of the author.
1. *Backster's polygraph.* In 1966 Cleve Backster, a polygraph
expert, conducted experiments in which he attached a lie detector
to a leaf of a plant and discovered that the plant showed reactions
similar to those of humans.
2. *Osiris, Krishna, Tézcatlipóca.* Osiris was the Egyptian god of
fertility, who suffered, died, rose to life immortal, and became the
god of the underworld and the judge of the dead. Krishna is one of
the most widely worshiped of the Hindu deities. Tézcatlipóca was
one of the principal Aztec gods, known as the creator and the god of
night, music, and the dance.

Robert Hayden

RUNAGATE RUNAGATE[1]

I.

Runs falls rises stumbles on from darkness into darkness
and the darkness thicketed with shapes of terror
and the hunters pursuing and the hounds pursuing
and the night cold and the night long and the river
5 to cross and the jack-muh-lanterns beckoning beckoning
and blackness ahead and when shall I reach that somewhere
morning and keep on going and never turn back and keep on going

Runagate

     Runagate

10   Runagate

Many thousands rise and go
many thousands crossing over

                        O mythic North
                  O star-shaped yonder Bible city

15 Some go weeping and some rejoicing
some in coffins and some in carriages
some in silks and some in shackles

           Rise and go or fare you well

No more auction block for me
20 no more driver's lash for me

     If you see my Pompey, 30 yrs of age,
     new breeches, plain stockings, negro shoes;
     if you see my Anna, likely young mulatto
     branded E on the right cheek, R on the left,
     catch them if you can and notify subscriber.
25   Catch them if you can, but it won't be easy.
     They'll dart underground when you try to catch them,
     plunge into quicksand, whirlpools, mazes,
     turn into scorpions when you try to catch them.

"Runagate Runagate" by Robert Hayden from SELECTED POEMS.
Copyright © 1966 by Robert Hayden. Reprinted by permission of
October House Inc.
1. *Runagate,* a runaway; in this case a runaway slave.

30 And before I'll be a slave
I'll be buried in my grave

North star and bonanza gold
I'm bound for the freedom, freedom-bound
and oh Susyanna don't you cry for me

35   Runagate

                    Runagate

II.

Rises from their anguish and their power,

Harriet Tubman,[2]

woman of earth, whipscarred,
40   a summoning, a shining

Mean to be free

And this way the way of it, brethren brethren,
way we journeyed from Can't to Can.
Moon so bright and no place to hide,
45   the cry up and the patterollers riding,
hound dogs belling in bladed air.
And fear starts a-murbling, Never make it,
we'll never make it. *Hush that now,*
and she's turned upon us, levelled pistol
50   glinting in the moonlight:
Dead folks can't jaybird-talk, she says;
you keep on going now or die, she says.

Wanted   Harriet Tubman   alias The General
alias Moses   Stealer of Slaves

55 In league with Garrison Alcott Emerson
Garrett Douglass Thoreau John Brown[3]

contd.

---

2. *Harriet Tubman* (1820?–1913), a fugitive slave who led other
slaves to freedom. Estimates of the number of slaves she freed have
ranged from sixty to three hundred.
3. *Garrison . . . John Brown,* leading abolitionists.

Robert Hayden

Armed and known to be Dangerous

Wanted   Reward   Dead or Alive

      Tell me, Ezekiel, oh tell me do you see
60   mailed Jehovah coming to deliver me?

Hoot-owl calling in the ghosted air,
five times calling to the hants in the air.
Shadow of a face in the scary leaves,
shadow of a voice in the talking leaves:

65   Come ride-a my train

      Oh that train, ghost-story train
      through swamp and savanna movering movering,
      over trestles of dew, through caves of the wish,
      Midnight Special on a sabre track movering movering,
70   *first stop Mercy and the last Hallelujah.*

Come ride-a my train

Mean mean mean to be free.

FREDERICK DOUGLASS

*Born a slave, Frederick Douglass (1817–1895)
escaped from his master's home in Maryland to
Massachusetts, where an extemporaneous speech
against slavery won him work as a lecturer. Fearing
capture as a fugitive, he journeyed to Britain
where his speeches did much to enlist British sympathy for the Abolitionist cause. In the meantime,
an Abolitionist group in the United States raised
enough money to pay for his freedom, and in 1847
he returned to this country. As a free man, Douglass
established and edited the* North Star, *a stanchly
abolitionist newspaper. His influential editorials
and eloquent speeches did much to further the cause
of the antislavery movement, and today Douglass is
recognized as perhaps the most outstanding Negro
leader of his century.*

When it is finally ours, this freedom, this liberty,
    this beautiful
and terrible thing, needful to man as air,
usable as earth; when it belongs at last to all,
when it is truly instinct, brain matter, diastole,
    systole,
5 reflex action; when it is finally won; when it is more
than the gaudy mumbo jumbo of politicians:
this man, this Douglass, this former slave, this
    Negro
beaten to his knees, exiled, visioning a world
where none is lonely, none hunted, alien,
10 this man, superb in love and logic, this man
shall be remembered. Oh, not with statues' rhetoric,
not with legends and poems and wreaths of
    bronze alone,
but with the lives grown out of his life, the lives
fleshing his dream of the beautiful, needful thing.

from

"WORDS IN THE MOURNING TIME"

V

*Oh, what a world we make,
oppressor and oppressed.*

Our world—
this violent ghetto, slum
5 of the spirit raging against itself.

We hate kill destroy
in the name of human good
our killing and our hate destroy.

"Frederick Douglass" by Robert Hayden from SELECTED POEMS.
Copyright © 1966 by Robert Hayden. Reprinted by permission of
October House Inc.
"Words in the Mourning Time, part V" by Robert Hayden from
WORDS IN THE MOURNING TIME. Copyright © 1970 by Robert Hay-
den. Reprinted by permission of October House Inc.

Robert Hayden

A PLAGUE OF STARLINGS

(Fisk Campus)
Evenings I hear
the workmen fire
into the stiff
magnolia leaves,
5 routing the starlings
gathered noisy and
befouling there.

Their scissoring
terror like glass
10 coins spilling breaking
the birds explode
into mica sky
raggedly fall
to ground rigid
15 in clench of cold.

The spared return,
when the guns are through,
to the spoiled trees
like choiceless poor
20 to a dangerous
dwelling place,
chitter and quarrel
in the piercing dark
above the killed.

25 Mornings, I pick
my way past death's
black droppings:
on campus lawns
and streets
30 the troublesome
starlings
frost-salted lie,
troublesome still.

And if not careful
35 I shall tread
upon carcasses
carcasses when I
go mornings now
to lecture on
40 what Socrates,
the hemlock hour nigh,
told sorrowing
Phaedo and the rest
about the migratory
45 habits of the soul.[1]

"A Plague of Starlings" by Robert Hayden from WORDS IN THE MOURNING TIME. Copyright © 1970 by Robert Hayden. Reprinted by permission of October House Inc.
1. *Socrates . . . the soul.* Socrates (c.470 B.C.–399 B.C.), the Greek philosopher, was indicted for "impiety" and sentenced to die. As was customary in Athens, he died by drinking hemlock, a poison. On his deathbed he told his friends that the soul is an unchanging thing and will survive the body.

FOR EXPLORATION

The Night-Blooming Cereus

1. (a) Why do those who watch the blooming cereus speak in whispers? (b) What is it about the swelling bud that suggests both miracle and mystery? (c) In what ways is the blooming both grotesque and beautiful?

2. (a) What imagery in the poem reinforces the "tribal sentience, focused energy of will" that characterizes life? (b) What is particular about the cereus that gives its flowering such "plangency"?

Runagate, Runagate

1. Both parts of this poem use a variety of voices and rhythms, intermixed with descriptive passages. (a) What are the effects of the first seven lines? How do the language and imagery work to create these? (b) Who or what is the speaker in lines 21–29? What impression of slave-owner and runaway slave does it present? (c) Who are the speakers in lines 41–52? What is the situation? Who is in command? What impression do you have of her? How do the lines that follow (53–58) support this impression? (d) What types of song do lines 59–72 recall? What, literally, is the "train" referred to? Does the use of language in this section give the impression of movement? How so?

2. This poem catches a variety of emotions—among them fear, hope, determination. Discuss the alternation of these throughout the poem. What emotional note does the poem end on?

3. (a) What signs of harshness, suffering, or brutality do you find in the poem? (b) By contrast, what kinds of hope does the "mythic North" offer? (c) Is there any suggestion in the poem that this hope might itself be "mythic"?

CREATIVE RESPONSE

Prepare a dramatic reading of this poem in which various voices speak, assigning the passages to individual readers, and the descriptive passages to one reader. You might want to score the final lines (59–72) for choral reading.

Frederick Douglass

1. How does this poem envision freedom? From what is it distinguished? How might this freedom be characterized as an "ordinary" rather than a "special" human state?

2. What in Frederick Douglass makes him representative of this freedom? How will his example realize itself?

A Plague of Starlings

1. (a) What impact does the second stanza have on you? (b) How are imagery and sound used to create this effect? (c) How might terror be "scissoring"? (d) How might birds tumbling from trees be like "glass coins spilling breaking"?

2. In what ways might the starlings be like the "choiceless poor"? Extend this analogy in as much detail as the poem permits.

3. (a) What is meant by the comment that the starlings, troublesome when alive, are "troublesome still"? (b) In what sense was Socrates "troublesome"? (Read a short account of his death in an encyclopedia, if unfamiliar with the story.) How was his situation similar to the starlings'?

4. What implications does the word "migratory," in the next to last line, have?

Robert Hayden 1913 /

Robert Earl Hayden has been writing and publishing his poetry since 1940, but not until 1966 did he receive the attention his work merits. In that year he was awarded the prize for English language poetry at the First World Festival of Negro Arts at Dakar, Senegal. In presenting the award, the judges described Hayden as "a remarkable craftsman, a striking singer of words" whose "extraordinary talent makes itself known in almost every line. . . ."

In 1970 he received the Russell Loines Award, presented by the National Institute of Arts and Letters. In 1972 he was a nominee for the National Book Award in poetry.

Hayden was born in Detroit, Michigan, and received his higher education at Wayne State University and the University of Michigan. Before accepting his present position as a professor of English at the University of Michigan, he worked as a drama and music critic for the *Michigan Chronicle* and for more than twenty years as a teacher of English and creative writing at Fisk University. He has also been Bingham Professor of English at the University of Louisville and Visiting Poet at the University of Washington.

Hayden's poetry, though influenced by his background, is not shaped by it. His poems are marked by an intensity of feeling and a lack of false sentiment, a creative use of language and a strong desire to communicate clearly with the reader, a love of mankind and an angry denunciation of its pettinesses.

Among Hayden's publications are *A Ballad of Remembrance* (1962), *Selected Poems* (1966), and *Words in the Mourning Time* (1970). He has also edited *Kaleidoscope: Poems by American Negro Poets* (1967) and is co-editor of *A Source Book of Afro-American Literature.*

Robert Lowell

FOR THE UNION DEAD

"Relinquunt Omnia Servare Rem Publicam."[1]

The old South Boston Aquarium stands
in a Sahara of snow now. Its broken windows are
    boarded.
The bronze weathervane cod has lost half its scales.
The airy tanks are dry.

5 Once my nose crawled like a snail on the glass;
my hand tingled
to burst the bubbles
drifting from the noses of the cowed, compliant
    fish.

My hand draws back. I often sigh still
10 for the dark downward and vegetating kingdom
of the fish and reptile. One morning last March,
I pressed against the new barbed and galvanized

fence on the Boston Common. Behind their cage,
yellow dinosaur steamshovels were grunting
15 as they cropped up tons of mush and grass
to gouge their underworld garage.

Parking spaces luxuriate like civic
sandpiles in the heart of Boston.
A girdle of orange, Puritan-pumpkin colored girders
20 braces the tingling Statehouse,

shaking over the excavations, as it faces Colonel
    Shaw
and his bell-cheeked Negro infantry
on St. Gaudens' shaking Civil War relief,[2]
propped by a plank splint against the garage's
    earthquake.

25 Two months after marching through Boston,
half the regiment was dead;
at the dedication,
William James[3] could almost hear the bronze
    Negroes breathe.

Their monument sticks like a fishbone
30 in the city's throat.
Its Colonel is as lean
as a compass-needle.

He has an angry wrenlike vigilance,
a greyhound's gentle tautness;
35 he seems to wince at pleasure,
and suffocate for privacy.

He is out of bounds now. He rejoices in man's
    lovely,
peculiar power to choose life and die—
when he leads his black soldiers to death,
40 he cannot bend his back.

On a thousand small town New England greens,
the old white churches hold their air
of sparse, sincere rebellion; frayed flags
quilt the graveyards of the Grand Army of the
    Republic.[4]

Reprinted with the permission of Farrar, Straus & Giroux, Inc. and Faber and Faber Limited from FOR THE UNION DEAD by Robert Lowell, copyright © 1960 by Robert Lowell.
1. *"Relinquunt . . . Publicam."* They sacrificed all to serve the state. [*Latin*]
2. *Colonel Shaw . . . War relief.* In 1897 Augustus Saint-Gaudens (1848–1907), an American sculptor, completed a monument honoring Robert G. Shaw (1837–1863), the colonel of the first Negro regiment in the Civil War.
3. *William James* (1842–1910), a psychologist and philosopher who taught at Harvard. As a substitute for war, he suggested conscripting boys for projects of manual labor.
4. *Grand Army of the Republic,* an organization established in 1866 by Union veterans of the Civil War in order to preserve friendships, honor fallen comrades, aid widows and the handicapped, and increase pensions.

The stone statues of the abstract Union Soldier
grow slimmer and younger each year—
wasp-waisted, they doze over muskets
and muse through their sideburns . . .

Shaw's father wanted no monument
except the ditch,
where his son's body was thrown
and lost with his "niggers."

The ditch is nearer.
There are no statues for the last war here;
on Boylston Street, a commercial photograph
shows Hiroshima[5] boiling

over a Mosler Safe, the "Rock of Ages"
that survived the blast. Space is nearer.
When I crouch to my television set,
the drained faces of Negro school-children rise
        like balloons.

Colonel Shaw
is riding on his bubble,
he waits
for the blessèd break.

The Aquarium is gone. Everywhere,
giant finned cars nose forward like fish;
a savage servility
slides by on grease.

5. *Hiroshima*, a city in Japan. On August 6, 1945, the United States dropped the first atomic bomb here which caused approximately 130,000 casualties and devastated 90 percent of the city.

FOR EXPLORATION

1. (*a*) What did the fish in the aquarium mean to the speaker when he was a boy? (*b*) What has since happened to the aquarium? (*c*) What changes are taking place on Boston Common? What attitude does the speaker take toward these? (*d*) How do these changes affect the memorial to Colonel Shaw and his infantry?

2. (*a*) How are Colonel Shaw and his infantry portrayed on the memorial plaque? (*b*) In what ways is the plaque related to other memorials?

3. (*a*) What other changes—specifically in warfare—have taken place since Shaw's time, as alluded to in the poem? How do these realities affect the meaning of war monuments? How might they explain the phrases "the ditch is nearer" and "space is nearer"?

4. (*a*) What is the significance of Colonel Shaw's waiting "for the blessed break" in his bubble? What forces might cause this break? (*b*) In what way is this "bubble" related to war monuments and their portrayal of war?

5. What is the tone of the last four lines? What attitude toward modern life do they reveal?

Robert Lowell   1917 /

Robert Lowell's poetry has been received enthusiastically from the start. In 1947 he received a Pulitzer Prize, in 1960 a National Book Award, and in 1962 the Bollingen Translation Prize. He is regarded as one of the new poets of the mid-century who might influence the literature of his generation. Although his poems are greatly influenced by his Catholicism, they range over a wide diversity of subjects.

Lowell was raised in Boston and educated at Harvard and Kenyon College in Ohio. During World War II he was drafted but filed as a conscientious objector and went to prison. He later served as the Consultant in Poetry to the Library of Congress and now teaches at Harvard.

John Ciardi

THE GIFT

In 1945, when the keepers cried *kaput*,
Josef Stein, poet, came out of Dachau[1]
like half a resurrection, his other
eighty pounds still in their invisible grave.

5 Slowly then the mouth opened and first
a broth, and then a medication, and then
a diet, and all in time and the knitting mercies,
the showing bones were buried back in flesh,

and the miracle was finished. Josef Stein,
10 man and poet, rose, walked, and could even
beget, and did, and died later of other causes
only partly traceable to his first death.

He noted—with some surprise at first—
that strangers could not tell he had died once.
15 He returned to his poet in the library, drank his beer,
published three poems in a French magazine,

and was very kind to the son who at last was his.
In the spent of one night he wrote three propositions:
That Hell is the denial of the ordinary. That nothing
     lasts.
20 That clean white paper waiting under a pen

is the gift beyond history and hurt and heaven.

"The Gift" from 39 POEMS by John Ciardi. © 1959, Rutgers, The
State University. Reprinted by permission of the author.
1. *Dachau,* a town near Munich; the site of a German concentration camp during Hitler's regime.

ON FLUNKING A NICE BOY OUT OF SCHOOL

I wish I could teach you how ugly
decency and humility can be when they are not
the election of a contained mind but only
the defenses of an incompetent. Were you taught
5 meekness as a weapon? Or did you discover,
by chance maybe, that it worked on mother
and was generally a good thing—
at least when all else failed—to get you over
the worst of what was coming. Is that why you bring
10 these sheepfaces to Tuesday?
                    They won't do.
It's three months work I want, and I'd sooner have it
from the brassiest lumpkin in pimpledom, but have it,
than all these martyred repentances from you.

"*On Flunking a Nice Boy Out of School*" from PERSON TO PERSON by John Ciardi, copyright 1964 by Rutgers, the State University. Reprinted by permission of the author.

FOR EXPLORATION

The Gift

1. (a) What is the literal meaning of the statement that Josef Stein came out of Dachau "like half a resurrection"? (b) What other connotations are there in this phrase? What in the poem supports your view?

2. What significance do Stein's three propositions have in terms of his experience?

On Flunking a Nice Boy Out of School

1. (a) Which of the boy's characteristics is the speaker criticizing? Is he critical of those qualities themselves or the way the boy uses them? (b) How in fact does the boy use them? In what ways might his mind not be "contained"?

2. Would you consider the speaker in this poem to be harsh and unsympathetic? Why or why not?

John Ciardi   1916 /

John Ciardi was born in Boston of Italian immigrant parents. He received his bachelor's degree from Tufts College and then received a scholarship to the University of Michigan. By working part-time as a busboy, he was able to earn his expense money at Michigan and receive his master's degree. He taught for a time at Harvard and Rutgers but left the academic world in 1961 to devote full time to his literary career. Since 1956, he has been the poetry editor of the *Saturday Review*.

Ciardi's poetic strength lies in the diversity and fluency of his work. He addresses himself to the body of general readers hoping that some of them will develop more than merely a general interest in poetry. Perhaps because of the battles fought in the ethnic neighborhoods of Boston, Ciardi believes that childhood and adolescence are the most violent times of life. This belief is reflected in some of his poems.

Robert Fitzgerald

THE IMPRISONED

I

The newsvendor with his hut and crutch
And black palm polished by pennies
Chinked me swiftly my worn-out silver;
Then I went underground.
5   Many went down there,
Down blowing passages and dimness where
Rocketing cars were sucked out of sound in the tunnel.

A train came and expired, opening slots to us
All alacritous moving in voiceless numbers,
10 Haunch to haunch, elbow to hard elbow.

One would sleep, gaping and sagged in a corner,
One might wish for a seat by the girl yonder;
Each a-sway with his useless heavy headpiece.

II

Tenements: "islands" in the ancient city.
15 Neither under the old law nor the new
Could any insulation make them gentle.

Here I retired, here I did lay me down—

Beyond the washing lines reeled in at evening,
Beyond the roofpots and the lightless skylights,
20 The elevated grated round a curve
To pick up pitch diminishing toward silence—
And took my ease amid that hardihood:
The virago at her sill obscenely screeching
Or the lutanist plucking away at "My Lady Greensleeves."[1]

"The Imprisoned" by Robert Fitzgerald, SPRING SHADE, POEMS 1931–1970. Copyright 1943 by Robert Fitzgerald. Reprinted by permission of New Directions Publishing Corporation.
1. "My Lady Greensleeves," an English folksong.

III

25 The down beat, off beat, beat.
A hopped up drummer's perfect
Tocking periodicity and abandon.
Cush a cush cush a cush. Whang.
Diddle di daddle di yup yup
30 Whisper to me daddy. On the
Down, the down beat, beat.

The spot's on blondie, see her croon,
See that remarkable subtle pelvic
Universal joint softly rolling.
35 Honey take it sweet and slow,
Honey, take your time.
Roll those eyes and send, baby, send.

And swing it. O cats
Express your joys and savoir faire
40 You hot lick connoisseurs: shake
A laig like New Orleans. Or

Rumba. O you Arthur Murray,[2] O you Murray boys
With your snappy steward jackets keeping young,
Steer and sway, you accomplished dancers.
45 Won't you come over to my table.
Meet Rosemary. This is Rosemary.

IV

The manhole disks were prone shields of morning
Where the sun greeted the avenue.
O lumbering conveyances! O yellow
50 Gliding of cabs, thousand-footed dimpling stir!
The fresh net placed on the fair hair!

The steel shutters removed at Tiffany's[3]
And the doorman pulling his beige gloves on;

---

2. *Arthur Murray,* founder of the Arthur Murray Dance Studios, a
nationwide network of schools that teach the popular dances of the
day.
3. *Tiffany's,* a famous jewelry store in New York City.

The elevator boy holding down his yawn
55 And the cool engineer with his briefcase;

The sun striking over the void city room
And the first hasteners through the concourse;

The riveter walking out on the flaking plank
And the welder donning his goggles;

60 The steel drawer sliding from the office file
And the receptionist fixing her lipline;

The towsled showgirl a-drool on the pillow
And the schoolyard filling with cries;

The roominghouse suicide at peace by the gasjet
65 And the nun smiling across the ward—

Against the shine of windows, visual
Madness of intersecting multitudes,
Their speech torn to bits in the torrent.

Robert Fitzgerald   1910 /

Although Robert Fitzgerald was born in Geneva, New York, he grew up in Springfield, Illinois, and later attended Harvard. After his graduation from college, he went to New York to live and worked as a reporter for the *New York Herald Tribune.* After that he became a staff writer at *Time* magazine and then poetry reviewer for the *New Republic.* He then turned to teaching. He first taught at Sarah Lawrence College, then at Princeton, and now he is teaching at Harvard.

About his own poetry, Fitzgerald has said, "I have been independent and trustful of my own powers. Poetry can be at least an elegance, at most a revelation, and I have worked as opportunity offered between these limits. Eliot was and remains a great touchstone and irritant. The Greek Masters have been before me often, and more lately so has Dante. I hold by constructive beauty, energy of language, depth of life."

FOR EXPLORATION

1. How does each section of the poem illustrate an aspect of imprisonment? Who are the "imprisoned" in each case?
2. Compare section II of this poem with Gwendolyn Brooks' "The Explorer" (page M 236). What similarities of imagery do you find? Do you find any differences in tone? What?
3. To what extent does the "imprisonment" seem physical? (Note the imagery in sections I and IV.) To what extent does it seem spiritual? What means of "escape" are implied?

Robert A. Davis

DUST BOWL[1]

These were our fields.
Now no flower blooms,
No grain grows here
Where earth moves in every wind.

5 No birds nest in these trees.
No fruit hangs
Where the boughs stretch bare
In the sun.

The dust sifts down—blows in.
10 Our mouths are filled.
The dust moves across,
And up and around the dust moves

In our waking—our sleeping—
In our dreams.

"*Dust Bowl*" by Robert A. Davis from I AM THE DARKER BROTHER
ed. by Arnold Adoff.
1. *Dust Bowl*, areas of the prairie states that suffer from dust storms
which carry off the topsoil.

FOR EXPLORATION

1. (*a*) Describe how the sound effects (onomatopoeia and internal rhyme) and rhythm contribute to the poem. (*b*) Experiment with variant readings until you find one you like best.
2. Does the poem seem to say as much through pure sound as through the literal meanings of the words it employs? Why or why not?

Robert A. Davis 1917 /

Robert A. Davis was born in Mobile, Alabama. In his youth the family moved north and he attended high school in Chicago. He then studied at the University of Chicago and the Chicago Christian College. He has since contributed to magazines and been active in theatre productions.

Lawrence Ferlinghetti

DOG

The dog trots freely in the street
and sees reality
and the things he sees
are bigger than himself
5 and the things he sees
are his reality
Drunks in doorways
Moons on trees
The dog trots freely thru the street
10 and the things he sees
are smaller than himself
Fish on newsprint
Ants in holes
Chickens in Chinatown windows
15 their heads a block away
The dog trots freely in the street
and the things he smells
smell something like himself
The dog trots freely in the street
20 past puddles and babies
cats and cigars
poolrooms and policemen
He doesn't hate cops
He merely has no use for them
25 and he goes past them
and past the dead cows hung up whole
in front of the San Francisco Meat Market
He would rather eat a tender cow
than a tough policeman
30 though either might do
And he goes past the Romeo Ravioli Factory
and past Coit's Tower[1]
and past Congressman Doyle
He's afraid of Coit's Tower
35 but he's not afraid of Congressman Doyle
although what he hears is very discouraging
very depressing
very absurd
to a sad young dog like himself
40 to a serious dog like himself

"Dog" by Lawrence Ferlinghetti, A CONEY ISLAND OF THE MIND. Copyright © 1958 by Lawrence Ferlinghetti. Reprinted by permission of New Directions Publishing Corporation and Laurence Pollinger Limited.
1. *Coit's Tower*, a memorial to San Francisco's volunteer firemen, built on top of Telegraph Hill in 1933.

But he has his own free world to live in
His own fleas to eat
He will not be muzzled
Congressman Doyle is just another
45 fire hydrant
to him
The dog trots freely in the street
and has his own dog's life to live
and to think about
50 and to reflect upon
touching and tasting and testing everything
investigating everything
without benefit of perjury
a real realist
55 with a real tale to tell
and a real tail to tell it with
a real live
          barking
                    democratic dog
60 engaged in real
                    free enterprise
with something to say
                    about ontology
something to say
65   about reality
                    and how to see it
                              and how to hear it
with his head cocked sideways
                    at streetcorners
70 as if he is just about to have
                    his picture taken
                              for Victor Records
          listening for
                    His Master's Voice[2]
75   and looking
               like a living questionmark
                         into the
                         great gramaphone
                    of puzzling existence
80 with its wondrous hollow horn
          which always seems
          just about to spout forth
                    some Victorious answer
          to everything

---

2. *His Master's Voice.* The trademark of the RCA Victor company
was a picture of a dog, seated, with his head cocked, listening to the
horn of an old phonograph. Underneath the picture was a notation
indicating the dog was listening to "His Master's Voice."

Lawrence Ferlinghetti

14

Don't let that horse
                    eat that violin
          cried Chagall's[1] mother
                              But he
5   kept right on
                              painting
And became famous
And kept on painting
                    The Horse With Violin In Mouth
10 And when he finally finished it
he jumped up upon the horse
                              and rode away
              waving the violin
And then with a low bow gave it
15 to the first naked nude he ran across
And there were no strings
                              attached

"14" by Lawrence Ferlinghetti, A CONEY ISLAND OF THE MIND.
Copyright © 1958 by Lawrence Ferlinghetti. Reprinted by permission of New Directions Publishing Corporation, and Laurence Pollinger Limited.
1. *Chagall,* Marc Chagall (1889–   ), a Russian painter who has lived mainly in France. He uses flower and animal symbols and draws his main subject matter from Jewish folklore.

FOR EXPLORATION

Dog

1. (*a*) In what ways could the dog's world be described as "free"? (*b*) How does his "realistic" view put things we normally take seriously in a humorous light? Give two examples.

2. Toward the end the poet uses several philosophical terms and brings up the question of "puzzling existence." Would you characterize the dog as philosophical or non-philosophical? Does he bother much about puzzling over things? How do his actions reflect on human philosophizing?

14

1. What types of whimsical action and language do you find in this poem?

2. Does Chagall seem bound by the laws of logic or common sense? What kind of imaginative world does his painting project?

3. The horse that Chagall jumps on is a fantastic blend of a real horse and the horse in the painting. What kind of blend do you find in the words "naked nude"?

ALEXANDER CALDER "COMPOSITION," 1953—WHITNEY MUSEUM OF AMERICAN ART, NEW YORK, GIFT OF MRS. MILTON WEILL

Lawrence Ferlinghetti 1919 /

Lawrence Ferlinghetti was born in New York but spent part of his childhood in France with an aunt when his parents died. He received a bachelor's degree from the University of North Carolina, a master's degree from Columbia University, and a doctorate from the Sorbonne in Paris. After World War II, he worked for *Time* magazine.

Then he went to San Francisco, where he now lives. There he founded the City Lights Bookstore, the center of San Francisco's avant-garde literary life, and the publishing company for City Lights Books and the Pocket Poets Series.

Ferlinghetti is one of the oldest members of the Beat Generation. He is a poet who speaks out—who protests, exclaims, exhorts. The material, tone, and phrasing of his poems are taken from everyday life; the poems are composed to be read aloud.

by Robert Hayden

American Poetry Today

American poetry at the present time exhibits great creative energy and a variety of styles and themes. As in the earlier decades of the century, poets continue to experiment with form and language, and poetry has become increasingly free in structure, increasingly "realistic" in subject matter. "Open" forms of "free" verse—that is, poetry without definite metrical pattern—is a characteristic mode of the period, although it is not the only one. Many outstanding poets still use meter and rhyme, but they, like their experimental contemporaries, are more influenced by the rhythms and textures of natural speech than by the old prosodic requirements. The prevalent feeling among most poets today is that all areas of human experience are appropriate for poetry. Hence, materials that in the past were considered at best too mundane for poetry and at worst offensive and improper are now freely used.

In preceding centuries critics and poets themselves were often concerned with the problem of an appropriate vocabulary for poetry—poetic diction. Slang and coarse expressions, common in recent poetry, were not approved by the arbiters of literary taste, although such major British poets as Shakespeare and William Blake frequently went beyond the limits of elegance and refinement. William Wordsworth, in the nineteenth-century England, held that poetry should be written in the language of "common men." The Scottish poet Robert Burns used dialect and folk expressions in his poems about Scottish life. Gerard Manley Hopkins (in late nineteenth-century England) frequently employed terms from the workaday world as well as outmoded and even made-up words.

Walt Whitman was undoubtedly the most daring of these early innovators. His *Leaves of Grass* offended many readers who considered his diction rough and "barbaric" and his references to the body, to sex, indelicate. In his efforts to encompass everything he did not hesitate to make use of slang and the vernacular—the language of "common men." And he was a pioneer in the use of free verse, rejecting conventional meters and stanza patterns in favor of a more flexible and individual kind of poetry.

Twentieth-century poets have gone much further in regard to diction and subject matter than Whitman. In order to get away from the "literary," poets like Allen Ginsberg and Le Roi Jones have employed slang and "four-letter" words, and they have sometimes consciously resorted to triteness and banality in order to bring their poems closer to everyday life and speech. The results are not always admirable or even interesting. Modern poets feel free to use any word that contributes to the expression of a theme or idea. The concept of a special vocabulary for poetry—"poetic diction"—has long since been abandoned.

Much of the poetry published in our country in recent years can be classified as the poetry of social awareness. It is poetry with a purpose and registers the social and moral pressures of our times. The Vietnam War, racial strife, such national tragedies as the assassinations of John and Robert Kennedy and Martin Luther King—all these have inspired poetic response.

The emergence of a so-called school of Black Poetry in America has been one of the significant literary developments of the modern period. Although the Harlem Renais-

LEVERTOV

JONES

FERLINGHETTI

CRUZ

CREELEY

sance of the 1920's brought certain Afro-American poets into prominence, it was not until the intensification of the civil rights struggle during the 1960's that a separate group of black poets began to take shape. Avowedly nationalistic (that is, racially proud) and scornful of western aesthetics, these poets continued the protest tradition, historically associated with Negro writers. But they were more radical in outlook than their predecessors. Unlike the Harlem group, they rejected entry into the mainstream of American literature as a desirable goal. They insisted that their poetry could not be judged by white standards, urging its importance as an expression of black consciousness.

Le Roi Jones—the most influential of the young activist poets—Don. L. Lee, Nikki Giovanni, Sonia Sanchez, Mari Evans, Etheridge Knight, and David Henderson[1] attune their lyres to the "black aesthetic." Not yet satisfactorily defined, this term, originating in the sixties, may be interpreted as a sense of the spiritual and artistic values of blackness. It is, perhaps, a logical (some would say "chauvinistic"), reaction to negative American racial attitudes. Perhaps the concept is best summarized by the slogan "Black is beautiful." Those who accept this point of view regard Negro subject matter as their exclusive domain, feeling that only those who have shared "black experience" can articulate it. Older poets whose work shows some alignment with the new Black Poetry include Margaret Walker and Gwendolyn Brooks, winner of the Pulitzer Prize in 1950.

Whether poetry should be valued primarily for the unique inner experience it can provide or for its effectiveness as political or social statement is a question that often recurs in discussions of the true function of the art today.

. . . . .

It has been impossible, of course, to do more than sketch in the main lines of poetic development. But even from so brief an account as this we can gain, perhaps, some idea of the directions our poetry has taken. Changes in attitude toward the function of poetry, experimentation, the use of materials once thought unpoetic have largely determined its course. Yet the formal and traditional have never been completely discarded, though they have been modified by the tastes and the preoccupations of the age.

American poets have frequently been criticized for their negative view of life in general and of American society in particular. It is true that many of them have given voice to doubt and pessimism. Yet the act of creation itself is an act of faith, a kind of affirmation, and the poetry of disillusionment often implies a moral concern with things as they ought to be, a vision of something better than we have.

The present century is a time of expanding consciousness, a time when new frontiers are being opened and new possibilities of life and art investigated. The concepts of God and the universe, of man and society are in process of revision. Poetry can offer us no solutions to our dilemmas, nor is it intended to, but it can help us understand ourselves at this stage of human evolution. It can make us aware. And it can give us a special kind of joy.

1. These poets are included in the Scott, Foresman record album, *Spectrum in Black*.

William Stafford

THE CONCEALMENT: ISHI, THE LAST WILD INDIAN

A rock, a leaf, mud, even the grass
Ishi[1] the shadow man had to put back where it was.
In order to live he had to hide that he did.
His deep canyon he kept unmarked for the world,
5 and only his face became lined, because no one saw it
and it therefore didn't make any difference.
If he appeared, he died; and he was the last. Erased
footprints, berries that purify the breath, rituals
before dawn with water—even the dogs roamed a land
10 unspoiled by Ishi, who used to own it, with his aunt
and uncle, whose old limbs bound in willow bark finally
stopped and were hidden under the rocks, in sweet leaves.

We ought to help change that kind of premature suicide,
the existence gradually mottled away till the heartbeat
15 blends and the messages all go one way from the world
and disappear inward: Ishi lived. It was all right
for him to make a track. In California now where his opposites
unmistakably dwell we wander their streets

And sometimes whisper his name—
20 "Ishi."

William Stafford 1914 /

William Stafford was raised in Kansas and received his education at the University of Kansas and the University of Iowa. During World War II he was a conscientious objector and is still active in pacifist organizations. He has taught at Manchester College in Indiana and San Jose State College in California, and is presently Professor of Literature at Lewis and Clark College in Portland, Oregon.

In commenting on his own poetry, Stafford has said, "My poetry seems to me direct and communicative, with some oddity and variety. It is usually not formal. It is much like talk, with some enhancement. Often my poetry is discursive and reminiscent, or at least is that way at one level: it delivers a sense of place and event; it has narrative impulses. Forms are not usually much evident, though tendencies and patterns are occasionally flirted with. . . . The voice I most consistently hear in my poetry is my mother's voice."

"*The Concealment: Ishi, the Last Wild Indian*" from THE RESCUED YEAR by William Stafford. Copyright © 1965 by William E. Stafford. Reprinted by permission of Harper & Row, Publishers, Inc.
1. *Ishi.* The Yana Indians were a tribe which was so mauled by white settlers, they had finally taken to complete concealment as the only possible means of survival. In 1911, Ishi, the last surviving member of the tribe, came down out of the California hills and was fortunately befriended by anthropologist Alfred Kroeber.

FOR EXPLORATION

1. In what way was Ishi's life a kind of "premature suicide"?

2. How did Ishi treat the land? Is there any contrast implied in his actions?

3. Who are Ishi's "opposites"? In what sense do we "wander their streets"?

4. (a) Why do we "sometimes whisper his name"? Why the hushed tone? (b) For what might Ishi stand as a reminder?

Henry Dumas

THOUGHT

Hate is also creative:
it creates more hate.

ROSE JUNGLE

(to Hale Chatfield)
For thirty-one years he planted roses,
until the withered structure of the house
became thorned flesh.
At night he would lie
5 exhausted and crucified.

For thirty-one years he had planted.
From the road I could see only
a mountain of roses growing wild.

"Why don't you train the stems
10 to bow?" I asked.

"The wind is the better teacher," he said.

"Why don't you trim their arms?"

"In due time these arms will
embrace the earth.
15 I will not lessen their love."

FOR EXPLORATION

Rose Jungle
How is the way the man treats his roses in this poem
similar to the way Ishi treated his canyon?

Thought

CREATIVE RESPONSE

Use these two lines as the title for an essay or free-verse
poem on a subject you think appropriate.

Henry Dumas   ? / 1968

Henry Dumas was born in Arkansas and came to Harlem in
New York when he was ten years old. He served in the Air
Force and attended Rutgers University. Among the journals
which have published his poetry are *Freedomways, Negro
Digest,* and *Umbra;* and he wrote one novel. In an interview, Dumas once said, "I am very much concerned about
what is happening to my people and what we are doing
with our precious tradition." In May of 1968, Henry
Dumas was shot and killed in New York City.

Mona Van Duyn

POSTCARDS FROM CAPE SPLIT

I

"What is that flower?" we asked right away. What a sight!
From the rocks of the beach all the way up the hill to our house,
and all around the house and on either side of the road,
a solid ocean of flowers, shifting in the wind, shifting
5 in shades of pink like strokes of a brush. Heliotrope.
Pinky-white masses of bloom on five-foot red stems.
"My father brought it here," our landlady says.
"'Be careful of heliotrope,' they told him, 'it spreads like a
          weed.'"
It has taken the hill and the house, it is on its way down the road.
10 Little paths are scythed through heliotrope to the sea,
from the house to the outhouse, from the road to the house,
and a square of back yard is cut away from the flowers.
"The heliotrope is taking my raspberry patch,"
the neighbor tells us, and, snuggled in heliotrope,
15 the kitchen gardens fight for their viney lives,
one here, one there. You can't even see them until
you're right on their edge, leaning over the heliotrope.

II

Everything looks like the sea but the sea.
The sea looks like a lake
20 except when fucus is dumped on its low-tide border
like heaps of khaki laundry left out to rot—
this seems a capacity for waste that is worthy of an ocean.
But the diningroom floor looks like the sea,
wide old boards, painted dark green,
25 that heave and ripple in waves.
Light hits the crest of each board and gives it a whitecap.

The house saves everything,
crutches and children's sleds, painted cups without handles,
chairs without seats, dried sweetgrass, fir tips in pillows.
30 It must be almost as old as it looks—
the father of our seventy-year-old landlady built it.
It is buffed by the salt winds to elephant color.

From TO SEE, TO TAKE by Mona Van Duyn. Copyright © 1967 by
Mona Van Duyn. Reprinted by permission of Atheneum Publishers.
Appeared originally in *Tambourine*.

One goes on vacation to housekeep another way.
I have made a chart of the tides,
35 which are now a part of my order for a few weeks.
I have learned the perverse ways of this house—
sink and refrigerator in the kitchen,
stove, dishes and table in the diningroom.
I have tied back white net curtains,
40 still creased from display in the dimestore.
I have found paths through heliotrope
to each new neighbor.

III

We move in a maze of villages—
Addison, East Addison, South Addison,
45 Machias, East Machias and Machiasport.
(The *ch* is pronounced *ch*, and not *k*.)
The lobsters and cheese are at South Addison,
the doctor, the bakery and the liquor store are at Machias,
the nearest post office and, they say, frozen chicken livers
50 are at Addison, the seafood cannery is at East Machias.
East Addison and Machiasport we have so far been able to ignore.

The kitchen in this house is papered in villages.
Five villages from floor to ceiling, I don't know how many
across the wall. There is no place to locate one's self.
55 Still, because the dog snores by the oilstove, the brown
sparrow-size birds squeak cheerily in a spruce by the outhouse,
little toy boats are out on the sea after lobsters, the sun
is warm and the heliotrope is blowing like waves,
because, my God, it *is* pleasant here,
60 we can surely live uncentered for three weeks,
gleaning a little from one village, a little from another.

IV

Who would believe that we could learn to cook, drink, bathe,
shave, fill the dog's bowl, the icecube tray, the vase
for wildflowers, and keep ourselves in clean clothes and towels
65 on two buckets of water a day? Of course we steam mussels
and lobsters in, drive the dog into, wade in, and gaze upon
the sea, and that saves on our freshwater needs.
Each morning we take our two buckets, go down the road
to the landlord's house, walk in the back door
70 (as we were told to do) and get our water
and a hot donut, or a story about the old times here.
But we want to be self-sufficient the rest of the day,
neither past nor people between us and the ocean,
and so we have learned this new skill for the summer.

contd.

75 But what a small thirst one has, in summer, for the everyday water,
whereas, for the salty stranger, from here to the horizon
at high tide is no more than we can drink in
in a single day.

V

There are thirty-five stalks of corn in our garden.
80 Our landlord is trying to raise some corn this year.
He has staked and tied every stalk
to hold it against the sea winds.
Our landlady dopes the tassels with liniment
to keep the raccoons off.
85 Except for its corn and its heliotrope wall,
our garden is just like others all over the Cape:
four rows of potatoes,
two rows of string beans,
one row each of peas and beets,
90 one row of squash,
and one row of dahlias.

The man from across the bar
brought us a sea-moss pudding
in a silver dish.

VI

95 Our landlord's youngest son, the lobsterman,
comes in his lobstering boots, turned halfway down,
to fix our oilstove. I am dazzled by the man in boots.
It is as if a heron stood in my diningroom.

His father sits in a rocker by his kitchen stove,
100 knitting the twine innards for lobster traps
and saying, "When we were young I'd go out in a skiff,
why, right off here, and spear a half bushel of flounder
while She cooked breakfast. We had dried fish all winter,
and they was *some good*, I tell you." The day's light changes.

105 We drove inland a ways, through the Blueberry Barrens.
Mile after mile, from road to the far mountains
of furzy wasteland, flat. You almost miss it.
Suddenly, under that empty space, you notice
the curious color of the ground. Blue mile, blue mile,
110 and then a little bent-over group of Indians
creeping down string-marked aisles. Blue mile, blue mile,
and then more Indians, pushing their forked dustpans.
It looks like a race at some country picnic, but lost
in that monstrous space, under that vacant sky.

115 Why am I dazzled? It is only another harvest.
The world blooms and we all bend and bring
from ground and sea and mind its handsome harvests.

ANDREW WYETH "APRIL WIND," 1952—WADSWORTH ATHENEUM, HARTFORD, CONNECTICUT—GIFT OF MR. AND MRS. JOSEPH R. SWAN

Mona Van Duyn 1921 /

Mona Van Duyn was born and educated in Iowa. She was raised in Waterloo, Iowa, and attended the University of Northern Iowa and the University of Iowa. She is now a lecturer in English at Washington University in St. Louis and the Poetry Consultant for the Washington University Library Modern Literature Collection. In addition, she is co-editor with her husband of *Perspective: A Quarterly of Literature.*

Van Duyn's poetry contains rhyme schemes that are definite and often complex. Her poems are homely and sophisticated, colloquial and formal, serious and witty— all at the same time.

FOR EXPLORATION

The six sections of this poem can each be interpreted as reports (postcards) from a person who finds herself responding to rhythms and sensations different from those she has been used to. Interpret each section in terms of the last two lines of the poem. How does each indicate a stage in her voyage of discovery? What has she discovered?

Denise Levertov

FEBRUARY EVENING IN NEW YORK

As the stores close, a winter light
   opens air to iris blue,
   glint of frost through the smoke,
   grains of mica, salt of the sidewalk.
5 As the buildings close, released autonomous
   feet pattern the streets
   in hurry and stroll; balloon heads
   drift and dive above them; the bodies
   aren't really there.
10 As the lights brighten, as the sky darkens,
   a woman with crooked heels says to another
      woman
   while they step along at a fair pace,
   "You know, I'm telling you, what I love best
   is life. I love life! Even if I ever get
15   *to be old and wheezy—or limp! You know?*
   Limping along?—I'd still . . ." Out of hearing.
To the multiple disordered tones
   of gears changing, a dance
   to the compass points, out, four-way river.
20 Prospect of sky
   wedged into avenues, left at the ends of streets,
   west sky, east sky: more life tonight! A range
   of open time at winter's outskirts.

Denise Levertov   1923 /

Denise Levertov was born in England, where she was edu-cated privately. It was here that she first began to write poetry, but her early writing was influenced by a roman-ticism that was popular in England at that time. During World War II she served as a nurse. At the end of the war she married an American and in 1948 came to this country to live.

In America Levertov came under the influence of William Carlos Williams, Ezra Pound, and H.D. The result is her concentration on the particulars of her own experience. At the same time, there is a strong element of inwardness; thus, the particulars of the outward experience are met by responses from within. Her poems are concrete, precise, intense, and shaped; they present compact and intensely immediate perceptions of people, things, and feelings.

Denise Levertov, WITH EYES AT THE BACK OF OUR HEADS. Copyright © 1959 by Denise Levertov Goodman. Reprinted by permission of New Directions Publishing Corporation.

FOR EXPLORATION

1. (a) What is the scene presented in this poem? What imagery delineates it? (b) What is the "four-way river" referred to in line 19? (c) Does the scene seem to constrict people and nature? How or how not?

2. (a) How are the inhabitants of this scene presented? (b) How do the words of the "woman with crooked heels" comment on the condition of these people?

Robert Creeley

"DO YOU THINK . . ."

Do you think that if
you once do what you want
to do you will want not to do it.

Do you think that if
there's an apple on the table
and somebody eats it, it
won't be there anymore.

Do you think that if
two people are in love with one another,
one or the other has got to be
less in love than the other at
some point in the otherwise happy relationship.

Do you think that if
you once take a breath, you're by
that committed to taking the next one
and so on until the very process of
breathing's an endlessly expanding need
almost of its own necessity forever.

Do you think that if
no one knows then whatever
it is, no one will know and
that will be the case, like
they say, for an indefinite
period of time if such time
can have a qualification of such time.

Do you know anyone,
really. Have you been, really,
much alone. Are you lonely,
now, for example. Does anything
really matter to you, really, or
has anything mattered. Does each
thing tend to be there, and then not
to be there, just as if that were it.

Do you think that if
I said, *I love you*, or anyone
said it, or you did. Do you
think that if you had all
such decisions to make and could
make them. Do you think that
if you did. That you really
would have to think it all into
reality, that world, each time, new.

"*Do You Think*" (copyright © 1971 Robert Creeley) is reprinted from THE DAY BOOK by Robert Creeley. Reprinted by permission of Charles Scribner's Sons.

Robert Creeley   1926 /

Born in Arlington, Massachusetts, Robert Creeley was educated at Harvard, Black Mountain College, and the University of New Mexico. Prior to accepting his present position of Professor of English at the State University of New York, he taught at Black Mountain College and was one of the founders of the *Black Mountain Review*, a progressive literary journal.

From the beginning, Creeley has had a keen regard for colloquial American speech. He has limited his production of poetry almost exclusively to short lyrics and has refused to admit social and political themes to his work. He is a superb technician and has been a personal influence on many other writers.

FOR EXPLORATION

1. (*a*) Answer as many of the questions in the poem as you can. (*b*) Are there any questions in the poem you cannot answer? Why? (*c*) Where do you think the poet's line of questioning is leading? How might the title of the poem be appropriate here?

2. Interpret this poem in terms of this statement: "An unquestioning acceptance of the universe creates a view of the world in which nothing matters because things simply are or aren't, and that's all there is to it."

Imamu Amiri Baraka
(LeRoi Jones)

EACH MORNING

*(SECTION 4 FROM "HYMN
FOR LANIE POO")*

      Each morning
      I go down
      to Gansevoort St.[1]
      and stand on the docks.
5   I stare out
      at the horizon
      until it gets up
      and comes to embrace
      me. I
10 make believe
      it is my father.
      This is known
      as genealogy.

Copyright © 1965 by Imamu Amiri Baraka. Reprinted from NEW
NEGRO POETS used with permission of the author and the Ronald
Hobbs Literary Agency.
1. *Gansevoort St.*, a street on the waterfront in New York City.

Le Roi Jones   1934 /

Although he considers himself primarily a poet, Le Roi
Jones also writes essays, novels, short stories, plays, and
jazz articles. He grew up in Newark, New Jersey, and received his degree from Howard University in Washington,
D.C. It was while serving with the Strategic Air Command
that he decided to become a writer.

Jones is often identified as the angry young man of the
ghetto. In 1967 he was arrested as a leader of the Newark
ghetto riots. After the riots, he led forces to rebuild the
area and improve the conditions there. To some people
his poetry seems homicidal, to others it seems caustic and
biting, and to still others it seems delicate and gentle.

PREFACE TO A
TWENTY VOLUME SUICIDE NOTE

Lately, I've become accustomed to the way
The ground opens up and envelops me
Each time I go out to walk the dog.
Or the broad edged silly music the wind
5 Makes when I run for a bus—

Things have come to that.

And now, each night I count the stars,
And each night I get the same number.
And when they will not come to be counted
10 I count the holes they leave.

Nobody sings anymore.

And then last night, I tiptoed up
To my daughter's room and heard her
Talking to someone, and when I opened
15 The door, there was no one there . . .
Only she on her knees,
Peeking into her own clasped hands.

"Preface to a Twenty Volume Suicide Note" by LeRoi Jones. Copyright © 1961 by LeRoi Jones. Reprinted by permission of Corinth Books Inc.

FOR EXPLORATION

Each Morning

How is the word "genealogy" used in this poem? Ironically? Literally? Humorously? What attitude does the speaker have toward formal family pedigrees? With what does he identify?

Preface to a Twenty Volume Suicide Note

1. The first ten lines of the poem use exaggerated language (hyperbole) to make a point about the speaker's condition. (*a*) What is that condition? (*b*) What is the speaker's attitude toward his condition?
2. Do you think the speaker's discovery of his daughter "talking to someone" has made any difference? How?

Michael S. Harper

MOVIN' WES

Gone from us
this guitar
where the bull resides
his heat
5 gone from us,
Movin' Wes rides
his beginnings:

Wes, guitar, Movin' Wes:
Charlie Christian
10 Movin' Wes
Leadbelly, Movin' Wes
John Lee Hooker
Movin' Wes
B. B. King, Movin' Wes
15 Wes Montgomery,[1]
Movin' Wes:

Shaped like a heart
this guitar is its own organ;
its gnarled hands
20 bled octaves
in men's veins,
their children
the stickpin controls:
Movin' Wes:

25 Gone from us,
electronic ears
tune on
Movin' Wes:

Unrecorded,
30 Movin' Wes
blew with Trane[2]
"Favorite Things"
so hard, out there,
guitar became man:
35 Movin' Wes:

Instrument
Favorite Things
all alive:
Movin' Wes:

"Movin' Wes" by Michael S. Harper from HISTORY IS YOUR OWN HEARTBEAT. © 1971 by Michael S. Harper. Reprinted by permission of University of Illinois Press.
1. *Charlie Christian . . . Wes Montgomery*. The musicians mentioned in the second stanza are famous jazz and blues guitarists. Christian, perhaps the first great jazz guitarist, and Montgomery, also highly regarded by jazz critics as well as fellow musicians, both died at early ages. The phrase "Movin' Wes" is a pun on Montgomery's name.
2. *unrecorded, Movin' Wes blew with Trane*. Toward the end of his life, Wes Montgomery played with saxophonist John Coltrane ("Trane") and his group. The poet apparently was present when the two musicians improvised on Rogers and Hammerstein's song, "My Favorite Things." Though Coltrane and Montgomery never made a record together, the poet is probably refering to the fact that this session, like so many other excellent live performances, went unrecorded and possibly even unnoticed.

Michael S. Harper 1938 /

Born in Brooklyn, New York, Michael S. Harper lived for a number of years in California where he was a postal clerk and teacher. His poems began appearing in print when he was in his early twenties and his first published volume was *Dear John, Dear Coltrane* in 1970. He has been associated with a number of colleges and is now teaching at Brown University. He was awarded one of the ten prizes for 1972 which the National Institute and its affiliate, The American Academy of Arts and Letters, bestows to encourage writers and help them to continue their creative work.

FOR EXPLORATION

1. (*a*) What metaphors are used to describe Wes' guitar? How do these reflect on his music? (*b*) What might the phrase "guitar became man" mean in terms of these metaphors?
2. Read the poem aloud. How does its movement help convey its subject?

Victor Hernández Cruz

SNAPS

monday night
the
winters
grow colder
5 colder than this

just the projects
on fridays
so good
sometimes the moon
10 so clear
head to the river
soft noise
of moving water
a ship passing
15 tugboats
so near
the bright lights
talking to us
in red & blue.

ALONE / DECEMBER / NIGHT

it's been so long
speaking to people
who think it all
too complex
5 stupidity in their eyes
&
it's been so long
so far from the truth
so far from a roof
10 to talk to
or a hand to touch
or anything to really
love

it's been so long
15 talking to myself
alone
in the night
listening to a music
that is me.

"*Snaps*" and "*Alone/december/night.*" Copyright © 1969 by Victor Hernández Cruz. Reprinted from SNAPS, by Victor Hernández Cruz, by permission of Random House, Inc.

FOR EXPLORATION

Snaps
1. "Snaps" seems, in its opening lines, to be about weather. (*a*) Is it possible to read the poem as a revelation of the speaker's "spiritual weather"? (*b*) How might the title, suggestive of the common expression "cold snap," be related to this reading of the poem?
2. Contrast the two stanzas, and indicate the elements that contribute to the differences in effect.

Alone/December/Night
Is this a poem about loneliness, in the sense of longing for contact with someone else? If so, what kind of contact is desired? Or is this a poem about being alone and the satisfactions of "listening to a music that is me"?

Victor Hernández Cruz   1949 /

Victor Hernández Cruz, the youngest poet represented in this anthology, was born in Puerto Rico and came to New York City when he was four years old. His poetry has appeared in *Evergreen Review, Umbra,* and *For Now, Down Here.* In 1968 Random House published his first book of poems, *Snaps.*

OVERLEAF: ROOM 2, 1966 BY LUCAS SAMARAS—ALBRIGHT-KNOX ART GALLERY, BUFFALO, N.Y., GIFT OF SEYMOUR H. KNOX

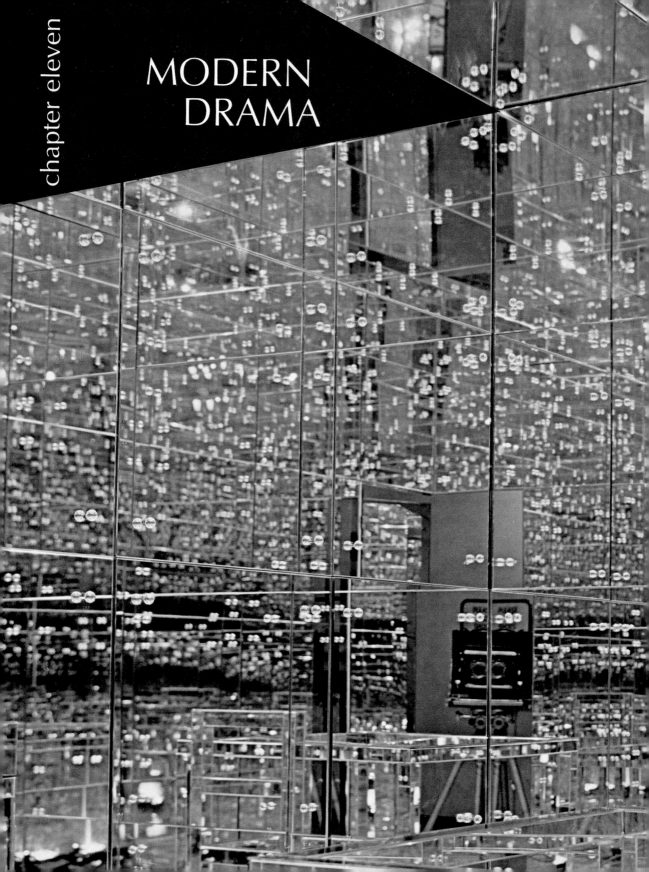

MODERN DRAMA

The Glass Menagerie

by Tennessee Williams

THE GLASS MENAGERIE was produced by Eddie Dowling and Louis J. Singer at the Playhouse Theatre, New York City, on March 31, 1945, with the following cast:

THE MOTHER .Laurette Taylor
HER SON . . . . .Eddie Dowling
HER DAUGHTER . . . . .Julie Haydon
THE GENTLEMAN CALLER . . . . .Anthony Ross

SCENE

An alley in St. Louis.

PART I: Preparation for a Gentleman Caller.
PART II: The Gentleman Calls.
TIME: Now and the Past.

Setting designed and lighted by JO MIELZINER.
Original Music composed by PAUL BOWLES.
Staged by MR. DOWLING and MARGO JONES.

THE GLASS MENAGERIE, by Tennessee Williams. Copyright 1945 by Tennessee Williams and Edwina D. Williams. Reprinted by permission of Random House, Inc. and Elaine Greene Ltd. for Secker & Warburg, Ltd.

CAUTION: Professionals and amateurs are hereby warned that THE GLASS MENAGERIE, being fully protected under the copyright laws of the United States of America, the British Empire, including the Dominion of Canada, and all other countries of the Copyright Union, is subject to royalty. All rights, including professional, amateur, motion picture, recitation, lecturing, public reading, radio and television broadcasting, and the rights of translation into foreign languages, are strictly reserved. Particular emphasis is laid on the question of readings, permission for which must be obtained in writing from the author's agent. All inquiries (except for amateur rights) should be addressed to the author's agent, Audrey Wood, c/o Ashley Famous Agency, Inc., 1301 Avenue of the Americas, New York, N. Y. 10019.

The amateur acting rights of THE GLASS MENAGERIE are controlled exclusively by the DRAMATISTS PLAY SERVICE, INC., 440 Park Avenue South, New York, N. Y. 10016. No amateur performance of the play may be given without obtaining in advance the written permission of the Dramatists Play Service, Inc., and paying the requisite fee.

Note on Incidental Music

Music used in the original production of this play, composed by Paul Bowles, is on a long playing (33⅓ RPM) record. The use of this record in the play requires a production fee of $5.00 a performance, which is payable to the Service.

The record may be ordered through the DRAMATISTS PLAY SERVICE at $6.75, packing and carrying charges included.

As indicated in the text, victrola records used on-stage and dance music off-stage, are left to the discretion of the individual producer.

STAGING THE PLAY

Practical Suggestions by the Publisher

In issuing this new text of *The Glass Menagerie*, intended primarily for producing groups, a few words from us would seem called for. We urge all who are going to direct and mount the play to read these notes with care.

The present edition differs from the book of the play as first issued by Random House: the dialogue itself has to some extent been revised by the author, and the stage directions likewise. The latter have been drastically changed in order to guide the director and actor.

Mr. Williams' careful directions and explanations throughout the text will prove most helpful in that they crystallize and explain various moods which are to be sought, and while some of these directions are very specific, others are intended rather as guides to the creation of the necessary atmosphere. As the author has stated in his *Production Notes*, the play "can be presented with unusual freedom of convention."

The text printed in this book is a faithful indication of the way the play was produced in New York and on the road, but nonprofessional directors are advised to follow the actual means of presentation which seems to them most effective. In other words, such producers are offered any of a variety of different means of production, the only point to be stressed being that the production should of course adhere closely to the spirit of the play as written by the author.

For instance, the use of the two scrim curtains described in the stage directions may not be thought the best means of achieving that air of unreality that is often called for; the black-outs as described in the stage directions may be discarded for the occasional fall of the house curtain; Mr. Bowles' music (especially arranged on a long playing record which we can furnish—see copyright page), although carefully cued into the text, need not necessarily be used at the precise places indicated by the music cues. It should be further stated that although the music on this record was that used for the professional production in New York, it is not absolutely essential that it should be used in this play at all. It is, however, highly recommended both by the author and by ourselves.

Special Note on Music Record: Some producers find it difficult to fit the music cues as indicated in this text into the record. Bear in mind that the director is given almost complete leeway as to where the incidental music shall be used.

A few other points may be here indicated: the actual shape of the fire-escape landing may be modified; the alley-way at the left of the stage as indicated in the stage diagram, prepared especially for this acting edition by Mr. Jo Mielziner, on Page 325 M, need not (and probably will not) be used at all, and the one or two entrances mentioned as being made in that alley-way can very easily be made in the similar alley to the right of the stage; the music as played in the dance hall down right may be chosen from among the popular dance tunes of the 1920's, without reference to this or that particular title, while the same thing applies to the records used by Laura on the phonograph. While the exact position of each door and piece of furniture is described in the stage directions and shown in the stage diagram, the director should be permitted considerable leeway in making his own changes in such matters.

In a word, the present text gives all the hints, suggestions and actual directions for production, but provided the director, having studied what is here printed, wishes to use other means to achieve a complete and unified production according to his own views, he should be encouraged to do so.

It should certainly be made clear to most directors that too great concern over certain technical details is not only unnecessary, but may easily interfere with the totality of effect to be sought throughout the entire play. For example, the glass figures which are Laura's "menagerie" need be no more than small clear glass objects which can be barely distinguished by the audience, presumably a few small cheap ornaments that can be bought at any ten-cent store.

The only off-stage sound effects of any complexity or importance are the thunder and distant church bells as described in the stage directions.

DRAMATISTS PLAY SERVICE, INC.

AUTHOR'S PRODUCTION NOTES

Being a "memory play," *The Glass Menagerie* can be presented with unusual freedom of convention. Because of its considerably delicate or tenuous material, atmospheric touches and subtleties of direction play a particularly important part. Expressionism and all other unconventional techniques in drama have only one valid aim, and that is a closer approach to truth. When a play employs unconventional techniques, it is not, or certainly shouldn't be, trying to escape its responsibility of dealing with reality, or interpreting experience, but is actually or should be attempting to find a closer approach, a more penetrating and vivid expression of things as they are. The straight realistic play with its genuine frigidaire and authentic ice-cubes, its characters that speak exactly as its audience speaks, corresponds to the academic landscape and has the same virtue of a photographic likeness. Everyone should know nowadays the unimportance of the photographic in art: that truth, life, or reality is an organic thing which the poetic imagination can represent or suggest, in essence, only through transformation, through changing into other forms than those which were merely present in appearance.

These remarks are not meant as a preface only to this particular play. They have to do with a conception of a new, plastic theatre which must take the place of the exhausted theatre of realistic conventions if the theatre is to resume vitality as a part of our culture.

THE MUSIC

Another extra-literary accent in this play is provided by the use of music. A single recurring tune, "The Glass Menagerie," is used to give emotional emphasis to suitable passages. This tune is like circus music, not when you are on the grounds or in the immediate vicinity of the parade, but when you are at some distance and very likely thinking of something else. It seems under those circumstances to continue almost interminably and it weaves in and out of your preoccupied consciousness; then it is the lightest, most delicate music in the world and perhaps the saddest. It expresses the surface vivacity of life with the underlying strain of immutable and inexpressible sorrow. When you look at a piece of delicately spun glass you think of two things: how beautiful it is and how easily it can be broken. Both of those ideas should be woven into the recurring tune, which dips in and out of the play as if it were carried on a wind that changes. It serves as a thread of connection and allusion between the narrator with his separate point in time and space and the subject of his story. Between each episode it returns as reference to the emotion, nostalgia, which is the first condition of the play. It is primarily Laura's music and therefore comes out most clearly when the play focuses upon her and the lovely fragility of glass which is her image.

THE LIGHTING

The lighting in the play is not realistic. In keeping with the atmosphere of memory, the stage is dim. Shafts of light are focused on selected areas or actors, sometimes in contradistinction to what is the apparent center. For instance, in the quarrel scene between Tom and Amanda, in which Laura has no active part, the clearest pool of light is on her figure. This is also true of the supper scene, when her silent figure on the sofa should remain the visual center. The light upon Laura should be distinct from the others, having a peculiar pristine clarity such as light used in early religious portraits of female saints or madonnas. A certain correspondence to light in religious paintings, such as El Greco's,[1] where the figures are radiant in atmosphere that is relatively dusky, could be effectively used throughout the play. (It will also permit a more effective use of the screen.) A free, imaginative use of light can be of enormous value in giving a mobile, plastic quality to plays of a more or less static nature.

NOTES ON THE CHARACTERS

AMANDA WINGFIELD (the mother): A little woman of great but confused vitality, clinging frantically to another time and place. Her characterization must be carefully created, not copied from type. She is not paranoiac, but her life is paranoia.[2] There is much to admire in Amanda, and as much to love and pity as there is to laugh at. Certainly she has endurance and a kind of heroism, and though her foolishness makes her unwittingly cruel at times, there is tenderness in her slight person.

LAURA WINGFIELD (her daughter): Amanda, having failed to establish contact with reality, continues to live vitally in her illusions, but Laura's situation is even graver. A childhood illness has left her crippled, one leg slightly shorter than the other, and held in a brace. This defect need not be more than suggested on the stage. Stemming from this, Laura's separation increases till she is like a piece of her own glass collection, too exquisitely fragile to move from the shelf.

TOM WINGFIELD (her son): And the narrator of the play. A poet with a job in a warehouse. His nature is not remorseless, but to escape from a trap he has to act without pity.

JIM O'CONNOR (the gentleman caller): A nice, ordinary, young man.

T. W.

---

1. *El Greco* (el grek′ō), late sixteenth-century painter who used perspective and lighting not to achieve a photographic likeness but for expressive effects.

2. *paranoiac . . . paranoia.* Paranoia is a form of insanity characterized by elaborate delusions. Williams is saying that Amanda is not insane, but that her life is out of contact with reality.

The Glass Menagerie

by Tennessee Williams

Act One

SCENE 1

The Wingfield apartment is in the rear of the building, one of those vast hive-like conglomerations of cellular living-units that flower as warty growths in over-crowded urban centers of lower middle-class population and are symptomatic of the impulse of this largest and fundamentally enslaved section of American society to avoid fluidity and differentiation and to exist and function as one interfused mass of automatism. The apartment faces an alley and is entered by a fire-escape, a structure whose name is a touch of accidental poetic truth, for all of these huge buildings are always burning with the slow and implacable fires of human desperation. The fire-escape is included in the set—that is, the landing of it and steps descending from it. (Note that the stage L. alley may be entirely omitted, since it is never used except for Tom's first entrance, which can take place stage R.) The scene is memory and is therefore nonrealistic. Memory takes a lot of poetic license. It omits some details, others are exaggerated, according to the emotional value of the articles it touches, for memory is seated predominantly in the heart. The interior is therefore rather dim and poetic. (CUE #1. As soon as the house lights dim, dance-hall music heard on-stage R. Old popular music of, say 1915-1920 period. This continues until Tom is at fire-escape landing, having lighted cigarette, and begins speaking.)

AT RISE: *At the rise of the house curtain, the audience is faced with the dark, grim rear wall of the Wingfield tenement. (The stage set proper is screened out by a gauze curtain, which suggests the front part, outside, of the building.) This building, which runs parallel to the footlights, is flanked on both sides by dark, narrow alleys which run into murky canyons of tangled clotheslines, garbage cans and the sinister lattice-work of neighboring fire-escapes. (The alleys are actually in darkness, and the objects just mentioned are not visible.) It is up and down these side alleys that exterior entrances and exits are made, during the play. At the end of Tom's opening commentary, the dark tenement wall slowly reveals (by*

means of a transparency) the interior of the ground-floor Wingfield apartment. (Gauze curtain, which suggests front part of building, rises on the interior set.) Downstage is the living-room, which also serves as a sleeping room for Laura, the day-bed unfolding to make her bed. Just above this is a small stool or table on which is a telephone. Up-stage, C., and divided by a wide arch or second proscenium with transparent faded portieres (or second curtain, "second curtain" is actually the inner gauze curtain between the living-room and the dining-room, which is up-stage of it), is the dining-room. In an old-fashioned what-not in the living-room are seen scores of transparent glass animals. A blown-up photograph of the father hangs on the wall of the living-room, facing the audience, to the L. of the archway. It is the face of a very handsome young man in a doughboy's First World War cap. He is gallantly smiling, ineluctably smiling, as if to say, "I will be smiling forever." (Note that all that is essential in connection with dance-hall is that the window be shown lighting lower part of alley. It is not necessary to show any considerable part of dance-hall.) The audience hears and sees the opening scene in the dining-room through both the transparent fourth wall (this is the gauze curtain which suggests outside of building) of the building and the transparent gauze portieres of the dining-room arch. It is during this revealing scene that the fourth wall slowly ascends, out of sight. This transparent exterior wall is not brought down again until the very end of the play, during Tom's final speech. The narrator is an undisguised convention of the play. He takes whatever license with dramatic convention as is convenient to his purposes.

Tom enters dressed as a merchant sailor from alley, stage L. (i.e., stage R. if L. alley is omitted), and strolls across the front of the stage to the fire-escape. (This is the fire-escape landing shown in diagram on page 325 M. Tom may lean against grillwork of this as he lights cigarette.) There he stops and lights a cigarette. He addresses the audience.

COURTESY OF THE LINCOLN PARK THEATRE; PHOTOS BY WILLIAM FRANKLIN MCMAHON

TOM. I have tricks in my pocket—I have things up my sleeve—but I am the opposite of the stage magician. He gives you illusion that has the appearance of truth. I give you truth in the pleasant disguise of illusion. I take you back to an alley in St. Louis. The time that quaint period when the huge middle class of America was matriculating from a school for the blind. Their eyes had failed them, or they had failed their eyes, and so they were having their fingers pressed forcibly down on the fiery Braille alphabet of a dissolving economy.—In Spain there was revolution.—Here there was only shouting and confusion and labor disturbances, sometimes violent, in otherwise peaceful cities such as Cleveland—Chicago—Detroit. . . . That is the social background of this play . . . The play is memory. (MUSIC CUE #2) Being a memory play, it is dimly lighted, it is sentimental, it is not realistic.—In memory everything seems to happen to music. —That explains the fiddle in the wings. I am the narrator of the play, and also a character in it. The other characters in the play are my mother, Amanda, my sister, Laura, and a gentleman caller who appears in the final scenes. He is the most realistic character in the play, being an emissary from a world that we were somehow set apart from.—But having a poet's weakness for symbols, I am using this character as a symbol—as the long-delayed but always expected something that we live for.—There is a fifth character who doesn't appear other than in a photograph hanging on the wall. When you see the picture of this grinning gentleman, please remember this is our father who left us a long time ago. He was a telephone man who fell in love with long distance—so he gave up his job with the telephone company and skipped the light fantastic out of town. . . . The last we heard of him was a picture postcard from the Pacific coast of Mexico, containing a message of two words—"Hello—Good-bye!" and no address. (LIGHTS UP IN DINING-ROOM. *Tom exits R. He goes off downstage, takes off his sailor overcoat and skull-fitting knitted cap and remains off-stage by dining-room R. door for his entrance cue. Amanda's voice becomes audible through the portieres—i.e., gauze curtains separating dining-room from living-room. Amanda and Laura are seated at a drop-leaf table. Amanda is sitting in C. chair and Laura in L. chair. Eating is indicated by gestures without food or utensils. Amanda faces the audi-*ence. *The interior of the dining-room has lit up softly and through the scrim—gauze curtains—we see Amanda and Laura seated at the table in the upstage area.*)

AMANDA. You know, Laura, I had the funniest experience in church last Sunday. The church was crowded except for one pew way down front and in that was just one little woman. I smiled very sweetly at her and said, "Excuse me, would you mind if I shared this pew?" "I certainly would," she said, "this space is rented." Do you know that is the first time that I ever knew that the Lord rented space. (*Dining-room gauze curtains open automatically.*) These Northern Episcopalians! I can understand the Southern Episcopalians, but these Northern ones, no. (*Tom enters dining-room R., slips over to table and sits in chair R.*) Honey, don't push your food with your fingers. If you have to push your food with something, the thing to use is a crust of bread. You must chew your food. Animals have secretions in their stomachs which enable them to digest their food without mastication, but human beings must chew their food before they swallow it down, and chew, chew. Oh, eat leisurely. Eat leisurely. A well-cooked meal has many delicate flavors that have to be held in the mouth for appreciation, not just gulped down. Oh, chew, chew—chew! (*At this point the scrim curtain—if the director decides to use it—the one suggesting exterior wall, rises here and does not come down again until just before the end of the play.*) Don't you want to give your salivary glands a chance to function?

TOM. Mother, I haven't enjoyed one bite of my dinner because of your constant directions on how to eat it. It's you that makes me hurry through my meals with your hawk-like attention to every bite I take. It's disgusting—all this discussion of animal's secretion—salivary glands—mastication! (*Comes down to arm-chair in living-room R., lights cigarette.*)

AMANDA. Temperament like a Metropolitan star! You're not excused from this table.

TOM. I'm getting a cigarette.

AMANDA. You smoke too much.

LAURA. (*Rising.*) Mother, I'll bring in the coffee.

AMANDA. No, no, no, no. You sit down. I'm going to be the colored boy today and you're going to be the lady.

LAURA. I'm already up.

AMANDA. Resume your seat. Resume your seat. You keep yourself fresh and pretty for the gentlemen callers. (*Laura sits.*)

LAURA. I'm not expecting any gentlemen callers.

AMANDA. (*Who has been gathering dishes from table and loading them on tray.*) Well, the nice thing about them is they come when they're least expected. Why, I remember one Sunday afternoon in Blue Mountain when your mother was a girl . . . (*Goes out for coffee,* U. R.)

TOM. I know what's coming now! (*Laura rises.*)

LAURA. Yes. But let her tell it. (*Crosses to* L. *of daybed, sits.*)

TOM. Again?

LAURA. She loves to tell it.

AMANDA. (*Entering from* R. *in dining-room and coming down into living-room with tray and coffee.*) I remember one Sunday afternoon in Blue Mountain when your mother was a girl she received—seventeen—gentlemen callers! (*Amanda crosses to Tom at armchair* R., *gives him coffee, and crosses* C. *Laura comes to her, takes cup, resumes her place on* L. *of day-bed. Amanda puts tray on small table* R. *of day-bed, sits* R. *on day-bed. Inner curtain closes, light dims out.*) Why sometimes there weren't chairs enough to accommodate them all and we had to send the colored boy over to the parish house to fetch the folding chairs.

TOM. How did you entertain all those gentlemen callers? (*Tom finally sits in armchair* R.)

AMANDA. I happened to understand the art of conversation!

TOM. I bet you could talk!

AMANDA. Well, I could. All the girls in my day could, I tell you.

TOM. Yes?

AMANDA. They knew how to entertain their gentlemen callers. It wasn't enough for a girl to be possessed of a pretty face and a graceful figure—although I wasn't slighted in either respect. She also needed to have a nimble wit and a tongue to meet all occasions.

TOM. What did you talk about?

AMANDA. Why, we'd talk about things of importance going on in the world! Never anything common or coarse or vulgar. My callers were gentlemen—all! Some of the most prominent men on the Mississippi Delta—planters and sons of planters! There was young Champ Laughlin. (MUSIC CUE #3.) He later became Vice-President of the Delta Planters'

Bank. And Hadley Stevenson; he was drowned in Moon Lake.—My goodness, he certainly left his widow well provided for—a hundred and fifty thousand dollars in government bonds. And the Cutrere Brothers—Wesley and Bates. Bates was one of my own bright particular beaus! But he got in a quarrel with that wild Wainwright boy and they shot it out on the floor of Moon Lake Casino. Bates was shot through the stomach. He died in the ambulance on his way to Memphis. He certainly left his widow well provided for, too—eight or ten thousand acres, no less. He never loved that woman; she just caught him on the rebound. My picture was found on him the night he died. Oh and that boy, that boy that every girl in the Delta was setting her cap for! That beautiful (MUSIC FADES OUT) brilliant young Fitzhugh boy from Greene County!

TOM. What did he leave his widow?

AMANDA. He never married! What's the matter with you—you talk as though all my old admirers had turned up their toes to the daisies!

TOM. Isn't this the first you've mentioned that still survives?

AMANDA. He made an awful lot of money. He went North to Wall Street and made a fortune. He had the Midas touch—everything that boy touched just turned to gold! (*Gets up.*) And I could have been Mrs. J. Duncan Fitzhugh—mind you! (*Crosses* L. C.) But—what did I do?—I just went out of my way and picked your father! (*Looks at picture on* L. *wall. Goes to small table* R. *of day-bed for tray.*)

LAURA. (*Rises from day-bed.*) Mother, let me clear the table.

AMANDA. (*Crossing* L. *for Laura's cup, then crossing* R. *for Tom's.*) No, dear, you go in front and study your typewriter chart. Or practice your shorthand a little. Stay fresh and pretty! It's almost time for our gentlemen callers to start arriving. How many do you suppose we're going to entertain this afternoon? (*Tom opens curtains between dining-room and living-room for her. These close behind her, and she exits into kitchen* R. *Tom stands* U. C. *in living-room.*)

LAURA. (*To Amanda, off-stage.*) I don't believe we're going to receive any, Mother.

AMANDA. (*Off-stage.*) Not any? Not one? Why, you must be joking! Not one gentleman caller? What's the matter? Has there been a flood or a tornado?

LAURA. (*Crossing to typing table.*) It isn't a flood. It's

not a tornado, Mother. I'm just not popular like you were in Blue Mountain. Mother's afraid that I'm going to be an old maid. (MUSIC CUE #4.) (Lights dim out. Tom exits U. C. in blackout. Laura crosses to menagerie R.)

Act One

SCENE 2

Scene is the same. Lights dim up on living-room. Laura discovered by menagerie, polishing glass. Crosses to phonograph, plays record.[1] She times this business so as to put needle on record as MUSIC CUE #4 ends. Enter Amanda down alley R. Rattles key in lock. Laura crosses guiltily to typewriter and types. (Small typewriter table with typewriter on it is still on stage in living-room L.) Amanda comes into room R. closing door. Crosses to armchair, putting hat, purse and gloves on it. Something has happened to Amanda. It is written in her face: a look that is grim and hopeless and a little absurd. She has on one of those cheap or imitation velvety-looking cloth coats with imitation fur collar. Her hat is five or six years old, one of those dreadful cloche hats that were worn in the late twenties and she is clasping an enormous black patent-leather pocketbook with nickel clasps and initials. This is her fulldress outfit, the one she usually wears to the D.A.R.[2] She purses her lips, opens her eyes very wide, rolls them upward and shakes her head. Seeing her mother's expression, Laura touches her lips with a nervous gesture.

LAURA. Hello, Mother, I was just . . .

AMANDA. I know. You were just practicing your typing, I suppose. (*Behind chair* R.)

LAURA. Yes.

AMANDA. Deception, deception, deception!

LAURA. (*Shakily.*) How was the D.A.R. meeting, Mother?

AMANDA. (*Crosses to Laura.*) D.A.R. meeting!

LAURA. Didn't you go to the D.A.R. meeting, Mother?

AMANDA. (*Faintly, almost inaudibly.*) No, I didn't go to any D.A.R. meeting. (*Then more forcibly.*) I didn't have the strength—I didn't have the courage. I just wanted to find a hole in the ground and

crawl in it and stay there the rest of my entire life. (*Tears type charts, throws them on floor.*)

LAURA. (*Faintly.*) Why did you do that, Mother?

AMANDA. (*Sits on* R. *end of day-bed.*) Why? Why? How old are you, Laura?

LAURA. Mother, you know my age.

AMANDA. I was under the impression that you were an adult, but evidently I was very much mistaken. (*She stares at Laura.*)

LAURA. Please don't stare at me, Mother! (*Amanda closes her eyes and lowers her head. Pause.*)

AMANDA. What are we going to do? What is going to become of us? What is the future? (*Pause.*)

LAURA. Has something happened, Mother? Mother, has something happened?

AMANDA. I'll be all right in a minute. I'm just bewildered—by life . . .

LAURA. Mother, I wish that you would tell me what's happened!

AMANDA. I went to the D.A.R. this afternoon, as you know; I was to be inducted as an officer. I stopped off at Rubicam's Business College to tell them about your cold and to ask how you were progressing down there.

LAURA. Oh . . .

AMANDA. Yes, oh—oh—oh. I went straight to your typing instructor and introduced myself as your mother. She didn't even know who you were. Wingfield, she said? We don't have any such scholar enrolled in this school. I assured her she did. I said my daughter Laura's been coming to classes since early January. "Well, I don't know," she said, "unless you mean that terribly shy little girl who dropped out of school after a few days' attendance?" "No," I said, "I don't mean that one. I mean my daughter, Laura, who's been coming here every single day for the past six weeks!" "Excuse me," she said. And she took down the attendance book and there was your name, unmistakable, printed, and all the dates you'd been absent. I still told her she was wrong. I still said, "No, there must have been some mistake! There must have been some mix-up in the records!" "No," she said, "I remember her perfectly now. She was so shy and her hands trembled so that her fingers

---

1. While *Dardanella* was used in the professional production, any other popular record of the 20's may be substituted. It should be a worn record.
2. *D.A.R.,* Daughters of the American Revolution, a society of women who can claim descent from Americans who fought in the Revolutionary War.

couldn't touch the right keys! When we gave a speed-test—she just broke down completely—was sick at the stomach and had to be carried to the washroom! After that she never came back. We telephoned the house every single day and never got any answer.'' (*Rises from day-bed, crosses* R. C.) That was while I was working all day long down at that department store, I suppose, demonstrating those— (*With hands indicates brassiere.*) Oh! I felt so weak I couldn't stand up! (*Sits in armchair.*) I had to sit down while they got me a glass of water! (*Laura crosses up to phonograph.*) Fifty dollars' tuition. I don't care about the money so much, but all my hopes for any kind of future for you—gone up the spout, just gone up the spout like that. (*Laura winds phonograph up.*) Oh, don't *do* that, Laura!—Don't play that victrola!

LAURA. Oh! (*Stops phonograph, crosses to typing table, sits.*)

AMANDA. What have you been doing every day when you've gone out of the house pretending that you were going to business college?

LAURA. I've just been going out walking.

AMANDA. That's not true!

LAURA. Yes, it is, Mother, I just went walking.

AMANDA. Walking? Walking? In winter? Deliberately courting pneumonia in that light coat? Where did you walk to, Laura?

LAURA. All sorts of places—mostly in the park.

AMANDA. Even after you'd started catching that cold?

LAURA. It was the lesser of two evils, Mother. I couldn't go back. I threw up on the floor!

AMANDA. From half-past seven till after five every day you mean to tell me you walked around in the park, because you wanted to make me think that you were still going to Rubicam's Business College?

LAURA. Oh, Mother, it wasn't as bad as it sounds. I went inside places to get warmed up.

AMANDA. Inside where?

LAURA. I went in the art museum and the bird-houses at the Zoo. I visited the penguins every day! Sometimes I did without lunch and went to the movies. Lately I've been spending most of my afternoons in the Jewelbox, that big glass house[3] where they raise the tropical flowers.

AMANDA. You did all that to deceive me, just for deception! Why? Why? Why? Why?

LAURA. Mother, when you're disappointed, you get that awful suffering look on your face, like the pic-

ture of Jesus' mother in the Museum! (*Rises.*)

AMANDA. Hush!

LAURA. (*Crosses* R. *to menagerie.*) I couldn't face it. I couldn't. (MUSIC CUE #5.)

AMANDA. (*Rising from day-bed.*) So what are we going to do now, honey, the rest of our lives? Just sit down in this house and watch the parades go by? Amuse ourselves with the glass menagerie? Eternally play those worn-out records your father left us as a painful reminder of him? (*Slams phonograph lid.*) We can't have a business career. (END MUSIC CUE #5.) No, we can't do that—that just gives us indigestion. (*Around* R. *day-bed.*) What is there left for us now but dependency all our lives? I tell you, Laura, I know so well what happens to unmarried women who aren't prepared to occupy a position in life. (*Crosses* L., *sits on day-bed.*) I've seen such pitiful cases in the South—barely tolerated spinsters living on some brother's wife or a sister's husband—tucked away in some mousetrap of a room—encouraged by one in-law to go on and visit the next in-law—little birdlike women —without any nest—eating the crust of humility all their lives! Is that the future that we've mapped out for ourselves? I swear I don't see any other alternative. And I don't think that's a very pleasant alternative. Of course—some girls *do* marry. My goodness, Laura, haven't you ever liked some boy?

LAURA. Yes, Mother, I liked one once.

AMANDA. You did?

LAURA. I came across his picture a while ago.

AMANDA. He gave you his picture too? (*Rises from day-bed, crosses to chair* R.)

LAURA. No, it's in the year-book.

AMANDA. (*Sits in armchair.*) Oh—a high-school boy.

LAURA. Yes. His name was Jim. (*Kneeling on floor, gets year-book from under menagerie.*) Here he is in ''The Pirates of Penzance.''[4]

AMANDA. (*Absently.*) The what?

LAURA. The operetta the senior class put on. He had a wonderful voice. We sat across the aisle from each other Mondays, Wednesdays and Fridays in the auditorium. Here he is with a silver cup for debating! See his grin?

---

3. *big glass house,* conservatory at the St. Louis zoo. Williams emphasizes the identification of Laura with the delicate flowers and the fragile, glass building.
4. *The Pirates of Penzance,* an operetta by the famous English team of William S. Gilbert (1836–1911) and Sir Arthur Sullivan (1842–1900)

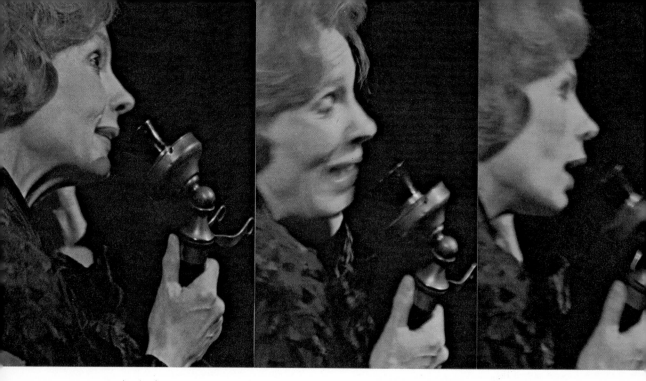

AMANDA. So he had a grin, too! (*Looks at picture of father on wall behind phonograph.[5] Hands yearbook back.*)

LAURA. He used to call me—Blue Roses.

AMANDA. Blue Roses? What did he call you a silly name like that for?

LAURA. (*Still kneeling.*) When I had that attack of pleurosis—he asked me what was the matter when I came back. I said pleurosis—he thought that I said "Blue Roses." So that's what he always called me after that. Whenever he saw me, he'd holler, "Hello, Blue Roses!" I didn't care for the girl that he went out with. Emily Meisenbach. Oh, Emily was the best-dressed girl at Soldan. But she never struck me as being sincere . . . I read in a newspaper once that they were engaged. (*Puts yearbook back on a shelf of glass menagerie.*) That's a long time ago—they're probably married by now.

AMANDA. That's all right, honey, that's all right. It doesn't matter. Little girls who aren't cut out for business careers sometimes end up married to very nice young men. And I'm just going to see that you do that, too!

LAURA. But, Mother—

AMANDA. What is it now?

LAURA. I'm—crippled!

AMANDA. Don't say that word! (*Rises, crosses to C. Turns to Laura.*) How many times have I told you never to say that word! You're not crippled, you've just got a slight defect. (*Laura rises.*) If you lived in the days when I was a girl and they had long graceful skirts sweeping the ground, it might have been considered an asset. When you've got a slight disadvantage like that, you've just got to cultivate something else to take its place. You have to cultivate charm—or vivacity—or *charm!* (*Spotlight on photograph.[6] Then dim out.*) That's the only thing your father had plenty of—charm! (*Amanda sits on day-bed. Laura crosses to armchair and sits.*) (MUSIC CUE #6.) (*Blackout.*)

Act One

SCENE 3

SCENE: *The same. Lights up again but only on R. alley and fire-escape landing, rest of the stage dark. (Typewriter table and typewriter have been taken offstage.) Enter Tom, again wearing merchant sailor overcoat and knitted cap, in alley R. As MUSIC CUE #6 ends, Tom begins to speak.*

SCENE 2 **5.** In the original production this photo was a life-sized head. It lights up from time to time as indicated. The illumination may, if desired, be omitted. If used, it lights here.
6. See note 5 above.

TOM. *(Leans against grill of fire-escape, smoking.)* After the fiasco at Rubicam's Business College, the idea of getting a gentleman caller for my sister Laura began to play a more and more important part in my mother's calculations. It became an obsession. Like some archetype of the universal unconscious,[1] the image of the gentleman caller haunted our small apartment. An evening at home rarely passed without some allusion to this image, this spectre, this hope. . . . And even when he wasn't mentioned, his presence hung in my mother's preoccupied look and in my sister's frightened, apologetic manner. It hung like a sentence passed upon the Wingfields! But my mother was a woman of action as well as words. (MUSIC CUE #7.) She began to take logical steps in the planned direction. Late that winter and in the early spring—realizing that extra money would be needed to properly feather the nest and plume the bird—she began a vigorous campaign on the telephone, roping in subscribers to one of those magazines for matrons called "The Homemaker's Companion," the type of journal that features the serialized sublimations of ladies of letters who think in terms of delicate cup-like breasts, slim, tapering waists, rich creamy thighs, eyes like wood-smoke in autumn, fingers that soothe and caress like soft, soft strains of music. Bodies as powerful as Etruscan sculpture. *(He exits down* R.

into wings. Light in alley R. *is blacked out, and a head-spot falls on Amanda, at phone in living-room.* MUSIC CUE #7 *ends as Tom stops speaking.)*

AMANDA. Ida Scott? *(During this speech Tom enters dining-room* U. R. *unseen by audience, not wearing overcoat or hat. There is an unlighted reading lamp on table. Sits* C. *of dining-room table with writing materials.)* This is Amanda Wingfield. We missed you at the D.A.R. last Monday. Oh, first I want to know how's your sinus condition? You're just a Christian martyr. That's what you are. You're just a Christian martyr. Well, I was just going through my little red book, and I saw that your subscription to the "Companion" is about to expire just when that wonderful new serial by Bessie Mae Harper is starting. It's the first thing she's written since "Honeymoon for Three." Now, that was unusual, wasn't it? Why, Ida, this one is even lovelier. It's all about the horsey set on Long Island and a debutante is thrown from her horse while taking him

1. *archetype of the universal unconscious,* a key portion of the psychological theory of Carl G. Jung (1875–1961), eminent German medical psychologist. It was his belief that everyone inherits images of experiences that are typical for all mankind. According to Jung's theory, these images are what give people their idea, for example, of what a mother or father should be, and they exert a powerful influence on behavior. Tom satirically suggests that the image of the "typical gentleman caller" began to dominate his mother's thinking in the manner of one of these universal archetypes.

over the jumps at the—regatta. Her spine—her spine is injured. That's what the horse did—he stepped on her. Now, there is only one surgeon in the entire world that can keep her from being completely paralyzed, and that's the man she's engaged to be married to and he's tall and he's blond and he's handsome. That's unusual, too, huh? Oh, he's not perfect. Of course he has a weakness. He has the most terrible weakness in the entire world. He just drinks too much. What? Oh, no, Honey, don't let them burn. You go take a look in the oven and I'll hold on . . . Why, that woman! Do you know what she did? She hung up on me. *(Dining-room and living-room lights dim in. Reading lamp lights up at same time.)*

LAURA. Oh, Mother, Mother, Tom's trying to write. *(Rises from armchair where she was left at curtain of previous scene, goes to curtain between dining-room and living-room, which is already open.)*

AMANDA. Oh! So he is. So he is. *(Crosses from phone, goes to dining-room and up to Tom.)*

TOM. *(At table.)* Now what are you up to?

AMANDA. I'm trying to save your eyesight. *(Business with lamp.)* You've only got one pair of eyes and you've got to take care of them. Oh, I know that Milton was blind, but that's not what made him a genius.

TOM. Mother, will you please go away and let me finish my writing?

AMANDA. *(Squares his shoulders.)* Why can't you sit up straight? So your shoulders don't stick through like sparrows' wings?

TOM. Mother, please go busy yourself with something else. I'm trying to write.

AMANDA. *(Business with Tom.)* Now, I've seen a medical chart, and I know what that position does to your internal organs. You sit up and I'll show you. Your stomach presses against your lungs, and your lungs press against your heart, and that poor little heart gets discouraged because it hasn't got any room left to go on beating for you.

TOM. What in hell . . . ! *(Inner curtains between living-room and dining-room close. Lights dim down in dining-room. Laura crosses, stands C. of curtains in living-room listening to following scene between Tom and Amanda.)*

AMANDA.[2] Don't you talk to me like that—

TOM. —am I supposed to do?

AMANDA. What's the matter with you? Have you gone out of your senses?

TOM. Yes, I have. You've driven me out of them.

AMANDA. What is the matter with you lately, you big—big—idiot?

TOM. Look, Mother—I haven't got a thing, not a single thing left in this house that I can call my own.

AMANDA. Lower your voice!

TOM. Yesterday you confiscated my books! You had the nerve to—

---

2. Tom and Amanda remain in dining-room throughout their argument.

AMANDA. I did. I took that horrible novel back to the library—that awful book by that insane Mr. Lawrence.[3] I cannot control the output of a diseased mind or people who cater to them, but I won't allow such filth in my house. No, no, no, no, no!

TOM. House, house! Who pays the rent on the house, who makes a slave of himself to—!

AMANDA. Don't you dare talk to me like that! *(Laura crosses D. L. to back of armchair.)*

TOM. No, *I* mustn't say anything! *I've* just got to keep quiet and let you do all the talking.

AMANDA. Let me tell you something!

TOM. I don't want to hear any more.

AMANDA. You will hear more—*(Laura crosses to phonograph.)*

TOM. *(Crossing through curtains between dining-room and living-room. Goes up stage of door* R. *where, in a dark spot, there is supposedly a closet.)* Well, I'm not going to listen. I'm going out. *(Gets out coat.)*

AMANDA. *(Coming through curtains into living-room, stand* C.*)* You are going to listen to me, Tom Wingfield. I'm tired of your impudence.—And another thing—I'm right at the end of my patience!

TOM. *(Putting overcoat on back of armchair and crossing back to Amanda.)* What do you think I'm at the end of, Mother? Aren't I supposed to have any patience to reach the end of? I know, I know. It seems unimportant to you, what I'm *doing*—what I'm trying to do—having a difference between

them! You don't think that.

AMANDA. I think you're doing things that you're ashamed of, and that's why you act like this. *(Tom crosses to day-bed and sits.)* I don't believe that you go every night to the movies. Nobody goes to the movies night after night. Nobody in their right minds goes to the movies as often as you pretend to. People don't go to the movies at nearly midnight and movies don't let out at two A.M. Come in stumbling, muttering to yourself like a maniac. You get three hours' sleep and then go to work. Oh, I can picture the way you're doing down there. Moping, doping, because you're in no condition.

TOM. That's true—that's very, very true. I'm in no condition!

AMANDA. How dare you jeopardize your job? Jeopardize our security? How do you think we'd manage—? *(Sits armchair* R.*)*

TOM. Look, Mother, do you think I'm *crazy* about the *warehouse?* You think I'm in love with the Continental Shoemakers? You think I want to spend fifty-five years of my life down there in that—*celotex interior!* with *fluorescent tubes?!* Honest to God, I'd rather somebody picked up a crow-bar and battered out my brains—than go back mornings! But I *go!* Sure, every time you come in yelling that bloody *Rise and Shine!* Rise and shine!! I think how lucky dead people are! But I get up. *(Rises from day-bed.)* I *go!* For sixty-five dollars a month I give up all that I dream of doing and being *ever!* And you say that is all I think of. Oh, God! Why, Mother, if self is all I ever thought of, Mother, I'd be where *he* is—GONE! *(Crosses to get overcoat on back of armchair.)* As far as the system of transportation reaches! *(Amanda rises, crosses to him and grabs his arm.)* Please don't grab at me, Mother!

AMANDA. *(Following him.)* I'm not grabbing at you. I want to know where you're going now.

TOM. *(Taking overcoat and starts crossing to door* R.*)* I'm going to the movies!

AMANDA. *(Crosses* C.*)* I don't believe that lie!

TOM. *(Crosses back to Amanda.)* No? Well, you're right. For once in your life you're right. I'm not going to the movies. I'm going to opium dens! Yes, Mother, opium dens, dens of vice and criminals'

---

3. *Mr. Lawrence*, D. H. Lawrence (1885–1930), English novelist and poet. Some of his works aroused considerable protest on moral grounds. The artistic merit of much of his work, however, is unquestioned.

hang-outs, Mother. I've joined the Hogan gang. I'm a hired assassin, I carry a tommy-gun in a violin case! I run a string of cathouses in the valley! They call me Killer, Killer Wingfield, I'm really leading a double life. By day I'm a simple, honest warehouse worker, but at night I'm a dynamic czar of the underworld. Why, I go to gambling casinos and spin away a fortune on the roulette table! I wear a patch over one eye and a false moustache, sometimes I wear green whiskers. On those occasions they call me—El Diablo![4] Oh, I could tell you things to make you sleepless! My enemies plan to dynamite this place some night! Some night they're going to blow us all sky-high. And will I be glad! Will I be happy! And so will you be. You'll go up—up—over Blue Mountain on a broomstick! With seventeen gentlemen callers. You ugly babbling old witch! *(He goes through a series of violent, clumsy movements, seizing his overcoat, lunging to* R. *door, pulling it fiercely open. The women watch him, aghast. His arm catches in the sleeve of the coat as he struggles to pull it on. For a moment he is pinioned by the bulky garment. With an outraged groan he tears the coat off again, splitting the shoulder of it, and hurls it across the room. It strikes against the shelf of Laura's glass collection, there is a tinkle of shattering glass. Laura cries out as if wounded.)*

LAURA. My glass!—menagerie . . . *(She covers her face and turns away.* MUSIC CUE #8 *through to end of scene.)*

AMANDA. *(In an awful voice.)* I'll never speak to you again as long as you live unless you apologize to me! *(Amanda exits through living-room curtains. Tom is left with Laura. He stares at her stupidly for a moment. Then he crosses to shelf holding glass menagerie. Drops awkwardly on his knees to collect fallen glass, glancing at Laura as if he would speak, but couldn't. Blackout. Tom, Amanda and Laura exit in blackout.)*

Act One

SCENE 4

The interior is dark. Faint light in alley R. *A deep-voiced bell in a church is tolling the hour of five as the scene commences.*

Tom appears at the top of R. *alley. After each solemn boom of the bell in the tower he shakes a little toy noisemaker or rattle as if to express the tiny spasm of man in contrast to the sustained power and dignity of the Almighty. This and the unsteadiness of his advance make it evident that he has been drinking. As he climbs the few steps to the fire-escape landing light steals up inside. Laura appears in night-dress, entering living-room from* L. *door of dining-room, observing Tom's empty bed (day-bed) in the living-room. Tom fishes in his pockets for door-key, removing a motley assortment of articles in the search, including a perfect shower of movie-ticket stubs and an empty bottle. At last he finds the key, but just as he is about to insert it, it slips from his fingers. He strikes a match and crouches below the door.*

TOM. *(Bitterly.)* One crack—and it falls through!

(Laura opens door R.*)[1]*

LAURA. Tom! Tom, what are you doing?

TOM. Looking for a door-key.

LAURA. Where have you been all this time?

TOM. I have been to the movies.

LAURA. All this time at the movies?

TOM. There was a very long program. There was a Garbo picture and a Mickey Mouse and a travelogue and a newsreel and a preview of coming attractions. And there was an organ solo and a collection for the milk-fund—simultaneously—which ended up in a terrible fight between a fat lady and an usher!

LAURA. *(Innocently.)* Did you have to stay through everything?

TOM. Of course! And, oh, I forgot! There was a big stage show! The headliner on this stage show was Malvolio the Magician. He performed wonderful tricks, many of them, such as pouring water back and forth between pitchers. First it turned to wine and then it turned to beer and then it turned to whiskey. I know it was whiskey it finally turned into because he needed somebody to come up out of the audience to help him, and I came up—both shows! It was Kentucky Straight Bourbon. A very generous fellow, he gave souvenirs. *(He pulls from his back pocket a shimmering rainbow-colored scarf.)* He gave me this. This is his magic scarf. You can have it, Laura. You wave it over a canary cage

---

SCENE 3 **4.** *El Diablo* (el di äb′lō), the devil. [*Spanish*]
SCENE 4 **1.** Next few speeches are spoken on fire-escape landing.

and you get a bowl of gold-fish. You wave it over the gold-fish bowl and they fly away canaries. . . . But the wonderfullest trick of all was the coffin trick. We nailed him into a coffin and he got out of the coffin without removing one nail. *(They enter.)* There is a trick that would come in handy for me— get me out of this 2 by 4 situation! *(Flops onto day-bed and starts removing shoes.)*

LAURA. Tom—shhh!

TOM. What're you shushing me for?

LAURA. You'll wake up Mother.

TOM. Goody goody! Pay'er back for all those "Rise an' Shines." *(Lies down groaning.)* You know it don't take much intelligence to get yourself into a nailed-up coffin, Laura. But who in hell ever got himself out of one without removing one nail? *(As if in answer, the father's grinning photograph lights up. Laura exits up L. Lights fade except for blue glow in dining-room. Pause after lights fade, then clock chimes six times. This is followed by the alarm clock. Dim in fore-stage.)*

Act One

SCENE 5

Scene is the same. Immediately following. The churchbell is heard striking six. At the sixth stroke the alarm clock goes off in Amanda's room off R. of dining-room and after a few moments we hear her calling, "Rise and shine! Rise and shine! Laura, go tell your brother to rise and shine!"

TOM. *(Sitting up slowly in day-bed.)* I'll rise—but I won't shine. *(The light increases.)*

AMANDA. *(Offstage.)* Laura, tell your brother his coffee is ready. *(Laura, fully dressed, a cape over her shoulders, slips into living-room. Tom is still in bed, covered with blanket, having taken off only shoes and coat.)*

LAURA. Tom!—It's nearly seven. Don't make Mother nervous. *(He stares at her stupidly. Beseechingly.)* Tom, speak to Mother this morning. Make up with her, apologize, speak to her!

TOM. *(Putting on shoes.)* She won't to me. It's her that started not speaking.

LAURA. If you just say you're sorry she'll start speaking.

TOM. Her not speaking—is that such a tragedy?

LAURA. Please—please!

AMANDA. *(Calling offstage R. from kitchen.)* Laura, are you going to do what I asked you to do, or do I have to get dressed and go out myself?

LAURA. Going, going—soon as I get on my coat! *(She rises and crosses to door R.)* Butter and what else? *(To Amanda.)*

AMANDA. *(Offstage.)* Just butter. Tell them to charge it.

LAURA. Mother, they make such faces when I do that.

AMANDA. *(Offstage.)* Sticks and stones can break our bones, but the expression on Mr. Garfinkel's face won't harm us! Tell your brother his coffee is getting cold.

LAURA. *(At door R.)* Do what I asked you, will you, will you, Tom? *(He looks sullenly away.)*

AMANDA. Laura, go now or just don't go at all!

LAURA. *(Rushing out R.)* Going—going! *(A second later she cries out. Falls on fire-escape landing. Tom springs up and crosses to door R. Amanda rushes anxiously in from dining-room, puts dishes on dining-room table. Tom opens door R.)*

TOM. Laura?

LAURA. I'm all right. I slipped, but I'm all right. *(Goes up R. alley, out of sight.)*

AMANDA. *(On fire-escape.)* I tell you if anybody falls down and breaks a leg on those fire-escape steps, the landlord ought to be sued for every cent he ——*(Sees Tom.)* Who are you? *(Leaves fire-escape landing, crosses to dining-room and returns with bowls, coffee cup, cream, etc. Puts them on small table R. of day-bed, crosses to armchair, sits. Counts 3. MUSIC CUE #9. As Tom reenters R., listlessly for his coffee, she turns her back to him, as she sits in armchair. The light on her face with its aged but childish features is cruelly sharp, satirical as a Daumier print. Tom glances sheepishly but sullenly at her averted figure and sits on day-bed next to the food. The coffee is scalding hot, he sips it and gasps and spits it back in the cup. At his gasp, Amanda catches her breath and half turns. Then catches herself and turns away. Tom blows on his coffee, glancing sidewise at his mother. She clears her throat. Tom clears his. He starts to rise. Sinks back down again, scratches his head, clears his throat again. Amanda coughs. Tom raises his cup in both hands to blow on it, his eyes staring over the rim of it at his mother for several moments. Then he slowly sets the cup down and awkwardly and hesitantly rises from day-bed.)*

TOM. *(Hoarsely.)* I'm sorry, Mother. I'm sorry for all those things I said. I didn't mean it. I apologize.

AMANDA. (*Sobbingly.*) My devotion has made me a witch and so I make myself hateful to my children!

TOM. No, you don't.

AMANDA. I worry so much, I don't sleep, it makes me nervous!

TOM. (*Gently.*) I understand that.

AMANDA. You know I've had to put up a solitary battle all these years. But you're my right hand bower! Now don't fail me. Don't fall down.

TOM. (*Gently.*) I try, Mother.

AMANDA. (*With great enthusiasm.*) That's all right! You just keep on trying and you're bound to succeed. Why, you're—you're just full of natural endowments! Both my children are—they're very precious children and I've got an awful lot to be thankful for; you just must promise me one thing.

(MUSIC CUE #9 STOPS.)

TOM. What is it, Mother?

AMANDA. Promise me you're never going to become a drunkard!

TOM. I promise, Mother. I won't ever become a drunkard, Mother.

AMANDA. That's what frightened me so, that you'd be drinking! Eat a bowl of Purina.

TOM. Just coffee, Mother.

AMANDA. Shredded Wheat Biscuit?

TOM. No, no, Mother, just coffee.

AMANDA. You can't put in a day's work on an empty stomach. You've got ten minutes—don't gulp! Drinking too-hot liquids makes cancer of the stomach. . . . Put cream in.

TOM. No, thank you.

AMANDA. To cool it.

TOM. No! No, thank you, I want it black.

AMANDA. I know, but it's not good for you. We have to do all that we can to build ourselves up. In these trying times we live in, all that we have to cling to is—each other. . . . That's why it's so important to—Tom, I—I sent out your sister so I could discuss something with you. If you hadn't spoken I would have spoken to you. (*Sits down.*)

TOM. (*Gently.*) What is it, Mother, that you want to discuss?

AMANDA. Laura! (*Tom puts his cup down slowly.* MUSIC CUE #10.)

TOM. —Oh.—Laura . . .

AMANDA. (*Touching his sleeve.*) You know how Laura is. So quiet but—still water runs deep! She notices things and I think she—broods about them. (*Tom looks up.*) A few days ago I came in and she was crying.

TOM. What about?

AMANDA. You.

TOM. Me?

AMANDA. She has an idea that you're not happy here.

(MUSIC CUE #10 STOPS.)

TOM. What gave her that idea?

AMANDA. What gives her any idea? However, you do act strangely. (*Tom slaps cup down on small table.*) I—I'm not criticizing, understand that! I know your ambitions do not lie in the warehouse, that like everybody in the whole wide world—you've had to—make sacrifices, but—Tom—Tom—life's not easy, it calls for—Spartan endurance! There's so many things in my heart that I cannot describe to you! I've never told you but I—loved your father . . .

TOM. (*Gently.*) I know that, Mother.

AMANDA. And you—when I see you taking after his ways! Staying out late—and—well, you had been drinking the night you were in that—terrifying condition! Laura says that you hate the apartment and that you go out nights to get away from it! Is that true, Tom?

TOM. No. You say there's so much in your heart that you can't describe to me. That's true of me, too. There's so much in my heart that I can't describe to you! So let's respect each other's—

AMANDA. But why—why, Tom—are you always so restless? Where do you go to, nights?

TOM. I—go to the movies.

AMANDA. Why do you go to the movies so much, Tom?

TOM. I go to the movies because—I like adventure. Adventure is something I don't have much of at work, so I go to the movies.

AMANDA. But, Tom, you go to the movies entirely too much!

TOM. I like a lot of adventure. (*Amanda looks baffled, then hurt. As the familiar inquisition resumes he becomes hard and impatient again. Amanda slips back into her querulous attitude toward him.*)

AMANDA. Most young men find adventure in their careers.

TOM. Then most young men are not employed in a warehouse.

AMANDA. The world is full of young men employed in warehouses and offices and factories.

TOM. Do all of them find adventure in their careers?

AMANDA. They do or they do without it! Not everybody has a craze for adventure.

TOM. Man is by instinct a lover, a hunter, a fighter,

and none of those instincts are given much play at the warehouse!

AMANDA. Man is by instinct! Don't quote instinct to me! Instinct is something that people have got away from! It belongs to animals! Christian adults don't want it!

TOM. What do Christian adults want, then, Mother?

AMANDA. Superior things! Things of the mind and the spirit! Only animals have to satisfy instincts! Surely your aims are somewhat higher than theirs! Than monkeys—pigs——

TOM. I reckon they're not.

AMANDA. You're joking. However, that isn't what I wanted to discuss.

TOM. (Rising.) I haven't much time.

AMANDA. (Pushing his shoulders.) Sit down.

TOM. You want me to punch in red at the warehouse, Mother?

AMANDA. You have five minutes. I want to talk about Laura.

TOM. All right! What about Laura?

AMANDA. We have to be making some plans and provisions for her. She's older than you, two years, and nothing has happened. She just drifts along doing nothing. It frightens me terribly how she just drifts along.

TOM. I guess she's the type that people call home girls.

AMANDA. There's no such type, and if there is, it's a pity! That is unless the home is hers, with a husband!

TOM. What?

AMANDA. (Crossing D. R. to armchair.) Oh, I can see the handwriting on the wall as plain as I see the nose in front of my face! It's terrifying! More and more you remind me of your father! He was out all (Sits in armchair.) hours without explanation!— Then left! Good-bye! And me with the bag to hold. I saw that letter you got from the Merchant Marine. I know what you're dreaming of. I'm not standing here blindfolded. Very well, then. Then do it! But not till there's somebody to take your place.

TOM. What do you mean?

AMANDA. I mean that as soon as Laura has got somebody to take care of her, married, a home of her own, independent—why, then you'll be free to go wherever you please, (Rises, crosses to Tom.) on land, on sea, whichever way the wind blows you! But until that time you've got to look out for your sister. (Crosses R. behind armchair.) I don't say me

because I'm old and don't matter! I say for your sister because she's young and dependent. I put her in business college—a dismal failure! Frightened her so it made her sick at the stomach. I took her over to the Young People's League at the church. Another fiasco. She spoke to nobody, nobody spoke to her. (Sits armchair.) Now all she does is fool with those pieces of glass and play those worn-out records. What kind of a life is that for a girl to lead?

TOM. What can I do about it?

AMANDA. Overcome selfishness! Self, self, self is all that you ever think of! (Tom springs up and crosses R. to get his coat and put it on. It is ugly and bulky. He pulls on a cap with earmuffs.) Where is your muffler? Put your wool muffler on! (He snatches it angrily from the hook and tosses it around his neck and pulls both ends tight.) Tom! I haven't said what I had in mind to ask you.

TOM. I'm too late to——

AMANDA. (Catching his arm—very importunately. Then shyly.) Down at the warehouse, aren't there some—nice young men?

TOM. No!

AMANDA. There must be—some . . .

TOM. Mother——(Gesture.)

AMANDA. Find out one that's clean-living—doesn't drink and—ask him out for sister!

TOM. What?

AMANDA. For sister! To meet! Get acquainted!

TOM. (Stamping to door R.) Oh, my go-osh!

AMANDA. Will you? (He opens door. Imploringly.) Will you? (He starts out.) Will you? Will you, dear? (Tom exits up alley R. Amanda is on fire-escape landing.)

TOM. (Calling back.) Yes!

AMANDA. (Re-entering R. and crossing to phone. MUSIC CUE #11.) Ella Cartwright? Ella, this is Amanda Wingfield. First, first, how's that kidney trouble? Oh, it has? It has come back? Well, you're just a Christian martyr, you're just a Christian martyr. I was noticing in my little red book that your subscription to the "Companion" has run out just when that wonderful new serial by Bessie Mae Harper was starting. It's all about the horsey set on Long Island. Oh, you have? You have read it? Well, how do you think it turns out? Oh, no. Bessie Mae Harper never lets you down. Oh, of course, we have to have complications. You have to have complications—oh, you can't have a story without them—but Bessie Mae Harper always leaves you with such an uplift——What's the matter, Ella? You sound so mad. Oh, because it's seven o'clock in the morning. Oh, Ella, I forgot that you never got up until nine. I forgot that anybody in the world was allowed to sleep as late as that. I can't say any more than I'm sorry, can I? Oh, you will? You're going to take that subscription from me anyhow? Well, bless you, Ella, bless you, bless you, bless you. (MUSIC #11 *fades into* MUSIC CUE #11-A, *dance music, and continues into next scene. Dim out lights.* MUSIC CUE #11-A.)

Act One

SCENE 6

SCENE: *The same.—Only* R. *alley lighted, with dim light.*

TOM. (*Enters down* R. *and stands as before, leaning against grillwork, with cigarette, wearing merchant sailor coat and cap.*) Across the alley was the Paradise Dance Hall. Evenings in spring they'd open all the doors and windows and the music would come outside. Sometimes they'd turn out all the lights except for a large glass sphere that hung from the ceiling. It would turn slowly about and filter the dusk with delicate rainbow colors. Then the orchestra would play a waltz or a tango, something that had a slow and sensuous rhythm. The young couples would come outside, to the relative privacy of the alley. You could see them kissing behind ashpits and telephone poles. This was the compensation for lives that passed like mine, without change or adventure. Changes and adventure, however, were imminent this year. They were waiting around the corner for all these dancing kids. Suspended in the mist over Berchtesgaden, caught in the folds of Chamberlain's umbrella[1]—In Spain there was Guernica![2] Here there was only hot swing music and liquor, dance halls, bars, and movies, and sex that hung in the gloom like a chandelier and flooded the world with brief, deceptive rainbows. . . . While these unsuspecting kids danced to "Dear One, The World is Waiting for the Sunrise." All the world was really waiting for bombardments. (MUSIC #11-A *stops. Dim in dining-room: faint glow. Amanda is seen in dining-room.*)

AMANDA. Tom, where are you?

TOM. (*Standing as before.*) I came out to smoke. (*Exit R. into the wings, where he again changes coats and leaves hat.*)

AMANDA. (*Tom re-enters and stands on fire-escape landing, smoking. He opens door for Amanda, who sits on hassock on landing.*) Oh, you smoke too much. A pack a day at fifteen cents a pack. How much would that be in a month? Thirty times fifteen? It wouldn't be very much. Well, it would be enough to help towards a night-school course in accounting at the Washington U! Wouldn't that be lovely?

TOM. I'd rather smoke.

AMANDA. I know! That's the tragedy of you. This fire-escape landing is a poor excuse for the porch we used to have. What are you looking at?

TOM. The moon.

AMANDA. Is there a moon this evening?

TOM. It's rising over Garfinkel's Delicatessen.

AMANDA. Oh! So it is! Such a little silver slipper of a moon. Have you made a wish on it?

TOM. Um-mm.

AMANDA. What did you wish?

TOM. That's a secret.

AMANDA. All right, I won't tell you what I wished, either. I can keep a secret, too. I can be just as mysterious as you.

TOM. I bet I can guess what you wished.

AMANDA. Why, is my head transparent?

TOM. You're not a sphinx.

AMANDA. No, I don't have secrets. I'll tell you what I wished for on the moon. Success and happiness for my precious children. I wish for that whenever there's a moon, and when there isn't a moon, I wish for it, too.

TOM. I thought perhaps you wished for a gentleman caller.

AMANDA. Why do you say that?

TOM. Don't you remember asking me to fetch one?

---

1. *Berchtesgaden* (bārH′təs gä′dən) . . . *Chamberlain's umbrella.* Adolf Hitler was visited at Berchtesgaden, his mountain retreat, by Britain's Conservative Prime Minister, Neville Chamberlain, in 1938. Here Chamberlain, in an effort to avoid war, decided that Hitler should be allowed to annex part of Czechoslovakia in return for a pledge by Hitler to make no further aggression. Hitler's breaking of this pledge brought on World War II.
2. *In Spain there was Guernica.* Guernica (ger nē′kä), a town in northern Spain, was held by the democratic faction during the Spanish Civil War. It was bombed by German and Italian airplanes in 1937 at the direction of the leader of the Fascist faction, General Franco, and thus became a symbol of the cruelty of the Fascist overthrow of the Spanish republic.

AMANDA. I remember suggesting that it would be nice for your sister if you brought home some nice young man from the warehouse. I think that I've made that suggestion more than once.

TOM. Yes, you have made it repeatedly.

AMANDA. Well?

TOM. We are going to have one.

AMANDA. *What?*

TOM. A gentleman caller!

AMANDA. You mean you have asked some nice young man to come over? *(Rising from stool, facing Tom.)*

TOM. I've asked him to dinner.

AMANDA. You really did?

TOM. I did.

AMANDA. And did he—accept?

TOM. He did!

AMANDA. He did?

TOM. He did.

AMANDA. Well, isn't that lovely!

TOM. I thought that you would be pleased.

AMANDA. It's definite, then?

TOM. Oh, very definite.

AMANDA. How soon?

TOM. Pretty soon.

AMANDA. How soon?

TOM. Quite soon.

AMANDA. How soon?

TOM. Very, very soon.

AMANDA. Every time I want to know anything you start going on like that.

TOM. What do you want to know?

AMANDA. Go ahead and guess. Go ahead and guess.

TOM. All right, I'll guess. You want to know when the gentleman caller's coming—he's coming to-morrow.

AMANDA. Tomorrow? Oh, no, I can't do anything about tomorrow. I can't do anything about to-morrow.

TOM. Why not?

AMANDA. That doesn't give me any time.

TOM. Time for what?

AMANDA. Time for preparations. Oh, you should have phoned me the minute you asked him—the minute he accepted!

TOM. You don't have to make any fuss.

AMANDA. Of course I have to make a fuss! I can't have a man coming into a place that's all sloppy. It's got to be thrown together properly. I certainly have to do some fast thinking by tomorrow night, too.

TOM. I don't see why you have to think at all.

AMANDA. That's because you just don't know. *(Enter living-room, crosses to* C. *Dim in living-room.)* You just don't know, that's all. We can't have a gentle-man caller coming into a pig-sty! Now, let's see. Oh, I've got those three pieces of wedding silver left. I'll polish that up. I wonder how that old lace tablecloth is holding up all these years? We can't wear anything. We haven't got it. We haven't got anything to wear. We haven't got it. *(Goes back to door* R.*)*

TOM. Mother! This boy is no one to make a fuss over.

AMANDA. *(Crossing to* C.*)* I don't know how you can say that when this is the first gentleman caller your little sister's ever had! I think it's pathetic that that little girl has never had a single gentleman caller! Come on inside! Come on inside!

TOM. What for?

AMANDA. I want to ask you a few things.

TOM. *(From doorway* R.*)* If you're going to make a fuss, I'll call the whole thing off. I'll call the boy up and tell him not to come.

AMANDA. No! You mustn't ever do that. People hate broken engagements. They have no place to go. Come on inside. Come on inside. Will you come inside when I ask you to come inside? Sit down.
(Tom comes into living-room.)

TOM. Any particular place you want me to sit?

AMANDA. Oh! Sit anywhere. *(Tom sits armchair* R.*)* Look! What am I going to do about that? *(Looking at day-bed.)* Did you ever see anything look so sad? I know, I'll get a bright piece of cretonne. That won't cost much. And I made payments on a floor lamp. So I'll have that sent out! And I can put a bright cover on the chair. I wish I had time to paper the walls. What's his name?

TOM. His name is O'Connor.

AMANDA. O'Connor—he's Irish and tomorrow's Fri-day—that means fish. Well, that's all right, I'll make a salmon loaf and some mayonnaise dressing for it. Where did you meet him? *(Crosses to day-bed and sits.)*

TOM. At the warehouse, of course. Where else would I meet him?

AMANDA. Well, I don't know. Does he drink?

TOM. What made you ask me that?

AMANDA. Because your father did.

TOM. Now, don't get started on that!

AMANDA. He drinks, then.

TOM. No, not that I know of.

AMANDA. You have to find out. There's nothing I want

less for my daughter than a man who drinks.

TOM. Aren't you being a little bit premature? After all, poor Mr. O'Connor hasn't even appeared on the scene yet.

AMANDA. But he will tomorrow. To meet your sister. And what do I know about his character? *(Rises and crosses to Tom who is still in armchair, smooths his hair.)*

TOM. *(Submitting grimly.)* Now what are you up to?

AMANDA. I always did hate that cowlick. I never could understand why it won't sit down by itself.

TOM. Mother, I want to tell you something and I mean it sincerely right straight from my heart. There's a lot of boys who meet girls which they don't marry!

AMANDA. You know you always had me worried because you could never stick to a subject. *(Crosses to day-bed.)* What I want to know is what's his position at the warehouse?

TOM. He's a shipping clerk.

AMANDA. Oh! Shipping clerk! Well, that's fairly important. That's where you'd be if you had more get-up. How much does he earn? *(Sits on day-bed.)*

TOM. I have no way of knowing that for sure. I judge his salary to be approximtely eighty-five dollars a month.

AMANDA. Eighty-five dollars? Well, that's not princely.

TOM. It's twenty dollars more than I make.

AMANDA. I know that. Oh, how well I know that! How well I know that! Eighty-five dollars a month. No. It can't be done. A family man can never get by on eighty-five dollars a month.

TOM. Mother, Mr. O'Connor is not a family man.

AMANDA. Well, he might be some time in the future, mightn't he?

TOM. Oh, I see. . . . Plans and provisions.

AMANDA. You are the only young man that I know of who ignores the fact that the future becomes the present, the present the past, and the past turns into everlasting regret if you don't plan for it.

TOM. I will think that over and see what I can make of it!

AMANDA. Don't be supercilious with your mother! Tell me some more about this.—What do you call him? Mr. O'Connor, Mr. O'Connor. He must have another name besides Mr.——?

TOM. His full name is James D. O'Connor. The D. is for Delaney.

AMANDA. Delaney? Irish on both sides and he doesn't drink?

TOM. *(Rises from armchair.)* Shall I call him up and ask him? *(Starts toward phone.)*

AMANDA. *(Crossing to phone.)* No!

TOM. I'll call him up and tell him you want to know if he drinks. *(Picks up phone.)*

AMANDA. *(Taking phone away from him.)* No, you can't do that. You have to be discreet about that subject. When I was a girl in Blue Mountain if it was *(Tom sits on R. of day-bed.)* suspected that a young man was drinking and any girl was receiving his attentions—if any girl *was* receiving his attentions, she'd go to the minister of his church and ask about his character—or her father, if her father was living, then it was his duty to go to the minister of his church and ask about his character, and that's how young girls in Blue Mountain were kept from making tragic mistakes. *(Picture dims in and out.)*[3]

TOM. How come you made such a tragic one?

AMANDA. Oh, I don't know how he did it, but that face fooled everybody. All he had to do was grin and the world was bewitched. *(Behind day-bed, crosses to armchair.)* I don't know of anything more tragic than a young girl just putting herself at the mercy of a handsome appearance, and I hope Mr. O'Connor is *not* too goodlooking.

TOM. As a matter of fact he isn't. His face is covered with freckles and he has a very large nose.

AMANDA. He's not right-down homely?

TOM. No. I wouldn't say right-down—homely—medium homely, I'd say.

AMANDA. Well, if a girl had any sense she'd look for character in a man anyhow.

TOM. That's what I've always said, Mother.

AMANDA. You've always said it—you've always said it! How could you've always said it when you never even thought about it?

TOM. Aw, don't be so suspicious of me.

AMANDA. I am. I'm suspicious of every word that comes out of your mouth, when you talk to me, but I want to know about this young man. Is he up and coming?

TOM. Yes. I really do think he goes in for self-improvement.

AMANDA. What makes you think it?

TOM. He goes to night school.

AMANDA. Well, what does he do there at night school?

TOM. He's studying radio engineering and public speaking.

---

3. See note **5,** p. M 290.

AMANDA. Oh! Public speaking! Oh, that shows, that shows that he intends to be an executive some day—and radio engineering. Well, that's coming . . . huh?

TOM. I think it's here.

AMANDA. Well, those are all very illuminating facts. *(Crosses to back of armchair.)* Facts that every mother should know about any young man calling on her daughter, seriously or not.

TOM. Just one little warning, Mother. I didn't tell him anything about Laura. I didn't let on we had dark ulterior motives. I just said, "How about coming home to dinner some time?" and he said, "Fine," and that was the whole conversation.

AMANDA. I bet it was, too. I tell you, sometimes you can be as eloquent as an oyster. However, when he sees how pretty and sweet that child is, he's going to be, well, he's going to be very glad he was asked over here to have some dinner. *(Sits in armchair.)*

TOM. Mother, just one thing. You won't expect too much of Laura, will you?

AMANDA. I don't know what you mean. *(Tom crosses slowly to Amanda. He stands for a moment, looking at her. Then—)*

TOM. Well, Laura seems all those things to you and me because she's ours and we love her. We don't even notice she's crippled any more.

AMANDA. Don't use that word.

TOM. Mother, you have to face the facts; she is, and that's not all.

AMANDA. What do you mean "that's not all"? *(Tom kneels by her chair.)*

TOM. Mother—you know that Laura is very different from other girls.

AMANDA. Yes, I do know that, and I think that difference is all in her favor, too.

TOM. Not quite all—in the eyes of others—strangers —she's terribly shy. She lives in a world of her own and those things make her seem a little peculiar to people outside the house.

AMANDA. Don't use that word peculiar.

TOM. You have to face the facts.—She is.

AMANDA. I don't know in what way she's peculiar. *(MUSIC CUE #12, till curtain. Tom pauses a moment for music, then—)*

TOM. Mother, Laura lives in a world of little glass animals. She plays old phonograph records—and— that's about all———*(Tom rises slowly, goes quietly out the door R., leaving it open, and exits slowly up*

the alley. Amanda rises, goes on to fire-escape landing R., looks at moon.)*

AMANDA. Laura! Laura! *(Laura answers from kitchen R.)*

LAURA. Yes, Mother.

AMANDA. Let those dishes go and come in front! *(Laura appears with dish towel. Gaily.)* Laura, come here and make a wish on the moon!

LAURA. *(Entering from kitchen R. and comes down to fire-escape landing.)* Moon—moon?

AMANDA. A little silver slipper of a moon. Look over your left shoulder, Laura, and make a wish! *(Laura looks faintly puzzled as if called out of sleep. Amanda seizes her shoulders and turns her at an angle on the fire-escape landing.)* Now! Now, darling, wish!

LAURA. What shall I wish for, Mother?

AMANDA. *(Her voice trembling and her eyes suddenly filling with tears.)* Happiness! And just a little bit of good fortune! *(The stage dims out.)*

CURTAIN
End of Act One

Act Two

SCENE 7

SCENE: *The same.*

Inner curtains closed between dining-room and living-room. Interiors of both rooms are dark as at beginning of play. Tom has on the same jacket and cap as at first. Same dance-hall music as CUE #1, fading as Tom begins.

TOM. *(Discovered leaning against grill on fire-escape landing, as before, and smoking.)* And so the following evening I brought Jim home to dinner. I had known Jim slightly in high school. In high school, Jim was a hero. He had tremendous Irish good nature and vitality with the scrubbed and polished look of white chinaware. He seemed to move in a continual spotlight. He was a star in basketball, captain of the debating club, president of the senior class and the glee club, and he sang the male lead in the annual light opera. He was forever running or bounding, never just walking. He seemed always just at the point of defeating the law of gravity. He was shooting with such velocity through his adolescence that you would just logically expect him to arrive at nothing short of the White House by the time he was thirty. But Jim apparently ran into more interference after his graduation from high school because his speed had definitely slowed. And so, at this particular time in our lives he was holding a job that wasn't much better than mine. He was the only one at the warehouse with whom I was on friendly terms. I was valuable to Jim as someone who could remember his former glory, who had seen him win basketball games and the silver cup in debating. He knew of my secret practice of retiring to a cabinet of the washroom to work on poems whenever business was slack in the warehouse. He called me Shakespeare. And while the other boys in the warehouse regarded me with suspicious hostility, Jim took a humorous attitude toward me. Gradually his attitude began to affect the other boys and their hostility wore off. And so, after a time they began to smile at me too, as people smile at some oddly fashioned dog that trots across their path at some distance. I knew that Jim and Laura had known each other in high school because I had heard my sister Laura speak admiringly of Jim's voice. I didn't know if Jim would remember her or not. Because in high school Laura had been as unobtrusive as Jim had been astonishing. And, if he did remember Laura, it was not as my sister, for when I asked him home to dinner, he smiled and said, "You know, a funny thing, Shakespeare, I never thought of you as having folks!" Well, he was about to discover that I did. . . . (MUSIC CUE #13. *Tom exits* R. *Interior living-room lights dim in. Amanda is sitting on small table* R. *of day-bed sewing on hem on Laura's dress. Laura stands facing the door* R. *Amanda has worked like a Turk in preparation for the gentleman caller. The results are astonishing. The new floor lamp with its rose-silk shade is in place,* R. *of living-room next to wall, a colored paper lantern conceals the broken light fixture in the ceiling, chintz covers are on chairs and sofa, a pair of new sofa pillows make their ini-*

tial appearance. Laura stands in the middle of room with lifted arms while Amanda crouches before her, adjusting the hem of the new dress, devout and ritualistic. The dress is colored and designed by memory. The arrangement of Laura's hair is changed; it is softer and more becoming. A fragile, unearthly prettiness has come out in Laura; she is like a piece of translucent glass touched by light, given a momentary radiance, not actual, not lasting. Amanda, still seated, is sewing Laura's dress. Laura is standing R. *of Amanda.*)

AMANDA. Why are you trembling so, Laura?

LAURA. Mother, you've made me so nervous!

AMANDA. Why, how have I made you nervous?

LAURA. By all this fuss! You make it seem so important.

AMANDA. I don't understand you at all, honey. Every time I try to do anything for you that's the least bit different you just seem to set yourself against it. Now take a look at yourself. (*Laura starts for door* R.) No, wait! Wait just a minute—I forgot something. (*Picks two powder puffs from day-bed.*)

LAURA. What is it?

AMANDA. A couple of improvements. (*Business with powder puffs.*) When I was a girl we had round little lacy things like that and we called them "Gay Deceivers."

LAURA. I won't wear them!

AMANDA. Of course you'll wear them.

LAURA. Why should I?

AMANDA. Well, to tell you the truth, honey, you're just a little bit flat-chested.

LAURA. You make it seem like we were setting a trap.

AMANDA. We are. All pretty girls are a trap and men expect them to be traps. Now look at yourself in that glass. (*Laura crosses* R. *Looks at mirror, invisible to audience, which is in darkness up* R. *of* R. *door.*) See? You look just like an angel on a postcard. Isn't that lovely? Now you just wait. I'm going to dress myself up. You're going to be astonished at your mother's appearance. (END OF MUSIC CUE. *End of Music Cue leads into dance music,*[1] *which then leads in* MUSIC CUE #14, *a few lines below, at stage direction. Amanda exits through curtains upstage off* L. *in dining-room. Laura looks in mirror for a moment. Removes "Gay Deceivers," hides them under mattress of day-bed. Sits on small table* R. *of day-bed for a*

1. Optional. Not on regular record of incidental music to the play.

moment, goes out to fire-escape landing, listens to dance music, until Amanda's entrance. Amanda, off.) I found an old dress in the trunk. But what do you know? I had to do a lot to it but it broke my heart when I had to let it out. Now, Laura, just look at your mother. Oh, no! Laura, come look at me now! *(Enters dining-room L. door. Comes down through living-room curtain to living-room C. MUSIC CUE #14.)*

LAURA. *(Re-enters from fire-escape landing. Sits on L. arm of armchair.)* Oh, Mother, how lovely! *(Amanda wears a girlish frock. She carries a bunch of jonquils.)*

AMANDA. *(Standing C., holding flowers.)* It used to be. It used to be. It had a lot of flowers on it, but they got awful tired so I had to take them all off. I led the cotillion in this dress years ago. I won the cake-walk twice at Sunset Hill, and I wore it to the Governor's ball in Jackson. You should have seen your mother. You should have seen your mother how she just sashayed around *(Crossing around L. of day-bed back to C.)* the ballroom, just like that. I had it on the day I met your father. I had malaria fever, too. The change of climate from East Tennessee to the Delta—weakened my resistance. Not enough to be dangerous, just enough to make me restless and giddy. Oh, it was lovely. Invitations poured in from all over. My mother said, "You can't go any place because you have a fever. You have to stay in bed." I said I wouldn't and I took quinine and kept on going and going. Dances every evening and long rides in the country in the afternoon and picnics. That country—that country —so lovely—so lovely in May, all lacy with dogwood and simply flooded with jonquils. My mother said, "You can't bring any more jonquils in this house." I said, "I will," and I kept on bringing them in anyhow. Whenever I saw them I said, "Wait a minute, I see jonquils," and I'd make my gentlemen callers get out of the carriage and help me gather some. To tell you the truth, Laura, it got to be a kind of a joke. "Look out," they'd say, "here comes that girl and we'll have to spend the afternoon picking jonquils." My mother said, "You can't bring any more jonquils in the house, there aren't any more vases to hold them." "That's quite all right," I said, "I can hold some myself." Malaria fever, your father and jonquils. *(Amanda puts jonquils in Laura's lap and goes out on to fire-escape landing. MUSIC CUE #14 STOPS. THUNDER HEARD.)* I hope they get here before it starts to rain. I gave your brother a little extra change so he and Mr. O'Connor could take the service car home. *(Laura puts flowers on armchair R., and crosses to door R.)*

LAURA. Mother!

AMANDA. What's the matter now? *(Re-entering room.)*

LAURA. What did you say his name was?

AMANDA. O'Connor. Why?

LAURA. What is his first name?

AMANDA. *(Crosses to armchair R.)* I don't remember— Oh, yes, I do too—it was—Jim! *(Picks up flowers.)*

LAURA. Oh, Mother, not Jim O'Connor!

AMANDA. Yes, that was it, it was Jim! I've never known a Jim that wasn't nice. *(Crosses L., behind day-bed, puts flowers in vase.)*

LAURA. Are you sure his name was Jim O'Connor?

AMANDA. Why, sure I'm sure. Why?

LAURA. Is he the one that Tom used to know in high school?

AMANDA. He didn't say so. I think he just got to know him—*(Sits on day-bed.)* at the warehouse.

LAURA. There was a Jim O'Connor we both knew in high school. If that is the one that Tom is bringing home to dinner——Oh, Mother, you'd have to excuse me, I wouldn't come to the table!

AMANDA. What's this now? What sort of silly talk is this?

LAURA. You asked me once if I'd ever liked a boy. Don't you remember I showed you this boy's picture?

AMANDA. You mean the boy in the year-book?

LAURA. Yes, that boy.

AMANDA. Laura, Laura, were you in love with that boy?

LAURA. *(Crosses to R. of armchair.)* I don't know, Mother. All I know is that I couldn't sit at the table if it was him.

AMANDA. *(Rises, crosses L. and works up L. of day-bed.)* It won't be him! It isn't the least bit likely. But whether it is or not, you will come to the table— you will not be excused.

LAURA. I'll have to be, Mother.

AMANDA. *(Behind day-bed.)* I don't intend to humor your silliness, Laura. I've had too much from you and your brother, both. So just sit down and compose yourself till they come. Tom has forgotten his key, so you'll *have* to let them in when they arrive.

LAURA. Oh, Mother—*you* answer the door! *(Sits chair R.)*

AMANDA. How can I when I haven't even finished making the mayonnaise dressing for the salmon?

LAURA. Oh, Mother, please answer the door, don't make me do it! (*Thunder heard off-stage.*)

AMANDA. Honey, do be reasonable! What's all this fuss about—just one gentleman caller—that's all—just one! (*Exits through living-room curtains. Tom and Jim enter alley* R., *climb fire-escape steps to landing and wait outside of closed door. Hearing them approach, Laura rises with a panicky gesture. She retreats to living-room curtains. The doorbell rings. Laura catches her breath and touches her throat. More thunder heard off-stage.*)

AMANDA. (*Off-stage.*) Laura, sweetheart, the door!

LAURA. Mother, please, you go to the door! (*Starts for door* R., *then back.*)

AMANDA. (*Off-stage, in a fierce whisper.*) What is the matter with you, you silly thing? (*Enters through living-room curtains, and stands by day-bed.*)

LAURA. Please you answer it, please.

AMANDA. Why have you chosen this moment to lose your mind? You go to that door.

LAURA. I can't.

AMANDA. Why can't you?

LAURA. Because I'm sick. (*Crosses to* L. *end of day-bed and sits.*)

AMANDA. You're sick! Am I sick? You and your brother have me puzzled to death. You can never act like normal children. Will you give me one good reason why you should be afraid to open a door? You go to that door. Laura Wingfield, you march straight to that door!

LAURA. (*Crosses to door* R.) Yes, Mother.

AMANDA. (*Stopping Laura.*) I've got to put courage in you, honey, for living. (*Exits through living-room curtains, and exits* R. *into kitchen. Laura opens door. Tom and Jim enter. Laura remains hidden in hall behind door.*)

TOM. Laura—(*Laura crosses* C.) this is Jim. Jim, this is my sister Laura.

JIM. I didn't know that Shakespeare had a sister! How are you, Laura?

LAURA. (*Retreating stiff and trembling. Shakes hands.*) How—how do you do?

JIM. Well, I'm okay! Your hand's *cold*, Laura! (*Tom puts hats on phone table.*)

LAURA. Yes, well—I've been playing the victrola. . . .

JIM. Must have been playing classical music on it. You ought to play a little hot swing music to warm you up. (*Laura crosses to phonograph. Tom crosses up to Laura. Laura starts phonograph[2]—looks at Jim. Exits through living-room curtains and goes off* L.)

JIM. What's the matter?

TOM. Oh—Laura? Laura is—is terribly shy. (*Crosses and sits on day-bed.*)

JIM. (*Crosses down* C.) Shy, huh? Do you know it's unusual to meet a shy girl nowadays? I don't believe you ever mentioned you had a sister?

TOM. Well, now you know I have one. You want a piece of the paper?

JIM. (*Crosses to Tom.*) Uh-huh.

TOM. Comics?

JIM. Comics? Sports! (*Takes paper. Crosses, sits chair* R.) I see that Dizzy Dean[3] is on his bad behavior.

TOM. (*Starts to door* R. *Goes out.*) Really?

JIM. Yeah. Where are *you* going? (*As Tom reaches steps* R. *of fire-escape landing.*)

TOM. (*Calling from fire-escape landing.*) Out on the terrace to smoke.

JIM. (*Rises, leaving newspaper in armchair, goes over to turn off victrola. Crosses* R. *Exits to fire-escape landing.*) You know, Shakespeare—I'm going to sell you a bill of goods!

TOM. What goods?

JIM. A course I'm taking.

TOM. What course?

JIM. A course in public speaking! You know you and me, we're not the warehouse type.

TOM. Thanks—that's good news. What has public speaking got to do with it?

JIM. It fits you for—executive positions!

TOM. Oh.

JIM. I tell you it's done a helluva lot for me.

TOM. In what respect?

JIM. In all respects. Ask yourself: what's the difference between you and me and the guys in the office down front? Brains?—No!—Ability?—No! Then what? Primarily, it amounts to just one single thing——

TOM. What is that one thing?

JIM. Social poise! The ability to square up to somebody and hold your own on any social level!

AMANDA. (*Off-stage.*) Tom?

TOM. Yes, Mother?

AMANDA. Is that you and Mr. O'Connor?

TOM. Yes, Mother.

---

2. A worn record of *Dardanella* or some other popular tune of the 1920's.

3. *Dizzy Dean,* a famous baseball player.

AMANDA. Make yourselves comfortable.

TOM. We will.

AMANDA. Ask Mr. O'Connor if he would like to wash his hands?

JIM. No, thanks, ma'am—I took care of that down at the warehouse. Tom?

TOM. Huh?

JIM. Mr. Mendoza was speaking to me about you.

TOM. Favorably?

JIM. What do you think?

TOM. Well——

JIM. You're going to be out of a job if you don't wake up.

TOM. I'm waking up——

JIM. Yeah, but you show no signs.

TOM. The signs are interior. I'm just about to make a change. I'm right at the point of committing myself to a future that doesn't include the warehouse or Mr. Mendoza, or even a night school course in public speaking.

JIM. Now what are you gassing about?

TOM. I'm tired of the movies.

JIM. The movies!

TOM. Yes, movies! Look at them. (*He waves his hands.*) All of those glamorous people—having adventures—hogging it all, gobbling the whole thing up! You know what happens? People go to the *movies* instead of *moving*. Hollywood characters are supposed to have all the adventures for everybody in America, while everybody in America sits in a dark room and watches them having it! Yes, until there's a war. That's when adventure becomes available to the masses! Everyone's dish, not only Gable's! Then the people in the dark room come out of the dark room to have some adventures themselves—goody—goody! It's our turn now to go to the South Sea Island—to make a safari —to be exotic, far off . . . ! But I'm not patient. I don't want to wait till then. I'm tired of the movies and I'm about to move!

JIM. (*Incredulously.*) Move?

TOM. Yes.

JIM. When?

TOM. Soon!

JIM. Where? Where?

TOM. I'm starting to boil inside. I know I seem dreamy, but inside—well, I'm boiling! Whenever I pick up a shoe I shudder a little, thinking how short life is and what I am doing!—Whatever that means, I know it doesn't mean shoes—except as something

to wear on a traveler's feet! (*Gets card from inside coat pocket.*) Look!

JIM. What?

TOM. I'm a member.

JIM. (*Reading.*) The Union of Merchant Seamen.

TOM. I paid my dues this month, instead of the electric light bill.

JIM. You'll regret it when they turn off the lights.

TOM. I won't be here.

JIM. Yeah, but how about your mother?

TOM. I'm like my father. The bastard son of a bastard. See how he grins? And he's been absent going on sixteen years.

JIM. You're just talking, you drip. How does your mother feel about it?

TOM. Sh! Here comes Mother! Mother's not acquainted with my plans!

AMANDA. (*Off-stage.*) Tom!

TOM. Yes, Mother?

AMANDA. (*Off-stage.*) Where are you all?

TOM. On the terrace, Mother.

AMANDA. (*Enters through living-room curtain and stands C.*) Why don't you come in? (*They start inside. She advances to them. Tom is distinctly shocked at her appearance. Even Jim blinks a little. He is making his first contact with girlish Southern vivacity and in spite of the night-school course in public speaking is somewhat thrown off the beam by the unexpected outlay of social charm. Certain responses are attempted by Jim but are swept aside by Amanda's gay laughter and chatter. Tom is embarrassed but after the first shock Jim reacts very warmly. Grins and chuckles, is altogether won over. Tom and Jim come in, leaving door open.*)

TOM. Mother, you look so pretty.

AMANDA. You know, that's the first compliment you ever paid me. I wish you'd look pleasant when you're about to say something pleasant, so I could expect it. Mr. O'Connor? (*Jim crosses to Amanda.*)

JIM. How do you do?

AMANDA. Well, well, well, so this is Mr. O'Connor? Introduction's entirely unnecessary. I've heard so much about you from my boy. I finally said to him, "Tom, good gracious, why don't you bring this paragon to supper finally? I'd like to meet this nice young man at the warehouse! Instead of just hearing you sing his praises so much?" I don't know why my son is so stand-offish—that's not

Southern behavior. Let's sit down. *(Tom closes door, crosses* U. R., *stands. Jim and Amanda sit on day-bed, Jim,* R., *Amanda* L.*)* Let's sit down, and I think we could stand a little more air in here. Tom, leave the door open. I felt a nice fresh breeze a moment ago. Where has it gone to? Mmmm, so warm already! And not quite summer, even. We're going to burn up when summer really gets started. However, we're having—we're having a very light supper. I think light things are better fo'—for this time of year. The same as light clothes are. Light clothes and light food are what warm weather calls fo'. You know our blood get so thick during th' winter—it takes a while fo' us to adjust ou'selves—when the season changes. . . . It's come so quick this year. I wasn't prepared. All of a sudden—Heavens! Already summer!—I ran to the trunk an'—pulled out this light dress—terribly old! Historical almost! But feels so good—so good and cool, why, y' know——

TOM. Mother, how about our supper?

AMANDA. *(Rises, crosses* R. *to Tom.)* Honey, you go ask sister if supper is ready! You know that sister is in full charge of supper. Tell her you hungry boys are waiting for it. *(Tom exits through curtains and off* L. *Amanda turns to Jim.)* Have you met Laura?

JIM. Well, she came to the door.

AMANDA. She let you in?

JIM. Yes, ma'am.

AMANDA. *(Crossing to armchair and sitting.)* She's very pretty.

JIM. Oh, yes ma'am.

AMANDA. It's rare for a girl as sweet an' pretty as Laura to be domestic! But Laura is, thank heavens, not only pretty but also very domestic. I'm not at all. I never was a bit. I never could make a thing but angel-food cake. Well, in the South we had so many servants. Gone, gone, gone. All vestige of gracious living! Gone completely! I wasn't prepared for what the future brought me. All of my gentlemen callers were sons of planters and so of course I assumed that I would be married to one and raise my family on a large piece of land with plenty of servants. But man proposes—and woman accepts the proposal!—To vary that old, old saying a little bit—I married no planter! I married a man who worked for the telephone company!—That gallantly smiling gentleman over there! *(Points to picture)* A telephone man who

—fell in love with long-distance!—Now he travels and I don't even know where!—But what am I going on for about my—tribulations? Tell me yours—I hope you don't have any! Tom?

TOM. *(Re-enters through living-room curtains from off* L.*)* Yes, Mother.

AMANDA. What about that supper?

TOM. Why, supper is on the table. *(Inner curtains between living-room and dining-room open. Lights dim up in dining-room, dim out in living-room.)*

AMANDA. Oh, so it is. *(Rises, crosses up to table* C. *in dining-room and chair* C.*)* How lovely. Where is Laura?

TOM. *(Going to chair* L. *and standing.)* Laura is not feeling too well and thinks maybe she'd better not come to the table.

AMANDA. Laura!

LAURA. *(Off-stage. Faintly.)* Yes, Mother? *(Tom gestures re: Jim.)*

AMANDA. Mr. O'Connor. *(Jim crosses up* L. *to table and to chair* L. *and stands.)*

JIM. Thank you, ma'am.

AMANDA. Laura, we can't say grace till you come to the table.

LAURA. *(Enters* U. L., *obviously quite faint, lips trembling, eyes wide and staring. Moves unsteadily toward dining-room table.)* Oh, Mother, I'm so sorry. *(Tom catches her as she feels faint. He takes her to day-bed in living-room.)*

AMANDA. *(As Laura lies down.)* Why, Laura, you are sick, darling! Laura—rest on the sofa. Well! *(To Jim.)* Standing over the hot stove made her ill!—I told her that it was just too warm this evening, but——*(To Tom.)* Is Laura all right now?

TOM. She's better, Mother. *(Sits chair* L. *in dining-room. Thunder off-stage.)*

AMANDA. *(Returning to dining-room and sitting at table, as Jim does.)* My goodness, I suppose we're going to have a little rain! Tom, you say grace.

TOM. What?

AMANDA. What do we generally do before we have something to eat? We say grace, don't we?

TOM. For these and all Thy mercies—God's Holy Name be praised. *(Lights dim out.* MUSIC CUE #15.*)*

Act Two

SCENE 8

SCENE: *The same. A half-hour later. Dinner is coming to an end in dining-room.*
Amanda, Tom and Jim sitting at table as at end of last scene. Lights dim up in both rooms, and MUSIC CUE #15 *ends.*

AMANDA. *(Laughing, as Jim laughs too.)* You know, Mr. O'Connor, I haven't had such a pleasant evening in a very long time.

JIM. *(Rises.)* Well, Mrs. Wingfield, let me give you a toast. Here's to the old South.

AMANDA. The old South. *(Blackout in both rooms.)*

JIM. Hey, Mr. Light Bulb!

AMANDA. Where was Moses when the lights went out? Do you know the answer to that one, Mr. O'Connor?

JIM. No, ma'am, what's the answer to that one?

AMANDA. Well, I heard one answer, but it wasn't very nice. I thought you might know another one.

JIM. No, ma'am.

AMANDA. It's lucky I put those candles on the table. I just put them on for ornamentation, but it's nice when they prove useful, too.

JIM. Yes, ma'am.

AMANDA. Now, if one of you gentlemen can provide me with a match we can have some illumination.

JIM. *(Lighting candles. Dim in glow for candles.)* I can, ma'am.

AMANDA. Thank you.

JIM. *(Crosses back to* R. *of dining-room table.)* Not at all, ma'am.

AMANDA. I guess it must be a burnt-out fuse. Mr. O'Connor, do you know anything about a burnt-out fuse?

JIM. I know a little about them, ma'am, but where's the fuse box?

AMANDA. Must you know that, too? Well, it's in the kitchen. *(Jim exits* R. *into kitchen.)* Be careful. It's dark. Don't stumble over anything. *(Sound of crash off-stage.)* Oh, my goodness, wouldn't it be awful if we lost him! Are you all right, Mr. O'Connor?

JIM. *(Off-stage.)* Yes, ma'am, I'm all right.

AMANDA. You know, electricity is a very mysterious thing. The whole universe is mysterious to me.

Wasn't it Benjamin Franklin who tied a key to a kite? I'd like to have seen that—he might have looked mighty silly. Some people say that science clears up all the mysteries for us. In my opinion they just keep on adding more. Haven't you found it yet?

JIM. *(Re-enters* R.*)* Yes, ma'am. I found it all right, but them fuses look okay to me. *(Sits as before.)*

AMANDA. Tom.

TOM. Yes, Mother?

AMANDA. That light bill I gave you several days ago. The one I got the notice about?

TOM. Oh—yeah. You mean last month's bill?

AMANDA. You didn't neglect it by any chance?

TOM. Well, I——

AMANDA. You did! I might have known it!

JIM. Oh, maybe Shakespeare wrote a poem on that light bill, Mrs. Wingfield?

AMANDA. Maybe he did, too. I might have known better than to trust him with it! There's such a high price for negligence in this world today.

JIM. Maybe the poem will win a ten-dollar prize.

AMANDA. We'll just have to spend the rest of the evening in the nineteenth century, before Mr. Edison found that Mazda lamp!

JIM. Candle-light is my favorite kind of light.

AMANDA. That shows you're romantic! But that's no excuse for Tom. However, I think it was very nice of them to let us finish our dinner before they plunged us into everlasting darkness. Tom, as a penalty for your carelessness you can help me with the dishes.

JIM. *(Rising. Tom rises.)* Can I be of some help, ma'am?

AMANDA. *(Rising.)* Oh, no, I couldn't allow that.

JIM. Well, I ought to be good for *something.*

AMANDA. What did I hear?

JIM. I just said, "I ought to be good for something."

AMANDA. That's what I thought you said. Well, Laura's all by her lonesome out front. Maybe you'd like to keep her company. I can give you this lovely old candelabrum for light. *(Jim takes candles.)* It used to be on the altar at the Church of the Heavenly Rest, but it was melted a little out of shape when the church burnt down. The church was struck by lightning one spring, and Gypsy Jones who was holding a revival meeting in the village, said that the church was struck by lightning because the Episcopalians had started to have card parties right in the church.

JIM. Is that so, ma'am?

AMANDA. I never say anything that isn't so.

JIM. I beg your pardon.

AMANDA. (Pouring wine into glass—hands it to Jim.) I'd like Laura to have a little dandelion wine. Do you think you can hold them both?

JIM. I can try, ma'am.

AMANDA. (Exits U. R. into kitchen.) Now, Tom, you get into your apron.

TOM. Yes, Mother. (Follows Amanda. Jim looks around, puts wine-glass down, takes swig from wine decanter, replaces it with thud, takes wine-glass—enters living-room. Inner curtains close as dining-room dims out. Laura sits up nervously as Jim enters. Her speech at first is low and breathless from the almost intolerable strain of being alone with a stranger. In her speeches in this scene, before Jim's warmth overcomes her paralyzing shyness, Laura's voice is thin and breathless as though she has just run up a steep flight of stairs.)

JIM. (Entering holding candelabra with lighted candles in one hand and glass of wine in other, and stands.) How are you feeling now? Any better? (Jim's attitude is gently humorous. In playing this scene it should be stressed that while the incident is apparently unimportant, it is to Laura the climax of her secret life.)

LAURA. Yes, thank you.

JIM. (Gives her glass of wine.) Oh, here, this is for you. It's a little dandelion wine.

LAURA. Thank you.

JIM. (Crosses C.) Well, drink it—but don't get drunk. (He laughs heartily.) Say, where'll I put the candles?

LAURA. Oh, anywhere . . .

JIM. Oh, how about right here on the floor? You got any objections?

LAURA. No.

JIM. I'll just spread a newspaper under it to catch the drippings. (Gets newspaper from armchair. Puts candelabra down on floor C.) I like to sit on the floor. (Sits on floor.) Mind if I do?

LAURA. Oh, no.

JIM. Would you give me a pillow?

LAURA. What?

JIM. A pillow!

LAURA. Oh . . . (Puts wine-glass on telephone table, hands him pillow, sits L. on day-bed.)

JIM. How about you? Don't you like to sit on the floor?

LAURA. Oh, yes.

JIM. Well, why don't you?

LAURA. I—will.

JIM. Take a pillow! (Throws pillow as she sits on floor.) I can't see you sitting way over there. (Sits on floor again.)

LAURA. I can—see you.

JIM. Yeah, but that's not fair. I'm right here in the limelight. (Laura moves a little closer to him.) Good! Now I can see you! Are you comfortable?

LAURA. Yes. Thank you.

JIM. So am I. I'm comfortable as a cow! Say, would you care for a piece of chewing-gum? (Offers gum.)

LAURA. No, thank you.

JIM. I think that I will indulge. (Musingly unwraps it and holds it up.) Gee, think of the fortune made by the guy that invented the first piece of chewing-gum! It's amazing, huh? Do you know that the Wrigley Building is one of the sights of Chicago? —I saw it summer before last at the Century of Progress.[1]—Did you take in the Century of Progress?

LAURA. No, I didn't.

JIM. Well, it was a wonderful exposition, believe me. You know what impressed me most? The Hall of Science. Gives you an idea of what the future will be like in America. Oh, it's more wonderful than the present time is! Say, your brother tells me you're shy. Is that right, Laura?

LAURA. I—don't know.

JIM. I judge you to be an old-fashioned type of girl. Oh, I think that's a wonderful type to be. I hope you don't think I'm being too personal—do you?

LAURA. Mr. O'Connor?

JIM. Huh?

LAURA. I believe I will take a piece of gum, if you don't mind. (Jim peels gum—gets on knees, hands it to Laura. She breaks off a tiny piece. Jim looks at what remains, puts it in his mouth, and sits again.) Mr. O'Connor, have you—kept up with your singing?

JIM. Singing? Me?

LAURA. Yes. I remember what a beautiful voice you had.

JIM. You heard me sing?

LAURA. Oh, yes! Very often. . . . I—don't suppose— you remember me—at all?

---

1. *Century of Progress*, the world's fair held in Chicago in 1933–1934.

JIM. (*Smiling doubtfully.*) You know, as a matter of fact I did have an idea I'd seen you before. Do you know it seemed almost like I was about to remember your name. But the name I was about to remember—wasn't a name! So I stopped myself before I said it.

LAURA. Wasn't it—Blue Roses?

JIM. (*Grinning.*) Blue Roses! Oh, my gosh, yes—Blue Roses! You know, I didn't connect you with high school somehow or other. But that's where it was, it was high school. Gosh, I didn't even know you were Shakespeare's sister! Gee, I'm sorry.

LAURA. I didn't expect you to.—You—barely knew me!

JIM. But, we did have a speaking acquaintance.

LAURA. Yes, we—spoke to each other.

JIM. Say, didn't we have a class in something together?

LAURA. Yes, we did.

JIM. What class was that?

LAURA. It was—singing—chorus!

JIM. Aw!

LAURA. I sat across the aisle from you in the auditorium. Mondays, Wednesdays and Fridays.

JIM. Oh, yeah! I remember now—you're the one who always came in late.

LAURA. Yes, it was so hard for me, getting upstairs. I had that brace on my leg then—it clumped so loud!

JIM. I never heard any clumping.

LAURA. (*Wincing at recollection.*) To me it sounded like—thunder!

JIM. I never even noticed.

LAURA. Everybody was seated before I came in. I had to walk in front of all those people. My seat was in the back row. I had to go clumping up the aisle with everyone watching!

JIM. Oh, gee, you shouldn't have been selfconscious.

LAURA. I know, but I was. It was always such a relief when the singing started.

JIM. I remember now. And I used to call you Blue Roses. How did I ever get started calling you a name like that?

LAURA. I was out of school a little while with pleurosis. When I came back you asked me what was the matter. I said I had pleurosis and you thought I said Blue Roses. So that's what you always called me after that!

JIM. I hope you didn't mind?

LAURA. Oh, no—I liked it. You see, I wasn't acquainted with many—people . . .

JIM. Yeah. I remember you sort of stuck by yourself.

LAURA. I never did have much luck at making friends.

JIM. Well, I don't see why you wouldn't.

LAURA. Well, I started out badly.

JIM. You mean being——?

LAURA. Well, yes, it—sort of—stood between me . . .

JIM. You shouldn't have let it!

LAURA. I know, but it did, and I——

JIM. You mean you were shy with people!

LAURA. I tried not to be but never could——

JIM. Overcome it?

LAURA. No, I—never could!

JIM. Yeah. I guess being shy is something you have to work out of kind of gradually.

LAURA. Yes—I guess it——

JIM. Takes time!

LAURA. Yes . . .

JIM. Say, you know something, Laura? (*Rises to sit on day-bed* R.) People are not so dreadful when you know them. That's what you have to remember! And everybody has problems, not just you but practically everybody has problems. You think of yourself as being the only one who is disappointed. But just look around you and what do you see—a lot of people just as disappointed as you are. You take me, for instance. Boy, when I left high school I thought I'd be a lot further along at this time than I am now. Say, you remember that wonderful write-up I had in "The Torch"?

LAURA. Yes, I do! (*She gets year-book from under pillow* L. *of day-bed.*)

JIM. Said I was bound to succeed in anything I went into! Holy Jeez! "The Torch"! (*She opens book, shows it to him and sits next to him on day-bed.*)

LAURA. Here you are in "The Pirates of Penzance"!

JIM. "The Pirates"! "Oh, better far to live and die under the brave black flag I fly!" I sang the lead in that operetta.

LAURA. So beautifully!

JIM. Aw . . .

LAURA. Yes, yes—beautifully—beautifully!

JIM. You heard me then, huh?

LAURA. I heard you all three times!

JIM. No!

LAURA. Yes.

JIM. You mean all three performances?

LAURA. Yes!

JIM. What for?

LAURA. I—wanted to ask you to—autograph my program. (*Takes program from book.*)

JIM. Why didn't you ask me?

LAURA. You were always surrounded by your own friends so much that I never had a chance.

JIM. Aw, you should have just come right up and said, "Here is my——"

LAURA. Well, I—thought you might think I was——

JIM. Thought I might think you was—what?

LAURA. Oh——

JIM. (With reflective relish.) Oh! Yeah, I was beleaguered by females in those days.

LAURA. You were terribly popular!

JIM. Yeah . . .

LAURA. You had such a—friendly way——

JIM. Oh, I was spoiled in high school.

LAURA. Everybody liked you!

JIM. Including you?

LAURA. I—why, yes, I—I did, too. . . .

JIM. Give me that program, Laura. (She does so, and he signs it.) There you are—better late than never!

LAURA. My—what a—surprise!

JIM. My signature's not worth very much right now. But maybe some day—it will increase in value! You know, being disappointed is one thing and being discouraged is something else. Well, I may be disappointed but I am not discouraged. Say, you finished high school?

LAURA. I made bad grades in my final examinations.

JIM. You mean you dropped out?

LAURA. (Rises.) I didn't go back. (Crosses R. to menagerie. Jim lights cigarette still sitting on day-bed. Laura puts year-book under menagerie. Rises, picks up unicorn—small glass object—her back to Jim. When she touches unicorn, MUSIC CUE # 16-A.) How is—Emily Meisenbach getting along?

JIM. That kraut-head!

LAURA. Why do you call her that?

JIM. Because that's what she was.

LAURA. You're not still—going with her?

JIM. Oh, I never even see her.

LAURA. It said in the Personal section that you were —engaged!

JIM. Uh-huh. I know, but I wasn't impressed by that —propaganda!

LAURA. It wasn't—the truth?

JIM. It was only true in Emily's optimistic opinion!

LAURA. Oh . . . (Turns R. of Jim. Jim lights a cigarette and leans indolently back on his elbows smiling at Laura with a warmth and charm which lights her inwardly with altar candles. She remains by the glass menagerie table and turns in her hands a piece of glass to cover her tumult. CUT MUSIC #16-A.)

JIM. What have you done since high school? Huh?

LAURA. What?

JIM. I said what have you done since high school?

LAURA. Nothing much.

JIM. You must have been doing something all this time.

LAURA. Yes.

JIM. Well, then, such as what?

LAURA. I took a business course at business college . . .

JIM. You did? How did that work out?

LAURA. (Turns back to Jim.) Well, not very—well. . . . I had to drop out, it gave me—indigestion. . . .

JIM. (Laughs gently.) What are you doing now?

LAURA. I don't do anything—much. . . . Oh, please don't think I sit around doing nothing! My glass collection takes a good deal of time. Glass is something you have to take good care of.

JIM. What did you say—about glass?

LAURA. (She clears her throat and turns away again, acutely shy.) Collection, I said—I have one.

JIM. (Puts out cigarette. Abruptly.) Say! You know what I judge to be the trouble with you? (Rises from day-bed and crosses R.) Inferiority complex! You know what that is? That's what they call it when a fellow low-rates himself! Oh, I understand it because I had it, too. Uh-huh! Only my case was not as aggravated as yours seems to be. I had it until I took up public speaking and developed my voice, and learned that I had an aptitude for science. Do you know that until that time I never thought of myself as being outstanding in any way whatsoever!

LAURA. Oh, my!

JIM. Now I've never made a regular study of it— (Sits armchair R.) mind you, but I have a friend who says I can analyze people better than doctors that make a profession of it. I don't claim that's necessarily true, but I can sure guess a person's psychology. Excuse me, Laura. (Takes out gum.) I always take it out when the flavor is gone. I'll just wrap it in a piece of paper. (Tears a piece of paper off the newspaper under candelabrum, wraps gum in it, crosses to day-bed, looks to see if Laura is watching. She isn't. Crosses around day-bed.) I know how it is when you get it stuck on a shoe. (Throws gum under day-bed, crosses around L. of day-bed. Crosses R. to Laura.) Yep— that's what I judge to be your principal trouble. A lack of confidence in yourself as a person. Now I'm basing that fact on a number of your remarks and on certain observations I've made. For instance, that clumping you thought was so awful in high school. You say that you dreaded to go upstairs? You see what you did? You dropped out of school, you gave up an education all because of a little clump, which as far as I can see is practically non-existent! Oh, a little physical defect is all you have. It's hardly noticeable even! Magnified a thousand times by your imagination! You know what my strong advice to you is? You've got to think of yourself as *superior* in some way! (*Crosses* L. *to small table* R. *of day-bed. Sits. Laura sits in armchair.*)

LAURA. In what way would I think?

JIM. Why, man alive, Laura! Look around you a little and what do you see? A world full of common people! All of 'em born and all of 'em going to die! Now, which of them has one-tenth of your strong points! Or mine! Or anybody else's for that matter? You see, everybody excels in some one thing. Well—some in many! You take me, for instance. My interest happens to lie in electrodynamics. I'm taking a course in radio engineering at night school, on top of a fairly responsible job at the warehouse. I'm taking that course *and* studying public speaking.

LAURA. Ohhhh. My!

JIM. Because I believe in the future of television! I want to be ready to go right up along with it. (*Rises, crosses* R.) I'm planning to get in on the ground floor. Oh, I've already made the right connections. All that remains now is for the industry itself to get under way—full steam! You know, *knowledge*—ZSZZppp! *Money*—Zzzzzzpp! *POWER*! Wham! That's the cycle democracy is built on! (*Pause.*) I guess you think I think a lot of myself!

LAURA. No—o-o-o, I don't.

JIM. (*Kneels at armchair* R.) Well, now how about you? Isn't there some one thing that you take more interest in than anything else?

LAURA. Oh—yes . . .

JIM. Well, then, such as what?

LAURA. Well, I do—as I said—have my—glass collection . . . (MUSIC CUE #16-A.)

JIM. Oh, you do. What kind of glass is it?

LAURA. (*Takes glass ornament off shelf.*) Little articles of it, ornaments mostly. Most of them are little animals made out of glass, the tiniest little animals in the world. Mother calls them the glass menag-

erie! Here's an example of one, if you'd like to see it! This is one of the oldest, it's nearly thirteen. (*Hands it to Jim.*) Oh, be careful—if you breathe, it breaks! (THE BELL SOLO SHOULD BEGIN HERE. *This is last part of* CUE #16-A *and should play to end of record.*)

JIM. I'd better not take it. I'm pretty clumsy with things.

LAURA. Go on, I trust you with him! (*Jim takes horse.*) There—you're holding him gently! Hold him over the light, he loves the light! (*Jim holds horse up to light.*) See how the light shines through him?

JIM. It sure does shine!

LAURA. I shouldn't be partial, but he is my favorite one.

JIM. Say, what kind of a thing is this one supposed to be?

LAURA. Haven't you noticed the single horn on his forehead?

JIM. Oh, a unicorn, huh?

LAURA. Mmmm-hmmmmm!

JIM. Unicorns, aren't they extinct in the modern world?

LAURA. I know!

JIM. Poor little fellow must feel kind of lonesome.

LAURA. Well, if he does he doesn't complain about it. He stays on a shelf with some horses that don't have horns and they all seem to get along nicely together.

JIM. They do. Say, where will I put him?

LAURA. Put him on the table. (*Jim crosses to small table* R. *of day-bed, puts unicorn on it.*) They all like a change of scenery once in a while!

JIM. (C., *facing upstage, stretching arms.*) They do. (MUSIC CUE #16-B: *Dance Music.*) Hey! Look how big my shadow is when I stretch.

LAURA. (*Crossing to* L. *of day-bed.*) Oh, oh, yes—it stretched across the ceiling!

JIM. (*Crosses to door* R., *exits, leaving door open, and stands on fire-escape landing. Sings to music.* [*Popular record of day for dance-hall.*] *When Jim opens door, music swells.*) It's stopped raining. Where does the music come from?

LAURA. From the Paradise Dance Hall across the alley.

JIM. (*Re-entering room, closing door* R., *crosses to Laura.*) How about cutting the rug a little, Miss Wingfield? Or is your program filled up? Let me take a look at it. (*Crosses back* C. *Music, in dance hall, goes into a waltz. Business here with imagi-*

nary dance-program card.) Oh, say! Every dance is taken! I'll just scratch some of them out. Ahhhh, a waltz! *(Crosses to Laura.)*

LAURA. I—can't dance!

JIM. There you go with that inferiority stuff!

LAURA. I've never danced in my life!

JIM. Come on, try!

LAURA. Oh, but I'd step on you!

JIM. Well, I'm not made out of glass.

LAURA. How—how do we start?

JIM. You hold your arms out a little.

LAURA. Like this?

JIM. A little bit higher. *(Takes Laura in arms.)* That's right. Now don't tighten up, that's the principal thing about it—just relax.

LAURA. It's hard not to.

JIM. Okay.

LAURA. I'm afraid you can't budge me.

JIM. *(Dances around L. of day-bed slowly.)* What do you bet I can't?

LAURA. Goodness, yes, you can!

JIM. Let yourself go, now, Laura, just let yourself go.

LAURA. I'm——

JIM. Come on!

LAURA. Trying!

JIM. Not so stiff now—easy does it!

LAURA. I know, but I'm——!

JIM. Come on! Loosen your backbone a little! *(When they get to up-stage corner of day-bed—so that the audience will not see him lift her—Jim's arm tightens around her waist and he swings her around C. with her feet off floor about 3 complete turns before they hit the small table R. of day-bed. Music swells as Jim lifts her.)* There we go! *(Jim knocks glass horse off table. MUSIC FADES.)*

LAURA. Oh, it doesn't matter——

JIM. *(Picks horse up.)* We knocked the little glass horse over.

LAURA. Yes.

JIM. *(Hands unicorn to Laura.)* Is he broken?

LAURA. Now he's just like all the other horses.

JIM. You mean he lost his——?

LAURA. He's lost his horn. It doesn't matter. Maybe it's a blessing in disguise.

JIM. Gee, I bet you'll never forgive me. I bet that was your favorite piece of glass.

LAURA. Oh, I don't have favorites—*(Pause.)* much. It's no tragedy. Glass breaks so easily. No matter how careful you are. The traffic jars the shelves and things fall off them.

JIM. Still I'm awfully sorry that I was the cause of it.

LAURA. I'll just imagine he had an operation. The horn was removed to make him feel less—freakish! *(Crosses L., sits on small table.)* Now he will feel more at home with the other horses, the ones who don't have horns. . . .

JIM. *(Sits on arm of armchair R., faces Laura.)* I'm glad to see that you have a sense of humor. You know—you're—different than anybody else I know? (MUSIC CUE #17.) Do you mind me telling you that? I mean it. You make me feel sort of—I don't know how to say it! I'm usually pretty good at expressing things, but—this is something I don't know how to say! Did anybody ever tell you that you were pretty? *(Rises, crosses to Laura.)* Well, you are! And in a different way from anyone else. And all the nicer because of the difference. Oh, boy, I wish that you were my sister. I'd teach you to have confidence in yourself. Being different is nothing to be ashamed of. Because other people aren't such wonderful people. They're a hundred times one thousand. You're one times one! They walk all over the earth. You just stay here. They're as common as—weeds, but—you, well you're—*Blue Roses!*

LAURA. But blue is—wrong for—roses . . .

JIM. It's right for you!—You're pretty!

LAURA. In what respect am I pretty?

JIM. In all respects—your eyes—your hair. Your hands are pretty! You think I'm saying this because I'm invited to dinner and have to be nice. Oh, I could do that! I could say lots of things without being sincere. But I'm talking to you sincerely. I happened to notice you had this inferiority complex that keeps you from feeling comfortable with people. Somebody ought to build your confidence up—way up! and make you proud instead of shy and turning away and—blushing——*(Jim lifts Laura up on small table on "way up.")* Somebody—ought to—*(Lifts her down.)* somebody ought to—kiss you, Laura! *(They kiss. Jim releases her and turns slowly away, crossing a little D. R. Then, quietly, to himself: As Jim turns away, MUSIC ENDS.)* Gee, I shouldn't have done that—that was way off the beam. *(Gives way D. R. Turns to Laura. Laura sits on small table.)* Would you care for a cigarette? You don't smoke, do you? How about a mint? Peppermint—Life-Saver? My pocket's a regular drug-store. . . . Laura, you know, if I had a sister like you, I'd do the same thing as Tom. I'd bring fellows home to meet you. Maybe I shouldn't be saying this. That may not have been the idea in having me over. But what if it was? There's nothing wrong with that.—The only trouble is that in my case—I'm not in a position to——I can't ask for your number and say I'll phone. I can't call up next week end—ask for a date. I thought I had better explain the situation in case you—misunderstood and I hurt your feelings . . .

LAURA. *(Faintly.)* You—won't—call again?

JIM. *(Crossing to* R. *of day-bed, and sitting.)* No, I can't. You see, I've—got strings on me. Laura, I've—been going steady! I go out all the time with a girl named Betty. Oh, she's a nice quiet home girl like you, and Catholic and Irish, and in a great many ways we—get along fine. I met her last summer on a moonlight boat trip up the river to Alton, on the *Majestic.* Well—right away from the start it was—love! Oh, boy, being in love has made a new man of me! The power of love is pretty tremendous! Love is something that—changes the whole world. It happened that Betty's aunt took sick and she got a wire and had to go to Centralia. So naturally when Tom asked me to dinner—naturally I accepted the invitation, not knowing—I mean—not knowing. I wish that you would—say something. *(Laura gives Jim unicorn.)* What are you doing that for? You mean you want me to have him? What for?

LAURA. A—souvenir. *(She crosses* R. *to menagerie. Jim rises.)*

AMANDA. *(Off-stage.)* I'm coming, children. *(She enters into dining-room from kitchen* R.*)* I thought you'd like some liquid refreshment. *(Puts tray on small table. Lifts a glass.)* Mr. O'Connor, have you heard that song about lemonade? It's "Lemonade, lemonade,
Made in the shade and stirred with a spade—
And then it's good enough for any old maid!"

JIM. No, ma'am, I never heard it.

AMANDA. Why are you so serious, honey? *(To Laura.)*

JIM. Well, we were having a serious conversation.

AMANDA. I don't understand modern young people. When I was a girl I was gay about everything.

JIM. You haven't changed a bit, Mrs. Wingfield.

AMANDA. I suppose it's the gaiety of the occasion that has rejuvenated me. Well, here's to the gaiety of the occasion! *(Spills lemonade on dress.)* Oooo! I baptized myself. *(Puts glass on small table* R.

of day-bed.) I found some cherries in the kitchen, and I put one in each glass.

JIM. You shouldn't have gone to all that trouble, ma'am.

AMANDA. It was no trouble at all. Didn't you hear us cutting up in the kitchen? I was so outdone with Tom for not bringing you over sooner, but now you've found your way I want you to come all the time—not just once in a while—but all the time. Oh, I think I'll go back in that kitchen. *(Starts to exit* U. C.*)*

JIM. Oh, no, ma'am, please don't go, ma'am. As a matter of fact, I've got to be going.

AMANDA. Oh, Mr. O'Connor, it's only the shank of the evening! *(Jim and Amanda stand* U. C.*)*

JIM. Well, you know how it is.

AMANDA. You mean you're a young working man and have to keep workingmen's hours?

JIM. Yes, ma'am.

AMANDA. Well, we'll let you off early this time, but only on the condition that you stay later next time, much later——What's the best night for you? Saturday?

JIM. Well, as a matter of fact, I have a couple of time-clocks to punch, Mrs. Wingfield, one in the morning and another one at night!

AMANDA. Oh, isn't that nice, you're so ambitious! You work at night, too?

JIM. No, ma'am, not work but—Betty!

AMANDA. *(Crosses* L. *below day-bed.)* Betty? Who's Betty?

JIM. Oh, just a girl. The girl I go steady with!

AMANDA. You mean it's serious? *(Crosses* D. L.*)*

JIM. Oh, yes, ma'am. We're going to be married the second Sunday in June.

AMANDA. *(Sits on day-bed.)* Tom didn't say anything at all about your going to be married?

JIM. Well, the cat's not out of the bag at the warehouse yet. *(Picks up hat from telephone table.)* You know how they are. They call you Romeo and stuff like that.—It's been a wonderful evening, Mrs. Wingfield. I guess this is what they mean by Southern hospitality.

AMANDA. It was nothing. Nothing at all.

JIM. I hope it don't seem like I'm rushing off. But I promised Betty I'd pick her up at the Wabash depot an' by the time I get my jalopy down there her train'll be in. Some women are pretty upset if you keep them waiting.

AMANDA. Yes, I know all about the tyranny of

women! Well, good-bye, Mr. O'Connor. (*Amanda puts out hand. Jim takes it.*) I wish you happiness —and good fortune. You wish him that, too, don't you, Laura?

LAURA. Yes, I do, Mother.

JIM. (*Crosses* L. *to Laura.*) Good-bye, Laura. I'll always treasure that souvenir. And don't you forget the good advice I gave you. So long, Shakespeare! (*Up* C.) Thanks, again, ladies.—Good night! (*He grins and ducks jauntily out* R.)

AMANDA. (*Faintly.*) Well, well, well. Things have a way of turning out so badly —— (*Laura crosses to phonograph, puts on record.*) I don't believe that I would play the victrola. Well, well—well, our gentleman caller was engaged to be married! Tom!

TOM. (*Off.*) Yes, Mother?

AMANDA. Come out here. I want to tell you something very funny.

TOM. (*Entering through* R. *kitchen door to dining-room and into living-room, through curtains,* D. C.) Has the gentleman caller gotten away already?

AMANDA. The gentleman caller made a very early departure. That was a nice joke you played on us, too!

TOM. How do you mean?

AMANDA. You didn't mention that he was engaged to be married.

TOM. Jim? Engaged?

AMANDA. That's what he just informed us.

TOM. I'll be jiggered! I didn't know.

AMANDA. That seems very peculiar.

TOM. What's peculiar about it?

AMANDA. Didn't you tell me he was your best friend down at the warehouse?

TOM. He is, but how did I know?

AMANDA. It seems very peculiar you didn't know your best friend was engaged to be married!

TOM. The warehouse is the place where I work, not where I know things about people!

AMANDA. You don't know things anywhere! You live in a dream; you manufacture illusions! (*Tom starts for* R. *door.*) Where are you going? Where are you going? Where are you going?

TOM. I'm going to the movies.

AMANDA. (*Rises, crosses up to Tom.*) That's right, now that you've had us make such fools of ourselves. The effort, the preparations, all the expense! The new floor lamp, the rug, the clothes for Laura! All for what? To entertain some other girl's fiancé! Go to the movies, go! Don't think about us, a mother deserted, an unmarried sister who's crippled and has no job! Don't let anything interfere with your selfish pleasure! Just go, go, go—to the movies!

TOM. All right, I will, and the more you shout at me about my selfish pleasures, the quicker I'll go, and I won't go to the movies either. (*Gets hat from phone table, slams door* R., *and exits up alley* R.)

AMANDA. (*Crosses up to fire-escape landing, yelling.*) Go, then! Then go to the moon—you selfish dreamer! (MUSIC CUE #18. INTERIOR LIGHT *dims out. Re-enters living-room, slamming* R. *door. Tom's closing speech is timed with the interior pantomime. The interior scene is played as though viewed through soundproof glass, behind outer scrim curtain. Amanda, standing, appears to be making a comforting speech to Laura who is huddled on* R. *side of day-bed. Now that we cannot hear the mother's speech, her silliness is gone and she has dignity and tragic beauty. Laura's hair hides her face until at the end of the speech she lifts it to smile at her mother. Amanda's gestures are slow and graceful, almost dance-like, as she comforts her daughter. Tom, who has meantime put on, as before, the jacket and cap, enters down* R. *from off-stage, and again comes to fire-escape landing, stands as he speaks. Meantime lights are upon Amanda and Laura, but are dim.*)

TOM. I didn't go to the moon. I went much farther. For time is the longest distance between two places. . . . I left Saint Louis. I descended these steps of this fire-escape for the last time and followed, from then on, in my father's footsteps, attempting to find in motion what was lost in space. . . . I travelled around a great deal. The cities swept about me like dead leaves, leaves that were brightly colored but torn away from the branches. I would have stopped, but I was pursued by something. It always came upon me unawares, taking me altogether by surprise. Perhaps it was a familiar bit of music. Perhaps it was only a piece of transparent glass. . . . Perhaps I am walking along a street at night, in some strange city, before I have found companions, and I pass the lighted window of a shop where perfume is sold. The window is filled with pieces of colored glass, tiny transparent bottles in delicate colors, like bits of a shattered rainbow. Then all at once my sister touches my shoulder. I turn around and look into her eyes. . . . Oh, Laura, Laura, I tried to leave you behind me, but I am more faithful than I intended to be! I reach for a cigarette, I cross the street, I run into a movie or a bar. I buy a drink, I speak to the nearest stranger—anything that can blow your candles out!—for nowadays the world is lit by lightning! Blow out your candles, Laura . . . *(Laura blows out candles still burning in candelabrum and the whole interior is blacked out.)* And so—good-bye! *(Exits up alley* R. *Music continues to the end.)*

CURTAIN
(End of play.)

COURTESY OF THE LINCOLN PARK THEATRE, PHOTOS BY WILLIAM FRANKLIN MCMAHON

Many of the elements the dramatist uses in writing a play are the same as those used by, for example, the short-story writer. Most writers of both literary forms make use of a **plot** of limited length acted out by a number of **characters** in a definite **setting.** Yet to the reader the differences between a short story and a play are likely to seem more striking than the resemblances. A play is, after all, almost always written for presentation in a theater, and this fact accounts, to a large extent, for those differences.

When a person picks up a book, he meets the author directly through the printed words. When a person sits in a theater, however, the contact between author and spectator is less direct, since the person is actually confronted only by the stage itself and by the actors. In reading a play it is easy to lose sight of the full effect of these two aspects of the play, since neither stage nor actor is visually present to the reader. With some practice the reader can supply with his imagination the full effect that is obvious to the person sitting in the theater. But to do this the reader must know what to look for in the author's descriptions of set, lighting, and placement of actors, and also how the playwright goes about developing and judging the characters.

Staging Understanding the author's use of staging is especially important today because modern playwrights have a wide variety of theatrical styles from which to choose. There are two reasons for this variety. First, since the time of the great Norwegian dramatist Henrik Ibsen (1828–1906), playwrights have frequently experimented with radically new ways of writing plays. Each of these new ways demanded its own theatrical style—a manner of staging which would complement the new literary form. Thus, for example, the so-called **realist** drama was associated with realistic techniques of staging; the **expressionist** drama demanded techniques for going beneath the surface reality to expose mental life—devices which have come to be called **expressionistic.** Contemporary playwrights, Americans in particular, have usually not been content to follow exclusively any one of these experimental ways of writing. Instead they have often created modes of writing, and, in the matter of staging, they have used a combination of staging techniques developed by earlier schools of play writing. A second source of the variety in staging is experimentation with stage design and methods of acting by famous producers.

Schools of Play Writing Most persistent among the modern schools of play writing is that for which Ibsen himself was most noted: **realism.** Realists felt that pre-Ibsen drama showed men as being more noble, more beautiful, more powerful than they really are. For this they substituted a drama that shows ordinary men, struggling against the unspectacular and unpleasant problems of ordinary life, and

succeeding no better than men ordinarily do. The staging that has become associated with realist drama can be described as the living room of a household in which the "fourth wall" has been turned into a one-way mirror: the audience can see in, but the characters cannot see out. In the room the audience discovers appropriate furnishings, often specified in great detail by the author. The set is not designed to dazzle the spectator with its beauty, but to imitate the worn, or vulgarly ostentatious, or dilapidated surroundings that are often encountered in reality. The set reflects the ugliness, meanness, or triviality that the typical realist believes surrounds the lives of most people. The reader is, of course, expected to recognize the kind of contribution these elements make to the play as a whole.

Playwrights who saw the basic human condition in a different light than the realists did began searching for other dramatic forms almost as soon as realism became popularly established. The **symbolists'** aim was to do justice to the beauty and deeper realities of man's life. The use of symbolic characters and, especially, symbolic settings was of primary importance in evoking feelings that could not be expressed in literal terms. Pure symbolist drama did not prove to be a lasting form, but later dramatists have found some elements of symbolist drama useful. The reader of contemporary plays must therefore be alert to the possible use of characters to symbolize whole classes of men, for example, or the use of symbolic settings or stage properties by which the author suggests things about characters which they cannot tell about themselves.

Expressionists agreed largely with the realists that in its outward aspect modern life is often empty, trivial, and oppressive; but they believed that much excitement and value could be found in modern life if one could only look inside of people. They presented this subjective life on the stage by presenting dreams, nightmares, memories—the whole internal drama of hopes, fears, and regrets common to all people. The representation of mental drama demanded special staging techniques: special lighting, exaggerated sound effects, use of scrims (a backdrop curtain that becomes transparent when lighted from behind), madly whirling stage platforms, and other appropriate nonrealistic devices. Expressionism, like symbolism, is no longer an active movement in the theater, but it has shown later dramatists the possibilities of presenting on stage what is going on in the mind of one of the characters. The flashback—showing something that happened in the past as remembered by one of the characters—has become widely used, even in motion pictures. In plays that employ expressionist techniques the reader must watch for the clues that will indicate the nature of what is happening—whether it is "real" action or "mental" action. He must also bear in mind that *how* a character dreams or remembers tells something about that character.

In the 1920's still another school of play writing was developed called **epic realism.** Epic realists agree with antirealist schools that realism itself is too restricted. They believe that since a play is not life, but is really a play, anything that can be done in a theater can be of legitimate use. Epic theater is frankly theatrical: actors address the audience, stylized gestures are used. Staging often calls for carrying titles on stage or flashing them on a screen, altering sets in mid-scene, and using sets that will allow the showing of action taking place at the same time but in different locales. These complexities of time and place, which can be made obvious on stage, call for additional care on the part of the reader.

All these theatrical forms are further complicated by the experiments of producers with methods of staging. Two of the most important are (1) the **empty stage,** which centers the attention of the audience on the characters themselves, and (2) the **plastic theater,** in which lighting is used to mold the actors into something resembling moving sculpture.

Most major American dramatists of this century have combined elements of staging from more than one of these styles, depending on each to add its own characteristic effect in reinforcing the central ideas of the play. Tennessee Williams' play *The Glass Menagerie*, in this chapter, is a good example of such a synthesis. The tenement setting, hemming in the lives of the characters, is in the **realistic** tradition. At least one of the characters, the fire-escape entrance, and the collection of glass animals are explicitly **symbolic.** Nearly the whole play is the memory of one of the characters, and is to that extent **expressionistic** in form. Techniques used by **epic realists** include: a character who addresses the audience as narrator and the showing of simultaneous scenes in two rooms. And Williams uses the light-modeling of the **plastic theater** to show how memory colors the thing remembered.

Characters However complex theatrical style may be, it remains only one aspect of the play. The center of interest remains in the characters. The dramatist must succeed in communicating two things by means of these characters: (1) the feelings and attitudes of the characters themselves, and (2) his judgment on the characters and their attitudes. This fact is obvious in the typical Western. Here there are basically two characters: the hero and the villain. The villain will do anything to gain a selfish advantage, but the hero lives and fights strictly by the code. This is most dramatically revealed in the final crucial situation, but the attitudes of the villain and hero are made clear from the beginning, even by look, dress, and bearing. Given such clearly good and bad characters, the judgment of them for the most part is obvious.

The literary dramatist, on the other hand, must make a more complex judgement, and make it about more complex characters. If, for example, a character who demonstrates many virtues suddenly commits an act of dishonesty, the audience or reader wants to know how to feel about this character. Are the circumstances of the act such that he can be excused, or does he merely become pitiful, or laughable, or wretched, or disgusting? These judgments are not obvious; the dramatist must use every means at his disposal to communicate exactly the shade of feeling which he thinks is right. It is in his ability to communicate to an audience his judgment on the characters he has created—and to make this judgment one that the audience will accept as being in harmony with the characters—that the playwright most surely shows his mastery of drama.

DISCUSSION

In the first part of a play, the dramatist's objective must usually be to make his characters introduce themselves. To do this without seeming awkward, he must involve them in events in which they will naturally reveal enough of their past and of their personalities so that the audience can understand their present situation and their attitudes toward it. Review the first three scenes: Which character is most fully revealed in each scene? What dramatic situation does the author create to make the character reveal himself? Is the situation plausible?

The basic situation in which all the characters are placed is simply the Wingfield family involvement. What special conditions exist in the Wingfield family that make it an especially trying situation for these characters? How are these conditions revealed early in the play? What are the involvements among the members of the entire·family as they are revealed in the first three scenes?

Each of the characters has a private world into which he sometimes retreats when the real world becomes unbearable. What kinds of situations does each character find unpleasant? What is the nature of the private world into which each retreats?

FOR EXPLORATION

Act I, Scene 1

1. Reread the description of the setting at the beginning of Scene 1 (page 285 M). (*a*) What do you learn about the condition of the Wingfield family from this setting? (*b*) What feeling does it convey?

2. (*a*) What two functions does Tom have in the play? (*b*) What difference in temperament do you notice between Tom as Narrator and Tom as Character? (*c*) What is meant by Tom's remark, "The play is memory"?

3. How is the fact that there is tension in the family revealed at the outset?

4. (*a*) What do you learn about Amanda's past in this scene? (*b*) How does she view her past? (*c*) What indications are there that her past was not exactly as she remembers it?

Scene 2

1. What do you learn about Laura in this scene?

2. (*a*) In what ways does it appear Amanda has been trying to help Laura? (*b*) Why have her efforts failed? (*c*) What alternative does Amanda decide upon toward the end of this scene? (*d*) What are the prospects, at this point, for the success of her plan? Explain.

Scenes 3 and 4

1. (*a*) What is the source of the fight between Tom and his mother? (*b*) Why is Tom discontented?

2. (*a*) Amanda calls Tom selfish. To what extent is her accusation fair, to what extent unfair? (*b*) Tom apparently thinks that his mother is making unfair demands upon him. To what extent is this true, to what extent untrue?

Scene 5

1. How does Amanda go about implementing the plan she has formed?

2. (*a*) Why does Amanda attempt to sell magazines by telephone? (*b*) What does this show about her character? (*c*) What effect does the episode create?

Scene 6

1. Humor is much more obvious when a play is performed than when it is read. There is humor throughout *The Glass Menagerie*, but in this scene it predominates. (*a*) Point out how Tom teases his mother with his announcement. (*b*) How might the actors point up the humor of this scene? (*c*) Quote some lines that are particularly funny.

2. (*a*) How does this scene advance the action? (*b*) What indication is there of the fate of Amanda's plan?

DISCUSSION

In the final part of the play the dramatist usually presents the main characters in a climactic situation. This situation is one in which he can best reveal the strength and weakness of the characters and of their ways of looking at things. It is here that the author's judgment is fully revealed. In this play Jim's visit brings about the climactic situation. Because he is an up-and-coming employee of the shoe company, because Laura was in love with him at school, and because he is the "gentleman caller," Jim represents a typically threatening situation to each of the other characters. How does Jim's visit to the Wingfield home bring about a situation that is trying to Tom, Laura, and Amanda?

Williams has said that what happens to a person is not so important as the attitude with which he meets it. How does each character react to the threat that Jim represents—to what extent does each retreat into his private world? To what extent does each try to face the situation realistically?

FOR EXPLORATION

Act II, Scenes 7 and 8

1. Explain how Laura feels and why she reacts as she does at each of the following points: (*a*) her mother tells her to let Jim in; (*b*) she starts to join Jim and the family at dinner; (*c*) Jim joins Laura in the parlor; (*d*) Jim dances with her and kisses her; (*e*) Jim explains that he is engaged.
2. Describe Jim O'Connor, paying particular attention to: (*a*) Tom's description of him (page M 286, column a, paragraph 1) as "an emissary from a world that we were some-how set apart from"; (*b*) Jim's reaction to Amanda; (*c*) his view of himself; (*d*) his reasons for liking Tom and Laura; (*e*) the fairness of his treatment of Laura.
3. (*a*) What is Amanda's reaction to the failure of her plan? (*b*) How does this affect your attitude toward her?
4. Why has Laura's image haunted Tom since his leaving home?

CREATIVE RESPONSE

1. Discuss the symbolism of each of the following, what each shows about a character or characters and their problems:

> Amanda's dress
> The glass menagerie
> The candelabrum and its history
> Blue roses

2. Reread Emerson's essay "Traveling." (page C 132) Then, in class, consider Tom's last speech. Would Tom agree with Emerson's views? Disagree? How? Why?

PROP LIST

Glass Swan and unicorn, and other glass ornaments
Yearbook (program in book)
Cigarette and matches
Folded newspaper
Typewriter and table; chair; charts
3 dinner plates—forks—bread—beans
Ash-tray
Alarm clock
Rattle, muffler and scarf
2 pillows for couch
2 powder puffs

Vase
Telephone
Lace tablecloth, 3 dinner plates, 4 sets silverware, candelabra, decanter (colored water), 2 wine glasses, silver coffee pot and sugar and creamer, 4 cups and saucers
Newspaper
Jonquils
Chewing-gum
Pencil
Life-savers (mints)

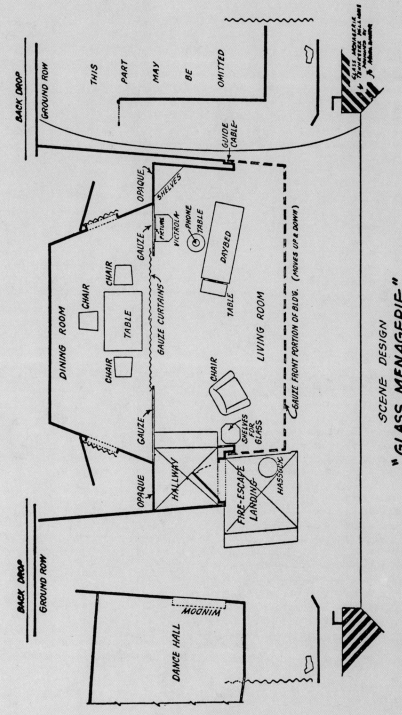

SCENE DESIGN

"GLASS MENAGERIE"

Tennessee Williams   1914 /

JILL KREMENTZ

The first play of Tom ("Tennessee") Williams to appear on Broadway was a sensational flop. For four years thereafter he worked at odd jobs around the country, returning to the theater in 1945 to captivate first Chicago and then New York with *The Glass Menagerie*.

Thomas Lanier Williams was born in Columbus, Mississippi, the son of a shoe salesman and the grandson of an Episcopalian clergyman. The family moved to St. Louis when Tom's father was transferred there. Tom's one ambition was to write, and his aim when he entered college was to learn to do so. But since the elder Williams saw writing as a slow and precarious way of making a living, Tom was recalled from college after little more than a year and sent to work in the shoe factory. Determined to fulfill his dreams of becoming a writer, Tom labored over his manuscripts until two or three o'clock every night. A nervous breakdown ended his shoe-business career. Eventually he returned to college and received an A.B. degree from the University of Iowa in 1938.

In *The Glass Menagerie* Tennessee Williams drew heavily upon the impressions of his early life. The Southern background, the distasteful job, the yearning to write, the drab surroundings—all these are based on memories. The success of this drama established Williams as a playwright. The intense concentration on writing which he had developed in his youth made him a prolific writer, turning out an average of one play every two years. A remarkable number of these have been of high quality and have met with great success, both at home and abroad. They have won him two Pulitzer Prizes and three New York Drama Critics' Circle Awards. And they have established his reputation as one of the foremost playwrights of the contemporary stage.

GLOSSARY OF LITERARY TERMS

ADAPTATION, the redoing of a literary work to fit another genre or audience. For example, many novels, such as *War and Peace,* have been adapted for the movies.

ALLEGORY, a narrative in which characters, action, and sometimes *setting* represent abstract concepts or moral qualities to form a consistent pattern of meaning in a one-to-one relationship.

ALLITERATION, repetition of consonant sounds at the beginnings of words or accented syllables.

ALLUSION, a brief, often indirect, reference to a person, event, or work of art.

AMBIGUITY, the expression of an idea to suggest more than one meaning. Deliberate and effective, ambiguity enriches the meaning of the passage in which it occurs; accidental or ineffective, it blurs the meaning.

ANACHRONISM, placing something at a time or place contrary to historical fact.

ANALOGY, a comparison made between two, frequently dissimilar, items or situations in order to provide insight into the nature of one or both of them.

ANAPEST, three-syllable metrical *foot,* consisting of two unaccented syllables followed by an accented syllable.

ANASTROPHE, inversion of the usual order of the parts of a sentence.

ANTAGONIST, a character who opposes the *protagonist,* often the villain.

ANTI-HERO, a kind of *protagonist* who lacks the conventional heroic qualities; he is frequently an outsider who passively observes the futile lives of those about him. See *hero, romantic hero.*

APHORISM, a short, pithy saying.

APOSTROPHE, a *figure of speech* in which an absent person, an abstract concept, or an inanimate object is addressed directly.

APOTHEGM, a brief saying, terse and pointed; a maxim.

ARCHETYPE, an image, story-pattern, or character type which recurs frequently and evokes strong, often unconscious associations in the reader. For example: the wicked witch, the enchanted prince, the sleeping beauty, and the fairy godmother are widely dispersed throughout folk literature, and appear in slightly different forms in poetry, drama, and novels.

ASSONANCE, repetition of vowel sound.

ATMOSPHERE, the prevailing emotional aura or *tone* of a literary work.

BALLAD, a narrative song passed on in the oral tradition. The ballad *stanza* usually consists of four lines alternating iambic *tetrameter* and *trimeter* and rhyming the second and fourth line. (See *literary ballad.*)

BILDUNGSROMAN, German term ("novel of formation") designating a story depicting the hero's maturing, or movement from childhood to manhood, in a spiritual, educational, or emotional sense.

BLANK VERSE, unrhymed iambic pentameter, ten-syllable lines with five unstressed syllables alternating with five stressed syllables. An unstressed syllable begins the line.

BROADSIDE, a large sheet of paper printed on one side (like a handbill). During earlier periods, some works of literature were distributed as broadsides.

BURLESQUE, a means of ridiculing people, actions, or literary works by mimicking.

CAESURA, pause in a line of verse.

CARICATURE, exaggeration of prominent features of appearance or character.

CARPE DIEM, "seize the day" (Latin), the name applied to a theme frequently found in *lyric* poetry: make the most of youth while you are young.

CATASTROPHE, a term sometimes applied to the ending of a *tragedy,* where the *conflict* is resolved and the actions resulting from the *climax* are completed.

CATHARSIS, a word used by Aristotle in his *Poetics* to describe the desired effect of *tragedy,* the "purgation" of the emotions of pity and fear; that is, in feeling pity and fear for the *tragic hero,* the viewer's own emotional tensions are released and temporarily resolved.

CHARACTERIZATION, *techniques* used by the writer in creating a character.

CLASSIC, in the special sense, the art and literature of Greece and Rome; in the general sense, art and literature of any time recognized as of the highest excellence.

CLASSICAL TRAGEDY, the tragedies of ancient Greece and Rome; those dealing with Greek and Roman subjects; and those written according to the "rules" of tragic drama derived from Aristotle. Such classically constructed plays enjoyed a great revival in the seventeenth and eighteenth centuries.

CLICHÉ, an expression or phrase that is so overused as to become trite.

CLIMAX. As a term of dramatic structure, this refers to the decisive point in a play, where the action changes course and begins to resolve itself. The word is also used to describe the point of highest emotional intensity in a play.

COMEDY, a play written to amuse the audience. In addition to arousing laughter, comic writing often appeals to the intellect. Thus the comic mode has often been used to "instruct" the audience about the follies of certain social conventions and human foibles, as in *satire.*

COMEDY OF MANNERS, a comedy in which the humor arises largely from violations of the conventions of a sophisticated society.

CONCEIT, an elaborate and surprising *figure of speech* comparing two very dissimilar things.

CONFLICT, the struggle that grows out of the interplay between two opposing forces. The four basic kinds of conflict are: (1) a person against another person; (2) a person against nature; (3) a person against society; (4) two elements within a person struggling for mastery.

CONNOTATION, the emotional associations surrounding a word, as opposed to its literal meaning. (See *denotation, diction*.)

CONSONANCE, the repetition of consonant sounds (within a line of poetry, usually).

CONVENTION, any artful *technique* widely accepted as appropriate to a given type of literature.

COUPLET, a *verse form* of two rhyming lines.

CRITICISM, the analysis of works of literature for the purpose of understanding and evaluating them. Criticism is sometimes confined to *explication*.

DACTYL, three-syllable metrical *foot*, consisting of one accented syllable followed by two unaccented syllables.

DENOTATION, the strict, literal meaning of a word. (See *connotation, diction*.)

DENOUEMENT, the final untying of the *plot*.

DEUS EX MACHINA, literally, "god from a machine"—as in ancient Greek drama, in which a god was lowered onto the stage in a machine; now, any element suddenly introduced into a literary work to resolve a situation.

DIALECT, the imitation of regional speech in writing, using altered, phonetic spelling.

DIALOGUE, the conversation between two of more people represented in a literary work. Dialogue can serve many purposes, among them: (1) *characterization* (of those speaking and spoken of); (2) *exposition*; (3) the creation of *mood*; (4) the advancement of *plot*; (5) the development of a *theme*; (6) a comment on the action.

DICTION, the particular choice of words made in a literary work. This choice considers both the *connotative* and the *denotative* meanings of a word and the level or type of usage.

DRAMA, a story told by means of characters speaking *dialogue*, usually for presentation in a theater.

DRAMATIC IRONY, a situation in which facts known to the reader and some of the characters are unknown to other characters.

DRAMATIC MONOLOGUE, poem in which the speaker addresses one or more persons who are present but whose replies are not recorded.

DRAMATIC POINT OF VIEW. See *point of view*.

ELEGY, a traditional poetic form that treats of death, or some other grave topic, in a formal, philosophic way.

END RHYME, the rhyming of words at the ends of lines of verse. (Compare *internal rhyme*.)

END-STOPPED, a term applied to a verse line or a couplet which contains a complete thought, thus necessitating the use of a semicolon or a period at the end.

EPIC, a long narrative poem—originally handed down in oral tradition, later a traditional literary form—dealing with national heroes, having a world-wide or cosmic setting, and written in a deliberately ceremonial style. By extension, *epic* may refer to any writing with similar qualities.

EPIGRAM, originally, an inscription; later, any very short, highly polished verse or saying, usually ending with a witty turn.

EPILOGUE, concluding section added to a work, serving to round out or interpret it.

EPISODE, an incident in the course of a *plot* which has a unity of its own.

ESSAY, a brief piece of nonfiction which presents a personal point of view either through informal discourse or formal analysis and argument.

EXPLICATION, the explanation of a literary text derived from close reading and careful internal analysis.

EXPOSITION, the beginning of a work of fiction, wherein the author sets the *atmosphere* and *tone*, and provides the reader with the information he will need in order to understand the unfolding of the *plot*.

EXTENDED METAPHOR, a comparison that is used throughout an entire work or a large portion of it.

FABLE, a brief tale, in which the characters are often animals, told to point out a *moral* truth.

FALLING ACTION, the action in a narrative which represents the working out of the decisive action of the *climax*.

FANTASY, a work which takes place in an unreal world, concerns incredible characters, or employs physical and scientific principles not yet discovered.

FARCE, a type of *comedy* which depends for its effect on outlandish situations rather than on witty *dialogue, plot*, and character.

FIGURES OF SPEECH, specific devices, such as *metaphors* and *similes*, used to gain renewed meaning through imaginative transformations.

FLASHBACK, interruption of the narrative to show an episode that happened prior to that particular point in the story.

FOIL, a character whose traits are the opposite of those of another character.

FOLKLORE, the customs, legends, songs, and tales of a people or nation.

FOOT, a metrical division consisting of one accented syllable and all unaccented syllables associated with it. (Exception: the *spondee*.)

FORESHADOWING, a hint given to the reader of what is to come.

FRAME, a narrative device presenting a story or group of stories within the frame of a larger narrative.

FREE VERSE, a type of poetry which differs from conventional verse forms in being "free" from a fixed pattern of *meter* and *rhyme*, but using *rhythm* and other poetic devices.

GENRE, a form or type of literary work. For example, the *novel*, the short story, and the poem are all genres. The term is a very loose one, however, so that subheadings under these three would themselves also be called genres, e.g., the *picaresque novel*, the tale, the *epic* poem.

GOTHIC NOVEL, type of novel which aims at evoking terror through a gloomy *setting* and sensational, supernatural action.

HAIKU, a seventeen-syllable Japanese verse form with vivid images and compressed, subtle meaning.

HERO, the chief male character in an imaginative work. Since in popular use the word also connotes a person with certain noble qualities, the more neutral term *protagonist* is often preferred.

HEROIC COUPLET, a pair of rhymed verse lines in *iambic pentameter*.

HEROIC SIMILE, a *simile* sustained for several lines and giving a *connotation* of the heroic in nature or quality.

HEROINE, the chief female character in an imaginative work, the female *protagonist*.

HEXAMETER, a verse line of six *feet*.

HOMILY, a sermon, or serious moral talk.

HUMOURS, in medieval and Renaissance literature, the body fluids that shaped temperament and behavior—blood, choler, black bile, and phlegm.

HYPERBOLE, a *figure of speech* involving great exaggeration for expressive or comic effect.

IAMB, two-syllable metrical *foot* consisting of one unaccented syllable followed by one accented syllable.

IDYL or IDYLL, a *pastoral poem*.

IMAGERY, the sensory details which provide vividness and immediacy and tend to evoke in the reader a complex of emotional suggestions which abstract language does not.

IMPERFECT RHYME, *slant rhyme* in which the vowel sounds are not quite identical.

IN MEDIAS RES, "in the middle of things"; for example, in a traditional epic the opening scene may begin in the middle of the action.

INTERNAL RHYME, rhyming words within, rather than at the end of, lines.

INVOCATION, the call on the muse for help and inspiration found at the beginning of traditional *epic* poems.

IRONY, a term used to describe any situation where two meanings or interpretations are at odds. In verbal irony the actual meaning of a statement is different, often opposite, from what the statement literally says. Irony of situation refers to an occurrence which is contrary to what is expected or appropriate.

LEGEND, a traditional story about a particular person, place, or deity, often popularly accepted as history.

LITERARY BALLAD, a *ballad* composed in the traditional form in order to achieve the feeling of folk art.

LOCAL COLOR, detailed representation in fiction of *setting*, speech, and customs of a particular region.

LYRIC, a short poem intended mainly to express feelings, thoughts, or a state of mind.

MAXIM, a brief saying embodying a *moral*. (Compare *aphorism* and *proverb*.)

MELODRAMA, a type of *tragedy* with an exaggerated *plot* and *stereotyped* characters, whose credibility are sacrificed for emotional response.

METAPHOR, a *figure of speech* involving an implied comparison. (Compare *simile*.)

METAPHYSICAL POETRY, poetry exhibiting a highly intellectual style which is witty, subtle, and sometimes fantastic, particularly in spinning out *conceits*. See especially John Donne and other seventeenth-century poets.

METER, the patterns of stressed and unstressed syllables used in poetry.

MICROCOSM, literally, "little world," an object or a situation which reflects in miniature a pattern implicit in the world as a whole.

MOCK EPIC, a *satire* using the form of an *epic* poem to develop a trivial incident.

MONOLOGUE, an extended speech given by one speaker.

MOOD, the prevailing emotional aura of a literary work.

MORAL, the lesson taught in a work such as a *fable*. A moral suggests that the reader act in a certain way.

MOTIF, a character, incident, or idea that recurs frequently in various works or in various parts of the same work.

MOTIVATION, the portrayal of circumstances and aspects of personality which make a character's actions and reactions appear believable or inevitable to the reader.

MYTH, a traditional tale of unknown authorship involving gods or other supernatural beings; often attempts to express some interpretation of an aspect or phenomenon of the natural world.

NARRATOR, the teller of a story, usually either an anonymous voice used by the author, or a character in the story itself.

NATURALISM, writing that depicts events as rigidly determined by the forces of heredity and environment. The world described tends to be a bleak and and hopeless place.

NEOCLASSICISM, writing that shows the influence of Greek and Roman *classics*, as, for example, eighteenth-century British literature.

NOVEL, a long work of prose fiction dealing with characters, situations, and *settings* that imitate those of real life.

NOVELLA, a brief tale, especially the early tales of French and Italian writers which are considered to be the form which engendered the later *novel*. *Novella* is also used as a synonym for novelette, or short novel.

OBJECTIVE CORRELATIVE, a set of objects or *images* which, in a work of literature, carry or arouse the emotion the author wishes to convey.

OCTAVE, first eight lines of a *sonnet*, particularly the Italian sonnet.

ODE, a long *lyric* poem, formal in style and complex in form, often written for a special occasion.

OMNISCIENT POINT OF VIEW. See *point of view.*

ONOMATOPOEIA, words used in such a way that the sound of the words imitates the sound of the thing spoken about.

PARABLE, a brief fictional work which concretely illustrates an abstract idea. It differs from a *fable* in that the characters in it are generally people rather than animals; and it differs from an *allegory* in that its characters do not necessarily represent abstract qualities.

PARADOX, a statement that seems to be self-contradictory but which turns out to have valid meaning.

PARALLEL, a likeness, usually in pattern or structure (of a sentence, character, situation, etc.).

PARODY, a kind of *burlesque* aimed particularly at making the style of an author ridiculous.

PASTORAL POETRY, a conventional form of *lyric* poetry using an idealized picture of rural life.

PATHOS, the quality of literature which evokes pity.

PENTAMETER, metrical line of five *feet.*

PERSONA, the mask or voice which a writer assumes in a particular work.

PERSONIFICATION, the representation of ideas, animals, or objects as human beings, by endowing them with human qualities.

PICARESQUE NOVEL, an episodic narrative, generally comic or satiric, portraying a ''picaro'' (Spanish for ''rogue''), or rascal, who lives by his wits and who undergoes little or no change through his adventures.

PLOT, in the simplest sense, a series of happenings in a literary work; but often used to refer to the action as it is organized around a *conflict* and builds through complication to a *climax* followed by a *denouement* or resolution.

POINT OF VIEW, the relation assumed between the teller of a story and the characters in it. The teller, or *narrator*, may himself be a character; or he may be a remote and anonymous voice to be identified, more or less, with the author. A writer who describes, in the third person, both the thoughts and the actions of his characters is said to use the *omniscient point of view;* one who describes only what can be seen, like a newspaper reporter, is said to use the *dramatic point of view.* A narrator's attitude toward his subject is also capable of much variation: it can range from one of apparent indifference to one of extreme conviction and feeling. When a narrator appears to have some bias regarding his subject, it becomes especially important to determine whether he and the author are to be regarded as the same person.

PROLOGUE, section of a work preceding the main part, serving as an introduction.

PROP, short for property, any kind of movable piece used in staging a play.

PROPAGANDA, writing which directly advocates a certain doctrine as the solution to some social or political problem.

PROTAGONIST, the leading character in a literary work.

PROTOTYPE, the original or the pattern from which subsequent works of literature (or elements in literature) derive. Sometimes called a model or archetype.

PROVERB, a brief, traditional saying. (Compare *aphorism* and *maxim.*)

PUN, simultaneous use of two or more different senses of the same word or different words with the same sound (homonyms) for expressive or humorous effect.

QUATRAIN, verse *stanza* of four lines.

QUIBBLE (rare), a play on words.

REALISM, a way of representing life as it seems to the common reader. Material selected tends to deal with ordinary people in everyday experiences.

REFRAIN, the repetition of one or more lines in each *stanza* of a poem.

RHETORIC, conventional *techniques* used in prose to heighten an effect. The term is sometimes used to disparage overblown language.

RHYME, exact repetition of sounds in at least the final accented syllables of two or more words.

RHYME SCHEME, any pattern of *rhymes* in a *stanza* which is a conventional pattern or which is repeated in another stanza.

RHYTHM, usually refers to sound patterns in poetry, but also often to patterns found in both poetry and prose, produced by a recurrence of sounds, *images, themes,* types of sentence structure, and feelings.

RISING ACTION, the building of tension between opposing characters or forces toward a *climax.*

ROMANCE, a long narrative in *verse* or prose that originated in the Middle Ages. Its main elements are adventure, love, and magic.

ROMANTIC HERO, the traditional hero-figure who possesses great courage, a strong sense of dedication, and other admirable qualities.

ROMANTICISM, unlike *realism,* stresses man's glory and freedom rather than his limitations. Generally speaking, romantic writers take an optimistic view of individuals; they prefer to stress the past over the present, and to dwell on the exciting, the exotic, and the beautiful.

SARCASM, the use of exaggerated praise to imply dispraise. Similar to *irony,* but more specific in intent, and heavier, less subtle in tone.

SATIRE, the *technique* which employs wit to ridicule a subject, usually some social institution or human foible, with the intention to inspire reform.

SESTET, the concluding six lines of a *sonnet,* particularly the Italian sonnet.

SETTING, the literal place and time in which the action of a work of fiction occurs, as opposed to the emotional aura evoked by the work.

SIMILE, a *figure of speech* involving a comparison made explicit by the use of the word *like* or *as.* (Compare *metaphor.*)

SLANT RHYME, *imperfect rhyme* in which the vowel sounds are not quite identical.

SOLILOQUY, a dramatic *convention* which allows a character to speak his thoughts aloud, apparently unheard by others who may be on stage.

SONNET, a *lyric* poem with a traditional form of fourteen *iambic pentameter* lines and one of several fixed *rhyme* schemes.

SPONDEE, metrical *foot* of two accented syllables.

SPRUNG RHYTHM, metrical form which prescribes only the number of accented syllables in a line.

STAGE DIRECTION, a dramatist's direction as to how scenes are to be set, how lines are to be spoken, and how his play is to be produced.

STANZA, a group of lines which are set off and form a division in a poem, sometimes interconnected by *rhyme* scheme.

STEREOTYPE, an expression, character, or plot that embodies only the conventional and expected, and thus possessing no individuality or particularity.

STREAM OF CONSCIOUSNESS, the recording of a character's flow of thought without any apparent attempt at clarification.

STRUCTURE, the pattern, outline, or "blue-print" which underlies a finished work of literature. An analysis of structure is an important aspect of *explicating* and understanding a literary work.

STYLE, the distinctive handling of language by a given author, involving the specific choices he makes with regard to *diction, syntax, figurative language,* etc.

SUBPLOT, a *plot* of secondary importance carried on in partial or complete independence of the main plot.

SURREALISM, a term used in both painting and literature to apply to incongruous and dreamlike *images* and sequences which are associated with the unconscious.

SYMBOLISM, the use in literature of objects or events to represent something other than themselves, frequently abstract ideas or concepts.

SYNTAX, sentence structure.

TECHNIQUE, the craftsmanship used by an author to give his work form and meaning. Also, a specific literary device, such as *symbolism* or *satire,* may be referred to as a technique.

TEMPO, rate of movement, speed.

TERZA RIMA, verse form with a three-line *stanza* rhyming aba, bcb, cdc, etc.

TETRAMETER, metrical line of four *feet.*

THEME, a central idea developed in a literary work.

TONE, the attitude and feelings of an author expressed in a given work, by such things as word choice and arrangement.

TRAGEDY, dramatic or narrative writing in which the *protagonist* suffers disaster after a serious and significant struggle, but faces his downfall in such a way as to attain heroic stature. According to Aristotle, tragedy evokes—and thus purges—the emotions of pity and fear.

TRAGIC FLAW, flaw of character in a tragic *hero* which precipitates his downfall.

TRIMETER, metrical line of three *feet.*

TROCHEE, metrical *foot* made up of one accented syllable followed by an unaccented syllable.

UNITIES. Classical dramatic criticism insisted that a good play must have (a) a unified action, taking place during (b) a single continuous time, in (c) one place. These criteria are known as the three *unities.*

UNITY, the quality achieved by an artistic work when all its elements are so interrelated as to form a complete whole.

VERSE. In its most general sense *verse* is a synonym of *poetry. Verse* also may be used to refer to poetry carefully composed as to *rhythm* and *rhyme* scheme, but of inferior literary value. Finally, *verse* may mean a single line of poetry.

Glossary
COMPLETE PRONUNCIATION KEY

The pronunciation of each word is shown just after the word, in this way: **ab bre vi ate** (ə brē′vē āt). The letters and signs used are pronounced as in the words below. The mark ′ is placed after a syllable with primary or strong accent, as in the example above. The mark ′ after a syllable shows a secondary or lighter accent, as in **ab bre vi a tion** (ə brē′vē ā′shən).

Some words, taken from foreign languages, are spoken with sounds that otherwise do not occur in English. Symbols for these sounds are given at the end of the table as "Foreign Sounds."

a	hat, cap	j	jam, enjoy	th	thin, both
ā	age, face	k	kind, seek	ŦH	then, smooth
ä	father, far	l	land, coal		
		m	me, am		
				u	cup, butter
b	bad, rob	n	no, in	u̇	full, put
ch	child, much	ng	long, bring	ü	rule, move
d	did, red				
				v	very, save
e	let, best	o	hot, rock	w	will, woman
ē	equal, see	ō	open, go	y	young, yet
ėr	term, learn	ô	order, all	z	zero, breeze
		oi	oil, voice	zh	measure, seizure
		ou	house, out		
f	fat, if				
g	go, bag			ə represents:	
h	he, how				a in about
		p	paper, cup		e in taken
		r	run, try		i in April
i	it, pin	s	say, yes		o in lemon
ī	ice, five	sh	she, rush		u in circus
		t	tell, it		

foreign sounds

Y as in French *du*. Pronounce ē with the lips rounded as for English ü in **rule.**

œ as in French *peu*. Pronounce ā with the lips rounded as for ō.

N as in French *bon*. The N is not pronounced, but shows that the vowel before it is nasal.

H as in German *ach*. Pronounce k without closing the breath passage.

From *Thorndike-Barnhart High School Dictionary* by E. L. Thorndike and Clarence L. Barnhart. Copyright © 1968 by Scott, Foresman and Company. Reprinted by permission.

PARTS OF SPEECH

n.	noun	*adj.*	adjective	*prep.*	preposition
v.	verb	*adv.*	adverb	*conj.*	conjunction
pron.	pronoun			*interj.*	interjection

ETYMOLOGY KEY

<	from, derived from, taken from	**gen.**	genitive
?	possibly	**lang.**	language
abl.	ablative	**masc.**	masculine
accus.	accusative	**neut.**	neuter
cf.	compare	**pp.**	past participle
dial.	dialect	**ppr.**	present participle
dim.	diminutive	**pt.**	past tense
fem.	feminine	**ult.**	ultimately
		var.	variant

LANGUAGE ABBREVIATIONS

AF	Anglo-French (=Anglo-Norman, the dialect of French spoken by the Normans in England, esp. 1066-c.1164)	ME	Middle English (1100–1500)
		Med.	Medieval
		Med.Gk.	Medieval Greek (700–1500)
Am.E	American English (originating in U.S.)	Med.L	Medieval Latin (700–1500)
Am.Ind.	American Indian	MF	Middle French (1400–1600)
Am.Sp.	American Spanish	MHG	Middle High German (1100–1450)
E	English	MLG	Middle Low German (1100–1450)
F	French	NL	New Latin (after 1500)
G	German	O	Old
Gk.	Greek (from Homer to 300 A.D.)	OE	Old English (before 1100)
Gmc.	Germanic (parent language of Gothic, Scandinavian, English, Dutch, German)	OF	Old French (before 1400)
		OHG	Old High German (before 1100)
		Pg.	Portuguese
HG	High German (speech of Central and Southern Germany)	Scand.	Scandinavian (one of the Germanic languages of Northern Europe before Middle English times; Old Norse unless otherwise specified)
Hindu.	Hindustani (the commonest language of India)		
Ital.	Italian	Skt.	Sanskrit (the ancient literary language of India, from the same parent language as Persian, Greek, Latin, Germanic, Slavonic, and Celtic)
L	Latin (Classical Latin 200 B.C.–300 A.D.)		
LG	Low German (speech of Northern Germany)	Sp.	Spanish
		VL	Vulgar Latin (a popular form of Latin, the main source of French, Spanish, Italian, Portuguese, and Romanian)
LGk.	Late Greek (300–700)		
LL	Late Latin (300–700)		
M	Middle		

ab a lo ne (ab/ə lō/nē), *n.* an edible mollusk, with a large, rather flat shell. The bright-colored lining of its shell is made into buttons and ornaments. [Am. E; < Am.Sp. *abulón* < Am.Indian *aulun*]

ab er ra tion (ab/ə rā/shən), *n.* 1. wandering from the right path or usual course of action. 2. deviation from a standard or ordinary type; abnormal structure or development. 3. temporary mental disorder. 4. the failure of a lens or mirror to bring to a single focus the rays of light coming from one point. Aberration causes a blurred image or an image with a colored rim.

a bet (ə bet/), *v.,* **a bet ted, a bet ting.** encourage or help, especially in something wrong: *One man did the actual stealing, but two others abetted him.* [< OF *abeter* arouse < L *ad-* + Gmc. *bētan* cause to bite] **—a bet/ment,** *n.* **—a bet/tor, a bet/ter,** *n.* **—Syn.** support.

a bey ance (ə bā/əns), *n.* temporary inactivity; state of suspended action: *The judge held the question in abeyance until he had the information necessary to make a decision.* [< AF *abeiance* expectation < L *ad-* at + VL *batare* gape]

ab hor (ab hôr/), *v.,* **-horred, -hor ring.** shrink away from with horror; feel disgust or hate for; detest: *Some people abhor snakes.* [< L *abhorrere* < *ab-* from + *horrere* shrink, bristle with fear] **—ab hor/rer,** *n.* **—Syn.** loathe, abominate. **—Ant.** admire.

ab hor rence (ab hôr/əns or ab hor/əns), *n.* a feeling of very great hatred; horror; disgust.

ab hor rent (ab hôr/ənt), *adj.* causing horror; disgusting; hateful. **—ab hor/rent ly,** *adv.*

ab ject (ab/jekt), *adj.* 1. wretched; miserable: *abject poverty.* 2. deserving contempt; degraded: *an abject flatterer.* 3. slavish: *abject submission.* [< L *abjectus,* pp. of *abjicere* < *ab-* down + *jacere* throw] **—ab ject/ly,** *adv.* **—Syn.** 2. contemptible, despicable.

a bra sion (ə brā/zhən), *n.* 1. place scraped or worn by rubbing: *Abrasions of the skin are painful.* 2. a scraping off; a wearing away by rubbing. [< L *abrasio, -onis* < *abradere*]

ab ro gate (ab/rə gāt), *v.,* **-gat ed, -gat ing.** 1. abolish or annul (a law or custom) by an authoritative act; repeal: *The 21st amendment to the Constitution, permitting the manufacture of intoxicating liquor, abrogated the 18th amendment, which prohibited it.* 2. do away with. [< L *abrogare* < *ab-* away + *rogare* demand] **—ab/ro ga/tion, —ab/ro ga/tor,** *n.*

a byss (ə bis/), *n.* 1. a bottomless or immeasurably deep space. 2. anything too deep to be measured; lowest depth. 3. the chaos before the Creation. [< L < Gk. *abyssos* < *a-* without + *byssos* bottom]

ac cede (ak sēd/), *v.,* **-ced ed, -ced ing.** 1. give in; agree (*to*): *Please accede to my request.* 2. come (*to*); attain (to an office or dignity): *When the king died, his oldest son acceded to the throne.* 3. become a party (*to*): *Our government acceded to the treaty.* [< L *accedere* < *ad-* to + *cedere* come]

ac cliv i ty (ə kliv/ə tē), *n., pl.* **-ties.** an upward slope (of ground). [< L *acclivitas* < *acclivis, acclivus* ascending < *ad-* toward + *clivus* rising ground]

ac co lade (ak/ə lād/), *n.* 1. a tap on the shoulder with the flat side of a sword given in making a man a knight. Formerly an embrace or kiss was given instead. 2. praise; recognition. [< F < Ital. *accollata* an embrace about the neck < L *ad-* to + *collum* neck]

ac qui esce (ak/wē es/), *v.,* **-esced, -esc ing.** give consent by keeping silent; submit quietly: *We acquiesced in their plan because we could not suggest a better one.* [< F < L *acquiescere* < *ad-* to + *quiescere* to rest] **—Syn.** accede, assent.

ac qui es cence (ak/wē es/ns), *n.* consent without making objections; agreeing or submitting quietly.

a cute (ə kyüt/), *adj.* 1. having a sharp point. 2. sharp and severe: *A toothache can cause acute pain.* 3. brief and severe. An acute disease like pneumonia reaches a crisis within a short time. 4. keen: *Dogs have an acute sense of smell. An acute thinker is clever and shrewd.* 5. high in pitch; shrill: *Some sounds are so acute that we cannot hear them.* 6. having the mark (´) over it. 7. less than a right angle. [< L *acutus,* pp. of *acuere* sharpen] **—a cute/ly,** *adv.* **—a cute/ness,** *n.*

ad mo ni tion (ad/mə nish/ən), *n.* act of admonishing; warning; advice concerning the faults a person has shown or may show. [< L *admonitio, -onis* < *ad-* to + *monere* warn]

af fec ta tion (af/ek tā/shən), *n.* 1. behavior that is not natural: *Her little affectations seem silly.* 2. outward appearance; pretense: *an affectation of ignorance.*

af fi da vit (af/ə dā/vit), *n.* statement written down and sworn to be true. An affidavit is usually made before a judge or notary public. [< Med.L *affidavit* he has stated on oath]

af fin i ty (ə fin/ə tē), *n., pl.* **-ties.** 1. natural attraction to a person or liking for a thing: *an affinity for dancing.* 2. person to whom one is especially attracted. 3. resemblance; likeness. 4. force that attracts certain chemical elements to others and keeps them combined. [< F *af(f)inité* < L *affinitàs* < *ad-* on + *finis* boundary]

ag gre gate (*v.* ag/rə gāt; *n., adj.* ag/rə git or ag/rə gāt), *v.,* **-gat ed, -gat ing,** *n., adj.* **—v.** 1. gather together in a mass or group; collect; unite. 2. amount to: *The money collected will aggregate $1000.* **—n.** 1. mass of separate things joined together; collection. 2. total: *The aggregate of all the gifts was $100.* 3. **in the aggregate,** together; as a whole. **—adj.** 1. gathered together in one mass or group. 2. total. [< L *aggregare* < *ad-* to + *grex* flock] **—ag/gre gate ly,** *adv.*

a lac ri ty (ə lak/rə tē), *n.* 1. brisk and eager action; liveliness: *Although the man was very old, he still moved with alacrity.* 2. cheerful willingness. [< L *alacritas* < *alacer* brisk] **—a lac/ri tous,** *adj.*

a lar um (ə ler/əm or ə lar/əm), *n. Archaic.* alarm.

al bur num (al bėr/nəm), *n.* the lighter, softer part of wood between the inner bark and the harder center of a tree; sapwood. [< L *alburnum* < *albus* white]

al che mist (al/kə mist), *n.* man who studied a combination of chemistry and magic in the Middle Ages. Alchemists tried to turn cheaper metals into gold and to find the elixir of life.

al i ment (al/ə mənt), *n.* food; nourishment. [< L *alimentum* < *alere* nourish]

al oe (al/ō), *n., pl.* **-oes.** 1. plant having a long spike of flowers and thick, narrow leaves, that grows in South Africa and other warm, dry climates. 2. *U.S.* century plant. 3. **aloes,** *pl.* a bitter drug made from the dried juice of the leaves of certain aloes. [< L < Gk.]

➤ **Aloes,** the drug, is plural in form and singular in use: *Aloes is sometimes used as a tonic.*

am ber gris (am/bər grēs/ or am/bər gris), *n.* a waxlike, grayish substance that comes from sperm whales. Ambergris is used in making perfumes. [< F *ambre gris* gray amber]

am bi dex tri an (am/bə dek/strē ən), *n.* one who is able to use both hands equally well. [< LL *ambidexter* < L *ambi-* both + *dexter* right]

am bi gu i ty (am/bə gyü/ə tē), *n., pl.* **-ties.** 1. possibility of two or more meanings. 2. word or expression that can have more than one meaning.

am u let (am/yə lit), *n.* some object worn as a magic charm against evil. [< L *amuletum*]

a nach ro nism (ə nak/rə niz əm), *n.* 1. act of putting a person, thing, or event in some time where he or it does not belong: *It would be an anachronism to speak of George Washington riding in an automobile.* 2. something placed or occurring out of its proper time. [< F < Gk. *anachronismos* < *ana-* backwards + *chronos* time]

a nal o gous (ə nal/ə gəs), *adj.* 1. alike in some way; similar; comparable. 2. in biology, corresponding in function, but not in structure and origin. **—a nal/o gous ly,** *adv.*

an a logue (an/ə lôg or an/ə log), *n.* something analogous.

an ar chism (an/ər kiz/əm), *n.* 1. the political theory that all systems of government and law are harmful. Believers in anarchism think that government and laws prevent individuals from reaching their greatest development. 2. practice or support of this belief. 3. lawlessness.

an ar chist (an/ər kist), *n.* person who wants to overthrow established governments and have a world without rulers and laws.

an i mos i ty (an/ə mos/ə tē), *n., pl.* **-ties.** violent hatred; ill will; active dislike or enmity: *Gossips soon earn the animosity of their neighbors.* [< L *animositas* < *animosus* spirited]

an ni hi late (ə nī′ə lāt), v., **-lat ed,** **-lat ing.** 1. destroy completely; wipe out of existence. 2. bring to ruin or confusion. [< LL *annihilare* < L *ad-* + *nihil* nothing]

an ni hi la tion (ə nī′ə lā′shən), n. complete destruction.

a nom a lous (ə nom′ə ləs), adj. departing from the common rule; irregular; abnormal: *A position as head of a department, but with no real authority, is anomalous.* [< LL < Gk. *anomalos* < *an-* not + *homalos* even]

a nom a ly (ə nom′ə lē), n., pl. **-lies.** 1. departure from a general rule; irregularity. 2. something abnormal: *A dog with six legs is an anomaly.*

an ti phon (an′tə fon), n. 1. psalm, hymn, or prayer sung or chanted in alternate parts. 2. verses sung or chanted in response in a church service. [< LL < Gk. *antiphona* sounding in response < *anti-* opposed to + *phone* sound]

an tiph o nal (an tif′ə nl), adj. like an antiphon; sung or chanted alternately. —n. book of antiphons.

an ti podes (an tip′ə dēz), n. pl. two opposites or contraries.

an tiq ui ty (an tik′wə tē), n., pl. **-ties.** 1. oldness; great age. 2. times long ago; early ages of history. Antiquity usually refers to the period from 5000 B.C. to 476 A.D. 3. people of long ago. 4. **antiquities,** pl. **a.** things from times long ago. **b.** customs and life of olden times.

ap a thy (ap′ə thē), n., pl. **-thies.** 1. lack of interest or desire for activity; indifference: *The miser heard the old beggar's story with apathy.* 2. lack of feeling. [< L < Gk. *apatheia* < *a-* without + *pathos* feeling]

a phid (ā′fid or af′id), n. a very small insect that lives by sucking juices from plants; plant louse. [< NL *aphis, aphidis*]

ap per cep tion (a′pər sep′shən), n. 1. assimilation of a new perception by means of a mass of ideas already in the mind. 2. clear perception; full understanding. [< F *aperception* < NL. Related to *perception.*]

a poth e o sis (ə poth′ē ō′sis), n., pl. **-ses** (-sēz). 1. raising of a human being to the rank of a god; deification: *The apotheosis of the emperor became a Roman custom.* 2. glorification; exaltation. 3. a glorified ideal. [< L < Gk. *apotheosis,* ult. < *apo-* + *theos* god]

ap pel la tion (ap′ə lā′shən), n. 1. name; title. In "John the Baptist," the appellation of *John* is the *Baptist.* 2. act of calling by a name.

ap prise (ə prīz′), v., **-prised, -pris ing.** inform; notify; advise. Also, **apprize.** [< F *appris,* pp. of *apprendre* learn < L *apprehendere*]

ap pro ba tion (ap′rə bā′shən), n. 1. approval; favorable opinion. 2. sanction. [< L *approbatio, -onis* < *approbare* approve]

ap ro pos (ap′rə pō′), adv. 1. fittingly; opportunely. 2. **apropos of,** with regard to. —adj. fitting; suitable; to the point: *an apropos remark.* [< F *à propos* to the purpose]

ar a besque (ar′ə besk′), n. an elaborate and fanciful design of flowers, leaves, geometrical figures, etc. —adj. 1. carved or painted in arabesque. 2. like arabesque; elaborate; fanciful. [< F < Ital. *arabesco* < *Arabo* Arab]

ar che type (är′kə tīp), n. an original model or pattern from which copies are made, or out of which later forms develop: *That little engine is the archetype of huge modern locomotives.* [< L < Gk. *archetypon,* neut. of *archetypos* original]

ar chi di a co nal (är′ki di ak′ə nal), adj. concerning an archdeacon or the position of archdeacon. [< LL *archidiacon(us)* archdeacon]

ar du ous (är′jü əs), adj. 1. hard to do; requiring much effort; difficult: *an arduous lesson.* 2. using up much energy; strenuous: *an arduous effort to learn the lesson.* 3. hard to climb; steep: *an arduous hill.* [< L *arduus* steep] —**ar′du ous ly,** adv. —**ar′du ous ness,** n.

ar raign (ə rān′), v. 1. bring before a law court for trial: *The tramp was arraigned on a charge of stealing.* 2. call in question; find fault with. [< AF *arrainer* < VL < L *ad-* to + *ratio* account] —**ar raign′er,** n. —**Syn.** 2. accuse.

ar rears (ə rirz′), n. pl. 1. money due but not paid; debts. 2. unfinished work; things not done on time. 3. **in arrears,** behind in payments, work, etc. [< OF *arere* < LL *ad retro* to the rear]

as pi rate (v. as′pə rāt; adj., n. as′pər it), v., **-rat ed, -rat ing,** adj., n. —v. 1. begin a word or syllable with an *h*-sound, as *hwot* (spelled *what*). 2. pronounce (a stop) with a following or accompanying puff of air. *P* is aspirated in *pin* but not in *tip.* —adj. pronounced with a breathing or *h*-sound. The *h* in *here* is aspirate. —n. an aspirated sound. English *p* is an aspirate in *pat,* but not in *tap.* [< L *aspirare*]

as sail (ə sāl′), v. 1. set upon with violence; attack: *assail a fortress.* 2. set upon vigorously with arguments, abuse, etc. [< OF *asalir* < VL *adsalire* < L *ad-* at + *salire* leap] —**as sail′a ble,** adj.

as sid u ous (ə sij′ü əs), adj. careful and attentive; diligent. [< L *assiduus* < *assidere* sit at] —**as sid′u ous ly,** adv.

a stern (ə stèrn′), adv. 1. at or toward the rear of a ship. 2. backward. 3. behind.

a sun der (ə sun′dər), adv. in pieces; into separate parts. —adj. apart; separate. [OE *on sundran*]

at ten u ate (ə ten′yü āt), v., **-at ed, -at ing.** 1. make or become thin or slender. 2. weaken; reduce. 3. make less dense; dilute. [< L *attenuare* < *ad-* + *tenuis* thin]

aught[1] (ôt), n. anything: *You may go for aught I care.* —adv. in any way; to any degree; at all: *Help came too late to avail aught.* [OE *āwiht* < *ā-* ever + *wiht* a thing]

aught[2] (ôt), n. zero; cipher; nothing. [< *naught; a naught* taken as *an aught; naught,* OE *nāwiht* < *nā* no + *wiht* a thing]

au re o la (ô rē′ə lə), n. aureole.

au re ole (ôr′ē ōl), n. 1. encircling radiance; halo. 2. a ring of light surrounding the sun. [< L *aureola (corona)* golden (crown) < *aurum* gold]

hat, āge, fär; let, ēqual, tèrm;
it, īce; hot, ōpen, ôrder;
oil, out; cup, pút, rüle;
ch, child; ng, long; sh, she;
th, thin; ᴛʜ, then; zh, measure;

ə represents *a* in about, *e* in taken,
i in pencil, *o* in lemon, *u* in circus.

< = from, derived from, taken from.

au to crat (ô′tə krat), n. 1. ruler having absolute power over his subjects. 2. person having unlimited power over a group of persons. [< Gk. *autokrates* < *auto-* self + *kratos* strength]

au to crat ic (ô′tə krat′ik), adj. of or like an autocrat; absolute in authority; ruling without checks or limitations. —**au′to crat′i cal ly,** adv.

au tom a tis m (ô tom′ə tiz əm), n. action not controlled by the will; involuntary action; automatic action.

au ton o mous (ô ton′ə məs), adj. self-governing; independent. —**au ton′o mous ly,** adv.

au ton o my (ô ton′ə mē), n., pl. **-mies.** 1. self-government; independence. 2. a self-governing community. [< Gk. *autonomia* < *auto-* of oneself + *nomos* law]

a vail (ə vāl′), v. 1. be of use or value to: *Money will not avail you after you are dead.* 2. help: *Talk will not avail without work.* 3. **avail oneself of,** take advantage of; profit by; make use of. —n. use; help; benefit: *Crying is of no avail now.* [apparently < *a-* to (< OF < L *ad-*) + *vail* < F < L *valere* be worth]

av ar ice (av′ər is), n. greedy desire for money or property. [< OF < L *avaritia* < *avarus* greedy] —**Syn.** greed. —**Ant.** generosity.

av o ca tion (av′ə kā′shən), n. 1. something that a person does besides his regular business; minor occupation; hobby: *Mr. Brown is a lawyer, but writing stories is his avocation.* 2. *Informal.* regular business; occupation. [< L *avocatio, -onis* < *avocare* < *ab-* away + *vocare* to call]

ax le tree (ak′səl trē′), n. crossbar that connects two opposite wheels. The wheels turn on or with its ends.

az ure (azh′ər), n. 1. blue; sky blue. 2. the clear blue color of the unclouded sky. —adj. blue; sky blue. [< OF *l'azur* the azure < Arabic < Persian *lajward* lapis lazuli]

ba nal (bā′nl or bə nal′), adj. commonplace; trite; trivial. [< F *banal* < *ban* proclamation < Gmc.; original sense "of feudal service"; later, "open to the community"] —**ba′nal ly,** adv. —**Syn.** hackneyed.

bare sark (bâr′särk), n., berserker, or fierce Norse warrior. [< Scand. var. of *berserkr*]

ba roque (bə rōk′), *adj.* 1. having to do with a style of art and architecture that prevailed in Europe from about 1550 to the late 18th century, characterized by use of curved forms and lavish ornamentation. 2. tastelessly odd; fantastic; grotesque. 3. irregular in shape: *baroque pearls.* —*n.* a baroque style. [< F < Pg. *barroco* irregular]

bas-re lief (bä′ri lēf′), *n.* carving or sculpture in which the figures project only slightly from the background. [< F < Ital. *bassorilievo* low relief]

Beaux Arts (bō zär′; *Fr.* bō ZAR′), *adj.* 1. concerning a style of architecture usually associated with the École des Beaux-Arts in Paris. This elaborate style was characterized by ornamental features of the 16th-18th centuries, and was popular in France at the end of the 19th century, and in the U.S. at the beginning of the 20th. 2. pertaining to the École des Beaux-Arts. 3. the fine arts.

beck (bek), *n.* 1. motion of the head or hand meant as a call or command. 2. **at one's beck and call**, a. ready whenever wanted. b. under one's complete control. —*v.* beckon to. [< *beck*, v., short for *beckon*]

be di zen (bi dī′zn or bi diz′n), *v.* dress in gaudy clothes; ornament with showy finery. [< *be-* + *dizen*]

be guile (bi gīl′), *v.*, **-guiled, -guil ing.** 1. deceive; cheat: *His pleasant ways beguiled me into thinking that he was my friend.* 2. take away from deceitfully or cunningly. 3. entertain; amuse. 4. while away (time) pleasantly. —**be guil′er**, *n.* —**Syn.** 1. delude.

be hoof (bi hüf′), *n.* use; advantage; benefit: *The father toiled for his children's behoof.* [OE *behōf* need]

bel li cose (bel′ə kōs), *adj.* warlike; fond of fighting. [< L *bellicosus* < *bellum* war]

be nig nant (bi nig′nənt), *adj.* 1. kindly; gracious: *a benignant ruler.* 2. favorable; beneficial. —**be nig′nant ly**, *adv.*

be queath (bi kwēтн′), *v.* 1. give or leave (property, etc.) by a will: *The father bequeathed the farm to his son.* 2. hand down to posterity: *One age bequeaths its civilization to the next.* [OE *becwethan* < *be-* to, for + *cwethan* say]

big ot ry (big′ə trē), *n., pl.* **-ries.** bigoted conduct or attitude; intolerance. —**Syn.** prejudice.

bil let (bil′it), *n.* 1. a thick stick of wood. 2. bar of iron or steel. [< F *billette*, dim. of *bille* log, tree trunk]

bit tern (bit′ərn), *n.* a small kind of heron that lives in marshes and has a peculiar booming cry. [< OF *butor*]

black leg (blak′leg′), *n.* 1. *Informal.* swindler. 2. *Brit.* worker who takes a striker's job. 3. an infectious, usually fatal disease of cattle and sheep.

blithe (blīтн or blīth), *adj.* gay; happy; cheerful. [OE *blithe*] —**blithe′ly**, *adv.* —**blithe′ness**, *n.*

blun der buss (blun′dər bus), *n.* 1. a

short gun with a wide muzzle. It is no longer used. 2. person who blunders. [alteration of Dutch *donderbus* thunder box]

bob bin (bob′ən), *n.* reel or spool for holding thread, yarn, etc. Bobbins are used in spinning, weaving, machine sewing, and lacemaking. Wire is also wound on bobbins. [< F *bobine*]

bob ma jor (bob mā′jər), *n.* a chime sequence rung on eight bells.

bole (bōl), *n.* trunk of a tree. [< Scand. *bolr*]

bond man (bond′mən), *n., pl.* **-men.** 1. slave. 2. serf in the Middle Ages.

bot tom ry (bot′əm rē), *n., pl.* **-ries.** contract by which a shipowner mortgages his ship to get money to make a voyage. If the ship is lost, the lender loses the money. [< *bottom* ship, after Dutch *bodemerij*]

bour geois (bur zhwä′), *n., pl.* **-geois,** *adj.* —*n.* person of the middle class. —*adj.* 1. of the middle class. 2. like the middle class; ordinary. [< F *bourgeois* < LL *burgensis* < *burgus* fort < Gmc. Doublet of BURGESS.]

bourn[1] or **bourne** (bôrn), *n.* a small stream; brook. [OE *burna*]

bourn[2] or **bourne**[2] (bôrn, bûrn), *n.* 1. *Archaic.* boundary; limit. 2. goal. [< F *borne.* Akin to *bound*[3].]

bow (bou), *n.* 1. the forward part of a ship, boat, or airship. 2. person who rows with the oar nearest the bow of a boat. [probably of LG or Scand. origin. Akin to *bough.*]

bow sprit (bou′sprit′), *n.* pole or spar projecting forward from the bow of a ship. Ropes from it help to steady sails and masts. [probably < LG or Dutch]

bra va do (brə vä′dō), *n.* a great show of boldness without much real courage; boastful defiance without much real desire to fight. [< Sp. *bravada* < *bravo.*]

bra vu ra (brə vyùr′ə), *n.* 1. piece of music requiring skill and spirit in the performer. 2. display of daring; attempt at brilliant performance; dash; spirit. [< Ital. *bravura* bravery]

buck ler (buk′lər), *n.* 1. a small, round shield. 2. protection; defense. [< OF *boucler*, originally, one with a boss < *boucle* boss < L *buccula*]

bul ly rag (bùl′ē rag′), *v.*, **-ragged, -rag ging.** *Informal.* bully; tease; abuse.

bur den (bėrd′n), *n.* 1. the main idea or message: *The value of peace was the burden of the President's speech.* 2. a repeated verse in a song; chorus; refrain. [< OF *bourdon* humming, drone of bagpipe < LL *burda* pipe]

cairn (kern or karn), *n.* pile of stones heaped up as a memorial, tomb, or landmark. [< Scotch Gaelic *carn* heap of stones]

cal dron (kôl′drən), *n.* a large kettle or boiler. Also, **cauldron.** [< OF *caudron* < L *caldus* hot]

cam bric (kām′brik), *n.* a fine, thin linen or cotton cloth. [from *Cambrai*, France]

camp meeting (kamp mē′ting), *n.* a religious gathering held outdoors or in a tent, usually lasting several days.

can did (kan′did), *adj.* 1. frank; sincere: *candid reply.* 2. fair; impartial: *a candid decision.* [< L *candidus* white] —**can′did ly**, *adv.* —**Syn.** 1. truthful, straightforward.

cane brake (kān′brāk′), *n.* thicket of cane plants.

can ker (kang′kər), *n.* 1. a spreading sore, especially one in the mouth. 2. disease of plants that causes slow decay. 3. anything that causes decay, rotting, or gradual eating away. 4. cankerworm. —*v.* infect or be infected with canker; decay; rot. [OE *cancer* < L *cancer* crab, tumor, gangrene. Doublet of CANCER, CHANCRE.]

can ton flan nel (kan′ton flan′l), *n., adj.,* a type of cotton cloth, with short, soft fibers, or nap on one side. [after CANTON, China]

ca pri cious (kə prish′es), *adj.* guided by one's fancy; full of unreasonable notions; changeable; fickle: *A spoiled child is often capricious.* —**ca pri′cious ly**, *adv.* —**ca pri′cious ness**, *n.*

cap tious (kap′shəs), *adj.* hard to please; faultfinding. [< L *captiosus* < *capere* take] —**cap′tious ly**, *adv.* —**cap′tious ness**, *n.* —**Syn.** carping, contentious.

car bun cle (kär′bung kəl), *n.* 1. a very painful, inflamed swelling under the skin. 2. pimple. 3. a smooth, round garnet or other deep-red jewel. [< L *carbunculus* < *carbo* coal]

car nage (kär′nij), *n.* slaughter of a great number of people. [< F < Ital. *carnaggio* < L *caro* flesh]

carrion crow (kar′ē ən krō), 1. the common European crow. 2. a black vulture of the southern United States.

cat a lep sy (kat′l ep′sē), *n.* kind of fit during which a person loses consciousness and the power to feel, and his muscles become rigid. [< LL *catalepsis* < Gk. *katalepsis* seizure < *kata-* down + *lambanein* seize]

cat a lep tic (kat′l ep′tik), *adj.* 1. of catalepsy. 2. having catalepsy. —*n.* person who has catalepsy.

cat head (kat′hed′), *n.* beam on a ship's side near the bow. The anchor is hoisted and fastened to it.

cha grin (shə grin′), *n.* a feeling of disappointment, failure, or humiliation. —*v.* cause to feel chagrin. [< F *chagrin* grained leather, vexation < Turkish *çāghri* rump of a horse; shift of meaning comes from idea of being ruffled (cf. *gooseflesh*).] —**Syn.** *n.* mortification, vexation.

chap ar ral (chap′ə ral′), *n.* in the southwestern United States, a thicket of low shrubs, thorny bushes, etc. [Am.E.; < Sp. *chaparral* < *chaparro* evergreen oak]

chap man (chap′mən), *n., pl.* **-men.** *Brit.* peddler. [OE *cēapman* < *cēap* trade + *man* man]

char la tan (shär′lə tən), *n.* person who pretends to have more knowledge or skill than he really has; quack. [< F < Ital. *ciarlatano*, apparently < *cerretano* < *Ceretto*, town in Italy] —**Syn.** imposter, cheat.

chat tel (chat′l), *n.* a movable possession; piece of property that is not real estate.

Furniture, automobiles, slaves, and animals are chattels. [< OF *chatel* < L *capitale*, neut. of *capitalis*. Doublet of CAPITAL and CATTLE.]

chi me ra or **chi mae ra** (kə mir′ə or kī mir′ə), *n., pl.* **-ras.** 1. Often, **Chimera.** in Greek legend, a monster with a lion's head, a goat's body, and a serpent's tail, supposed to breathe out fire. 2. a horrible creature of the imagination. 3. an absurd or impossible idea; wild fancy: *The hope of changing dirt to gold was a chimera.* [< F *chimère* < L < Gk. *chimaira* she-goat]

chrys a lis (kris′ə lis), *n., pl.* **chrys a lis es, chry sal i des** (krə sal′ə dēz). 1. form of an insect when it is in a case; pupa. A butterfly has this inactive form after it has been a caterpillar or larva and before it becomes a winged adult. 2. the case; cocoon. 3. stage of development or change. [< L < Gk. *chrysallis* golden sheath < *chrysos* gold]

churl ish (chér′lish), *adj.* rude; surly: *a churlish reply.* —**churl′ish ly,** *adv.* —**churl′ish ness,** *n.*

cir cum lo cu tion (sér′kəm lō kyü′shən), *n.* a roundabout way of speaking: *"The wife of your father's brother" is a circumlocution for "Your aunt."* [< L *circumlocutio, -onis* < *circum* around + *loqui* speak]

clar i on (klar′ē ən), *adj.* clear and shrill. —*n.* 1. a trumpet with clear, shrill tones. 2. *Poetic.* sound made by this trumpet. 3. *Poetic.* a clear, shrill sound like it. [< Med.L *clario, -onis* < L *clarus* clear]

clink er (kling′kər), *n.* 1. piece of the rough, hard mass left in a furnace or stove after coal has been burned; large, rough cinder. 2. a very hard brick. 3. mass of bricks fused together. 4. slag. [< Dutch *klinker* brick < *klinken* ring]

clo ven (klō′vən), *v.* a pp. of **cleave**[1]. —*adj.* split; divided.

cloven foot, cloven hoof.

clo ven-foot ed (klō′vən fůt′id), *adj.* 1. having cloven feet. 2. devilish.

cloven hoof, hoof divided into two parts. Cows have cloven hoofs. The Devil is supposed to have cloven hoofs.

cloy (kloi), *v.* 1. weary by too much, too sweet, or too rich food. 2. weary by too much of anything pleasant. [ME *acloy, ancloy* drive a nail into, stop up, fill full < OF *encloyer* < en- in (< L *in-*) + *clou* nail (< L *clavus*)] —**Syn.** 2. surfeit, pall.

co ad ju tor (kō aj′ə tər or kō′ə jü′tər), *n.* 1. assistant; helper. 2. bishop appointed to assist a bishop. [< LL < L *co-* with + *adjutor* helper < *adjuvare* < *ad-* + *juvare* help]

co a lesce (kō′ə les′), *v.,* **-lesced, -lesc ing.** 1. grow together. 2. unite into one body, mass, party, etc.; combine: *The thirteen colonies coalesced to form a nation.* [< L *coalescere* < *co-* together + *alescere* grow]

co her ent (kō hir′ənt), *adj.* 1. logically connected; consistent in structure and thought: *A sentence that is not coherent is hard to understand.* 2. sticking together; holding together. —**co her′ent ly,** *adv.*

col lat er al (kə lat′ər əl), *adj.* 1. parallel; side by side. 2. related but less important; secondary; indirect. 3. in a parallel line of descent; descended from the same ancestors, but in a different line: *Cousins are collateral relatives.* 4. additional. 5. secured by stocks, bonds, etc. —*n.* 1. a collateral relative. 2. stocks, bonds, etc., pledged as security for a loan. [< Med.L *collateralis* < *com-* + L *lateralis* lateral] —**col lat′er al ly,** *adv.*

col lo ca tion (kol′ō kā′shən), *n.* arrangement: *the collocation of words in a sentence.*

comb er (kō′mər), *n.* 1. person or thing that combs. 2. wave that rolls over or breaks at the top.

com min gle (kə ming′gəl), *v.,* **-gled, -gling.** mingle together; blend.

com mis er ate (kə miz′ə rāt′), *v.,* **-at ed, -at ing.** feel or express sorrow for; sympathize with; pity. [< L *commiserari* < *com-* + *miser* wretched]

con ci sion (kən sizh′ən), *n.* 1. conciseness; expression of much in few words. 2. *Obs.* a cutting or mutilation. [< L *concisus,* pp. of *concidere* < *com-* + *caedere* cut]

con fla gra tion (kon′flə grā′shən), *n.* a big fire: *A conflagration destroyed most of the city.* [< L *conflagratio, -onis* < *conflagrare* < *com-* up + *flagrare* burn]

con jec ture (kən jek′chər), *n., v.,* **-tured, -tur ing.** —*n.* 1. formation of an opinion admittedly without sufficient evidence for proof; guessing. 2. a guess. —*v.* guess. [< L *conjectura* < *conjicere* < *com-* together + *jacere* throw] —**con jec′tur a ble,** *adj.* —**con jec′tur er,** *n.* —**Syn.** *n.* 2. supposition. —*v.* suppose.

con joint (kən joint′), *adj.* 1. joined together; united; combined. 2. formed by two or more in combination; joint. [< F *conjoint,* pp. of *conjoindre*] —**con joint′ly,** *adv.*

con ju ra tion (kon′jə rā′shən), *n.* 1. act of invoking by a sacred name. 2. a magic form of words used in conjuring; magic spell. 3. practice of magic: *In the fairy tale, the princess was changed into a toad by conjuration.* 4. *Archaic.* a solemn appeal.

con jure (kun′jər or kon′jər *for 1-6;* kən jür′ *for 7),* **-jured, -jur ing.** 1. **conjure up, a.** cause to appear in a magic way. **b.** cause to appear in the mind. 2. compel (a spirit, devil, etc.) to appear or disappear by magic words. 3. summon a devil, spirit, etc. 4. cause to be or happen by magic or as if by magic. 5. practice magic. 6. perform tricks by skill and quickness in moving the hands. 7. make a solemn appeal to; request earnestly; entreat: *I conjure you not to betray your country.* [< OF < L *conjurare* make a compact < *com-* together + *jurare* swear]

con nate (kon′āt), *adj.* 1. in existence from the beginning; inborn. 2. related by origin or source. 3. in accord with nature. [< LL *connāt(us)* ptp. of *connasci* to be born concurrently with] —**con nate ly,** *adv.* —**con nate ness,** *n.* —**con na tion** (kə nā′shən), *n.*

con san guin i ty (kon′sang gwin′ə tē), *n.* relationship by descent from the same

hat, āge, fär; let, ēqual, tèrm; it, īce; hot, ōpen, ôrder; oil, out; cup, pút, rüle; ch, child; ng, long; sh, she; th, thin; ŦH, then; zh, measure;

ə represents *a* in about, *e* in taken, *i* in pencil, *o* in lemon, *u* in circus.

< = from, derived from, taken from.

parent or ancestor; relationship by blood: *Brothers and cousins are united by ties of consanguinity.*

con so nant (kon′sə nənt), *n.* 1. any letter of the alphabet that is not a vowel. 2. sound that such a letter represents. —*adj.* 1. harmonious; in agreement; in accord. 2. agreeing in sound. 3. consonantal. [< L *consonans, -antis,* ppr. of *consonare* < *com-* together + *sonare* sound] —**con′so nant ly,** *adv.*

con temn (kən tem′), *v.* treat with contempt; despise; scorn. [< L *contemnere* < *com-* + *temnere* disdain, orginally, cut]

con ten tious (kən ten′shəs), *adj.* 1. quarrelsome; fond of arguing; given to disputing: *A contentious person argues and disputes about trifles.* 2. characterized by contention: *a contentious campaign.* —**con ten′tious ly,** *adv.* —**con ten′tious ness,** *n.*

con tral to (kən tral′tō), *n., pl.* **-tos,** *adj.* —*n.* 1. the lowest woman's voice. 2. in music, a part to be sung by the lowest woman's voice. 3. person who sings this part. —*adj.* of or for a contralto. [< Ital. *contralto* < *contra-* counter to (< L) + *alto* high < L *altus*]

con tra ri e ty (kon′trə rī′ə tē), *n., pl.* **-ties.** 1. state or quality of being contrary. 2. something contrary; contrary fact or statement.

con triv ance (kən trī′vəns), *n.* 1. thing invented; mechanical device. 2. act or manner of contriving. 3. power or ability of contriving. 4. plan; scheme.

co nun drum (kə nun′drəm), *n.* 1. riddle whose answer involves a pun or play on words. "When is a door not a door?" is a conundrum. *Answer:* "When it's ajar." 2. any puzzling problem. [origin unknown]

con vul sion (kən vul′shən), *n.* 1. a violent, involuntary contracting and relaxing of the muscles; spasm: *The sick child's convulsions frightened its mother.* 2. fit of laughter. 3. a violent disturbance: *The country was undergoing a political convulsion.*

co pi ous (kō′pē əs), *adj.* 1. plentiful; abundant. 2. containing much matter. 3. containing many words. [< L *copiosus* < *copia* plenty < *copis* well supplied < *co-* with + *ops* resources] —**co′pi ous ly,** *adv.* —**co′pi ous ness,** *n.* —**Syn.** ample.

cop y book (kop′ē bůk′), *n.* book with models of handwriting to be copied in learning to write. —*adj.* commonplace; conventional; ordinary.

cor nice (kôr′nis), *n., v.,* **-niced, -nic ing.**

—*n.* 1. an ornamental molding that projects along the top of a wall, pillar, building, etc. 2. molding around the walls of a room just below the ceiling. —*v.* furnish or finish with a cornice. [< F < Ital. < Med.Gk. *koronis* copestone < Gk. *koronis* something bent]

co rol la (kə rol′ə), *n.* the internal envelope or floral leaves of a flower usually of some color other than green; the petals. [< L *corolla* garland, dim. of *corona* crown]

cor pu lent (kôr′pyə lənt), *adj.* fat. [< L *corpulentus* < *corpus* body]

co til lion (kə til′yən), *n.* Esp. U.S. a dance with complicated steps and much changing of partners, led by one couple. [< F *cotillon*, originally, petticoat, dim. of *cotte* coat]

coun te nance (koun′tə nəns), *n.*, *v.*, -nanced, -nanc ing. —*n.* 1. expression of the face: *His angry countenance frightened us all.* 2. face; features: *The king had a noble countenance.* 3. approval; encouragement: *He gave countenance to our plan, but no active help.* 4. calmness; composure. 5. keep one's countenance, a. be calm; not show feeling. b. keep from smiling or laughing. 6. lose countenance, get excited. 7. put out of countenance, embarrass and confuse; make uneasy and ashamed. —*v.* approve or encourage: *Mother countenanced the boys' friendship.* [< OF *contenance* < Med.L *continentia* demeanor < L *continentia* self-control < *continere*] —Syn. *n.* 1, 2. visage. 3. support.

cov e nant (kuv′ə nənt), *n.* 1. a solemn agreement between two or more persons or groups to do or not to do a certain thing; compact. 2. Covenant, a. agreement signed by Scotch Presbyterians and members of the English Parliament in 1643. It established the Presbyterian Church in England. b. an earlier agreement signed by Scotch Presbyterians in 1638, for the defense of the Presbyterian faith. 3. in the Bible, the solemn promises of God to man; compact between God and man. 4. a legal contract; formal agreement that is legal. 5. Covenant, Covenant of the League of Nations. —*v.* solemnly agree (to do certain things). [< OF *covenant* < *covenir* < L *convenire.*]

cov et (kuv′it), *v.* desire eagerly (something that belongs to another). [< OF *coveitier*, ult. < L *cupere* desire] —cov′et er, *n.*

cov et ous (kuv′ə təs), *adj.* desiring things that belong to others. —cov′et ous ly, *adv.* —cov′et ous ness, *n.* —Syn. greedy, avaricious.

cov ey (kuv′ē), *n.*, *pl.* -eys. 1. brood of partridges, quail, etc. 2. a small flock; group. [< OF *covée* < *cover* incubate < L *cubare* lie]

cre du li ty (krə dü′lə tē or krə dyü′lə tē), *n.* a too great readiness to believe.

cre o sote (krē′ə sōt), *n.*, *v.*, -sot ed, -sot ing, —*n.* 1. an oily liquid with a penetrating odor, obtained by distilling wood tar, used to preserve wood and in cough medicine. 2. a similar substance obtained from coal tar. —*v.* treat with creosote. [originally, a meat preservative; < Gk. *kreo-* (for *kreas* flesh) + *soter* savior < *sozein* save]

cru ci ble (krü′sə bəl), *n.* 1. container in which metals, ores, etc., can be melted. 2. a severe test or trial. [< Med.L *crucibulum* originally, night lamp]

cryp tic (krip′tik), *adj.* having a hidden meaning; secret; mysterious: *a cryptic message.* [< LL *crypticus* < Gk. *kryptikos* < *kryptos* hidden] —cryp′ti cal ly, *adv.*

dap ple (dap′əl), *adj.*, *n.*, *v.*, -pled, -pling. —*adj.* spotted: *a dapple horse.* —*n.* 1. a spotted appearance or condition. 2. animal with a spotted or mottled skin. —*v.* mark or become marked with spots. [cf. Scand. *depill* spot]

de bauch (di bôch′), *v.* 1. lead away from duty, virtue, or morality; corrupt morally; seduce. 2. corrupt; pervert; deprave. —*n.* 1. excessive indulgence in sensual pleasures; excess in eating or drinking. 2. bout or period of debauchery. [< F *débaucher* entice from duty] —de bauch′er, *n.* —de bauch′ment, *n.*

deb au chee (di′bôch ē′), *n.* an intemperate, corrupt, dissipated, or depraved person.

de bauch er y (di bô′chər ē), *n.*, *pl.* -er ies. 1. excessive indulgence in sensual pleasures. 2. seduction from duty, virtue, or morality.

de bil i ty (di bil′ə tē), *n.*, *pl.* -ties. weakness. [< L *debilitas* < *debilis* weak]

de cal co ma ni a (di kal′kə mā′nē ə), *n.* 1. design or picture treated so that it will stick fast to glass, wood, etc. 2. process of decorating glass, wood, etc., by applying these designs or pictures. [< F *décalcomanie* < *décalquer* transfer a tracing + *manie* mania]

de cid u ous (di sij′ü əs), *adj.* 1. falling off at a particular season or stage of growth: *deciduous leaves, deciduous horns.* 2. of trees, shrubs, etc., shedding leaves annually. Maples, elms, and most oaks are deciduous trees. [< L *deciduus* < *decidere* < *de-* + *cadere* fall]

dec or ous (dek′ər əs or di kôr′əs), *adj.* well-behaved; acting properly; in good taste; dignified. [< L *decorus* < *decor* seemliness, comeliness] —dec′o rous ly, *adv.* —dec′or ous ness, *n.*

de fer (di fer′), *v.*, -ferred, -fer ring. put off; delay. [< L *differre.* Doublet of DIFFER.] —Syn. postpone.

def er ence (def′ər əns), *n.* 1. a yielding to the judgment or opinion of another; courteous submission. 2. great respect. 3. in deference to, out of respect for the wishes or authority of.

de file (di fīl′), *v.*, -filed, -fil ing, *n.* —*v.* march in a line. —*n.* a narrow way or passage through which troops can march only in narrow columns; steep and narrow valley. [< F *défilé*, special use of pp. of *défiler* march by files < *dé-* off + *file* file[1]]

deft (deft), *adj.* skillful; nimble: *The fingers of a violinist or surgeon are deft.* [var. of *daft*] —deft′ly, *adv.* —deft′ness, *n.*

de i cide (dē′i sīd′), *n.*, 1. the killer of a god. 2. the killing of a god. [< L *dei* (form of *deus* god) + *cid* (form of *caedere* to kill, to cut)] —de′i ci′dal, *adj.*

de i ty (dē′ə tē), *n.*, *pl.* -ties. 1. god or goddess. 2. divine nature; being a god. 3. the Deity, God. [< F *déité* < L *deitas* < *deus* god]

de lu sive (di lü′siv), *adj.* misleading; deceptive; false.

de mean (di mēn′), *v.* lower in dignity or standing; humble. [< *de-* down + *mean*; formed after *debase*]

de mean or (di mē′nər), *n.* way a person looks and acts; behavior; conduct; manner. [ME *demenure* < *demenen* behave < OF *demener.*]

dem i cul ver in (dem′ē kul′vər in), *n.* a type of long, heavy cannon, used in the 16th and 17th centuries, with an approximately 4$\frac{1}{2}$ inch barrel, that fired about 10 pounds of shot. [< F *demicoulevrine*]

dem i john (dem′i jon), *n.* a large bottle of glass or earthenware enclosed in wicker. [< F *dame-jeanne* Lady Jane]

de mo ni ac (di mō′nē ak), *adj.* 1. of demons. 2. devilish; fiendish. 3. raging; frantic. 4. possessed by an evil spirit. —*n.* person supposed to be possessed by an evil spirit.

de mo ni a cal (dē′mə nī′ə kəl), *adj.* demoniac. —de′mo ni′a cal ly, *adv.*

de noue ment or **dé noue ment** (dā′nü män′), *n.* solution of a plot in a play, a story, etc.; outcome; end. [< F *dénouement* < *dénouer* untie < L *dis-* + *nodus* knot]

de prav i ty (di prav′ə tē), *n.*, *pl.* -ties. 1. wickedness; corruption. 2. a corrupt act; bad practice.

dep re cate (dep′rə kāt), *v.*, -cat ed, -cat ing. express strong disapproval of; plead against; protest against: *Lovers of peace deprecate war.* [< L *deprecari* plead in excuse, avert by prayer < *de-* + *precari* pray] —dep′re cat′ing ly, *adv.* —dep′re ca′tor, *n.*

➤ **deprecate, depreciate.** Do not confuse *deprecate*, meaning to express strong disapproval of, with *depreciate*, meaning to lessen in value or price. Contrast these sentences: *I feel I must deprecate the course the club is following. Naturally a car depreciates after a number of years of service.*

dep re ca to ry (dep′rə kə tô′rē or dep′rə kə tō′rē), *adj.* 1. deprecating. 2 *Informal.* apologetic.

de range (di rānj′), *v.*, -ranged, -rang ing. 1. disturb the order or arrangement of; throw into confusion. 2. make insane. [< F *déranger* < *dé-* (< L *dis-*) + *ranger* range]

der vish (der′vish), *n.* a Moslem monk or friar. **Dancing dervishes** have a religious ceremony in which they dance and spin about violently. **Howling dervishes** chant and shout loudly. [< Turkish *dervīsh* < Persian *darvīsh*]

des ic cate (des′ə kāt), *v.*, -cat ed,

-cat ing. 1. dry thoroughly. **2.** preserve by drying thoroughly. [< L *desiccare* < *de-* out + *siccus* dry] **—des′ic ca′tion,** *n.*
➤ **desiccate.** Observe the proper meaning of this word. Because desiccated foods have often been cut into small pieces, people sometimes suppose that *desiccate* means cut up or shred.

des ti tu tion (des′tə tü′shən or des′tə tyü′shən), *n.* **1.** destitute condition; extreme poverty. **2.** state of being without; lack.

de ter rent (di tėr′ənt), *adj.* deterring; restraining. **—***n.* something that deters: *Fear of consequences is a common deterrent from wrongdoing.*

dex ter i ty (dek ster′ə tē), *n.* **1.** skill in using the hands. **2.** skill in using the mind; cleverness.

di a dem (dī′ə dem), *n.* **1.** crown. **2.** an ornamental band of cloth formerly worn as a crown. **3.** royal power, authority, or dignity. [< L < Gk. *diadema* < *diadeein* < *dia-* across + *deein* bind]

di a bol ic (dī′ə bol′ik), *adj.* **1.** devilish; like the Devil; very cruel or wicked; fiendish. **2.** having to do with the Devil or devils. [< LL *diabolicus* < Gk. *diabolikos* < *diabolos.* See DEVIL.] **—di′a bol′i cal ly,** *adv.*

di a bol i cal (dī′ə bol′ə kl), *adj.* diabolic.

di as to le (dī as′tə lē), *n.* the normal, rhythmical dilation of the heart, especially that of the ventricles. [< LL < Gk. *diastole* expansion < *dia-* apart + *stellein* send]

dic tum (dik′təm), *n., pl.* **-tums, -ta. 1.** a formal comment; authoritative opinion: *The dictum of the critics was that the play was excellent.* **2.** maxim; saying. [< L *dictum* (thing) said, pp. neut. of *dicere* say]

dif fi dence (dif′ə dəns), *n.* lack of self-confidence; shyness.

dif fi dent (dif′ə dənt), *adj.* lacking in self-confidence; shy. [< L *diffidens, -entis,* ppr. of *diffidere* < *dis-* + *fidere* trust] **—dif′fi dent ly,** *adv.*

di lap i da tion (də lap′ə dā′shən), *n.* a falling to pieces; decay; ruin; tumble-down condition: *The house was in the last stage of dilapidation.*

di late (dī lāt′), *v.,* **-lat ed, -lat ing. 1.** make or become larger or wider: *The pupils of John's eyes dilated when the light got dim.* **2.** speak or write in a very complete or detailed manner. [< L *dilatare* < *dis-* apart + *latus* wide]

dil et tan te (dil′ə tan′tē or dil′ə tänt′), *n., pl.* **-tes, -ti. 1.** lover of the fine arts. **2.** person who follows some art or science as an amusement or in a trifling way. **3.** trifler. [< Ital. *dilettante* < *dilettare* < L *delectare*]

dire ful (dīr′fəl), *adj.* dire; dreadful; terrible. **—dire′ful ly,** *adv.* **—dire′ful ness,** *n.*

dirge (dėrj), *n.* a funeral song or tune. [contraction of L *dirige* direct (imperative of *dirigere,* first word in office for the dead]

dis a vow (dis′ə vou′), *v.* deny that one knows about, approves of, or is responsible for; disclaim: *The prisoner disavowed the confession bearing his signature.*

dis com fi ture (dis kum′fi chər), *n.* **1.** a

---

complete overthrow; defeat; rout. **2.** defeat of plans or hopes; frustration. **3.** confusion.

dis con so late (dis kon′sə lit), *adj.* without hope; forlorn; unhappy; cheerless. [< Med.L *disconsolatus* < L *dis-* + *consolatus,* pp. of *consolari* < *com-* + *solari* soothe] **—dis con′so late ly,** *adv.* **—discon′so late ness,** *n.* **—Syn.** dejected, sad.

dis cre tion (dis kresh′ən), *n.* **1.** freedom to judge or choose: *Making final plans was left to the president's discretion.* **2.** quality of being discreet; good judgment; carefulness in speech or action; wise caution. **—Syn. 1.** choice.

dis par i ty (dis par′ə tē), *n., pl.* **-ties.** inequality; difference: *There will be a disparity in the accounts of the same event given by several people.*

dis pas sion ate (dis pash′ə nit), *adj.* free from emotion or prejudice; calm; impartial: *To a dispassionate observer, the drivers of both cars seemed equally at fault.* **—dis pas′sion ate ly,** *adv.*

dis pu ta tious (dis′pyə tā′shəs), *adj.* fond of disputing; inclined to argue. **—dis′pu ta′tious ly,** *adv.* **—dis′pu ta′tious ness,** *n.* **—Syn.** quarrelsome.

dis sev er (di sev′ər), *v.* sever; separate.

dis si pate (dis′ə pāt), *v.,* **-pat ed, -pat ing. 1.** spread in different directions; scatter. **2.** disappear or cause to disappear; dispel: *The sun dissipated the mists.* **3.** spend foolishly; waste on things of little value: *The extravagant son soon dissipated his father's fortune.* **4.** indulge too much in evil or foolish pleasures. [< L *dissipare* < *dis-* in different directions + *sipare* throw]

dis si pa tion (dis′ə pā′shən), *n.* **1.** a dissipating or being dissipated. **2.** amusement; diversion, especially harmful amusements. **3.** too much indulgence in evil or foolish pleasures; intemperance.

dis trait (dis trā′), *adj.* not paying attention; absentminded. [< F *distrait,* pp. of *distraire* distract]

di verge (də vėrj′ or dī vėrj′), *v.,* **-verged, -verg ing. 1.** move or lie in different directions from the same point; branch off: *Their paths diverged at the fork in the road.* **2.** differ; vary; deviate. [< LL *divergere* < *dis-* in different directions + *vergere* slope]

Syn. 1. Diverge, deviate, digress mean to turn or move in a different direction. **Diverge** means to branch out in different directions like a Y from a main or old path or way: *Our paths diverged when we left school.* **Deviate** means to turn aside in one direction from a normal or regular path, way of thinking or acting, rule, etc.: *The teacher deviated from her custom and gave us no homework.* **Digress** applies chiefly to turning aside from the main subject while speaking or writing: *I lose interest if an author digresses too much.*

di vers (dī′vərz), *adj.* several different; various. [< OF < L *diversus,* pp. of *divertere*]

di verse (də vėrs′), *adj.* **1.** different; un-

---

hat, āge, fär; let, ēqual, tėrm; it, īce; hot, ōpen, ôrder; oil, out; cup, pút, rüle; ch, child; ng, long; sh, she; th, thin; ᴛʜ, then; zh, measure;

ə represents *a* in about, *e* in taken, *i* in pencil, *o* in lemon, *u* in circus.

< = from, derived from, taken from.

---

like. **2.** varied: *A person of diverse interests can talk on many subjects.* [var. of *divers;* now regarded as immediately from L *diversus*] **—di verse′ness,** *n.*

div i na tion (div′ə nā′shən), *n.* **1.** act of foreseeing the future or foretelling the unknown. **2.** a skillful guess or prediction.

dog ger el (dô′gər əl), *n.* very poor poetry; poetry that is not artistic in form or meaning. **—***adj.* **1.** of or like doggerel; not artistic; poor. **2.** of verse, comic in style and irregular in form. [ME; origin uncertain]

dog mat ic (dôg mat′ik), *adj.* **1.** having to do with dogma; doctrinal. **2.** asserting opinions as if one were the highest authority; positive; overbearing. **3.** asserted without proof. **—dog mat′i cal ly,** *adv.*

do min ion (də min′yən), *n.* **1.** supreme authority; rule; control. **2.** territory under the control of one ruler or government. **3.** a self-governing territory. **4. Dominion,** between 1926 and 1947, a self-governing part of the British Empire. Such a nation is now known as a member of the British Commonwealth of Nations. [< obsolete F < Med.L *dominion, -onis,* alteration of L *dominium* ownership]

dor mant (dôr′mənt), *adj.* **1.** sleeping. **2.** quiet as if asleep. **3.** inactive: *The plant bulbs were dormant during the cold of winter.* [< OF *dormant,* ppr. of *dormir* sleep < L *dormire*]

dough ty (dou′tē), *adj.,* **-ti er, -ti est.** brave; valiant; strong. [OE *dohtig* < *dugan* be good] **—dough′ti ness,** *n.*

dray (drā), *n.* a low, strong cart for hauling heavy loads. **—***v.* transport or carry on a cart. [OE *dræge* dragnet < *dragan* draw]

drop sy (drop′sē), *n.* an abnormal accumulation of watery fluid in certain tissues or cavities of the body. [var. of *hydropsy* < OF *idropisie* < L *hydropisis* < Gk. *hydrops* < *hydor* water]

duc tile (duk′təl), *adj.* **1.** capable of being hammered out thin or drawn out into a wire: *Gold and copper are ductile metals.* **2.** easily molded or shaped: *Wax is ductile.* **3.** easily managed or influenced; docile. [< F < L *ductilis* < *ducere* lead]

dudg eon (duj′ən), *n.* **1.** anger; resentment. **2. in high dudgeon,** very angry; resentful. [origin unknown]

dwine (dwīn), *v.i.,* **dwined, dwin ing.** to diminish; fade; dwindle. [ME; OE *dwin(an)* to waste away]

dys pep si a (dis pep′sē ə), *n.* poor digestion; indigestion. [< L < Gk. *dyspepsia* < *dys-* bad + *pep-* cook, digest]

---

ef face (ə fās′), v., **-faced, -fac ing.** 1. rub out; blot out; do away with; destroy; wipe out: *The inscriptions on many ancient monuments have been effaced by time. It takes many years to efface the unpleasant memories of a war.* 2. keep (oneself) from being noticed; make inconspicuous: *The shy boy effaced himself by staying in the background.* [< F *effacer* < *es-* (< *ex-*) away + *face* face < L *facies* form] —**ef face′a ble,** adj.

ef fi ca cy (ef′ə kə sē), n., pl. **-cies.** power to produce a desired effect or result; effectiveness. [< L *efficacia* < *efficere* accomplish]

ef flu vi um (i flü′vē əm), n., pl. **-vi a** or **-vi ums.** 1. an unpleasant vapor or odor. 2. vapor; odor. [< L *effluvium* a flowing out < *effluere*]

ef fuse (i fyüz′), v., **-fused, -fus ing.** pour out; spill; shed. [< L *effusus,* pp. of *effundere* < *ex-* out + *fundere* pour]

e lix ir (i lik′sər), n. 1. substance supposed to have the power of changing lead, iron, etc., into gold or of lengthening life indefinitely, sought for by the alchemists of the Middle Ages. 2. a universal remedy; cure-all. 3. medicine made of drugs or herbs mixed with alcohol and syrup. [< Med.L < Arabic *al-iksīr* (def. 1), probably < Gk. *xerion* drying powder used on wounds < *xeros* dry]

e ma ci ate (i mā′shē āt), v., **-at ed, -at ing.** make unnaturally thin; cause to lose flesh or waste away: *A long illness had emaciated the invalid.* [< L *emaciare* < *ex-* + *macies* leanness]

em bra sure (em brā′zhər), n. 1. an opening in a wall for a gun, with sides that spread outward to permit the gun to swing through a greater arc. 2. a slanting off of the wall at an oblique angle on the inner sides of a window or door. [< F *embrasure* < *embraser* widen an opening]

en cum brance (en kum′brəns), n. 1. anything that encumbers; hindrance; obstruction; burden. 2. a dependent person; child. 3. claim, mortgage, etc., on property. Also, **incumbrance.**

en fran chise (en fran′chīz), v., **-chised, -chis ing.** 1. give the right to vote: *The 19th amendment to the Constitution enfranchised American women.* 2. set free; release from slavery or restraint. —**en fran′chis er,** n.

en fran chise ment (en fran′chiz mənt), n. 1. an enfranchising. 2. being enfranchised.

e nig ma (i nig′mə), n. 1. a puzzling statement; riddle: *To most of the audience the philosopher seemed to speak in enigmas.* 2. a baffling or puzzling problem, situation, person, etc.: *The queer behavior of the child was an enigma even to her parents.* [< L *aenigma* < Gk. *ainigma* < *ainissesthai* speak darkly < *ainos* fable]

en trench (en trench′), v. 1. surround with a trench; fortify with trenches. 2. establish firmly: *Exchanging gifts at Christmas is a custom entrenched in peo-*

ple's minds. 3. trespass; encroach; infringe: *Do not entrench upon the rights of others.* Also, **intrench.**

e phem er al (i fem′ər əl), adj. lasting for only a day; lasting for only a very short time; very short-lived. [< Gk. *ephemeros* liable to be cut short < *epi-* subject to + *hemera* the day (of destiny)]

ep i thet (ep′ə thet), n. a descriptive expression; adjective or noun, or even a clause, expressing some quality or attribute: *In "crafty Ulysses" and "Richard the Lion-Hearted" the epithets are "crafty" and "the Lion-Hearted."* [< L < Gk. *epitheton* added < *epi-* on + *tithenai* place]

e pit o me (i pit′ə mē), n. 1. a condensed account; summary. An epitome contains only the most important points of a literary work, subject, etc. 2. some thing or part that is typical or representative of the whole: *Solomon is often spoken of as the epitome of wisdom.* [< L < Gk. *epitome* < *epithemnein* cut short < *epi-* into + *temnein* cut]

e qua nim i ty (ē′kwə nim′ə tē or ek′wə nim′ə tē), n. evenness of mind or temper; calmness: *A wise man bears misfortune with equanimity.* [< L *aequanimitas* < *aequus* even + *animus* mind, temper] —**Syn.** composure.

e quiv o cal (i kwiv′ə kəl), adj. 1. having two or more meanings; intentionally vague or ambiguous: *His equivocal answer left us uncertain as to his real opinion.* 2. undecided; uncertain: *The result of the experiment was equivocal and proved nothing.* 3. questionable; rousing suspicion: *The stranger's equivocal behavior made it unlikely that anyone would trust him.* [< LL *aequivocus* ambiguous < L *aequus* equal + *vocare* call] —**e quiv′o cal ly,** adv. —**Syn.** 1. doubtful. —**Ant.** 1. clear, evident, definite.

es cri toire (es′krə twär′ or es′krə twär), n. a writing desk. [< F < LL *scriptorium* < L *scribere* write]

es cu lent (es′kyə lənt), adj. suitable for food; edible. [< L *esculentus* < *esca* food]

e ther e al (i thir′ē əl), adj. 1. light; airy; delicate: *Her ethereal beauty made her seem more like a spirit than a human being.* 2. not of the earth; heavenly. 3. of or having to do with the upper regions of space. 4. of or having to do with the ether diffused through space. Also, **aethereal.** —**e the′re al ly,** adv. —**Syn.** 1. intangible.

eu phe mism (yü′fə miz′əm), n. 1. use of a mild or indirect expression instead of one that is harsh or unpleasantly direct. 2. a mild or indirect expression used in this way. "Pass away" is a common euphemism for "die." The name *Eumenides* for the Furies was a euphemism. [< Gk. *euphemismos* < *euphemizein* speak with fair words < *eu-* good + *pheme* speaking]

→ **euphemism, euphuism.** *Euphemism* is a world-wide trait, the effect of superstition, squeamishness, tact, or kindness. *Euphuism,* in its exact sense, was a passing fad; in a broader sense it includes tendencies to artificiality which may be shown by individuals. *Euphuism* relates to a sus-

tained style; *euphemism* to a particular expression.

ev a nes cent (ev′ə nes′nt), adj. tending to disappear or fade away; able to last only a short time.

e vince (i vins′), v., **e vinced, e vinc ing.** 1. show clearly: *The dog evinced its dislike of strangers by growling.* 2. show that one has (a quality, trait, etc.). [< L *evincere* < *ex-* out + *vincere* conquer]

ev i ta ble (ev′i tə bəl), adj. avoidable, [< L *ēvitāre* equiv. to ē+ *vitāre* to avoid]

ex cres cence (ek skres′ns), n. 1. an unnatural growth; disfiguring addition. Warts are excrescences on the skin. 2. a natural outgrowth. Fingernails are excrescences.

ex e cra tion (ek′sə krā′shən), n. 1. abhorrence; loathing; detestation. 2. a cursing. 3. a curse: *The mob shouted angry execrations.* 4. person or thing execrated.

ex hort (eg zôrt′), v. urge strongly; advise or warn earnestly: *The preacher exhorted his congregation to live better lives.* [< L *exhortari* < *ex-* + *hortari* urge strongly] —**ex hort′er,** n.

ex pe di en cy (ek spē′dē ən sē), n., pl. **-cies.** 1. usefulness; suitability for bringing about a desired result; desirability or fitness under the circumstances. 2. personal advantage; self-interest: *The crafty lawyer was influenced more by expediency than by the love of justice.*

ex pe di ent (ek spē′dē ənt) adj. 1. fit for bringing about a desired result; desirable or suitable under the circumstances. 2. giving or seeking personal advantage; based on self-interest. —n. means of bringing about a desired result: *Having no ladder or rope, the prisoner tied sheets together and escaped by this expedient.* [< L *expediens, -entis,* ppr. of *expedire* to free from a net, set right < *ex-* out + *pes* foot] —**ex pe′di ent ly,** adv. —**Syn.** adj. 1. advantageous, profitable, advisable. —n. shift, device.

ex tort (ek stôrt′), v. obtain (money, a promise, etc.) by threats, force, fraud, or illegal use of authority. Blackmailers try to extort money from their victims. [< L *extortus,* pp. of *extorquere* < *ex-* out + *torquere* twist] —**ex tort′er,** n.

ex u ber ant (eg zü′bər ənt), adj. 1. very abundant; overflowing; lavish: *exuberant health, good nature, or joy; an exuberant welcome.* 2. profuse in growth; luxuriant: *the exuberant vegetation of the jungle.* [< L *exuberans, -antis,* ppr. of *exuberare* grow luxuriantly < *ex-* thoroughly + *uber* fertile] —**ex u′ber ant ly,** adv.

fa cil i ty (fə sil′ə tē), n., pl. **-ties.** 1. absence of difficulty; ease: *The facility of communication is far greater now than it was a hundred years ago.* 2. power to do anything easily, quickly, and smoothly. 3. something that makes an action easy; aid; convenience: *Ropes, swings, and sand piles are facilities for play.* 4. easy-going quality; tendency to yield to others. —**Syn.** 1. easiness. 2. knack, readiness.

fag ot (fag′ət), n. 1. bundle of sticks or twigs tied together: *He built the fire with* *fagots.* **2.** bundle of iron rods or pieces of iron or steel to be welded. —*v.* **1.** tie or fasten together into bundles; make into a fagot. **2.** ornament with fagoting. [< OF]

fain (fān), *Archaic and Poetic.* —*adv.* by choice; gladly. —*adj.* **1.** willing, but not eager; forced by circumstances. **2.** glad; willing. **3.** eager; desirous. [OE *fægen*]

fane (fān), *n. Archaic and Poetic.* temple; church. [< L *fanum* temple]

far i na ceous (far′ə nā′shəs), *adj.* consisting of flour or meal; starchy; mealy. *Cereals, bread, and potatoes are farinaceous foods.*

fat u ous (fach′ü əs), *adj.* stupid but self-satisfied; foolish; silly. [< L *fatuus* foolish] —**fat′u ous ly,** *adv.* —**fat′u ous ness,** *n.* —**Syn.** See **foolish.**

feign (fān), *v.* **1.** put on a false appearance of; make believe; pretend: *Some animals feign death when in danger.* **2.** make up to deceive; invent falsely: *feign an excuse.* **3.** imagine: *The phoenix is a feigned bird.* [< OF *feign-*, stem of *feindre* < L *fingere* form] —**Syn. 1.** assume, affect, simulate.

fer rule (fer′əl or fer′ül), *n.* a metal ring or cap put around the end of a cane, wooden handle, umbrella, etc., for strength and protection. Also, **ferule.** [earlier *verrel,* < OF *virelle* < L *viriola,* dim. of *viriae* bracelets; form influenced by L *ferrum* iron]

fer ule (fer′əl or fer′ül), *n.* ferrule.

fe tish (fē′tish or fet′ish), *n.* **1.** any material object supposed to have magic power. **2.** anything regarded with unreasoning reverence or devotion: *Some people make a fetish of style.* [< F *fétiche* < Pg. *feitço* charm, originally adj.; artificial < L *facticius.* Doublet of FACTITIOUS.]

fi as co (fē as′kō), *n., pl.* **-cos** or **-coes.** failure; breakdown. [< F < Ital. *fiasco,* literally, flask; development of meaning uncertain]

fice (fīs), *n.* a feist, or small, bad-tempered dog.

fil i al (fil′ē əl), *adj.* of a son or daughter; due from a son or daughter: *The children treated their parents with filial respect.* [< LL *filialis* < L *filius* son] —**fil′i al ly,** *adv.*

fil let (fil′it; *n. 3 and v. 2, usually* fi lā′ or fil′ā), *n.* **1.** a narrow band, ribbon, etc., put around the head to keep the hair in place or as an ornament. **2.** a narrow band or strip of any material. Fillets are often used between moldings, the flutes of a column, etc. **3.** slice of fish, meat, etc., without bones or fat; filet. —*v.* **1.** bind or decorate with a narrow band, ribbon, strip, etc. **2.** cut (fish, meat, etc.) into fillets. [< F *filet,* dim. of *fil* < L *filum* thread]

flume (flüm), *n.* **1.** a deep, narrow valley with a stream running through it. **2.** a large, inclined trough or chute for carrying water. Flumes are used to transport logs or to furnish water for power. [< OF *flum* < L *flumen* river < *fluere* flow]

foi ble (foi′bəl), *n.* a weak point; weakness: *Talking too much is one of her foibles.* [< F *foible,* older form of modern *faible* feeble] —**Syn.** failing, frailty.

for mi car y (fôr′mə ker′ē), *n., pl.*

-**car ies.** an ant colony. [< ML *formicāri(us)* pertaining to ants]

foun tain head (foun′tən hed′), *n.* **1.** source of a stream. **2.** an original source.

free boot er (frē′bü′tər), *n.* pirate; buccaneer. [< Dutch *vrijbuiter* < *vrij* free + *buit* booty]

fresh et (fresh′it), *n.* **1.** flood caused by heavy rains or melted snow. **2.** rush of fresh water flowing into the sea. [< *fresh* flood, stream or pool of fresh water + -*et*]

frip per y (frip′ər ē), *n., pl.* **-per ies.** **1.** cheap, showy clothes; gaudy ornaments. **2.** a showing off; foolish display; pretended refinement: *Affectations of manner and speech are mere frippery.* [< F *friperie,* ult. < *frepe* rag]

fu cus (fyü′kəs), *n., pl.* **-ci**(-sī), **-cuses.** alga or seaweed of the genus *Fucus.*

furze (ferz), *n.* gorse, a low, prickly, evergreen shrub with yellow flowers, common on waste lands in Europe. [OE *fyrs*]

fyce See *fice.*

gaf fle (gaf′l), *v.* to enchain or bind up. [var. of cable: < F < Provençal < L *capulum* halter]

gall (gôl), *v.* **1.** make or become sore by rubbing: *The rough strap galled the horse's skin.* **2.** annoy; irritate. —*n.* **1.** a sore spot on the skin caused by rubbing. **2.** cause of annoyance or irritation.

gam bit (gam′bit), *n.* way of opening a game of chess by purposely sacrificing a pawn or a piece to gain some advantage. [< F < Provençal *cambi* an exchange]

gar ru lous (gar′ə ləs), *adj.* **1.** talking too much about trifles. **2.** using too many words. [< L *garrulus* < *garrire* chatter] —**gar′ru lous ly,** *adv.* —**gar′ru lous-ness,** *n.* —**Syn. 1.** talkative, loquacious.

gauche (gōsh), *adj.* awkward; clumsy; tactless. [< F *gauche* left] —**gauche′ly,** *adv.* —**gauche′ness,** *n.*

gaunt (gônt), *adj.* **1.** very thin and bony; with hollow eyes and a starved look: *Hunger and suffering make people gaunt.* **2.** looking bare and gloomy; desolate; forbidding; grim. [origin uncertain] —**gaunt′ly,** *adv.* —**gaunt′ness,** *n.* —**Syn. 1.** lean, spare, lank.

gen e sis (jen′ə sis), *n., pl.* **-ses** (-sēz). origin; creation; coming into being. [< L < Gk.]

gird (gerd), *v.,* **girt** or **gird ed, gird ing.** **1.** put a belt or girdle around. **2.** fasten with a belt or girdle. **3.** surround; enclose. **4.** get ready for action: *The soldiers girded themselves for battle.* **5.** clothe; furnish; endue. [OE *gyrdan*]

grape shot (grāp′shot′), *n.* cluster of small iron balls formerly used as a charge for cannon.

gra tu i tous (grə tü′ə təs or grə tyü′ə-təs), *adj.* **1.** freely given or obtained; free. **2.** without reason or cause; unnecessary; uncalled-for. —**gra tu′i tous ly,** *adv.* —**gra tu′i tous ness,** *n.* —**Syn. 2.** unwarranted.

gre gar i ous (grə ger′ē əs or grə gar′ē-əs), *adj.* **1.** living in flocks, herds, or other groups: *Sheep and cattle are gregarious.*

hat, āge, fär; let, ēqual, tèrm; it, īce; hot, ōpen, ôrder; oil, out; cup, pút, rüle; ch, child; ng, long; sh, she; th, thin, тн, then; zh, measure;

ə represents *a* in about, *e* in taken, *i* in pencil, *o* in lemon, *u* in circus.

< = from, derived from, taken from.

---

2. fond of being with others. **3.** of or having to do with a flock or crowd. [< L *gregarius* < *grex* flock] —**gre gar′i ous-ly,** *adv.* —**gre gar′i ous ness,** *n.*

guile (gil), *n.* crafty deceit; craftiness; sly tricks: *A swindler uses guile; a robber uses force.* [< OF < Gmc. Akin to *wile*] —**Syn.** cunning, wiliness, trickery. —**Ant.** honesty.

gun wale (gun′l), *n.* the upper edge of a ship's or boat's side. Also, **gunnel.** [< *gun* + *wale* a plank; because formerly used to support the guns]

---

her biv or ous (her biv′ə rəs), *adj.* feeding on grass or other plants. Cattle are herbivorous animals. [< NL *herbivorus* < L *herba* herb + *vorare* devour]

hi er o glyph (hi′ər ə glif), *n.* hieroglyphic.

hi er o glyph ic (hī′ər ə glif′ik), *n.* **1.** picture of an object standing for a word, idea, or sound; character or symbol standing for a word, idea, or sound. The ancient Egyptians used hieroglyphics instead of an alphabet like ours. **2.** any writing that uses hieroglyphics. **3.** a secret symbol. **4.** letter or word that is hard to read. **5. hieroglyphics,** *pl.* writing that is hard to read. —*adj.* **1.** of or written in hieroglyphics. **2.** symbolical. **3.** hard to read. [< LL *hieroglyphicus* < Gk. *hieroglyphikos* < *hieros* sacred + *glyphe* carving] —**hi′er o glyph′i cal ly,** *adv.*

his tri on ic (his′trē on′ik), *adj.* **1.** having to do with actors or acting. **2.** theatrical; insincere. [< L *histrionicus* < *histrio* actor]

hoar y (hôr′ē), *adj.,* **hoar i er, hoar i est.** **1.** white or gray. **2.** white or gray with age. **3.** old; ancient. —**hoar′i ness,** *n.*

hogs head (hogz′hed′), *n.* **1.** a large barrel that contains from 100 to 140 gallons. **2.** a liquid measure equal to 63 gallons. [not known why so called]

hos tler (os′lər or hos′lər), *n.* person who takes care of horses at an inn or stable. Also, **ostler.** [var. of *ostler* < OF *hostelier* < *hostel*.]

hu bris (hyü′bris, hü′-), *n.* excessive arrogance. Also, **hybris.** —**hu bris tic,** *adj.* [< Gk: insolence]

hull (hul), *n.* **1.** body or frame of a ship. Masts, sails, and rigging are not part of the hull. **2.** the main body or frame of a seaplane, airship, etc. **3. hull down,** so far away that the hull is below the horizon. —*v.* strike or pierce the hull of (a ship) with a shell, torpedo, etc.

ig no ble (ig nō′bəl), *adj.* 1. mean; base; without honor: *To betray a friend is ignoble.* 2. of low birth. [< L *ignobilis* < *in-* not + OL *gnobilis* noble] —**ig no′ble ness**, *n.* —**ig no′bly**, *adv.* —**Syn.** 1. degraded, dishonorable, contemptible. —**Ant.** 1. noble.

il lu sive (i lü′siv), *adj.* due to an illusion; unreal; misleading; deceptive. —**il lu′sive ly**, *adv.* —**il lu′sive ness**, *n.*

il lu so ry (i lü′sər ē), *adj.* illusive.

im mit i ga ble (i mit′ə gə bəl), *adj.* that which cannot be made milder or lessened. [< L *mitigare mitis* gentle]

im mu ta ble (i myü′tə bəl), *adj.* never changing; unchangeable. —**im mu′ta bly**, *adv.* —**Syn.** unalterable, permanent.

im pal pa ble (im pal′pə bəl), *adj.* 1. that cannot be perceived by the sense of touch: *Sunbeams are impalpable. A thread of a spider's web is so thin as to be almost impalpable.* 2. very hard for the mind to grasp: *impalpable distinctions.* —**im pal′pa bly**, *adv.*

im pi ous (im′pē əs or im pi′əs), *adj.* not pious; not having or not showing reverence for God; wicked; profane. —**im′pi ous ly**, *adv.* —**im′pi ous ness**, *n.*

im pre ca tion (im′prə kā′shən), *n.* 1. act of calling down curses, evil, etc. 2. a curse.

im pute (im pyüt′), *v.,* **-put ed, -put ing.** consider as belonging; attribute; charge (a fault, etc.) to a person; blame: *I impute his failure to laziness.* [< L *imputare* < *in-* in + *putare* reckon] —**im put′a ble**, *adj.*

in cre ment (in′krə mənt), *n.* 1. increase; growth. 2. amount by which something increases. [< L *incrementum* < *increscere.*]

in cu bus (in′kyə bəs or ing′kyə bəs), *n., pl.* **-bi** (-bī) or **-bus es.** 1. an evil spirit supposed to descend upon sleeping persons. 2. nightmare. 3. an oppressive or burdensome thing: *This debt will be an incubus until I have paid it.* [< Med.L (def. 1), LL (def. 2) < L *incubare* < *in-* on < *cubare* lie]

in cul cate (in kul′kāt), *v.,* **-cat ed, -cat ing.** impress by repetition; teach persistently. [< L *inculcare,* originally, trample in, ult. < *in-* in + *calx* heel] —**in cul′ca tor**, *n.*

in ef fa ble (in ef′ə bəl), *adj.* 1. not to be expressed in words; too great to be described in words. 2. that must not be spoken. [< L *ineffabilis,* ult. < *in-* not + *ex-* out + *fari* speak] —**in ef′fa bly**, *adv.*

in ef face a ble (in′ə fās′ə bəl), *adj.* that cannot be rubbed out or wiped out. —**in′ef face′a bly**, *adv.*

in e luc ta ble (in′i luk′tə bəl), *adj.* unavoidable; inescapable. [< L *ineluctabil(is)* equiv. to IN + *elucta(ri)* to surmount] —**in′e luc′ta bil′i ty**, *n.* —**in′e luc′ta bly**, *adv.*

in ex o ra ble (in ek′sər ə bəl), *adj.* relentless; unyielding; not influenced by prayers or entreaties: *The forces of nature are inexorable.* [< L *inexorabilis* < *in-* not + *ex-* successfully + *orare* entreat] —**in ex′o ra bly**, *adv.* —**Syn.** unrelenting.

in gen u ous (in jen′yü əs), *adj.* 1. frank; open; sincere. 2. simple; natural; innocent. [< L *ingenuus,* originally, native, free born] —**in gen′u ous ly**, *adv.* —**in gen′u ous ness**, *n.* —**Syn.** 1. candid. 2. naïve.

in or di nate (in ôrd′n it), *adj.* much too great; excessive; unrestrained. [< L *inordinatus* < *in-* not + *ordo* order]

in or di nate ly (in ôrd′n it lē), *adv.* excessively.

in ter ne cine (in′tər nē′sn or in′tər nē′sin), *adj.* 1. destructive to both sides. 2. deadly; destructive. [< L *internecinus* < *internecere* kill < *inter-* between + *nex* slaughter]

in ter stice (in tėr′stis), *n., pl.* **-sti ces** (-stə siz). a small or narrow space between things or parts; chink. [< LL *interstitium* < L *inter-* between + *stare* to stand]

in trin sic (in trin′sik), *adj.* belonging to a thing by its very nature; essential; inherent: *The intrinsic value of a dollar bill is only that of a piece of paper.* [< F < Med.L *intrinsecus* internal < L *intrinsecus* inwardly]

in vid i ous (in vid′ē əs), *adj.* likely to arouse ill will or resentment; giving offense because unfair or unjust. [< L *invidiosus* < *invidia* envy. Related to *envy.*] —**in vid′i ous ly**, *adv.* —**in vid′i ous ness**, *n.* —**Syn.** hateful.

jad ed (jā′did), *adj.* 1. worn out; tired; weary. 2. dulled from continual use; surfeited; satiated: *a jaded appetite.*

jit ney (jit′nē), *n., pl.* **-neys.** *U.S. Slang.* 1. automobile that carries passengers for a small fare. It usually travels along a regular route. 2. a five-cent piece; nickel. [Am.E; origin uncertain]

Jug ger naut (jug′ər nôt), *n.* 1. idol of the Hindu god Krishna, pulled around on a huge car. Devotees of the god are said to have thrown themselves under the wheels to be crushed to death. 2. something to which a person blindly devotes himself or is cruelly sacrificed. [< Hindu. *Jagannāth* < Skt. *Jagannātha* lord of the world]

jux ta pose (juk′stə pōz′), *v.,* **-posed, -pos ing.** put close together; place side by side. [< F *juxtaposer* < L *juxta* beside + F *poser* place]

keel (kēl), *n.* 1. the main timber or steel piece that extends the whole length of the bottom of a ship or boat. 2. *Poetic.* ship. 3. part in an airplane or airship resembling a ship's keel. 4. **on an even keel,** horizontal. —*v.* 1. turn upside down; upset. 2. **keel over. a.** turn over or upside down; upset. **b.** fall over suddenly. **c.** *Informal.* faint. [< Scand. *kjölr*]

kine (kin), *n.pl. Archaic* or *Dialect.* cows; cattle. [earlier *kyen,* formed after pattern of *oxen* < OE *cȳ,* pl. of *cū* cow]

knell (nel), *n.* 1. sound of a bell rung slowly after a death or at a funeral. 2. a warning sign of death, failure, etc.: *Their refusal rang the knell of our hopes.* 3. a mournful sound.

lab y rinth (lab′ə rinth), *n.* 1. a place through which it is hard to find one's way; maze. 2. a confusing, complicated arrangement. 3. a confusing, complicated state of affairs. 4. **Labyrinth,** in Greek mythology, the maze built by Daedalus for King Minos of Crete. The Minotaur was kept there. 5. the internal ear. [< L < Gk. *labyrinthos*]

las si tude (las′ə tüd or las′ə tyüd), *n.* lack of energy; weakness; weariness. [< L *lassitudo* < *lassus* tired]

last (last), *n.* 1. block shaped like a person's foot, on which shoes and boots are formed or repaired. 2. **stick to one's last,** pay attention to one's own work; mind one's own business. —*v.* form (shoes and boots) on a last. [OE *lǣste* < *lǣst* track]

la tent (lāt′nt), *adj.* present but not active; hidden; concealed: *latent germs of disease, latent powers, latent ability.* [< L *latens, -entis,* ppr. of *latere* lie hidden] —**la′tent ly**, *adv.*

Syn. Latent, potential mean existing as a possibility or fact, but not now showing itself plainly. **Latent** means actually existing as a fact, but lying hidden, not active or plainly to be seen at the present time: *The power of a grain of wheat to grow into a plant remains latent if it is not planted.* **Potential** means existing as a possibility and capable of coming into actual existence or activity if nothing happens to stop development: *That boy has great potential ability in science.*

letters patent See *patent.*

lig a ture (lig′ə chür or lig′ə chər), *n., v.,* **-tured, -tur ing.** —*n.* 1. anything used to bind or tie up; bandage, cord, etc. 2. thread, string, etc., used to tie up a bleeding artery or vein. 3. a binding or tying up. 4. in music, a slur or a group of notes connected by a slur. 5. two or three letters joined in printing. Æ and ffl are ligatures. —*v.* bind or tie up with a ligature. [< LL *ligatura* < L *ligare* bind]

light er (līt′ər), *n.* a flat-bottomed barge used for loading and unloading ships. —*v.* carry (goods) in a flat-bottomed barge. [< *light* or ? < Dutch *lichter*]

lim pid (lim′pid), *adj.* clear; transparent: *limpid water, limpid eyes.* [< L *limpidus*] —**lim′pid ly**, *adv.*

lin e a ment (lin′ē ə mənt), *n.* part or feature; part or feature of a face with attention to its outline. [< L *lineamentum* < *linea* line]

lin tel (lin′tl), *n.* a horizontal beam or stone over a door, window, etc., to support the structure above it. [< OF *lintel,* ult. < L *limes, limitis* boundary]

li ti gious (lə tij′əs), *adj.* 1. having the habit of going to law. 2. offering material for a lawsuit; that can be disputed in a court of law. 3. of lawsuits. [< L *litigiosus* < *litigium* dispute < *litigare.*]

lor gnette (lôr nyet′), *n.* 1. eyeglasses mounted on a handle. 2. opera glass. [< F *lorgnette* < *lorgner* look sidelong at, eye < OF *lorgne* squinting]

lu cid (lü′sid), *adj.* 1. easy to understand: *a lucid explanation.* 2. shining; bright. 3. sane: *An insane person sometimes has*

lucid intervals. 4. clear; transparent: *a lucid stream.* [< L *lucidus* < *lux* light] —**lu′cid ly,** *adv.*

lu cid i ty (lü sid′ə tē), *n.* lucid quality or condition.

mace (mās), *n.* **1.** a war club used in the Middle Ages. **2.** staff used as a symbol of authority. [< OF < VL *mattea* < L *matteola* kind of hammer]

mac e rate (mas′ə rāt′), *v.,* **-at ed, at ing. 1.** soften by soaking for some time. Flowers are macerated to extract their perfume. **2.** cause to grow thin. **3.** become thin; waste away. [< L *macerare* soften] —**mac′er a′tion,** *n.*

mac ro cosm (mak′rə koz′əm), *n.* the universe. [< F < Med.L *macrocosmus* < Gk. *makros* great + *kosmos* world]

man di ble (man′də bəl), *n.* **1.** jaw; especially, the lower jaw. **2.** either part of a bird's beak. **3.** organ in insects for seizing and biting. [< L *mandibula* < *mandere* chew]

man i fest (man′ə fest), *adj.* apparent to the eye or to the mind; plain; clear. —*v.* **1.** show plainly; reveal; display. **2.** prove; put beyond doubt. —*n.* list of a ship's cargo. [< L *manifestus* palpable < *manus* hand + ? *fers-* seize] —**man′i fest′ly,** *adv.* —**Syn.** *adj.* obvious, evident, unmistakable. —*v.* **1.** exhibit, disclose, evidence.

man i fes ta tion (man′ə fə stā′shən), *n.* **1.** a manifesting. **2.** being manifested. **3.** thing that manifests: *A brave deed is a manifestation of courage.* **4.** a public demonstration.

met a mor phose (met′ə môr′fōz), *v.,* **-phosed, -phos ing.** change in form; transform: *The witch metamorphosed people into animals.*

met a mor pho sis (met′ə môr′fə sis), *n.,* *pl.* **-ses** (-sēz). **1.** change of form. Tadpoles become frogs by metamorphosis; they lose their tails and grow legs. **2.** the changed form. **3.** a noticeable or complete change of character, appearance, or condition. [< L < Gk. *metamorphosis,* ult. < *meta-* over + *morphe* form]

mi as ma (mi az′mə), *n.,* *pl.* **-mas, -ma ta** (-mə tə). poisonous vapor rising from the earth and infecting the air. The miasma of swamps was formerly supposed to cause disease. [< NL < Gk. *miasma* pollution < *miainein* pollute]

mi cro cosm (mī′krō koz′əm), *n.* **1.** a little world; universe in miniature. **2.** man thought of as a miniature representation of the universe. [< F < LL *microcosmus* < LGk. *mikros kosmos* little world]

mien (mēn), *n.* manner of holding the head and body; way of acting and looking: *George Washington had the mien of a soldier.* [probably < *demean;* influenced by F *mine* expression < Celtic] —**Syn.** bearing, demeanor, appearance.

milk leg (milk leg), *n.* a painful swelling of the leg caused by clots in the veins.

mis an thrope (mis′ən thrōp), *n.* hater of mankind; person who dislikes or distrusts human beings. [< Gk. *misanthropos* < *miseein* hate + *anthropos* man]

moil (moil), *v.* work hard; drudge. —*n.* **1.** hard work; drudgery. **2.** trouble; confusion. [< OF *moillier* moisten < L *mollis* soft]

mon o lith (mon′l ith), *n.* **1.** a single large block of stone. **2.** monument, column, statue, etc., formed of a single large block of stone. [< L < Gk. *monolithos* < *monos* single + *lithos* stone]

mon o lith ic (mon′l ith′ik), *adj.* of a monolith; being a monolith.

mort main (môrt′mān), *n.* an inalienable possession; the condition of lands or tenements held without right to sell them or give them away. [< OF *mortemain,* translation of Med.L *mortua manus* dead hand; with reference to corporations as not being persons]

mum mer (mum′ər), *n.* **1.** person who wears a mask, fancy costume, or disguise for fun. **2.** actor. [< OF *momeur* < *momer* mask oneself]

mum mer y (mum′ər ē), *n.,* *pl.* **-mer ies. 1.** performance of mummers. **2.** any useless or silly show or ceremony. [< OF *mommerie*]

mu nif i cent (myü nif′ə sənt), *adj.* extremely generous. [< *munificence*] —**mu nif′i cent ly,** *adv.* —**Syn.** bountiful, bounteous, lavish, liberal.

mur phy (mėr′fē), *n.,* *pl.* **-phies.** a type of potato.

mus ket oon (mus′ki tün′), *n.* a type of short musket with a large opening.

mu ta tion (myü tā′shən), *n.* **1.** change; alteration. **2.** a new feature that appears suddenly in animals or plants and can be inherited. **3.** a new variety of animal or plant formed in this way. **4.** umlaut. [< L *mutatio, -onis* < *mutare* change]

ne ol o gism (ni ol′ə jiz əm), *n.* **1.** use of new words or new meanings for old words. **2.** a new word; new meaning for an old word. [< F < Gk. *neos* new + *logos* word]

nim bus (nim′bəs), *n.,* *pl.* **-bus es, -bi** (-bī). **1.** a light disk or other radiance about the head of a divine or sacred person in a picture. **2.** a bright cloud surrounding a god, person, or thing. **3.** a rain cloud. [< L *nimbus* cloud]

nos trum (nos′trəm), *n.* **1.** medicine made by the person who is selling it; quack remedy; patent medicine. **2.** a pet scheme for producing wonderful results; cure-all. [< L *nostrum* ours]

ob se qui ous (əb sē′kwē əs), *adj.* polite or obedient from hope of gain or from fear; servile; fawning: *Obsequious courtiers greeted the king.* [< L *obsequiosus,* ult. < *ob-* after + *sequi* follow] —**ob se′qui ous ly,** *adv.* —**ob se′qui ous ness,** *n.* —**Syn.** slavish.

ob strep er ous (əb strep′ər əs), *adj.* **1.** noisy; boisterous. **2.** unruly; disorderly. [< L *obstreperus* < *ob-* against + *strepere* make a noise] —**ob strep′er ous ly,** *adv.* —**ob strep′er ous ness,** *n.* —**Syn. 1.** clamorous, vociferous.

hat, āge, fär; let, ēqual, tėrm;
it, īce; hot, ōpen, ôrder;
oil, out; cup, pùt, rüle;
ch, child; ng, long; sh, she;
th, thin; ŦH, then; zh, measure;

ə represents *a* in about, *e* in taken,
i in pencil, *o* in lemon, *u* in circus.

< = from, derived from, taken from.

ob tru sive (əb trü′siv), *adj.* inclined to obtrude; intrusive. —**ob tru′sive ly,** *adv.* —**ob tru′sive ness,** *n.* —**Syn.** meddlesome, officious.

oc cult (ə kult′ or ok′ult), *adj.* **1.** beyond the bounds of ordinary knowledge; mysterious. **2.** outside the laws of the natural world; magical: *Astrology and alchemy are occult sciences.* [< L *occultus* hidden, pp. of *occulere* < *ob-* up + *-celere* cover] —**Syn. 1.** secret, hidden, mystic.

on tol o gy (on tol′ə jē), *n.* that part of philosophy that deals with the nature of reality. [< NL *ontologia* < Gk. *on, ontos* being + *-logos* treating of]

op pro bri ous (ə prō′brē əs), *adj.* expressing scorn, reproach, or abuse: *Coward, liar, and thief are opprobrious names.* [< LL *opprobriosus*] —**op pro′bri ous ly,** *adv.*

op pro bri um (ə prō′brē əm), *n.* disgrace or reproach caused by shameful conduct; infamy; scorn; abuse. [< L *opprobrium,* ult. < *ǫb-* at + *probrum* infamy, reproach]

o ri el (ôr′ē əl), *n.* a bay window projecting from the outer face of a wall. [< OF *oriol* porch]

os ten si ble (os ten′sə bəl), *adj.* apparent; pretended; professed: *Her ostensible purpose was borrowing sugar, but she really wanted to see the new furniture.* [< F < L *ostendere* show < *ob-* toward + *tendere* stretch]

os ten ta tion (os′ten tā′shən), *n.* a showing off; display intended to impress others. [< L *ostentatio, -onis,* ult. < *ob-* toward + *tendere* stretch] —**Syn.** parade, pomp. —**Ant.** modesty, reserve, simplicity.

ost ler (os′lər), *n.* hostler.

o yer and ter mi ner (ō′yər, oi′ər; tėr′mə nər), *Law.* any of the higher criminal courts (in certain states). [ME<AF,c. OF *oir*<L *audīre* to hear + to determine]

pall (pôl), *n.* **1.** a heavy cloth of black, purple, or white velvet spread over a coffin, a hearse, or a tomb. **2.** a dark, gloomy covering: *A pall of smoke shut out the sun from the city.* [OE *pæll* < L *pallium* cloak]

pal li ate (pal′ē āt), *v.,* **-at ed, -at ing. 1.** lessen without curing; mitigate: *palliate a disease.* **2.** make appear less serious; excuse: *palliate a fault.* [< L *palliare* cover with a cloak < *pallium* cloak]

pal li a tion (pal′ē ā′shən), *n.* **1.** a palliating. **2.** thing that palliates; excuse.

pal pa ble (pal′pə bəl), *adj.* 1. readily seen or heard and recognized; obvious: *a palpable error.* 2. that can be touched or felt. [< LL *palpabilis* < L *palpare* feel] —**Syn.** 1. perceptible, plain, evident, manifest. 2. tangible.

pan o ply (pan′ə plē), *n., pl.* **-plies.** 1. a complete suit of armor. 2. complete equipment or covering. [< Gk. *panoplia* < *pan-* all + *hopla* arms]

pan e gyr ist (pan′ə jir′ist or pan′ə-jir′ist), *n.* person who praises enthusiastically or extravagantly.

par si mo ny (pär′sə mō′nē), *n.* extreme economy; stinginess. [< L *parsimonia* < *parcere* to spare]

passe men terie (pas men′ trē), *n.,* ornamental trimmings. [F < *passeman* railing < Sp. *pasamano*]

pas til (pas′til), *n.* pastille.

pas tille (pas tēl′), *n.* 1. a flavored or medicated lozenge. 2. a small roll or cone of aromatic paste, burnt as a disinfectant, incense, etc. 3. pastel for crayons. 4. a crayon made from pastel. [< F < L *pastillus* roll, aromatic lozenge, dim. of *panis* bread]

pat ent (*n., adj. 1, v.* pat′nt, *esp. Brit.* pāt′nt; *adj. 2, 3* pāt′nt or pat′nt), *n.* 1. a government grant to a person by which he is the only one allowed to make or sell a new invention for a certain number of years. 2. invention that is patented. 3. an official document from a government giving a right or privilege. —*adj.* 1. given or protected by a patent. 2. evident; plain: *It is patent that cats dislike dogs.* 3. open. —*v.* get a patent for. [< L *patens, -entis,* ppr. of *patere* lie open] —**pat′ent a ble,** *adj.*

pat ri mo ny (pat′rə mō′nē), *n., pl.* **-nies.** 1. property inherited from one's father or ancestors. 2. property belonging to a church, monastery, or convent. 3. any heritage. [< OF < L *patrimonium* < *pater* father]

pelf (pelf), *n.* money or riches, thought of as bad or degrading. [< OF *pelfre* spoils]

pen u ry (pen′yə rē), *n.* great poverty. [< L *penuria*]

per fi dy (per′fə dē), *n., pl.* **-dies.** a breaking faith; base treachery; being false to a trust. [< L *perfidia,* ult. < *per-* + *fides* faith]

per i anth (per′ē anth), *n.* envelope of a flower, including the calyx and the corolla. [< NL < Gk. *peri-* around + *anthos* flower]

per spi cu i ty (per′spə kyü′ə tē), *n.* clearness in expression; ease in being understood. —**Syn.** lucidity, plainness.

per ti nac i ty (pert′n as′ə tē), *n.* great persistence; holding firmly to a purpose, action, or opinion.

phan tasm (fan′taz′əm), *n.* 1. thing seen only in one's imagination; unreal fancy: *the phantasms of a dream.* 2. a supposed appearance of an absent person, living or dead. 3. a deceiving likeness (of some-

thing). [< L < Gk. *phantasma* image, ult. < *phainein* show. Doublet of PHANTOM.]

phan tas ma go ri a (fan taz′mə gô′rē ə or fan taz′mə gō′rē ə), *n.* 1. a shifting scene of real things, illusions, imaginary fancies, deceptions, and the like: *the phantasmagoria of a dream.* 2. show of optical illusions in which figures increase or decrease in size, fade away, and pass into each other. [< Gk. *phantasma* image + ? *agora* assembly] —**phan tas′ma gor′-ic;** —**i cal,** *adj.*

phi lol o gy (fə lol′ə jē), *n.* 1. an older name for linguistics. 2. the study of literary and other records. [< L < Gk. *philologia,* ult. < *philos* loving + *logos* word, speech, story]

phleg mat ic (fleg mat′ik), *adj.* 1. sluggish; indifferent. 2. cool; calm: *John is phlegmatic; he never seems to get excited about anything.* [< LL *phlegmaticus* < Gk. *phlegmatikos* < *phlegma*] —**phleg mat′i cal ly,** *adv.*

plan gent (plan′jənt), *adj.* 1. the beating sound of waves. 2. loudly resounding. [< L *plangēns* lament] —**plan′gen cy,** *n.*

pleach (plēch), *v.* interweave (growing branches, vines, etc.); entwine. [< OF *plechier,* ult. < L *plectere* weave]

ple be ian (pli bē′ən), *n.* 1. one of the common people of ancient Rome. 2. one of the common people. 3. a common, vulgar person. —*adj.* 1. of the plebeians. 2. belonging or having to do with the common people. 3. common; vulgar. [< L *plebeius* < *plebs* the common people]

plinth (plinth), *n.* 1. the lower, square part of the base of a column. 2. a square base of a pedestal. [< L < Gk. *plinthos*]

polemic divinity See *polemics.*

po lem ics (pə lem′iks), *n.* art or practice of disputation or controversy, especially in theology.

pol y tone (pol′ē tōn′), *n.* in music, the use of more than one key at the same time. [< OF < Ital. *poppa* < L *puppis* stern]

poop (püp), *n.* 1. deck at the stern above the ordinary deck, often forming the roof of a cabin. 2. stern of a ship. —*v.* of a wave, break over the stern of (a ship). [< OF < Ital. *poppa* < L *puppis* stern]

porte-co chere or **porte-co chère** (pôrt′kō shār′ or pōrt′kō shār′), *n.* 1. porch at the door of a building under which carriages and automobiles stop so that persons getting in or out are sheltered. 2. entrance for carriages, leading into a courtyard. [< F *porte-cochère* coachgate]

por ten tous (pôr ten′təs), *adj.* 1. indicating evil to come; ominous; threatening. 2. amazing; extraordinary. —**por ten′tous ly,** *adv.* —**por ten′tous ness,** *n.* —**Syn.** 1. foreboding. 2. wonderful, marvelous.

por tiere or **por tière** (pôr tyer′), *n.* curtain hung at a doorway. [< F *portière* < *porte* door]

pos se co mi ta tus (pos′ē kom′i tā′-təs, -tā′-), *n.* 1. the body of men that a sheriff or country officer may call together for assistance. 2. a body of men called into such service. [< ML *posse* power < L *comitāt(us)* escort]

pos ter i ty (po ster′ə tē), *n.* 1. genera-

tions of the future: *If we burn up all the coal in the world, what will posterity do?* 2. all of a person's descendants. [′< L *posteritas* < *posterus.*]

pos tu late (*n.* pos′chə lit; *v.* pos′chə lāt), *n., v.,* **-lat ed, -lat ing.** —*n.* something taken for granted or assumed as a basis for reasoning; a fundamental principle; necessary condition: *One postulate of geometry is that a straight line may be drawn between any two points.* —*v.* 1. take for granted; assume without proof as a basis of reasoning; require as a fundamental principle or necessary condition. 2. require; demand; claim. [< L *postulatum,* originally pp. neut. of *postulare* demand] —**pos′tu la′tion,** *n.*

pow der mon key (pou′dər mung′kē), *n.* 1. in former times the boy on warships who carried powder to the guns. 2. the man in charge of explosives in a situation requiring their use.

pre ci os i ty (presh′ē os′ə tē), *n., pl.* **-ties.** too much refinement; affectation. [< F *préciosité* < *précieux* precious]

pre ëm i nent or **pre-em i nent** (prē-em′ə nənt), *adj.* standing out above all others; superior to others. [< L *praeeminens, -entis,* ppr. of *praeeminere* < *prae-* before + *eminere* stand out] —**pre ëm′i-nent ly, pre-em′i nent ly,** *adv.*

pre ëmpt or **pre-empt** (prē empt′), *v.* 1. secure for someone else can; acquire or take possession of beforehand: *The cat had preëmpted the comfortable chair.* 2. settle on (land) with the right to buy it before others. [< *preëmption*] —**pre-ëmp′tor, pre-emp′tor,** *n.*

pres age (*n.* pres′ij; *v.* pri sāj′), *n., v.,* **pre saged, pre sag ing.** —*n.* 1. sign felt as a warning; omen. 2. a feeling that something is about to happen. —*v.* 1. give warning of; predict: *Some people think that a circle around the moon presages a storm.* 2. have or give a prophetic impression (of). [< L *praesagium,* ult. < *prae-* before + *sagus* prophetic] —**pre sag′er,** *n.*

pre sen ti ment (pri zen′tə mənt), *n.* a feeling or impression that something is about to happen; vague sense of approaching misfortune; foreboding. [< MF *presentiment,* ult. < L *prae-* before + *sentire* to sense]

pre ter nat ur al (prē′tər nach′ər əl), *adj.* 1. out of the ordinary course of nature; abnormal. 2. due to something above or beyond nature; supernatural. [< Med.L *praeternaturalis,* ult. < L *praeter-* beyond + *natura* nature] —**pre′ter nat′u ral-ly,** *adv.*

pri mor di al (pri môr′dē əl), *adj.* 1. existing at the very beginning; primitive. 2. original; elementary. [< L *primordialis* < *primordium* beginning]

pro di gious (prə dij′əs), *adj.* 1. very great; huge; vast: *The ocean contains a prodigious amount of water.* 2. wonderful; marvelous. [< L *prodigiosus* < *prodigium* prodigy, omen] —**pro di′gious ly,** *adv.* —**pro di′gious ness,** *n.*

pro lix i ty (prō lik′sə tē), *n.* too great length; tedious length of speech or writing.

pro pi ti ate (prə pish′ē āt), *v.,* **-at ed, -at ing.** prevent or reduce the anger of;

win the favor of; appease or conciliate. [< L *propitiare*, ult. < *propitius* propitious. See PROPITIOUS.] —**pro pi'ti a'tor**, *n.*

pro pi ti a to ry (prə pish'ē ə tôr'ē), *adj.* intended to propitiate; making propitiation; conciliatory: *a propitiatory offering.*

pro pi tious (prə pish'əs), *adj.* **1.** favorable: *propitious weather for our trip.* **2.** favorably inclined; gracious. [< L *propitius*, originally, falling forward < *pro-* forward + *petere* go toward] —**pro pi'tious ly**, *adv.* —**pro pi'tious ness**, *n.* —**Syn. 1.** auspicious, promising.

pu er ile (pyü'ər əl), *adj.* foolish for a grown person to say or do; childish. [< L *puerilis* < *puer* boy] —**Syn.** juvenile, immature.

pule (pyül), *v.*, **puled, pul ing.** cry in a thin voice, as a sick child does; whimper; whine. [? imitative]

pun cheon (pun'chən), *n.* **1.** a large cask for liquor. **2.** amount that it holds. **3.** slab of timber, or a piece of a split log, with the face roughly smoothed. **4.** a short upright piece of wood in the frame of a building. [< OF *poinchon*, ult. < L *pungere* pierce]

purl (pèrl), *v.* flow with rippling motions and a murmuring sound: *A shallow brook purls.* —*n.* a purling motion or sound. [? < Scand. (Norwegian) *purla*]

put cha min *n.* early form of persimmon.

py tho ness (pī'thə nis), *n.* **1.** priestess of Apollo at Delphi, who gave out the answers of the oracle. **2.** prophetess. [earlier *phytoness* < OF < LL *phythonissa* < *phyto* familiar spirit < Gk. *phyton*]

quaff (kwäf, kwaf), *v.* drink in large draughts; drink freely. —*n.* a quaffing. [origin uncertain]

quer u lous (kwer'ə ləs), *adj.* **1.** complaining; faultfinding. **2.** fretful; peevish. [< L *querulus* < *queri* complain] —**quer'u lous ly**, *adv.* —**quer'u lous ness**, *n.* —**Syn. 2.** petulant.

ram i fi ca tion (ram'ə fə kā'shən), *n.* **1.** dividing or spreading out into branches or parts. **2.** branch; part.

rec on dite (rek'ən dīt), *adj.* **1.** hard to understand; profound. **2.** little known; obscure. [< L *reconditus*, pp. of *recondere* store away, ult. < *re-* back + *com-* up + *dare* put]

rec ti tude (rek'tə tüd or rek'tə tyüd), *n.* upright conduct or character; honesty; righteousness. [< LL *rectitudo* < L *rectus* straight]

rec re ant (rek'rē ənt), *adj.* **1.** cowardly. **2.** disloyal; traitorous. —*n.* **1.** coward. **2.** traitor. [< OF *recreant* confessing oneself beaten, ult. < L *re-* back + *credere* believe]

re dress (*v.* ri dres'; *n.* rē'dres or ri dres'), *v.* set right; repair; remedy. —*n.* a setting right; reparation; relief: *Any man deserves redress if he has been injured unfairly.* [< F *redresser* < *re-* again + *dresser* straighten, arrange]

reef (rēf), *n.* part of a sail that can be rolled or folded up to reduce its size. —*v.* **1.** reduce the size of (a sail) by rolling or folding up a part of it. **2.** reduce the length of (a topmast, bowsprit, etc.) by lowering, etc. [< Scand. *rif* rib, reef. Cf. *reef.*]

ref lu ent (ref'lü ənt), *adj.* flowing back; ebbing. [< L *refluens, -entis*, ppr. of *refluere* flow back < *re-* back + *fluere* flow]

re ful gent (ri ful'jənt), *adj.* shining brightly; radiant; splendid: *a refulgent sunrise.* [< L *refulgens, -entis*, ppr. of *refulgere* < *re-* back + *fulgere* shine]

re pine (ri pīn'), *v.*, **-pined, -pin ing.** be discontented; fret; complain. [< *re-* + *pine*]

re tort (ri tôrt'), *n.* container used for distilling or decomposing substances by heat. [< Med.L *retorta*, originally fem. pp. of L *retorquere* throw back < *re-* back + *torquere* twist]

riv en (riv'ən), *adj.* torn apart; split. —*v.* a pp. of *rive.*

ru di ment (rü'də mənt), *n.* **1.** part to be learned first; beginning: *the rudiments of grammar.* **2.** something in an early stage; an organ or part incompletely developed in size or structure: *the rudiments of wings on a baby chick.* [< L *rudimentum* < *rudis* rude]

saf fron (saf'rən), *n.* **1.** an orange-yellow coloring matter obtained from a kind of crocus. Saffron is used to color and flavor candy, drinks, etc. **2.** an autumn crocus with purple flowers having orange-yellow stigmas. **3.** an orange yellow. —*adj.* orange-yellow. [< F *safran*, ult. < Arabic *za'farān*]

sa ga cious (sə gā'shəs), *adj.* **1.** wise in a keen, practical way; shrewd. **2.** intelligent. [< L *sagax, -acis*] —**sa ga'cious ly**, *adv.* —**sa ga'cious ness**, *n.* —**Syn. 1.** astute, perspicacious.

sa gac i ty (sə gas'ə tē), *n.*, *pl.* **-ties.** keen, sound judgment; mental acuteness; shrewdness. —**Syn.** acumen, perspicacity.

sal u tar y (sal'yə ter'ē), *adj.* **1.** beneficial: *The teacher gave the boy salutary advice.* **2.** good for the health; wholesome: *Walking is a salutary exercise.* [< L *salutaris* < *salus* good health] —**Syn. 1.** profitable, useful.

san dal wood (san'dl wùd'), *n.* **1.** a fragrant wood used for making boxes, fans, etc., and burned as incense. **2.** the tree that it comes from. [< *sandal* < Med.L *sandalum*, ult. < Skt. *candana*) + *wood*]

san guine (sang'gwən), *adj.* **1.** naturally cheerful and hopeful: *a sanguine disposition.* **2.** confident; hopeful: *sanguine of success.* **3.** having a healthy red color; ruddy: *a sanguine complexion.* **4.** in the old physiology, having an active circulation, a ruddy color, and a cheerful and ardent disposition. **5.** sanguinary. [< L *sanguineus* < *sanguis* blood] —**san'guine ly**, *adv.* —**Syn. 1.** optimistic.

sav in or **sav ine** (sav'ən), *n.* **1.** a juniper shrub whose tops yield an oily drug used in medicine. **2.** this drug. **3.** any of various junipers, such as the red cedar. [ult. < L *sabina*, originally adj., Sabine]

scin til la tion (sin'tl ā'shən), *n.* **1.** a

hat, āge, fär; let, ēqual, tèrm;
it, īce; hot, ōpen, ôrder;
oil, out; cup, pùt, rüle;
ch, child; ng, long; sh, she;
th, thin; ᴛʜ, then; zh, measure;

ə represents *a* in about, *e* in taken,
i in pencil, *o* in lemon, *u* in circus.

< = from, derived from, taken from.

sparkling; a flashing. **2.** a spark; flash.

sco ri a (skô'rē ə or skō'rē ə), *n.*, *pl.* **-ri ae** (-rē ē). **1.** slag or refuse left from ore after the metal has been melted out. **2.** cinderlike lava. [< L < Gk. *skoria* < *skor* dung]

scull (skul), *n.* **1.** oar worked with a side twist over the end of a boat to make it go. **2.** one of a pair of oars used, one on each side, by a single rower. **3.** act of propelling by sculls. **4.** a light racing boat for one or more rowers. —*v.* propel (a boat) by a scull or by sculls. [ME; origin unknown]

scut (skut), *n.* a short tail, especially that of a rabbit or deer. [< Scand. *skutr* stern]

sear (sir), *v.* **1.** burn or char the surface of: *The hot iron seared his flesh.* **2.** make hard or unfeeling: *That cruel man must have a seared conscience.* **3.** dry up; wither. **4.** become dry, burned, or hard. [OE *sēarian*, *v.* < *sēar*, adj.] —*n.* mark made by searing. —*adj.* dried up; withered. [OE *sēar*, adj.]

sen tience (sen'shəns), *n.* capacity for feeling: *Some people believe in the sentience of flowers.*

sere (sir), *adj.* sear. [var. of *sear*]

shale (shāl), *n.* a fine-grained rock, formed from clay or mud, that splits easily into thin layers. [OE *scealu* shell]

shal lop (shal'əp), *n.* a small, light open boat with sail or oars. [< F *chaloupe* < Dutch *sloepe*. Doublet of SLOOP.]

share (sher or shar), *n.* plowshare. [OE *scear*]

shib bo leth (shib'ə lith), *n.* any test word, watchword, or pet phrase of a political party, a class, sect, etc. [< Hebrew *shibbōleth* stream; used as a password by the Gileadites to distinguish the fleeing Ephraimites, because they could not pronounce *sh*. Judges 12:4-6]

shoat (shōt), *n.* a young pig able to feed itself. Also, **shote.** [origin uncertain]

sib yl (sib'əl), *n.* **1.** any of several prophetesses that the ancient Greeks and Romans consulted about the future. **2.** prophetess; fortuneteller; witch. [< L < Gk. *Sibylla*]

sil la bub (sil'ə bub), *n.* dessert made of cream, eggs, and wine sweetened and flavored. Also, **syllabub.** [origin uncertain]

si mil i tude (sə mil'ə tüd or sə mil'ə tyüd), *n.* **1.** similarity; likeness; resemblance. **2.** comparison: *She could think of no similitude to describe the sunset.* **3.** copy; image. [< L *similitudo* < *similis* like]

sloop (slüp), *n.* sailboat having one mast, a mainsail, a jib, and sometimes other sails.

[< Dutch *sloep*, earlier *sloepe*. Doublet of SHALLOP.]

slug gard (slug′ərd), *n.* a lazy, idle person. —*adj.* lazy; idle. [ult. < *slug*]

smi lax (smī′laks), *n.* 1. a twining, trailing plant or vine, much used by florists in decoration. 2. any of a large group of woody vines with prickly stems, umbrella-shaped clusters of flowers, and blackish or red berries. [< L < Gk.]

smirch (smėrch), *v.* make dirty; soil with soot, dirt, dust, dishonor, disgrace, etc. —*n.* a dirty mark; blot; stain. [ME *smorch*; ? < OF *esmorcher* torture, ult. < L *ex*-(intensive) + LL *mordicare* bite]

so journ (*v.* sō jėrn′ or sō′jėrn; *n.* sō′jėrn), *v.* stay for a time: *The Israelites sojourned in the land of Egypt.* —*n.* a brief stay. [< OF *sojorner*, ult. < L *sub* under + *diurnus* of the day] —**so journ′er,** *n.*

sol stice (sol′stis), *n.* either of the two times in the year when the sun is at its greatest distance from the celestial equator. In the Northern Hemisphere, June 21 or 22, the **summer solstice,** is the longest day of the year and December 21 or 22, the **winter solstice,** is the shortest. In the Southern Hemisphere the solstices are reversed. [< OF < L *solstitium*, ult. < *sol* sun + *sistere* stand still]

so no rous (sə nôr′əs), *adj.* 1. giving out or having a deep, loud sound. 2. full and rich in sound. 3. having an impressive sound; high-sounding: *sonorous phrases, a sonorous style.* [< L *sonorus*, ult. < *sonus* sound] —**so no′rous ly,** *adv.*

spar (spär), *n., v.,* **sparred, spar ring.** —*n.* 1. a stout pole used to support or extend the sails of a ship; mast, yard, gaff, boom, etc., of a ship. 2. the main beam of an airplane wing. —*v.* provide (a ship) with spars. [ME *sparre.* Cf. Scand. *sparri,* M Dutch *sparre.*]

spate (spāt), *n.* 1. Brit. flood; freshet. 2. a very heavy downpour of rain. 3. a sudden outburst: *a spate of words.* [ME; related to OE *spātan* spit]

spe cious (spē′shəs), *adj.* 1. seeming desirable, reasonable, or probable, but not really so; apparently good or right, but without real merit: *The teacher saw through John's specious excuse.* 2. making a good outward appearance in order to deceive: *His dishonest actions showed him to be nothing but a specious hypocrite.* [< L *speciosus* < *species* appearance] —**spe′cious ly,** *adv.* —**spe′cious ness,** *n.*

spur i ous (spyur′ē əs), *adj.* 1. not coming from the right source; not genuine; false; sham: *a spurious document.* 2. illegitimate. [< L *spurius*] —**spu′ri ous ly,** *adv.* —**spu′ri ous ness,** *n.*

squill (skwil), *n.* plant of the lily family, whose onionlike bulb is used in medicine. [< L *squilla,* var. of *scilla* < Gk. *skilla*]

squire ar chy (skwīər′är kē), *n.* 1. a group of landed gentry. 2. the social class composed of landed gentry. —**squire arch′al, squire ar′chi cal,** *adj.*

stanch (stänch), *adj.* 1. firm; strong: *stanch walls, a stanch defense.* 2. loyal; steadfast: *a stanch friend, a stanch supporter of the law.* 3. watertight: *a stanch boat.* Also, **staunch.** [< OF *estanche,* fem. < *estanchier.*] —**stanch′ly,** *adv.* —**stanch′ness,** *n.* —**Syn.** 2. constant, true, faithful, steady, unswerving.

staunch (stônch), *v., adj.* stanch. —**staunch′ly,** *adv.* —**staunch′ness,** *n.*

stern (stėrn), *n.* the hind part of a ship or boat. [probably < Scand. *stjörn* steering]

stern post (stėrn′pōst′), *n.* the principal piece of timber or iron in the stern of a ship. Its lower end is fastened to the keel, and it usually supports the rudder.

stile (stīl), *n.* 1. step or steps for getting over a fence or wall. 2. turnstile. 3. a vertical piece in a door, paneled wall, etc. [OE *stigel*; related to *stigan* climb]

strait en (strāt′n), *v.* 1. limit by the lack of something; restrict. 2. make narrow. 3. Archaic. confine; confine within narrow limits. 4. in straitened circumstances, needing money badly.

sub ter fuge (sub′tər fyüj), *n.* trick, excuse, or expedient used to escape something unpleasant: *The girl's headache was only a subterfuge to avoid taking the examination.* [< LL *subterfugium,* ult. < L *subter-* from under + *fugere* flee] —**Syn.** artifice, ruse.

suc cinct (sək singkt′), *adj.* expressed briefly and clearly; expressing much in few words; concise. [< L *succinctus,* pp. of *succingere* tuck up clothes for action < *sub-* up + *cingere* gird] —**suc cinct′ly,** *adv.* —**suc cinct′ness,** *n.* —**Syn.** compressed, condensed, terse.

suc cor (suk′ər), *n., v.* help; aid. [< OF *sucurs,* ult. < L *succurrere* run to help < *sub-* up (to) + *currere* run]

suc cour (suk′ər), *n., v.* Esp. Brit. succor.

su per car go (sü′pər kär′gō), *n., pl.* **-goes** or **-gos.** officer on a merchant ship who has charge of the cargo and the business affairs of the voyage. [earlier *supracargo* < Sp. *sobrecargo*]

su per cil i ous (sü′pər sil′ē əs), *adj.* haughty, proud, and contemptuous; disdainful; showing scorn or indifference because of a feeling of superiority: *The duchess looked down at the workman with a supercilious stare.* [< L *superciliosus* < *supercilium* eyebrow.] —**su′per cil′i ous ly,** *adv.*

su per sede (sü′pər sēd′), *v.,* **-sed ed, -sed ing.** 1. take the place of; cause to be set aside; displace: *Electric lights have superseded gas lights in most homes.* 2. fill the place of; replace: *A new governor superseded the old one.* [< L *supersedere* be superior to, refrain from < *super-* above + *sedere* sit] —**su′per sed′er,** *n.*

sup pli ant (sup′lē ənt), *adj.* asking humbly and earnestly: *He sent a suppliant message for help.* —*n.* person who asks humbly and earnestly: *She knelt as a suppliant at the altar.* [< F *suppliant,* ppr. of *supplier* < L *supplicare.*] —**sup′pli ant ly,** *adv.*

sup pli cant (sup′lə kənt), *n., adj.* suppli-

ant. [< L *supplicans, -antis,* ppr. of *supplicare.*]

sup pli ca tion (sup′lə kā′shən), *n.* 1. a supplicating. 2. a humble and earnest request or prayer: *Supplications to God arose from all the churches of the besieged town.*

suppositious See *supposititious.*

sup pos i ti tious (sə poz′ə tish′əs), *adj.* 1. put by fraud in the place of another; pretended; false; not genuine. 2. hypothetical; supposed. [< L *supposititius,* ult. < *sub-* under + *ponere* place] —**sup pos′i ti′tious ly,** *adv.*

sus te nance (sus′tə nəns), *n.* 1. food: *He has gone for a week without sustenance.* 2. means of living; support: *He gave money for the sustenance of a poor family.* [< OF *sustenance* < *sustenir* sustain < L *sustinere.*]

swain (swān), *n.* Archaic or Poetic. 1. lover. 2. a young man who lives in the country. [< Scand. *sveinn* boy]

syl lo gism (sil′ə jiz əm), *n.* 1. a form of argument or reasoning, consisting of two statements and a conclusion drawn from them. *Example:* All trees have roots; an oak is a tree; therefore, an oak has roots. 2. reasoning in this form; deduction. [< L < Gk. *syllogismos,* originally, inference, ult. < *syn-* together + *logos* a reckoning]

syl lo gis tic (sil′ə jis′tik), *adj.* of or having to do with syllogism; using syllogisms.

syn the sis (sin′thə sis), *n., pl.* **-ses.** 1. combination of parts or elements into a whole. *Synthesis* is the opposite of *analysis.* 2. formation of a compound or a complex substance by the chemical union of its elements, combination of simpler compounds, etc. Alcohol, ammonia, and rubber can be artificially produced by synthesis. [< L < Gk. *synthesis* < *syn-* together + *theinai* put]

sy rin ga (sə ring′gə), *n.* shrub with fragrant white flowers blooming in early summer; mock orange. [< NL *syringa* < Gk. *syrinx, -ingos* shepherd's pipe]

sys to le (sis′tlē), *n.* the normal rhythmical contraction of the heart. [< NL < Gk. *systole* contraction < *syn-* together + *stellein* wrap]

taff rail (taf′rāl′), *n.* a rail around a ship's stern. [< Dutch *tafereel* panel, dim. of *tafel* table]

tal low (tal′ō), *n.* the hard fat from sheep, cows, etc., used for making candles and soap. —*v.* smear with tallow. [ME *talgh*]

tan gen tial (tan jen′shəl), *adj.* 1. of or having to do with a tangent. 2. being a tangent. 3. in the direction of a tangent. 4. diverging. 5. slightly connected.

tarn (tärn), *n.* Brit. a small lake or pool in the mountains. [< Scand. *tjörn*]

Tar ta rus (tär′tə rəs), *n.* in Greek mythology: **a.** a place of punishment below Hades. **b.** the underworld; Hades. [< L < Gk. *Tartaros*]

te mer i ty (tə mer′ə tē), *n.* reckless boldness; rashness. [< L *temeritas* < *temere* heedlessly] —**Syn.** foolhardiness, audacity. —**Ant.** caution, wariness.

te na cious (ti nā′shəs), *adj.* 1. holding fast: *the tenacious jaws of a bulldog, a person tenacious of his rights.* 2. stubborn; persistent: *a tenacious salesman.* 3. able to remember: *a tenacious memory.* 4. holding fast together; not easily pulled apart. 5. sticky. [< L *tenax, -acis* < *tenere* hold] —**te na′cious ly,** *adv.* —**Syn.** 2. obstinate. 3. retentive.

ten u i ty (ten ū′ə tē or ti nü′ə tē), *n.* rarefied condition; thinness; slightness.

ten u ous (ten′yü əs), *adj.* 1. thin; slender. 2. not dense: *Air ten miles above the earth is very tenuous.* 3. having slight importance; not substantial. [< L *tenuis* thin] —**ten′u ous ly,** *adv.* —**ten′u ous ness,** *n.*

ter ma gant (tėr′mə gənt), *n.* a violent, quarreling, scolding woman. —*adj.* violent; quarreling; scolding. [ult. < OF *Tervagan,* fictitious Moslem deity]

tinc ture (tingk′chər), *n., v.,* **-tured, -tur ing.** —*n.* 1. solution of medicine in alcohol: *tincture of iodine.* 2. trace; tinge. 3. color; tint. —*v.* 1. give a trace or tinge to. 2. color; tint. [< L *tinctura* < *tingere* tinge]

tip pet (tip′it), *n.* 1. scarf for the neck and shoulders with ends hanging down in front. 2. a long, narrow, hanging part of a hood, sleeve, or scarf. [probably < *tip*]

tip ple (tip′əl), *v.,* **-pled, -pling,** *n.* —*v.* drink (alcoholic liquor) often. —*n.* an alcoholic liquor. [origin uncertain. Cf. Norwegian *tipla* drip, tipple]

tit u lar (tich′ə lər), *adj.* 1. in title or name only: *He is a titular prince without any power.* 2. having a title. 3. having to do with a title. [< L *titulus* title]

ton so ri al (ton sô′rē əl), *adj. Often used humorously.* of or having to do with a barber or his work. [< L *tonsorius,* ult. < *tondere* to shear]

tor pid (tôr′pid), *adj.* 1. dull; inactive; sluggish. 2. not moving or feeling. Animals that hibernate become torpid in winter. 3. numb. [< L *torpidus* < *torpere* be numb] —**tor′pid ly,** *adv.* —**tor′pid ness,** *n.* —**Syn.** 1. lethargic, apathetic.

tor por (tôr′pər), *n.* torpid condition. [< L *torpor* < *torpere* be numb]

trans mog ri fy (trans mog′rə fī, tranz-), *v.* to transform or change in appearance. —**trans mog′ti fi ca′tion,** *n.*

trav ail or **tra vail** (trav′āl or trə vāl′), *n.* 1. toil; labor. 2. trouble; hardship. 3. the pains of childbirth. —*v.* 1. toil; labor. 2. suffer the pains of childbirth. [< OF *travail,* ult. < LL *tripalium* (spelled *trepalium*) torture device, probably ult. < L *tri-* three + *palus* stake]

trem u lous (trem′yə ləs), *adj.* 1. trembling; quivering. 2. timid; fearful. [< L *tremulus* < *tremere* tremble. Doublet of TREMOLO.] —**trem′u lous ly,** *adv.* —**trem′u lous ness,** *n.* —**Syn.** 1. shaking, vibrating.

trep i dan cy (trep′ə dan′sē), *n.* a trepidation.

trep i da tion (trep′ə dā′shən), *n.* 1. nervous dread; fear; fright. 2. a trembling. [< L *trepidatio, -onis,* ult. < *trepidus* alarmed]

trist ful (trist′fəl), *adj., Archaic.* filled with sorrow. [< late ME < F *triste* sad + -FUL]

trunk hose (trungk′hōz), full, baglike breeches reaching halfway down the thigh, or lower. Trunk hose were worn in the 16th and 17th centuries.

tulle (tül), *n.* a thin, fine silk net, used for veils, etc. [from *Tulle,* French town]

tum brel or **tum bril** (tum′brəl), *n.* 1. a farmer's cart. 2. cart that carried prisoners to be executed. 3. a two-wheeled covered cart for carrying ammunition and military tools. [probably < OF *tomberel* cart < *tomber* fall < Gmc.]

tur bid (tėr′bid), *adj.* 1. muddy; thick; not clear: *a turbid river.* 2. confused; disordered: *a turbid imagination.* [< L *turbidus* < *turba* turmoil] —**tur′bid ly,** *adv.* —**tur′bid ness,** *n.*

twain (twān), *n., adj. Archaic or Poetic.* two [OE *twēgen*]

ul ster (ul′stər), *n.* a long, loose, heavy overcoat.

u na nim i ty (yü′nə nim′ə tē), *n.* complete accord or agreement. —**Syn.** harmony.

un con cil i a to ry (un′kən sil′ē ə tôr′ē), *adj.* not soothing; annoying. [< L *conciliare* council]

un gen dered (un jen′dərd), *adj.* unconceived; unbegotten. [< L *generāre* to beget]

un gorge (un′gôrj′), *v.* 1. to starve; famish. 2. to vomit. 3. to empty out, deplete. [un + OF *gorge* throat, ult. < LL *gurges* throat, jaws < L *gurges* abyss, whirlpool]

un re quit ed (un′ri kwīt′əd), *adj.* 1. unreturned; unrewarded.

un tram meled (un tram′ld), *adj.* not hindered; not restrained; free.

up braid (up braid′), *v.* find fault with; blame; reprove: *The captain upbraided his men for falling asleep.* [OE *upbregdan* < *upp* up + *bregdan* weave, braid] —**Syn.** reproach.

ur ban i ty (ėr ban′ə tē), *n., pl.* **-ties.** 1. courtesy; refinement; elegance. 2. smooth politeness.

ur sine (ėr′sīn or ėr′sən), *adj.* 1. of or having to do with bears; bearlike. 2. covered with bristlelike hairs: *ursine caterpillars.* [< L *ursinus* < *ursus* bear]

ux o ri ous (uks ô′rē əs or uks ō′rē əs), *adj.* excessively or foolishly fond of one's wife. [< L *uxorius* < *uxor* wife] —**ux o′ri ous ness,** *n.*

va gar y (və ger′ē or vā′gə rē), *n., pl.* **-gar ies.** 1. an odd fancy; extravagant notion: *the vagaries of a dream.* 2. odd action; caprice; freak: *the vagaries of women's fashions.* [probably < L *vagari* wander < *vagus* roving]

ver dure (vėr′jər), *n.* 1. fresh greenness. 2. a fresh growth of green grass, plants, or leaves. [< OF *verdure,* ult. < L *viridis* green]

ver i ty (ver′ə tē), *n., pl.* **-ties.** 1. truth.

hat, āge, fär; let, ēqual, tėrm; it, īce; hot, ōpen, ôrder; oil, out; cup, pùt, rüle; ch, child; ng, long; sh, she; th, thin; ᴛʜ, then; zh, measure;

ə represents *a* in about, *e* in taken, *i* in pencil, *o* in lemon, *u* in circus.

< = from, derived from, taken from.

2. a true statement or fact. 3. reality. [< L *veritas* < *verus* true]

ver nac u lar (vər nak′yə lər), *n.* 1. a native language; language used by the people of a certain country or place. 2. everyday language; informal speech. 3. language of a profession, trade, etc.: *the vernacular of the lawyers.* —*adj.* 1. used by the people of a certain country, place, etc.; native: *English is our vernacular tongue.* 2. of or in the native language, rather than a literary or learned language. [< L *vernaculus* domestic, native < *verna* home-born slave]

ves tig i al (ve stij′ē əl), *adj.* 1. remaining as a vestige of something that has disappeared. 2. in biology, no longer fully developed or useful.

vit re ous (vit′rē əs), *adj.* 1. glassy; like glass: *vitreous china.* 2. having to do with glass. 3. made from glass. [< L *vitreus* < *vitrum* glass]

vor tex· (vôr′teks), *n., pl.* **-tex es** or **-ti ces.** 1. a whirling mass of water, air, etc., that sucks in everything near it; whirlpool; whirlwind. 2. whirl of activity or other situation from which it is hard to escape: *The two nations were unwillingly drawn into the vortex of war.* [< L *vortex,* var. of *vertex*]

vo tar y (vō′tər ē), *n., pl.* **-ries.** 1. person devoted to something; devotee: *He was a votary of golf.* 2. person bound by vows to a religious life. [< L *votum* vow]

vo tive (vō′tiv), *adj.* promised by a vow; given, etc., because of a vow. [< L *votivus* < *votum* vow]

wax (waks), *v.,* **waxed, waxed** or *(Poetic)* **wax en, wax ing.** 1. grow bigger or greater; increase: *The moon waxes till it becomes full, and then wanes.* 2. become: *The party waxed merry.* [OE *weaxan*]

with al (wiᴛʜ ôl′ or with ôl′), *Archaic.* —*adv.* with it all; as well; besides; also: *The lady is rich and fair and wise withal.* —*prep.* with. [< *with* + *all*]

wiz ened (wiz′nd), *adj.* dried up; withered; shriveled: *a wizened apple, a wizened face.* [pp. of dialectal *wizen,* OE *wisnian* shrivel]

wont (wunt), *adj.* accustomed: *He was wont to read the paper at breakfast.* —*n.* custom; habit: *He rose early, as was his wont.* [originally pp., ult. < OE *wunian* be accustomed]

wraith (rāth), *n.* 1. ghost of a person seen before or soon after his death. 2. specter; ghost. [? < Scand. *vörthr* guardian]

GENERAL INDEX

Names of authors represented in the text appear in capital letters. Page numbers immediately following an author's name refer to biographical information. Titles of selections printed in the text are italicized.